KU-663-605

Police Law

Fifteenth Edition

Richard Card LLB LLM Hon LLD FRSA
Emeritus Professor of Law
De Montfort University, Leicester

The late **Jack English** OBE QPM MA
Ex-Assistant Chief Constable, Northumbria Police
Ex-Director of the Central Planning, Instructor Training and
Police Promotion Examinations Unit
Ex-Chief Examiner to the Police Promotions Examinations Board

OXFORD
UNIVERSITY PRESS

OXFORD
UNIVERSITY PRESS

Great Clarendon Street, Oxford, OX2 6DP,
United Kingdom

Oxford University Press is a department of the University of Oxford.
It furthers the University's objective of excellence in research, scholarship,
and education by publishing worldwide. Oxford is a registered trade mark of
Oxford University Press in the UK and in certain other countries

© Oxford University Press 2017

The moral rights of the authors have been asserted

First Edition published in 1985
Fourteenth Edition published in 2015
Fifteenth Edition published in 2017

Impression: 1

All rights reserved. No part of this publication may be reproduced, stored in
a retrieval system, or transmitted, in any form or by any means, without the
prior permission in writing of Oxford University Press, or as expressly permitted
by law, by licence or under terms agreed with the appropriate reprographics
rights organization. Enquiries concerning reproduction outside the scope of the
above should be sent to the Rights Department, Oxford University Press, at the
address above

You must not circulate this work in any other form
and you must impose this same condition on any acquirer

Crown copyright material is reproduced under Class Licence
Number C01P0000148 with the permission of OPSI
and the Queen's Printer for Scotland

Published in the United States of America by Oxford University Press
198 Madison Avenue, New York, NY 10016, United States of America

British Library Cataloguing in Publication Data

Data available

Library of Congress Control Number: 2014959664

ISBN 978-0-19-878680-1

Printed in Great Britain by
Clays Ltd, St Ives plc

Links to third party websites are provided by Oxford in good faith and
for information only. Oxford disclaims any responsibility for the materials
contained in any third party website referenced in this work.

Preface

When Jack English and I wrote the first edition of this book 30 years ago, our aims were to cover comprehensively, and in terms easily understood by those who had received no legal training, those areas of the law and legal procedure with which all police officers are concerned. The material included in *Police Law* and its appendices has been prepared in a way which recognises the ordinary needs of police officers, of those in legal advice agencies, and of members of the public who wish to refer to a legal text. Now in its 15th edition, the work remains true to its original aims.

This is the fourth edition of this book which I have prepared on my own following Jack English's untimely death in January 2010.

Jack was born in 1931. He became a police cadet at the age of 16. He rose steadily through the ranks, achieving the highest-ever mark in his Inspectors' promotion examination, and was promoted into the training department in 1965. 1968 saw another promotion, this time to Chief Inspector at Whitley Bay, the place at which he would settle and stay for the remainder of his life. In 1971 Jack was seconded to the regional training centre at Dishforth in North Yorkshire and on completion of that secondment he took up the position of head of the Examinations Unit at Ryton on Dunsmore, near Coventry, which included promotion to Superintendent. A few years later the unit moved to Harrogate and the newly formed Central Planning Unit was established with Jack as its head. Following regular success at the Central Planning Unit, Jack finally reached the rank of Assistant Chief Constable and in 1984 he was awarded the Queen's Police Medal for services to the police. Jack retired from the police service in 1985, in which year he was awarded the OBE. Jack enjoyed 57 happy years of marriage to Jeanne and was a strong family man.

For 25 years Jack and I worked closely together producing new editions of *Police Law*. Jack's imprint can be found throughout this edition. He was an utterly reliable colleague in every respect. Always entertaining, he was a joy to work with.

The previous edition, published in 2015, has been extensively amended in consequence of the many subsequent legislative changes.

I wish to thank all those who have assisted me in various ways in the production of this edition. In particular, I would like to thank my wife, Rachel, for her assistance with the manuscript, Lucy Alexander, Paul Tompsett, Geraldine Ferguson, Deborah Hey and Nicola Lennon for their help in the production of the book, and the publishers for compiling tables of cases and statutes.

As a result of the large amount of legislation which continues to be made, the increasing size of *Police Law* edition by edition has become a concern. Recent editions have become physically unwieldy. The solution to this is twofold. First, a small number of specific items which previously appeared in the text have been moved to the companion website. Among these items are those which do not have national application, matters of considerable detail not suited to the text to which they refer, and matters of minor importance. Reference to them, and to their inclusion on the companion website, is made at the appropriate points in the text. Second, as in the previous edition, some areas of law previously contained in chapters which reader feedback has shown are of less importance to most police officers are excluded from the body of the book, and are contained in five appendices which appear on the companion website. In this respect, I wish to thank a range of readers at all levels and with varying interests for their advice about the contents of this book. The topics, revised as necessary, which now appear as appendices to *Police Law* on the companion website are:

Appendix 1 Public Service Vehicles
Appendix 2 Goods Vehicles
Appendix 3 Immigration
Appendix 4 Animals, Birds and Plants
Appendix 5 Game, Deer and Fish.

The companion website also contains regular updates to the chapters contained in the book. It can be found at <http://www.oup.com/>.

The law is stated as it was on 20 June 2016, except that I have included then existing statutory provisions which are to come into force before the anticipated publication date of this book. European Union law currently has a considerable impact on our criminal law. Following the referendum vote in June 2016 in favour of leaving the EU, the UK government announced its intention to do so. Once the UK government has served the formal notice to the EU Council under Article 50 of the Lisbon Treaty of its intention to leave (which it is not expected to do until 2017), there will be a two-year period in which to negotiate a new treaty setting out the arrangements for the UK's withdrawal. Any legislation in the meantime in consequence of the decision to withdraw will not come into force until the end of that period. It is important to note that there will therefore be no consequential change in the application to the UK of EU legislation until two years has elapsed after service of the Article 50 notice. The nature and extent of the impact of the UK leaving the EU will not be clear until the withdrawal treaty has been negotiated.

It is common for Parliament to enact provisions which do not come into force, if ever, until a long time after enactment. Where the commencement date of a relevant provision is not known, the provision does not generally appear in the text but does appear at the appropriate point on the companion website. In such a case, there is normally a signposting reference in the text.

Most of the offences described are only triable summarily (ie in a magistrates' court). Where this is not the case, it is indicated that the offence is triable only on indictment (ie in the Crown Court) or triable either way (ie in the Crown Court or a magistrates' court). The absence of such an indication means that the offence is summary only.

1 September 2016   Richard Card

Contents

Table of Primary Legislation

The European Convention on Human Rights is tabled under Sch 1 of the Human Rights Act 1998

Table of Secondary Legislation

Abbreviations

AA 1967	Abortion Act 1967
ABH	actual bodily harm
ACPO	Association of Chief Police Officers
ADBA	American Dog Breeders' Association
AETR	European agreement concerning the work of crews of vehicles engaged in international transport
AHA 1981	Animal Health Act 1981
ASB	anti-social behaviour
A-sBA 2003	Anti-social Behaviour Act 2003
A-sB,C&PA 2014	Anti-social Behaviour, Crime and Policing Act 2014
ASBO	Anti-social behaviour order
AWA 2006	Animal Welfare Act 2006
BA 1976	Bail Act 1976
BA 2010	Bribery Act 2010
BNA 1981	British Nationality Act 1981
BTP	British Transport Police
CA 2003	Communications Act 2003
CAA 1981	Criminal Attempts Act 1981
CAA 1984	Child Abduction Act 1984
CA(YP)A 1997	Confiscation of Alcohol (Young Persons) Act 1997
CBL	children's barred list
CBO	criminal behaviour order
CCA 2013	Crime and Courts Act 2013
CDA 1971	Criminal Damage Act 1971
CDA 1998	Crime and Disorder Act 1998
CEA	civil enforcement area
C(IC)A 2003	Crime (International Co-operation) Act 2003
CJA 1967	Criminal Justice Act 1967
CJA 1988	Criminal Justice Act 1988
CJA 2003	Criminal Justice Act 2003
CJCA 2015	Criminal Justice and Courts Act 2015
C&JA 2009	Coroners and Justice Act 2009
CJIA 2008	Criminal Justice and Immigration Act 2008
CJPA 2001	Criminal Justice and Police Act 2001
CJPOA 1994	Criminal Justice and Public Order Act 1994
CLA 1967	Criminal Law Act 1967
CLA 1977	Criminal Law Act 1977
CMA 1990	Computer Misuse Act 1990
CMCHA 2007	Corporate Manslaughter and Corporate Homicide Act 2007
CNEA 2005	Clean Neighbourhoods and Environment Act 2005

CPC	Certificate of Professional Competence
CPIA 1996	Criminal Procedure and Investigations Act 1996
CPM	Commissioner of Police of the Metropolis
CPN	community protection notice
CPS	Crown Prosecution Service
CSO	community support officer
C-TA 2008	Counter-Terrorism Act 2008
CYPA 1933	Children and Young Persons Act 1933
CYPA 1969	Children and Young Persons Act 1969
CYP(HP)A 1955	Children and Young Persons (Harmful Publications) Act 1955
DA 1991	Deer Act 1991
DA 2005	Drugs Act 2005
DBS	Disclosure and Barring Service
DDA 1991	Dangerous Dogs Act 1991
DDES(E&W)O 2015	The Dangerous Dogs Exemption Schemes (England and Wales) Order 2015
D(FL)A 1996	Dogs (Fouling of Land) Act 1996
DPA 1998	Data Protection Act 1998
DPP	Director of Public Prosecutions
DSCC	Defence Solicitor Call Centre
DVLA	Driver and Vehicle Licensing Agency
DVPN	domestic violence protection notice
DVPO	domestic violence protection order
DVSA	Driver and Vehicle Standards Agency
EA	Environment Agency
EA 1875	Explosives Act 1875
EC	European Community
ECE	UN Economic Commission for Europe
ECHR	European Convention on Human Rights
EEA	European Economic Area (see p 334)
ELPB	Elected Local Policing Body
EPA 1990	Environmental Protection Act 1990
ESA 1883	Explosive Substances Act 1883
EU	European Union
FA 2006	Fraud Act 2006
FCA 1981	Forgery and Counterfeiting Act 1981
FiA 1968	Firearms Act 1968
Fi(A)A 1997	Firearms (Amendment) Act 1997
FLA 1996	Family Law Act 1996
F(O)A 1991	Football (Offences) Act 1991
FR 2004	Fireworks Regulations 2004
FSA 1989	Football Spectators Act 1989
GBH	grievous bodily harm
GCHQ	Government Communications Headquarters

GRC	gender recognition certificate
GV(LO)A 1995	Goods Vehicles (Licensing of Operators) Act 1995
HA 1980	Highways Act 1980
HA 2004	Hunting Act 2004
HHCA 1939	House to House Collections Act 1939
HMIC	Her Majesty's Inspectors of Constabulary
HRA 1998	Human Rights Act 1998
IA 1971	Immigration Act 1971
IAA 1999	Immigration and Asylum Act 1999
IDA 2010	Identity Documents Act 2010
ID(C)A 1981	Indecent Displays (Control) Act 1981
IPCC	Independent Police Complaints Commission
ISO	individual support order
KA 1997	Knives Act 1997
LA 1872	Licensing Act 1872
LA 2003	Licensing Act 2003
LGV	large goods vehicle
LPB	local policing body
MCA 1980	Magistrates' Courts Act 1980
MDA 1861	Malicious Damage Act 1861
MDA 1971	Misuse of Drugs Act 1971
MHA 1983	Mental Health Act 1983
MOPC	Mayor's Office for Policing and Crime
MPV	mechanically propelled vehicle
MSA 2015	Modern Slavery Act 2015
MV(DL)R 1999	Motor Vehicles (Driving Licences) Regulations 1999
MV(IR)R 2011	Motor Vehicles (Insurance Requirements) Regulations 2011
MV(IR)(I, R and D)R 2011	Motor Vehicles (Insurance Requirements) (Immobilisation, Removal and Disposal) Regulations 2011
MV(WSBCFS)R 1993	Motor Vehicles (Wearing of Seat Belts by Children in Front Seats) Regulations 1993
MV(WSB)R 1993	Motor Vehicles (Wearing of Seat Belts) Regulations 1993
NCA	National Crime Agency
NHS	National Health Service
NSPCC	National Society for Prevention of Cruelty to Children
OAPA 1861	Offences against the Person Act 1861
OPA 1959	Obscene Publications Act 1959
PA 1871	Pedlars Act 1871
PA 1911	Perjury Act 1911

PA 1996	Police Act 1996
PACE	Police and Criminal Evidence Act 1984
PATR 2008	Police Appeals Tribunal Rules 2008
PBA 1992	Protection of Badgers Act 1992
PCA 1953	Prevention of Crime Act 1953
PCA 1978	Protection of Children Act 1978
PCA 2002	Proceeds of Crime Act 2002
P&CA 2009	Policing and Crime Act 2009
PCC	Police and Crime Commissioner
P(C)R 2012	Police (Conduct) Regulations 2012
P(CM)R 2012	Police (Complaints and Misconduct) Regulations 2012
PCV	passenger-carrying vehicle
PEA 1977	Protection from Eviction Act 1977
PFA 2012	Protection of Freedoms Act 2012
PHA 1997	Protection from Harassment Act 1997
PII	public interest immunity
PNC	Police National Computer
PND	penalty notice for disorder
POA 1936	Public Order Act 1936
POA 1986	Public Order Act 1986
P(P)R 2008	Police (Performance) Regulations 2008
PPVA 1981	Public Passenger Vehicles Act 1981
PRA 2002	Police Reform Act 2002
PRSRA 2011	Police Reform and Social Responsibility Act 2011
PSA 2016	The Psychoactive Substances Act 2016
RD(A)A 1978	Refuse Disposal (Amenity) Act 1978
RDVR 1986	Removal and Disposal of Vehicles Regulations 1986
RIPA 2000	Regulation of Investigatory Powers Act 2000
RNLI	Royal National Lifeboat Institution
RSA 2006	Road Safety Act 2006
RSPB	Royal Society for the Protection of Birds
RTA 1988	Road Traffic Act 1988
RTOA 1988	Road Traffic Offenders Act 1988
RTRA 1984	Road Traffic Regulation Act 1984
RTSA 2003	Railway and Transport Safety Act 2003
RV(C&U)R 1986	Road Vehicles (Construction and Use) Regulations 1986
RV(DRM)R 2001	Road Vehicles (Display of Registration Marks) Regulations 2001
RV(R&L)R 2002	Road Vehicles (Registration and Licensing) Regulations 2002
SCA 2015	Serious Crime Act 2015
SE(CA)A 1985	Sporting Events (Control of Alcohol, etc) Act 1985
SI	statutory instrument
SMD	scrap metal dealer

SMDA 2013	Scrap Metal Dealers Act 2013
SOA 1956	Sexual Offences Act 1956
SOA 2003	Sexual Offences Act 2003
SOCPA 2005	Serious Organised Crime and Police Act 2005
SOPO	sexual offences prevention order
SRA	Solicitors Regulatory Authority
StOA 1959	Street Offences Act 1959
SVGA 2006	Safeguarding of Vulnerable Groups Act 2006
TA 1968	Theft Act 1968
TA 1978	Theft Act 1978
TA 1985	Transport Act 1985
TA 2000	Terrorism Act 2000
TA 2006	Terrorism Act 2006
TEN	temporary events notice
TfL	Transport for London
TMA 2004	Traffic Management Act 2004
TPIMA 2011	Terrorism Prevention and Investigation Measures Act 2011
TSR&GD 2016	Traffic Signs Regulations and General Directions 2016
TULR(C)A 1992	Trade Union and Labour Relations (Consolidation) Act 1992
TWA 1992	Transport and Works Act 1992
UKBA	UK Border Agency
UKBA 2007	UK Borders Act 2007
UKVI	UK Visas and Immigration
VA 1824	Vagrancy Act 1824
V(C)A 2001	Vehicles (Crime) Act 2001
VCRA 2006	Violent Crime Reduction Act 2006
VERA 1994	Vehicle Excise and Registration Act 1994
VOO	violent offender order
WAO	witness anonymity order
WM(P)A 1996	Wild Mammals (Protection) Act 1996
YCC	youth conditional caution
YJCEA 1999	Youth Justice and Criminal Evidence Act 1999

CHAPTER 1
General Principles

This book deals with those branches of the law of particular relevance to police officers in England and Wales.

SOURCES

There are two principal sources of English law: legislation and common law.

Legislation

In modern times legislation has played a preponderant part in the branches of the law dealt with in this book.

Statute

'Statute' has traditionally meant an Act of the UK Parliament. Except for the very few common law offences, all serious offences are defined by statute, as are many minor offences. By and large the law relating to police powers, criminal procedure and evidence is derived from statute.

Since 2011, the National Assembly for Wales has had power to enact its own Acts, which only apply in relation to Wales, on any matter within its legislative competence, which is limited to 21 devolved areas. The devolved areas do not include criminal justice and the impact of the Acts of the Assembly on Police Law is marginal.

Subordinate legislation

A statute may give power to some body, such as the Queen in Council, a minister of the UK government, the Welsh Ministers (ie the ministers of the Welsh assembly Government) or a local authority or other public body, to make Orders in Council, regulations, or byelaws (respectively), and prescribe for their breach. Subordinate legislation made at central government level is normally required to be made by way of 'statutory instrument'.

Common law

Common law is that part of the law which is not the result of legislation, ie it is the law which has been developed by the decisions and rulings of the judges.

Very few offences are now governed and defined by the common law. Moreover, the judges do not now have the capacity to create new offences or widen existing ones. Examples of common law offences are murder, manslaughter and conspiracy to defraud.

Although almost all offences are now governed by legislation, the general principles of criminal liability dealt with later in this chapter are derived from the common law.

The common law has been built up on the basis of the doctrine of precedent, under which the reported decisions of certain courts are more than just authoritative legal statements whose effect is persuasive, since they can be binding (ie must be applied) in subsequent cases. In the context of courts with criminal jurisdiction, the following have binding effect: decisions of the Supreme Court (and of the House of Lords, which was the supreme court of appeal until 2009), the Court of Appeal (Criminal Division), a divisional court of the Queen's Bench Division of the High Court, and a judge sitting in the Administrative Court of that Division. Each of these courts has a criminal jurisdiction limited to appeals. Whether or not one of their decisions is binding in a particular case depends on the relative standing of the court which made the decision and the court in which that decision is subsequently cited. The reason is that the doctrine of precedent depends on the principle that the courts form a hierarchy which, in the case of courts with criminal jurisdiction, is in the following descending order: *Supreme Court (House of Lords), Court of Appeal (Criminal Division), divisional court, judge in the Administrative Court,* Crown Court and magistrates' courts. The basic rule is that a decision by one of the courts italicised is binding on those courts below that in which it was given and, save in exceptional circumstances, will be followed by a court of equal status. A decision which is not binding under the above rules is nevertheless of persuasive authority, and may be cited to a court in a subsequent case.

European Union law

This currently has a considerable impact on our criminal law. In order for breach of EU legislation to be an offence in English law, an Act of Parliament or subordinate legislation to this effect is required. Following the referendum vote in June 2016 in favour of leaving the EU, and once the UK government has served the formal notice to the EU Council under Article 50 of the Lisbon Treaty of its intention to leave (which it is not expected to do until 2017), there will be a two-year period in which to negotiate a new treaty setting out the arrangements for the UK's withdrawal. Any legislation in the meantime in consequence of the decision to withdraw will not come into force until the end of that period. It is important to note that there will therefore be no consequent change in the application to the UK of EU legislation until two years has elapsed after service of the Article 50 notice. The nature and extent of the impact of the UK leaving the EU will not be clear until the withdrawal treaty has been negotiated.

European Convention on Human Rights and the Human Rights Act 1998

The European Convention on Human Rights (ECHR), taken together with the Human Rights Act 1998 (HRA 1998), is of major importance.

Impact of HRA 1998

There has for a considerable time been a right of individual petition to the European Court of Human Rights in Strasbourg against a breach by the UK of a right under the ECHR. Under HRA 1998, remedies are available in the courts of England and Wales in respect of breach of a Convention right set out in Sch 1 (the Convention rights). The Convention does not automatically take priority over English law. Our courts have not been given a power to disapply an inconsistent Act of Parliament (primary legislation), but the effect of the main provisions in the Act comes close to permitting disapplication.

On the other hand, subordinate legislation incompatible with a Convention right can sometimes be quashed.

The Convention rights The Convention rights specified in HRA 1998, Sch 1 include rights:

(a) to life (ECHR, art 2);
(b) not to be subjected to torture or inhuman or degrading treatment or punishment (art 3);
(c) not to be deprived of liberty save in specified cases, eg after conviction or lawful arrest, and in accordance with a procedure prescribed by law (art 5);
(d) to a fair trial (including the presumption of innocence) (art 6);
(e) to respect for private and family life (art 8);
(f) to freedom of thought, conscience and religion (art 9);
(g) to freedom of expression (art 10); and
(h) to freedom of assembly and association (art 11).

The exercise of the last four rights may be restricted by the law on specified grounds if this is necessary in a democratic society (for example in the interests of national security, for the prevention of disorder or crime, for the protection of health or morals or for the protection of the rights and freedoms of others).

By ECHR, art 14 the enjoyment of the Convention rights must be secured without discrimination on any ground such as sex, race, opinion, national or social origin or other status.

In determining a question which has arisen in connection with a Convention right, our courts must take into account the case law of the European Court of Human Rights.

Statutory interpretation Acts of Parliament and other legislation must, so far as possible, be read and given effect to in a way which is compatible with the Convention rights. The courts, where necessary, will prefer a strained but possible interpretation which is consistent with Convention rights to one more consistent with the statutory words themselves.

Declaration of incompatibility If a court is unable to interpret a statutory provision compatibly with a Convention right, it will have to proceed as normal. The issue of incompatibility can be raised on appeal. As far as criminal cases are concerned, if satisfied that a provision of primary legislation (Act of Parliament) is incompatible with a Convention right, a judge of the Administrative Court, a divisional court, the Court of Appeal or the Supreme Court may then make a declaration of incompatibility. The court may also make such a declaration in respect of a provision of other legislation which is so incompatible if satisfied that (disregarding the possibility of revocation) the primary legislation prevents removal of that incompatibility.

If a declaration of incompatibility is made, the government and Parliament are not required to take remedial action.

Unlawful acts It is unlawful for a 'public authority', a term which includes a police officer, to act in a way incompatible with a Convention right, unless:

(a) as a result of one or more provisions of primary legislation, the authority could not have acted differently; or
(b) in the case of one or more provisions of, or made under, primary legislation which cannot be read or given effect in a way which is compatible with the Convention rights, the authority was acting so as to give effect to or enforce those provisions.

This provides some protection for police officers who act in accordance with the law as it stands at the moment in question.

A person who is a victim of such an unlawful act may bring civil legal proceedings against a public authority in respect of any act by that authority. A court may grant such relief or remedy (including compensatory damages) or make such an order as it considers appropriate within the terms of HRA 1998.

GENERAL PRINCIPLES OF CRIMINAL LIABILITY

Criminal liability

There are two elements of criminal liability:

(a) the outward conduct which must always be proved against the defendant (hereafter 'D') (the actus reus, 'the legally blameworthy act'); and

(b) the state of mind which, apart from in exceptional offences, it must be proved that D had at the time of the relevant conduct (the mens rea, the 'legally blameworthy state of mind').

Of course, the definition of these two things varies from offence to offence, but if the relevant conduct and state of mind can be proved by the prosecution D is guilty unless he can rely successfully on a defence.

Actus reus

It would be wrong to think that proof of the relevant conduct required for an offence is limited to proof of an act on the part of D. There are two reasons.

First, some offences can be committed (and, indeed, some can only be committed) by a failure to do a particular act on the part of a person who was under a legal duty to do that act; an example of such an offence is that of failing to provide a specimen of breath for analysis, without reasonable excuse, when required to do so under the Road Traffic Act 1988, s 7. It should also be noted that there are some offences whose definitions require neither an act nor an omission but simply the existence of a state of affairs on the part of D; an example is the offence of being found drunk in a public place, contrary to the Licensing Act 1872, s 12.

The second reason why more than an act on D's part must be proved is that rarely, if ever, is a mere act (or omission or state of affairs) sufficient for criminal liability for a substantive offence. The definitions of offences often specify surrounding circumstances which are essential to render the act, etc criminal. Sometimes the definition requires a consequence to result from the act or omission, such as the consequence in murder that another human being dies unlawfully. The need to prove that a requisite consequence resulted from D's act or omission is known as the requirement of causation. The legal rules about causation are dealt with on p 690 in relation to homicide offences, but the principles described there are also generally applicable to the other offences with a causation requirement. The specified circumstances and/or consequences of an offence are part of its actus reus.

Mens rea

Mens rea is not concerned with whether D had an evil mind or knowledge of the wrongfulness of the act. D's ignorance of the criminal law is no defence, nor generally is the fact that D did not regard his conduct as immoral or know that it was so regarded by the bulk of society.

The expression mens rea refers to the state of mind expressly or impliedly required by the definition of the offence charged. This varies from offence to offence, but typical instances are intention, recklessness, knowledge and belief.

Intention

A number of offences require D to have acted with a particular intention: in murder D must have acted with intent unlawfully to kill, or cause grievous bodily harm to, another human being; in theft D must have dishonestly appropriated another's property with intent permanently to deprive him of it. Generally speaking, 'intention' refers to a state of mind in relation to a potential consequence of one's act. In some crimes, that consequence must actually result in order for there to be criminal liability; in others, such as theft, it is not necessary that the intended consequence should occur.

In law, a person 'intends' a consequence of his conduct if it is his aim or purpose to achieve it. A person who does not have the aim or purpose of bringing about a particular consequence may nevertheless be found to have intended that consequence if it is proved that it was virtually certain to result from his conduct and he foresaw that it was virtually certain to result.

Recklessness

In some offences 'recklessness', either as to the consequence required for the actus reus, or as to a requisite circumstance of it, or as to some other risk, suffices for criminal liability as an alternative to some other mental state such as intention or knowledge.

A person acts recklessly with respect to:

(a) a circumstance when he is aware of a risk that it exists, or will exist;
(b) a consequence when he is aware of a risk that it will occur,

and it is, in the circumstances known to him, unreasonable to take the risk.

Transferred malice

Provided that D intends the specified consequence to occur, or (where recklessness suffices) is reckless as to that consequence occurring, it is irrelevant that the actual object of that consequence is not the person or property whom D intends to harm, or is reckless as to harming. Thus, if D fires a gun intending to kill X, it is irrelevant that the person killed is Y. D will have intended to kill another human being, and will therefore have acted with mens rea for murder. This is called the doctrine of transferred malice.

Knowledge

Many offences require 'knowledge' as to the material circumstances (ie the circumstances specified for the actus reus). A person knows that a circumstance exists if he is certain that it exists.

Belief

In some offences 'belief' as to the material circumstances is required. A person believes that a circumstance exists if he is virtually certain that it does.

Statutory expressions

In some statutes the mens rea requirement, in whole or part, is denoted by adverbs such as 'wilfully', 'maliciously' or 'dishonestly'. These terms have acquired special meanings in law; see further pp 408, 535, 652 and 914.

Effect of inadvertence or mistake

If D lacks the requisite intention, recklessness or other state of mind because he did not think about the matter in issue or made a mistake which prevented him having that state of mind, D is not guilty of the offence, however unreasonable his inadvertence or mistake. Of course, the more unreasonable an allegation of inadvertence or mistake is, the less likely it is that the allegation will be accepted by the jury or magistrates.

Proof of a state of mind

In proving whether D had a requisite state of mind, regard must be had:

(a) to the statements of D; and
(b) to the conduct and circumstances of D, and the presence of any motive, since these *may* give rise to the inference that he had the necessary state of mind.

In addition, the Criminal Justice Act 1967, s 8 provides that a court or jury in determining whether a person has committed an offence:

(a) is *not bound* in law to infer that he intended or foresaw a result of his actions by reason only of its being a natural and probable consequence of those actions, but
(b) must decide whether he did intend or foresee that result by reference to all the evidence, drawing such inferences from the evidence *as appear proper* in the circumstances.

Knowledge or belief as to a circumstance *may be* inferred from proof that D was wilfully blind as to it (ie D realised the risk that it might exist but deliberately refrained from making inquiries).

Strict liability

In the case of many, generally minor, offences, the courts have held that a person can be convicted despite having no type of mens rea as to a particular element of the actus reus (or sometimes even though he had no type of mens rea as to any element). These offences are known as offences of 'strict liability'.

All but three offences of strict liability are statutory offences. Clearly, an offence is not one of strict liability if the statutory definition expressly uses a word such as 'intentionally', 'recklessly' or 'knowingly'. The fact that a statutory definition does not use any word importing the concept of mens rea does not necessarily mean that the offence is one of strict liability; it depends on whether or not the courts are prepared to imply a requirement of mens rea into the definition. The basic rule is that, where a statute is silent on the point, it is presumed that Parliament intended a requirement to prove mens rea (so that the offence is not one of strict liability), unless this is rebutted by clear evidence that Parliament intended the contrary.

Justifications

An offence is not committed if D has a legal justification such as the use of reasonable force in the prevention of crime, effecting a lawful arrest, self-defence or defence of property (see Chapter 23) which renders the conduct lawful. Police officers are often empowered to do something which would otherwise be an offence. Such powers are another example of a legal justification.

Infancy

A child under 10 is irrebuttably presumed not to be guilty of an offence.

Insanity

Everyone is presumed sane until the contrary is proved. The mere fact that a person is medically insane is no defence, but a person proved to be legally insane has a defence. The test of insanity for the purposes of legal responsibility is provided by the *M'Naghten Rules*, which comprise three elements which must be proved by D (unless it is the prosecution which alleges insanity). At the time of the conduct in question:

(a) *D must have been suffering from a 'disease of the mind'*, ie an impairment of the mental faculties of reason, memory and understanding due to a disease as opposed to some external factor like a blow on the head;

(b) *D must have been suffering a 'defect of reason' due to disease of the mind*, ie a deprivation of reasoning power (as opposed to momentary confusion or absent-mindedness); and

(c) *as a result, D must not have known the physical nature and quality of his act or, if he did know this, not have known he was doing 'a legal wrong'.* The mere fact that, because of a defect of reason due to a disease of the mind, D acted under an irresistible impulse is not enough.

It has been held by a divisional court that the defence of insanity is not available where the offence charged is an offence of strict liability as to every element of the actus reus, ie one where no mens rea is required.

Defendants found not guilty by reason of insanity in the Crown Court must be made subject to one of three orders, one of which is indefinite detention in hospital until this is no longer necessary for the protection of the public.

Automatism

Generally, it is a defence that D was in a state of automatism at the time of the act in question. An act is done in a state of automatism if it is done by the muscles without any control of the mind (eg a reflex action, or a spasmodic or convulsive act) or if it is done during a state involving lost consciousness (eg concussion, or a hypoglycaemic coma resulting from insulin taken by a diabetic). Where the automatism directly results from a *disease* the relevant defence is insanity, not automatism.

D does not have to prove the defence of (non-insane) automatism. Instead he simply has the burden of adducing sufficient evidence to raise the issue; D's evidence will very rarely be sufficient unless it is supported by medical evidence. If D adduces sufficient evidence, he must be acquitted unless the prosecution disproves the alleged automatism.

Sometimes, non-insane automatism is self-induced in that it results from something done or not done by D (as where a diabetic becomes an automaton as a result of taking insulin, or, having taken insulin, failing to eat sufficiently thereafter). In such a case, D cannot be convicted of an 'offence of specific intent' (which is defined below). Nor can he be convicted of an 'offence of basic intent' (below), *unless* either the automatism was caused by his voluntary intoxication *or*, before becoming an automaton, D was aware that something done or not done was likely to make him aggressive, unpredictable or uncontrollable (as opposed simply to becoming unconscious), and he deliberately disregarded the risk.

Intoxication

The rules relating to the effect of intoxication in criminal liability are the same whether the intoxication was caused by drink or drugs. Intoxication is not in itself a defence. It is no excuse that because of intoxication D's power to judge between right and wrong, or to exercise self-control, was impaired.

Voluntary intoxication

In most cases a person's intoxication is regarded as 'voluntary'. Intoxication is voluntary if it results from knowingly taking alcohol or some other drug. There are two exceptions: intoxication is not voluntary where it is caused by something taken under and in accordance with medical advice, or where it is caused by a non-dangerous drug (ie a sedative or soporific drug), provided that D is not aware of the risk of becoming unpredictable or aggressive when taking it. These cases of involuntary intoxication are dealt with below.

Where D was voluntarily intoxicated, D may rely on the intoxication as evidence that he lacked mens rea if, but only if, the offence requires proof of a specific intent. Even if an offence is one of specific intent, an intoxicated, mistaken belief that he is acting in self-defence or the like will not excuse D. Where an offence is one of basic intent, D may be convicted of it if he was voluntarily intoxicated at the time of his conduct, even though because of his intoxication he did not have the mens rea required for that offence, and even though he was then in a state of automatism, provided that he would have been aware of the risk in question had he been sober. However, the fact that an offence is one of basic intent does not prevent D relying on evidence of his voluntary intoxication as evidence that his act (as opposed to its consequences) was an 'accident', such as where he stumbles into someone in an intoxicated state.

The following have been held to be offences of specific intent: murder; wounding or causing grievous bodily harm with intent contrary to the Offences Against the Person Act 1861 (OAPA 1861), s 18; theft; robbery; burglary with intent to steal; and attempt to commit an offence.

Conversely, the following are examples of offences of basic intent: manslaughter; maliciously wounding or inflicting grievous bodily harm contrary to OAPA 1861, s 20; assault occasioning actual bodily harm; assault on a constable in the execution of his duty; sexual assault; taking a conveyance without lawful authority; and criminal damage contrary to CDA 1971, s 1(1) or (2) (unless only an intentional offence is alleged).

Involuntary intoxication

The situation is different where a person is involuntarily intoxicated. Intoxication is involuntary in the two exceptional cases outlined four paragraphs above, and also where it is not self-induced (as where a person has been secretly drugged).

Where he was involuntarily intoxicated, D can use evidence of this intoxication as evidence that he lacked the mens rea for the offence in question (whether or not it is an offence of specific intent). However, if it can be proved that D had the necessary mens rea when the offence was committed, it is no defence that involuntary intoxication led him to commit an offence which he would not have committed when sober, and this is so even though, because of the intoxication, he acted under an irresistible impulse.

Duress

The defences of duress by threats and duress of circumstances are restricted to cases where D was impelled to act as he did because, on the facts as he reasonably believed them to be, he had good cause to believe that he or someone for whom he felt responsible was subject to a threat of imminent death or serious physical injury unless he acted as he did to avoid the threatened harm. The defence of duress by threats deals with the case where the threat comes from another person and, expressly or impliedly, is in the form of an order to do a particular, nominated act or suffer the harm; the defence of duress of circumstances deals with the case where the threat of death or serious physical injury is of any other type (as where the threat comes from the surrounding circumstances).

The threat must be such that an ordinary, sober person of reasonable firmness sharing D's characteristics would have responded as D did. Because this 'ordinary person' is someone of reasonable firmness he is not invested with a characteristic of D which did not make D less able to resist the threat than an ordinary person of reasonable firmness. In addition, the ordinary person of reasonable firmness is not invested with a characteristic of D, such as pliancy, vulnerability to pressure or timidity, since it would be a contradiction in terms to invest an ordinary person with these. On the other hand, if D is in a category of persons who might be less able to resist pressure than people outside that category, the characteristic which puts him in that category may be a relevant one. Obvious examples are age (a young person may not be as robust as a mature person); pregnancy (added fear for the unborn child); serious physical disability (may inhibit self-protection); and a recognised mental illness or psychiatric condition (may make the person more susceptible to pressure).

The defences of duress by threats and duress of circumstances are not applicable in respect of conduct committed after a threat has ceased to be operative or if D could have neutralised the threat by seeking police protection. With a few exceptions, the defences are available in respect of any offence. The principal exceptions are murder and attempted murder.

The defence of duress by threats is not available to a person who foresaw or ought to have foreseen that voluntary association with other people involved a risk of being subjected to any compulsion by threat of violence. Thus, the defence is not available to a person who joins a criminal gang, knowing that other members might bring pressure to bear on him to rob someone, and who is subsequently put under such pressure.

PARTIES TO A CRIME

Perpetrators

A perpetrator is otherwise known as the principal. The perpetrator is normally the person who, with the relevant mens rea, commits the actus reus of the offence, eg by firing the fatal shot in murder, or having intercourse in rape. Of course, there can be more than one perpetrator, as where a group of men enter a building as trespassers in order to steal therein; in such a case there are said to be joint perpetrators of the offence.

A person who makes use of an innocent agent in order to procure the commission of an offence is the perpetrator of the offence, even though he does nothing with his own hands. Thus, a person who kills another by posting a time bomb to him which is delivered by an innocent postman, or who employs a child under ten (the age of criminal responsibility) to remove goods from a shop, may be convicted of murder or theft, as the case may be, if he acts with the appropriate mens rea.

Accomplices

A person who aids, abets, counsels or procures the commission of an offence (an accomplice) is liable to be tried and punished for that offence as a principal offender.

Aiding, abetting, counselling and procuring

The terms 'aiding' and 'abetting' are often used together, but they refer to different things; 'aid' describes the activity of a person who assists the perpetrator to commit the principal offence, and 'abet' describes the activity of a person who encourages the perpetrator to commit it, whether or not in either case present at the time of commission. Although liability as an accomplice does not require an agreement between an alleged accomplice and the perpetrator, an agreement between the two is by its nature a form of encouragement by the former. 'Counsel', which means 'encourage', does not add anything strictly but is used to describe encouragement before the commission of the principal offence. A person 'procures' the commission of an offence where he sets out to see that it is committed and takes appropriate steps to produce its commission.

It can be seen from the above that basically there must be some assistance or encouragement by a person in the commission of an offence by another before he can be convicted as an accomplice to it. That assistance or encouragement must be given before, or at the time of, the commission of the offence. Someone who assists the perpetrator after the commission of an offence is not liable as a party to it, but one who assists the perpetrator to escape detection or arrest may commit the offence of assisting offenders (see Chapter 38).

Mens rea

The mens rea required of an accomplice is not the same as that required of the perpetrator of the principal offence. Instead, what is required to be proved is an intent to assist or encourage the commission by the perpetrator of the act which constitutes or results in the principal offence.

This requires the following to be proved against an alleged accomplice:

(a) intentional assistance or encouragement, with knowledge that it was capable of assisting or encouraging the commission of the principal offence;
(b) knowledge of the facts necessary to constitute the principal offence;
(c) an intention to assist or encourage the perpetrator to commit the principal offence with the mens rea required for it. The alleged accomplice is not required to know the details of that offence.

Where a party to a joint criminal venture to commit an offence intentionally perpetrates a further offence in doing so, another party to the venture is liable for the further offence only if he intends to assist or encourage the perpetrator in committing the further offence in accordance with the above rules. When the further offence is murder, but the person is not guilty of it as an accomplice under the above rules, he may be convicted of constructive manslaughter if he has intentionally assisted in or encouraged the unlawful act from which the victim died and any sober and reasonable person would realise that it carried the risk of some harm resulting.

Miscellaneous points

A person who cannot in law perpetrate a particular offence may nevertheless be con-victed as an accomplice to it. For example, a woman can be convicted of rape as an ac-complice where she has encouraged or assisted a man to rape another woman.

Where D is alleged to be an accomplice to an offence, the charge may allege that he aided, abetted, counselled or procured it, and he will be convicted if he is proved to have participated in one or more of these four ways.

Vicarious liability

Vicarious liability means liability for the acts of another person which D has not authorised and of which he was ignorant.

Vicarious *criminal* liability is exceptional; it is imposed only on employers and, in some cases, certain other people with a similar status. It arises in three ways:

(1) Where a statute expressly states that a specified person is vicariously liable for the prohibited act of another. This is rare.
(2) Where a statutory strict liability offence uses a word like 'use' or 'sell' which con-notes an activity which can be performed by an employee on behalf of his em-ployer, an employer can be vicariously liable for a prohibited 'using', etc by the employee in the course of his employment.
(3) Certain statutes impose duties on someone who is a licensee and make it an offence for someone with that status knowingly to contravene them. If a licen-see completely delegates his statutory responsibilities to someone else such as an employee, and the delegate knowingly contravenes one of these duties, the conduct and the state of mind of the delegate are imputed to the person with the specified status, who is consequently vicariously liable for the offence in question.

CORPORATE LIABILITY

A company or other corporate body may be criminally liable:

(a) on the basis of vicarious liability (above); or
(b) for breach of a statutory duty, such as that imposed on it as an 'occupier' of prem-ises or as an 'employer', etc,

in the same way as a natural person. The offences to which these principles apply are essentially ones of strict liability.

A company or other corporate body may also be liable for most offences (murder is a notable exception) requiring proof of mens rea where the acts and state of mind of an individual who physically committed the offence can be attributed to it. In the case of a *common law offence*, such as conspiracy to defraud, such attribution is only possible in respect of a person who is a 'controlling officer', ie someone who represents the 'directing mind and will' of the corporation (such as a director). Whether or not the conduct of a particular employee of a corporation can be attributed to the cor-poration for the purposes of criminal liability for a *statutory offence* depends on the proper construction of the particular rule of law concerned; a particular statute may be interpreted so that the act and state of mind of someone lower down the company or other corporate body's hierarchy can be attributed to it.

EXEMPTION FROM CRIMINAL LIABILITY

The Diplomatic Privileges Act 1964 provides that ambassadors and Commonwealth High Commissioners, members of their families, and their administrative and technical staff and their families are immune from arrest and criminal proceedings whilst in the UK in that capacity. There is no immunity for a member of the family who is a UK national. Members of the service staff also have immunity but only in respect of acts in the course of their duties. A report should be sent to the Diplomatic Protection Group of the Metropolitan Police where a person dealt with for an offence claims diplomatic immunity; a copy will be forwarded to the Foreign and Commonwealth Office for advice as to whether the offender has immunity.

The Consular Relations Act 1968 grants immunity from criminal proceedings to career consular officers and members of their administrative or technical staff in the exercise of consular functions. As well as this, career consular officers may not be arrested or detained pending trial unless the offence is grave and the detention is authorised by a competent judicial authority. Honorary consular officers are not immune from the jurisdiction of our criminal courts nor from arrest or detention.

CHAPTER 2
Elements of Criminal Procedure

INSTITUTION OF CRIMINAL PROCEEDINGS

Responsibility for prosecutions

Prosecutions (criminal proceedings) are normally instituted on behalf of:

(a) a police force;
(b) the Director of Public Prosecutions (DPP); or
(c) a body with statutory powers to do so in specific matters, such as the Serious Fraud Office, a Secretary of State or a local authority.

The DPP is the head of the Crown Prosecution Service (CPS). The DPP is under the general supervision of the Attorney General. The DPP's functions are discharged on his behalf and under his direction by Crown Prosecutors working in the CPS.

Where prosecutions are instituted on behalf of a police force (whether by a police officer or other person) the DPP is obliged to take over their conduct.

By way of exception, and with the qualifications below, the DPP is not obliged to take over a prosecution instituted on behalf of the police for a range of minor offences such as the following:

> fixed penalty road traffic offences (eg speeding); failing to comply with a traffic direction; failing to stop, report an accident, or give information or documents; using or keeping a vehicle without a vehicle licence; careless or inconsiderate driving; criminal damage, not including arson and only if the value of the property involved is no more than £5,000; low-value shoplifting (goods under £200 in value); being drunk in a highway, other public place, or licensed premises; throwing fireworks in a thoroughfare; trespassing or throwing stones on the railway; disorderly behaviour while drunk in a public place; behaviour likely to cause harassment, alarm or distress; depositing and leaving litter; contravention of a prohibition or failure to comply with a requirement imposed by or under fireworks regulations or making false statements; knowingly giving a false alarm of fire; failing to give a sample for the purposes of testing for the presence of Class A drugs; and failing to attend an assessment following testing for the presence of Class A drugs. With one exception, all these offences are summary offences. The exception is criminal damage, which is an indictable (either way) offence.

The rule that the DPP is not obliged to take over a prosecution instituted on behalf of the police for any of the above offences does not apply if the proceedings are commenced by the defendant (D) being charged by a custody officer at a police station, or if D is under 16 when the proceedings are commenced. In addition, the rule ceases to apply:

(a) if a case summary or copy of the witness statement(s) upon which the prosecution intends to rely in the event that the court proceeds under the 'pleading guilty by post' procedure (p 22: which is not available in respect of criminal damage) is not served with the requisition or summons; or

(b) if a case summary or copy of the witness statement(s) upon which the prosecution intends to rely if D pleads guilty is not served with a requisition or summons in respect of criminal damage; or

(c) if at any time a magistrates' court begins to receive evidence, other than evidence in proceedings held in D's absence or under the 'pleading guilty by post' procedure, or evidence adduced in an attempt to avoid a 'totting up' disqualification; or

(d) if a magistrates' court indicates that it is considering imposing a custodial sentence.

There is generally nothing to prevent a private individual or an organisation which is not governmental or public from instituting and conducting criminal proceedings, and such 'private' prosecutions are occasionally instituted. The DPP may take over a private prosecution even if his purpose is to offer no evidence against D in the public interest and thereby to abort those proceedings.

A qualification to the general rule that a police officer, a private individual or an official of a public or private body may institute criminal proceedings is that there are offences where proceedings for an offence may only be instituted by or with the consent of the Attorney General or of the DPP. In the latter case, the DPP's functions can, of course, be exercised by a Crown Prosecutor on the DPP's behalf. Where proceedings for an offence may only be instituted by or with the consent of the Attorney General or of the DPP, this is indicated at the appropriate point in this book. Such a requirement does not prevent D's arrest or remand in custody or on bail but if the requisite consent has not been given before the hearing at which D indicates his plea or intended plea the subsequent proceedings will be null and void.

Alternatives to prosecutions

Traditionally, the criminal process has involved prosecution, trial (if D pleaded not guilty) and sentence. Other methods are increasingly being used to deal quickly and proportionately with low-level, often first-time, offending.

Where the offender admits the offence the following out-of-court disposals are available in an appropriate case:

(a) community resolution, which involves the offender making amends, eg by offering an apology, making reparation (such as fixing damage) or paying compensation, usually when the victim agrees that he does not want more formal action to be taken. See further the provisions about the 'community remedy' on p 285, which seek to ensure that the victim has a say in the out-of-court punishment of offenders;

(b) a cannabis or khat warning in respect of simple possession;

(c) simple cautions (p 178);

(d) youth cautions (p 180);

(e) conditional cautions (p 181); and

(f) youth conditional cautions (p 182).

In addition, whether or not the offender admits his guilt, many road traffic offences can be dealt with by the issue (and satisfaction) of a fixed penalty notice, and so may over a score or so of offences involving 'disorderly behaviour' (a penalty notice for disorder: PND). The former are dealt with in Chapter 11, and the latter at the end of this chapter. (There are also other offences in respect of which penalty notices may be issued under other legislation and by officials not associated with the police.)

Ways of instituting criminal proceedings

Criminal proceedings may be instituted in one of four ways:

(1) a 'relevant prosecutor' may institute criminal proceedings against a person (D) by issuing a document (a written charge) which charges D with an offence. Where a relevant prosecutor issues a written charge, it must at the same time issue:
   (a) a requisition securing D's presence before a magistrates' court (if necessary by an arrest under warrant), or
   (b) a single justice procedure notice;
(2) a person may institute criminal proceedings by laying an information alleging that D has, or is suspected of having, committed an offence and then securing D's presence before a magistrates' court by a summons or by an arrest under a warrant. This method of instituting criminal proceedings by laying an information for the purpose of obtaining a summons is no longer available to a relevant prosecutor authorised to issue a requisition;
(3) by an arrest under a warrant, followed by a charge; or
(4) by an arrest without a warrant, followed by a charge.

Relevant prosecutors

A 'relevant prosecutor' is:

(a) a police force;
(b) the DPP;
(c) the Attorney General;
(d) the Director of the Serious Fraud Office;
(e) the Commissioners for Revenue and Customs, or of Inland Revenue;
(f) the Director General of the National Crime Agency;
(g) a Secretary of State;
(h) any person specified in an order made by the Secretary of State. The following have been so specified:
   (i) Transport for London;
   (ii) a local authority (other than a parish council or its equivalent);
   (iii) the Environment Agency, and the National Resources Body for Wales;
   (iv) a railway operator (for the purposes of prosecuting a 'railway offence', essentially a railway byelaw offence);
   (v) a Croydon, Manchester or Nottingham tramcar operator;
   (vi) a television licensing enforcement body (for the purposes of enforcing a 'relevant offence');

or, in each case above, a person authorised by such a body or person to institute criminal proceedings.

An order under (h) in the list above specifying a person must also specify whether that person and a person authorised by that person to institute criminal proceedings:

(a) are authorised to issue written charges, requisitions and single justice procedure notices; or
(b) are authorised to issue only written charges and single justice procedure notices.

Transport for London (TfL) and a person so authorised by TfL are authorised to issue written charges, requisitions and single justice procedure notices. The other persons listed in (ii)–(vi), or persons so authorised by them, are only authorised to issue written charges and single justice procedure notices. If they wish to proceed otherwise than by such a notice, they must proceed by going down the laying of information route referred to at (2) on p 15.

Written charge or information

A written charge or information must contain:

(a) a statement of the offence which describes the offence 'in ordinary language' and (if the offence is created by statute) identifies the legislation that creates it; and
(b) sufficient particulars of the conduct constituting the commission of the offence to make clear what the prosecutor alleges against D.

Where a number of incidents, taken together, amount to a course of conduct (having regard to the time, place or purpose of commission), those incidents may be included in the allegation. Moreover, a single document may contain more than one charge.

By the Magistrates' Courts Act 1980 (MCA 1980), s 127, a written charge or information relating to an offence triable only summarily cannot generally be tried unless it has been laid within six months from the time when the offence was committed. An example of an exception to this general rule is provided by the Vehicle Excise and Registration Act 1994, which permits an information (or written charge) to be laid in respect of offences of using or keeping a vehicle without a vehicle licence up to three years after the commission of the offence. The general rule does not apply to an information (or written charge) relating to an offence which is triable on indictment. There is no set time limit in the case of such an offence, unless its parent statute expressly provides one.

Requisition, single justice procedure notice or summons

A requisition requires the person on whom it is served to appear before a magistrates' court to answer the written charge.

A single justice procedure notice requires the person on whom it is served to serve on the designated officer for a magistrates' court specified in the notice a written notification stating:

(a) whether he desires to plead guilty or not guilty; and
(b) if he desires to plead guilty, whether or not he desires to be tried in accordance with the 'trial by single justice on the papers' provisions below.

Where a relevant prosecutor issues a written charge and a requisition, both documents must be served on the person concerned, and a copy of both must be served on the appropriate court officer. A corresponding rule applies where a relevant prosecutor issues a written charge and a single justice procedure notice. If a single justice procedure notice is served on a person, the relevant prosecutor must:

(a) at the same time serve on him such documents as prescribed by Criminal Procedure Rules; and
(b) serve copies of those documents on the designated officer specified in the notice.

A summons is a written order issued by a justice of the peace or by a justices' clerk (or authorised assistant) on behalf of a justice. It is directed to the person named in an information and requires him to appear before a magistrates' court to answer the charge against him.

A requisition or summons must contain a notice setting out when and where D must attend the court, and must specify each offence in respect of which it has been issued.

Additionally, a summons must identify the issuing court, and a requisition must identify the person under whose authority it is issued.

Other types of summonses

These are mentioned here for convenience.

Summonses for a breach of the peace

A summons may also be issued as a result of a complaint. A complaint is a written or verbal allegation made before a justice in respect of anything which is within the civil jurisdiction of a magistrates' court to make an order. Of particular importance to a police officer is the fact that a complaint may be made to the effect that a person has committed a breach of the peace. Breach of the peace is not in itself a criminal offence. If the complaint is proved, that person may be bound over to keep the peace. A magistrates' court has jurisdiction to hear any complaint.

Summonses in respect of a witness

Where a justice of the peace or justices' clerk (or authorised assistant) is satisfied that any person in England or Wales, or outside the British Isles, is likely to be able to give material evidence, or to produce any document or thing likely to be material evidence, at the summary trial of a written charge or information or the hearing of a complaint by a magistrates' court, and it is in the interests of justice to issue a summons to secure the attendance of that person to give evidence or produce the document or thing, the justice may issue a summons requiring that person to attend before the court to give evidence or to produce the thing or document. Unlike other summonses, such a summons may not be served by post. A justice may refuse to issue a witness summons if he is not satisfied that the application was made as soon as reasonably practicable after D pleaded not guilty. Crown Courts are also empowered to issue witness summonses in prescribed circumstances.

Service of requisitions, single justice procedure notices or summonses

A requisition, single justice procedure notice or summons may be served on an individual:

(a) by handing it to him (except that if he is under 18, it must be handed to a parent, guardian, or other appropriate adult if such a person is readily available);
(b) by leaving it at the appropriate address for service (ie an address in England and Wales where it is reasonably believed that he will receive it); or
(c) by sending it to that address by first class post or by the equivalent of first class post;

and may be served on a corporation:

(i) by handing it to a person holding a senior position in that corporation;
(ii) by leaving it at the appropriate address for service (ie the corporation's principal office in England and Wales, and if there is no readily identifiable principal office then any place in England and Wales where it carries on its activities or business); or
(iii) by sending it to that address by first class post or the equivalent of first class post.

In addition, service of a requisition, single justice procedure notice or summons can be effected by the use of document exchange (DX) or by electronic means.

Service by document exchange   Where the person to be served has given a DX box number, and has not refused to accept service by DX, a requisition, single justice procedure notice or summons may be served:

(a) by addressing it to that person at that DX box number; and
(b) leaving it at the DX at which the addressee has that DX box number, or a DX at which the person serving it has a DX box number.

Service by electronic means   Where the person to be served has given an electronic address and has not refused to accept service at that address, or is given access to an electronic address at which a document may be deposited and has not refused to accept service by the deposit of a document at that address, a requisition, single justice procedure notice or summons may be served:

(a) by sending it by electronic means to that electronic address; or
(b) by depositing it at an electronic address to which the recipient has been given access and:
  (i)   in every case, making it possible for the recipient to read the document, or view or listen to its content, as the case may be;
  (ii)   unless the court otherwise directs, making it possible for the recipient to make and keep an electronic copy of the document; and
  (iii) notifying the recipient of the deposit of the document (which notice may be given by electronic means).

Where a document is so served, the person serving it need not provide a paper copy as well.

A document served by handing it over is served on the day it is handed over. Unless something different is shown, a document served on a person by any other method is served:

(a) in the case of a document left at an address, on the next business day after the day on which it was left;
(b) in the case of a document sent by first class post or by the equivalent of first class post, on the second business day after the day on which it was posted or dispatched;
(c) in the case of a document served by DX, on the second business day after the day on which it was left at a DX as permitted under the above rule;
(d) in the case of a document served by electronic means:
  (i)   on the day on which it is sent by sending it by electronic means to the address which the recipient has given, if that day is a business day and if it is sent by no later than 14.30 on that day;
  (ii)   on the day on which notice of its deposit is given, if that day is a business day and if that notice is given by no later than 14.30 that day; or
  (iii) otherwise, on the next business day after it was sent or such notice was given; and
(e) in any case, on the day on which the addressee responds to it, if that is earlier.

Unless something different is shown, a document produced by a computer system for dispatch by post is to be taken as having been sent by first class post, or by the equivalent of first class post, to the addressee on the business day after the day on which it was produced.

Proof of service is usually by means of a certificate of service signed by the person who effected the service, explaining how and when service was made.

A requisition, single justice procedure notice or summons may be served, in accordance with rules of court, in Scotland or Northern Ireland. The same is true vice versa in respect of a Northern Irish summons. A Scottish citation may be served in England and Wales in the same way as may be done in Scotland.

Special provision is made as to service on a person outside the UK by the Crime (International Co-operation) Act 2003 and the Criminal Procedure Rules 2015, and as to service on an overseas company by the Companies Act 2006, s 1139.

Warrants of arrest

A justice of the peace may issue a warrant to arrest when a written information is laid before him to the effect that a person has, or is suspected of having, committed an offence.

No such warrant may be issued for the arrest of an adult unless:

(a) the offence to which the warrant relates is an indictable offence or is punishable with imprisonment, or
(b) as from a day to be appointed, his address is not sufficiently established for a summons, or a written charge or requisition, to be served on him.

Where the offence charged is an indictable offence:

(a) a warrant may be issued at any time notwithstanding that a requisition or summons has previously been issued; and
(b) a warrant may be issued upon a copy of a written charge (rather than an information) being laid by a relevant prosecutor after the previous issue of a written charge and requisition.

Where a person who is not a relevant prosecutor authorised to issue requisitions lays an information in respect of:

(a) a 'qualifying offence' alleged to have been committed outside the UK or
(b) an offence of attempting, conspiring or encouraging or assisting the commission of such an offence where it is alleged that the qualifying offence was, or would have been, committed outside the UK,

no arrest warrant may be issued without the consent of the DPP. A 'qualifying offence' means an offence under the Criminal Justice Act 1988, s 134 (torture: see p 666), the Aviation Security Act 1982, ss 1, 2, or 6 (hijacking, etc), or the Aviation and Maritime Security Act 1990, s 1 (endangering safety at aerodromes) or ss 9 to 14 (hijacking ships, etc) or certain other offences (eg grave breaches of Geneva Conventions and offences relating to nuclear material) over which the UK has asserted jurisdiction regardless of where in the world the offence is committed and regardless of the nationality of D or the victim. These provisions are designed to make it more difficult to arrest in this country foreign ministers and officials who are suspected by groups such as Amnesty International of being war criminals.

Arrest warrants issued by judicial authorities in EU countries may be executed in the UK.

An arrest warrant directs its addressee: (a) to arrest the accused; and (b) bring him before the magistrates' court named in it. However, by way of exception in respect of (b), an arrest warrant may be endorsed with a direction that on arrest the person to be arrested shall be released on bail, with or without sureties. This is known as 'backing for bail'.

An arrest warrant may be executed anywhere in England and Wales by any constable. Alternatively, it may be executed by an authorised civilian enforcement officer or an approved enforcement agency.

An arrest warrant remains in force until executed or withdrawn. If the original is lost a justice may issue a replacement.

As to charging a person arrested under a warrant, see Chapter 5.

Other warrants

For the sake of completeness, mention is made of some other warrants which may be issued by a justice or magistrates' court on an information being laid.

Warrant to arrest a witness   Such a warrant may be issued by a justice, who is satisfied that a person who could give material evidence, etc is unlikely to attend court voluntarily. Such a warrant will only be issued where a summons would be ineffective.

Warrants of control or commitment   Under MCA 1980, s 76, a magistrates' court may issue a warrant of control or of commitment where a person is in default of payment of a sum adjudged to be paid by a conviction or order of a magistrates' court.

A warrant of control empowers an authorised civil enforcement officer or approved enforcement agency to take control of goods (other than 'exempt goods') and sell them to recover that sum. 'Exempt goods' include the defaulter's clothing, bedding, furniture, household equipment and household provisions, and (up to an aggregate value of £1,350) items or equipment necessary for use by the defaulter for his trade, employment or education. It is an offence under MCA 1980, s 78(4) for any person to remove the goods, or the marks placed on them to signify seizure.

A warrant of commitment orders the defaulter to be arrested and committed to prison. It may be issued *either* where it appears on the return to a warrant of control that the defaulter's assets are insufficient to pay the amount outstanding *or* instead of a warrant of control. If the magistrates' court considers this expedient, it may fix a term of imprisonment and suspend the issue of the warrant until such time and on such conditions as it thinks fit. A receipt must be obtained for the defaulter when he is handed over to a prison pursuant to a warrant of commitment.

Search warrant   This type of warrant is discussed in Chapter 3.

Execution of warrants

A warrant of arrest, or of control, or of commitment, or a search warrant, may be executed anywhere in England and Wales by any person to whom it is directed, or by any constable acting in his police area.

In addition, by the Criminal Justice and Public Order Act 1994, s 136 a warrant issued in England, Wales or Northern Ireland for the arrest or commitment of a person (or a like warrant issued in Scotland) may, without endorsement, be executed in one of the other home countries by a constable of a police force of the country of issue or of the country of execution or by a British Transport Police constable, as well as by any other persons within the directions of the warrant. As in the case of other arrest warrants, a constable who arrests the person named in the warrant is not liable for false imprisonment if that person is in fact innocent of the offence, unless there is malice on the part of the constable.

A search warrant may not be executed by a person entitled to execute it who does not have it in his possession at the time.

The following types of warrant may be executed by a constable, although he is not in possession of the warrant:

(a) warrant to arrest a person in connection with an offence;
(b) warrant under the armed forces legislation (desertion, etc);
(c) warrant relating to the non-appearance of a defendant, warrants of control, warrants of commitment and warrants issued to arrest a potentially unwilling witness;
(d) warrant of arrest under the Family Law Act 1996, s 47(8) (failure to comply with occupation order or non-molestation order); and
(e) warrant of arrest under the Powers of Criminal Courts (Sentencing) Act 2000, Sch 1, para 3(2) (offender referred to court by youth offender panel).

However, a warrant referred to in this paragraph must, on the demand of the person concerned, be shown to him as soon as practicable.

Entry to execute warrants

The Police and Criminal Evidence Act 1984 (PACE), s 17 permits a constable to enter and search premises, including any vehicle, vessel, aircraft or tent, in specified circumstances for the purpose of executing a warrant of arrest issued in connection with or arising out of criminal proceedings, or a warrant of commitment issued under the MCA 1980, s 76. See p 69.

Arrest without a warrant, followed by charge

This is dealt with later in Chapters 3 and 5.

CLASSIFICATION OF OFFENCES BY METHOD OF TRIAL

Offences can be classified as indictable offences or summary offences, according to their mode of trial.

'Indictable offence' means an offence which, if committed by an adult, is triable in the Crown Court, whether it is exclusively so triable (eg murder or robbery) or triable either way, ie in the Crown Court or a magistrates' court (eg unlawful wounding or fraud).

'Summary offence' means an offence which, if committed by an adult, is triable only in a magistrates' court (eg most driving offences).

The vast majority of offences are summary ones. *Where an offence is indictable (whether triable only on indictment or triable either way) this will be stated at an appropriate point in the text. Otherwise, it should be assumed that the offence is only summary.*

COURTS OF CRIMINAL JURISDICTION

There are two methods of trying persons accused of criminal offences. One is by judge and (almost invariably) jury in the Crown Court; the other is summarily by a magistrates' court without a jury. With a few exceptions, all criminal proceedings in the Crown Court begin in a magistrates' court since a defendant (D) tried in the Crown Court must normally have been sent for trial there by a magistrates' court.

Magistrates' courts

A magistrates' court is normally composed of two or three justices of the peace, but some functions can be discharged by a single justice. A notable exception is the trial by a single justice on the papers procedure described on p 23.

The normal sittings of a magistrates' court take place in a properly appointed courthouse on appointed days of the week. On other occasions, or in other places, a court may sit as an occasional court but with quite limited powers. A District Judge (Magistrates' Courts), a legally qualified, salaried magistrate, may sit alone and has all the powers of two lay justices.

The court is advised by a legally qualified justices' clerk. Some matters authorised to be done by, to or before a single justice may be done before a justices' clerk or an assistant clerk.

A magistrates' court has jurisdiction in relation to a range of civil matters, some of which are described later in this book.

In criminal matters a magistrates' court has jurisdiction in relation to the following matters.

Offences triable summarily only

A magistrates' court has jurisdiction to try any summary offence alleged to have been committed by a person who appears or is brought before the court.

A person appearing before a magistrates' court does so either in answer to a requisition or summons, or under arrest.

Guilty plea   A person (D) who appears before the court will have the charge read over to him and will be asked if he pleads guilty or not guilty. If D pleads guilty the court must be satisfied that it is a clear and unequivocal plea. On a plea of guilty being entered, the court may convict without hearing evidence. In practice, however, the facts of the case are outlined by the prosecution, and D or his legal representative is at liberty to dispute those facts should he wish to do so and may also put before the court any mitigating facts which he feels that the court should consider before passing sentence. Usually the court will also hear any evidence by the prosecutor of any previous recorded convictions of D and of his general character in order to enable it to decide the appropriate penalty. D may also ask the court to take into consideration, when passing sentence, other offences which he has committed.

Pleading guilty by post   In the case of many offences triable summarily only, the Magistrates' Courts Act 1980 (MCA 1980), s 12 permits pleas of guilty to be entered at a magistrates' court (or where D is 16 or 17 when the summons or requisition is issued, at a youth court) without the necessity for D to attend the proceedings, or for any witnesses to be called. There are certain conditions which must be met in respect of the offence:

(a) the proceedings must be by way of requisition or summons;
(b) the offence must not be one specified by the Secretary of State;
(c) D, when served with the requisition or summons for the offence, must also have
     been served with:
     (i)   a notice explaining the prescribed procedure;
     (ii) *either* a concise statement of such facts relating to the charge as will be placed
           before the court if D pleads guilty without appearing before the court, *or* a
           copy of such signed written statement(s) complying with the Criminal Justice
           Act 1967, s 9(2)(b) ((a) on p 251) (proof by written statement) as will be so
           placed in those circumstances; and

(iii) if any information relating to D (ie information relevant to sentence) will, or may in the circumstances, be placed before the court by or on behalf of the prosecutor, a notice containing or describing the information; and

(d) D or his solicitor must have notified the designated officer that he wishes to plead guilty. On receipt of this notification, the officer will inform the prosecutor.

Where D does not appear and proof of service of the documents referred to in (c) is given, the court may hear and dispose of the case in the absence of D, the prosecutor or both. The documents are read to a court before a conviction is registered. The court is not required to conduct the proceedings in open court.

Should D appear even though the notification referred to in (d) has been received, the court may, with his consent, proceed as just described but D may make oral submissions with a view to mitigation of sentence, in place of any written submission which he may have sent.

Trial by single justice on the papers   MCA 1980, s 16A provides for such a trial. Under it, a magistrates' court which may consist of a single justice may try a written charge on the papers if the offence charged is a summary offence not punishable with imprisonment, and the defendant (D) was at least 18 when charged. The following conditions must be satisfied:

(a) *the following documents must have been served on D:*
  (i) *a written charge;*
  (ii) *a single justice procedure notice; and*
  (iii) *a summary of the prosecution's evidence, and a copy of any written statements (as described on p 22);*
  and service of all of the documents must have been effected at the same time;
(b) *if any information relevant to sentence relating to D will or may in the circumstances be placed before the court by or on behalf of the prosecutor, a notice containing or describing the information must have been served on D;*
(c) *separate notices for D's use if D wants to plead guilty, if D wants to plead guilty but wants the case dealt with at a hearing by a court consisting of more than one justice, or if D wants to plead not guilty, must have been served on D; and*
(d) *D must not have not served on the designated officer specified in the single justice procedure notice (the designated officer) within 21 days after service of the above documents, a written notification stating either:*
  (i) *a desire to plead not guilty; or*
  (ii) *a desire not to be tried in accordance with the trial by a single justice on the papers provisions.*

The court may not hear any oral evidence and may consider only the contents of the following:

(a) the documents specified in (a) to (c) above ('the specified documents');
(b) any document containing information described in a notice served on D at the same time as the specified documents, provided a copy of the notice has been served on the designated officer; and
(c) any written submission that D makes with a view to mitigation of sentence.

The court may disregard a written submission that is not served on the designated officer within the above 21-day period.

The court is not required to conduct the proceedings in open court. It may try the charge in the absence of the parties and, if a party appears, must proceed as if the party were absent.

If D served on the designated officer a written notification stating a desire to plead guilty and to be tried in accordance with the trial by a single justice on the papers provisions, the court may try the charge as if D had pleaded guilty.

The court may not remand D.

If a magistrates' court decides, before D is convicted of the offence, that it is not appropriate to convict D in proceedings conducted in accordance with the above provisions, the court may not try or continue to try the charge in that way.

A magistrates' court may not try a written charge in accordance with the above provisions if, at any time before the trial, D or D's legal representative on his behalf gives notice to the designated officer that D does not desire to be tried in accordance with them.

If a magistrates' court may not try or continue to try a written charge in accordance with the above provisions because the *italicised conditions* on p 23 are not satisfied or because it decides that it is inappropriate to convict D in accordance with the above provisions or because a notice has been given that D does not desire to be tried in accordance with them, the magistrates' court must:

(a) adjourn the trial, if it has begun; and
(b) issue a summons directed to D requiring him to appear before a traditional magistrates' court for the trial of the written charge. A magistrates' court issuing such a summons may consist of a single justice.

If a magistrates' court decides, after D is convicted of the offence, that it is not appropriate to try the written charge in accordance with the above provisions, the court may not continue to try the charge in that way. If a magistrates' court trying a written charge in accordance with the above provisions proposes, after D is convicted of the offence, to order him to be disqualified under the Road Traffic Offenders Act 1988, s 34 or s 35 (pp 382, 385), it must give D the opportunity to make representations about the proposed disqualification, and, if he indicates a wish to make such representations, the court may not continue to try the case in accordance with the above provisions. In either case, the court must adjourn the trial and issue a summons directed to D requiring him to appear before a traditional magistrates' court to be dealt with in respect of the offence in the normal way.

Not guilty plea   If D pleads not guilty the court must hear the evidence and, at the request of either party, the court will order all witnesses out of court so that evidence may be presented independently. The proceedings will be opened by the prosecution outlining the facts of the case and calling its witnesses one by one to give evidence to the court. Each witness will either take the oath or affirm, and will give evidence during examination-in-chief. After the prosecution has asked questions to introduce and identify the witness, it may not ask leading questions in relation to the facts in issue. Leading questions are those which may usually be answered 'yes' or 'no'. For example, a prosecutor may not ask, 'Did you see the defendant standing outside the premises at 2 East Street?' but instead should ask, 'Where was the defendant when you saw him?'

When a witness has given evidence for the prosecution he may be *cross-examined* by the defence upon any aspect of the evidence which he has given. Leading questions may be asked. Questions put in cross-examination (a) must be calculated to elicit answers which are directly relevant to an issue in the case, or (b) must be calculated to test the credibility of the evidence or to diminish its value. In respect of (a), cross-examination is not limited to matters arising during the examination-in-chief; it may relate to anything relevant to an issue in the case. Questions may be asked in respect of new facts unexpectedly introduced in the witness's testimony which do not form part of the cross-examining side's case and could not reasonably have been anticipated.

At the conclusion of the cross-examination the prosecution has a right to *re-examine* the witness upon *any new facts* which have come to light, or to clear up ambiguities which might have arisen, during cross-examination. Leading questions may not be put, nor may new evidence be introduced.

D or his legal representative may then address the court, whether or not he calls witnesses. PACE 1984, s 79, which also applies to trials in the Crown Court, requires that, if the defence intends to call two or more witnesses to the facts of the case and those witnesses include D, D must be called before the other witness or witnesses unless the court in its discretion otherwise directs. Such a direction is likely where, for instance, a witness is to speak of an occurrence before the matters about which D is to give evidence.

When a witness for the defence, including D, has given his evidence, he may be cross-examined by the prosecution and may then be re-examined by the defence on any new facts or ambiguities which have arisen during the cross-examination.

When the prosecution and defence have finished calling their evidence, each side has a right to address the court (except that the prosecution does not have the right if D has not called witnesses and is not legally represented), the prosecution's closing speech coming before that of the defence.

The court may adjourn to consider its verdict and may seek the advice of its clerk by specific request. If it decides to convict, its pronouncement of this verdict will usually be followed by evidence by the prosecutor of any previous recorded convictions of D and of his general character in order to enable the court to decide on the appropriate penalty. A plea in mitigation may be made by D or his legal representative. D may also take the opportunity to ask the court to take into consideration, when passing sentence, other offences which he has committed.

Before beginning to try an offence, or at any time during such proceedings, a magistrates' court may adjourn the proceedings to a time which it fixes. It may remand D, either in custody or on bail. If the remand is in custody, the remand will be for a maximum of eight clear days; if D is allowed bail, the remand may be for longer with the consent of both parties. Remands may be for longer periods after conviction where the proceedings are adjourned for a medical report or for other enquiries to be undertaken.

Offences triable either way: where to be tried

An offence which is triable either way may be tried either on indictment in the Crown Court or summarily in a magistrates' court. Where it is tried depends on the following rules.

Indication of intended plea Unless a notice has been given under the Crime and Disorder Act 1998 (CDA 1998), s 51B or s 51C (below), where someone aged 18 or over (D) appears or is brought before a magistrates' court charged with an either-way offence, the court must cause the charge to be written down, if this has not already been done, and to be read to D. The court must explain to D that he may indicate whether (if the offence were to proceed to trial) he would plead guilty or not guilty, and that if he indicates that he would plead guilty:

(a) the court must proceed as if the proceedings constituted from the beginning the summary trial of the offence, and the court had asked whether he pleaded guilty or not guilty; and

(b) he may be committed for sentence to the Crown Court if the court is of the opinion that a Crown Court sentence should be available.

The court must then ask D whether (if the offence were to proceed to trial) he would plead guilty or not guilty. If he indicates that he would plead guilty the court must proceed as if the proceedings constituted from the beginning the summary trial of the offence and D had pleaded guilty. If the court is of the opinion that one of the specified grounds exists the court may commit D in custody or on bail to the Crown Court for sentence.

Special provision is made in the case of a person who, by reason of disorderly conduct before the court, makes it impracticable to proceed in that manner. In such a case, a court may proceed in D's absence but in the presence of his legal representative who may make the choices in relation to mode of trial.

If D (or his legal representative) indicates that he would plead not guilty, or fails to indicate how he would plead, the court must go on to the next stage.

Allocation of trial proceedings   The next stage is that the court must decide in 'allocation of trial proceedings' whether the offence appears to be more suitable for summary trial or for trial on indictment. Before making a decision the court must give the prosecutor an opportunity to disclose any previous convictions (including convictions under the law of another EU member state for an offence corresponding to an offence under English law), and both parties must be given an opportunity to make representations about the mode of trial. The court must consider whether the sentencing powers of a magistrates' court would be adequate for the offence(s), together with the representations made by both parties.

Where a summary trial appears to be more suitable the court must explain to D that summary trial appears to be more suitable and that he can either consent to be so tried or, if he wishes, be tried on indictment and that, if tried summarily and convicted, he may be committed to a Crown Court for sentence. At this stage, D may request an indication of whether a custodial or a non-custodial sentence would be more likely to be imposed if he were to be tried summarily and plead guilty. The court may or may not give such an indication. If it does, it must ask D whether, on the basis of the indication, he wishes to change his plea. If D indicates that he would plead guilty the court must proceed to summary trial. Where the court does not give an indication as to sentence, or D does not indicate that he would plead guilty, the court must ask D whether he consents to summary trial or wishes to be tried on indictment. If he consents, the court must proceed to summary trial. In a case where a court has indicated whether or not a custodial sentence would be imposed no court may impose such a sentence unless that possibility was indicated. There is only one exception; it relates to the second type of committal for sentence described on p 28.

If D does not consent to summary trial, or the court decides that the offence appears to be more suitable for trial on indictment, or the prosecution requests that the offence be tried on indictment, the court must proceed to send D to the Crown Court for trial.

Children and young persons   The above provisions about indication of intended plea and allocation of proceedings do not apply in the case of a child or young person (ie someone under 18), but similar provisions apply in respect of an indication of intended plea. As to sending a juvenile to the Crown Court, see below and pp 27 and 29.

Notice under CDA 1998, s 51B or 51C   If a notice is served on a magistrates' court under CDA 1998, s 51B or s 51C, the effect is that the magistrates must forthwith send D, regardless of his age, to the Crown Court for trial; they cannot allocate the case for summary trial if the offence is an either-way one. By s 51B, in *serious or complex fraud cases* a notice may be given by a designated authority (the DPP, the Director of the Serious Fraud Office, or the Secretary of State) in respect of an indictable offence where the authority is satisfied that there is sufficient evidence for the person charged to be put on trial and that a case of fraud of such seriousness or complexity is revealed making it appropriate that the management of the case should, without delay, be taken over by the Crown Court. By s 51C, in *certain offences involving child witnesses*, the DPP may give such a notice if he is of the opinion that the evidence is sufficient for the person to be put on trial for the offence; that a child would be called as a witness at the trial; and that, for the purpose of avoiding prejudice to the welfare of the child, the case should be taken over by the Crown Court and proceed without delay. The offences are sexual offences; those which involve an assault on, or injury or a threat of injury to, a person; cruelty to a person under 16; making, etc indecent photographs etc of a child; kidnapping, false imprisonment or child abduction; slavery, servitude, or forced or compulsory labour; human trafficking; and encouragement or assistance, attempt or conspiracy to commit, aiding, abetting, counselling, procuring or inciting such offences. For these purposes a child is a person who is under the age of 17, or a person of whom a video recording was made when he was under the age of 17 with a view to its admission as evidence-in-chief in the trial.

Sending cases to Crown Court for trial

Where an *adult* (D) appears or is brought before a magistrates' court charged with an offence which is triable on indictment only, or where (under the above provisions) an offence triable either way is not to be tried by a magistrates' court, or where a notice under CDA 1998, s 51B or s 51C has been given, the court must send D forthwith to the Crown Court for trial. It may at the same time send D for trial for any related either-way offence, and for a related summary offence if it satisfies the 'requisite conditions', namely is punishable with imprisonment or involves obligatory or discretionary disqualification from driving. Other adult persons who are jointly charged with D with an either-way offence for which D is sent for trial must be sent for trial if they appear before the magistrates' court on the same occasion as D (and may be so sent if they appear later). If another such adult is so sent in respect of an either-way offence with which he is jointly charged with D, he must also be sent for trial in respect of any either-way offence, or any summary offence which meets the 'requisite conditions', related to that offence. In addition, where a court sends an adult for trial in this way, it must (if it considers it necessary in the interests of justice) also send for trial a child or young person who is jointly charged with the adult with an indictable offence for which the adult is sent for trial, or an indictable offence related to that offence. If it does, it may also send the child or young person for trial for any related either-way offence or any related summary offence which meets the 'requisite conditions', if it considers it necessary to do so in the interests of justice.

Generally, *children and young persons* have to be tried summarily in a youth court (or sometimes a magistrates' court other than a youth court); see below. However, in the following cases a person under 18 may be sent to the Crown Court for trial. The first, mentioned above, is where such a person is charged jointly with an adult with an indictable offence for which the adult is sent for trial, or an indictable offence related to that offence. The second is where a child or young person appears or is brought before a magistrates' court charged with an offence for which any of the following conditions is satisfied:

(a) the offence is one of homicide;

(b) the offence is one of a number of particular types of offence of possessing a prohibited weapon and the accused young person was aged 16 or 17 when he committed it;

(c) the offence is one in respect of which a long period of detention may be ordered and the court considers that such a sentence ought to be possible;

(d) a notice has been served under CDA 1998, s 51B or s 51C in respect of the child or young person; or

(e) the offence is a 'specified offence', namely one of a range of violent or sexual offences, and it appears to the magistrates' court that if the defendant child or young person is found guilty of the offence the criteria for an extended sentence would be met.

If one of the conditions (a)–(e) is satisfied, the magistrates' court must send the child or young person for trial. In such a case, it may also send the child for trial for any related indictable offence or any relevant summary offence which meets the 'requisite conditions'.

Where a court sends a child or young person for trial in such a case it may also send for trial an adult person who is jointly charged with an either-way offence or a related either-way offence or a related summary offence which meets the 'requisite conditions'.

The court is required to give notice of the offence or offences for which a person is sent for trial and the place at which the trial is to take place. A copy of this notice must be served on D and given to the Crown Court.

Live television links at certain preliminary hearings

Under CDA 1998, s 57B, where it appears to a magistrates' court before which a preliminary hearing is to take place that the defendant (D) is likely to be held in 'custody' (a term which does not include police detention but does include secure juvenile accommodation) during a preliminary hearing, the court may require D to attend the hearing via a live link from the place where he is held.

Section 57B also applies to a preliminary hearing in the Crown Court.

A magistrates' court may also make a live link direction under s 57C where D is in police detention at a police station in connection with the offence in question and appears likely to remain there until the beginning of the preliminary hearing, or where D is at a police station in answer to live link bail (see p 173) in connection with the offence.

A live link direction may not be given under s 57C unless the court is satisfied that it is not contrary to the interests of justice to give the direction.

Committal for sentence

Where a person aged 18 or over (or his legal representative) has indicated an intention to plead guilty to an either-way offence and the magistrates' court considers that the offence, or the combination of the offence and one or more offences associated with it, was so serious that the Crown Court should have the power to deal with him, the court may commit him, in custody or on bail, to the Crown Court for sentence for that offence and any related either-way offences to which he has also pleaded guilty. Similar provisions are made in respect of children and young persons.

There are special provisions in respect of dangerous adult offenders who have been convicted on a summary trial of an offence triable either way. If it appears to the court that the 'dangerous offender criteria' would be met for the imposition of extended sentences, the court must commit the offender in custody or on bail to the Crown Court for sentence. Similar provision is made in respect of dangerous young offenders, although there is simply a power (rather than an obligation) to commit in such a case.

In all cases, the Crown Court may deal with the offender in any way in which it could have dealt with him had he been tried and convicted before that court.

Youth courts

A youth court is a summary court (ie a magistrates' court) and is composed of justices who are specially appointed because of their qualifications. It sits for the purpose of hearing any charge against a child or young person or to exercise any other jurisdiction conferred on youth courts by the Courts Act 2003 or any other enactment.

The general public do not have a right of access to proceedings in a youth court.

A magistrates' court before which a person under 18 (hereafter described as a 'juvenile') appears charged with an offence which, in the case of an adult, is triable only on indictment or triable either way must deal with it *summarily* unless provisions on pp 27–8 relating to a juvenile apply.

With certain exceptions, no charge against a juvenile may be heard summarily by a magistrates' court other than a youth court. The exceptions, which allow trial by an 'adult' magistrates' court, are:

(a) where the juvenile is charged jointly with an adult;
(b) where an adult is charged with aiding, abetting, counselling, procuring, allowing, or permitting an offence with which a juvenile is charged;
(c) where a juvenile is charged with aiding, etc an offence committed by an adult;
(d) where the fact that the person is a juvenile is discovered in the course of proceedings in a magistrates' court; and
(e) where the charge against a juvenile arises out of circumstances which are the same as, or are connected with, those which give rise to an offence by an adult (eg a theft by a youth and a handling by an adult).

The law recognises the specialist nature of youth courts by requiring a Crown Court or adult magistrates' court which finds a juvenile guilty of an offence other than homicide to send the case to a youth court for sentencing as if that juvenile had been found guilty by that court, unless satisfied that it would be undesirable to do so. In effect, subject to that exception, they must send the case to the youth court for sentence to be passed.

The 'pleading guilty by post' provisions described on pp 22–3 do not generally apply to proceedings in a youth court. The only exception is where D is aged 16 or 17 when the requisition or summons is issued.

The sentencing powers of courts generally are limited in relation to children and young persons.

Crown Court

The Crown Court has jurisdiction over all offences which are triable only on indictment and also over offences triable either way in respect of which D has been sent for trial on indictment. Trials on indictment are heard with a jury who determine the issue of guilt after a direction on the relevant law by the judge. A trial can be without a jury where there is a risk of jury tampering.

Indictable offences are divided into three classes for the purposes of trial in the Crown Court; these classes depend on the seriousness of the offence. When sending a person to a Crown Court, magistrates' courts will send him to the appropriate tier of the Crown Court according to this classification.

A person who has been convicted by a magistrates' court may appeal to the Crown Court against sentence if he pleaded guilty, or against conviction or sentence if he pleaded not guilty. Appeals are heard by a court consisting of a judge and no more than four justices of the peace. The Crown Court also deals with people committed to it by a magistrates' court for sentence. These cases are determined by a judge sitting alone.

The Central Criminal Court in London is a Crown Court.

Queen's Bench Division of the High Court

One function of the High Court is to hear appeals on points of law from magistrates' courts or from the Crown Court in respect of appeals from magistrates' courts to the Crown Court. Such an appeal is known as appeal by case stated, since the magistrates' court or Crown Court is asked to 'state a case', that is set out its reasons for its finding on the basis of its interpretation of the law in relation to the facts found by it. The High Court is not concerned with any form of retrial.

Cases of the above type are dealt with by the Administrative Court, which is part of the Queen's Bench Division. They are heard by a divisional court or a single judge. A divisional court consists of two (or sometimes three) judges.

Judicial review

Judges in the Administrative Court also deal with the *judicial review* of the decisions of a magistrates' court, the Crown Court in its appellate capacity or a range of other bodies. In such cases the court will examine whether there was authority or power by which the decision made could have been properly reached; whether the procedure followed the rules of natural justice; or whether the exercise of discretion was lawful. Thus the court is not examining the correctness of the decision on its merits but whether it was lawfully and reasonably reached.

Court of Appeal (Criminal Division)

Appeals to this division are normally heard by a court consisting of three judges.

If convicted of an offence on indictment before the Crown Court, a person may appeal to this court against *conviction* with the leave of the Court of Appeal or the trial judge. On an appeal against conviction, the Court of Appeal can dismiss the appeal, allow it and quash the conviction, or substitute a conviction for another offence if it appears that D should have been convicted of that offence, rather than the one of which he was actually convicted. If fresh evidence has come to light, the court may order a new trial. It may also do so in any other case where the interests of justice so require.

A person convicted on indictment before the Crown Court may appeal against *sentence* with the leave of the Court of Appeal, and so may a person who has been sentenced by the Crown Court on committal for sentence. On *appeal* against sentence, the Court of Appeal may vary a sentence but cannot increase it. However, the Attorney General may (in certain cases) refer a sentence to the Court of Appeal with its leave if it appears to him to be unduly lenient. On such a reference, the court may impose a more severe sentence.

CJA 2003, Part 9 permits a prosecutor to appeal to the Court of Appeal in relation to any ruling made by the judge within a trial on indictment, other than a ruling that a jury be discharged. Following notice, proceedings may be adjourned and the judge's ruling has no effect within the period of adjournment. Such an appeal may only be made against one ruling but in the case of a submission of 'no case to answer' other rulings may be specified which are related to that submission.

Supreme Court

The Supreme Court took over the House of Lords' judicial functions in 2009.

The Supreme Court is the highest court in the land and hears criminal appeals from the Court of Appeal or the Queen's Bench Division, but only where:

(a) the court has certified that a question of law of general public importance is involved; and

(b) the court or the Supreme Court is satisfied that the point of law is one which ought to be considered by the Supreme Court; and

(c) leave to appeal to the Supreme Court has been given by the court or the Supreme Court itself.

JURISDICTION OF ARMED SERVICE AUTHORITIES TO DEAL WITH CRIMINAL OFFENCES

The Acts relating to armed service personnel make provisions for concurrent jurisdiction in respect of civil and service courts. As a result, arrangements have been made between civilian and military prosecuting and investigating authorities governing how they will work together, decide issues of jurisdiction and, where necessary, decide how an allegation will be investigated.

PENALTY NOTICES FOR 'DISORDERLY BEHAVIOUR'

The Criminal Justice and Police Act 2001 (CJPA 2001), s 2 provides that a constable who has reason to believe that someone aged 18 or over has committed a 'penalty offence' *may* issue a 'penalty notice for disorder' (PND). (Note the comment at p 14.)

If the penalty offence is a 'relevant penalty offence', ie a penalty offence in relation to which there is an approved educational course, the constable may issue a penalty notice with an education option. A PND with an education option is a penalty notice that also offers recipients the opportunity to discharge their liability to be convicted of the penalty offence by paying for and completing an approved educational course related to the offence for which notice was given. An approved educational course means a course run as part of an educational course scheme established by the chief constable.

Penalty offences

'Penalty offences' under CJPA 2001 fall into two groups:

Offence-creating provision	Description of offence
First group	
Explosives Act 1875, s 80	Throwing fireworks in a thoroughfare
Criminal Law Act 1967, s 5(2)	Wasting police time or giving a false report
Criminal Justice Act 1967, s 91	Disorderly behaviour while drunk in a public place
Theft Act 1968, s 1	Theft (limited by *guidance* to retail thefts of goods not exceeding £100 inc VAT in value)

Offence-creating provision	Description of offence
Criminal Damage Act 1971, s 1(1)	Destroying or damaging property (limited by *guidance* to damage not exceeding £300)
Misuse of Drugs Act 1971, s 5(2)	Possession of various forms of cannabis and cannabis derivatives, etc
Public Order Act 1986, s 5	Behaviour likely to cause harassment, alarm or distress
Licensing Act 2003, s 141	Sale of alcohol to person who is drunk
Licensing Act 2003, s 146(1), (3)	Sale of alcohol to person under 18
Licensing Act 2003, s 149(3), (4)	Purchase of alcohol on behalf of person under 18, etc
Licensing Act 2003, s 151	Delivery of alcohol to person under 18 or allowing such delivery
Communications Act 2003, s 127(2)	Using a public electronic communications network in order to cause annoyance, inconvenience, or needless anxiety
Fireworks Act 2003, s 11	Contravention of a prohibition or failure to comply with a requirement imposed by or under fireworks regulations or making false statements
Fire and Rescue Services Act 2004, s 49	Knowingly giving a false alarm to person acting on behalf of a fire and rescue authority
Second group	
Licensing Act 1872, s 12	Being drunk in a highway, other public place, or licensed premises
Parks Regulation (Amendment) Act 1926, s 2(1) so far as it creates an offence against Parks Regulation Act 1872 relating to Royal Parks and Other Open Spaces Regulations 1997:	Failing to comply with, or contravening, those Regulations by:
(a) reg 3(3)	Littering
(b) reg 3(4)	Cycling except on park road or designated area
(c) reg 3(6)	Dog fouling
British Transport Commission Act 1949, s 55	Trespassing on a railway
British Transport Commission Act 1949, s 56	Throwing stones, etc at trains or other things on railways
Misuse of Drugs Act 1971, s 5(2)	Possession of khat and any preparation or other product containing khat

Offence-creating provision	Description of offence
Environmental Protection Act 1990, s 87	Depositing and leaving litter
Licensing Act 2003, s 149(1)	Purchase of alcohol by person under 18 on relevant premises
Licensing Act 2003, s 150	Consumption of alcohol by a person under 18 on relevant premises or allowing such consumption

Amount of penalty

The Penalties for Disorderly Behaviour (Amount of Penalty) Order 2002 prescribes penalties of £90 for the first group of offences, and £60 for the second group.

Effect of penalty notice

CJPA 2001, s 4 provides that, if a PND is given to a person (A) under s 2, and A asks to be tried for the alleged offence in the specified manner before the end of the suspended enforcement period (21 days beginning with the date the notice was given), proceedings may be brought against him. If, in the case of a PND that is not one with an education option, by the end of the suspended enforcement period the penalty has not been paid, and A has not made a request to be tried, a sum equal to one and a half times the amount of the penalty may be registered under s 8 for enforcement against A as a fine. In the case of a PND with an education option, a sum equal to one and a half times the amount of the penalty may be registered under s 8 for enforcement against A as a fine if, by the end of the suspended enforcement period:

(a) (i) A does not ask to attend an approved educational course relating to the offence to which the notice relates,
    (ii) A does not pay the penalty, or
    (iii) A does not request to be tried; or
(b) (i) A has asked to attend an approved education course, and
    (ii) A does not, in accordance with regulations, pay the course fee, start such a course, or complete such a course.

General restrictions on proceedings

The relevant provisions are in CJPA 2001, s 5.

Proceedings for the offence to which a PND relates may not be brought during the suspended enforcement period. If the penalty is paid before the end of the suspended enforcement period, no proceedings may be brought for the offence.

Proceedings for an offence to which a PND with an education option relates may not be brought against a person who has, by the end of the suspended enforcement period, asked to attend an approved educational course relating to the offence, unless (b) above applies. If the person to whom a PND with an education option is given:

(a) completes, in accordance with regulations, an approved educational course relating to the offence to which the notice relates, and
(b) pays the course fee in accordance with those regulations,

no proceedings may be brought for the offence.

Miscellaneous points

The provisions in respect of registration of penalties and sums payable in default, and enforcement, are the same as those provided in relation to the more widely available fixed penalties for road traffic offences; see Chapter 11.

It is not intended that a PND should always be issued in respect of the specified cases; the constable has discretion. PNDs are designed for minor and straightforward cases. More serious cases should be dealt with by using the traditional criminal process.

Community support officers and accredited persons may be designated or accredited to issue PNDs under CJPA 2001: see pp 292 and 294–5. An accredited person may not issue a notice in respect of those offences, of criminal damage, and of the other two offences involving drunkenness in a public place.

The issue of a PND for an offence and the payment of the penalty under it is only a bar to proceedings for the offence specified in the notice. Payment of the penalty is not an admission of guilt for that offence or any proof that it has been committed by A. It does not prevent proceedings against A for another offence. This is of obvious importance where it subsequently becomes apparent that that offence was committed in the course of the same incident.

A victim should be consulted about the possibility of a PND being given, but a witness cannot insist that the case is disposed of in a particular way. The Ministry of Justice issued guidance on PNDs in 2014.

CHAPTER 3
Police Powers

The description of police powers in this book focuses on the powers of police officers, ie 'constables' (members of police forces hold the status of constable, whatever their rank, and special constables). This is done for convenience because it must not be forgotten that some powers possessed by constables are exercisable by police civilians and accredited persons as explained on pp 291–5.

Conduct in breach or in excess of a relevant statutory or common law power may constitute a breach of a 'Convention right' under the Human Rights Act 1998 and may cause the police officer concerned to be liable in civil law or in criminal law. It may also result in disciplinary proceedings and render inadmissible evidence obtained as a result (pp 255 and 267).

Police powers must be used fairly, responsibly, with respect for the people to whom they apply and without unlawful discrimination. Under the Equality Act 2010, s 149, when police officers are carrying out their functions, they must have due regard to the need to eliminate unlawful discrimination, harassment, and victimisation; to advance equality of opportunity between people who share a relevant protected characteristic and people who do not; and to take steps to foster good relations between those persons. The 'protected characteristics' are age, disability, gender re-assignment, race, religion or belief, sex, sexual orientation, pregnancy, and maternity.

PACE

Throughout this book, but particularly in this and the next four chapters, references are made to the Police and Criminal Evidence Act 1984, hereafter PACE. Its provisions are law and therefore must be followed. Although non-compliance by a police officer is not in itself an offence or civil wrong, it may render unlawful the exercise of a police power or other conduct. It may also result in disciplinary proceedings or render inadmissible evidence obtained by it (pp 255 and 267).

PACE CODES OF PRACTICE

PACE, s 66 requires the Secretary of State to issue Codes of Practice, approved by both Houses of Parliament, in connection with the exercise of a wide range of powers by police officers. The Secretary of State may at any time revise a Code of Practice then in force. Such a revision does not require the approval of the Houses of Parliament, although it may be submitted for approval, but it must at least be laid before Parliament.

Eight PACE Codes of Practice have been issued and revised. They apply throughout England and Wales. They are: Code A (stop and search); Code B (search and seizure); Code C (detention, treatment and questioning of persons); Code D (identification); Code E (audio recording of interviews); Code F (visual recording of interviews);

Code G (arrest); and Code H (detention, treatment and questioning of persons detained under the Terrorism Act 2000, s 41 and Sch 8).

Annexes to a Code are provisions of the Code but guidance notes printed with the Code are technically not. They are, however, frequently referred to by the courts when considering whether there has been a breach of a Code.

The powers covered by the Codes must be used fairly, responsibly, with respect for people suspected of committing offences, and without unlawful discrimination.

Apart from the PACE Codes of Practice, there are a number of codes under other statutes which are referred to at the appropriate points.

Compliance with PACE Codes

The provisions of the PACE Codes are not law but they should be followed. By s 67(11), the Codes are admissible in evidence and may be taken into account by a court where relevant to any question in the proceedings. Conduct by a police officer which involves a breach of a Code may result in disciplinary proceedings.

Any person with police powers conferred by a designation or accreditation under the Police Reform Act 2002 (see pp 291–5) must have regard to relevant provisions of a Code in the exercise of powers and duties.

Breach of a Code's provisions does not of itself give rise to criminal or civil proceedings (s 67(10)). Evidence obtained in a way involving a breach of a Code may be ruled inadmissible.

Wherever the Codes require the prior authority or agreement of an officer of at least inspector or superintendent rank, a sergeant is treated as holding the rank of inspector, and a chief inspector as holding the rank of superintendent, if he has been authorised by a superintendent to perform the functions of the higher rank (PACE, s 107).

Gender-related issues

All searches and procedures should be carried out with courtesy, consideration and respect for the person concerned.

Certain provisions of the PACE Codes explicitly state that searches and other procedures may only be carried out by, or in the presence of, persons of the same sex as the person subject to the search or other procedure.

Annexes to Codes A, C and H contain general provisions dealing with the implications of this in respect of transgender individuals (including transsexuals) and transvestites. Police officers should show particular sensitivity when dealing with such persons. While there is no agreed definition of '*transgender*' (or 'trans'), it is generally used as an umbrella term to describe people whose gender identity (self-identification as being a woman, man, neither or both) differs from the sex they were registered as at birth. The term includes, but is not limited to, transsexual people. '*Transsexual*' means a person who is proposing to undergo, is undergoing, or has undergone a process (or part of a process) for the purpose of gender re-assignment by changing physiological or other attributes of that person's sex. This includes aspects of gender such as dress and title. '*Transvestite*' means a person of one gender who dresses in the clothes of a person of the opposite gender; a transvestite does not live permanently in the gender opposite to that person's birth sex.

Legally, the *gender* (and, accordingly, the sex) of an individual (P) is P's gender as registered at birth unless P possesses a gender recognition certificate (GRC), in which case P's gender is the acquired gender.

When establishing whether someone should be treated as being male or female the following approach, designed to minimise embarrassment and secure the person's co-operation, should be followed:

(1) The person (P) must not be asked whether P has a GRC.
(2) If there is no doubt as to whether P should be treated as being male or female, P should be dealt with as being of that sex.
(3) If at any time (including during the search or carrying out the procedure) there is doubt as to whether P should be treated or continue to be treated as being male or female:
    (a) P should be asked what gender P considers P to be. If P expresses a preference to be dealt with as a particular gender, P should be asked to indicate and confirm a preference by signing the custody record or, if a custody record has not been opened, the search record or the officer's notebook. Subject to (b) below, P should be treated according to that preference;
    (b) if there are grounds to doubt that the preference in (a) accurately reflects P's predominant lifestyle, eg if P asks to be treated as a woman but documents and other information make it clear that P lives predominantly as a man, P should be treated according to what appears to be P's predominant lifestyle;
    (c) if P is unwilling to express a preference, efforts should be made to determine P's predominant lifestyle and P should be treated as such;
    (d) if none of the above apply, P should be dealt with according to what reasonably appears to have been P's sex as registered at birth.

Once a decision has been made about which gender P is to be treated as having, each officer responsible for the search or procedure should where possible be advised before the search or procedure of any doubt as to P's gender and P should be informed the doubts have been disclosed.

Where the gender of P is established, the decision should be recorded either on the search record or in the officer's notebook, or, if applicable, in P's custody record. Where P elects which gender P considers P to be but is not treated in accordance with that preference, the reason must be recorded.

Information about an application for a GRC or about a successful applicant's gender before it became that person's acquired gender is 'protected information' and must not be disclosed by a police officer or police staff in contravention of the Gender Recognition Act 2004. Disclosure includes making a record which is read by others.

POLICE POWERS DESCRIBED IN THIS CHAPTER

Police powers are dealt with in the following order in this chapter:

(a) stop and search;
(b) road check;
(c) arrest;
(d) entry and search in relation to an arrest;
(e) search under a search warrant;
(f) interception of communications, surveillance and the conduct and use of 'covert human intelligence sources'; and
(g) authorisation of action in respect of property.

A judge in the Administrative Court has held that, where a police officer effects a stop, search or arrest under a power to do so, which the officer is justified in using, there is no requirement at common law for him to be aware of the legal origin of that power in order for its exercise to be lawful. The judge went on to express the point as follows:

> There is no requirement to call the statutory provision or the correct section or subsection to mind at the moment a police officer exercises any power of stop, arrest or search in order for its exercise to be lawful. An act is not unlawful because a police officer does not ask himself or forgets which power he had, provided that he had the power to do what he did with knowledge and belief which he had.

POWERS TO STOP AND SEARCH

Various statutes (eg PACE, s 1) give *every* constable (p 288) the power on reasonable suspicion to stop and search for particular articles, for example stolen or prohibited articles, controlled drugs, firearms, and poaching equipment.

Stop and search by a constable may be authorised under the Criminal Justice and Public Order Act 1994, s 60 (see p 44) if the necessary reasonable belief exists.

Code A: the Code of Practice for the Exercise by Police Officers of Statutory Powers of Stop and Search, and by Police Officers and Police Staff of Requirements to Record Public Encounters applies to the above powers of stop and search and also to:

(a) powers to search a person who has not been arrested in the exercise of a power to search premises; and
(b) specified powers in the Terrorism Prevention and Investigation Measures Act 2011 (TPIMA 2011), Sch 5, paras 6, 8 and 10 (see Chapter 28 on the companion website) to search an individual who has not been arrested.

On the other hand, Code A does not apply to the powers of stop and search under PACE, s 6 (powers of constables employed by statutory undertakers (bodies authorised by statute to carry out any railway, road transport, inland navigation, or harbour undertaking) on premises of statutory undertaker), or under the Aviation Security Act 1982, s 24B (hijacking), or to searches carried out for the purposes of examination under the Terrorism Act 2000 (TA 2000), Sch 7 (port and border controls) and to which the Code of Practice for Examining Officers issued under that Act applies, or to the powers of stop and search to which the Code of Practice issued under TA 2000, s 47AB (p 780) applies.

It must be emphasised that nothing in the provisions about stop and search affects the ability of an officer to speak to or question a person in the ordinary course of his duties without detaining the person or exercising any element of compulsion. When a police officer is trying to discover whether, or by whom, an offence has been committed he may question anyone from whom useful information might be obtained, subject to the restrictions imposed by Code C (Chapter 4). A person's unwillingness to reply does not alter this entitlement, but in the absence of a power to arrest or to detain in order to search, the person is free to leave at will and cannot be compelled to remain with the officer.

Power under PACE, s 1 to stop and search

PACE, s 1(2) states that a constable:

(a) may search any person or vehicle ('vehicle' includes vessels, aircraft and hovercraft), *and* anything which is in or on a vehicle, for stolen or prohibited articles or an article to which PACE, s 1(8A) applies or any firework to which s 1(8B) applies; and

(b) may detain persons or vehicles for the purpose of such a search.

Section 1(3) provides that a constable only has this power to search if he has *reasonable grounds for suspecting* (see further p 40) that he will find stolen or prohibited articles or an article to which s 1(8A) applies or any firework to which s 1(8B) applies; he must of course have such grounds *before* carrying out a search. Reasonable force may be used in the exercise of these powers, but every effort should be made to persuade a person to co-operate and force should only be used as a last resort. A compulsory search may only be made if it is established that the person is unwilling to co-operate.

The courts have held that the test of lawfulness of a search under s 1 is:

(a) whether the searching constable suspected that he would find stolen or prohibited articles or anything to which s 1(8A) or (8B) applies;

(b) assuming that that constable had the necessary suspicion, whether there was reasonable cause for that suspicion; and

(c) if the answer to (a) and (b) is 'yes', whether that constable exercised his discretion to make a search in accordance with the general principles for the exercise of executive discretion, ie the decision to search must have been made taking into account relevant matters and excluding irrelevant ones, it must have been made for a proper purpose, and it must not have been one that no reasonable constable (taking account of the relevant matters) could have made.

It is not necessarily essential that the searching constable reasonably suspect each and every individual member of a group to be carrying a prohibited article, etc before he can search the individual members of the group. A divisional court has held that, if (a) and (b) above have been satisfied in respect of the group, the issue in relation to searching the individual members goes to (c), namely whether the constable's decision to search the individuals, given his suspicion, reasonably held, went beyond the bounds of decision open to him under (c) in the circumstances in question.

Where a police officer has reasonable grounds to suspect that a person is in innocent possession of a specified article, the power to stop and search exists notwithstanding that there would be no power of arrest. However, every effort should be made to secure the voluntary production of the article before the power is resorted to.

A *'prohibited article'* is defined by s 1(8) as:

(a) an offensive weapon, defined by s 1(9) as any article made or adapted for use for causing injury to persons, or intended by the person having it with him for such use by him or by some other person; or

(b) an article made or adapted for use in the course of or in connection with an offence of burglary, theft, taking a conveyance without authority, fraud, or destroying or damaging property, or intended by the person having it with him for such use by him or by some other person.

An *article to which PACE, s 1(8A) applies* is any article with a blade or point in relation to which a person has committed, or is committing or is going to commit, an offence under the Criminal Justice Act 1988, s 139 or s 139AA.

An *article to which s 1(8B) applies* is any firework which a person possesses in contravention of a prohibition imposed by the Fireworks Regulations 2004 referred to on p 616. '*Firework*' means a device which is a firework for the purposes of the relevant British Standard specification or which would be if intended as a form of entertainment.

Places in which powers to search can be exercised

PACE, s 1(1) states that a constable may exercise any powers under s 1:

(a) in any place to which at the time when he proposes to exercise the power the public or any section of the public has access, on payment or otherwise, as of right or by virtue of express or implied permission; or

(b) in any other place to which people have ready access at the time when he proposes to exercise the power but which is not a dwelling.

Persons have a right to use streets and highways; they have express permission to access cinemas, theatres or football grounds subject to paying an entry fee. There is an implied permission for persons to enter buildings to carry out business transactions with the owners, and even to use a footpath to a dwelling house for the purpose of paying a *lawful call* upon the householder.

'Place to which people have ready access' in (b) is wide in meaning. It extends the power of search to any place (other than a dwelling) to which the public have access in fact, whether lawfully or not, for example a private field or grounds into which people regularly gain access as trespassers.

Section 1(4) states that, if a person is in a garden or yard occupied with, and used for, the purposes of a dwelling or on other land so occupied and used, a constable may not search him under s 1 unless the constable has reasonable grounds for believing that:

(a) he does not reside in the dwelling; and

(b) he is not in the place in question with the express or implied permission of a person who resides in the dwelling.

Similar restrictions apply to the search of a vehicle (or anything in or on it) in a garden, yard or land occupied with and used for the purpose of a dwelling. By s 1(5), a constable may not search it unless he has reasonable grounds for believing that:

(a) the person in charge of the vehicle does not reside in the dwelling; and

(b) the vehicle is not in the place in question with the express or implied permission of a person who resides in the dwelling.

In effect, the only places in which a constable cannot exercise s 1 powers are dwelling houses, the curtilage of dwelling houses if the person or vehicle is there lawfully, or any other place which is secure and does not permit ready access.

Seizure of articles

PACE, s 1(6) provides that suspected stolen or prohibited articles, or an article suspected to be one to which s 1(8A) or s 1(8B) applies, found in a search may be seized.

Reasonable suspicion

Code A gives the following guidance on what may be 'reasonable suspicion' for the purposes of statutory powers of stop and search which require a reasonable suspicion. 'Reasonable suspicion' requires (a) that the officer suspects that the relevant matter is satisfied, and (b) that there are reasonable grounds for that suspicion.

'Suspicion' exists where a person thinks that there is a possibility, which is more than fanciful, that the relevant matter is satisfied. It can be contrasted with 'belief' which requires more than mere suspicion, since belief refers to having no substantial doubt about the matter in question.

General

The test of reasonable suspicion must be applied to the particular circumstances in each case and is in two parts:

(a) the officer must have formed a *genuine* suspicion in his own mind that he will find the object for which the search power being exercised allows him to search; and
(b) the suspicion that the object will be found must be *reasonable*. This means that there must be an objective basis for that suspicion based on facts, information and/or intelligence which are relevant to the likelihood that the object in question will be found, so that a reasonable person would be entitled to reach the same conclusion based on the same facts and information and/or intelligence.

Officers must therefore be able to explain the basis for their suspicion by reference to intelligence or information about, or some specific behaviour by, the person concerned.

The exercise of the 'reasonable suspicion stop and search powers' depends on the likelihood that the person searched is in possession of an item for which he may be searched; it does not depend on the person concerned being suspected of committing an offence in relation to the object of the search. A police officer who has reasonable grounds to suspect that a person is in *innocent possession* of a stolen or prohibited article, controlled drug or other item for which the officer is empowered to search, may stop and search the person even though there would be no power of arrest. This provision would apply when a child under the age of criminal responsibility (10 years) is suspected of carrying any such item; he would be in innocent possession of it, even if he knew he had it. It is not uncommon for children under 10 to be used by older children and adults to carry stolen property, drugs and weapons and, in some cases, firearms, for the criminal benefit of others, either in the hope that police may not suspect they are being used for carrying the items, or knowing that, if they are suspected of being couriers and are stopped and searched, they cannot be arrested or prosecuted for any criminal offence. The availability of stop and search powers in such a case therefore allow the police to intervene effectively to break up criminal gangs and groups that use young children to further their criminal activities.

A guidance note to Code A states that whenever a child under 10 is suspected of carrying unlawful items for someone else, or is found in circumstances which suggest that his welfare and safety may be at risk, the facts should be reported and actioned in accordance with established force safeguarding procedures. This will be in addition to treating the child as a potentially vulnerable or intimidated witness in respect of his status as a witness to the serious criminal offence(s) committed by those using him as courier. Safeguarding considerations will also apply to other persons aged under 18 who are stopped and searched under any of the powers to which Code A applies.

Personal factors can never support reasonable grounds for suspicion

Reasonable suspicion can never be supported on the basis of personal factors. This means that unless the police have information or intelligence which *provides a description* of a person suspected of carrying an article for which there is a power to stop and search, the following *cannot be used*, alone or in combination with each other, or in combination with any other factor, as the reason for stopping and searching any individual, including any vehicle which he is driving or in which he is being carried:

(a) a person's physical appearance with regard, for example, to any of the 'relevant protected characteristics' set out in the Equality Act 2010, s 149 (see p 35), or the fact that the person is known to have a previous conviction; and

(b) generalisations or stereotypical images that certain groups or categories of people are more likely to be involved in criminal activity.

Reasonable grounds for suspicion based on information and/or intelligence

Reasonable grounds for suspicion should normally be linked to accurate and current intelligence or information relating to articles for which there is a power to stop and search being carried by individuals or being in vehicles in any locality. This would include reports from members of the public or other officers describing:

(a) a person who has been seen carrying such an article or a vehicle in which such an article has been seen;
(b) crimes committed in relation to which such an article would constitute relevant evidence, for example, property stolen in a theft or burglary, an offensive weapon or bladed or sharply pointed article used to assault or threaten someone or an article used to cause criminal damage to property.

Searches based on accurate and current intelligence or information are more likely to be effective. Targeting searches in a particular area at specified crime problems not only increases their effectiveness but also minimises inconvenience to law-abiding members of the public. It also helps in justifying the use of searches both to those who are searched and to the public. This does not, however, prevent stop and search powers being exercised in other locations where such powers may be exercised and reasonable suspicion exists.

Reasonable grounds for suspicion and searching groups

Where there is reliable information or intelligence that members of a group or gang habitually carry knives unlawfully or weapons or controlled drugs, and wear a distinctive item of clothing or other means of identification (eg jewellery, insignias, tattoos or other features known to identify members of the particular gang or group) in order to identify themselves as members of that group or gang, that distinctive item of clothing or other means of identification may provide reasonable grounds to stop and search any person believed to be a member of that group or gang.

A similar approach would apply to particular organised protest groups where there is reliable information or intelligence:

(a) that the group in question arranges meetings and marches to which one or more members bring articles intended to be used to cause criminal damage and/or injury to others in support of the group's aims;
(b) that at one or more previous meetings or marches arranged by that group, such articles have been used and resulted in damage and/or injury; and
(c) that on the subsequent occasion in question, one or more members of the group have brought with them such articles with similar intentions.

These circumstances may provide reasonable grounds to stop and search any members of the group to find such articles. A guidance note to Code A states that a decision to search individuals believed to be members of a particular group or gang must be judged on a case-by-case basis according to the circumstances applicable at the time of the proposed searches and, in particular, having regard to: (i) the number of items suspected of being carried; (ii) the nature of those items and the risk they pose; and (iii) the number of individuals to be searched. A group search will only be justified if it is a necessary and proportionate approach based on the facts and having regard to the nature of the suspicion in these cases. The extent and thoroughness of the searches must not be excessive. The size of the group and the number of individuals it is proposed to search will be a key factor and steps should be taken to identify those who are to be searched to avoid unnecessary inconvenience to unconnected members of the public who are also present. The onus is on the police to be satisfied and to demonstrate that their approach to the decision to search is in pursuit of a legitimate aim, necessary and proportionate.

Reasonable grounds for suspicion based on behaviour, time and location

Reasonable suspicion may also exist without specific information or intelligence and on the basis of the behaviour of a person. For example, if an officer encounters someone on the street at night who is obviously trying to hide something, the officer may (depending on the other surrounding circumstances) base such suspicion on the fact that this kind of behaviour is often linked to stolen or prohibited articles being carried. An officer who forms the opinion that a person is acting suspiciously or that he appears to be nervous must be able to explain, with reference to specific aspects of the person's behaviour or conduct which he observed, why he formed that opinion. A hunch or instinct which cannot be explained or justified to an objective observer can never amount to reasonable grounds.

Securing public confidence and promoting community relations

All police officers must recognise that searches are more likely to be effective and legitimate and to secure public confidence when their reasonable grounds for suspicion are based on a range of objective factors. The overall use of these powers is more likely to be effective when up-to-date and accurate intelligence or information is communicated to officers and they are well informed about local crime patterns. Local senior officers have a duty to ensure that those under their command who exercise stop and search powers have access to such information, and the officers exercising the powers have a duty to acquaint themselves with that information.

Questioning to decide whether to carry out a search

An officer who has reasonable grounds for suspicion may detain the person concerned in order to carry out a search. Before carrying out the search the officer may ask questions about the person's behaviour or presence in circumstances which gave rise to the suspicion. As a result of questioning the detained person, the reasonable grounds for suspicion necessary to detain that person may be confirmed or, because of a satisfactory explanation, be dispelled. Questioning may also reveal reasonable grounds to suspect the possession of a different kind of unlawful article from that originally suspected. However, reasonable grounds for suspicion cannot be provided retrospectively by such questioning during a person's detention or by refusal to answer any questions asked.

If, as a result of questioning before a search, or other circumstances which come to the attention of the officer, there cease to be reasonable grounds for suspecting that an article of a kind for which there is a power to stop and search is being carried, no search may take place. In the absence of any other lawful power to detain, the person is free to leave at will and must be so informed.

There is no power to stop or detain a person in order to find grounds for a search. Police officers have many encounters with members of the public which do not involve detaining people against their will and do not require any statutory power for an officer to speak to a person. However, if reasonable grounds for suspicion emerge during such an encounter, the officer may detain the person to search him, even though no grounds existed when the encounter began. As soon as detention begins, and before searching, the officer must inform the person that he is being detained for the purpose of a search and take action in accordance with the procedure set out on pp 47–8.

Authorisation of stop and search in anticipation of violence or after violence

The Criminal Justice and Public Order Act 1994 (CJPOA 1994), s 60 provides further powers to stop and search. Section 60(1) provides that where a police officer of the rank of inspector or above (see end of p 45 and top of p 46) reasonably *believes* (p 56):

(a)   that incidents involving serious violence may take place in any locality in his police area, and that it is expedient to give an authorisation under s 60 to prevent their occurrence; or
(b)   that
   (i)   an incident involving serious violence has taken place in England and Wales in his police area;
   (ii)   a dangerous instrument or offensive weapon used in the incident is being carried in any locality in his police area by a person; and
   (iii)   it is expedient to give an authorisation under s 60 to find the instrument or weapon; or
(c)   that persons are carrying dangerous instruments or offensive weapons in any locality in his police area without good reason,

he may give an authorisation that the powers conferred by the section are to be exercised at any place within that locality for a specified period not exceeding 24 hours.

The *Best Use of Stop and Search Scheme* (to which all local police forces signed up in 2014, although only 26 per cent of them were fully compliant at the last survey) deals, among other things, with s 60 authorisations. The survey indicated that 95 per cent of forces were compliant in this respect. Under the *Scheme*, the authorising officer must reasonably believe that incidents of violence *will* take place, rather than may (as a possibility) take place as stated in (a).

'Offensive weapon' in (b) is extended in the case of an incident of the kind mentioned in (b) to include 'any article used in the incident to cause or threaten injury to any person or otherwise to intimidate'.

The extent of a 'locality' within which these powers may be exercised will differ in relation to the nature of the incident. An anticipated serious disorder at a pub would be in a small 'locality' while one within a housing estate would be in an extensive 'locality'. Provided it is proved that thought has been given to defining the locality, a court is unlikely to rule that the authorisation was invalid. The authorising officer should not set a geographical area which is wider than that he believes necessary for the purpose of the authorisation's objective. The locality must be carefully specified and officers must be aware of the geographical area enclosed. If the powers are to be used in response to a threat or incident which straddles police force areas, an officer from each of the forces affected must give an authorisation.

Although s 60(1) provides for initial authorisation to last for up to 24 hours, under the *Best Use of Stop and Search Scheme* forces will limit the maximum duration to 15 hours, with the possibility of an extension of that initial authorisation by a maximum of nine hours (ie up to the statutory maximum of 24 hours).

Whether or not it is expedient to give an authorisation may involve consideration of the effectiveness of other powers, and the resources available to deal with the type of incidents which might arise. Provided that such judgements are made in good faith, a court is unlikely to interfere.

Although the word 'necessary' does not appear in s 60(1), the effect of the European Convention on Human Rights, art 8 is that an authorisation made under s 60 must be made only if the officer believes that it is necessary, as well as expedient, to prevent serious violence, or to find dangerous instruments or offensive weapons after an incident involving serious violence, or to apprehend persons carrying weapons.

The period during which these powers may be exercised must be the minimum considered necessary to deal with the risk of violence or the carrying of knives or offensive weapons.

Where an inspector gives an authorisation he must, as soon as it is reasonably practicable to do so, cause an officer of or above the rank of superintendent to be informed.

The authorisation may be extended once only for a further 24 hours on the authority of an officer of or above the rank of superintendent, where expedient, having regard to offences committed, or reasonably suspected to have been committed, in connection with an activity falling within the authorisation. Thereafter further use of the powers requires a new authorisation. The same comments about necessity and the maximum duration under the *Best Use of Stop and Search Scheme* apply to extension in the same way as they apply to initial authorisations.

Police powers

Stop and search   Where an authorisation is in force under CJPOA 1994, s 60 a constable in uniform is empowered:

(a) to stop any pedestrian and search him and anything carried by him, for offensive weapons or dangerous instruments; and
(b) to stop any vehicle and search the vehicle, its driver and any passenger for offensive weapons or dangerous instruments.

A driver of a vehicle which has been stopped is entitled to obtain a written statement to that effect, if he applies within 12 months. The same rights apply to pedestrians or a passenger in a vehicle.

These stops and searches may be carried out *whether or not* the *constable in question* has any grounds for suspecting that the person or vehicle is carrying weapons or articles of the specified kind. A constable may seize any dangerous instrument or any article which he has reasonable grounds for suspecting to be an offensive weapon. A 'dangerous instrument' is one which has a blade or is sharply pointed; a vehicle includes a 'caravan'; and an 'offensive weapon' is as defined by PACE, s 1(9) (see p 39). A person carries a dangerous instrument or an offensive weapon if he has it in his possession.

The selection of persons and vehicles under s 60 to be stopped and, if appropriate, searched should reflect an objective assessment of the nature of the incident or weapon in question and the individuals and vehicles thought likely to be associated with that incident or those weapons. The powers under s 60 must not be used to stop and search persons and vehicles for reasons unconnected with the purpose of the authorisation. When selecting persons and vehicles to be stopped in response to a specific threat or incident, officers must take care not to discriminate unlawfully against anyone on the grounds of any of the protected characteristics (set out on p 35).

The fact that individual constables are not required to have any reasonable grounds for suspicion has made the s 60 stop and search powers among the most controversial stop and search powers. For this reason, under the *Best Use of Stop and Search Scheme* police forces raises the level of officer required for an initial authorisation or extension to that of assistant Chief Constable, or Commander in the case of the Metropolitan Police or the City of London Police, or above.

Require removal of masks, etc   Where an authorisation under CJPOA 1994, s 60 is in force in relation to any locality, by s 60AA(2) a constable in uniform is given the power in that locality:

(a) to require any person to remove any item (eg a face mask) which the constable reasonably believes that person is wearing wholly or mainly for the purpose of concealing his identity; and
(b) to seize any item which the constable reasonably believes any person intends to wear wholly or mainly for that purpose.

Where an authorisation under s 60 is not in force in relation to a locality, an authorisation may be given by an inspector (or above) for the exercise of the powers under s 60AA(2) if he reasonably believes that activities may take place in any locality in his police area that are likely (if they take place) to involve the commission of offences, and that it is expedient, in order to prevent or control the activities to give the following authorisation. In such a case that officer may authorise under s 60AA(3) that the powers under s 60AA(2) shall be exercisable at any place within that locality for a specified period not exceeding 24 hours. Where it then appears to a superintendent that, in view of offences which have been, or are reasonably suspected to have been, committed in connection with the activities to which the authorisation relates, he may direct that the authorisation continues in force for a further 24 hours. Where an inspector gives the initial authorisation under s 60AA(3), as soon as practicable he must inform a superintendent (or above).

Further points

In the case of the British Transport Police references to a 'locality' or to 'a locality in his police area' are references to any locality in or in the vicinity of any policed premises, or to the whole or any part of such premises.

An authorisation under CJPOA 1994, ss 60 or 60AA must be in writing and signed and must specify the grounds for it, the locality and the period during which the powers are exercisable. There is one exception: an authorisation under (b) on p 44 need not be given in writing where it is not practicable to do so but any oral authorisation must state the matters which otherwise would have to be specified in respect of an authorisation under s 60 and must be recorded in writing as soon as practicable.

An extension of the initial 24-hour period must be signed by its maker, or where that is not practicable, recorded in writing as soon as practicable.

As indicated above, an officer exercising the power to require the removal of a face covering must reasonably believe that someone is wearing the item wholly or mainly for the purpose of concealing his identity. There is no power to stop and search for a face covering. However, a face covering may be seized if it is discovered when searching for something else, or is seen to be carried in circumstances in which an officer reasonably believes it is intended to be used for the purpose of concealing identity.

Under the *Best Use of Stop and Search Scheme*, forces must communicate with the public in the areas where a s 60 authorisation is to be put in place. They must do so in advance (where practicable) and afterwards. The public need to be informed of the purpose and outcome of each s 60 operation.

A person who fails to stop or (as the case may be) to stop his vehicle when required to do so by a constable exercising these powers commits an offence (s 60(8)). Failure to remove an item when required is an offence (s 60AA(7)).

Authorisation of stop and search for the prevention of terrorism

This is dealt with in Chapter 28 (see p 782).

Power to stop and search at aerodromes

The Aviation Security Act 1982, s 24B permits a constable to search without warrant any person, vehicle, or aircraft in an aerodrome, or anything which is in or on such a vehicle or aircraft, for stolen or prohibited articles, provided that he has reasonable grounds for suspecting that he will find such articles. For the purposes of carrying out such a search, a constable may enter any part of an aerodrome; detain a person, vehicle, or aircraft; and board any vehicle or aircraft. He may seize any article which he has reasonable grounds for suspecting to be a stolen or prohibited article.

For these purposes, a 'prohibited article' is an article made or adapted for use in the course of or in connection with criminal conduct, or intended by the person having it with him for such use. 'Criminal conduct' means conduct which constitutes an offence in the part of the UK in which the aerodrome is situated, or would constitute an offence in that part of the UK if it occurred there.

Section 24B does not authorise entry into a dwelling.

Searches where no power to search

An officer must not search a person, even with his consent, where no power to search is applicable. Code A specifies, as a sole exception, that an officer does not require a specific power to search persons with their consent given as a condition of entry to sports grounds or other premises.

Where it transpires that search is not required or is impracticable

PACE, s 2(1) provides that, if a constable detains a person or vehicle in the exercise of the power under s 1 or any similar power to stop and search, he need not subsequently carry out that search if it appears to him that no search is required or that a search is impracticable. These circumstances will frequently arise: a person will often be detained on valid grounds for the purpose of a search and then satisfy the constable of his bona fides by answering his questions, or because of other circumstances which come to the attention of the officer. In such a case it is unnecessary to search and the detention will not be unlawful merely because the search was not carried out.

Procedure before carrying out a search

The following procedure is provided by Code A. Before any search of a detained person or attended vehicle takes place the officer must take reasonable steps, if not in uniform, to show his warrant card to the person to be searched or in charge of the vehicle to be searched, and whether or not in uniform, to give that person the following information:

(a) that he is being detained for the purposes of a search;
(b) the officer's name (except in the case of enquiries linked to the investigation of terrorism, or otherwise where the officer reasonably believes that giving his name might put him in danger, in which case a warrant or other identification number must be given and the name of the police station to which the officer is attached);
(c) the legal search power which is being exercised; and
(d) a clear explanation of the object of the search in terms of the article or articles for which there is a power to search; and in the case of:
  (i) the power under the Criminal Justice and Public Order Act 1994, s 60, the nature of the power, the authorisation and the fact that it has been given;
  (ii) the powers under the Terrorism Prevention and Investigation Measures Act 2011 (TPIMA 2011) Sch 5, the fact that a TPIM notice is in force or is being served (as the case may be), and the nature of the power being exercised. (For a search for compliance purposes, the search warrant must be produced and the person provided with a copy.);
  (iii) all other powers requiring reasonable suspicion, the grounds for that suspicion;
(e) that he is entitled to a copy of the record of the search if one is made if he asks within three months from the date of the search and:
  (i) if he is not arrested and taken to a police station as a result of the search and it is practicable to make the record on the spot, that immediately after the search is completed he will be given, if he requests, either a copy of the record, or a receipt which explains how he can obtain a copy of the full record or access to an electronic copy of the record, or
  (ii) if he is arrested and taken to a police station as a result of the search, that the record will be made at the station as part of his custody record and he will be given, if he requests, a copy of his custody record which includes a record of the search as soon as practicable whilst he is at the station.

A divisional court has held that a failure to take the above reasonable steps renders a search unlawful.

The above requirements apply even if the police officer reasonably believes that the suspect is about to dispose of the item in question. The Court of Appeal has suggested that they can be satisfied by simply saying, eg 'Jones, Central; drug search; spit it out'.

Because non-compliance with the requirements renders a search unlawful, a suspect who obstructs the search or resists it will not be guilty of assaulting or obstructing a police officer in the execution of his duty.

The person should also be given information about police powers to stop and search and the individual's rights in these circumstances.

If the person to be searched, or in charge of a vehicle to be searched, does not understand what is being said, or there is any doubt about his ability to understand English, the officer must take reasonable steps to bring to that person's attention his rights and any relevant provisions of Code A. If that person is deaf or cannot understand English and has someone with him, the officer must establish whether that person can interpret or otherwise help him to give the required information.

A constable asking a person to remove a mask pursuant to the CJPOA, s 60AA is not performing a search, so the above requirements do not apply.

Conduct of search

Every reasonable effort must be made to minimise the embarrassment that a person being searched may experience. By PACE, s 2(8) a person may be detained for a search for such time as is reasonably required to permit a search to be carried out either at the place where the person or vehicle was first detained or nearby.

The co-operation of the person to be searched must always be sought, even if he initially objects to being searched. A forcible search may be made only if it has been established that the person is unwilling to co-operate (eg by opening a bag) or resists. A judge in the Administrative Court has held that a pat-down search does not constitute a forcible search, and that neither does placing a hand on a person's body without applying pressure. Reasonable force may be used as a last resort, but only if this is necessary to detain the person or to search him. The length of time for which a person or vehicle may be detained will depend on the circumstances, but it must be reasonable and not extend beyond the time taken for the search.

Code A states that, where the exercise of the power requires reasonable suspicion, the extent of the search will be related to the nature of the article sought and the circumstances. If a person is seen to put an offensive weapon into a particular pocket, then, unless there are grounds for suspecting that it has been moved elsewhere, the search must be confined to that pocket; whereas, if the article sought may easily be concealed anywhere on the person, the search may have to be more thorough.

The term 'nearby' in PACE, s 2(8) is not defined but it is submitted that it should be interpreted quite narrowly. To move a vehicle from a congested spot into a side street, or a person from the public gaze into an alley, would be a reasonable action to take and would not prevent the search from being 'nearby'.

An officer who is not in uniform may not stop a vehicle for the purpose of a search.

Removal of clothing

Code A restricts searches in public to a 'superficial examination of outer clothing'. A constable is not authorised under PACE, s 1, or under any other power of stop and search, to *require* a person to remove any of his clothing in public other than an outer coat, jacket, or gloves, or under CJPOA 1994, s 60AA (see p 46: power to require the removal of any item worn to conceal identity). Where there might be religious sensitivities about asking someone to remove a face covering, as in the case of a Muslim woman, the police officer should permit the item to be removed out of public view (for example, in a police van or police station if there is one nearby). Where practicable, the item should be removed in the presence of an officer of the same sex and out of sight of anyone of the opposite sex. A search in public of clothing which has not been removed must be restricted to a superficial examination of outer garments. This does not prevent an officer placing his hands inside the pockets of outer clothing, or feeling around the inside of collars, socks, and shoes if this is reasonably necessary. Subject to the restrictions upon removal of headgear, a person's hair may be searched in public.

If, on reasonable grounds, a more extensive search than a superficial examination of outer clothing is considered necessary (eg by requiring a person to take off a T-shirt or headgear) it must be done out of view of the public, for example in a police van or a police station if there is one nearby. Any search involving more than the removal of an outer coat, jacket or gloves, headgear or footwear, or any other item concealing identity, may only be made by an officer of the same sex as the person searched and may not be made in the presence of anyone of the opposite sex (see p 36) unless the person being searched specifically requests it.

Searches which involve exposure of intimate parts of the body must not be conducted as a routine extension of a less thorough search simply because nothing is found in the course of the initial search. Searches involving such exposure may be carried out only at a nearby police station or other nearby location which is out of the public view.

A search in a street itself should be regarded as being in public, even though the street is empty at the time the search begins. As a search of a person in public should be a superficial examination of outer clothing, such searches should be completed as soon as possible.

Recording requirements

Searches which do not result in an arrest

A record of the search must be made, electronically or on paper, unless there are exceptional circumstances making this wholly impracticable (eg in situations involving public disorder or when the recording officer's presence is urgently required elsewhere). If a record is to be made, the officer carrying out the search must make the record on the spot unless this is not practicable, in which case the officer must make the record as soon as practicable after the search is completed.

If the record is made at the time, the person searched or in charge of the vehicle searched must be asked if he wants a copy; if he does, he must be given immediately (a) a copy of the record, or (b) a receipt which explains how he can obtain a copy of a full record or access to an electronic copy of the record.

An officer is not required to provide a copy of the full record or a receipt at the time if he is called to an incident of higher priority. In such a situation, the officer should consider giving the person details of the station which he may attend for a copy of the record. A receipt may take the form of a simple business card which includes sufficient information to locate the record should the person ask for a copy, for example the date and place of the search, a reference number, or the name of the officer who carried out the search (unless the exception below in the case of terrorism investigations applies).

Searches which result in an arrest

If a search results in a person being arrested and taken to a police station, the officer carrying out the search must ensure that a record of the search is made as part of the custody record. The custody officer must then ensure that the person is asked if he wants a copy of the record, and if he does, that he is given a copy as soon as practicable.

The requirement to make the record of the search as part of the person's custody record does not apply if the person is granted 'street bail' after arrest (p 64) to attend a police station and is not taken in custody to the police station. An arrested person's entitlement to a copy of the search record which is made as part of his custody record does not affect his entitlement to a copy of his custody record or any other provisions of PACE Code C: the Code of Practice for the Detention, Treatment, and Questioning of Persons by Police Officers about custody records.

Record of search

The record of a search must always include the following information:

(1) *A note of the self-defined ethnicity, and, if different, the ethnicity as perceived by the officer making the search, of the person searched or of the person in charge of the vehicle searched (as the case may be).*

Officers should record the self-defined ethnicity of every person stopped according to the categories used in the 2001 census question listed in Annex B to Code A. The person should be asked to select one of the five main categories representing broad ethnic groups and then a more specific cultural background from within this group. The ethnic classification should be coded for recording purposes using the coding system in Annex B. An additional 'Not stated' box is available but should not be offered to respondents explicitly. Officers should be aware and explain to members of the public, especially where concerns are raised, that this information is required to obtain a true picture of stop and search activity and to help improve ethnic monitoring, tackle discriminatory practice, and promote effective use of the powers. If the person gives what appears to the officer to be an 'incorrect' answer (eg a person who appears to be white states that he is black), the officer should record the response that has been given and then record his own perception of the person's ethnic background by using the Police National Computer (PNC) classification system. If the 'Not stated' category is used the reason for this must be recorded on the form.

(2) *The date, time and place the person or vehicle was searched.*

(3) *The object of the search in terms of the article or articles for which there is a power to search.*

(4) *In the case of:*

   (a) *the power under the Criminal Justice and Public Order Act 1994, s 60, the nature of the power, the authorisation, and the fact that it has been given;*

   (b) *the powers under TPIMA 2011, Sch 5, the fact that a TPIM notice is in force or is being served (as the case may be), and the nature of the particular power being exercised.* In addition, for a search for compliance purposes, the date of the search warrant, and the fact that it was produced and a copy provided must be recorded, and the warrant must also be endorsed by the constable executing it to state whether anything was found and whether anything was seized;

   (c) *all other powers requiring reasonable suspicion, the grounds for that suspicion.*

(5) *Subject to one exception, the identity of the officer carrying out the search.*

   Where a stop and search is carried out by more than one person the identity of all the officers must be recorded in the record. The exception referred to is that the names of police officers are not required to be shown on the search record or any other record required to be made under Code A in the case of enquiries linked to the investigation of terrorism or otherwise where an officer reasonably believes that recording names might endanger the officers. In such cases the record must show the officers' warrant or other identification number and duty station.

For the purposes of completing the search record, there is no requirement to record the name, address and date of birth of the person searched or the person in charge of a vehicle which is searched and the person is under no obligation to provide this information. In addition, the person should not be asked to provide the information for the purpose of completing the record.

A record is required for each person and each vehicle searched. However, only one record is required where a person who is in a vehicle is searched in addition to the vehicle, and the object and grounds of the search are the same. Where only a vehicle is searched, the self-defined ethnic background of the person in charge of the vehicle must be recorded, unless the vehicle is unattended.

The record of the grounds for making a search must, briefly but informatively, explain the reason for suspecting the person concerned, by reference to information and/or intelligence about, or some specific behaviour by, the person concerned.

Where officers detain an individual with a view to performing a search, but the need to search is eliminated as a result of questioning the person detained, a search should not be carried out (see p 43) and a record is not required.

Encounters not governed by statutory powers

Code A no longer contains the national recording requirement (and associated provisions) in respect of such encounters (request in public place to account) which used to be specified. A person who is asked to account for himself should, if he requests, be given information about how he can report his dissatisfaction about how he has been treated.

Unattended vehicles

If an unattended vehicle, or anything in or on it, is searched the constable is required to leave a notice:

(a) stating that he has searched it;
(b) giving the name of the police station to which he is attached;
(c) stating that any application for compensation for any damage caused by the search may be made to that police station; and
(d) stating that the person in charge of the vehicle may obtain a copy of the record of the search (if there is one) if he asks for it within three months.

The notice should explain how (if applicable) an electronic copy of the record may be accessed. The notice must be left inside the vehicle (or on it, if things have been searched without opening it). A vehicle which has been searched must, if practicable, be left secure.

Monitoring and supervising the use of stop and search powers

General

Supervising officers must monitor the use of stop and search powers and should consider whether there is evidence of such powers being exercised on the basis of stereotyped images or inappropriate generalisations. They must satisfy themselves that officers are acting in accordance with Code A. They must also examine whether the records reveal any trends or patterns which give cause for concern, and, if they recognise such trends, take appropriate action. Senior officers with area or force-wide responsibilities must also monitor such matters on a broader basis. Disproportionate use in relation to particular sections of the community should be investigated. Arrangements must be made, in consultation with local policing bodies, for records to be scrutinised by community representatives. Such scrutiny must take account of an individual's right to confidentiality.

Suspected misuse of power by individual officers

Police supervisors must monitor the use of stop and search powers by individual officers to ensure that they are being applied appropriately and lawfully, eg direct supervision of the exercise of the powers, examining stop and search records and asking the officer to account for the way in which he conducted and recorded particular searches, or through complaints about a stop and search that the officer has carried out. Where a supervisor identifies issues with the way that an officer has used a stop and search power, the facts of the case will determine whether the standards of professional behaviour as set out in the Code of Ethics (p 298) have been breached and which formal action is pursued. Improper use might be a result of poor performance of a conduct matter, which will require the supervisor to take timely and appropriate action such as performance or misconduct procedures.

Search and seizure powers of community support officers

If their designation so provides, community support officers may exercise specified powers to search and seize. All references to 'officers' in the provisions about records and related matters include community support officers so designated.

POWERS TO CONDUCT A ROAD CHECK

Statutory power

PACE, s 4 governs the conduct of road checks by police officers for the purpose of ascertaining whether a vehicle is carrying:

(a) a person who has committed an offence other than a road traffic offence or a vehicle excise offence;
(b) a person who is a witness to such an offence;
(c) a person intending to commit such an offence; or
(d) a person unlawfully at large.

A 'road check' consists of the exercise in a locality of the power conferred by RTA 1988, s 163 (power of a constable in uniform to stop a mechanically propelled vehicle or pedal cycle on a road) in such a way as to stop all vehicles or vehicles selected by any criterion.

PACE, s 4 is mainly concerned with setting up road checks to arrest actual or intending criminals or escaping prisoners. The purpose of the check will be to stop all vehicles or selected vehicles. It may be that the person the officers are seeking to arrest is known to be in a black Volkswagen Golf and therefore only vehicles similar to that description will be stopped. Section 4 does not in any way affect an officer's powers to deal with road traffic matters and he may stop as many vehicles as he thinks necessary for that purpose. An officer who wishes to stop a single vehicle, which he reasonably suspects may be carrying a person who has committed or intends to commit an offence, etc, may do so under the powers given by RTA 1988, s 163, which are unaffected in such circumstances.

Authorisation of road checks

A road check must be authorised in writing. Normally, the authorisation must be given by an officer of the rank of superintendent or above. PACE, s 4 limits the instances in which authorisation may be given. An officer may only authorise a road check under s 4:

(a) for the purpose specified in (a) above, if he has reasonable grounds:
  (i) for believing that the offence is an indictable offence; and
  (ii) for suspecting that the person is, or is about to be, in that locality in which vehicles would be stopped if the road check were authorised;

(b) for the purpose specified in (b) above, if he has reasonable grounds for believing that the offence is an indictable offence;
(c) for the purpose specified in (c) above, if he has reasonable grounds:
  (i) for believing that the offence is an indictable offence; and
  (ii) for suspecting that the person is, or is about to be, in that locality in which vehicles would be stopped if the road check were authorised;
(d) for the purpose specified in (d) above, if he has reasonable grounds for suspecting that the person is, or is about to be, in that locality.

If it appears to an officer below the rank of superintendent that a road check is required as a matter of urgency for one of the above purposes, he may authorise it, but that officer must, as soon as practicable:

(a) make a written record of the time of authorisation; and
(b) cause a superintendent (or above) to be informed.

The superintendent (or above) may then authorise, in writing, the road check to continue. If he decides it should not continue, he must record the fact that it took place, and its purpose (including any relevant indictable offence).

Time limits, records and searches

The maximum period for which a road check may be authorised is seven days, but written authorisation may be given for a further period not exceeding seven days if a superintendent (or above) believes that a road check ought to continue.

The authorisation may be for a road check to be carried out throughout the 24 hours of each day, or may be limited to specified times.

The record (ie written authorisation) which must be kept of a road check must show:

(a) the period during which the road check is authorised to continue;
(b) the name of the officer who authorised it;
(c) the purpose of the road check (including any relevant indictable offence); and
(d) the locality in which vehicles are to be stopped.

The person in charge of a vehicle stopped in a road check is entitled to obtain a written statement *of the purpose* of the road check if he applies for it within 12 months.

PACE does not give direct powers to a constable to search a vehicle stopped in a road check. However, he is empowered to do so:

(a) if he has reasonable grounds for suspecting that it contains stolen or prohibited articles (PACE, s 1); or
(b) for the purpose of arresting someone for an offence or certain other offences if he has reasonable grounds to suspect that the person is there (PACE, s 17); or
(c) under powers granted by any other statute, eg the Firearms Act 1968.

Common law powers

The power under PACE, s 4 does not affect or replace the existing common law power to set up road checks where an imminent breach of the peace is reasonably apprehended.

Having stopped the vehicle under this power, the police may also search it thereunder. Anyone who insists on continuing his journey is liable to arrest under the common law power to arrest for an apprehended breach of the peace (see p 60).

Clearly, where the imminent breach of the peace would involve the commission of an indictable offence a road check can be operated either under PACE, s 4 or under the common law power. The procedural safeguards laid down for s 4 road checks do not, of course, apply to those under the common law power.

Prevention of terrorism: police cordons and prohibitions or restrictions on parking

TA 2000, ss 33 to 36 and 48 to 51 provide powers to impose a police cordon and to prohibit or restrict parking for the purposes of a 'terrorist investigation' (as defined by TA 2000, s 32). These provisions are discussed in Chapter 28 (see pp 778 and 791).

POWERS TO ARREST

An arrest (see p 61) may be authorised by a warrant or be lawfully made without warrant. The law relating to the issue and execution of warrants of arrest issued by a justice of the peace was explained in Chapter 2. The law relating to arrest without warrant is as follows.

ARREST WITHOUT WARRANT: CONSTABLES

PACE, s 24, supplemented by PACE Code G: the Code of Practice for the Statutory Power to Arrest by Police Officers, deals with this.

A lawful arrest under s 24 requires two elements:

(a) a person's involvement, or attempted involvement, or suspected involvement, in the commission of a criminal offence; and
(b) reasonable grounds for believing that the person's arrest is necessary for one of a number of specified reasons.

Involvement or suspected involvement in the commission of an offence

By PACE, s 24(1) to (3):

(1) A constable may arrest without warrant:
   (a) anyone who is *about to* commit an offence;
   (b) anyone who *is in* the act of committing an offence;
   (c) anyone whom *he has reasonable grounds for suspecting to be about* to commit an offence;
   (d) anyone whom *he has reasonable grounds for suspecting to be* committing an offence.
(2) If a constable has *reasonable grounds for suspecting* that an offence *has been* committed he may arrest without warrant anyone whom *he has reasonable grounds* to suspect of being guilty of it.
(3) If an offence *has been committed*, a constable may arrest without warrant:
   (a) anyone who *is* guilty of the offence;
   (b) anyone whom *he has reasonable grounds for suspecting to be* guilty of it.

'Suspicion' exists where a person thinks that there is a possibility, which must be more than fanciful, that the relevant matter is satisfied.

There must be some reasonable, objective grounds for the suspicion, based on known facts or information which are relevant to the likelihood that the offence has been or will be committed and to the fact that the person to be questioned committed it or will commit it. There may be grounds for arresting a suspect on the sole basis of the word of an informant but any police officer should treat that information with considerable reserve.

As in the case of most other police powers where phrases like 'reasonable grounds for suspecting' are used, it is not enough that such reasonable grounds for suspicion exist; the constable must actually suspect the matter in question. The Court of Appeal has emphasised that whether a police officer has reasonable grounds for suspicion depends on the information which he has, but that information need not be based on first-hand knowledge. So long as it comes from a source which it is reasonable to rely on, it can form the basis of a reasonable suspicion; the officer is not required to check it. The Court of Appeal has held that, when an arresting officer's suspicion is formed on the basis of a PNC entry, that entry is likely to provide him with a reasonable suspicion. An officer instructed to arrest a person but without being given reasonable grounds to suspect that person's guilt cannot assume that his superior who instructed him must have other information providing reasonable grounds which has not been disclosed to him.

See also the comments on pp 40–3 about 'reasonable suspicion'.

The necessity criteria

By PACE, s 24(4), the power of arrest without warrant conferred by s 24(1) to (3) is only exercisable if the constable has *reasonable grounds for believing* that it is *necessary* for specified reasons (the 'necessity criteria' set out in s 24(5)) to arrest the person. There must not only be reasonable grounds for believing the relevant matter but also the constable must actually believe that matter. 'Belief' is more than 'suspicion'; it refers to having no substantial doubt about the relevant matter. As a divisional court has pointed out, the concept of necessity requires more than that an arrest is merely desirable or convenient for one of the specified reasons.

If there were no reasonable grounds at the time of the arrest, which is the crucial time, that defect cannot be cured subsequently by the custody officer considering that there were reasonable grounds when the arrested person was presented before him.

The Court of Appeal has held that an arresting officer is not required actively to consider all possible courses of action alternative to arrest. The effect of s 24(4), it held, is that (a) the officer must believe arrest to be necessary for one of the reasons specified in s 24(5); and (b) that belief must be objectively reasonable; there is not a third requirement actively to consider all possible courses of action alternative to arrest.

The specified reasons are set out in s 24(5) as follows:

(a) to enable the name of the person in question to be ascertained (in the case where the constable does not know, and cannot readily ascertain, the person's name, or has reasonable grounds for doubting whether a name given by the person as his name is his real name);

(b) correspondingly as regards the person's address;

(c) to prevent the person in question:

    (i)   causing physical injury to himself or any other person;

    (ii) suffering physical injury;

    (iii) causing loss of or damage to property;

    (iv) committing an offence against public decency (but only where members of the public going about their normal business cannot reasonably be expected to avoid the person in question); or

    (v)   causing an unlawful obstruction on the highway;

(d) to protect a child or other vulnerable person from the person in question;

(e) to prevent any prosecution for the offence from being hindered by the disappearance of the person in question, as where there are reasonable grounds for believing that if the person is not arrested he will not attend court, or that street bail after arrest would be insufficient to deter the suspect from trying to evade prosecution;

(f) to allow the prompt *and* effective investigation of the offence or of the conduct of the person in question. A divisional court has held that 'prompt' must be considered in context, taking account of all the relevant circumstances, and that 'effective' is not the same as efficient or cost-effective but means tending to achieve its purpose.

Head (f) may include cases such as:

(i) where there are reasonable grounds to believe that the person concerned:
- (*a*) has made false statements;
- (*b*) has made statements which cannot readily be verified;
- (*c*) has presented false evidence;
- (*d*) may steal or destroy evidence;
- (*e*) may make contact with co-suspects or conspirators;
- (*f*) may intimidate or threaten or make contact with witnesses; or
- (*g*) may have information which may be obtained by questioning; or

(ii) when considering arrest in connection with an indictable offence there is a need to:
- (*a*) enter and search any premises occupied or controlled by a person;
- (*b*) search the person;
- (*c*) prevent contact with others; or
- (*d*) take fingerprints, footwear impressions, samples or photographs of the suspect; or

(iii) to ensure compliance with statutory drug testing requirements.

Code G: the Code of Practice for the Statutory Power of Arrest by Police Officers adds the following points set out in the next three paragraphs.

An arrest interferes with the right to liberty recognised by the European Convention on Human Rights, art 5. The power must be used fairly, responsibly, with respect for the suspect and without unlawful discrimination. It remains an operational decision at the discretion of the officer as to:

(a) which one or more of the necessity criteria (if any) applies to the individual; and

(b) *if any of the criteria do apply*, whether to arrest, grant street bail after arrest, report for written charge, etc, issue a penalty notice, or take any other action that is open to the officer.

In applying the criteria, the arresting officer has to be satisfied that at least one of the reasons supporting the need for arrest is satisfied.

Applying the necessity criteria requires the constable to examine and justify the reason or reasons why a person needs to be arrested or (as the case may be) further arrested.

The circumstances that may satisfy those criteria remain a matter for the operational discretion of individual officers. In considering the individual circumstances, the constable must take into account the situation of the victim, the nature of the offence, the circumstances of the suspect, and the needs of the investigative process.

A police officer must consider carefully the necessity to arrest when deciding whether or not to do so. For example, not every refusal to provide a name and address at the officer's first request necessitates an arrest. Such a refusal should be followed by an explanation of the consequences of a continued refusal to provide an identity and an address which the officer believes to be true, and only if there is a continued refusal to provide such an identity and address should the arrest be made. However, a divisional court has accepted that where a person, whose name was unknown to a constable, was reasonably suspected by the constable of having committed an offence, these requirements were satisfied by the questions, 'What is your name?' and 'What is your address?' followed by a refusal to answer. In the event of refusal to answer, the offender should be told that he is being arrested in relation to the particular offence *and* for refusing to give his name and address.

PACE, s 30(7) requires that a person arrested by a constable at a place other than a police station must be released without bail if a constable is satisfied, before the person arrested reaches a police station, that there are no grounds for keeping him under arrest or releasing him on bail. This means, for example, that a person arrested on the grounds that a satisfactory name and address have not been provided must instantly be released if that information is subsequently provided. A record of such a release must be made as soon as practicable after the release.

Action to be taken in relation to an arrest

See p 61 below.

Limits on powers resulting from arrest

The powers available to an officer as a result of an arrest—for example, entry and search of premises (with exceptions), holding a person incommunicado, setting up road checks—are only available in respect of an indictable offence.

ARREST WITHOUT WARRANT: OTHER PERSONS

PACE, s 24A provides that:

(1) A person other than a constable may arrest without warrant:
    (a) anyone who is in the act of committing an indictable offence;
    (b) anyone whom he has reasonable grounds for suspecting to be committing an indictable offence.
(2) Where an indictable offence has been committed, a person other than a constable may arrest without warrant:
    (a) anyone who is guilty of that offence;
    (b) anyone whom he has reasonable grounds for suspecting to be guilty of it.
(3) The power of arrest conferred by (1) and (2) is only exercisable if:
    (a) the person making the arrest has reasonable grounds for believing that for any of the reasons mentioned in (4) it is necessary to arrest the person in question; and
    (b) it appears to the person making the arrest that it is not reasonably practicable for a constable to make it instead.
(4) The reasons are to prevent the person in question:
    (a) causing physical injury to himself or any other person;
    (b) suffering physical injury;
    (c) causing loss of or damage to property; or
    (d) making off before a constable can assume responsibility for him.

The above provisions do not apply in relation to an offence under the Public Order Act 1986, Parts III or IIIA (racial, etc hatred offences). Nor do they apply to the arrest inside a polling station of a person who has committed or is suspected of committing an offence of personation.

As can be seen, the conditions under which an arrest can be made by some 'other person' are more limited than in the case of a constable. The reason in (4)(d) is included because of the power given to community support officers to detain persons with a view to handing them over to a constable.

OTHER POWERS OF ARREST WITHOUT WARRANT

Specific statutory power of arrest without warrant

PACE preserves a small number of specific powers of arrest, such as those under the Bail Act 1976, s 7 (Chapter 5) and the Immigration Act 1971, s 24 (Appendix 3 on the companion website).

Cross-border powers of arrest

CJPOA 1994, s 137 provides that, where it appears to a constable that it would have been lawful for him to have exercised the power had the suspected person been in England or Wales, a constable of an English or Welsh police force, who has reasonable grounds for suspecting that an offence has been committed or attempted in England and Wales and that the suspected person is in Scotland or Northern Ireland, may arrest without warrant the suspected person wherever he is in Scotland or Northern Ireland. Constables who are members of the police services in Scotland or Northern Ireland have a similar power of arrest within England and Wales in respect of offences committed or attempted in Scotland or Northern Ireland respectively. These powers may be exercised in England and Wales and Scotland (but not Northern Ireland) by a British Transport Police officer. Thus, for example, such an officer can arrest someone in Scotland for an offence committed in England or Wales.

Where a person is arrested in Scotland or Northern Ireland under s 137, he must be taken to the nearest convenient designated police station in England or Wales or to a designated police station in a police area where the offence is being investigated. This must be done as soon as reasonably practicable.

Arrest of service personnel—absentees without leave and deserters

Under the Armed Forces Act 2006, s 314, a constable who is a member of a police force or of the Ministry of Defence police has power to arrest without warrant any person whom he has reasonable cause to suspect of being a person subject to service law who has deserted or is absent without leave. Warrants authorising such arrests may also be issued by justices of the peace. Whether or not a person so arrested admits to being an absentee or deserter he *must* be brought before a court as soon as practicable. Where a court is satisfied that such a person is a deserter or absentee, it will remand him in custody to await a service escort unless he is also in custody for some other reason.

Immediately such an arrest has been effected, the appropriate service authority must be informed and provided with all particulars of the case, stating whether the identity of the person arrested is disputed and whether his behaviour is refractory (non-compliant). Details of escort arrangements should be noted. Where an escort arrives before the court rises the person concerned can be handed over immediately, thereby avoiding his committal to prison or to other civil custody. Where the escort is likely to arrive quite soon, the court will usually commit such a person to police custody. The court must provide a certificate giving details of the serviceman's arrest (or surrender, see below).

Absentees frequently surrender to the police, having simply overstayed their leave. Such persons need not be taken before a magistrates' court but they may be if this is desirable for any reason. In such a case the court will remand the person in custody to await a service escort, subject to the same rules as just set out. Where an absentee serviceman is not taken before a court, a certificate must be made out by the police officer who causes the serviceman to be handed over to the escort. If the certificate is incorrectly completed or is not signed by the officer in charge of the police station, it is inadmissible in evidence at a subsequent court martial.

In all such cases of arrest or surrender the appropriate authority to be informed is as follows:

(a) in the case of the Royal Navy or Royal Marines, HMS *Nelson*, Portsmouth PO1 3HH (Metropolitan Police report to Naval Provost Marshal, London);
(b) in the case of the Army or Royal Air Force, the Service Police Crime Bureau, Royal Military Police.

On occasions the service authorities may issue a warrant to arrest a serviceman. In such a case, the serviceman should be arrested and handed to a service escort. He need not be placed before a court unless he is to be dealt with for some other reason. The appropriate certificate must be handed over to the escort.

Power to arrest at common law

At common law a police officer or anyone else has power to arrest without warrant in certain circumstances, and this power is not affected by PACE. The common law power exists:

(a) where a breach of the peace is committed by the person arrested in the presence of the person making the arrest; or
(b) where no breach of the peace has occurred in the presence of the person making the arrest, but he reasonably believes that such a breach by the person arrested is actually imminent.

'Breach of the peace' is not an offence in itself. It is defined on p 703.

These common law powers of arrest are important to police officers. They are in no way restricted by the nature of the place in which the breach of the peace occurs or is anticipated. The arrest within the above terms is a preventive measure and should be effected wherever it is necessary to preserve the peace, even on private premises and even if no member of the public is present. If two men are fighting, that is a breach of the peace regardless of all other considerations and an arrest by anyone who sees it occur is justified. It might be that the stage at which a fight actually occurs has not been reached but a constable reasonably believes that it will occur in the immediate future; in such a case he may arrest those in dispute. Likewise, where an actual fight might have been discontinued but a constable reasonably believes that the argument is not at an end and that the fight is likely to be resumed, and a breach of the peace to occur, an arrest is justified.

Once a constable reasonably foresees a breach of the peace, he is entitled to remain on premises in which, until that time, he has been a trespasser.

Since a breach of the peace does not necessarily require anyone to be acting, or threatening to act, unlawfully, the power to arrest for breach of the peace is not limited to cases where unlawful conduct occurs, or is suspected or anticipated. By way of a limit on the arrest of those who are not acting unlawfully, the Court of Appeal has set out four factors to be considered in such a case.

(1) There must be a real and present threat to the peace justifying depriving a citizen, not at the time acting unlawfully, of his liberty.
(2) The threat must come from the person arrested.
(3) The conduct must clearly interfere with the rights of others and its natural consequence must be 'not wholly unreasonable violence' from a third party.
(4) The conduct of the person to be arrested must be unreasonable.

OTHER POINTS ABOUT ARREST

The nature of an arrest

An arrest involves deprivation of a person's liberty to go where one pleases as an initial stage of the criminal process. Some recent decisions have said that there cannot be an arrest unless the person depriving the other of liberty intends to arrest him and tells him that he is under arrest and informs him of the offence for which he is being arrested. In terms of the last two points this is clearly wrong, because PACE states that these factors are necessary for an arrest to be lawful (as opposed to being necessary for an arrest). A police officer who physically restrains someone or restricts his movements but does not at that time intend or purport to arrest him, eg because he simply wants to detain him temporarily to establish his identity, is criminally and civilly liable for false imprisonment (and in the first case, for assault), even if he would have been justified in arresting that person; there is no power to detain someone short of an arrest.

An arrest is normally effected by the seizing or the touching of a person's body with a view to his detention. It is possible, however, to effect an arrest merely by words if they bring to the person's notice that he is under restraint and will be compelled to remain, and he submits to that compulsion. Where unreasonable force is used to effect an arrest the arrest is unlawful.

If the arrest occurs outside, it is probable that some form of physical restraint will be applied as the constable will be anxious to ensure that his prisoner does not escape. However, if the person arrested is a quiet, elderly person who is not physically capable of such escape, physical restraint would be unnecessary and undesirable. In the same way, persons already in custody who are arrested for other offences do not require a show of restraint, nor would it serve any purpose.

Information to be given on arrest

PACE, s 28 provides that where a person is arrested, otherwise than by being informed that he is under arrest, the arrest is unlawful unless, as soon as practicable after his arrest, the person arrested is informed that he is under arrest. This is so whether or not the fact of his arrest is obvious. In addition, no arrest is lawful unless the person arrested is informed of the ground for arrest at the time of arrest, or as soon as practicable thereafter. This is a separate requirement from that just mentioned. It applies regardless of whether the ground for arrest is obvious. An arrested person must be given sufficient information to enable him to understand that he has been deprived of his liberty and the reason for his arrest, eg when a person is arrested on suspicion of committing an offence, he must be informed of the suspected offence's nature and when and where it was committed. He must also be informed of the reason or reasons why arrest is considered necessary. Vague or technical language should be avoided. The adequacy of the information must be judged objectively having regard to the information reasonably available to the arresting officer.

While it is preferable that the person arrested is informed of the precise offence for which he is being arrested, for example: 'I am arresting you for an offence of burglary which I have seen you commit', this is not essential (although the ground given must be a valid one). It suffices if, by the use of commonplace language, he is informed of the type of offence for which he is being arrested, so that he has the opportunity to give information which would avoid the arrest. Thus, where a constable making an arrest reasonably suspected that the offence was theft, handling, or taking a conveyance (a car), her statement that she was arresting the suspect for unlawful possession of a car was held to be sufficient. The Court of Appeal has held that the requirements of s 28 are satisfied where a suspect is arrested by one officer, but informed by another of the reason for his arrest.

Section 28 exempts an officer from the necessity to give either item of information if it was not reasonably practicable to do so by reason of the person's escape before the information could be given.

Caution

Code G requires that a person must be cautioned upon arrest for an offence unless:

(a) it is impracticable to do so by reason of his condition or behaviour at the time; or

(b) he has already been cautioned immediately prior to arrest and before questions, or further questions, were put to him under Code C (p 112) as a person suspected of an offence.

The caution must be in the following terms:

'You do not have to say anything. But it may harm your defence if you do not mention when questioned something which you later rely on in court. Anything you do say may be given in evidence.'

Records of arrest

A police officer who makes an arrest for an offence must record in his pocket book or by any other method used for recording information:

(a) the nature and circumstances of the offence leading to arrest;

(b) the reason or reasons why arrest was necessary;

(c) the giving of the caution; and

(d) anything said by the person at the time of arrest.

The record should be made at the time of the arrest unless impracticable to do so. If not made at the time, it must be completed as soon as possible thereafter.

On arrival at the police station, or after being arrested at a police station, the arrested person must be brought before the custody officer as soon as practicable. The custody officer must open a custody record and the information given by the arresting officer on the circumstances and reason or reasons for arrest must be recorded as part of the custody record. As an alternative, a copy of the entry made by the officer (as required above) may be attached to the custody record. The custody record stands as a record of the arrest.

Young people

A guidance note in Code C states that someone under 18 should not be arrested at his place of education unless this is unavoidable. In the event of this happening, the principal or his nominee must be informed.

Arrest elsewhere than at a police station

PACE, s 30(1) and (1A) requires that, where a person is arrested by a constable for an offence (or is taken into custody by a constable having been arrested for an offence by someone other than a constable) at any place other than a police station, he must be taken to a police station as soon as practicable. The policy of s 30 is to bring the arrested person within the protective rules of Code C as soon as practicable. A deliberate breach of s 30(1) and (1A) may lead to evidence obtained during the delay being excluded on the ground that the fairness of the proceedings has been affected. Section 30(1) and (1A) is subject to the rules below concerning release on street bail or without bail. The inclusion of 'as soon as practicable' allows for the circumstances in which it would be unrealistic to take such a person directly to a police station. This is expressly recognised by s 30(10) and (10A), which provides that a constable may delay taking an arrested person to a police station (or releasing him on bail) if that person's presence elsewhere is necessary in order to carry out such investigations as it is reasonable to carry out immediately; in such a case any questions put to the arrested person should be confined to those investigations. Thus, where a person is arrested for a theft which he was seen to commit but the property was not in his possession when arrested after a chase, a constable carrying out one of the duties of his office, to protect property, could quite properly retrace the route of the chase with his prisoner in order to recover the stolen property as soon as possible.

If there is any delay in taking an arrested person to a police station, the reason must be recorded on first arrival there or, as the case may be, when he is released on bail. With certain exceptions, the police station to which the person arrested must be taken under s 30 must be a *designated police station* (s 30(2)). This term is explained in Chapter 5, but in essence it refers to a police station approved for the purpose of detention of prisoners. In exceptional circumstances, a person arrested may be taken to *any police station*. These circumstances are where:

(a) the constable is working in a locality covered by a police station which is not a designated police station; or

(b) he is a constable belonging to a police force maintained by an authority other than a local policing body (eg the British Transport Police) (s 30(4)).

The exception at (a) recognises that a 'designated police station' may be many miles from the place at which an arrest is made. If a person is arrested for an offence in respect of which he is likely to be released on bail more or less immediately, it would be unrealistic to require him to be taken to a designated police station many miles from the scene of the arrest. Neither exception applies if it appears to the constable that it may be necessary to keep the arrested person in police detention for more than six hours. In that case the person arrested must be taken to a *designated* police station (s 30(3)).

In addition, by s 30(5), any constable may take an arrested person to *any* police station if:

(a) the constable has arrested him without the assistance of any other constable and no other constable is available to assist him; or
(b) the constable has taken him into custody from a person other than a constable without the assistance of any other constable and no other constable is available to assist him,

and (in either case) it appears to the constable that he will be unable to take the arrested person to a designated police station *without the arrested person injuring himself, the constable or some other person.*

When the person is arrested and taken to a non-designated police station, and there is no officer present at that police station to act as a custody officer, the inspector at that designated police station to which that person would have been taken must be informed. If the first police station to which an arrested person is taken is not a designated police station, he must be taken to a designated police station within six hours unless he is previously released (s 30(6)).

A separate custody record must be opened as soon as practicable for each person who is brought to a police station under arrest. Custody records are discussed in the next chapter.

Release without bail

A person arrested by a constable at a place other than a police station may be released without bail if a constable is satisfied before that person reaches a police station that there are no grounds for keeping him under arrest or releasing him from bail under PACE, s 30A (s 30(7) and (7A)). The constable must record the fact of the release as soon as practicable (s 30(8) and (9)).

Bail elsewhere than at a police station

PACE, s 30A provides that a constable may release on bail ('street bail') a person who has been arrested for an offence by a constable, or taken into custody after arrest by someone other than a constable, at any time before he arrives at a police station. Such a person must be required to attend at a police station. Where a constable releases such a person (A) on bail:

(a) no recognisance for A's surrender to custody may be taken from him;
(b) no security for A's surrender to custody may be taken from him or from anyone else on his behalf;
(c) A may not be required to provide a surety or sureties for his surrender to custody; and
(d) no requirement to reside in a bail hostel may be imposed as a condition of bail.

Subject to (a)–(d) above, a constable may impose, as conditions of bail, requirements which he considers to be necessary:

(a) to secure that A surrenders to custody;
(b) to secure that A does not commit an offence while on bail;
(c) to secure that A does not interfere with witnesses or otherwise obstruct the course of justice, whether in relation to himself or any other person;
(d) for A's own protection or, if A is under the age of 17, for A's own welfare or in A's own interests.

No other requirements may be imposed as a condition of bail.

Where conditions are applied to street bail under s 30A, the person released on bail (A) has the right to apply for variation of the conditions to a custody officer or to a magistrates' court (ss 30CA, 30CB).

By s 30B, a notice in writing must be given to A by the constable granting bail. The notice must state the offence for which A was arrested and the ground on which he was arrested. The notice *must* inform A that he is required to attend a police station. It *may* also specify the police station at which A is required to attend, and the time of attendance. Where bail has been granted subject to conditions under s 30A, the above notice must specify the requirements imposed by those conditions; must explain the provisions relating to variation of conditions; and, if it does not specify the police station at which A is required to attend, must specify a police station at which A may request a variation by a custody officer. (If the police station and time of attendance are not stated in the notice referred to above, a further written notice containing that information must be sent later. An amended notice may be sent requiring attendance at a different police station or at a different time.)

Section 30C provides that the requirement to attend a police station may be cancelled by written notice and that, if A is required to attend a non-designated police station, he must be released or taken to a designated police station not more than six hours after his arrival. Nothing in the Bail Act 1976 applies to bail under s 30A, nor do the provisions of PACE prevent re-arrest without warrant of a person released on bail under s 30A if new evidence justifying a further arrest has come to light since his release.

By s 30D, a constable may arrest without warrant a person who has been released on bail under s 30A but:

(a) fails to attend the specified police station at the appointed time; or
(b) is reasonably suspected by the constable to have broken a condition of bail.

A person so arrested must be taken to any police station as soon as practicable after the arrest. An arrest under s 30D is treated as an arrest for the purposes of s 30 (above) and s 31 (below).

Arrest for a further offence

Where a person is under arrest at a police station for an offence and it appears that, if released, he would be liable to arrest for some other offence, PACE, s 31 requires that he be arrested for that other offence. The usual procedures to be followed after an arrest must be carried out; the person must be told that he is being arrested for that other offence and what the reasons are for that arrest, and he must be cautioned. This must be done whether or not it is intended to release him at that time.

POWERS OF ENTRY AND SEARCH IN RELATION TO AN ARREST

Search and seizure on arrest for an offence

Search

PACE, s 32(1) provides that, where a person has been *arrested elsewhere than at a police station*, a constable may search him if the constable has reasonable grounds for believing that the arrested person may present a danger to himself or others.

Section 32(2) goes further and also empowers a constable in such a case, whether or not he has such grounds:

(a) to *search* the *arrested person* for anything which he might use to assist him to escape from lawful custody or which might be evidence relating to an offence (s 32(2)(a)); *and*
(b) if the offence for which he has been arrested is an indictable offence, to *enter and search* any *premises* in which he was when arrested or immediately before he was arrested for evidence relating to the offence (s 32(2)(b)).

This power to search only extends to a search which is reasonably required for the purpose of discovering any such thing or any such evidence. A constable may not search a person under (a) unless he has reasonable grounds for believing that the person may have concealed on him anything for which a search is permitted under (a) (s 32(5)). Similarly, a constable may not search premises under (b) unless he has reasonable grounds for believing that there is evidence for which a search is permitted under (b) on the premises (s 32(6)).

The power in (a) gives statutory authority to 'on the spot' searches at the time of an arrest. That search may be for weapons or dangerous articles, for things which might assist escape, or for things which might be evidence of an offence. The power to search for evidence is particularly important since, if such property is not recovered at the time of such arrest, it is likely to be disposed of by the arrested person if an opportunity presents itself.

'*Premises*' in (b) and elsewhere in the PACE provisions in this chapter includes any place and, in particular, includes any vehicle, vessel, aircraft or hovercraft, any offshore installation, any renewable energy installation and any tent or movable structure.

PACE, s 32(7) deals with the problem in relation to (b) of communal occupation (including bedsit premises) by stating that where there are two or more separate dwellings, the search must be limited to the dwelling in which the arrest took place or in which the arrested person was immediately before his arrest *and* any part of the premises which the occupier of the dwelling uses in common with the other occupiers of other dwellings comprised in the premises. In the case of a bedsit, therefore, the constable would be able to search the room in which the arrested person was found and the common kitchen and lounge area used by all of the residents. This is useful because, for example, a thief occupying one room, on seeing the approach of a constable, might enter a communal part of the premises and conceal the stolen property there. A divisional court has stated that there is no decisive test to determine when a place of occupation is to be treated as divided into separate dwellings and that each case must be decided on its own facts. In the case in question, the bedrooms which homeless people had a licence to occupy for a day in a local authority hostel, each of which had a lock, were separate dwellings, because each licensee had a sufficient degree of exclusive possession.

The powers under s 32 do not authorise the removal of clothing in a public place other than an outer coat, jacket or gloves, but they do authorise a search of a person's mouth (s 32(4)).

Section 32 does not provide any general powers of search either of persons or premises when an arrest is made. The particular circumstances described in s 32 must exist. If someone is arrested for a sexual assault and is known to be of a non-violent disposition, there are no grounds for an 'on the spot' search; nor would there be, in most circumstances, reason to search premises unless articles had been used in the commission of the offence.

Seizure from a person

A constable searching under PACE, s 32(1) may seize and retain anything which he has reasonable grounds for believing that the person searched might use to cause physical injury to himself or another (s 32(8)).

A constable searching a person under PACE, s 32(2)(a) may seize and retain anything, other than an item subject to legal privilege (see p 73), if he has reasonable grounds for believing that the person might use it to escape from lawful custody or that it is evidence of an offence or has been obtained in consequence of the commission of an offence (s 32(9)).

The Criminal Justice and Police Act 2001 (CJPA 2001), s 51 provides additional powers of seizure from the person which apply to the power of seizure under PACE, s 32.

CJPA 2001, s 51(1) deals with the case where a person (P) carrying out a lawful search of another person finds something which he reasonably believes may be, or may contain, something for which he is authorised to search and to seize. It provides that if, in the circumstances, *it is not reasonably practicable for it to be determined whether what P has found (or its contents) is (or are) something which he is entitled to seize*, P's powers of seizure include seizing so much of what he has found as is necessary to remove from the place of the search to enable that to be determined.

Section 51(2) provides a power of seizure where a person carrying out a lawful search of someone finds anything ('the seizable property') which he would be entitled to seize but for its being comprised in something else that he has (apart from s 51(2)) no power to seize. Section 51(2) provides that where:

(a) the power under which that person would have power to seize the seizable property is a power to which s 51 applies; and

(b) in all the circumstances *it is not reasonably practicable for the seizable property to be separated, at the time and place of the search, from that in which it is comprised,*

that person's power of seizure includes power to seize both the seizable property and that from which it is not reasonably practicable to separate it.

The factors to be taken into account when considering whether it is reasonably practicable to achieve one of the things italicised in s 51(1) or (2) are the same as in s 50(3) (seizure from premises: below), with the modifications necessary to recognise that s 51 applies to a search of a person.

Where a person exercises this power of seizure under s 51, he must give written notice to the person from whom such property is seized:

(a) specifying what has been seized;

(b) specifying the grounds under which the power was exercised;

(c) setting out the effect of ss 59–61 (remedies and safeguards);

(d) specifying the name and address of the person to whom any application for the return of the seized property must be made; and
(e) specifying the name and address of the person to whom an application may be made to be allowed to attend the initial examination of the seized property which must be held to determine how much of it is property for which the person seizing had a power to search (s 52(4)).

A divisional court has held that non-compliance with s 52 does not necessarily render unlawful a seizure under ss 50 (below) or 51; it is a factor to be considered by the court on an application under s 59 (p 88), or in judicial review proceedings, or under PACE, s 78 (exclusion of unfair evidence) in any later trial.

Section 51 also applies to a number of other powers of seizure from the person listed in CJPA 2001, Sch 1, Part 2, some of which are referred to later in this book.

Seizure from premises

The powers of seizure under PACE, s 19 (p 86) apply to a search of premises under PACE, s 32(2)(b).

In addition, the CJPA 2001, s 50(1) deals with situations where a person who is lawfully on any premises finds objects on those premises which he reasonably believes to contain something for which he is authorised to search and in respect of which there would be a power of seizure under s 32 or under one of the more than 70 other statutory provisions listed in CJPA 2001, Sch 1, Part 1 to which s 50 applies. Some of these are referred to later in this book. Section 50(1) provides that if, in the circumstances, *it is not reasonably practicable for it to be determined whether what the person has found (or its contents) is (or are) something which he is entitled to seize*, his powers of seizure include seizing so much of what he has found as is necessary to remove from the premises to enable that to be determined.

Section 50(2) provides a power of seizure where a person lawfully on any premises finds anything on those premises ('the seizable property') which he would be entitled to seize but for its being comprised in something else that he has (apart from s 50(2)) no power to seize. Section 50(2) provides that where:

(a) the power under which that person would have power to seize the seizable property is a power to which s 50 applies; and
(b) in all the circumstances it is not reasonably practicable *for the seizable property to be separated in those premises from that in which it is comprised,*

that person's power of seizure includes power to seize both the seizable property and that from which it is not reasonably practicable to separate it.

Section 50(3) states that the factors to be taken into account in considering whether it is reasonably practicable to achieve one of the things italicised in s 50(1) or (2) are confined to:

(a) how long it would take to carry out the determination or separation on those premises;
(b) the number of persons who would be required to carry out that determination or separation on those premises within a reasonable period;
(c) whether the determination or separation would (or would if carried out on those premises) involve damage to property;
(d) the apparatus or equipment that it would be necessary or appropriate to use for the carrying out of the determination or separation; and
(e) in the case of separation, whether the separation:

    (i) would be likely, or

    (ii) if carried out by the only means that are reasonably practicable on those prem-
ises, would be likely,

to prejudice the use of some or all of the separated seizable property for the purpose
for which something seized under the power in question is capable of being used.

Where a power of seizure under s 50 has been exercised, written notice containing
the same information as under s 52(4) must be given to the occupier, or some other
person on the premises who is in charge (s 52(1) and (2)). Where there is no person on
the premises a notice must be attached, in a prominent place, to the premises (s 52(3)).

Examination and return of property seized under ss 50 or 51

CJPA 2001, s 53 requires that at a subsequent initial examination, which must take place
as soon as reasonably practicable, property seized under ss 50 or 51 which does *not*
fall within (a) to (c) below must be separated from the rest of the seized property and
returned as soon as reasonably practicable. Property does not have to be returned if:

(a) it is property for which there was a power of search and it is not an item subject to
legal privilege (p 73);

(b) there are reasonable grounds for believing that it is property obtained in consequence of an offence, or evidence in relation to any offence, and that it is necessary
for it to be retained in order to prevent its concealment, loss, alteration or destruction; or

(c) it is property which cannot be reasonably practically separated from that in
(a) or (b).

By ss 54 or 55, property subject to legal privilege and excluded or special procedure
material (p 74) must be returned unless its retention is authorised by the grounds set
out in (b) or, where comprised in something else, it cannot reasonably practicably be
separated from other property whose return is not required or which satisfies (b).

Entry to premises to effect an arrest, etc

PACE abolished all the common law rules which gave a constable power to enter
premises without a warrant, except that the power still exists at common law to enter
premises to deal with a breach of the peace or to prevent it (pp 703–4).

    PACE, s 17 provides that, without prejudice to any other enactment, a constable may
enter and search any premises (as defined on p 66) for the purpose:

(a) of executing a warrant of arrest issued in connection with or arising out of criminal
proceedings, or a warrant of commitment issued under the Magistrates' Courts Act
1980, s 76;

(b) of arresting someone for an indictable offence;

(c) of arresting someone for an offence under the Public Order Act 1936, s 1 (prohibited uniforms), the Public Order Act 1986, s 4 (fear or provocation of violence),
RTA 1988, s 4 (driving, etc under the influence of drink or drugs) or s 163 (failure
to stop when required to do so by a police constable in uniform), the Transport
and Works Act 1992, s 27 (drink or drugs on public guided transport systems), or
the Animal Welfare Act 2006, ss 4, 5, 6(1) or (2), 7, and 8(1) or (2) (unnecessary
suffering, mutilation, docking of tails, administering poisons, and animal fighting);

(d) of arresting someone for an offence under CJPOA 1994, s 76 (failure to comply
with an interim possession order), the Criminal Law Act 1977, ss 6 to 8, or 10

(offences of entering and remaining on property), or the Legal Aid, Sentencing and Punishment of Offenders Act 2012, s 144 (squatting in a residential building)—in these cases the arresting constable must be in uniform;

(e) of arresting, in pursuance of the Children and Young Persons Act 1969, s 32(1A), any child or young person who has been remanded to local authority accommodation or youth detention accommodation;

(f) of arresting someone for an offence to which the Animal Health Act 1981, s 61 applies (powers of entry and search in relation to rabies offences);

(g) of recapturing someone who is, or is deemed for any purpose to be, unlawfully at large while liable to be detained:

    (i) in a prison, young offender institution, secure training centre or secure college; or

    (ii) in pursuance of the Powers of Criminal Courts (Sentencing) Act 2000, s 92 (detention of children and young persons guilty of grave crimes), in any other place;

(h) of recapturing someone unlawfully at large whom he is pursuing (ie chasing); or

(i) of saving life or limb or preventing serious damage to property. A divisional court has held that the words 'life or limb' are wide enough to cover saving someone from himself as well as saving someone from a third party.

Except in the case of (i), the powers of entry and search under PACE, s 17: (a) are only exercisable where a constable has reasonable grounds for believing that the person whom he is seeking is on the premises, and (b) are limited in respect of premises consisting of two or more dwellings in the same way as with the powers to search under s 32 described on p 66.

A search under s 17 may only be made to the extent reasonably required for the purpose for which the power of entry is required. The courts have ruled that, when exercising his right of entry by force under s 17, a police officer must give any occupant present the reason why he is seeking entry even if that reason is apparent in the circumstances. Otherwise the forcible entry will be unlawful, unless circumstances make giving reasons impossible, impracticable or undesirable. If the real reason is to arrest a person inside for an offence, for instance, it is insufficient to tell the occupants that the officer wishes to 'speak to' that person about the offence.

Entry, search and seizure after an arrest

Entry and search

PACE, s 18(1) empowers a constable to enter and search any premises (as defined on p 66) which *are* occupied or controlled by a person under arrest for an indictable offence before that person is taken to a police station or released on street bail, if he has reasonable grounds for suspecting that there is on the premises evidence, other than items subject to legal privilege (p 73), which relates to that offence or to another indictable offence connected with or similar to that offence (eg, if the person has been arrested for burglary, the proceeds of other burglaries or large-scale theft, but not drugs). A search under s 18 is only permitted to the extent reasonably required for the purpose of discovering such evidence (s 18(3)). Because the power under s 18 only applies to premises *occupied or controlled* by the arrested person, a search of premises not so occupied or controlled is unlawful—even if they are reasonably believed to be so occupied or controlled (eg because the arrested person has given a false name and address).

Unless the following exception applies, a search under s 18 may not be made without the written authorisation of an officer of the rank of inspector (or above). The exception is that such a search may be carried out by a constable without an authorisation before a person is taken to a police station or released on street bail if the presence of that person elsewhere is necessary for the effective investigation of the offence (s 18(4)–(5A)). In such a case, the constable who conducts the search must notify an inspector (or above) of it as soon as practicable. PACE Code B: the Code of Practice for Searches of Premises by Police Officers and the Seizure of Property Found by Police Officers on Persons or Premises provides that if possible the authorising officer should record the authority on the Notice of Powers and Rights (which should be given or left as explained on p 84). The record of the grounds for the search and the nature of the evidence sought should be made in the custody record if there is one. Otherwise it should be made in the officer's pocket book, or the search record.

If the person in occupation or control of the premises is in police custody at the time that the search is carried out, the record must be made in the custody record.

An officer who proposes to enter and search premises under a written authorisation under s 18 must explain to the occupier, in so far as it is practicable to do so, the reason why he intends so to act. Failure to do so will render his subsequent conduct unlawful. A divisional court has held that simply offering to show the written authorisation at a window to an occupier who refused to come to the window was insufficient; the reason must be stated.

The effect of PACE, s 18 is that if a television retailer is arrested in the living quarters above his shop premises on a charge of theft of television sets, the constable would be empowered to search not only his living quarters but also the shop premises after arrest as they are premises 'occupied or controlled' by that person.

A search of any person who has not been arrested, which is carried out during a search of premises, must be carried out in accordance with Code A.

Seizure

A constable may seize and retain anything on the premises for which he may search under the above power. (Although a vehicle, vessel or tent is 'premises' for the purpose of PACE, this does not prevent the seizure of the vehicle, vessel or tent itself.) The additional powers of seizure under CJPA 2001, s 50 (see p 68) apply to this power of seizure.

POWERS TO SEARCH UNDER A SEARCH WARRANT

Power to issue warrant

Many statutes provide *particular* powers to enter and search premises under the authority of a warrant. An example is provided by the Terrorism Act 2000, Sch 5 referred to on p 76. In addition, PACE, s 8 provides justices with a *general* power to issue warrants to enter and search premises (as defined on p 66).

Applications for a search warrant are served on the court officer (or the court, if the court office is closed), and not on a person who would be affected by the warrant. Applications are heard in private, unless the court otherwise directs, in the absence of any person who would be affected by the warrant.

Search warrants under PACE, s 8

Requirement for issue of search warrant under s 8

PACE, s 8(1) provides that if, on an application made by a constable, a justice of the peace is satisfied that there are reasonable grounds for believing:

(a) that an indictable offence (or a 'relevant offence' under the Immigration Act 1971) has been committed; and

(b) that there is material on premises mentioned in PACE, s 8(1A) (below) which is likely to be of substantial value (whether by itself or with other material) to the investigation of the offence; and

(c) that the material is likely to be relevant (ie admissible) evidence; and

(d) that it does not consist of or include items subject to legal privilege, excluded material or special procedure material (described on p 74); and

(e) that *any* of the conditions specified in s 8(3) below applies, in relation to each set of premises specified in the application;

he may issue a warrant authorising a constable to enter and search the premises.

A divisional court has held that a computer and its hard disc are 'material' for the purposes of s 8(1).

Section 8(1A) provides that the 'premises' mentioned in (b) above are:

(a) one or more sets of premises specified in the application (in which case the application is for a 'specific premises warrant'); or

(b) any premises occupied or controlled by a person specified in the application, including such sets of premises as are so specified (in which case the application is for an 'all-premises warrant').

Section 8(1B) provides that, if the application is for an all-premises warrant, the justice of the peace must also be satisfied:

(a) that, because of the particulars of the offence referred to in s 8(1)(a) above, there are reasonable grounds for believing that it is necessary to search premises occupied or controlled by the person in question which are not specified in the application in order to find the material referred to in s 8(1)(b) above; and

(b) that it is not reasonably practicable to specify in the application all the premises which he occupies or controls and which might need to be searched.

These additional provisions assist in the investigation of serious organised crime. Crime syndicates may occupy or control many sets of premises and the search of one might lead to the discovery of other premises upon which the material being sought is situated. Provided that the search continues within buildings which are within the syndicate's control, it will be authorised by an 'all-premises warrant'.

It is vital to remember that the justice must be satisfied that all the requirements in s 8(1)(a) to (d) above are satisfied. If that is so, then it is necessary for him to be satisfied of the existence of any one of the conditions set out in s 8(3) referred to in s 8(1) (e) above, namely:

(a) that it is not practicable to communicate with any person entitled to grant entry to the premises;

(b) that it is practicable to communicate with a person entitled to grant entry to the premises but it is not practicable to communicate with any person entitled to grant access to the evidence;

(c) that entry to the premises will not be granted unless a warrant is produced; or
(d) that the purpose of the search may be frustrated or seriously prejudiced unless a constable arriving at the premises can secure immediate entry to them.

If the application for the warrant does not identify which of these conditions is being relied on, the issue of the warrant will be unlawful.

Condition (a) would apply if there was no one occupying the premises at the time; (b) would apply if, for example, there was a caretaker to a block of flats who had master keys and who could therefore allow access but would have no right to grant access to the material; (c) would apply in the usual circumstances in which a warrant is sought; and (d) in circumstances in which the nature of the evidence is such that it could be easily disposed of if the occupier was aware of police interest. 'Practicable' in (a) and (b) does not simply mean feasible or physically possible. The circumstances must also be considered, eg the nature of the inquiries and the persons subject to them.

The obtaining of a search warrant is never to be treated as a formality. All the material necessary to justify the grant of the warrant should be contained in the information on the application form, which must identify which of the conditions in s 8(3) is being relied on. However, a divisional court has held that information grounding a warrant need not be disclosed in the warrant if that would not be in the public interest, even though the withholding of information might mean that the subject of the warrant cannot see how the warrant can be lawful.

A divisional court has held that, as a matter of good practice, the applicant for a search warrant under s 8 should, save in exceptional circumstances, be an officer directly involved in the investigation.

Items for which a search warrant under PACE, s 8 should not be sought

As noted above, a search warrant may not be sought under s 8 where the material in question may consist of or include items prima facie subject to legal privilege, excluded material or special procedure material. In such a case, application should be made to a judge under the provisions of PACE, Sch 1 described below.

Various terms included in PACE, s 8(1) are defined by ss 10 to 13 as follows.

Items subject to legal privilege   These are defined as:

(a) communications between a professional legal adviser and client (or representative) made in connection with the giving of legal advice;
(b) communications between a professional legal adviser and client (or representative), or between any such adviser or his client (or representative) and any other person, made in contemplation of legal proceedings and for the purpose of them; and
(c) items enclosed with or referred to in such communications.

A solicitor's record of appointments and attendances, therefore, is not subject to legal privilege. The exemption relating to items subject to legal privilege only applies if the material is in the possession of a person entitled to possess it. Items held with the intention of furthering a criminal purpose are specifically excluded from being subject to legal privilege, even though that intention does not exist on the part of the holder (eg a solicitor) but does on the part of another (eg a solicitor's client). The High Court has held that the retention of a small amount of legally privileged material inadvertently seized during a search does not render the execution of the search warrant unlawful.

Excluded material   This means:

(a) personal records (ie documentary and other records relating to the health of an individual or counselling given to him) acquired or created by a person in the course of a trade, business, etc or for the purpose of any paid or unpaid office and held in confidence by him;
(b) human tissue or tissue fluid taken for diagnosis or medical treatment and held in confidence; or
(c) journalistic material (ie material acquired or created for the purpose of journalism and held by the person acquiring or creating it for that purpose) consisting of documents or other records and held in confidence.

Special procedure material   This means:

(a) journalistic material, other than excluded material, and
(b) material, other than items subject to legal privilege and excluded material, held in confidence and acquired or created in the course of any trade, business, etc.

Production orders and search warrants under PACE, Sch 1

Although a justice may not issue a search warrant under PACE, s 8 in respect of material of any of the three types set out above, s 9 recognises that there may be occasions in which it is necessary to enter premises and search for excluded material or special procedure material by providing that a constable may obtain access to such material by making an application under Sch 1. Section 9 does not provide for access to items subject to legal privilege.

At the time of writing, the powers to make a production order or issue a warrant under PACE, Sch 1 are exercisable only by a circuit judge, but when amendments are brought into force the powers will also be exercisable by a judge of the High Court, a recorder, a qualifying judge advocate or a district judge (Magistrates' Courts). For convenience, 'judge' is used hereafter to cover the existing and future positions.

Under Sch 1, a judge may make a 'production order' or, in certain cases, issue a search warrant in respect of excluded material or special procedure material.

These provisions are intended to protect the confidence of the maker or holder of the record, etc, and not that of the suspect. Consequently, it is open to the maker or holder voluntarily to disclose the material. It is only where there is no consent on his part to do so that the special provisions of s 9 and Sch 1 come into play.

Production order

The basic order which a judge may issue under PACE, Sch 1 is a 'production order'. An application for such an order must be made by a constable. The person who has custody of the material—but not the suspected person unless he is in custody of the material—must be notified of the application (and of the material sought) and allowed to attend the hearing of the application and make representations. The Supreme Court has held that this means that each party should know what material the other party is asking the judge to take into account in making his decision and should have a fair opportunity to respond to it.

A production order requires the person apparently in possession of the material in question *either* to produce it to the constable for him to take away *or* to give the constable access to it not later (*in either case*) than the end of a seven-day period from the date of the order or the end of such longer period as the order may specify.

Where the material consists of information stored in electronic form, an order to produce has effect as an order to produce the material in a form in which it can be taken away and in which it is visible and legible, and an order to give access has effect as an order to give a constable access to the material in a form in which it is visible and legible.

The making of a production order depends on one or other of two sets of 'access conditions' being fulfilled. If the judge is satisfied of this, he may (not must) make a production order.

The two sets of access conditions   The first set of access conditions is fulfilled if:

(a) there are reasonable grounds for believing that:
  (i)   an indictable offence has been committed;
  (ii) there is material which consists of special procedure material or includes special procedure material and does not also include excluded material on premises specified in the application, or on premises occupied or controlled by a person specified in the application (including all such premises on which there are reasonable grounds for believing that there is such material as it is reasonably practicable so to specify);
  (iii) the material is likely to be of substantial value (whether by itself or together with other material) to the investigation in connection with which the application is made; and
  (iv) the material is likely to be relevant evidence;
(b) other methods of obtaining the material:
  (i)   have been tried without success; or
  (ii) have not been tried because it appeared that they were bound to fail; and
(c) it is in the public interest having regard:
  (i)   to the benefit likely to accrue to the investigation if the material is obtained; and
  (ii) to the circumstances under which the person in possession of the material holds it,
  that the material should be produced or that access to it should be given.

The second set of access conditions is met if:

(a) there are reasonable grounds for believing that there is material which consists of or includes special procedure material or excluded material on premises specified in the application or on premises occupied or controlled by a person specified in the application (including all such premises on which there are reasonable grounds for believing that there is such material as it is reasonably practicable so to specify);
(b) prior to the enactment of PACE, s 9, a search of such premises for that material could have been authorised by the issue of a warrant to a constable under an enactment other than Sch 1; and
(c) the issue of such a warrant would have been appropriate.

It will be noted that the second set of access conditions is not limited to cases where it is reasonably believed that an indictable offence has been committed.

A production order can be made even if it infringes or might infringe the privilege against self-incrimination of the person ordered to make production.

A divisional court has held that, before granting the application, the judge must be satisfied that it is substantially the last resort, ie that other practicable methods of obtaining the material have been exhausted without success.

Search warrant

The requirement of notice, together with the seven (or more) days' grace referred to above, gives a person time to dispose of incriminating material.

PACE, Sch 1 provides that a judge, on application by a constable, may issue a specific premises or all-premises search warrant in two types of case.

First, a judge may do so if satisfied that:

(a) either set of access conditions is met; and
(b) any of the four further conditions is also met in relation to each set of premises specified in the application:
  (i)   that it is not practicable to communicate with any person entitled to grant entry to the premises;
  (ii)   that it is practicable to communicate with a person entitled to grant entry to the premises but it is not practicable to communicate with any person entitled to grant access to the material;
  (iii) that the material contains information which is subject to a statutory restriction on disclosure or obligation of secrecy and is likely to be disclosed in breach of it if a warrant is not issued;
  (iv)   that service of notice of an application for a production order may seriously prejudice the investigation.

A search warrant (as opposed to a production order) will not be granted in practice in respect of a solicitor's office, unless proceeding by way of production order might seriously prejudice the investigation.

Second, a judge may also issue a search warrant under Sch 1 if satisfied that:

(a) the second set of access conditions is met; and
(b) a production order relating to the material has not been complied with.

The judge may not issue an all-premises warrant under Sch 1 unless he is satisfied:

(a) that there are reasonable grounds for believing that it is necessary to search premises occupied or controlled by the person in question which are not specified in the application, as well as those which are, in order to find the material in question; and
(b) that it is not reasonably practicable to specify all of the premises which he occupies or controls which might need to be searched.

Code B requires that an inspector (or above) be present and in charge of a search under a warrant issued under PACE, Sch 1 or TA 2000, Sch 5 (below). The Code also contains further provisions concerning such a search.

Search warrants under Terrorism Act 2000, Sch 5

By TA 2000, Sch 5, a constable may apply to a justice of the peace for the issue of a warrant for the purposes of a terrorist investigation authorising a constable to enter specified premises, to search those premises and persons found there, and to seize and retain relevant material. The 'premises' may be one or more sets of premises specified in the application (in which case the application is for a 'specific premises' warrant); or any premises occupied or controlled by a person specified in the application, including such sets of premises as are so specified (in which case the application is for an 'all-premises' warrant). A search warrant under the present provision does not authorise the seizure and retention of items subject to legal privilege.

Code A points out that, although the power to search persons found on premises to which a search warrant issued under TA 2000, Sch 5 applies does not require prior specific grounds to suspect that the person to be searched is in possession of an item for which there is an existing power to search, it is still necessary to ensure that the selection and treatment of those searched under these powers is based upon objective factors connected with the search of the premises, and not upon personal prejudice.

Schedule 5 also provides for production orders and search warrants in respect of excluded or special procedure material for the purposes of a terrorist investigation.

For a prospective power of a constable to remove and retain a document to ascertain whether it is one that may be seized under TA 2000, Sch 5, see Chapter 28 on the companion website.

Procedure before application is made for a search warrant or a production order

The relevant provisions are contained in Code B. Where information is received appearing to justify an application for any search warrant or for a production order, the officer concerned must take reasonable steps to check that the information is accurate, recent, and not provided maliciously or irresponsibly. An application is not permitted on the basis of information from an anonymous source where corroboration has not been sought. The nature of the articles and their location must be established as specifically as possible.

The officer must also make reasonable inquiries to establish what, if anything, is known about the likely occupier of the premises and the nature of the premises themselves, and whether they have previously been searched (and, if so, how recently); he must also obtain any other information relevant to the application.

An application to a justice of the peace for a search warrant or to a judge for a search warrant or production order may not be made without the signed written authority of an inspector (or above) or, in a case of urgency where no officer of this rank is readily available, the senior officer on duty. Where the application is made to a judge under TA 2000, Sch 5 it must be supported by a signed written authority from a superintendent (or above). In addition, other than in a case of urgency, the community relations officer must be consulted before a search takes place which might have an adverse effect on police/community relations. In urgent cases, the local police community liaison officer should be informed of the search as soon as possible after it has been made.

The making of an application

Between them, PACE, s 15 and Code B provide the following rules for *all* search warrants. An application for a search warrant must be supported by information in writing, specifying:

(a) the enactment under which the application is made;
(b) (i)   whether the warrant is to authorise entry and search of:
     (a) one set of premises, or
     (b) if the application is under PACE s 8, or Sch 1, more than one set of specified premises or all premises occupied or controlled by a specified person;
    (ii) the premises to be searched;
(c) the object of the search;

(d) the grounds on which the application is made (including, when the purpose of the search is to find evidence of an alleged offence, an indication of how the evidence relates to the investigation);

(e) where the application is under s 8 or Sch 1, for a single warrant to enter and search:
  (i) more than one set of specified premises, the officer must specify each set of premises which it is desired to enter and search;
  (ii) all premises occupied or controlled by a specified person, the officer must specify:
    (*a*) as many sets of premises which it is desired to enter and search as it is reasonably practicable to specify,
    (*b*) the person who is in occupation or control of those premises and any others which it is desired to search,
    (*c*) why it is necessary to search more premises than those which can be specified, and
    (*d*) why it is not reasonably practicable to specify all the premises which it is desired to enter and search;

(f) whether an application under s 8 is for a warrant authorising entry and search on more than one occasion; if so, the officer must state the grounds for this and whether the desired number of entries authorised is unlimited or a specified maximum;

(g) that there are no reasonable grounds for believing that material to be sought:
  (i) consists of or includes items subject to legal privilege (when applying to a justice of the peace or a judge); or
  (ii) consists of or includes excluded material or special procedure material (when applying to a justice of the peace);
  however, this does not affect the additional powers of seizure in the Criminal Justice and Police Act 2001 (material to be sifted and examined elsewhere—see pp 68–9);

(h) if applicable, a request for the warrant to authorise a person or persons to accompany the officer who executes the warrant.

Although the identity of an informant need not be disclosed, the officer must be prepared to deal with questions about the accuracy of previous information provided by that source or other related matters. The Court of Appeal has held that an applicant for a search warrant under PACE, s 8 must make a full and frank disclosure of material facts within his knowledge; in effect, the applicant for the warrant must put on a 'defence hat' and ask himself what, if he was representing the person who would be affected by the warrant, he would say to the justice, and then state it.

A divisional court has held that police officers would be well advised to seek legal advice before applying for a search warrant under Sch 1, especially if the material sought is more than likely to contain legally privileged material. It added that the application must:

(a) set out each of the statutory requirements which has to be satisfied in the particular case before the warrant in question can be granted, although only the route (p 75) to a warrant which has been selected in a particular case should be dealt with;

(b) explain how each of the relevant requirements is satisfied by setting out all the relevant facts relied on, including all facts and matters which are said to show that a particular 'reasonable belief' is justified and (in the case of the first set of access conditions) why it is in the public interest for the material to be produced (having regard to (c) in the third paragraph on p 75);

(c) state whether there might be a claim for legal privilege in respect of any communication sought and, if so, how and why that would arise together with precise details of the arrangements which are to be taken to ensure that there will be an independent supervising lawyer present at the time of the search;

(d) make full and frank disclosure (as in the previous paragraph).

An application under TA 2000, Sch 5 must indicate why a production order would be inappropriate.

The constable must answer on oath any question asked by the justice or judge. If an application is refused, no further application may be made for a warrant to search those premises unless supported by additional grounds.

The search warrant

PACE, s 8(1C) provides that a warrant may authorise entry to and search of premises on more than one occasion if, on the application, the justice of the peace is satisfied that it is necessary to authorise multiple entries in order to achieve the purpose for which he issues the warrant. PACE, s 8(1D) provides that, if multiple entries are so authorised, the number of entries authorised may be unlimited, or limited to a maximum.

Section 8(2) authorises a constable to seize and retain anything for which a search has been authorised.

Although PACE distinguishes between a 'specific premises warrant' and an 'all-premises warrant', a single warrant may include both types provided that the relevant information is given in the application.

By s 15(6), a warrant (which term includes a schedule to the warrant):

(a) must specify:
    (i) the name of the person who applies for it (it is not enough to state, for example, that the applicant is 'the paedophile intelligence unit'),
    (ii) the date on which it is issued,
    (iii) the enactment under which it is issued, and
    (iv) each set of premises to be searched, or (in the case of an all-premises warrant) the person who is in occupation or control of premises to be searched, together with any premises under his occupation or control which can be specified and which are to be searched; and

(b) must identify, so far as is practicable, the articles or persons to be sought. (The purpose of (b) is to enable anyone interested in the execution of the warrant to know the limits of the powers granted, and to enable him to challenge the lawfulness of the seizure of a particular item.)

In relation to (a)(iv), if the police want to keep information about the search of other sets of premises from the occupier, separate warrants should be obtained; alternatively, the addresses of the other sets of premises can be redacted. A divisional court has held that whether or not a warrant satisfies the requirements of s 15(6) must be judged exclusively by reference to the terms of the warrant and not by reference to any other source such as the information supporting the grant of the warrant.

A search based on a warrant which does not satisfy the requirements of s 15(6) is unlawful.

Section 15(7) provides that there must be two copies of a specific premises warrant which specifies only one set of premises and does not authorise multiple entries. In the case of any other warrant, as many copies as are reasonably required may be made.

Where a warrant authorises multiple entries it must specify whether the number of entries authorised is unlimited, or limited to a specified maximum.

A divisional court has held that 'a copy' of a search warrant means a full copy, and that therefore a copy which omitted the premises to be searched and left that information to be filled in by hand in respect of particular premises by the officer executing the warrant on those premises was not a valid copy of the warrant.

Execution of a search warrant

PACE, s 15(1) provides that an entry on or search of premises under a search warrant is unlawful and there is no right to retain anything seized, unless ss 15 (above) and 16 are complied with. Section 16 sets out the following provisions which apply to all search warrants.

A warrant may be executed by any constable. A warrant may authorise a person, other than a constable or designated person, to accompany the constable who executes the warrant (s 16(2)), for example an expert in a particular field to help accurately identify the material sought. Such a person has the same powers as a constable in relation to the execution of the warrant and the seizure or (prospectively) detention of anything to which it relates, but may exercise them only in the company, and under the supervision, of a constable (s 16(2A), (2B)). Entry and search must be within three calendar months of issue (s 16(3)) (or within the period specified in the enactment under which the warrant is issued, if shorter) and must be at a reasonable hour unless this would frustrate the purpose of the search (s 16(4)). However, this does not apply to warrants issued under TA 2000, Sch 5, which are exercisable only within 24 hours of issue. Section 16(3A) covers the execution of all-premises warrants. It provides that in the case of an all-premises warrant, no premises which are not specified in the warrant may be entered or searched unless an inspector (or above) has in writing authorised them to be entered. Section 16(3B) provides that no premises may be entered or searched for the second or any subsequent time under a warrant which authorises multiple entries unless an inspector (or above) has authorised that entry in writing. Code B provides that the inspector (or above) referred to in s 16(3A) and (3B) must not be involved in the investigation.

A divisional court has held that, where a search warrant authorises entry 'on one occasion' to search for specified goods, the word 'occasion' does not equal one day, or require the search to be completed in one calendar day. Thus, it is not a breach of such a warrant for the police to occupy the premises for a number of days while the search is carried out.

Where the occupier of the premises is present, the constable must, when seeking to execute a search warrant:

(a) identify himself (by warrant or other identification number in the case of terrorism inquiries) and, if not in uniform, show his warrant card (but in so doing in the case of terrorism inquiries, he need not reveal his name);

(b) produce the warrant to the occupier; and

(c) supply him with a copy of it.

The constable must act likewise in relation to a person apparently in charge of the premises in the absence of the occupier.

A divisional court has held that requirements (a) to (c) existed so that the occupier of premises might know that those who executed a search warrant had lawful authority to do so and could see before the search began what property might be seized under the search warrant. It held that a failure by a constable executing a search warrant to hand over a copy of it until after the search had been completed was unlawful as being in breach of the requirements. Likewise, another divisional court has held that a search was unlawful where a warrant stated that the premises to be searched were described in an attached schedule but the copy given to the occupier did not include the schedule. This would be the case even if an uncertified photocopy of the schedule was attached to the warrant.

In any other case, the constable must leave a copy of the warrant in a prominent place on the premises.

The premises may only be searched to the extent required for the purpose for which the warrant was issued. A divisional court has held that a breach of this provision does not necessarily render the entirety of an entry, search and seizure unlawful.

A divisional court has held that an independent supervising lawyer should be present at a search where there is a potential issue as to legal professional privilege.

The Court of Appeal has held that the Equality Act 2010 requires the police to make reasonable adjustments to the practice of conducting searches in spoken English so that it does not have a detrimental effect on deaf persons, eg by adopting a policy of a sign language interpreter on standby every time there is a search of premises of a person known or believed to be deaf, or taking other reasonable steps, such as having available officers skilled in lip reading and sign language.

Save in exceptional circumstances the media should not be invited to be present when a search warrant (or any other investigative procedure) is being executed, nor should they be invited to police briefings prior to the execution of a warrant, because reports emanating from such involvement are liable to prejudice a fair trial.

SEIZURE

A constable who is searching any person or premises under any statutory power or with the consent of the occupier may seize anything, other than a legally privileged item, which:

(a) is covered by a warrant;

(b) the officer has reasonable grounds for believing is evidence of an offence or has been obtained in consequence of the commission of an offence, but only if seizure is necessary to prevent the item(s) being concealed, lost, disposed of or tampered with; or

(c) is covered by the powers in CJPA 2001 allowing an officer to seize property and retain it for sifting or examination elsewhere.

GENERAL PROVISIONS ON ENTRY, SEARCH, SEIZURE, ACCESS AND RETENTION

In addition to the specific rules already described, Code B lays down a number of rules which apply to searches by police of premises (as defined on p 66), whether those of the suspect or anyone else including the victim:

(a) undertaken for the purposes of an investigation into an alleged offence, with the occupier's consent, other than searches made in the following circumstances:

(i) routine scenes-of-crime searches;

(ii) calls to a fire or burglary made by or on behalf of an occupier or searches following the activation of fire or burglar alarms;

(iii) searches where it is unnecessary to seek consent because in the circumstances this would cause disproportionate inconvenience to the person concerned;

(iv) bomb threat calls;

(b) under powers conferred by PACE, ss 17 (entry to arrest/search), 18 (entry and search after arrest) and 32 (search on arrest);

(c) undertaken in pursuance of any search warrant issued in accordance with PACE, ss 15 or 16; or

(d) under any other police power to enter premises with or without a search warrant for any purpose connected with the investigation into an alleged or suspected offence or with the enforcement of a TPIM notice.

The exception for routine scenes-of-crime searches ceases to apply if the search develops into more than just a routine scenes-of-crime search. At that point, at the latest, Code B applies.

Entry other than with consent

The officer in charge must first attempt to communicate with the occupier or any other person entitled to grant access to the premises by explaining the authority under which he seeks entry to the premises and ask the occupier to allow him to do so, unless:

(a) the premises are unoccupied;

(b) the occupier and any other person entitled to grant access are absent; or

(c) there are reasonable grounds to believe that to alert the occupier or any other person entitled to grant access by attempting to communicate with him would frustrate the object of the search or endanger the officers concerned or other persons.

The circumstances in (c) might exist where there are known to be a number of persons on the premises all of whom are suspected of being involved in the offence, any of whom could dispose of the evidence whilst these procedures are being followed; or, in the case of entry to search for an armed criminal, where danger might arise if he was warned of imminent arrest. Although, in the circumstances in (c), an officer need not comply with the requirements as to identification, production of his warrant card (if not in uniform) and search warrant (if any) before effecting entry, he must do so before conducting the search (except that if the search is under a search warrant it is enough if he gives a copy of the search warrant at the first reasonable opportunity).

Unless (c) applies, where the premises are occupied, the officer in charge of the search must before the search begins:

(i)   identify himself (by warrant or other identification number in a terrorist investigation) and, if not in uniform, show his warrant card (although he may do so without revealing his name in a terrorist investigation);

(ii) state the purpose of the search and the grounds for undertaking it; and

(iii) identify and introduce any person accompanying the officer on the search (such persons should carry identification for production on request) and briefly describe that person's role in the process.

Searches with consent

Code B provides that, if it is proposed to search premises with the consent of a person (X) entitled to grant entry, the consent must, if practicable, be in writing.

Before seeking such consent the officer in charge must state the purpose of the search and its extent. This information must be as specific as possible, particularly regarding the articles or persons sought and the parts of the premises to be searched. X must be clearly informed that he is not obliged to consent, that any consent may be withdrawn at any time, including before the search starts or while it is underway, and that anything seized may be produced in evidence. If, at the time, X is not suspected of an offence the officer must tell him so when stating the purpose of the search. An officer cannot enter and search premises or continue to search premises if consent has been given under duress or is withdrawn before the search is completed.

In the case of a lodging house or other similar accommodation, a search should not be made on the basis solely of the landlord's consent.

It is unnecessary to seek consent where this would cause disproportionate inconvenience to the person concerned, for example where it is reasonable to assume that innocent occupiers would agree to, and expect that, police would take the proposed action. Examples are where a suspect has fled from the scene of the crime and it is necessary quickly to check surrounding gardens and the like to see whether he is hiding; or where police have arrested someone in the night after a pursuit and it is necessary to make a brief check of gardens along the route of the pursuit to see whether stolen or incriminating articles have been found.

Use of force

Where the police are acting under a warrant or under one of the above statutory powers, reasonable and proportionate force may be used if necessary in the following cases if the officer in charge is satisfied that the premises are those specified in the warrant:

(a) where the occupier or another person entitled to grant access has refused to allow entry;

(b) where it is impossible to communicate with such a person;

(c) where the premises are known to be unoccupied or the occupier, etc is known to be absent; or

(d) where there are reasonable grounds to believe that to do so would frustrate the object of the search or endanger someone.

It is permissible to restrict the movement of occupants to one room while another room is being searched.

Designated persons

If a power conferred on a designated person under the Police Reform Act 2002, Part 4:

(a) allows reasonable force to be used when exercised by a police officer, a designated person exercising that power has the same entitlement to use force; and

(b) includes power to use force to enter premises, that power is not exercisable by that designated person except:

　(i)　in the company and under the supervision of a police officer; or

　(ii)　for the purpose of:

　　(*a*)　saving life or limb; or

　　(*b*)　preventing serious damage to property.

Notice of Powers and Rights

Under Code B, an officer conducting a search of premises under a search warrant issued under PACE or TA 2000 or under a power given by PACE (see (a) below), or with the occupier's consent, must, unless it is impracticable to do so, provide the occupier with a copy of a notice in a standard format:

(a) specifying whether the search is made under warrant, or with consent, or in the exercise of powers under PACE, ss 17, 18, or 32;

(b) summarising the extent of the powers of search and seizure conferred in PACE and other relevant legislation as appropriate;

(c) explaining the rights of the occupier and of the owner of property seized;

(d) explaining that compensation may be payable in appropriate cases for damage caused in entering and searching premises, and giving the address to which an application should be directed; and

(e) stating that a copy of Code B is available for consultation at any police station.

If the occupier is present, copies of the notice, and of the warrant (if the search is made under warrant), should if practicable be given to him before the search begins, unless the officer in charge of the search reasonably believes that to do so would frustrate the object of the search or endanger the officers concerned or other persons. If the occupier is not present, copies of the notice, and of the warrant where appropriate, should be left in a prominent place on the premises or appropriate part of the premises and should be endorsed with the names of the officer in charge of the search and of his police station and the date and time of the search. The officer's warrant number, not his name, should be given in the case of a terrorism investigation. The warrant itself should be endorsed to show that this has been done.

Conduct of searches

Code B provides as follows.

Premises may be searched only to the extent necessary to achieve the object of the search, having regard to the size and nature of what is sought. This means that a search cannot be made in places where the articles specified in a warrant could not possibly be found or for longer than necessary to find those articles. For example, a warrant to search for television sets would not authorise the examination of the contents of small drawers.

A search may not continue under the authority of a warrant once everything specified in it has been found, or the officer in charge is satisfied that things specified are not on the premises.

The search must be conducted with due consideration for the property and privacy of the occupier, and with no more disturbance than necessary. Reasonable force may only be used to conduct the search where it is necessary because the co-operation of the occupier cannot be obtained or is insufficient for the purpose. An occupier must not be discouraged or prevented from securing the services of a friend, neighbour, or other person to witness the search, unless the officer in charge has reasonable grounds to believe that this would seriously hinder the investigation or endanger the officers concerned or other people. A search need not be unreasonably delayed for this purpose. If the premises have been entered by force the officer in charge must satisfy himself, before leaving, that they are secured either by arranging for the occupier or his agent to be present or by any other appropriate means.

A person need not be cautioned before being asked questions solely concerned with the proper and effective conduct of a search; for example, to locate the key to a locked drawer or otherwise to seek co-operation during the search. If questioning goes beyond this point it may amount to an interview and would require the associated safeguards.

In determining when to make a search, the officer in charge must always give regard to the time of day at which the occupier is likely to be present, and should not search at a time when the occupier or any other person on the premises is likely to be asleep unless this is unavoidable. If the wrong premises are mistakenly searched, everything possible should be done to allay any sense of grievance. In appropriate cases assistance should be given to obtain compensation.

The local police/community consultative group or its equivalent should be informed as soon as practicable after a search where there is reason to believe that it might have had an adverse effect on relations between the police and the community.

Records of searches

Code B requires that, if premises have been searched, a record of the search must be made. That record must be made by or on behalf of the officer in charge of the search, on his return to the police station. The record must include:

(a) the address of the premises;
(b) the date, time and duration of the search;
(c) the authority for it (including a copy of the warrant and the written authority to apply for it, or the written consent where the search was made thereunder);
(d) the names of officer(s) in charge of, and of the other officers and authorised persons conducting, the search (except inquiries linked to the investigation of terrorism, or where it is reasonably believed that disclosing their names might endanger them; here the record must state the warrant or other identification number and duty station of each officer and any identification of any police staff);
(e) the names of any persons on the premises (if known);
(f) any grounds for refusing the occupier's request to have someone present during the search;
(g) a list of articles seized (or a note of its location) and, if not covered by a warrant, the reason for seizure;
(h) whether force was used and, if so, the reason;
(i) a list of any damage caused, and the circumstances in which it was caused;
(j) if applicable, the reason it was not practicable to give the occupier a copy of the 'Notice of Powers and Rights'; and
(k) when the occupier was not present, the place where copies of the Notice of Powers and Rights and search warrant were left on the premises.

Search registers must be maintained at each sub-divisional or equivalent police station and the above record must be made, copied, or referred to in the register.

On each occasion when premises are searched under a warrant, the warrant must be endorsed to show:

(a) whether any articles specified in the warrant were found and the address where found;
(b) whether any other articles were seized;

(c) the date and time at which it was executed and, if present, the name and address of the occupier, or if he was not present, the name of the person in charge of the premises;

(d) the names of the officers who executed it and any authorised persons who accompanied them (except in the case of inquiries linked to the investigation of terrorism, in which case the warrant or other identification number and duty station of each officer concerned, and any identification number of police staff, should be given); and

(e) whether a copy, together with a copy of the Notice of Powers and Rights, was handed to the occupier; or whether it was endorsed as required (see p 84).

A warrant must be returned to the appropriate person within three months from issue or sooner on completion of the search(es) authorised by it. The appropriate person is:

(a) if the warrant was issued by a justice of the peace, the designated officer for the local justice area; or

(b) if it was issued by a judge, the appropriate officer of the court from which he issued it.

General powers of seizure

PACE, s 19 gives the police wide powers of seizure in addition to those otherwise provided by the Act or elsewhere. It provides that a constable lawfully on any premises (as defined on p 66) (eg with the occupier's consent) may seize anything on the premises if he has reasonable grounds for believing that:

(a) it has been obtained in consequence of the commission of an offence; or

(b) it is evidence in relation to an offence which he is investigating or any other offence; *and* (in either case)

(c) it is necessary to seize it in order to prevent it from being concealed, lost, altered or destroyed.

Although a vehicle, vessel or tent is premises for the purpose of PACE, the reference to anything 'on the premises' does not prevent the seizure of a vehicle, vessel or tent as a whole.

In the same circumstances (ie (a) to (c)), a constable may require any information stored in any electronic form and accessible from the premises to be produced in a form in which it can be taken away and in which it is legible or from which it can readily be produced in such a form.

Section 19 also provides that no relevant statutory power of seizure authorises the seizure of an item which the constable has reasonable grounds for believing to be subject to legal privilege as defined on p 73. Generally, a constable will have to examine an item to test a claim to legal privilege and, if no claim is made, the constable will not have reasonable grounds for believing it to be privileged until he has examined it. If the constable later obtains reasonable grounds, the item must be returned forthwith, but the seizure does not become unlawful.

A divisional court has held that, where property has been obtained by an unlawful search and is stored at a police station, s 19 cannot be relied on to enable a constable to seize it there and thereby to convert unlawful possession into lawful possession.

Additional powers of seizure

The additional powers of seizure under CJPA 2001, s 50 and related provisions (see p 68) apply where there is a right of seizure under a search warrant or under PACE, ss 18, 19 and 32.

Record of seizure and access

PACE, s 21 provides that a constable who seizes anything *under any statutory power* must, on request, provide within a reasonable time the occupier of premises where it was seized or a person who had custody or control of the thing immediately before seizure with a record of what he seized.

Section 21 also provides for access to a thing which has been seized, and for the photographing or copying of it, by a person who had custody or control of it immediately before seizure.

Retention

Unless a court exercises a statutory power of forfeiture of property on conviction, the situation is as follows.

PACE, s 22 provides that anything seized or taken away under s 19 may be retained so long as is necessary in all the circumstances. 'So long as necessary' in s 22 means so long as necessary for carrying out the purposes for which the powers of seizure under s 19 are conferred. In particular, anything seized under s 19 for the purposes of a criminal investigation may be retained (unless a photograph or copy would suffice) for use as evidence at a trial for an offence, or for forensic examination or investigation in connection with an offence. Moreover, anything may be retained to establish its owner, where there are reasonable grounds for believing that it has been obtained in consequence of the commission of an offence.

Section 22 has been construed by the Court of Appeal as meaning that, if the police consider that, for 'criminal law enforcement purposes' (ie the four matters set out in (a) to (d) on pp 220–1), it is necessary to retain a DNA profile derived from a swab taken under s 19 from a scene of crime, they cannot use it for any other unconnected purpose. Thus, for example, the police cannot disclose a profile for use to resolve a paternity issue in civil proceedings.

Nothing seized on the grounds that it may be used:

(a) to cause physical injury;
(b) to damage property;
(c) to interfere with evidence; or
(d) to assist in escape from police detention or lawful custody

may be retained after the person from whom it was seized has been freed from detention or custody or has been bailed.

There is no power to retain seized property for any purpose other than that for which it was originally seized.

Any person who had custody or control of property immediately prior to its seizure must, if it is retained, be provided on request within a reasonable time with a list or description of the property, and he or his representative must be allowed supervised access to examine the property or have it photographed or copied (or must be provided with a photograph or copy) within a reasonable time and at his own expense, unless the officer in charge of the investigation has reasonable grounds for believing that this would prejudice the investigation of the offence or criminal proceedings, or lead to the commission of an offence by providing access to unlawful material such as pornography. A record of such grounds must be made if access is denied.

The Court of Appeal has ruled that the police may retain seized property:

(a) for a short period, after detention under s 22 is no longer necessary, while they consider their position; or

(b) so long as necessary in all the circumstances after the CPS has decided not to prosecute but a private prosecution is being contemplated or taking place.

According to a divisional court, s 22 does not entitle the police, once an investigation is over, to retain CCTV footage on the basis that its owner might use it to identify someone in order to carry out a revenge attack.

A person claiming property seized by the police may apply for its possession to a magistrates' court under the Police (Property) Act 1897 and should, where appropriate, be advised of this procedure. The court has a discretion under the 1897 Act. Hence, although the police cannot rely on PACE, s 22 to retain property, there may be circumstances where its return should be refused, eg where it would encourage or assist someone in a criminal act.

In addition to the provisions in PACE 1984, s 22, retention of seized property is also governed by CJPA 2001, s 56. Section 56 applies to property seized by any constable who is lawfully on premises (or by a person authorised by a search warrant to accompany a constable), and to property seized by a constable carrying out a lawful search of any person. Retention of such property is authorised by s 56 if there are reasonable grounds for believing that it is property obtained in consequence of the commission of an offence and that its retention is necessary to prevent it being concealed, lost, damaged, altered or destroyed. The power under s 56 also extends to property that is believed to be evidence in relation to any offence where its retention is required for the same purposes.

By CJPA 2001, s 59, any person with a relevant interest in property seized under CJPA 2001 ss 50 or 51 (pp 67–9) or under any other statutory powers of seizure conferred on a constable may apply to a judge of the Crown Court for its return on the grounds that there was no power of seizure, or that the seized material contains matter subject to legal privilege or contains excluded or special procedure material, as defined on p 74. The term 'any person with a relevant interest in property' refers to the person from whom the property was seized, any person with an interest in it or any other person if he had custody or control of it immediately before the seizure.

INTERCEPTION OF COMMUNICATIONS, AND ACQUISITION AND DISCLOSURE OF COMMUNICATIONS DATA

Interception of telecommunications and public postal services

The Regulation of Investigatory Powers Act 2000 (RIPA 2000), Part I, Chapter 1 (ss 1–21) is aimed at protecting the confidentiality of public postal services and public telecommunications systems, and some private telecommunication systems which are attached to a public system. It is an indictable (either way) offence under s 1(1) (public postal services and public telecommunication systems) and s 1(2) (private telecommunication systems) intentionally and without lawful authority to intercept a communication in the course of its transmission by one of these means. 'Transmission' includes the period when a transmissions system stores a communication in such a manner as to enable the intended recipient to access it (eg where it is stored on voicemail); this is so even if it has been accessed by him. However, in the case of a private system, an interceptor does not commit an offence if he is a person with a right to control the operation or use of the system, which means the right to authorise or forbid the operation or use of the system, *or* if he has the express or implied consent of such a person to make the interception. In the case of the interception of a communication made by means of a public telecommunications system, a civil sanction has been provided to deal with cases of interceptions without lawful authority which do not constitute the above offence.

The recording by a covert listening device in a motor car of one person's voice speaking on a telephone is not an interception. Nor is the audio recording by an undercover police officer of a telephone conversation with a suspect, although it does amount to surveillance (dealt with below).

RIPA 2000 makes special provisions for the issue of *interception warrants* and provides for lawful interception without an interception warrant where one or more of the parties has consented (eg calls received from kidnappers). Such an interception will be authorised as surveillance, rather than by means of an interception warrant.

The Regulation of Investigatory Powers (Interception of Communications: Code of Practice) Order 2016 brought into force a revised code of practice relating to the interception of communications, to which anyone exercising or performing a power or duty to which the Code applies must have regard.

Acquisition and disclosure of communications data

RIPA 2000, Part 1, Chapter 2 (ss 21–25) provides a regulatory framework for access to and handling of 'communications data' (ie data about the use made of a communication service which may be comprised in an attachment to a communication, or which exists independently of a communication, as opposed to the content of a communication—which is dealt with by Chapter 1).

There are powers under separate legislation for the retention of communications data subject to safeguards.

SURVEILLANCE, AND CONDUCT AND USE OF 'COVERT HUMAN INTELLIGENCE SOURCES'

Surveillance and 'covert human intelligence sources'

RIPA 2000, Part II (ss 26–48) deals with these matters. It creates a regulatory framework for three types of activity: directed surveillance; the use of covert human intelligence sources; and intrusive surveillance. A fundamental feature of each of these is that it is 'covert'.

Each of the three types of activity involves a different authorisation procedure. RIPA 2000, s 27 provides that conduct falling within one of these three types is lawful if it is authorised and carried out in accordance with the authorisation. No civil liability will be incurred in respect of conduct 'incidental' to such lawful conduct, which is not in itself conduct in respect of which an authorisation or warrant is capable of being granted under a relevant enactment and might reasonably have been expected to be sought. A 'relevant enactment' means the RIPA 2000; the Intelligence Services Act 1994, s 5 (warrants for the intelligence services); or an enactment contained in the Police Act 1997 (PA 1997), Part III (powers of covert entry and interference with property by the police).

Directed surveillance

Surveillance is directed if it is *covert*, but *not intrusive*, and is undertaken:

(a) for the purpose of a specific investigation or a specific operation;
(b) in such a manner as is likely to result in the obtaining of private information about a person (whether or not one specifically identified for the purposes of the investigation or operation); and
(c) otherwise than by way of an immediate response to events or circumstances the nature of which is such that it would not be reasonably practicable for an authorisation under RIPA 2000, Part II to be sought for the carrying out of the surveillance.

'Private information' includes any information relating to a person's private or family life.

Surveillance is *covert* if it is carried out in a manner that is calculated to ensure that the persons who are subject to the surveillance are unaware that it is or may be taking place.

Surveillance is *intrusive* if, and only if, it is covert surveillance that is carried out in relation to anything taking place on any residential premises (a police cell is such) or in any private vehicle (a police vehicle is not a private vehicle) and involves the presence of an individual on the premises or in the vehicle or is carried out by means of a surveillance device. However, there are qualifications to this. Surveillance is *not intrusive* if it involves no more than the placing of a vehicle location device, or it is surveillance involving the interception of a communication which is sent by, or intended for, a person who has consented to the interception. In addition, it is *not intrusive* if it is carried out by a device which is not present upon the residential premises or private vehicle concerned, unless the device is such that it consistently provides information of the same quality and detail as might be expected to be obtained from a device which was actually present on the premises or in the vehicle. Lastly, surveillance by devices designed to catch TV licence dodgers is neither directed nor intrusive.

By RIPA 2000, s 28, a 'designated person' may grant an authorisation for the carrying out of directed surveillance if he believes it is necessary on specified grounds, including national security, the prevention or detection of crime, and the prevention of disorder. The designated person must believe that the authorised surveillance is proportionate to what is sought to be achieved by it.

Among the persons designated for the purposes of s 28 (and s 29, below, with the exceptions on pp 92–3) are police officers of the rank of superintendent (inspector in urgent cases). For the purposes of the grant of an authorisation that combines an authorisation under ss 28 or 29 and an authorisation for carrying out intrusive surveillance (see p 93), the Secretary of State is the person designated for the purpose.

A written authorisation has effect for three months. Urgent oral authorisations or written authorisations granted by a person who is entitled to act only in urgent cases only have effect for 72 hours, unless renewed.

Code of practice

The Regulation of Investigatory Powers (Covert Surveillance and Property Interference: Code of Practice) Order 2014 brought into force a revised code of practice relating to covert surveillance which applies to directed surveillance.

Use of a covert human intelligence source

A person is a covert human intelligence source if:

(a) he establishes or maintains a personal or other relationship with a person, for the covert purpose of facilitating:
    (i) the covert obtaining of information or the provision of access to information to another person; or
    (ii) the covert disclosure of information obtained by the use of such a relationship or in consequence of such a relationship;
(b) he covertly uses such a relationship to obtain information or to provide such access; or
(c) he covertly discloses information obtained by the use of such a relationship, or as a consequence of the existence of such a relationship.

The 'use of a covert human intelligence source' refers to inducing, asking or assisting a person to engage in the conduct of such a source, or to obtain information by means of such a source.

A purpose is covert in relation to the establishment or maintenance of a personal or other relationship only if the relationship is conducted in a manner that is calculated to ensure that one of the parties to the relationship is unaware of the purpose. A relationship is used covertly, and information obtained is disclosed covertly, only if it is used or disclosed in a manner that is calculated to ensure that one of the parties to the relationship is unaware of the use or disclosure in question.

RIPA 2000, s 29 governs the authorisation of a covert human intelligence source. An authorisation is generally valid for 12 months; for exceptions see pp 90 and 92. It may be granted by a designated person (see pp 90 and 92–3).

The criteria which apply to the grant of an authorisation for directed surveillance also apply to covert surveillance. However, there are additional requirements concerning satisfactory arrangements for the supervision of the source depending on whether or not a source is a source of a relevant collaborative unit, and there are further requirements where matters subject to legal privilege are involved, and also about records relating to the use of the source.

The Regulation of Investigatory Powers (Covert Human Intelligence Sources: Matters Subject to Legal Privilege) Order 2010 (the 2010 Order) applies where any conduct that is, or is to be, authorised in an authorisation under s 29 consists in any activities involving conduct of a source, or the use of a source to:

(a) obtain matters,
(b) provide access to another person to any matters, or
(c) disclose matters,

subject to legal privilege (as defined on p 73).

An authorisation for such conduct must not be granted or renewed unless it satisfies the additional requirements set out on p 93. Such conduct is referred to hereafter as 'specified conduct'.

Where a single authorisation under s 29 authorises conduct to which the 2010 Order applies and other conduct falling within RIPA 2000, Part II, the additional requirements only apply in relation to those parts of the combined authorisation which authorise obtaining, giving access to, or disclosing matters subject to legal privilege.

Notification and prior approval regime

The Regulation of Investigatory Powers (Covert Human Intelligence Sources: Relevant Sources) Order 2013 introduced a notification and prior approval regime in respect of an authorisation of a covert human intelligence source under RIPA 2000, s 29 (s 29 authorisation) where that source is a *'relevant source'*. 'Relevant source' means a covert human intelligence source holding an office, rank or position with a listed law-enforcement body, including a police force maintained under the Police Act 1996, the City of London Police Force, the Metropolitan Police Force, the Ministry of Defence Police and the British Transport Police.

Notification   The Order requires a person granting a s 29 authorisation for the conduct or use of a relevant source to give notice of that grant to an ordinary Surveillance Commissioner (ie a Commissioner appointed by the Prime Minister under the Police Act 1997, Part III), save where the authorisation is for the grant or renewal of a 'long-term authorisation' (defined below). The notice must be given or transmitted electronically in writing. It must specify the grounds for the authorisation and the conduct authorised.

Prior approval   must be sought from an ordinary Surveillance Commissioner in respect of the grant or renewal of a long-term authorisation. Specified criteria apply, both in respect of any request for approval and the Commissioner's decision. There is an appeal mechanism where a request for prior approval is refused.

Long-term authorisation   A s 29 authorisation for the conduct or use of a relevant source is a long-term authorisation if the periods mentioned in (a) and (b) below, when taken together, exceed 12 months:

(a) *the period for which the relevant source will be authorised under the authorisation,* having regard to a provision that, where the period(s) in respect of which a relevant source has previously been authorised is less than 12 months in total, any further authorisation will cease to have effect, unless renewed, at the end of a period of 12 months less the total period for which the source has previously been authorised, but disregarding any period of authorisation which ceased to have effect more than three years prior to the intended commencement date of the authorisation; and
(b) *any period or periods for which the relevant source has previously been authorised as a source in relation to the same investigation or operation,* other than
   (i) a period or periods where the authorisation was granted orally or by a person whose entitlement to act is confined to urgent cases, or
   (ii) any period of authorisation which ceased to have effect more than three years prior to the intended commencement date of the authorisation referred to in (a).

The 12-month period is reduced to three months in respect of authorisations involving access to legally privileged material.

With respect to the calculation of the relevant period, any period for which the relevant source has previously been authorised as a source in relation to the same investigation or operation prior to 1 January 2014 is disregarded save for any period in relation to an authorisation that is extant on that date.

Who can authorise?   An authorisation of a relevant source who holds an office, rank or position in a police force may be made by an assistant chief constable, or by a commander in the case of the City of London or Metropolitan Police Forces. In urgent cases, an authorisation of a relevant source may be made by a superintendent instead of such a senior officer.

A long-term authorisation of a relevant source who holds an office, rank or position in a police force may only be made by a chief constable, the Commissioner of the City of London Police or an assistant commissioner of the Metropolitan Police Service.

Matters subject to legal privilege: additional requirements

The additional requirements where matters subject to legal privilege are involved are as follows in relation to police operations.

Before a person grants or renews an authorisation for specified conduct, he must in accordance with arrangements made by an ordinary Surveillance Commissioner give or transmit electronically written notice to the Commissioner. The notice must state that the requisite approval is sought and include the specified matters.

An authorisation for conduct to which the 2010 Order applies must not be granted or renewed until it has been approved by the Commissioner and written notice of the Commissioner's decision to approve the grant or renewal of the authorisation has been given or transmitted electronically.

The Commissioner must give his approval to the grant or renewal of the authorisation if, and only if, satisfied that there are reasonable grounds for believing that the authorisation is necessary and the requirements of proportionality and satisfactory arrangements which apply to authorisations are met.

Where an authorisation authorises conduct to which the 2010 Order applies, it has effect for three months.

An authorisation will specify the conduct which is authorised and require that it is carried out in accordance with the authorisation. In the case of informants the authorisation will be specific to the individual and the particular investigation.

Code of Practice

The Regulation of Investigatory Powers (Covert Human Intelligence Sources: Code of Practice) Order 2014 brought into force a revised code of practice which must be observed by a person exercising or performing a power or duty to which the code applies.

Intrusive surveillance

As already stated, surveillance is *intrusive* if, but only if, it is *covert* surveillance (see above) carried out in relation to anything taking place on any residential premises (a police cell is such) or in any private vehicle (a police vehicle is not a private vehicle), and involves the presence of an individual on the premises or in the vehicle or is carried out by means of a surveillance device.

Directed surveillance that is carried out in relation to anything taking place on so much of a police station, court building, lawyer's business premises, or a prison or similar place as is, at any time during the surveillance, used for the purpose of legal consultations is also treated as intrusive surveillance.

RIPA 2000, s 32 states that intrusive surveillance authorisations may be granted by the Secretary of State (valid for six months) and senior authorising officers (chief constables and equivalents, plus assistant commissioners of the Metropolitan Police) (three months). Such authorisations will only be granted where it is believed that this is necessary in the interests of national security or of the economic well-being of the UK, or for the purpose of preventing or detecting serious crime, *and* that the authorised surveillance is proportionate to what is sought to be achieved.

Authorisations valid for 72 hours for intrusive surveillance may be granted under s 34, by the appropriate deputy chief constable or an assistant chief constable who is designated to act, or their equivalents (specified as a commander in the Metropolitan Police) in urgent cases where it is not reasonably practicable for the senior authorising officer to do so.

When a police authorisation for intrusive surveillance is granted or cancelled, notice must be given to an ordinary Surveillance Commissioner.

Except in cases of urgency, the approval of an ordinary Surveillance Commissioner is needed before a police authorisation for intrusive surveillance may take effect.

The Regulation of Investigatory Powers (Covert Surveillance and Property Interference: Code of Practice) Order 2014 brought into force a revised code of practice relating to covert surveillance which applies to intrusive surveillance.

AUTHORISATION OF ACTION IN RESPECT OF PROPERTY

PA 1997, Part III introduced a system whereby authorisations may be given in respect of entry on or interference with property or with wireless telegraphy. No act carried out in accordance with an authorisation is unlawful. Although authorisations may be given by 'authorising officers' (which term includes, among others, a chief constable, the Commissioner or an Assistant Commissioner of Police of the Metropolis, and the Commissioner of the City of London Police) they are subject in some cases to approval by the Chief Commissioner or a Commissioner appointed under PA 1997, Part III by the Prime Minister.

The law is as follows where the authorising officer is a chief constable, or the Commissioner or an Assistant Commissioner of the Metropolitan Police, or the Commissioner of the City of London Police. Where an authorising officer believes:

(a) that it is necessary for the action specified to be taken to prevent or detect serious crime; and

(b) that that action is proportionate to what the action seeks to achieve,

he may authorise:

(i)   the taking of such action, in respect of such property in his police area (or area specified in a collaboration agreement with another force), as he may specify;

(ii) the taking of such action in respect of property outside that area for the purpose of maintaining or retrieving any equipment, apparatus or device the placing of which in the relevant area has been authorised under PA 1997, Part III or RIPA 2000, Part II (above); or

(iii) the taking of such action in that area as he may specify, in respect of wireless telegraphy.

Provision is made for authorisations to be given by specified senior officers (assistant chief constables or commander in the case of police forces) where it is not reasonably practicable for an authorising officer or his designated deputy to consider an application for an authorisation.

Authorisations must be in writing, although in urgent cases they may be given orally. Unless renewed, they cease to have effect after 72 hours if given orally, or by someone other than the actual authorising officer or his designated deputy. In any other case an authorisation may last for three months. An authorisation may be renewed for a further three months by the authorising officer.

The Regulation of Investigatory Powers (Covert Surveillance and Property Interference: Code of Practice) Order 2014 provides guidance on entry on or interference with property or with wireless telegraphy by public authorities under PA 1997, Part III.

As soon as is reasonably practicable, the giving, renewal or cancellation of an authorisation must be notified to a Commissioner appointed under PA 1997, Part III.

Where the person who gives an authorisation believes that any of the property specified in it is used wholly or mainly as a dwelling or as a bedroom in a hotel, or constitutes office premises, or that the action authorised is likely to result in someone acquiring knowledge of legally privileged matters (p 73), confidential personal information or confidential journalistic material, the authorisation is ineffective until approved by a Commissioner and the person who gave the authorisation has been notified of that approval. However, this does not apply in a case of urgency.

Confidential personal information is (a) personal information which a person has acquired or created in the course of any trade, business, profession or other occupation, or for the purpose of any paid or unpaid office, and which he holds in confidence, and (b) communications as a result of which personal information is so acquired or created and is held in confidence.

Confidential journalistic material is (a) material acquired or created for the purposes of journalism which is in the possession of persons who acquired or created it for those purposes, is held in confidence and has been continuously held (by one or more persons) subject to such an undertaking, restriction or obligation since it was first acquired or created for those purposes; and (b) communications as a result of which information is acquired for those purposes and so held.

CHAPTER 4

Police Questioning and the Rights of Suspects

INTRODUCTION

Code C

In this and the following chapter, frequent reference is made to PACE Code C: the Code of Practice for the Detention, Treatment and Questioning of Persons by Police Officers. This Code applies to persons in custody at police stations, whether or not they have been arrested, and (except for its provisions as to reviews and extensions of detention) to those who have been removed to a police station as a place of safety under the Mental Health Act 1983, ss 135 (warrant to search for and remove mental patients) and 136 (mentally disordered persons found in public places) as a last resort. Persons who are voluntarily at police stations must be treated with no less consideration.

Code C does not apply to the following persons in custody:

(a) persons arrested on warrants issued in Scotland by police officers under the Criminal Justice and Public Order Act 1994 (CJPOA 1994), s 136 (p 20), or arrested or detained without warrant by officers from a police force in Scotland under s 137. In these cases, police powers and duties and the person's rights and entitlements whilst at a police station in England and Wales are the same as those in Scotland;

(b) persons arrested for the purpose of fingerprinting under the Immigration and Asylum Act 1999, s 142;

(c) persons whose detention is authorised by an immigration officer under the Immigration Act 1971, Sch 2 or 3 or the Immigration and Asylum Act 2002, s 62;

(d) persons who are convicted or remanded prisoners held in police cells on behalf of the prison service; and

(e) persons detained for searches under stop and search powers except as required by PACE Code A (stop and search).

No part of Code C applies to a detained person:

(a) to whom PACE Code H (Terrorism) (p 36) applies because:
   (i) he is detained following arrest under the Terrorism Act 2000 (TA 2000), s 41 and not charged, or
   (ii) an authorisation has been given for post-charge questioning of him as a terrorist suspect—matters dealt with in Chapter 28;

(b) to whom the Code of Practice for Examining Officers and Review Officers applies because he is detained for examination under TA 2000, Sch 7.

Nothing in Code C requires the identity of officers or other police staff to be recorded or disclosed if the persons concerned reasonably believe that recording or disclosing their names might put them in danger. In such cases they must use their warrant or other identification number and the name of their police station.

Where Code C requires the prior authority or agreement of an officer of at least inspector or superintendent rank, that authority may be given by a sergeant or chief inspector, respectively, authorised to perform the functions of the higher rank by a superintendent (or above).

If an officer suspects, or is told, that a person may be mentally disordered or otherwise mentally vulnerable, that person must be treated as such for the purposes of PACE Codes C, D (identification) and H, in the absence of clear evidence to dispel that suspicion. Mental vulnerability includes alcoholic incapacity and sleep deprivation.

If a person appears to be under 17, he must, in the absence of clear evidence that he is older, be treated as a juvenile for the purposes of Code C and any other PACE Code.

If a person appears to have attained the age of 17 and to be under 18, he must, in the absence of clear evidence that he is older, be treated as a 17-year-old for the purposes of Code C and any other PACE Code.

Evidence obtained in breach of the procedures set out below is liable to be excluded in any subsequent court proceedings. In addition, a failure to comply with Code C may lead to a disciplinary offence.

Custody officer

Code C makes frequent reference to 'the custody officer'; such references include any police officer performing the functions of a custody officer. References in the Code to a police officer include a 'designated person' (ie a person designated under the Police Reform Act 2002, (p 291)) acting in the exercise or performance of the powers and duties conferred or imposed by their designation. Nothing in the Code prevents a custody officer from allowing civilian support staff who are not designated persons to carry out individual procedures or tasks at the police station if the law allows. However, the officer remains responsible for making sure the procedures and tasks are carried out correctly in accordance with the Codes of Practice. Any such civilian must be a person employed by a police force and under the direction and control of the Chief Officer, or employed by a person with whom a force has a contract for the provision of services relating to persons arrested or otherwise in custody.

A custody officer must perform the functions in Code C as soon as practicable. A custody officer is not in breach of the Code if delay is justifiable (as where a large number of suspects are brought to a police station simultaneously to be placed in custody, or interview rooms are all in use, or there are difficulties in contacting the appropriate adult, solicitor or interpreter) and reasonable steps are taken to prevent unnecessary delay. The custody record must show when a delay has occurred and the reason.

Appropriate adult

Code C (and the other Codes referred to in this chapter) refer to 'the appropriate adult'.
In the case of a *juvenile*, 'the appropriate adult' means:

(a) his parent or guardian (or, if he is in care, the care authority or organisation). 'In care' covers all cases where a juvenile is 'looked after' by a local authority under the Children Act 1989; or

(b) a local authority social worker; or

(c) failing either of the above, another responsible adult aged 18 or over who is not a police officer or employed by the police.

These provisions also apply to someone called to fulfil the role of appropriate adult for a 17-year-old.

A person, including a parent or guardian, should not be the appropriate adult if he is suspected of involvement in the offence in question, is the victim, is a witness, is involved in the investigation or has received admissions. If the parent or guardian of a juvenile or 17-year-old is estranged from him, he should not be asked to be the appropriate adult if the juvenile or 17-year-old expressly and specifically objects to his presence. The fact that a parent participates in questioning a juvenile, etc during the interview does not disqualify the parent from being the appropriate adult. If a juvenile or 17-year-old admits an offence to a social worker or member of a youth offending team other than when that person is acting as the appropriate adult, another appropriate adult should be appointed.

Although 'the appropriate adult' is referred to in the singular, cases can arise where it is appropriate for more than one adult to be present as 'appropriate adults' during the interview of a juvenile, etc, as where both parents are present or where a parent with language difficulties is present and a second adult is present to assist in questions of language.

In the case of a person *who is mentally disordered or mentally handicapped*, 'the appropriate adult' means:

(a) a relative, guardian or other person responsible for his care or custody; or
(b) someone who has experience of dealing with persons who are mentally disordered or mentally vulnerable (ie because of their mental state or capacity they may not understand the significance of what is said, of questions or of their replies) but who is not a police officer or employed by the police; or
(c) failing either of the above, some other responsible adult aged 18 or over who is not a police officer or employed by the police.

In the case of people who are mentally disordered or otherwise mentally vulnerable it may in some cases be more satisfactory if the appropriate adult is someone who has experience or training in their case rather than a relative lacking such qualifications. However, if the person himself prefers a relative to a better-qualified stranger, his wishes should if practicable be respected.

A solicitor or independent custody visitor who is present at the police station in a professional capacity may not act as the appropriate adult.

A person should always be given an opportunity, when the appropriate adult is called to a police station, to consult privately with a solicitor in the absence of the appropriate adult if he wishes to do so. The appropriate adult is not subject to legal privilege.

DOCUMENTATION

Code C provides as follows.

When a person is brought to a police station under arrest, or is arrested at a police station having attended there voluntarily, or attends a police station in answer to bail, he must be brought before the custody officer as soon as practicable after arrival, or following arrest at the police station. This equally applies to designated and non-designated police stations. Such a person is 'at a police station' if he is anywhere upon the premises or enclosed yards forming part of the premises.

As stated in Chapter 3, a separate custody record must be opened as soon as practicable for each person who is brought to a police station under arrest or who is arrested at the police station, having attended there voluntarily.

Where the arresting officer is not physically present when a detainee is brought to the police station, the arresting officer's account must be made available to the custody officer remotely or by a third party on the arresting officer's behalf. All information which is required to be recorded under Code C must be recorded as soon as practicable in the custody record unless otherwise specified. Any audio or visual recording made in the custody area is not part of the custody record. It is a matter for the custody officer to determine whether a record should be made of the property a detained person has with him or had taken from him on arrest. Any record made is not required to be kept as part of the custody record but the custody record should be noted as to where such a record exists. Whenever a record is made the detainee must be allowed to check and sign it as correct. Any refusal to sign must be recorded.

Where a person is answering street bail, the custody officer should link any documentation held in relation to the arrest with the custody record and any further action must be recorded in accordance with the Code.

In the case of any action requiring the authority of an officer of a specified rank, his name and rank must be recorded in the custody record, *except where the person is detained under TA 2000, or where there are reasonable grounds to believe that naming the officer would endanger him (in which case the record must state the officer's warrant or other identification number and duty station).*

All entries in the custody record must be timed and signed by the maker. In the case of a record held on a computer, this should be timed and contain the operator's identification. Warrant or other identification numbers and the name of the duty station should be used rather than names in the cases italicised above where the special rule applies.

If someone is arrested and taken to a police station as a result of a search in the exercise of any stop and search power to which Code A or the 'search powers code' issued under TA 2000 applies, the officer carrying out the search is responsible for ensuring that the record of the stop and search is made as part of the custody record. The custody officer must then ensure that the person is asked if he wants a copy of the search record and, if he does, that he is given a copy as soon as practicable.

The custody officer is responsible for the accuracy and completeness of the custody record and for ensuring that the record (or a copy) accompanies a detained person if he is transferred to another police station. The record must show the time of, and reason for, a transfer and the time a person is released from detention. The detainee's solicitor and appropriate adult must be permitted to inspect the custody record as soon as practicable after arrival at the police station and at any other time during his detention. When someone leaves police detention or is taken to court, he or his legal representative or appropriate adult must be given, on request, a copy of the custody record as soon as practicable. This entitlement lasts for twelve months after release.

The fact and time of any refusal by any person to sign a custody record when asked to do so in accordance with Code C must be recorded.

INITIAL ACTION

Detained persons: normal procedure

When a person is brought to a police station under arrest or arrested at the station having gone there voluntarily, the custody officer must ensure that he is told clearly about the right to be informed about the offence and (as the case may be) any further offences for which he is arrested while in custody and why he has been arrested and detained, and about the following continuing rights which may be exercised at any stage during the period in custody:

(a) the right to have someone informed of his arrest;
(b) the right to consult privately with a solicitor and that free independent legal advice is available;
(c) the right to consult the PACE codes;
(d) if applicable, the right to interpretation and translation and the right to communicate with his High Commission, Embassy or Consulate.

The detainee must also be given a written notice:

(a) setting out:
  • the above rights;
  • the arrangements for obtaining legal advice;
  • the right to a copy of the custody record;
  • the right to remain silent as set out in the caution in the terms set out on p 113;
  • the right to have access to materials and documents which are essential to effectively challenging the lawfulness of his arrest and detention for any offence and (as the case may be) any further offences for which he is arrested whilst in custody;
  • the maximum period for which the detainee may be kept in police detention without being charged, when detention must be reviewed and when release is required;
  • the right to medical assistance in accordance with the requirements on pp 143–6;
  • the right, if prosecuted, to have access to the evidence in the case before his trial;
(b) briefly setting out his entitlements while in custody.

The detainee must be given an opportunity to read the notice and be asked to sign the custody record to acknowledge receipt of these notices. An 'easy read' illustrated version should also be provided if available.

The custody officer must:

(a) record the offence(s) that the detainee has been arrested for and the reason(s) for the arrest;
(b) note on the custody record any comment the detainee makes in relation to the arresting officer's account but must not invite comment. If the arresting officer is not physically present when the detainee is brought to a police station, the arresting officer's account must be made available to the custody officer remotely or by a third party on the arresting officer's behalf. If the custody officer authorises a person's detention, he must record the grounds for detention in the detainee's presence and, at the same time, inform the detainee of them unless he is incapable of understanding, or is (or may become) violent, or in urgent need of medical attention. In such a case, the information must be given as soon as practicable. The detainee must be informed of the grounds for his detention before he is questioned about any offence;
(c) note any comment the detainee makes in respect of the decision to detain him but must not invite comment;
(d) not put specific questions to the detainee regarding his involvement in any offence, nor in respect of any comments he may make in response to the arresting officer's account or the decision to place him in detention. Such an exchange is

likely to constitute an interview and require the associated safeguards set out on pp 116–17.

These provisions also apply to any further offences and grounds for detention coming to light while the person is detained.

Documents and materials essential to effectively challenging the lawfulness of the detainee's arrest and detention must be made available to the detainee or his solicitor. (Documents and materials will be 'essential' for this purpose if they are capable of undermining the reasons and grounds which make the detainee's arrest and detention *necessary*.) The decision about whether particular documents or materials must be made available for this purpose rests with the custody officer who determines whether detention is necessary, in consultation with the investigating officer who has the knowledge of the documents and materials in a particular case necessary to inform that decision. A note should be made in the detainee's custody record of the fact that documents or materials have been made available under this provision and when. The investigating officer should make a separate note of what is made available and how it is made available in a particular case. This provision also applies (with modifications) for the purposes of the provisions about reviews and extensions of detention, and charging detained persons.

The custody officer or other custody staff as directed by him must:

(a) ask the detainee (i) whether at this time he would like legal advice, or wants someone informed of his detention, and (ii) to confirm his decisions in these respects;

(b) determine whether the detainee is, or might be, in need of medical treatment or attention, or requires an appropriate adult, help to check documentation, or an interpreter, and record the decision in this respect.

Where any of these duties have been carried out by custody staff, the outcomes must, as soon as practicable, be reported to the custody officer.

If the appropriate adult (where one is involved) is already at the police station, the above provisions must be complied with in the appropriate adult's presence; if he is not at the station when they are complied with, they must be complied with again in the presence of the appropriate adult when he arrives and a copy of the notice given to the detainee must also be given to the appropriate adult.

When these needs are determined, the custody officer is responsible for initiating an assessment to consider whether the detainee is likely to present specific risks to custody staff or himself. This should always include a Police National Computer (PNC) check. It may be necessary for him to consult and involve others, for example the arresting officer or an appropriate healthcare professional. Risk assessments must follow a structured process which clearly defines the categories of risk to be considered and the results must be incorporated in the detainee's custody record. The *Detention and Custody Authorised Professional Practice* produced by the College of Policing provides detailed guidance on risk assessments and identifies key risk areas which should always be considered. The custody officer must ensure those responsible for the detainee's custody are appropriately briefed about the risks. The content of any risk assessment and any resulting analysis need not be shown to the detainee or any person acting on his behalf. However, information should not be withheld from anyone acting on his behalf, if to do so might put him at risk. The custody officer is responsible for implementing the response to any specific risk assessment.

Detained persons—special groups

If a person appears to be blind or seriously visually impaired or unable to read, deaf, or unable to speak, or to have difficulty orally because of a speech impediment, he should be treated as such for the purpose of Code C in the absence of clear evidence to the contrary.

If a person is blind, seriously visually impaired or unable to read, the custody officer must ensure that his solicitor, a relative, the appropriate adult, or some other person likely to take an interest in him (and not involved in the investigation) is available to help in checking any documentation. Where Code C requires consent or signing, then the person who is assisting may be asked to sign instead, if the detained person so wishes. However, there is no requirement that the appropriate adult be called solely to assist in checking and signing documentation for a person who is not a juvenile or mentally disordered or otherwise mentally vulnerable.

If the detainee appears not to speak or understand English, or to have a hearing or speech impediment, the custody officer must ensure that:

(a) without delay, an interpreter is called for assistance in the initial action referred to on pp 99–101. If the detainee appears to have a hearing or speech impediment, the reference to 'interpreter' includes appropriate assistance necessary to comply with the required initial action;

(b) in addition to the continuing rights set out on p 100, the detainee is told clearly about his right to interpretation and translation;

(c) the written notice given to the detainee referred to on p 100 is in a language the detainee understands and includes the right to interpretation and translation together with information about the provisions referred to on pp 134–9, which explain how the right applies; and

(d) if the translation of the notice is not available, the information in the notice is given through an interpreter and a written translation provided without undue delay.

If the detainee is a citizen of an independent Commonwealth country or a national of a foreign country, including the Republic of Ireland, the custody officer must ensure that in addition to the continuing rights set out above, the detainee is informed as soon as practicable about his rights of communication with his High Commission, Embassy or Consulate set out on p 112. This right must be included in the written notice given to the detainee referred to above.

If the detainee is a juvenile or 17-year-old, the custody officer must ascertain the identity of a person responsible for the detainee's welfare, for example his parent or guardian, local authority with care, or someone who has temporarily assumed responsibility for his welfare, and must, as soon as practicable, inform that person of the arrest, the reason and the place of detention.

If a juvenile or 17-year-old is known to be subject to a court order under which a person or organisation is given any degree of statutory responsibility to supervise or otherwise monitor him, reasonable steps must also be taken to notify that person or organisation (the 'responsible officer'). The responsible officer is normally a member of a youth offending team, except in the case of a curfew order which involves electronic monitoring, when the monitoring contractor is normally the responsible officer.

If the detainee is a juvenile, a 17-year-old, mentally handicapped or otherwise mentally vulnerable, the custody officer must, as soon as practicable, inform the appropriate adult of the grounds of detention and the person's whereabouts, and ask that the adult come to see the detainee.

The above requirements to inform apply even if Annex B (p 104) applies.

Persons attending a police station or elsewhere voluntarily

PACE, s 29 provides that where, for the purpose of assisting with an investigation, a person attends voluntarily at a police station or at any other place where a constable is present, or accompanies a constable to a police station or any other place without having been arrested, he is entitled to leave at will unless he is placed under arrest. If the interview is at 'any other place' where the interviewer requires the person's informed consent to remain (eg that person's home) 'entitled to leave' means 'entitled to require the interviewer to leave'. If, during an interview, it is decided that it is necessary to arrest him, he must be informed at once that he is under arrest and given the grounds and reasons (see p 61), and be brought before the custody officer at that police station or one to which he is then taken. The same rules apply thereafter as in the case of other detainees. The interviewer's responsibilities include determining whether the suspect requires an interpreter and the provision of interpretation and translation services (as to which, see pp 134–9).

Code C goes further, requiring that, at any stage at which a person voluntarily attending is cautioned, the officer must tell him that he is not under arrest and is free to leave and must remind him of his right to free, independent legal advice. The police should assist a 'volunteer' who asks how he should go about obtaining such advice. The person must also be given a copy of the notice explaining the arrangements for obtaining legal advice, told that the right to legal advice includes the right to speak with a solicitor on the telephone and asked if he wants advice. If advice is requested, the interviewer is responsible:

(a) for securing its provision without delay by contacting the Defence Solicitor Call Centre (DSCC), and

(b) for ensuring that the provisions of Codes C, E and F concerning the conduct and recording of interviews of suspects and the rights and entitlements and safeguards for suspects who have been arrested are followed insofar as they can be applied to suspects who are not under arrest.

Head (b) includes:

(i) informing the suspect of the offence and, as the case may be, any further offences, he is suspected of committing (with the grounds and reasons) and his right to be so informed;

(ii) the caution;

(iii) determining whether he requires an appropriate adult and help to check documentation; and

(iv) determining whether he requires an interpreter and the provision of interpretation and translation services and informing him of that right,

but does not include any requirement to provide a written notice in addition to that above which concerns the arrangements for obtaining legal advice.

Persons answering street bail

When someone is answering street bail, the custody officer should link any documentation held in relation to arrest with the custody record. Any further action must be recorded on the custody record.

Alleged failure to give information about rights to suspect

If a complaint is made by or on behalf of a suspect who has been cautioned that the requisite information and (as the case may be) access to records and documents has not been provided, the matter must be reported to an inspector to deal with as a complaint for the purposes of the provisions on pp 133 and 146 if the challenge is made during an interview.

RIGHT NOT TO BE HELD INCOMMUNICADO

Notification of detention

A detainee has a right under PACE, s 56 to have someone informed at public expense and as soon as practicable of his detention. However, this extends only to one friend, relative or other person who is known to him or is likely to take an interest in his welfare. If the person cannot be contacted, the detainee may choose up to two alternatives. If they cannot be contacted the custody officer may allow further attempts. If a person is moved from one police station to another, the right to have someone informed of his whereabouts arises again.

Delay

PACE, s 56, together with Annex B to Code C, provides that a delay in informing someone may be authorised by an inspector (or above) where the person is in police detention for an indictable offence and has not been charged with it. Such authorisation may only be given in two types of case. The first is where the inspector has reasonable grounds for believing that telling the person named of the arrest will:

(a) lead to interference with, or harm to, evidence connected with an indictable offence or interference with or physical harm to other persons; or
(b) lead to the alerting of other persons suspected of having committed such an offence but not yet arrested for it; or
(c) hinder the recovery of any property obtained as a result of such an offence.

The second type of case is that an inspector may authorise delay where he has reasonable grounds for believing that the person detained for an indictable offence has benefited from his criminal conduct (decided in accordance with the Proceeds of Crime Act 2002, Part 2) and that the recovery of the value of the property constituting that benefit will be hindered by telling the named person of the arrest.

If a delay is authorised, the detainee must be informed, as soon as practicable, of the reason for it and the reason must be noted on his custody record. If given orally, the authorisation must be confirmed in writing as soon as practicable. When the reasons for delay have been removed, for example by the arrest of other persons, the detainee must be asked if he wishes to exercise the right to communicate (and the custody record must be noted accordingly) and any request to communicate must be granted. The right to communicate cannot be delayed for more than 36 hours.

Any delay authorised under the above provisions should be proportionate and last no longer than necessary.

Visits, letters and phone calls

If a detainee agrees, he may, at the discretion of the custody officer, receive visits from friends, family, or others likely to take an interest in his welfare, or in whose welfare the detainee has an interest. Where inquiries by interested persons are received concerning his whereabouts, the information must be given if the detainee agrees and an inspector (or above) has not authorised delay in the release of such information. The custody officer must exercise his discretion as to visits in the light of the availability of sufficient manpower to supervise a visit and any possible hindrance to the investigation.

The detainee must also be supplied on request with writing material. Letters and messages must be sent (at his expense) as soon as practicable, but all letters, other than those to his solicitor, may be read. The detainee may speak for a reasonable time to one person on the telephone. Whether or not the call can be made at police expense is a matter for the custody officer's discretion. Unless the call is to a solicitor, a police officer may listen to the call and may terminate it if it is being abused. The detainee must be cautioned that what he says in a letter, call or message (other than to his solicitor) may be read or listened to and may be given in evidence. An interpreter may make a call on behalf of a detainee.

Where an inspector (or above) considers that the sending of a letter or the making of a telephone call might result in any of the consequences referred to in the list on p 104, and the person is detained in connection with an indictable offence, that officer can deny or delay the exercise of either or both these privileges.

Any delay or denial of these rights should be proportionate and should last no longer than necessary.

Prisoners

Where a prisoner has been transferred to police custody for specific purposes and periods under the Crime (Sentences) Act 1997, Sch 1, the exercise of the above rights is subject to any additional conditions specified in the transfer direction for the purpose of regulating his contact and communication with others whilst in police custody.

Documentation

A record must be kept of:

(a) any request made in relation to matters of communication and of the action taken in consequence of that request;
(b) letters or messages sent, calls made, or visits received; and
(c) any refusal by the detainee to have information about himself or his whereabouts given to an outside inquirer. The detainee must be asked to countersign the record accordingly.

LEGAL ADVICE

By PACE, s 58 a person arrested and held in police custody is entitled, if he so requests, to consult a solicitor privately at any time. This is a fundamental right. Unless Annex B (delay) applies, all detainees must be informed of this right. Code C provides that the consultation may be in person, in writing or by telephone, and that free independent legal advice is available.

A detainee has a right to free legal advice and to be represented by a solicitor. What follows explains the arrangements which enable detainees to obtain legal advice. The arrangements also apply, with appropriate modifications, to persons attending a police station or other location voluntarily who are cautioned prior to being interviewed.

When a detainee asks for free legal advice, the Defence Solicitor Call Centre (DSCC) must be informed of the request.

Free legal advice will be limited to telephone advice provided by CDS Direct if a detainee is:

(a) detained for a non-imprisonable offence;
(b) arrested on a bench warrant for failing to appear and being held for production at court (except where the solicitor has clear documentary evidence available that would result in the client being released from custody);
(c) arrested for drink-driving (driving/in charge with excess alcohol or while unfit through drink, or failing to produce a specimen); or
(d) detained in relation to breach of police or court bail conditions,

unless one or more exceptions apply, in which case the DSCC should arrange for advice to be given by a solicitor at the police station.

Examples of exceptions are:

(a) the police want to interview the detainee or carry out an identification parade;
(b) the detainee needs an appropriate adult, is unable to communicate over the telephone or alleges serious maltreatment by the police;
(c) the investigation includes another offence not included in the list;
(d) the solicitor to be assigned is already at the police station.

When free advice is not limited to telephone advice, a detainee can ask for free advice from a solicitor he knows or, if he does not know a solicitor or the solicitor he knows cannot be contacted, from the duty solicitor.

To arrange free legal advice, the police should telephone the DSCC. The call centre will decide whether legal advice should be limited to telephone advice from CDS Direct, or whether a solicitor known to the detainee or the duty solicitor should speak to the detainee.

When a detainee wants to pay for legal advice himself:

(a) the DSCC will contact a solicitor of his choice on his behalf;
(b) he may, when free advice is only available by telephone from CDS Direct, still speak to a solicitor of his choice on the telephone for advice but the solicitor would not be paid by legal aid and may ask him to pay for the advice;
(c) he should be given an opportunity to consult a specific solicitor or another solicitor from that solicitor's firm. If this solicitor is not available, he may choose up to two alternatives. If these alternatives are not available, the custody officer has discretion to allow further attempts until a solicitor has been contacted and has agreed to provide advice;
(d) he is entitled to a private consultation with his chosen solicitor on the telephone or the solicitor may decide to come to the police station;
(e) if his chosen solicitor cannot be contacted, the DSCC may still be called to arrange free legal advice.

Apart from carrying out duties necessary to implement these arrangements, an officer must not advise the suspect about any particular firm of solicitors.

In the case of a juvenile, 17-year-old, or mentally disordered or otherwise mentally vulnerable person, an appropriate adult (pp 97–8) should consider whether legal advice from a solicitor is required. If a juvenile, etc indicates that legal advice is not required the appropriate adult has the right to ask for a solicitor to attend if this would be in the best interests of the person. However, the juvenile, etc cannot be forced to see the solicitor if he is adamant that he does not wish to do so.

Whenever legal advice is requested (and unless delay is permitted under Annex B), the custody officer must act without delay to secure the provision of such advice. If the detainee declines to exercise his right to speak to a solicitor in person, the officer should point out that the right to legal advice includes the right to speak with a solicitor on the telephone. If the detainee continues to waive his right, or a detainee whose right to free legal advice is limited to telephone advice from CDS Direct declines to exercise that right, the officer should ask him why. Any reasons must be recorded on the custody record or the interview record as appropriate. Once it is clear that a person neither wishes to speak to a solicitor in person, nor by telephone, he should cease to be asked his reasons.

Except as allowed in the case of persons arrested under TA 2000, s 41 (see p 791), if the requirement for privacy of consultation is compromised because what is said or written by the detainee or the solicitor for the purpose of the giving or receiving of legal advice is overheard, listened to or read by others without the informed consent of the detainee, the right will effectively have been denied. Where a detainee speaks to a solicitor on the telephone, he should be allowed to do so in private unless this is impractical because of the design and layout of the custody area or the location of the telephones.

Delay

Access to legal advice may be delayed if the person is in police detention for an indictable offence, has not yet been charged, and a superintendent (or above) authorises the delay. An oral authorisation must be confirmed in writing as soon as practicable. Delay may only be authorised in two types of case specified in Annex B to Code C.

The first is where the superintendent (or above) has reasonable grounds for believing that access to a solicitor at a time when the detainee wishes to have access will:

(a) lead to interference with or harm to evidence connected with an indictable offence or interference with or physical injury to other persons; or
(b) lead to the alerting of other persons suspected of having committed such an offence but not yet arrested for it; or
(c) hinder the recovery of any property obtained as a result of such an offence.

The Court of Appeal has held that an authorisation on such a ground can only be justified by reference to specific circumstances, including evidence as to the person detained or the *actual solicitor* sought to be consulted. Thus, if it is believed that a particular solicitor may bring about one of the consequences at (a) to (c) above, that belief would only be relevant to that particular solicitor and would not apply to others selected by the detainee.

The second type of case is that a superintendent (or above) may authorise delay where he has reasonable grounds to believe that the person detained for an indictable offence has benefited from his criminal conduct (decided in accordance with the Proceeds of Crime Act 2002, Part 2) and that the recovery of the value of the property constituting that benefit will be hindered by the exercise of the right to consult a solicitor privately.

Access to a solicitor may not be delayed on the ground that he might advise the detainee not to answer any questions or that he was initially asked to attend by someone other than the detainee, provided the detainee wishes to see him. In the latter case the detainee must be told that the solicitor has come to the police station at another person's request, and must be asked to sign the custody record to signify whether or not he wishes to see the solicitor.

If delay is authorised the detainee must be told the reason and the reason must be noted in his custody record as soon as practicable. Once the reason for delay ceases, no further delay in permitting access to a solicitor is permissible and the detainee must be asked if he wishes to exercise his right to legal advice (and the custody record must be noted accordingly). *In any case* the detainee must be permitted to consult a solicitor within 36 hours from the 'relevant time' (a term defined on pp 159–60).

Where a delay has been authorised under Annex B and an interview takes place during it, a court or jury may not draw adverse inferences from a suspect's silence.

Arrival of solicitor at police station

Unless Annex B applies, when a solicitor arrives at a police station to see a particular person, that person must be informed of his arrival whether or not he is being interviewed, and asked if he wishes to see the solicitor. This applies even if the detainee has declined legal advice or, having requested it, subsequently agreed to be interviewed without receiving advice. The attendance and the detainee's decision must be recorded. Where a consultation is permitted, a solicitor is entitled to be present whilst the detainee is interviewed if the detainee so wishes.

Accredited or probationary representatives

For the purposes of Code C, a 'solicitor' is a person who holds a current practising certificate, or an accredited or probationary representative included on the register of representatives maintained by the Legal Aid Agency.

An accredited or probationary representative sent to provide advice on an actual solicitor's behalf must be admitted to the police station for this purpose, unless an inspector (or above) considers that such a visit will hinder the investigation of crime and directs otherwise. (Hindering the investigation of crime does not include giving the detainee proper legal advice.) In determining this issue, an inspector must take into account in particular whether the identity or status of the accredited or probationary representative has been satisfactorily established; whether he is of suitable character to provide legal advice (a person with a criminal record is unlikely to be suitable unless the conviction was for a minor offence and is not of recent date); and any other matters in any written letters of authorisation provided. The Court of Appeal has held that a chief constable is not entitled to make a blanket order banning a particular solicitor's probationary representative from all police stations in his area. He may advise his officers that a particular representative is likely to hinder an investigation but the officer dealing with the case must decide whether, in the particular circumstances, the representative should be excluded.

If an inspector refuses access to an accredited or probationary representative or a decision is taken that such a person must not remain at an interview, he must forthwith notify the solicitor on whose behalf that person was to have acted, or was acting, and give him an opportunity of making other arrangements. The detainee must also be informed and the custody record noted. If an inspector considers that a particular firm of solicitors is persistently sending probationary representatives who are unsuited to provide legal advice, he should inform a superintendent (or above), who may wish to take the matter up with the Solicitors Regulation Authority (SRA).

Removal of 'solicitor'

A 'solicitor' may only be required to leave an interview if his conduct is such that the investigating officer is unable properly to put questions to the suspect.

The solicitor's only role in the police station is to protect and advance the legal rights of his client. On occasions this may require the solicitor to give advice which has the effect of avoiding his client giving evidence which strengthens a prosecution case. The solicitor may intervene to seek clarification or to challenge an improper question to his client or the manner in which it is put, or to advise his client not to reply to particular questions, or if he wishes to give his client further legal advice. He may only be required to leave if his approach or conduct prevents or unreasonably obstructs proper questions being put to the detainee or his response being recorded, as where a solicitor answers on his client's behalf or provides written replies for his client to quote. If the investigating officer considers that a solicitor is acting in such a way, he will stop the interview and consult a superintendent (or above), if one is readily available, and otherwise an officer not below the rank of inspector who is not concerned with the investigation. After speaking to the solicitor the officer who has been consulted will decide whether or not the interview should continue in the presence of the solicitor. If he decides that it should not, the detainee will be given an opportunity to consult another solicitor before the interview continues and that solicitor will be given an opportunity to be present.

Code C points out that the removal of a solicitor from an interview is a serious step and, if it occurs, the superintendent (or above) who took the decision will consider whether the incident should be reported to the SRA (and to the Legal Aid Agency in the case of a duty solicitor). If the decision was taken by an officer below the rank of superintendent, a superintendent (or above) must consider whether to make such a report. A note of guidance in the Code points out that where an officer takes the decision to exclude a solicitor, he must be in a position to satisfy the court that the decision was properly made. In order to do this, he may need to witness what is happening himself.

Other points

In the absence of compelling reasons, delaying access to a solicitor is likely to amount to a breach of the right to a fair trial under the European Convention on Human Rights, art 6.

Any request for legal advice, and the action taken on it, must be recorded in the custody record. If a person has asked for legal advice and an interview has commenced in the absence of his solicitor, etc (or the solicitor, etc is required to leave) a record must be made in the interview record.

A detainee who wants legal advice *may not be interviewed or continue to be interviewed* until he has received it unless:

(a) a delay has been authorised in accordance with Annex B to Code C set out above (see p 107), in which case the restriction on drawing adverse inferences from silence (see p 114) will apply because the detainee is not allowed an opportunity to consult a solicitor; or

(b) a superintendent (or above) has reasonable grounds to believe that:
   (i) the consequent delay might lead to interference with, or harm to, evidence or other people, or to serious loss of, or damage to, property, or to alerting

other people suspected of having committed an offence but not yet arrested; or might hinder the recovery of property obtained in consequence of the offence; or

(ii) when a solicitor, including a duty solicitor, has been contacted and has agreed to attend, awaiting his arrival would cause unreasonable delay to the process of investigation;

in which instances the restriction upon drawing adverse inferences from silence (p 114) will apply; or

(c) the solicitor nominated or selected from a list by the detainee cannot be contacted, has previously indicated that he does not wish to be contacted, or having been contacted has declined to attend, and the detainee has been advised of the Duty Solicitor Scheme but has declined to ask for the duty solicitor, in which instances the restriction upon drawing inferences from silence will not apply because the detainee has been allowed an opportunity to consult a solicitor; or

(d) the detainee changes his mind about wanting legal advice or (as the case may be) about wanting a solicitor present at the interview and states that he no longer wishes to speak to a solicitor. In this case, the interview may be started or continued without delay provided that:

(i) an inspector (or above) asks the detainee why he has changed his mind, and makes reasonable efforts to ascertain the solicitor's expected time of arrival and to inform the solicitor that the suspect has stated that he wishes to change his mind and the reason (if given);

(ii) the detainee's reason for his change of mind (if given) and the outcome of the action in (i) are recorded in the custody record;

(iii) the detainee after being informed of the outcome of the action in (i) confirms in writing that he wants the interview to proceed without speaking or further speaking to a solicitor or (as the case may be) without a solicitor being present and does not wish to wait for a solicitor by signing an entry to this effect in the custody record;

(iv) an inspector (or above) is satisfied that it is proper for the interview to proceed in these circumstances, and

(a) gives authority in writing for the interview to proceed; if the authority is not recorded in the custody record, the officer must ensure that the custody record shows the date and time of the authority and where it is recorded, and

(b) takes or directs the taking of reasonable steps to inform the solicitor that the authority has been given and the time when the interview is expected to commence, and records or causes to be recorded the outcome of this action in the custody record;

(v) when the interview starts and the interviewer reminds the suspect of his right to legal advice, the interviewer must ensure that the following is recorded in the written interview record or the interview record made in accordance with PACE Code E (audio recording) or F (visual recording with sound):

(a) confirmation that the detainee has changed his mind about wanting legal advice or (as the case may be) about wanting a solicitor present and the reasons for it if given;

(b) the fact that authority for the interview to proceed has been given and, with the usual exception, the name of the authorising officer;

(c) that, if the solicitor arrives at the station before the interview is completed, the detainee will be so informed without delay and a break will be taken to allow him to speak to the solicitor if he wishes, unless (b) above applies;

(d) that, at any time during the interview, the detainee may again ask for legal advice and that, if he does, a break will be taken to allow him to speak to the solicitor, unless (a), (b), or (c) applies.

In these circumstances there will be no restriction on drawing adverse inferences from silence because the detainee is allowed an opportunity to consult a solicitor if he wishes.

If (a) applies, where the reason for authorising the delay ceases to apply, there may be no further delay in permitting the exercise of the right in the absence of a further authorisation unless (b), (c) or (d) applies. Where (b)(i) applies, once sufficient information has been obtained to avert the risk, questioning must cease until the detainee has received legal advice unless (a), (b)(ii), (c) or (d) applies. Where (c) applies, the interview may be started or continued without further delay provided that an inspector (or above) has agreed. Where (d) applies, the interview may be started or continued without further delay provided that the detainee has given an agreement in writing, or on recording media, to being interviewed without receiving legal advice and that an inspector (or above), having inquired into the detainee's reasons for his change of mind, has given authority for the interview to proceed. Confirmation of the detainee's agreement, his change of mind, his reasons where given, and the name of the authorising officer, except where it might endanger the officer to do so, must be recorded in writing or in the interview record made in accordance with Code E or F, at the beginning or recommencement of the interview. Such authorisation can be given over the telephone, if the authorising officer is able to satisfy himself as to the reason for the detainee's change of mind and is satisfied that it is proper to continue the interview in those circumstances.

In considering whether awaiting the arrival of a solicitor would cause unreasonable delay (see (b) above), the superintendent should, where practicable, ask the solicitor for an estimate of the time he is likely to take in coming to the station, and relate this to the time for which detention is permitted, to whether a required period of rest is imminent, and to the requirements of other investigations in progress. If the solicitor says that he is on his way or that he will set off immediately, it will not normally be appropriate to begin an interview before he arrives. If it appears that it will be necessary to begin an interview before the solicitor's arrival he should be given an indication of how long the police could wait so that he has the opportunity to make arrangements for someone else to provide legal advice.

A breach of the requirement that detainees should generally be allowed access to a solicitor does not necessarily justify exclusion of evidence obtained at the interview. Where a challenge is made, the court must establish whether a request was made and whether it had been refused. If this is so it must then consider whether a delay in compliance with such a request was permissible under the above rules. If it was not, the court must then consider whether the evidence obtained at the interview should be excluded under s 76 (confessions) or s 78 (unfairly obtained evidence (pp 255–6 and 267)) or by any rule of common law.

The Supreme Court has decided that the effect of art 6 of the European Convention on Human Rights is that legal advice must be available not only to a person in custody but also to anyone else who has been 'charged' for the purposes of art 6, which occurs where the person's situation has been substantially affected. This situation is likely to occur where questions are addressed to a person which the police have reason to think may well elicit an incriminating response, ie when he has ceased to be a potential witness and become a suspect. However, even if someone not in police custody has been 'charged' in this sense, this does not necessarily mean that he has been deprived of a fair trial contrary to art 6; it would simply be a circumstance to be taken into account when considering whether he has been so deprived.

ALIENS, ETC

Code C provides that a detainee who is a citizen of an independent Commonwealth country or a foreign national is entitled on request to communicate at any time with his High Commission, Embassy or Consulate. Such a person must be informed as soon as practicable of this right and asked if he wants his High Commission, etc told of his whereabouts and the grounds for his detention. Such a request should be acted on as soon as practicable.

A detainee who is a national of a country with which a consular treaty is in force requiring notification of arrest (for the list of countries, see <https://gov.uk/government/publications/table-of-consular-conventions-and-mandatory-notification-obligations>) must also be informed that, with the following qualification, notification of his arrest will be sent to his High Commission, etc as soon as practicable, whether or not he requests it. The qualification is that, if the detainee claims that he is a refugee or has applied or intends to apply for asylum, the custody officer must ensure that UK Visas and Immigration (UKVI) is informed as soon as practicable of the claim. UKVI will then determine whether compliance with relevant international obligations requires notification of the arrest to be sent and will inform the custody officer as to what action police need to take.

Consular officers may visit to advise one of their nationals and those visits must take place out of the hearing of a police officer.

A record must be made:

(a) when a detainee is informed of the above rights and of any requirement to notify under a consular treaty;
(b) of any communications with a High Commission, etc; and
(c) of any communications with UKVI about a detainee's claim to be a refugee or to be seeking asylum and the resulting action taken by police.

CAUTIONS

When a caution must be given

Code C provides as follows.

A person whom there are grounds to suspect of an offence must be cautioned before any questions about an offence, or further questions if the answers provide the grounds for suspicion, are put to him if either his answer or silence (ie failure or refusal to answer or answer satisfactorily) may be given in evidence to a court in a prosecution. The grounds for suspicion must be reasonable grounds, based on known facts or relevant information. Cautions may be given in the Welsh language where use of the Welsh language is appropriate.

A person need not be cautioned if questions are put to him for other purposes, for example:

(a) solely to establish his identity or his ownership of any vehicle; or
(b) to obtain information in accordance with any relevant statutory requirement;
(c) in furtherance of the proper and effective conduct of a search (for example, to determine the need to search in the exercise of powers to stop and search or to seek co-operation while carrying out a search); or
(d) to seek verification of a written record.

Whenever a person not under arrest is initially cautioned, or is reminded that he is still under caution after a break, he must at the same time be told that he is not under arrest, and be informed about how (see p 103) he may obtain legal advice. The officer must point out that the right to legal advice includes the right to speak with a solicitor over the telephone. The officer must ask the person whether he wishes to do so.

A person who is arrested, or further arrested, must be informed that he is under arrest and given the grounds for that arrest. He must also be cautioned unless it is impracticable because of his condition or behaviour at the time, or unless he has already been cautioned immediately before arrest.

Since Code C obliges police officers to administer a caution if the answer to a question may be offered in evidence in criminal proceedings, it is necessary to caution motorists when pointing out to them that they have committed an offence as their reply is almost certainly going to be relevant to the proceedings. Indeed, although there is no direct requirement to caution when informing a person that he will be reported for an offence, the admissibility of his reply in evidence may depend upon whether or not he has been cautioned at some stage. Practice may still require that such a reply is included in an officer's report and, if this is so, the offender should be cautioned at some stage before he makes it.

Nothing in Code C requires a caution to be given or repeated when informing a person not under arrest that he may be prosecuted for an offence. However, a court will not be able to draw any inferences under the Criminal Justice and Public Order Act 1994, s 34 (pp 258–9), if the person was not cautioned.

The caution prescribed by Code C is:

'You do not have to say anything. But it may harm your defence if you do not mention when questioned something which you later rely on in court. Anything you do say may be given in evidence.'

Minor deviations do not constitute a breach of this requirement provided that the sense of the caution is preserved.

Other forms of caution are prescribed for use where the restriction on drawing adverse inferences from silence applies (see pp 114–15).

After any break in questioning under caution, the person being questioned must be made aware he remains under caution. If there is any doubt the relevant caution should be given again in full.

When, despite being cautioned, a person fails to co-operate or to answer particular questions which may affect his immediate treatment, he should be informed of any relevant consequences and that those consequences are not affected by the caution. Examples are when a person's refusal to provide his name and address when charged may make him liable to detention, or when his refusal to provide particulars in accordance with a statutory requirement, such as under the Road Traffic Act 1988, may amount to an offence or may make him liable to a further arrest.

Special warnings under CJPOA 1994, ss 36 and 37

When a suspect who is interviewed at a police station or authorised place of detention after arrest fails or refuses to answer certain questions, or to answer them satisfactorily, *after due warning*, a court or jury may draw such inferences as appear proper under CJPOA 1994, ss 36 and 37 (pp 261–2). Such inferences may only be drawn when:

(a) the restriction on drawing adverse inferences from silence (p 000) does not apply; and

(b) the suspect is arrested by a constable and fails or refuses to account for any objects, marks, or substances, or marks on such objects, found on his person, or in or on his clothing or footwear, or otherwise in his possession, or in the place where he is arrested; or

(c) an arrested suspect was found by a constable at a place at or about the time the offence for which he was arrested is alleged to have been committed, and he fails or refuses to account for his presence at that place.

When the restriction on drawing adverse inferences from silence applies, the suspect may still be asked to account for any of the matters in (b) or (c) but the special warning described in the next paragraph will not apply and must not be given.

For an inference to be drawn when a suspect fails or refuses to answer a question about one of these matters or to answer it satisfactorily, the suspect must first be given the *special warning*. He must be told in ordinary language the following *specified information*: (a) what offence is being investigated; (b) what fact he is being asked to account for; (c) that this fact may be due to him taking part in the commission of the offence; (d) that a court may draw a proper inference if he fails or refuses to account for this fact; and (e) that a record is being made of the interview and it may be given in evidence if he is brought to trial.

Cautions when the restriction on drawing adverse inferences from silence applies

CJPOA 1994, ss 34, 36 and 37 (pp 258–9 and 261–2) describe the conditions under which adverse inferences can be drawn from a person's failure or refusal to say anything about his involvement in the offence when interviewed, or on being charged or informed that he may be prosecuted. These provisions are subject to an overriding *restriction* on the ability of a court or jury to draw inferences from a person's silence. This restriction applies:

(a) to any detainee at a police station who, before being interviewed, or charged, or informed that he may be prosecuted, has:
   (i)   asked for legal advice;
   (ii) not been allowed an opportunity to consult a solicitor, as in Code C; and
   (iii) not changed his mind about wanting legal advice;
   (Condition (ii) will apply when a detainee who has asked for legal advice is interviewed before speaking to a solicitor, but will not apply if the detained person declines to ask for the duty solicitor.)

(b) to anyone charged with, or informed that he may be prosecuted for, an offence who:
   (i) has had brought to his notice a written statement made by another person or the content of an interview with another person which relates to that offence;
   (ii) is interviewed about that offence; or

(iii) makes a written statement about that offence.

Where a requirement to caution arises at a time when the restriction on drawing adverse inferences from silence applies, the caution must be:

'You do not have to say anything, but anything you do say may be given in evidence.'

Whenever the restriction begins or ceases to apply after a caution has been given, the person must be re-cautioned in the appropriate terms. The changed position in relation to inferences and the fact that the previous caution no longer applies must be explained to the detainee in ordinary language.

Code C suggests, in a guidance note, that where the restriction on drawing adverse inferences begins to apply it should be explained that the caution previously given no longer applies because after caution the detainee asked to speak to a solicitor but has not yet had an opportunity to do so (restriction (a)), or because the detainee has been charged with or informed that he will be prosecuted for the offence (restriction (b)). He should be informed that this means that, from now on, adverse inferences cannot be drawn at court and his defence will not be harmed just because he chooses to say nothing. He should be asked to note that the new caution does not say anything about his defence being harmed.

Where restriction (a) ceases to apply before or at the time the person is charged or informed that he may be prosecuted, the detainee should be told that the caution previously given no longer applies, and that this is because after that caution he has been allowed an opportunity to speak to a solicitor. He should be told to listen carefully as the caution now being given explains how his defence at court may be affected by his choosing to say nothing.

Special groups

The *specified information* referred to on p 114 must not be given to a suspect who is vulnerable (ie a juvenile or a 17-year-old or someone who is mentally disordered or otherwise mentally vulnerable) unless the appropriate adult is present.

If such a vulnerable person is cautioned in the absence of the appropriate adult, the caution must be repeated in the appropriate adult's presence.

General

It is important that the appropriate caution is given; if an inappropriate one is chosen the court is liable to exclude evidence subsequently obtained.

Where there is a break in questioning under caution the officer in charge must ensure that the person being questioned is aware that he remains under caution; if there is any doubt the caution should be given again in full when the interview resumes. This is important because the officer may have to satisfy a court that the person understood that he was still under caution when the interview resumed.

If it appears that a person does not understand what the caution means, the officer who has given it should go on to explain it in his own words.

If a person is not under arrest when an initial caution (or reminder) is given, the officer must tell him that he is not under arrest and is not obliged to remain with the officer. The officer must also tell him that he is free to leave if he wishes *and remind him that he may obtain free legal advice* if he wishes. See further p 103.

Documentation

A record must be made when a caution is given, either in the officer's pocket book (or by other methods used for recording information) or in the interview record as appropriate.

INTERVIEWS

General provisions concerning interviews

What is an 'interview'?

Code C defines an interview as 'the questioning of a person regarding his involvement or suspected involvement in a criminal offence or offences which, by virtue of the Code, is required to be carried out under caution'. For example, where, after arresting a man for possessing an offensive weapon, police officers asked him in the police car why he had the knife and he told them there had been some trouble and that he had it for his own protection, it was held that this amounted to an interview for the purposes of Code C, so that a record should have been made of it.

Procedures undertaken under the Road Traffic Act 1988, s 7 (pp 516–18) or the corresponding provisions under the Transport and Works Act 1992 and the Railways and Transport Safety Act 2003 (p 532 and Chapter 15 on the companion website) do not constitute interviews for the purposes of the Code. An informal conversation at or near the scene of a crime is not an 'interview', but it will be if it descends into detailed questioning.

Action

Before a person is interviewed, he and, if he is represented, his solicitor must be given sufficient information to enable them to understand the nature of the offence, and why he is suspected of committing it, in order to allow for the effective exercise of the rights of the defence. However, whilst the information must always be sufficient for the person to understand the nature of any offence, this does not require the disclosure of details at a time which might prejudice the criminal investigation. The decision about what needs to be disclosed for the purpose of this requirement therefore rests with the investigating officer who has sufficient knowledge of the case to make that decision. What is sufficient will depend on the circumstances of the case, but it should normally include, as a minimum, a description of the facts relating to the suspected offence that are known to the officer, including the time and place in question. The officer who discloses the information must make a record of what was disclosed, and when it was disclosed. This record may be made in the interview record, his pocket book or other form provided for this purpose.

Following a decision to arrest a suspect, he must not be interviewed about the relevant offence except at a police station (or other authorised place of detention) unless the consequent delay would be likely:

(a) to lead to interference with or harm to evidence connected with an offence, or interference with or physical harm to other persons, or serious loss of, or damage to, property; or

(b) to lead to the alerting of other persons suspected of having committed an offence but not yet arrested for it; or

(c) to hinder the recovery of property obtained in consequence of the commission of an offence.

Interviewing in any of these exceptions should cease once the relevant risk has been averted or the necessary questions have been put in order to attempt to avert that risk.

Immediately prior to the commencement or recommencement of any interview at a police station (or other authorised place of detention), the interviewing officer must remind the suspect of his entitlement to free legal advice and that the interview can be delayed for him to obtain legal advice (unless one of the exceptions where delay is permitted applies (see p 107)).

At the beginning of an interview carried out in a police station, the interviewing officer, after cautioning the suspect, must put to him any significant statement or silence which occurred in the presence and hearing of a police officer or civilian interviewer before the start of the interview and which has not been put to the suspect in the course of a previous interview, and must ask him whether he confirms or denies that earlier statement or silence and whether he wishes to add anything. This does not prevent an interviewer from putting significant statements and silences to a suspect again at a later stage of a further interview. A 'significant statement' is one which appears capable of being used in evidence against the suspect, in particular a direct admission of guilt. A 'significant silence' is a failure or refusal to answer a question or answer satisfactorily when under caution which might, allowing for the restriction on drawing adverse inferences from silence, give rise to an inference under CJPOA 1994. The interviewing officer must ensure that all such reminders are noted in the record of the interview.

No interviewer may try to obtain answers to questions or to elicit a statement by the use of oppression. Except as provided by Code C, no police officer may indicate, except in answer to a direct question, what action will be taken on the part of the police if the interviewee answers questions, makes a statement or refuses to do either. If the interviewee asks the officer directly what action will be taken in the event of his answering questions, making a statement or refusing to do either, the officer may inform him what action the police propose to take in that event provided that the action is itself proper and warranted.

An interview concerning an offence with which the interviewee has not been charged or for which he has not been informed that he may be prosecuted must cease when:

(a) the officer in charge of the investigation is satisfied that all relevant questions to obtain accurate and reliable information about the offence have been put to the interviewee, including giving an opportunity for an innocent explanation to be put forward and asking any questions to test the accuracy or reliability of such explanation (eg to clear up ambiguities);

(b) the officer in charge of the investigation has taken account of any other available evidence; and

(c) the officer in charge of the investigation, or (in the case of a detained suspect) the custody officer, reasonably believes that there is sufficient evidence to provide a realistic prospect of conviction for that offence if the interviewee was prosecuted.

This does not, however, prevent officers in revenue cases or acting under the money laundering confiscation provisions from inviting suspects to complete a formal question and answer record after the interview is concluded.

In addition, according to the Court of Appeal, provided the officer has an open mind and is prepared not to charge (or not to refer to another officer responsible for charging) if the suspect produces a convincing account, the interviewer may proceed in order to see whether the suspect can produce an explanation.

Interview records

An accurate record must be made of each interview with a suspect, whether or not the interview takes place at a police station. The record must state the place of the interview, the times of its start and end, any breaks in it, and the names of those present. The requirement to record names of those present is subject to the special rule on p 96.

An interview record:

(a) enables the prosecutor to make informed decisions;

(b) is capable of being exhibited to an officer's witness statement and used pursuant to the Criminal Justice Act 1967, s 9 (see p 251);

(c) enables the prosecutor to comply with advance disclosure rules; and

(d) where the record is accepted by the defence, facilitates the conduct of the case by the prosecution, the defence and the court.

The record must be made on the forms provided or in the interviewer's pocket book or in accordance with PACE Code E: the Code of Practice on Audio Recording Interviews with Suspects or PACE Code F: the Code of Practice on Visual Recording with Sound of Interviews with Suspects. Codes E and F do not apply to interviews with persons detained under the Terrorism Act 2000, s 41 or Sch 7, or post-charge questioning authorised under the Counter-Terrorism Act 2008, s 22, both dealt with in Chapter 28, which are subject to separate Codes.

Audio recording and video recording

Interviews to be recorded   Code E states that, with the exceptions mentioned below, audio recording must normally be used for any interview:

(a) *with a person cautioned under Code C, in respect of any indictable offence (whether indictable-only or triable either way)* **except when:**

    (i)   that person has been arrested and the interview takes place elsewhere than at a police station in accordance with Code C for which a written record would be required;

    (ii) *(a)* it is not reasonably practicable to audio record the interview, or continue to do so, because of equipment failure or the unavailability of a suitable interview room or recording equipment; and *(b)* the authorising officer reasonably considers that the interview or its continuation should not be delayed until the problem has been rectified. In such a case, the interview must be recorded or continue to be recorded in writing in accordance with Code C, the authorising officer must record the specific reasons for not audio recording and the interviewer is responsible for ensuring that the written interview record shows the date and time of the authority, the authorising officer and when the authority is recorded. The authority not to audio record the interview must be given by the custody officer in the case of a detained suspect, or a sergeant (or above) in the case of a suspect who has not been arrested and who is attending a police station or elsewhere voluntarily; or

    (iii) the following four conditions in the Annex to Code E are satisfied, in which case the interview must be conducted and recorded in writing, in accordance with Code C. The four conditions are that:

        (*a*) the person has not been arrested;

        (*b*) the interview takes place elsewhere than at a police station;

(c) the indictable offence in respect of which the person has been cautioned is one of the following: possession of khat or cannabis (other than cannabis oil), contrary to the Misuse of Drugs Act 1971, s 5(2); low-value shoplifting, contrary to the Theft Act 1968, s 1; criminal damage, contrary to the Criminal Damage Act 1971, s 1(1); and an attempt to commit one of these offences; and

(d) the general requirements and relevant specific requirements are satisfied.

The *general requirements* are that: *(i)* the person (S) suspected of committing the offence appears to be at least 18; does not require an appropriate adult; appears to be able to appreciate the significance of questions and their answers; does not appear unable to understand what is happening because of drink, drugs, illness or condition; and does not require an interpreter in accordance with Code C; *(ii)* it appears that the commission of the offence has not resulted in any injury to any person or involved any realistic threat or risk of injury to any person, and has not caused any substantial financial or material loss to an individual's private property; *(iii)* S's arrest is not necessary in order to investigate the offence; and *(iv)* S is not being interviewed about any other offence.

The *specific requirements* where S has been cautioned in respect of possession of khat or cannabis (other than cannabis oil) are that a police officer experienced in the recognition of the physical appearance, texture and smell of khat or cannabis (as the case may be) is able to say that the substance found in S's possession by him or by another officer not so experienced is one or other of those drugs, and the quantity found is consistent with personal use by the suspect and does not provide any grounds to suspect an intention to supply others.

The *specific requirements* where S has been cautioned in respect of low-value theft are that the value of the property stolen does not exceed £100 inclusive of VAT; that the stolen property has been recovered and remains fit for sale unless the items stolen comprised drink or food and have been consumed; and that S is not employed (whether paid or not) by the person or organisation to which the property belongs.

The *specific requirements* where S has been cautioned in respect of criminal damage are that it appears to the officer that the value of the criminal damage does not exceed £300, and that S is not employed (whether paid or not) by the person or organisation to which the property belongs.

If it appears to the interviewing officer, before the conclusion of an interview to which the Annex applies, that any of the general or relevant specific requirements have ceased to apply, the Annex ceases to apply. The person being interviewed must be so informed and a break in the interview must be taken. The reason must be recorded in the interview record and the continuation of the interview must be audio recorded in accordance with Code E. For the purposes of the continuation, the provisions of Code E about commencement of interviews (the first paragraph under the heading *Commencement of interviews* on p 126) and the corresponding passage on p 130 apply.

The present exemption (ie under (iii): p 118) means that on-the-street disposals for the specified offences will not breach the requirements of Code E. Its purpose is to support the policy which gives police options for dealing with low-level offences quickly and non-bureaucratically in a proportionate manner;

(b) *which takes place as a result of an interviewer exceptionally putting further questions to a suspect about an indictable offence (whether indictable-only or triable either way) after he has been charged with, or told that he may be prosecuted for, that offence;* or

(c) *in which an interviewer wants to tell a person, after he has been charged with, or informed he may be prosecuted for, an indictable offence (whether indictable-only or triable either way), about any written statement or interview with another person.*

There is no requirement visually to record interviews, but Code F suggests that it might be appropriate to choose to do so in the three cases in italics above and also when the interview is with, or in the presence of, a deaf, deaf/blind or speech-impaired person who uses sign language to communicate, or where the presence of the appropriate adult is required, or where the suspect or his representative requests it.

If a detainee refuses to go into or remain in a suitable interview room, and the custody officer considers, on reasonable grounds, that the interview should not be delayed the interview may, at the custody officer's discretion, be conducted in a cell using portable recording equipment or, if none is available, recorded in writing as in Code C. The reasons for this must be recorded.

In the application of Code E to the conduct and recording of an interview of a suspect who has not been arrested, note that:

(a) references to the 'custody officer' include references to an officer of the rank of sergeant (or above) not directly involved in the investigation of the offence(s);

(b) if the interview takes place elsewhere than at a police station, references to 'interview room' include any place or location which the interviewer is satisfied will enable the interview to be conducted and recorded in accordance with Code E and where the suspect is present voluntarily; and

(c) provisions in addition to those which expressly apply to such interviews must be followed insofar as they are relevant and can be applied in practice.

An interviewer who is not sure, or has any doubt, about the suitability of a place or location of an interview to be carried out elsewhere than at a police station should consult an officer of the rank of sergeant (or above) for advice.

The whole of an audibly or visually recorded interview must be so recorded, including the taking and reading back of any statement. If, during the course of any audibly or visually recorded interview, it becomes apparent that the interview should be conducted under the terrorism code for video recording of interviews, the interview should continue in accordance with the relevant code.

The recording of interviews must be carried out openly. It must be made clear to the suspect that there is no opportunity to interfere with the equipment or recording media. Where the recording is not by secure digital network, the 'master recording' will be sealed before it leaves the presence of the suspect. A master recording may be either one of two recording media used in a twin-deck/drive machine or the only medium used in a single-deck/drive machine. A second medium will be used as a working copy and it may be either the other medium in the case of a twin-deck/drive machine, or a copy of the master used in a single-deck/drive machine. Such a copy must be made in the presence of the suspect and without the master recording leaving his sight.

As to the procedure for audio or video recording, see pp 126–33.

Written record

Written interview records must be signed and timed by the maker.

Any written record must be made during the interview, unless in the investigating officer's view this would not be practicable or would interfere with the conduct of the interview, and must constitute either a verbatim record or, failing this, an account of the interview which adequately and accurately summarises it. If the record is not made during the interview, it must be made as soon as practicable thereafter and the reason must be recorded in the interview record.

Checking the interview record

Unless it is impracticable, the person interviewed must be given the opportunity to read the interview record and to sign it as correct or to indicate the respects in which he considers it inaccurate. When a suspect agrees to read records of interviews and of other comments and to sign them as correct, he should be asked to endorse the record with words such as 'I agree that this is a correct record of what was said' and add his signature. Where the suspect does not agree with the record, the officer should record the details of any disagreement and then ask the suspect to read these details and then sign them to the effect that they accurately reflect his disagreement.

If the person concerned cannot read, or refuses to read the record or to sign it, the senior police officer present must read it over to him and ask him whether he would like to sign it as correct or to indicate the respects in which he considers it inaccurate. The police officer must then certify on the interview record itself what has occurred.

If the interview is audibly or visually recorded the arrangements set out in Code E or Code F apply (see pp 128, 131 and 132).

Records of comments outside interview

A written record must be made of any comments made by a suspected person, including unsolicited comments, which are outside the context of a formal interview but which might be relevant to the offence. A judge in the Administrative Court has held that this requirement does not apply only to incriminating comments or only where a caution has been given. Any such record must be timed and signed by the maker. Where practicable the person must be given the opportunity to read that record and to sign it as correct or to indicate the respects in which he considers it inaccurate. Any refusal to sign must be recorded.

Vulnerable persons

A juvenile or 17-year-old or a mentally disordered or vulnerable person must not be interviewed regarding his involvement or suspected involvement in a criminal offence or offences, or be asked to provide or sign a written statement under caution or record of an interview, in the absence of the appropriate adult, subject to the special provisions below about urgent interviews authorised by a superintendent.

A juvenile, 17-year-old or someone who is mentally disordered or vulnerable may be particularly open to suggestion. Consequently, special care must always be exercised in questioning such a person, and it is important to obtain corroboration of any facts admitted wherever possible.

A juvenile or 17-year-old may only be interviewed at his place of education in exceptional circumstances and then only when the principal or his nominee agrees and is present. Every effort should be made to contact both the parents, or other person responsible for his welfare, and the appropriate adult (if a different person). A reasonable time should be allowed to enable the appropriate adult to attend. Where this would cause undue delay, and unless the offence is against the educational establishment, the principal or his nominee can act as the appropriate adult for the purposes of the interview.

An interview is an indivisible process. A failure to involve the appropriate adult in some part of it is a breach of Code C and may render the whole of the interview inadmissible.

If an appropriate adult is present at an interview, he must be told that he is not expected to act simply as an observer. He must also be informed that the purposes of his presence are:

(a) to advise the person being interviewed and to observe whether or not the interview is conducted fairly and properly; and
(b) to facilitate communication with the person being interviewed.

If a person is blind, seriously visually impaired, or unable to read, the custody officer must ensure that his solicitor, relative, the appropriate adult or some other person likely to take an interest in him (and not involved in the investigation) is available to help in checking any documentation. Where Code C requires consent or signing, then the person who is assisting may be asked to sign instead, if the detained person so wishes. However, there is no requirement that the appropriate adult be called solely to assist in checking and signing documentation in such circumstances.

If the appropriate adult or the person's solicitor is present during the interview, he should also be given an opportunity to read and sign the interview record or any written statement taken down during the interview. Any refusal to sign when asked must itself be recorded on the interview record. If the interview is audibly or visually recorded the arrangements set out in Code E or Code F apply.

Vulnerable suspects: urgent interviews at police stations

The following interviews may take place only if a superintendent (or above) considers that delaying the interview will lead to one of the consequences (potential interference, harm, loss, etc) set out at (b)(i) on pp 109–10, and is satisfied that the interview would not significantly harm the person's physical or mental state:

(a) an interview of a juvenile, 17-year-old, or person who is mentally disordered or otherwise mentally vulnerable without the appropriate adult being present;
(b) an interview of anyone other than in (a) who appears unable to:
    (i)   appreciate the significance of questions and his answers; or
    (ii) understand what is happening because of the effects of drink, drugs or any illness, ailment or condition;
(c) an interview, without an interpreter being present, of a person whom the custody officer has determined requires an interpreter (p 134) which is carried out by an interviewer speaking the suspect's own language or (as the case may be) otherwise establishing effective communication which is sufficient to enable the necessary questions to be asked and answered in order to avert the consequences referred to above.

These interviews may not continue once sufficient information has been obtained to avert the consequences referred to above. A record must be made of the grounds for any decision urgently to interview a person.

Interviews in police stations

Code C provides that if a police officer wishes to interview a detained person, or to conduct inquiries which require the presence of a detained person, it is the custody officer who must decide whether to deliver his prisoner into that officer's custody. An investigating officer who is given custody of a detainee takes over responsibility for the detainee's care and safe custody until he returns the detainee to the custody officer when he must report the manner in which he complied with the Code whilst having custody of the detainee.

In any period of 24 hours a detained person must be allowed a continuous period of at least eight hours' rest, free from questioning, travel or any interruption by police officers in connection with the investigation concerned. This period should normally be at night or other appropriate time which takes account of when the detainee last slept or rested. If a detainee is arrested at a police station after going there voluntarily, the 24-hour period runs from the time of arrival at the police station. The period of rest may not be interrupted or delayed except:

(a) when there are reasonable grounds for believing that not delaying or interrupting that period would:
  (i)   involve a risk of harm to people or serious loss of, or damage to, property;
  (ii) delay unnecessarily the detainee's release from custody;
  (iii) otherwise prejudice the outcome of the investigation;
(b) at the request of the detainee, his appropriate adult, or his legal representative;
(c) when a delay or interruption is necessary in order to comply with the legal obligations and duties under Code C relating to reviews and extensions of detention or as to the care and treatment of detained persons who are intoxicated or in need of clinical treatment and attention.

If such a period of rest is interrupted in accordance with (a), a fresh period must be allowed. Interruptions under (b) and (c) do not require that a fresh period be allowed.

As far as practicable, an interview must take place in a properly heated, lit, and ventilated interview room. The detained person must not be required to stand.

A suspect whose detention without charge has been authorised under PACE, because his detention is necessary so that he may be interviewed with a view to obtaining evidence of the offence for which he was arrested, may choose not to answer questions. However, the police do not require a suspect's consent to interview him for this purpose. If a suspect takes steps to prevent an interview, such as refusing to leave his cell, or trying to leave the interview room, he must be cautioned and be told that refusal to co-operate could lead to the interview taking place in the cell and that such failure to co-operate may be given in evidence. A further invitation should then be given to co-operate by going to the interview room.

With the italicised exception on p 96, before the start of an interview, each interviewing officer must identify himself and any other officers present to the interviewee.

In all interviews, there must be breaks at the recognised meal times and there must also be short breaks for refreshment at intervals of approximately two hours, subject to the interviewing officer's discretion to delay a break if there are reasonable grounds for believing that it would:

(a) involve a risk of harm to persons or serious loss of, or damage to, property; or
(b) delay unnecessarily the person's release from custody; or
(c) otherwise prejudice the investigation.

Meal breaks should normally last at least 45 minutes and shorter breaks after two hours should last at least 15 minutes. If a break is delayed as permitted by Code C and prolongs the interview, a longer break should then be provided. If there is a short interview, and a subsequent short interview is contemplated, the length of the break may be reduced if there are reasonable grounds to believe that this is necessary to avoid any of the consequences set out at (a) to (c) above.

A record must be made of times during which a detainee was not in the custody of the custody officer, and why; of any reason for refusal to deliver the detainee out of that custody; of any reason why it was not practicable to use an interview room; and of any action taken in consequence of a refusal to be interviewed.

Written statements under caution

All written statements made at police stations under caution must be written on the forms provided for the purpose. All written statements under caution must be taken in accordance with the rules in Annex D to Code C ((1)–(12) below). Before a person makes a written statement under caution at a police station he must be reminded about the right to legal advice. It is not normally necessary to ask for a written statement if the interview was recorded in writing, and the record signed, or audibly or visually recorded in accordance with Code E or Code F respectively.

Written by a person under caution

(1) A person must always be invited to write down himself what he wants to say.
(2) A person who has not been charged with, or informed that he may be prosecuted for, any offence to which the statement relates, must:
   (a) unless the statement is made at a time when the restriction on drawing adverse inferences from silence applies, be asked to write out and sign the following before writing what he wants to say:

   'I make this statement of my own free will. I understand that I do not have to say anything but that it may harm my defence if I do not mention when questioned something which I later rely on in court. This statement may be given in evidence.';

   (b) if the statement is made at a time when the restriction on drawing adverse inferences from silence applies, he must be asked to write out and sign the following before writing what he wants to say:

   'I make this statement of my own free will. I understand that I do not have to say anything. This statement may be given in evidence.'

(3) When a person, on the occasion of being charged with, or informed that he may be prosecuted for, any offence, asks to make a statement which relates to any such offence and wants to write it he must, unless the restriction on drawing adverse inferences from silence applied when he was so charged or informed that he might be prosecuted, be asked to write out the words in bold above and sign them before writing what he wants to say. If the restriction on drawing adverse inferences from silence applied when the person was so charged or informed that he would be prosecuted, he must be asked to write out the words italicised above and sign them before writing what he wants to say.

(4) Where a person, who has already been charged with or informed that he may be prosecuted for any offence, asks to make a statement which relates to any such

offence and wants to write it, he must be asked to write out and sign the words italicised above before writing what he wants to say.

(5) Any person writing his own statement must be allowed to do so without any prompting except that a police officer or civilian interviewer may indicate to him which matters are material or question any ambiguity in the statement.

Written by a police officer or other police staff

(6) If a person says that he would like someone to write it for him, a police officer or other member of police staff must write the statement.

(7) If the person has not been charged with, or informed that he may be prosecuted for, any offence to which the statement he wants to make relates, he must, before starting, be asked to sign, or make his mark, to the appropriate one of the following endorsements.

(a) Unless the statement is made at a time when the restriction on drawing adverse inferences from silence applies, the endorsement is:

'I, ..., wish to make a statement. I want someone to write down what I say. I understand that I do not have to say anything but that it may harm my defence if I do not mention when questioned something which I later rely on in court. This statement may be given in evidence.'

(b) If the statement is made at a time when the restriction on drawing adverse inferences from silence applies, the endorsement is:

'I, ..., wish to make a statement. I want someone to write down what I say. I understand that I do not have to say anything. This statement may be given in evidence.'

(8) If, on the occasion of being charged with or informed that he may be prosecuted for any offence, the person asks to make a statement which relates to any such offence, he must before starting be asked to sign, or make his mark to, the following as appropriate. Unless the restriction on drawing adverse inferences from silence applied when he was so charged or informed that he may be prosecuted, the words are the same as in (7)(a). If the restriction on drawing adverse inferences from silence applied when he was so charged or informed that he may be prosecuted, the words are the same as in (7)(b).

(9) If, having already been charged with or informed that he may be prosecuted for any offence, a person asks to make a statement which relates to such an offence, he must, before starting, be asked to sign or make his mark to the form of words in (7)(b).

(10)The person writing the statement must take down the exact words spoken by the person making it and he must not edit or paraphrase it. Any questions that are necessary (eg to make it more intelligible) and the answers given must be recorded contemporaneously on the statement form.

(11)When the writing of a statement is finished the person making it must be asked to read it and to make any corrections, alterations or additions he wishes. When he has finished reading it he must be asked to write and sign or make his mark on the following certificate at the end of the statement:

'I have read the above statement, and I have been able to correct, alter, or add anything I wish. This statement is true. I have made it of my own free will.'

(12)If the person making the statement cannot read, or refuses to read it, or to write the above-mentioned certificate at the end of it or to sign it, the person taking the statement must read it over to him and ask him whether he would like to correct, alter or add anything and put his signature or make his mark at the end. The person taking the statement must then certify on the statement itself what has occurred.

Audio-recorded interviews

Code E provides as follows.

Recording and sealing master recordings

Recording of interviews must be carried out openly to instil confidence in its reliability as an impartial and accurate record of the interview.

One recording, the master recording, will be sealed in the suspect's presence. The master recording is any of the recordings made by a multi-deck/drive machine or the only recording made by a single-deck/drive machine. The working copy is one of the other recordings made by a multi-deck/drive machine or a copy of the master recording made by a single-deck/drive machine. *This paragraph does not apply to interviews recorded using a secure digital network (SDN) (see below).*

The identity of officers or police staff conducting interviews need not be recorded or disclosed if the interviewer reasonably believes recording or disclosing his name might put him in danger. In these cases interviewers should use warrant or other identification numbers and the name of their police station. Such instances and the reasons for them must be recorded in the custody record or the interviewer's pocket book.

A sign or indicator which is visible to the suspect must show when the recording equipment is recording.

Commencement of interview

When the suspect is brought into the interview room the interviewer must, without delay, but in sight of the suspect, load the audio recorder with new recording media and set it to record. 'Recording media' means any removable, physical audio-recording medium (such as magnetic tape, optical disc or solid state memory) which can be played or copied. The recording media must be unwrapped or opened in the suspect's presence. *This paragraph does not apply to interviews recorded using a SDN.*

The interviewer must then:

(a) explain that the interview is being audibly recorded and point out the sign or indicator which shows that the recording equipment is activated and recording;

(b) give his name and rank and the name and rank of any other interviewer present, except in the case described on p 96;

(c) ask the suspect and any other person present (eg a solicitor) to identify themselves;

(d) state the date, time of commencement, and place of the interview; and

(e) *except where the recording uses a SDN*, state that the suspect will be given a notice about what will happen to the recording.

Any person entering the interview room after the interview has commenced must be invited by the interviewer to identify himself for the purpose of the audio recording and state the reason why he has entered the interview room.

The interviewer must:

(a) caution the suspect, as provided by Code C; and

(b) if the suspect is detained, remind him of his entitlement to free legal advice, as set out in Code C; or

(c) if the suspect is not detained under arrest, explain this and his entitlement to free legal advice, as set out in Code C.

The interviewer must then put to the suspect any 'significant statement or silence' (as to which see p 117) which occurred before the start of the audibly recorded interview, and must ask him whether he confirms or denies that earlier statement or silence or whether he wishes to add anything.

The reader is reminded that a special warning must be given before inferences can be drawn under CJPOA 1994, ss 36 or 37 and of the fact that adverse inferences cannot be drawn where legal advice has been requested but has not yet been received.

Objections

If the suspect or appropriate adult raises objections to the interview being audibly recorded at the outset, or during the interview, or during a break in the interview, the interviewer must explain that the interview is being audibly recorded and that Code E requires the objections to be recorded on the audio recording. When any objections have been recorded or the suspect or appropriate adult has refused to have his objections recorded, the interviewer may turn off the recorder. In this eventuality, he must say that he is turning off the recorder and give his reasons for doing so and then turn it off. The interviewer must then make a written record of the interview in accordance with Code C. If, however, the interviewer reasonably considers that he may proceed to put questions to the suspect with the audio recorder still on, he may do so. He should bear in mind that a decision to continue recording against the wishes of the suspect may be the subject of comment in court.

If a suspect indicates that he wishes to tell an interviewer about matters not directly connected with the offence of which he is suspected and that he is unwilling for these matters to be recorded, he must be given the opportunity to tell the police officer about these matters after the conclusion of the formal interview.

Changing recording media

Where recording media are coming to an end, the interviewer must inform the suspect and round off that part of the interview. If the interviewer leaves the room for a second set of recording media, the suspect should not be left unattended. The interviewer will remove the recording media and insert new ones which must be unwrapped or otherwise opened in the suspect's presence. Recording media must be marked with an identification number immediately they are removed from the recorder.

The above paragraph does not apply to a recording using a SDN as this does not use removable media; nor do the paragraphs below relating to breaks in interview, equipment failure, removing recording media, the conclusion of the interview, after the interview and master recording security.

Taking a break during the interview

When a break is taken, that fact must be recorded on the audio recording together with the reason for it and the time it was taken. If the interview room is vacated by the suspect, the recording media must be removed from the recorder and the procedures (below) for the conclusion of the interview followed.

When a break is a short one and both the suspect and the interviewer remain in the interview room, the recording may be stopped. There is no need to remove the recording media. The time of recommencement of the interview must be recorded.

Whenever there has been a break in questioning under caution the interviewer must remind the person being questioned of his right to legal advice, if he has not exercised it, and that he remains under caution. If there is a doubt, the caution must be renewed. The interviewer must bear in mind that he may have to satisfy a court that the person realised that the caution still applied. He may also have to show that nothing occurred during a break in an interview or between interviews which influenced the suspect's recorded evidence. In view of this, he should consider, at recommencement or at a subsequent interview, summarising on recording media the reason for the break and confirming this with the suspect. As to lengths of breaks, see p 123.

Equipment failure

In the event of an equipment failure which can be rectified quickly, for example by inserting new recording media, this must be done following the prescribed procedures about the changing of recording media. When the recording is resumed, the interviewer must record the reason and the time the interview recommences. Where the further use of the audio recorder is impossible and no alternative is readily available, the interview may continue without being audibly recorded but the authority of the custody officer or, if the suspect has not been arrested, a sergeant (or above) must be sought.

Where the media or recording equipment fail during the interview the interviewer should stop the interview immediately. Where part of the interview is unaffected by the error and is still accessible on the media, those media must be copied and sealed in the suspect's presence and the interview recommenced using new equipment/media as required. Where the content of the interview has been lost in its entirety the media should be sealed in the suspect's presence and the interview begun again.

Removing recording media

When recording media are removed from the recorder during the interview, they must be retained and the procedures which apply to them at the conclusion of the interview (below) followed.

Conclusion of the interview

At the conclusion of the interview, the suspect must be offered the opportunity to clarify anything he has said and asked if there is anything he wishes to add. At the conclusion of the interview, including the taking and reading back of any written statement, the time must be recorded and the audio recorder stopped.

The master recording must then be sealed with a master recording label and treated as an exhibit. The interviewer must sign the label and ask the suspect and any third party to sign it also. If either, or both, refuse to sign the label, an inspector (or above), or if one is not available, the custody officer, or, if the suspect has not been arrested, a sergeant (or above), must be called in to the interview room and asked to sign it.

The suspect must be handed a notice explaining the use which will be made of the audio recording and the arrangements for access to it and explaining that a copy of the audio recording will be supplied as soon as practicable (or as otherwise agreed with him or on the order of a court) if he is charged or informed that he will be prosecuted.

After the interview

The interviewer must make a note in his pocket book: (a) that the interview has taken place and was audibly recorded; (b) of the time it commenced, its duration, and date; and (c) of the identification number of the master recording. Where no proceedings follow in respect of the person whose interview was recorded the recording media must nevertheless be kept securely as required by Code E. Where proceedings follow, the interviewer must prepare a written record of the interview and sign it. Any such record should be made in accordance with the national guidelines for police officers, police staff and CPS prosecutors concerned with the preparation, processing and submission of prosecution files. Before preparing it the interviewer may refresh his memory by listening to the working copy of the recording media to check its accuracy. The interview record must be exhibited to any written statement prepared by the interviewer. If the interviewer's evidence of the interview is accepted by the defence, the evidence must refer to the fact that the interview was audio recorded and may be presented to the court in the form of the interview record. Where the interviewer's evidence is not accepted by the defence, the interviewer must refer to the fact that the interview was audibly recorded and produce the master recording medium of the whole interview, as an exhibit, informing the court of any transcription which has been made of which he is aware.

Master recording security

The officer in charge of each police station at which interviews with suspects are recorded or, as the case may be, where recordings of interviews carried out elsewhere than at a police station are held must make arrangements for master recordings to be kept securely and their movements accounted for on the same basis as material which may be used for evidential purposes, in accordance with force standing orders. A police officer must not break the seal on a master recording required for criminal trial or appeal proceedings, except in the presence of a representative of the CPS. In such a case, the defendant, or his legal adviser, must be informed and be given a reasonable opportunity to be present. If either is present, he must be invited to reseal and sign the master recording. If not present, or in the event of refusal, this will be done by the representative of the CPS. If the recording has been delivered to the Crown Court following sending for trial, the Crown Prosecutor will apply to the Chief Clerk of the Crown Court for the release of the media for unsealing by the Crown Prosecutor.

The chief officer of police is responsible for establishing arrangements for breaking the seal of the master copy where no criminal proceedings result, or the criminal proceedings to which the interview relates have been concluded and it becomes necessary to break the seal. These arrangements should be those which the chief officer considers are reasonably necessary to demonstrate to the person interviewed and any other party who may wish to use or refer to the interview record that the master copy has not been tampered with and that the interview record remains accurate.

With the italicised exception below, a representative of each party must be given a reasonable opportunity to be present when the seal is broken and the master recording copied and re-sealed. If one or more of the parties is not present when the master copy seal is broken because he cannot be contacted or refuses to attend, or in the case italicised below, arrangements should be made for an independent person such as a custody visitor to be present. Alternatively, or as an additional safeguard, arrangement should be made for a film or photographs to be taken of the procedure.

A person need not be given an opportunity to be present when:

- *it is necessary to break the master copy seal for the proper and effective further investigation of the original offence or the investigation of some other offence; and*
- *the officer in charge of the investigation has reasonable grounds to suspect that allowing an opportunity might prejudice any such an investigation or criminal proceedings which may be brought as a result or endanger any person.*

The italicised words could apply, for example, when one or more of the outcomes or likely outcomes of the investigation might be: (i) the prosecution of one or more of the original suspects; (ii) the prosecution of someone previously not suspected, including someone who was originally a witness; and (iii) any original suspect being treated as a prosecution witness and when premature disclosure of any police action, particularly through contact with any parties involved, could lead to a real risk of compromising the investigation and endangering witnesses.

Recording interviews by secure digital network (SDN)

The term 'secure digital network' means a computer network system which enables an original interview recording to be stored, as a digital multimedia file or a series of such files, on a secure file server which is accredited in accordance with the UK Government Protective Marking Scheme.

Code E applies to such recordings. The differences in procedure are described below.

Commencement of interview

When the suspect is brought into the interview room, the interviewer must, without delay and in the sight of the suspect, switch on the recording equipment and enter the information accessory to log on to the secure network and start recording. The interviewer must then inform the suspect that the interview is being recorded using a SDN and that recording has commenced. In addition to explaining that the interview is being audibly recorded and saying the other things required by Code E at the commencement of an interview (see pp 126–7), the interviewer must also inform the person that:

(a) he will be given access to the recording of the interview in the event that he is charged or informed that he will be prosecuted, but if he is not charged or informed that he will be prosecuted he will only be given access as agreed with the police or on the order of a court;

(b) he will be given a written notice at the end of the interview setting out his rights to access the recording and what will happen to the recording.

Taking a break during interview

When a break is taken, the fact that a break is to be taken, the reason for it, and the time must be recorded on the audio recording. The recording must be stopped and the procedures for the conclusion of an interview followed. When the interview recommences the above procedures for commencing a SDN recorded interview must be followed to create a new file to record the continuation of the interview. The time the interview recommences must be recorded on the audio recording.

Failure of recording equipment

Where there is an equipment failure which can be rectified quickly, for example by commencing a new SDN recording, the procedure laid down in the previous paragraph must be followed. On resumption, the interviewer must explain what has happened and record the time of recommencement. Where it is not possible to continue on the SDN the interview should be recorded on removable audio-recording media as described on p 128, unless the necessary equipment is not available. In the event of such unavailability, the interview may continue without being audibly recorded and the consent of the custody officer or, if the suspect has not been arrested, a sergeant (or above) should be sought.

Conclusion of the interview

At the conclusion of the interview, the suspect must be given the opportunity to clarify anything he has said and asked if there is anything that he wants to add.

In addition, at the conclusion of the interview, including after the taking and reading back of any written statement:

(a) the time must be orally recorded;

(b) the suspect must be handed a notice which explains: how the audio recording will be used; the arrangements for access to it; and that if he is charged or informed that he will be prosecuted, he will be given access to the recording of the interview either electronically or by being given a copy on removable recording media, but if he is not charged or informed that he will be prosecuted, he will only be given access as agreed with the police or on the order of a court;

(c) the suspect must be asked to confirm that he has received a copy of the notice and, should he fail to acknowledge receipt, the interviewer will state for the recording that a copy of the notice has been provided to the suspect and that he has refused to accept it or has refused to acknowledge receipt; and

(d) the time must be recorded and the interviewer must inform the suspect that the recording is being saved to the secure network; the saving of the recording must be done in the presence of the suspect who should be told that the interview is terminated.

The notice referred to in (b) should provide a brief explanation of the SDN and how access is strictly limited to the recording. The notice should also explain the access rights of the suspect, his legal representative, the police and the prosecutor to the recording of the interview. Space should be provided on the form to insert the date and the file reference number for the interview.

After the interview

The interviewer must make a note in his pocket book that the interview has taken place and was audibly recorded, the time it commenced, its duration, and date, and the original recording's identification number. If no proceedings follow in respect of the person whose interview was recorded, the recordings must be kept securely as set out below. Any written record should be made in accordance with the national guidelines and the advice referred to on p 129.

Security of SDN interview records

Interview record files are stored in read-only format on non-removable storage devices, for example hard disc drives, to ensure their integrity. The recordings are first saved locally to a secure non-removable device before being transferred to the remote network device. If for any reason the network connection fails, the recording remains on the local device and will be transferred when the network connections are restored.

Access to interview recordings, including copying to removable media, must be strictly controlled and monitored to ensure that access is restricted to persons who have been given specific permission to access them for specified purposes when this is necessary. Such persons may, for example, be police officers and CPS lawyers involved in the preparation of any prosecution case, and persons interviewed if they have been charged or informed they may be prosecuted and their legal representatives.

Visual recording of interviews

Police officers may choose to visually record, with sound, interviews with suspects (see p 118); if they do, they must have regard to the terms of Code F.

Where an interviewing officer wishes to make a visual recording on removable media, the rules which govern the conduct of visually recorded interviews largely follow those applicable to audibly recorded interviews which do not involve a SDN. The recording must be carried out openly to instil confidence in its reliability as an impartial and accurate record of the interview. The cameras should be placed in the interview room so as to ensure coverage of as much of the room as possible. When the recording medium is placed in the recorder and it is switched on to record, the correct date and time, in hours, minutes and seconds, will be superimposed automatically, second by second, during the whole recording. The master copy must be sealed before leaving the presence of the suspect. A second copy will be used as a working copy. The usual safeguards apply to identification of officers where it is reasonably believed that identification might endanger the officers. Such officers will be seated with their backs to the camera and must use their warrant number and the name of the police station to which they are attached.

The procedure concerning the explanation and identification of persons present is the same as that which applies to audio recording. Similar provisions also apply to objections.

Should the recording media run out before the interview is concluded further certified recording media will be used. As recording media near completion, a suspect should be warned and allowed to wind up that part of the interview. A suspect must not be left alone in the room while further recording media are sought. Care must be taken when a number of recording media have been used to ensure that they are properly identified.

When a break is taken, the fact that a break is to be taken, the reason for it, and the time must be recorded on the visual record. Thereafter, the same 'taking a break provisions' apply as set out on p 127 in respect of audio recordings.

Provisions corresponding to those on p 128 apply in the event of equipment failure.

At the conclusion of the interview, the master must be sealed with a label and treated as an exhibit. The label should be signed by the interviewer who should ask the suspect and any other person present to sign also. If no other such person will sign, an inspector (or above) should be asked to do so and, if no such officer is available, the custody officer or, if the suspect has not been arrested, a sergeant (or above) should sign the label. In addition, the suspect will be given a notice which explains the use to which the recording will be put and the arrangements for access to it. The notice will also advise the suspect that a copy of the recording will be supplied as soon as practicable if he is charged or informed that he will be prosecuted.

The same procedures apply, in relation to the security of the master copy and the breaking of the seal on a master copy which is required for criminal trial or appeal procedures, as apply in the case of audio-recording media.

Where an officer wishes to make a visual recording with sound of an interview using a SDN which does not use removable media, the above provisions will not apply to the SDN recording. Instead, the requirement and provisions for the audio recording of interviews using a SDN set out in Code E should be applied to the visual recording of interviews as if references to audio recordings of interviews included references to visual recordings with sound.

Where a person raises objections to an interview being visually recorded the interviewer must explain that the objection must be recorded on the visual recording. When any objections have been visually recorded, or the person refuses to have his objections so recorded, the interviewer must say that he is turning off the recorder, giving his reasons for doing so. If a separate audio recording is being made, the interviewer must ask the person to record the reasons for refusal to agree to visual recording. If the person objects to audio recording, the provisions of Code E relating to objections by suspects will apply.

Complaints

If, during an interview at a police station, the detained person makes a complaint concerning a matter covered by Code C, Code E or Code F, it must be recorded in the interview record and the interviewing officer must inform the custody officer who must deal with it in accordance with Code C (see p 146). (These obligations also apply if it comes to the interviewer's notice that the interviewee may have been treated improperly.) Where the interview is being audibly recorded or visually recorded with sound, the recording should be left running until the custody officer has entered the room and has spoken to the interviewee. Continuation or termination of the interview should be at the discretion of the interviewing officer pending action by an inspector.

Where, during the course of an interview which is being recorded, a complaint is made about a matter not connected with Code C, Code E or Code F, the decision to continue the interview or terminate it is at the discretion of the interviewing officer. If continued, the officer must inform the complainant that the complaint will be brought to the attention of the custody officer at the conclusion of the interview, which must be done as soon as practicable thereafter.

Other points

The custody record must show the times during which the prisoner was not in the custody of the custody officer and the reason why he was removed from his custody; if a request for the delivery of a prisoner out of that custody was refused, the reason for refusal must be recorded. Decisions to defer breaks must be recorded, with grounds, in the interview record. Assuming he is still at the police station when it is made, the person interviewed must be allowed to read the interview record and to sign it as being correct or to indicate what he considers to be inaccurate, but no person may be kept in custody for this sole purpose.

In conclusion, it should be noted that the Codes of Practice do not prevent a police officer from asking questions at the scene of a crime to elicit an explanation which could provide the arrested person with the opportunity to show that he is innocent. The reason is obvious: since the questions are not asked with a view to establishing admissions on which proceedings can be founded, there is technically no interview for the purposes of the Codes. If, in the course of asking such questions, a suspect makes a confession, it is prima facie admissible (even if the suspect is a juvenile and no appropriate adult is present).

In addition, there is no universal rule that, whenever there is a breach of a Code of Practice in a police interview, all subsequent interviews must be tainted and evidence of them excluded. Such a rule would fetter a judge's discretion under PACE, s 78 (p 267), which depends upon the facts of the particular case.

INTERPRETERS

General

Chief officers of police are responsible for making arrangements to provide appropriately qualified independent persons to act as interpreters and to provide translations of essential documents for:

(a) detained suspects who the custody officer has determined require an interpreter, and
(b) suspects who are not under arrest but are cautioned and who the interviewer has determined require an interpreter. In these cases, the responsibilities of the custody officer are, if appropriate, assigned to the interviewer. An interviewer who has any doubts about whether an interpreter is required or about how the provisions about interpreters should be applied to a suspect who is not under arrest should seek advice from an officer of the rank of sergeant (or above).

If the suspect has a hearing or speech impediment, references to 'interpreter' and 'interpretation' include appropriate assistance necessary to establish effective communication with that person. With regard to persons in Wales, nothing in Code C or any other Code affects the application of the Welsh Language Schemes produced by police and crime commissioners in Wales in accordance with the Welsh Language Act 1993.

The arrangements must comply with the minimum requirements set out in an EU Directive on the right to interpretation and translation in criminal proceedings, which is designed to safeguard the fairness of the proceedings, in particular by ensuring that suspected or accused persons have knowledge of the cases against them and are able to exercise their right of defence. The provisions of Code C implement the requirements for those to whom Code C applies. Chief officers have discretion when determining the individuals or organisations they use to provide interpretation and translation services for their forces, provided that these services are compatible with the requirements of the Directive. One example which chief officers may wish to consider is the Ministry of Justice Framework Agreement for interpretation and translation services.

All reasonable attempts should be made to make the suspect understand that interpretation and translation will be provided at public expense.

Interviewing suspects: foreign languages

Unless a superintendent (or above) considers that delay will lead to one of the consequences set out on p 107 (urgent interviews), in which case the same rules apply as in the case of interviews with vulnerable suspects (p 122), a suspect who requires an interpreter because he does not appear to speak or understand English must not be interviewed in the absence of a person capable of interpreting.

An interpreter should also be called if a juvenile or 17-year-old is interviewed and his parent or guardian, present as the appropriate adult, does not appear to speak or understand English, unless the interview is urgent and a superintendent (or above) considers that delay will lead to the consequences set out on p 107.

When a written record of the interview is made, the interviewer must make sure that the interpreter makes a note of the interview at the time in the person's language for use in the event of the interpreter being called to give evidence, and certifies its accuracy. The interviewer should allow sufficient time for the interpreter to note each question and answer after each is put, given and interpreted. The person should be allowed to read the record or have it read to him and to sign it as correct or indicate the respects in which he considers it inaccurate. If an audio or visual record of the interview is made, the arrangements in Code E or Code F apply.

In the case of a person making a statement under caution to a police officer or other police staff other than in English:

(a) the interpreter must record the statement in the language it is made;
(b) the person must be invited to sign it;
(c) an official English translation must be made in due course.

Interviewing suspects who have a hearing or speech impediment

Unless a superintendent (or above) considers that delay will lead to one of the consequences set out on p 107, a suspect who requires an interpreter or other appropriate assistance to enable effective communication with him because he appears to have a hearing or speech impediment must not be interviewed in the absence of an independent person capable of interpreting or without that assistance.

An interpreter should also be called if a juvenile or 17-year-old is interviewed and his parent or guardian, present as the appropriate adult, appears to have a hearing or speech impediment, unless the interview is urgent and a superintendent (or above) considers that delay will lead to the consequences set out on p 107.

The interviewer must ensure that the interpreter is allowed to read the interview record and certify its accuracy in the event of the interpreter being called to give evidence. If an audio or visual record of the interview is made, the arrangements in Code E or Code F apply.

Additional rules for detained persons

If the detainee cannot communicate with a solicitor under his entitlement to legal advice because of language, hearing or speech difficulties, an interpreter must be called. A police officer or any other police staff may not be used for this purpose.

After the custody officer has determined that a detainee requires an interpreter and following the initial action referred to in pp 99–101, arrangements must also be made for an interpreter to:

(a) explain (i) the grounds and reasons for any authorisation for the detainee's continued detention, before or after charge, and (ii) any information about the authorisation given to the detainee by the authorising officer and which is recorded in the custody record;
(b) be present at the magistrates' court for the hearing of an application for a warrant of further detention or any extension or further extension of such warrant to explain (i) any grounds and reasons for the application and (ii) any information about the authorisation of the detainee's further detention given to him by the court; and
(c) explain any offence with which the detainee is charged or for which he is informed that he may be prosecuted and any other information about the offence given to him by or on behalf of the custody officer.

Translations of essential documents

Written translations, oral translations and oral summaries of essential documents in a language the detainee understands must be provided in accordance with the following provisions:

Essential documents comprise records required to be made in accordance with Code C which are relevant to decisions to deprive a person of his liberty, to any charge, and to any record considered necessary to enable a detainee to defend himself in criminal proceedings and to safeguard the fairness of the proceedings. Passages of essential documents which are not relevant need not be translated. It is not necessary to disclose information in any translation which is capable of undermining or otherwise adversely affecting any investigative processes, for example by enabling the suspect to fabricate an innocent explanation or to conceal lies from the interviewer.

The Table of Essential Documents below lists the documents considered essential for the purposes of Code C and when (subject to the provisions below) written translations must be created and provided.

	Essential Documents for the Purposes of this Code	*When Translation to be Created*	*When Translation to be Provided*
(i)	The grounds for each of the following authorisations to keep the person in custody as they are described and referred to in the custody record: (a) authorisation for detention before and after charge given by the custody officer and by the review officer; (b) authorisation to extend detention without charge beyond 24 hours given by a superintendent; (c) a warrant of further detention issued by a magistrates' court and any extension(s) of the warrant; (d) an authority to detain in accordance with the directions in a warrant of arrest issued in connection with criminal proceedings including the court issuing the warrant.	As soon as practicable after each authorisation has been recorded in the custody record.	As soon as practicable after the translation has been created, whilst the person is detained or after he has been released. *There is no power under PACE to detain a person or to delay his release solely to create and provide a written translation of any essential document.*
(ii)	Written notice on charge showing particulars of the offence charged or the offence for which the suspect has been told he may be prosecuted.	As soon as practicable after the person has been charged or reported.	As soon as practicable after the person has been charged or reported.

	Essential Documents for the Purposes of this Code	When Translation to be Created	When Translation to be Provided
(iii)	Written interview records. Written statement under caution.	To be created contemporaneously by the interpreter for the person to check and sign.	As soon as practicable after the person has been charged or told he may be prosecuted.

The custody officer may authorise an oral translation or oral summary of documents (i) to (ii) in the table (but not (iii)) to be provided (through an interpreter) instead of a written translation. Such an oral translation or summary may only be provided if it would not prejudice the fairness of the proceedings by in any way adversely affecting or otherwise undermining or limiting the ability of the suspect in question to understand his position and to communicate effectively with police officers, interviewers, solicitors and appropriate adults with regard to his detention and the investigation of the offence in question and to defend himself in the event of criminal proceedings. The quantity and complexity of the information in the document should always be considered, and specific additional consideration given if the suspect is mentally disordered or otherwise mentally vulnerable or is a juvenile or a 17-year-old. The reason for the decision must be recorded.

Subject to the next three paragraphs, a suspect may waive his right to a written translation of the essential documents described in the table but only if he does so voluntarily after receiving legal advice or having full knowledge of the consequences and gives his unconditional and fully informed consent in writing.

The suspect may be asked if he wishes to waive his right to a written translation, and before giving his consent he must be reminded of his right to legal advice and asked whether he wishes to speak to a solicitor.

No police officer or police staff should do or say anything with the intention of persuading a suspect who is entitled to a written translation of an essential document to waive that right. No police officer or police staff shall indicate to any suspect, except to answer a direct question, whether the period for which he is liable to be detained, or, if not detained, the time taken to complete the interview, might be reduced: (a) if he does not ask for legal advice before deciding whether he wishes to waive his right to a written translation of an essential document; or (b) if he decides to waive his right to a written translation of an essential document. There is no power under PACE to detain a person or to delay his release solely to create and provide a written translation of any essential document.

For the purpose of the waiver:

(a) The consent of a person who is mentally disordered or otherwise mentally vulnerable is only valid if the information about the circumstances under which he can waive the right, the reminder about his right to legal advice, and his consent are given in the presence of the appropriate adult. Someone must be present to fulfil the role of the appropriate adult when a 17-year-old is given the requisite information and reminder and gives his consent to waive his right. The consent of his parent or guardian is not required.

(b) The consent of a juvenile is only valid if his parent's or guardian's consent is also obtained unless the juvenile is under 14, when his parent's or guardian's consent is sufficient in its own right, and the requisite information and reminder and the juvenile's consent are also given in the presence of the appropriate adult (who may or may not be a parent or guardian).

The detainee, his solicitor or appropriate adult may make representations to the custody officer that a document which is not included in the table is essential and that a translation should be provided. The request may be refused if the officer is satisfied that the translation requested is not essential for the purposes described in italics above.

If the custody officer has any doubts about

(a) providing an oral translation or summary of an essential document instead of a written translation;
(b) whether the suspect fully understands the consequences of waiving his right to a written translation of an essential document; or
(c) refusing to provide a translation of a requested document,

the officer should seek advice from an inspector (or above).

Action taken in accordance with the above provisions must be recorded in the detainee's custody record or interview record as appropriate.

Complaints

If a detainee complains that he is not satisfied with the quality of interpretation, or of a translation, the custody officer, or (as the case may be) the interviewer, is responsible for deciding whether a different interpreter should be called, or a different translation provided, in accordance with the procedures set out in the arrangements made by the chief officer.

Decisions not to provide interpretation and translation

If a suspect challenges a decision:

(a) made by the custody officer or (as the case may be) by the interviewer, that he does not require an interpreter; or
(b) not to provide a different interpreter or another translation, or not to translate a requested document,

the matter must be reported to an inspector to deal with as a complaint (see pp 133 and 146) if the challenge is made during an interview.

Documentation

The following must be recorded in the custody record or, as applicable, the interview record:

(a) action taken to call an interpreter;
(b) action taken when a detainee is not satisfied about the standard of interpretation or translation provided;
(c) when an urgent interview is carried out in the absence of an interpreter;

(d) when a detainee has been assisted by an interpreter for the purpose of providing or being given information or being interviewed;

(e) action taken in accordance with the prescribed procedure when:

    (i) a written translation of an essential document is provided;

    (ii) an oral translation or oral summary of an essential document is provided instead of a written translation and the authorising officer's reason(s) why this would not prejudice the fairness of the proceedings;

    (iii) a suspect waives his right to a translation of an essential document;

    (iv) representations that a document which is not included in the table above is essential and that a translation should be provided are refused and the reason for the refusal.

CHAPTER 5

Treatment, Charging and Bail of Detainees

GENERAL

Whenever PACE Code C (see p 96) requires a person to be given certain information he does not have to be given it if he is incapable at the time of understanding what is said to him or if he is violent or in urgent need of medical attention, but he must be given it as soon as practicable.

Where video cameras are installed in the custody area, suspects and other people entering should be informed by prominently placed notices that cameras are in use. Any request by a suspect or other person to have video cameras switched off should be refused.

A reference to a 'juvenile' is to someone apparently under 17. See, further, as to this reference and any reference to a '17-year-old', p 97. In respect of a reference to 'appropriate adult' and 'appropriate consent', see pp 97 and 208 respectively.

RECEPTION OF ARRESTED PERSONS AT POLICE STATIONS

Designated police stations

PACE, s 35(1) requires that the chief officer of police designates the police stations in his area which are to be used for the purpose of detaining arrested persons; his duty is to designate police stations which appear to him to provide sufficient accommodation for detaining arrested persons. By s 35(2A) the Chief Constable of the British Transport Police may designate police stations which (in addition to those designated under s 35(1)) may be used for the purpose of detaining arrested persons.

Custody officers

Where a station is designated under s 35(1) or (2A), s 36(1), (2) and (3) requires that one or more custody officers must be appointed by the relevant chief officer of police or his nominee. They must be of the rank of sergeant (or above), but s 36(4) allows another officer of any rank to perform the duties of a custody officer under PACE at a designated police station if such an officer is not readily available to perform those duties. Such an officer is only not 'readily available' if he is not actually at the police station and cannot, without much difficulty, be fetched there.

None of the functions of a custody officer in relation to a person may be performed by an officer who at the time when the function falls to be performed is involved in the investigation of an offence for which that person is in police detention at that time, except that this does not prevent a custody officer:

(a) performing any function assigned to custody officers by PACE, or by a code of practice issued under PACE;
(b) carrying out the duty imposed on custody officers by PACE, s 39 (below);
(c) doing anything in connection with the identification of a suspect; or
(d) doing anything under the Road Traffic Act 1988, s (breath, blood or urine specimens).

Where an arrested person is taken to a non-designated police station any officer not concerned in the investigation of the offence may, by PACE, s 36(7), assume the responsibilities of a custody officer. If no such officer is available, it may be the arresting officer.

Custody officer's duties

A custody officer's duties are laid down by PACE, ss 37 to 39. Basically, and this is provided for by s 39, he is responsible for persons in detention, for ensuring that they and their property are treated in accordance with PACE and Code C, and for maintaining a chronological and contemporaneous record of every aspect of a person's treatment whilst in detention. These responsibilities cannot be overstated. The provisions in relation to detention are quite complex and the requirements for such a log mean that omissions in the keeping of it cannot be corrected. If a duty is carried out but not recorded, the failure to record as required by the Codes is sufficient to raise the issue of disciplinary proceedings. Sections 37 and 38 are dealt with on p 163 and p 168 respectively.

Where PACE and its Codes require that certain things are done by a custody officer, the requirement also applies to a police officer other than a custody officer who is performing the functions of a custody officer.

Where a person has been arrested, a custody officer does not have to satisfy himself that the arrest is lawful before he can hold the arrested person in lawful custody.

A custody officer is required to perform the functions specified in Code C as soon as is practicable. A custody officer is not in breach of the Code in the event of delay provided that the delay is justifiable and that every reasonable step is taken to prevent unnecessary delay.

This provision covers cases where, for example, a large number of suspects are brought into the police station simultaneously to be placed in custody, or interview rooms are all being used, or where there are difficulties in contacting the appropriate adult, solicitor or interpreter. The custody record must indicate where a delay has occurred and the reason why.

Police detention

A person is stated by PACE, s 118 to be in police detention for the purposes of the Act if:

(a) he has been taken to a police station after being arrested for an offence, or after being arrested by a police officer under the Terrorism Act 2000 (TA 2000), s 41 on reasonable suspicion of being a terrorist; or
(b) he is arrested at a police station after attending voluntarily at the station or accompanying a constable to it,

and he is detained there or is detained elsewhere in the charge of a constable.

In most circumstances, of course, a person's detention begins under (a) on arrival at a police station under arrest. If a person is subsequently removed from a police station, for example to attend an identification parade or to visit the scene of a crime or on transfer to another station, he is in detention whilst he remains in the charge of a constable. This is important when periods of detention are to be considered by custody officers. By way of an exception, s 118 provides that a person who is at a court after being charged is not in police detention for the purposes of the Act.

As already stated, a separate custody record must be opened as soon as practicable for each person detained at a police station.

Limitations on police detention

PACE, s 34 provides that a person arrested for an offence (as opposed to a breach of the peace, which is not an offence) must not be kept in police detention, except in accordance with the provisions outlined below. However, no person in police detention may be released except on the authority of a custody officer.

Section 34 requires that if at any time a custody officer:

(a) becomes aware, in relation to any person in police detention at that station, that the grounds for the detention of that person have ceased to apply; and

(b) is not aware of any other grounds on which the continued detention of that person could be justified under the provisions of the Act,

the custody officer must order his immediate release from custody. However, a person who was unlawfully at large when arrested must not be released under these provisions.

A person released in these circumstances must be released without bail, unless it appears to the custody officer that there is a need for further investigation of any matter in connection with which he was detained at any time during the period of his detention, or that in respect of any such matter proceedings may be taken against him or he may be given a youth caution (which is only possible where the offender is under 18), in which case he must be released on bail.

An investigating officer may bring facts to the notice of a custody officer but issues of further detention or release are to be decided by the custody officer. It will be appreciated that custody officers may find themselves in dispute with officers of senior rank in respect of detention issues. If this occurs the superintendent responsible for the police station must be consulted.

For the above purposes and for the purposes of the detention provisions of PACE (ss 34–51) in general, a person who:

(a) attends a police station to answer bail under s 30A (p 64),

(b) returns to a police station to answer to bail granted under the detention provisions, or

(c) is arrested under PACE, ss 30D or 46A (pp 65 and 176),

is to be treated as arrested for an offence and that offence is the offence in connection with which he was granted bail. (This is, however, subject to the rule (p 177) whereby periods when a person has been on bail are excluded from the calculation of the time when the person is in police detention.) The above provision does not apply in relation to a person who is granted bail subject to the duty to attend at a police station appointed by the custody officer for proceedings in relation to a live link direction or any preliminary hearing in relation to which such a direction is given, and who either attends a police station to answer to such bail, or is arrested under s 46A for failing to do so. Provision as to the treatment of such persons is made by s 46ZA (p 173).

Conditions of detention

(1) So far as practicable, not more than one person shall be detained in each cell.

(2) Cells in use must be adequately heated, cleaned and ventilated. They must be adequately lit, subject to such dimming as is compatible with safety and security to allow people detained overnight to sleep. No additional restraints should be used within a locked cell unless absolutely necessary, and then only approved restraint equipment which is reasonable and necessary in the circumstances having regard to the detainee's demeanour and with a view to ensuring his safety and the safety of others. If the detainee is deaf, mentally disordered or otherwise mentally vulnerable, particular care must be taken when deciding whether to use any form of approved restraints.

(3) Blankets, mattresses, pillows and other bedding supplied should be of a reasonable standard and in a clean and sanitary condition.

(4) Access to toilet and washing facilities must be provided.

(5) If it is necessary to remove a person's clothes for the purpose of investigation, for hygiene or health reasons or for cleaning, replacement clothing of a reasonable standard of comfort and cleanliness must be provided. A person must not be interviewed unless adequate clothing has been offered to him.

(6) At least two light meals and one main meal must be offered in any period of 24 hours. Drinks should be provided at meal times and on reasonable request between meal times. Meals should, so far as practicable, be offered at recognised meal times, or at other times that take account of when the detainee last had a meal. Whenever necessary, advice must be sought from the appropriate healthcare professional (clinically qualified person working within the scope of his practice) on medical or dietary matters. As far as practicable, meals provided must offer a varied diet and meet any special dietary needs or religious beliefs that a person may have. At the custody officer's discretion, the detainee may also have meals supplied by his family or friends at his or their own expense. However, especially in the case of a person detained under the Terrorism Act 2000 (TA 2000), immigration detainees and others likely to be detained for an extended period, a custody officer is entitled to take account of the risk of items being concealed in any food or package and of his (the officer's) duties and responsibilities under food handling arrangements.

(7) Brief outdoor exercise must be offered daily if practicable.

(8) A juvenile or 17-year-old must not be placed in a police cell, unless no other secure accommodation is available and the custody officer considers that it is not practicable to supervise him if he is not placed in a cell or the custody officer considers that a cell provides more comfortable accommodation than other secure accommodation in the police station.

(9) A juvenile or 17-year-old must not be placed in a cell with a detained adult.

Care and treatment of detainees

Detainees should be visited at least every hour. If no reasonably foreseeable risk was identified in a risk assessment, a sleeping detainee need not be awakened. A person suspected of being under the influence of drink or drugs or having swallowed drugs, or whose level of consciousness causes concern, must, subject to any clinical directions given by the appropriate healthcare professional, be visited and roused at least every half-hour, have his condition assessed and clinical treatment arranged if appropriate. His condition must be assessed by entering the cell, calling his name and shaking him gently, before asking his name and where he lives as well as where he thinks he is. He should be asked to open his eyes and to lift one arm and then the other. These provisions apply to a person in police custody by order of a magistrates' court under the Criminal Justice Act 1988 (CJA 1988), s 152 to facilitate the recovery of evidence where that person has been charged with drug possession or drug trafficking and is suspected of having swallowed the drugs. In the case of the healthcare needs of a person who has swallowed drugs, the custody officer, subject to any clinical direction, should consider the necessity for rousing every half-hour. This does not negate the need for regular visiting of the suspect in the cell.

It is important to remember that a person who appears to be drunk or behaving abnormally might be suffering from illness or the effects of drugs or may have sustained injury (particularly a head injury) which is not apparent, and that someone addicted to certain drugs may experience harmful effects within a short time of being deprived of their supply. Consequently, police officers should always err on the side of caution when in doubt about calling an appropriate healthcare professional, and act with all due speed. A detainee may be dependent upon certain drugs, including alcohol, and may experience harmful effects within a short time of being deprived of their supply. In these circumstances an appropriate healthcare professional should be consulted or an ambulance should be called. A record must be made of any intoxicating liquor supplied. Annex G to Code C limits the circumstances in which persons under the influence of drink or drugs, or whose mental state is affected in some other way, may be interviewed.

Should the custody officer feel in any way concerned about a detainee's condition, the officer must arrange for medical treatment.

For detailed guidance on matters concerning detainee healthcare and treatment and associated forensic issues, see the *Detention and Custody Authorised Professional Practice* produced by the College of Policing.

Documentation

A record must be kept of replacement clothing and meals offered. If a juvenile or 17-year-old is placed in a cell, the reason must be recorded. The use of any restraints, the reason for such use and any arrangements for enhanced supervision must be recorded.

Clinical treatment and attention

(1) A custody officer must make sure that a detainee receives appropriate clinical attention as soon as reasonably practicable if that person appears to be suffering from physical illness or mental disorder or to be in need of clinical attention or is injured. This applies even if no request for such attention has been received or if clinical attention has already been received elsewhere. The custody officer must also consider the need for clinical attention in relation to those suffering from the effects of alcohol or drugs.

These rules about seeking medical attention are not intended to delay the transfer of a person to a place of safety under MHA 1983, s 136 (mentally disordered persons found in public places), where that is applicable. A mentally disordered or otherwise mentally vulnerable person, *detained under the MHA 1983, s 136*, must be assessed as soon as possible. A police station should only be used as a place of safety under s 136 (or s 135 (warrant to search for and remove mental patients)) as a last resort; a hospital or care home is a more appropriate place. The MHA 1983 Code of Practice provides more detailed guidance about arranging assessments under s 136 and transferring detainees from police stations to other places of safety. Where an assessment takes place, the custody officer must consider whether an appropriate healthcare professional should be called to conduct an initial check on the detainee. This applies particularly where there is likely to be any significant delay in the arrival of a suitably qualified medical practitioner.

(2) If it appears to the custody officer, or he is told, that a person brought to the police station under arrest may be suffering from an infectious disease or condition, reasonable steps must be taken to safeguard the health of the detainee and others. Advice must be sought from an appropriate healthcare professional. The person and his property may be isolated pending clinical direction.

(3) If a detainee requests a clinical examination, an appropriate healthcare professional must be called as soon as practicable. If a safe and appropriate healthcare plan cannot be provided, the police surgeon's advice must be sought.

(4) If a detainee is required to take or apply any medication in compliance with clinical directions prescribed before his detention, the custody officer must consult the appropriate healthcare professional prior to the use of the medication; such consultation and its outcome must be noted in the custody record. The custody officer is responsible for the safekeeping of any medication and for ensuring that the detainee is given the opportunity to take or apply prescribed or approved medication. However, no police officer may administer medicines which are also controlled drugs subject to the Misuse of Drugs Regulations 2001, Schs 1, 2 or 3. A detainee may administer controlled drugs to himself only under the personal supervision of the registered medical practitioner authorising their use or other appropriate healthcare professional. The custody officer may supervise the self-administration or authorise other custody staff to supervise the self-administration of drugs listed in Schs 4 or 5, if he has consulted the appropriate healthcare professional authorising their use and both are satisfied self-administration will not endanger the detainee, police officers, or anyone else.

(5) Where appropriate healthcare professionals administer drugs or other medication, or supervise self-administration, it must be within the scope of their practice as defined by their professional body.

(6) If a detainee has in his possession, or claims to need, medication relating to a heart condition, diabetes, epilepsy, or a condition of comparable potential seriousness then, even though (1), above, may not apply, the advice of the appropriate healthcare professional must be obtained.

A record must be made in the custody record of any complaint made, together with a record of any clinical attention received, and of any request for a clinical examination under (3) and arrangements made in response. A note should also be made of any injury, ailment or condition causing such arrangements to be made, together with clinical directions and advice or clarifications given by a healthcare professional. Where applicable, a note should be made of responses made when attempting to rouse a detainee. Should a healthcare professional not record his clinical findings in the custody record, a note must be made in it of where the findings are recorded. Information necessary to ensure ongoing care and well-being of a detainee must be recorded openly in the custody record. A custody record must include all medication in the possession of a detainee on his arrival, together with a note of medication which he claims to need.

Whenever an appropriate healthcare professional is consulted, the custody officer must ask for an opinion concerning risks or problems which need to be taken into account when making a decision about detention, when to carry out an interview if applicable and the need for safeguards. Any doubts concerning directions, particularly in relation to the frequency of visits, must be cleared up.

Nothing in the above provisions prevents the police from calling an appropriate healthcare professional to examine a detainee for the purpose of obtaining evidence relating to an offence in which he is suspected of being involved.

Complaints about treatment

If a complaint is made by or on behalf of a detainee about his treatment since his arrest, or it comes to the notice of any officer that he may have been treated improperly, a report must be made as soon as practicable to an inspector (or above) who is not connected with the investigation. If the matter concerns a possible assault or the unreasonable use of force, the appropriate healthcare professional must also be called as soon as practicable; a record must be made of any arrangements made.

A record must be made of any complaint reported under the above provisions, together with any relevant remarks by the custody officer.

Independent custody visitors for places of detention

The Police Reform Act 2002, s 51 requires local policing bodies to make arrangements for detainees to be visited by independent custody visitors. The arrangements may provide rights of access to police stations; examination of records; meetings with detainees; and the inspection of facilities. Access to a detainee may be denied if:

(a) it appears to an inspector (or above) that there are grounds for doing so at the time that it is requested;
(b) those grounds are specified within the arrangements; and
(c) the procedural requirements imposed by the arrangements in relation to a denial of access are complied with.

Local policing bodies must ensure:

(a) that the arrangements require independent custody visitors who visit a suspected terrorist detainee (ie someone detained under TA 2000, s 41 (p 791)) to submit a report on that visit; and
(b) that a copy of the report is sent to the independent reviewer of terrorism legislation.

In addition, the arrangements may empower independent custody visitors to listen to audio recordings or view video recordings of police interviews with a suspected terrorist detainee, but a visitor may be denied access to these recordings, whether in whole or in part, on the same basis as above.

The Secretary of State has issued a code of practice as to the carrying out of functions under the arrangements. The notice of rights and entitlements given to detainees explains that 'visitors' are members of the community who are allowed access to police stations unannounced to ensure that detainees have access to their rights. It explains that a detainee does not have a right to see an independent custody visitor and that he cannot request to see one; that such a visitor acts independently of the police to check that welfare rights are protected; and that the detainee does not have to speak to such a visitor if he does not wish to do so.

Information to be given to detainees

When the custody officer authorises the detention of a person who has not been charged, he is required by PACE, s 37 to make, as soon as practicable, a written entry on the custody record of the grounds which exist for detention. This must be done in the person's presence and he must be informed at that time of those grounds. If he is asleep he must be woken and told. (However, if at that time a person is incapable of understanding what is said to him or is violent or likely to be so, or is in urgent need of medical treatment, the information may be given as soon as practicable, and in any case before he is questioned for the offence.) At the same time the detainee must be informed clearly of the rights set out on pp 99–100 and the other functions referred to there must be carried out.

Communication with others

See Chapter 4.

Access to legal advice

See Chapter 4.

Searching and retention of property

PACE, s 54 charges the custody officer with a duty to ascertain the property which a person has with him when he is:

(a) brought to a police station after being arrested elsewhere or after being committed to custody by an order or a sentence of a court; or
(b) arrested at a police station or detained there:
    (i) under s 37 (p 163),
    (ii) when answering police bail,
    (iii) for failing to answer police bail, or
    (iv) as a person treated by s 46ZA (p 173) as arrested and charged for an offence for which he has been granted live link bail.

A detainee may be searched to the extent considered necessary if the custody officer considers it necessary to ascertain the property which that person has with him, but an intimate search (pp 150–2) may not be carried out for this purpose under s 54. A strip search (ie one involving the removal of more than outer clothing) is only permissible if the custody officer reasonably considers that the detainee might have concealed an article which he would not be allowed to keep under the provision below. A strip search, however, may only be carried out if the necessary requirements set out later in this chapter (see pp 149–50) are satisfied.

The custody officer may record all or any of the items which he finds. In the case of an arrested person, this may be done in the custody record.

Articles other than those subject to legal privilege (eg letters from solicitors, etc) may be seized and retained. However, clothes and personal effects (which do not include cash) may only be seized if the custody officer believes that they may be used by the person:

(a) to cause physical injury to himself or another;
(b) to damage property;

(c) to interfere with evidence;

(d) to assist him to escape,

or if the custody officer has *reasonable grounds* for believing that they may be evidence of an offence.

There will be some difficult decisions to be taken by custody officers who are required to allow a person in custody to retain property of a personal, non-dangerous character. Is a woman's handbag mirror likely to cause harm? It will not do so whilst it remains in its original condition but it will certainly do so if it is broken. This, perhaps, leads to a second question for the custody officer: is the woman in a mental state which might lead her to attempt to take her own life? Whatever decision the officer takes, he should apply his mind carefully to the particular situation which confronts him. If personal articles are retained by the custody officer he must explain why.

Section 54 also provides that a constable may at any time search a person who is in custody at a police station, or is in police detention otherwise than at a police station, in order to ascertain whether he has with him any articles which he could use for any of the purposes in (a)–(d) above. A constable may seize and detain anything found in such a search, except that clothes and personal effects may only be seized in the same circumstances as mentioned above.

Any search under s 54 must be by a constable of the same sex as the detainee.

Where articles are seized under s 54, the person must be told the reason unless he is violent or likely to be violent or is incapable of understanding. Items which are seized on the grounds that they may be used to cause injury or damage, interfere with evidence or assist escape must be returned when the person is released from police detention. Code C states that the custody officer is responsible for the safekeeping of property taken from a person.

Search and examination to ascertain identity

A detainee at a police station may be searched or examined to establish:

(a) whether he has any marks, features or injuries that would tend to identify him as a person involved in the commission of an offence; or

(b) his identity.

Where the appropriate consent has been withheld, or it is not practicable to obtain it, PACE, s 54A permits an inspector (or above) to authorise the search and/or examination of a detainee to find marks under (a). If the person concerned has refused to identify himself or the officer has reasonable grounds for suspecting that the person is not who he claims to be, an inspector (or above) may authorise a non-consensual search and/or examination to establish identity under (b). Either authorisation may be given orally but must be confirmed in writing as soon as is practicable.

Any identifying mark (including features and injuries) which is found may be photographed with consent, or if such consent is withheld or it is not practicable to obtain it, without consent. 'Photographed' covers the use of any means by which a visual image may be produced.

Such searches, examinations, and taking of photographs may only be conducted or taken by constables of the same sex as the person concerned, who may use reasonable force. An intimate search may not be carried out under the authority of s 54A. An examination of the mouth is a non-intimate search and therefore may be undertaken by a constable. A dentist has no power to conduct such examination without consent under these provisions.

Photographs taken under s 54A may be used by, or disclosed to, any person for any purpose relating to the prevention or detection of crime, the investigation of an offence, or the conduct of a prosecution. They may be retained after use or disclosure but may not be used or disclosed except for a related purpose.

The references to 'crime' in s 54A include conduct which is an offence (whether under UK law or the law of a country or territory outside the UK) or which is or corresponds to conduct which would be an offence in the UK if it all took place in any part of the UK.

When a person is searched, examined or photographed under the above provisions, he must be informed of the:

(a) purpose of the search;
(b) grounds on which the relevant authority, if applicable, has been given; and
(c) purposes for which the photograph may be used, disclosed or retained.

This information must be given before the search or examination commences or the photograph is taken, except if the photograph is to be taken covertly.

A record must be made when a detainee is searched or examined, or a photograph of him, or any identifying marks found on him, is taken. The record must include the:

(a) identity (subject to the usual exclusion) of the officer carrying out the search or examination, or taking the photograph;
(b) purpose of the search, examination or photograph and the outcome;
(c) detainee's consent to the search, examination or photograph, or the reason the person was searched, examined or photographed without consent; and
(d) giving of any authority, the grounds for giving it and the authorising officer.

If force is used when searching, examining, or taking a photograph in accordance with s 54A, a record must be made of the circumstances and those present.

SEARCHES

Strip searches

A strip search is any search involving the removal of more than outer clothing; outer clothing includes shoes and socks. Code C states that, for a strip search to take place, the custody officer must believe it necessary to remove an article which the detainee would not be allowed to keep, which there is reasonable suspicion the person might have concealed. Strip searches should not be routinely carried out where there is no reason for suspicion that articles have been concealed.

Conduct

The following procedures must be observed when strip searches are conducted:

(1) A police officer carrying out a strip search must be the same sex as the person searched.
(2) The search must take place in an area where the suspect cannot be seen by anyone who does not need to be present, or by a member of the opposite sex (except the appropriate adult who has specifically been requested by the person being searched).
(3) Except in cases of urgency, where there is a risk of serious harm to the person detained or to others, whenever a strip search involves exposure of intimate parts of the body, there must be at least two people present other than the person searched, and if the

search is of a juvenile, 17-year-old, or mentally disordered or vulnerable person, one of the people must be the appropriate adult. Except in urgent cases, a search of a juvenile or 17-year-old may take place in the absence of the appropriate adult only if he signifies in that adult's presence that he prefers to be searched in that adult's absence and that adult agrees. A record must be made of the signification and signed by the appropriate adult. The presence of more than two people, other than the appropriate adult, may be permitted only in the most exceptional circumstances.

(4) The search must be conducted with proper regard to the sensitivity and vulnerability of the detainee in these circumstances. Every reasonable effort must be made to secure co-operation and minimise embarrassment. Detainees who are searched should not normally be required to have all their clothes removed at the same time; for example, a person should be allowed to remove clothing above the waist and re-dress before removing further clothing.

(5) Where necessary to assist the search, the suspect may be required to hold his or her arms in the air or to stand with his or her legs apart and to bend forward so that a visual examination may be made of the genital and anal areas provided that no physical contact is made with any body orifice.

(6) If, during a search, articles are found, the person must be asked to hand them over. If articles are found within any body orifice other than the mouth, and the person refuses to hand them over, their removal would constitute an intimate search which must be carried out in accordance with the provisions of the Code set out below.

(7) A strip search should be conducted as quickly as possible, and the suspect allowed to dress as soon as the procedure is complete.

Documentation

A note should be made on the custody record of a strip search. It should record the parts of the body searched, who searched, the reason it was considered necessary to undertake it, those present and any result.

Intimate searches

An intimate search is a search which consists of the physical examination of a person's body orifices other than the mouth, ie the nose, ears, anus and vagina. The intrusive nature of such searches means the actual and potential risks associated with intimate searches must never be underestimated. Intimate searches are governed by PACE, s 55. Before an intimate search is authorised, every effort must be made to persuade a detainee to hand over the article. Whenever possible, a registered medical practitioner or registered nurse should be asked to make a risk assessment. The authorising officer must consider whether the grounds for believing that an article is concealed are reasonable. In cases of doubt, advice should be sought from a superintendent.

Authorisation

An intimate search must be authorised by an inspector (or above). To authorise such a search that officer must have reasonable grounds for believing that the detainee may have concealed on himself:

(a) an article which he could, and might, use to cause physical injury to himself or others at the police station; or

(b) a Class A drug which he intended to supply to another or to export;

and that, in either case, an intimate search is the only practicable means of removing it.

The authorisation of an intimate search may be given orally or in writing, but if orally it must be confirmed in writing as soon as practicable.

An *intimate drug offence search* may not be carried out without appropriate written consent. Before a detainee is asked to give such consent he must be warned that if he refuses without good cause his refusal may harm his case if it comes to trial. The following form of words may be used to give such a warning:

> 'You do not have to allow yourself to be searched but I must warn you that if you refuse without good cause, your refusal may harm your case if it comes to trial.'

In appropriate cases the warning may be given in a specified Welsh version. The warning may be given by a police officer or member of police staff. In the case of juveniles, 17-year-olds, and mentally vulnerable or mentally disordered detainees, the seeking and giving of consent must take place in the presence of the appropriate adult. A juvenile's consent is only valid if his parent's or guardian's consent is also obtained, unless the juvenile is under 14 (in which case his parent's or guardian's consent is sufficient in its own right). Someone fulfilling the role of the appropriate adult must be present when the warning is given to a 17-year-old and his consent to a drug offence search is sought and given, but the consent of his parent or guardian is not required. If not legally represented, the detainee must be reminded of his entitlement to legal advice, and the reminder must be noted in the custody record. Before the search begins, a constable or a designated detention officer must inform the person of the authorisation and the grounds for giving it and for believing that the item cannot be removed without an intimate search.

Where appropriate consent to a drug offence search is refused without good cause, a court or jury in any proceedings which follow may draw such inferences from that refusal as appear proper.

Execution

Intimate searches may take place only at:

(a) a police station (but not if it is a drug offence search);
(b) a hospital;
(c) a surgery; or
(d) other medical premises.

Before an intimate search takes place, the reasons why it is considered necessary must be explained to the person to be searched and he must be reminded of his entitlement to have legal advice and the reminder must be noted in the custody record.

An intimate drug offence search may only be carried out by a registered medical practitioner or registered nurse. The same is the case for other intimate searches, unless an inspector (or above) considers that it is not practicable and the search takes place because there are reasonable grounds for believing that an article which could cause physical injury to the detainee or others at the police station has been concealed, in which case it must be carried out by a constable of the same sex and the reason for the impracticability must be recorded. A proposal for a search to be carried out by someone other than a registered medical practitioner or a registered nurse must only be considered as a last resort where the risks involved in retention of the item outweigh those associated with its removal. With the exception in the next paragraph, no one of the opposite sex, other than a doctor or nurse, may be present, nor anyone whose presence is unnecessary, but a minimum of two people, other than the person searched, must be present during the search.

An intimate search at a police station of a juvenile, or person who is mentally disordered or vulnerable, must take place in the presence of the appropriate adult of the same sex (unless the person specifically requests the presence of a particular adult of the opposite sex who is readily available). The search of a juvenile may take place in the absence of the appropriate adult only if the juvenile signifies in the adult's presence that he prefers it to be done in his absence and that adult agrees. A record should be made of the signification and signed by the appropriate adult. The requirement in this paragraph also applies in respect of a 17-year-old.

Documentation

After an intimate search has been carried out, an entry must be made as soon as practicable on the custody record, stating the authorisation to carry out the search; the grounds for the authorisation and for believing that the article could not be removed without an intimate search; which parts of the detainee's body were searched; who carried out the search; who was present; and the result. Where the intimate search is a drug offence search, a record must be made of the necessary warning and the fact that appropriate consent was given or (as the case may be) refused, and if refused, the reason given for the refusal.

The powers of seizure in respect of articles found are the same as those which apply to other searches. If an intimate search is carried out by a police officer, the reason why it was impracticable for a registered medical practitioner or a registered nurse to conduct it must be recorded.

X-rays and ultrasound scans

PACE, s 55A provides that where an inspector (or above) has reasonable grounds for believing that a person arrested for an offence and in police detention may have swallowed a Class A drug (p 865), and was in possession of it with the appropriate criminal intent before his arrest, he may authorise an X-ray or an ultrasound scan (or both) to be taken. An X-ray or ultrasound scan must not take place without the appropriate consent in writing. The detainee must be told beforehand by a police officer or designated detention officer of the authorisation and its grounds. Before being asked for his consent he must be warned that an unjustified refusal may harm his case if it comes to trial. This warning may be given by a police officer or member of police staff. In the case of juveniles, 17-year-olds, and mentally vulnerable or mentally disordered detainees, the notification of the authorisation and its grounds, and the seeking and giving of consent must take place in the presence of the appropriate adult. A *juvenile's* consent is only valid if his parent's or guardian's consent is also obtained, unless the juvenile is under 14 (in which case his parent's or guardian's consent is sufficient in its own right). A detainee who is not legally represented must be reminded of his entitlement to have free legal advice, and the reminder noted in the custody record. The provisions in relation to the inferences which may be drawn where consent to an intimate drug offence search is refused also apply to refusals to permit X-rays and ultrasound scans to be carried out.

An X-ray or ultrasound scan may only be carried out by a suitably qualified person at a hospital, a doctor's surgery or at some place used for medical purposes.

If authority is given for an X-ray or an ultrasound scan (or both), consideration should be given to asking a registered medical practitioner or registered nurse to explain to the detainee what is involved and to allay any personal concerns about the effect which such examinations may have upon him. If appropriate consent is not given, evidence of the explanation may, if the case comes to trial, be relevant to determining whether the detainee had good cause for refusing.

A record must be made as soon as practicable in the detainee's custody record of the authorisation, its grounds, the warning, the giving (or otherwise) of the appropriate consent, and the details of the X-ray or scan (if carried out).

TESTING FOR PRESENCE OF CLASS A CONTROLLED DRUGS

When permitted

PACE, s 63B permits the taking of urine or non-intimate samples from someone *for the purpose of ascertaining whether he has any specified Class A drug (ie cocaine and diamorphine (heroin), their salts, and any preparation containing either drug or its salts)* in his body where:

(a) either the arrest condition or the charge condition is met;
(b) both the age condition and the request condition are met; and
(c) the notification condition is met in relation to the arrest condition, the charge condition or the age condition (as the case may be).

The arrest condition is that the person concerned has been arrested for an offence but has not been charged with that offence and either:

(a) that offence is a 'trigger offence' (theft, attempted theft, robbery, attempted robbery, burglary, attempted burglary, aggravated burglary, taking a motor vehicle or other conveyance without authority, aggravated vehicle-taking, fraud, possessing articles used in frauds and making or supplying articles used in frauds, attempted fraud, handling stolen goods or attempted handling, going equipped for stealing, etc, and an offence under the Misuse of Drugs Act 1971 (if committed in respect of a specified Class A drug) of producing or supplying a controlled drug, possessing a controlled drug, or possessing a controlled drug with intent to supply, and begging or persistent begging contrary to the Vagrancy Act 1824, ss 3 or 4 respectively); or
(b) an inspector (or above), who has reasonable grounds for suspecting that the misuse by that person of any specified Class A drug caused or contributed to the offence, has authorised such a sample to be taken.

The charge condition is either:

(a) that the person concerned has been charged with a trigger offence; or
(b) that the person concerned has been charged with an offence and an inspector (or above), who has reasonable grounds for suspecting that the misuse by that person of any specified Class A drug caused or contributed to the offence, has authorised the sample to be taken.

The age condition is:

(a) if the arrest condition is met, that the person concerned is 18 or over; or
(b) if the charge condition is met, that he is 14 or over.

The request condition is that a police officer has requested the person concerned to give the sample (which in the case of a juvenile or 17-year-old must be done in the presence of the appropriate adult).

The notification condition is that:

(a) the relevant chief officer has been notified by the Secretary of State that appropriate arrangements have been made for the police area as a whole, or for the particular police station, in which the person is in police detention; and
(b) the notice has not been withdrawn.

Where a sample is taken from a person who satisfies the arrest condition, no other sample may be taken during the same continuous period of detention, but if the charge condition is met during that period, the sample already taken must be treated as one taken after charge. This must be recorded in the custody record.

In circumstances in which a person is arrested for a first offence which satisfies the arrest condition but not the charge condition, and he would normally be liable to be released from custody before a sample is taken but he remains in custody by reason of arrest for another offence not falling within the arrest condition, a sample may be taken before the end of a period of 24 hours following his *initial* arrest.

A sample must not be taken from a person in custody unless he is brought before the custody officer. It may only be taken by a person authorised by the Police and Criminal Evidence Act 1984 (Drug Testing of Persons in Police Detention) Prescribed Persons Regulations 2001, viz a police officer, a person employed by a local policing body, or chief officer of police, or by a contractor engaged by such a body or chief officer, whose duties include taking samples for testing for the presence of specified Class A drugs. A sample may be taken from a juvenile or 17-year-old only in the presence of the appropriate adult.

Disclosure of information obtained

Information obtained from a sample taken under s 63B may be disclosed:

(a) for the purpose of informing any decision about granting bail in criminal proceedings to the person concerned, or about the giving of a conditional caution or a youth conditional caution (YCC);
(b) where the person concerned is in police detention or is remanded in or committed to custody by an order of a court or has been granted such bail, for the purpose of informing any decision about his supervision;
(c) where the person concerned is convicted of an offence, for the purpose of informing any decision about the appropriate sentence to be passed by a court and any decision about his supervision or release;
(d) for the purpose of:
    (i)   an initial or follow-up assessment which the person concerned is required to attend;
    (ii) proceedings against the person concerned for an offence of failing to attend such an assessment; or
    (iii) ensuring that appropriate advice and treatment is made available to the person concerned.

Procedure

A request for a sample must be preceded by an explanation (a) of its *purpose*; (b) that failure without good cause to provide a sample may make the person requested liable to prosecution; and (c) where the taking of the sample has been authorised by an inspector (or above) under (b) of the arrest condition or of the charge condition (see p 153), of the grounds for the authorisation. In addition, the person requested must be reminded of his right to have someone informed of his arrest; of his right to consult privately with a solicitor; of the availability free of charge of independent legal advice; and of the right to consult the relevant code of practice. When warning a person who is asked to provide a urine or non-intimate sample in these circumstances, the following form of words may be used (an alternative warning in Welsh is provided):

> 'You do not have to provide a sample, but I must warn you that if you fail or refuse without good cause to do so, you will commit an offence for which you may be imprisoned, or fined, or both.'

Custody officers may authorise continued detention for up to six hours from the time of charge to enable a sample to be taken.

Where the warning and information are given to a juvenile or 17-year-old, this must be done in the presence of the appropriate adult, as must the taking of the sample.

Where a sample is taken following authorisation by an inspector (or above), the authorisation and the grounds for suspicion must be recorded in the custody record. An authorisation given by an inspector may be given orally but must subsequently be confirmed in writing as soon as practicable. Details of authorisations and the giving of warnings must be recorded, together with the time of charge and the time at which a sample was given.

A person who fails without good cause to give any sample which may be taken from him is guilty of an offence under s 63B(8).

Assessment of misuse of drugs after positive drug test

Initial assessment

Where an analysis of a sample reveals the presence of a Class A drug a police officer may, at any time before the person's release, require a person of 18 or over to attend an 'initial assessment' and to remain for its duration. A qualified 'initial assessor' will seek to establish dependency or a tendency to misuse any specified Class A drug and whether the person will benefit from further assessment or advice. If an initial assessor finds that a follow-up assessment is appropriate, he must inform the person of the time and place at which it is to take place, confirm this in writing, and warn the person of the consequences of failing to attend.

Follow-up assessment

The police officer may, at the same time as he imposes a requirement on the detainee to attend an initial assessment, require the person to attend a follow-up assessment and to remain for its duration. The officer must inform the detainee that the second requirement will cease to have effect, if at the initial assessment he is informed that a follow-up assessment is not necessary. A follow-up interview will be concerned with a 'care plan'.

Attendance at assessments

A constable must inform the detainee (to be confirmed in writing) that failure to attend either or both forms of assessment, and to remain there for its duration without good cause, may result in prosecution. This must be done prior to release from custody and a record must be made in the custody record.

The Drugs Act 2005, s 12(2) provides that a person who is required to attend an initial assessment commits an offence if he fails, without good cause, to attend at the specified time and place, or attends but fails to remain for the duration of the assessment. Where such a failure occurs, any requirement imposed in relation to a follow-up assessment ceases to have effect. It is an offence against s 14(3) to fail, without good cause, to attend a follow-up assessment or to fail to attend for its duration. These offences are not committed if a subsequent analysis of a sample reveals that a specified Class A drug was not present in the person's body. This is because any requirement imposed ceases to have effect.

Any sample taken may not be used for any purpose other than to ascertain whether the person has a Class A drug in his body. It can be disposed of as clinical waste unless it is to be sent for further analysis in cases where the test result is disputed at the point when the result is known, for example on the basis that medication has been taken, or for quality assurance purposes.

REVIEWS AND MAXIMUM PERIODS OF POLICE DETENTION

The following rules do not apply where a person has been arrested as a suspected terrorist under TA 2000, s 41. In such a case TA 2000, Sch 8 (pp 799–800) applies.

Reviews

PACE, s 40 requires periodic reviews of the detention of each person in police detention. The review will be carried out:

(a) in the case of a person who has been arrested *and charged*, by the custody officer; and
(b) in the case of a person who has been arrested *but not charged*, by an inspector (or above) who has not been directly involved in the investigation.

The officer by whom the review is carried out is called the 'review officer'.

There will be some designated police stations at which the custody officer will be an officer of the rank of inspector. Where this is so he could carry out both of the above functions.

PACE, s 40 is precise in relation to when these reviews must be carried out:

(a) the first review must be not later than *six hours* after the detention was first authorised;
(b) the second review must be not later than *nine hours* after the first; and
(c) subsequent reviews must be at intervals of *not more than nine hours*.

There is, however, a limited power to postpone a review (see p 159).

Failure to carry out a review in accordance with these rules renders the previously lawful detention unlawful and entitles the detainee to damages for false imprisonment.

The review officer is responsible under s 40 for determining whether or not a person's detention continues to be necessary.

The case of a person who has been arrested but not charged

Here the review officer must proceed as follows:

(1) Where the person was detained because he was not in a fit state to be charged or released without charge (with or without bail), for example because he was under the influence of drink or drugs, the review officer must consider whether he is now in a fit state to be charged or released. If he is, one or other of these courses must be

adopted. If he is not, further detention may be authorised, but consideration should be given to whether there is sufficient evidence to charge him with an offence.

(2) Where, although there is then insufficient evidence to charge him, the detention of the person has been authorised by the custody officer on the basis that there are reasonable grounds to believe that his detention without charge is necessary to secure or preserve evidence relating to an offence for which he is under arrest or to obtain such evidence by questioning him, the review officer may authorise further detention if this is necessary on the same basis.

The review of the detention of a person who has been arrested but not charged may be conducted in person or (under s 40A) remotely by video-conferencing or telephone discussion with persons at the police station where the arrested person is detained. The use of a telephone is not permitted if the reviewer has access to the use of video-conferencing facilities that enable him to communicate with persons in the other police station (s 40A(2) and PACE (Remote Reviews of Detention) Regulations 2014).

Subject to this, the decision on which form of communication is to be used is a matter for the review officer, who must take full account of the detainee's needs. The benefits of carrying out a review in person should always be considered, based on the particular circumstances with specific additional consideration if the person is:

(a) a juvenile or 17-year-old (in which case his actual age should also be considered),
(b) suspected of being mentally vulnerable,
(c) in need of medical attention for other than routine minor ailments, or
(d) subject to presentational or community issues around his detention.

Where a review is conducted by video-conferencing facilities or over the telephone, the review officer must require another officer at the station to carry out the review officer's functions under s 40 and Code C by making any record connected with the review in the detainee's custody record in the presence of the detainee (if applicable) and giving the detainee information about the review.

A video-conferencing or telephone review may be terminated by the review officer at any stage in favour of a review in person, and a record should be made of such a decision.

Before deciding whether to authorise continued detention the review officer must give an opportunity to make representations about the detention to: the detainee, unless he is asleep; the detainee's solicitor, if available; and the appropriate adult. Other people with an interest in the detainee's welfare may also make representations at the authorising officer's discretion.

The case of a person who has been charged

The person must be released, either on bail or without bail, unless:

(a) his name and address cannot be ascertained or there are reasonable grounds to doubt the name and address given; or
(b) in the case of an imprisonable offence, there are reasonable grounds to believe that his detention is necessary to prevent him committing an offence; or
(c) in the case of a non-imprisonable offence, there are reasonable grounds to believe that his detention is necessary to prevent him causing physical injury to any person or loss of or damage to property; or
(d) in the case where a drug sample may be taken (p 153), there are reasonable grounds to believe that his detention is necessary for a sample to be taken; or

(e) there are reasonable grounds to believe that he will fail to answer bail or that his detention is necessary to prevent him interfering with the administration of justice or with police investigations or for his own protection; or

(f) in the case of an arrested juvenile, his detention is necessary in his own interests.

Before deciding whether to authorise continued detention the review officer must give an opportunity to make representations about the detention to: the detainee (unless the detainee is asleep); the detainee's solicitor if available at the time; and the appropriate adult if available at the time.

Other people having an interest in the detainee's welfare may also make representations at the authorising officer's discretion.

General

Representations may be made orally in person, or by telephone or in writing (including email). The authorising officer, however, may refuse to hear oral representations from the detainee if the officer considers him unfit to make representations because of his condition or behaviour.

Any comment the detainee may make if the decision is to keep him in detention must be recorded and, if applicable, the review officer must be informed of the comment as soon as practicable. No officer may put specific questions to the detainee regarding his involvement in any offence, nor in respect of any comments he may make when given the chance to make representations or in response to the decision to keep him in detention. Such an exchange is likely to constitute an 'interview' and would require the safeguard of the Code's provisions concerning interviews generally.

Before conducting a review the review officer must ensure that the detainee is reminded of his entitlement to free legal advice, unless he is asleep. This reminder must be noted in the custody record.

The review officer must determine what documents and materials are essential (p 101) to effectively challenging the lawfulness of the detention, and these must be made available to the detainee.

The detainee need not be woken for the review. If the detainee is likely to be asleep at the latest time when a review or extension authorisation may take place, the review officer should bring it forward, if possible, so that the detainee may make representations without being woken up.

If, after considering any representations, the review officer authorises the detention of a person (whether charged or not) to continue, the review officer must make a written record of the grounds for the detention as soon as practicable. A detainee who is asleep at a review and whose continued detention is authorised must be informed about the decision and reason as soon as practicable after waking.

Where a person is in police custody in circumstances which are not subject to statutory review, for example:

(a) someone arrested on warrant for failure to answer to bail or for breach of a condition of bail;

(b) someone in police custody under the Crime (Sentences) Act 1997 for a specific purpose and period;

(c) a convicted or remanded prisoner held on behalf of the Prison Service;

(d) someone detained:
   (i)   to prevent him causing a breach of the peace;
   (ii) on behalf of Immigration Enforcement; or

(iii) under CJA 1988, s 152 by order of a magistrates' court to facilitate the recovery of evidence where that person has been charged with drug possession or trafficking and is suspected of having swallowed drugs,

it is advised that reviews take place periodically to ensure that the power to detain still applies and that detention conditions are being complied with. Such reviews may be conducted by a sergeant.

Postponement of review

PACE, s 40 allows for the postponement of a review:

(a) if, having regard to all the circumstances at the latest time for the review, it is impracticable to carry out the review at that time; or
(b) if at that time the detainee is being questioned by a police officer and the review officer is satisfied that an interruption of the questioning for the purpose of carrying out the review would prejudice the particular investigation; or
(c) if at that time no review officer is readily available.

If a review is postponed it must be carried out as soon as practicable after the normal latest time for it. The reason for any postponement must be recorded in the custody record. The postponement of a review does not affect the time at which any subsequent review must be carried out. Thus, a second review must be carried out nine hours after the latest time at which the first review should have taken place, which time is six hours after the detention was first authorised.

Where the person whose detention is under review has not been charged before the time of the review, the first two paragraphs under the heading 'Duties of custody officer before charge' on p 163 apply with the substitution of 'a person whose detention is under review' for 'person . . . arrested', and of 'review officer' for 'custody officer', and with the addition of 'asleep' in the list referred to at s 37(4)–(6).

Documentation

A record must be made as soon as practicable of the outcome of each review: if a detainee was asleep when his continued detention was authorised, a record must be made of when he was informed and by whom. The grounds for, and the extent of, any delay in conducting a review must be recorded and reasons for there being a telephone, etc review must also be recorded, together with the place where the review officer was, and the method by which representations were made.

Limits on period of detention without charge

PACE, s 41 provides that a person must not be kept in police detention for more than 24 hours without being charged, except that detention beyond that period may be authorised in certain circumstances by a superintendent (or above) (s 42) or by a magistrates' court (ss 43 and 44). The maximum period of detention without charge is 96 hours, but is only 24 hours where an offence is not indictable.

Calculation of period of detention

PACE, s 41 refers to the 'relevant time', which is the time from which the detention of a particular person is to be calculated. This may be:

(a) in the case where a person, whose arrest is sought in one police area in England and Wales, is arrested in another area, and is not questioned in the area in which he is arrested about the offence for which he has been arrested, *the time at which the person arrives at the first police station in the area in which his arrest is sought, or the time 24 hours after that person's arrest, whichever is the earlier;*

(b) in the case of a person arrested outside England and Wales, *the time at which that person arrives at the first police station to which he is taken in the police area in England and Wales in which the offence for which he is arrested is being investigated, or the time 24 hours after the time of that person's entry into England and Wales, whichever is the earlier;*

(c) in the case of a person who attends voluntarily at a police station, or who accompanies a constable to a police station without having been arrested, and is arrested at the police station, *the time of his arrest;*

(d) in the case of a person who attends a police station to answer bail under s 30A (released on street bail without attending a police station), *the time when he arrives at a police station;* and

(e) in any other case, *the time at which the person arrested arrives at the first police station to which he is taken after arrest, unless he is in detention in an area* in England and Wales and his arrest for an offence is being sought *in some other police area* in England and Wales and he is taken to that second area for the purpose of investigating that offence, without being questioned in the first area in order to obtain evidence in relation to it. In such a case the 'relevant time' will be the time 24 hours after he leaves the place where he is detained in the first area or the time at which he arrives at the first police station to which he is taken in the second area, whichever is the earlier.

Section 41 provides a safeguard in relation to a person in police detention who, whilst detained, is arrested for a second offence. The time does not start running again with his arrest for the second offence. It also provides for instances in which a person in police detention is removed to a hospital for medical treatment. Normally the period commencing with his journey to hospital and ending with his arrival back in police custody does not count towards his 24 hours in police custody; in effect, the clock may be stopped. However, any period, either during his journey or whilst in hospital, during which he is questioned by a police officer for the purpose of obtaining evidence in relation to an offence, is included in his period of police detention.

Release from detention after 24 hours

Section 41 provides that, subject to the following paragraph, if a person has not been charged after 24 hours in police detention he *must* be released either on bail or without bail. A person so released must not be re-arrested without a warrant for the same offence unless new evidence justifying a further arrest has come to light since his release, but this does not prevent his arrest for failure to surrender to police bail. It is submitted that evidence justifying further arrest would have to be substantial, probably sufficient in itself to justify arrest.

Release after 24 hours is not required if continued detention is authorised or a warrant of further detention is issued under the powers next discussed.

Authorisation of continued detention

The relevant provisions are set out by PACE, s 42. Where a superintendent (or above) who is responsible for a police station at which a person is detained has reasonable grounds for believing that:

(a) the detention of that person without charge is necessary to secure or preserve evidence relating to an offence for which he is under arrest or to obtain such evidence by questioning him;

(b) an offence for which he is under arrest is an *indictable* offence; and

(c) the investigation is being conducted diligently and expeditiously,

he may authorise the keeping of that person in police detention for a period expiring at or before 36 hours after the relevant time.

This may not be done if the person has been in detention for more than 24 hours from the relevant time when the authorisation of continued detention is sought, nor may such an authorisation be given before the second review of that person's detention, that is the review at 15 hours after detention was first authorised. If the first period of continued detention given does not take the detention time fully to 36 hours (a superintendent will not necessarily authorise an additional 12 hours), a further period may be authorised if the conditions in the previous paragraph are satisfied, up to the maximum of 36 hours. This further period may be authorised at any time during the first extension, and even though more than 24 hours has elapsed from the relevant time.

The detainee must be informed on all occasions of the grounds for his continued detention and the custody record must be endorsed with them. Before deciding whether to authorise continued detention, the officer responsible must give an opportunity to make representations about the detention to the detainee, or his solicitor if available, and the appropriate adult if available. Any other person having an interest in the detainee's welfare may also make representations at the discretion of the officer authorising continued detention. Representations may be made orally or in writing. During consideration of authorisations of continued detention, specific questions must not be put to a detainee regarding his involvement in an offence or in respect of any comments which he makes. Such an exchange could be considered to be an interview. Before conducting a review the officer responsible must ensure that the detainee is reminded of his entitlement to free legal advice. This reminder must be noted in the custody record. The person (unless he is asleep), or the detainee's solicitor if available to attend in person or contactable by telephone or other electronic means at the time of the review, must be given an opportunity by the review officer to make representations to him concerning the detention. If, when an extension of detention is authorised, the detainee has not yet exercised his right to have some person informed of his detention, or his right of access to legal advice, the custody officer must inform him of his rights, decide whether he shall be permitted to exercise them, and record his decision in the custody record. Any comment made by a detainee about an authorisation of continued detention must be recorded and, if applicable, the authorising superintendent must be informed of the comment as soon as practicable.

Detaining a juvenile, 17-year-old or mentally vulnerable person for longer than 24 hours is dependent upon the circumstances of the case and with regard to the person's special vulnerability, the legal obligation to provide an opportunity for legal representations to be made prior to a decision about extending detention, the need to consult and consider the views of the appropriate adult, and any alternatives to police custody.

A person who has been the subject of continued detention must be released, with or without bail, not later than 36 hours after the relevant time, unless he has been charged, or unless his continued detention is authorised or otherwise permitted by a warrant of further detention (below). Such a person may not be re-arrested without warrant for the same offence unless new evidence justifying a further arrest has come to light since his release, but this does not apply to a person who fails to surrender to police bail.

Warrant of further detention

Such a warrant is governed by PACE, s 43. A magistrates' court may issue a warrant of further detention following an application on oath by a constable which is supported by a written information. The court must be satisfied that there are reasonable grounds for believing that further detention is justified. A person's further detention is only justified for the purpose of s 43 (or s 44 (below)) if the conditions set out on pp 160–1 in relation to s 42 are satisfied.

The detainee must be given a copy of the information and he must be brought before the court. If he is not legally represented, but wishes such representation, the court must adjourn for this to be done and he may be kept in detention during the adjournment.

An application for a warrant of further detention may be made at any time before the expiry of 36 hours after the 'relevant time', or, if it is not practicable for the magistrates' court to sit at that time but it will sit during the six hours following that period, at any time before the expiry of those six hours. In the latter case, the detainee may be kept in police detention until the application is heard, and the custody officer must record in the custody record the fact that (and the reason why) he was detained for more than 36 hours after the relevant time. It is not sufficient for the police to have the application on the court lists for hearing within the sitting of the court. The application must be brought to the notice of the court before the end of the relevant period.

If an application for a warrant of further detention is made after the expiry of 36 hours after the relevant time, and it would have been reasonable for the police to make it before the expiry of that period, the court must dismiss the application. Where on an application for a warrant of further detention a magistrates' court is not satisfied that there are reasonable grounds for believing that the further detention of the person to whom the application relates is justified, it must:

(a) refuse the application; or
(b) adjourn the hearing of it until not later than 36 hours after the relevant time (in which case the detainee may be kept in police detention during the adjournment).

Where an application is refused, the person to whom the application relates must forthwith be charged or released, either on bail or without bail, but he need not be released:

(a) before the expiry of 24 hours after the relevant time; or
(b) before the expiry of any longer period for which his continued detention is or has been authorised under s 42 above.

Where an application is refused, no further application may be made for a warrant of further detention in respect of the person in question, unless supported by evidence which has come to light since the refusal.

A warrant of further detention must state the time of issue and the period of detention which it authorises, which must not be longer than 36 hours.

A 'magistrates' court' in the present context (and in that of s 44) is a court consisting of two or more justices, sitting otherwise than in open court for the purpose of these provisions.

Where a warrant of further detention is issued, the person must be released from police detention, with or without bail, on or before the expiry of the warrant unless he is charged. He may not be re-arrested for the same offence unless new evidence has come to light since his arrest, but this does not apply to a person who fails to surrender to police bail.

Extension of warrant of further detention

This is dealt with by PACE, s 44. A magistrates' court may extend a warrant of further detention, on an application made in the same way as under s 43, if satisfied that there are reasonable grounds for believing that further detention is justified. The extension may not exceed 36 hours or end later than 96 hours after the relevant time. If an extension ends earlier than 96 hours after that time, it may be further extended, provided that the extension ends no later than 96 hours after that time.

The provisions under s 43 ('Warrant of further detention') apply equally to an application under s 44.

Where an application for an extension is refused, the person to whom the application relates must forthwith be charged or released, either on bail or without bail. However, he need not be released before the expiry of any period for which a warrant of further detention has previously been extended or further extended.

General

When an application is made under ss 43 or 44, the detainee:

(a) must be brought to court for the hearing of the application;
(b) is entitled to be legally represented if he wishes, in which case the provisions about delay on p 107 cannot apply; and
(c) must be given a copy of the information which supports the application and states:
    (i) the nature of the offence for which the person to whom the application relates has been arrested;
    (ii) the general nature of the evidence on which the person was arrested;
    (iii) what inquiries about the offence have been made and what further inquiries are proposed;
    (iv) the reasons for believing continued detention is necessary for the purposes of the further inquiries.

A record must be made of the outcome of any determination whether to extend the maximum detention period without charge or an application for a warrant of further detention or its extension. Where an authorisation of continued detention has been given, the record must show the length of time by which the detention was extended or further extended. The same applies where a warrant (or extension) of further detention is granted.

Provision of essential documents

The officer reviewing the need for detention without charge (s 40), or (as the case may be) the officer considering the need to extend detention without charge from 24 to 36 hours (s 42), is responsible, in consultation with the investigating officer, for deciding which documents and materials are essential (p 00) and must be made available to the detainee or his solicitor. The same applies when an application is made under s 43 or 44 for a warrant of further detention or an extension thereof.

DUTIES OF CUSTODY OFFICER BEFORE CHARGE

PACE, s 37 states that, where a person has been arrested without warrant, or on a warrant which is not endorsed for bail, the custody officer must determine whether he has sufficient evidence to charge him with the offence for which he was arrested.

The person may be detained at a police station for such period as is necessary for him to make that decision. The custody officer must record on the custody record the offence(s) for which the detainee has been arrested (and the reasons). He should also note on the custody record any comment the person may make in relation to the arresting officer's account but should not invite comment. Section 37(2) provides that, if there is insufficient evidence of an offence, the custody officer must release that person either with or without bail, unless he has reasonable grounds for believing that detention is necessary to secure or preserve evidence of the offence or to obtain evidence by questioning him.

If the custody officer has reasonable grounds for so believing, he may authorise the arrested person to be kept in police detention. If he authorises a person's detention, he must, as soon as practicable, record the grounds in the custody record. This written record must be made in the presence of the arrested person and at that time that person must be informed by the custody officer of the grounds for detention, unless the arrested person is incapable of understanding what is said to him, violent or likely to become violent, or in urgent need of medical attention (s 37(4)–(6)). In any event, he must inform the detainee of the grounds as soon as practicable and in any case before that person is then questioned about any offence. The custody officer must note on the custody record any comment the person may make in respect of the decision to detain him but may not invite comment, nor may he put specific questions to the person concerning his involvement in any offence, nor in respect of any comments he may make in response to the investigating officer's account or the decision to place him in detention. Such an exchange is likely to constitute an interview and would require the necessary safeguards.

Section 37(7) provides that, if the custody officer determines that he has sufficient evidence to charge the person arrested for the offence for which he was arrested, that person must:

(a) be released without charge and on bail, or kept in police detention, for the purpose of enabling the DPP (in practice, a Crown Prosecutor) to make a decision about charging or cautioning him;

(b) be released without charge and on bail but not for that purpose;

(c) be released without charge and without bail; or

(d) be charged.

By way of exception, if the person arrested is not in a fit state to be dealt with in this way (eg because he is under the influence of drink or drugs), he may be kept in police detention until he is in a fit state.

By s 37(7A), the decision as to how a person is to be dealt with under s 37(7) is that of the custody officer, but in making that decision the custody officer must have regard to the DPP's *Guidance on Charging* below.

In relation to (a), it should be noted that Crown Prosecutors are often located at police stations to enable charge decisions to be taken relatively quickly. CPS Direct operates an out-of-hours service linked to the police by a high speed IT and telephony system.

If a person is dealt with under (a), the custody officer must inform him that he is being released, or as the case may be, detained, to enable the DPP (in practice, a Crown Prosecutor) to make a decision about charging or cautioning him. In such a case, an officer involved in the investigation must send to the CPS such information as is specified in the DPP's *Guidance on Charging*. A Crown Prosecutor must decide whether there is sufficient evidence to charge the person; must then decide whether he should be charged or given a simple caution, conditional caution, youth caution or youth conditional caution; and, if so, state the offence. The Crown Prosecutor must notify the officer of his decision, at which stage the person must be charged (which constitutes the institution of criminal proceedings by the DPP), cautioned, or told that he has been released from his bail. If a person is arrested for a breach of bail granted under these circumstances he may be charged or released without charge, either on bail or without bail. The custody officer may subsequently appoint a different time, or an additional time, at which the person must attend a police station. A person who surrenders to such bail may be kept in police detention to enable him to be dealt with.

If a person is released without charge under (b) or (c), and a decision has not yet been taken whether he should be prosecuted, the custody officer must inform him of this. A person released without charge and without bail may be dealt with by one of the available alternatives to prosecution (see p 14).

DPP's *Guidance on Charging*

Under the DPP's *Guidance on Charging*, the situation is as follows.

A custody officer may charge:

(a) any *summary only* offence (and criminal damage where the value of the loss or damage is less than £5,000) irrespective of plea;

(b) any offence of retail theft (shoplifting) or attempted retail theft irrespective of plea provided it is suitable for sentence in the magistrates' court; and

(c) any *either-way offence* anticipated as a guilty plea and suitable for sentence in a magistrates' court, provided it is not:

    (i)   a case requiring the consent of the DPP or Law Officer;

    (ii)   a case involving a death;

    (iii) connected with terrorist activity or official secrets;

    (iv) classified as hate crime or domestic violence under CPS Policies;

    (v)   an offence of violent disorder or affray;

    (vi) causing grievous bodily harm or wounding, or actual bodily harm;

    (vii) a Sexual Offences Act offence committed by or upon a person under 18;

    (viii) an offence under the Licensing Act 2003.

A guilty plea may be anticipated where either:

(a) the suspect has made a clear and unambiguous admission to the offence and has said nothing that could be used as a defence, or

(b) the suspect has made no admission but has not denied the offence or otherwise indicated it will be contested and the commission of the offence and identification of the offender can be established by reliable evidence or the suspect can be seen clearly committing the offence on a good quality visual recording.

A case may be considered suitable for sentence in a magistrates' court unless:

(a) the loss or damage relating to the charge is more than £5,000 or would exceed that sum if more than one offence is charged (or taken into consideration), or

(b) the overall circumstances of the offence are so serious that the court may decide that a sentence of more than six months' imprisonment justifies sending the case to the Crown Court, or

(c) the offence has been committed whilst the suspect was subject to a Crown Court order then in force.

A Crown Prosecutor must make charging decisions in respect of any *offence triable only on indictment, any either-way offence not suitable for sentence in a magistrates' court or not anticipated as a guilty plea, and the offences specified in (c)(i)–(viii) above*. The offence must be referred to a Crown Prosecutor for this purpose.

In a case where any offences under consideration for charging by the police include any offence which must be referred to a Crown Prosecutor under the *Guidance* then all offences in the case will be referred to a Crown Prosecutor to consider which should be charged.

By way of qualification to the last two paragraphs, a police inspector may authorise the charging of an offence that should be referred to a Crown Prosecutor under the *Guidance* where the continued detention of the suspect after charge is justified and where it will not be possible to obtain a Crown Prosecutor's authority to charge before the expiry of any relevant PACE time limit applicable to the suspect. Any cases so charged under this provision must be referred to a Crown Prosecutor as soon as possible following charge and not later than the time proposed for the first appearance before a magistrates' court.

Police officers should anticipate the PACE custody time limits and seek a charging decision in good time.

Other points

Where the offence for which the person is arrested is one in relation to which a sample could be taken for a drug test under PACE, s 63B (see p 153), and the custody officer is required by s 37(2) to release that person and decides to release him on bail or decides in pursuance of s 37(7) to release that person without charge on bail, the detention of that person may be continued to enable such a sample to be taken, but this does not permit a person to be detained for more than 24 hours after the relevant time (as defined on pp 159–60).

Regulations made under PACE, s 45A may provide for the functions relating to an arrested person taken to, or answering bail at, a non-designated police station (which, in the case of an arrested person taken to a designated police station, are a custody officer's functions under PACE, s 37) to be exercised by video link facilities. No regulations for this purpose are in force at the time of writing.

CHARGING DETAINEES

Procedures

When the officer in charge of the investigation reasonably believes that there is sufficient evidence to provide a realistic prospect of a detainee's conviction, he must without delay inform the custody officer who will be responsible for considering whether or not the detainee should be charged. Where a person has been detained for more than one offence it is permissible to delay informing the custody officer until these conditions are satisfied in respect of all of the offences. If the detainee is a juvenile, a 17-year-old or mentally disordered or vulnerable, any resulting action must be carried out in the presence of the appropriate adult (if present at the time). There is no power under PACE to detain a person and delay action solely to await the arrival of the appropriate adult. Reasonable efforts should therefore be made to give the appropriate adult sufficient notice of the time the decision (charge, etc) is to be implemented so that he can be present.

If the appropriate adult is not, or cannot be, present at that time, the detainee should be released on bail to return for the decision to be implemented when the adult is present, unless the custody officer determines that the absence of the appropriate adult makes the detainee unsuitable for bail for this purpose.

Where a custody officer determines in accordance with the DPP's *Guidance on Charging* that there is sufficient evidence to charge the detainee, he may detain that person for no longer than is reasonably necessary to decide how that person is to be dealt with under PACE, s 37(7) (see p 164), including, where appropriate, consultation with the duty prosecutor. The period is subject to the maximum period determined by ss 41 to 44 ('Limits on period of detention without charge'). Where a reference is made to the CPS a custody officer is responsible for ensuring that all specified information is sent with that reference.

Where a person is arrested under the provisions of the Criminal Justice Act 2003 (CJA 2003) allowing a person to be re-tried after being acquitted of a specified serious offence a superintendent (or above) who has not been directly involved in the investigation is responsible for determining whether the evidence is sufficient to charge.

Where a Crown Prosecutor is unable to make a charging decision based upon the information available at the time, a detainee may be released without charge or on bail. A detainee should be informed of the circumstances of such a decision.

Unless the restriction on drawing adverse inferences from silence applies (see p 114), a detainee who is charged or informed that he may be prosecuted for an offence must be cautioned in the relevant terms set out on p 113. If the restriction does apply, the alternative terms of the caution set out on p 115 must be used. The detainee must also be given a written notice showing particulars of the offence charged, which must include the name of the officer (with the usual exception: p 96) and the case reference number. The charge must be stated in simple terms but must show the precise offence in law. The notice must begin with the following words:

'You are charged with the offence(s) shown below' [and be followed by the appropriate caution in the particular circumstances].

Where applicable a copy of the notice must be given to the appropriate adult.

If, after these procedures have been carried out, a police officer wishes to tell a detainee about any written statement or interview with another person relating to the offence, the detainee must either be handed a true copy of the written statement or have the content of the interview record brought to his attention. Nothing must be done to invite a reply or comment except to caution the detainee that he does not have to say anything, but that anything he does say may be given in evidence, and to remind him of his right to legal advice. If the detainee cannot read, the document may be read to him. In relevant cases, the appropriate adult must be given a copy of the document, or the interview record must be brought to his attention.

When a *juvenile* is charged with an offence and the custody officer authorises his continued detention after charge, the custody officer must arrange for the juvenile to be taken into the care of a local authority to be detained pending appearance in court unless he certifies that:

(a) for any juvenile, it is impracticable to do so; or
(b) in the case of a juvenile at least 12 years old, no secure accommodation is available and other accommodation would not be adequate to protect the public from serious harm from that juvenile.

Questioning after charge

Further questions relating to the offence may not generally be asked of a person after he has been charged with that offence, or informed that he may be prosecuted for it. Exceptions are: where they are necessary to prevent or minimise harm or loss to some other person or to the public, or to clear up ambiguity in a previous answer or statement; or where it is in the interests of justice that the person should have put to him (and have the opportunity to comment upon) new information concerning the offence; or where he volunteers to make a further statement. This could occur where a detainee mentions that property stolen was sold to a second party, or where a reference is made to a day of the week but no date is given, or where the name of a street is given without mention of the town. It could also occur where it would be advantageous to the detainee and in the interests of justice for him to have another offence taken into consideration by the court, should he be prepared to admit responsibility. In such cases the detainee must be cautioned before further questions are put that he does not have to say anything, but that anything he does say may be given in evidence, and the caution must be written at the head of any statement made. He must be reminded of his right to legal advice.

The giving of a warning or the service of a notice of intended prosecution required by the Road Traffic Offenders Act 1988, s 1 does not amount to informing a detainee that he may be prosecuted for an offence and so does not preclude further questioning in relation to that offence.

For a special provision under the terrorism legislation, see p 806.

Documentation

A record must be made of anything a detainee says when he is charged. Questions put in an interview after a charge and answers given must be recorded in full during the interview on the forms provided and the record must be signed by the detainee or, if he refuses, by the interviewer and any third parties present. If the questions are audibly recorded or visually recorded the arrangements set out in Code E or Code F apply.

DUTIES OF CUSTODY OFFICER AFTER CHARGE

PACE, s 38 requires that, when a person arrested otherwise than under a warrant endorsed for bail is charged with an offence, the custody officer, subject to the Criminal Justice and Public Order Act 1994 (CJPOA 1994), s 25 (p 174), must order his release from police detention, either on bail or without bail, *unless* the charge is murder or unless the following special rules apply. The Court of Appeal has held that the provisions of s 38 (described here and in the following paragraphs) do not apply where a person is in custody solely because he has been arrested for breach of his bail conditions contrary to the Bail Act 1976, s 7.

Arrested person not a juvenile

PACE, s 38 provides that if the person charged (D) is not a juvenile the custody officer (CO) must order his release from police detention, with or without bail, unless:

(a) D's name and address cannot be ascertained or the CO has reasonable grounds for doubting the truth of a name or address provided; or

(b) the CO has reasonable grounds for believing that D will fail to appear in court to answer bail;

(c) if D was arrested for an imprisonable offence, the CO has reasonable grounds for believing that the detention of D is necessary to prevent him from committing an offence;

(d) in a case where a sample may be taken from D under PACE, s 63B (see p 153), the CO has reasonable grounds for believing that the detention of D is necessary to enable a sample to be taken from him;

(e) if D was arrested for a non-imprisonable offence, the CO has reasonable grounds for believing that the detention of D is necessary to prevent him from causing physical injury to any other person or from causing loss of or damage to property;

(f) the CO has reasonable grounds for believing that the detention of D is necessary (i) to prevent D from interfering with the administration of justice or with the investigation of offences or of a particular offence; or (ii) for D's own protection.

Arrested person a juvenile

PACE, s 38 provides that if the person charged (JD) is a juvenile (ie a person appearing to be under 18) the custody officer (CO) must order JD's release from police detention, with or without bail, *unless* one of the above grounds applies or the CO has reasonable grounds for believing that JD should be detained in the interests of his welfare. In the case of (d) this only applies if JD has reached the minimum age specified by s 63B (at present 14).

Section 38 also requires that, where the CO authorises JD to be kept in police detention, the CO must secure that JD is to be taken to local authority accommodation unless the CO certifies:

(a) that by reason of such circumstances as are specified in the certificate, it is impracticable to do so. This requires a statement of the reasons, but detailed reasons are not required; or

(b) where JD is 12 or over, that no secure accommodation is available and that keeping him in other local authority accommodation would not be adequate to protect the public from serious harm from him.

Such a certificate must be produced to the court before which JD is first brought thereafter. The Court of Appeal has held that a failure to do so does not in itself render the detention unlawful.

In a case where JD is charged with a violent or sexual offence, the reference in (b) to protecting the public from serious harm is to protection from death or serious personal injury, whether physical or psychological, occasioned by further such offences by him.
'*Sexual offence*' in this context means an offence:

(a) under the Protection of Children Act 1978 (indecent photographs of children);

(b) under any provision of the Sexual Offences Act 2003, Part 1, except s 71 (sexual activity in a public lavatory); or

(c) conspiracy or attempt to commit any of these offences.

'*Violent offence*' means an offence contained in a list of 76 offences against the person, firearms offences, explosives offences, public order offences and road traffic offences which lead, or are intended or likely to lead, to a person's death or to physical injury, and include an offence which is required to be charged as arson (whether or not it would otherwise fall within this definition).

Except as provided above, neither JD's behaviour nor the nature of the offence charged provides grounds for the CO to decide that it is impracticable to arrange for the transfer to local authority care on the grounds of impracticability. Similarly, the lack of secure local authority accommodation does not make it impracticable to transfer him. The availability of secure accommodation is only a factor in relation to a juvenile aged 12 or over when the local authority accommodation would not be adequate to protect the public from serious harm from him.

Detention

If the release of a person arrested is not required by PACE, s 38, the CO may authorise him to be kept in police detention, but he may not authorise an adult to be so detained for a sample to be taken under PACE, s 63B after a six-hour period running from the charge.

Where the CO authorises a person who has been charged to be kept in police detention he must, as soon as practicable, record the grounds (ie reasons) in the custody record in that person's presence, unless the usual exceptions (see p 147) apply.

PACE, s 46 requires that where a person: (a) is charged with an offence; and (b) after being charged, is kept in police detention or (in the case of a juvenile) is detained by a local authority, he must be brought before a magistrates' court as soon as practicable, and in any event not later than the first sitting after he is charged (or, if he is to be brought before a magistrates' court in another local justice area, not later than the first sitting of that court after his arrival in that area). If the person is to be brought before a magistrates' court in another area, he must be removed to that area as soon as practicable for the above purpose.

If no magistrates' court is due to sit on the day the person is charged (or on the day he arrives in the other area) or on the next day, the custody officer must inform the designated officer for a local justice area that there is a person in the area who has been detained after charge, and that officer must arrange for a sitting of a magistrates' court not later than the day next following the day on which he is charged (or, if he has been transferred to another area, the day next following the day of his arrival in that area). Christmas Day, Good Friday, and any Sunday do not count as 'days next following' for this purpose; thus, for example, the day next following Saturday is Monday.

None of the above provisions requires a person who is in hospital to be brought before a court if he is not well enough.

BAIL

Bail of arrested person (police bail)

When an investigating officer brings a person arrested for an offence before the custody officer, the custody officer may decide that there is insufficient evidence to justify a charge and that there is unlikely to be other evidence obtained; or that there is enough evidence to charge at that stage; or that there is not sufficient evidence available at that stage to charge the prisoner, but that there probably will be when further inquiries have been made. If the first of the decisions is reached the prisoner must be released at once without charge. If the second decision is reached the detainee may be released on bail if he is charged or pending a decision by a Crown Prosecutor (p 164). If the third decision is reached, he may be released on bail if there are no further grounds for keeping him in custody.

PACE, s 47 provides that, for the purposes of police bail, 'bail' refers to bail subject to a duty:

(a) to appear at a magistrates' court at such time and such place as the custody officer may appoint;
(b) to attend at such police station and at such time as the custody officer may appoint for the purposes of (i) proceedings relating to a live link direction (p 28), and (ii) any preliminary hearing in relation to which any such direction is given; or
(c) to attend at such police station at such time as the custody officer may appoint for purposes other than those mentioned at (b).

Release on police bail: general

PACE, s 47 states that a release on police bail must be a release on bail granted in accordance with the Bail Act 1976 (BA 1976).

By BA 1976, ss 3 and 3A, a custody officer releasing a person on bail and without charge pending a decision of the DPP (in practice, a Crown Prosecutor) or after charge has power to require him to comply with such conditions on bail as appear to him to be necessary:

(a) to secure that the person:
   (i)   surrenders to custody;
   (ii) does not commit an offence whilst on bail;
   (iii) does not interfere with witnesses or otherwise obstruct the course of justice whether in relation to himself or any other person; or
(b) for the protection of the person concerned or, if he is under 18, for his own welfare or in his own interests.

However, the custody officer does not have power to impose a requirement to reside in a bail hostel. A custody officer would not have sufficient time to make the necessary inquiries before such a condition might properly be imposed.

The combined effect of provisions in BA 1976, s 3 is to permit the following additional requirements to be made of a person before he is released on bail:

(a) he may be required:
   (i) to provide a surety or sureties (see below) to ensure his surrender to custody;
   (ii) to give security for his surrender which may be given by him or on his behalf;
(b) if a parent or guardian of a person under 17 consents to be surety for him, the parent or guardian may be required to ensure that the juvenile complies with conditions imposed under (a)(i)–(iii) above, except that no such condition may be imposed where a juvenile will be 17 before the time appointed for surrender, and that a parent or guardian may not be required to secure compliance with any requirement to which his consent does not extend and may not, in respect of those requirements to which his consent does extend, be bound in a sum greater than £50.

Where a custody officer has granted bail in criminal proceedings, he or another custody officer serving at the same police station may vary the condition of bail at the request of the person bailed, and in doing so he may impose conditions or more onerous conditions.

BA 1976, s 5 provides that, where a custody officer grants bail or varies any conditions of bail, or imposes conditions in respect of bail, he must make a record of the decision and, if requested by the person in question, give that person a copy of the record as soon as practicable; in practice this is always done. Sections 5 and 5A provide that, where a custody officer imposes conditions in granting bail or varies any condition of bail, he must give reasons for doing so. This is to enable the person concerned to consider requesting the custody officer to vary those conditions. A note of the custody officer's reasons for imposing (or varying) conditions must be made in the custody record and a copy must be given to the person concerned.

A person who is bailed enters into a promise to appear as prescribed. That promise cannot be set against a recognisance from him that, if he fails to appear, a specific sum of money shall be forfeit. Instead BA 1976 provides its own penalties for non-appearance. In serious cases it may be necessary for a defendant to find one or more 'sureties', that is persons who *undertake to secure his attendance*. This is done by each surety entering a recognisance to forfeit a specified sum to the Crown in the event of the non-attendance of the accused. By the Magistrates' Courts Act 1980, s 43, the magistrates' court before whom the person is bailed to appear may enlarge the recognisances of any sureties.

Police bail of person not charged

The custody officer, when the investigating officer brings the person detained before him, may decide under PACE, s 37 to release the detainee on bail, such bail being conditioned upon his appearance at a police station at a given time, as opposed to appearing at a court. The custody officer may reach this decision because he considers that there is not sufficient evidence at that stage to charge the detainee, but that there probably will be when further inquiries have been made. Alternatively, he may consider that there is sufficient evidence to charge the detainee but decide under s 37 to release him on bail pending a decision by the DPP (in practice, a Crown Prosecutor) about charging or for some other purpose. The requirement to attend at a police station may be cancelled at any time by notice in writing from the custody officer.

Section 47(1B) provides that no application by the prosecutor may be made for a reconsideration of a custody officer's decision to grant bail where a person:

(a) is released under s 37 without charge on bail, or
(b) is released without charge on bail following arrest for breach of bail granted under s 37:
    (i) to enable the DPP (in practice, a Crown Prosecutor) to make a decision about charging, or
    (ii) for some other purpose.

Where a person is released on conditional bail in such circumstances, that person will not be entitled to apply to a magistrates' court for bail, but may seek variation of such conditions.

Police bail after charge

By PACE, s 47(3A), where a custody officer grants bail subject to a duty to appear before a magistrates' court, he must appoint for the appearance:

(a) a date which is not later than the first sitting of the court after the person is charged with the offence; or
(b) where he is informed by the designated officer for the relevant local justice area that the appearance cannot be accommodated until a later date, that later date.

The Magistrates' Courts Act 1980, s 43 enables a magistrates' court to fix a later time for appearance before it.

Alternatively, the custody officer may bail the person charged to attend a police station pursuant to a live link direction (p 28).

Live link police bail

Section 46ZA provides that a defendant answering live link bail is not to be treated as being in police detention, except where, at any time before the beginning of proceedings in relation to a live link direction at a preliminary hearing, he is told by a constable that a live link will not be available, or where the court determines not to give a live link direction. In such a circumstance, the defendant is to be treated as arrested for and charged with the offence for which he was granted bail, and as if he had been so charged when that circumstance first applied to him. A person arrested under s 46A for failing to attend at a police station to answer to live link bail, and who is brought to such a station, is to be treated as if he had been arrested for and charged with the offence for which he was granted bail and had been so charged when brought to the station.

By s 54B, a constable may search at any time any person who is at a police station to answer to live link bail; and any article in the possession of such a person. If the constable reasonably believes a thing in the person's possession ought to be seized on any of the grounds that it:

(a) may jeopardise the maintenance of order in the police station;
(b) may put the safety of any person in the police station at risk; or
(c) may be evidence of, or in relation to, an offence,

the constable may seize and retain it or cause it to be seized and retained. Anything so seized and retained must be recorded. Such a search may only be conducted by a constable of the same sex as the person concerned. An intimate search may not be carried out under the authority of s 54B.

Section 54C empowers a constable to retain a thing seized under s 54B until the person from whom it was seized leaves the police station. However, retention beyond that point of time is permissible in two cases:

(a) a constable may retain something seized under s 54B in order to establish the thing's lawful owner, where there are reasonable grounds for believing that it has been obtained in consequence of the commission of an offence; or
(b) where the thing may be evidence of, or in relation to, an offence, a constable may retain it for use as evidence at a trial or for forensic examination or for investigation, if a photograph or copy would be insufficient for that purpose.

Arrest warrant endorsed for bail

The MCA 1980, s 117 allows a person arrested on a warrant endorsed for bail to be released on bail (ie admitted to bail 'on the spot') without being taken to a police station, provided that the endorsement for bail does not demand sureties. If sureties are required, the person must be taken to a police station.

Bail by a court

Section 4 of BA 1976 states that, when a person who is accused of an offence appears before a magistrates' court or the Crown Court in the course of, or in connection with, the proceedings for the offence, or when he applies to a court for bail or for a variation of the conditions of bail in connection with the proceedings, he must be granted bail if none of the exceptions specified in Sch 1 (below) applies. However, this is subject to the provisions of CJPOA 1994, s 25 (bail for defendant charged with or convicted of murder, attempted murder or manslaughter, or any offence under the Sexual Offences Act 2003, ss 1, 2, 4, 5, 6, 8, 30 and 31 (involving rape, non-consensual penetration or sexual activity, the same activity with children under 13 and mentally disordered persons), or an attempt to commit any such offence, after a previous conviction for such an offence (or an equivalent offence in another EU state) only to be granted if there are exceptional circumstances justifying it). Section 25 also applies to a police officer considering the grant of bail in such circumstances.

Bail may only be granted by a Crown Court judge to a person charged with murder.

In taking decisions under BA 1976, Sch 1, a court must have regard, so far as it is relevant, to any misuse of a controlled drug by the defendant.

Exceptions to right to bail: imprisonable offences

An imprisonable offence is one which is punishable in the case of an adult with imprisonment.

The following exceptions to the right to bail apply under BA 1976, Sch 1, Part I, where the offence or one of them is imprisonable, except that they do not apply where the offence or each of them is triable only summarily or where the offence is criminal damage or aggravated vehicle-taking only involving damage where the value of the damage is less than £5,000.

(1) Bail need not be granted if the court is satisfied that there are *substantial grounds for believing that the defendant (D), if released on bail (whether subject to conditions or not), would:*
    (a) *fail to surrender to custody; or*
    (b) *commit an offence while on bail; or*
    (c) *interfere with witnesses or otherwise obstruct the course of justice, whether in relation to himself or any other person.*
This exception does not apply if D falls within (7) (below), unless the court is satisfied as mentioned there. In addition, this exception does not apply where:
    (a) **D has attained the age of 18,**
    (b) **D has not been convicted of an offence in the proceedings, and**
    (c) **it appears to the court that there is no real prospect that D will be sentenced to a custodial sentence in the proceedings.**

(2) Bail need not be granted if the court is satisfied that there *are substantial grounds for believing that D, if released on bail (whether subject to conditions or not), would commit an offence while on bail by engaging in conduct that would, or would be likely to, cause (a) physical or mental injury to an associated person, or (b) an associated person to fear physical or mental injury.*

(3) Where the offence is an indictable offence (including an either-way offence), D need not be granted bail if it appears that D was on bail in criminal proceedings on the date of the offence. This provision does not apply in the circumstances shown in bold above in respect of (1).

(4) Bail need not be granted by the court:
    (a) if it is satisfied that D should be kept in custody for his own protection or, if a child or young person (ie under 18), for his own welfare; or

(b) if he is in custody under a court order or in pursuance of any authority under the Armed Forces Act 2006; or

(c) if the court is satisfied that there has not been time to obtain sufficient information upon which a decision about bail may be made.

(5) D need not be granted bail if, having previously been released on bail in, or in connection with, the proceedings, he has been arrested under BA 1976, s 7. This provision does not apply in the circumstances printed in bold above in respect of (1).

(6) A person charged with murder must not be granted bail unless the court is of the opinion that there is *no significant risk of him committing, while on bail, an offence that would, or would be likely to, cause physical or mental injury to any person other than himself.*

(7) An alleged drug offender aged 18 or over who is charged may not be granted bail (unless the court is of the opinion that there is *no significant risk of his committing an offence while on bail*) where:

(a) a drug test indicates the presence of a Class A drug;

(b) the offence is one of possession of a Class A drug *or* the court is satisfied that there are substantial grounds for believing that the misuse of a Class A drug caused or contributed to that offence or provided its motivation; and

(c) the person concerned does not agree to a dependency/propensity to misuse assessment, or has undergone such assessment but does not agree to participate in any relevant follow-up offered.

However, these provisions only apply in areas where facilities are in place.

In taking decisions about the words italicised in heads (1), (2), (6), and (7), the court must have regard to the nature and seriousness of the offence; the character, antecedents, associations and community ties of D; D's record in respect of previous grants of bail; the strength of the evidence available (except where the case is merely being adjourned for inquiries or a report); and if there are substantial grounds for believing that D, if released on bail, would commit an offence while on bail, the risk that D may do so by engaging in conduct that would, or would be likely to, cause physical or mental injury to any person other than D.

BA 1976, Sch 1, Part IA applies where *the imprisonable offence (or each of them) is a summary offence or where the offence is criminal damage, or aggravated vehicle-taking only involving damage, and the value of the damage is less than £5,000.*

BA 1976, Sch 1, Part IA provides that D need not be granted bail if:

(a) there has been a previous failure to surrender to bail and the court believes that this will occur again;

(b) D was on bail when the offence was committed and the court believes that, if released on bail, he would commit an offence while on bail;

(c) the court is satisfied that there are substantial grounds for believing that, if released on bail, D would commit an offence by engaging in conduct likely to cause physical or mental injury, or fear of such injury, to an associated person;

(d) the court is satisfied that D should be kept in custody for his own protection, or, if under 18, for his own welfare;

(e) D is in custody under the sentence of a court or of an officer under the Armed Forces Act 2006;

(f) having been released on bail in proceedings for the same offence, D has been arrested under BA 1976, s 7 for absconding or breaking conditions of his bail, and the court is satisfied that there are substantial grounds for believing that if released on bail (with or without conditions) D would fail to surrender, commit an offence while on bail, interfere with witnesses or otherwise obstruct the course of justice;

(g) it has not been practical to obtain enough information to take the decisions required by Part 1A due to lack of time since the proceedings began; or

(h) the drug-users exception (see (7) above) applies.

Heads (a), (b) and (f) do not apply in relation to bail where:

(i)   D has attained the age of 18,

(ii) D has not been convicted of an offence in those proceedings, and

(iii) it appears to the court that there is no real prospect that D will be sentenced to a custodial sentence in the proceedings.

Exceptions to right to bail: non-imprisonable offences

BA 1976, Sch 1, Pt II provides that D charged with a non-imprisonable offence need not be granted bail if (a), (d) or (e) immediately above applies. Head (a) only applies where D is under 18, or has been convicted in the proceedings of an offence.

D need not be granted bail if, having been released on bail in proceedings for the offence, D has been arrested under BA 1976, s 7 (arrest for absconding or breaking conditions of bail), and the court is satisfied that there are substantial grounds for believing that if released on bail (with or without conditions) D would, or would be likely to, cause physical or mental injury to an associated person, or to cause an associated person to fear physical or mental injury.

D need not be granted bail if:

(a) he is under 18, or has been convicted in the proceedings of an offence;

(b) having been released on bail in proceedings for the offence, D has been arrested under BA 1976, s 7; and

(c) the court is satisfied that there are substantial grounds for believing that, if released on bail (with or without conditions), D would fail to surrender to custody, commit an offence on bail or obstruct the course of justice (eg witness intimidation).

Conditions

In granting bail a court may impose conditions for a number of specified purposes, including those specified for the purposes of conditional police bail.

CJA 2003 makes provision for an appeal to the Crown Court by the person concerned against the imposition of conditions relating to residence, provision of surety or giving a security, curfew, electronic monitoring or contact.

Breach of requirements of live link bail or other bail subject to duty to attend police station: arrest, etc

PACE, s 46A empowers a constable to arrest without warrant any person who, having been released on bail subject to a duty to attend at a police station, fails to attend at that police station at the time appointed for him to do so. In addition, a person who has been released on bail under s 37, or who has been released on bail after being arrested while on bail granted under s 37, may be arrested without warrant by a constable if he has reasonable grounds for suspecting that the person has broken any conditions of his bail.

Such a person must be taken to that police station as soon as practicable after his arrest.

Section 46A(1ZA) and (1ZB) has the effect of extending the power of arrest under s 46A to cover the case where a defendant attends a police station for a live link bail hearing, but (a) leaves the police station before the beginning of the proceedings relating to the live link hearing without informing a constable that he does not intend to give his consent to the direction, or (b) refuses to be searched under PACE, s 54B.

Section 47(2) provides that nothing in BA 1976 prevents a re-arrest without warrant of a person released on bail subject to a duty to appear at a police station if new evidence justifying a further arrest has come to light since his release. If such a person is re-arrested the detention provisions in PACE apply as if he has been arrested for the first time, but this does not apply to a person arrested under s 46A for failure to surrender to police bail at a police station, or who has surrendered to that bail and who accordingly is deemed to have been arrested for that offence, or to a person who is treated under s 46ZA as if he had been arrested.

MCA 1980, s 43 permits the enforcement of the recognisance of any surety for a person granted bail which is conditioned upon appearance at a police station in the same way as if conditioned on appearance at a magistrates' court.

PACE, s 47(6) provides that, where a person who has been granted police bail and either has attended at a police station or has been arrested under s 46A is detained at a police station, any previous time in custody must be included in any calculation of detention time and any time during which he was on bail must not be so included. In practice, his old custody record will be continued.

Breach of bail by person under duty to surrender into custody of court: arrest

BA 1976, s 7 provides a power to arrest without warrant. A person (D) who has been released on bail in criminal proceedings and is under a duty to surrender into the custody of a court may be arrested without warrant by a constable if:

(a) the constable has reasonable grounds for believing that D is not likely to surrender to custody, or

(b) the constable has reasonable grounds for believing that D is likely to break any of the conditions of his bail or has reasonable grounds for suspecting that D has broken any of those conditions; or

(c) in a case where D was released on bail with one or more sureties, if a surety notifies a constable in writing that D is unlikely to surrender to custody, and that for that reason the surety wishes to be relieved of his obligations as a surety.

Unless D was arrested within 24 hours of the time appointed for surrender to custody, D must be brought before a justice as soon as practicable and in any event within 24 hours. Christmas Day, Good Friday and any Sunday are excluded from the calculation of 24 hours. If arrested within 24 hours of the surrender time, D must be brought before the court at which he was to have surrendered to custody.

Failure to surrender: offence

By BA 1976, s 6, a person (D) who has been bailed commits an offence if he fails without reasonable cause to surrender to custody as required. 'Surrender to custody' means surrendering into the custody of the court by entering the dock or of a constable (according to the requirements of the grant of bail) 'at the appointed time and place' and not 'at or about' the appointed time. Consequently, it is no defence that D was only slightly late. Moreover, if D had reasonable cause for failing to surrender at the appropriate time, D commits an offence if he fails to surrender to custody at the appointed place as soon after the appointed time as is reasonably practicable.

It is for D to prove 'reasonable cause'.

Where D has been released on bail by a court and subsequently fails to surrender to custody, D must be brought before the court at which proceedings in respect of which bail was granted are to be heard. No written charge should be issued to commence proceedings for such failure. The court in question should initiate proceedings for an offence of failing to surrender to bail on its own motion, following an express invitation by the prosecutor. On the other hand, where D has been bailed from a police station to appear before a magistrates' court, proceedings for an offence of failure to surrender to bail should be initiated by way of charging him.

Remand to police custody

By MCA 1980, s 128, a magistrates' court has power to remand a person for a period not exceeding three clear days (24 hours if a person under 18) to 'detention at a police station' where there is a need to question him about other offences. Section 128 also requires that such a person must not be kept in detention at a police station unless there is a need for him to be detained for the purpose of inquiries into other offences. If he is kept in such detention, he must be brought back to the magistrates' court which committed him as soon as the need for detention for the purpose of inquiries ceases. Such a person must be treated as a person in detention for the purposes of PACE (and therefore he must be treated in accordance with Code C and his detention must be subject to reviews as prescribed by PACE).

CAUTIONS AS ALTERNATIVE TO PROSECUTIONS

The various types of cautions are among the alternatives to prosecution referred to on p 14. They are available where someone admits to committing an offence. They form part of an offender's criminal record. Offenders must be made aware of this before agreeing to accept one of these cautions.

Simple cautions

A simple caution can be offered by a police officer to someone aged 18 or over.

Under the Criminal Justice and Courts Act 2015 (CJCA 2015), s 17(2), where the offence is *triable only on indictment*, a police officer may not give a simple caution except:

(a) in exceptional circumstances relating to the person or the offence, and
(b) with the consent of the DPP (given by a Crown Prosecutor).

In the case of *other offences*, the police may—subject to CJCA 2015, s 17(3) or (4)—make a decision to offer a simple caution without reference to a Crown Prosecutor, unless the DPP's *Guidance* (p 164) requires the case to be so referred. Whenever a case is referred to a Crown Prosecutor, the Crown Prosecutor's decision is binding on the police. Where the relevant requirements in CJCA 2015, s 17(3) or (4) (below) are not met, the offender must be charged with the offence.

By CJCA 2015, s 17(3), where the offence is a specified *either-way* offence, a police officer may not give a simple caution except in exceptional circumstances relating to the person or the offence. The following offences are specified in the Criminal Justice and Courts Act 2015 (Simple Cautions) (Specification of Either-Way Offences) Order 2015, viz an offence under:

(a) the Children and Young Persons Act 1933, s 1(1);
(b) the Prevention of Crime Act 1953, s 1(1) or 1A(1);
(c) the Sexual Offences Act 1956, s 14(1) or 15(1) (indecent assault on woman/man respectively: both repealed), where the victim of the offence was under the age of 16 at the time of the offence;
(d) the Indecency with Children Act 1960, s 1(1) (repealed);
(e) the Firearms Act 1968, s 19, where the offence was committed in relation to a firearm within the meaning of s 57(1) and is triable either way;
(f) the Misuse of Drugs Act 1971, s 4(2) or (3) or 5(3), where the offence was committed in relation to a Class A drug and is triable either way;
(g) the Protection of Children Act 1978, s 1(1);
(h) the Customs and Excise Management Act 1979, ss 50(2) and (3), 68(2), 107(1) or 170(2) in connection with a prohibition having effect by virtue of the Misuse of Drugs Act 1971, s 3(1), where the offence was committed in relation to a Class A drug and is triable either way;
(i) the Criminal Justice Act 1988, ss 139(1), 139A(1) or (2), 139AA(1) or 160(1);
(j) the Sexual Offences (Amendment) Act 2000, s 3(1) (abuse of position of trust) (repealed);
(k) the Nationality, Immigration and Asylum Act 2002, s 145(1), (2) or (3) (traffic in prostitution) (repealed);
(l) the Sexual Offences Act 2003, ss 3(1) or 4(1) and (5), where the victim of the offence was under the age of 16 at the time of the offence;
(m) the Sexual Offences Act 2003, ss 7(1), 8(1) and (3), 9(1) and (3), 10(1) and (3), 11(1), 12(1), 14(1), 15(1), 16(1), 17(1), 18(1), 19(1), 25(1) and (4)(b), 25(1) and (5), 26(1) and (4)(b), 26(1) and (5), 47(1) and (4)(b), 47(1) and (5), 48(1), 49(1), 50(1), 57(1), 58(1), 59(1) or 59A(1) (ss 57-59A (sexual trafficking) repealed);
(n) the Coroners and Justice Act 2009, s 62(1);
(o) the Modern Slavery Act 2015, s 1 or 2.

By CJCA 2015, s 17(4), where:

(a) the offence is a summary offence or an either-way offence not specified above; and
(b) in the two years before the commission of the offence the person concerned has been convicted of, or cautioned for, a similar offence,

a police officer may not give him a simple caution except in exceptional circumstances relating to the person, the offence committed or the previous offence. (For the purposes of (b), a person has been 'cautioned for' an offence if he has been given a simple caution, a conditional caution, a youth caution or a youth conditional caution.)

By CJCA 2015, s 17(5), it is for a police officer not below a rank specified in the Criminal Justice and Courts Act 2015 (Simple Cautions) (Specification of Police Ranks) Order 2015 to determine whether there are exceptional circumstances for the purposes of s 17(2), (3) or (4), and whether a previous offence is similar to the offence admitted for the purposes of s 17(4). Such a determination must be made in accordance with guidance to be issued by the Secretary of State. The ranks are as follows:

Determination	Minimum rank
Whether there are exceptional circumstances for the purposes of s 17(2)	Superintendent
Whether there are exceptional circumstances for the purposes of s 17(3) or s 17(4), or whether a previous offence is similar to the offence admitted for the purposes of s 17(4)	Inspector

Whatever the offence, a simple caution must not be offered to someone who has not admitted committing the offence, or who does not agree to accept it. In such a case, the offender must be charged with the offence. A simple caution may only be given if the decision-maker is satisfied that there is sufficient evidence to charge the offender (ie sufficient to provide a realistic prospect that the offender would be convicted). In addition, a simple caution must not be given if the decision-maker considers that it is in the public interest for the offender to be prosecuted. Although the victim should be consulted, he cannot insist that the case is disposed of in a particular way.

Simple cautions do not have a statutory basis, although their existence is recognised by a number of statutes. The Ministry of Justice has issued guidance, *Simple Cautions for Adult Offenders*, which should be applied to all decisions relating to simple cautions. The guidance should be used in conjunction with the DPP's *Guidance on Charging* referred to at p 164.

Youth cautions

A constable may give a child or young person (ie someone under 18) (Y) a youth caution under CDA 1998, s 66ZA if:

(a) he decides that there is sufficient evidence to charge Y with an offence,

(b) Y admits to the constable that Y committed the offence, and

(c) the constable does not consider that Y should be prosecuted or given a youth conditional caution (YCC) (below) in respect of the offence.

Unlike a simple (adult) caution, Y's agreement to the caution is not required. A youth caution may only be given if the decision-maker is satisfied that it would not be in the public interest to prosecute or offer a YCC (below).

Although the victim should be consulted, he cannot insist that the case is disposed of in a particular way.

A youth caution must be given in the presence of an appropriate adult.

The constable must explain in ordinary language to Y and to the appropriate adult the effect of a youth caution, and any guidance which has been given.

The Secretary of State has issued guidance (*Youth Cautions: Guidance for Police Officers and Youth Offending Teams*) as to the circumstances in which it is appropriate to give youth cautions, the places where youth cautions may be given, the form which youth cautions are to take, and the manner in which they are to be given and recorded.

Reference to youth offending team

CDA 1998, s 66ZB provides as follows.

If a constable gives a youth caution to a person (Y), he must as soon as practicable refer Y to a youth offending team (YOT). On a referral, the YOT must assess Y, and unless they consider it inappropriate to do so, must arrange for Y to participate in a rehabilitation programme.

If Y has not previously been referred under the above provision and has not previously been given a YCC, the YOT may assess Y, and may arrange for Y to participate in a rehabilitation programme.

If:

(a) a person who has received two or more youth cautions is convicted of an offence committed within two years beginning with the date of the last of those cautions, or
(b) a person who has received a YCC followed by a youth caution is convicted of an offence committed within two years beginning with the date of the youth caution,

the court:

(i) must not conditionally discharge him in respect of the offence unless it is of the opinion that there are exceptional circumstances relating to the offence or him that justify it doing so, and
(ii) where it does so, must state in open court that it is of that opinion and its reasons for that opinion.

A youth caution given to a person, and a report on a failure by a person to participate in a rehabilitation programme, may be cited in criminal proceedings in the same circumstances as a conviction of the person may be cited.

Conditional cautions

Conditional cautions: adults

CJA 2003, Part 3 (ss 22–27) makes provision for 'conditional cautions'. An authorised person (ie a constable, investigating officer or person authorised by a relevant prosecutor (as defined below)) may give a conditional caution to a person aged 18 or over if:

(a) he has evidence that the person has committed the offence;
(b) a relevant prosecutor (the DPP (Crown Prosecutor) or the like) or the authorised person has decided that there is sufficient evidence to charge him and that a conditional caution should be given;
(c) the person admits to committing the offence;
(d) the authorised person has explained the effect of the conditional caution to the offender and has warned him that failure to comply with any of the conditions may result in a prosecution for the offence; and
(e) the offender has signed a document which contains details of the offence; an admission of guilt; his consent to being given a conditional caution; and the conditions attached to the caution.

Although the victim should be consulted, he cannot insist that the case is disposed of in a particular way.

The conditions which may be attached to such a caution are those which have one or more of the following objects:

(a) facilitating the rehabilitation of the offender;
(b) ensuring that the offender makes reparation for his offence; and
(c) punishing the offender.

Typical conditions are payment of compensation, letters of apology, or drink or drugs referral interventions. CJA 2003, Part 3 provides that the conditions may include a condition that the offender pays a financial penalty (but only in respect of offences or descriptions of offences prescribed by the Secretary of State) which must not exceed one-quarter of the maximum fine to which the offender would have been liable on summary conviction or £250, whichever is the smaller.

The CJA 2003 (Conditional Cautions: Financial Penalties) Order 2013 provides that a financial penalty condition may be attached to the following descriptions of offence and that the amount listed against each description of offence is the maximum penalty which may be specified in such a condition:

Any summary offence	£50
Any either-way offence	£100
Any indictable-only offence	£150

A conditional caution given to a 'relevant foreign offender' may have conditions attached to it that have the object of bringing about his departure from the UK and/or ensuring that he does not return to the UK, whether or not these are in addition to conditions with objects specified above. A 'relevant foreign offender' means someone in respect of whom (a) directions for removal from the UK have been, or may be, given under the Immigration Act 1971, Sch 2 or the Immigration and Asylum Act 1999, s 10, or (b) a deportation order is in force under the Immigration Act 1971, s 5.

Before deciding what conditions to attach to a conditional caution, a relevant prosecutor or the authorised person must make reasonable efforts to obtain the views of the victim (if any) of the offence, and in particular the victim's views as to whether the offender should carry out any of the actions listed in the community remedy document (as to which see p 285). *If the victim expresses the view that the offender should carry out a particular action listed in the community remedy document, the prosecutor or authorised person must attach that as a condition unless it seems to the prosecutor or authorised person that it would be inappropriate to do so.* Where there is more than one victim and they express different views, or for any other reason the italicised words do not apply, the prosecutor or authorised person must nevertheless take account of any views expressed by the victim (or victims) in deciding what conditions to attach to the conditional caution.

The Secretary of State has issued a revised Conditional Cautioning Code of Practice and the DPP has issued a revised *Guidance on Adult Conditional Cautioning.* Provision is made for the National Probation Service to provide assistance in deciding whether conditional cautions should be given, the conditions which might be attached and the supervision and rehabilitation of persons so cautioned.

If an offender fails, without reasonable excuse, to comply with any of the conditions attached to the conditional caution, criminal proceedings may be instituted for the original offence and the document signed by him referred to above is admissible in evidence in those proceedings. The caution ceases to have effect with the institution of proceedings.

Youth conditional cautions

The Crime and Disorder Act 1998 (CDA 1998), s 66A provides for youth conditional cautions (YCCs). The Secretary of State has issued a Code of Practice for such cautions. The YCC provisions apply to those aged 10 or over but under 18. A YCC can be given by an 'authorised person' (as defined on p 181) to an offender aged 10 or over but under 18 where five requirements are satisfied. These requirements are essentially the same as those in respect of 'Conditional cautions: adults' as set out at (a)-(e) on p 181, substituting 'YCC' for 'conditional caution'. The requisite explanation and warning must be given in the presence of the appropriate adult.

The conditions which may be attached must have one or more of these objects:

(a) facilitating the offender's rehabilitation;
(b) ensuring that he makes reparation;
(c) punishing him.

A condition may be attached that the offender attend at a specified place at a specified time (but not for more than 20 hours, excluding attendance required for the purpose of rehabilitation). In addition, a condition requiring the payment of a financial penalty may be attached to a YCC if the offence committed is a prescribed offence. The CDA 1998 (Youth Conditional Cautions: Financial Penalties) Order 2013 prescribes any summary offence, any offence triable either way, and any offence triable on indictment. The 2013 Order also prescribes the maximum penalties which may be attached to a YCC:

Description of offence	Offender 14 or over but under 18	Offender 10 or over but under 14
Any summary offence	£30	£15
Any either-way offence	£50	£25
Indictable only offence	£75	£35

There is a duty to consult victims; its terms are identical to those relating to adult conditional cautions, above.

If a YCC is given by an authorised officer, he must refer the offender to a youth offending team as soon as possible.

If the offender fails without reasonable excuse to comply with any of the conditions attached to a YCC he may be prosecuted for the offence in question whereupon the YCC ceases to exist. The document signed by the young offender referred to above is admissible in evidence in proceedings for the offence.

Arrest for failure to comply

CJA 2003, s 24A(1), applied to YCCs by CDA 1998, s 66E, provides that, where a constable has reasonable grounds for believing that the offender has failed, without reasonable excuse, to comply with any of the conditions attached to a conditional caution or a YCC, he may arrest him without warrant. A person so arrested must be:

(a) charged with the offence in question;
(b) released without charge and on bail to enable a decision to be made as to whether he should be charged with the offence (in which case the custody officer must inform him that he is being released pending such a decision); or
(c) released without charge and without bail (with or without any variation in the conditions attached to the caution) (s 24A(2)).

The requirements of s 24A(2) also apply:

(i) where a person who, having been released on bail under (b) above, returns to a police station to answer bail or is otherwise in police detention at a police station;

(ii) where a person who, having been released on bail elsewhere than at a police station, attends to answer that bail or is otherwise in police detention; and

(iii) where a person has been arrested for failure to answer to police bail.

Section 24A(2) does not require a person who falls within (i) or (ii) above, and is in police detention in relation to another matter, to be so released if he is liable to be kept in detention in relation to that other matter.

A person arrested under s 24A, or any other person to whom s 24A(2) applies, may be kept in police detention:

(a) to enable him to be dealt with in accordance with s 24A(2) (and this includes power to keep him in detention if necessary for the purpose of investigating whether he has failed, without reasonable excuse, to comply with any of the conditions attached to his conditional caution); or

(b) where applicable, to enable a custody officer to appoint a different or additional time for answering to police bail.

Where a person is not in a fit state to be so dealt with, he may be kept in police detention until he is.

CJA 2003, s 24B provides that certain provisions in PACE (those dealing with limitations on police detention, duties of a custody officer, records kept by a custody officer, duties and responsibilities of custody officers, x-rays, and ultrasound scans) apply, with modifications, to persons arrested for suspected breach of a conditional caution or a YCC as they do to offenders arrested in respect of an offence.

PACE, ss 30 to 31, 34, 36, 37(4)–(6), 38, 39 and 55A apply (with any necessary modifications) to a person arrested under CJA 2003, s 24A.

CHAPTER 6

Identification Methods

Identification by witnesses who saw the crime committed may be made in a video identification, identification parade or similar procedure. There may also be an identification by fingerprints or footwear impressions, or by body samples and impressions. The relevant PACE Code of Practice (Code D: the Code of Practice for the Identification of Persons by Police Officers) is concerned with these methods. The Code is also concerned with the keeping of records and with the taking of photographs of arrested people.

GENERAL PRINCIPLES

PACE Code D provides certain general principles, in addition to those set out in the third paragraph of p 35, which apply to all methods by which identification can be made. It provides that:

(1) References to a police officer include a person designated under the Police Reform Act 2002 (p 291) acting in the exercise or performance of powers or duties under his designation.

(2) Where a record is made of any action requiring the authority of an officer of a specified rank, the name (except in the case of terrorism inquiries, or where it is reasonably believed that it might be a source of danger, in which cases his warrant or other identification number and his police station should be used) and rank of the officer must be included in the record.

(3) All records must be timed and signed by the maker. This is subject to the same exceptional provision as in (2).

(4) In the case of a detained person, records must be made in the custody record unless otherwise specified.

(5) If an officer suspects, or is told, that a person may be mentally disordered or otherwise mentally vulnerable, that person must be treated as such, in the absence of clear evidence to dispel that suspicion.

(6) If a person appears to be under 17, he must, in the absence of clear evidence that he is older, be treated as a juvenile.

(7) If a person appears to have attained the age of 17 and to be under 18, he must, in the absence of clear evidence that he is older, be treated as a 17-year-old.

(8) Where the consent of the suspect to a procedure is required, the consent of a mentally disordered or mentally vulnerable suspect is only valid if given in the presence of the appropriate adult; and in the case of a juvenile (but not a 17-year-old) his parent or guardian must consent in addition to the juvenile himself (unless he is under 14, in which case his parent or guardian's consent suffices in its own right).

(9) Where a person is blind or seriously visually impaired or unable to read, the custody officer or identification officer must ensure that his solicitor, a relative, the appropriate adult or some other person likely to take an interest in him (and not involved in the investigation) is available to help in checking any documentation.

Where Code D requires written consent or signification, the person assisting may be asked to sign if the detained person so wishes.

(10) If any information concerning the processes of an identification must be given to or sought from a suspect, it must be given or sought in the presence of the appropriate adult if the suspect is mentally disordered or mentally vulnerable, or a juvenile or 17-year-old. If the appropriate adult is not present when the information is first given or sought, the procedure must be repeated in his presence when he arrives. If the suspect is deaf or there is doubt about his hearing ability or his ability to understand, the information must be given through an interpreter.

(11) Any procedure in Code D involving the participation of a witness who is or appears to be mentally disordered, otherwise mentally vulnerable, a juvenile or a 17-year-old should take place in the presence of a pre-trial support person unless the witness states that he does not want a support person to be present. A support person must not be allowed to prompt any identification of a suspect by a witness. The support person should not be (or not be likely to be) a witness in the investigation.

The terms 'appropriate adult' and 'solicitor' where they appear above have the same meaning as in Code C (see pp 97–8 and 108).

Persons other than police officers, who are police staff but not 'designated persons', may be allowed to carry out procedures or tasks at the police station if the law allows. Such persons must be employees under the control of the chief officer of police or employed by a person contracted to provide services relating to persons arrested or otherwise in custody. The custody officer or the officer given custody must ensure that Code D is complied with.

IDENTIFICATION AND RECOGNITION OF SUSPECTS

In Code D, the material under this heading is divided into two parts:

(a) Part A: Identification of a suspect by an eye-witness;
(b) Part B: Evidence of recognition by showing films, photographs and other images.

Part A: identification of a suspect by an eye-witness

Part A applies when an eye-witness has seen someone committing the crime or has seen someone in any other circumstances which tend to prove or disprove his involvement in the crime—for example, close to the scene of the crime, immediately before or immediately after it was committed. Part A sets out the procedures to be used to test the ability of that eye-witness to identify a person suspected of involvement in the offence as the person whom he saw on the previous occasion.

(Code D states that, while it concentrates on visual identification procedures, it does not preclude the police making use of aural identification procedures, such as a 'voice identification parade', where they judge that appropriate.)

A guidance note to Code D points out that the eye-witness identification procedures in Part A should not be used to test whether a witness can recognise a person as someone he knows and would be able to give evidence of recognition along the lines that 'On (describe date, time, location) I saw an image of an individual who I recognised as AB'. In these cases, the procedures in Part B apply. Except where stated, the provisions of Part A do not apply to the procedures described in Part B and the guidance note.

A record of the description of the suspect (S) as first given by a potential witness must be made and kept in a form which enables details of that description to be accurately produced from it, in a visible and legible form, which can be given to S or to his solicitor in accordance with Code D. Unless otherwise specified, the record must be made before the witness takes part in any identification procedures. A copy must be provided to S or his solicitor before any procedures under the Code are carried out.

Methods where the suspect is known and available

Where the identity of S is known to the police and he is available, the methods of visual identification which may be used are:

(1) *Video identification* (where the witness is shown video images of a known suspect, together with similar images of other people who resemble him: see p 191). Moving images must be used unless S has unusual features and the identification officer does not consider that replication of a physical feature can be achieved or that it is possible to conceal the location of the feature on the image of S. The identification officer may then decide to make use of video identification but using still images.

(2) *Identification parade* (where the witness sees S in a line of other people who resemble S: see p 193).

(3) *Group identification* (where the witness sees S in an informal group of people: see p 195).

(4) *Confrontation by a witness* (where S is directly confronted by the witness: see p 198).

A suspect is 'known' if there is sufficient information known to the police to justify the arrest of a particular person (the 'suspect') for suspected involvement in the offence. A suspect is 'available' if he is immediately available to take part in the procedure or will become available in a reasonably short time and is willing to take an effective part in at least one of the identification procedures.

The arrangements for, and conduct of, the four methods of identification are the responsibility of an officer *not below the rank of inspector* who must *not be involved in the investigation;* he is called the 'identification officer' (IO). Unless otherwise specified, the IO may allow another officer or a member of police staff to make arrangements for, and to conduct any of, these identification procedures. The IO must supervise such persons effectively.

No officer or any other person involved with the investigation may take any part in these procedures beyond the extent required by the procedures, or act as the IO. There will be a breach of this prohibition, not only if an officer investigating an offence participates in the actual identification process, but also if he takes the witness to the police station at which an identification is to be attempted. This does not prevent an IO from consulting the officer in charge of an investigation to determine which procedure to use.

Circumstances in which an identification procedure must be held

Whenever:

(a) a witness has identified a suspect or purported to have identified him prior to any identification procedure having been held; or

(b) there is a witness available, who expresses an ability to identify S, or where there is a reasonable chance of the witness being able to do so, and he has not been given an opportunity to identify S in any procedure,

and S disputes being the person the witness claims to have seen, an identification procedure must be held unless it is impracticable or would serve no useful purpose in proving or disproving whether the S was involved in committing the offence, as where S admits being at the scene of the crime and gives an account of what took place and the eye-witness does not see anything which contradicts that, or where it is not disputed that S is already known to the witness who claims to have recognised S when seeing him commit the crime.

An identification procedure may also be held if the officer in charge of an investigation considers it would be useful.

Identification procedures must be held as soon as practicable.

Selecting an identification procedure

If an identification procedure is to be held, S must initially be offered by the officer in charge a video identification, unless:

(a) this is impracticable, or
(b) an identification parade is practicable and more suitable, or
(c) a group identification is practicable and more suitable than the other two methods.

The IO and the officer in charge of the investigation must discuss which option is to be offered. An identification parade may not be practicable because of factors such as the number of witnesses, their state of health, availability and travelling requirements. A video identification would normally be more suitable if, in a particular case, it could be arranged and completed sooner than an identification parade. Before an option is offered S must also be reminded of his entitlement to have free legal advice.

Where S refuses the offer of one of these procedures he must state his reason and may obtain advice from his solicitor and appropriate adult if present. All such persons must be allowed to make representations as to why another identification procedure should be used. These matters must be recorded. After consideration of such reasons and representations the IO must, if appropriate, arrange for an alternative which he considers to be suitable and practicable to be offered to S. If he decides that it is not suitable and practicable to offer an alternative, his reasons must be recorded.

Notice to suspect

Before a video identification, an identification parade or a group identification is arranged, the following must be explained to S:

(a) the purpose of the video identification, identification parade or group identification;
(b) S's entitlement to free legal advice;
(c) the procedures for holding it (including S's right to have a solicitor or friend present);
(d) that S does not have to take part in a video identification, identification parade or group identification;
(e) that, if S does not consent to and take part in a video identification, identification parade or group identification, his refusal may be given in evidence in any subsequent trial and police may proceed covertly without his consent or make other arrangements to test whether a witness can identify him;

(f) whether, for the purpose of the video identification procedure, images of S have previously been obtained and, if so, that S may co-operate in providing further suitable images to be used instead;

(g) where appropriate, the special arrangements for juveniles, 17-year-olds, or mentally disordered or mentally vulnerable persons;

(h) that should S significantly alter his appearance between being offered an identification procedure and any attempt to hold it, this may be given in evidence and the IO may then consider other forms of identification;

(i) that a moving image or photograph may be taken of S when he attends for any identification procedure;

(j) whether the witness has been shown photographs, a computerised or artist's composite likeness or similar likeness or picture by the police;

(k) that if S changes his appearance before an identification parade it may not be practicable to arrange one on the day in question or subsequently and, because of his changed appearance, the IO may consider alternative methods of identification; and

(l) that S or his solicitor will be provided with details of the description of S as first given by any witnesses who are to attend the video identification, identification parade, group identification or confrontation.

S must also be given a written 'Notice to Suspect' containing this information and a reasonable opportunity to read it. S must then be asked to sign a second copy of the notice to indicate if he is willing to participate in the making of a video or an identification parade or group identification. The IO must retain the signed copy.

The above duties of an IO may be performed by the custody officer or any other officer not involved in the investigation if:

(a) it is proposed to release S in order that an identification procedure can be arranged and carried out (as where S is bailed to attend an identification parade) and an inspector is not available to act as IO before S leaves the station, or

(b) it is proposed to keep S in police detention while the procedure is arranged or carried out, and waiting for an inspector to act as IO would cause unreasonable delay.

Where the IO and the officer in charge of the investigation have reasonable grounds to suspect that, if given the above information and Notice, S would take steps to avoid being seen by a witness in any identification procedure, the IO may arrange for images of S for use in a video identification procedure to be obtained before giving the information and Notice. If this is done, S may co-operate in providing new images to be used instead, if suitable.

A witness must not be shown photographs, or photofit, identikit or similar pictures if the identity of S is known to the police and S is available to take part in a video identification, an identification parade or a group identification.

Where the suspect is known but not available

Where a known suspect is not available or has ceased to be available, the IO may make arrangements for a video identification in accordance with Code D. If necessary, the IO may follow the video identification procedures but using *still* images. Any suitable moving or still images may be used and these may be obtained covertly if necessary; covert activity must be limited to that which is necessary. Alternatively, the IO may make arrangements for a group identification. He may arrange a confrontation where no other option is available. The requirements for the giving of information to, and seeking it from, S, or for S to have the opportunity to view the images before they are shown to a witness, do not apply if S's lack of co-operation prevents the necessary action.

These provisions would apply where a known suspect deliberately makes himself unavailable in order to delay or frustrate arrangements being made for obtaining evidence. They enable any suitable images of S (moving or still) which are available (eg from custody and other CCTV systems) or can be obtained to be used in a video identification.

Where the identity of the suspect is not known

In such cases, a witness may be taken to a neighbourhood or place to see whether he can identify the person whom he saw on the relevant occasion. Although there can be no control over the general mix of people, their age, sex, race and general description or manner of dress, the principles governing the formal identification procedures must be followed so far as practicable. For example:

(1) Where practicable, a record should be made of any description of S given by the witness, before he is asked to make an identification.

(2) The witness's attention should not be directed towards any individual unless this is unavoidable. This does not prevent a witness being told to look carefully at people who are around, or to look towards a group or in a particular direction if this appears necessary to ensure that the witness does not overlook a possible suspect simply because the witness is looking in the opposite direction and also to enable him to make comparisons between any suspect and others in the area.

(3) Where there is more than one witness, every effort should be made to keep them separate and witnesses should be taken to see whether they can identify a person independently.

(4) Once there is sufficient information to justify the arrest of a particular individual, for example after a witness makes a positive identification, the formal identification procedures must be adopted for any other witnesses in relation to that individual.

(5) The officer or police staff accompanying the witness must record in his pocket book the action taken as soon as practicable and in as much detail as possible. That record should include the date, time and place of the previous occasion when the witness claims to have seen S; where any identification was made; how it was made and the conditions at the time (eg, the distance which the witness was from S, the weather and light); if the witness's attention was drawn to S; the reason for this; and anything said by the witness or S about the identification or the conduct of the procedure.

If the identity of a suspect is not known, the showing of photographs, or photofit, identikit or similar pictures must be in accordance with Annex E to Code D (see p 199).

Documentation

A record must be made of any video identification, identification parade, group identification or confrontation. Where an IO considers that it is impracticable to hold a video identification or identification parade requested by S, the reasons must be recorded and explained to S. So must a victim's failure or refusal to co-operate in a video identification, identification parade or group identification. If applicable, the grounds for obtaining images must be recorded. Any records relating to these procedures must be made on the forms provided.

Execution: video identification

The following rules are laid down by Annex A to Code D as to how video identification should be carried out.

General

The arrangements for obtaining and ensuring the availability of a suitable set of images to be used in a video identification must be the responsibility of an IO who has no direct involvement with the case.

The set of images must include S and at least eight other people who, so far as possible, resemble S in age, general appearance, and position in life. Only one suspect may appear on any set unless there are two suspects of roughly similar appearance, in which case they may be shown together with at least 12 other people.

If S has an unusual physical feature, for example a facial scar, tattoo or distinctive hairstyle or hair colour which does not appear on the images of the other people available to be used, steps may be taken, electronically or otherwise, to:

(a) conceal the location of the feature on the images of S and the other people; or
(b) replicate that feature on the images of the other people.

The IO has discretion to choose whether to conceal or replicate the feature and the method to be used. If an unusual physical feature has been described by the witness, the IO should, if practicable, have that feature replicated. If it has not been described, concealment may be more appropriate.

If a feature is concealed or replicated, the reason and whether the feature was concealed or replicated must be recorded.

If the witness requests to view an image where an unusual physical feature has been concealed or replicated without that feature being concealed or replicated, the witness may be allowed to do so.

The images used to conduct a video identification must, so far as possible, show S and other people in the same positions or carrying out the same sequence of movements. They must also show S and other people under identical conditions unless the IO reasonably believes:

(a) that because of S's failure or refusal to co-operate or other reasons, this is not practicable; or
(b) that any difference in the conditions would not direct a witness's attention to any individual image.

The reason why identical conditions were not practicable must be recorded.

Provision must be made for each person filmed to be identified by number. If police officers are filmed, any numerals or other identifying badges must be concealed. If a prison inmate is filmed, either as a suspect or not, either all or none of the persons filmed should be in prison clothing.

S or his solicitor, friend, or appropriate adult must be given a reasonable opportunity to see the complete set of images before it is shown to any witness. If S has a reasonable objection to the set of images or any of its participants, he must be asked to state his reason. If practicable, steps must be taken to remove the grounds for objection. If this is not practicable, S and/or his representative must be told why his objections cannot be met. The objection, the reason given for it and why it cannot be met must be recorded.

Before the images are shown, S or his solicitor must be provided with the details of the first description of S by any witnesses who are to attend the video identification. S or his solicitor must also be allowed to view any material released to the media by the police for the purpose of recognising or tracing S, provided this is practicable and would not unreasonably delay the investigation.

Where practicable, S's solicitor must be given reasonable notification of the time and place that it is intended to conduct the video identification in order that a legal representative may attend. S may not be present when the film is shown to a witness. In the absence of a person representing S the viewing itself must be recorded on video. No unauthorised person may be present.

Conduct of video identification

The IO must ensure that, before they see the set of images, witnesses cannot communicate with each other about the case, see any of the images, see, or be reminded of, any photograph or description of S or be given any other indication as to S's identity, or overhear a witness who has seen the material. There must be no discussion with the witness about the composition of the set of images and the witness must not be told whether a previous witness has made any identification.

Only one witness may see the set of images at a time. Immediately before the images are seen, the witness must be told that the person he saw might or might not appear in the images he is shown and that if he cannot make a positive identification he should say so. The witness must be advised that at any point he may ask to see a particular part of the set of images or to have a particular image frozen for him to study. Furthermore, it should be pointed out to the witness that there is no limit on how many times he can view the whole set of images or any part of them. However, he should be asked to refrain from making any decision until he has seen the entire set at least twice.

Once the witness has seen the whole set of images at least twice and has indicated that he does not want to view the images or any part of them again, the witness must be asked to say whether the individual he saw in person on an earlier occasion has been shown and, if so, to identify him by number. The witness will then be shown that image to confirm the identification.

Care must be taken not to direct the witness's attention to any one individual image, or to give any other indication of S's identity. Where a witness has previously made an identification by photographs, or a photofit, identikit or similar picture, the witness must not be reminded of such a photograph or picture once a suspect is available for identification by other means in accordance with Code D. Neither must the witness be reminded of any description of S.

Each witness must be asked after the procedure whether he has seen any broadcast or published films or photographs or any description of suspects relating to the offence; his reply must be recorded.

Image security and destruction

The IO must ensure that all relevant material containing sets of images used for a specific identification procedure is kept securely and its movement accounted for. In particular, no one involved in the investigation against S may be permitted to view the material prior to its being shown to any witness.

Like any other photograph taken in accordance with PACE, s 64A (p 225), where a video film has been made all copies of it must be destroyed with the exceptions set out on p 226. An opportunity of witnessing the destruction must be given to S, if he so requests within five days of being cleared or informed that he will not be prosecuted.

Documentation

A record must be made of all those participating in or seeing the set of images whose names are known to the police.

A record of the conduct of the video identification must be made on the forms provided. This must include anything said by the witness about the identification or the conduct of the procedure and any reasons why it was not practicable to comply with any provisions of Code D governing the conduct of a video identification.

Identification parades

Identification parades must be carried out in accordance with Annex B to Code D, which provides as follows.

A suspect must be given a reasonable opportunity to have a solicitor or friend present, and he must be asked to indicate his wishes in this respect on a second copy of the 'Notice to Suspect'. A parade may take place in a normal room or in one equipped with a screen permitting witnesses to see members of the parade without being seen.

Before the parade takes place S or his solicitor must be provided with the details of the first description of S by any witnesses who are to attend. S or his solicitor should be allowed to view any material released to the media by the police for the purpose of recognising or tracing S, provided it is practicable to do so and would not unreasonably delay the investigation.

Cases involving prison inmates

If a prison inmate is required for identification, and there are no security problems about his leaving the establishment, he may be asked to participate in an identification parade or video identification.

A parade may be conducted in a Prison Department establishment. If it is, it must be conducted as far as practicable under normal parade rules. Members of the public must make up the parade unless there are serious security or control objections to their admission to the establishment. In such cases, or if a video or group identification is arranged within the establishment, other inmates may participate.

If S is an inmate he should not be required to wear prison clothing for the parade unless the other persons taking part are other inmates in prison clothing or are members of the public who are prepared to wear prison clothing for the occasion.

Conduct of an identification parade

Immediately before the parade, S must be reminded of the procedure governing its conduct and given the appropriate caution (pp 113 and 115). All unauthorised persons must be excluded from the place where the parade is held.

Once the parade has been formed, everything afterwards in respect of it must take place in the presence and hearing of S and of any interpreter, solicitor, friend or appropriate adult who is present (unless the parade involves a screen, in which case everything said to or by any witness must be said in the hearing and presence of S's solicitor, friend, or appropriate adult or be video recorded). No investigating officer should enter the room where the parade is being held.

The parade must consist of at least eight persons (other than S) who, so far as possible, resemble S in age, height, general appearance, and position in life. Where a suspect has an unusual physical feature, for example a facial scar or tattoo or distinctive hairstyle or hair colour, which cannot be replicated on other members of the identification parade, steps may be taken to conceal the location of that feature on S and other members of the parade if S and his solicitor or appropriate adult agree. A plaster or a hat may achieve such an objective. It is also permissible to take reasonable steps in good faith to make non-suspects resemble S by the use of make-up, provided there is no objection.

One suspect only may be included in a parade unless there are two suspects of roughly similar appearance, in which case they may be paraded together with at least 12 other persons. In no circumstances may more than two suspects be included in one parade, and where there are separate parades they must be made up of different persons.

Where all members of a similar group are possible suspects, separate identification parades must be held for each member of the group unless there are two suspects of similar appearance. Where police officers in uniform form an identification parade, numerals or other identifying badges must be concealed.

When S arrives, he must be asked whether he has any objection to the arrangements for the parade or to any of the other participants in it and to state reasons for any objection made. S may obtain advice from his solicitor or friend, if present, before the parade proceeds. If he has a reasonable objection to the arrangements or to any of the participants, steps must, where practicable, be taken to remove the grounds for objection. Where this is impracticable, the officer must explain to S why his objection cannot be met and the objection, the reason for it and why it cannot be met must be recorded on the forms provided.

S may select his own position in the line. Where there is more than one witness, the IO must tell S, after each witness has left the room, that he can if he wishes change position. Each position must be clearly numbered, whether by means of a numeral laid on the floor in front of each parade member or by other means.

Appropriate arrangements must be made to ensure, before they attend the parade, that witnesses are not able to:

(a) communicate with each other or overhear a witness who has already seen the parade;
(b) see any member of the parade;
(c) see, or be reminded of, any photograph or description of S, nor given any other indication of his identity; or
(d) see S, either before or after the parade.

The person conducting a witness to the parade must not discuss with him its composition; in particular, he must not disclose whether a previous witness has made any identification.

Witnesses must be brought in one at a time. Immediately before a witness inspects the parade, he must be told that the person he saw might or might not be on the parade and that if he cannot make a positive identification he should say so. The witness must also be told that he should not make any decision before looking at each member of the parade at least twice. When the officer or police staff member conducting the procedure is satisfied that the witness has properly looked at each member of the parade, he must ask him whether the person he saw in person on an earlier relevant occasion is on the parade and, if so, to indicate the number of the person concerned. Where this takes place behind a screen it is desirable for the witness to be asked to make a note of the number of the person identified so that he may give direct evidence of that fact. However, if a witness is unable to recall that number at a subsequent trial, evidence from the person who conducted the parade as to the number indicated by the witness is admissible as there is statutory authority for its admission. If the witness makes an identification after the parade has ended, S and, if present, his solicitor, interpreter, or friend must be informed. Where this occurs, consideration should be given to allowing the witness a second opportunity to identify S.

If a witness wishes to hear any parade member speak, or to see him adopt any specified posture or move, the witness must first be asked whether he can identify any persons on the parade on the basis of appearance only. When the request is to hear members of the parade speak, the witness must be reminded that the participants in the parade have been chosen on the basis of physical appearance only. Members of the parade may then be asked to comply with the witness's request to hear them speak or to see them move or adopt any specified posture.

If the witness requests that the person indicated by him remove anything used to conceal the location of an unusual physical feature, that person may be asked to remove it.

Each witness must be asked after the parade whether he has seen any broadcast or published films or photographs or any description of suspects relating to the offence; his reply must be recorded.

When the last witness has left, S must be asked whether he wishes to make any comments on the conduct of the parade.

Documentation

A video recording of the parade must normally be taken. Where this is impracticable, a colour photograph must be taken. A copy of the video or photograph must be supplied, on request, to S or his solicitor within a reasonable time. The rules about the destruction and retention of such a video or photograph are the same as those described on pp 225–6.

If any person is asked to leave the parade because he is interfering with its conduct, the circumstances must be recorded. A record must be made of all those present at an identification parade whose names are known to the police. A record of the conduct of the parade must be made on the forms provided, including anything said by the witness or S about any identifications or the conduct of the procedure, and any reasons why it was not practicable to comply with any provision of Code D.

Group identification

Group identification must be carried out in accordance with Annex C to Code D, which provides as follows.

General

A group identification may take place either with S's consent and co-operation or covertly without his consent.

The location is a matter for the IO, although he may take into account representations made by a suspect, or his appropriate adult, solicitor or friend. It should be somewhere where other people are passing by, or waiting around informally, in groups so that S is able to join them and is capable of being seen at the same time as others in the group, for example where people are leaving an escalator, walking through a shopping centre, or in queues. Where group identification is carried out covertly, its location depends on where S can be found (along with a number of other people). A suitable location might be a route regularly travelled by S, including buses, trains and public places frequented by him.

In selecting the location, the IO must consider the general appearance and number of persons likely to be present. In particular, he must reasonably expect that persons broadly similar to S will appear from time to time during the period of the witness's observation. A group identification need not be held where the IO believes that, because of S's unusual appearance, none of the practicable locations is likely to make the identification fair.

Immediately after a group identification (whether with or without S's consent) a colour photograph or a video should be taken of the scene, where practicable, so as to give a general impression of the scene and the number of people present. Alternatively, if practicable, the group identification may be video recorded. If such a photograph or video is impracticable, then a photograph or film of the scene may be made later when practicable.

If, at the time of the identification, S is on his own rather than in a group, it remains a group identification.

Before the group identification takes place S or his solicitor must be provided with details of the first description of S by any witness attending it, and should be allowed to view any material released to the media for the purpose of recognising or tracing S, provided that it is practicable to do so and it will not unreasonably delay the investigation. After the procedure each witness must be asked whether he has seen any broadcast or published films or photographs or any descriptions of suspects relating to the offence; his reply must be recorded.

Group identification with the consent of the suspect

S must be given a reasonable opportunity to have a solicitor or friend present. He must be asked to indicate his wishes on a second copy of the Notice to Suspect. The witness, person carrying out the procedure, S's solicitor, appropriate adult, friend, and any interpreter for the witness may be concealed from the sight of the persons in the group if this facilitates the identification. The person conducting a witness to the location must not discuss the forthcoming group identification nor disclose whether a previous witness has made an identification.

Anything said to or by a witness during the procedure regarding the identification must be said in the presence and hearing of those at the procedure. Witnesses who have not yet attended the identification must not be able: (a) to communicate with each other about the case or overhear a witness who has already been given an opportunity to see S in the group; (b) to see S; or (c) to see or be reminded of any photograph or description of S or to be given any other indication of his identity. Witnesses must be brought to the place singly and must be told that the person they saw might or might not be in the group and that if they cannot make a positive identification they should say so. The witness must then be asked to observe the group; the manner of doing so will depend upon whether the group is stationary or moving.

Moving group   When the group in which S is to appear is moving, for example leaving an escalator, the following provisions apply.

If two or more suspects consent to a group identification, they should each be subject to different identification procedures, which may be conducted consecutively. The person conducting the procedure must ask the witness to observe the group and ask him to point out anyone he thinks he saw on the earlier occasion. S should then be allowed to take up whatever position in the group he prefers. When an identification is made, the witness must, where practicable, be asked to take a closer look to confirm identification. If this is impracticable, or the witness is unable to confirm the identification, the witness must be asked how sure he is that the person is the relevant person. The duration of the identification process must be such as the person conducting the procedure reasonably believes necessary for the witness to be able to make comparisons between S and other individuals of broadly similar appearance.

Stationary group   When the group in which S is to appear is stationary, for example people in a queue, the following provisions apply.

If two or more suspects consent to a group identification, there should generally be two separate procedures. However, if they are of broadly similar appearance, they may appear in the same group. Separate stationary group identifications must consist of different people.

S may select his position. Where there is more than one witness, S must be told, out of sight and hearing of any witness, that he may change his position. The witness must be asked to pass along or amongst the group and to look at each person at least twice before making an identification. Once the witness has done so, he must be asked if the person he saw previously is in the group and to indicate that person by any means considered appropriate by the person conducting the identification. If this is not practicable, the witness will be asked to point out that person. He must, where practicable, be asked to take a closer look and confirm his identification. If this is impracticable, he must be asked how sure he is that the person is the one seen on the earlier occasion.

Rules common to moving and stationary groups   An unreasonable delay by S in joining the group, or (having joined the group) his deliberate self-concealment from the sight of the witness, may be considered as a refusal to co-operate in the identification.

Where a witness identifies someone other than S, that person should be asked if he is prepared to give his name and address. He is not obliged to do so. There is no duty to record persons present in the group or at the place where the procedure is conducted.

At the end of the procedure S must be asked to comment on the conduct of the procedure. Unless previously informed, S must be told of any identifications made by witnesses.

Group identifications without suspect's consent

These should, so far as possible, follow the rules set out above. As such an identification will take place without S's knowledge, no solicitor, etc will be present. Any number of suspects may be identified at the same time.

Group identifications in police stations

These must only take place for reasons of security or safety, or because it is impracticable to hold them elsewhere. The group identification may be in a room equipped with a one-way screen, or elsewhere in a police station. Safeguards applicable to identification parades must be followed where practicable.

Group identifications involving prison inmates

These may only take place in a prison or police station. They must follow the procedure which is applicable to group identifications in a police station. Where a group identification takes place in a prison, other inmates may participate. If S is in prison clothing, all persons taking part must be so dressed.

Documentation

Where a photograph or video is taken a copy must be supplied on request to S or his solicitor within a reasonable time. Such material must be destroyed in accordance with the rules described on p 226. A record of the conduct of the identification must be made on the forms provided, and must include anything said by the witness or suspect about any identification or the conduct of the procedure and any reason why it was impracticable to comply with any of the relevant provisions of the Code.

Confrontation by a witness

A confrontation does not require S's consent.

The rules concerning confrontation, which are set out in Annex D to Code D, are simple.

Before the confrontation takes place:

(a) the witness must be told that the person he saw might or might not be the person he is to confront and that if he cannot make a positive identification he should say so;

(b) S or his solicitor must be provided with the details of the first description of S given by any witness who is to attend the confrontation.

Where a broadcast or publication has been made for the purpose of recognition and tracing of suspects, S or his solicitor should also be allowed to view any material released by the police to the media, provided that it is practicable to do so and would not unreasonably delay the investigation.

Force cannot be used to make S's face visible to a witness.

S must be confronted independently by each witness, who must be asked 'Is this the person?' If the witness identifies the person but is unable to confirm the identification he must be asked how sure he is that the person is the person he saw on the earlier relevant occasion. Confrontation must take place in the presence of S's solicitor, interpreter, or friend, unless this would cause unreasonable delay.

The confrontation should normally take place in the police station, either in a normal room or one equipped with a screen permitting a witness to see S without being seen. In both cases, the procedures are the same, except that a room equipped with a screen may be used only when S's solicitor, friend or appropriate adult is present or the confrontation is recorded on video.

After the confrontation each witness must be asked whether he has seen any broadcast or published films or photographs or any descriptions of suspects relating to the offence; his reply must be recorded.

Informal identification

Informal evidence of identification may be admitted provided that the evidence was obtained in good faith and has no adverse effect on the fairness of the proceedings.

Where a suspect and a witness are well known to each other, there is less need for any formal out-of-court identification procedure to be used. However, where S asks for a parade, the procedure is governed by Code D and the failure to provide one may result in the exclusion of evidence, whether S and the witness were previously known to one another or not.

Part B: evidence of recognition by showing films, photographs, and other images

Part B of Code D's section on the identification and recognition of suspects applies when, *for the purposes of obtaining evidence of recognition,* any person, including a police officer, views the image of an individual in a film, photograph or other visual medium, and is asked whether he recognises that individual as someone he knows. Except as stated, these separate provisions are not subject to the eye-witness identification procedures described in Part A.

A guidance note states that the admissibility and value of evidence of recognition obtained when carrying out the procedures in Part B may be compromised if before the person is recognised, the witness who has claimed to know that person is given or is made, or becomes aware of, information about that person which was not previously known to him personally but which he has purported to rely on to support his claim that the person is in fact known to him.

Part B provides that the films, photographs and other images must be shown on an individual basis to avoid any possibility of collusion and, to provide safeguards against mistaken recognition, the showing must as far as possible follow the procedures for video identification *if S is known* (see p 191) or the procedure in Annex E for identification by photographs *if S is not known.*

Annex E provides as follows.

A sergeant (or above) must be responsible for supervising and directing the showing of photographs, but the actual showing may be done by a constable or police staff. The supervising officer must confirm that the first description of S given by the witness has been recorded before the witness is shown the photographs. If he is unable to confirm that the description has been recorded, he must postpone the showing.

Only one witness may be shown photographs at any one time. He must be given as much privacy as practicable and must not be allowed to communicate with any other witness in the case. Not less than 12 photographs must be shown at a time, which, as far as possible, must all be of a similar type.

When the witness is shown photographs, he must be told that the photograph of the person whom he has said that he has previously seen might or might not be among them and that if he cannot make a positive identification he should say so. The witness must be told not to make a decision until he has viewed at least 12 photographs. He must not be prompted or guided in any way but must be left to make any selection without help. If a witness makes a positive identification from photographs then, unless the person identified is otherwise eliminated from the inquiries or is not available, other witnesses must not be shown photographs. However, both they and the witness who has made the identification must be asked to attend a video identification, identification parade or group identification unless there is no dispute about the identification of S. If the witness makes a selection but is unable to confirm the identification the person showing the photographs must ask him how sure he is that the photograph indicated is the person that he saw on a previous occasion.

Where the use of a computerised or artist's composite likeness or similar likeness has led to there being a known suspect who can be asked to participate in a video identification, an identification parade, or a group identification, that likeness may not be shown to other potential witnesses.

When a witness attending a video identification, an identification parade or a group identification has previously been shown photographs or computerised or artist's composite likeness or similar likeness, S and his solicitor must be informed of this fact before the video identification, identification parade or group identification takes place. The officer in charge of the investigation is responsible for informing the IO of this fact.

None of the photographs used may be destroyed, whether or not an identification is made, since they may be required for production in court. The photographs should be numbered and a separate photograph taken of the frame or part of the album from which the witness made an identification as an aid to reconstituting it.

Documentation

Part B requires that a record of the circumstances and conditions under which the person is given an opportunity to recognise the individual must be made and that the record must include a record of:

(a) whether the person knew or was given information concerning the name or identity of any suspect;
(b) what the person has been told before the viewing about the offence, the person(s) depicted in the images, or the offender and by whom;
(c) how and by whom the witness was asked to view the image or look at the individual;
(d) whether the viewing was alone or with others, and if with others the reason for it;
(e) the arrangements under which the person viewed the film or saw the individual and by whom those arrangements were made;
(f) whether the viewing of any images was arranged as part of a mass circulation to police and the public or for selected persons;
(g) the date, time and place that images were viewed or further viewed or the individual was seen;
(h) the times between which the images were viewed or the individual was seen;
(i) how the viewing of images or sighting of the individual was controlled and by whom;
(j) whether the person was familiar with the location shown in any images or the place where he saw the individual and if so, why; and
(k) whether or not on this occasion, the person claims to recognise any image shown, or any individual seen, as being someone known to him, and if he does:
   (i)   the reason,
   (ii) the words of recognition,
   (iii) any expressions of doubt,
   (iv) what features of the image or the individual triggered the recognition.

The above record may be made by:

(a) the person who views the image or sees the individual and makes the recognition; or
(b) the officer or police staff in charge of showing the images to the person or in charge of the conditions under which the person sees the individual.

The Court of Appeal has recognised that such a formal procedure cannot be expected where recognition occurs in an informal context, but it stated that there should be something in the nature of an audit trail that will assist the assessment of its reliability.

Showing films and photographs of incidents and information released to the media

Films, photographs (including video recordings by security cameras) or other images may be shown to the public through the national or local media, or to police officers, for the purposes of recognition and tracing suspects. However, when such material is shown to obtain evidence of recognition, the procedures in Part B apply.

IDENTIFICATION BY FINGERPRINTS AND FOOTWEAR IMPRESSIONS

PACE, ss 61 and 61A and Code D deal with the taking of fingerprints (which term includes palmprints) and footwear impressions. These provisions do not apply in respect of someone arrested as a suspected terrorist under TA 2000, s 41 or someone subject to Terrorist Prevention and Investigation Measures; separate rules apply to such a person (see Chapter 28).

Fingerprints: consent

A person's fingerprints may be taken only with the appropriate consent (which must be in writing if given at a police station) or (in the circumstances set out below) without the appropriate consent. As to 'appropriate consent', see p 208.

Where fingerprints are taken at a police station with the appropriate consent, the person must be informed that they may be subject to a speculative search against other fingerprints. A record must be made of these matters and that the person has been so informed.

Taking fingerprints without consent

Powers to take fingerprints from a person over the age of 10 without the appropriate consent are provided by PACE, s 61. This provides that fingerprints may be taken without the appropriate consent from a person:

(1) If he is detained at a police station in consequence of his arrest for a recordable offence (see p 209) or because he has been charged with such an offence or informed that he will be reported for it, and he has not had his fingerprints taken in the course of the investigation of the offence by the police (s 61 (3) and (4)). *(By s 61(3A), where such a person has had his fingerprints taken in the course of the investigation by the police, this does not prevent a second set of prints from being taken if the first did not constitute a full set or are of unsatisfactory quality for their purpose.)*

(2) Where he has answered to bail to appear at a court or police station, if the court, or an inspector (or above), authorises them to be taken (s 61(4A)). This may be done where the court or officer reasonably believes that a person who has surrendered to bail is not the person admitted to bail and the person bailed has been previously fingerprinted, or the person who has answered to bail claims to be a different person from the person who had his fingerprints taken on a previous occasion.

(3) If he has been arrested for a recordable offence and released, and:
   (a) in the case of a person who is on bail, he has not had his fingerprints taken in the course of the investigation; or
   (b) in any case, he has had his fingerprints taken in the course of that investigation but (i) the first set did not constitute a full set or are of unsatisfactory quality for

their purpose, or (ii) s 61(5C) applies. Section 61(5C) applies where the investigation was discontinued but subsequently resumed, and before that resumption the fingerprints were destroyed pursuant to s 63D(3) (p 214) (s 61(5A)).

(4) If, not detained at a police station, he has been charged with a recordable offence or informed that he will be reported for such an offence and:

   (a) he has not had his fingerprints taken in the course of the investigation; or

   (b) he has had his fingerprints taken in the course of that investigation but (i) the first set did not constitute a full set or are of unsatisfactory quality for their purpose; or (ii) s 61(5C) applies (s 61(5B)).

(5) If he has been convicted of a recordable offence (or been found not guilty by reason of insanity or found under a disability but to have done the act charged) or he has been cautioned for an admitted recordable offence (s 61(6)). Fingerprints may only be taken under this provision (a) if the person has not had his fingerprints taken since he was convicted or cautioned, or (b) if he has had his fingerprints taken since then but s 61(3A) applies (s 61(6ZA)). Fingerprints may only be taken under s 61(6) with the authorisation of an inspector (or above), who may only give such an authorisation if satisfied that taking the fingerprints is necessary to assist in the prevention or detection of crime.

(6) If a constable reasonably suspects that the person is committing or attempting to commit an offence, or has committed or attempted to commit an offence, and the name of the person is unknown to, and cannot be readily ascertained by the constable, or the constable has reasonable grounds for doubting whether a name furnished by the person as his name is his real name (s 61(6A)). This provision will apply to taking fingerprints at a police station or any other place. Before the power under s 61(6A) is exercised, the constable should:

   (a) inform the person of the nature of the suspected offence and why he is suspected of committing it;

   (b) give him a reasonable opportunity to establish his real name before deciding that his name is unknown, etc or that there are reasonable grounds to doubt that a name which he has given is his real name;

   (c) as applicable, inform the person of the reason why his name is not known, etc or of the grounds for doubting that a name which he has given is his real name, including, for example, the reason why a particular document the person has produced to verify his real name, is not sufficient.

   The taking of fingerprints by virtue of s 61(6A) does not count for the purposes of PACE as taking them in the course of an investigation of an offence by the police. Fingerprints taken under this power will have to be destroyed as soon as the purpose for which they were taken has been achieved. They will not be retained or added to IDENT1 (the national automated fingerprint system). The reason for s 61(6A) is that the police may now use mobile digital fingerprint readers which are connected to IDENT1. This enables the taking of fingerprints (of two fingers) at a place other than a police station. These can immediately be checked to assist an officer in deciding upon a course of action.

(7) If:

   (a) the person has been 'convicted' of an offence under the law in force in a country territory outside England and Wales;

   (b) the act constituting the offence would constitute a qualifying offence if done in England and Wales (whether or not it constituted such an offence when the person was convicted); and

(c) either (i) the person has not had his fingerprints taken on a previous occasion under the present provision, or (ii) he has had his fingerprints so taken on a previous occasion but s 61(3A) applies (s 61(6D) and (6E)).

A 'conviction' for these purposes includes a finding equivalent to one of not guilty by reason of insanity or of disability but that the act charged was committed. Fingerprints may only be so taken with the authorisation of an inspector (or above), who must be satisfied that taking the fingerprints is necessary to assist in the prevention or detection of crime (s 61(6F) and (6G)).

A 'qualifying offence' means the common law offences of murder, manslaughter, false imprisonment, kidnapping, or indecent exposure, an offence of indecent exposure under the Vagrancy Act 1824, s 4 or Town Police Clauses Act 1847, s 28 (both offences now repealed), the Offences Against the Person Act 1861, ss 4, 16, 18, 20–24 or 47, the Explosive Substances Act 1883, ss 2 or 3, the Infant Life Preservation Act 1929, s 1, the Children and Young Persons Act 1933, s 1, the Infanticide Act 1938, s 1, the Sexual Offences Act 1956, s 12 or 13 (repealed) (unless other party 16 or over and consenting), any other section of the Sexual Offences Act 1956 (largely repealed) other than ss 18 and 32, the Mental Health Act 1959, s 128 (repealed), the Indecency with Children Act 1960, s 1 (repealed), the Sexual Offences Act 1967, s 5 (repealed), the Criminal Law Act 1967, s 4 (in relation to murder), the Firearms Act 1968, ss 16–18, the Theft Act 1968, ss 8, 10 or (where fatal accident involved) s 12A, the Genocide Act 1969, s 1(1) (repealed), the Criminal Damage Act 1971, s 1 (where required to be charged as arson), the Criminal Law Act 1977, s 54 (repealed), the Protection of Children Act 1978, s 1, the Aviation Security Act 1982, s 1, the Child Abduction Act 1984, s 2, the Prohibition of Female Circumcision Act 1985, s 1 (repealed), the Public Order Act 1986, s 1, the Aviation and Maritime Security Act 1990, s 9, the Sexual Offences (Amendment) Act 2000, s 3 (repealed), the International Criminal Court Act 2001, s 51, the Female Genital Mutilation Act 2003, ss 1–3, the Sexual Offences Act 2003, ss 1–19, 25, 26, 30–41, 47–50, 52, 53, 57–59A (repealed), 61–67, 69 and 70, the Domestic Violence, Crime and Victims Act 2004, s 5, or the Modern Slavery Act 2015, s 2, an offence listed under the Counter-Terrorism Act 2008 (C-TA 2008), s 41, aiding, abetting, counselling or procuring one of the above offences, attempting or conspiring to commit any of them, or an offence of encouraging or assisting crime in relation to any of them.

Any power under PACE, s 61 to take fingerprints without the appropriate consent must be exercised by a constable. Reasonable force may be used.

Before any fingerprints are taken without the appropriate consent under any power under PACE, s 61, the person must be informed of:

(a) the reason why his fingerprints are to be taken;
(b) the power under which they are to be taken;
(c) the fact that the relevant authority has been given where it is required;
(d) where the fingerprints are taken at a police station (or, in the case of (2) and (6), elsewhere), that his fingerprints may be the subject of a speculative search against other fingerprints; and
(e) that his fingerprints may be retained in accordance with the relevant provisions unless they were taken under the power in (6) when they must be destroyed after they have been checked.

A record must be made as soon as possible of these matters and of the fact that the person has been so informed. If a person is detained at a police station when the fingerprints are taken, the reason must be noted on his custody record. If force is used a record must be made of the circumstances and those present.

Taking footwear impressions

PACE, s 61A provides that, with the exceptions below, no impression of a person's footwear may be taken without the appropriate consent. Consent to the taking of an impression of a person's footwear must be in writing if it is given at a time when he is at a police station.

Where a person is detained at a police station, a footwear impression may be taken without appropriate consent from a person over the age of 10 if:

(a) he is detained in consequence of his arrest for a recordable offence (p 209), or has been charged with a recordable offence, or informed that he will be reported for a recordable offence, and

(b) he has not had an impression taken of his footwear in the course of the investigation of the offence by the police.

Reasonable force may be used. A record must be made as soon as possible of the reason for the non-consensual taking and, if force is used, of the circumstances and those present. If a person mentioned in (a) has already had an impression of his footwear taken in the course of the investigation of the offence, that fact must be disregarded if the impression taken previously is incomplete, or is not of sufficient quality to allow satisfactory analysis, comparison or matching (whether in the case in question or generally). An impression taken without the appropriate consent must be taken by a constable.

In all cases where a footwear impression is taken, the person must be informed that the impression may be retained and may be the subject of a speculative search, and this must be recorded as soon as practicable. If the person is at a police station, the fact must be recorded in the custody record.

IDENTIFICATION BY INTIMATE SAMPLES AND NON-INTIMATE SAMPLES

PACE, ss 62 and 63 contain the basic provisions in this area, but (within the terms of these sections) it is Code D which sets out the detailed procedures. The powers set out below do not apply in respect of a suspected terrorist arrested under TA 2000, s 41 or of someone subject to Terrorism Prevention and Investigation Measures; separate rules apply to such a person (see Chapter 28).

Intimate samples

An intimate sample means a sample of blood, semen, or any other tissue fluid, urine, or pubic hair, a dental impression, or a swab taken from any part of a person's genitals or from a person's body orifices other than the mouth. Intimate samples are governed by PACE, s 62.

An intimate sample may be taken from a person in police detention only with the appropriate consent (p 208) in writing and with the requisite authorisation (below) (s 62(1)).

An intimate sample may be taken from a person not in police detention if: (a) in the course of an investigation into an offence, two or more non-intimate samples have been taken which have proved unsuitable or insufficient for a particular form of analysis, (b) the requisite authorisation is given, and (c) the appropriate written consent is given (s 62(1A)).

In these two cases an intimate sample may only be taken if an inspector (or above) authorises it to be taken because he has reasonable grounds for suspecting the involvement of the person in a recordable offence (p 209) and for believing that the sample will tend to confirm or disprove this involvement.

An intimate sample may also be taken from a person with the appropriate written consent where:

(a) two or more non-intimate samples suitable for the same means of analysis have been taken from the person under s 63(3E) and (3F) (persons convicted of offence outside England and Wales, etc) but have proved insufficient; and

(b) an inspector (or above), who must be satisfied that taking the sample is necessary to assist in the prevention or detection of crime, authorises it to be taken (s 62(2A)).

Before an intimate sample is taken from a person:

(1) He must be informed:
   (a) of the reason;
   (b) that authorisation has been given and the provisions under which it has been given; and
   (c) that a sample taken at a police station may be the subject of a speculative search.

   The reason referred to in (a) must include, except in a case where the sample is taken under s 62(2A), a statement of the nature of the offence in which it is suspected that the person has been involved. After an intimate sample has been taken from a person, the following must be recorded as soon as practicable: the matters referred to in (a) and (b); if the sample was taken at a police station, the fact that the person has been informed as specified in (c); and the fact that the appropriate consent was given.

(2) He must be warned that a refusal without good cause may harm his case in any proceedings against him. The Code suggests the use of the following words:

   'You do not have to provide this sample/allow this swab or impression to be taken, but I must warn you that if you refuse without good cause, your refusal may harm your case if it comes to trial.'

   The warning must be recorded.

(3) He must be reminded of his entitlement to free legal advice. The giving of this reminder must be recorded in the custody record if the person is in police custody.

In any proceedings for an offence, a court may draw such inferences as appear proper from a refusal, without good cause, to consent to the taking of an intimate sample.

An intimate sample, other than a sample of urine, may only be taken from a person by a registered medical practitioner or a registered nurse or registered paramedic. A dental impression may only be taken by a registered dentist.

Non-intimate samples

There are separate provisions, contained in PACE, s 63, for the taking of a *non-intimate sample*.

A non-intimate sample means hair, other than pubic hair, which includes hair plucked by the root; a sample taken from a nail or under a nail; a swab taken from any part of the body other than a part from which a swab taken would be an intimate sample; saliva; or a 'skin impression' which means any record, other than a fingerprint, which is a record, in any form and produced by any method, of the skin pattern and any other physical characteristics or features of the whole, or any part of, a person's foot or any other part of the body.

Where hair samples are taken for the purpose of DNA analysis (rather than for other purposes such as making a visual match) the suspect (S) should be permitted a reasonable choice as to where the hairs are to be taken from. When hairs are plucked they should be plucked individually unless S prefers otherwise; no more should be plucked than the plucker reasonably considers necessary for a sufficient sample.

Except in the following cases, a non-intimate sample may be taken from a suspect only with the appropriate consent (p 208) in writing. The exceptional cases are:

(1) A non-intimate sample may be taken from a person without the appropriate consent if:

    (a) he is in detention as a result of an arrest for a recordable offence (p 209), and he has not had a non-intimate sample of the same type and from the same part of the body taken in the course of the investigation of the offence by the police, or he has had such a sample taken but it proved insufficient (s 63(2A)–(2C)); or

    (b) he is being held in custody by the police on the authority of a court, and an inspector (or above) has authorised it to be taken without consent (s 63(3)). Such authorisation may only be given where that officer has reasonable grounds to suspect that the offence in question is a recordable offence and that the sample will tend to confirm or disprove S's involvement in it. An authorisation must not be given if the non-intimate sample concerned consists of a skin impression and such an impression has already been taken in the course of the investigation of the offence and that impression did not prove to be insufficient. Where such authorisation is given, S must be informed, before it is taken, of the grounds on which it has been given, including the nature of the suspected offence. He must also be told that any sample taken may be the subject of a speculative search.

(2) A non-intimate sample may be taken from a person without the appropriate consent if he has been arrested for a recordable offence and released and:

    (a) in the case of a person who is on bail, he has not had a non-intimate sample of the same type and from the same part of the body taken from him in the course of the investigation of the offence by the police; or

    (b) in any case, he has had a non-intimate sample taken from him in the course of that investigation but (i) it was not suitable for the same means of analysis, or (ii) it proved insufficient in quantity or quality for a particular form of analysis, or (iii) s 63(3AA) applies (s 63(3ZA)). Section 63(3AA) applies where the investigation was discontinued but subsequently resumed, and before that resumption any DNA profile derived from the sample was destroyed pursuant to s 63D(3) (p 214) and the sample itself was destroyed pursuant to s 63R(4), (5) or (12) (pp 219 and 220).

(3) A non-intimate sample may be taken without the appropriate consent from any person (whether or not he is in police detention or held in custody by the police on the authority of a court) if:

(a) he has been charged with a recordable offence or informed that he will be reported for such an offence; and

(b)   (i) he has not had a non-intimate sample taken from him in the course of the investigation; or

(ii) he has had a non-intimate sample taken from him, but it proved unsuitable or insufficient, or s 63(3AA) applies; or

(iii) he has had a non-intimate sample taken from him in the course of the investigation and the sample has been destroyed pursuant to s 63R (p 219) or any other enactment, and it is disputed, in relation to any proceedings relating to the offence, whether a DNA profile (ie information derived from a DNA sample) relevant to the proceedings is derived from the sample (s 63(3A)). A 'DNA sample' means any material that has come from a human body and consists of or includes human cells.

(4) A non-intimate sample may be taken from a person without the appropriate consent if:

(a) he has been convicted (see below) of a recordable offence, or he has been given a caution in respect of an admitted recordable offence, and

(b) either of the conditions mentioned in s 63(3BA) is met (s 63(3B)), viz:

(i) a non-intimate sample has not been taken from him since the conviction or caution; or

(ii) such a sample has been taken from him since then but it was not suitable for the same means of analysis, or it proved insufficient.

A non-intimate sample may only be so taken with the authorisation of an inspector (or above), who must be satisfied that taking the sample is necessary to assist in the prevention or detection of crime.

(5) A non-intimate sample may be taken without appropriate consent from a person detained following acquittal on the grounds of insanity or a finding of unfitness to plead (s 63(3C)).

(6) A non-intimate sample may be taken without the appropriate consent from a person if:

(a) under the law in force in a country or territory outside England and Wales the person has been convicted of an offence under that law;

(b) the act constituting the offence would constitute a qualifying offence (see p 203) if done in England and Wales (whether or not it constituted such an offence when the person was convicted); and

(c) either:

(i) the person has not had a non-intimate sample taken from him on a previous occasion under the present provision, or

(ii) he has had such a sample taken from him on a previous occasion under it but the sample was not suitable for the same means of analysis, or it proved insufficient (s 63(3E), (3F)).

A non-intimate sample may only be so taken with the authorisation of an inspector (or above), who must be satisfied that taking the sample is necessary to assist in the prevention or detection of crime.

A 'conviction' for these purposes includes a finding equivalent to one of not guilty by reason of insanity or of disability but that the act charged was committed.

Reasonable force may be used to take a non-intimate sample without S's consent under the above provisions.

Before any non-intimate sample is taken without the appropriate consent, the person must be informed of:

(a) the reason for taking it;
(b) the power under which it is taken;
(c) the fact that the relevant authorisation (where required) has been given.

The 'reason' for taking the sample must include a statement of the nature of the suspected offence, except in cases under s 63(3B), (3E), or (3F).

Before a non-intimate sample is taken with or without consent at a police station, the person must be warned:

(i)   that his sample or information derived from it may be the subject of a speculative search against other samples and information derived from them; and
(ii) that his sample and the information derived from it may be retained in accordance with the relevant provisions.

A record must be made as soon as practicable of the matters in (a) to (c) and that the person was informed of them and given the two warnings. If force is used a record must be made of the circumstances and those present.

General

Where clothing needs to be removed in circumstances likely to cause embarrassment, no person of the opposite sex (see p 36) who is not a medical practitioner or registered healthcare professional may be present (unless, in the case of a juvenile, 17-year-old, or mentally disordered or mentally handicapped person, that person specifically requests the presence of a particular adult of the opposite sex who is readily available), nor shall anyone whose presence is unnecessary. However, in the case of a juvenile or 17-year-old this is subject to the overriding proviso that such a removal of clothing may take place in the absence of the appropriate adult only if the juvenile or 17-year-old signifies in that adult's presence that he prefers the search to be done in his absence and the appropriate adult agrees.

As to the destruction of samples: see p 219.

IDENTIFICATION BY FINGERPRINTS, FOOTWEAR IMPRESSIONS, AND SAMPLES: GENERAL POINTS

The following general points apply to all these types of identification.

Appropriate consent

'Appropriate consent', in relation to someone, means:

(a) if the person is aged 17 or over, the consent of that person;
(b) if the person is aged 14 to 16, the consent of that person and his parent or guardian; and
(c) if the person is aged under 14, the consent of his parent or guardian.

A *note* to Annex F (destruction and speculative searches) of Code D contains specimen endorsements in relation to the appropriate consent:

(a) in respect of the case where fingerprints, footwear impressions or samples are re-quested for the purpose of elimination or as a part of an intelligence-led screening and to be used only for that purpose:

'I consent to my [fingerprints/footwear impressions being taken for elimination pur-poses/DNA/mouth swab being taken for forensic analysis—as the case may be].

I understand that the [fingerprints/footwear impressions/swab] will be destroyed at the end of the case and that my [fingerprints/footwear impressions/profile] will only be com-pared to the [fingerprints/footwear impressions/crime stain profile] from this enquiry.

I have been advised that the person taking the [fingerprints/footwear impressions/ sample] may be required to give evidence and/or provide a written statement to the po-lice in relation to the taking of it.'

(b) in respect of the case where fingerprints, footwear impressions, or samples are re-quired to be retained for future use (ie speculative search):

'I consent to my [fingerprints/footwear impressions/DNA sample and information de-rived from it—as the case may be] being retained and used only for the purposes related to the prevention and detection of crime, the investigation of an offence, or the conduct of a prosecution either nationally or internationally.

I understand that my [fingerprints/footwear impressions/this sample] may be checked against other [records/DNA records] held by, or on behalf of, relevant law enforcement authorities, either nationally or internationally.

I understand that once I have given my consent for my [fingerprints/footwear impres-sions/sample] to be retained and used I cannot withdraw this consent.'

However, Annex F *itself* is no longer up to date and should not be referred to.

Recordable offence

Some provisions refer to a 'recordable offence'. The following offences are recordable:

(a) any offence punishable with imprisonment (regardless of any statutory prohibition or restriction on the punishment of young offenders);

(b) persistently loitering or soliciting for the purposes of prostitution (Street Offences Act 1959, s 1);

(c) tampering with a motor vehicle (RTA 1988, s 25);

(d) unauthorised sale or disposal of tickets for a designated football match, and touting for car hire services (CJPOA 1994, ss 166(1) and 167);

(e) giving intoxicating liquor to a child under five, exposing children under 12 to risk of burning, and failing to provide for safety of children at entertainments (Children and Young Persons Act 1933, ss 5, 11 and 12);

(f) being drunk in a public place (Criminal Justice Act 1967, s 91);

(g) failing to deliver up authority to possess prohibited weapon or ammunition, pos-session of assembled shotgun by unsupervised person under 15, and possession of air weapon or ammunition for air weapon by unsupervised person under 14 (Firearms Act 1968, ss 5(6), 22(3) and (4));

(h) trespassing in daytime in search of game, refusal by such trespasser to give name and address, and five or more found armed in daytime in search of game and using violence or refusing to give name and address (Game Act 1831, ss 30, 31 and 32);

(i) being drunk in a highway or public place (Licensing Act 1872, s 12);

(j) obstructing authorised person exercising various powers under the Licensing Act 2003 (LA 2003, ss 59(5), 96(5), 108(3) and 179(4));

(k)   failing to notify licensing authority of change of name or rules of club, or of convictions, and failing to notify court of the holding of a personal licence (LA 2003, ss 82(6), 123(2) and 128(6));

(l)   keeping alcohol on premises for unauthorised sale, etc, allowing disorderly conduct on premises, selling alcohol to drunken person, obtaining it for such a person, failing to leave licensed premises, keeping smuggled goods, and allowing unaccompanied children on certain premises (LA 2003, ss 138(1), 140(1), 141(1), 142(1), 143(1), 144(1) and 145(1));

(m)   selling alcohol to children, allowing sale to, purchase by or on behalf of children, allowing consumption by or delivery to children, sending a child to obtain alcohol, delivering alcohol to children, and allowing unsupervised sale by children (LA 2003, ss 146(1) and (3), 147(1), 149(1), (3) and (4), 150(1) and (2), 151(1), (2) and (4), 152(1), and 153(1));

(n)   making false statements in applications for licences, etc (LA 2003, s 158(1));

(o)   allowing premises to remain open following a closure order (LA 2003, s 160(4));

(p)   making false statement in relation to an application for sex establishment licence (Local Government (Miscellaneous Provisions) Act 1982, Sch 3);

(q)   falsely claiming professional qualification (Nursing and Midwifery Order 2001, art 44);

(r)   taking or destroying game or rabbits by night (Night Poaching Act 1828, s 1);

(s)   wearing police uniform with intent to deceive, and unlawful possession of police uniform (Police Act 1996, s 90(2) and (3));

(t)   conduct likely to cause harassment, alarm or distress, failing to give notice of public procession, failing to comply with condition imposed on public procession, taking part in prohibited public procession, failing to comply with a condition imposed on a public assembly, taking part in a trespassory assembly and failing to comply with directions relating to such an assembly (Public Order Act 1986, ss 5, 11, 12(5), 13(8), 14(5), 14B(2) and 14C(3));

(u)   failing to co-operate with preliminary test (RTA 1988, s 6);

(v)   in connection with designated sporting events, (i) allowing alcohol to be carried on public vehicle, (ii) being drunk on such a vehicle, (iii) allowing alcohol to be carried in some other vehicles, (iv) being drunk at designated sports ground (Sporting Events (Control of Alcohol, etc) Act 1985, ss 1(2), 1(4), 1A(2), 2(2));

(w)   at designated football match, (i) throwing missiles, (ii) indecent or racialist chanting and (iii) going on to the playing area (Football (Offences) Act 1991, ss 2, 3 and 4);

(x)   taking or riding a pedal cycle without the owner's consent (Theft Act 1968, s 12(5));

(y)   purchasing or hiring a crossbow (or part) by person under 17, and unsupervised possession by person under 17 (Crossbows Act 1987, ss 2 and 3);

(z)   begging, and persistent begging (Vagrancy Act 1824, ss 3 and 4);

(aa)   individual subject to a banning order (i) failing to comply with requirement to report, etc, (ii) knowingly or recklessly providing false or misleading information in support of application for exemption from a reporting requirement (Football Spectators Act 1989, ss 19(6) and 20(10));

(bb)   soliciting, and paying for sexual services of prostitute subjected to force (SOA 2003, ss 51A and 53A).

Fingerprints and samples: requirement to attend

PACE, Sch 2A provides as follows.

Fingerprints

A constable may require a person to attend a police station for the purpose of taking his fingerprints under s 61(5A) (see pp 201–2). This power may not be exercised in a case within s 61(5A)(b)(i) (fingerprints taken on previous occasion insufficient, etc) after six months from the day on which the appropriate officer was informed that s 61(3A) (p 201) applied. The 'appropriate officer' means the officer investigating the offence for which the person was arrested. In addition, this power may not be exercised in a case falling within s 61(5A)(b)(ii) (fingerprints destroyed in a case where an investigation has been interrupted) after the end of a six-month period beginning with the day on which the investigation was resumed.

A constable may require a person to attend a police station for the purpose of taking his fingerprints under s 61(5B) (see p 202). This power may not be exercised after six months from:

(a) in a case within s 61(5B)(a) (fingerprints not taken previously in the course of investigation), the day on which the person was charged or informed that he would be reported;

(b) in a case within s 61(5B)(b) (fingerprints taken on previous occasion insufficient, etc), the day on which the appropriate officer was informed that s 61(3A) applied. The 'appropriate officer' means the officer investigating the offence for which the person was charged or informed that he would be reported; or

(c) in a case where fingerprints have been destroyed when the investigation was interrupted, the day on which the investigation was resumed.

A constable may require a person to attend a police station for the purpose of taking his fingerprints under s 61(6) (fingerprints of convicted or cautioned person) (see p 202). Where the condition in s 61(6ZA)(a) is satisfied (fingerprints not taken since conviction or caution), this power may not be exercised after two years from the day on which the person was convicted or cautioned. Where the condition in s 61(6ZA)(b) is satisfied (fingerprints taken on previous occasion insufficient, etc), this power may not be exercised after two years from the day on which an officer of the investigating police force was informed that s 61(3A) applied. These provisions do not apply where the offence is a qualifying offence (see p 203) (whether or not it was such an offence at the time of the conviction or caution).

A constable may require a person to attend a police station for the purpose of taking his fingerprints under s 61(6D), (6E) (pp 202–3).

Intimate samples

A constable may require a person to attend a police station for the purpose of taking an intimate sample from him under s 62(1A) (see p 205) if, in the course of the investigation of an offence, two or more non-intimate samples suitable for the same means of analysis have been taken from him but have proved insufficient.

A constable may require a person to attend a police station for the purpose of taking a sample from him under s 62(2A) (see p 205) if two or more non-intimate samples suitable for the same means of analysis have been taken from him under s 63(3E), (3F) (see p 207) but have proved insufficient.

Non-intimate samples

A constable may require a person to attend a police station for the purpose of taking a non-intimate sample from him under s 63(3ZA) (see p 206). This power may not be exercised in a case falling within s 63(3ZA)(b) (sample taken on a previous occasion not suitable, etc) after six months from the day on which the appropriate officer was informed of the matters specified in s 63(3ZA)(b)(i) or (ii). The 'appropriate officer' means the officer investigating the offence for which the person was arrested. Where a sample, and any DNA profile, have been destroyed in a case where an investigation has been interrupted, the power to require attendance for the taking of a non-intimate sample may not be exercised after the end of a six-month period beginning with the day on which the investigation was resumed.

A constable may require a person to attend a police station for the purpose of taking a non-intimate sample from him under s 63(3A) (see p 207). This power may not be exercised in a case falling within s 63(3A)(a) (sample has not been taken previously since conviction or caution) after six months from the day on which the person was charged or informed that he would be reported. The above power may not be exercised in a case falling within s 63(3A)(b) (sample taken on a previous occasion not suitable, etc) after six months from the day on which the appropriate officer was informed of the matters specified in s 63(3A)(b)(i) or (ii). The 'appropriate officer' means the officer investigating the offence for which the person was charged or informed that he would be reported.

A constable may require a person to attend a police station for the purpose of taking a non-intimate sample from him under s 63(3B) (see p 207). Where the first condition in s 63(3BA) is satisfied (sample has not been taken since conviction or caution), this power may not be exercised after two years from the day on which the person was convicted or cautioned. Where the second condition in s 63(3BA) is satisfied (sample taken on a previous occasion not suitable, etc), the above power may not be exercised after two years from the day on which an appropriate officer was informed that the sample was unsuitable or insufficient. The 'appropriate officer' means an officer of the police force which investigated the offence in question. These time limits do not apply where the offence is a qualifying offence (see p 203).

A constable may require a person to attend a police station for the purpose of taking a non-intimate sample from him under s 63(3E), (3F) (see p 207).

Multiple exercise of power in respect of fingerprints or non-intimate samples

Where fingerprints or a non-intimate sample have been taken from a person under s 61 or s 63 (as the case may be) on two occasions in relation to any offence, he may not be required to attend a police station to have another set of prints or sample sample taken from him under the relevant section in relation to that offence on a subsequent occasion without the authorisation of an inspector (or above). The fact of the authorisation, and the reasons for giving it, must be recorded as soon as practicable after it has been given.

General

A power conferred by Sch 2A to require a person to attend a police station for taking fingerprints or a sample under any provision of PACE may be exercised only where the fingerprints or sample may be taken from the person under that provision (and, in particular, if any necessary authorisation for taking the fingerprints or sample under that provision has been obtained). A requirement under Sch 2A must (except in urgent cases) give at least seven days within which to attend the police station; and may require attendance at a specified time of day or between specified times of day. In urgent cases, a shorter period may be specified if authorised by an inspector (or above). The fact of such authorisation and the reasons for giving it must be recorded as soon as practicable. In specifying a period of time or times of day for attendance, the constable must consider whether the fingerprints or sample could reasonably be taken at a time when the person is for any other reason required to attend the police station. The time, etc at which the person must attend may be varied by written agreement between him and the constable.

The information and recording requirements referred to on pp 203–4 p 205 (fingerprints), (intimate samples) and the last paragraph on p 208 (non-intimate samples) are applied by Code D to fingerprints taken under Sch 2A.

A constable may arrest without warrant a person who has failed to comply with a requirement under Sch 2A. A guidance note to Code D states that, to justify the arrest without warrant of a person for non-compliance with a requirement under Sch 2A, the officer making the requirement, or confirming in writing an agreed variation of it, should be prepared to explain how, when and where the requirement was made or the variation was confirmed and what steps were taken to ensure that the person understood what to do and the consequences of not complying with the requirement.

Speculative searches

PACE, s 63A(1) provides that, where someone has been arrested on suspicion of being involved in a recordable offence (p 209), or has been charged with a recordable offence, or has been informed that he will be reported for a recordable offence, fingerprints, footwear impressions, or samples or the information derived from samples taken under any power conferred by PACE from the person may be subjected to speculative searches, ie checked against:

(a) other fingerprints, footwear impressions or samples to which the person seeking to check has access and which are held by or on behalf of any one or more relevant law enforcement agencies (eg a police force or NCA), or are held in connection with or as a result of an investigation of an offence;

(b) information derived from other samples if the information is contained in records to which the person seeking to check has access and which are held as described in (a).

Where:

(a) fingerprints, impressions of footwear or samples have been taken from any person in connection with the investigation of an offence but otherwise than in circumstances to which s 63A(1) applies, and

(b) that person has given his consent in writing to the use in a speculative search of the fingerprints, of the impressions of footwear, or of the samples and of information derived from them,

the fingerprints, etc and that information may be checked against any of the fingerprints, etc or information mentioned in (a) or (b) of s 63A(1) (s 63A(1C)). A consent given for the above purposes cannot be withdrawn (s 63A(1D)).

Section 63A(1E) and (1F) provide respectively that where fingerprints or samples have been taken:

(a) under ss 61(6) or 63(3B) (persons convicted, etc), or

(b) under ss 61(6D), 62(2A), or 63(3E), (3F) (offences outside England and Wales, etc),

the fingerprints or samples, or information derived from the samples, may be subjected to a speculative search.

Fingerprints taken by virtue of s 61(6A) ((6) on p 202: reasonable suspicion that person whose name is not known is committing or has committed an offence, etc) may be checked against other fingerprints to which the person seeking to check has access and which are held by, or on behalf of, any one or more relevant enforcement authorities or which are held in connection with or as a result of an investigation of an offence.

DESTRUCTION, RETENTION AND USE OF FINGERPRINTS, FOOTWEAR IMPRESSIONS AND DNA PROFILES SUBJECT TO PACE

PACE, ss 63D to 63U, which came into effect on 31 October 2013, deal with this. Subject to any exceptions noted under the headings below, ss 63D to 63U apply in respect of material taken, or (in the case of a DNA profile) derived from a sample taken, before 31 October 2013, as if the material were taken on or after that date.

Destruction rule for fingerprints and DNA profiles

PACE, s 63D deals with the destruction of:

(a) fingerprints:
    (i) taken from a person under any power conferred by PACE (as described earlier in this chapter), or
    (ii) taken by the police, with the consent of the person from whom they were taken, in connection with the investigation of an offence by the police, and
(b) a DNA profile derived from a DNA sample (p 207) taken as mentioned in (a)(i) or (ii).

Fingerprints and DNA profiles to which s 63D applies ('s 63D material') must be destroyed if it appears to the responsible chief officer of police that:

(a) the taking of the fingerprint or, in the case of a DNA profile, the taking of the sample from which the DNA profile was derived, was unlawful, or
(b) the fingerprint was taken, or, in the case of a DNA profile, was derived from a sample taken, from a person in connection with that person's arrest and the arrest was unlawful or based on mistaken identity.

(Notwithstanding (a), any fingerprints which were taken (and any DNA profile which was derived from a sample taken) before 31 October 2013 may be retained if they were taken from a person who:

(a) was convicted of a recordable offence (pp 209 and 221) (other than an excluded offence (as defined on p 215)) and
(b) at the time the fingerprints or sample were taken, gave purported consent to them being taken.)

The 'responsible chief officer of police' is the chief officer of police for the police area:

(i) in which the material concerned was taken or derived, or
(ii) in the case of a DNA profile, in which the sample from which the DNA profile was derived was taken (s 63D(2)).

In any other case, s 63D material must be destroyed unless it is retained under any power conferred by ss 63E to 63O (including those sections as applied by s 63P) (s 63D(3)). However, that material taken, or (in the case of a DNA profile) derived from a sample taken, before 31 October 2013 which has been identified by a law-enforcement agency as requiring consideration of whether it should be retained by virtue of a national security determination under s 63M (p 218) is not subject to destruction until 31 October 2016. Section 63D material which ceases to be retained under such a power may continue to be retained under any other such power which applies to it.

Nothing in s 63D prevents a speculative search, in relation to s 63D material, from being carried out within such time as may reasonably be required for the search if the responsible chief officer of police considers the search to be desirable.

Modification of s 63D destruction rules for particular circumstances

Retention of s 63D material pending investigation or proceedings

PACE, s 63E provides that s 63D material taken (or, in the case of a DNA profile, derived from a sample taken) in connection with the investigation of an offence in which it is suspected that the person to whom the material relates has been involved may be retained until the conclusion of the investigation of the offence or, where the investigation gives rise to proceedings against the person for the offence, until the conclusion of those proceedings (for example, the time when charges are dropped or when a verdict is returned).

Further retention of s 63D material: persons arrested for or charged with a qualifying offence

PACE, s 63F deals with the case where s 63D material:

(a) relates to a person who is arrested for, or charged with, or informed that he will be reported for, a qualifying offence (see p 203) but is not convicted (p 221 below) of that offence, and

(b) was taken (or, in the case of a DNA profile, derived from a sample taken) in connection with the investigation of the offence.

If the person has previously been convicted of a recordable offence (see p 209) which is not an excluded offence, or is so convicted before the material is required to be destroyed by virtue of s 63F, the material may be retained indefinitely (s 63F(2)). An 'excluded offence', in relation to a person, means a recordable offence:

(a) which:
    (i) is not a qualifying offence,
    (ii) is the only recordable offence of which the person has been convicted, and
    (iii) was committed when the person was aged under 18, and

(b) for which the person was not given a sentence of imprisonment or detention for five years or more.

If a person is convicted of more than one offence arising out of a single course of action, those convictions are treated as a single conviction for the above purposes.

Otherwise, by s 63F(3), material falling within s 63F(4) or (5) may be retained until the end of the retention period below.

Material falls within s 63F(4) if it:

(a) relates to a person who is charged with a qualifying offence but is not convicted of that offence, and

(b) was taken (or, in the case of a DNA profile, derived from a sample taken) in connection with the investigation of the offence.

Material falls within s 63F(5) if:

(a) it relates to a person who is arrested for a qualifying offence but is not charged with that offence,

(b) it was taken (or, in the case of a DNA profile, derived from a sample taken) in connection with the investigation of the offence, and

(c) the Commissioner for the Retention and Use of Biometric Material has consented to the retention of the material concerned.

In its application to material taken, or (in the case of a DNA profile) derived from a sample taken, before 31 October 2013, s 63F has effect as if the words 'or (5)' in s 63F(3) were omitted, and as if s 63F(5) and s 63G (below) were omitted.

The retention period is three years beginning with the date on which (as the case may be):

(a) the fingerprints were taken, and

(b) the DNA sample from which the profile was derived was taken (or, if the profile was derived from more than one DNA sample, the date on which the first of those samples was taken).

The responsible chief officer of police or a specified chief officer of police may apply within a three-month period ending on the last day of the retention period to a District Judge (Magistrates' Courts) for an order extending the retention period for an additional two years. Appeal lies to the Crown Court against an extension order, or a refusal to make such an order. A 'specified chief officer of police' means:

(i)   the chief officer of the police force of the area in which the person from whom the material was taken resides, or

(ii) a chief officer of police who believes that the person is in, or is intending to come to, the chief officer's police area.

Consent of Commissioner   Section 63G provides as follows in relation to the consent of the Commissioner for the Retention and Use of Biometric Material referred to above. The responsible chief officer of police may apply in writing to the Commissioner for consent to the retention of s 63D material which falls within s 63F(5)(a) and (b). An application may be made on one of two bases:

(a) that the material was taken (or, in the case of a DNA profile, derived from a sample taken) in connection with the investigation of an offence where any alleged victim (or intended victim) of the offence was, at the time of the offence, under the age of 18, a vulnerable adult, or associated with the person to whom the material relates; or

(b) that the material is not material to which (a) relates, but the retention of the material is necessary to assist in the prevention or detection of crime.

The responsible chief officer of police must give the person to whom the material relates (P) written notice of an application under s 63G, and the right to make representations. The notice may, in particular, be given to P by leaving it at his usual or last known address (whether residential or otherwise), by sending it to P by post at that address, or by sending it to P by email or other electronic means. There is no need to give notice if the whereabouts of P is not known and cannot, after reasonable inquiry, be ascertained.

On such application the Commissioner may consent to the retention of material to which the application relates if he considers that it is appropriate to retain the material. Before deciding whether or not to give consent, the Commissioner must consider any representations by P which are made within 28 days beginning with the day on which the notice is given.

Retention of s 63D material: persons arrested for or charged with a minor offence

PACE, s 63H deals with the retention of s 63D material which:

(a) relates to a person who:
  (i) is arrested for, or charged with, or informed that he will be reported for, a recordable offence other than a qualifying offence (see p 203), and
  (ii) if arrested for, or charged with, or informed that he will be reported for, more than one offence arising out of a single course of action, is not also arrested for or charged with a qualifying offence, and
  (iii) is not convicted of the offence or offences in respect of which he is arrested or charged, and
(b) was taken (or, in the case of a DNA profile, derived from a sample taken) in connection with the investigation of the offence or offences in respect of which the person is arrested or charged.

If, in such a case, the person has previously been convicted of a recordable offence which is not an excluded offence (see p 215), the material may be retained indefinitely.

If a person is convicted of more than one offence arising out of a single course of action, the convictions are treated as a single conviction for the above purpose.

Retention of material: persons convicted of a recordable offence

PACE, s 63I provides that:

(a) s 63D material (other than material to which s 63K (below) applies) which:
  (i) relates to a person who is convicted of a recordable offence (pp 209 and 221), and
  (ii) was taken (or, in the case of a DNA profile, derived from a sample taken) in connection with the investigation of the offence, or
(b) material taken under s 61(6) (see p 202) or 63(3B) (see p 207) which relates to a person who is convicted of a recordable offence,

may be retained indefinitely.

Retention of material: persons convicted of an offence outside England and Wales

PACE, s 63J provides that:

(a) fingerprints taken from the person under s 61(6D), (6E) (power to take fingerprints without consent in relation to offences outside England and Wales: see pp 202–3), or
(b) a DNA profile derived from a DNA sample taken from the person under s 62(2A) or 63(3E), (6F) (powers to take intimate and non-intimate samples in relation to offences outside England and Wales: see pp 205 and 207),

which relates to a person who is convicted (p 209) of an offence under the law of any country outside England and Wales may be retained indefinitely.

Retention of s 63D material: exception for persons under 18 convicted of first minor offence

PACE, s 63K deals with the case where s 63D material, which relates to a person (P) who:

(a) is convicted (p 000) of a recordable offence other than a qualifying offence,
(b) has not previously been convicted of a recordable offence, and

(c) is under 18 at the time of the offence,

was taken (or, in the case of a DNA profile, derived from a sample taken) in connection with the investigation of the offence.

Section 63K(2)–(4) provides as follows:

(a) where P is given a custodial sentence in respect of the offence, the material may be retained until the end of the period consisting of the term of the sentence plus five years (if sentence less than five years), or indefinitely (if the sentence is five years or more);
(b) where P is given a sentence other than a relevant custodial sentence in respect of the offence, the material may be retained until the end of the period of five years beginning with the date on which (as the case may be):
  (i) the fingerprints were taken, and
  (ii) the DNA sample from which the profile was derived was taken, or, if the profile was derived from more than one DNA sample, the date on which the first of those samples was taken.

However, if, before the end of the relevant period, P is again convicted of a recordable offence, the material may be retained indefinitely.

Retention of s 63D material: persons given a penalty notice

PACE, s 63L provides that, where s 63D material relates to a person who is given a penalty notice under the Criminal Justice and Police Act 2001 and in respect of whom no proceedings are brought for the offence to which the notice relates, and was taken (or, in the case of a DNA profile, derived from a sample taken) from the person in connection with the investigation of that offence, the material may be retained for two years beginning with the date on which (as the case may be):

(a) the fingerprints were taken,
(b) the DNA sample from which the profile was derived was taken, or, if the profile was derived from more than one DNA sample, the date on which the first of those samples was taken.

Retention of s 63D material for purposes of national security

PACE, s 63M provides that s 63D material may be retained for as long as a national security determination made by the responsible chief officer of police (ie a determination that the retention of any such material is necessary for the purposes of national security) has effect in relation to it. Such a determination must be made in writing, has effect for a maximum of two years, and may be renewed.

Retention of s 63D material given voluntarily

PACE, s 63N provides that fingerprints, or a DNA profile derived from a DNA sample, taken from a person with his consent, may be retained until they or it has fulfilled the purpose for which taken or derived.

Such material which relates to a person who is convicted of a recordable offence, or who has previously been convicted of a recordable offence (other than a person who has only one 'exempt conviction'), may be retained indefinitely. A conviction is exempt if it is in respect of a recordable offence, other than a qualifying offence, committed when the person is under 18.

If a person is convicted of more than one offence arising out of a single course of action, the convictions are treated as a single conviction for the above purpose.

Retention of s 63D material with consent

By PACE, s 63O, fingerprints (other than fingerprints taken under s 61(6A) (see p 202)) to which s 63D applies, and a DNA profile to which s 63D applies, may be retained for so long as the person to whom the material relates consents to its retention in writing. Such consent can be withdrawn at any time.

Retention of s 63D material in connection with different offence

If s 63D material is taken (or, in the case of a DNA profile, derived from a sample taken) from a person (X) in connection with the investigation of an offence, and X is subsequently arrested for, or charged with a different offence, or convicted of or given a penalty notice for a different offence, ss 63E to 63O (above) and ss 63Q and 63T (below) have effect in relation to the material as if the material were also taken (or, in the case of a DNA profile, derived from a sample taken):

(a) in connection with the investigation of the different offence,
(b) on the date on which X was arrested for that offence (or charged with it, or given a penalty notice for it, if he was not arrested) (s 63P).

Destruction of copies of s 63D material

This is dealt with by PACE, s 63Q. If fingerprints are required by s 63D to be destroyed, any copies of the fingerprints held by the police must also be destroyed. If a DNA profile is required by s 63D to be destroyed, no copy may be retained by the police except in a form which does not include information which identifies the person to whom the DNA profile relates.

Destruction rules for samples and footwear impressions

Destruction of samples

PACE, s 63R provides as follows. Samples taken under any power conferred by PACE, or taken by the police, with the person's consent, in connection with the investigation of an offence, must be destroyed if it appears to the responsible chief officer of police (p 214) that:

(a) the taking of the samples was unlawful, or
(b) the samples were taken from a person in connection with that person's arrest and the arrest was unlawful or based on mistaken identity (s 63R(2)).

Where neither (a) nor (b) applies, (i) a DNA sample so taken must be destroyed as soon as a DNA profile has been derived from the sample, or if sooner, before the end of six months beginning with the date on which the sample was taken; and (ii) any other sample so taken must be destroyed before the end of six months beginning with the date on which it was taken (s 63R(4) and (5)).

The responsible chief officer of police may apply to a District Judge (Magistrates' Courts) for an order to retain a sample beyond the date on which it would otherwise be required to be destroyed by virtue of (i) or (ii) if the sample was taken from a person in connection with the investigation of a qualifying offence (p 203), and the responsible chief officer of police considers that the following condition is met. The condition is that, having regard to the nature and complexity of other material that is evidence in relation to the offence, the sample is likely to be needed in any proceedings for the offence for the purposes of disclosure to, or use by, a defendant, or responding to any challenge by a defendant in respect of the admissibility of material that is evidence on which the prosecution proposes to rely. Such application must be made before the date on which the sample would otherwise be required to be destroyed.

If, on such an application, the District Judge is satisfied that the above condition is met, he may make an order which allows the sample to be retained for 12 months beginning with the date on which the sample would otherwise be required to be destroyed, and may be renewed (on one or more occasions) for a further period of not more than 12 months from the end of the period when the order would otherwise cease to have effect. An application for such an order (other than an application for renewal) may be made without notice of the application having been given to the person from whom the sample was taken, and may be heard and determined in private in the absence of that person. A sample retained by virtue of such an order must not be used other than for the purposes of any proceedings for the offence in connection with which the sample was taken (s 63R(11)). A sample that ceases to be retained by virtue of such an order must be destroyed (s 63R(12)).

Section 63R does not prevent a speculative search, in relation to samples to which it applies, from being carried out within such time as may reasonably be required for the search if the responsible chief officer of police considers the search to be desirable. Section 63R has not been brought into force for the purpose of its application to samples that are, or may become, disclosable under the Criminal Procedure and Investigations Act 1996 or its attendant Code of Practice.

In its application to samples taken before 31 October 2013, s 63R has effect as if it did not apply:

(a) to samples that are, or may become, disclosable under the Criminal Procedure and Investigations Act 1996 or its associated Code of Practice (p 274); or
(b) to samples which
   (i) were taken by the police, with the consent of the person from whom they were taken, in connection with the investigation of an offence by the police, and
   (ii) are or may be required for purposes related to the identification of a missing person.

Destruction of footwear impressions

PACE, s 63S provides that impressions of footwear taken from a person under any power conferred by PACE, or taken by the police, with the person's consent, in connection with the investigation of an offence, must be destroyed, with the proviso that they may be retained for as long as is necessary for purposes related to the prevention or detection of crime, the investigation of an offence or the conduct of a prosecution.

Supplementary provision for material subject to PACE

Use of retained material

PACE, s 63T deals with the use of material to which PACE, s 63D, 63R or 63S applies. 'Use of material' includes allowing any check to be made against it and disclosing it to any person.

Any material to which s 63D, 63R or 63S applies must not be used other than:

(a) in the interests of national security,
(b) for the purposes of a terrorist investigation (see p 778),

(c) for purposes related to the prevention or detection of crime, the investigation of an offence or the conduct of a prosecution, or

(d) for purposes related to the identification of a deceased person or of the person to whom the material relates.

For the purposes of s 63T, the reference to crime includes a reference to any conduct which constitutes one or more criminal offences (whether under the law of England and Wales or of any other country or territory), or is, or corresponds to, any conduct which, if it all took place in England and Wales, would constitute one or more criminal offences, and the references to an investigation and to a prosecution include references, respectively, to any investigation outside England and Wales of any crime or suspected crime and to a prosecution brought in respect of any crime in a country or territory outside England and Wales.

Material which is required by s 63D, 63R or 63S to be destroyed must not at any time after it is required to be destroyed be used in evidence against the person to whom the material relates, or for the purposes of the investigation of any offence.

Exclusions for certain regimes

PACE, ss 63D to 63T do not apply to biometric data held under the Terrorism Act 2000, Sch 8 or the Terrorism Prevention and Investigation Measures Act 2011, Sch 6 (Chapter 28) (PACE, s 63U). A broadly equivalent regime for the destruction, retention and use of such material operates under these statutes (see pp 795–9 and Chapter 28 on the companion website respectively).

Nor do PACE, ss 63D to 63T apply to material which is or may become disclosable under *the Criminal Procedure and Investigations Act 1996 or its associated Code of Practice* (p 274), or to material taken from someone which relates to another person (s 63U).

A sample which is or may become disclosable under the italicised provisions above, which would otherwise be required to be destroyed under s 63R, must not be used other than for the purposes of any proceedings for the offence in connection with which the sample was taken, and once the italicised provisions above no longer apply the sample must be destroyed (s 63U).

Other supplementary provisions

Cautions treated as convictions

For the purposes of PACE, ss 63D to 63T above, any reference to a person who is convicted of an offence includes a reference to a person who has been given a caution (or, if under 18 at the time, a warning or reprimand (now abolished)), or to a person who has been found not guilty by reason of insanity or found to be under a disability and to have done the act charged.

Spent conviction rules do not apply

PACE, s 65B(2) provides that the provisions of PACE about fingerprints, samples, etc apply irrespective of the Rehabilitation of Offenders Act 1974 (under which certain convictions and cautions are treated as being spent, and therefore disregarded for most purposes, after the end of a specified expiry period). However, a person is not to be treated as having been convicted of an offence if that conviction is a conviction or caution for the repealed offences of buggery or gross indecency between men and the Secretary of State has ordered it to be disregarded (s 65B(3)).

Inclusion of DNA profiles on National DNA Database

A DNA profile derived from a DNA sample which is retained under PACE, ss 63E to 63L (including those sections as applied by s 63P) will have to be recorded on the National DNA Database (s 63AA). This provision puts on a statutory footing the pre-existing National DNA Database, as does s 63AB, which requires the Secretary of State to make arrangements in respect of the National DNA Database Strategy Board, whose role is to oversee the National DNA Database. The Board is required to issue guidance about the destruction of DNA profiles taken or retained under the above provisions of PACE in accordance with which chief officers of police must act, and may issue guidance about applications under s 63G (p 216).

Commissioner for the Retention and Use of Biometric Material

The Protection of Freedoms Act 2012, s 20 provides for the appointment of a Commissioner for the Retention and Use of Biometric Material, whose functions are to keep under review determinations under PACE, s 63M and corresponding terrorism provisions (see Chapter 28) made by chief officers of police and others that the fingerprints and DNA profiles of a person are required to be retained for national security purposes and the use to which fingerprints and DNA profiles so retained are being put. The Secretary of State has issued guidance about the making or renewing of such determinations, to which regard must be had.

To enable the Commissioner to discharge his functions, s 20 requires persons making national security determinations to notify the Commissioner in writing of the making of a determination, including the reasons for it, and to provide such other information as the Commissioner may require.

The Commissioner has power under s 20 to order the destruction of the fingerprints and DNA profile held pursuant to it where satisfied that it is not necessary for any material retained under the determination to be so retained. There is no appeal against such a ruling by the Commissioner save by way of judicial review. The Commissioner may not order the destruction of material that could otherwise be retained pursuant to any other statutory provision.

The Commissioner must also keep under review the retention and use in accordance with PACE, ss 63A and 63D to 63T (or the corresponding terrorism provisions) of any material to which s 63D or 63R (or corresponding terrorism provisions) applies and any copies of any material to which s 63D (or corresponding terrorism provision) applies.

DESTRUCTION, RETENTION AND USE OF NATIONAL SECURITY MATERIAL NOT SUBJECT TO EXISTING STATUTORY RESTRICTIONS

This is dealt with by C-TA 2008, ss 18–18E, which came into force on 31 October 2013 in respect of fingerprints and DNA samples taken, held or (in the case of a DNA profile) derived from a sample taken on or after that date. C-TA 2008, ss 18–18E apply from 31 October 2015 to such material taken, held or derived under the C-TA 2008 before 31 October 2013.

The basic provision is s 18, which applies to fingerprints (as defined on p 201), DNA samples (p 207) and DNA profiles that:

(a) are held for the purposes of national security by a law enforcement authority under the law of England and Wales or Northern Ireland, and

(b) are not held subject to existing statutory restrictions.

Such material is described as 's 18 material'.

'Law enforcement authority' means:

(a) a police force,
(b) NCA,
(c) HM Revenue and Customs Commissioners, or
(d) a foreign authority so far as exercising functions which correspond to those of a police force, or otherwise involve criminal investigation or prosecution.

The prime example of material not held subject to 'existing statutory restrictions' is material on the counter-terrorism DNA database maintained by the Metropolitan Police which comprises DNA material and fingerprints obtained from crime scenes, covert surveillance or from foreign police or intelligence services.

Destruction of material

By C-TA 2008, s 18, material must be destroyed if it appears to the responsible officer that the material has not been:

(a) obtained by the law enforcement authority pursuant to an authorisation under the Police Act 1997, Pt III (p 94);
(b) obtained by the law enforcement authority in the course of surveillance, or use of a covert human intelligence source, authorised under the Regulation of Investigatory Powers Act 2000, Part II (p 89);
(c) supplied to the law enforcement authority by another law enforcement authority; or
(d) otherwise lawfully obtained or acquired by the law enforcement authority for any of the purposes mentioned in s 18D below.

In any other case, ie where the s 18 material has been so obtained, s 18 material must be destroyed unless it is retained by the law enforcement authority under any power conferred by s 18A or 18B (non-DNA samples: below), but this is subject to a rule that a DNA sample to which s 18 applies must be destroyed as soon as a DNA profile has been derived from the sample, or, if sooner, before the end of the period of six months beginning with the date on which it was taken.

Section 18 material which ceases to be retained under a power conferred by s 18A or s 18B may continue to be retained under any other such power which applies to it.

Section 18 does not prevent s 18 material from being the subject of a speculative search within such time as may reasonably be required for the check, if the responsible officer considers the check to be desirable.

Retention of material: general

By C-TA 2008, s 18A, s 18 material which is *not a DNA sample* and relates to a person who has no previous convictions or only one exempt conviction may be retained by the law enforcement authority until the end of the specified retention period. The retention period is three years beginning with the date on which (as the case may be):

(a) the fingerprints were taken, and
(b) the DNA sample from which the profile was derived was taken (or, if the profile was derived from more than one DNA sample, the date on which the first of those samples was taken).

A person 'has no previous convictions' if he has not previously been convicted in England and Wales or Northern Ireland of a recordable offence (see p 209 and the corresponding Northern Irish legislation), and 'convicted' is defined in the same way as on p 221. 'Spent convictions' are treated in the same way as under PACE, s 65B(2) and (3). A 'conviction' is exempt if it is in respect of a recordable offence, other than a qualifying offence, committed when the person was under 18. A qualifying offence has the meaning as in p 203 and a corresponding meaning in Northern Ireland. Convictions of more than one offence arising out of a single course of action are treated as a single conviction for the purposes of calculating under s 18A whether the person has been convicted of only one offence.

Section 18 material which is *not a DNA sample* and relates to a person who has previously been convicted of a recordable offence (other than a single exempt conviction), or is so convicted before the material is required to be destroyed by virtue of s 18A, may be retained indefinitely.

Section 18 material which is *not a DNA sample* may be retained indefinitely if it is held by the law enforcement authority in a form which does not include information identifying the person (P) to whom the material relates, and the authority does not know, and has never known, the identity of P. Where s 18 material is being so retained by a law enforcement authority, and the authority comes to know the identity of P, and P has no previous convictions or only one exempt conviction, the material may be retained by the authority until the end of the period of three years beginning with the date on which the P's identity comes to be known by the authority.

Retention for purposes of national security

C-TA 2008, s 18B provides that s 18 material which is *not a DNA sample* may be retained for as long as a national security determination made by the responsible officer has effect in relation to it.

A national security determination is made if the responsible officer (ie the chief officer of police in relation to the material obtained or acquired by a police force in England and Wales) determines that it is necessary for any such s 18 material to be retained for the purposes of national security. A national security determination must be written, has effect for a maximum of two years and may be renewed.

Destruction of copies

C-TA 2008, s 18C provides that, if fingerprints are required by s 18 to be destroyed, any copies of the fingerprints held by the law enforcement authority concerned must also be destroyed. If a DNA profile is required by s 18 to be destroyed, no copy may be retained by the law enforcement authority concerned except in a form which does not include information which identifies the person to whom the DNA profile relates.

Use of retained material

By C-TA 2008, s 18D, s 18 material must not be used other than for the same purposes as under PACE, s 63T (p 220).

Subject to this, s 18 material may be subjected to a speculative search if the responsible officer considers the check to be desirable.

Material which is required by s 18 to be destroyed must not at any time after it is required to be destroyed be used in evidence against the person to whom the material relates, or for the purposes of the investigation of any offence.

The references above to using material have the same meaning as under PACE, s 63T (p 220), and so does the reference to crime (with the substitution of 'UK' for 'England and Wales').

PHOTOGRAPHS

(a) Persons detained at a police station

PACE, s 64A provides powers to take a photograph of a detainee with the appropriate consent (p 208), or without such consent where it is withheld or it is impracticable to obtain consent.

(b) Otherwise than at a police station

Section 64A also authorises the taking of a photograph elsewhere than at a police station with the appropriate consent, or without such consent where it is withheld or it is impracticable to obtain it, if the person has been:

(a) arrested by a constable for an offence;
(b) taken into custody by a constable after a citizen's arrest;
(c) required to wait by a community support officer;
(d) given a fixed penalty notice by a constable or designated community support officer or accredited person by virtue of his accreditation; or
(e) given a direction to leave and not return to a specified location for up to 48 hours by a constable (under the Anti-social Behaviour, Crime and Policing Act 2014, s 35).

General to (a) and (b)

For these purposes, the term 'photograph' includes a moving image. A photograph obtained without the appropriate consent may be obtained by making a copy of an image taken on a camera system installed anywhere in a police station. In the event of non-co-operation, where it is not possible to take the photograph covertly, reasonable force may be used to take the photograph. The use of reasonable force to take the photograph of a suspect elsewhere than at a police station must be carefully considered.

Only a police officer may take a photograph under s 64A. The officer may require the person to remove anything worn on, or over, all or any part of the head or face. In the event of non-compliance, the officer may remove the item or substance. In order to obtain a suspect's consent and co-operation to remove an item of religious headwear to take a photograph, a constable should consider whether in the situation the removal of the headwear and the taking of the photograph should be by an officer of the same sex as the person. It would be appropriate for these actions to be conducted out of public view.

The suspect must be informed of the reason for taking the photograph and the purposes for which it may be used. This must be done beforehand, unless the photograph is taken covertly or by making a copy of an image (in which cases he must be informed as soon as practicable thereafter).

A photograph so taken may be used or disclosed only for purposes related to the prevention or detection of crime (including a foreign crime corresponding to one under UK law), the investigation of an offence, the conduct of a prosecution or the enforcement of a sentence.

After being so used or disclosed, a photograph may be retained but may only be used or disclosed for the same purposes. Its retention is subject to the guidance on retention contained in the section of the College of Policing's Authorised Professional Practice relating to the Management of Police Information (MOPI), with which chief officers are required to comply by the Code of Practice on MOPI, issued by the Secretary of State.

(c) Persons voluntarily at a police station

When there are reasonable grounds for suspecting the involvement of a person in a criminal offence, but that person is at a police station voluntarily and not detained, the above provisions apply, except that force may not be used to take the person's photograph.

Destruction of photographs

Code D provides that the photograph of a person which is not taken in accordance with the provisions under headings (a) or (b) above or under PACE, s 54A (see p 148) must be destroyed (together with any negatives and copies) unless he:

(a) is charged with, or informed that he may be prosecuted for, or is prosecuted for a recordable offence (p 209);
(b) is cautioned for a recordable offence; or
(c) gives informed, written consent to the photograph being retained.

Such a person must be given an opportunity to witness the destruction or to have a certificate confirming destruction, if he so requests within five days of notification that the destruction is required.

Documentation

A record must be made of the identity of the photographer (with the usual exceptions), the purpose of the photograph and its outcome, and the detainee's consent (or the reason for taking the photograph without consent).

CHAPTER 7

The Law of Criminal Evidence

The law of criminal evidence determines two things:

(a) the means by which the facts in issue are proved in a court; and
(b) those facts which may (or may not) be proved in a court.

CLASSIFICATION OF EVIDENCE

Certain rules of evidence apply specifically to a particular class of evidence only. Evidence may be classified as follows.

Direct evidence and circumstantial evidence

Direct evidence is evidence which (if believed) directly establishes a particular fact in issue itself. For example, the existence of a firearm alleged to have been possessed by the defendant (D) may be proved by its production in court and the fact that he was in possession of it may be proved by a statement from a person who claims to have discovered D in possession.

Circumstantial evidence is evidence of a fact or facts from which a fact in issue may be inferred. Suppose that D is charged with murder. If an eye-witness gives evidence that he saw D fire a gun at the victim, this is direct evidence of a fact in issue. On the other hand, evidence that D was seen in possession of a gun near the scene of the crime shortly before it was committed is circumstantial evidence since it is evidence of a fact from which the fact in issue (that D fired the gun) may be inferred.

Oral evidence, documentary evidence and real evidence

Oral evidence

Most evidence given in a court is oral evidence. This consists of statements made in court by witnesses concerning matters of which they have knowledge, such as something which they have seen, or heard, or smelt or touched.

Normally, oral evidence must be given on oath (ie sworn). However, where it is not possible to administer the oath in the manner appropriate to the religious beliefs of the witness (W), or where he objects to being sworn, W may make a solemn affirmation.

Determination of whether a witness should be sworn   The question whether W may be sworn is determined by the court as follows in accordance with the Youth Justice and Criminal Evidence Act 1999 (YJCEA 1999), s 55.

W may not be sworn unless he has reached 14 and he has sufficient appreciation of the solemnity of the occasion and of the particular responsibility to tell the truth which is involved in taking an oath. If W is able to give intelligible testimony, he is presumed to have sufficient appreciation if no evidence is adduced to the contrary. If such evidence is adduced, it is for the party seeking to have W sworn to prove on the balance of probabilities that W has reached 14 and has sufficient appreciation of the specified matters.

Such issues must be dealt with in the absence of the jury.

Reception of unsworn evidence   YJCEA 1999, s 56 deals with a person of any age who is competent to give evidence in criminal proceedings (see p 233) but is not permitted to be sworn by s 55. It provides that the evidence of such a person may be given unsworn. A deposition of unsworn evidence may be accepted as if it had been given on oath.

Unsworn evidence may also be given by a person called simply to produce a document.

Evidence by live link   CJA 2003, Part 8 (ss 51–56) provides as follows.

A 'live link' is a live television link or other arrangement by which a witness, while at a place in the UK which is outside the building where the proceedings are being held, is able to see and hear a person at the place where the proceedings are being held and to be seen and heard by the defendants, judge and/or justices, jury (if any), legal representatives and any interpreter.

A witness (other than D) may, if the court so directs, give evidence through a live link in criminal proceedings whether at a trial or during an appeal. The court may give such a direction on its own motion or on the application of a party. It cannot make a direction unless it has been notified by the Secretary of State that suitable facilities are available in the area where the proceedings will take place. The court must be satisfied that it is in the interests of the efficient or effective administration of justice for this to take place. In deciding whether to give a direction, the court must consider all the circumstances, including the availability of the witness, the need to attend in person, the importance of the evidence and the views of the witness, the suitability of facilities, and whether giving a direction might inhibit a party to the proceedings from effectively testing the witness's evidence. If the court refuses an application it must state in open court its reasons for doing so.

When such a direction is in force the witness may not give evidence by any other means.

Where a magistrates' court wishes to give such a direction and facilities are not available at any place where it can lawfully sit, the court may sit at any place appointed for the purpose of receiving such evidence and this may be outside its local justice area.

Evidence by video recording   For video-recorded evidence under the 'special measures provisions', see pp 238–40. In addition, CJA 2003, ss 137 and 138, which are not yet in force, make provision for video-recorded evidence-in-chief by a witness other than D in respect of an offence triable only on indictment or a prescribed either-way offence. They are dealt with in Chapter 7 on the companion website.

Refreshing memory   Witness statements are usually recorded well in advance of trial. Recognising the difficulties associated with refreshing memory from an audio or video recording, CJA 2003, s 139 states that a witness giving evidence in criminal proceedings may refresh his memory from a document made or verified by him at an earlier time provided that:

(a) he states in his oral evidence that the document records his recollections of the matter at that earlier time; and

(b) his recollection of the matter is likely to have been significantly better at that time than it is at the time of his oral evidence.

Where two witnesses have acted together (and this is common in the case of police officers) they may refresh their memories from notes which they made together.

Hostile witness   If, during a trial in a Crown Court, a witness gives evidence which is hostile to the side calling him (it must be 'hostile' as opposed to unfavourable), that evidence may be contradicted by other evidence or, with the leave of the judge, it may be proved that the witness, on another occasion, made a statement which is inconsistent with his present testimony.

Documentary evidence

It is a general rule that the contents of a document (a term which includes not only a written document but also a map or drawing, photograph, disc, tape or the like, and any film or the like) may be proved only by production of the original or an admission as to its contents (primary evidence). However, there are now so many exceptions to this general rule that it has lost much of its importance. When one of these exceptions applies, secondary evidence (eg a copy authenticated in a way approved by the court or oral evidence) of the contents of the document may be given.

The principal exceptions whereby secondary evidence of the contents of a document may be given are as follows:

(1) Where the original is proved to have been lost or destroyed, secondary evidence of the contents may be given.
(2) The contents of public documents can always be proved by means of secondary evidence, although some statutes providing this exception for a particular type of public document limit the nature of this secondary evidence. A 'public document' is a document prepared for the purpose of the public making use of it and being able to refer to it. Examples are Registers of Births, Deaths and Marriages, the contents of which can be proved by a copy of an entry certified by a person who has lawful custody of the register. Judicial notice is taken of Acts of Parliament and their contents, ie they do not have to be proved by evidence. A statutory instrument is proved by production of the Queen's Printer's copy.
(3) By the Bankers' Books Evidence Act 1879, ss 3–5, an examined copy of any entry in a banker's book kept in the ordinary course of business is admissible as prima facie evidence of such entry.

Certain statutory provisions specially provide for evidence to be given by the production of a document. Examples appear in the discussion of the exceptions to the rule against hearsay.

Real evidence

Real evidence is the production of an object for the inspection of the court or jury. Where a document is produced as evidence of the matter contained in it, as opposed to proof of its physical existence, it is, as we have just seen, documentary evidence. The firearm which was produced by a witness in the example quoted earlier is real evidence. So, it has been held, is a computer printout recording attempts to enter a website. Police officers frequently give evidence of having recovered stolen property; this is oral evidence. When the property is produced for inspection in court, this is real evidence.

Original evidence and hearsay evidence

Original evidence is evidence of a fact by 'first-hand' evidence of it. Hearsay evidence is 'second-hand' evidence, since it consists of any representation of fact or opinion made by whatever means (eg orally, in writing, or by conduct (such as a nod of the head)) by a person, otherwise than in oral evidence in the particular proceedings, which is tendered as evidence to establish the matter stated in it. As an example, a policeman's notebook containing a statement about a stabbing is hearsay evidence of the stabbing. It must be emphasised that not all evidence of what someone else stated is hearsay. If it is produced merely to prove the fact that it was stated, as opposed to being produced with the object of establishing the truth of what was stated, it is original evidence and not hearsay evidence. If D says that he acted under a threat to kill him made by Y, evidence of what he said is original evidence because it is produced as evidence that Y uttered a threat, but if a witness says that X had told him that Y had broken the windows of a greenhouse, this is hearsay evidence since it is produced as evidence of the truth of what X stated, ie that Y had broken the windows.

The distinction between original evidence and hearsay evidence is important, because hearsay evidence is inadmissible in criminal cases unless its admission is permitted under a variety of rules.

PROOF

The general rule is that the prosecution must prove the existence of any fact on which it relies. There are, however, certain facts which do not need to be proved.

Facts which may be established by means other than proof

Judicial notice

The court may take 'judicial notice' of certain matters which are so notorious or well known that evidence of their existence need not be adduced. One does not have to prove that beer is intoxicating, for example, as this is a matter of general knowledge, whereas it may be necessary to prove that a less well-known drink is intoxicating.

Presumptions

Sometimes there is a presumption of *law* that if a particular fact is proved some other fact *must* be presumed to exist. There are two kinds of presumption of law: irrebuttable and rebuttable.

When the presumption is irrebuttable, no evidence can be received to contradict the presumed fact. An example of an irrebuttable presumption of law is provided by the rule that a child under 10 is incapable of committing an offence.

Where there is a rebuttable presumption of law against D, the jury (or magistrates) must find that the presumed fact existed unless (depending on the presumption) D proves the contrary on the balance of probabilities, or there is evidence raising a doubt that the presumption is rebutted (in which case the prosecution will have to disprove that evidence beyond reasonable doubt). An example of a rebuttable presumption of law is that mechanical instruments are in proper working order, in the absence of evidence to the contrary.

Presumptions of law must be distinguished from presumptions of *fact*. When a jury (or magistrates' court) *may* find that a particular fact (the presumed fact) exists on proof of some other fact, the presumption is one of fact. Presumptions of fact arise in a wide range of cases, because they are suggested by common sense. For example, if D is seen driving a car immediately after an accident, it may be inferred that he was driving at the time of the accident. As a moment's thought shows, presumptions of fact are merely particular and frequently occurring instances of the operation of circumstantial evidence since the nature of circumstantial evidence is that it consists of facts from which other facts may be presumed to exist.

Formal admissions

A formal admission of a fact *dispenses with the need* for proving that fact since it is conclusive evidence of that fact as against the party admitting it. Provision is made for formal admissions, by or on behalf of either prosecution or defence, by the Criminal Justice Act 1967, s 10. Such a formal admission may be made before or at the proceedings. Unless made in court, it must be made in writing and signed by the person making it (or by an officer of the company if made by a company).

CJA 2003, s 118 preserves the common law rules under which in criminal proceedings:

(a) an admission made by D's agent (eg solicitor or counsel), or
(b) a statement made by a person to whom D refers a person for information,

is admissible as evidence against D of any matter stated.

The burden of proof

The burden of proof is often described as the 'persuasive' or 'legal' burden. The general rule is that the prosecution has the burden of proving D's guilt beyond reasonable doubt. In more detail, the position is as follows. The prosecution must prove beyond reasonable doubt that D committed the actus reus of the offence charged with the requisite mens rea. In relation to defences, D normally has the burden of adducing sufficient evidence to raise a defence (an evidential burden); if he does so it is then for the prosecution to disprove the alleged defence beyond reasonable doubt.

Exceptionally, D has the burden of proving a defence on the balance of probabilities. The burden of proof is imposed on D in the following cases:

Defence of insanity   This was outlined in Chapter 1.

Express statutory provision   A statute sometimes provides that it is a defence if D proves certain facts. For example, under the Homicide Act 1957, s 2, D has the burden of proving the defence of diminished responsibility on a charge of murder.

Provisos and exemptions in statutory offences   Where a statute governing any offence provides any exception, exemption, proviso, excuse or qualification, as where it prohibits the doing of an act save in specified circumstances (or by persons of specified classes, or with specified qualifications, or with the licence or permission of specified authorities), the onus of proving such an exception, exemption, etc is impliedly cast on D. This rule is provided in the case of summary proceedings by the Magistrates' Courts Act 1980, s 101, and applies in the case of trial on indictment by virtue of the common law. In exceptional cases, however, the rule will not apply if the court construes the legislation as only imposing an evidential burden.

Rebuttable presumption of law against the defendant where the defendant bears the burden of proving that the presumption is rebutted   We dealt with this on p 230.

Placing a persuasive burden on D may be incompatible with the presumption of innocence guaranteed by the European Convention on Human Rights, art 6(2), depending on the nature of the provision which imposes that burden. In each case it depends on whether imposing a persuasive burden serves a legitimate aim and is a justifiable and proportionate response to it; if not it will be incompatible. The Human Rights Act 1998, s 3 gives the courts a liberal power of statutory interpretation which enables them to read an express or implied statutory requirement for D to prove something as simply imposing an evidential burden on D if this makes the provision compatible with the Convention when it would not otherwise be so.

Corroboration

'Corroboration' is evidence from a source (or sources) independent of the witness whose evidence is to be corroborated which confirms or supports that evidence in some material particular. Corroboration is not generally required as a matter of law. This means that, generally, although corroboration may aid proof, it is possible for the prosecution to discharge its burden of proof by adducing only one item of evidence.

There are, however, exceptional circumstances in which corroboration is required by statute or may be necessary as a matter of practice.

Corroboration required by statute

In cases under this heading the relevant fact is not proved on uncorroborated evidence given on behalf of the prosecution. These cases are:

(a) perjury and other offences under the Perjury Act 1911; and
(b) speeding contrary to the Road Traffic Regulation Act 1984, s 89.

Discretion to give corroboration warning

A judge has a *discretion* to give a warning to the jury about the danger of convicting on the uncorroborated evidence of a witness. For it to be appropriate for a warning to be given, there must be an evidential basis for suggesting that a witness is unreliable; mere suggestions by counsel do not provide such a basis.

Proof of convictions and acquittals

The Police and Criminal Evidence Act 1984 (PACE), s 73 provides that, where the fact that a person has in the UK or in any other EU member state been convicted or acquitted of an offence, otherwise than by a Service court, is admissible in evidence, it may be proved by producing a certificate of conviction or acquittal relating to that offence, and proving that the person named in the certificate is the person whose conviction or acquittal for the offence is to be proved. The certificate must be signed by the 'proper officer' of the court of conviction or acquittal, ie the designated officer in the case of a magistrates' court in England and Wales; the clerk of the court, his deputy, or any other person with custody of the court record in the case of any other court in the UK; or, in relation to a court in another EU state, the officer of the foreign court who equates to a certificate-signatory in the UK. A document purporting to be such a certificate is presumed to be such until the contrary is proved. Where such a certificate is relied on to prove a conviction against D, it must be proved by the prosecution beyond reasonable doubt that D is the person named in that certificate. In respect of any foreign conviction not covered by s 73, there is a corresponding provision in the Evidence Act 1851, s 7. This refers to 'examined copies' or 'authenticated copies' of the foreign court's conviction records.

PACE, s 73 supplements other previous provisions. The Criminal Procedure Act 1865, s 6 provides that if, on a witness being lawfully questioned about a conviction, there is a denial or refusal to answer, the cross-examining party may prove the conviction. To do so, the procedure under s 73 will have to be followed. The Road Traffic Offenders Act 1988, s 31 provides that, where a person is convicted of an offence involving obligatory or discretionary disqualification, any previous conviction for a driving offence endorsed on his driving record is prima facie evidence of that conviction.

In any proceedings where evidence is admissible of the fact that D has committed an offence, he is rebuttably presumed by PACE, s 74 to have committed it if he is proved to have been convicted (ie found guilty) of it by a UK court, by an EU court or by a Service court outside the UK.

Section 74 also provides that the fact that a person *other than* D has been convicted in the UK or any other EU member state or by a Service court outside the UK is admissible in evidence for the purpose of proving that that person committed that offence, where evidence of his having done so is admissible. If that conviction is proved that person is rebuttably presumed to have committed it. However, where D is jointly charged with others who have pleaded guilty, proof of the convictions of those others, in circumstances where the jury is encouraged to rely on that evidence in determining D's guilt, is liable to be held inadmissible by reason of its adverse effect upon the fairness of the proceedings in accordance with PACE, s 78. As to s 78, see p 267.

Although it is possible to prove previous convictions by adducing Police National Computer (PNC) records admitted under CJA 2003, s 117 (see p 248), s 117 cannot be relied on so as to make admissible details on the PNC about the offences (as opposed to the dates of convictions, the offences charged, and the sentences).

COMPETENCE, COMPELLABILITY AND PRIVILEGE

Who can give evidence? Who is obliged to? When is a witness entitled to refuse to answer questions? The answers to these questions are to be found respectively in the law relating to competence to give evidence, to compellability to give evidence and to various types of privilege.

Competence

YJCEA 1999, s 53 provides that anyone, of whatever age, is competent to give evidence in criminal proceedings unless he is unable to understand questions put to him as a witness, or unable to answer them in a way which can be understood. The Court of Appeal has emphasised that this alone is the test of competence, and that a witness need not understand the special importance that the truth should be told in court, and the witness need not understand every single question or give a readily understandable answer to every question. A witness may need the assistance of 'special measures' (see p 236).

A person charged in criminal proceedings is not competent to give evidence *for the prosecution* (whether or not he is the only person, or is one of two or more persons, charged in the proceedings). This reference to a person charged in criminal proceedings does not include a person who is not, or is no longer, liable to be convicted of any offence in the proceedings (whether because of a guilty plea, or otherwise).

Under s 54, questions of competence are decided by the court and in the absence of the jury if there is one. The party calling the witness must satisfy the court that the witness, on the balance of probabilities, is competent to give evidence.

As a general rule a witness who is competent is also compellable.

Compellability of D's spouse or civil partner

PACE, s 80 deals with the 'compellability' of the *spouse or civil partner of a defendant* to give evidence.

In any proceedings, the spouse or civil partner (W) of a person charged in the proceedings is compellable to give evidence *on behalf of that person*, unless he or she (ie W) is also charged in those proceedings.

In addition, provided that he or she (ie W) is not also charged in those proceedings, W is compellable to give evidence *on behalf of any other person charged in those proceedings*, but only in respect of any specified offence with which that other person is charged, *or to give evidence for the prosecution*, but only in respect of any specified offence with which any person is charged in the proceedings. In relation to W, an offence is a specified offence for these purposes if:

(a) it involves an assault on, or injury or a threat of injury to, W or a person who was at the material time under 16;
(b) it is a sexual offence alleged to have been committed in respect of a person who was at the material time under 16; or
(c) it consists of encouraging or assisting, attempting or conspiring to commit, or of aiding, abetting, counselling or procuring the commission of, an offence under (a) or (b).

The Court of Appeal has held that (a) is judged by reference to the legal nature of the offence (ie the offence charged must in itself encompass the real possibility of an assault, or injury or threat of injury), and not its factual circumstances; thus, an offence of threatening to damage another's property fell outside (a), even though in the circumstances there was a threat of injury, because the legal nature of that offence did not involve the real possibility of an assault, or injury or threat of injury.

For the purposes of (b), a 'sexual offence' is an offence under:

(a) the Protection of Children Act 1978 (taking, etc indecent photographs, etc of a child);
(b) the Sexual Offences Act 2003, Part 1 (ss 1–79);
(c) the Sexual Offences Act 1956 or the Indecency with Children Act 1960, both of which have been repealed; or
(d) an offence under the Modern Slavery Act 2015, s 2 (human trafficking) committed with a view to exploitation consisting of or including 'sexual exploitation' (as defined on pp 672–3).

The references above to a person charged in any proceedings do not include a person who is not, or is no longer, liable to be convicted of any offence in the proceedings (whether as a result of pleading guilty or for any other reason).

The failure of a spouse or civil partner of a person charged in any proceedings to give evidence in the proceedings may not be commented on by the prosecution.

An ex-spouse or ex-civil partner is compellable to give evidence as if he or she had never been married to the defendant.

Privilege

Self-incrimination

A person required to answer questions or produce something may refuse to do so on the grounds that the evidence might incriminate him. Exceptions to this rule are created by a number of statutes concerned with drink-driving, the care and protection of children, and investigations carried out by the Serious Fraud Office. However, there are restrictions in relation to the use of evidence obtained within SFO investigations.

Lawyer/client

Communications between a qualified lawyer and his client which are concerned with the giving of legal advice or as to the presentation of material, and those between a qualified lawyer, his client and a third party which are concerned with litigation and legal advice, are privileged. Privilege is not afforded in respect of such communications in the furtherance of crime or fraud. In addition, where such communications are disclosed from other sources (document coming into possession of police) or where privilege is waived by the lawyer's client, such evidence may be given.

Exclusion of evidence on grounds of public interest immunity

Evidence held by the prosecution may need to be excluded from disclosure at trial or in preliminary proceedings (and from pre-trial disclosure to the defendant) by the court on grounds that its disclosure is not in the public interest. Such material is said to be excluded on the basis of public interest immunity (PII). The approach to be taken where such immunity is claimed is as follows:

(1) Does the material weaken the prosecution case or strengthen the defence case? If it does not, it should not be disclosed. If it does, the 'golden rule' is that disclosure should be made unless PII prevents it.

(2) In determining whether the golden rule can be derogated from, the court must consider whether there is a real risk of serious prejudice to an important public interest. If there is not, PII does not apply and the material must be disclosed.

(3) If the material does give rise to such a risk, the court must consider whether D's interests can be protected without disclosure or whether disclosure can be ordered in a way which would adequately protect the public interest and the interests of the defence. This requires the court to consider whether the prosecution should formally admit what the defence sought to establish or whether limited disclosure could be ordered.

(4) If the court is minded to order limited disclosure it must consider whether what it proposes in order to protect D's interest and the public interest represents the minimum derogation to protect the public interest. If it does not, fuller disclosure should be ordered.

(5) If limited disclosure might render the trial process unfair to D, fuller disclosure should be ordered even if this leads to the discontinuance of the prosecution case. The court must keep the issue of unfairness under review as the trial proceeds.

Where a claim of PII is successful no adverse inference may be drawn from the witness's failure to give evidence. Notice should be given of an intention to claim such privilege.

PII may apply to many police matters: information relied upon for the issue of search warrants; reports to the DPP; the disclosure of the identity of informants or the siting of police observation posts. PII may also apply to files relating to the investigation of complaints (although disclosure of working papers and reports prepared by investigating officers may be ordered where the public interest in disclosure outweighs that in preserving confidentiality) and to disciplinary matters connected with the police. On the other hand, any written complaint made about the conduct of a police officer is not privileged. Nor can privilege be claimed in respect of statements made within a police 'grievance' procedure alleging unlawful discrimination.

PROTECTION OF WITNESSES

Special measures directions in case of vulnerable and intimidated witnesses (other than defendants)

The relevant provisions about such directions are in YJCEA 1999, Part 2, Ch 1, ss 16–33C.

Eligibility for special measures

Witnesses who are eligible for assistance on grounds of age or incapacity   A witness in criminal proceedings may be eligible under YJCEA 1999, ss 16 or 17 for assistance by special measures to help him in giving his evidence.

Section 16 provides that a witness (W) (*other than the defendant* (D)) is eligible for such assistance if:

(a) W is *under 18 at the time of the hearing* (the time when a court must decide whether he is eligible for such assistance); or
(b) if the court considers that the quality of the evidence given by W is likely to be diminished by reason of W:
   (i) suffering from mental disorder within the meaning of the Mental Health Act 1983; or
   (ii) otherwise having a significant impairment of intelligence and social functioning; or
   (iii) having a physical disability or suffering from physical disorder.

References to the quality of W's evidence are to its quality in terms of completeness, coherence and accuracy. 'Coherence' refers to W's ability in testifying to give answers which address the questions put to him and can be understood both individually and collectively (ie in relation to a particular question and to his evidence generally).

Where the age of a witness who is the complainant in respect of an offence under the Sexual Offences Act 2003, Part 1 (ss 1 to 79), the Protection of Children Act 1978, s 1, the Criminal Justice Act 1988, s 160 (indecent photographs of children) or the Modern Slavery Act 2015, s 1 or 2 (slavery, etc; trafficking) is uncertain, and there are reasons to believe that the witness is under 18, that witness is presumed to be under 18.

Witnesses eligible for assistance on ground of fear or distress about testifying   YJCEA 1999, s 17 provides that a witness in criminal proceedings (*other than* D) is eligible for assistance by special measures where the court is satisfied that the quality of evidence given by him is likely to be diminished by reason of fear or distress on his part in connection with testifying in the proceedings. In determining whether it is so satisfied, the court must consider in particular:

(a) the nature and the alleged circumstances of the offence to which the proceedings relate;

(b) W's age;
(c) such of the following matters as appear relevant:
  (i) W's social and cultural background and ethnic origins;
  (ii) W's domestic and employment circumstances; or
  (iii) W's religious beliefs or political opinions, if any;
(d) any behaviour towards W on the part of:
  (i) D;
  (ii) members of the family or associates of D; or
  (iii) any other person who is likely to be a defendant or a witness in the proceedings.

Where the complainant in respect of an offence under the Sexual Offences Act 2003, Part 1 (ss 1 to 79) or the Modern Slavery Act 2015, s 1 or 2 is a witness in proceedings relating to that offence (or another offence), there is a presumption that the witness is eligible for assistance by special measures unless the witness waives that entitlement.

There is a presumption that a witness in proceedings relating to a relevant offence involving weapons (or to a relevant offence and any other offences) is eligible for assistance by special measures, unless the witness waives that entitlement. For these purposes, an offence is a relevant offence if it is an offence described in YCEA 1999 Sch 1A, viz:

(a) murder, or manslaughter, where it is alleged that *a firearm or knife* was used to cause the death in question, or where it is alleged that:
  (i) D was carrying such a weapon during the commission of the offence, and
  (ii) a person other than D knew or believed during the commission of the offence that D was carrying such a weapon;
(b) an offence under the Offences Against the Person Act 1861, ss 18, 20, 38 or 47 where it is alleged that *a firearm or knife* was used to commit the offence in question, or in a case where it is alleged that (i) or (ii) above applies;
(c) an offence under the Prevention of Crime Act 1953, s 1 or s 1A or the Criminal Justice Act 1988, s 139 or s 139A or s 139AA (which deal with having an offensive weapon or bladed or pointed article in public places or schools or threatening with such an article);
(d) an offence under the Firearms Act 1968, ss 1, 2(1), 3, 4, 5(1), 5(1A), 16, 16A, 17, 18, 19, 20, 21, 21A, or 24A;
(e) an offence under the Violent Crime Reduction Act 2006, ss 28, 32 or 36.

For the above offences see Chapters 19, 23 and 25.

The reference in (a) and (b) to an offence ('offence A') includes a reference to:

(i) an attempt or conspiracy to commit offence A in a case where it is alleged that the attempt or conspiracy was to commit offence A in a manner or circumstances described in (a) or (b);
(ii) an offence under the Serious Crime Act 2007, Part 2 (encouraging or assisting crime) in relation to which offence A is the offence (or one of them) which the person intended or believed would be committed in a case where it is alleged that the person intended or believed offence A would be committed in the manner or circumstances described in (a) or (b); and
(iii) aiding, abetting, counselling or procuring the commission of offence A in a case where it is alleged that offence A was committed, or the act or omission charged in respect of offence A was done or made, in the manner or circumstances described in (a) or (b).

A reference in (c)–(e) to an offence ('offence A') includes a reference to:

(i)   an attempt or conspiracy to commit offence A;
(ii) an offence under the Serious Crime Act 2007, Part 2 in relation to which offence A is the offence (or one of the offences) which the person intended or believed would be committed; and
(iii) aiding, abetting, counselling or procuring the commission of offence A.

Special measures direction

By YJCEA 1999, s 18 a range of special measures is made potentially available to witnesses in criminal proceedings who are eligible for special measures under s 16 or s 17. The 'special measures' are set out in detail by ss 23 to 30 (below).

Special measures direction relating to eligible witness   YJCEA 1999, s 19(2) provides that, once a court has determined that a witness is eligible for special measures, it must then determine whether any of those measures (or a combination of them) would be likely to improve the quality of the witness's evidence and, if so, determine which of those measures would be likely to maximise so far as practicable the quality of his evidence. Having made this second determination, it must give a 'special measures' direction in relation to the measure or measures so determined. An exception to this approach is provided by s 21.

Special provisions relating to child witnesses   YJCEA 1999, s 21 provides special protection for one type of person eligible for 'special measures' under s 16: 'a child witness' (ie someone under 18 at the time of the hearing). It provides that, where in making a determination under s 19, a court determines that a witness (W) is a 'child witness', it must first have regard to the following provisions. Under them the 'primary rule' is that in respect of W it must give a special measures direction providing for a video recording of his evidence-in-chief to be admitted (unless this is contrary to the interests of justice) and providing for any evidence given by him which is not by means of video recording (whether in chief or otherwise) to be given by means of a live link. The primary rule does not apply to the extent that the court is satisfied that compliance with it would not be likely to maximise the quality of W's evidence so far as practicable (whether because the application to that evidence of one or more other special measures available in relation to the witness would have that result or for any other reason).

If W informs the court of his wish that the primary rule should not apply or should apply only in part, the primary rule does not apply to the extent that the court is *satisfied that not complying with the rule would not diminish the quality of W's evidence*. Where, as a consequence of all or part of the primary rule being disapplied under this provision, W's evidence or any part of it would fall to be given as testimony in court, the court must give a special measures direction for W to be screened from D when giving the evidence or that part of it. However, this screening requirement is subject to two limitations:

(a)   if W informs the court of his wish that the requirement should not apply, the requirement should not apply to the extent that the court *is satisfied that not complying with it would not diminish the quality of W's evidence*; and
(b)   the requirement does not apply to the extent that the court is satisfied that screening would not be likely to maximise the quality of W's evidence so far as practicable.

In making a decision under the italicised provisions, the court must take into account the following factors (and any others it considers relevant):

(a) W's age and maturity;
(b) W's ability to understand the consequences of giving evidence otherwise than in accordance with the requirements of the primary rule or a screening requirement (as the case may be);
(c) the relationship (if any) between W and D;
(d) W's social and cultural background and ethnic origins;
(e) the nature and alleged circumstances of the offence to which the proceedings relate.

Only after it has had regard to the above provisions must the court have regard to s 19(2) (above).

If W is not under 18 at the hearing but was under 18 when a video recording of his evidence-in-chief was made, YJCEA 1999, s 22 provides that the primary rule applies, *so far as relating to the giving of a direction for the recording to be admitted.*

Special provisions relating to sexual offences

YJCEA 1999, s 22A makes special provisions relating to the trial of a sexual offence (or a sexual offence and other offences) *in the Crown Court where the complainant is a witness (eligible for special measures) in the proceedings and is not under 18 at the time of the hearing.* (If the complainant is under 18, s 21 applies.) *Where it applies,* s 22A establishes a rule in favour of admitting the complainant's video-recorded evidence-in-chief. Section 22A does not mean that such evidence is inadmissible in a magistrates' court, but merely that there is no rule in favour of admitting it.

For these purposes, a 'sexual offence' means an offence under the Sexual Offences Act 2003 (SOA 2003), Part 1 (ss 1–79), any 'relevant superseded offence' (ie a corresponding offence superseded by SOA 2003, Part 1) or an offence under the Modern Slavery Act 2015 (MSA 2015), s 2 (human trafficking) committed with a view to exploitation consisting of or including 'sexual exploitation' (as defined on pp 672–3).

The operation of s 22A is as follows:

(a) If a party to the proceedings applies for a special measures direction in relation to the complainant, that party may request that the direction provide for a video recording of an interview of the complainant to be admitted as evidence-in-chief of the complainant.
(b) If the court determines that the complainant is eligible for assistance by virtue of s 16 (see (b) on p 236) or s 17 (see p 236), it must give such a special measures direction in relation to the complainant, unless:
    (i) it considers that in the interests of justice the recording should not be admitted; or
    (ii) it is satisfied that compliance with such a direction would not be likely to maximise the quality of the complainant's evidence so far as practicable (whether because the application to that evidence of one or more other special measures available in relation to the complainant would have that result or for any other reason).

Special measures available

The special measures are:

(1) *Screening (s 23)* Screens may be authorised to shield W from D (but the judge, jury, justices, a legal representative from each side, any interpreter, and any person appointed to assist W must be able to see him).

(2) *Evidence by live link (s 24)* Usually this will be done by closed-circuit television but any technology is permitted. Where a live link direction is given, evidence may not be given in any other way without the consent of the court. A divisional court has held that evidence being given in this way does not breach D's human right to a fair trial.

(3) *Evidence given in private (s 25)* The court may be cleared of non-essential personnel but this measure is only available in relation to a sexual offence (as defined above) or an offence under MSA 2015, s 1 (slavery, etc), or when the court reasonably believes that someone has tried to intimidate, or will try to intimidate, W. At least one news reporter must be allowed to remain.

(4) *Removal of wigs and gowns (s 26)* This applies to the judiciary as well as legal representatives.

(5) *Video-recorded evidence-in-chief (s 27)* Where this special measure is directed, it will provide for a video recording of an interview of W to be admitted in evidence-in-chief. However, the direction may not provide for a video recording, or part of it, to be admitted if its admission would not be in the interests of justice. If it is decided to permit only an edited version to be shown, the court must consider whether the exclusion of part of the recording is prejudicial. A court may later exclude a recording if its making is not properly proved, but may nevertheless admit it in such circumstances. The party tendering the evidence must call W, unless a special measures direction provides for cross-examination under s 28 (below) or the parties have agreed to non-attendance. W may not without the permission of the court give evidence-in-chief otherwise than by means of the recording as to any matter which, in the opinion of the court, is dealt with in his recorded testimony. In giving such permission, the court may direct that the evidence is given by W by means of a live link.

(6) *Video-recorded cross-examination or re-examination (s 28)* The relevant provisions are not yet generally in force. At the time of writing they are being trialled at Kingston-upon-Thames, Leeds and Liverpool Crown Courts where W is under 16 and is eligible for special measures under head (a) of s 16 or is eligible under head (b) of s 16. It is expected that s 28 will be fully rolled out nationally from 2017. When s 28 is fully and nationally in force, the law will be as follows. Where a special measures direction provides for video recording of W's evidence-in-chief to be admitted, the special measures direction may also provide that W may be cross-examined before trial and that that cross-examination (and any re-examination) may be recorded for use at trial. This will not occur in the physical presence of D, although D will be able to see and hear it and to communicate with his legal adviser (live link). Nor need it take place in the physical presence of the judge or magistrates and the defence and prosecution legal representatives, although they must be able to see and hear the examination and to communicate with those present. However, a judge or magistrate must control the proceedings and this person will normally be the trial judge or magistrate. Where a recording has been made of the examination of W under the above power, W may not be subsequently cross-examined or re-examined in respect of his evidence unless the court makes a further direction to this effect. Such a further direction may only be given: (a) where the proposed cross-examination is sought by a party to the proceedings as a result of having become aware since the original recording of a matter which he could not with reasonable diligence have ascertained by then, or (b) where it is in the interests of justice to do so.

The following two additional measures under ss 29 and 30 are available only in the case of someone eligible for special measures under s 16:

Examination of witness through intermediary (s 29) An intermediary is an interpreter or someone else whom the court approves to communicate to W the questions asked in court, and then to communicate W's answers. The intermediary may also explain such questions or answers, if necessary to facilitate understanding. An intermediary will normally be a specialist. An intermediary can act however and wherever the examination is conducted. The judge or magistrates, and at least one legal representative for each side, should be able to see and hear W and to communicate with the intermediary. The jury must be able to see and hear W unless the evidence is video recorded.

Aids to communication (s 30) A special measures direction may require a witness to be provided with an appropriate device to assist communication.

General Evidence given using any of the special measures set out above must be treated in the same way as oral evidence. However, the judge may give such warning to the jury as he considers necessary to ensure fairness to D.

If a witness who would normally be sworn gives unsworn evidence by means of a video recording, that evidence is admissible. However, where a person authorised to administer an oath is present, the evidence could be taken under oath in appropriate cases.

The *Criminal Practice Directions* require that the party who made the application to admit video-recorded evidence-in-chief must edit the recording in accordance with the judge's directions and send a copy of the edited recording to the appropriate officer of the Crown Court and to every other party to the proceedings.

Where a video recording is to be adduced during proceedings before a Crown Court, it must be produced and proved by the interviewer, or any other person who was present at the interview with the witness at which the recording was made. The parties may agree to accept a written statement in lieu of the attendance of such a person. The party adducing the video recording must arrange for the operation of the video-playing equipment.

Failure so to prepare, which leads to an adjournment for this to be done, may lead to an appropriate award for costs.

Best practice in questioning child and vulnerable witnesses

The Ministry of Justice has published assistance for those dealing with witnesses subject to special measures and for those preparing video-recorded interviews, *Achieving Best Evidence in Criminal Proceedings: Guidance on Interviewing Victims and Witnesses, and Guidance on Using Special Measures*.

The guidance is primarily aimed at police officers conducting visually-recorded interviews with vulnerable, intimidated and significant witnesses, those tasked with preparing and supporting such witnesses during the criminal justice process and those involved at the trial, both in supporting and questioning the witness in court. While the guidance is advisory, compliance with *Achieving Best Evidence* and effective training is likely to maximise the quality of interviews with such witnesses and is likely to benefit the interviewer, the witness, practitioners, and the courts alike. Where there has been a breach of *Achieving Best Evidence* an interview will only be inadmissible if the court cannot be sure that the witness has given a credible and accurate account.

Evidence of vulnerable defendant

YJCEA 1999, s 33A allows a court, on the application of the defendant (D), to direct that D's evidence should be given over a live link. The court must be satisfied that it would be in the interests of justice for D to give evidence through a live link, and:

(a) if D is under 18, that his ability to participate effectively as a witness giving oral evidence is compromised by his level of intellectual ability or social functioning, and that use of a live link would enable him to participate more effectively as a witness;

(b) if D is 18 or over, that he is unable to participate in the proceedings effectively as a witness in court giving oral evidence because he has a mental disorder or a significant impairment of intelligence and social function, and that use of a live link would enable him to participate more effectively as a witness.

Section 33A is intended to provide a structured approach to decision-making and to ensure that the giving of evidence in this way is reserved for exceptional cases. Where a juvenile is concerned the test is less strict as there is no reference to mental disorder or impairment.

Where a direction has been given under s 33A, D must give all his oral evidence through a live link and cross-examination should be carried out by the same means.

A divisional court has held that the courts have a common law duty to appoint an intermediary to help a child defendant (or, indeed, an adult defendant) follow the proceedings and give evidence where he would otherwise not have a fair trial.

When brought into force, s 33BA will provide for a vulnerable defendant to give evidence through an intermediary. It is dealt with in Chapter 7 on the companion website.

Protection of witnesses from cross-examination by defendant in person

Complainants in proceedings for sexual offences

YJCEA 1999, s 34 provides that no person charged with a sexual offence may in any criminal proceedings cross-examine in person a witness who is a complainant, either in connection with the offence, or in connection with any other offence (of whatever nature) with which that person is charged in the proceedings. Here, 'sexual offence' means any offence under the Sexual Offences Act 2003 (SOA 2003), Part 1 (ss 1–79), any 'relevant superseded sexual offence' ie (a corresponding offence superseded by ss 1–79), or one under MSA 2015, s 1 committed with a view to sexual exploitation.

Child complainants and other witnesses who are children

In relation to an offence to which it applies, YJCEA 1999, s 35 makes similar provisions concerning a 'protected witness'. A 'protected witness' is a witness who:

(a) either is a complainant or a witness to the offence; and

(b) either is a child or falls to be cross-examined after giving evidence-in-chief as a child.

Section 35 applies to any offence under SOA 1956, ss 33–36 (brothels), the Protection of Children Act 1978 (taking, etc indecent photographs, etc of a child), SOA 2003, Part 1 (ss 1–79) or any 'relevant superseded enactment', or MSA 2015, ss 1 and 2. For the purposes of YJCEA 1999, s 35, where an offence is under one of these pieces of legislation, a 'child' is someone under 18.

Section 35 also applies to kidnapping, false imprisonment, child abduction (Child Abduction Act 1984, ss 1 or 2), cruelty to children (Children and Young Persons Act 1933, s 1) or any offence involving an assault on, or injury (or a threat of injury) to, any person. For the purposes of these other specified offences, a 'child' is someone under 14.

Direction prohibiting cross-examination

YJCEA 1999, s 36, which is not limited to the sexual offences or other offences to which s 35 applies, permits a court to prohibit an unrepresented defendant from cross-examining witnesses in other cases, where the provisions of ss 34 and 35 do not apply. This may be done where the court is satisfied that the quality of the evidence given by the witness on cross-examination is likely to be diminished if cross-examination is undertaken or continued by the defendant in person, and would be likely to be improved if a direction was given, and that such a prohibition will not be contrary to the interests of justice.

The term 'witness' does not include any other person who is charged with an offence within the proceedings.

Representation of such persons for the purpose of cross-examination

Where D is prohibited from cross-examining a witness under the provisions of YJCEA 1999, ss 34, 35 or 36, the court must invite D to appoint a legal representative to cross-examine on his behalf. If no such appointment is made within the prescribed time limits, the court must consider whether it is necessary, in the interests of justice, for the witness to be cross-examined by a legal representative. If the court considers that it is necessary, it must appoint a legal representative. Such a court-appointed representative will not have been instructed by D and will not, therefore, be responsible to him. Material relating to the proceedings must be made available to an appointee.

Warning to the jury

Where D is prevented from cross-examining a person by virtue of ss 34, 35 or 36, the judge must give the jury such warning as he considers necessary to ensure that D is not prejudiced:

(a) by any inferences which might be drawn from the fact that he has been prevented from cross-examining in person;

(b) where the witness has been cross-examined by a legal representative appointed by the court, by the fact that such cross-examination was carried out by a representative other than a person acting as D's own legal representative.

Witness anonymity

The Coroners and Justice Act 2009 (C&JA 2009), ss 86–95 provide for the making of witness anonymity orders (WAOs) in criminal proceedings, on the application of the prosecutor or the defendant (D).

A WAO is an order that requires such specified measures to be taken in relation to a witness (W) in criminal proceedings as the court considers appropriate to ensure that the identity of W is not disclosed in or in connection with the proceedings.

A court may make a WAO only if it is satisfied that conditions A to C below are all met.

Condition A is that the measures to be specified in the order are necessary in order:

(a) to protect the safety of W or another person or to prevent any serious damage to property; or
(b) to prevent real harm to the public interest (whether affecting the carrying on of any activities in the public interest or the safety of a person involved in carrying on such activities, or otherwise).

Condition B is that, having regard to all the circumstances, the taking of those measures would be consistent with D receiving a fair trial.

Condition C is that the importance of W's testimony is such that in the interests of justice W ought to testify and:

(a) W would not testify if the proposed order were not made, or
(b) there would be real harm to the public interest if W were to testify without the proposed order being made.

When deciding whether conditions A to C are met in the case of an application for a WAO, the court must have regard to the following considerations:

(a) the general right of a defendant in criminal proceedings to know the identity of a witness;
(b) the extent to which the credibility of W would be a relevant factor when the weight of his identity comes to be assessed;
(c) whether evidence given by W might be the sole or decisive evidence implicating D;
(d) whether W's evidence could be properly tested without his identity being disclosed;
(e) whether there is any reason to believe that W has a tendency to be dishonest, or has any motive to be dishonest in the circumstances of the case; and
(f) whether it would be reasonably practicable to protect W's identity by any means other than by making a WAO specifying the measures that are under consideration by the court.

The court must also have regard to other matters it considers relevant.

MEANS OF PROOF WHICH MAY BE INADMISSIBLE

Opinion

Opinion evidence is generally inadmissible because it is the function of the court or jury, and not of a witness, to draw conclusions from the facts proved. If a witness alleges that a particular driver was at fault and caused an accident, that evidence is inadmissible because that is the issue which the court or jury must decide. A fine line can sometimes exist between 'opinion' and 'fact', and for this reason evidence as to the identification of a person or thing (which must always be an opinion to some extent) is admissible. In addition, by way of exception to the general rule, the following opinion evidence of experts is admissible:

(a) opinion evidence of experts on matters (outside the knowledge or experience of a jury) of a scientific, technical or artistic nature, such as doctors of medicine, forensic scientists, metallurgists or literary experts: a police officer can be an expert under this heading in appropriate circumstances; for example, the opinion evidence of a police officer that a quantity of drugs was too great for personal use was held admissible as expert evidence because the officer based his opinion on his 17 years' experience and on published and unpublished material;

(b) opinion evidence from persons who are experts in handwriting comparison; and

(c) opinion evidence by a lawyer shown to have knowledge of a particular system of foreign law.

An expert witness should provide independent, objective assistance to the court in relation to matters within his expertise, and should never assume the role of advocate. An expert is obliged to act in the cause of justice. His duties are owed to the court and override any obligation to those instructing him or by whom he is paid. Consequently, for example, if an expert instructed by the prosecution carries out a test, or knows that a test has been carried out in his laboratory, which casts doubt on his opinion, he must disclose this to his instructing solicitor, who must disclose it to the defence.

Hearsay

As said on p 230, hearsay evidence is 'second-hand' evidence since it consists of any representation of fact or opinion made by whatever means (eg orally, in writing or by conduct) by a person otherwise than in oral evidence in the particular proceedings which is tendered as evidence of any matter stated *in it*. Hearsay evidence is inadmissible, unless its admission is permitted under a variety of rules, because the law of evidence generally requires a fact to be proved by direct evidence of it.

Of course, as already indicated, not all evidence of what someone other than a witness said or wrote is hearsay. If it is produced merely to prove the fact that it was said or written, as opposed to establishing a matter contained in the oral or written statement, it is original evidence and not hearsay evidence, and therefore admissible if relevant to the facts in issue. This distinction can be illustrated as follows.

If a witness says that the deceased, while in hospital with injuries from which he unexpectedly died, told him, 'Fred did this to me', this is hearsay evidence since it is produced as evidence of the truth of what the deceased stated, ie that Fred caused the injuries.

By way of contrast, it is not necessarily hearsay evidence for evidence to be called to show that D said that he had acted under a threat of death made by Jones, or for a witness to say 'Mrs Bird complained to me that Tate had fondled her breasts'. This is original evidence of the fact that a threat or complaint had been made. The latter statement is, however, hearsay if it is intended to show the fact that the sexual offence has been committed.

The rule against hearsay evidence has gradually been whittled away, culminating in CJA 2003, Part 11, Chapter 2 (ss 114–136) which abolished the common law rules about hearsay evidence and created a set of rules about its admissibility. It should be noted that hearsay evidence does not have to be shown to be reliable or independently verified before it can be admitted under these rules.

The cases where a statement is admissible in criminal proceedings as evidence of the truth of its contents under an exception to the rule against hearsay are as follows.

Admissibility of hearsay evidence: the basic provisions

CJA 2003, Part 11, Chapter 2 commences in s 114 by stating in s 114(1) that hearsay evidence is admissible in criminal proceedings as evidence of any matter stated if, but only if s 114(1)(a), (b), (c) or (d) applies:

(a) a statutory provision makes it admissible (considered below);

(b) any rule of law preserved by s 118 (pp 231 and 252–3) makes it admissible;

(c) all parties to the proceedings agree to it being admissible; or

(d) the court is satisfied that it is in the interests of justice for it to be admissible.

The Court of Appeal has held that an agreement can be inferred in appropriate circumstances for the purposes of s 114(1)(c) from a failure by a party to object to the admissibility of the hearsay evidence.

In deciding under s 114(1)(d) whether it is in the interests of justice, the court must have regard to the following factors (and any others it considers relevant):

(i)   how much probative value the statement has in relation to a matter in issue (ie how much value is it in determining the matter) or how valuable it is for understanding other evidence;

(ii)   what other evidence has been, or can be, given on the matter or evidence mentioned in (i);

(iii)   how important the matter or evidence mentioned in (i) is in the context of the case as a whole;

(iv)   the circumstances in which the statement was made;

(v)   how reliable the maker of the statement appears to be;

(vi)   how reliable the evidence of the making of the statement appears to be;

(vii)   whether oral evidence of the matter stated can be given and, if not, why it cannot;

(viii) the amount of difficulty involved in challenging the statement; and

(ix)   the extent to which the difficulty would be likely to prejudice the party facing it (s 114(2)).

A court does not have to reach a conclusion about all nine of these factors in order to admit hearsay evidence under (d). The Court of Appeal has held that s 114(1)(d) must be cautiously applied in the case of an absent witness who does not fall within s 116 ('Witness unavailable': p 247); otherwise the conditions in s 116 would be circumvented.

The European Court of Human Rights, agreeing with the Supreme Court, has held that where hearsay evidence is the sole or decisive evidence against D its admission does not automatically breach the right to a fair trial under the European Convention on Human Rights, art 6. In the case of such a statement, there will not be a breach if there are sufficient counterbalancing factors, including strong procedural safeguards, that permit a proper assessment of the reliability of the hearsay evidence. The safeguards in English law, particularly the hearsay provisions of CJA 2003, are—if properly applied—sufficiently strong safeguards to ensure fairness.

The Court of Appeal has held that an anonymous witness statement made by a person whose identity is not known at all cannot be admitted under the hearsay rules in CJA 2003, Part 11, Chapter 2.

CJA 2003, Part 11, Chapter 2 does not affect the exclusion of evidence of a statement on grounds other than the fact that it is hearsay. For example, a confession (a type of admissible hearsay) might be excluded under the provisions of PACE.

CJA 2003, s 115 provides that, for the purposes of CJA 2003, Part 11, Chapter 2, references to a 'statement' are to any representation of fact or opinion made by a person by whatever means, including a representation made in a sketch, photofit or other pictorial form. By s 115, a 'matter stated' is one to which CJA 2003, Part 11, Chapter 2 applies only if the purpose (or one of the purposes) of the maker of the statement appears to have been to cause another person to believe the matter or to cause another person to act or a machine to operate on the basis that the matter is as stated. As a result a statement which was not made with such a purpose, but from which a fact may be inferred, is not hearsay evidence and is admissible. Examples would be a statement made in a secret diary or in a text to another person mentioning a fact that the texter believes the other knows. This reverses the old law of hearsay, under which such a statement was hearsay.

The exceptions to the hearsay rule to which (a) and (b) above relate are as follows.

Witness unavailable

CJA 2003, s 116 provides that in criminal proceedings a statement which is not made in oral evidence in the proceedings is admissible in evidence as evidence of any matter stated if:

(a) oral evidence given by the person making the statement would be admissible as evidence of that matter;
(b) the person who made the statement is identified to the satisfaction of the court; and
(c) that person:
   (i) is dead;
   (ii) is unfit to be a witness because of his bodily or mental condition;
   (iii) is outside the UK and it is not reasonably practicable to secure his attendance;
   (iv) cannot be found although such steps as it is reasonably practicable to take to find him have been taken; or
   (v) through fear does not give (or continue to give) oral evidence in the proceedings, either at all, or in connection with the subject matter of the statement, and the court gives leave for the statement to be given in evidence.

'Unfit to be a witness' in (c)(ii) applies not only to a person's physical inability to attend a court but also to his mental capacity when there to give evidence. The Court of Appeal has said that there is nothing to prevent the written evidence of a witness being admitted where he is too ill to give evidence at the time of the trial, even though his evidence is the only evidence against D.

'Cannot be found' in (c)(iv) includes 'cannot be contacted'.

'Fear' in (c)(v) is to be widely construed and (for example) includes fear of the death or serious injury of another person or of financial loss. There must, if possible, be direct evidence (of fear) from the witness. However, the evidence of fear may, for example, be given by a police officer. Nonetheless, it is important to establish that the fear existed at the time of the trial. Before a court can properly be satisfied as to the requirements, it should be informed of what steps have been taken to persuade the witness to attend or to alleviate his fears. Leave to admit may only be given under (c)(v) where the court considers that the statement ought to be admitted in the interests of justice, having regard to its contents, to the risk of unfairness and, in appropriate cases, to the fact that a special measures direction could be made in relation to the person making the statement, and to any other relevant circumstances.

Any condition in (c)(i)–(v) which is in fact satisfied will be treated as not having been satisfied if any of the circumstances described in (c) have effectively been caused by the person in support of whose case it is sought to admit the statement, or by any person acting on his behalf, in order to prevent the person referred to in (c) from giving oral evidence in the proceedings (whether at all or in connection with the subject matter of the statement). It is irrelevant whether the steps which had the relevant effect were taken before or after the commencement of the proceedings.

Business and other documents

CJA 2003, s 117 provides that in criminal proceedings a statement contained in a document is admissible as evidence of any matter stated if:

(a) oral evidence given in the proceedings would be admissible as evidence of that matter;

(b) the following requirements are satisfied:

   (i) the document or the part containing the statement was created or received by a person in the course of a trade, business, profession or other occupation, or as the holder of a paid or unpaid office;

   (ii) the person who supplied the information contained in the statement (the relevant person) had, or may reasonably be supposed to have had, personal knowledge of the matters dealt with; and

   (iii) each person (if any) through whom the information was supplied from that relevant person to the person mentioned in (i) received the information in the course of a trade, business, profession or other occupation, or as the holder of a paid or unpaid office; and

(c) additional requirements are satisfied where the statement was prepared for the purpose of pending or contemplated criminal proceedings, or for a criminal investigation, but was not obtained pursuant to a request under the Crime (International Co-operation) Act 2003, s 7, or an order under the Criminal Justice Act 1988, Sch 13 (overseas evidence). The additional requirements referred to are any of the five conditions set out at (c) under the heading 'Witness unavailable' on p 247 above, or that the relevant person cannot reasonably be expected to have any recollection of the matters dealt with in the statement (having regard to the length of time since he supplied the information and all other circumstances).

The persons mentioned in (b)(i) and (ii) may be the same person. Thus, for example, a note made by an operator working for a paging company that messages had been left for a customer would be admissible under s 117.

Section 117 is obviously sensible. It would be unnecessarily burdensome, and sometimes stultifying, if oral evidence was always required from a person who was either the creator or keeper of the document, or the supplier of the information contained in the document.

As a result of s 117, entries in a police officer's notebook (or a computerised crime record produced by a police officer) are admissible if the terms of s 117 are satisfied. An example of a case where s 117 was satisfied is where a man presented a stolen debit card at a supermarket checkout and a supervisor saw him making off in a car, the registered number of which she noted; a record made by a second supervisor, at the dictation of the first, was held to be a document created or received in the course of a business, profession, etc for these purposes; the fact that she could recall other matters which occurred at the time (such as the colour of the offender) did not mean that she could be expected to remember the registered number of the car.

It is important to note the limitations of s 117. For example, where a shopper had left the offending vehicle's registration number on the damaged car's windscreen after it had been hit in a supermarket car park and that number had been reported in the police incident log after it had been given by the girlfriend of the owner of the damaged car, the Court of Appeal held that the information in the log should not have been admitted under s 117 because the girlfriend had not received it in the course of trade or business and therefore condition (b)(iii) was not satisfied. The Court of Appeal added that the police record would have been admissible under the rule relating to the admissibility of multiple hearsay (see condition (c) under s 121 on p 250).

A statement is not admissible under s 117 if the court makes a direction to that effect, which it can do if satisfied that the statement's reliability as evidence is doubtful, either in its contents, the source of its information, the way or circumstances in which the information was supplied or received, or the way in which the document was created or received.

Inconsistent statements

CJA 2003, s 119 provides that, where a witness (W) in criminal proceedings gives oral evidence and admits making a previous inconsistent statement, or a previous inconsistent statement made by W is proved to have been made, the previous statement is admissible as evidence of any matter in respect of which oral evidence would be admissible. Thus, the fact that W made a previous inconsistent statement does not merely affect W's credibility but it is also some evidence of the truth of the facts which W had previously stated. Evidence may be admitted to show that W has made a statement which is inconsistent with the evidence he has given.

Other previous statements of a witness

Where it is suggested that a witness (W) in criminal proceedings has fabricated oral evidence, a previous statement by W is admissible not only on the issue of credibility but also to prove the truth of the matters previously stated. This is the effect of CJA 2003, s 120(2), which states that any previous statement which W has made is admissible in evidence as evidence of any matter which it contains.

In addition, s 120(3) provides that where W refreshes his memory from a written document and is cross-examined on a statement in that document, and the document is in consequence received in evidence, that statement in the document will become evidence of any matter stated in it. Section 120(3) does not make admissible as truth of the matters stated a statement made in a written document in circumstances where a re-reading of a previous out-of-court document has failed to refresh W's memory when giving oral evidence at the trial. The situation where W has made a previous statement when the matters were fresh in his memory, but does not remember them at the time of the trial, even when he has attempted to refresh his memory, is dealt with specifically by (b) in the following provisions.

By s 120(4)–(7) a previous statement is also admissible as evidence of the facts contained in it if W states that he made the statement and believes it to be true and any one of the following conditions applies:

(a) that the statement describes or identifies a person, object, or place;
(b) that it was made by W when the matters stated were fresh in his memory, and he cannot reasonably be expected to remember the matters stated well enough to give oral evidence of them; or
(c) that:
    (i) W claims to be a victim of an offence to which the proceedings relate,
    (ii) the statement consists of a complaint by W about conduct which (if proved) would constitute the offence (or part of it),
    (iii) the complaint was not made as a result of a threat or promise, and
    (iv) W gives oral evidence in respect of the matter before the statement is adduced.

Additional requirements for admissibility of multiple hearsay

'Multiple hearsay' refers to the case where the witness has no personal knowledge of the matter stated to him, but repeats a hearsay statement made to him by another, as where X makes a statement to Y who repeats it to Z. Repetition of the statement by Z is multiple (or second-hand) hearsay, whereas if Y gave the statement in evidence it would be first-hand hearsay. CJA 2003, s 121 provides that a hearsay statement is not admissible to prove the fact that an earlier hearsay statement was made unless:

(a) either of the statements is admissible under s 117 (business and other documents), 119 (inconsistent statements) or 120 (other previous statements by a witness), or

(b) all parties agree to its admissibility, or

(c) the court is satisfied that the value of the evidence in question, taking into account how reliable the statement appears to be, is so high that the interests of justice require the later statement to be admissible for that purpose.

CJA 2003, ss 116, 117, 119 and 120: general provisions concerning capability to make statements

CJA 2003, s 123 provides as follows.

A statement made under s 116 (cases where a witness is unavailable), s 119 or s 120 is not admissible in evidence if it was made by a person who did not have the 'required capability' at the time that he made the statement.

In the case of a statement made under s 117 such a statement is not admissible so far as the requirements of para (b) (see p 248) are concerned (created or received by the particular persons in the course of their business, etc) if any person who, in order to satisfy the requirements, must have supplied or received the information concerned (or created or received the document or part concerned) did not at the time have the required capability, or if that person cannot be identified but cannot reasonably be assumed to have had the required capability at that time.

A person has the 'required capability' if he is capable of understanding questions put to him about the matter and of giving answers which can be understood. Where such capability is disputed, the fact must be determined in the absence of the jury (if there is one) and expert evidence may be received as well as that of any person to whom the statement was made. The burden of proof lies upon the party seeking to adduce the statement and the standard of proof is the balance of probabilities.

Evidence from computer records

The ordinary law on evidence applies to computer evidence. In the absence of evidence to the contrary, courts will presume that the computer system was working correctly. If there is evidence that it might not have been, the party seeking to introduce the evidence will need to prove that it was working. Such proof can be satisfied by the evidence of a person familiar with the operation of the computer, who need not be a computer expert. The House of Lords has held that evidence by a store detective that computerised cash tills were working satisfactorily was admissible where it was apparent from the nature of her evidence that she was thoroughly familiar with the operation of the tills and the central computer, even though she did not understand the technical operation of the computer.

CJA 2003, s 129 provides that, where a representation of fact is generated by a machine and depends for its accuracy on information supplied by a person, the representation will only be admissible as evidence of the fact where it is proved that the information was accurate. This is not directly related to proof of the reliability of the machine, but is associated, in that there is a requirement to show that accurate information was fed into the machine.

Procedural rules

A party who wants to introduce hearsay evidence under ss 114(1)(d) (evidence admissible in the interests of justice), 116 (witness unavailable), 117 (head (c) statement prepared for criminal proceedings) or 121 (multiple hearsay) (see pp 246, 247, 248 and 250 respectively) must give notice in accordance with the Criminal Procedure Rules 2015, Part 20; see Chapter 7 on the companion website.

Evidence by certificate

The Criminal Justice Act 1948, s 41 provides that a certificate signed by a constable or qualified person certifying that a plan or drawing exhibited in criminal proceedings is a plan or drawing made by him of an identified place or object specified in the certificate, and that the plan or drawing is correctly drawn to a scale so specified, is evidence of the relative position of things shown on the plan or drawing. The plan, etc is admissible to the same extent that oral evidence would be admissible. A 'qualified person' means a registered architect or a chartered engineer of one of certain types.

In order for the certificate to be admissible, a copy of such a plan, etc must be served on D at least seven days before the hearing. Moreover, if D serves the appropriate notice that he requires the attendance of the person who signed the certificate, the certificate will not be admissible.

Proof by written statements

The Criminal Justice Act 1967, s 9 provides for the admissibility of written statements in criminal proceedings. It states that a written statement signed by the person who made it is admissible as evidence to the like extent as oral evidence given by that person. There are certain conditions which must be satisfied:

(a) the statement must contain a declaration by that person to the effect that it is true to the best of his knowledge or belief and that he has made the statement knowing that, if it were tendered in evidence, he would be liable to prosecution if he wilfully stated in it anything which he knew to be false or did not believe to be true;

(b) before the hearing at which the statement is tendered in evidence, a copy of the statement must be served, by or on behalf of the party proposing to tender it, on each of the other parties to the proceedings; and

(c) none of the other parties or their solicitors must, within the relevant period, have served a notice on the party so proposing objecting to the statement being tendered in evidence under the section.

Conditions (b) and (c) do not apply if the parties agree before or during the hearing that the document shall be so tendered.

In practice, statement forms carried by police officers incorporate the declaration at (a) so that the evidence of any witness can be offered in written form if it is accepted by the other side.

'The relevant period' in (c) is defined by the Criminal Procedure Rules 2015, Part 16. It is the period of seven days after service of the statement unless:

(i) the court extends that time limit;

(ii) the 'pleading guilty by post' provisions apply, in which case the time limit is the later of seven days after service of the statement or seven days before the hearing date; or

(iii) the trial by single justice on the papers procedure applies, in which case the time limit is 21 days after service of the statement.

It has been held that 'statement' in s 9 means the written assertion of facts made by the person who signed the document, and that what is required by (a) is that the written assertion of facts is contained in a document in identical terms to those in the signed document. Thus, it was irrelevant that the copy of the statement which had been served on D had not been signed by the maker of the written statement; the important thing was that the assertions of facts in the copy were identical to those in the signed statement.

The Criminal Procedure Rules 2015, Part 16 additionally require the statement to contain:

(a) the witness's (W's) age, if under 18; and

(b) if W cannot read the statement, a signed declaration by someone else that that person read it to W.

In addition, where the statement refers to a document or object as an exhibit, the statement must clearly identify that document or object.

Regardless of this procedure having been carried out, the party whose witness it is may nevertheless call that person to give evidence and the court may require that that person attend to give evidence.

Proof of convictions and acquittals

The provisions relating to how such proof may be established, discussed above (p 232), afford another exception to the rule against hearsay.

Statements received as part of the res gestae

A statement is part of the res gestae if it is so closely associated in time, place and circumstances with the fact in issue that it can be said to be part of the same transaction. At common law, under the 'res gestae rule', a statement which is part of the res gestae is admissible if the conditions set out below are satisfied.

The res gestae rule is specifically preserved by CJA 2003, s 118, which preserves any rule of law under which, in criminal proceedings, a statement is admissible as evidence of any matter stated if:

(a) the statement was made by a person so emotionally overpowered by an event that the possibility of concoction or distortion can be disregarded;

(b) the statement accompanied an act which can be properly evaluated as evidence only if considered in conjunction with the statement; or

(c) the statement relates to a physical sensation or mental state (such as intention or emotion).

Thus, an oral statement made by a person involved in an unusual, startling or exciting event is admissible as part of the res gestae as evidence of the facts stated, provided it was so clearly made spontaneously that, in the light of the circumstances, the possibility of concoction or distortion can be disregarded. If the issue is one of murder it is probable that a victim's statement 'don't shoot, Sidney', which was made as (or immediately before) the gun was fired, would be admissible as part of the res gestae, although it is hearsay, and that likewise the victim's agitated shout immediately afterwards, 'Look what you've done. Get a doctor, quick', would be admissible. Where a man was stabbed and, whilst being given first aid treatment by a constable, named his attackers, this evidence was admitted as a part of the res gestae at D's trial after the declarant had died.

Confessions

Although hearsay, a confession is generally admissible. The law relating to confessions is dealt with below. At this point, it needs to be noted that the exception of confessions from the hearsay rule has been held to apply to the case where, in the course of a routine inquiry, a police officer asks someone to identify himself and that person does so by saying 'I am Robin Hood of 15 High Street'. If, in later proceedings against that person the officer cannot independently identify Robin Hood of 15 High Street as the person who spoke to him on the previous occasion, the officer may testify that this person had said 'I am Robin Hood of 15 High Street', despite the fact that this is hearsay, because it amounts to a confession. However, the jury must be directed to be sure that it was D who gave the identification on the previous occasion.

These rules are specifically preserved by CJA 2003, s 118.

Public information

CJA 2003, s 118 preserves the rule of law which permits, in criminal proceedings, the admissibility of:

(a) facts of a public nature stated in published works dealing with matters of a public nature (eg histories, scientific works, dictionaries, maps), or
(b) facts stated in public documents (eg public registers, and returns under public authority with respect to matters of public interest), or in court records, treaties, etc, or
(c) evidence as to a person's age or date or place of birth in a birth certificate.

Expert reports

An expert report is admissible in evidence in criminal proceedings, whether or not the person making it attends to give oral evidence. However, if it is proposed that the maker of the report will not give oral evidence, the report is only admissible with the leave of the court. In determining whether to give leave, the court must have regard to the contents of the report; the reasons why it is proposed that oral evidence will not be given; the likely risk to fairness in relation to D; and any other relevant circumstance. An 'expert report' is one written by a person dealing wholly or mainly with matters on which he is (or if living would be) qualified to give expert evidence.

This common law rule is preserved by CJA 2003, s 118.

Reputation

CJA 2003, s 118 preserves the common law rules whereby, in criminal proceedings, hearsay evidence of a person's reputation is admissible for the purpose of proving his good or bad character, but only in so far as it allows the court to treat such evidence as proving his good or bad character.

Section 118 also preserves the common law rules about the admissibility of evidence of reputation or family tradition for the purpose of proving pedigree or the existence of a marriage, the existence of any public or general right, or the identity of any person or thing. The use of these rules will be rare.

Supplementary points about hearsay

Credibility of hearsay evidence   By CJA 2003, s 124, a challenge may be made to the credibility of the maker of a statement admitted in criminal proceedings as hearsay evidence if he does not give oral evidence in the proceedings. In certain circumstances, the person against whom the hearsay evidence has been admitted may produce evidence to discredit the maker of the statement or to show that he has contradicted himself.

Stopping case where hearsay evidence unconvincing   A judge has the duty under CJA 2003, s 125 to stop a case and either direct acquittal, or (if the judge considers that there ought to be a re-trial) discharge the jury, if the prosecution case is based wholly or partly on an out-of-court statement which is *so unconvincing that, considering its importance to the case against D, a conviction would be unsafe*. If any untested out-of-court statement is not shown to be reliable and it is a statement which is part of the central body of evidence without which the case cannot proceed, the italicised words will be satisfied.

A magistrates' court would have a similar duty to that under s 125 in the above circumstances.

General discretion to exclude hearsay evidence   CJA 2003, s 126 gives a court a discretion to exclude a statement as evidence of a matter stated if the statement was made otherwise than in oral evidence in the proceedings, and the court is satisfied that the case for excluding the statement, taking account of the danger that to admit it would result in undue waste of time, substantially outweighs the case for admitting it, taking account of the value of the evidence. This is in addition to any discretion under PACE, s 78 (p 267) or any other power of a court to exclude evidence.

CONFESSIONS

Confession by one defendant: evidence against co-defendant?

An out-of-court confession by *one defendant is not evidence against another co-defendant* unless the co-defendant expressly or impliedly adopts the statements contained in it. There are qualifications to this statement. First, the House of Lords has held that, when in a joint trial of two or more for an offence alleged to have been committed jointly, proof of the guilt of one of the defendants, A, is essential in proving the case against another of them, B, and the evidence against A consists solely of his own out-of-court confession, then A's confession will be admissible as evidence, not only against A but also against B in so far as the fact of A's guilt of itself establishes B's guilt. Second, an out-of-court accusation against a co-defendant contained in a confession is *capable* of being admitted as hearsay evidence if it falls within CJA 2003, s 114(1)(d) (interests of justice for evidence to be admissible: p 246).

Confession by defendant as evidence against him

For the purposes of the rules which follow, a 'confession' is defined by PACE, s 82 as including 'any statement wholly or partly adverse to the person who made it, whether made to a person in authority or not and whether made in words or otherwise'. A wholly exculpatory statement is not a confession for these purposes. Because of the phrase 'in words or otherwise', a defendant's confession may simply consist of a gesture of acceptance of a statement adverse to him made by another. Statements made which are intended to vindicate a suspect, for example, where he gives explanations intended to justify his possession of goods, and if taken to be true, would do so, do not amount to a confession, even if they are later shown to be false or inconsistent with the maker's evidence. In such a case, however, a record should be made as soon as possible; the reason for there being no contemporaneous notes should be recorded and the suspect should be given an opportunity to check the record.

PACE, s 76(1) allows a confession by D to be given in evidence against him in so far as that confession is relevant to a matter in issue in the proceedings and has not been excluded by the court under s 76(2) on the basis explained below. Thus, if D makes a confession to an offence of burglary and mentions involvement in an offence of wounding on another occasion, his confession to burglary will be admissible at his trial for that offence since it is relevant to a matter in issue, but if he has not also been charged with wounding, his confession to wounding is not admissible since it is not relevant to a matter in issue in the proceedings.

Exclusion

If it is represented by D (or by D's counsel), on the basis of some credible, more than insignificant or trivial evidence, that a confession by D was, or may have been, obtained by oppression or in consequence of anything said or done which was likely to render the confession unreliable, the court must not allow the confession to be given in evidence against that person except in so far as the prosecution proves beyond reasonable doubt that the confession (notwithstanding that it might be true) was not obtained by these means.

PACE, s 76(2) provides that a *confession by oppression must always be excluded.* 'Oppression' includes torture, inhuman or degrading treatment, and the use of threats or violence. Apart from this, 'oppression' bears its ordinary dictionary meaning, namely, 'the exercise of power or authority in a burdensome, harsh, or wrongful manner; unjust or cruel treatment'. It will almost inevitably involve some impropriety on the part of the questioner. The fact that a confession has been obtained in circumstances involving a breach of a code of practice does not in itself constitute oppression. However, bullying questioning may exceptionally amount to oppression.

Section 76(2) also provides that a *confession must be excluded if it was obtained in consequence of anything said or done which was likely, in the circumstances existing at the time, to render unreliable any confession which might be made by D in consequence thereof.* An example of something which will be held to be likely to render a confession unreliable is making an untrue inducement to bring about a confession (eg 'if you confess, the matter will go no further'). Another example is the use of hostile and intimidating interview techniques. For such a likelihood of unreliability to be found there is no need for any hint of impropriety. Where a suspect was mentally handicapped and was interviewed without an adult person being present, it was held that once it had been established that there had been a breach of PACE Code C, the onus was on the prosecution to satisfy the judge beyond reasonable doubt that the confession was not obtained in breach of s 76(2). The circumstances existing at the time were all important in relation to reliability.

Where it is shown that there has been aggressive and hostile questioning it becomes a matter of degree as to whether the threshold is passed beyond which the behaviour of police officers has made the confession unreliable in all circumstances. However, all the circumstances must be examined. In the course of an interview concerning drug offences an officer interjected, implying that if the suspect (D) did not tell the truth he would be held in custody. Some 16 minutes later D confessed to an offence. The trial judge refused to exclude his confession being satisfied that D was astute, had experience of being interviewed at a police station, and that his will had not been broken. He had continued to deny other offences. The Court of Appeal endorsed the trial judge's decision.

It has not yet been decided whether interviewing a drug addict when he is withdrawing falls within the present provision. However, the Court of Appeal has held that, if it is, the question of 'likely to be rendered unreliable' depends on whether or not the addict was fit to be interviewed in the sense that his answers could be relied upon in the circumstances. This, the court held, is a matter for those present at the time. The court held that, where experienced police officers considered a person fit to be interviewed and a doctor who saw him after the interview was of the same opinion, there was no reason to believe that a confession was likely to be unreliable.

Facts discovered as a result of inadmissible confession   PACE, s 76(4) provides that, even if a confession, or a part of it, is excluded under the above provisions, this does not affect the admissibility in evidence:

(a) of any facts discovered as a result of the confession; or
(b) where the confession is relevant as showing that D speaks, writes or expresses himself in a particular way, of so much of the confession as is necessary to show that he does so.

The effect of (a) is as follows. If evidence of a fact is discovered as a result of a confession, or part of a confession, and that confession, or a relevant part of it, is excluded under s 76(2), that evidence may nevertheless be adduced by the prosecution. However, no reference should be made to the fact that the discovery was the result of a confession; only D, or someone acting on his behalf, may disclose this. Thus, if D is arrested for thefts of motor cars and makes a confession which includes details of the persons to whom he sold the vehicles, and that confession is excluded, the prosecution may give evidence of the recovery of the vehicles from those persons but it may not mention that they were discovered as a result of the excluded confession.

The effect of (b) is that, if there is something in a confession, or part, excluded under s 76, which shows that D writes, speaks or expresses himself in a particular manner, and this serves, for example, to identify him with whoever committed the offence, so much of the confession as is necessary to show the characteristic referred to is admissible.

Confessions given in evidence for co-defendant

PACE, s 76A provides that a confession, as defined by s 82, made by a defendant may be given in evidence for a co-defendant in so far as it is relevant to a matter in issue unless excluded by the court on one of the two grounds under s 76. If it is alleged that one of them applies, the co-defendant seeking to rely on the confession must prove on the balance of probabilities that the confession was not obtained by oppression, etc. The Court of Appeal has held that s 76A does not apply so as to permit evidence of a confession to be given when D who gave the confession has pleaded guilty and is therefore not on trial with the co-defendant; s 76A it said, is designed to cater for the joint trial of the defendant and co-defendant.

The fact that a confession is wholly or partly excluded under s 76A does not affect the admissibility in evidence of the matters referred to in s 76(4).

Confessions by the mentally handicapped

PACE, s 77 is concerned with confessions, as defined by s 82, made by mentally handicapped defendants. Where the case against D depends wholly or substantially upon his confession and the court is satisfied that he is mentally handicapped and that the confession was not made in the presence of an independent person, the jury must be warned of, or the magistrates' court must heed, the special need for caution before convicting D in reliance on the confession. A police officer or member of police staff is not an independent person in this context. Generally speaking, to question a suspect in the absence of an independent person amounts to a breach of PACE Code C.

In establishing whether D is mentally handicapped it is not appropriate to attempt to take figures provided by intelligence tests in one case and then to apply them slavishly to another in order to define some rigid line, the crossing of which would lead automatically to the exclusion of confession evidence. Each case must be looked at on its own facts.

Of course, if a mentally handicapped person's confession is obtained by oppression or by words or conduct likely to make it unreliable (as in a case where D confessed at a fifth interview after 36 hours' detention and without having received any legal advice), the confession will be inadmissible under s 76.

Procedure—video- or audio-recorded confessions: Crown Court

The procedure to be followed in preparation for proceedings in the Crown Court in relation to video or audio recordings of police interviews with suspects is laid down in the *Criminal Practice Directions*. The recording should be produced and proved by the interviewing officer, or any other officer who was present at the interview; the prosecution must ensure that someone is available to operate any video or audio equipment; and counsel must indicate to the operator the parts of a recording which it may be necessary to play.

DEFENDANT'S RIGHT OF SILENCE

The Criminal Justice and Public Order Act 1994 (CJPOA 1994), ss 34 to 37 permit a court or jury to draw such inferences from D's failure to mention facts as appear proper. The circumstances, generally, in which such inferences may be drawn are:

(a) where D has failed, when questioned under caution or on being charged or officially informed that he may be prosecuted (or after being charged when questioned under the Counter-Terrorism Act 2008, s 22), to mention facts later relied upon as part of his defence, and which it is reasonable to expect him to have mentioned (s 34);

(b) where D fails, without good cause, to give evidence or answer questions at trial (s 35);

(c) where an arrested person fails or refuses to account for possession of objects, substances or marks when requested to do so (s 36);

(d) where an arrested person fails or refuses to account for his presence at a particular place, when requested to do so (s 37).

By s 38, an adverse inference drawn under ss 34 to 37 cannot be the sole basis for a finding of a case to answer, or for a finding of guilt. As a result, the importance of ss 34 to 37 is that an adverse inference under them may enable the judge, jury or magistrates to find that other evidence, when considered with the adverse inference, enables them to be sure beyond reasonable doubt of the truth and accuracy of that other evidence and, in consequence, of D's guilt.

When evidence is to be offered and admissibility

Subject to any directions given by the court, evidence which tends to establish the particular failure may be given before or after the evidence which tends to establish the fact which D is alleged to have failed to mention. Thus, where an interview is concerned with D's possession of a stolen watch, evidence of his failure to offer an explanation for his possession of it may be given before, or after, evidence of it being found in his possession. In most circumstances, the most appropriate time will be after evidence of his possession of the property has been given. These provisions do not prejudice the admissibility of evidence of his silence or other reaction which would otherwise be admissible (eg reaction to things said in his presence and hearing which relate to his involvement in an offence).

Effect of defendant's silence when questioned under caution or on being charged, etc

The relevant provision is contained in CJPOA 1994, s 34, which applies in relation to:

(a) the determination of applications for dismissal of charges made by a person sent to the Crown Court for trial;
(b) the determination of the issue of whether a person accused of an offence (of whatever type) has a case to answer; and
(c) the determination of whether a person is guilty of the offence charged.

By s 34, where, *in the circumstances* existing at the time, D could reasonably have been expected:

(a) when questioned under caution to discover whether or by whom the offence was committed; or
(b) when charged with it or officially informed that he might be prosecuted for it; or
(c) when questioned under the Counter-Terrorism Act 2008, s 22 after being charged,

to have mentioned a fact (as opposed to theory, possibility or speculation) on which he later relies in his defence, a judge, jury or magistrate may draw such inferences as appear proper from D's failure. The Court of Appeal has held that 'in the circumstances' includes such matters as the time of day, and D's age, experience, mental capacity, state of health, sobriety, tiredness, knowledge and personality, and legal advice, which might all be relevant. It has also held that s 34 does not permit an adverse inference to be drawn from D's failure to leave his police cell to be interviewed because this does not fall within the ambit of 'being questioned'. In addition, the Court has held that a person who, when questioned, gives the interviewing officer a prepared statement from which he does not depart when giving evidence at his subsequent trial has 'mentioned facts' and therefore falls outside s 34, notwithstanding that the prepared statement was not given in response to questioning and that he said 'no comment' to all subsequent police questions.

The rule that an inference may only be drawn from a failure to mention facts which D could have been reasonably expected to mention when questioned requires an assessment of the situation at the time of that questioning, not with the benefit of hindsight as at the date of trial. An inference cannot be drawn from a failure to mention a fact of which D was unaware when questioned.

Section 34 does not apply in a case where D was at a police station at the time of the failure if he had not been allowed an opportunity to consult a solicitor prior to being questioned, charged or informed that he might be prosecuted.

It should be noted that there are significant areas of overlap between the rule under s 34 and the rules under ss 36 and 37 (dealt with below). In addition, they share the similarity that drawing an adverse inference under them may infringe the European Convention on Human Rights, art 6 (right to a fair trial). Whether or not it does must be determined in the light of all the circumstances of the case, including any explanation offered for the silence and the compulsion inherent in the situation.

Unlike ss 36 and 37, s 34 is not confined to the questioning of persons who are under arrest. In addition, ss 36 and 37 operate irrespective of whether a fact is relied upon as part of the defence, or irrespective of whether any defence is in fact made. By contrast, it is this reliance which is at the heart of s 34. Lastly, under s 36 or s 37, a constable is under a duty to explain the effect of the requirement in ordinary language, while the key prerequisite in s 34 is the formal caution.

There will be 'reliance' on a fact, even though D does not give evidence at his trial, if D relies on a fact by evidence through a witness on his behalf or through cross-examination of a prosecution witness.

Where D follows a solicitor's advice to remain silent, the ultimate question for the jury remains under s 34 whether the facts relied on at the trial were facts which D could reasonably have been expected to mention at interview. If they were not, that is the end of the matter. If the jury consider that D genuinely depended on the advice, that is not necessarily the end of the matter. It might still not have been reasonable for him to depend on the advice, or the advice might not have been the true explanation for his silence, the true reason being that he had no or no satisfactory explanation consistent with innocence to give.

Although under the PACE Code C an under-18-year-old or mentally vulnerable suspect (hereafter 'vulnerable suspect') must not be interviewed in the absence of an appropriate adult, except in the case of an urgent interview, s 34 is not confined to questioning that amounts to an 'interview'. However, a note to that Code states that vulnerable suspects may be particularly prone to provide information which is unreliable, misleading or self-incriminating. It goes on to state that special care should always be taken when questioning such a person. This must be true with equal force in respect of any failure to state facts. There is also the distinct possibility that such a person will not understand the significance of the caution, or believe that an obligation to answer exists. For these reasons, considerable caution should be exercised in drawing an inference from a failure of a vulnerable suspect to disclose facts subsequently relied upon, certainly in questioning which occurs in the absence of an appropriate adult.

The Court of Appeal has discouraged prosecutors from too readily seeking to activate s 34. Its mischief, it said, was primarily directed at the positive defence following a 'no comment' and/or 'ambush' defence. Where that was not the case, the Court warned against the further complicating of trials and summings-up by invoking s 34.

Effect of defendant's silence at trial

CJPOA 1994, s 35 deals with the case where D fails to give evidence or refuses without good reason to answer a question. It does not apply where:

(a) D's guilt is not in issue, or
(b) it appears to the court (from evidence, and not just from a submission by an advocate) that D's physical or mental condition makes it undesirable (and not just difficult) for D to be called upon to give evidence.

For the purposes of (a), D's guilt will not be in issue if he has pleaded guilty and the hearing is merely concerned to resolve matters relevant to sentencing. Nor will it be in issue in preliminary hearings or in issues concerning the admissibility of evidence. Where the defence wish to rely on (b) they must adduce evidence on the issue referred to in (b).

Where s 35 applies, the court must, at the conclusion of the evidence for the prosecution, satisfy itself (in the presence of the jury where applicable) that D is aware that:

(a) the stage has been reached at which evidence can be given for the defence;
(b) he can, if he wishes, give evidence; and
(c) if he chooses not to give evidence, or, having been sworn, without good cause refuses to answer any question, it will be permissible for the court or jury to draw such inferences as appear proper from such failure or refusal.

This rule will not apply if, at the conclusion of the evidence for the prosecution, it is established that D will give evidence.

For the purposes of (c), a refusal will be taken to be without good cause where a person, having been sworn, refuses to answer any question, unless:

(a) he is entitled to refuse to answer the question by virtue of any enactment, whenever passed or made, or on the ground of privilege; or
(b) the court in the exercise of its general discretion excuses him from answering it.

The privilege against self-incrimination and the common law doctrine of legal professional privilege therefore apply. Outside such matters 'good cause' may be limited to relevance and propriety and perhaps where a question may be considered oppressive.

Where s 35 applies, the jury or magistrates in determining whether D is guilty of the offence charged may draw such inferences as appear proper from D's failure to give evidence or his refusal, without good cause, to answer any question.

The Court of Appeal has ruled that, apart from the two exceptions included in s 35 (ie D's guilt not in issue and D's physical or mental condition), it was open to a jury or magistrates to decline to draw an inference from silence where the circumstances of the case justified such a course. However, there had to be some evidential basis, or exceptional factors, making that a fair course to take. The inferences permitted by s 35 were only such as 'appear proper'.

The Court of Appeal has highlighted the need for a jury to be told that:

(a) the burden of proof remains on the prosecution;
(b) D is entitled to remain silent;
(c) an inference cannot by itself prove guilt;
(d) the jury must be satisfied that the prosecution has established a case to answer before drawing such an inference; and

(e) if, despite any evidence relied upon to explain silence or in the absence of any such evidence, the jury concludes that silence can only sensibly be attributed to D's having no answer, or none that would stand up to cross-examination, they may draw an adverse inference.

Effect of defendant's failure or refusal to account for objects, marks, etc

CJPOA 1994, s 36 is the relevant provision. Where:

(a) a person is arrested by a constable and there is:
  (i)   on his person; or
  (ii) in or on his clothing or footwear; or
  (iii) otherwise in his possession; or
  (iv) in any place in which he is at the time of his arrest,
  any object, substance or mark, or there is any mark on any such object; and
(b) that or another constable investigating the case reasonably believes that the presence of the object, substance or mark may be attributable to the participation of the person arrested in the commission of an offence specified by the constable; and
(c) the constable informs the person so arrested that he so believes, and requests him to account for the presence of the object, substance or mark; and
(d) the person fails or refuses to do so,

then if, in any proceedings (of the type to which s 34 applies) for the offence so specified, evidence of those matters is given, the judge, jury or magistrates, as appropriate, may draw such inferences from the failure or refusal as appear proper. These provisions of s 36 apply to the condition of clothing or footwear as they apply to a substance or mark thereon. They do not apply unless D was told in ordinary language by the constable when making the request in (c) what the effects of s 36 would be if he failed or refused to comply with the request.

An inference may not be drawn under s 36 where D was at an authorised place of detention (a police station or other authorised place) at the time of the failure or refusal, if he had not been allowed an opportunity to consult a solicitor prior to the request being made.

The provisions of s 36 do not preclude the drawing of inferences from a failure or refusal to account for objects, marks, etc which could properly be drawn apart from s 36.

Effect of defendant's failure or refusal to account for presence at a particular place

CJPOA 1994, s 37 provides that, in the circumstances below, in proceedings of the type to which s 34 applies, a judge, jury or magistrates may draw such inferences as appear proper from D's failure or refusal to account for certain matters. Such inferences are permitted where:

(a) a person arrested by a constable was found by him at a place at or about the time the offence for which he was arrested is alleged to have been committed; and

(b) that or another constable investigating the offence reasonably believes that the presence of the person at that place and at that time may be attributable to his participation in the commission of the offence; and

(c) the constable informs the person that he so believes, and requests him to account for his presence; and

(d) the person fails or refuses to do so.

Section 37 does not apply unless D was told in ordinary language by the constable when making the request in (c) what the effects of s 37 would be if he failed or refused to comply with the request.

An inference may not be drawn under s 37 where D was at an authorised place of detention (see above) if he had not been allowed an opportunity to consult a solicitor prior to the request being made.

Once again, the provisions of s 37 do not prevent the drawing of any other inference from a refusal or failure to account which could properly be drawn apart from s 37.

EVIDENCE AS TO CHARACTER

By the defendant of his good character

D may always give evidence of his good character.

D's good character may be relevant to his credibility and to the likelihood that he would commit the offence (propensity). The judge must give a direction to the jury as to the relevance of good character to credibility and propensity if D has an absolute good character (no convictions or cautions recorded, or other reprehensible conduct alleged) or effective good character (conviction or cautions recorded but old, minor and irrelevant to the charge, and the judge decides that in all the circumstances it is fair to treat D as of good character).

If D has convictions or cautions which are not in the same category as the offence alleged, and is not judged to be of effective good character and adduces them under head (b) of CJA 2003, s 101 (p 264), for example to found an argument that he has no propensity for the type of offence alleged, he is not entitled to a good character direction in respect of credibility and propensity, but the judge has a discretion to give any part of the direction if fairness dictates.

If D has no previous convictions or cautions but other misconduct is relied on by the prosecution, the judge may weave comments about D's residual good character into a direction about the relevance of D's bad character.

Bad character

Evidence of bad character is only admissible if the relevant provisions of CJA 2003, Part 11, Ch 1 (below) are satisfied.

CJA 2003, s 98 provides that references in the relevant provisions to a person's 'bad character' are to evidence of, or of a disposition towards, misconduct on his part, *other than evidence which*:

(a) *has to do with the alleged facts of the offence with which D is charged, or*

(b) *is evidence of misconduct in connection with the investigation or prosecution of that offence.*

'Misconduct' refers to the commission of an offence or other reprehensible behaviour. 'Reprehensible behaviour' is clearly intended to include conduct which is scandalous, disgraceful, dishonest or improper, without being criminal. Behaviour for which a person has been charged with an offence can clearly amount to misconduct even if the prosecution is later dropped or the person is acquitted.

In relation to exception (a), the Court of Appeal has held that for evidence 'to do' with the alleged facts of the offence there must be a nexus in time between that offence and the evidence of misconduct; the evidence must be reasonably contemporaneous and closely associated with the alleged facts. However, the Court has subsequently held that there is no 'nexus in time requirement' where the evidence relates to incidents alleged to have created the motive for the offence; such evidence therefore falls within the exception.

The Court of Appeal has held that exception (b) is not limited to misconduct by the prosecuting authorities and that it could be said to encompass evidence of intimidation or blackmail by a co-defendant which could be said to be connected with the prosecution or investigation of the offence.

Where the evidence falls within either of the italicised exceptions it is admissible without more ado; it does not have to pass through any of the gateways under ss 100 (non-defendants) or 101 (defendants).

Evidence of non-defendant's bad character

CJA 2003, s 100 provides that, in criminal proceedings, evidence of the bad character of any person other than D is admissible *only* if:

(a) it is important explanatory evidence;
(b) it has substantial probative value in relation to a matter which is in issue in the proceedings and is of substantial importance in the context of the case as a whole; or
(c) all parties in the proceedings agree to its admissibility.

Section 100 applies to a witness, victim or any other person.

As to (a), 'important explanatory evidence' has the same meaning as it does in respect of s 101 (p 265).

In relation to (b), evidence of a non-defendant's bad character would be of probative value if it assisted in establishing an issue one way or another. In assessing the probative value of evidence for the purposes of (b) the court must have regard to the following factors (and any other relevant factors):

(i) the nature and number of the events, or other things, to which the evidence relates;
(ii) when those events or things are alleged to have happened or existed;
(iii) where (*a*) the evidence is evidence of a person's misconduct, and (*b*) it is suggested that the evidence has probative value by reason of similarity between that misconduct and other alleged misconduct, the nature and extent of the similarities and the dissimilarities between each of the alleged instances of misconduct;
(iv) where (*a*) the evidence is evidence of a person's misconduct, (*b*) it is suggested that that person is also responsible for the misconduct charged, and (*c*) the identity of the person responsible for the misconduct charged is disputed, the extent to which the evidence shows or tends to show that the same person was responsible each time.

As a result of (b) and the above provisions, evidence of a non-defendant's bad character may be admitted, for example, as evidence of *his* propensity to commit the offence in question or of his credibility as a witness.

The Court of Appeal has held that a police report recording unproven allegations against a non-defendant of criminal behaviour is most unlikely to have substantial probative value; first, it is, at best, hearsay, and it would fall to be judged by reference to the rules for the admission of hearsay and (given the difficulties of assessing such evidence) it would be rare for it to be judged of substantial probative value; second, if there is no complainant prepared to support the allegation, that robs it of a great deal of probative value.

Except in the case of (c), evidence of the bad character of a non-defendant may only be given with the leave of the court.

A party who wants to introduce evidence of a non-defendant's bad character must make an application in accordance with the Criminal Procedure Rules 2015, Part 21; see Chapter 7 on the companion website.

Evidence of defendant's bad character

CJA 2003, s 101 deals with such matters.

By s 101, evidence of D's bad character is admissible in criminal proceedings only if one of the following seven gateways is satisfied:

(a) all parties agree to its being admissible;
(b) it is evidence adduced by D himself or is given in answer to a question asked by him during cross-examination and intended to elicit it;
(c) it is important explanatory evidence;
(d) it is relevant to an 'important matter' (ie a matter of substantial importance in the context of the case as a whole) in issue between D and the prosecution;
(e) it has 'substantial probative value' (ie an enhanced capability of proving or disproving) in relation to an 'important matter' in issue between D and a co-defendant;
(f) it is evidence to correct a false impression given by D; or
(g) D has made an attack on another person's character.

Evidence must not be admitted under gateways (d) or (g) if D has made an application to exclude it and the judge or magistrates' court considers that the admission of the evidence would have such an adverse effect on the fairness of the proceedings that it ought not to admit it. The test to be applied is the same as that set out in PACE, s 78 (p 267). On such an application, regard must be had, in particular, to the time which has passed between the matters to which the evidence relates and the matters forming the subject of the offence charged.

By CJA 2003, s 108, which applies in addition to s 101, in proceedings for an offence by D when aged 21 or over, evidence of D's conviction for an offence when under 14 is not admissible unless both offences are triable only on indictment and the interests of justice require the evidence to be admissible.

Where D's conviction under 14 was for an offence under the law of a country outside England and Wales ('the previous offence') and that offence would be an offence under the law of England and Wales ('the corresponding offence') if done in England and Wales at the time of the proceedings with which D is now charged, the previous offence is regarded as triable only on indictment if the corresponding offence is so triable.

Gateway (c): important explanatory evidence

For the purpose of gateway (c) under CJA 2003, s 101, evidence is important explanatory evidence if, in its absence, the jury or court would find it impossible or difficult properly to understand other evidence in the case, and its value for understanding the case as a whole is substantial. In an assault case, for example, evidence may be given that D (who claims that he acted in self-defence) has previously made unprovoked attacks on the victim.

Gateway (d): important matter in issue between defendant and prosecution

CJA 2003, s 103(1) provides that, for the purposes of gateway (d), matters in issue between D and the prosecution *include*:

(a) the question whether D has a 'propensity' to commit offences of the kind with which he is charged, except where his having that propensity makes it no more likely that he is guilty of the offence; and

(b) the question whether D has a propensity to be untruthful, except where it is not suggested that D's case is untruthful in any respect.

In respect of (b), the Court of Appeal has held that the question whether D has a propensity to be untruthful will not normally be describable as an 'important matter in issue between D and the prosecutor'; the only circumstance where there is likely to be an important issue as to whether D has a propensity to be untruthful is where telling lies is an important element of the offence, and even then the propensity is only likely to be significant if the lying was in the context of committing criminal offences (in which case evidence is likely to be admissible under (a)).

Section 103(2) provides that, where (a) applies, D's propensity to commit offences of the kind with which he is charged may (without prejudice to any other way of doing so) be established by evidence of a previous conviction for an offence of the same description as that with which D is charged, or an offence of the same category as that offence. For these purposes, two offences are of the same description as each other if the statement of the offence in a written charge or indictment would, in each case, be in the same terms, and two offences are of the same category if they are of the same *category of offences as prescribed by order*. The CJA 2003 (Categories of Offences) Order 2004 prescribes two categories of offence: one category is specified offences against the Theft Acts 1968 and 1978, and the other is specified offences against the Sexual Offences Act (SOA) 2003 where the victim was under 16. They are offences under the Theft Act 1968, ss 1, 8, 9 (if theft intended, committed or attempted), 10 (if the above type of offence under s 9 involved), 12, 12A, 22, or 25; the Theft Act 1978, s 3; or, provided complainant under 16, the Sexual Offences Act 2003, ss 1, 2, 3, 4, 5, 6, 7, 8, 9, 10, 14, 16, 17, 25, 26, 30, 31, 34, 35, 38, or 39; and aiding, abetting, counselling or procuring, encouraging or assisting, or attempting the commission of such an offence. The sexual offences category also includes corresponding offences superseded by the Sexual Offences Act 2003.

By CJA 2003, s 103(3), s 103(2) does not apply if the court is satisfied, by reason of the length of time since the conviction or for any other reason that it would be unjust for it to apply.

CJA 2003, s 103(7) provides that where:

(a) D has been convicted of an offence under the law of any country outside England and Wales ('the previous offence'), and

(b) the previous offence would constitute an offence under the law of England and Wales ('the corresponding offence') if it were done in England and Wales at the time of the trial for the offence with which D is now charged ('the current offence'),

then for the purpose of determining for the purposes of s 103(2) whether the previous offence and the current offence are of the same description or category:

(i) the previous offence is of the same description as the current offence if the corresponding offence is of that same description, as set out in the 2004 Order referred to above;

(ii) the previous offence is of the same category as the current offence if the current offence and the corresponding offence belong to the same category of offences as prescribed by the 2004 Order.

Similar provision is also made by s 103(10) in respect of a conviction of an offence under a foreign service law which would constitute an offence under the law of England and Wales or a service offence if done in England and Wales by a member of HM forces.

In referring to offences of the same description or category, CJA 2003, s 103(2) is not exhaustive of the types of conviction which may be relied on to show evidence of propensity to commit offences of the kind charged. Indeed, the provision is not limited to previous convictions; the fact that D has previously asked for offences to be taken into consideration can be admitted.

Gateway (e): substantial probative value in relation to an important matter in issue between the defendant and co-defendant

This is intended to deal with 'cut-throat' defences. CJA 2003, s 104 provides that evidence relevant to whether D has a propensity to be untruthful is admissible on that basis under (e) only if the nature or conduct of his defence is such as to undermine the co-defendant's defence. Only evidence adduced by the co-defendant or by a witness in cross-examination by the co-defendant is admissible under (e).

Gateway (f): correcting a false impression

CJA 2003, s 105 provides that, for the purposes of gateway (f), D gives a false impression if he is responsible for the making of an express or implied assertion which is apt to give a false or misleading assertion about D, and that evidence to correct such an impression is evidence which has probative value in correcting it.

D is treated as responsible for the making of an assertion if it is made by D in the proceedings, or by a defence witness, or by any witness in response to a question by D which was intended or likely to elicit it, or if it was made by D when questioned under caution or on being charged with the offence, or if it was made out-of-court by any person and D adduces evidence of it.

The Court of Appeal has held that gateway (f) is concerned with attempting to mislead the court in a way that goes beyond denying the offence. The false impression has to be one which is given to the court.

Gateway (g): attack on another person's character

By CJA 2003, s 106, D attacks the character of another person if he adduces evidence to the effect that this person has committed any offence or has behaved in a reprehensible way, or if he asks questions in cross-examination which are intended or likely to elicit such evidence, or if evidence is given of an imputation about the other person by D on being questioned under caution before charge or on being charged or informed that he might be prosecuted. Where evidence of D's bad character has been admitted as a result of his attack upon the character of another person, it can be used, if relevant, to establish a propensity on the part of D to commit offences of the type with which he is charged.

Assumption of truth in assessment of relevance or probative value

CJA 2003, s 109 provides that any reference in the Act's provisions about bad character to the relevance or probative value of evidence is a reference to its relevance or probative value on the assumption that it is true. However, in assessing the relevance or probative value of an item of evidence, a court need not assume that evidence is true if it appears, on the basis of material before it, that no court or jury could reasonably find it to be true.

Notice of introduction of evidence of a defendant's bad character

A party who wants to introduce evidence of a defendant's bad character must serve notice in accordance with the Criminal Procedure Rules 2015, Part 21; see Chapter 7 on the companion website.

Spent convictions, etc

The provisions of the Rehabilitation of Offenders Act 1974 whereby an offender's convictions become 'spent' and the offender is thereafter treated as if he had not been convicted do not prevent the admissibility in criminal proceedings of evidence relating to a spent conviction which is otherwise admissible (s 7). A similar rule applies in respect of spent cautions (Sch 2). A person who has a conviction or caution for the abolished offence of buggery or the abolished offence of gross indecency between men which has been ordered to be disregarded by the Secretary of State under the Protection of Freedoms Act 2012, s 92 is to be treated as if he had not committed, or been charged with, or prosecuted for, or convicted of, or sentenced for, or cautioned for, that offence. In particular, no evidence is admissible to prove any of these matters and he is not, in any court proceedings, to be asked (and, if asked, is not to be required to answer) any question relating to his past which cannot be answered without acknowledging or referring to the conviction or caution or any circumstances ancillary to it (s 96).

Proof of a conviction

See p 232.

EXCLUSION OF UNFAIR EVIDENCE

The purpose of all the rules concerning the gathering of evidence and the manner of its presentation in court is to ensure absolute fairness to an accused person. PACE, s 78 provides that, in any proceedings, a judge or magistrates' court may refuse to allow evidence (including confessions) on which the prosecution proposes to rely to be given if it appears that, having regard to all the circumstances, including the circumstances in which the evidence was obtained, the admission of the evidence would have *such an adverse effect on the fairness of the proceedings that the court ought not to admit it.* 'Fairness of the proceedings' is directed primarily to fairness of the actual conduct of the proceedings but it is not strictly limited to this.

Evidence obtained by a breach by the police of PACE or one of the Codes of Practice does not necessarily render evidence inadmissible under s 78, but it will if it has such an adverse effect on the fairness of the proceedings that it ought not to be admitted.

The issue is whether there has been a significant and substantial breach. There is no general requirement for the breach to have been committed deliberately or in bad faith before evidence is excluded under PACE, s 78. Bad faith on the part of police officers will usually lead to the exclusion of evidence (bad faith may make significant and substantial a breach which might not otherwise be so), but evidence may be excluded even though the police acted in good faith if there is a significant and substantial breach of police powers.

An example of the operation of s 78 is provided by a case where a person had been convicted on evidence based solely on a confession obtained after police had falsely pretended that his fingerprints had been found at the scene of the crime; the Court of Appeal ruled that such evidence should have been excluded under s 78 on the ground that it posed a threat to the fairness of proceedings. Another example is provided by various cases where evidence obtained after a significant and substantial breach of the provisions described in Chapter 4 relating to the right to legal advice or to the conduct of an interview has been excluded on the ground that in the circumstances of the case it would be unfair to admit it.

Section 78 does not affect the common law powers of a court to exclude evidence on the basis that its prejudicial effect is likely to be greater than its probative value, and to exclude self-incriminatory evidence unfairly obtained from the defendant after the commission of the alleged offence. Although s 78 goes much further than the common law power, particularly because it significantly widens the discretion to exclude evidence which has been unfairly or unlawfully obtained, there is one context in which the common law power is more extensive than s 78. This is where the evidence in question has already been adduced. Section 78 does not apply in this context, but if the evidence ought not to have been admitted the court may, under the common law power, take any necessary steps to prevent an injustice, whether by directing the jury to ignore the offending evidence or, if necessary, by discharging the jury.

Sometimes, in cases of unfairness to D, it is more appropriate for the court to stay proceedings on the grounds of an abuse of process on the basis that a fair trial would not be possible or, if it would, that a trial would be contrary to the public interest in the integrity of the criminal justice system, for example because the actions of the police threaten a basic human right. One such case recognised by the House of Lords is police entrapment, ie luring D into committing an offence and then seeking to prosecute him. Alleged entrapment does not prevent D seeking to have the evidence obtained by entrapment excluded as inadmissible, but it must be borne in mind that the tests are different. In staying proceedings the test is that just stated; under s 78 it is whether admitting the evidence would have such an adverse effect on the fairness of proceedings that the evidence ought not to be admitted. The House of Lords has held that in entrapment cases a stay of proceedings should normally be regarded as the appropriate response.

DISCLOSURE OF EVIDENCE

The disclosure provisions of the Criminal Procedure and Investigations Act 1996

The Criminal Procedure and Investigations Act 1996 (CPIA 1996), Part 1 (ss 1 to 21) contains provisions relating to the advance disclosure of material which apply where:

(a) a person charged with a summary offence pleads not guilty;

(b) a person of 18 or over charged with an either-way offence, in respect of which a court proceeds to summary trial, pleads not guilty; or

(c) a person under 18 charged with an indictable offence, in respect of which a court proceeds to summary trial, pleads not guilty.

The provisions also apply where a person is charged with an indictable offence and is sent for trial in the Crown Court.

For the purpose of the disclosure provisions, 'material' refers to material of all kinds, and in particular refers to information, and to objects of all descriptions.

Initial duty of prosecutor to disclose

By s 3, the prosecutor must:

(a) disclose to the defendant (D) previously undisclosed prosecution material which might reasonably be considered capable of undermining the prosecution case, or of assisting the case for D; or

(b) give to D a written statement that there is no material of a description mentioned in (a).

Material must not be so disclosed to the extent that the court, on an application by the prosecutor, concludes that it is not in the public interest to disclose it and orders accordingly. At the same time as he acts under s 3, the prosecutor must give D any schedule of non-sensitive material previously given to him by the disclosure officer (p 275) (s 4).

Information need not be disclosed by the prosecutor to the extent that the court, on the prosecutor's application, concludes it is not in the public interest to disclose it and orders accordingly. Nor should it be disclosed if its disclosure is prohibited under the Regulation of Investigatory Powers Act 2000. The Court of Appeal has held that the disclosure responsibilities imposed on the prosecution by the disclosure provisions cannot be sidestepped by not making an enquiry. It stated that a police officer who believes that a person may have information which might undermine the case for the prosecution or assist the case for the suspect or defendant cannot decline to make enquiries of that person in order to avoid the need to disclose what the person might say. The Court therefore allowed appeals against conviction where there had been a failure to disclose a complaint by a prosecution witness against a police officer in case the result of the investigation should require disclosure.

The Court of Appeal has stated by way of guidance that full disclosure, under s 3, of material which is not part of the formal case against D, and which either weakens its case or strengthens D's, is essential to avoid a miscarriage of justice. The prosecution is not, however, required to disclose material which is neutral or adverse to D. Especially in large and complex cases, investigating and prosecuting agencies must apply their respective case management and disclosure strategies and policies and be transparent with the defence and the courts about how the prosecution has approached complying with its disclosure obligations in the context of the individual case. The defence will be expected to play their part in defining the real issues in the case, and will be invited to participate in defining the scope of the reasonable searches that may be made of any digitally stored material by the investigator to identify material that may reasonably be expected to undermine the prosecution case or assist the defence. It is not the duty of the prosecution to comb through all the material in its possession on the look-out for anything which may conceivably or speculatively assist the defence.

Compulsory disclosure by defendant

The relevant provisions are in CPIA 1996, s 5. Where cases are to be tried on indictment, and the prosecutor complies (or purports to comply) with his initial duty of disclosure, and provided that D has received documents containing the prosecution's case, D is required to provide the court and the prosecutor during the relevant period (p 273) with a defence statement.

By s 6A(1), a defence statement must be in writing and set out the nature of D's defence, including any particular defences which are to be relied upon; indicate the matters of fact on which D takes issue with the prosecution, and why he takes issue; set out the matters of fact on which D intends to rely for the purposes of his defence; and indicate any point of law (including any point as to the admissibility of evidence or an abuse of process) which D wishes to take and any authority upon which he intends to rely. The Court of Appeal has held that if D raises no positive case at all in a defence statement but *simply* requires the prosecution to prove its case, there is no failure to comply with s 6A. It also held that both legal professional privilege and D's privilege against self-incrimination have survived s 6A. Section 6A requires D to disclose what is going to happen at the trial. It does not compel disclosure of his confidential discussions with his advocate. Nor is D obliged to incriminate himself.

Any defence statement which includes an alibi is required by s 6A(2) to give *the name, address and date of birth of any witness D believes is able to give evidence in support of the alibi, or as many of those details as are known to D, and any other information in his possession which might assist in identifying or finding any such witness where such details are not known to D at that time.* Evidence in support of an alibi is evidence tending to show that, by reason of D's presence at a particular place or area at a particular time, D was not, or was unlikely to have been, at the place where the offence is alleged to have been committed at the time of its alleged commission.

Where a defence statement identifies an alibi witness under s 6A(2) or where D gives a notice under s 6C (p 272) indicating that he intends to call an identified witness at his trial, guidance is provided by a code of practice to police officers and others charged with the duty of investigating offences in relation to arranging and conducting interviews of persons notified. The Code of Practice for Arranging and Conducting Interviews of Witnesses Notified by the Accused provides as follows.

If an investigator wishes to interview a witness identified as above, the witness must be asked whether he consents to being interviewed and informed that:

(a) an interview is being requested following his identification by D as a proposed witness under ss 6A(2) or 6C;
(b) he is not obliged to attend the interview;
(c) he is entitled to be accompanied by a solicitor; and
(d) a record will be made of the interview and he will be sent a copy of it.

If the witness (W) consents to being interviewed, W must be asked whether he:

(a) wishes to have a solicitor present;
(b) consents to a solicitor attending on behalf of D, as an observer; and
(c) consents to a copy of the record being sent to D. If he does not consent, W must be informed that the effect of disclosure requirements in criminal proceedings may nevertheless require the prosecution to disclose the record to D (and any co-defendant) in the course of the proceedings.

The investigator must notify D or D's legal representatives:

(a) that the investigator requested an interview with W;
(b) whether W consented to the interview; and
(c) if W consented to the interview, whether he also consented to a solicitor attending on behalf of D, as an observer.

If D is not legally represented in the proceedings, and if W consents to a solicitor attending the interview on behalf of D, D must be offered a reasonable opportunity to appoint a solicitor to attend it.

The investigator must nominate a reasonable date, time and venue for the interview and notify W of them and any changes to them.

If W has consented to the presence of D's solicitor, D's solicitor must be notified that the interview is taking place, invited to observe and provided with reasonable notice of the date, time, and venue of the interview and any changes.

The identity of the investigator conducting the interview must be recorded. He must have sufficient skills and authority, commensurate with the complexity of the investigation, to discharge his functions effectively. He must not conduct the interview if that is likely to result in a conflict of interest, for instance if he is the victim of the alleged crime which is the subject of the proceedings. The advice of a more senior officer must always be sought if there is doubt as to whether a conflict of interest precludes an individual conducting the interview. If thereafter the doubt remains, the advice of a prosecutor must be sought.

D's solicitor may only attend the interview as an observer if W has consented to his presence as an observer. Provided that D's solicitor was given reasonable notice of the date, time and place of the interview, the fact that D's solicitor is not present will not prevent the interview from being conducted. If W at any time withdraws consent to D's solicitor being present at the interview, the interview may continue without the presence of D's solicitor.

Where W has indicated that he wishes to appoint a solicitor to be present, that solicitor must be permitted to attend the interview.

If W is under 18 or is mentally disordered or otherwise mentally vulnerable, he must be interviewed in the presence of an appropriate person.

A record must be made of the interview, wherever it takes place. It must be made, where practicable, by audio recording or by visual recording with sound, or otherwise in writing. Any written record must be made and completed during the interview, unless this would not be practicable or would interfere with the conduct of the interview, and must constitute either a verbatim record of what has been said or, failing this, an account of the interview which adequately and accurately summarises it. If a written record is not made during the interview it must be made as soon as practicable after its completion. Written interview records must be timed and signed by the maker.

The Code concludes by providing that a copy of the record must be given, within a reasonable time of the interview, to:

(a) W, and
(b) if W consents, to D or D's solicitor.

Any police officer or other person charged with the duty of investigating offences who arranges or conducts such an interview must have regard to the Code. Any provision of the Code or any failure to have due regard to the Code, either of which is relevant to any question arising in civil or criminal proceedings, can be taken into account by a court or tribunal conducting those proceedings in deciding that question.

Voluntary disclosure by defendant

By CPIA 1996, s 6, where the case is to be tried summarily, and the prosecutor complies (or purports to comply) with his initial duty of disclosure, D or his solicitor *may* give a defence statement to the prosecutor during the relevant period. If he does so, he must also give the statement to the court.

Notification of intent to call witnesses

By CPIA 1996, s 6C, referred to on p 270, D must give the court and the prosecutor notification of his intention to call witnesses, together with their identity or details which might lead to their identification. Changes must be notified.

Continuing duty of disclosure by prosecutor

After the prosecutor has complied (or purported to comply) with his initial duty of disclosure, the prosecutor remains under a continuing duty under CPIA 1996, s 7A, up to the time of acquittal, conviction or a decision not to proceed with the case, to keep under review whether there is any undisclosed prosecution material which might reasonably be considered capable of undermining the case for the prosecution against D or of assisting D's case. If there is, the prosecution must disclose it as soon as reasonably practicable.

Where D gives a defence statement under s 5 or 6, as a result of which the prosecutor is required by the above provision to make any disclosure, or further disclosure, the prosecutor must do so within the relevant period. If he considers that he is not so required he must give D a written statement to that effect within that period.

Application by defendant for further disclosure

Following compliance (or purported compliance) by the prosecutor with the provision just mentioned, or a failure by the prosecutor to comply with a duty under that provision to disclose, and provided that D has given a defence statement under CPIA 1996, s 5 or 6, D may apply to the court under s 8 for the disclosure of material which he reasonably believes is required to be disclosed to him but has not been. An order for further disclosure can only be made in respect of material: (a) in the possession of the prosecution in connection with the case against D, or (b) which the prosecutor has inspected or is entitled to inspect in pursuance of the CPIA 1996 (s 23(1)) Code of Practice (p 274), or (c) of which in pursuance of that Code the prosecutor is entitled to have a copy. An order for further disclosure cannot be made against a third party.

Failure in disclosure by defendant

CPIA 1996, s 11 deals with this. It applies in the three cases set out below.

The first case is where s 5 applies and D:

(a) fails to give an initial defence statement; or
(b) gives one out of time; or
(c) sets out inconsistent defences in his defence statement; or
(d) puts forward at his trial a defence which differs from that set out in a defence statement, relies on a matter which, in breach of s 6A, was not mentioned in his

defence statement, adduces evidence in support of an undisclosed alibi, or calls a witness to support an alibi about whom he made no disclosure in his defence statement.

The second case is where s 6 applies, D gives an initial defence statement, and D gives that statement after the end of the relevant period for doing so, or does any of the things mentioned in (c) or (d) above.

The third case is where D gives a witness notice but does so after the relevant period for doing so, or at his trial calls a witness (other than himself) not included or adequately identified in a witness notice.

In these three cases, the judge, or any other party (in some cases only with the judge's leave), may make such comment as appears appropriate. In addition, the judge or jury may draw such inferences as appear proper in deciding whether D is guilty of the offence concerned, but a person may not be convicted solely on the basis of such an inference.

Time limits

The CPIA 1996 (Defence Disclosure Time Limits) Regulations 2011 provide that the relevant period for compulsory disclosure by D (CPIA 1996, s 5), voluntary disclosure by D (s 6), or notification of intent to call defence witnesses (s 6C) begins with the day on which the prosecutor complies or purports to comply with the prosecutor's initial duty of disclosure (s 3), and that:

(a) in respect of summary proceedings, the relevant period for s 6 and s 6C expires at the end of 14 days beginning with the first day of the relevant period;

(b) in respect of proceedings in the Crown Court, the relevant period for s 5 and s 6C expires at the end of 28 days beginning with the first day of the relevant period.

Where such a period expires on a weekend, Christmas Day, Good Friday or a bank holiday, the relevant period is extended so as to expire on the next day which is not such a day.

The Regulations also provide that on an application by D the court may extend, or further extend, the relevant period by so many days as it specifies, if it is satisfied that it would be unreasonable to require D to give a defence statement under s 5 or s 6, or give notice under s 6C, as the case may be, within the relevant period. D's application must be made within the relevant period, specify the ground on which it is made and state the number of days by which D wishes the relevant period to be extended. There is no limit to the number of applications for an extension.

The Regulations do not prescribe a particular period of time in relation to disclosure by the prosecution. However, s 13 requires such disclosure as soon as is reasonably practicable after the relevant specified event, for example the service of copies of the evidence served on a person sent for trial.

Common law disclosure rules

Common law rules about disclosure by the prosecution still apply in two types of case:

(a) where the investigation began before 1 April 1997 (when the statutory—CPIA 1996—disclosure provisions came into force); and

(b) at any stage in the process when the statutory provisions do not apply, ie after the institution of proceedings but before D pleads guilty or not guilty in a magistrates' or youth court, or is sent for trial, and after a conviction.

The prosecution's *common law* duty of disclosure is more limited than under CPIA 1996. Before the statutory provisions apply, the prosecutor must be alive to the need to make advance disclosure of materials of which he is aware and that might reasonably assist D with the early preparation of his case or at a bail hearing.

Police procedure

Police procedure is controlled by the CPIA 1996 (s 23(1)) Code of Practice. In summary:

The officer in charge of an investigation

The officer in charge of an investigation is any police officer involved in the conduct of a criminal investigation. All investigators are responsible for the recording and retention of materials and this includes negative material resulting from the interview of persons who could give no positive evidence. The officer in charge of an investigation must make such material available to the disclosure officer. While the officer in charge of an investigation may delegate tasks to other investigators, he remains responsible for ensuring that the duties relating to disclosure are properly carried out. All reasonable enquiries, whether pointing towards or away from a suspect must be investigated. Where material is held on a computer, the investigating officer must decide which factors may reasonably be inquired into.

Where an investigating officer believes that other parties may be in possession of relevant material which has not been obtained he may invite those persons to retain the material in case a request for disclosure is received. The disclosure officer should inform the prosecutor that those persons have the material. There is no requirement to make speculative enquiries; there must be some reason to believe that the persons concerned have relevant material.

Material which might be relevant to a criminal investigation but is not recorded must be held in a durable or retrievable form. Information must be recorded at the time at which it is obtained or as soon as is practicable thereafter. There is no requirement to take a statement where it would not otherwise be taken. The investigator has a duty to retain material obtained in a criminal investigation which might be relevant to the investigation. Where material which previously has been examined but not retained becomes relevant, the officer in charge of an investigation must take steps to obtain it or ensure that it is retained. The duty to retain material includes:

(a) crime reports of all descriptions;
(b) custody records;
(c) records derived from tapes of telephone messages containing descriptions of an alleged offence or offenders;
(d) final versions of witness statements (and draft versions if they differ) together with exhibits retained;
(e) interview records in any form with witnesses, potential witnesses or suspects;
(f) communications between police and experts (eg forensic scientists);
(g) records of first descriptions of suspects; and
(h) material casting doubt upon the reliability of a witness.

In addition, the duty to retain material which might be relevant to the investigation includes in particular the duty to retain material which may satisfy the test for prosecution disclosure, such as information provided by D which indicates an explanation for the offence with which he is charged, and material casting doubt on the reliability of a confession or a prosecution witness.

All such material which may be relevant to the investigation must be retained until a decision has been taken whether to institute proceedings against a person for an offence. If proceedings are instituted the material must be retained until the proceedings result in conviction or acquittal or a decision not to proceed has been taken. Where there is a conviction, material must be retained until the person is released from custody, or, in other circumstances, six months from the date of conviction. If a convicted person is released from custody within six months of conviction the material must be retained until the six months has elapsed. Where an appeal is lodged, material must be retained until the appeal is determined.

The disclosure officer

The disclosure officer is the person responsible for examining material retained by the police during an investigation; revealing material to the prosecutor during the investigation and any criminal proceedings resulting from it, and certifying that he has done this; and disclosing material to D at the request of the prosecutor. In any criminal investigation, one or more deputy disclosure officers may be appointed to assist the disclosure officer, and such a deputy may perform any of the above functions of the disclosure officer.

The functions of the disclosure officer may be carried out by the investigator or officer in charge of the investigation. Indeed, the functions of all three roles may be carried out by one person. Where this is not done there must be full consultation between both officers. The disclosure officer is the link between the investigators and the Crown Prosecution Service and is responsible for providing the material for 'primary disclosure' and performing any other tasks required by the prosecutor. He must ensure, by liaison with the officer in charge of the case where that is a different person, that all material is made available for examination.

The disclosure officer, the officer in charge of an investigation or an investigator may seek advice from the prosecutor concerning which items are relevant to the investigation. Material which may be so relevant, which has been retained in accordance with the Code, and which the disclosure officer believes will not form a part of the prosecution case must be listed on a schedule. This process will differ depending on whether the case is likely to be heard in the magistrates' court or the Crown Court.

Magistrates' courts   If D is charged with a summary offence or an either-way offence that is likely to remain in the magistrates' court, and a guilty plea is anticipated as likely, a schedule or streamlined disclosure certificate is not required. Where there is material which the prosecution is obliged to disclose (before its statutory duty arises) under its common law duty, the certification on the Police Report (MG5/SDF) must be completed. If, contrary to the expectation of a guilty plea being entered, D pleads not guilty at the first hearing, the disclosure officer must ensure that the streamlined disclosure certificate is prepared and submitted as soon as is reasonably practicable after that happens.

If D is charged with a summary offence or an either-way offence that is likely to remain in the magistrates' court, and a not guilty plea is anticipated as likely, a streamlined disclosure certificate must be completed in like form to that in the Annex to the Code.

In every case, irrespective of the anticipated plea, if there is material known to the disclosure officer that might assist the defence with the early preparation of their case or at a bail hearing (for example, a key prosecution witness has relevant previous convictions or a witness has withdrawn his or her statement), a note must be made on the MG5 (or other format agreed under the National File Standards). The material must be disclosed to the prosecutor who will disclose it to the defence if he thinks it meets this test.

If there is no material which might fall to be disclosed as undermining the prosecution case or assisting the defence, the officer should complete the appropriate entry on the streamlined disclosure certificate. If there is any sensitive unused material the officer should complete a sensitive material (defined below) schedule (MG6D or similar) and attach it to the prosecution file. In exceptional circumstances, when its existence is so sensitive that it cannot be listed, it should be revealed to the prosecutor separately.

Crown Court   For cases to be held in the Crown Court, the unused material schedules (MG6 series) are used. The disclosure officer must ensure that a schedule is prepared in the following circumstances: (a) D is charged with an offence which is triable only on indictment; or (b) D is charged with an offence which is triable either way, and it is considered that the case is likely to be tried on indictment. Material which the disclosure officer does not believe is sensitive must be listed on a schedule of non-sensitive material. The schedule must include a statement that the disclosure officer does not believe the material is sensitive.

For indictable-only cases or either-way cases sent to the Crown Court, schedules MG6 C, D and E should be completed to facilitate service of the MG6C with the prosecution case, wherever possible. The disclosure officer should ensure that each item of material is listed separately on the schedule, and is numbered consecutively. The description of each item should make clear the nature of the item and should contain sufficient detail to enable the prosecutor to decide whether he needs to inspect the material before deciding whether or not it should be disclosed. In some enquiries it may not be practicable to list each item of material separately. For example, there may be many items of a similar or repetitive nature. These may be listed in a block and described by quantity and generic title. Even if some material is listed in a block, the disclosure officer must ensure that any items among that material which might satisfy the test for prosecution disclosure are listed and described individually.

Sensitive material—Crown Court   Any material which is believed to be sensitive either must be listed on a schedule of sensitive material or, in exceptional circumstances where its existence is so sensitive that it cannot be listed, it should be revealed to the prosecutor separately. If there is no sensitive material, the disclosure officer must record this fact on a schedule. Sensitive material is material, the disclosure of which, the disclosure officer believes, would give rise to a real risk of serious prejudice to an important public interest. Examples of sensitive material are specified in the Code. They range from material relating to national security to material given in confidence, and include material relating to informants or undercover police officers, premises used for police surveillance, methods of detecting crime or the private life of a witness. The full list of specified examples is set out in Chapter 7 on the companion website.

In exceptional circumstances, where an investigator considers that material is such that revelation by means of a schedule entry is inappropriate (and this will apply only where compromising the material would be likely to lead directly to the loss of life, or directly threaten national security) the existence of the material may be revealed to the prosecutor separately.

Revelation of material to prosecutor   As noted above, certain unused material must be disclosed to D at common law if it would assist the defence with the early preparation of their case or at a bail hearing. Such material must be revealed to the prosecutor for service on the defence with the initial details of the prosecution case.

In anticipated not guilty plea cases for hearing in the magistrates' court the disclosure officer must give the streamlined disclosure certificate to the prosecutor at the same time as he gives the prosecutor the file containing the material for the prosecution case.

In cases sent to the Crown Court, wherever practicable, the disclosure officer should give the schedules concerning unused material to the prosecutor at the same time as the prosecution file in preparation for the first hearing and any case management that the judge may wish to conduct at that stage.

The disclosure officer should draw the attention of the prosecutor to any material an investigator has retained (including material listed in a block in Crown Court cases) which may satisfy the test for prosecution disclosure in the Act, and should explain why he has come to that view.

Where material is in a form other than in writing, it should be given to the prosecutor in a form agreed between the disclosure officer and the prosecutor.

Subsequent action by disclosure officer   When a streamlined disclosure certificate is prepared for magistrates' court cases, or a schedule of non-sensitive material is prepared for Crown Court cases, the disclosure officer may not know exactly what material will form the case against D. In addition, the prosecutor may not have given advice about the likely relevance of particular items of material. Once these matters have been determined, the disclosure officer must give the prosecutor, where necessary, an amended certificate or schedule unless he is informed in writing by the prosecutor that the prosecutor intends to disclose the material to the defence.

As already mentioned, a continuing duty is imposed on the prosecutor, for the duration of criminal proceedings against D, to disclose material which might reasonably be considered to undermine the case for the prosecution, or which might assist D. After a defence statement has been given or details of the issues in dispute have been recorded on the effective trial preparation form, the disclosure officer must look again at the material retained and must bring any material which might have this effect to the attention of the prosecutor.

The disclosure officer must certify that to the best of his knowledge and belief all relevant material which has been retained and made available to him has been revealed to the prosecutor. Further certification must follow subsequent developments.

Disclosure of material to D

Other than early disclosure under the common law duty, in the magistrates' court, the schedule in the Annex to the Code (and any relevant unused material to be disclosed under it) will be disclosed to D either at the hearing where a not guilty plea is entered, or as soon as possible following a formal indication from D or his representative that a not guilty plea will be entered at the hearing.

If material has not already been copied to the prosecutor, and he requests its disclosure to D on the grounds that it satisfies the criteria for disclosure or a court has ordered its disclosure, the disclosure officer must disclose it to D. If material has been copied to the prosecutor, and it is so disclosed, it is a matter for agreement as to who should make the disclosure. Disclosure by the disclosure officer must be made by the provision of a copy or an opportunity to inspect it. Where a request is made for the provision of a copy of inspected material it must be given by the disclosure officer unless he considers that it is not practicable to do so (eg because the material consists of an object which cannot be copied, or because the volume of material is too great), or that it is not desirable (eg where the material is a statement by a child witness in relation to a sexual offence). Where information is recorded other than in writing, it is for the disclosure officer to decide whether it should be given in its original form or by means of a transcript certified as a true record.

If a court concludes that an item of sensitive material satisfies the prosecution disclosure test and that the interests of the defence outweigh the public interest in withholding disclosure, the material must be disclosed if the case is to proceed. The court, however, may in such circumstances direct that parts of the material be blanked out, or that the documents be summarised, or that the prosecutor make an admission concerning the substance of the material under CJA 1967, s 10.

CHAPTER 8

The Police

ORGANISATION OF POLICE FORCES

Unless otherwise indicated, the provisions referred to below are contained in the Police Reform and Social Responsibility Act 2011 (PRSRA 2011), Part 1.

England and Wales are divided into police areas. Those areas are:

(a) the police areas listed in the Police Act 1996 (PA 1996), Sch 1 (which may be increased or reduced in number or extent by the Secretary of State);
(b) the Metropolitan Police district; and
(c) the City of London police area.

Police areas listed in PA 1996, Sch 1

Police and crime commissioners

Subject to the qualification referred to on p 280, there must be a police and crime commissioner (PCC) for each police area. Such commissioners are elected and hold office for four years.

Functions of police and crime commissioners

A PCC must secure the maintenance of the police force for his police area, and secure that the police force is efficient and effective. The PCC must hold the chief constable to account for the exercise of:

(a) the chief constable's functions and duties, including:
  (i) the exercise of the duties to have regard to the police and crime plan (see p 283) issued by the PCC and to the strategic policing requirement and codes of practice issued by the Secretary of State;
  (ii) the effectiveness and efficiency of the chief constable's arrangements for co-operating with other persons in the exercise of the chief constable's functions; and
  (iii) the exercise of duties relating to equality and diversity that are imposed on the chief constable by any enactment; and
(b) the functions of persons under the direction and control of the chief constable.

A PCC has a number of other functions referred to below.

Neither a PCC, nor a member of his staff, is personally liable for his conduct in the exercise of his functions unless it is shown to have been otherwise than in good faith.

Deputy commissioners, etc

A PCC may appoint a deputy commissioner and may arrange for the deputy commissioner to exercise most of the PCC's functions.

A PCC may arrange for any person eligible for appointment as a deputy commissioner to exercise some of the PCC's functions.

Scrutiny of police and crime commissioners

Each police area outside the London area must have a police and crime panel with the duties set out below. Such a panel is composed of councillors appointed by local authorities in England and by the Secretary of State in Wales. Provision is made for a panel to co-opt additional members.

A police and crime panel has various powers of scrutiny including:

(a) reviewing or scrutinising decisions or other action by the PCC in connection with the discharge of his functions, and making reports or recommendations to the PCC with respect to such discharge;

(b) reviewing the draft police and crime plan, or draft variation, devised by the PCC, and making a report or recommendations on it to him;

(c) reviewing the PCC's annual report, and making a report or recommendations on it to the PCC;

(d) reviewing the precept proposed by the PCC and (if necessary) vetoing it;

(e) scrutinising, via a confirmation hearing, the proposed appointment by the PCC of a deputy commissioner or the PCC's chief executive or the PCC's chief finance officer. The PCC is not bound by the panel's recommendation about the proposed appointment; and

(f) scrutinising the PCC's proposed appointment of a chief constable or the PCC's requirement of a chief constable to retire or resign (see below).

Suspension of police and crime commissioner   A police and crime panel may suspend the PCC if it appears to the panel that the PCC has been charged in the British Isles with an offence carrying a maximum term of imprisonment exceeding two years. If the PCC is subsequently convicted of any imprisonable offence his office becomes vacant.

Acting police and crime commissioner   The police and crime panel for a police area must appoint a member of the PCC's staff to act as PCC (ie to be 'acting PCC') if no person holds the office of PCC, or the PCC is incapacitated or suspended.

Replacement of some police and crime commissioners by elected mayors

The Cities and Local Government Devolution Act 2016 enables the functions of a PCC to be transferred to an elected mayor. This can be achieved as a result of generic provisions (to be applied by secondary legislation to individual areas agreeing deals) which, among other things, (a) enable public authority functions to be conferred on a combined authority, (b) enable the Secretary of State by order to provide for an elected mayor for the combined authority's area, and (c) enable the Secretary of State by order to provide for the mayor for the combined authority's area to exercise functions of a PCC in relation to it in place of the PCC.

In an order under (c), the Secretary of State may provide that the mayor may exercise all PCC functions or a limited number. However, there are some functions that must always be exercisable by the mayor (including holding the relevant chief constable to account and issuing a police and crime plan). There are also a number of essential matters that, where PCC functions are transferred to a mayor, the Secretary of State must put in place. These include enabling the mayor to appoint a deputy mayor for PCC functions, requiring the establishment of a scrutiny panel for policing matters and giving the panel the power to suspend the mayor from exercising PCC functions.

The Secretary of State has made an order under (b) and (c) in respect of the Greater Manchester Combined Authority. The mayor of that combined authority will exercise

PCC functions in relation to its area from 8 May 2017. There will be no PCC for the area from that date.

Chief constable

Appointment, suspension and removal   Each police force must have a chief constable appointed by the PCC. A police and crime panel must hold a public confirmation in respect of a proposed appointment and may veto that appointment.

The PCC may suspend from duty the chief constable or require him to resign or retire. A PCC's proposal to require a chief constable to retire or resign is subject to scrutiny by the police and crime panel but the panel can only make recommendations and cannot veto the proposal.

Functions   Subject to any provision in a collaboration agreement, a police force, and the civilian staff of a police force, are under the direction and control of the chief constable of the force.

Deputy and assistant chief constables

Each police force must have one or more deputy chief constables and one or more assistant chief constables. The chief constable must consult the PCC before appointing a person to be a deputy chief constable or an assistant chief constable. Those officers are 'senior police officers'. The chief constable of a police force may suspend from duty a deputy chief constable or an assistant chief constable or require him to resign or retire.

A deputy chief constable (or, where there is more than one, the most senior (as designated by the chief constable after consulting the PCC), or if he is absent, incapacitated, or suspended, the next most senior) may exercise any or all of the powers and duties of the chief constable during any absence, incapacity or suspension from duty of the chief constable, or during any vacancy in the office of chief constable, or at any other time with the chief constable's consent.

The chief constable must, after consulting the PCC, designate a particular assistant chief constable to exercise any or all of the chief constable's powers if both the chief constable and his deputy (or deputies) are absent, incapacitated, or suspended or those posts are all vacant.

Metropolitan Police District

The Mayor's Office for Policing and Crime

A body with the name 'The Mayor's Office for Policing and Crime' (MOPC) whose occupant is the Mayor of London, elected every four years, is established for the Metropolitan Police District. This body has replaced the Metropolitan Police Authority.

The MOPC has the same functions as a PCC (above and below), with the substitution of 'Mayor's Office for Policing and Crime' for 'police and crime commissioner/ PCC' and 'Commissioner of Police of the Metropolis' for 'chief constable'.

Neither the occupant of the MOPC, nor a member of his staff, is personally liable for his conduct in the exercise of his functions unless it is shown to have been otherwise than in good faith.

The MOPC may appoint a Deputy Mayor for Policing and Crime and arrange for that Deputy Mayor to exercise most of the function of the MOPC. The MOPC may not appoint the Deputy Mayor until after the end of a confirmation hearing process, or if (after that process) the London Assembly vetoes the appointment of the candidate on the ground that the candidate is not an Assembly member.

The MOPC may also appoint someone who is not the Deputy Mayor for Policing and Crime to exercise some functions of the MOPC.

Scrutiny of Mayor's Office for Policing and Crime

The London Assembly must arrange for the following functions to be discharged on its behalf by a particular committee of the Assembly (the 'police and crime panel'):

(a) reviewing the draft police and crime plan given to the Assembly by the MOPC and making a report or recommendations on the draft plan to the MOPC;
(b) keeping under review the exercise of the functions of the MOPC, insofar as the Assembly is not otherwise required to do so; and
(c) holding a confirmation hearing in respect of appointment of the Deputy Mayor for Policing and Crime by the MOPC.

Commissioner of Police of the Metropolis

The Commissioner of Police of the Metropolis (CPM) is appointed by the Queen on the recommendation of the Secretary of State. Before recommending a person for appointment as the Commissioner the Secretary of State must have regard to any recommendations made by the MOPC. The CPM holds office at Her Majesty's pleasure.

The MOPC may, with the approval of the Secretary of State, suspend the CPM or require him to resign or retire.

The Secretary of State may require the MOPC to exercise the power to require the CPM to retire or resign, or (if the Secretary of State considers that suspension is necessary for the maintenance of public confidence in the Metropolitan Police Force) to suspend the CPM. Where it is proposed to require the exercise of the power to require retirement or resignation, one or more persons must be appointed by, and report to, the Secretary of State after holding an inquiry.

Subject to any provision in a collaboration agreement, the Metropolitan Police Force, and the civilian staff of the Metropolitan Police Force, are under the direction and control of the CPM.

Deputy and Assistant Commissioners

The Metropolitan Police Force has one Deputy Commissioner of Police of the Metropolis, who is appointed and holds office in the same way as the Commissioner, except that before recommending a person for appointment the Secretary of State must also consult the CPM as well as any representations made by the MOPC. The rules about suspending the Deputy CPM, or requiring him to retire or resign are the same as those which apply to the CPM.

The Deputy CPM may exercise any or all of the powers and duties of the CPM:

(a) during any absence, incapacity or suspension from duty of the CPM,
(b) during any vacancy in the office of CPM, or
(c) at any other time, with the consent of the CPM.

The Deputy CPM may not act by virtue of (a) or (b) for a continuous period exceeding three months, except with the consent of the Secretary of State.

The Metropolitan Police Force must have one or more Assistant Commissioners of Police of the Metropolis, one or more Deputy Assistant Commissioners of Police of the Metropolis, and one or more Commanders. These officers are appointed by the CPM. The CPM must consult the MOPC before appointing a person to one of these offices. These officers ('senior Metropolitan Police officers') may be suspended by the

CPM. After consulting the MOPC, the CPM may require a senior Metropolitan Police officer to resign or retire. An Assistant Commissioner of Police of the Metropolis may exercise any of the powers and duties of the CPM with his consent.

Other functions and duties of elected local policing bodies

A police and crime commissioner or the Mayor's Office for Policing and Crime is an 'elected local policing body'.

Police and crime plans

The elected local policing body (ELPB) must issue a police and crime plan within the financial year in which each four-yearly election is held and must do so as soon as practicable after taking office. In addition, it may, at any time, issue or vary a police and crime plan. In issuing or varying a police and crime plan, an ELPB must have regard to the strategic policing requirement issued by the Secretary of State (below).

A police and crime plan is a plan which sets out, in relation to the planning period, a number of matters, including:

(a) the ELPB's police and crime objectives;
(b) the policing of the police area which the chief officer of police is to provide;
(c) the financial and other resources which the ELPB is to provide to the chief officer of police for the exercise of his functions.

Before issuing or varying a police and crime plan, an ELPB must consult the relevant chief officer of police and the relevant police and crime panel on a draft plan.

If, and to any extent that, the plan or variation differs from the draft plan, the ELPB must consult the relevant chief officer before issuing or varying the plan.

A plan or variation of it must be published.

After consulting the persons representing the views of the Association of Police and Crime Commissioners, the Mayor's Office, the National Police Chiefs' Council (NPCC), and other persons as thought fit, the Secretary of State may give guidance to ELPBs about matters to be dealt with in these plans, and such bodies must have regard to it.

An ELPB and a chief officer of police must have regard to the police and crime plan, and to any guidance issued by the Secretary of State about how this duty to do so is to be complied with.

Duties when carrying out functions

In carrying out functions, an ELPB must have regard not only to the local policing plan (see above) but also:

(a) to the views of people in the ELPB's area about policing in that area;
(b) in a particular financial year, to any report or recommendations made by the relevant police and crime panel on the annual report for the previous financial year; and
(c) any financial code of practice issued by the Secretary of State.

Police fund

Each ELPB must keep a 'police fund' into which all receipts must be paid and from which all expenditure must be paid. The Secretary of State, for each financial year, makes a grant from central funds for the purposes of each ELPB. The remainder of the finance will be met from other grants from the Secretary of State (for capital expenditure or expenditure on safeguarding national security) or local authorities, precepts on local authorities and gifts and loans.

City of London police area

The provisions of PRSRA 2011, Part 1 do not apply to this area.

The Common Council of the City of London continues to be the police authority for the City of London police area.

The head of the City of London Police is the Commissioner of Police for the City of London. Its other senior officers are an Assistant Commissioner and a Commander.

Ranks below senior officers

Appointments and promotions to any rank below that of assistant chief constable (or commander) are made by the chief constable (or Commissioner of Police for the Metropolis or Commissioner of City of London Police). Those ranks are chief superintendent, superintendent, chief inspector, inspector, sergeant and constable.

The role of the Secretary of State

The Secretary of State's principal police-related functions are as follows.

Strategic policing requirement

Although the courts have ruled that chief officers of police must carry out their duties independently, so that there may be no suggestion of direct government control in relation to law enforcement, by PA 1996, s 37A, the Secretary of State is required, from time to time, to issue the 'strategic policing requirement' which sets out what, in the Secretary of State's view, are:

(a) national threats (ie threats to national security, public safety, public order, or public confidence so grave as to be of national importance, or threats which can be countered effectively or efficiently only by 'national policing capabilities' (ie the ability of all English and Welsh police forces)); and

(b) appropriate national policing capabilities to counter those national threats.

A chief officer of police must, in exercising the functions of chief officer, have regard to the strategic policing requirement.

Before issuing the strategic policing requirement, the Secretary of State must obtain the advice of the Association of Police and Crime Commissioners and the NPCC, and must consult such other persons as the Secretary of State thinks fit.

Power to give directions

By PA 1996, ss 40 and 40A, the Secretary of State may direct a local policing body (an ELPB or the Common Council of the City of London) to take specified measures to remedy any defect or potential defect in the discharge of its functions or those of its police force. When directing specified measures, the Secretary of State may require an action plan.

Regulation-making powers

PA 1996, s 53A empowers the Secretary of State to make regulations requiring police forces in England and Wales to adopt particular procedures or practices. If the College of Policing, having consulted the National Crime Agency, submits to the Secretary of State a draft of regulations under s 53A, the Secretary of State must make regulations in terms of the draft unless the Secretary of State considers that:

(a) doing so would impair the efficiency or effectiveness of the police, or
(b) it would be unlawful, or for some other reason wrong, to do so.

By PA 1996, s 50, the Secretary of State may, after consultation, make regulations as to the government, administration and conditions of service of police forces. If the College of Policing submits to the Secretary of State draft regulations with respect to police ranks, qualification for appointment for promotion, probationary periods or the maintenance of personal records of members of police forces, the Secretary of State must make regulations in terms of the draft unless the Secretary of State considers that (a) or (b) above applies. The Secretary of State may not make regulations with respect to any of these matters unless the text of the regulations has been prepared or approved by the College of Policing.

PA 1996, s 53 enables the Secretary of State to make regulations as to the standard and provision of police equipment. The Secretary of State may not make such regulations unless their text has been prepared or approved by the College of Policing.

Crime and disorder strategies

The Crime and Disorder Act 1998, ss 5 to 7 makes provision for crime and disorder reduction partnerships in each district council area in England, and each county or county borough area in Wales, in a police area to formulate and implement crime and disorder strategies.

The members of such a partnership are the 'responsible authorities', ie the council, every chief officer of police whose police area is in the council's area, every provider of probation services, every fire and rescue authority, and every clinical commissioning group (England) or Local Health Board (Wales) in that area.

In England, two or more areas may be combined by an agreement made by the ELPB or the Secretary of State (City of London) and the responsible authorities.

The community remedy document

The Anti-social Behaviour Crime and Policing Act 2014 (A-s B, C&PA 2014), s 101 requires each local policing body to prepare a community remedy document for its area.

A community remedy document is a list of actions, any of which might, in the opinion of the local policing body (LPB)—ie PCC, MOPC or Common Council of the City of London—be appropriate (in terms of rehabilitation, reparation or punishment) in a particular case to be carried out by a person who:

(a) has engaged in anti-social behaviour (as defined on p 723) or has committed an offence, and
(b) is to be dealt with for that behaviour or offence without court proceedings.

In preparing or revising the document the LPB must also consult:

(a) the chief officer of police;
(b) the district council (England) or county council or county borough council (Wales).

An LPB must agree the community remedy document for its area, and any revised document, with the chief officer of police and must then publish it.

Collaboration agreements

These are dealt with by PA 1996, ss 22A–23H.

A collaboration agreement is a written agreement containing provision about one or more of the following:

(a) the discharge of functions of members of a police force ('force collaboration provision');
(b) support by a policing body for another policing body ('policing body collaboration provision');
(c) support by a policing body for the police force which another policing body is responsible for maintaining ('policing body and force collaboration provision').

A 'policing body' means an ELPB, the Common Council of the City of London, the British Transport Police Authority and the Civil Nuclear Police Authority.

Such an agreement may be made by two or more policing bodies, or by the chief officers of police of one or more police forces and two or more policing bodies.

Force collaboration provision in a collaboration agreement involving police forces may, in particular, consist of provision for the joint discharge of functions by members of police forces; for members of a police force to discharge functions in another force's area; for members of a police force to be provided to another force. A collaboration agreement involving police forces may provide for a member of a police force, or a civilian employee, to be under the direction and control of a chief officer specified in or determined in accordance with the agreement.

Policing body collaboration provision, or policing body and force collaboration provision, in a collaboration agreement involving policing bodies may, in particular, consist of provision:

(a) for support to be provided jointly by two or more policing bodies;
(b) for support to be provided for two or more policing bodies or forces jointly;
(c) for a policing body to provide support to another policing body or to a force maintained by another policing body.

Where a force collaboration provision, contained in a collaboration agreement, is about the discharge of functions by designated civilian employees of one police force for the purposes of another police force, the force collaboration agreement must specify:

(a) the functions which the designated civilian employees (ie designated under PRA 2002, s 38 (p 291)) are permitted by the collaboration agreement to discharge for the purposes of the assisted force, and
(b) any restrictions or conditions on that permission for the designated civilian employees to discharge those functions.

The force collaboration agreement must not permit the designated civilian employees to discharge functions for the purposes of the assisted police force unless those employees are, by virtue of the relevant s 38 designation, authorised to discharge those functions for the purposes of the assisting force. The force collaboration provision does not authorise the designated civilian employees to discharge functions for the purposes of the assisted police force; such authorisation depends on a designation by the chief officer of the assisted force.

The Secretary of State may, by order, require a specified police function to be exercised in relation to all police areas, or all police areas apart from any specified in the order, in accordance with police collaboration provision. The Secretary of State has specified the provision of police air support as such a function in relation to all police areas.

The Secretary of State may give one or more chief officers or policing bodies binding directions about collaboration agreements. The person or persons to whom it is to be given must be consulted in advance. A direction may, in particular, require or prohibit the making or varying of a collaboration agreement, or require the making of a collaboration agreement of a specified description to be considered, or specify terms to be included, or not included, in collaboration agreements. A direction may relate to a particular agreement, agreements of a particular description, or agreements in general.

After consulting the parties to an agreement, the Secretary of State may terminate a collaboration agreement by notice to these parties.

National Police Chiefs' Council

The NPCC, established under a force collaboration agreement, co-ordinates operational policing and collaboration amongst forces at the national level.

Her Majesty's Inspectors of Constabulary

PA 1996, ss 54 and 55 and Sch 4A govern Her Majesty's Inspectors of Constabulary (HMIC), who are appointed by the Queen.

HMIC must inspect, and report on the efficiency and effectiveness of, every police force maintained for a police area.

The local policing body for a police area (ie PCC, MOPC, or the Common Council of the City of London) may at any time request HMIC to carry out, at its expense, an inspection of a police force maintained for that police area. The request may include a request for the inspection to be confined to a particular part of the force in question, to particular matters or to particular activities of that force. The Secretary of State has a corresponding power to request an inspection of a police force maintained for any police area; the only difference is that the inspection is not at the expense of the relevant local policing body.

Where such an inspection leads to a conclusion that the force, or a part of it, or the local policing body, is not efficient or effective, or will cease to be so unless remedial action is taken, the Secretary of State may give a direction under ss 40 or 40A to the relevant local policing body to take such remedial measures as are specified in the direction. These measures may include the submission of an action plan.

The chief inspector of constabulary must in each year submit to the Secretary of State a report on the carrying out of inspections and the Secretary of State must lay a copy of that report before Parliament. Such a report must include the chief inspector's assessment of the efficiency and effectiveness of policing for the year reported on.

PA 1996, Sch 4A permits an inspector of constabulary to delegate any of his functions (to such extent as he may determine) to another public authority. The inspectors of constabulary may act jointly with another public authority where it is appropriate.

JURISDICTION OF CONSTABLES

In law every member of a police force holds the office of constable, whatever his rank. Although he is not 'a member of a police force', so does a special constable.

PA 1996, s 30 provides that every member of a police force or a special constable has all the powers and privileges of a constable throughout England and Wales and the adjacent UK waters. 'UK waters' means the sea and other waters within the seaboard limits of the territorial seas.

REPRESENTATION

The Superintendents' Association and the Police Federation represent the interests of the various members of police forces at the relevant ranks. A member of a police force is not permitted to be a member of a trade union, or of any association having as one of its objects control or influence over pay, pensions or conditions of service of any police force. However, persons who were members of trade unions before joining the police force may retain that membership with the approval of their chief constable.

LIABILITY

Civil liability

A constable will be liable to pay damages if his conduct is unlawful in civil law, as where he commits a tort, acts in breach of a Convention right under the Human Rights Act 1998 or unlawfully discriminates. Examples of a tort are the torts of battery, false (unlawful) imprisonment and negligence. Negligence requires that there is a duty of care owed to the victim, that the conduct in question falls below the standard of care expected and that reasonably foreseeable injury was caused as a result of the conduct.

PA 1996, s 88 states that a chief officer of police is vicariously liable in civil law for any unlawful conduct of his constables in the performance or purported performance of their duties. This means that civil claims may be pursued against a chief officer, as well as against (or instead of against) the officer alleged to have committed a wrongful act or to have failed to comply with a duty of care owed to another. The chief officer can even be liable for the off-duty unlawful conduct of a constable if it was committed at a time when the constable was apparently acting in his capacity as a constable. It has been held in the High Court that a chief officer is not necessarily liable for conduct in the purported performance of a constable's duties if the conduct was clearly for a purpose unrelated to the constable's duties—as where he offers not to report an illegal immigrant in return for sexual favours. Special provision is made by PA 1996, s 97 in relation to officers seconded to central service; it is the Secretary of State (and not their chief constable) who is vicariously liable for their unlawful conduct.

The House of Lords has held that, save in exceptional circumstances, no action lies in tort against a constable or his chief constable for injury caused to a person (X) by a negligent act or omission in the course of the operational duties of investigating, detecting or suppressing crime, or apprehending the offender. A subsequent decision of the Supreme Court is to like effect to that of the House of Lords. The Supreme Court held that the police do not owe a duty of care to a specific member of the public (X) where they were aware, or ought reasonably to have been aware, of a threat to his life or physical safety, or where they had been given apparently credible information by him that an identifiable third party presented a specific and imminent threat to his life or physical safety. Thus a constable or his chief constable would not be liable, in respect of a negligent act or omission, for injury caused to X when the threat was put into action.

A constable conducting disciplinary proceedings (or his chief constable) cannot be liable in tort to the officer under investigation if he negligently conducts the proceedings or acts in breach of his duty under the relevant regulations (see p 319). As a matter of public policy, chief constables are not generally liable to their subordinates who are injured by rioters in the course of controlling serious public disorder. Nor are they liable to a person in respect of whom they provide inaccurate information for criminal records purposes. Under the provisions of the Sexual Offences Act 2003 and Anti-social Behaviour, Crime and Policing Act 2014 relating to closure notices and orders in respect of premises, neither a constable nor his chief officer is liable in tort for anything done or omitted in the course of a constable's performance of his functions thereunder unless the act or omission is shown to have been in bad faith. This does not prevent damages being awarded if the act or omission was unlawful because of the Human Rights Act 1998 (p 3).

Neither a constable nor his chief constable is liable to someone who suffers injuries in a foreseeable attempt to escape, nor to a road user for injuries caused by a constable's failure to give warnings of hazards of which the constable was aware but for which he was not responsible.

The Court of Appeal has upheld the award of damages under the Human Rights Act 1998 on the ground that, in certain circumstances, the police are under a 'human rights duty' to conduct investigations into particularly severe violent acts (such as those in question) in a timely and efficient manner, which they had not in the case in question. The Court of Appeal noted that the State's duty to conduct an official investigation into alleged ill-treatment by private individuals in order to identify those responsible was inherent in the European Convention on Human Rights, art 3 (right not to be subjected to inhuman treatment). The energy required of the State to combat or redress such ill-treatment was variable. More was required at the top end of the scale to comply with art 3 than at the bottom end. At what might be called the lower end of the scale where injury happened through the negligence of private individuals, the State's provision of a judicial system of civil remedies would often suffice. Serious violent crime by private individuals was of a different order: higher up the scale. In those cases, a proper criminal investigation by the State was required. Not every allegation of ill-treatment which met the art 3 threshold called for a full criminal investigation. There would be cases, for example, where all the facts were known, or where the victim did not want the police involved, which might, depending on the details, yield the conclusion that a full criminal investigation was unnecessary or inappropriate or disproportionate.

A constable or his chief officer may be liable under the Equality Act 2010 for discrimination on grounds of race, sex, sexual orientation, gender reassignment, age, disability, religious belief, marriage or civil partnership, pregnancy, or maternity.

Any costs or damages awarded against a chief officer on the grounds of his vicarious liability must be paid out of police funds. Those awarded against the constable concerned may be paid or part-paid from police funds at the discretion of the local policing body, and it has been held that they should be so paid if the constable acted in good faith.

Criminal liability

A constable is, of course, subject to the ordinary criminal law. There are, however, two offences worthy of note here.

First, a constable will commit the common law offence of misconduct in a public office if, while acting as such, he wilfully neglects to perform his duty and/or wilfully misconducts himself to such a degree as to amount to an abuse of the public's trust in the office holder, without reasonable excuse or justification. The offence is triable only on indictment.

Second, a 'police constable' listed below commits an offence contrary to the Criminal Justice and Courts Act 2015, s 26(1), if he exercises the powers and privileges of a constable improperly, and knows or ought to know that the exercise is improper. The offence is triable only on indictment.

Section 26 applies to a constable or special constable of a police force in England and Wales; a British Transport Police Force (BTP) constable or special constable; a Civil Nuclear Constabulary or Ministry of Defence Police constable; and a National Crime Agency officer designated as having the powers and privileges of a constable.

For the purposes of s 26, a police constable exercises the powers and privileges of a constable improperly if:

(a) he exercises a power or privilege of a constable for the purpose of achieving:
  (i) a benefit for himself, or
  (ii) a benefit or a detriment for another person, and
(b) a reasonable person would not expect the power or privilege to be exercised for the purpose of achieving that benefit or detriment.

'Benefit' and 'detriment' mean any benefit or detriment, whether or not in money or other property and whether temporary or permanent.

A police constable is to be treated as exercising the powers and privileges of a constable improperly where:

(i) he fails to exercise a power or privilege of a constable, the purpose of the failure is to achieve a benefit or detriment described in (a) above, and a reasonable person would not expect a constable to fail to exercise the power or privilege for the purpose of achieving that benefit or detriment; or
(ii) he threatens to exercise, or not to exercise, a power or privilege of a constable, the threat is made for the purpose of achieving a benefit or detriment described in (a) above, and a reasonable person would not expect a constable to threaten to exercise, or not to exercise, the power or privilege for the purpose of achieving that benefit or detriment.

The above references to exercising, or not exercising, the powers and privileges of a constable include performing, or not performing, the duties of a constable.

IMPERSONATION, ETC AND CAUSING DISAFFECTION AMONGST MEMBERS OF A POLICE FORCE

Impersonation

A person who, with intent to deceive, impersonates a member of a police force (including the BTP or Civil Nuclear Constabulary) or a special constable appointed for a police area or of the BTP, or makes any statement or does any act calculated falsely to suggest that he is such a member or constable, commits an offence against PA 1996, s 90(1). It is also an offence against s 90(2) for a person who, not being a member of a police force or a special constable, wears any article of police uniform in circumstances where it gives him an appearance so nearly resembling that of a member of a police force as to be calculated to deceive. Section 90(3) makes it an offence to possess an article of police uniform, unless it was obtained lawfully and is possessed for a lawful purpose.

Causing disaffection

A person who causes, or attempts to cause, or does any act calculated to cause, disaffection amongst members of any police force, or induces, or attempts to induce, or does any act calculated to induce, any member of a police force to withhold his services commits an offence against PA 1996, s 91(1). The section also applies to special constables appointed for a police area and members of the BTP or Civil Nuclear Constabulary as it does to members of a police force.

EXERCISE OF POLICE POWERS BY CIVILIANS

PRA 2002, s 38 authorises a chief officer of police to designate a relevant employee as an officer who is under his direction and control as:

(a) a community support officer (CSO);
(b) an investigating officer;
(c) a detention officer;
(d) an escort officer.

For these purposes, 'relevant employee' means:

(a) in the case of:
  (i) a police force maintained for an area listed in PA 1996, Sch 1, or
  (ii) the police force maintained for the Metropolitan Police District,
  a member of the civilian staff of that force;
(b) in the case of any other police force, a person who:
  (i) is employed by the police authority maintaining that force, and
  (ii) is under the direction and control of the chief officer making the designation.

A person designated under s 38 has the powers and duties conferred or imposed on him by the designation as well as (in the case of a CSO) any standard duties and powers conferred on such an officer by an order made by the Secretary of State. The complete range of powers and duties which may be conferred or imposed by a designation are set out in PRA 2002, Sch 4.

A community support officer

A person designated as a CSO has the standard powers and duties of a CSO conferred by the Police Reform Act (Standard Powers and Duties of Community Support Officers) Order 2007 made by the Secretary of State under PRA 2002, s 38A, in addition to any powers conferred on him by designation as set out in Sch 4, Part 1.

The standard powers and duties of a CSO are set out in the Schedule to the 2007 Order, which makes the following powers in PRA 2002, Sch 4, Part 1 standard powers:

(a) issue of fixed penalty notices under the (i) Road Traffic Offenders Act 1988, s 54 in respect of footway-cycling or (ii) Environmental Protection Act 1990, s 88 in respect of litter. Such offences are also 'relevant fixed penalty offences';

(b) requirement of name and address if the CSO has reason to believe that the person has committed a 'relevant offence' (ie a relevant fixed penalty offence (above and below), or an offence which appears to have caused injury, alarm or distress to another, or any damage to another's property, or certain other offences) or a relevant licensing offence. It is an offence to fail to comply with such a requirement. (In addition, a designation *may* provide a power permitting a CSO who is so designated and who has made a requirement for a name and address to require the other person to remain with him for a period, not exceeding 30 minutes, for the arrival of a constable, where the CSO has reasonable grounds for suspecting that the person has given a false or inaccurate name or address. When making that requirement, the officer may enforce it by a gesture. The alleged offender may elect to accompany the CSO to a police station as an alternative to waiting. Such a person, on arrival at a police station, is under a duty to remain there until his custody is transferred to a constable. Failure to wait, or making off, is an offence. A designation *may* also empower search of a person asked to wait or the use of reasonable force to prevent an individual making off when subject to a requirement to give his name and address or while accompanying the officer to a police station);

(c) requirement of name and address of person reasonably believed to have been active or to be acting in an anti-social manner;

(d) requirement of name and address under RTA 1988, ss 165 or 169 (power to require name and address following failure to comply with a traffic direction or failure by a pedestrian to comply with a direction given by a police officer or a traffic officer respectively);

(e) exercise of a constable's powers to deal with alcohol consumption in breach of a public spaces protection order (a designation may give an associated power of search and seizure);

(f) exercise of a constable's powers to confiscate alcohol or tobacco from a young person (a designation may give an associated power of search and seizure);

(g) seizure of a controlled drug or a psychoactive substance found in someone's possession (a designation may give an associated power of search and seizure);

(h) entry to save life or limb or prevent serious damage to property;

(i) seizure of vehicles used to cause alarm, etc (entry to premises to do so only in company, and under supervision, of a constable);

(j) exercise of powers in respect of abandoned vehicles;

(k) stopping pedal cycles in respect of reasonably believed specified offence;

(l) control of traffic for purposes other than escorting a load of exceptional dimensions;

(m) carrying out road checks;

(n) placing traffic signs;

(o) exercise of constable's powers under the Terrorism Act 2000, s 36 in cordoned areas;

(p) exercise of specified stop, search and seizure powers under the Terrorism Act 2000, s 47A; and

(q) photographing persons arrested, detained, or given fixed penalty notices.

Examples of powers which may be conferred on a CSO are as follows.

A designation may confer on a CSO the power to issue prescribed fixed penalty notices in respect of the following '*relevant fixed penalty offences*':

(a) under the Criminal Justice and Police Act 2001 (CJPA 2001) (fixed penalty notices for offences of disorder), except in relation to offences of theft against the Theft Act 1968, s 1, and of leaving litter against the Environmental Protection Act 1990 (EPA 1990), s 87;

(b) under education legislation, in respect of failure to secure attendance of a pupil at school or of the presence of an excluded pupil in a public place;

(c) under the Anti-social Behaviour Act 2003, s 43, in respect of graffiti or fly-posting;

(d) under the Anti-social Behaviour Crime and Policing Act 2014, ss 43 or 68, in respect of failure to comply with a community protection notice or failure to comply with a public spaces protection order, respectively;

(e) under legislation in London in respect of unauthorised street trading;

(f) under the Road Traffic Offenders Act 1988, s 54 in respect of specified offences.

A designation may confer on a CSO power to issue a community protection notice.

In addition, a designation may confer on a CSO the same powers as a constable under PACE, s 19 (general powers of seizure) and ss 21 and 22 (access, copying and retention). It may also confer the power to direct a person to leave an area and to surrender property, to remove truants and excluded pupils to designated premises, to serve closure notices for licensed premises persistently serving children, to enter to investigate licensing offences, to stop vehicles for testing, to control traffic for purposes of escorting a load of exceptional dimensions, and to require the production of authority, name, address and signature, under the House to House Collections Act 1939.

An investigating officer

A designation may empower an investigating officer to exercise the powers under the Police and Criminal Evidence Act 1984 (PACE), s 8 to apply for a warrant to enter and search premises to be issued to him and to seize and retain articles found during a search. The safeguards, etc provided by PACE in relation to searches apply equally to an officer so designated. A designation may permit a search warrant to be issued, and executed, under the Theft Act 1968, s 26 or the Misuse of Drugs Act 1971, s 23, by an officer in respect of whom the designation applies these provisions. A designation may give the powers of a constable under PACE, s 9(1) (access to excluded and special procedure material) to an investigating officer. The various procedural matters prescribed by PACE in relation to such matters apply to such an officer. Powers under PACE, ss 18, 19 and 21 to enter, search, seize and copy things seized may also be given by a designation, as may powers to arrest for a further offence someone who is at a police station under arrest for another offence. In addition, a designation may give powers under CJPOA 1994 to require arrested persons to account for certain matters, or powers under the UK Borders Act 2007, ss 44, 45 and 46 to enter and search premises and to seize nationality documents where a person, who is suspected of not being a British citizen, has been arrested on suspicion of having committed an offence under that Act. Authorised persons have the same search-and-seize powers as are possessed by an investigating officer whom they accompany.

A detention officer

A designation may authorise a detention officer: to require a person to attend a police station for the taking of a sample or fingerprints (and to take those fingerprints without consent); to photograph a detained person; to carry out intimate or non-intimate searches; to search a person answering live link bail; to carry out a search and examination to establish identity (including the taking of a photograph of an identifying mark); to take impressions of footwear; and to carry out a search of someone attending a police station to answer live link bail, and to seize articles found.

A designation may authorise a detention officer to keep under control detainees at a police station (or to assist others in doing so) and to secure that persons in detention do not escape; reasonable force may be used for these purposes. A designation may authorise a detention officer to carry out specified duties to give information in relation to intimate searches, X-rays and ultrasound scans carried out in respect of Class A drug searches.

An escort officer

An escort officer may be designated to take an arrested person to a police station or to escort a person in police detention. An escort officer designated to escort a person in police detention may also use reasonable force to keep the detainee under control. A designated escort officer remains in control until the detainee is handed over to the custody officer or other responsible person, and may use reasonable force to prevent that person escaping and to keep him under his control. A designated escort officer may carry out an intimate search of the detainee.

Community safety accreditation schemes

PRA 2002, s 40 authorises a chief officer to establish and maintain a 'community safety accreditation scheme' for the exercise in his area, by persons accredited by him under s 41, of powers related to community safety and security and (in co-operation with the local police) combating crime and disorder, public nuisance, and other forms of anti-social behaviour. Any such scheme must contain provisions for arrangements to be made with employers who are carrying on a business in the police area for those employers to supervise the carrying out of such functions for the purposes of which accreditation powers are provided. Chief officers must ensure that the employer has made satisfactory arrangements for the handling of complaints relating to the exercise of those powers.

The powers which may be conferred on accredited persons are set out in PRA 2002, Sch 5, namely powers to give fixed penalty notices:

(a) under CJPA 2001, except in respect of offences of drunkenness, theft, criminal damage or leaving litter (contrary to EPA 1990, s 87);
(b) in respect of offences relating to cycling on a footpath, failing to secure attendance of a pupil at school, being an excluded pupil in a public place, graffiti or fly-posting, and litter under EPA 1990, s 88.

Accredited persons may also be given powers to deal with alcohol consumption in a designated public place, confiscation of liquor or tobacco from those under 18, abandoned vehicles, stopping vehicles for testing, and controlling traffic for the purpose of escorting a load of exceptional dimensions.

Accredited persons may be authorised to require names and addresses in relation to certain traffic offences, to control traffic and to photograph persons given fixed penalty notices.

Accreditation of weights and measures inspectors

PRA 2002, s 41A provides that weights and measures inspectors (trading standards officers) may be accredited ('an accredited officer') by a chief officer of police. An accredited officer may be accredited to issue fixed penalty notices under CJPA 2001, to require the name and address of someone reasonably believed to have committed a fixed penalty offence for the purposes of CJPA 2001 and/or to photograph someone to whom he has given such a notice. The powers may only be exercised by such an accredited officer in the exercise of his duties as a trading standards officer. Section 41B authorises the Secretary of State to apply these provisions related to an accredited officer to persons of a description specified by order.

General

A designated person or person accredited under PRA 2002, s 41 or s 41A must produce evidence of his designation or accreditation if requested to do so when exercising one of his powers. In addition, such a person is restricted in the exercise of powers to times when he is wearing approved uniform or badge. However, a police inspector (or above) may direct a particular investigating officer not to wear uniform for the purposes of a particular operation.

PRA 2002, s 46(1) provides that it is an offence to assault a designated person, an accredited person, an accredited inspector, or a person assisting a designated or accredited person or an accredited inspector, in each case in the execution of his duty. By s 46(2), it is an offence to resist or wilfully obstruct such a person.

Under s 46(3) a person commits an offence if, with intent to deceive, he

(a) impersonates a designated person, an accredited person or an accredited inspector;
(b) makes any statement or does any act calculated falsely to suggest that he is such a person; or
(c) makes any statement or does any act calculated falsely to suggest that he has powers of such a person that exceed his actual powers.

These auxiliary personnel must have regard, in the discharge of their duties, to the provisions of the PACE Codes of Practice. A person lawfully in the custody of such a person must be treated as in police detention.

Where any power exercised by one of the above types of person includes power to use reasonable force to enter premises, that power may only be exercised in the company, and under the supervision, of a constable, or to save life or limb or to prevent serious damage.

NATIONAL POLICE ORGANISATIONS

National Crime Agency

The Serious Organised Crime Agency was abolished by the Crime and Courts Act 2013 (CCA 2013) and replaced by the National Crime Agency (NCA) in October 2013. The NCA is not a police force but is mentioned here for convenience.

The NCA is focused on organised crime, economic crime, border policing and child protection. It has both a strategic and operational role, and powers to instruct local police forces.

The provisions relating to the NCA are contained in CCA 2013, Part 1 (ss 1–116) and Schs 1–7.

The NCA is under the direction and control of its Director General, who is appointed by the Secretary of State.

The NCA consists of the NCA officers, ie the Director General of the NCA, persons appointed by the Director General as NCA officers, persons seconded to the NCA to serve as NCA officers, and NCA specials (ie persons appointed by the Director General as NCA officers on a part-time basis).

If a person with operational powers, for example a constable (other than a special constable), Revenue and Customs officer, or immigration officer, becomes an NCA officer, his existing powers are suspended during the time when he is an NCA officer. This does not apply to a member of the British Transport Police, Civil Nuclear Constabulary, or Ministry of Defence Police who is an NCA officer by virtue of a secondment.

The Director General may make arrangements for NCA officers to be seconded to a UK police force. An NCA officer who is so seconded is under the direction and control of the chief officer of the police force (but is not a member of the police force).

Functions

The NCA has:

(a) the 'crime-reduction function';
(b) the 'criminal intelligence function';
(c) the functions relating to the recovery of assets conferred by the Proceeds of Crime Act 2002; and
(d) the other functions conferred by CCA 2013 (eg assistance to a foreign government) and by other enactments.

The crime-reduction function is the function of securing that efficient and effective activities to combat organised crime and serious crime are carried out (whether by the NCA, other law enforcement agencies or other persons). It does not include the function of the NCA itself prosecuting offences.

The criminal intelligence function is the function of gathering, storing, processing, analysing and disseminating information that is relevant to activities to combat any kind of crime, or relevant to exploitation proceeds investigations or orders.

For these purposes, a reference to activities to combat crime is a reference to:

(a) the prevention and detection of crime;
(b) the investigation and prosecution of offences;
(c) the reduction of crime; and
(d) the mitigation of the consequences of crime.

Strategic priorities

The Secretary of State must determine strategic priorities for the NCA. In determining them, the Secretary of State must consult the Director General, a range of specified persons with an official interest in the NCA's work, and any other persons whom the Secretary of State deems appropriate.

Operations

The Director General has operational control. He has the power to decide which particular operations are to be mounted by the NCA officer, and how such operations are to be conducted.

In exercising his functions, the Director General must have regard to:

(a) any strategic priorities for the NCA;
(b) the annual plan for the exercise of the NCA's functions (which must be agreed with the Secretary of State); and
(c) the framework document (which is issued by the Secretary of State and deals with ways in which the NCA is to operate and ways in which it is to be administered).

Operational powers

The Secretary of State may designate the Director General as a person having one or more of the following:

(a) the powers and privileges of a constable;
(b) the powers of an officer of Revenue and Customs;
(c) the powers of an immigration officer;

but may only do so if required or authorised by specified provisions.

The Director General may designate any other suitable NCA officer as a person having one or more of the above operational powers and privileges.

It is an offence to resist or wilfully obstruct a designated officer acting in the exercise of an operational power, or a person assisting him in the exercise of such a power (CCA 2013, Sch 5, para 21), or to assault such a designated officer or such a person (Sch 5, para 22).

A person commits an offence if, with intent to deceive:

(a) he impersonates a designated officer;
(b) he makes any statement or does any act calculated falsely to suggest that he is a designated officer; or
(c) he makes any statement or does any act calculated falsely to suggest that he has powers as a designated officer that exceed the powers he actually has (Sch 5, para 23).

Mutual assistance

Voluntary arrangements may be made in relation to mutual assistance between the NCA and police forces. Where there is a failure to agree, the Secretary of State may direct the Director General to provide specified assistance to a police force; or (as the case may be) the Director General, with the Secretary of State's consent, may require the chief officer of a police force, etc to provide specified assistance to the NCA.

Inspections and complaints

Her Majesty's Inspectors of Constabulary must carry out inspections of the NCA. They must also carry out an inspection of the NCA if requested to do so by the Secretary of State either generally or in respect of a particular matter. Following an inspection they must report to the Secretary of State on the efficiency and effectiveness of the NCA either generally or regarding the particular matter.

The National Crime Agency (Complaints and Misconduct) Regulations 2013 provide for the basis on which the IPCC has oversight of complaints and other matters relating to the conduct of an NCA officer. The Regulations broadly reflect the provisions in the text from p 298 relating to persons serving with a police force, with modifications where necessary to reflect differences between the NCA and the police.

Liability of the NCA for unlawful acts

The NCA is liable in respect of unlawful conduct by an NCA officer in the same manner as an employer is liable in respect of unlawful conduct of employees in the course of their employment. In addition, the NCA is also liable where there is unlawful conduct by a constable or other person which occurs when that person is carrying out, or purporting to carry out, functions whilst seconded to the NCA to serve as an NCA officer, or whilst provided for the assistance of the NCA.

College of Policing

The College of Policing is the professional body for the police in England and Wales. The Anti-social Behaviour, Crime and Policing Act 2014, ss 123 to 130 establish the legislative basis for the College to discharge its responsibilities.

The purpose of the College of Policing is to support the fight against crime and protect the public by ensuring professionalism in policing. It aims to do this through the delivery of five key areas of responsibility:

(a) setting standards and developing guidance and policy for policing;
(b) building and developing the research evidence base for policing;
(c) supporting the professional development of police officers and staff;
(d) supporting the police, other law enforcement agencies and those involved in crime reduction to work together; and
(e) identifying and developing the ethics and values of the police.

The College may, with the approval of the Secretary of State, issue codes of practice relating to the discharge of their functions by chief officers of police (PA 1996, s 39A). Under this power, it has issued a Code of Practice for the Principles and Standards of Professional Behaviour for the Policing Profession of England and Wales (the 'Code of Ethics') <http://www.college.police.uk/What-we-do/Ethics/Documents/Code_of_Ethics.pdf>.

HANDLING OF COMPLAINTS AND CONDUCT MATTERS, ETC RELATING TO PERSONS SERVING WITH THE POLICE

There are three ways to enter the system dealing with these matters. The first is via a complaint about the conduct of someone serving with the police (ie a member of a police force (whatever his rank), a civilian employee of a police force or a special constable). The second concerns circumstances where there has not been a complaint but where there is an indication that someone serving with the police either committed a criminal offence or behaved in a way which would justify disciplinary proceedings (a 'conduct matter'). The third relates to a 'death or serious injury (DSI) matter', which arises where there has been no complaint or conduct but the circumstances are such that a person has died or suffered serious injury and the police are involved in one or more defined ways. While the following account deals with these matters by reference to police officers it must not be forgotten that the system applies to chief officers of police and anyone serving under the direction or control of a chief officer of police.

By the Independent Police Complaints Commission (Complaints and Misconduct) (Contractors) Regulations 2015, for the purposes of the provisions of the Police Reform Act 2002 (PRA 2002) relating to the above, and of the Police (Complaints and Misconduct) Regulations 2012 (P(CM)R 2012) referred to below, a contractor, sub-contractor of a contractor, or an employee of a contractor or sub-contractor is to be treated as a person serving with the police. A 'contractor' in this context means a person who has entered into a contract with a local policing body or a chief officer of police to provide services to a chief officer.

The foundations of the system

PRA 2002 established the Independent Police Complaints Commission (IPCC). The investigation of many complaints is carried out by police forces. Investigations may be carried out by a person serving with the police (of the force concerned or any other force), or a member of staff of the NCA. There is no requirement that the investigator must be a police officer. In addition, the IPCC is empowered to carry out its own investigation of complaints and to supervise or manage other investigations.

Under PRA 2002, s 9 and Sch 2, the IPCC consists of a chairman (appointed by the Queen) and not less than five other members (appointed by the Secretary of State).

The functions of the IPCC include securing the maintenance by the IPCC itself, and by police and crime commissioners, etc and chief officers, of suitable arrangements for:

(a) the handling of complaints about the conduct of persons serving with the police;
(b) the recording of matters from which it appears that there may have been conduct by such persons which constitutes or involves a criminal offence or behaviour justifying disciplinary proceedings;
(c) the recording of matters from which it appears that a person has died or suffered serious injury during, or following, contact with a person serving with the police; and
(d) the manner in which such complaints or any such matters are investigated or otherwise handled and dealt with.

The IPCC is required to enter into arrangements with the chief inspector of constabulary for the purpose of securing co-operation between the IPCC and the HMIC.

The provisions of PRA 2002, Sch 3 (below) about complaints or conduct matters apply to a complaint or conduct matter relating to the direction and control of a police force by a chief officer of police (or a person for the time being carrying out his functions). Such a matter is referred to in Sch 3 as a 'direction and control matter'.

The IPCC, its officers and employees have equivalent powers to use directed or intrusive surveillance, to use covert human intelligence sources, and to enter property to interfere with property or wireless telegraphy, to those exercisable by the police (see Chapter 3).

Complaints: introductory points

As will be seen, various functions relating to complaints relating to persons serving with the police are carried out by the 'appropriate authority'. The 'appropriate authority' is the chief officer of police of the person under his direction and control who is subject to the complaint. (The chief officer may delegate his powers and duties in respect of complaints to an officer above the rank of chief superintendent (or, in the case of local resolution below, to anyone serving with the force).) Where a complaint relates to the chief officer, his local policing body (PCC, MOPC, or Common Council of the City of London, as the case may be) is the 'appropriate authority'.

By PRA 2002, s 12, a 'complaint' is any complaint, written or otherwise, about the conduct of a person serving with the police which is made by:

(a) a member of the public claiming to be the person in relation to whom the conduct took place;
(b) any other member of the public claiming to have been adversely affected by the conduct;
(c) a member of the public claiming to have witnessed the conduct; or
(d) a person acting on behalf of a person in (a) to (c) above.

A judge in the Administrative Court has held that the word 'conduct' in PRA 2002, s 12 (and elsewhere in PRA 2002) does not carry with it the notion that the behaviour had to be of a particular quality, good or bad; 'conduct' in PRA 2002 is not limited to bad behaviour, misconduct or personal misconduct.

For the purposes of the provisions about complaints, (b) does not include a complaint made by or on behalf of a person who claims to have been adversely affected as a result only of having seen or heard the conduct, or any of its alleged effects, unless:

(i) it was only because *that person* was physically present, or sufficiently nearby, when the conduct took place or the effects occurred that he was able to see or hear the conduct or its effects; or

(ii) the adverse effect is attributable to, or was aggravated by, the fact that the person in relation to whom the conduct took place was already known to the person claiming to have suffered the adverse effect.

A person is taken to have witnessed conduct only if he acquired his knowledge in a manner which would make him a competent witness capable of giving admissible evidence, or if he has in his possession or under his control anything which would constitute admissible evidence.

A person within (a) to (c) is not taken to have authorised another to act on his behalf unless that other person is designated by the IPCC as a person through whom a complaint may be made, or is a person who has been authorised in writing by the person on behalf of whom he is acting.

Handling of complaints

PRA 2002, Sch 3, Part 1 deals with this.

Duties to preserve evidence relating to complaints

Where a complaint about the conduct of a person serving under his direction or control is submitted to a chief officer of police, or that chief officer becomes aware that such a complaint has been made to the IPCC or to a local policing body, he must, as soon as reasonably practicable, take any steps appearing to him to be desirable to obtain or preserve evidence relating to the conduct complained of. The term 'a person serving under his control and direction' includes members of a police force, local policing body employees under the direction and control of a chief officer, and special constables.

Initial handling and recording of complaints

Where a complaint is made to the IPCC, it must notify the appropriate authority, unless it considers that there are exceptional circumstances that justify its not doing so.

Where a complaint is made to a local policing body and it determines that it is not the appropriate authority it must notify the chief officer who is the appropriate authority in relation to the person against whom the complaint was made. Where a complaint is made to a chief officer and he determines that he is not the appropriate authority, because the complaint relates to an officer in another force or to the chief officer himself, he must notify the appropriate authority.

Where notification of a complaint is given to an appropriate authority, the person who gave the notification must notify the complainant.

If a local policing body or chief officer determines that he is the appropriate authority in relation to a complaint, or if he is notified that he is, he must record the complaint. However, a complaint need not be recorded where the subject matter of the complaint has been, or is already being, dealt with by means of criminal or disciplinary proceedings, where the complaint has been withdrawn or (the courts have held) where the complaint lacks the degree of specificity without which a sensible proportionate investigation would be impossible.

There is no need to record any complaint about any conduct if it is considered that the complaint falls within a description of complaints specified in the Police (Complaints and Misconduct) Regulations 2012 (P(CM)R 2012), namely:

(a) the matter is already the subject of a complaint made by or on behalf of the same complainant;

(b) the complaint discloses neither the name and address of the complainant or other interested parties and such a name or address cannot reasonably be ascertained;

(c) the complaint is vexatious, oppressive or otherwise an abuse of the complaints procedures; or

(d) the complaint is repetitious or fanciful.

Non-notification or recording of a complaint

Where a complaint has been received by, or notified to, an appropriate authority and the authority decides to take no action in relation to recording it, or notifying the appropriate authority, it must notify the complainant of the decision, the grounds for it, and the complainant's right of appeal. The complainant has a right of appeal to the IPCC against that decision. If the IPCC thinks that action should have been taken, it must give directions to the appropriate authority which are binding. All parties must be notified. P(CM)R 2012 govern the procedures to be followed.

The right of appeal referred to under this heading is not available where:

(a) there is no need to record the complaint because it relates to criminal or disciplinary proceedings or has been withdrawn; or

(b) the complaint relates to a direction and control matter, and the appeal relates to a failure by a local policing body.

Reference of complaints to the IPCC

A complaint must be referred to the IPCC if:

(a) it alleges that the conduct complained of has resulted in death or serious injury;

(b) it is of a description specified in P(CM)R 2012; or

(c) the IPCC notifies the appropriate authority that it requires the matter to be referred for consideration.

P(CM)R 2012 provide that a complaint of serious assault, a serious sexual offence, serious corruption, a criminal offence or behaviour which is liable to lead to a disciplinary sanction and which in either case was aggravated by discriminatory behaviour on the grounds of race, sex, religion or other status identified in guidance issued by the IPCC, murder or an offence carrying seven or more years' imprisonment are complaints for the purposes of (b) above.

In cases other than those in which reference is mandatory, the appropriate authority may refer a complaint to the IPCC if it considers that it would be appropriate to do so in view of the gravity of the subject matter or other exceptional circumstances. Such references may be made regardless of the fact that the complaint is already being considered by the IPCC. Such action must be notified to the complainant and, except where any future investigation may be prejudiced, to the person complained against. In addition, where a death or serious injury matter comes to the attention of a local policing body, or a chief officer who is the appropriate authority, the matter must be recorded and if this has not been done the IPCC may direct that it be done. Following the investigation of such matters a report will be submitted and the IPCC may make recommendations or give advice. Where such an investigation reveals a conduct matter (a criminal or disciplinary offence) the matter will be treated as a conduct matter.

Where a complaint relates to a direction and control matter, and it is not a case where the appropriate authority must refer the complaint to the IPCC, the appropriate authority may refer the complaint to the IPCC under those provisions only if the IPCC consents.

Where a complaint is referred to the IPCC, the IPCC must determine whether or not investigation of the complaint is necessary. Where it considers that investigation is unnecessary, it may refer the complaint back to the appropriate authority to be dealt with under the rules under the following heading, and inform the complainant and (unless this might prejudice an investigation of the complaint) the person complained against that it has done so.

Handling of complaints by the appropriate authority

Where a complaint has been recorded by the appropriate authority, it must determine whether or not the complaint is suitable for being subjected to local resolution. If the appropriate authority determines that the complaint is suitable for being subjected to local resolution, it must make arrangements for it to be so subjected. If the appropriate authority determines that the complaint is not so suitable, it must make arrangements for the complaint to be investigated by the authority on its own behalf.

A determination that a complaint is suitable for being subjected to local resolution may not be made unless the appropriate authority is satisfied that:

(a) the conduct complained of (even if proved) would not justify the bringing of any criminal or disciplinary proceedings against the person whose conduct is complained of; and

(b) the conduct complained of (even if proved) would not involve the infringement of a person's rights under the European Convention on Human Rights, art 2 (right to life) or 3 (prohibition of inhuman or degrading treatment).

The above provisions do not apply to a complaint if it is one that has been, or must be, referred to the IPCC (see p 301), unless the complaint is for the time being:

(a) referred back to the authority under the provisions referred to in the third paragraph on this page; or

(b) the subject of a determination by the IPCC as to the form of an investigation referred to under the heading 'Power of the IPCC to determine the form of an investigation' (p 308).

Where (b) applies, a determination that the complaint is suitable for being subjected to local resolution may not be made without the IPCC's approval.

Disapplication of requirements

Where a complaint has been recorded, and not referred to the IPCC, and the appropriate authority considers that it should be handled otherwise than in accordance with the procedures set out in PRA 2002, Sch 3, or that no action should be taken in relation to that complaint, and that the complaint falls within a description of complaints specified in P(CM)R 2012, the appropriate authority may handle the complaint in whatever manner (if any) it thinks fit. The specified description of complaints is where the appropriate authority considers that:

(a) the incident is more than 12 months old and there is no good reason for the delay;
(b) the matter is already the subject of a complaint by or on behalf of the complainant;
(c) the complaint does not disclose the name and address of the complainant or other interested party and such an address cannot reasonably be ascertained;
(d) the complaint is vexatious, oppressive or otherwise an abuse of the complaint procedures;
(e) the complaint is repetitious; or
(f) it is not reasonably practicable to investigate the complaint.

The appropriate authority is not required to apply for (and obtain) permission from the IPCC to handle the complaint in an alternative manner, except in a case where the complaint:

(a) has been, or must be, referred to the IPCC, and has been referred back to the authority, or
(b) is the subject of a determination as to the form of an investigation (see 'Handling of complaints by the appropriate authority' (above)).

Where the appropriate authority has decided to handle the case in an alternative manner, it must notify the complainant of this.

Where an application to the IPCC for permission to handle the case in an alternative manner has been made, the appropriate authority must notify the complainant of this.

Where the complaint is to be handled in whatever manner (if any) the authority thinks fit (whether or not the IPCC's permission is needed), the authority need do no more under Sch 3 than preserve the evidence, and may take any action which it considers appropriate, or no action at all.

Where the appropriate authority is required to apply to the IPCC for permission to handle the complaint in an alternative manner, and does so, and the IPCC does not grant permission, the appropriate authority must consider whether the complaint is suitable for local resolution.

The complainant has a right of appeal to the relevant appeal body against any decision by the appropriate authority to handle the complaint otherwise than in accordance with Sch 3 or to take no action in relation to it. By way of exception, the complainant has no right of appeal if the appeal relates to a decision for which the IPCC has given permission, or the complaint relates to a direction and control matter. The relevant appeal body is:

(a) the IPCC, where the relevant complaint falls within a description of complaints specified in regulations made by the Secretary of State; or
(b) the chief officer of police who is the appropriate authority in relation to the relevant complaint, in any other case.

The procedural rules for an appeal are set out in P(CM)R 2012.

On such an appeal, the relevant appeal body must:

(a) determine whether any decision by the appropriate authority should have been taken in the case in question; and
(b) if the relevant appeal body finds in the complainant's favour, give such binding directions as it thinks appropriate to the local policing body or chief officer as to the action to be taken for handling the complaint in accordance with Sch 3 or otherwise.

However, this provision does not apply where a particular chief officer of police is both the person in respect of whose decision the appeal is made and the relevant appeal body in relation to the appeal. In such a case:

(i)   the appeal must determine whether any decision taken by the appropriate authority should have been taken in the case in question; and

(ii) if the appeal finds in the complainant's favour, the chief officer of police must take such action as the chief officer thinks appropriate for handling the complaint in accordance with Sch 3 or otherwise.

Local resolution of complaints

Where there is to be a local resolution of a complaint, the arrangements made by the appropriate authority for subjecting a complaint to local resolution may include the appointment of a person, who is serving with the police and is under the direction and control of the chief officer of police of the relevant force, to secure the local resolution of the complaint. P(CM)R 2012 deal with the procedural requirements. Any statement made for the purpose of such resolution is not admissible in any subsequent criminal, civil or disciplinary proceedings except to the extent that it consists of an admission relating to a matter which has not been subjected to local resolution.

If, after attempts to achieve local resolution, it appears to the appropriate authority that local resolution is impossible, or that the matter is unsuitable for local resolution, it must arrange for an investigation, and any attempt at local resolution must be discontinued. Such an attempt must also be discontinued if there is a requirement for the matter to be referred to the IPCC or it is otherwise referred. Any person who has been involved in an attempt at local resolution is barred from participation in subsequently investigating the complaint.

Appeals relating to complaints dealt with other than by investigation

Unless the complaint relates to a direction and control matter, the complainant has a right of appeal to the 'relevant appeal body' (as defined on p 303) against the outcome of any complaint that is subjected to local resolution or handled otherwise than in accordance with Sch 3. P(CM)R 2012 deal with the procedural requirements.

On such an appeal, the relevant appeal body must:

(a) determine whether the outcome of the complaint is a proper outcome; and

(b) if the relevant appeal body finds in the complainant's favour, give such binding directions as it thinks appropriate to the appropriate authority as to the action to be taken in relation to the complaint.

However, this provision does not apply if a chief officer of police is the relevant appeal body in relation to the appeal. In such a case:

(i)   the appeal must determine whether the outcome of the complaint is a proper outcome; and

(ii) if the appeal finds in the complainant's favour, the chief officer of police must take such action as the chief officer thinks appropriate in relation to the complaint.

Withdrawn and discontinued complaints

P(CM)R 2012 provide that, where an appropriate authority receives written notification, signed by the complainant or by his solicitor or other authorised agent, that he withdraws his complaint or does not wish any further action to be taken, that withdrawal must be recorded. The procedures will be discontinued unless the appropriate authority decides, notwithstanding the withdrawal, to treat the matter as a recordable conduct matter (p 306), in which case the provisions of Sch 3, Part 2 below apply.

Circumstances in which an investigation or other procedure may be suspended

The IPCC or the appropriate authority may suspend any investigation or other procedure which, if it were to continue, would prejudice any criminal proceedings. The IPCC, however, may direct an appropriate authority to continue an investigation if of the view that it is in the public interest to do so.

Where the investigation of a complaint has been suspended pending the outcome of criminal proceedings, the IPCC or the appropriate authority must contact the complainant after that outcome to establish whether or not he wishes the investigation to continue. If he does not wish to do so, or fails to reply within 21 days, the IPCC or the appropriate authority must decide whether or not it is in the public interest to treat the complaint as a recordable conduct matter.

Handling of conduct matters

PRA 2002, Sch 3, Part 2 deals with this.

As already stated, a 'conduct matter' is a matter which is not and has not been the subject of a complaint but in respect of which there is an indication that the person serving with the police might have committed a criminal offence or might have behaved in a manner which would justify disciplinary proceedings.

Conduct matters arising in civil proceedings

Where a local policing body or a chief constable has received notification that civil proceedings have been brought by a member of the public against it or him, or are likely to be brought, and it appears that these proceedings would involve a conduct matter, it or he should follow a similar procedure as in respect of a complaint about determining the appropriate authority (and, if necessary, notifying that authority). The appropriate authority must determine whether the matter is one which it or he is required to refer to the IPCC (see p 306) or is one which it would be appropriate to so refer. If it or he determines that the matter is, it or he must record the matter. In any other case, the appropriate authority must determine whether the matter falls within a description of matters specified in regulations made by the Secretary of State. If it determines that it does not, it or he must record the matter. Otherwise, the appropriate authority may (but need not) record the matter. In a case where the appropriate authority:

(a) records a matter under the above provisions, and
(b) is not required to refer the matter to the IPCC (see p 306) and does not do so,

the appropriate authority may deal with the matter in such other manner (if any) as it or he may determine.

Recording, etc of conduct matters in other cases

Where a conduct matter comes (otherwise than as arising in civil proceedings) to the attention of a local policing body or chief officer of police in some other way from that just mentioned and it is conduct:

(a) which appears to have resulted in the death of any person;
(b) as a result of which a member of the public has been adversely affected; or

(c) which is (i) a serious assault; (ii) a serious sexual assault; (iii) serious corruption; (iv) a criminal offence or behaviour liable to lead to a disciplinary sanction and which in either case was aggravated by discriminatory behaviour on the grounds of race, sex, religion, or other status identified in guidance by the IPCC; (v) murder or an offence carrying a maximum of seven or more years' imprisonment; (vi) *conduct whose gravity or other exceptional circumstances make it appropriate to record the matter in which the conduct is involved*; or (vii) conduct alleged to have taken place in the same incident as one in which conduct within (i) to (v) is alleged,

the appropriate authority must determine whether the matter is one which it or he is required to refer to the IPCC (see p 306), or is one which it would be appropriate to so refer. If the appropriate authority determines that it is, it or he must record the matter.

In any other case, the appropriate authority must determine whether the matter is a 'repetitious conduct matter' (ie a conduct matter concerning substantially the same matter as a previous complaint or conduct matter with no significant fresh information and no fresh evidence not reasonably available at the previous time). If it determines that it is not, the matter must be recorded. If the appropriate authority determines that the matter is a repetitious conduct matter, it may (but need not) record the matter. Where the appropriate authority:

(a) records a matter under the above provisions, and
(b) is not required to refer the matter to the IPCC and does not do so,

the appropriate authority may deal with the matter in such other manner (if any) as it or he may determine.

No conduct matter which has already been dealt with by means of criminal or disciplinary proceedings need be recorded.

The IPCC may direct the appropriate authority to record a matter that has come to its attention and that it considers to be a 'recordable conduct matter' if it has not otherwise been recorded. A 'recordable conduct matter' is a conduct matter which must be recorded under this or the previous heading by the appropriate authority or has been so recorded.

Duties to preserve evidence relating to conduct matters

The appropriate authority must, as soon as practicable, obtain and preserve evidence related to a recordable conduct matter.

Reference of conduct matters to the IPCC

The same matters as in (c) at the top of this page besides that italicised must be referred as in the case of complaints and there are similar arrangements in respect of voluntary references. Similar conditions apply in relation to notifications to interested parties.

Where reference has been made, it is the duty of the IPCC to decide whether or not an investigation is necessary. Where an investigation is considered unnecessary, it may refer the matter back to the appropriate authority to be dealt with in such manner (if any) as the authority determines.

P(CM)R 2012 deal with the recording and reference of conduct matters. Those matters are similar to those applying in the case of a complaint, together with conduct the gravity of which, or other exceptional circumstances, make it appropriate to record such conduct.

Delegation of powers and duties by chief officer

A chief officer may delegate all or any of his powers or duties above in relation to handling conduct matters to:

(a) a senior officer (ie an officer above the rank of chief superintendent), in the case of a complaint or conduct matter concerning the conduct of a senior officer, and
(b) a member of a police force of at least the rank of chief inspector, in any other case,

or to a police staff member who, in the opinion of the chief officer, is of at least a similar level of seniority.

A chief officer may not delegate any such power or duty to a person whose involvement in the role could reasonably give rise to a concern as to whether he could act impartially.

Handling of death and serious injury matters

PRA 2002, Sch 3, Part 2A deals with this.

A 'death or serious injury matter' ('DSI matter') means circumstances (other than those which are or have been the subject of a complaint or which amount to a conduct matter) in or in consequence of which a person has died or has sustained serious injury and in relation to which one or other of the following requirements is satisfied:

(a) at the time of the death or serious injury the person had been arrested by a person serving with the police and had not been released from that arrest, or was otherwise detained in the custody of a person serving with the police, or
(b) at or before that time the person—directly or indirectly—had contact with a person serving with the police who was acting in the execution of his duties and there is an indication that the contact may directly or indirectly have caused or contributed to the death or serious injury.

Duty to record DSI matters

Where a DSI matter comes to the attention of the local policing body or chief officer who is the appropriate authority in relation to that matter, the appropriate authority must record that matter.

If it appears to the IPCC:

(a) that any matter that has come to its attention is a DSI matter, but
(b) that that matter has not been recorded by the appropriate authority,

the IPCC may direct the appropriate authority to record that matter, and that authority must comply with the direction.

Duty to preserve evidence relating to DSI matters

Where:

(a) a DSI matter comes to the attention of a local policing body, and
(b) the relevant officer in relation to that matter is the chief officer of the force maintained by that local policing body,

that body must secure that all appropriate steps are taken, both initially and thereafter, to obtain and preserve evidence relating to that matter.

Where:

(a) a chief officer becomes aware of a DSI matter, and
(b) the relevant officer in relation to that matter is a person under his direction and control,

he must take all such steps as appear appropriate as soon as practicable to obtain and preserve evidence relating to that matter. After that, he must, until he is satisfied that it is no longer necessary to do so, continue to take the steps from time to time appearing appropriate for obtaining and preserving evidence relating to the matter.

A local policing body must comply with all such directions as may be given to it by the IPCC in relation to the performance of its duty to obtain and preserve evidence relating to the matter.

The chief officer must take all such specific steps for obtaining or preserving evidence relating to any DSI matter as he may be directed to take by the local policing body maintaining his force or by the Commission.

Reference of DSI matters to the IPCC

The appropriate authority must refer a DSI matter to the IPCC by the end of the day, whether or not a working day, following the day on which the IPCC directs a referral or the matter comes to the attention of the relevant authority.

Duties of the IPCC on reference

The IPCC must, in the case of every DSI matter referred to it by a local policing body or a chief officer, determine whether or not it is necessary for the matter to be investigated. Where the IPCC determines that it is unnecessary for a DSI matter to be investigated, it may if it thinks fit refer the matter back to the appropriate authority to be dealt with by that authority in such manner (if any) as that authority may determine.

Investigations and subsequent proceedings

PRA 2002, Sch 3, Part 3 deals with these.

Power of the IPCC to determine the form of an investigation

Where a complaint, recordable conduct matter, or DSI matter has been referred to the IPCC and it decides that an investigation is necessary, the form of the investigation will depend upon the seriousness of the case and the public interest but must consist of:

(a) an investigation by the appropriate authority on its own behalf;
(b) an investigation by that authority under the supervision of the IPCC;
(c) an investigation by that authority under the management of the IPCC; or
(d) an investigation by the IPCC.

The form of the investigation may be changed by the IPCC at any time and the IPCC may give directions to that effect.

Investigations by the appropriate authority on its own behalf

The appropriate authority must appoint a person serving with the police (whether under the direction and control of the chief officer of police of the relevant force or of another force) or an NCA officer to investigate the complaint or matter.

Under P(CM)R 2012 no one may be appointed to carry out an investigation by the authority on its own behalf *or when the investigation is supervised or managed by the IPCC* (below):

(a) unless he has an appropriate level of knowledge, skills and experience to plan and manage the investigation,
(b) if there could be any reasonable appearance of bias,
(c) if he works, directly or indirectly, under the management of the person being investigated, and
(d) where the person concerned is a senior officer, if he is the chief officer of the police force concerned, or a member of the same force as the officer concerned.

Heads (c) and (d) do not apply in a case where the investigation is of a complaint in relation to a direction and control matter. Where the investigation is of a complaint in relation to a direction or control matter, the fact that a person:

(i) works, directly or indirectly, under the management of the person whose conduct is being investigated; or
(ii) is the chief officer of the police force concerned or a member of the same force as the officer concerned,

does not, without more, constitute reasonable grounds for concern as to whether that person could act impartially for the purposes of (b).

Where the person being investigated is a chief officer, no one under the chief officer's direction and control may be appointed to carry out the investigation.

Investigations supervised by the IPCC

The IPCC may require that no appointment as an investigating officer may be made without its approval. If an appointment has already been made a further approved appointment must be made as soon as practicable.

The person appointed to investigate the complaint or matter must comply with directions from the IPCC which are authorised by regulations.

Investigations managed by the IPCC

The same conditions apply as apply in the case of supervised investigations with the addition that the investigator must be under the direction and control of the IPCC.

Investigations by the IPCC itself

The IPCC must designate a member of its own staff to take charge of the investigation on its behalf; it must also designate other members of its staff to assist that person. Any member of the IPCC's staff so designated who does not already have all the powers and privileges of a constable throughout England and Wales and the adjacent UK waters has, for the purposes of carrying out the investigation and all purposes connected with it, all those powers and privileges of a constable. Where PACE or PACE Code B or C requires the exercise of a power to be authorised by a police officer of or above a specified rank, the exercise of that power by a member of IPCC staff may be authorised by a member of IPCC staff who is of or above the relevant grade specified in the IPCC (Investigation of Offences) Order 2014.

The IPCC may serve upon any person an information notice requiring him to provide it with information that it reasonably requires for the purposes of an investigation by the IPCC itself. However, an information notice must not require a person to provide information that might incriminate him, or to provide an item subject to legal privilege, or to make a disclosure that would be prohibited by the Regulation of Investigatory Powers Act 2000, Part 1, Chapter 2 (p 89), or to provide information that was provided to the person by, or by an agency of, the government of a foreign country or territory where that government does not consent to the disclosure. An information notice may not require a postal or telecommunications operator to provide communications data.

If a person who has received an information notice fails or refuses to provide the information required by the notice, or knowingly or recklessly provides information in response to the notice that is false in a material respect, the IPCC may certify to the High Court that he has failed to comply with the notice. The High Court may then inquire into the matter and, after hearing any witness who may be produced, and after hearing any statement in defence, deal with the person as if he had committed a contempt of court.

Where the IPCC receives under an information notice specified sensitive information (intelligence service information, intercept information, or information obtained (directly or indirectly) from a government department whose disclosure might damage national security or international relations, or the UK's economic interests), it must not disclose the information, or the fact that it has received it, unless the relevant authority consents to the disclosure. Where the IPCC discloses to another person such information, or the fact that it has received it, that person must not disclose that information or that fact unless the relevant authority consents to the disclosure.

Special procedure where investigation relates to a police officer or special constable

Where it appears to an investigating officer that there is an indication that a member of a police force or a special constable under investigation may have committed a criminal offence, or behaved in a manner which would justify the bringing of disciplinary proceedings, the investigator must certify the investigation as one subject to special requirements and make a severity assessment as soon as reasonably practicable in relation to the conduct. A similar requirement is included in relation to the investigation of a recordable conduct matter, in which case such an assessment must be made as soon as reasonably practicable after it is recorded. A 'severity assessment' is an assessment as to whether the conduct, if proved, would amount to misconduct or gross misconduct, and if the conduct were to become the subject of disciplinary proceedings, the form which those proceedings would be likely to take. The appropriate authority must be consulted in respect of the assessment. Such assessments may be revised and if so, the person concerned must be notified.

Following such an assessment, the person under investigation must be given a written notice (unless the investigator considers that doing so might prejudice the investigation or any other investigation, including in particular, any criminal investigation), containing information prescribed by P(CM)R 2012.

Under P(CM)R 2012, the person appointed to investigate must notify the person under investigation in writing of his appointment and the notification must state:

(a) the conduct that is the subject matter of the allegation and how that conduct is alleged to fall below the Standards of Professional Behaviour (set out in Chapter 8 on the companion website);

(b) that there is to be an investigation into the matter, and the identity of the investigator;

(c) the investigator's assessment of whether that conduct, if proved, would amount to misconduct or gross misconduct;

(d) whether, if the matter was referred to misconduct proceedings, those would be likely to be a misconduct meeting or a misconduct hearing;

(e) that, if the likely form of any misconduct proceedings to be held changes, further notice (with reasons) will be given;

(f) that he has the right to seek advice from his staff association or any other body and of the effect of provisions permitting him to choose to have a police officer, police staff member, or, where he is member of a police force, someone nominated by his staff association to act as his police friend;

(g) the effect of reg 18 (officer concerned or police friend must provide any relevant statement or notice within 10 working days of written notification referred to above unless period extended) and of PRA 2002, Sch 3, para 19C (duty to consider submissions from person whose conduct is being investigated) and of the Police (Conduct) Regulations 2012 (P(C)R 2012), reg 7(1) to (3) (legal or other representation); and

(h) that, while he does not have to say anything, it may harm his case if he does not mention when interviewed or when providing any information under reg 18 or P(C)R 2012, reg 22 (procedure on receipt of notice of referral to misconduct proceedings) something which he later relies on in any misconduct proceedings, special case hearing, appeal meeting or appeal hearing.

P(CM)R 2012 go on to provide that, if the investigator revises his assessment of the conduct or his determination of the likely form of any misconduct proceedings to be taken, the investigator must, as soon as practicable, give the person concerned written notice of that revised assessment.

As indicated above, the officer concerned or police friend must provide documents for the investigator within 10 clear working days. The officer concerned must attend an interview with the investigator. The investigator must, if reasonably practicable, agree a date for any interview with the officer but may specify a date in the absence of agreement, but that date may be postponed by agreement.

Interviews of serving officers as witnesses during investigations

A 'serving officer' (ie a member of a police force, special constable or member of police staff) who may be a witness to a matter under investigation undertaken or managed by the IPCC can be required to attend an interview with the investigator. The rules about fixing a date correspond with those mentioned in the previous paragraph.

Procedure where conduct matter revealed during DSI investigation

If, during an investigation into a DSI matter, it appears to the investigating officer that there is an indication that the person (P) whose conduct is in question may have committed a criminal offence or behaved in a way justifying disciplinary proceedings, he must make a submission to that effect to the IPCC (if the IPCC appointed him) or to the appropriate authority (if it appointed him). If the appropriate authority or the IPCC (as the case may be) determines that there is such an indication, it must act as follows:

(a) in the case of the IPCC, notify the appropriate authority and send it a copy of the submission;

(b) in the case of the appropriate authority, if it is not the appropriate authority in relation to P, it must notify the other authority of its determination and send it a copy of the submission, and, in any event, it must notify the IPCC of its determination and send it a copy of the submission.

Once notified, the appropriate authority must record the DSI matter as a conduct matter, and the investigating officer must continue the investigation thereafter as a conduct matter investigation.

Restrictions on proceedings pending the conclusion of an investigation

No criminal or disciplinary proceedings may be brought in relation to any matter subject to an investigation (unless it has been discontinued) until the appropriate authority has certified the case as a 'special case' or a report has been submitted to the IPCC or the appropriate authority. However, these provisions do not apply to proceedings by the Director of Public Prosecutions (DPP) in exceptional cases where delay is undesirable.

Accelerated procedure in special cases

There is an accelerated procedure in respect of a complaint or a recordable conduct matter in 'special cases'. These are where the investigating officer believes that the appropriate authority would be likely to consider that there is sufficient written evidence to establish on the balance of probabilities that the police officer or special constable in question is guilty of gross misconduct and that his dismissal without delay is in the public interest. In such cases the investigator must submit a report to the appropriate authority before the completion of the investigation to enable disciplinary proceedings to be brought earlier than would otherwise have been possible. The DPP should be consulted in such cases and he may order the continuation of the investigation regardless of the disciplinary proceedings. It is difficult to see how any following trial for an alleged criminal offence will not be affected by the outcome of disciplinary proceedings in respect of which there are reduced standards of proof and majority verdicts.

Power to discontinue an investigation

The IPCC may by order require the discontinuance of the investigation of a complaint or matter if (whether on the application of the appropriate authority or otherwise) it appears to the IPCC that:

(a) the complaint or matter is of a description specified in P(CM)R 2012, and
(b) discontinuance of the investigation is within the IPCC's power.

The appropriate authority that is investigating a complaint or matter may discontinue the investigation if it appears to that authority that:

(a) the complaint or matter is of a description specified in P(CM)R 2012, and
(b) discontinuance of the investigation is not within the IPCC's power.

For the above purposes:

(a) the descriptions of conduct or matter specified by P(CM)R 2012 are any complaint or matter:
  (i)   in which the complainant refuses to co-operate to the extent that it is not reasonably practicable to continue the investigation;
  (ii) which the appropriate authority has determined is suitable for local resolution;
  (iii) which is vexatious, oppressive or otherwise an abuse of the procedures for dealing with complaints, conduct matters or DSI matters;
  (iv) which is repetitious; or

(v) which is such as to make it not reasonably practicable to proceed with the investigation;
(b) discontinuance of the investigation of a complaint is within the IPCC's power if (i) the investigation is being undertaken by the appropriate authority on its own behalf and the complaint is one required to be referred to the IPCC under the provisions (p 301); or (ii) the investigation is under the supervision or management of the IPCC;
(c) discontinuance of the investigation of a matter other than a complaint is within the IPCC's power if the investigation is under the supervision or management of the IPCC.

Where the investigation is being conducted by the IPCC itself, the IPCC may only discontinue it if the complaint or matter falls within (a) immediately above.

Where an investigation is discontinued *by order* of the IPCC, the IPCC may give the appropriate authority directions as to steps (specified in P(CM)R 2012) to be taken and may itself take such steps of a description specified in P(CM)R 2012 as it considers appropriate for the purposes connected with the discontinuance, and neither the appropriate authority nor the IPCC may take any further action in accordance with Sch 3 in relation to that complaint or matter. Where the appropriate authority decides (ie otherwise than by order of the IPCC) to discontinue an investigation, the appropriate authority may take such steps (specified in P(CM)R 2012) as it considers appropriate in connection with the discontinuance, and neither the appropriate authority nor the IPCC may take any further action in accordance with Sch 3 in relation to that complaint or matter.

The IPCC or the appropriate authority (as the case may be) must notify the complainant (if the investigation is of a complaint) and every person entitled to be kept informed about the investigation of the discontinuance.

Except if the complaint relates to a direction and control matter, the complainant has a right of appeal to the relevant appeal body against any discontinuance decision by the appropriate authority.

The relevant appeal body is:

(a) the IPCC, where the relevant complaint falls within a description of complaints specified in P(CM)R 2012 or
(b) the chief officer of police who is the appropriate authority in relation to the relevant complaint, in any other case.

On such an appeal, the relevant appeal body must:

(a) determine whether any decision taken by the appropriate authority should have been taken; and
(b) if the relevant appeal body finds in the complainant's favour, give such binding directions as the relevant appeal body thinks appropriate to the local policing body or chief officer as to the action to be taken for investigating the complaint.

If, however, a particular chief officer of police is both the person in respect of whose decision an appeal is made and the relevant appeal body in relation to the appeal:

(i) the appeal must determine whether any decision taken by the appropriate authority should have been taken in the case in question; and
(ii) if the appeal finds in the complainant's favour, the chief officer of police must take such action as the chief officer thinks appropriate for investigating the complaint.

P(CM)R 2012 deal with the procedural requirements which apply before and after a discontinuance decision is taken and as to appeals against such a decision.

Final reports on investigations

On completion of an investigation of a complaint or conduct matter, the investigating officer must submit his report to the appropriate authority. Where the investigation was supervised or managed by the IPCC, the investigating officer must send a report to the IPCC and a copy to the appropriate authority. Where the IPCC carries out the investigation itself, the investigating officer must report to the IPCC. In all of these cases, the investigator is not prevented by any obligation of secrecy from including all such matters in his report as he thinks fit.

The report must provide an accurate summary of the evidence; attach or refer to any relevant document; and indicate the investigator's opinion as to whether there is a case to answer in respect of misconduct or gross misconduct, or whether there is no case to answer.

Action by the IPCC in response to an investigation report

Where the IPCC receives a report on an investigation which it has supervised, managed or carried out itself, it must send a copy to the appropriate authority and determine whether or not a criminal offence is disclosed. If it considers that such an offence is disclosed it must notify the DPP and send him a copy of the report, and it must notify the appropriate authority of this notification. The DPP must notify the IPCC of his decision to take, or not to take, action in respect of the matter or matters investigated. If criminal proceedings are brought by the DPP, the IPCC must inform, in the case of a complaint, the complainant and every person entitled to be kept informed in relation to the complaint; in the case of a recordable conduct matter, every person entitled to be kept informed of that matter must be informed. On receipt of the report of an investigation supervised, managed or carried out by itself, the IPCC must also notify the appropriate authority that it must:

(a) determine in accordance with regulations:
  (i) whether any person to whose conduct the investigation related has a case to answer in respect of misconduct or gross misconduct or has no case to answer;
  (ii) whether or not any such person's performance is unsatisfactory; or
  (iii) what action (if any) the authority is required to, or will in its discretion, take in respect of the matters dealt with in the report, and
(b) determine what other action (if any) the authority will in its discretion take in respect of those matters.

On receipt of such a notification the appropriate authority must make those determinations and submit a memorandum to the IPCC which sets out the determinations the authority has made, and, if it has decided that disciplinary proceedings should not be brought, sets out its reasons for so deciding. On receipt of the memorandum, the IPCC must determine whether or not to make recommendations under the provisions on pp 317–8 about duties with respect to disciplinary proceedings, and make such recommendations (if any) as it thinks fit. The complainant and other entitled persons must be informed of the report's findings, the IPCC's determination and the recommended action.

Action by appropriate authority in response to an investigation report

The appropriate authority must determine whether an investigation report submitted or sent to it indicates that a criminal offence may have been committed by the person whose conduct has been investigated, and that it is appropriate for the report to be considered by the DPP. If it determines that it has, it must notify the DPP and send a copy of the report. It must notify the complainant and every other person entitled to be kept informed of its determination and of a reference to the DPP. If the DPP brings criminal proceedings, the appropriate authority must notify the above persons.

On receipt of an investigation report, the appropriate authority must also:

(a) determine:
    (i) whether any person to whose conduct the investigation related has a case to answer in respect of misconduct or gross misconduct or has no case to answer;
    (ii) whether or not such person's performance is unsatisfactory; and
    (iii) what action (if any) the authority is required to, or will in its discretion, take in respect of the matters dealt with in the report, and
(b) determine what other action (if any) the authority will in its discretion take in respect of those matters.

The complainant and other entitled persons must be informed of the report's findings, the authority's determinations and the complainant's right of appeal. Except so far as it may be otherwise directed by regulations, an appropriate authority may (notwithstanding any obligation to secrecy imposed by any rule of law) give such a person notification of the findings by sending the person a copy of the report.

Final reports on DSI investigations and actions in response

On completion of an investigation into a DSI matter in respect of which neither the IPCC nor the appropriate authority has made a determination (see p 000) that a person serving with the police (P) *may* have committed a criminal offence or behaved in a way justifying disciplinary proceedings, the investigating officer must send a report to the IPCC and a copy to the appropriate authority. The IPCC must then determine whether the report indicates P may have committed a criminal offence or so behaved. If it determines that the report does so indicate, it must notify the appropriate authority which must record the matter as a conduct matter and the investigating officer must investigate the matter as a conduct matter investigation.

If the IPCC determines that the report does not indicate that P may have committed a criminal offence or so behaved, it may notify the appropriate authority that it must determine whether or not P's performance is unsatisfactory, and what action (if any) the authority will take in respect of P's performance. Having made those determinations, the appropriate authority must submit a memorandum to the IPCC stating them. On receipt of it, the Commission must (a) consider it and whether the appropriate authority has made appropriate determinations, (b) determine whether or not to make recommendations of the type referred to on p 317, and (c) make such recommendations (if any) as it thinks fit.

Complaints or conduct matters concerning officers who are no longer serving or whose identity cannot be ascertained

By P(CM)R 2012, where a complaint or conduct matter is recorded against an ex-officer, the preceding conditions apply as if they did not include a requirement on the part of the appropriate authority to determine whether disciplinary proceedings should be brought.

P(CM)R 2012 also make it clear that, where a complaint or conduct matter relates to the conduct of an unidentified person, all provisions concerning notices to be given to such a person and the determination of whether or not there may be criminal liability or liability to disciplinary proceedings do not apply.

Appeals with respect to an investigation

Unless the complaint relates to a direction and control matter, a complainant whose complaint has been investigated by the appropriate authority on its own behalf or under the supervision of the IPCC has a right of appeal to the *relevant appeal body*:

(a) on the grounds that he has not been provided with adequate information about the findings of the investigation or any proposals in relation to the taking or not taking of action;

(b) against the findings of the investigation;

(c) against a determination by the appropriate authority that a person investigated has a case to answer in respect of misconduct or gross misconduct or has no case to answer, or that his performance is, or is not, unsatisfactory;

(d) against any determination of the appropriate authority to take, or not to take, action in respect of any of the matters dealt with in the report; and

(e) against a determination by the appropriate authority about whether a criminal offence may have been committed and whether the case should be considered by the DPP, as a result of which it is not required to send the DPP a copy of the report.

The relevant appeal body is the IPCC, where the relevant complaint falls within a description of complaints specified in P(CM)R 2012. Otherwise it is the chief officer of police who is the appropriate authority in relation to the relevant complaint.

The complaints specified by P(CM)R 2012 are any complaint:

(a) about the conduct of a senior officer;

(b) in the case of which the appropriate authority is unable to satisfy itself, from the complaint alone, that the conduct complained of (if it were proved):

 (i) would not justify the bringing of criminal or misconduct proceedings against a person serving with the police; or

 (ii) would not involve the infringement of a person's rights under the European Convention on Human Rights, art 2 (right to life) or 3 (inhuman or degrading treatment);

(c) that has been, or must be, referred to the IPCC;

(d) arising from the same incident as a complaint to which (a), (b), or (c) applies;

(e) to any part of which (a), (b), (c), or (d) applies.

The relevant appeal body must notify all persons concerned that an appeal with respect to an investigation has been lodged. If such an appeal is brought, the IPCC may require the appropriate authority to submit a memorandum specifying whether it has made a determination of the type referred to in (c) in the second paragraph on p 316; whether any action is proposed to be taken (and, if it is, specifying the nature of that action); where no disciplinary proceedings are proposed, specifying the reasons for so deciding; and, where a determination of the type referred to in (e) in the second paragraph on p 316 has been made, the reasons for it. In addition, where the investigation was carried out by the appropriate authority on its own behalf, and the IPCC so requires, the IPCC must be supplied with a copy of the report of the investigation.

If the relevant appeal body considers that the complainant has not been provided with adequate information:

(a) where the IPCC is the relevant appeal body, the IPCC must direct the appropriate authority to provide such information; and

(b) where the appropriate authority is the relevant appeal body, that authority must take such steps as it considers appropriate for securing that the complainant is properly informed.

If, in a case where the IPCC is the relevant appeal body, the IPCC determines that the findings of the investigation need to be reconsidered, it must either:

(a) review those findings without an immediate further investigation; or
(b) direct that the complaint be re-investigated; and

in a case where the appropriate authority is the relevant appeal body, that authority must re-investigate the complaint.

Where the relevant appeal body determines that the appropriate authority has not made a determination as to whether there is a case to answer that the relevant appeal body considers appropriate, or determines that the appropriate authority has not made a determination as to whether or not there is unsatisfactory performance, or determines that the appropriate authority is not proposing to take appropriate action, the situation is as follows:

(a) if the IPCC is the relevant appeal body, it may make such recommendations as it thinks fit;
(b) if the chief officer of police is the relevant appeal body, he must take such steps as he thinks fit in relation to bringing disciplinary proceedings.

Any determination or recommendation made by the relevant appeal body as a result of determining an appeal must be notified to all persons concerned.

P(CM)R 2012 deal with the appeal procedures relating to an appeal.

Review and re-investigations following an appeal

On a review of the findings of an investigation based upon the existing report, the IPCC may:

(a) uphold the findings in whole or in part;
(b) give the appropriate authority such directions as to the review by the authority of the findings, as to the information to be provided to the complainant, and generally in respect of the handling of the matter in future, as it thinks fit; or
(c) direct that the complaint be re-investigated in a specified form.

All persons concerned must be informed by the IPCC of any such determination or direction.

Duties with respect to disciplinary proceedings

Certain duties are imposed on the appropriate authority in the case of any investigation where it has given, or is required to give, notification to entitled persons of its proposed action (p 315), or it has submitted, or is required to submit, a memorandum to the IPCC setting out its determination and proposed action (pp 314, 315, and 316).

Subject to any recommendations or directions given by the IPCC, the authority must take any action notified and, where that action consists of or includes disciplinary proceedings, it must secure that those proceedings are taken to a proper conclusion.

Where a memorandum has been submitted to the IPCC, the IPCC may recommend to the appropriate authority in respect of a person serving with the police that:

(a) the person has a case to answer in respect of misconduct or gross misconduct or has no case to answer;

(b) the person's performance is or is not unsatisfactory;
(c) disciplinary proceedings in the form specified are brought in respect of the person's conduct, or efficiency or effectiveness; and
(d) any disciplinary proceedings brought are modified so as to deal with such aspects of that person's conduct, or efficiency or effectiveness, as may be specified.

The appropriate authority is then obliged to notify the IPCC as to whether it accepts the recommendation and (if it does) to set out its proposed steps.

Where the appropriate authority has submitted, or is required to submit, a memorandum to the IPCC about whether or not the person's performance is satisfactory, and about any proposed action, the IPCC may make a recommendation to the appropriate authority that the performance of the person is, or is not, satisfactory, and that action of the form specified in the recommendation is taken in respect of his performance. The appropriate authority must notify the IPCC on whether it accepts the recommendation and (if it does) must set out its proposed steps to give effect to it.

Where the appropriate authority does not take steps to carry out the IPCC's recommendations, the IPCC may direct it to do so, setting out the steps to be taken, and the authority must comply. The IPCC must supply a statement of its reasons for giving such a direction. The authority must keep the IPCC informed of the action which it takes.

Information for complainant, etc about disciplinary recommendations

The complainant, and all other persons entitled to be informed of such matters, must be notified by the IPCC of any steps which it recommends to be taken by the appropriate authority unless the authority has not notified its acceptance of the recommendation. If the appropriate authority notifies the IPCC that it does not accept the recommendations, or fails to effect them, the IPCC must determine what further steps, if any, should be taken. The IPCC must also notify such persons of any determination not to take further steps or of the outcome of a determination to take further steps.

Recommendations by the IPCC and requirement to respond

The provisions below apply where the IPCC has received a report on completion of an investigation of (a) a complaint or conduct matter supervised or managed by the IPCC (p 314), (b) a complaint or conduct matter by the Commission itself (p 314), or (c) a DSI matter that is not also conduct matter (p 315). They also apply where the IPCC has made a determination on an appeal relating to a complaint dealt with other than by investigation (p 304), or an appeal with respect to an investigation (p 316).

In such cases, the IPCC may make a recommendation in relation to a matter dealt with in the report or appeal. The recommendation may be made to any person if it is made:

(a) following the receipt of a report relating to a DSI matter, or to a conduct matter or complaint of a type specified in the P(CM)R 2012 (which includes a matter relating to—or a complaint alleging—an incident where someone has died or suffered serious injury, a serious assault or sexual assault, serious corruption, or a matter or complaint which the IPCC required the appropriate authority to refer to it); or
(b) following a determination on an appeal relating to a complaint of a type specified in those Regulations.

In any other case, the recommendation may be made only to a person serving with the police, or to a local policing body.

Where the Commission makes such a recommendation, it must publish the recommendation and send a copy of it to the specified person or body relevant in relation to the addressee of the recommendation.

A person to whom a recommendation is made must, within 56 days, provide to the IPCC a response in writing stating what action he has taken or proposes to take in response, or why the person has not taken, or does not propose to take, any action in response. On receiving a response, the IPCC must, within 21 days, publish the response, and send a copy of it to anyone who was sent a copy of the recommendation, unless the person giving the response has, at that time, made representations asserting that the requirements of publication and disclosure should not apply to the response, or to particular parts of it. On receiving such representations, the IPCC may decide that the response should not be published, or that only parts of it should be published, or that the response should not be disclosed, or that only parts of the response should be disclosed. Where, following a decision on representations, the IPCC decides to publish or disclose a response (in whole or in part), it must do so only after the person giving the response has been informed of the Commission's decision. Where a local policing body or a chief officer makes a response, the body or officer must, at the time the IPCC publishes the response, also publish the response (to the same extent as published by the IPCC) and the recommendation referred to above.

HANDLING OF COMPLAINTS AND CONDUCT MATTERS, ETC IN RELATION TO POLICE AND CRIME COMMISSIONERS AND THE LIKE

The Elected Local Policing Bodies (Complaints and Misconduct) Regulations 2012 set out the functions of police and crime panels and the IPCC in relation to the handling of complaints and other matters concerning the conduct of police and crime commissioners, deputy commissioners, the holder of the Mayor's Office for Policing and Crime, and the Deputy Mayor for Policing and Crime. The Regulations set out the process to be followed in dealing with these complaints and matters. They also provide for complaints alleging criminal conduct, and all conduct matters (those matters which indicate that criminal conduct may have occurred), to be referred to the IPCC and investigated either by the IPCC itself or a police force under the management of the IPCC. The Regulations provide for any other complaint to be resolved informally by the police and crime panel, except in the case of the holder of the Mayor's Office for Policing and Crime, or the Deputy Mayor for Policing and Crime if that person is a member of the London Assembly (in which cases the complaint will be passed to the monitoring officer of the Greater London Authority, who is responsible for dealing with complaints about the conduct of the Mayor and other Assembly members). The Regulations are modelled on the provisions of PRA 2002 and associated regulations about the handling of complaints and conduct matters in relation to persons serving with the police. In some instances, the Regulations apply those provisions, with or without modifications.

POLICE DISCIPLINARY OR PERFORMANCE PROCEEDINGS

The Police (Conduct) Regulations 2012 govern disciplinary procedures in respect of misconduct by police officers and special constables. Matters connected with unsatisfactory performance or attendance are dealt with by the Police (Performance)

Regulations 2012. In addition, the Police Appeals Tribunal Rules 2012 provide for appeals to the Police Appeals Tribunal against findings and specific outcomes resulting from the procedures set out in the two sets of regulations.

The very detailed provisions under these Regulations are set out in Chapter 8 on the companion website.

RESTRICTIONS UPON PRIVATE LIVES OF MEMBERS OF POLICE FORCES

General

The Police Regulations 2003 impose a number of general restrictions upon the private lives of members of a police force. Schedule 1 to the Regulations lists the restrictions:

(1) A member of a police force must at all times abstain from any activity which is likely to interfere with the impartial discharge of his duties, or which is likely to give rise to the impression amongst members of the public that it might so interfere.

(2) A member of a police force must not take any active part in politics, nor belong to any organisation specified or described in a determination of the Secretary of State.

(3) A member of a police force must not reside at premises which are not for the time being approved by his chief officer of police.

(4) A member of a police force must not, without the previous consent of his chief officer, receive a lodger in a house or quarters with which he is provided by the local policing body or sublet any part of the house or quarters.

(5) A member of a police force must not, unless he has previously given notice to his chief officer, receive a lodger in a house in which he resides and in respect of which he receives a rent allowance or sublet any part of the house.

(6) A member of a police force must not wilfully refuse or neglect to discharge any lawful debt.

While not representing a 'restriction', the Police Regulations provide that every serving member of a police force must provide a DNA sample via a hair, oral fluid or a mouth swab when directed to do so by his chief officer of police. Such samples (or information derived from them) must be kept separate from samples (or information derived from them) taken under the provisions of PACE, s 63 described on p 206. Such samples (or information derived from them) are to be used for elimination purposes—ie for the purposes of establishing that a sample recovered from a crime scene does not originate from a police officer dealing with the crime. This includes checking DNA profiles recovered from crime scene samples against the profiles of individual police officers, and also wholesale checking of the database of police officers' profiles against the National DNA Database. Samples of a member of a police force taken in accordance with the regulation must be destroyed before the end of the period of six months beginning with the date on which they were taken. The information derived from samples of a member of a police force so taken, and all copies and records thereof, must be destroyed within 12 months of that member leaving the service.

In addition, the Police Regulations provide the power to test a urine or oral fluid sample for controlled drugs in respect of officers who give cause to suspect that they have used such drugs, of probationers, of officers whose work involves dealing with drugs and of officers selected in accordance with a routine of random testing. In the case of that routine, a power to test breath for alcohol is also provided. The Secretary of

State is given power to set out in a determination the consequences of testing positive in any of these situations.

Business interests

For the following purposes, a person has a 'business interest' if:

(a) being a member of a police force, he holds any office or employment for hire or gain (otherwise than as such a member) or carries on any business; or

(b) being a member of a police force or a relative of a member, he holds or possesses a pecuniary interest in a liquor or betting and gaming licence or permit (or certain similar types of licence) in his force area.

The Police Regulations 2003 require a member of a police force to give notice to his chief officer in writing of any actual or proposed business interest of himself or of a relative, ie his spouse or civil partner (not separated), cohabitee, parent, child or sibling, unless that interest has previously been disclosed. However, in the case of a business interest held by a relative, the duty to notify arises only where the member is of the opinion that the interest could interfere with the discharge of his duties. On receipt of notification, the 'appropriate officer' (a person responsible for maintaining professional behaviour standards who has been authorised by the chief constable) must decide whether or not that business interest is compatible with the member's duties as a police officer. In making his decision, an appropriate officer must have regard to whether, as a result of the interest, the officer's conduct fails, or would fail, to meet the appropriate standard in the statutory Standards of Professional Behaviour (set out in Chapter 8 on the companion website).

Where the appropriate officer is minded to decide that the business interest is not compatible, or is not compatible unless conditions are imposed, he must:

(a) notify the member in writing of this preliminary view and the reasons for it;

(b) give the member the opportunity to make representations in writing, at a meeting, or both, at the discretion of the member; and

(c) take any such representations into account.

Whether or not such notification is given, the appropriate officer must, within 28 days of receipt of the member's notice, notify the member of his decision. Where the decision is that the business interest is not compatible, or is not compatible unless conditions are imposed, the notification must:

(a) include a statement of the reasons for the decision;

(b) be accompanied by copies of any document on which the officer relies in support of the decision; and

(c) inform the member of the existence of the right of appeal to the chief officer.

Where, on such an appeal, it appears to the chief officer that the member has adduced substantive reasons why he should be permitted to have the business interest, or why conditions should not be imposed, or that in reaching his determination the appropriate officer failed to apply fair procedures, he may remit the matter back to the appropriate officer for redetermination. Otherwise he must determine the appeal.

Where a business interest has been held by the appropriate officer to be incompatible with continued membership of the force, and either no appeal has been made or such an appeal has been made and the chief officer has upheld the decision of the appropriate officer, the decision of the appropriate officer is regarded as a lawful order for the purposes of the Standards of Professional Behaviour and, in the event of any failure to abide by the decision, as though the appropriate authority had determined under the Police (Conduct) Regulations 2012 that the member had a case to answer in respect of gross misconduct.

The above functions of the chief officer may be exercised only by the chief officer personally or by an acting chief officer.

PROBATIONARY SERVICE

The Police Regulations 2003 provide that a member of a police force appointed in the rank of constable is on probation for such period as the Secretary of State determines. This rule applies to all members of a police force appointed in the rank of constable other than a member who transfers to the force from another force, having completed the required period of probation therein. The rule also applies to a direct entry superintendent or inspector appointed in that rank. Where, in the opinion of the chief officer of police (which term hereafter includes an Assistant Commissioner in the Metropolitan Police), the period of probation was seriously interrupted by a period of absence from duty, by reason of injury or illness, probation may be extended for a longer period, not exceeding 12 months, as determined in the particular circumstances. Such an extension may be made after the expiry of the initial probationary period if the probationer was on sick leave at the time of expiry. It may also be extended for other reasons. The power to extend a period of probation may be delegated to an assistant chief constable, but a decision to dispense with the services of a constable may only be taken by the chief officer himself.

A member of a police force appointed in the rank of constable who transfers from one force to another and has already successfully completed not less than one year of probationary service in that or any other police force will thereafter be on probation for one year (unless extended as above). However, the chief officer may reduce this period, provided that the total probationary service is not less than two years.

Where someone, having ceased to be a member of a police force at some time after satisfactorily completing his probationary period, returns to police service as a member of a police force he must be on probation for six months.

This period of probationary service is used to establish whether or not a person is fitted mentally and physically to perform the duties of his office. A probationer may be discharged at any time if his chief officer considers that he is not mentally or physically so fitted. The word 'mentally' is not used to indicate a level of academic acceptability. The demands of the job can be considerable and the pressures can be too much for those who are not equipped to handle certain situations.

The chief officer may also dispense with the services of a probationer if he considers that he is not likely to become an efficient or well-conducted constable (or superintendent or inspector, as the case may be). A judge in the Administrative Court has held that this power to discharge does not apply where the reason is the misconduct of the probationer; the only way in which a probationer can be dismissed on grounds of misconduct is as a result of formal misconduct proceedings.

Where a chief officer is considering dispensing with the services of a probationer under these regulations, the probationer must be shown any report containing judgements and opinions on him. However, it has been held that where the grounds for dispensing with his services are that, in the opinion of medical officers, he is too overweight to carry out his duties satisfactorily, there would be no purpose in such action as any further observation could not alter the decision.

DATA PROTECTION

The Data Protection Act 1998 (DPA 1998) is concerned with the regulation of processing of information relating to individuals, including the obtaining, holding, use or disclosure of such information.

Principles

Unless exempted by the Act, a 'data controller' is obliged to comply with certain 'data protection principles' in relation to all 'personal data' in relation to which he is data controller. A 'data controller' is a person who (alone or jointly or in common with others) determines the purposes for which and the way in which any personal data are, or are to be, processed. It follows that each chief constable is a data controller.

The 'data protection principles' are:

(1) Personal data must be processed fairly and lawfully and, in particular, must not be processed unless:
   (a) the data subject (DS) has given his consent, or the processing is necessary for the performance of a contract to which DS is a party (or for the taking of steps at the request of DS with a view to entering into a contract), or is required by law, or is necessary to protect the vital interests of DS, or is necessary in the interests of the administration of justice, or in certain other cases, and
   (b) in the case of 'sensitive personal data' (eg an individual's racial origin, political or religious belief, health or commission (or alleged commission) of an offence), DS has given his explicit consent, or the processing is necessary for exercising or performing any right or duty imposed by law on the data controller in connection with employment, or is necessary to protect the vital interests of DS (if the consent of DS cannot be given or cannot reasonably be expected to be obtained), or is necessary in the interests of justice, or in certain other cases.

   The application of this principle does not usually apply to the processing of personal data for the purpose of preventing or detecting crime.
(2) Personal data must be obtained only for one or more specified and lawful purposes, and may not be further processed in any manner incompatible with it or them.
(3) Personal data must be adequate, relevant and not excessive in relation to the purpose or purposes for which processed.
(4) Personal data must be accurate and, where necessary, kept up to date.
(5) Personal data processed for any purpose or purposes may not be kept longer than necessary for it or them.
(6) Personal data must be processed in accordance with the rights of data subjects under the DPA 1998.
(7) Appropriate technical and organisational measures must be taken against unauthorised or unlawful processing of personal data and against accidental loss or destruction of, or damage to, personal data.
(8) Personal data must not be transferred to a country or territory outside the EEA (ie outside the EU, Iceland, Liechtenstein and Norway) unless that country or territory ensures an adequate level of protection for the rights and freedoms of data subjects in relation to the processing of personal data.

'Data' means information which:

(a) is being processed by means of equipment operating automatically in response to instructions given for that purpose;
(b) is recorded with the intention that it should be processed by means of such equipment;
(c) is recorded as part of a relevant filing system or with the intention that it should form part of a relevant filing system;
(d) does not fall within paragraphs (a), (b) or (c) but forms part of an educational, health or accessible public record of a prescribed type; or
(e) is recorded information held by a public authority and does not fall within (a) to (d).

'Personal data' means data which relate to a living individual who can be identified:

(a) from those data, or
(b) from those data and other information which is in the possession of, or is likely to come into the possession of, the data controller,

and includes any expression of opinion about the individual and any indication of the intentions of the data controller or any other person in respect of the individual.

There is no statutory constraint on the purposes for which personal data may be retained, other than that a purpose must be lawful. In particular, the police are entitled to retain personal data relating to convictions, including spent convictions and cautions, however old or minor, not only for core purposes (the prevention and detection of crime, the investigation and apprehension of offenders, or the maintenance of law and order) but also for non-core purposes (eg to supply accurate records of convictions to the CPS or the courts).

Registration

'Data controllers' must register with the Information Commissioner in order for 'personal data' to be processed if that personal data falls within types (a) or (b) *of the definition of 'data' above*, but not (normally) in the case of the other types of data. Thus, the manual files retained within command and control systems do not require registration, but data stored on the Police National Computer does.

By DPA 1998, s 21(1), it is an indictable (either way) offence to process personal data of the above types unless an entry in respect of the data controller has been registered.

Unlawful obtaining, etc of personal data

DPA 1998, s 55(1) provides that it is an offence knowingly or recklessly, without the consent of the data controller, to:

(a) obtain or disclose personal data or the information contained in personal data; or
(b) procure the disclosure to another person of the information contained in personal data.

It is a defence to show:

(a) that the obtaining, disclosing or procuring:

    (i) was necessary to prevent or detect crime (as where the data is passed from one police force to another for this purpose); or

    (ii) was required or authorised by or under any law or court order;

(b) that the defendant reasonably believed that he had in law the right to obtain or disclose the data or information or, as the case may be, to procure the disclosure of the information to the other person;

(c) that he reasonably believed that he would have had the consent of the data controller if the data controller had known of the obtaining, disclosing or procuring and the circumstances of it;

(d) from a day to be appointed, that he acted:

    (i) for the special purposes (ie the purposes of journalism, artistic purposes and literary purposes),

    (ii) with a view to the publication by any person of any journalistic, literary or artistic material, and

    (iii) in the reasonable belief that in the particular circumstances the obtaining, disclosing or procuring was justified as being in the public interest; or

(e) that in the particular circumstances the obtaining, disclosing or procuring was justified as being in the public interest.

By s 55(4), a person who sells personal data is guilty of an offence if he has obtained the data in contravention of s 55(1). Section 55(5) provides that a person who offers to sell personal data commits an offence if he has obtained it in contravention of s 55(1) or if he subsequently does so.

Offences under s 55 are indictable (either way) offences.

Prohibition of requirement as to production of certain records

DPA 1998, s 56(1) provides that a person must not, in connection with:

(a) the recruitment of another person as an employee;

(b) the continued employment of another person; or

(c) any contract for the provision of services to him by another person,

require that other person or a third party to supply him with a relevant record or to produce a relevant record to him.

Likewise, s 56(2) provides that a person concerned with the provision (for payment or not) of goods, facilities or services to the public or a section of the public must not, as a condition of providing or offering to provide any goods, facilities or services to another person, require that other person or a third party to supply him with a relevant record or to produce a relevant record to him.

Breach of either of these provisions is an indictable (either way) offence. A 'relevant record' in these provisions includes any record of a conviction or caution obtained by a data subject from a data controller who is a chief officer of police or the Director General of NCA.

Section 56(1) and (2) do not apply to a person who shows that:

(a) the imposition of the requirement was required or authorised by or under any enactment, by any rule of law or by the order of a court; or

(b) in the particular circumstances the imposition of the requirement was justified as being in the public interest (which it will not be if the alleged justification is that it would assist in the prevention or detection of crime; in such a case one of the various types of certificate of criminal record under the Police Act 1997, Part V will be available from the Disclosure and Barring Service (DBS)).

Limit on prosecutions

No proceedings may be instituted for an offence under DPA 1998 except by the Information Commissioner or by or with the consent of the DPP.

CHAPTER 9

Traffic: General Provisions

TERMINOLOGY

Mechanically propelled vehicle

The means of propulsion may be petrol, diesel, gas, steam, or electricity. Whether or not a vehicle is mechanically propelled is a question of fact. A broken-down motor car remains a mechanically propelled vehicle; it is irrelevant that it might not be driven at that particular time. Before a vehicle can cease to be a mechanically propelled vehicle it must be in such a condition or in such circumstances that there is no reasonable prospect of it ever being driven again. Where a vehicle has been immobilised the extent of the immobilisation is the critical factor when considering whether it remains a mechanically propelled vehicle. A motor car in a scrap yard, stripped of all of its mechanical means of propulsion and without any reasonable prospect of the restoration of motive power, is obviously not a mechanically propelled vehicle. However, a motor car similarly stripped down in a garage to effect repairs remains a mechanically propelled vehicle as there is a reasonable prospect of it being restored to its former mobility.

The Road Traffic Act 1988 (RTA 1988), ss 1–4, 34, 163 and 170, referred to later, do not apply to a mechanically propelled single-person invalid carriage *whose unladen weight does not exceed 254 kgs, as long as it is being used by someone with a physical defect or physical disability, by someone taking it to or from repair, by a manufacturer testing or demonstrating it, by a seller demonstrating it or by someone giving training in its use.*

Motor vehicle

This is defined by RTA 1988, s 185 as a mechanically propelled vehicle intended or adapted for use on a road. The words *'intended or adapted for use on a road'* are important. 'Adapted' does not mean 'altered'; it simply means 'fit and apt'. Some vehicles are quite obviously 'mechanically propelled' but they are not 'intended or adapted for use on a road'.

Whether or not a mechanically propelled vehicle is intended or adapted for use on a road depends on whether a reasonable person looking at the vehicle would say that one of its uses is general use on a road. On this basis, for example, it has been held that two types of motorised scooter known as a 'Segway' and a 'Go-ped' were motor vehicles within s 185. A 'Segway' consisted of a small gyroscopically stabilised platform mounted on two wheels, on which the traveller stood, powered by a battery driven electric motor. A vertical joy-stick was used to steer. Speed was controlled by leaning forward (to go faster) or standing up straight (to slow down). A divisional court held that, although the expectations, advice and intentions of the manufacturer were that it should not be used on a road, they did not provide the answer to the question whether a Segway was a motor vehicle; the judge had not been wrong in concluding that a Segway was a motor vehicle within s 185. A 'Go-ped' consisted of a small foot platform attached to a sub-frame on which the person using the Go-ped would stand. Its engine gave it a maximum speed of 20 mph. The braking system was such that it could not stop the vehicle if it was travelling at any great speed, or in an emergency situation. Severe braking caused the rear wheel to lift from the road surface. A divisional court said that the roadworthiness of a conveyance or its capability to be used safely on a road were not conclusive in relation to whether or not its use on a road was contemplated. There was no obvious place in which a Go-ped could be used, other than on a road. It could not travel on rough ground, or on soft or uneven surfaces. Regardless of the fact that the manufacturers said that it was not to be used on a road, it would be and the reasonable person would recognise that to be so.

The above test does not depend on the owner's or manufacturer's intention. Unless there is evidence of regular use on a road, the particular use to which the vehicle is put at the time is irrelevant to the above test. In one case, a dumper truck, which was used on a site for the transport of material around that site and was occasionally driven on adjoining roads for short distances, was held not to be a motor vehicle because there was no proof of general (as opposed to occasional) use on roads. On the other hand, in another case, a Euclid earth scraper, which was primarily used to dig up earth on a building site and carry that earth under its own power to other places, was held to be intended for use on a road when evidence of its general use on roads and of its capability of reaching a speed of 45 mph was given.

RTA 1988, s 189 expressly provides that pedestrian-controlled lawnmowers and 'electrically assisted pedal cycles' (p 432) are not motor vehicles. Mechanically propelled single-person invalid carriages are expressly stated not to be motor vehicles for the purposes of the Road Traffic Regulation Act 1984 and RTA 1988, except in relation to RTA 1988, s 22A (p 407), if the conditions italicised on p 327 are satisfied.

A mechanically propelled vehicle originally manufactured for use on a road may cease to be a 'motor vehicle' for the purposes of s 185 if it is subsequently altered, but only if such alterations are very substantial.

Road

This is defined by RTA 1988, s 192 as meaning any highway and any other road to which the public has access and including bridges over which a road passes.

Highway

A 'highway' is defined by the common law. It is a way over which there exists a public right of passage on foot, riding, accompanied by a beast of burden or with vehicles and cattle. The term is therefore wide enough to embrace public footpaths, bridleways, and carriageways, defined below. It is presumed that the boundary of the highway is defined by the buildings, hedges, fences, walls or the like along its route. Consequently, grass verges are generally a part of the highway. If, for example, a fence behind a grass verge was erected by the highway authority it would clearly mark the limits of the highway. If it was erected by an adjoining landowner this would not necessarily be so.

A footpath is a highway over which the public has a right of way on foot alone.

A bridleway is a highway over which the public has a right of way while on foot, on horseback or leading a horse. By the Countryside Act 1968, s 30, the public also has a right to ride a pedal bicycle on a bridleway (provided that the cyclist gives way to pedestrians and persons on horseback). The right to ride a pedal cycle on a bridleway may be controlled by a local authority order. There may be a right on some bridleways to drive animals; such bridleways may be referred to locally as 'droves' or 'driftways'.

A carriageway is a way constructed or comprised in a highway, being a way (other than a cycle track) over which the public has a right of way on foot, on horseback, or with vehicles or cattle.

Road

Apart from a highway, 'road' in the road traffic legislation means any road (ie a definable way for passage between two points) to which the public has access. The essential factor is whether or not, as a question of fact, the public in general has access to the road. A private road leading to a farmhouse, which was maintained by the farmer, has been held to be a 'road' on evidence being offered that there was no gate and that it was regularly used by persons who had no business at the farm. Likewise, a divisional court has held that justices were entitled to find that tarmacked roadways across a caravan park to a beach, which had road markings and were easily definable as routes leading from one point to another on a map and to which the public had unrestricted access, were 'roads'.

It has been decided that any road may be regarded as a road to which the public has access if members of the public are to be found on it who have not obtained access either by overcoming a physical obstruction or in defiance of a prohibition, express or implied. A pavement which is partly publicly owned and partly privately owned is a road if the public has access to the whole of it. It is essential to show that the public in general has access. Access which is restricted to certain classes of person is not usually sufficient to make a road 'public'.

Where a road within a housing estate has not been adopted by the local authority, the determining factor is not whether the road is repairable at public expense but whether the public has access to it. If members of the public are seen there, and their presence is tolerated, it is a road.

The House of Lords has ruled that a road is provided for the purpose of moving from one place to another as opposed to parking a car. It said that even though a part of a car park might be made up of routes giving access to parking bays this, by itself, was not enough if those routes merely gave access to parking bays and were not for the purpose of travelling from one place to another.

REGISTRATION

All vehicles used or kept on roads in the UK must be registered with the Secretary of State. A 'vehicle' for this purpose is a mechanically propelled vehicle, or anything (whether or not a vehicle) that has been, but has ceased to be, a mechanically propelled vehicle. All records relating to vehicles are retained by the Driver and Vehicle Licensing Agency (DVLA) at Swansea (or Coleraine, in the case of Northern Ireland).

The Road Safety Act 2006 (RSA 2006), s 49A contains a provision for the disclosure by the Secretary of State to chief officers of police and certain other persons and bodies of information in foreign registers of vehicles which has been obtained.

The Road Vehicles (Registration and Licensing) Regulations (RV(R&L)R) 2002 provide a single set of Regulations for the whole of the UK.

The Vehicle Excise and Registration Act 1994 (VERA 1994), s 21 provides that it is the duty of the Secretary of State to register a vehicle on the first issue by him of a vehicle licence or a nil licence (ie a licence for a vehicle exempt from excise duty), or where particulars in respect of the vehicle are received by the Secretary of State from a motor dealer before the first licence is issued. The registration mark assigned to a vehicle must be fitted in the prescribed manner. Since it is the Secretary of State's responsibility to register vehicles, the use of an unregistered vehicle on a road simply constitutes the offence of use without a vehicle licence.

RV(R&L)R 2002, reg 10 authorises the Secretary of State to register a vehicle in either the Great Britain or Northern Ireland records as he considers appropriate and to issue a registration document. He may require the keeper of a vehicle to produce it for inspection or to produce other evidence that the vehicle accords with the particulars furnished with the application. If he is not satisfied that the vehicle accords with the particulars, he may refuse to issue a registration document or replacement registration document.

VEHICLES: REGISTRATION DOCUMENTS AND MARKS

Registration document

When the Secretary of State registers a vehicle a registration document is issued and, unless a registration mark has already been assigned by a motor dealer who has received a 'block' of marks, a registration mark is assigned to that vehicle. Even if a vehicle is exempt from the requirement to be licensed, it must still be registered. A registration document contains the registered particulars of the vehicle and the name and address of the person shown in the register as the owner or keeper of the vehicle. The Secretary of State has power to issue, without charge and on surrender of the existing registration document, a registration document which complies with Community Directive 1999/37/EC in relation to dimensions, composition and the information to be contained in it.

On first registration of a vehicle registered in another member state of the EU or in Gibraltar, the Secretary of State must retain for not less than six months the former registration document surrendered and notify the appropriate member state or Gibraltar in which the vehicle was previously registered.

The Secretary of State may issue a registration document in a microprocessor smart card format and may issue that type of registration document without charging a fee where the old type of document is surrendered. The Secretary of State may issue a replacement registration document where a registration document has, or may have been, lost, stolen, destroyed or damaged, or it contains any particulars that have become illegible; see Chapter 9 on the companion website.

The registered owner of a vehicle is not necessarily its legal owner, and possession of a registration document is not in itself proof of ownership.

By reg 12, the keeper of a vehicle must produce a registration document for inspection if required to do so at any reasonable time by a constable or person acting on the Secretary of State's behalf. There are no provisions for later production.

VERA 1994, s 28A requires a person *using* a vehicle in respect of which a registration document has been issued to produce it for inspection by a constable or a person authorised by the Secretary of State (who must produce his authority). Failure to do so is an offence. However, no offence is committed if the person produces the document personally at a police station specified by him within seven days or as soon as is reasonably practicable. Nor is an offence committed if a vehicle is on lease or hire, and the vehicle is not registered (nor required to be registered) in the name of the lessee or hirer, and he personally produces appropriate evidence of the lease or hire agreement in the same way as just described. However, he must reasonably believe (or it must be reasonable for him to expect) that the lessor, etc is able to produce, or require production of, the registration document.

Notification of change of ownership

RV(R&L)R 2002, regs 22–24 are concerned with changes of ownership affecting vehicles.

Where there is a 'private' sale or transfer of a vehicle, ie to a person other than a vehicle trader, the registered keeper must give to the new keeper the part of the registration document which provides for particulars of a new keeper, and must forthwith deliver to the Secretary of State on the remainder of the registration document, or otherwise in writing, or, if the Secretary of State thinks fit, orally by telephone or by electronic means, the following information:

(a) the name and address of the new keeper;
(b) the date of transfer; and
(c) a declaration by him that this information is correct to the best of his knowledge (reg 22).

A 'vehicle trader' is a person who:

(i) holds a trade licence;
(ii) carries on business as a dealer in, or auctioneer or dismantler of, motor vehicles; or
(iii) in relation to a particular vehicle is a finance company which has repossessed it under a repossession order, or an insurer which has acquired it in satisfaction of a total loss claim.

Where the new keeper is a vehicle trader, the *registered keeper* must forthwith provide the Secretary of State with:

(i) the name and address of the vehicle trader;
(ii) the date of the transfer to the vehicle trader; and
(iii) a declaration by himself that the transfer occurred on the specified date.

The Secretary of State may, if he thinks fit, accept a notification or declaration made orally by telephone or by electronic means, and in any other case it must be made on that part of the registration document relating to the transfer to a vehicle trader, or otherwise in writing (reg 23).

Where the new keeper is a vehicle trader, the *trader* must, on or before the appropriate date, notify the Secretary of State of the transfer of the vehicle to him, and the date on which he became its keeper. The 'appropriate date' is the earliest of the following days:

(a) the day of the trader's first use of the vehicle on a public road otherwise than under a trade licence;
(b) the day on which the trader first keeps it on such a road; or
(c) the day following the expiry of a three-month period beginning with the day on which the vehicle was last kept by someone who was not a vehicle trader.

If there is a transfer to another vehicle trader within the three-month period the registration document must be transferred with the vehicle (reg 24).

Where a vehicle trader transfers the vehicle to a person *other than another vehicle trader or transfers the vehicle to another trader outside the three-month period,* he must forthwith deliver to the Secretary of State the following:

(a) the name and address of the new keeper;

(b) the date of transfer; and

(c) a declaration as to the correctness of the details under (a) and (b) (reg 24).

The Secretary of State may, if he thinks fit, accept a notification or declaration under reg 24 made orally by telephone or by electronic means, and in any other case a notification on or before the appointed day must be made on that part of the registration document relating to a change of keeper and in any other case, on that part, or otherwise in writing (reg 24).

Where all parts of the registration document have been, or may have been, lost, stolen or destroyed, the new keeper *whether or not a trader* must submit an application to the Secretary of State for a new registration document and send the prescribed fee. If the new keeper can produce that part of the registration document which is to be given to the new keeper, no fee need be sent.

Failure to comply with any of the above requirements is an offence under VERA 1994, s 59(1). It is not a continuing offence and therefore the time limitation upon proceedings runs from the day of the transfer of the vehicle. If, therefore, a period of six months has passed since the transfer of a vehicle no proceedings may be taken against either of the parties to the transaction if they have failed to comply with the requirement to notify the Secretary of State forthwith.

Notification of other changes

An owner of a registered vehicle who changes his name or address is required by RV(R&L)R 2002, reg 18 forthwith to notify the Secretary of State. Where the registration document has been, or may have been, lost, stolen or destroyed, notification must be accompanied by an application for the issue of a registration document and a fee. Such a notification or application may, if the Secretary of State thinks fit, be made orally by telephone or by electronic means and in any other case, except where the registration document has been, or may have been, lost, stolen or destroyed, a notification must be accompanied by the registration document. A notification may be made on the registered keeper's behalf by a vehicle trader by whom the vehicle is sold or to whom the vehicle is disposed of.

In the event of a vehicle being sent permanently out of the UK the registered keeper is required by reg 17 immediately to notify the Secretary of State of that fact. The Secretary of State may, if he thinks fit, accept such a notification by electronic means. A notification may be made on the registered keeper's behalf by a vehicle trader by, or to whom, the vehicle is sold or disposed of.

Regulation 17A requires that where an 'end-of-life' vehicle is transferred to an authorised treatment facility (facility operating under a waste disposal site licence) the facility must, in addition to issuing a 'certificate of destruction' to the last holder/owner of the vehicle, inform the Secretary of State of the issue of that certificate. No further records may then be made which are related to that vehicle.

Regulation 16 is concerned with procedures which must be followed when any alteration to a vehicle renders the particulars in the registration document incorrect, as where it is resprayed a different colour or has a different engine fitted. Notification of the alteration must be given to the Secretary of State:

(a) by the registered keeper; or

(b) on behalf of the registered keeper, by a vehicle trader to whom the vehicle is sold or by whom the vehicle is disposed of.

Where the registration document has been, or may have been, lost, stolen or destroyed, such a notification must be accompanied by an application for the issue of a new registration document, and a fee. Any such notification or application may, if the Secretary of State thinks fit, be made orally by telephone or by electronic means and in any other case, except where the registration document is lost, stolen or destroyed, a notification must be accompanied by the registration document.

Non-compliance with any of the above requirements is an offence under VERA 1994, s 59(1).

Offence of using incorrectly registered vehicle

VERA 1994, s 43C(1) and (2) provides that it is an offence to use a vehicle on a public road or in a public place if excise duty is chargeable in respect of it, or it is an exempt vehicle which requires a nil licence (pp 342–5), where the name and address of its keeper are not recorded in the register, or any particulars recorded in the register are incorrect.

It is a defence under s 43C(3) for the defendant (D) to show that there was no reasonable opportunity, before the material time, to furnish:

(a) the name and address of the keeper of the vehicle; or
(b) particulars correcting the incorrect particulars.

It is a defence under s 43C(4) for D to show:

(a) that he had reasonable grounds for believing, or it was reasonable for him to expect, that the name and address of the keeper or the other particulars of registration (as the case may be) were correctly recorded in the register; or
(b) that any prescribed exception is met. No such exception has been prescribed.

Registration marks

Generally

The Secretary of State has power to assign to a vehicle:

(a) a registration mark on initial registration;
(b) a new registration mark in place of its existing one; and
(c) whether on first registration or not, a registration mark previously assigned to another vehicle.

The Secretary of State may also grant to a person the right to retain a registration number by transferring it from one vehicle registered in that person's name to another such vehicle.

The Road Vehicles (Display of Registration Marks) Regulations 2001 (RV(DRM)R 2001) deal with the forms of registration marks and the manner in which they are fixed to vehicles.

Regulation 10 and Sch 2 introduce a mandatory requirement for the use of registration plates made of retro-reflecting material conforming to British Standard specification BS AU 145a or an equivalent standard laid down by a European Economic Area (EEA) state on all vehicles first registered on or after 1 September 2001, and on all vehicles registered before that date but on or after 1 January 1973 if an existing plate is replaced. Regulation 10 and Sch 2 also set out the requirements for vehicles registered on or after 1 January 1973 and before 1 September 2001 in other circumstances (reflex-reflecting plates conforming to British Standard specification BS AU 145a or an equivalent standard laid down by an EEA state) but such vehicles *may* carry the forms of plates prescribed for vehicles first registered on or after 1 September 2001. In either case they must have black characters on a white background on a front plate; and black characters on a yellow background on a rear plate. The EEA comprises all EU member states plus Iceland, Liechtenstein and Norway.

Schedule 2 also deals with vehicles registered before 1 January 1973. It provides as follows. Where a plate is constructed so that it may be illuminated from behind by virtue of the translucency of its characters they must be white translucent characters on a black background, and when illuminated the characters must appear white against a black background. Where a plate is not so constructed, it must *either* comply with BS AU 145 carrying black characters on a white background at the front and black characters on a yellow background at the rear, *or* be white, silver, or light grey letters and numbers on a black surface which are indelibly inscribed on the plate and cannot readily be detached.

Permitted layouts

RV(DRM)R 2001, reg 13 and Sch 3 govern this. Registration marks in any non-permitted format are unlawful. The marks may be, for example, a group consisting of two letters and two numbers followed by a group of three letters (eg DE51 ABC); a group consisting of a single letter and not more than three numbers followed by a group of three letters (eg A123 ABC); a group of three letters followed by a group consisting of not more than three numbers and a single letter (eg ABC 123A); a group of four numbers followed by a single letter or a group of two letters (eg 1234 A, 1234 AB); a group of not more than three numbers followed by a group of not more than three letters (eg 123 ABC, 123 AB, 12 A); a group of not more than three letters followed by a group of not more than three numbers (eg ABC 123, AB 123, A 12); a single letter or group of two letters followed by a group of four numbers (eg A 1234, AB 1234); and in Northern Ireland, a group of three letters followed by a group of four numbers (ABZ 1234) or a group of four numbers followed by a group of three letters (eg 1234 ABZ).

It is not necessary that these letters and numbers all follow one another. The plates may be square, permitting the letters and characters to be placed in two or three rows, except that plates containing three rows of characters are not permitted on vehicles first registered on or after 1 September 2001 or a replacement plate fixed to a vehicle first registered before then but on or after 1 January 1973. Plates containing all of the letters and numbers in a straight line are not permitted on motor cycles.

Character sizes and fonts

RV(DRM)R 2001, reg 14 and Sch 3 deal with the size and spacing of characters. Regulation 14 provides that the registration marks of vehicles must be 79 mm high. In respect of vehicles first registered before 1 September 2001 the registration marks may be 78 mm high instead of 79 mm, except where the vehicle was first registered on or after 1 January 1973 and the mark is displayed on a new registration plate. By way of further exception, the required height is 64 mm in relation to a motor cycle, motor tricycle, quadricycle, agricultural machine, works truck or road roller. The width of characters, spacing and margins are all precisely prescribed by Table B in Sch 3.

Regulation 14A applies special rules to a vehicle imported into the UK which does not have EC Whole Vehicle Type Approval and is so constructed that the area available for the fixing of the registration plate precludes the display on the plate of a registration mark in conformity with the requirements of reg 14. In such a case the prescribed height of characters is 64 mm; the width (except for the letter 'I' or figure '1') must be 44 mm; the width of every part of a stroke and the spacing of characters within a group must be 10 mm, the vertical spacing between groups of characters and the width of a margin between the mark and the top and lateral sides of the registration plate must not be less than 5 mm; and the space between the bottom of the mark and the bottom of the registration plate must not be less than 13 mm.

Regulation 12(2) permits deviation from the prescribed height of characters provided that the deviation is not more than 1 mm either way. In the case of other dimensions, including spaces, the permitted deviation is 0.5 mm either way.

Regulation 15 and Sch 4 deal with the font of characters displayed on a registration plate fixed to a vehicle first registered on or after 1 September 2001, or on a new registration plate fixed to any other vehicle (except where the vehicle was first registered before 1 January 1973). They require that each of the characters must be in the prescribed font. In relation to other cases, characters must be in the prescribed font or in a style which is substantially similar to the prescribed font so that the character is easily distinguishable but, in the latter case, characters must not be formed in italic script (or other script which is not vertical), or in script in which the curvature or alignment of the lines of the strokes is substantially different from the prescribed font, or in script using multiple or a broken stroke or in such a way that a character, or characters, appear like a different character or characters. A character will not be treated as substantially different solely on the grounds that it has, or does not have, serifs (small lines at the extremity of a main stroke).

Fixing of rear registration plates: post-1938 vehicles

RV(DRM)R 2001, reg 5 (which applies to all vehicles first registered on or after 1 October 1938 other than works trucks, road rollers, and agricultural machines) requires a rear registration plate to be fixed on the rear of the vehicle or (where it is towing a trailer) to the rear of the trailer or the rearmost trailer. However, where a vehicle or trailer has been constructed for rear plates to be fixed in accordance with relevant European type approval Directives, the plate may be fixed in the space provided in accordance with the Directives. Regulation 9 requires a plate of the present type to be lit in accordance with the regulation when used on a road between sunset and sunrise.

Unless fitted in a space provided in accordance with a European type approval Directive, a rear registration plate must be fitted vertically (or, if that is not reasonably practicable, as close to vertical as is reasonably practicable) in such a position that the characters are easily distinguishable from a distance of 22 m (where the characters are of a width of 57 mm); 21.5 m (where the characters are of a width of 50 mm); and 18 m (where the characters are of a width of 44 mm). Regulation 9 provides that, except where it is fitted and lit in accordance with European type approval requirements, a rear plate must be lit so that it is easily distinguishable from a distance of 18 m, but 15 m is substituted where the characters are of a width of only 44 mm.

Fixing of front registration plates: post-1938 vehicles

RV(DRM)R 2001, reg 6 deals with registration plates on a vehicle first registered on or after 1 October 1938, with the same exceptions as above in relation to rear plates. It requires that a front registration plate must be fixed vertically (or if that is not reasonably practicable, as close to vertical as is reasonably practicable) so that its characters are easily distinguishable from the rest of the plate in normal daylight. Regulation 6 requires that, in the case of motor cycles or motor tricycles which do not have a body of a type which is characteristic of the body of a four-wheeled vehicle, there must not be a front registration plate if the vehicle was first registered on or after 1 September 2001. A front registration plate need not be fitted if such a vehicle was registered before that date.

Pre-1938 vehicles, works trucks, road rollers and agricultural machines

RV(DRM)R 2001, reg 7 deals with registration plates fitted to the front of vehicles registered before 1 October 1938 and to their rear (and the rear of any trailer or rear-most trailer). It requires vertically fitted plates which are easily distinguishable.

There are similar provisions in respect of reasonable practicability and distinguishability of the characters on a plate as under regs 5 and 6. Likewise, there is no need for a front plate to be fitted to a motor bicycle or motor tricycle. The lighting requirements of reg 9 apply to the rear plates of these vehicles.

Regulation 8 is concerned with works trucks, road rollers and agricultural machines. Registration plates must be fitted vertically on both sides of the vehicle and on its rear, so that the characters on the mark are easily distinguishable from the sides and rear respectively. When the vehicle is towing a trailer and the plate is not fixed to the sides of the vehicle, a plate must be fixed on the trailer (or rearmost trailer) so that the characters of the mark are easily distinguishable from behind the trailer. In the case of a towing machine which is an agricultural machine (tractor, off-road tractor, light agricultural vehicle, agricultural engine or mowing machine) the plate displayed on the trailer may be that of any agricultural machine kept by the keeper of the towing vehicle. The lighting requirements of reg 9 do not apply to these vehicles.

Use of reflex-reflecting material and other impediments to true photographs

RV(DRM)R 2001, reg 11 prohibits the application of reflex-reflecting material to any part of the registration plate or the treatment of the plate in such a way as to cause the registration mark to become retro-reflective. In addition, it requires that the surface of a registration plate must not comprise nor incorporate any design, pattern or texture, or be treated in any way which gives to any part of the plate the appearance of a design, pattern or texture. It also prohibits any treatment of a registration plate which has the effect of making it less distinguishable or would prevent or impair the making of a true photograph. The use of a screw or bolt or other fixing device in a manner which has the effect of changing the appearance or legibility of any characters of a registration mark, or would impair the making of a true photograph, is also prohibited.

GB plates

RV(DRM)R 2001, reg 16 provides that no material other than a registration mark and the following material may be displayed on a registration plate. 'The following material' refers to the international distinguishing sign of the UK ('GB') *or* (unless the vehicle is recorded in the part of the register relating to Northern Ireland) the displayed letters denoting in full or by a specified abbreviation one of the constituent countries of Great Britain, Great Britain (as a whole), or the United Kingdom (as a whole) accompanied by an image of the Union Flag or the national flag of one of those countries. Thus, registration marks may identify vehicles as belonging to the UNITED KINGDOM (UK), GREAT BRITAIN (GB), ENGLAND (ENG), SCOTLAND (SCO), or WALES/CYMRU (CYM) by capital letters or (except GB) a mixture of initial capital letters followed by lower case and by the respective flags of those nations.

Exemptions

RV(DRM)R 2001, regs 3 and 18 exempt small purpose-built invalid carriages and pedestrian-controlled vehicles from the requirement to carry registration marks. The use of old-style number plates on 'classic' vehicles is also exempt from the Regulations.

Breach of the Regulations: offences

VERA 1994, s 59(1) provides that a contravention of, or a failure to comply with, RV(DRM)R 2001 is an offence. An offence under s 59(1) is a fixed penalty offence if it relates to a failure to fix prescribed registration marks to a vehicle in accordance with the regulations relating to the size, shape and character of registration marks.

Offences relating to registration marks

VERA 1994, ss 42(1) and 43(1) provide, respectively, that, if a registration mark is not fixed on a vehicle as required by s 23, or if a registration mark is obscured or has become not easily distinguishable, the driver (or, if it is not being driven, its keeper) is guilty of an offence. D has a defence to a charge under s 42(1) if he proves that he had no reasonable opportunity to register the vehicle and that it was being driven for the purpose of being registered (s 42(4)). D has a defence to a charge under s 43 if he proves that he took all reasonably practicable steps to prevent the mark being obscured, etc (s 43(4)).

Forgery, fraud or falsity

VERA 1994, s 44(1) and (2) makes it an indictable (either way) offence to forge, alter, fraudulently use, fraudulently lend, or fraudulently allow another to use, a registration mark.

Registration plates

Regulation of suppliers of registration plates

V(C)A 2001, Part 2 is concerned with the regulation of suppliers of registration plates.

By s 17(1), a person commits an offence if he carries on business as a registration plate supplier without being registered with the Secretary of State. A person carries on a business as a registration plate supplier if his business consists wholly or partly in selling registration plates and he is not exempt from the provisions of the Act. The Vehicles Crime (Registration of Registration Plate Suppliers) Regulations 2008, reg 3 exempts a dealer in vehicles who has arranged a first registration in the UK on behalf of the intended purchaser or keeper, or where the registration plate was not fixed to the vehicle by the dealer or on his behalf.

Under s 18, on receipt of any prescribed fee, the Secretary of State must supply information from the register of registration plate suppliers on request by any person (subject to exceptions provided by regulations). Where a request is so made, and subject to any prescribed exception and fee, the Secretary of State must supply the information in the form of a certified copy of the register or of an extract from it. Any such certified copy is evidence of the matters mentioned in it. The Secretary of State may make all the information contained in the register, or prescribed parts of it, available for use by constables, civilian employees (ie members of the civilian staff of a police force or persons employed by the Common Council of the City of London who are under the direction and control of the Commissioner of the City of London Police) in the investigation of offences against Part 2. Regulations limit the further disclosure by constables of information to which they have been given access.

By s 19(3), a person who, in applying for registration, makes a statement which he knows to be false in a material particular, or recklessly makes a statement which is so false, commits an offence. On conviction, a court may make an order under s 20 providing for the removal of the entry relating to him in the register, and/or prohibiting him from making an application for registration within a period not exceeding five years specified by the court.

Under s 21, the Secretary of State may cancel a person's registration if satisfied that the person is not carrying on the business of a registration plate dealer and has not, while registered, been doing so for the past 28 days, but may not do so without serving notice under s 22 and allowing time for representations. An appeal lies to a magistrates' court within 21 days.

Information to be obtained from prospective purchasers of plates

The Vehicles Crime (Registration of Registration Plate Suppliers) Regulations 2008 require registered persons who are in the course of selling registration plates to obtain prescribed information from the prospective purchasers before the completion of the sale. They also require registered persons to keep records of prescribed matters.

The information to be obtained by a registered supplier from a prospective purchaser is prescribed by reg 6. He is required to obtain:

(a) where the prospective purchaser is a partnership or is one or more partners of a partnership (or a limited liability partnership (LLP) or registered company) purchasing on behalf of such an organisation, the firm's name and the address of the principal place of business (the registered name and office, and principal place of business if different, in the case of a LLP or company);

(b) where the prospective purchaser is not as set out above at (a), the purchaser's name and residential or other address;

(c) where a person is acting as an agent for a prospective purchaser, the name and address of that agent;

(d) the registration mark to be displayed on the plate;

(e) the connection of the prospective purchaser with the registration mark or the vehicle on which the registration plate is intended to be fixed.

The information in (a)–(c) must be verified by the registered person. This must be done by reference to one of the following documents listed in Part 1 of the Schedule to the Regulations:

(a) a valid driving licence containing a photograph;

(b) a valid driving licence (whether or not issued in the UK);

(c) a registration document or registration certificate provided it is also used to verify the prospective purchaser's connection with the registration mark or vehicle (see below);

(d) a valid passport whether or not it is issued in the UK;

(e) a valid national identity card (whether or not issued in the UK);

(f) a valid debit card or credit card issued by a bank or building society;

(g) a police warrant card;

(h) a valid armed forces identity card;

(i) a dated bill or statement of account issued in respect of the supply of gas, electricity, water or telecommunications services to premises at a specified address;

(j) a dated council tax bill or statement of account;

(k) a dated bill or statement of account issued in respect of rates payable in Northern Ireland; or

(l) a dated statement relating to an account held at a bank or building society.

If not dated, documents referred to in (i) to (l) must relate to a period ending no earlier than six months before that time.

In addition, the registered person must verify the purchaser's connection with the registration mark or the vehicle by one of the following documents listed in Part 2 of the Schedule to the 2008 Regulations: the registration document or registration certificate, or that part of such document or certificate relevant to the transfer of a vehicle; a certificate of entitlement to a registration mark; a retention document relating to the right of retention of a registration mark; a vehicle licensing reminder issued to the registered keeper; a temporary registration certificate; an authorisation issued by the Secretary of State for the purchase of a number plate; or an authorisation for the purchase of the number plate issued by a company owning more than one vehicle stating that it holds the registration document or the registration certificate and giving the reference number of that document or certificate.

By V(C)A 2001, s 25(3), a person who contravenes any provision in reg 6 commits an offence, unless he shows that he took all reasonable steps and exercised all due diligence to avoid committing the offence.

Regulation 7 of the 2008 Regulations requires a registered person to keep records at his principal place of business or at any other premises at which he carries on the business of a registration plate supplier. Records must be retained for a period of three years from the date of registration. Such records must contain:

(a) the information required by reg 6;

(b) the registration mark displayed on the registration plate (where not recorded under (a)); and

(c) details of all documents used for verification in accordance with reg 6 and those details must include:

  (i) in the case of a document listed in Part 1 of the Schedule which is used for verification, such particulars or numbers (if any) appearing on the document as purport to make it, or those particulars or numbers (or both), unique to the purchaser and which, in the case of a driving licence, must be the driver number, or

  (ii) in the case of a registration document or certificate the reference number of that document, and in the case of an authorisation to purchase the number plate, issued by a company owning more than one vehicle, the reference number referred to in that document.

Failure to comply with these provisions as to records is an offence against V(C)A 2001, s 24(4), unless the defendant shows that he took all reasonable steps and exercised all due diligence to avoid committing the offence.

Supplementary provisions and offences

V(C)A 2001, s 26 empowers a constable, or person authorised by the Secretary of State or the local authority for the area, to enter and inspect the registered premises of registered persons at any reasonable time. The constable or authorised person has power to require production of, and to inspect, any plates kept at the premises and any records which are required to be kept under V(C)A 2001, Part 2, and to take copies or extracts. Provision is also made for the issue to a constable or authorised person of a warrant.

While force may not be used to obtain entry in normal circumstances, it may be used in the exercise of the constable or authorised person's powers under the authority of a warrant. When effecting entry without a warrant, a constable or authorised person must, if required by or on behalf of the owner or occupier or person in charge of the premises, produce evidence of identity, and of his authority for entering, before doing so. This also applies to an authorised person when executing a warrant. Section 26(7) also creates an offence of obstruction of an authorised person in the exercise of his powers under the section. The Secretary of State is authorised to prosecute offenders.

A person registered under V(C)A 2001, Part 2 is required by s 27 to give notice of changes of circumstances. Section 27(4) creates the offence of failure to do so. The same due diligence defence as is set out above in relation to ss 24 and 25 is available to a person accused of this offence.

Section 28 is concerned with counterfeit registration plates and those which do not conform with regulations. It creates three offences:

(a) selling a plate or other device which is not a registration plate as a registration plate, knowing that it is not such a plate or being reckless as to whether it is a registration plate (s 28(1));

(b) selling a plate or other device which is not a registration plate because the mark does not comply with regulations or is displayed otherwise than as permitted by regulations (s 28(1A)); and

(c) supplying a plate, device or other object to a person who is carrying on a business which consists wholly or partly in unlawful activity contrary to (a) or (b) and he knows or reasonably suspects that the plate, device or other object will be used for the purposes of that other person's unlawful activities (s 28(2)).

Section 29(1) creates the offence of supplying a plate, device or other object to an unregistered person (other than an exempt person to be defined by regulations) who is carrying on a business which consists wholly or partly in selling registration plates, knowing or reasonably suspecting that the plate, device or other object will be used for the purpose of that other person's business as a registration plate or as part of a registration plate.

LICENSING

VERA 1994, s 1 provides that vehicle excise duty must be charged in respect of:

(a) every mechanically propelled vehicle that:
   (i)   is registered under the Act, or
   (ii) (if not so registered) is used, or kept, on a public road.
   As we have seen, it is not necessary to prove that such a vehicle was intended or adapted for use on roads. Any mechanically propelled vehicle, including a go-kart, which is actually used or kept on a public road requires a vehicle licence regardless of whether or not it was intended or adapted for use on a road; and

(b) every thing (whether or not it is a vehicle) that has been, but has ceased to be, a mechanically propelled vehicle and:
   (i)   is registered under the Act, or
   (ii) (if not so registered) is used, or kept, on a public road.

Vehicle excise duty charged in respect of a vehicle is paid on a vehicle licence.

By s 5, certain vehicles (exempt vehicles: pp 342–5) are exempt from duty, although they must generally have a nil licence (p 345).

Where a vehicle for which a vehicle licence is in force is transferred by the holder of the licence to another person, the licence is to be treated for the purposes of ss 29 and 31A below as no longer in force.

In the rest of VERA 1994 'vehicle' means a mechanically propelled vehicle or any thing (whether or not it is a vehicle) that has been, but has ceased to be, a mechanically propelled vehicle.

Offences of using or keeping unlicensed vehicle

VERA 1994, s 29(1) provides that if any person *uses* or *keeps* a vehicle for which no vehicle licence or trade licence (see p 348) is in force, he is guilty of an offence.

Section 29(2A) provides that the offence under s 29(1) does not apply if the vehicle is an exempt vehicle requiring a nil licence and such a licence is in force, or if it is an exempt vehicle not required by regulations to have a nil licence (pp 342–5).

Section 29(1) does not apply if (a) the vehicle is neither being used or kept on a public road, (b) the requisite particulars and statutory declaration (the statutory off-road notification (SORN)) have been furnished and provided, and (c) the terms of that declaration have not been breached (s 29(2B)). In relation to the SORN, RV(R&L)R 2002, reg 26 and Sch 4 require that, where a person does not renew a vehicle licence on expiry, or keeps an unlicensed vehicle, he must make a required declaration to the Secretary of State (in writing, orally or by electronic means) not later than the day upon which the licence ceases to be in force (or three months after such expiry in the case of motor traders). The declaration is to the effect that (except for use under a trade licence) (a) the vehicle is not intended for the time being to be used or kept on a public road and (b) a licence will be taken out before any such use. It is an offence under VERA 1994, s 59(1) to fail to make such a declaration. If there is a transfer of such a vehicle during an unlicensed period and a licence is not taken out, a required declaration must be made by the new owner.

In addition, s 29(1) does not apply if the vehicle is kept by a motor trader or vehicle tester at his business premises (s 29(2C)).

Section 29(2E) provides that a defendant is not entitled to the benefit of any of these exceptions from s 29(1) unless evidence is adduced which is sufficient to raise an issue with respect to that exception, but where evidence is so adduced it is for the prosecution to prove beyond reasonable doubt that the exception does not apply.

Offence of being registered keeper of unlicensed vehicle

If a registered vehicle does not have a vehicle licence or trade licence in force the registered keeper is guilty of an offence contrary to VERA 1994, s 31A(1), unless it is an exempt vehicle of one of the types referred to in s 29(2A) above. However, s 31B provides a number of exceptions. The registered keeper does not commit an offence under s 31A if *at the relevant time*:

(a) he is not the person keeping the vehicle and, if previously he was the person keeping it, he has by the relevant time complied with *any requirements to furnish particulars which apply on not renewing a licence, or when keeping an unlicensed vehicle;*
(b) he is keeping the vehicle, it is neither kept nor used on a public road and he has complied with any requirement italicised in (a);
(c) the vehicle has been stolen and has not been recovered, and within 14 days he has notified a member of a police force with prescribed details about the theft; or

(d) the period of 'grace days' has not expired since the expiry of the last licence and a
     licence is taken out within the 14 'grace days'.

RV(R&L)R 2002, reg 26A deals with the 'requirements to furnish particulars', etc referred to in (a). They are the requirements in relation to the surrender or destruction of
a registration document; delivery of a registration document to the Secretary of State;
notification of transfer to a vehicle trader; and notification by a vehicle trader of a sale
or transfer.

Definitions and other general points

Uses

This term is described in Chapter 10. An employer is liable for use by his employee even
though blamelessly unaware of what the employee is doing. It is not good practice to
proceed against the employee in normal circumstances.

Keeps

VERA 1994, s 62 states that a person keeps a vehicle on a public road if he causes it
to be on such a road for any period, no matter how short, when it is not in use there.
If the description 'use' cannot be applied to the vehicle's presence on the road at any
particular time, it is 'kept' on that road by any person who causes it to be there. It is a
question of fact in each case who that person is. It may be a driver who has parked it
there whilst the vehicle still remains under his control. It may be the owner who allows
it to remain in a back street unlicensed, or it may be some person in temporary possession. If an unlicensed vehicle is repaired at a garage and placed outside on the road by
the proprietor when the repairs have been effected, the garage proprietor is keeping the
vehicle on a road without there being a vehicle licence in force.

Public road

A public road is one which is repairable at public expense. Whether or not a road is
repairable at public expense can be established by the local authority who will be able
to say whether it has been 'adopted' in the sense that a highway authority is responsible for its maintenance under the Highways Act 1980 or another enactment. In most
instances, particular reference to authorities is unnecessary as the road concerned is
commonly known to be a public road and justices are entitled to apply their knowledge
to such matters. Inquiries are advisable when use on roads within new housing estates
is alleged, as the roads may still be the responsibility of the builder if development work
is still continuing or has recently finished.

Licence is in force

The prosecutor invariably offers evidence of the lack of a vehicle licence but this does
not strictly need to be proven. Once (a)(i) or (ii) or (b)(i) or (ii) on p 340 is established,
the defendant must prove that it was licensed. A 'licence' in this context includes a trade
licence (p 348). Where a licence is obtained by means of a cheque which is dishonoured
the licence is void from the time of issue on notice from the Secretary of State.

Exempt vehicle

Vehicles which are exempt from the need for a licence are listed in VERA 1994, Sch 2.
  The most significant exemptions relate to light passenger vehicles with low CO_2
emissions, ie a passenger-carrying vehicle with four or more wheels and no more

than eight seats plus the driver's. A light passenger vehicle first registered (in any country) after 28 February 2001 but before 1 April 2017 is an exempt vehicle if its applicable CO_2 emissions figure does not exceed 100 g/km. A light passenger vehicle first registered (in any country) after 28 February 2001 but before 1 April 2017 is an exempt vehicle for the appropriate period if its applicable CO_2 emissions figure exceeds 100 g/km but does not exceed 130 g/km. 'The appropriate period' is the period for which (if the vehicle were not an exempt vehicle) the first vehicle licence for it would (if taken out) have effect. A light passenger vehicle first registered (in any country) on or after 1 April 2017 is an exempt vehicle if it has an applicable CO_2 emissions figure of 0 g/km, provided that its price does not exceed £40,000 and that it is less than six years since its first registration.

Other significant exemptions from the necessity to be licensed are police vehicles, fire engines, ambulances and health service vehicles, veterinary ambulances, invalid carriages not exceeding 508 kg, vehicles for export, vehicles imported by members of foreign armed forces, vehicles which are used only for purposes related to agriculture, horticulture or forestry and are on public roads only in passing between different areas of land occupied by the same person and the distance so travelled on public roads in doing so does not exceed 1.5 km, off-road tractors, agricultural engines, hedge and verge-cutting tractors, mowing machines, electrically propelled vehicles (except a light passenger vehicle first registered after 1 April 2017, whose price exceeds £40,000), snow ploughs and gritters.

A vehicle used by or for persons with particular disabilities may, in certain circumstances, be exempt.

A vehicle constructed *before 1 January 1976* is exempt, except:

(a) a vehicle for which an annual rate is specified in Sch 1, Parts III, V, VI, VII and VIII (buses, recovery vehicles, vehicles used for exceptional loads, haulage vehicles and goods vehicles); or

(b) a special vehicle (other than a digging machine, works truck, mobile crane, mobile pumping vehicle or road roller) where:
  (i) it is designed or adapted for use for the conveyance of goods or burden of any description (or for use with a semi-trailer attached);
  (ii) it is put to a commercial use on a public road; and
  (iii) that use is not a use for the conveyance of goods or burden of any description (or in a case where that use is a use with a semi-trailer attached, the semi-trailer is not used for the conveyance of goods or burden of any description).

As from 1 April 2017, the italicised words above will be replaced by the following text: 'during the 12-month period beginning with 1 April in any year if it was constructed more than 40 years before 1 January in that year'.

A 'recovery vehicle' is a vehicle which is constructed or permanently adapted primarily for any one or more of the purposes of lifting, towing and transporting a disabled vehicle. A vehicle is not a recovery vehicle if at any time it is used for a purpose other than:

(a) the recovery of a disabled vehicle;

(b) the removal of a disabled vehicle from where it became disabled to premises where it is to be repaired or scrapped;

(c) the removal of a disabled vehicle from premises where it was taken for repair, to other premises where it is to be repaired or scrapped;

(d) carrying fuel and other liquids required for its propulsion and tools and other art-icles required for the operation of or in connection with integral or permanently mounted apparatus designed to lift, tow or transport a disabled vehicle;

(e) carrying any person who, immediately before a vehicle became disabled, was the driver of or a passenger in that vehicle, together with his personal effects, from the premises at which the vehicle is to be repaired or scrapped to his original intended destination;

(f) at the request of either a constable or a local authority empowered to remove a vehicle from a road, removing such vehicle to a place nominated by him or it;

(g) proceeding to a place at which the vehicle will be available for use for either of the purposes specified in (a) and (b) and remaining temporarily at such a place so as to be available for such use;

(h) proceeding from:
  (i) a place where the vehicle has remained temporarily so as to be available for such use; or
  (ii) a place where the vehicle has recovered a disabled vehicle; or
  (iii) any premises mentioned in (b) or (c).

Where a recovery vehicle is being used to recover a disabled vehicle or to remove such a vehicle from the place where it has become disabled to a place for repair or for being scrapped, certain uses are permitted which would otherwise take the vehicle out-side the definition of a recovery vehicle:

(a) the carriage of a person who, immediately before the vehicle became disabled, was the driver of or a passenger in the vehicle;

(b) the carriage of any goods which, immediately before the vehicle became disabled, were being carried in the vehicle; or

(c) repairing a disabled vehicle where it became disabled or at a place to which it had been removed for safety reasons after becoming disabled; or

(d) drawing or carrying one trailer if the trailer was, immediately before a vehicle be-came disabled, being drawn or carried by it (VERA 1994, Sch 1 and RV(R&L)R 2002, Sch 7).

A vehicle is not a recovery vehicle at any time when it is used to recover more than two vehicles.

A 'special vehicle' is:

(a) a vehicle which has a revenue weight exceeding 3,500 kg and is a digging machine, mobile crane, mobile pumping vehicle, works truck or road roller;

(b) a vehicle designed or adapted for use for the conveyance of goods or burden of any description, but not so used, or not so used for hire or reward or in connection with a trade or business; or

(c) a vehicle designed or adapted for use with a semi-trailer attached but which is not so used or, if it is used, the semi-trailer is not used for the conveyance of goods or burden of any description.

'Digging machines' are machines designed for use for trench digging, excavating or shovelling which are used on public roads for such a purpose or for getting to or from the place where they will so operate.

'Mobile cranes' are cranes used on public roads only in connection with work in the immediate vicinity of that road or in travelling to or from that place.

A 'works truck' is a goods vehicle (other than a straddle carrier) designed for use on private premises and used on public roads only for carrying goods between such premises and a vehicle on a road in the immediate vicinity, or in passing from one part of any such premises to another or to other private premises in the immediate vicinity, or in connection with roadworks while at or in the immediate vicinity of the site of such works. 'Immediate vicinity' connotes a very considerable degree of closeness. Divisional Courts have held that the use of a works truck more than one and a half miles away from premises, or even six-tenths of a mile away from premises, was not in the immediate vicinity of them.

A nil licence is required in respect of all the above exempt vehicles.

An electrically assisted pedal cycle (see p 432) is also an exempt vehicle.

When used for particular purposes, a vehicle may also be exempt for that purpose only. One case is where the vehicle is used only for the purpose of submitting it by prior arrangement for examination or re-examination for a test certificate (or a vehicle weight test or vehicle identity check) or of taking it from such an examination or re-examination. This exemption also applies to a charge of 'keeping'. Thus, if a driver parks whilst on his way to the testing station simply for the purpose of buying something in a shop, such 'keeping' of the vehicle on a public road is exempt because it is still possible to say that the vehicle was on the road *solely* for the purpose of going to the testing station. Another exemption is where the vehicle is used in the course of an examination; another is where, having been refused a test certificate, a vehicle is taken by prior arrangement for repair, etc.

A foreign vehicle is exempt if brought temporarily into the UK by a non-UK resident. The term 'foreign' includes vehicles from the Isle of Man and the Channel Islands. A visitor from abroad may purchase a vehicle in this country with the intention of exporting it and then use it here without licensing it before taking it out of Great Britain. Northern Ireland licences are treated as licences issued here. RV(R&L)R 2002, Sch 5 exempts vehicles imported by members of visiting forces, members of a headquarters or other organisation, or a dependant of such a person. This exemption lasts for a period of 12 months only.

Documentary evidence of commission of offence of using or keeping

The Road Traffic Offenders Act 1988 (RTOA 1988), s 20 provides that evidence of a fact relevant to proceedings for an offence to which it applies may be given by the production of a record produced by a prescribed device, accompanied by a certificate as to the circumstances in which it was produced, signed by a constable or a person authorised by or on behalf of a chief officer of police. An offence under VERA 1994, s 29 is prescribed as an offence to which RTOA 1988, s 20 applies and in respect of it a prescribed device is one designed or adapted to register:

(a) an image of a vehicle and its registration mark; and
(b) the time at which the image is registered,

and to record that information if, according to data stored by or otherwise accessible by the device, that vehicle is unlicensed. See p 442 for more about s 20.

Duration and issue of licence

Vehicle licences may be issued for a period of 12 months or for six months in the case of (a) vehicles in respect of which the annual rate of duty exceeds £50, and (b) tractive units for which the 'tractive unit: special case' annual rate of duty is £10. In addition, where an application is made for a vehicle licence, the Secretary of State may issue a temporary licence for 14 days or such other period as is prescribed by regulations. Other than temporary licences, licences are valid from the first day of the month on which they are taken out. An application may be made out by any person who must make a declaration and furnish particulars which are prescribed. V(C)A 2001 extended the provisions of VERA 1994 to permit the Secretary of State to require, in addition to the declaration and particulars originally required by VERA 1994, s 7, any other document or evidence prescribed. This is intended to counter the practice of 'ringing' stolen vehicles to assume the identity of legitimate vehicles.

The traditional paper-based licence is no longer issued. Reliance is now placed on DVLA's electronic vehicle register and use of tools like Automatic Number Plate Recognition to ensure that vehicles are correctly licensed and that vehicle excise duty has been paid.

The licence is issued to the vehicle, not the applicant, and it does not authorise that person to use or keep any other vehicle. On the sale of a vehicle an application must be made to DVLA for a rebate of duty; the licence cannot be transferred with the vehicle.

Supplement payable on late renewal

A supplement of £80 is payable where a licence for a vehicle has expired and no vehicle licence is issued for the vehicle before the expiry of a period of one month from the date of expiry of the licence and no 'statutory off-road notification' has been made. That sum may be reduced to £40 if it is paid within 28 days of the registered keeper being notified by the Secretary of State that a supplement may or has become payable. This supplement is payable by the person in whose name the vehicle is registered at the date of expiry of the licence by reason of whose late renewal the supplement became payable.

Annual rates of duty

Vehicle licences cost differing amounts depending upon the nature of the vehicle and its particular use. VERA 1994, Sch 1 sets out the various rates of duty but the actual amounts of the rates are set out in the Finance Acts and are regularly changed.

Immobilisation of unlicensed vehicles

The Vehicle Excise Duty (Immobilisation, Removal and Disposal of Vehicles) Regulations 1997 authorise the immobilisation and removal of stationary unlicensed vehicles in places other than the curtilage of a dwelling in circumstances in which an 'authorised person' (a person, such as a police officer or local authority employee, authorised by the Secretary of State) has reason to believe that an offence is being committed under VERA 1994, s 29(1) (using or keeping unlicensed vehicle: p 341). Such persons are given power to enter any such place for the purpose of enforcement.

The vehicle may be wheelclamped where it stands, or moved to another place and wheelclamped there. This may be done by the authorised person or a person acting under his direction. An immobilisation notice must be fixed to the vehicle indicating that the device has been fitted, warning that no attempt should be made to move the vehicle until it has been released from the device, and providing other information, including the charge for release, removal and disposal. Before an authorised person can release such a vehicle:

(a) the prescribed 'release charge' must be paid; and
(b) (i) evidence must be produced that no offence contrary to s 29(1) was being committed at the time of clamping or removal;
   (ii) a vehicle licence for the vehicle must be in force;
   (iii) the prescribed 'surety payment' (a sum payable where no such licence is in force) must be made; or
   (iv) a declaration must be made to the effect that a licence was in force at the specified time, that a statutory off-road notification (SORN) was in force or that the vehicle was an exempt vehicle which did not require a nil licence.

A voucher will be issued to a person who makes a 'surety payment'. Where a licence cannot be obtained immediately the 'surety payment' permits the vehicle to be used unlicensed for a period of 24 hours. The payment will be refunded if a claim to a refund is made within 15 days and a vehicle licence is then in force.

The Regulations authorise the removal of a vehicle which has been clamped for a period of 24 hours without release; it may be removed to the custody of an authorised 'custodian'. Where this has been done, a removal fee will be charged additionally, together with charges for storage.

The 1997 Regulations create the following offences:

(a) unauthorised removal of or interference with an immobilisation notice: reg 7(1) and (2);
(b) unauthorised removal, or attempted removal, of an immobilisation device: reg 7(3);
(c) false declaration with a view to securing release of vehicle from an immobilisation device: reg 8(2);
(d) false declaration with a view to securing possession of impounded vehicle: reg 13(1);
(e) making declaration in connection with obtaining voucher or refund relating to a surety payment, knowing that it is false or in a material respect misleading: reg 16(1) and (3); and
(f) forgery, fraudulent alteration, fraudulent use, or the fraudulent lending, of a voucher relating to surety payment: reg 16(2) and (3).

The offences under (c), (d), (e) and (f) are indictable (either way) offences.

Offences related to vehicle licences

The most common offences committed contrary to VERA 1994 are:

(a) using or keeping a vehicle without having in force a vehicle licence or trade licence in respect of it: s 29(1) (p 341);
(b) making, in connection with an application for the issue of a vehicle licence, a declaration which to the knowledge of the defendant (D) is false or in a material respect misleading: s 45(1);
(c) supplying or producing false information or documents which D knows are (or is reckless as to their being) false or in a material respect misleading in relation to the design weight of a vehicle (for the purposes of establishing the revenue weight): s 45(3A);
(d) forgery, alteration or use of a certificate (design weight certificate) with intent to deceive, or lending or allowing such a certificate knowing or believing that it will be used for deception, or without reasonable excuse making or possessing a document so resembling such a certificate as to be calculated to deceive: s 45(3B).

An offence under (b), (c) or (d) is an indictable (either way) offence.

Proceedings for offences and admissibility of evidence

VERA 1994, s 47 provides that proceedings for offences of using, etc without a licence, of using a trade licence outside permitted uses (see p 350) and of using a licensed vehicle for a purpose which attracts a higher rate of duty than that paid can only be instituted by the Secretary of State or a constable; such a person is known as the authorised prosecutor. Moreover, no prosecution may be instituted by a constable for these offences without the approval of the Secretary of State; proof of such approval is required at the outset of proceedings in court.

Proceedings instituted by an authorised prosecutor for one of the above offences or for an offence under s 44 or 45 (forgery or false statements, etc) may be instituted within six months from the date on which sufficient evidence came to the prosecutor's knowledge to warrant proceedings, subject to a maximum limit of three years from the commission of the offence. This means that, if the Secretary of State institutes proceedings as the authorised prosecutor, the six-month time limit runs from the time when the required evidence came to his knowledge.

The six-month limit replaces the normal rule requiring that proceedings for summary offences be taken within six months from the commission of the offence. Section 47 allows proof of the date upon which evidence came to the knowledge of the authorised prosecutor, or proof that the Secretary of State has approved the institution of a prosecution by a constable, to be given by means of a certificate signed by or on behalf of the authorised prosecutor or, as the case may be, the Secretary of State. Such a certificate is conclusive evidence of the facts stated, and is deemed to be properly signed unless the contrary is proved.

Section 52 allows certified extracts from DVLA records to be admissible to the same extent as oral evidence. Evidence may therefore be offered of the last date upon which a vehicle was licensed by means of such a certified extract.

Section 46 requires that, where an offence under s 29 above or s 34 (p 350) is alleged to have been committed in relation to a particular vehicle, the person keeping the vehicle must give such information as he may be required by or on behalf of a chief officer of police or the Secretary of State to give as to the identity of any person concerned in the offence. Failure to do so is an offence under s 46(4), unless the keeper proves that he did not know, and could not with reasonable diligence have ascertained, the identity of the person(s) concerned (s 46(6)). A divisional court has held that where there is evidence of using or keeping a vehicle on a road and a notice has been sent in accordance with s 46 to which the keeper does not respond, the justices should draw an adverse inference from the failure to respond and that this, coupled with the other evidence of using or keeping, is sufficient to support a conviction under s 46. The requirement to respond also extends to any person other than a 'keeper', and (in the case of a s 29 offence) to the person alleged to have been using the vehicle. Both types of person commit an offence under s 46(4) if they fail to give such information as to identity as it is in their power to give. A request under s 46 is, in practice, made by serving on a person a form requiring the specified information. A reply to such a request must be made in writing.

TRADE LICENCES

Without modification, the requirement that all vehicles which are registered, or which are used or kept on a road, should be individually licensed under VERA 1994 would cause considerable problems for motor traders, through whose hands many vehicles pass, most of which are retained for a short period of time. The purpose of trade licences is to permit traders temporarily to use vehicles for restricted purposes without the necessity for licensing in the manner described above. Trade licences are inexpensive and in consequence their permitted uses are carefully defined.

Who may apply for a trade licence?

By VERA 1994, s 11, a motor trader may apply to the Secretary of State for a licence to cover all vehicles which are from time to time temporarily in his possession in the course of his business as a motor trader. Any motor trader who is a manufacturer may also be granted a licence for the purpose of allowing him to carry out research and development work in the course of his business as a manufacturer, and for all other vehicles which are from time to time submitted to him by other manufacturers for testing on roads in the course of that business.

The term 'motor trader' means a manufacturer or repairer of, or dealer in, vehicles. A person is treated as a dealer in vehicles if he carries on a business consisting wholly or mainly of collecting and delivering vehicles.

A person whose business is that of modifying vehicles (by fitting accessories or otherwise) or of 'valeting' vehicles (which means the thorough cleaning of a vehicle prior to first registration or in order to prepare it for sale, and includes removing wax and grease from the exterior, engine and interior) is also a 'motor trader'.

A vehicle tester may also apply for a trade licence to cover his use of vehicles submitted to him for testing in the course of his business. A vehicle tester is a person, other than a motor trader, who regularly in the course of his business engages in the testing on roads of vehicles belonging to other persons.

Persons who satisfy the Secretary of State that they intend to commence business as motor traders or vehicle testers may also take out trade licences.

Trade licences may be taken out for a period of 12 months. Shorter-term licences are also available but are seldom used. There is nothing to prevent a motor trader from holding more than one licence to permit use of more than one vehicle at any one time.

Trade plates

The holder of a trade licence is issued with a set of two plates (which are generally referred to as 'trade plates') in respect of each licence held. These plates consist of red letters on a white background and show the registration mark assigned to the holder of the licence. One plate must be displayed to the front of the vehicle, and the other to the rear, in the same way as a registration plate. If the trader satisfies the Secretary of State that the vehicles which he will use in the course of his business will include motor cycles as well as other vehicles, he may be issued with a single additional plate for the motor cycles only. Trade licences for motor cycles only are much cheaper. The plates remain the property of the Secretary of State and must be returned when the trader ceases to be the holder of the licence.

Non-permitted uses of trade licences

VERA 1994, s 12 provides that the holder of a trade licence is not entitled by virtue of *that* licence:

(a) to use more than one vehicle at any one time; or
(b) to use any vehicle for any purpose other than a permitted one (see below); or
(c) to keep any vehicle on a road if it is not being used thereon.

It is an offence, contrary to s 34(1), for the holder of a trade licence to use on a public road a greater number of vehicles than permitted by his licence (or licences), or to use a vehicle for a non-permitted purpose. Section 34(1) also punishes using a trade licence for the purposes of keeping on a public road a vehicle which is not being used at that time.

Restrictions on use of trade licences

RV(R&L)R 2002, Sch 6 provides that the holder of a trade licence must not permit any person to display trade plates on a vehicle other than one which that person is using for the purpose of the licence-holder's business (Sch 6, para 5), or other than when the vehicle is being used for one or more of the prescribed permitted purposes (Sch 6, para 6). However, this does not prevent a person driving a vehicle on a road with the consent of the licence-holder, when the vehicle is being used for the licence-holder's business. Thus, an employee may drive vehicles in the course of his employer's (the licence-holder's) business. Breach of Sch 6, para 5 or 6 is an offence contrary to VERA 1994, s 59(1).

Permitted purposes

The use of vehicles by a motor trader under a trade licence is controlled by RV(R&L)R 2002, regs 38 to 42 and Sch 6, breach of which is an offence under VERA 1994, s 59(1).

Regulation 38 and Sch 6 prescribe the purposes for which the holder of a trade licence may use a vehicle by virtue of a trade licence. Those purposes do not include the carrying of any person on the vehicle or any trailer drawn by it except a person carried in connection with such a purpose. The prescribed purposes are without prejudice to the provisions of VERA 1994, s 11, which specify classes of vehicle for which a trade licence is a licence, in relation respectively to a motor trader who is a manufacturer of vehicles, any other motor trader and a vehicle tester.

Schedule 6, para 10 authorises a motor trader who is the holder of a trade licence to use a vehicle on a public road for purposes which meet each of the following requirements:

(a) business purposes, as specified by para 11;
(b) purposes specified by para 12; and
(c) purposes that do not include the conveyance of goods or burden of any description except specified loads (as defined by para 13).

Business purposes, para 11

A vehicle is used for 'business purposes' if used for purposes connected with the motor trader's business:

(a) as a manufacturer or repairer of or dealer in:
  (i) vehicles; or
  (ii) trailers carried on in conjunction with his business as a motor trader;
(b) of modifying vehicles (whether by the fitting of accessories or otherwise); or
(c) of valeting vehicles.

Paragraph 12 purposes

A vehicle is used for a para 12 purpose if it is used:

(a) for the test or trial of the vehicle, or its accessories or equipment, in the ordinary course of construction, modification or repair, or after completion;

(b) for proceeding to or from a public weighbridge to ascertain its unladen weight, or to or from any place for its registration or inspection by someone acting on the Secretary of State's behalf;

(c) for its test or trial for the benefit of a prospective purchaser, including going either to or from a place of such test or trial at the instance of the prospective purchaser;

(d) for its test or trial for the benefit of a person interested in promoting publicity in regard to the vehicle, including going either to or from a place of such test or trial at the instance of such a person;

(e) for delivering it to a purchaser;

(f) for demonstrating the operation of the vehicle or its accessories or equipment when handed over to a purchaser;

(g) for delivering it between parts of the motor trader's own premises or to the premises of another manufacturer, dealer or repairer or bringing it back from there directly to his own premises;

(h) for proceeding to or from a workshop where a body, or a special type of equipment or accessories, is to be or has been fitted to it or where it is to be or has been painted, valeted or repaired;

(i) for proceeding from the premises of a manufacturer, repairer or dealer to a railway station, airfield or shipping dock for the purpose of transportation, or for proceeding to such premises from a railway station, etc to which it has been transported;

(j) for proceeding to or from any garage, auction room or storage place where vehicles are usually stored or offered for sale and at which the vehicle is to be or has been stored or offered for sale as the case may be;

(k) for proceeding to or from a place of testing; or

(l) for proceeding to a place to be broken up or otherwise dismantled.

The use of a vehicle with a trailer is regarded as the use of a single vehicle under the licence.

Specified loads

Schedule 6, para 13 defines the 'specified loads' referred to in para 10 above as follows:

(a) a load which is carried by a vehicle being used for the purpose of testing or demonstrating the vehicle, or its accessories or equipment, within the terms of (b), (d), (e) or (g), above, and is carried solely for that purpose, and which is returned to the place of loading without having been removed from the vehicle (except in the case of an accident or for demonstrating its operation to a purchaser when handed over to him, or when the load consists of water, fertiliser or refuse);

(b) in the case of a vehicle which is being delivered or collected and is being used for a relevant purpose (as described in (f) to (k) above), a load consisting of another vehicle used or to be used for travel to or from the place of delivery or collection;

(c) any load built in as a permanent part of the vehicle or permanently attached to it;

(d) in the case of a vehicle which is being used for a purpose falling within (h), (i) or (j) above, a load which consists of a trailer or of parts, accessories or equipment designed to be fitted to the vehicle and of tools for fitting them.

Comment on Sch 6, paras 10–13

The effect of these provisions is simply to prohibit the carriage of goods on vehicles being used under a trade licence in all but the narrowest of circumstances. It may be that a 'test and trial' will necessarily involve the use of a vehicle with a load. If so, the provisions limit the carriage of the load to the duration of that trial. In most circumstances in which a goods vehicle is observed being used under a trade licence while carrying a load, an offence will be committed. Some vehicles have what might be described as built-in loads, such as essential engineering equipment, and vehicles which are on their way to have accessories, etc fitted may carry these accessories, etc with them for that purpose. None of these loads is being carried for a commercial purpose connected with the use of the vehicle in the accepted sense of the word 'commercial'.

Research and vehicle testing purposes

RV(R&L)R 2002, Sch 6, paras 14 and 15 deal respectively with manufacturers' research vehicles and use by vehicle testers. The first restricts use to manufacturers for research and development purposes and the second restricts testing to vehicles and trailers drawn thereby, or any accessory or equipment on the vehicle or trailer, in the course of a business as a vehicle tester.

No other permitted purposes

The above purposes are the only permitted purposes for which vehicles may be used under a trade licence, and even then only in the course of the business of the holder. If an employee used the trade plates and licence to remove his own private car to a paint shop for spraying, not in the course of his employer's business, the use would be unlawful. If the holder of the licence used under trade plates a vehicle which was in his possession in the course of his business to visit a cinema in the evening, that use of the motor vehicle would be unlawful as it would not be in the course of his business as a motor trader.

Other trade plate offences

Breach of the regulations relating to loads or passengers is also an offence under VERA 1994, s 34(1).

RV(R&L)R 2002, Sch 6, para 3 provides that the holder of a licence must not, or must not permit any person to, exhibit on any vehicle any trade plate which has been altered, defaced, mutilated, or added to, upon which the figures or particulars have become illegible, or upon which the colour has been altered by fading or otherwise. Breach of such prohibition is an offence contrary to VERA 1994, s 59(1).

By VERA 1994, s 44(1) and (2), forgery, fraudulent alteration or use, or fraudulent lending or allowing to be used by any other person, of a trade plate is an indictable (either way) offence. So is the false declaration under s 45(1) (p 347), which also applies in respect of an application for a trade licence.

DRIVING LICENCES, PENALTY POINTS AND DISQUALIFICATION

Driving licences

The licensing of drivers of motor vehicles is dealt with by RTA 1988, Part III (ss 87 to 109C) and the Motor Vehicles (Driving Licences) Regulations 1999 (MV(DL)R 1999).

For driving licence purposes, motor vehicles are divided by MV(DL)R 1999 into various categories and sub-categories and it is essential that licences are checked, not only to establish the identity of the driver, but also to ascertain that he is authorised to drive the particular vehicle in which he is found. Amendments made to MV(DL)R 1999 with effect from 19 January 2013 provide for the introduction of new categories and sub-categories of vehicles (principally mopeds and motor cycles). The categories and sub-categories of vehicles for licensing purposes is set out in MV(DL)R 1999, Sch 2 as follows:

Category or sub-category	*Class of vehicle included*	*Additional categories and sub-categories covered*
	Part 1	
	A licence authorising the driving of motor vehicles of a class included in a category or sub-category shown in Part 1 may be granted to a person who is entitled thereto by virtue of:	
	(a) holding or having held a full licence, full Northern Ireland licence, full British external licence, full British Forces licence, exchangeable licence (p 379) or Community licence (p 377) authorising the driving of vehicles of that class, or	
	(b) having passed a test for a licence authorising the driving of motor vehicles of that class or a Northern Ireland or Gibraltar test corresponding to such a test.	
AM	Mopeds: two- or three-wheel vehicles with a maximum design speed (MDS) not exceeding 45 km/h (excluding those with MDS less than 25 km/h) and light quadricycles: quadricycles with unladen mass not exceeding 350 kg (excluding batteries in case of electric vehicles), MDS not exceeding 45 km/h, and engine capacity not exceeding 50 cc (spark ignition) or maximum net power output not exceeding 4 kw (other internal combustion engine) or maximum continuous rated power not exceeding 4 kw (electric motor)	Q

(continued)

Category or sub-category	Class of vehicle included	Additional categories and sub-categories covered
A	Motor bicycles and motor tricycles: motor vehicles with three symmetrically arranged wheels with MDS exceeding 45 km/h and engine capacity exceeding 50 cc (if internal combustion engine)	Q, AM, A1, A2 and K
A1	A sub-category of A comprising A1 motor cycles: motor bicycles with engine capacity not exceeding 125 cc, power not exceeding 11 kw and power to weight ratio (PWR) not exceeding 0.1 kw/kg and A1 motor tricycles: motor tricycles with power not exceeding 15 kw	Q and AM
A2	A sub-category of A comprising A2 motor cycles: motor bicycles of power not exceeding 35 kw, PWR not exceeding 0.2 kw/kg and not being derived from a vehicle of more than double its power	Q, AM and A1
A3	A sub-category of A comprising (a) A3 motor cycles: motor bicycles (i) of power exceeding 35 kw or PWR exceeding 0.2 kw/kg, or (ii) of power not exceeding 35 kw with PWR not exceeding 0.2 kw/kg and derived from a vehicle of more than double the particular cycle's power; and (b) A3 motor tricycles: motor tricycles with power exceeding 15 kw	Q, AM, A1, A2 and K
B	Motor vehicles, other than vehicles included in category Q, AM, A, F, or K, having maximum authorised mass (MAM) not exceeding 3.5 tonnes and designed and constructed for not more than 8 passengers in addition to the driver, including: (a) combination of any such vehicle and trailer where trailer has MAM not exceeding 750 kg, and (b) combination of any such vehicle and trailer where MAM of combination does not exceed 3.5 tonnes	Q, AM, F, and K
B + E	Combinations of motor vehicle (being tractor vehicle in category B) and trailer or semi-trailer where (a) combination does not fall within category B or B96; and (b) MAM of trailer or semi-trailer does not exceed 3.5 tonnes	None
C	Motor vehicles having MAM exceeding 3.5 tonnes, other than vehicle falling within category D, F, G, or H, designed and constructed for the carriage of no more than 8 passengers in addition to the driver, and including such vehicle drawing trailer having MAM not exceeding 750 kg	None

(continued)

Category or sub-category	Class of vehicle included	Additional categories and sub-categories covered
C1	A sub-category of C comprising motor vehicles having MAM exceeding 3.5 tonnes but not exceeding 7.5 tonnes, designed and constructed for the carriage of no more than 8 passengers in addition to the driver, and including such vehicle drawing trailer having MAM not exceeding 750 kg	None
D	Motor vehicles designed and constructed for the carriage of more than eight passengers in addition to the driver, including such vehicle drawing trailer having MAM not exceeding 750 kg	None
D1	A sub-category of D comprising motor vehicle designed and constructed for the carriage of not more than 16 passengers not including the driver with maximum length not exceeding 8m, and including such vehicle drawing a trailer with MAM not exceeding 750 kg	None
C + E	Combination of motor vehicle and trailer where the tractor vehicle is in category C but the combination does not fall within that category	B + E
C1 + E	A sub-category of C + E comprising combinations of motor vehicle in category B, or in sub-category C1, and trailer or semi-trailer where combination's MAM is no more than 12 tonnes and: (a) if tractor vehicle is in category B, MAM of trailer or semi-trailer exceeds 3.5 tonnes, or (b) if tractor vehicle is in sub-category C1, MAM of trailer or semi-trailer exceeds 750 kg	B + E
D + E	Combination of motor vehicle and trailer where tractor vehicle is in category D but the combination does not fall into that category	B + E
D1 + E	A sub-category of D + E comprising any combination of motor vehicle and trailer where: (a) tractor vehicle is in sub-category D1, and (b) MAM of trailer exceeds 750 kg but not the unladen weight of the tractor vehicle	B + E
F	Agricultural or forestry tractors, including any such vehicle drawing trailer but excluding any motor vehicle included in category H	K
G	Road rollers	None
H	Track-laying vehicles steered by their tracks	None

(continued)

Category or sub-category	Class of vehicle included	Additional categories and sub-categories covered
K	Mowing machines, not falling within category A, or vehicle controlled by pedestrian	None

Part 2

A licence authorising the driving of motor vehicles of a class included in any category or sub-category shown in Part 2 may not be granted to a person unless, at a time before 1 January 1997:

(a) *in the case of a person applying for a full licence, (i) he held a full licence authorising the driving of motor vehicles of that class or a class which by virtue of MV(DL)R 1999 corresponds to a class included in that category or sub-category, or (ii) he passed a test which at the time it was passed authorised the driving of motor vehicles of such a class or a Northern Ireland test corresponding to such a test;*

(b) *in the case of a person applying for a provisional licence, he held a provisional licence authorising the driving of vehicles of that class or a class which by virtue of MV(DL)R 1999 corresponds to a class included in that category or sub-category*

Category or sub-category	Class of vehicle included	Additional categories and sub-categories covered
C1 + E (8.25 tonnes)	A sub-category of category C + E comprising combinations of motor vehicle and trailer in sub-category C1 + E where MAM of trailer exceeds 750 kg and may exceed unladen weight of tractor vehicle, and MAM of combination does not exceed 8.25 tonnes	None
D1 (not hire or reward)	A sub-category of category D comprising motor vehicles in sub-category D1 driven otherwise than for hire or reward	None
D1 + E (not hire or reward)	A sub-category of D + E comprising motor vehicles in sub-category D1 + E where: (a) motor vehicle driven otherwise than for hire or reward, and (b) MAM of trailer exceeds 750kg and may exceed unladen weight of tractor vehicle	None
L	Vehicle propelled by electrical power	None

Part 3

Category or sub-category	Class of vehicle included	Additional categories and sub-categories covered
B1 (invalid carriage)	A sub-category of category B comprising motor vehicles which are invalid carriages	None

(continued)

Category or sub-category	Class of vehicle included	Additional categories and sub-categories covered
	Part 4	
	A licence authorising the driving of motor vehicles of a class shown in column 2 of Part 4 opposite a former category or former sub-category (as the case may be) shown in column 1 may not be granted to a person unless, before 19 January 2013, that person held a licence authorising the driving of motor vehicles of that class or passed a test for a licence authorising the driving of motor vehicles of that class	
Former sub-category B1 (vehicle with three or four wheels and unladen weight not exceeding 550 kg)	Motor vehicles having four wheels and unladen weight not exceeding 550 kg, except light quadricycles	None
Former category B + E (as column 2)	Combination of motor vehicle and trailer where tractor vehicle is in category B and MAM of trailer exceeds 3.5 tonnes	None
Former sub-category D1 (as column 2)	Motor vehicles having more than 8 but not more than 16 seats in addition to driver's seat with maximum length exceeding 8m and including any such vehicle drawing trailer with MAM not exceeding 750 kg	None
Former sub-category D1 + E (as column 2)	Combination of motor vehicle and trailer where: (a) tractor vehicle is in former sub-category D1, (b) MAM of trailer exceeds 750 kg but not unladen weight of tractor vehicle, (c) MAM of combination does not exceed 12 tonnes, and (d) trailer is not used for carriage of passengers	None

(continued)

Category or sub-category	Class of vehicle included	Additional categories and sub-categories covered
Former category P (vehicles having fewer than four wheels, MDS not exceeding 50 km/h and, if internal combustion engine, not exceeding 50 cc)	Motor vehicle with fewer than four wheels, MDS exceeding 45 km/h but not exceeding 50 km/h and, if internal combustion engine, maximum 50 cc	None

Part 5

Category or sub-category	Class of vehicle included	Additional categories and sub-categories covered
Q These would be mopeds but for maximum speed limit of 25 km/h	Category Q vehicles: motor vehicle with less than four wheels which: (a) if propelled by internal combustion engine, has a cylinder capacity not exceeding 50 cc and, if not equipped with pedals capable of propelling vehicle, MDS not exceeding 25 km/h; and (b) if not propelled by internal combustion engine, has MDS not exceeding 25 km/h A licence authorising the driving of category Q vehicles may not be granted to a person unless he is entitled to be granted a full licence authorising the driving of motor vehicles of a class included in category AM, A, or B, or category P vehicles.	None

Part 6

Category or sub-category	Class of vehicle included	Additional categories and sub-categories covered
B96	Combinations of motor vehicle and trailer where: (a) tractor vehicle is in category B, (b) MAM of trailer exceeds 750 kg, (c) MAM of combination exceeds 3.5 tonnes but not 4.25 tonnes A B96 licence is only granted if person holds or has held a Community licence to drive B96 vehicle	None

So far as vehicles of category B1 (invalid carriages) are concerned, MV(DL)R 1999, reg 5 provides that no licence may be issued for that sub-category to a person who did not hold one for a B1 vehicle or a corresponding class before 12 November 1999.

The term 'maximum authorised mass' has the same meaning:

(a) in relation to goods vehicles as 'permissible maximum weight' (defined on p 375); and

(b) in relation to any other vehicle or trailer as 'maximum gross weight' in the Road Vehicles (Construction and Use) Regulations 1986, reg 3(2), namely the weight which the vehicle is designed or adapted not to exceed when on a road.

MV(DL)R 1999 parallel categories of vehicle with the previous categories under earlier regulations. The 1999 Regulations provide that licences (whether full or provisional) granted before 1 January 1997 or 19 January 2013, as the case may be, are valid in respect of the new categories of vehicle, as set out in the table to the regulations.

Where a licence (whether full or provisional) granted before 19 January 2013 authorises the driving of:

(a) standard motor bicycles only, or
(b) standard motor bicycles and side-car combinations only,

any reference in that licence to motor vehicles in category A (save for those in sub-category A1) is a reference:

(i) where the standard access period (two years commencing on the day when the test to drive a standard motor bicycle was passed excluding any period of disqualification or any period when the licence was not in force) has not expired, to motor vehicles in sub-category A2; and

(ii) where that period has expired, to motor vehicles in category A.

Entitlement on passing a test

MV(DL)R 1999, reg 43 provides that, where a person passes a test prescribed in respect of any category for a licence which authorises the driving of motor vehicles included in that category or in a sub-category of that category, the Secretary of State must grant him a licence authorising him to drive vehicles of all classes included in that category or sub-category unless his licence is restricted to such vehicles fitted with automatic transmission, or vehicles specially adapted for the disabled, in which cases his entitlement will be so restricted. Such holders are also authorised to drive those vehicles shown in column 3 above as additional categories or sub-categories with the same limitations as set out above, should the test have been taken on those types of vehicle. However, where the additional category is Q, AM, F or K the limitation in respect of 'automatics' will not apply.

In relation to a person passing the test of competence to drive a vehicle in category B on or after 1 February 2001, a licence to drive a vehicle in category B does not confer entitlement to drive vehicles in category Q or category AM unless that licence-holder *either* held at the date of that test a valid certificate of successful completion of an approved training course for motor cyclists, *or* holds a valid certificate of successful completion of an approved course for motor cyclists furnished after that date.

Where a person has passed the test of competence to drive a vehicle in category AM in a three-wheeled moped or light quadricycle, reg 44A provides for the grant of a licence restricted to three- or four-wheeled vehicles in category AM.

When licence-holder reaches the prescribed age

Full driving licences issued to those who have passed the appropriate test are granted until the holder reaches 70. After that, the licence can be renewed for three-year periods. Those licences which authorise the holder to drive prescribed goods or passenger-carrying vehicles are renewable on the holder's 45th birthday, or after five years, whichever is the longer, or where the licence is issued to a person between 45 and 65 for the period ending on his 66th birthday or after five years, whichever is the shorter. A licence granted after the age of 65 will remain in force for one year only.

Other licences

RTA 1988, s 88 provides that it is lawful for a person to drive provided that the driver has held a driving licence, a Community licence (p 377), a Northern Irish licence, a British external licence or British forces licence, or an exchangeable licence (p 379), for the class of vehicle in question or a corresponding licence, and a 'qualifying application' for a licence under Part III of the Act which includes that time has been received. This provision does not apply where the application received was made as a result of, or in anticipation of, the expiry of a disqualification on or after 26 April 2013 which is relevant to the licence applied for, was made by a 'high-risk offender' (p 374), and where the Secretary of State has notified the applicant that he must be medically assessed. The effect is that a high-risk driver will not be able to obtain a new licence before it is granted following a successful medical assessment.

Grant of licences

RTA 1988, s 97(1) requires the Secretary of State to issue a licence to a person who: (a) meets the relevant residence requirement, (b) applies in the prescribed manner, (c) pays the appropriate fee, (d) supplies necessary evidence to support his application, and (e) is not disqualified or otherwise barred from obtaining the licence. The Secretary of State may revoke the licence of someone if it appears that he is not lawfully resident in the UK.

By s 97A, a person meets the relevant residence requirements if, on the date the application is made:

(a) in the case of an application that is made by the holder of a Community licence (p 377), the applicant is lawfully resident in the UK and:
   (i) is also normally resident in the UK, or
   (ii) has been attending a course of study in the UK during the period of six months ending on that date;
(b) in the case of an application that is made by the holder of an exchangeable licence (p 379), the applicant is normally and lawfully resident in Great Britain but has not been so resident for more than the prescribed period;
(c) in the case of an application for a provisional licence, the applicant is lawfully resident in Great Britain and the Secretary of State is satisfied that the applicant will remain so for not less than 185 days; and
(d) in any other case, the applicant is normally and lawfully resident in Great Britain.

For the purposes of s 97A, a person is not lawfully resident in Great Britain or the UK if the person requires leave to enter or remain in the UK but does not have it.

Section 98 requires the licence to be in the form of a photocard of a description specified by the Secretary of State, or in such other form as he may specify. Photocard licences were introduced in 1998, but existing licences remain in force until they expire or the holder's details expire. Where a photocard licence is issued an applicant must supply the Secretary of State with a photograph which is a current likeness of him and with a specimen signature which can be electronically recorded and reproduced on the licence. If any other form of licence is granted, the holder must forthwith sign the licence in ink. Defaced or lost licences may be replaced by the Secretary of State. If a lost licence is subsequently found it must be returned to the authority. By s 99, where a photocard licence remains in force after the end of the administrative validity period, its holder must nevertheless surrender the licence to the Secretary of State not later than the end of that period. The period will be five years for a licence to drive any prescribed class of goods vehicles or passenger-carrying vehicle, except that it is ten years for any licence issued before 19 January 2013 and in some other cases. If a licence expires before the end of the standard five- or ten-year period (for instance in the case of licences issued for shorter periods on medical grounds), its administrative validity period will end on the expiry date of the licence. Subject to exceptions, the surrender of a photocard will be followed by the grant of a new one.

By s 89(1), a person applying for the first time for a full driving licence authorising the driving of a motor vehicle must:

(a) have passed a UK driving test within the previous two years;
(b) hold (or have held) a Community licence; or
(c) hold an exchangeable licence,

authorising the driving of vehicles of that or a corresponding class.

Disqualification of persons under age

A person may be disqualified from driving a particular class of vehicle by reason of age. A person is disqualified from holding or obtaining a licence to drive a motor vehicle of a particular class if he is under the age applicable to that class of vehicle. The minimum ages at which persons may drive particular classes of vehicles are listed by RTA 1988, s 101, which provides that a person below the minimum age to drive a particular class of vehicle is disqualified from holding a licence to drive that class of vehicle. The requirements of s 101 are amplified by MV(DL)R 1999, reg 9. The minimum ages are as follows:

(a) *16 years*:
  (i) invalid carriage,
  (ii) vehicle in category AM (moped and light quadricycle) or category Q,
  (iii) agricultural or forestry tractor, provided it is a wheeled vehicle not exceeding 2.45 m in width and driven without a trailer (other than a two-wheeled or close-coupled four-wheeled trailer not exceeding 2.45 m in width); the driver must have passed a test for category F or be proceeding to or from such a test, or
  (iv) a small vehicle (as defined in (b)(ii) below) driven without a trailer attached where the driver of the vehicle is a person:
    (*a*) who has received an award of the higher rate component of the disability living allowance, which was in force immediately before his 16th birthday, provided he has made a claim for a personal independence payment under the Welfare Reform Act 2012, Pt 4; or
    (*b*) who is in receipt of such a personal independence payment which includes the mobility component at the enhanced rate;
(b) *17 years*:
  (i) A1 motor cycle or A1 motor tricycle,
  (ii) small vehicle, which means a motor vehicle (other than an invalid carriage, or a vehicle in category AM or category Q, or a motor tricycle) which:
    (*a*) is not constructed or adapted to carry more than nine persons inclusive of the driver, and

(*b*) has a maximum gross weight not exceeding 3.5 tonnes, and includes a combination of such a vehicle and a trailer, but does not include a motor tricycle or light quadricycle,

(iii) incomplete large vehicle not exceeding 3.5 tonnes, or

(iv) road roller which is not steam propelled, whose unladen weight does not exceed 11.69 tonnes, which has no pneumatic, soft or elastic tyres, and which is not constructed or adapted to carry a load other than equipment of the vehicle;

(c) *18 years*:

(i) medium-sized goods vehicle, which means a motor vehicle constructed or adapted to carry or haul goods and not adapted to carry more than nine persons inclusive of the driver, with a permissible maximum weight exceeding 3.5 tonnes but not 7.5 tonnes, and includes a combination of such a vehicle and a trailer where the relevant maximum weight of the trailer does not exceed 750 kg. However, the age of 21 applies if such a vehicle is drawing a trailer and the maximum authorised mass of the combination exceeds 7.25 tonnes,

(ii) motor-vehicle-and-trailer combination of sub-category C1 + E the maximum authorised mass of which does not exceed 7.5 tonnes,

(iii) motor vehicle of a class included in category C or C + E where that person:

(*a*) has an initial qualification (Certificate of Professional Competence (CPC) (see Appendix 1 on the companion website)) to drive a vehicle of that class;

(*b*) has been issued by the Secretary of State with a document authorising him to drive the relevant vehicle for a specified period of up to 12 months while undertaking a vocational training course; or

(*c*) is using the vehicle in the course of a lesson leading to the grant of a licence or a CPC test;

(iv) motor vehicle of a class included in category C or C + E where being used by the fire service or for maintaining public order or is undergoing road tests for repair or maintenance purposes,

(v) motor-vehicle-and-trailer combination which is in sub-category C1 + E and the maximum authorised mass of the combination does not exceed 12 tonnes,

(vi) motor vehicle of a class included in category D or D + E, other than sub-category D1 of D1 + E, where the person driving the vehicle:

(*a*) has an initial qualification authorising him to drive motor vehicles of that class and is either (*i*) engaged in the carriage of passengers on a regular service over a route which does not exceed 50 km, or (*ii*) is not engaged in the carriage of passengers;

(*b*) is using the vehicle in the course of a driving lesson or driving test for the purpose of obtaining a driving licence or CPC; or

(*c*) has been issued by the Secretary of State with a document authorising him to drive the relevant vehicle for a specified period of up to 12 months while undertaking a vocational training course;

(vii) motor vehicle of a class included in sub-category D1 (more than eight but not more than 16 seats in addition to driver's seat) or D1 + E, where:

(*a*) the person driving the vehicle has an initial qualification authorising him to drive vehicles of that type, in which case (*i*) or (*ii*) of (*a*) in (vi) do not apply, or

(*b*) one of (*b*) or (*c*) in (vi) applies; or

(viii) incomplete large vehicle exceeding 3.5 tonnes but not exceeding 7.5 tonnes;

(d) *19 years:* A2 motorcycle;

(e) *20 years*: motor vehicle of a class included in category D or D + E, other than sub-category D1 or D1 + E, where the driver has an initial qualification authorising him to drive motor vehicles of that class and is engaged in the carriage of passengers otherwise than on a regular service restricted to 50 km;

(f) *21 years*:

    (i) motor vehicle of a class included in category D or D + E, other than sub-category D1 or D1 + E, where the vehicle is being used by the fire service or for maintaining public order or is undergoing road tests for repair and maintenance purposes, and

    (ii) all other motor vehicles not referred to in (a) to (g);

(g) *24 years*:

    (i) A3 motorcycle or A3 motor tricycle,

    (ii) subject to (c)(vi) and (e), a motor vehicle of a class included in category D or D + E, other than sub-category D1 or D1 + E, save where the vehicle is being used by the fire service or for maintaining public order or is undergoing road tests for repair and maintenance purposes, or in respect of a person under the age of 24 who was entitled to a licence to drive a vehicle of that class before 19 January 2013, in which case the minimum age is 21.

The regulations permit members of the armed services, aged 17 or over, to drive A2 or A3 motorcycles, A3 motor tricycles and medium and large goods vehicles which are owned by the Secretary of State for Defence and are being used subject to his orders. Clearly this exemption is not a general one and the nature of the use of the vehicle at the time must be taken into account.

A1 motorcycles or A1 motor tricycles, A2 motorcycles, and A3 motorcycles can be ridden at 16, 18, and 20 respectively in the case of a person holding a Community licence authorising the driving of vehicles of that particular sub-category. An A3 motorcycle or A3 motor tricycle can be driven by a person at 21 where, for two or more years, he has held a full licence for A2 motorcycles. An A2 motorcycle or A3 motorcycle can be driven at 17 by someone who passed a test before 19 January 2013 in respect of a motorcycle (other than one with an engine with maximum net power output of 11kw or less) and the standard access period (p 359) has elapsed. An A3 motorcycle can be driven by a person who passed an appropriate driving test after 18 January 2013 on a vehicle of a class in category B or sub-category A2 or A3, and was entitled, before 19 January 2013, to a licence to drive a motor bicycle with an engine having a maximum net power output exceeding 25kw or a power to weight ratio exceeding 0.16kw per kg. An A3 motor tricycle can be driven at 17 by someone who was, before 19 January 2013, entitled to drive vehicles having three or four wheels and an unladen weight not exceeding 550kg.

Although these provisions appear to be complex at first sight, the vehicles with which police officers are generally concerned are motor cycles, private saloon cars, goods vehicles, and public service vehicles and the age limits which generally apply are as follows: mopeds may be ridden at 16, motor cycles (unless they are A2 or A3 motorcycles) and private cars at 17, vehicles between 3.5 tonnes and 7.5 tonnes at 18, and those in excess of 7.5 tonnes at 21 (18 in the circumstances described above in relation to initial qualifications) in most circumstances. Small passenger vehicles, which are generally private cars (as the seating of such a vehicle must not exceed nine) may be driven at 17. Passenger vehicles with more than nine seats, with the exceptions outlined, may only be driven by a person of 21; most vehicles of the 'Transit' type fall within this category.

Grant of licences

A person may apply for a driving licence at any time within two months of the date from which the licence will take effect. Where the application is for a large goods or passenger-carrying vehicle driver's licence, it must be made within three months of such date.

Full licences

Where the application is for a full licence, an applicant must satisfy the Secretary of State that he has passed a test at the time of his application. In support of his application he must produce a valid test certificate.

MV(DL)R 1999, Part III deals with the constituent parts of driving tests, and the certificates to be issued to those who take tests. It requires that a test for a licence to drive a category B vehicle (eg the typical private motor car) must be in accordance with reg 40(2A) or (2B).

Regulation 40(2A) provides that a test thereunder must consist of two parts: (a) the standard test of driving theory and the standard test of hazard perception; and (b) the practical test of driving skills and behaviour.

Regulation 40(2B) provides that a test thereunder must consist of three parts: (1) the safe road use test; (2) the abridged standard test of driving theory and the standard test of hazard perception; and (3) the practical test.

In either type of test the theory part must be passed before the practical part is taken.

Where a person has been awarded the Safe Road User Award before 1 May 2010, the test for a category B licence is conducted in two parts, parts (2) and (3) as mentioned above.

As to driving tests for licences for other types of vehicle, see p 369 (motor bicycles), and Appendix 1 (buses and lorries) on the companion website.

MV(DL)R 1999 include a requirement that, where a person produces to an examiner an appropriate licence which does not include a photograph, he must satisfy the person conducting the test as to his identity by producing a document to establish his identity as prescribed by Sch 6 (all of which have a photograph) or a document of a like nature. However, if the person's identity is clearly apparent from the facts known to, or other evidence in the possession of, the person conducting the test, this will be satisfactory.

Provisional driving licences

Full licences to drive a class of vehicle may only be granted to those who have passed the relevant driving test to drive that class of vehicle. Provisional licences are issued to those who wish to learn to drive motor vehicles and are issued subject to conditions set out in MV(DL)R 1999, reg 16. These conditions are concerned with the need for supervision, distinguishing marks, the drawing of trailers, and the carriage of passengers. However, these conditions do not apply where a provisional licence-holder has passed a test by virtue of which he is entitled to be granted a licence authorising him to drive a vehicle of the class then being driven.

Supervision   With the exceptions listed below, a provisional licence-holder must not drive or ride a motor vehicle otherwise than under the supervision of a qualified driver who is present with him in or on the vehicle (reg 16).

A person is a qualified driver if he:

(a) is 21 or over;
(b) holds a relevant licence (see below);

(c) has the relevant driving experience (see below); and

(d) in the case of a disabled driver, is supervising a provisional licence-holder who is driving a vehicle of a class included in categories B, C, D, C + E or D + E and would in an emergency be able to take control of the steering and braking functions of the vehicle in which he is a passenger.

However, for the purposes of supervising the holder of a provisional licence driving a vehicle of a class included in sub-category C1, C1 + E, D1 or D1 + E ('the learner vehicle') which the holder is authorised to drive by that licence, a person is not a qualified driver unless that person has, in addition to meeting the above requirements, passed a test in which the vehicle used in the practical test fell within the same sub-category as that of the learner vehicle.

Subject to provisions below relating to a disabled driver, a 'relevant licence' means a *full licence authorising the driving of vehicles of the same class as the vehicle being driven by the provisional licence-holder.* However, subject to the provisions relating to a disabled driver, where a person holds a full licence authorising the driving of vehicles of the same class as that being driven by the provisional licence-holder, which class is included in a category or sub-category specified in column 1 of the table below, and that person has held the licence for less than three years, 'relevant licence' has a special meaning. It means a full licence authorising:

(a) where that class of vehicle is included within any sub-category specified in column 1 of the table below, the driving of vehicles in the sub-category specified in column 2 which is opposite that sub-category; or

(b) where (a) above does not apply, the driving of vehicles in the category specified in column 2 of that table which is opposite the category specified in column 1 that includes the class of vehicle being driven by the provisional licence-holder.

For the above purposes, the term 'full licence' includes a Northern Ireland licence and a Community licence.

The table referred to above is as follows:

Column (1)	Column (2)
Categories and sub-categories which include the vehicle being driven by the provisional licence-holder	Categories and sub-categories authorised by the relevant licence
C	D
C1	D1
C + E	D + E
C1 + E	D1 + E
D	C
D1	C1
D + E	C + E
D1 + E	C1 + E

In the case of a (supervising) disabled driver who holds a licence authorising the driving of vehicles in category B, a relevant licence must authorise the driving of vehicles other than a quadricycle or vehicles in sub-category B1 (invalid carriages). A 'disabled driver' is a person who holds a relevant licence which is limited by virtue of a declaration made with his application for the licence or a notice under RTA 1988, s 92(5)(b) to vehicles of a particular class.

Where the above italicised definition of 'relevant licence' only applies, a person has '*relevant driving experience*' if he has held the relevant licence for a minimum period of three years. Where the definitions in (a) and (b) above apply, a person has *relevant driving experience* if he has held the relevant licence authorising the driving of vehicles:

(a) of the same class as the vehicle being driven by the provisional licence-holder for a minimum period of one year; and

(b) in the category or sub-category specified in column 2 of the table above for a minimum period of three years.

For the purpose of meeting the requirements in this paragraph the minimum period of time for holding a full licence may be met either by holding that licence continuously for that period or for periods amounting in aggregate to not less than that period.

A period before 1 May 2010 during which a person ('the supervising driver') has held a licence authorising the driving of vehicles included in sub-category C1, C1+E, D1 or D1+E may only be taken into account in assessing whether the supervising driver has the relevant driving experience to supervise the holder of a provisional licence driving such a vehicle if the supervising driver has passed a test before 1 May 2010 in which the vehicle used for the practical test fell within one of those sub-categories.

The conditions requiring that a qualified driver is over 21 and that he has relevant driving experience do not apply to a member of the armed forces of the Crown acting in the course of his duties. In addition, reg 8 provides that such a person may drive a dual-purpose vehicle (p 412) when it is being used to carry passengers for naval, military or air force purposes:

(a) where it does not exceed 3.5 tonnes, with a category B (not former sub-category B1 or sub-category B1) licence;

(b) where it exceeds 3.5 tonnes but does not exceed 7.5 tonnes, a C1 licence; and

(c) in any other case, a C licence (other than C1).

The supervisor's duty is to make up for any deficiencies in the skill of the learner; as part of his duty he must participate in the driving to such extent as could reasonably be expected to prevent danger to other persons or property. Because he has a right of control over the learner driver, a supervisor can be convicted as an accomplice to a driving offence committed by the learner driver if he deliberately fails to prevent it when he could reasonably have done so.

A provisional licence-holder is not required to be supervised while undergoing a test. Although an examiner will be with him, the examiner is there for the purpose of assessing his competence, not for the purpose of supervision (and therefore not for the purpose of interference when a lack of skill is evident). The examiner is not, therefore, similarly exposed to charges of aiding and abetting offences by the learner.

A provisional licence-holder is not required to be supervised if he:

(a) is driving a motor vehicle constructed to carry only one person which is not adapted to carry more than one person and which is a vehicle in sub-category B1 (invalid carriages), a motor tricycle, a motor vehicle having four wheels and an unladen weight not exceeding 550 kg, or a motor vehicle of a class included in category F, G, H or K;

(b) is driving a motor vehicle of a class included in former sub-category B1 which is adapted to carry only one person, and the licence-holder has at any time between 1 August 2002 and 1 March 2003 had the use of an NHS invalid carriage that was issued to him by reason of his having a relevant disability. Former sub-category B1 vehicles may have three or four wheels and an unladen weight not exceeding 550 kg;

(c) is riding a moped, or motor bicycle with or without a sidecar, a former category P vehicle, or a category Q vehicle; or

(d) is driving a motor vehicle, other than a vehicle of a class in category C, C + E, D or D + E, on a road in an exempted island (a term which covers small islands like Lundy and the Isles of Scilly other than St Mary's).

It follows, for example, that a small three- or four-wheeler with two seats requires a supervisor in order to be driven by a provisional licence-holder, whereas if it is constructed with only one seat it does not (unless it has since been adapted to carry more than one person). The removal of a seat from a two-seater does not alter the position since it will have been constructed with two. It must be emphasised that there is a total exemption for two-wheeled motor bicycles, whether fitted with a sidecar or not.

Other licence conditions   Motor vehicles which are driven or ridden by persons holding a provisional driving licence must display on the front and on the back of the vehicle the letter 'L' (or 'D' in Wales) in such a manner that it is clearly visible from a reasonable distance to other persons using the road. It is an offence under RTA 1988, s 87(1) for the holder of a provisional licence to drive a vehicle which is not so marked.

The drawing of trailers by a motor vehicle driven by the holder of a provisional licence is prohibited, except that the holder of a provisional licence may do so in relation to the category of vehicles specified if his provisional licence authorises the driving of a vehicle of a class included in category B + E, C + E, D + E or F (combination vehicles where the tractor falls in category B, C or D respectively but the combination does not, or agricultural or forestry tractors).

Holders of provisional licences authorising the driving of a moped, a motor bicycle with or without a sidecar, or a former category P vehicle, or a category Q vehicle, must not drive such a vehicle while carrying on it another person.

The holder of a provisional licence authorising the driving of a motor bicycle other than an A1 motor cycle must drive under the supervision of a 'direct access instructor' who is accompanying him on another motor bicycle or, if the instructor is suffering from a relevant disability of such a nature that he is unable to ride a two-wheeled vehicle, a three-wheeled vehicle in category AM or A; is able to communicate with him by radio other than a hand-held radio; is supervising only that person or, at the most, one additional provisional licence-holder; and is carrying a valid certificate issued by the Secretary of State. The 'learner' and the supervisor must both wear fluorescent or (during hours of darkness) luminous apparel.

The requirements concerning communication by radio do not apply to a person who has impaired hearing provided that a suitable means of communication with the instructor is arranged in advance. Direct access instructors hold additional qualifications in respect of larger motor cycles.

It is a condition of a provisional licence to drive a moped or A1 motor cycle that, when undergoing 'relevant training' (receiving professional tuition from a paid instructor in driving on a road after compulsory basic training), the holder of the licence cannot be in a group of more than three other such learners. Such an instructor must be present with him and riding a moped, A1 motor bicycle or former category P vehicle.

Offences

By RTA 1988, s 87(1), it is an offence for any person to drive on a road a motor vehicle of any class otherwise than in accordance with a licence authorising him to drive a motor vehicle of that class. Once the prosecution has proved that D has driven a motor vehicle on a road, the onus is upon D to prove that he is licensed to drive as this is a fact peculiarly within his own knowledge. It is desirable that there should be, where possible, a statutory demand for production of the relevant licence, but there is no obligation to do so.

It is an offence, under s 87(2), for a person to cause or permit another person to drive on a road a motor vehicle of any class otherwise than in accordance with a licence authorising that other person to drive a motor vehicle of that class. For the meaning of 'permit' and 'cause' see pp 415–6.

Section 3ZB provides the indictable (either way) offence of causing death by driving on a road when unlicensed. Disqualification for not less than 12 months is obligatory. It is irrelevant to an offence under s 3ZB that the risk of death resulting from the driving was unforeseen or unforeseeable. The Supreme Court has held that, to be guilty of an offence under s 3ZB, D must be shown to have done something other than simply putting his vehicle on the road so that it is there to be struck. It must be proved that there was something which he did or omitted to do by way of driving it which contributed in a more than minimal way to the death, and that thing must involve some element of fault (whether it amounts to careless or inconsiderate driving or is otherwise open to proper criticism). Thus, an unlicensed defendant is not guilty of an offence under s 3ZB if a car erratically driven by V crashes into D's carefully driven car and V is killed or if V jumps onto D's car as he drives under a bridge.

What constitutes 'driving' in relation to a motor vehicle is explained on p 486 and it is sufficient to bear in mind that the essence of 'driving' is the use of the driver's controls (or, at least, one of them) in order to control the movements of the vehicle, however that movement is produced, provided that what occurs can in any sense be described as driving.

It should be noted that, when a police officer discovers an offence of driving without a driving licence in circumstances in which the offender's driving would not have been in accordance with any licence that could have been granted to him, the police officer should include in the report reference to whether or not the conditions applicable to that licence were being complied with. The reason is that this is important to the court in relation to the penalty points awarded for the offence.

Motor bicycles: some special rules

Restrictions on provisional licences: two-wheeled vehicles   These are set out in MV(DL) R 1999, reg 15A. A provisional licence granted in respect of a vehicle in category AM or A is restricted to such vehicles as have no more than two wheels save where the applicant declares that he is suffering from a relevant disability of such a nature that he is unable to ride a vehicle which has two wheels. A provisional licence granted in respect of a vehicle with two wheels is restricted to vehicles of a class within category AM or A.

Approved training course   Motor cyclists and moped riders must undertake the two-part practical training which is applicable to them, within an approved training course for motor cyclists and moped riders. The first part is concerned with the basic handling and control of machines. The training for the first part can be undertaken without the necessity to ride on a road. The second part is the normal 'on the road' training to drive which takes place under the supervision of instructors.

A provisional licence does not authorise a person, before he has passed a test of competence to drive, to drive on a road a motor bicycle or moped, except where he has successfully completed an approved training course for motorcyclists or is undergoing training on such a course and is driving a motor bicycle or moped on a road as part of the training. Certificates will be issued to those who have successfully completed such courses.

A certificate is not valid:

(a) if the person to whom it is issued is at the time of issue ineligible to undertake the training course; and

(b) after whichever is the earliest of the following dates, namely:

(i) in a case where the person to whom the certificate was furnished is subsequently disqualified by order of a court under the RTOA 1988, s 36, the date on which the order is made,

(ii) in a case where the licence of the person to whom the certificate was furnished is subsequently revoked by the Secretary of State under the Road Traffic (New Drivers) Act 1995 (see p 387), the date on which the revocation has effect,

(iii) in a case where the certificate was issued before 1 February 2001, the last day of the period of three years beginning with the date of the certificate, or

(iv) in a case where the certificate was issued on or after 1 February 2001, the last day of the period of two years beginning with the date of the certificate.

MV(DL)R 1999, reg 69 provides that the requirement that a person is not authorised, unless he has passed a driving test of competence, to drive a motor bicycle on a road without having successfully completed an approved training course, does not apply to a person who is a provisional entitlement holder by virtue of having passed a test in respect of former category P (mopeds) on or after 1 December 1990 and before 19 January 2013, or passes the test in respect of category AM (mopeds and light quadricycles), and such a person is also exempt from the need to produce a certificate of such a pass on applying for a driving test to drive a motor bicycle. Similar exemptions exist in favour of persons resident on exempted islands (p 367).

The general proposition, that no person may be permitted to take a test of competence to drive a vehicle in category A (motor bicycles and motor tricycles) unless he produces the prescribed certificate of completion of an approved training course, is subject to the following qualifications contained in reg 69. It does not apply to a person who is for the time being the holder of a full licence for a class of vehicle included in category A in respect of a test of competence to drive a vehicle of any other class included in that category. Such a holder is also exempt from the restrictions imposed by RTA 1988, s 97(3) (which prevent the driving of a vehicle in category AM or category A on a road, by the holder of a provisional licence, before he has successfully completed an approved training course for motorcyclists) in respect of his driving of a vehicle of any class included in category AM or A. However, these qualifications do not apply in relation to the holder of a full licence authorising him only to drive a vehicle in category A having automatic transmission in respect of a test to drive vehicles with manual transmission or the driving of such a vehicle.

Driving test By MV(DL)R 1999, reg 40(1A), the driving test for a licence for a category AM or a category A vehicle must be conducted in three parts: (a) the standard test of driving theory and the standard test of hazard perception; (b) the manoeuvres test; and (c) the practical test. All three parts must be passed and must be passed in the same category or sub-category of vehicle. Test (a) must be passed before test (b) is taken and test (b) must be passed before test (c) is taken.

Entitlement upon passing a test to drive a category AM vehicle   MV(DL)R 1999, reg 44A provides that, where a person has passed a test for a licence authorising the driving of vehicles included in category AM, the Secretary of State must grant:

(a) in a case where the test was passed on a three-wheeled moped or a light quadri-cycle, a licence authorising the driving of all vehicles having three or four wheels included in category AM;

(b) in any other case, a licence authorising the driving of all vehicles included in category AM.

Full licence as provisional licence

RTA 1988, ss 98(2) provides that a full licence may act as a provisional licence for any other classes of vehicle, unless the holder is below the minimum age at which the other class of vehicle may be driven. However, by MV(DL)R 1999, reg 19, this does not apply to a full licence which is restricted to a specially adapted vehicle for a person with a physical disability, nor does it authorise a person who has not passed a moped or motor bicycle test to drive a former category P or a category Q vehicle.

MV(DL)R 1999, reg 19 provides that RTA 1988, s 98(2) applies as follows. It provides that the holder of a full licence which authorises the driving of motor vehicles of a class included in a category or sub-category specified in column (1) of the table below may drive motor vehicles:

(a) of other classes included in that category or sub-category, and

(b) of a class included in each category or sub-category specified, in relation to that category or sub-category, in column (2) of the table,

as if he were authorised by a provisional licence to do so.

Column (1)	*Column (2)*
Full licence held	Provisional entitlement included
AM	A, B, F and K
A1	A, B, F and K
A2	A, B, F and K
A3	B, F and K
B	A, B + E, G and H
C1	C1 + E
C	C1 + E, C + E
D1	D1 + E
D	D1 + E, D + E
F	Q, AM and B
G	H
H	G

In the case of a full licence granted before 19 January 2013 which authorises the driving of a class of standard motor bicycles, other than motor bicycles with an engine the maximum net power output of which is 11 kilowatts or less, such licences do not authorise the driving of an A3 motorcycle before the expiration of the standard access period described on p 359. Nor do they authorise the driving, as if authorised by a provisional licence, of vehicles of any class included in category B96.

Except to the extent indicated in the table, s 98(2) does not apply in so far as it authorises the full licence-holder to drive vehicles of any class included in category B + E, C + E, D + E or K or in sub-category B1 (invalid carriages), C1 or D1 (not for hire or reward).

Holders of full licences restricted to vehicles with automatic transmissions may use those licences as provisional licences to drive manually controlled vehicles of a category or sub-category as specified in the table above. A corresponding provision applies to holders of Community licences.

Physical fitness of drivers

RTA 1988, s 92 provides that an applicant for a driving licence must declare his physical fitness to drive, stating whether or not he is suffering, or has in the past suffered, from any relevant or prospective disability. The term 'disability' for the purposes of the section includes disease and the persistent use of drugs or alcohol, whether or not such misuse amounts to dependency, and:

(a) a *relevant disability* means (i) any *prescribed disability*, and (ii) *any other disability likely to cause* the driving of a vehicle by him to be a source of danger to the public; and

(b) prospective disability means any other disability which, by virtue of its intermittent or progressive nature, may become a disability of the type specified in (a) in course of time.

Subject to the provisions referred to below, the Secretary of State must refuse an applicant a licence if satisfied that the applicant is suffering from a relevant disability.

The Secretary of State must not refuse a licence on account of a relevant disability if the applicant has had a previous licence and his disability is one of absence of a limb, or deformity or loss of use of a limb provided that the condition has not become more acute, or if the application is for a provisional licence.

For the purposes of the prescribed disabilities, licences are divided into Group 1 and 2 licences. Group 1 licences are those for vehicles in categories AM, A, B, B + E, F, G, H, K and L and the former category N (vehicles travelling six or less miles on public roads per week between two pieces of land in same occupation). Group 2 licences cover the other categories of licence; the rules relating to them are more stringent.

In respect of Groups 1 and 2 licences, the disabilities prescribed for the purposes of (a) above are:

(i) severe mental disorder;

(ii) liability to sudden attacks of giddiness or fainting due to a heart condition for which a 'pacemaker' has been fitted. (A licence must not be refused if the Secretary of State is satisfied that the person's driving is unlikely to endanger the public and that that person has adequately arranged regular medical supervision and is conforming to those arrangements);

(iii) liability to sudden attacks of disabling giddiness or fainting for some other reason; or

(iv) persistent misuse of drugs or alcohol, whether or not such misuse amounts to dependency.

In respect of Group 1 licences, the following are *also prescribed* as relevant disabilities:

(a) *impairment of vision*, where the person concerned fails to meet the Group 1 visual acuity standard or Group 1 visual field standard, or (in the case of a person with diplopia or sight in only one eye) fails to meet the adaptation standard for those conditions. A Group 1 licence must not be refused on the basis that a person fails to meet the visual field standard, where prescribed conditions are met. For an account of these standards, see Chapter 9 on the companion website.

(b) *diabetes mellitus*. Where the person is being treated with medication which carries a risk of inducing hypoglycaemia and has experienced two or more episodes of severe hypoglycaemia during the previous one-year period, or has impaired awareness of hypoglycaemia, there are no qualifications; the grant of a licence must be refused. On the other hand, where the person is being treated with insulin, he must not be refused a Group 1 licence if he:
    (i) has had no more than one episode of severe hypoglycaemia during the past year;
    (ii) does not have impaired awareness of hypoglycaemia;
    (iii) can demonstrate an understanding of the risks of hypoglycaemia and adequate control of the condition;
    (iv) undertakes regular glucose monitoring;
    (v) is under regular medical review; and
    (vi) is a person in respect of whom the Secretary of State is satisfied that the driving of the vehicle in accordance with the licence is not likely to be a source of danger to the public.

(c) *epilepsy*, where the person concerned has had two or more epileptic seizures during the previous five-year period. 'Epilepsy' is defined as the occurrence of two or more unprovoked seizures over a period which exceeds 24 hours and 'epileptic seizure' means any such seizure. 'Unprovoked seizure' means a seizure which is not a provoked seizure; 'provoked seizure' means a seizure which has a recognisable causative factor which is reliably avoidable and which is not a medication adjustment seizure (ie a seizure occurring during and because of documented physician-advised substitution, reduction or withdrawal of anti-epilepsy medication).

An epileptic who satisfies specified conditions must not be refused a Group 1 licence if either he has been free from any unprovoked seizure during the immediately preceding one-year period or during that period he has suffered no unprovoked seizure other than a permitted seizure. As to the specified conditions and a 'permitted seizure', see Chapter 9 on the companion website.

(d) *an isolated seizure* is prescribed as a relevant disability in relation to a person:
    (i) in a case where there is an underlying causative factor that may increase future risk, where such a seizure has occurred during the previous one-year period; and
    (ii) in any other case, where such a seizure has occurred during the previous six-month period.
'Isolated seizure' means one or more unprovoked seizures occurring either over a single period not exceeding 24 hours, or over a period not exceeding 24 hours, where that period of seizure has occurred more than five years after the last unprovoked seizure.

A person (P) must not be refused a Group 1 licence on the ground of isolated seizure if:

  (i) (*a*) where there is an underlying causative factor that may increase future risk, P has had such a seizure more than one year immediately before the date when the licence is granted; and

        (*b*) in any other case, P has had such a seizure more than six months immediately before the date when the licence is granted;

  (ii) P has had no other unprovoked seizure since that seizure; and

  (iii) P satisfies the specified conditions in respect of an epileptic person.

In respect of Group 2 licences, the following are *also prescribed* as relevant disabilities:

(a) *impairment of vision*, where the person concerned fails to meet the Group 2 visual acuity and visual field standards or has sight in only one eye (with exceptions) or uncontrolled diplopia. The details are set out in Chapter 9 on the companion website;

(b) *diabetes mellitus*. Where the person is being treated with insulin or another medication which carries a risk of inducing hypoglycaemia and has experienced one or more episodes of severe hypoglycaemia during the previous one-year period, or does not have full awareness of hypoglycaemia, there are no qualifications; the grant of a licence must be refused.

A person must not be refused a Group 2 licence in the following cases:

  (i) where he is being treated with insulin and:

      (*a*) has undergone treatment with insulin for at least four weeks, has full awareness of hypoglycaemia, and has not, during the past year, had an episode of severe hypoglycaemia, and

      (*b*) regularly monitors his condition and, in particular, undertakes blood glucose monitoring at least twice daily and at times relevant to driving (and provides a signed declaration as to his understanding and preparedness to report significant changes in his condition, to follow medical advice, and to provide evidence as to monitoring); or

  (ii) where he is being treated with a medication which carries a risk of inducing hypoglycaemia, other than insulin, and has full awareness of hypoglycaemia; and

      (*a*) has not, during the previous year, had an episode of severe hypoglycaemia;

      (*b*) regularly monitors his condition and, in particular, undertakes blood glucose monitoring at least twice daily and at times relevant to driving (and provides a signed declaration as to his understanding and preparedness to report significant changes in his condition, to follow medical advice, and to provide evidence as to monitoring); and

      (*c*) a specialist confirms responsible diabetic control and minimal risk of impairment due to hypoglycaemia; and electronic monitoring is used;

(c) *liability to seizure other than epilepsy*;

(d) *epilepsy*, where two or more epileptic seizures have occurred, or the person concerned has been prescribed medication to treat epilepsy, during the previous ten-year period.

A person (P) must not be refused a Group 2 licence on the ground of epilepsy if:

  (i) in the case of a person whose last epileptic seizure was an isolated seizure (see below), P satisfies the following conditions:

      (*a*) *there has been an appropriate medical assessment by a neurologist (if required by the Secretary of State);*

      (*b*) *the Secretary of State is satisfied that the driving of a vehicle by P, in accordance with the licence, is not likely to be a source of danger to the public; and*

(c) *for at least a five-year period immediately preceding the date when the licence is granted P has been free from any unprovoked seizure, and has not been prescribed medication to treat epilepsy or a seizure;* or

(ii) in any other case, P satisfies conditions (*a*) and (*b*) just mentioned, and for at least a ten-year period immediately preceding the date when the licence is granted he has been free from any epileptic seizure, and has not been prescribed medication to treat epilepsy;

(e) an *isolated seizure*, where during the previous five-year period, such a seizure has occurred, or the person concerned has been prescribed medication to treat epilepsy or a seizure. The definition 'isolated seizure' in respect of a Group 2 licence is different from that given above in relation to a Group 1 licence in that *ten years* is substituted for five years in that definition.

A person must not be refused a Group 2 licence on the ground of an isolated seizure if the italicised conditions in (d) above are satisfied.

Further points about disability   By RTA 1988, s 93, existing licences (including Community licences of persons normally resident in Great Britain) may be revoked totally if such a disability as described above actually arises and an application for the licence would have had to be refused, or may be revoked and replaced with shorter-term licences if a prospective disability (as described above) arises.

Licences may be issued which allow the driving of vehicles of a special construction—for example, a vehicle fitted with hand controls for a person who has lost both legs—or they may allow driving subject to certain specified conditions.

Persons holding driving licences who suffer an actual or prescribed disability must notify the Secretary of State forthwith. Failure without reasonable excuse to do so is an offence under RTA 1988, s 94(3). Driving after such a failure is an offence under s 94(3A).

A person who holds a licence and drives a motor vehicle of the class authorised on a road commits an offence under s 92(10) if he knowingly made a false declaration in relation to a relevant disability to obtain the licence. A person who drives a motor vehicle on a road, otherwise than in accordance with a licence, commits an additional offence under s 94A(1) if a licence has earlier been refused or revoked on account of such a disability. These offences may also be committed by holders of Community licences normally resident in Great Britain.

Section 96(1) makes it an offence for a person to drive a motor vehicle on a road while his eyesight is such (whether through a defect which cannot be or one which is not for the time being sufficiently corrected, eg by the use of spectacles) that he cannot comply with any prescribed requirement as to eyesight.

A constable having reason to suspect a person driving a motor vehicle of committing a s 96(1) offence may require him to submit to an eyesight test; it is an offence under s 96(3) to refuse to submit to such a test.

Disabilities requiring medical investigation: high-risk offenders

RTA 1988, s 94 provides that, if prescribed circumstances obtain in relation to a person who is an applicant for, or the holder of, a driving licence or if the Secretary of State has reasonable grounds for believing that a person who is an applicant for, or the holder of, a licence may be suffering from a relevant or prospective disability (p 371), the Secretary of State may by notice in writing served on the applicant or holder require him to be medically assessed for the purpose of determining whether he suffers or has suffered from such a disability, or (except where the licence in question is a provisional one) require him to take such driving test as the Secretary of State directs.

The prescribed circumstances are that the person has been disqualified from driving by a court:

(a) by reason that the proportion of alcohol in his body equalled or exceeded two-and-a-half times the prescribed limit;

(b) by reason of failure, without reasonable excuse, to provide a specimen when required to do so pursuant to RTA 1988, s 7;

(c) by reason of failure, without reasonable excuse, to give permission for a laboratory test of a specimen of blood taken pursuant to RTA 1988, s 7A; or

(d) on two or more occasions within any period of ten years for drink-driving or driving while unfit through drink.

For the purposes of (a) and (b) a disqualification must not be taken into account unless it was ordered on or after 1 June 1990, and (d) does not apply to a person unless the last disqualification was ordered on or after that date. For the purposes of (c) a disqualification must not be taken into account unless it was ordered on or after 1 June 2013.

Licences to drive passenger-carrying vehicles or large goods vehicles

Definitions

There are two types of passenger-carrying vehicle (PCV).

A vehicle is a '*large PCV*' if it is used to carry passengers and is constructed or adapted to carry more than 16 passengers, whether or not for hire or reward. The various forms of large PCVs are included in variations of category D types of vehicles under MV(DL)R 1999.

A vehicle is a '*small PCV*' if it is used to carry passengers *for hire or reward* and constructed or adapted to carry more than eight but not more than 16 passengers. Small PCVs are category D1 type vehicles.

A large goods vehicle (LGV) is a motor vehicle (not being a medium-sized goods vehicle as defined at (c) on p 362) which is constructed or adapted to carry or to haul goods and the permissible maximum weight of which exceeds 7.5 tonnes. The permissible maximum weights of goods vehicles are as follows:

(a) in the case of a motor vehicle which neither is an articulated goods vehicle nor is drawing a trailer, the relevant maximum weight of the vehicle;

(b) in the case of an articulated goods vehicle:
   (i) when drawing only a semi-trailer, the relevant maximum train weight of the articulated goods vehicle combination;
   (ii) when drawing a trailer as well as a semi-trailer, the aggregate of the relevant maximum train weight of the articulated goods vehicle combination and the relevant maximum weight of the trailer;
   (iii) when drawing a trailer but not a semi-trailer, the aggregate of the relevant maximum weight of the articulated goods vehicle and the relevant maximum weight of the trailer;
   (iv) when drawing neither a semi-trailer nor a trailer, the relevant maximum weight of the vehicle;

(c) in the case of a motor vehicle (not being an articulated goods vehicle) which is drawing a trailer, the aggregate of the relevant maximum weight of the motor vehicle and the relevant maximum weight of the trailer.

The 'relevant maximum weight' of a goods vehicle is the maximum gross weight which is shown on the relevant plate of the vehicle. The relevant plate is always the Ministry plate if the vehicle has then been fitted with one. If it has not, then the relevant maximum weight will be shown on the vehicle.

The 'relevant maximum train weight' of an articulated goods vehicle combination is the gross weight of the unladen motor vehicle and its unladen trailer plus the maximum weight which the combination is permitted to carry. This is shown under the column marked 'gross train weight' on the plate attached to the vehicle.

Matters relating to the weights of goods vehicles are discussed further in Appendix 2 on the companion website.

A driving licence issued under RTA 1988, Part III (ss 87 to 109C) is required to cover the driving of PCVs or LGVs or any class thereof on a road. However, by RTA 1988, s 110, licences under Part III to drive such vehicles must be granted by the Secretary of State in accordance with Part IV (ss 110 to 122) and, in so far as they authorise the driving of PCVs or LGVs, are subject to Part IV as well as Part III.

Licensing requirements

By s 112, the Secretary of State may not grant a PCV driver's licence or LGV driver's licence unless satisfied, having regard to his conduct, that the applicant is a fit and proper person to hold the licence applied for. Any issue relating to an applicant's conduct may be referred to a traffic commissioner for a determination as to whether the applicant is, having regard to his conduct, a fit person to hold a PCV licence or LGV licence (s 113).

Someone who drives a PCV or LGV without holding a driving licence authorising the driving of a PCV or LGV of the class in question commits an offence under s 87(1), and so does a person who permits him to do so.

By s 114, it is an offence to fail without reasonable excuse to comply with conditions of a PCV or LGV licence

Other provisions of RTA 1988, Part IV are referred to on pp 389–90.

Exemptions

MV(DL)R 1999, reg 50(1) provides that the provisions of RTA 1988, Part IV and the provisions of MV(DL)R 1999, regs 54 (below) and 55, 56 and 57 (special provisions relating only to LGV and PCV drivers' licences) do not apply to LGVs of a classs included in categories F, G or H (some tractors, road rollers and track-laying vehicles) or sub-category C1 + E (8.25 tonnes), or to exempted vehicles. The list of other exempted vehicles is extensive, covering military vehicles, a variety of vehicles used in public works, industry and agriculture, articulated vehicles the unladen weight of which does not exceed 3.5 tonnes, unladen goods vehicles manufactured before 1 January 1960, and emergency vehicles. In addition, by reg 50(2) and (3), RTA 1988, Part IV and the provisions of regs 54 to 57 of the Regulations do not apply to:

(a) a PCV manufactured more than 30 years before the date upon which it is driven and not used for hire or reward or for the carriage of more than eight passengers;
(b) a PCV driven by a constable for the purpose of removing or avoiding obstruction to other road users or to other members of the public, for the purpose of protecting life or property (including the PCV and its passengers) or for other similar purposes.

LGV licences granted to persons under 21

These may be of two types. To permit those aged 18 or over but under 21 to be taught to drive a LGV within a training agreement, provisional trainee drivers' licences may be issued. Other learner drivers will be issued with a standard provisional driving licence.

MV(DL)R 1999, reg 54(1) provides that a LGV driver's licence granted to a person under 21 is subject to the following additional conditions.

A LGV trainee driver's licence is subject to the condition that its holder must not drive a LGV unless he is a registered employee of a registered employer, and the vehicle is a LGV to which his training agreement applies and which is owned or operated by that employer or by a registered LGV driver training establishment (reg 54(2)).

A full LGV driver's licence authorising the driving of a vehicle of category C is subject to the condition that its holder may not drive LGVs in category C + E (other than vehicles included in sub-category C1 + E whose maximum authorised mass does not exceed 7.5 tonnes) as if he were authorised to do so by a provisional licence before the expiry of six months commencing on the date on which he passed a test for category C (reg 54(4)). Thus, a trainee driver could pass a test for category C vehicles (exceeding 3.5 tonnes + trailer not exceeding 750kg) but would be unable to use his full licence for category C vehicles as a provisional licence in respect of category C + E vehicles (combinations of motor vehicles and trailers which fall outside category C) until he has held that full licence for a period of six months.

It is an offence to fail without reasonable excuse to comply with any of these conditions (RTA 1988, s 114(1)), or knowingly to cause or permit someone under 21 to do so (s 114(2)).

Other matters

Other matters relating to the driving of PCVs and LGVs are dealt with in Appendices 1 and 2 on the companion website.

Foreigners and driving licences

Community licence-holders

By RTA 1988, s 99A, a Community licence-holder (a holder of a licence issued within the EEA) may drive in Great Britain a motor vehicle of any class which he is authorised by his Community licence to drive, provided that he is not disqualified for holding or obtaining a licence under RTA 1988.

Thus, unlike other drivers from abroad, a Community licence-holder who becomes resident in Great Britain is authorised to drive here without the need to exchange his licence for a British licence within 12 months of becoming resident. He does, however, have a right to exchange his licence. Where matters of validity, standards of health and fitness, and disqualification are concerned, the exchange of licences is mandatory. A resident Community licence-holder is subject to the same medical requirements as holders of a British licence. A Community licence-holder resident in Great Britain who is authorised to drive medium-sized or large goods vehicles or passenger-carrying vehicles of any class must, within a period of 12 months' residence, deliver his licence to the Secretary of State and provide details prescribed by s 99B.

Drivers from abroad other than Community licence-holders

The Motor Vehicles (International Circulation) Order 1975, art 2 states that it is lawful for *a person resident outside the UK who is temporarily in Great Britain* to drive for a period of 12 months from the date of his last entry into the UK if he holds a Convention driving permit (see below) or a domestic driving permit of a country outside the UK authorising him to drive the vehicle in question, provided he is not disqualified (eg by age) for holding or obtaining a British licence.

What has just been said is subject to qualification in respect of large passenger-carrying vehicles, privately operated passenger-carrying vehicles (vehicles not used for carrying passengers for hire or reward which are constructed or adapted to carry more than eight but not more than 16 passengers), large goods vehicles and medium-sized goods vehicles (vehicles constructed or adapted to carry or haul a load which is not adapted to carry more than nine persons including the driver and exceeds 3.5 tonnes but does not exceed 7.5 tonnes). A holder of either type of permit may drive such a vehicle if he is resident in an EEA state, the Isle of Man, Jersey, or Guernsey. Other holders of such a permit may only drive such a vehicle if it has been temporarily brought into Great Britain. In the cases set out in this paragraph no other licence is required.

Generally, any person may cause or permit holders of such Convention or domestic driving permits to drive vehicles which they are authorised by their permit to drive. In the phrase 'temporarily in Great Britain', 'temporarily' is an element other than simply a time element. It involves a presence for casual purposes, for example a holiday, as contrasted with regular habits. For example, an overseas student studying here is not 'temporarily' resident here.

A Convention driving permit is usually referred to as an 'international driving licence'. In Britain it is issued by the AA or RAC. The term 'domestic driving permit' refers to the licence issued by the driver's own country and it is therefore lawful for a visitor to Great Britain to drive for a one-year period on the authority of his own, local driving licence. Article 2, above, merely recognises that persons visiting from abroad would experience difficulty in undertaking a test in Great Britain while they are temporarily in this country. These permits are treated as driving licences in every respect and a constable's powers to demand production of a licence and to demand the holder's date of birth apply equally to them.

MV(DL)R 1999, reg 80 makes the same provision for a person from abroad who becomes resident in Great Britain, the one-year period in this case running from when he became a resident. Someone from abroad who is in this country but who falls outside the term 'temporarily in Great Britain', for example an overseas student, will be resident in Great Britain.

The holder of a relevant permit who becomes resident in Great Britain and is not disqualified for holding or obtaining a licence in Great Britain is, during the one-year period after he becomes so resident, treated as the holder of a licence authorising him to drive all classes of small vehicles (generally vehicles not constructed or adapted to carry more than nine persons inclusive of the driver and vehicles not exceeding 3.5 tonnes, including a combination of such a vehicle and a trailer), motor cycles or mopeds which he is authorised to drive by that permit. A 'relevant permit' is a 'domestic driving permit', or a 'Convention driving permit'. Where a question arises as to whether a person is normally resident in Great Britain or the UK, a person is deemed to be normally resident if he shows that he will have lived there for not less than 185 days preceding a test appointment.

Persons who become resident in Great Britain and who hold British external licences granted in the Isle of Man, Guernsey or Jersey authorising the driving of large goods vehicles or passenger-carrying vehicles, and who are not disqualified for holding or obtaining a licence in Great Britain, may drive such vehicles under the authority of those licences for a one-year period from the date upon which they became resident.

People permitted to drive in this country under a domestic driving permit, etc who take out a provisional licence during the one-year period in order to take a driving test need not comply with the normal conditions applicable to a learner driver if they are still driving under the authority of their domestic permit, etc at the time (ie within the one-year period).

Exchangeable licences

Licences issued in Gibraltar and certain non-EEA countries designated by order under RTA 1988, s 108(2) by the Secretary of State are exchangeable by a holder resident in Great Britain for a British driving licence. The Secretary of State may designate a non-EEA country for the purpose of 'exchangeable licences' where he is satisfied that the driving test in that country is satisfactory. He may, however, restrict approval to the grant of exchangeable licences to particular circumstances, impose conditions to which they are subject and limit the exchanged licence to particular classes of vehicles. An up-to-date list of the countries specified by order is contained in the Driving Licences (Exchangeable Licences) (Amendment) Order 2013.

Production of driving licences

By virtue of RTA 1988, s 164(1), a constable or vehicle examiner (ie an examiner appointed under RTA 1988, s 66A by the Secretary of State (see p 435)) may demand the production of a driving licence by the following people:

(a) a person driving a motor vehicle on a road; or

(b) a person whom a constable or vehicle examiner has reasonable cause to believe has been the driver of a vehicle at the time when an accident occurred owing to its presence on a road; or

(c) a person whom a constable or vehicle examiner has reasonable cause to believe has committed an offence in relation to the use of a motor vehicle on a road; or

(d) a person supervising the holder of a provisional licence while the holder is driving a motor vehicle on a road; or

(e) a person whom the constable or vehicle examiner has reasonable cause to believe was supervising the holder of such a licence when an accident occurred owing to the presence of the vehicle on a road or when an offence is suspected of having been committed by the holder in relation to the use of a vehicle on a road.

When a licence is produced to a constable or vehicle examiner pursuant to a request under RTA 1988, s 164(1), he is entitled to ascertain the name and address of the holder of the licence, its date of issue, and the authority by which it was issued. Section 164(2) also provides a power whereby a constable may require a person (A) in circumstances prescribed by MV(DL)R 1999 to state his date of birth. These circumstances are:

(a) where A fails to produce forthwith for examination his driving licence on being required to do so by a constable; or

(b) where, on being so required, A produces a licence which the constable has reason to suspect:
    (i)   was not granted to A, or
    (ii) was granted to him in error, or
    (iii) contains an alteration in its particulars made with intent to deceive; or

(c) where, on being so required, A produces a licence in which the driver number has been altered, erased or defaced; or

(d) where A is a person supervising the holder of a provisional licence while he is driving a motor vehicle on a road, or is someone whom the constable reasonably suspects to have been supervising such a person when an accident occurred or an offence was committed, and the constable has reasonable cause to suspect that A is under 21.

Section 164(4A) provides that, where a constable to whom a provisional licence has been produced by a person driving a motor bicycle has reasonable cause to believe that the holder was not driving it as a part of the training being provided on a training course for motorcyclists, the constable may require him to produce the prescribed certificate of completion of such a course.

The term 'licence' means a licence under RTA 1988, Part III or a Community licence.

Police officers have direct access to details of driving licences and their holders through the Police National Computer.

Section 164(3) and (5) provide that:

(a) where a licence has been revoked by the Secretary of State but the holder has not surrendered it; or
(b) where the holder has failed to produce his licence to a court when lawfully required to do so; or
(c) where the Secretary of State has served notice on a Community licence-holder in pursuance of s 99C (relevant disability) or s 115A (conduct of holder of LGV or PCV Community licence) requiring delivery of the licence to him,

a constable or vehicle examiner may require the holder to produce them and on production may seize them.

A person who fails to produce his licence, or a certificate of completion of a training course for motorcyclists, or fails to state a date of birth, when required to do so under any of the provisions of s 164, commits an offence under s 164(6).

An offence of failing to produce a licence is not committed if the person produces a current receipt for the surrender of the licence issued under the fixed penalty procedure (see p 451) and, if required, produces the licence in person immediately on its return at a police station specified at the time of the request, or if within seven days of the request he produces the receipt in person at that police station and, if requested, produces the licence there in person immediately on its return. In addition, in proceedings for an offence of failing to produce a licence it is a defence for D to show that:

(a) within seven days after the production of his licence was required he produced it in person at such police station as may have been specified by him at the time its production was required; or
(b) he produced it in person there as soon as was reasonably practicable; or
(c) it was not reasonably practicable for him to produce it there before the day on which proceedings commenced.

If a licence is not produced at the time its production was required, it is the usual practice of the police to make out a form HO/RT1 which will be produced at the police station nominated by the driver, together with the licence. This is merely a practice followed by the police and there is no statutory requirement that this be done.

As to the power of seizure where a licence is not produced when required, see p 403.

Records

System of recording penalty points

Consequent on the abolition of the driving licence counterpart in Great Britain with effect from 8 June 2015, endorsements are no longer entered onto counterparts. They are instead entered solely onto an individual's electronic driving record, just as they had been previously in the case of unlicensed drivers and foreign drivers who did not have counterparts to their driving licences. Under the Road Traffic Offenders Act 1988 (RTOA 1988), s 97A, a 'driving record', in relation to a person, is defined as a record in relation to the person maintained by the Secretary of State and designed to be endorsed with particulars relating to offences committed by the person under the Traffic Acts (Road Traffic Act 1988, RTOA 1988 and Road Traffic Regulation Act 1984). An individual's driving record is maintained for the Secretary of State by the Driver and Vehicles Licensing Agency (DVLA), which is an executive agency of the Department for Transport. Endorsements placed on counterparts before 8 June 2015 are treated as endorsements placed on the driving record.

Under RTOA 1988, s 57A, the driving record of a person, whether or not he is a licence-holder, who has been given a fixed penalty notice for an offence carrying obligatory endorsement (see p 451), is endorsed, without the need for a court hearing, at the end of a suspended enforcement period unless he gives notice requesting a hearing and has not paid the fixed penalty.

Access to driver licensing records

The Motor Vehicles (Access to Driver Licensing Records) Regulations 2001, reg 2 provides that the purposes for which constables may be given access to information held by the Secretary of State and made available are:

(a) the prevention, investigation or prosecution of a contravention of any provision of the following enactments:
  (i) the RTA 1988;
  (ii) the RTOA 1988;
  (iii) the Road Traffic (Northern Ireland) Orders 1981 and 1995;
  (iv) the Road Traffic Offenders (Northern Ireland) Order 1996;
  (v) the Vehicle Drivers (Certificates of Professional Competence) Regulations 2007; and
(b) ascertaining whether a person has had an order made in relation to him under:
  (i) the Child Support Act 1991, s 40B(1) or (5) (disqualification from driving: further provisions);
  (ii) the Criminal Procedure (Scotland) Act 1995, ss 248A(1) (general power to disqualify offenders) or 248B(2) (power to disqualify fine defaulters); or
  (iii) the Crime (Sentences) Act 1997, ss 39(1) (offenders) or 40(2) (fine defaulters).

Regulation 3 provides that information to which constables have been given access may be further disclosed to an employee of a police authority, local policing body or chief officer of police for any purpose ancillary to, or connected with, the use of the information by constables.

In addition, RV(R&L)R 2002, reg 27 authorises the Secretary of State to make available particulars contained in the register to:

(a) a local authority for the purpose of an investigation of an offence or for any purpose connected with its activities as an enforcement authority under the Traffic Management Act 2004, Part 6 (see p 450);
(b) a chief officer of police;
(c) the Motor Insurers' Bureau in connection with its functions relating to the enforcement of the offence of keeping a vehicle which does not meet insurance requirements; or

(d) any person who can show satisfactory cause for requiring the information.

Regulation 28 authorises the Secretary of State to sell such particulars to such persons as he considers fit, provided that the information does not identify any person or contain anything enabling such identification.

Disqualification by a court and penalty points

Obligatory disqualification

RTOA 1988, s 34(1) deals with disqualification for driving following a conviction for an offence involving obligatory disqualification. On such a conviction, a court must order disqualification for at least a specified minimum period, unless the court for special reasons thinks fit to order a shorter period of disqualification or not to order disqualification at all. These offences, which are all offences under RTA 1988 unless otherwise indicated, are:

(a) manslaughter (common law offence);
(b) causing death by dangerous driving (s 1);
(c) causing serious injury by dangerous driving (s 1A);
(d) dangerous driving (s 2);
(e) causing death by careless or inconsiderate driving (s 2B);
(f) causing death by driving: unlicensed or uninsured drivers (s 3ZB);
(g) causing death by driving: disqualified drivers (s 3ZC);
(h) causing serious injury by driving: disqualified drivers (s 3ZD);
(i) causing death by careless driving when under the influence of drink or drugs (s 3A);
(j) driving or attempting to drive whilst unfit through drink or drugs (s 4(1));
(k) driving or attempting to drive with excess alcohol in breath, blood or urine (s 5(1)(a));
(l) driving or attempting to drive with a concentration of a specified controlled drug above the specified limit (s 5A(1)(a)) and (2);
(m) failure to provide specimen, or to allow it to be taken, for analysis (where specimen required to assess ability or alcohol or drug level, etc at time offender was driving or attempting to drive) (ss 7(6) and 7A(6));
(n) motor racing and speed trials on a public highway (s 12);
(o) aggravated vehicle-taking (Theft Act 1968, s 12A).

In the case of most of these offences, the specified minimum period of disqualification is 12 months. However, in the case of the offence of manslaughter, or an offence under RTA 1988, ss 1, 1A, 3ZC, 3ZD or 3A, it is two years. The same (two-year) minimum period applies in relation to a person on whom more than one disqualification for a fixed period of 56 days or more has been imposed within the three years immediately preceding the commission of the offence. However, a disqualification imposed as a result of an offence committed by using vehicles in the course of crime or in respect of a conviction for stealing or attempting to steal a motor vehicle, joyriding, or going equipped to steal, etc a motor vehicle, or attempting to commit any such offence, is disregarded for this purpose, as is an interim disqualification on committal for sentence.

If the conviction is for any of the above offences that are connected with the drink-driving laws, that is, an offence under RTA 1988, ss 3A, 4(1), 5(1)(a) or 5A(1)(a) and (2), referred to above, and there has been a previous conviction for such an offence within the preceding 10 years, a court *must* order disqualification for a period of not less than three years, unless there are special reasons for not doing so. The same applies to an offence under s 7(6) or 7A(6) where it involves obligatory disqualification.

Particulars of any disqualification must be endorsed on the driving record.

'*Special reasons*' are reasons special to the circumstances of the offence, as opposed to special to the offender. It is of no consequence that the loss of a driving licence will lose the offender his job, that he is a man of previous good character and/or that he has driven for many years without having been convicted of any motoring offence. The courts' approach is strict in this respect. They have refused to accept as special reasons the hardship to a country doctor and his patients or the problems caused for a disabled man. An example of a case where there would be reasons special to the offence is where someone has his supposed non-alcoholic drink 'laced' without his knowledge. In such a case, it is open to the court in its discretion to mitigate the period of disqualification, or not to disqualify at all, because of special reasons. Special reasons might have been found in the case of the country doctor if the country doctor had been called out to a man suffering a heart attack in circumstances in which no other doctor could reasonably have been summoned to attend.

Discretionary disqualification

RTOA 1988, s 34(2) deals with discretionary disqualification. Where a person is convicted of an offence which is shown in Sch 2 to the Act to be one which carries discretionary disqualification and either:

(a) the penalty points to be taken into account on that occasion number fewer than 12; or

(b) the offence is not one involving obligatory endorsement,

the court may disqualify for any period which it thinks fit. Disqualification may not be for an indefinite period, since the court must state the period of disqualification (although it may be for life). Particulars of any disqualification must be endorsed on the driving record. Offences which carry discretionary disqualification usually carry obligatory endorsement.

Extension of disqualification period where immediate custodial sentence also imposed

Under RTOA 1988, s 35A, where the offender has been sentenced to an immediate term of imprisonment for the offence for which he is ordered to be disqualified under s 34 or s 35 (pp 382–3 and 385), the court must add to the period of disqualification which it would otherwise have imposed under s 34 or s 35 an extension period (broadly, the custodial period which must be served). This is designed to require that the former period of disqualification takes effect after the offender's release from imprisonment.

Endorsement and penalty points

RTOA 1988, s 44 provides that, unless there are special reasons not to do so, where a person is convicted of an offence involving obligatory endorsement the court must order particulars of the conviction to be endorsed on his driving record and the endorsement must also include:

(a) if the court orders disqualification, particulars of the disqualification; or

(b) if the court does not order disqualification, particulars of the offence (including its date) and the number of penalty points to be attributed as shown in respect of the offence in RTOA 1988, Sch 2 (or, where a range of numbers is so shown, a number falling within the range).

It follows that, where an offender is convicted and the court imposes disqualification under RTOA 1988, s 34, no penalty points are to be attributed for that offence or any other offence in respect of which he is convicted on that occasion. This prevents the possibility of 'double disqualification'.

Where a person is convicted of two or more offences included in Sch 2, all of which are committed on the same occasion, the number of points awarded is generally the highest single figure applicable to one of those offences.

RTOA 1988, Sch 2 lists the offences which carry penalty points. Where a person is convicted for aiding and abetting offences involving obligatory disqualification the number of penalty points to be attributed to the offence is 10. The offences of causing death by dangerous driving; dangerous driving; causing death by driving: disqualified drivers; causing death by driving: unlicensed or uninsured drivers; causing death by careless driving when under the influence of drink or drugs; causing serious injury by dangerous driving; causing serious injury by driving: disqualified drivers; driving or attempting to drive vehicles when under the influence of drink or drugs or with excess alcohol in breath, blood or urine or with excess of a specified controlled drug in blood or urine; and failing to provide a specimen for analysis, all carry obligatory endorsement of 3–11 penalty points, in addition to obligatory disqualification, unless there are special reasons. However, as indicated above, if disqualification is ordered the licence will not be endorsed with penalty points.

The offence of failing to stop after an accident carries 5–10 points, as does that of failing to report an accident. Insurance offences carry 6–8, careless driving 3–9 and failing to co-operate with a preliminary test (eg of breath) 4. Any contravention of the construction and use regulations which constitutes an endorsable offence carries 3 points, as does a failure to comply with traffic directions, with the directions of school crossing patrols or with pedestrian crossing regulations. All offences of exceeding a speed limit carry 3–6 penalty points or 3 (fixed penalty). However, this is prospectively amended by RSA 2006, s 17 which extends the range of penalty points which may be given in respect of speeding to 2–6 or appropriate penalty points (fixed penalty). Offences concerned with driving licences carry 3–6 penalty points, except driving whilst disqualified by a court order which carries 6 points.

Unless there are special reasons for not doing so a court *must* endorse a person's licence if he is convicted of an offence shown in RTOA 1988, Sch 2 to be one in respect of which endorsement is obligatory.

Recognition of disqualification imposed in another EU state, Northern Ireland, etc

By virtue of the Crime (International Co-operation) Act 2003, Part 3, Chapter 1, which is currently in force only in respect of Ireland, where an individual normally resident in the UK is convicted in another EU member state of an offence of reckless or dangerous driving, drink-driving, speeding, driving while disqualified, or certain other offences, and is disqualified in that state for holding or obtaining a driving licence, and provided certain conditions are satisfied, the appropriate Minister in the UK must give a notice disqualifying that individual for holding or obtaining a licence for the unexpired period of the foreign disqualification beginning 21 days from the giving of the notice; where the unexpired period is less than one month the Minister is not required to give such a notice but may do so. The unexpired period of the foreign disqualification is the period of that disqualification less any period of that disqualification which is treated by regulations as having been served in the foreign state. By the Mutual Recognition of Driving Disqualifications (Great Britain and Ireland) Regulations 2008 the period to be treated for this purpose as having been served in Ireland starts on the day the disqualification became operative in Ireland and ends on the day immediately before the beginning of the 21-day notice period; any time during which the disqualification was suspended is disregarded in determining the period.

RTA 1988, s 102A provides that a person disqualified for holding or obtaining a driving licence by a court in Northern Ireland, the Isle of Man, any of the Channel Islands or Gibraltar is disqualified for holding or obtaining a licence in Great Britain for the period of the disqualification.

Obligatory disqualification for repeated offences

RTOA 1988, s 35 applies to an offence involving discretionary disqualification and obligatory endorsement and to an offence involving obligatory disqualification in respect of which no order is made under s 34. Section 35 requires that where, on conviction for such an offence, the award of the penalty points for the offence, together with those already endorsed on the licence, brings the total to 12, the offender must be disqualified for a minimum period of six months if the points have been accumulated within three years of the commission (and not the conviction) of the offence for which penalty points are then awarded, unless the court is satisfied that there are grounds for mitigating the normal consequences of the conviction and thinks fit to order a shorter period of disqualification or not to order disqualification. If the total is in excess of 12 this may be recognised by disqualification for a longer period. The minimum period is one year's disqualification if there is a previous disqualification in the above period, or two if there is more than one. No account is to be taken, as a ground for mitigating the normal consequences, of any circumstances which are alleged to make the offence or any of the offences not a serious one; nor of any hardship other than exceptional hardship; nor of any circumstances which, within the preceding three years, have already been taken into account in ordering the offender to be disqualified for a shorter period or not to be ordered to be disqualified at all. Exceptional hardship which would be caused to a person other than the offender (for example a dependent, invalid wife) may be taken into account.

It follows from the above rules that, even if a court decides not to order disqualification when it is discretionary in relation to the offence in question, because of mitigating circumstances, it may be required to disqualify under s 35 as a result of the 'totting-up' of the penalty points attributed for the offence with previous penalty points.

A person who is already the holder of a driving licence authorising him to drive a vehicle of a particular class is disqualified by RTA 1988, s 102 for holding another licence for that class of vehicle. This is to prevent a person from holding more than one licence. If he was able to do so he could share out his penalty points by holding two licences indicating different addresses.

Once the disqualification has been imposed the driving record is in effect wiped clean. However, 'wiping clean' is restricted to disqualification under s 35 for repeated offences. Where a disqualification is imposed under s 34 for a specific offence, the penalty points previously accumulated remain effective at the end of the period of disqualification until the expiry of three years from the date of the offence for which they were imposed.

Use of vehicle in commission of crime: discretion to disqualify

On conviction of an offender in the Crown Court of an offence punishable with imprisonment for a term of two years or more, or when sentencing such a person after his conviction before a magistrates' court for such an offence, the Crown Court, if satisfied that a motor vehicle was used (by the person convicted or anyone else) for the purpose of committing or facilitating the commission of the offence, may disqualify the person convicted for such a period as it thinks fit for holding or obtaining a licence to drive (Powers of Criminal Courts (Sentencing) Act 2000 (PCC(S)A 2000), s 147). 'Facilitation' will include use after the offence for disposal of property or avoiding apprehension or detection.

Where a court imposing disqualification under s 147 or s 146 below also imposes a custodial sentence it must add to the period of disqualification which it would otherwise have imposed an extension period (broadly the custodial period which must be served).

Disqualification: offenders in general

PCC(S)A 2000, s 146 empowers a court on conviction for *any* offence to order the offender to be disqualified.

Legislation also empowers a magistrates' court to order disqualification in a case of default in paying a fine.

Effect of an order of disqualification

RTOA 1988, s 37(1) provides that, where a licence-holder is disqualified by order of a court, the licence is to be treated as revoked with effect from the beginning of the period of disqualification. However, where the disqualification is for a fixed period shorter than 56 days in respect of an offence involving obligatory endorsement or where the order is made under s 26 (interim disqualification), this does not prevent the licence from again having effect at the end of the period of disqualification.

Removal of disqualification

RTOA 1988, s 42 provides that a person who has been disqualified by a court may apply to have the disqualification removed as follows:

(a) if the disqualification is for less than four years, after two years;
(b) if it is for less than ten but more than four years, when half the disqualification has expired; or
(c) in any other case (life or ten or more years), when five years have passed.

Disqualification until passing of driving test

RTOA 1988, s 36 provides that, where a person:

(a) is disqualified under s 34 (obligatory disqualification) on conviction for manslaughter by the driver of a motor vehicle, or for causing death by dangerous driving, or for causing serious injury by dangerous driving, or for dangerous driving, or for causing death by careless driving while under the influence of drink or drugs, or for causing death by driving: disqualified drivers, or for causing serious injury by driving: disqualified drivers, or
(b) is disqualified under ss 34 or 35 (repeated offences) in such circumstances or for such period as the Secretary of State may prescribe, or

(c) is convicted of an offence involving obligatory endorsement which may be prescribed by the Secretary of State,

the court must order him to be disqualified until he has passed the appropriate
driving test.

Where a person is disqualified under s 34 on conviction for any other offence carrying obligatory endorsement, the court may order him to be disqualified until he has
passed the appropriate driving test.

An order of disqualification until the passing of a driving test ends when a certificate
of competence is produced to the Secretary of State.

An extended driving test is required where a person is convicted of an offence involving obligatory disqualification or is disqualified under the totting-up provisions (RTOA
1988, s 35), and the ordinary driving test is required in any other circumstances.

A person disqualified until he has passed a driving test is permitted by s 37(3) to
take out a provisional licence, once any fixed period of disqualification has expired, in
which case he may drive under the conditions applicable to such a licence. A person
who drives under a provisional licence granted by virtue of s 37(3), but who does not
comply with the conditions attached to such a licence, commits an offence contrary to
RTA 1988, s 103(1), of driving whilst disqualified. A person charged with driving while
disqualified who relies on RTOA 1988, s 37(3) has the burden of proving that he is the
holder of a provisional licence and that he was driving in accordance with the provisions of such a licence.

Further provisions

Further provisions under RTOA 1988 about a reduction in penalty points or the disqualification period effective on successful completion of a training course are dealt
with in Chapter 9 on the companion website. The provisions about the reduction of
penalty points are not yet in force.

Revocation of licence of 'new driver'

Under the Road Traffic (New Drivers) Act 1995, where a qualified driver commits an
offence involving obligatory endorsement during his 'probationary period' (two years
from becoming a qualified driver) and the penalty points to be taken into account on
that occasion number six or more, the court must send the Secretary of State a notice
containing the particulars to be endorsed on the person's driving record together with
the licence. A similar requirement is made of a fixed penalty clerk, where a fixed penalty offence is involved. The Secretary of State must, by notice, revoke the new driver's
licence. Such a licence may not be granted (restored) until he has passed a relevant
driving test (ie re-test); the re-test must be within two years of that revocation. There
are similar provisions about the revocation of a provisional licence and test certificate
where the driver has not applied for a full licence.

The prescribed probationary period ends early:

(a) where an order is made under RTOA 1988, s 36 (disqualified until a test is
    passed); or
(b) where, after revocation of the licence (or provisional licence plus test certificate)
    by the Secretary of State (see above), the full licence is granted after the person has
    passed a re-test.

Obtaining licence, or driving, while disqualified

RTA 1988, s 103 creates two offences which can be committed by a person disqualified *by a court*: obtaining a licence while so disqualified (s 103(1)(a)), and driving a motor vehicle on a road whilst so disqualified (s 103(1)(b)).

RTA 1988, s 3ZC provides a more serious offence, triable only on indictment, of causing death by driving: disqualified driver. Section 3ZC provides that a person is guilty of an offence if he:

(a) causes the death of another person by driving a motor vehicle on a road; and
(b) at that time, is committing an offence under s 103(1)(b) of driving while disqualified.

Section 3ZD provides a similarly worded indictable (either way) offence, the only difference being that it relates to causing serious injury rather than death. 'Serious injury' means physical harm which amounts to grievous bodily harm for the purposes of the Offences Against the Person Act 1861 (p 652).

What is said on p 368 about an offence under s 3ZB is equally applicable to an offence under s 3ZC or 3ZD. As to disqualification on conviction, see p 382.

An order of disqualification remains valid unless it is suspended pending an appeal or is subsequently revoked. A subsequent revocation does not excuse driving whilst the order was in force. The prosecution must prove not only the order of disqualification (by means of certificate of conviction or entry in a court register), but that the person before the court is the person so disqualified. There is no prescribed way that the identification of D as the person disqualified must be proved; it can be proved by any admissible means. Proof of identity may be given, for example, by an admission under the Criminal Justice Act (CJA) 1967, s 10, or by evidence of a person who was present in court when the disqualification was imposed. In addition, a written statement made under CJA 1967, s 9, which refers to a person whom the deponent knew and stating that the deponent knew him under a particular name, may provide sufficient evidence of identification. It will normally be possible to establish a prima facie case on the basis of a match between the personal details of D and those recorded on the certificate of conviction. Indeed, where D has a highly unusual name it may not be necessary for the date of birth on the certificate to correspond with his. If D calls no evidence to contradict a prima facie case, it is open to the court to be satisfied that it has been proved that D was the person disqualified. In addition, if it is proper and fair to do so and warning has been given, a failure to give contradictory evidence can additionally give rise to an adverse inference under the Criminal Justice and Public Order Act 1994, s 35, dealt with on p 260.

Offender escaping consequences of endorsable offence by deception

RTOA 1988, s 49 covers the case where, in dealing with a person convicted of an endorsable offence (ie one involving obligatory or discretionary endorsement), a court was deceived regarding any circumstances that were or might have been taken into account in deciding whether, or for how long, to disqualify him. It provides that, if the deception constituted or was due to an offence committed by that person and he is convicted of *that* offence, the court has the same powers of disqualification as the court which was deceived. However, the court must take account of the order made by the first court on his conviction for the endorsable offence.

Revocation of passenger-carrying vehicle or large goods vehicle drivers' licences

RTA 1988, s 115 requires that a passenger-carrying vehicle or large goods vehicle driver's licence (p 375):

(a) must be revoked by the Secretary of State if, in relation to its holder, prescribed circumstances occur; or

(b) must be revoked or suspended by the Secretary of State if the holder's conduct is such as to make him unfit to hold such a licence. A divisional court has held that 'conduct' such as to make a driver 'unfit to hold such a licence' refers to conduct 'as a driver of a motor vehicle'.

Section 115A makes similar provision in respect of the holder of a LGV Community licence or a PCV Community licence where that person ceases to be authorised to drive a LGV or PCV (as the case may be).

The 'prescribed circumstances' referred to in (a) are set out in respect of a large goods vehicle driver's licence or a LGV Community licence by MV(DL)R 1999, reg 55. They are that, in the case of the holder of such a licence who is *under 21*, the holder has been convicted, or is by virtue of RTOA 1988, s 58 (*effect of endorsement without hearing under fixed penalty points provisions*) to be treated as if he had been convicted, of an offence as a result of which more than three penalty points are to be taken into account. Where such large goods vehicle licences are revoked, the cases in which such persons must be disqualified indefinitely or for a fixed period must be determined by the Secretary of State. Where it is determined that the disqualification shall be for a fixed period, such a person must be disqualified until he reaches 21 or for such longer period as the Secretary of State may determine. No corresponding provisions have been made in respect of large passenger-carrying vehicle licences.

Where the Secretary of State orders disqualification until a test is passed, the test must be a test for a licence authorising the driving of any class of vehicle in Category C (other than C1), C + E, D or D + E which, prior to his disqualification by order of the court, the offender was authorised to drive by his revoked licence.

By RTA 1988, s 117 or 117A respectively, where a person's licence is revoked under s 115 or s 115A the Secretary of State must order that that person be disqualified. A disqualification under s 117 for more than two years may be removed after two years if the disqualification is for less than four years, or after half the disqualification period if that period is between four and 10 years, or five years in any other case, provided the applicant for removal has not incurred any penalty points (while disqualified) (reg 57).

RTA 1988, s 117 is modified by MV(DL)R 1999, reg 56, which applies where large goods vehicle or passenger-carrying vehicle drivers' licences are treated as revoked by RTOA 1988, s 37 (effect of disqualification by order of court), so as to provide that, where the licence to be treated as revoked is a large goods vehicle driver's licence held by a person under 21, the Secretary of State must order that person to be disqualified either indefinitely or for a fixed period, and where the Secretary of State determines that it shall be for a fixed period, he must be disqualified until he reaches 21 or for such longer period as the Secretary of State determines. Where the licence revoked is held by *any other person*, or is a large passenger-carrying vehicle driver's licence:

(a) the Secretary of State may order that person to be disqualified either indefinitely or for a fixed period; or

(b) the Secretary of State may order him to be disqualified for holding or obtaining a full licence until he passes a test if it appears that, owing to that person's conduct, it is expedient to require him to comply with the prescribed conditions applicable to provisional licences until he passes a test. This does not apply where the licence is a provisional licence.

DRIVING WHEN UNLAWFULLY IN THE UK

As from a day to be appointed, a person will commit an offence contrary to the Immigration Act 1971, s 24C if he drives when unlawfully in the UK. Sections 24D and 24E provide associated enforcement powers.

MOTOR VEHICLE INSURANCE

Using, or causing or permitting use of, a motor vehicle on a road without insurance

RTA 1988, s 143(1) states that a person must not use, or cause or permit any other person to use, a motor vehicle on a road or other public place unless there is in force in relation to the use of that vehicle by that person or that other person, as the case may be, such a policy of insurance or such security in respect of third-party risks as complies with the requirements of RTA 1988, Part VI. By s 143(2), breach of s 143(1) is an offence. Section 143(4) states that Part VI does not apply to invalid carriages not exceeding 254 kg unladen weight; a mobility scooter is a type of invalid carriage. Since electrically assisted pedal cycles (p 432) are not motor vehicles (unless they fall outside the relevant regulations), the provisions dealing with insurance do not apply to them.

As in the case of driving without a driving licence, the onus is upon the defendant (D), if proved to have used a motor vehicle on a road or other public place, to prove the existence of insurance as this is a fact peculiarly within his knowledge. However, a divisional court has said that if the prosecution contends that D used the vehicle *in a way not permitted by that insurance* the prosecution must prove *this fact*.

For the meaning of 'road' and 'public place', see pp 328 and 487 respectively. The terms 'use', 'cause' and 'permit' are discussed in Chapter 10. Basically, a person who drives a vehicle 'uses' it, but 'using' is not limited to driving. 'Use' means 'have the use of', with the result that, for example, if someone parks a motor vehicle on a road he can be said to be using it while it is parked, and it has been held that this is so even though the vehicle has been totally immobilised. Where an employee drives a motor vehicle owned by his employer in the course of his employment, his employer is regarded in law as also using it. A person 'causes' a vehicle to be used when, being in a position to do so, he expressly orders or authorises the vehicle to be used; and he 'permits' a vehicle to be used when he allows another person to use it. In each case, of course, the use must be on a road or other public place without there being in force in relation to the use of the person using the vehicle a requisite third-party policy of insurance or security.

The prohibition in s 143(1) against using, or causing or permitting the use of, an uninsured vehicle is strict in the sense that it is no defence that D reasonably believed that he, or the person allowed, etc to drive, was covered by an insurance policy, etc. There is one exception: under s 143(3) it is a defence for a person charged with *using* an uninsured vehicle to prove that it did not belong to him and was not in his possession under a contract of hiring or loan, and that he was using it in the course of his employment and neither knew nor had reason to believe that it was not properly insured, etc.

Can a person be said to permit his vehicle to be used on a road or other public place without insurance when he has lent it out on the express condition that it should only be used if its use is covered by insurance and its subsequent use is not so covered? The law provides a rather odd answer. If the condition is directly communicated to the person who uses the vehicle without insurance, the person imposing the condition does not permit his vehicle to be used without insurance. This seems sensible. How can you permit something which you have expressly forbidden? Thus, it is somewhat surprising that a divisional court has held that, if the condition as to use being covered by insurance has not been directly communicated to the user but has been communicated to someone else, for example to someone who borrows the vehicle, with a view to it being driven by the user, and it is used in breach of that condition, the person imposing the condition does in law permit uninsured use.

A person cannot permit another's use if he was not in a position to forbid it. Thus A, who supervises B, a learner driver, in B's own car cannot be convicted of permitting its uninsured use.

Causing death by driving: uninsured drivers

RTA 1988, s 3ZB creates an indictable (either way) offence of causing death by driving when uninsured. The offence is committed when it is shown that D was using a motor vehicle on a road while uninsured or unsecured against third-party risks, contrary to s 143, and that the death of another person was caused by the driving of that vehicle. Disqualification for not less than 12 months is obligatory. See, further, p 382.

Keeping vehicle not meeting insurance requirements

RTA 1988, s 144A creates an offence of keeping a motor vehicle which does not meet the insurance requirements. No use on a road or other public place is required. A vehicle will meet the insurance requirements if it is covered by a policy of insurance or a security complying with RTA 1988 and either the policy or security, or a related certificate, identifies the vehicle covered by its registration mark or the policy or security covers any vehicle, or any particular type of vehicle, owned by the person named in it or a related certificate. There are no penalty points to be imposed for this offence.

Section 144B specifies exceptions which are generally the same as those set out in s 144 (vehicles of local authorities, the police, and National Health Service, etc: see p 382).

Section 144B provides further exceptions where the vehicle is no longer kept by the registered keeper, it is not kept for use on a road or other public place or it has been stolen. However, these exceptions only apply if a 'prior statement' has been made in respect of the vehicle. The Motor Vehicles (Insurance Requirements) Regulations (MV(IR)R) 2011, regs 2–4 set out the following requirements for the 'prior statement':

(1) In the case of the exception relating to a vehicle no longer kept by the registered keeper (RK):
   (a) where the vehicle has been sold or transferred by the RK (other than to be destroyed or sent permanently out of Great Britain) the RK must, by the relevant time and in relation to that vehicle, have furnished the information and documents and made the declarations in accordance with the appropriate requirements;

(b) where the vehicle has been sold or transferred by the RK for the purpose of its destruction, that keeper must, by the relevant time and in relation to that vehicle, have furnished the information and documents and made the prescribed declarations, or been given a certificate of destruction; and

(c) where the vehicle has been sent permanently out of Great Britain, the RK must, by the relevant time and in relation to that vehicle, have notified the Secretary of State of that fact (reg 2).

(2) In the case of the exception relating to a vehicle not kept for use on a road or other public place, the RK must, by the relevant time and in relation to that vehicle, have made a statutory off-road notification (SORN) (reg 3).

(3) In the case of the exception relating to a vehicle which has been stolen, the RK must, by the relevant time and in relation to that vehicle, have given notification of the theft to a member (or employee) of a police force (reg 4).

A further exception under RTA 1988, s 144B, to an offence under s 144A is that:

(a) the RK is at the relevant time keeping the vehicle;

(b) neither a licence nor a nil licence under VERA 1994 was in force on 31 January 1998;

(c) neither a licence nor a nil licence has been taken out for the vehicle for a period starting after that date; and

(d) the vehicle has not been used or kept on a public road after that date.

RTA 1988, s 144C authorises the Secretary of State to serve a fixed penalty notice on a person whom he believes to have committed an offence against s 144A. That penalty is £100 but it is reduced to £50 if that amount is paid within 21 days of notice being given that a s 144A offence has been committed.

Immobilisation, removal, and disposal

The Motor Vehicles (Insurance Requirements) (Immobilisation, Removal and Disposal) Regulations 2011 (MV(IR)(I, R and D) R 2011) provide for the clamping of vehicles by an authorised person (AP) who has reason to believe that a s 144A offence has been committed, and their removal and disposal. An AP is a person authorised by the Secretary of State for the purposes of MV(IR)(I, R and D)R 2011. An AP may be a local authority, an employee of a local authority, a member of a police force or any other person. Different persons may be authorised for different purposes, but a person who is an AP for the purposes of reg 14 (appeals: below) must not act as an AP for any other purpose (reg 3).

By reg 4, MV(IR)(I, R and D)R 2011 do not apply where:

(a) a current disabled person's badge is displayed on the vehicle;

(b) the vehicle appears to an AP to have been abandoned;

(c) the vehicle is a public service vehicle being used for the carriage of passengers;

(d) the vehicle is being used for the purpose of the removal of any obstruction to traffic, the maintenance, improvement or reconstruction of a public road, or the laying, erection, alteration, repair or cleaning in or near a road of any traffic sign or sewer or of any main, pipe or apparatus for the supply of gas, water or electricity, or of any telegraph or telephone wires, cables, posts or supports; or

(e) the vehicle is being used by a universal service provider in relation to the provision of a universal postal service and each side of the vehicle is clearly marked with the name of the universal service provider concerned.

Power to immobilise vehicles   Where an AP has reason to believe that a s 144A offence is being committed as regards a vehicle which is stationary on a road or other public place, he (or a person acting under his direction) may:

(a) fix an immobilisation device to the vehicle while it remains in the place where it is stationary, or

(b) move it from that place to another place on the same or another road or public place and fix an immobilisation device to it in that other place.

The exercise of this power does not prevent a prosecution for an offence under RTA 1988, Part VI (ss 143 to 162) (reg 5).

Where an immobilisation device is so fixed to a vehicle, the person fixing it must also fix to the vehicle an immobilisation notice which:

(a) indicates that the device has been fixed to the vehicle and warns that no attempt should be made to drive it or otherwise put it in motion until it has been released from the device;

(b) states the reason why the device has been fixed;

(c) specifies the steps to be taken to secure its release, including the charges payable under MV(IR)(I, R and D)R 2011 and the person to whom and the means by which those charges may be paid; and

(d) states the right of the owner, or person in charge of the vehicle at the time it was immobilised, to appeal, and specifies the steps to be taken and the address to which representations to an AP should be sent.

Except in relation to a vehicle which is the subject of a hiring agreement or a hire-purchase agreement, references to the 'owner' of a vehicle at a particular time in MV(IR)(I, R and D)R 2011 are to the person by whom it was then kept and the registered keeper (RK) at a particular time is to be taken, unless the contrary is shown, to be the person by whom the vehicle was kept at that time.

For the purposes of regs 5 (above), 11 (below) and 12 (below), 'owner', in relation to a vehicle which is the subject of a hiring agreement or hire-purchase agreement, means a person who is a party to such an agreement.

Release of immobilised vehicle (reg 6)   A vehicle to which an immobilisation device has been fixed in accordance with reg 5:

(a) may only be released by, or under the direction of, an AP; and

(b) subject to (a), is to be released:

   (i) where an AP is satisfied that the vehicle was immobilised in any of the circumstances specified in reg 4; or

   (ii) if the following two requirements are met, viz.

      (*a*) that the prescribed charge (£100) for the release of the vehicle from the immobilisation device is paid in any manner specified in the immobilisation notice, and

      (*b*) that, in accordance with any instructions specified in the immobilisation notice, prescribed evidence is produced which establishes that any person who proposes to drive the vehicle away will not in doing so be guilty of an offence under RTA 1988, s 143, and that the RK is not, at the point of release, guilty of a s 144A offence as regards the vehicle.

For the purposes of MV(IR)(I, R and D)R 2011, 'prescribed evidence' means any of the following: a policy or certificate of insurance, or a policy or certificate of security in respect of third party risks.

Removal of or interference with immobilisation notice or device   An immobilisation notice must not be removed or interfered with except by or under the authority of an AP; it is an offence to do so (reg 7(1) and (2)).

Any person who, without being authorised to do so in accordance with reg 6, removes or attempts to remove an immobilisation device fixed to a vehicle is guilty of an offence (reg 7(3)).

Other offences connected with immobilisation (reg 8)   Where MV(IR)(I, R and D)R 2011 would apply to a vehicle but for the fact that a current disabled person's badge is displayed on it and the vehicle was not, at the time it was stationary, being used:

(a) in accordance with the 'Badges Regulations' made under regulations under the Chronically Sick and Disabled Persons Act 1970 (p 460), and
(b) in circumstances falling within the Road Traffic Regulation Act 1984, s 117(1)(b) ((b) on p 463),

the person in charge of the vehicle at that time is guilty of an offence.

Removal of vehicles (reg 9)   Where an AP has reason to believe that a s 144A offence:

(a) is being committed as regards a vehicle which is stationary on a road or other public place, or
(b) was being committed as regards a vehicle at the time when an immobilisation device which is fixed to the vehicle was fixed to it and:
    (i) 24 hours have elapsed since the device was fixed to the vehicle, and
    (ii) the vehicle has not been released in accordance with MV(IR)(I, R and D) R 2011,

the AP, or a person acting under his direction, may remove the vehicle and deliver it to a person authorised by the Secretary of State to keep vehicles so removed ('the custodian').

Disposal of removed vehicle (reg 10)   The custodian of a vehicle delivered in accordance with reg 9 may dispose of it by selling it or dealing with it as scrap, as he thinks fit.

Where the owner of a vehicle has disclaimed all rights of ownership of that vehicle, it may be disposed of at any time.

In any other case, a vehicle must not be disposed of before:

(a) the end of a period, beginning with the date on which the vehicle was removed in accordance with reg 9, of either:
    (i) in the case of a vehicle of no economic value, seven days, or
    (ii) in any other case, 14 days;
(b) the custodian has, for the purpose of ascertaining the owner of the vehicle, taken steps to ascertain from GB records or, as the case may be, Northern Irish records, the name and address of the RK, or, if the vehicle does not carry a GB or Northern Irish registration mark, the custodian has made such inquiries as appear to be practicable to ascertain the identity of the owner of the vehicle, and
(c) either:
    (i) the custodian has failed to ascertain the name and address of the owner; or

(ii) the owner has failed to comply with a notice in accordance with the following requirements served on the owner by first class post. The requirements are that the notice must be a notice addressed to the owner which states:

(*a*) the registration mark and make of the vehicle;

(*b*) the place where the vehicle was found before it was immobilised;

(*c*) the place to which it has been removed;

(*d*) the steps to be taken to obtain possession of it in accordance with reg 12 (below); and

(*e*) that unless it is removed by the owner on or before the date as specified below, the custodian intends to dispose of it;

and requires the owner to remove the vehicle from the custody of the custodian:

(*f*) in the case of a vehicle which is of no economic value, within three days of the date on which the notice is served; or

(*g*) in any other case, within seven days of that date.

For these purposes, a vehicle is of no economic value if the custodian is satisfied that the total prescribed charges for the removal of the vehicle and its storage for seven days exceed the resale or scrap value of the vehicle.

Where it appears to a custodian of a vehicle that more than one person is the owner:

(a) the notice under (c)(ii) must be sent to all persons appearing to be the owner of the vehicle; and

(b) the vehicle may not be disposed of in accordance with the italicised words above unless all persons appearing to be owners have disclaimed all rights of ownership.

Except in relation to a vehicle which is the subject of a hiring agreement or a hire-purchase agreement, references to the 'owner' of a vehicle at a particular time are to the person by whom it was then kept and the RK at a particular time is to be taken, unless the contrary is shown, to be the person by whom the vehicle was kept at that time (reg 2).

For the purposes of regs 10 and 13, 'owner', in relation to a vehicle which is the subject of a hiring agreement or hire-purchase agreement, means the person who, being a party to such agreement, has given up possession of the vehicle in return for payment under the agreement.

Recovery of prescribed charges (reg 11)   Where a vehicle has been removed and delivered into the custody of a custodian in accordance with reg 9, the Secretary of State or the custodian may (whether or not any claim is made under reg 12 or 14 (below)) recover from the person who was the owner of the vehicle when the vehicle was removed the prescribed charges for:

(a) its removal and storage; and

(b) its disposal, if the vehicle has been disposed of.

The relevant prescribed charges are:

Removal of a vehicle where possession is taken within the first 24 hours of such removal	£100
Removal of vehicle where the above does not apply	£200
Storage of vehicle for each period of 24 hours or part thereof	£21
Disposal of vehicle	£50

For the above purposes, 'owner' has the same meaning as for the purposes of reg 5 (p 393).

Where, by virtue of (a) above, any sum is recoverable in respect of a vehicle by a custodian, the custodian is entitled to retain custody of it until that sum is paid.

Where:

(a) it appears to a custodian of a vehicle that more than one person is the owner; and
(b) one of those owners, or a person authorised by one of those owners, has gained possession of the vehicle under reg 12 (below),

then the owner who gained possession of the vehicle under reg 12 must be treated as the owner from whom the sum is recoverable (reg 11(3)).

Where:

(a) it appears to a custodian of a vehicle that more than one person is the owner; and
(b) one of those owners has made a claim under reg 13 that satisfies conditions (a), (b) and (c) in reg 13, set out below,

then the owner who made the claim under reg 13 must be treated as the owner from whom the sum is recoverable (reg (11(4)).

Where:

(a) it appears to a custodian of a vehicle that more than one person is the owner; and
(b) neither reg 11(3) nor reg 11(4) applies,

then those persons must be treated as jointly and severally liable for the prescribed charges (reg 11(5)).

Taking possession of a vehicle (reg 12)   A person ('the claimant') may take possession of a vehicle which has been removed and delivered to a custodian and has not been disposed of under reg 10, if:

(a) the claimant satisfies the custodian that the claimant is the owner of the vehicle (see p 393), or a person authorised by the owner to take possession of the vehicle;
(b) except where the claimant produces evidence that no s 144A offence was committed or the custodian is satisfied that MV(IR)(I, R and D)R 2011 did not apply to the vehicle at the time it was immobilised or removed, the claimant pays to the custodian:
  (i) the prescribed charge in respect of the removal of the vehicle; and
  (ii) the prescribed charge for the storage of the vehicle during the period it was in the custody of the custodian; and
(c) prescribed evidence is produced which establishes that:
  (i) any person who proposes to drive the vehicle away will not in doing so be guilty of an offence under RTA 1988, s 143; and
  (ii) that such person is not, at the point of release, guilty of a s 144A offence as regards the vehicle.

On giving the claimant possession of a vehicle pursuant to the above, the custodian must give the claimant a statement of the right of the owner, or person in charge of the vehicle at the time it was immobilised or (where it was not immobilised) it was removed, to appeal, of the steps to be taken in order to appeal and of the address to which representations to an AP made as mentioned in reg 14 should be sent.

Where it appears to a custodian of a vehicle that more than one person is the owner, or person authorised by the owner, the custodian must give possession of the vehicle to the first claimant who satisfies the conditions set out in (a), (b) and (c).

Claim by owner of a vehicle after its disposal (reg 13) If, after a vehicle has been disposed of by a custodian pursuant to reg 10, a person claims to have been the 'owner' (as defined for the purposes of reg 10: p 395) of the vehicle at the time when it was disposed of and:

(a) the person making the claim satisfies the custodian that that person was the owner of the vehicle at the time it was disposed of; and

(b) the claim is made before the end of the period of one year beginning with the date on which the vehicle was disposed of; and

(c) no previous claim in respect of the vehicle has been paid,

the custodian must pay that person an amount calculated by deducting from the proceeds of sale the prescribed charges for the removal, storage and disposal of the vehicle.

Where it appears to a custodian of a vehicle that more than one person is the owner, the custodian must treat the first person who makes a claim that satisfies the conditions set out in (a), (b) and (c) above as the owner for the purposes of reg 13.

Appeal (reg 14) Where a dispute has arisen because:

(a) a person ('the claimant') has paid a charge in accordance with reg 6 or 12 in order to secure the release or to obtain possession of a vehicle and alleges that the charge ('the disputed charge') should be refunded to him on the ground that, at the time the vehicle was immobilised or, where it was not immobilised, at the time it was removed:

    (i) a s 144A offence was not being committed (*ground 1*); or

    (ii) any of the circumstances specified in reg 4 applied to the vehicle (*ground 2*); and

(b) the person to whom the disputed charge was paid refuses to refund the charge,

the claimant may appeal against the refusal of a refund by sending, to the AP whose name is given for this purpose in the immobilisation notice under reg 5 or the statement under reg 12 of the right of the owner, etc, at the address so given, written representations stating the grounds on which a refund is claimed.

The AP to whom the appeal is made may disregard representations and evidence received later than 28 days from the date on which the vehicle was released, or as the case may be, on which possession was taken.

The AP must uphold the appeal if satisfied that:

(a) *ground 1* or *ground 2* has been established; and

(b) the disputed charge has not been refunded.

Where the AP upholds an appeal, he must inform the claimant of the decision and the Secretary of State must refund the disputed charge.

Where the AP rejects the appeal, he must inform the claimant of the decision and of the right to make a further appeal.

A claimant who has made an appeal to an AP may make a further appeal to a magistrates' court:

(a) if the claimant's appeal has been rejected and the further appeal is made within 28 days of the claimant being served with notification to that effect; or

(b) if the AP has not notified the claimant of the outcome of the appeal and 56 days have elapsed since the claimant appealed.

If the court finds that:

(a) *ground 1* or *ground 2* has been established; and
(b) the disputed charge has not been refunded,

it must order the Secretary of State to refund the disputed charge.

Provision of information

MV(IR)R 2011, reg 7 provides that the Motor Insurers' Information Centre must make available to the Secretary of State, for the purpose of enforcing the s 144A offence, information relating to vehicle insurance policies in the UK and to vehicles which are permitted to be used on the road without insurance.

Third-party insurance policies

Certificate of insurance

The requirement made by RTA 1988, s 143 is that there must be a policy of insurance (or a security: see later) in respect of third-party risks in accordance with Part VI (ie ss 143 to 162) of that Act in relation to the use of the vehicle by the person using it. By s 147, an insurer issuing a policy of insurance must deliver to the person insured a certificate of insurance in the prescribed form. Delivery of the certificate may be by electronic transmission, or via a website, with the insured's consent. 'Telephone insurance' is not valid; no certificate has been delivered at that time giving evidence of a contract between insurer and insured. Police officers frequently exercise discretion in circumstances in which a company has clearly accepted liability for third-party risks but some technicality has delayed delivery of a certificate. A cover note is a certificate.

What must be covered

RTA 1988, s 145 provides that, in order to comply with the requirements of Part VI, a policy must be issued by an 'authorised insurer' and must insure such person, persons or classes of persons as may be specified in it in respect of any liability which may be incurred by him or them in respect of the death of or bodily injury to any person (other than the driver) or damage to property up to a maximum value of £1,000,000 caused by, or arising out of, the use of the vehicle on a road or other public place in Great Britain.
    The policy must also cover him or them:

(a) in respect of any liability for the emergency treatment of persons injured;
(b) in the case of a vehicle normally based in Great Britain, in respect of any liability which may be incurred as a result of its use within the territory of any EU member state, according to the law on compulsory insurance against civil liability in that state or, if it would give higher cover, according to the law which would be applicable if the vehicle was used in Great Britain; and
(c) in the case of a vehicle normally based in another EU state, in respect of any liability which may be incurred as a result of the use of the vehicle in Great Britain if, under the law of that other state, he or they would be required to be insured in respect of a liability which would arise under it had the event occurred in that state, and the cover required by that law is higher than that required as indicated in (a).

Extent of cover

The nature of the policy held will be specified in the certificate. A policy covering use for social, domestic and pleasure purposes does not cover business use. However, to give a lift to a friend who is on business at the time is not a business use of the vehicle. To help move household goods for a friend without payment is not a business use, but it might be if payment was made. It is usual for non-business policies to exclude use for hire or reward, but RTA 1988, s 150 makes specific provisions for 'car-sharing' schemes. Provided that arrangements are made before the journey that payment is in respect of running costs and depreciation only, and that the vehicle used is not adapted to carry more than eight passengers, the use is not for hire or reward.

The extent of cover is the cover specified in the policy of insurance. In disputed cases this depends on the construction of the insurance policy rather than the views of the insurance company or its willingness to meet liabilities.

Some policies allow persons to drive with the permission of the insured person if such a person 'holds or has held a driving licence' and is not disqualified. If a person has at any time held a licence, whether full or provisional, it is sufficient in law to satisfy such a requirement. The terms of the policy will have to be examined in circumstances in which the class of vehicle which the person is licensed to drive is different to the class of vehicle which is being driven. If the policy demands that such a person holds or has held a licence to cover the same class of vehicle as is covered by the policy, then use by a person who does not hold (and has not held) such a licence will amount to uninsured use, unless the licence which he holds may act as a provisional one to cover use of the vehicle in question. Similarly, where a person has borrowed a vehicle subject to an implied limitation, of which he was aware, concerning the purpose for which the vehicle was to be driven, he does not have the consent of the owner for a purpose outside that limitation. Where, therefore, insurance cover was dependent upon the driver having 'the consent of the owner thereof', use outside that limitation was uninsured use.

The use of trailers in Great Britain does not expressly need to be covered in respect of third-party risks, whereas this is essential in other EU countries. However, the use of trailers in Great Britain is generally covered in all policies of insurance and would seem to be within the use of the motor vehicle in any case. Injury caused to a person by a trailer is certainly caused due to the use of the motor vehicle on a road or other public place.

Validity

When a policy has been taken out it remains in force until it expires or is validly set aside. If a disqualified driver obtains insurance by failing to disclose his disqualification, then, although such insurance is obtained by means of a false declaration, it remains valid until the company takes steps to set aside the policy. If the company does set it aside, this only invalidates the policy for the future.

It is the practice of some insurance companies to insert restrictive clauses in their policies which can affect their validity in particular circumstances. However, RTA 1988, s 148 states that the third-party requirement of s 143 must be covered by companies regardless of restrictions which might be inserted covering the age, mental or physical condition of a driver; the condition of the vehicle; the number of persons carried; the load; the times or areas of use; the horsepower cylinder capacity or value of the vehicle; the carrying of any special apparatus, or the carrying on the vehicle of special identification marks.

When a person is apprehended for taking motor vehicles without consent, it is good practice to check any certificate of insurance held by him in respect of motor vehicles. It is the terms of the policy which are important, not the moral implications. If his policy covers the use by him of another vehicle not owned by him or hired to him by a hire-purchase agreement, that policy will cover such use even though the vehicle has been taken illegally. It would be different if the use covered was similar but 'with the consent of the owner of such vehicle'.

Securities and other exemptions from insurance requirements

Securities

A security, rather than a policy of insurance, can satisfy the provisions of RTA 1988, Part VI if it satisfies certain conditions set out in s 146. The security must consist of an undertaking by the giver of the security (who must be an authorised insurer or some body of persons in the business of giving securities which has deposited with the Accountant General of the Senior Courts the sum of £500,000 in respect of that business). The undertaking must be to make good, subject to any conditions specified therein, any failure by the person covered by the security duly to discharge any third-party liability for which insurance would otherwise be required under Part VI of the Act. Use of securities is frequently made by large undertakings, such as bus companies, which would experience unnecessary difficulties in negotiating separate insurance in respect of a large fleet of vehicles. Although a person giving a security must deliver to the person to whom it is given a 'certificate of security', non-delivery of the certificate does not render the security of no effect.

Exemptions

The offences relating to use without third-party insurance or security, which are provided by RTA 1988, s 143, are subject to exemptions provided by s 144. Section 144 exempts from the requirement for third-party insurance or security:

(a) a vehicle owned by a local authority, a National Parks Authority or the Broads Authority at a time when it is being driven under the owner's control;

(b) a vehicle owned by a local policing body or police authority being driven under its control, or a vehicle driven by a person for police purposes by or under the direction of a police constable, or by a person employed by a local policing body, etc or by a member of the civilian staff of the police force; a police officer on duty using his own car for police purposes falls within this exemption;

(c) a vehicle being driven for salvage purposes pursuant to the Merchant Shipping Act 1995, Part IX;

(d) a vehicle owned by a health service body, or an ambulance owned by an NHS Trust, or NHS foundation trust, at a time when it is being driven under the owner's control;

(e) a vehicle made available by the Secretary of State or the Welsh Ministers to any person, body or local authority under the National Health Service Act 1977 at a time when it is being used within the terms on which it is being made available; or

(f) a vehicle used by the Care Quality Commission, at a time when the vehicle is being used under the owner's control.

The reasoning behind these exemptions is clear: the vehicles are either owned by or being used by undertakings which are in a position to meet liabilities which might be incurred. Crown vehicles appear to be similarly exempt, as RTA 1988, s 183, which deals with the application of the provisions of the Act to the Crown, does not mention s 143.

Fraud, forgery, etc

By RTA 1988, s 174(5), it is an indictable (either way) offence to make a false statement, or to withhold any material information, for the purpose of obtaining the issue of a certificate of insurance or security, or any other document which may be produced in lieu of such a certificate of insurance or security. Any person who issues such a document which to his knowledge is false in any material particular commits an offence against s 175(1).

The alternative documents to which s 174(5) refers are specified by the Motor Vehicles (Third-Party Risks) Regulations 1972, reg 7 as follows:

(a) duplicates of certificates of security;
(b) certificates of deposit;
(c) a certificate signed by a specified body, local policing body, police authority, etc; or
(d) in the case of a vehicle normally based in another EU country, or Norway or Switzerland, a document issued by the insurer in the prescribed form.

The making of false statements to obtain insurance is not uncommon. The disclosure of previous convictions for motoring offences, particularly those involving endorsement, can lead to high premiums which can be avoided by non-disclosure. In this context, the Rehabilitation of Offenders Act 1974 is important. The Act provides for convictions to become 'spent'. It also provides that where a question seeking information with respect to a person's previous convictions is put to him, otherwise than in proceedings before a judicial authority, the question must be treated as not relating to spent convictions and answers may be made accordingly. Most road traffic offences will have resulted in a fine and as a result will become spent after a period of 12 months.

It is not necessary to prove that the person who made the statement was aware of its falsity (or even of the risk that it might be false).

RTA 1988, s 173(1) makes it an indictable (either way) offence for a person, with intent to deceive, to forge, alter, use, lend for use, or allow to be used, a certificate of insurance or a document which may be used in lieu thereof. Section 173(1) also provides an indictable (either way) offence of making, or having in possession, with intent to deceive, any document or other thing so closely resembling a document or other thing of the above types as to be calculated (ie likely) to deceive. Uncompleted insurance forms can be documents for this purpose; so can an expired certificate, if used with intent to deceive.

Other requirements in respect of motor vehicle insurance

RTA 1988, s 154 requires any person against whom a claim is made in respect of any such liability as is required to be insured against by s 145 (see p 398) to provide particulars of his insurance cover in respect of that liability. It is an offence under s 154(2) to fail to do so without reasonable excuse, or wilfully to make a false statement in reply to such a demand. Section 154 allows the administrative officers of hospitals, etc to recover the cost of emergency treatment from vehicle insurers.

Persons temporarily in Great Britain

The Motor Vehicles (International Motor Insurance Card) Regulations 1971, reg 5 authorises a visitor to Great Britain to use his motor vehicle under the internationally recognised 'green card' insurance provision. 'Green cards' are referred to in the regulations as 'valid insurance cards'. A peculiarity of this provision is that a green card remains valid after the expiry date shown. This is to prevent the complications which would otherwise arise if holiday visitors decided to extend their stay. A constable's powers in respect of insurance certificates, etc apply to 'green cards'.

Certificates of insurance or security issued in Northern Ireland are, of course, valid in Great Britain.

Disclosure of vehicle insurance information to Secretary of State

SOCPA 2005, s 153 empowers the Secretary of State to make regulations requiring the Motor Insurers' Information Centre to make available 'relevant motor vehicle insurance information' to the Secretary of State for processing with a view to making the processed information available for use by police officers. 'Relevant motor vehicle insurance information' means information relating to vehicles whose use was, but is no longer, insured. The Disclosure of Vehicle Insurance Information Regulations 2005 require the provision of such information at such intervals as reasonably required. It must then be processed in a form which either (a) will be of assistance to a police officer in determining whether or not an offence of uninsured use of a vehicle has been committed, or (b) will enable chief officers of police to further process it to assist a police officer in determining whether such an offence has been committed. A constable may use the processed information to determine whether to demand production of evidence of insurance under RTA 1988, s 165. Processed information must not be disclosed other than for the purposes of proceedings.

Production of evidence of insurance

RTA 1988, s 165 states that a person:

(a) driving a motor vehicle, other than an invalid carriage, on a road; or
(b) whom a constable or vehicle examiner reasonably believes to have:
    (i) been the driver of such a motor vehicle on a road or other public place when an accident occurred, etc; or
    (ii) committed an offence in relation to the use of such a motor vehicle on a road,

must, on being required by a constable or vehicle examiner, give his name and address and the name and address of the owner of the vehicle, and produce for examination the relevant certificate of insurance (or electronic access to a copy of it where it was transmitted electronically or made available via a website by the insurer), etc. The Court of Appeal has held that the 'relevant certificate of insurance' is a certificate covering the driving of a vehicle, whether or not the vehicle is identified in the certificate (as where a borrower of the vehicle is driving it on his insurance). Failure to do any of these things is an offence. The usual provisions concerning production of documents apply, allowing seven days for production; or production as soon as reasonably practicable; or proof that production was not reasonably practicable before the day on which proceedings were instituted. The documents (unlike a driving licence) need not be produced in person.

The provisions of s 165 requiring a person to give his name and address and the name and address of the owner of the vehicle also apply to a supervisor of a provisional licence-holder in each of the circumstances set out above.

Police powers of seizure of vehicles being driven without a driving licence or insurance

RTA 1988, s 165A provides that:

(a) where a constable in uniform requires, under RTA 1988, s 164, the production of a licence (p 379), or under s 165, the production of evidence of insurance; and
(b) it is not produced; and
(c) the constable has reasonable grounds for believing that the vehicle was being driven in contravention of s 87(1) (requirement to have a driving licence) or s 143 (requirement to have insurance),

the constable may seize the vehicle and remove it.

Section 165A also provides that:

(a) where a constable in uniform has required, under s 163 (p 443), a person driving a motor vehicle to stop it; and
(b) there is a failure to do so, or a failure to do so for a sufficient time to allow the constable to make appropriate enquiries, and the constable has reasonable grounds for believing that the vehicle is being driven in contravention of s 87(1) (driving without licence) or s 143 (uninsured driving),

he may seize and remove it.

Section 165A empowers the constable to enter any premises (other than a private dwelling house) on which he has reasonable grounds for believing the vehicle to be in order to seize it. The constable may use reasonable force to seize and remove the vehicle or to enter premises to seize and remove it.

Before seizing a vehicle under s 165A, and provided it is practicable to do so, a constable must warn the person by whom it appears that the vehicle is, or was being, driven in contravention of either s 87(1) or s 143 that he will seize the vehicle if the relevant documents are not produced. On seizing a vehicle under s 165A, a constable must give a seizure notice (below) to the driver unless the circumstances make it impracticable to do so.

Where there has been a failure to stop, the power of seizure is valid for a period of 24 hours.

Retention and disposal of vehicles seized under powers provided by RTA 1988, s 165A

The Road Traffic Act 1988 (Retention and Disposal of Seized Motor Vehicles) Regulations 2005 provide for the retention, safe-keeping and disposal by an authorised person (AP), ie a constable or other person authorised by the chief officer of police, of vehicles seized under RTA 1988, s 165A.

Such a vehicle must be passed into and remain in the custody of an AP until the AP permits it to be removed from his custody by a person appearing to him to be the registered keeper or owner of the vehicle, or until it has been disposed of in accordance with the Regulations.

An AP must, as soon as is reasonably practicable after he has taken a vehicle into his custody, take such steps as are reasonably practicable to give a seizure notice to the person who is the registered keeper of the vehicle and to the owner, where that person appears to be someone different, unless (a) the AP is satisfied that a seizure notice has already been given, by a constable on seizing the vehicle, to the registered keeper and to the owner, where it appears that the owner is a different person; or (b) the vehicle has been released from his custody in accordance with the Regulations.

A seizure notice must contain information which can be or could have been ascertained from an inspection of the vehicle, or has been ascertained from another source, as to the registration mark and make of the vehicle. It also must include a statement as to the place of seizure and the place where the vehicle is now being kept; a requirement that the keeper or owner claim the vehicle from an AP on or before a date specified in the notice (not less than seven working days from the date upon which the notice is given); a statement that unless the vehicle is claimed on or before that date, an AP intends to dispose of it; a notice that charges are payable and that the vehicle may be retained until they are paid and a notice that the registered keeper or owner must either:

(a) produce at a specified police station a valid insurance certificate covering his use of that vehicle and a valid licence authorising him to drive that vehicle; or

(b) nominate for this purpose a third person who produces at a specified police station such a valid certificate and such a valid licence.

The notice must also make clear that the vehicle may be retained until (a) or (b) is satisfied.

A seizure notice may be given:

(a) by delivering it to the person to whom it is directed;

(b) in the case of the registered keeper, by leaving it at the registered address or by sending it by registered post to that address;

(c) in the case of the owner, by leaving it at his usual or last known address, or by sending it by registered post to that address;

(d) in the case of a body corporate, by delivering it to the secretary or clerk of the body at its registered or principal office, or by sending it by registered post addressed to that secretary or clerk at that office.

Where, before a relevant motor vehicle is disposed of, a person satisfies an AP that he is the registered keeper or owner of that vehicle, pays the appropriate charge and produces at a police station specified in the notice a valid insurance certificate covering his use of the vehicle and a valid driving licence authorising him to drive the vehicle (or such documents are produced by a nominated person), the AP must permit him to remove the vehicle from custody. An AP may consider any documentary evidence produced to him in determining whether a person who claims to be the owner of a motor vehicle is in fact the owner.

A person, who would otherwise be liable to pay the appropriate charge, is not liable to pay it if he was not driving the vehicle at the time when it was seized under s 165A; did not know that the vehicle was being driven at that time; had not consented to it being driven; and could not, by taking reasonable steps, have prevented it from being driven.

An AP is empowered to dispose of a vehicle if:

(a) where the registered keeper and the owner appear to be the same person, that person fails to comply with any requirement in the seizure notice, or an AP was not able, after taking reasonably practicable steps, to give a seizure notice to that person;

(b) where the owner and registered keeper appear to be different:

   (i) where the seizure notice was given to both of those persons, neither the registered keeper nor the owner complies with all the requirements of the seizure notice;

   (ii) where, having taken such steps as were reasonably practicable, the AP was only able to give a seizure notice to one of them, that person fails to comply with any requirement in that seizure notice; or

   (iii) where, after taking reasonably practicable steps, the AP was not able to give a seizure notice to either the registered keeper or the owner.

An AP may not dispose of a vehicle:

(a) during the period of 14 days starting with the date of seizure; or

(b) if that date has expired, until after a date specified in the seizure notice; or

(c) if not otherwise covered by (a) or (b), during the period of seven working days starting with the date on which the vehicle is claimed under the above provisions.

Where there is a disposal by way of sale, the net proceeds of that sale must be paid to any person who, within a one-year period beginning with the date of sale, satisfies an AP that at the time of the sale he was the owner of the vehicle. Where it appears that there may be more than one owner, the proceeds must be paid to such one of them as the AP thinks fit. The term 'net proceeds' refers to that part of the money remaining after the deduction of charges under the legislation.

INFORMATION AS TO IDENTITY OF DRIVER IN SPECIFIED CASES

The requirement to give information

RTA 1988, s 172(2) provides that where the driver of a vehicle is alleged to be guilty of an offence to which the section applies:

(a) the person keeping the vehicle must give such information as to the identity of the driver as he may be required to give by or on behalf of a chief officer of police. A requirement made with the express or implied authority of the chief officer is given on his behalf; and

(b) any other person must if required as stated above give any information which is in his power to give and may lead to the identification of the driver.

The expression 'any other person' includes the driver himself.

Section 172 applies to:

(a) all offences against RTA 1988, except an offence under Part V (driving instruction), or s 13 (promoting motoring events on highway), s 16 (wearing of protective headgear), s 51(2) (certain test conditions—goods vehicles), s 61(4) (certain type approval requirements), s 67(9) (obstructing a vehicle examiner), s 68(4) (failing to proceed to place of vehicle inspection), s 96 (driving with uncorrected defective eyesight), or s 120 (offence against regulations dealing with licensing of drivers of large goods vehicles and passenger-carrying vehicles);

(b) an offence under RTOA 1988, s 25 (information as to date of birth and sex after conviction), s 26 (interim disqualification), or s 27 (production of a licence on conviction);

(c) any offence against any other enactment relating to the use of vehicles on roads; and

(d) manslaughter by the driver of a motor vehicle.

A requirement may be made by way of written notice and served by post. Where it is so made it has effect as a requirement to give the information within the 28-day period beginning on the day on which the notice is served.

Where more than one individual is registered as the keeper of a vehicle (eg where husband and wife are joint keepers), a notice under s 172 may be sent to them jointly; if there is a failure to comply and no defence is shown under s 172(4) or (7)(b) (below) each is guilty of the offence under s 172(3) (below).

The offence

By RTA 1988, s 172(3), a person who fails to comply with such a requirement commits an offence. However, by s 172(4), a person who *keeps* the vehicle is not guilty of the offence if he shows that he did not know, and could not with reasonable diligence have ascertained, who the driver of the vehicle was. A divisional court has held that the answer to the question of whether the driver's identity was known or could have been ascertained with reasonable diligence is to be assessed from the date the requirement is made and not earlier; the keeper is not required to keep a written record of those to whom he lends the vehicle. Section 172(4) is subject to s 172(6) in the case of a corporate body; s 172(6) provides that s 172(4) does not apply unless the alleged offender also shows that no record of those who drove the vehicle was kept and that the failure to do so was reasonable. Any other person must be proved to have had the information within his power to give.

The fact that D does not know the driver's identity does not excuse him if he simply fails to respond to a requirement for information (as opposed to responding and saying that he does not know). There must be evidence of the notice and that a requirement under s 172 has been made. This can be done by annexing a copy of the notice and requirement to a written statement under CJA 1967, s 9. By s 172(7)(b), where the requirement is posted, D is not guilty of the offence if he shows that he gave the information as soon as reasonably practicable after the end of the 28-day period or that it had not been reasonably practicable for him to give it. A divisional court has held that it is not necessary to prove that D knew that he was required to provide the specified information, but that in an appropriate case D might be able to show that it was not reasonably practicable for him to be aware of the notice, in which case s 172(7)(b) would apply.

Procedure in respect of the notice

It is not necessary to specify the nature of the offence alleged to have been committed. Where a notice has been produced from an official source and has every appearance of authenticity, justices may draw an inference as to the validity of the notice.

A divisional court has held that the obligation to respond is an obligation to respond in the manner specified in the notice. Thus, for example, if the notice requires (as usual) that information be given in writing and signed, the obligation to respond is not satisfied by providing the required information by telephone.

Where (as usual) a requirement under RTA 1988, s 172(2) has been served by post, RTOA 1988, s 12 permits a court to accept a signed statement as evidence that the signatory was the driver of the vehicle at the time in question. A divisional court has held that where the name of the driver had been inserted in block capitals on the form sent to him, but there was no signature, this could not be a statement in writing purporting to be signed by D for the purposes of s 12 in the circumstances. On the other hand, where a registered keeper replied to a s 172(2) request by endorsing the form sent by the police, 'please see covering letter enclosed', and the letter was signed by him, a divisional court allowed an appeal by the keeper against his conviction for failing to provide the required information.

DANGEROUS ACTIVITIES

Dangerous parking

RTA 1988, s 22 makes it an offence to cause or permit a vehicle or trailer drawn by it to remain at rest on a road in such a position, or in such condition or in such circumstances, as to involve danger of injury to other persons. The danger may be caused by the manner of the parking, the condition of the bodywork, etc which may come into contact with persons, or other circumstances. It has been held that, where a vehicle has been parked without the brake being properly set and the vehicle moves and injures a pedestrian, the offence is committed.

Causing danger to road users

By RTA 1988, s 22A, a person commits an indictable (either way) offence if he intentionally and without lawful authority or reasonable cause:

(a) causes anything to be on or over a road; or
(b) interferes with a motor vehicle, trailer or cycle; or
(c) interferes (directly or indirectly) with traffic equipment,

in such circumstances that it would be obvious to a reasonable person that to do so would be dangerous. If the danger would have been obvious to a *reasonable* person, it is irrelevant that D was unaware of it. In relation to (b), it has been held that 'interferes' suggests 'tampering' with the vehicle and that a person who stands in front of a vehicle does not interfere with it.

'*Dangerous*' refers to danger either of injury to any person while on or near a road, or of serious damage to property on or near a road. In determining what would be 'obvious' to a reasonable person in a particular case, regard must be had not only to the circumstances of which he could be expected to be aware but also to any circumstances shown to have been within the knowledge of D.

With regard to (a) above, where persons are seen on a bridge over a motorway in possession of large pieces of concrete, and then are seen to *balance* these objects on the parapet, they certainly cause those objects to be over a road and it is submitted that it would be obvious to a reasonable person that what they are doing is dangerous. Protesters who erect a barrier across a road will not normally be guilty of an offence under s 22A if the barrier is solid and easily seen. Although their actions are otherwise unlawful, the essential element of 'danger' is normally missing in such circumstances. However, the stretching of a thin rope or wire across a road would cause the type of danger which the section seeks to outlaw.

A person who interferes with a vehicle's brakes or steering clearly interferes with it for the purposes of (b), above, in such circumstances that it would be obvious to a reasonable person that to do so would be dangerous. The Court of Appeal has held that interference with a vehicle, etc does not have to take place prior to its being driven, etc, nor does it have to have altered its physical state. Thus, conduct which interferes with a mechanical part of a vehicle, as where a passenger applies the handbrake of a moving car, interferes with the vehicle even though the interfering person is inside it. Interfering with the driver (eg grabbing him), as opposed to the vehicle, is not enough.

For the purposes of (c) above, 'traffic equipment' means:

(a) anything lawfully placed on or near a road by a highway authority;
(b) a traffic sign lawfully placed on or near a road by a person other than a highway authority;
(c) any fence, barrier or light lawfully placed on or near a road (i) to protect street works or undertakings, or (ii) by a constable or person acting on the instructions (whether general or specific) of a chief officer of police.

Any such thing placed on or near a road is, unless the contrary is proved, deemed to have been lawfully placed.

For another offence of dangerousness, see p 409.

LAW RELATING TO HIGHWAYS

Highways

The meaning of the term 'highway' for the purposes of the Highways Act 1980 (HA 1980) is given in HA 1980, s 328. Section 328 states that the term includes the whole or part of a highway other than a ferry or waterway. Where a highway passes over a bridge or through a tunnel, the bridge or tunnel is, for the purposes of the Act, a part of the highway. Section 328 does not define 'highway'; instead, that term is defined by common law (see p 328).

Obstruction of highway

By HA 1980, s 137(1), it is an offence for a person, without lawful authority or excuse, in any way wilfully to obstruct the free passage along the highway.

Whether or not there was an *obstruction* is a question of degree for a court to decide; a complete blockage of the highway is not required. Whether or not a use of the highway amounts to an obstruction depends upon whether or not it was unreasonable having regard to all the circumstances of the case, including where it occurs, its duration, its nature, its extent and its purpose, and whether there is an actual, as opposed to a potential, obstruction. Where a supermarket left trolleys in a pedestrian precinct for the convenience of shoppers there was an obstruction even though no complaint had been made by a member of the public. In another case there was held to be an obstruction where for 15 years a bridleway had been completely blocked by farm gates, tied by twine to hedges and held closed by a loop of twine, which could be opened easily. Simply to cause fear to users of a highway cannot amount to an obstruction. A divisional court so held in a case where D allowed his Rottweiler dogs to act in a menacing way behind a fence separating his land from a path constituting a highway. Pedestrians on the path were put in fear but, said the court, the highway was not obstructed.

The term *'wilfully'* in this context means that the particular obstruction was occasioned by some deliberate act which was freely carried out by D; consequently, a motorist who stops at a traffic light showing red does not wilfully obstruct the highway. In one case, a man who addressed a crowd, whose assembly interfered with traffic although traffic movement was not completely stopped, was held to have caused a wilful obstruction because, by the exercise of free will, he caused that obstruction to take place. On the other hand, if a queue forms outside a shop because many customers are attracted to it, it cannot be said that the shopkeeper has committed a deliberate and wilful act which caused the obstruction, as he is trading in a normal way. It would be different if the obstruction was caused because he was trading in an unusual way, for example through the window, as that unusual act would be wilful and would lead to an obstruction.

The question of whether or not a person has '*lawful authority or excuse*' will always be a question for the court to decide. Clearly, a road block established in accordance with PACE would have lawful authority. 'Lawful excuse' embraces activities lawful in themselves which are a reasonable use of the highway or incidental to the right of passage. On the other hand, the right to protest does not give a right to obstruct the highway; consequently there is no lawful authority or excuse for such obstruction.

Danger or annoyance on highway

HA 1980, s 161 makes it an offence for any person, without lawful authority or excuse:

(a) to deposit anything on a highway in consequence of which a user is injured or endangered (s 161(1)); or
(b) to light any fire on or over a highway which consists of or comprises a carriageway, or to discharge any firearm or firework within 50 feet of the centre of such a highway, if in consequence a user of the highway is injured, interrupted or endangered (s 161(2)).

Section 161A(1) prohibits a person from lighting a fire on any land not forming part of a highway which consists of or comprises a carriageway, or from directing or permitting such a fire to be lit, when in consequence a user of any highway which consists of or comprises a carriageway is injured, interrupted or endangered by, or by smoke from, that fire or any other fire caused by that fire. However, s 161A(2) provides a defence if it can be proved that at the time the fire was lit the person was satisfied on reasonable grounds that it was unlikely that users of any such highway would be injured, interrupted or endangered by the fire or by smoke from it, or from any other fire caused by it, and *either* that before or after the fire was lit he did all that he reasonably could to prevent the consequences *or* that he had reasonable excuse for not doing so. Section 161A is aimed at preventing smoke clouds, caused by straw burning in surrounding fields, blowing over motorways and main roads.

Section 161(4) punishes those who, without lawful authority or excuse, allow filth, lime or dirt, or other offensive matter or thing, to run on to a highway from any adjoining premises.

Section 161(3) prohibits the playing of football or any other game on a highway to the annoyance of a user of the highway. This offence creates many problems for police officers. Usually a complaint is received by telephone from a householder who wishes to complain that he is being annoyed by children playing football in the street. The offence is only committed when the game is 'to the annoyance of a user of the highway'; a person sitting in his house is not such a 'user'. A person who was not using the highway when annoyed cannot be subsequently annoyed by walking into the street unless the game continues to his annoyance when on the highway.

It is an offence contrary to s 162 to place, for any purpose, a rope, wire or other apparatus across a highway in such a manner as to be likely to cause danger to persons using the highway, unless D proves that he had taken necessary means to give adequate warning. A washing line in a back street with white sheets suspended from it certainly involves the stretching of a rope across the highway, but in the circumstances it can easily be proved that adequate warning was given. However, if the washing is taken in and only the rope is left, it will be harder to prove that the necessary steps were taken to give adequate warning.

Builders' skips

HA 1980, s 139 provides that a builder's skip must not be deposited on the highway without the permission of the highway authority; otherwise an offence is committed under s 139(3).

Such permission must be in writing; it is granted to a named person and the highway where the skip is to be located is specified. Each skip must be authorised on each occasion; a general permission to place skips is not possible. The authority may impose conditions on its permission. These may refer to the siting of the skip, its dimensions, the painting of the skip to make it visible, the care and disposal of its contents, the manner in which it is to be lighted or guarded and its removal at the end of the authorised period. Skips must be fitted with two oblong plates of diagonal red and yellow fluorescent or reflective material, similar to those fitted to heavy goods vehicles.

Section 139 also provides that, whatever the conditions imposed, an owner must secure that the skip is properly lit during the hours of darkness, that it is clearly and indelibly marked with the owner's name and with his telephone number or address, that it is removed as soon as possible after it has been filled, and that all conditions of the permission are complied with. Failure to do so is an offence under s 139(4) on the part of the owner. The term 'owner' in relation to a skip which is hired for a month or more, or one which is the subject of a hire-purchase agreement, means the person in possession of the skip under the hiring agreement.

Where the commission by any person of an offence under s 139 is due to the act or default of some other person, that other person is also guilty and may be convicted whether or not proceedings are taken against the first-mentioned person.

It is a defence to a charge under s 139 for D to prove that the commission of the offence was due to the act or default of another and that D took all reasonable precautions and exercised all due diligence to avoid the commission of the offence by himself or any other person under his control.

Section 140 provides that, regardless of whether or not permission has been obtained, the highway authority or a constable in uniform may require the owner of a skip to remove it, or reposition it, or cause it to be removed or repositioned. To fail to do so as soon as possible is an offence. A request by a constable must be made in person; a request by telephone, for example, is not sufficient.

Use of loudspeakers

The Control of Pollution Act 1974, s 62 bans the operation of loudspeakers in a street between 9 pm and 8 am the following morning for any purpose. It also bans their use at any other time for the purpose of advertising any entertainment, trade or business. Breach of these bans is an offence under s 62(1). The term 'street' means any highway and any other road, footway, square, or court which is for the time being open to the public. The ban is therefore effective both in built-up areas and in the country, provided, in either case, the loudspeaker is operated in a 'street'.

The exemptions to these provisions are predictable. They are: use for police, fire and rescue or ambulance purposes; by the Environment Agency (or the Natural Resources Body for Wales) or a water undertaking in the exercise of its functions, or by a local authority; 'in-vehicle' entertainments or announcements; telephones; use by showmen at a pleasure fair; and use in an emergency provided that the loudspeaker is operated so as not to give reasonable cause for annoyance to persons in the vicinity.

The most common exception to the general rule against the use of loudspeakers for advertising is in favour of those who have a loudspeaker fixed to a vehicle used for the conveyance of a perishable commodity for human consumption, which is used solely for the purpose of informing the public (by means other than words) that the commodity is on sale from the vehicle. Such a loudspeaker must be operated so as not to give reasonable cause for annoyance to persons in the vicinity and it may only be used between noon and 7 pm of the same day. Thus 'ice-cream chimes' can be used between these times, but at no other.

SPECIAL EVENTS ON ROADS

The Road Traffic Regulation Act 1984, ss 16A and 16B permit traffic authorities to make temporary orders restricting/prohibiting traffic in connection with sporting events, social events or entertainments on a road. By s 16C(1), contravention of such an order is an offence.

An order may not be made in relation to motor racing, and may only be made in respect of a motor 'competition or trial' or a bicycle race or time trial if authorised by or under RTA 1988, s 13 or s 31 (see pp 501 and 431).

OFF-ROAD DRIVING

RTA 1988, s 34(1) prohibits a person from driving a mechanically propelled motor vehicle, without lawful authority, on to or on any common land, moorland or land of any other description which is not a part of the road, or on any road which is a footpath, bridleway or restricted byway. However, s 34 provides that driving within fifteen yards of a road upon which a motor vehicle may be driven is not an offence if the driving is only for the purpose of parking. Nor is it an offence under s 34 for a person with an interest in the land, or a visitor to it, to drive to it along a road which before 2 May 2006 (England) or 16 November 2006 (Wales) was shown in a definitive map and statement as a road used as a public path. It is a defence to prove that the vehicle was driven for saving life, or extinguishing fire, or for dealing with any other similar emergency.

The Police Reform Act 2002, s 59 provides powers for the seizure of vehicles in prescribed circumstances: see p 492.

CHAPTER 10

Use of Vehicles

TERMINOLOGY

'Motor vehicle', 'mechanically propelled vehicle' (MPV), and 'road' have already been defined (pp 327–9). The following terms also used in this chapter are defined as set out below by the Road Traffic Act (RTA) 1988 and/or Road Vehicles (Construction and Use) Regulations 1986 (RV(C&U)R 1986).

A *'motor car'* is an MPV for the carriage of a load or passengers whose unladen weight does not exceed: (a) 3,050 kg (3 tonnes), if it is constructed solely for the carriage of passengers and adapted to carry no more than seven of them exclusive of the driver, or if it is constructed for the conveyance of goods; or (b) 2,540 kg (2.5 tonnes) in any other case.

A *'heavy motor car'* is an MPV (not being a motor car) constructed to carry a load, whether goods or passengers, and whose unladen weight exceeds 2,540 kg (2.5 tonnes). Although this definition covers buses and coaches, there are some requirements of the regulations which are specific to them. For this reason 'bus', 'large bus', and 'coach' are separately defined.

A *'bus'* is a motor vehicle constructed or adapted to carry more than eight seated passengers in addition to the driver, and a *'large bus'* is a vehicle constructed or adapted to carry more than 16 such passengers. A *'coach'* is a large bus with a maximum gross weight of more than 7.5 tonnes and a maximum speed exceeding 60 mph.

A *'dual-purpose vehicle'* is a vehicle constructed or adapted for the carriage both of passengers and of goods or burden, being a vehicle whose unladen weight does not exceed 2,040 kg, and which either:

(a) is so constructed or adapted that the driving power of the engine is, or can be, transmitted to all the wheels of the vehicle; or
(b) (i) is permanently fitted with a rigid roof;
    (ii) has at least one row of transverse, upholstered seats for two or more passengers permanently fitted;
    (iii) has on each side and at the rear a window or windows having an overall area of not less than 1,850 square cms on each side and not less than 770 square cms at the rear; and
    (iv) is such that the distance between the rearmost part of the steering wheel and the back-rests of the row of transverse seats in (ii) (or, if there is more than one such row of seats, the distance between the rearmost part of the steering wheel and the back-rests of the rearmost such row) is not less than one-third of the distance between the rearmost part of the steering wheel and the rearmost part of the floor of the vehicle.

A *'motor tractor'* is defined as a MPV which is not constructed itself to carry a load (other than one concerned with its own propulsion or maintenance) and the unladen weight of which does not exceed 7,370 kg. A *'locomotive'* is a similar vehicle, the unladen weight of which exceeds 7,370 kg (7.25 tonnes); there are two types: 'light locomotive'—unladen weight not exceeding 11,690 kg (11.5 tonnes), 'heavy locomotive'—unladen weight in excess of this.

ROAD VEHICLES (CONSTRUCTION AND USE) REGULATIONS 1986

RV(C&U)R 1986 are made under RTA 1988, s 41. They are divided into two main parts: Part II dealing with the construction, equipment and maintenance of motor vehicles and trailers, and Part IV dealing with the various uses of motor vehicles and trailers on roads.

The 'construction elements' of the regulations are aimed at manufacturers in the main, as they amount to specifications for vehicle production. Many of these provisions are being replaced in relation to most modern vehicles by requirements of an international nature relating to 'type approved' vehicles. The date of manufacture or first registration of vehicles will normally be the conclusive factor in deciding whether the 'construction elements' of RV(C&U)R 1986 apply, or those directed towards type approval. A vehicle which complies with the relevant type approval and has the relevant certificate of type approval or manufacturer's certificate of conformity to the type approval is exempt from certain of the 'construction elements'.

Certain special types of vehicle are authorised under the Road Vehicles (Authorisation of Special Types) General Order 2003 and do not have to comply with all of the requirements of the RV(C&U)R 1986. The clue to the nature of such vehicles lies within the term 'special'. The vehicles concerned are likely to be track-laying vehicles; those used for special engineering and maintenance purposes; military vehicles and vehicles used for life-saving operations.

The type approval system is backed up by two offences under RTA 1988, ss 63 and 65:

(a) using, or causing or permitting to be used, on a road, a vehicle subject in whole or part to compulsory type approval, without a certificate; and
(b) selling, supplying, offering to sell or supply, or exposing for sale a vehicle which does not have a certificate.

It is the provisions of RV(C&U)R 1986 about the equipment and maintenance, and use, of vehicles with which police officers are much more frequently concerned. They are dealt with on pp 416–26.

CONSTRUCTION AND USE OFFENCES: GENERAL

RTA 1988, ss 40A, 41A, 41B, 41D and 42 provide various offences which may be committed in relation to the use of a vehicle in a dangerous condition and/or in contravention of the RV(C&U)R 1986.

Using vehicle in dangerous condition

RTA 1988, s 40A makes it an offence for a person to use, cause or permit another to use a motor vehicle or a trailer on a road when:

(a) the condition of the motor vehicle or trailer, or of its accessories or equipment; or
(b) the purpose for which it is used; or
(c) the number of passengers carried by it, or the manner in which they are carried; or
(d) the weight, position or distribution of its load, or the manner in which it is secured,

is such that the use of the motor vehicle or trailer involves danger of injury to any person. The question of whether there was a danger for the purposes of s 40A is a matter which the court must consider by reference to the matters set out above.

Offences against s 40A carry discretionary disqualification; the endorsement of three penalty points is obligatory. However, if a s 40A offence is committed within three years of a previous conviction for such offence, disqualification is obligatory. Such obligatory disqualification will be for not less than six months.

Breach of requirements as to brakes, steering-gear or tyres

RTA 1988, s 41A makes it an offence for a person to:

(a) contravene or fail to comply with a construction and use requirement as to brakes, steering gear or tyres; or
(b) use on a road a motor vehicle or trailer which does not comply with such a requirement, or cause or permit a motor vehicle or trailer to be so used.

Offences against s 41A carry discretionary disqualification; the endorsement of three penalty points is obligatory.

Breach of requirement as to weight: goods and passenger vehicles

RTA 1988, s 41B punishes offences in relation to 'weight'. By s 41B(1), a person who:

(a) contravenes or fails to comply with a construction and use requirement as to any description of weight applicable to:
    (i) a goods vehicle; or
    (ii) a motor vehicle or trailer adapted to carry more than eight passengers; or
(b) uses on a road a vehicle which does not comply with such a requirement, or causes or permits a vehicle to be so used,

commits an offence. Where the alleged contravention relates to any description of weight applicable to a goods vehicle, it is a defence to prove either that the vehicle was going to or coming from a weighbridge, or, where the relevant weight limit is not exceeded by more than 5 per cent, that this weight was not exceeded at the time of loading and this load had not been added to (s 41B(2)). Those who contravene s 41B are not thereby liable to disqualification or endorsement.

Breach of requirements as to control of vehicle, mobile telephones, etc

RTA 1988, s 41D makes it an offence for a person to contravene or fail to comply with construction and use requirements as to a driver being in such a position that he can retain proper control of the vehicle, or a full view, or as to not using a mobile telephone (p 424). Such an offence carries discretionary disqualification; the endorsement of three penalty points is obligatory.

Breach of other construction and use requirements

RTA 1988, s 42 is concerned with contraventions of a construction and use requirement other than one dealt with by ss 41A, 41B and 41D. It provides that a person who:

(a) contravenes or fails to comply with such a requirement; or
(b) uses on a road a motor vehicle or trailer which does not comply with such a requirement, or causes or permits a motor vehicle or trailer to be so used,

commits an offence.

An offence of using on a road a trailer which does not comply with regulations is an offence distinct from that of using a defective motor vehicle.

Those who contravene s 42 are not liable to disqualification or to endorsement.

Use

This term should be given its ordinary meaning. A person uses a vehicle if he controls, manages or operates it, or otherwise has the use of it as a vehicle.

RTA 1988, ss 40A to 42 impose strict liability upon those who use motor vehicles in contravention of RV(C&U)R 1986; consequently, it is irrelevant that the defendant (D) did not know of the defect, etc, nor ought to have known of it.

In law, an employer can 'use' a vehicle in breach of RV(C&U)R 1986, even though he does not do so personally. This is because use of a vehicle by an employee in the course of his employment is regarded in law as use by the employer as well (and the employer can therefore be held vicariously liable for it, regardless of whether he caused or permitted it).

The appeal courts have consistently refused to impose vicarious liability for 'using' outside the employer/employee relationship. Where such a strict employer/employee relationship cannot be established, as where the use is by a contractor, a charge of 'causing' or 'permitting' must be considered.

Where a vehicle is hired out with a driver for use by another firm, the driver will usually remain the employee of the owner of the vehicle, so that a 'using' by the driver will be a 'using' by the owner. Thus, where a haulier (BRS) hired a vehicle together with its driver to another haulier for a period of five years, and that other haulier operated the vehicle under its own livery, BRS was held to be using that vehicle when it was found to be overloaded. BRS had been in the business of hiring out vehicles with drivers who remained their employees and the vehicles were being used in the course of that business. Similarly, where the driver of a vehicle who was employed by company A was ordered by telephone to pick up a return load on behalf of company B, company B being responsible for loading the vehicle, its documentation and the selection of route, a divisional court held that company A was guilty of using the vehicle when it was found to be overloaded.

As is apparent from the above, someone who lends his private motor car to his friend is not liable for 'using' that vehicle if RV(C&U)R 1986 are contravened by the friend.

Where a trailer is towed by another vehicle and the offence concerned relates to the trailer (eg a defective tyre or insecure load), the information or written charge should specify that it was the trailer which was defective or improperly used. This is essential where the tractor unit and the trailer are owned by different persons or companies.

Cause the use

This term, together with 'permitting the use', covers circumstances in which charges of aiding and abetting would otherwise normally be appropriate. To be guilty of causing the use of a vehicle in contravention of RV(C&U)R 1986, D must actually have known of the contravention in question, and have been in a position to exercise some control over the driver. To 'cause' involves some express or positive command or direction from the person 'causing' to the person 'using'. If the foreman of a haulage depot, knowing that a vehicle has a defective tyre, orders an employee to drive the vehicle, the foreman 'causes' the driver to commit the offence. He is in a position to give orders to the employee in relation to the use of the vehicle and does so, and he knows of the defect. In such a case the haulage company would also be guilty of using the vehicle as it was used on their business and knowledge is not an essential ingredient of that offence.

A person who tows another vehicle is causing it to be used on a road.

Permit the use

Like 'causing the use' of a vehicle, 'permitting' a vehicle to be used in contravention of RV(C&U)R 1986 requires proof that D actually knew of the contravention in question. However, the meaning of 'permitting' is much wider than the meaning of 'causing' because there does not need to be any express or positive mandate to use a motor vehicle by a person in a position to exercise control over the driver, and a general or particular permission to use a vehicle will be sufficient. However, for a person to be guilty of 'permitting', he must be in a position to forbid another person to use the vehicle.

Many employees are given general permission to use their employers' vehicles in any way they choose in their own time. Having given such a general permission, it is unlikely that such an employer will be liable for contraventions of the RV(C&U)R 1986 in respect of that vehicle, but in some circumstances he may. There is a distinction between knowledge that the vehicle is being used and knowledge that it is being used unlawfully. A sales representative may be given total use of a motor car. As a driver he will be responsible for its use in such contravention but his employers will not normally be liable for *permitting* such use, as they are unlikely to have knowledge of the particular unlawful use. This can be compared with the case where the driver is unlawfully using the vehicle in the course of his employment; there a charge of using will be appropriate.

Someone who lends his car to his friend permits him to use it. That permission does not extend to unlawful use of a warning instrument as no permission has been given in that respect. On the other hand, if the tyres were defective, it would be a question of fact as to whether the owner of the vehicle knew of the defect when permission was given to use it.

PARTICULAR REGULATIONS UNDER RV(C&U)R 1986, PART II

Brakes

The differing braking systems with which different types of vehicles must be fitted are dealt with in reg 15 (which applies to almost all vehicles with three or more wheels) and reg 16 and Sch 3 (which apply to motor bicycles and other vehicles). These provisions include exemptions from RV(C&U)R 1986 if type approval has been given. However, the fitting of various systems is not a matter of prime concern to police officers. On the other hand, the maintenance of brakes is. Regulation 18 deals with the maintenance of brakes and applies quite generally to braking systems (where fitted under these, or other, regulations).

Regulation 18(1) requires every braking system and the means of operation thereof fitted to a vehicle to be maintained in good and efficient working order, and properly adjusted. This applies to any vehicle to which a braking system is fitted, including a trailer which is not required to have a braking system fitted.

By reg 18(3) and (6), braking systems must be so maintained that service braking systems and secondary braking systems, and parking brakes, respectively, have pre-scribed braking efficiencies as set out in considerable detail in two tables in the regulations. The tables appear in Chapter 10 on the companion website.

Speedometer

By RV(C&U)R 1986, reg 35 every motor vehicle (with very limited exceptions) must be fitted with a speedometer. Regulation 35 also provides that speedometers fitted to vehicles first used after 1 April 1984 must indicate speed in both miles per hour and kilometres per hour; otherwise the indication given by a speedometer may be either in miles per hour or kilometres per hour. Instead of complying with reg 35, a vehicle may comply with the relevant Community Directive or ECE Regulation.

The following vehicles do not need to have speedometers fitted:

(a) invalid carriages, motor cycles not exceeding 100 cc, and works trucks (provided in each case they were first used before 1 April 1984);

(b) agricultural vehicles, not being a category T tractor (as defined on p 418), which are not driven at more than 20 mph;

(c) category T tractors which are not driven at more than 40 km/h;

(d) vehicles which legally or physically cannot exceed 25 mph; and

(e) vehicles first used before 1 October 1937.

Regulation 36 requires that a speedometer must be kept free from any obstruction which might prevent its being easily read and must at all times be maintained in good working order. On a charge involving a breach of this requirement, it is a defence to prove that the defect occurred in the course of the journey being then undertaken or that steps had already been taken to have repairs or replacements effected as soon as possible. These defences cover so many possibilities, and if alleged are so hard to dis-prove, that enforcement is almost limited to admitted long-standing defects in respect of which no repairs have been arranged or when the instrument registers incorrectly.

Mirrors

RV(C&U)R 1986, reg 33 sets out detailed requirements about the fitting of mirrors. Instead of complying with the above requirements about mirrors, a vehicle may comply with the relevant Community Directive or ECE Regulation. The various requirements are of particular relevance to the manufacturers and others in the motor trade.

Windscreen wipers and washers

By RV(C&U)R 1986, reg 34(1), all vehicles fitted with windscreens must be fitted with one or more efficient automatic windscreen wipers, unless the driver can obtain an adequate view to the front without looking through the windscreen, for example by opening the windscreen or looking over it (as is the case with many cars produced before the 1950s). Regulation 34(1) also requires that the wipers fitted must be capable of clearing the windscreen so that the driver has an adequate view of the road in front of both sides of the vehicle and to the front of the vehicle.

Regulation 34(6), which deals with maintenance, requires that every windscreen wiper required by the Regulations to be fitted is, at all times while the vehicle is used on a road, maintained in good and efficient working order and is properly adjusted. As stated, reg 34(1) demands one or more wipers. If the driver's wiper provides the view ahead and to both sides, as required, any other wiper is not subject to the maintenance requirement.

By reg 34(2), a windscreen washer must be fitted to any vehicle which requires one or more automatic wipers, except:

(a) an agricultural motor vehicle, not being a category T tractor, unless it is first used on or after 1 June 1986 and is driven at more than 20 mph;

(b) a category T tractor, unless it is first used on or after 1 June 1986 and is driven at more than 40 km/h;

(c) a vehicle incapable of exceeding 20 mph;

(d) a track-laying vehicle; or

(e) a vehicle being used to provide a local bus service.

The washer must be such that, in conjunction with the wipers, it is capable of cleaning the area of the windscreen swept by the blades of mud or similar deposits.

In the alternative to the above requirement, a vehicle may comply with the relevant Community Directive.

Audible warning instrument

The following provisions are made by RV(C&U)R 1986, reg 37.

All motor vehicles with a maximum speed of more than 20 mph must be fitted with a horn (but, in the case of an agricultural motor vehicle, only if it is being driven at more than 20 mph, and in the case of a category T tractor, only if it is being driven at more than 40 km/h). A category T tractor is a vehicle defined in EU Regulation 167/2013 and includes wheeled agricultural and forestry vehicles.

In the case of motor vehicles first used on or after 1 August 1973 the sound emitted by any horn must be continuous and uniform and not strident. This is to ensure that the horns of such vehicles give a sound which is not offensive to the ear.

With the exception of police vehicles, NCA vehicles, fire and rescue vehicles, vehicles used for ambulance purposes or for the purpose of providing a response to an emergency at the request of an NHS ambulance service, vehicles of HM Revenue & Customs used in the investigation of serious crime, and vehicles owned and operated by the Secretary of State for Defence and used by the special forces in response (or training or practising in responding) to a national security emergency, no motor vehicle may be fitted with a bell, gong, siren, or two-tone horn. However, vehicles may be fitted with an instrument or apparatus (not being a two-toned horn) to give a sound informing the public that goods are for sale from the vehicle; thus, ice-cream chimes, etc are not prohibited (but see also p 411). The rule against fitting gongs, etc does not apply to an anti-theft device nor to an alarm to summon help to a public service vehicle. Any anti-theft device fitted must have a cut-out limiting its use to five minutes. Where a horn can operate as an anti-theft device, such a cut-out must be fitted if the motor vehicle was first used on or after 1 October 1982.

A 'reversing alarm' fitted to a vehicle to warn persons that the vehicle is reversing or about to reverse or a 'boarding aid alarm' fitted to a bus to warn that a power-operated ramp or lift is in operation is exempted from the requirement that the sound of a warning instrument shall be continuous and uniform but it must not be strident. The sound emitted must be such that it is not likely to be confused with the sound emitted from a pedestrian crossing (reg 99). A reversing alarm may only be used on a stationary vehicle if the vehicle's engine is running and it is about to move backwards or the vehicle is in danger from another moving vehicle.

Horns and other audible warning instruments must be maintained in good and efficient working order at all times.

Instead of complying with the provisions mentioned above concerning the nature and maintenance of audible warning instruments, a vehicle may comply with the relevant Community Directive or ECE Regulation.

Regulation 99 provides that no person shall sound, or cause or permit to be sounded, the horn or other audible warning device of a motor vehicle when it is stationary on a road at any time. The only exception is when there is danger due to another moving vehicle on or near the road. In addition, it provides that no person shall sound, or cause or permit to be sounded, in a vehicle in motion on a restricted road, a horn, etc, between 23.30 and 07.00 on the following day. This does not, of course, apply to anti-theft alarms, reversing devices, or boarding aid alarms.

Silencer

By RV(C&U)R 1986, reg 54, every vehicle propelled by an internal combustion engine must be fitted with an exhaust system including a silencer, and the exhaust gases from the engine must not escape into the atmosphere without first passing through its silencer. Specified noise levels are prescribed but they are directed at the manufacturers. Instead of complying with the above provisions, a vehicle may comply with the relevant Community Directive or ECE Regulation. Regulation 54 also requires that every exhaust system and silencer must be maintained in good and efficient working order and must not after the date of manufacture be altered so as to increase the noise made by the escape of exhaust gases.

Although not directly concerned with silencers, regs 97 and 98 also deal with noise. Regulation 97 prohibits the use, etc of a motor vehicle in a manner so as to cause excessive noise which could reasonably have been avoided by the driver. Regulation 98 requires the driver of a stationary vehicle to stop the action of machinery attached to it, or forming part of the vehicle, so far as may be necessary for the prevention of noise or of exhaust emissions.

Wings

RV(C&U)R 1986, reg 63 requires the following to be fitted with wings or similar fittings to catch, as far as practicable, mud or water thrown up by the wheels:

(a) invalid carriages;
(b) heavy motor cars, motor cars and motor cycles, not being agricultural motor vehicles or pedestrian-controlled vehicles;
(c) agricultural motor vehicles, not being category T tractors, driven at more than 20 mph;

(d) category T tractors (p 418) driven at more than 40 km/h; and

(e) trailers.

The requirements in relation to trailers are restricted to the rear wheels, if the trailer has more than two wheels.

Works trucks, unfinished vehicles, broken-down vehicles, living vans, agricultural trailers not drawn in excess of 40 km/h and agricultural trailed appliances are exempt from the above requirements. Trailers used for or in connection with the carriage of round timber and the rear wheels of the motor vehicle parts of articulated vehicles whose semi-trailer is so used are also exempt.

Instead of complying with these requirements, a vehicle may comply with the relevant Community Directive.

Dangerous vehicles, etc

RV(C&U)R 1986, reg 100(1) requires that a motor vehicle, every trailer and all parts and accessories of such vehicle or trailer are at all times in such a condition that no danger is caused or is likely to be caused to any person in or on the vehicle or trailer or on a road. The provision is concerned with actual or likely danger; a mere possibility of danger is not enough.

Regulation 100(1) applies to a vehicle which in its manufactured condition is inherently likely to cause danger to other road-users, as well as to a vehicle which has become dangerous through lack of maintenance. In relation to the requirement that all parts and accessories must be in such condition that no danger is caused, it is immaterial that parts may be in reasonable condition if they are dangerous because they are not in working order. Separate and distinct offences are involved in using a defective motor vehicle and using a defective trailer. This equally applies to articulated vehicles.

Regulation 100(1) also requires that the number of passengers carried, or the manner of their carriage, is such that no danger is caused or is likely to be caused to any person in or on the vehicle or trailer or on a road.

Regulation 100(1) also requires that the weight, packing, distribution and adjustment of a load is such that no such danger is caused, or likely to be caused. This prohibition is really aimed at a badly loaded vehicle; insecure loads are dealt with by reg 100(2).

Regulation 100(2) requires that the load carried by a motor vehicle or trailer must at all times be so secured, if necessary by physical restraint other than its own weight, and be in such a position, that neither danger nor nuisance is likely to be caused to any person or property by reason of the load or any part of it falling or being blown from the vehicle or by reason of any other movement of the load or a part of it. In effect, this deals with insecure loads which for any reason cause danger or nuisance. It is necessary to specify which of these alternatives resulted from the insecurity of the load. Where a substantial part of a solid load falls onto a busy road there is little doubt that danger is caused. In circumstances where a goods vehicle, loaded with gravel, sheds part of its load steadily into the path of following traffic, there is no doubt that there is a breach of the requirement so to secure the load that no nuisance to persons or property is likely.

In considering whether a load has been adequately secured so that neither danger nor nuisance is likely to be caused one has to consider four things:

(a) the nature of the journey;
(b) the way in which the load was secured;
(c) the way in which the load was positioned; and
(d) the journey to be taken.

What might be secure for one journey in fine weather and on good roads might not be secure for another journey in poor weather and on less good roads. If the load is a high one, and too high to go under a bridge on the route, so that it is inevitable that the load will be knocked off, the load will not have been so secured that neither danger nor nuisance was likely.

Regulation 100(3) prohibits the use of a motor vehicle or trailer for any purpose for which it is so unsuitable as to cause danger or nuisance to any person on the vehicle or trailer, or on a road. The crucial question is whether the vehicle or trailer was unsuitable. If it is not properly loaded and it is the load which causes the danger or nuisance, this does not affect the suitability of the vehicle itself. In a case where an excavator which was loaded onto a trailer struck a bridge, it was held that the trailer did not become unsuitable when it was so loaded. It was the manner of the loading which was at fault; reg 100(1) was the relevant provision.

Most offences involving dangerous vehicles will now be charged under RTA 1988, s 40A (p 413) and not under s 42 for a breach of reg 100(1), since a conviction of an offence under s 40A involves the risk of discretionary disqualification and requires the obligatory endorsement of three penalty points. Where there is a conviction under s 42 for a breach of reg 100 there can be no disqualification or endorsement of the offender's driving licence.

Some aspects of reg 100(2) and (3) have also been overtaken by RTA 1988, s 40A as they also deal with elements related to danger being caused to persons in consequence of the use of the motor vehicle or trailer in the manner prohibited by s 40A.

Maintenance of glass

All glass or other transparent material fitted to motor vehicles is required, by RV(C&U) R 1986, reg 30(3), to be maintained in such condition that it does not obscure the vision of the driver while the vehicle is being driven on a road. This regulation is not limited to the windscreen but applies to all glass affecting the driver's vision, such as the rear window and side windows through which he needs to look.

Maintenance of fuel tank

By RV(C&U)R 1986, reg 39 a fuel tank on a motor vehicle must be maintained so that any leakage of liquid or vapour from it is adequately prevented (except that this does not prevent a tank being fitted with a pressure release valve). Instead of complying with these requirements, a vehicle may comply with the corresponding requirements contained in the relevant Community Directive or ECE Regulation.

Maintenance of tyres

Except as provided below, RV(C&U)R 1986, reg 27(1) prohibits the use, on a road, of a motor vehicle or trailer, a wheel of which is fitted with a pneumatic tyre, if:

(a) the tyre is unsuited to the use to which the vehicle or trailer is being put or to the type of tyres fitted to its other wheels;

(b) the tyre is wrongly inflated for such use;

(c) the tyre has a cut in excess of 25 mm or 10 per cent of the section width of the tyre, whichever is the greater, measured in any direction on the outside of the tyre and deep enough to reach the ply or cords;

(d) the tyre has a lump, bulge or tear caused by separation or partial failure of its structure;

(e) the tyre has a portion of the ply or cord exposed;

(f) the base of any groove which showed in the original tread pattern is not clearly visible;

(g) either—

   (i) the grooves of the tread pattern of the tyre do not have a depth of at least 1 mm throughout a continuous band measuring at least three-quarters of the breadth of the tread and round the entire outer-circumference of the tyre; or

   (ii) if the grooves of the original tread pattern of the tyre did not extend beyond three-quarters of the breadth of the tread, any groove which showed in the original tread pattern does not have a depth of at least 1 mm; or

(h) the tyre is not maintained in such condition as to be fit for the use to which the vehicle or trailer is being put or has a defect which might in any way cause damage to the surface of the road or damage to persons on or in the vehicle or to other persons using the road.

There are general exemptions from (a) to (g) in favour of agricultural trailers or trailed appliances, agricultural motor vehicles, not being category T tractors, which are not driven at more than 20 mph, category T tractors (p 418) which are not driven at more than 40 km/h, and broken-down vehicles being towed at a speed not exceeding 20 mph. In addition, (f) and (g) do not apply to:

(i) a passenger vehicle, other than a motor cycle, constructed or adapted to carry no more than eight seated passengers in addition to the driver;

(ii) a goods vehicle with a maximum gross weight which does not exceed 3,500 kg; or

(iii) a light trailer not falling within (ii),

first used on or after 3 January 1933. Instead, the grooves of the tread pattern must be of a depth of at least 1.6 mm throughout a continuous band comprising the central three-quarters of the breadth of the tyre and round the entire circumference of the tyre. Nor do (f) and (g) apply to three-wheelers not exceeding 102 kg with a maximum possible speed of 12 mph or less, nor to pedestrian-controlled works trucks. In addition, (g) does not apply to motor cycles not exceeding 50 cc.

It follows from these exemptions from (f) and (g) that the only vehicles to which (f) and (g) apply are large goods vehicles, motor cycles (except those just mentioned in relation to (g)), and other vehicles not included above.

Regulation 27(5) prohibits the fitting on a motor vehicle or trailer of a recut pneumatic tyre if its ply or cord has been cut or exposed in the process of recutting. Heavy-duty tyres fitted to goods vehicles can usually be recut without causing danger, but tyres fitted to saloon cars do not usually have sufficient thickness of rubber to accept the process.

Regulation 27(2) makes special provision to allow for the use of tyres designed to be used safely when deflated.

Special provision is made by reg 27(3) to allow passenger vehicles (not buses) to fit a temporary-use spare tyre, provided the vehicle does not exceed 50 mph.

Mixture of tyres

RV(C&U)R 1986, reg 26(1) provides that pneumatic tyres of different types of construction must not be fitted to the same axle of a vehicle. The regulation mentions three types of tyre:

(a) diagonal-ply tyres, which are commonly known as cross-ply tyres;
(b) bias-belted tyres, which are as above but have a reinforcing band around the outer circumference of the tyre under the tread, but on top of the cords; and
(c) radial-ply tyres.

Regulation 26(2) provides that a motor vehicle having only two axles must not be fitted with the following combinations of tyres:

(a) cross-plys or bias-belted tyres on the rear axle and radials on the front; or
(b) cross-ply on the rear axle and bias-belted on the front.

This regulation is designed to prevent a gripping tyre from being fitted to the 'steering' wheels, whilst a tyre which is not so stable is fitted to the rear.

Not to emit smoke, etc

RV(C&U)R 1986, reg 61(5) provides that no person shall use, or cause or permit to be used, on a road, a motor vehicle from which is emitted any smoke, visible vapour, grit, sparks or oily substance which causes, or is likely to cause, damage to property or injury or danger to any person who is, or who may reasonably be expected to be, on the road. This could occur where oil spillage made the road unsafe or fumes badly affected visibility.

Regulation 61(1) provides that a vehicle must be maintained so as not to emit any avoidable smoke or avoidable visible vapour.

CONDITIONS UNDER RV(C&U)R 1986, PART IV RELATING TO USE

Position to retain proper view and control

RV(C&U)R 1986, reg 104 provides that a driver must at all times be in such a position that he retains full control and has a full view of the road and traffic ahead. Someone who drove with a sheepdog on his lap has been held to be in breach of this provision.

Reversing

By RV(C&U)R 1986, reg 106, no person shall drive, or cause or permit to be driven, a motor vehicle backwards on a road further than may be requisite for the safety or reasonable convenience of the occupants of the vehicle or other traffic.

Unnecessary obstruction

RV(C&U)R 1986, reg 103 provides that a person in charge of a motor vehicle or trailer must not cause or permit it to stand on a road so as to cause any unnecessary obstruction. The various exemptions within local no-waiting orders in favour of goods vehicles which are loading or unloading has led to a belief by some van drivers that they may double park and even completely block roads for these purposes. This is not so. Any unreasonable use of the road which leads to the obstruction of other road users is an offence against reg 103. An obstruction can be caused by taking up so much of the road that normal two-way traffic is reduced to a one-way flow. In considering whether a particular use was reasonable or unreasonable, a court will apply its mind to the facts, including the duration of the obstruction, the nature of the place where it occurred, the purpose for which the vehicle was there and the *actual* (as opposed to potential) obstruction caused.

Parking facing the wrong way at night

RV(C&U)R 1986, reg 101 provides that, except with the permission of a uniformed police officer, a person must not cause or permit a motor vehicle to stand on a road between sunset and sunrise otherwise than with the left or nearside of the vehicle as close as may be to the edge of the carriageway. If lights are not displayed in a place where parking lights are required to be shown, two offences are committed.

The exemptions from the prohibition under reg 101 are predictable: vehicles being used for fire and rescue or police purposes; vehicles being used for ambulance purposes or for the purpose of providing a response to an emergency at the request of an NHS ambulance service; taxi stands and bus stops; one-way streets; emergency operations, etc.

Stopping engine and setting parking brake

RV(C&U)R 1986, reg 107 provides that no person shall leave, or cause or permit to be left, on a road, any motor vehicle which is not attended by a person duly licensed to drive it, unless the engine has been stopped and the parking brake effectively set. The exceptions include vehicles being used for fire and rescue authority or police purposes; vehicles being used for ambulance purposes or for the purpose of providing a response to an emergency at the request of an NHS ambulance service; and special vehicles which use their engines for particular operations other than the driving of the vehicle. Although there is a requirement to do two things, that is stop the engine and set the handbrake, the failure to carry out either of these operations completes the offence under RTA 1988, s 42.

Opening of doors

RV(C&U)R 1986, reg 105 provides that *no person* may open, or cause or permit to be opened, the door of a motor vehicle on a road so as to cause injury or danger to any person. It is not necessary to prove negligence: if the action causes injury or danger that is sufficient.

Mobile telephones

RV(C&U)R 1986, reg 110(1) prohibits the driving of a motor vehicle on a road if the driver is using a hand-held mobile telephone, or a hand-held device of any kind, other than a two-way radio, which performs an interactive communication function by transmitting and receiving data.

For the purposes of reg 110 a mobile telephone or device is classified as 'handheld' if it is, or must be, held at some point during the course of making or receiving a call or performing any other interactive communication function. The term 'interactive communication function' includes:

(a) sending or receiving oral or written messages, or
(b) facsimile documents, or
(c) still or moving images; and
(d) providing access to the internet.

The term 'two-way radio' refers to wireless telegraphy apparatus which is designed or adapted for the purpose of transmitting or receiving spoken messages and to operate on any frequency except a number of ranges. Such equipment is fitted to vehicles used by the emergency services and is therefore exempted from these provisions.

Regulation 110(2) prohibits causing or permitting any other person to drive a motor vehicle on a road while using a hand-held mobile telephone or hand-held device of the specified type. Regulation 110(3) forbids a person supervising a provisional licence holder to use a hand-held mobile telephone or such a hand-held device at a time when the provisional licence holder is driving a motor vehicle on a road.

Regulation 110(5) provides that there is no contravention of reg 110 where:

(a) the use is to call the emergency service on 112 or 999;
(b) it is in response to a genuine emergency; and
(c) it is unsafe or impracticable to cease driving in order to make the call, or for the provisional licence holder to cease driving while the call is made.

Trailers

RV(C&U)R 1986, reg 86 provides that, where a motor vehicle is drawing a trailer by means of a rope or chain, the length of the rope or chain must not exceed 4.5 m, and must not exceed 1.5 m unless the rope or chain is made clearly visible to other road users within a reasonable distance from either side.

Regulation 86A provides that trailers to which reg 15 (see p 416) applies, which are not fitted with an automatic stopping device operative in the event of separation, must not be used on a road unless a secondary coupling is attached to the drawing vehicle and its trailer in such a way that, in the event of separation, the drawbar of the trailer would be prevented from touching the ground and there would be some residual steering of the trailer.

Trailers to which reg 15 applies which are fitted with a device that is designed to stop the trailer automatically in the event of separation but is dependent on a secondary coupling must not be used on a road unless that coupling is properly attached to the drawing vehicle and trailer.

Trailers which are living vans and have less than four wheels (or have two close-coupled wheels on each side) are prohibited by reg 90 from being used for the carriage of passengers. The only exception is in favour of testing, when a repairer, etc may be carried in the van for that purpose.

Regulation 83 limits the number of trailers which may be drawn by a motor vehicle on a road. It limits locomotives to a maximum of three trailers, motor tractors to one laden trailer or two unladen trailers, and heavy motor cars and motor cars to one trailer. For the purposes of reg 83, a vehicle drawn by a steam-powered vehicle and which is used solely to carry water for the purpose of the drawing vehicle is not a trailer.

Miscellaneous

RV(C&U)R 1986, reg 53 provides that mascots, emblems, or other ornamental objects fitted to vehicles first used on or after 1 October 1937 must not be in such a position that they are likely to strike persons with whom the vehicle may collide unless the nature of the mascot is such that injury is not liable to be caused.

Regulation 109 provides that no person shall drive, or cause or permit to be driven, a motor vehicle on a road if the driver is in such a position as to be able to see, whether directly or by reflection, a television receiving apparatus or other cinematographic apparatus used to display anything other than information concerning the vehicle or its journey.

SEAT BELTS

RV(C&U)R 1986, regs 46 and 47 deal with the fitting of anchorage points and seat belts. These provisions are of particular relevance to manufacturers and others engaged in the motor trade.

Wearing of seat belts

The circumstances in which seat belts must be worn by passengers in motor vehicles are now prescribed in the Motor Vehicles (Wearing of Seat Belts) Regulations (MV(WSB) R) 1993 and the Motor Vehicles (Wearing of Seat Belts by Children in Front Seats) Regulations (MV(WSBCFS)R) 1993 and not by RV(C&U)R 1986. The 1993 Regulations implement the requirements of two Community Directives which apply to vehicles of less than 3.5 tonnes with four or more wheels and a design speed of more than 25 kph, and to large and small buses and light goods vehicles. One of the Directives requires additional measures in respect of the wearing of child-restraining devices and places obligations upon bus operators to require the wearing of seat belts fitted to large and small buses.

The offences committed by breaches of the Seat Belt Regulations are punishable under RTA 1988, ss 14 and 15 and not by RTA 1988, s 42. The requirements created by the 1993 Regulations are not always confined to the description of vehicles set out in the Directives.

Adult passengers

Subject to the exemptions below, MV(WSB)R 1993, reg 5 requires that every person:

(a) driving a motor vehicle (other than a two-wheeled motor cycle with or without a sidecar); or
(b) riding in a front or rear seat of a motor vehicle (other than a two-wheeled motor cycle with or without a sidecar)

must wear an adult seat belt. The regulation does not apply to a person under the age of 14, or if no adult belt is provided (driver) or available (passenger: see p 430).

Failure to comply with reg 5 is an offence under RTA 1988, s 14(3).

Regulation 6 provides the following exemptions from the requirement to wear a seat belt made by reg 5:

(a) a person holding a medical certificate to the effect that it is inadvisable for him to wear a seat belt;
(b) the driver of or a passenger in a motor vehicle constructed or adapted for carrying goods, while on a journey which does not exceed 50 metres and which is undertaken for the purpose of delivering or collecting anything;

(c)   a person performing a manoeuvre which includes reversing;

(d)   a qualified driver supervising a learner carrying out such a manoeuvre;

(e)   a person by whom a test of competence to drive is being conducted where wearing a seat belt would endanger himself or another person;

(f)   a person driving or riding in a vehicle being used for fire and rescue, or police or NCA purposes, or for carrying a person in lawful custody (who is also included in this exemption);

(g)   a person riding in a motor ambulance while the person is providing medical attention or treatment to a patient which due to its nature or the medical situation of the patient cannot be delayed;

(h)   the driver of a licensed taxi whilst being used to seek hire or answer a call, or when carrying a passenger for hire, or a private hire car whilst it is being used to carry a passenger for hire;

(i)   a person in a vehicle being used under a trade licence for investigating or remedying a fault;

(j)   a disabled person who is wearing a disabled person's belt; or

(k)   a person riding in a vehicle whilst in a procession organised by or on behalf of the Crown.

There are two other exemptions under reg 6.

First, a person who is riding in a vehicle which is participating in a procession which is held to mark or commemorate an event is exempt from the requirement to wear a seat belt if the procession is one commonly or customarily held in a police area or areas, or if notice in respect of the procession has been given in accordance with the Public Order Act 1986, s 11 (see p 715).

Second, the second seat belt requirement in reg 5, which relates to a person riding in a front or rear seat of a motor vehicle other than a two-wheeled motor cycle with or without a sidecar, does not apply to a person riding in a small or large bus which is being used to provide a 'local service' in a built-up area (ie entirely on restricted roads) or which is constructed or adapted for the carriage of standing passengers and on which the operator permits standing.

A 'local service' means a local service within the meaning of the Transport Act 1985 (TA 1985), ie a service, using one or more public service vehicles, for the carriage of passengers by road at separate fares other than:

(a)   a journey organised privately by persons acting independently of the vehicle operators, etc; or

(b)   a service within which every vehicle used is operated under a permit granted under TA 1985, s 19 (minibuses and buses operated by educational, religious, social, recreational and other beneficial bodies); or

(c)   a service in relation to which (except in an emergency) *either* the place where each passenger is set down is 15 miles or more, measured in a straight line, from the place where he was taken up *or* some point on the route between those places is 15 miles or more from that place or both (limited stop vehicles).

Front-seat child passengers

It is an offence, contrary to RTA 1988, s 15(1) and (2), for a person, without reasonable excuse, to drive a motor vehicle on a road if a child under 14 is in the front of that vehicle, unless the child is wearing a seat belt in conformity with MV(WSBCFS)R 1993, reg 5. Generally, it is irrelevant that a seat belt is not provided or available for the seat. The Regulations set out the rules with which a driver must conform. A 'front seat' is one which is wholly or partially in the front of the vehicle. The Regulations do not apply to two-wheeled motor cycles, with or without sidecars.

The description of the seat belts to be worn by front-seat child passengers set out in MV(WSBCFS)R 1993, reg 5 is as follows:

(a) in the case of a 'small child', the seat belt must be (i) a child restraint with a marking required under RV(C&U)R 1986, reg 47(7), or (ii) a child restraint approved by another EU member state, or (iii) a child restraint with markings required under UN Economic Commission for Europe (ECE) Regulation 129 about uniform provisions concerning the approval of enhanced child restraint systems if the markings indicate that it is suitable for his height, weight and age;

(b) in the case of a 'large child', the seat belt must be a child restraint as described in (a) (i) or (iii), or an adult belt.

For the purposes of the Regulations, a 'small child' is a child who is under 12 and under 135 cm in height, and a 'large child' is a child under 14 who is not a 'small child'. MV(WSBCFS)R, reg 7 exempts from these provisions:

(a) a 'small child' aged three or more who is riding in a bus and is wearing an adult belt if an appropriate seat belt is not available for him in the front or rear of the vehicle;

(b) a child for whom there is a medical certificate; or

(c) a disabled child who is wearing a disabled person's belt.

In addition, RTA 1988, s 15(1) does not apply in relation to a child riding in a bus which is being used to provide a 'local service' (p 427) in a built-up area or which is constructed or adapted for the carriage of standing passengers and on which the operator permits standing. The prohibition does not apply in relation to a 'large child' if no appropriate seat belt is available for him in the front of the vehicle.

RTA 1988, s 15(1A) requires that where:

(a) a child is in the front seat of a motor vehicle other than a bus;

(b) that child is in a rear-facing child restraining device; and

(c) the passenger seat where the child is placed is protected by a front air bag,

a person must not, without reasonable excuse, drive the vehicle on a road unless the air bag is deactivated. 'Deactivation' includes the case where a bag is designed or adapted in such a way that it cannot inflate enough to pose a risk of injury to a child travelling in a rear-facing child restraining device in the seat in question. It is an offence contrary to s 15(2) for the person to drive a motor vehicle in contravention of s 15(1A).

For the purposes of s 15, 'bus' means a motor vehicle with at least four wheels, constructed or adapted for the carriage of passengers, with more than eight seats in addition to the driver's seat, and with a maximum design speed exceeding 25 kph.

Rear-seat child passengers

RTA 1988, s 15(3) provides that a person must not, without reasonable excuse, drive a motor vehicle on a road if:

(a) a child under the age of three is in the rear of that motor vehicle; or

(b) a child of or over that age but under the age of 14 is in the rear of the motor vehicle and any seat belt is fitted in the rear of that vehicle,

unless the child is wearing a seat belt in conformity with MV(WSB)R 1993, reg 8. Regulation 8 is identical to the requirements which apply to children in front seats, ie MV(WSBCFS)R 1993, reg 5 (see above).

RTA 1988, s 15(3A) provides that a person must not, without reasonable excuse, drive a passenger car on a road where a child under the age of 12 and less than 150 cm in height is in the rear of the car and no seat belt is fitted in the rear of that car, but a seat in the front of the passenger car is provided with a seat belt and is not occupied by any person.

Exemption from these prohibitions is provided by MV(WSB)R 1993, regs 9 and 10. Regulation 9 provides that they do not apply where the motor vehicle is a large bus, or where the vehicle is a licensed taxi or licensed hire car in which (in each case) the rear seats are separated from the driver by a fixed partition. Regulation 10 provides that the prohibitions in s 15(3) and (3A) do not apply in relation to:

(a) a child for whom there is a medical certificate;
(b) a small child (p 428) aged under three who is riding in a licensed taxi or a licensed hire car if no appropriate seat belt is available for him in the front or rear of the vehicle;
(c) a small child aged three or more who is riding in a licensed taxi, a licensed hire car, or a small bus and wearing an adult belt if an appropriate seat belt is not available for him in the front or rear of the vehicle;
(d) a small child aged three or more who is wearing an adult belt and riding in a passenger car or light goods vehicle where the use of child restraints by the child occupants of two seats in the rear of the vehicle prevents the use of an appropriate seat belt for that child and no appropriate seat belt is available for him in the front of the vehicle;
(e) a small child who is riding in a vehicle being used for the purposes of the police, security or emergency services to enable the proper performance of their duty;
(f) a small child aged three or more who is wearing an adult belt and who, because of an unexpected necessity, is travelling a short distance in a passenger car or light goods vehicle in which no appropriate seat belt is available for him; or
(g) a disabled child who is wearing a disabled person's belt or whose disability makes it impracticable to wear a seat belt where a disabled person's belt is unavailable to him.

In addition, by reg 10, the prohibition in s 15(3) does not apply in relation to a child under three riding in a rear seat of a small bus. Nor does it apply to a small child aged three or more riding in the rear of a small bus if neither an appropriate seat belt nor an adult seat belt is available for him in the front or rear of the vehicle. In addition, it does not apply in relation to a 'large child' in any vehicle, if no appropriate seat belt is available for him in the rear of the vehicle. Lastly, the prohibition in s 15(3) does not apply to a child riding in a small bus which is being used to provide a 'local service' (p 427) in a built-up area (ie entirely on restricted roads) or which is constructed or adapted for the carriage of standing passengers and on which the operator permits standing.

Regulation 10 also provides that the prohibition in s 15(3A) does not apply to a child if no appropriate seat belt is available for him in the front of the vehicle.

For the purposes of the seat belt regulations, 'large buses' and 'small buses' are 'buses' as defined on p 428. The difference between them is that a large bus has a maximum laden weight exceeding 3.5 tonnes and a small bus has a maximum laden weight not exceeding 3.5 tonnes. A 'light goods vehicle' is a motor vehicle with at least four wheels, a maximum design speed of more than 25 kph, and a maximum laden weight not exceeding 3.5 tonnes. 'Small child' and 'large child' have the same meaning as in respect of 'child front seat passengers' (p 428).

Breach of RTA 1988, s 15(3) or (3A) is an offence under s 15(4).

'Availability' of seat belts

MV(WSB)R 1993, Sch 2, and MV(WSBCFS)R 1993, Sch 2, describe in the same terms the circumstances in which a seat belt will be regarded as not being available. They are where:

(a) another person is wearing the relevant belt;
(b) a child is occupying the relevant seat and wearing a child restraint which is an appropriate child restraint for that child and this renders use of the seat belt impracticable;
(c) a person holding a medical certificate is occupying the relevant seat;
(d) a disabled person (not being the person in question) is occupying the relevant seat and wearing a disabled person's belt and this renders use of the seat belt impracticable;
(e) by reason of his disability, it would not be practicable for the person in question to wear the relevant belt;
(f) the person in question is prevented from occupying the relevant seat by the presence of a child restraint which could not readily be removed without the aid of tools; or
(g) the relevant seat is so designed that it can be adjusted to increase the space available for goods and effects and when it is so adjusted the seat cannot be used.

TAMPERING WITH, OR HOLDING OR GETTING ON TO, VEHICLES

Tampering with motor vehicles

RTA 1988, s 25 provides that if, while a motor vehicle is on a road or on a parking place provided by a local authority, a person:

(a) gets on to the vehicle, or
(b) tampers with the brake or other part of its mechanism,

without lawful authority or reasonable cause he is guilty of an offence.

Holding or getting on to vehicle in order to be towed or carried

If, for the purpose of being carried, a person without lawful authority or reasonable cause takes or retains hold of, or gets on to, a motor vehicle or trailer while in motion on a road he is guilty of an offence under RTA 1988, s 26(1).

If, for the purpose of being drawn, a person takes or retains hold of a motor vehicle or trailer while in motion on a road he is guilty of an offence under s 26(2).

CYCLES

Use of motor cycles

RTA 1988, s 23 restricts the carriage of passengers on a motor bicycle to one person who must be carried sitting astride the cycle on a proper seat securely fixed to the vehicle behind the driver's seat. Interestingly, a pillion passenger need not be carried facing the front. The driver commits an offence if a passenger is carried in contravention of s 23. RV(C&U)R 1986, reg 102 prohibits the carriage of a passenger on a motor bicycle (whether it has a sidecar attached to it or not) on which there are not available suitable supports or rests for the feet for him.

RTA 1988, s 16 empowers the Secretary of State to make regulations requiring persons driving or riding on a specified type of motor cycle (other than in a sidecar) which is on a road to wear protective headgear. The type of headgear is prescribed by the Motor Cycles (Protective Helmets) Regulations 1998. For the purpose of these Regulations, 'motor cycle' means a motor bicycle, including one with a sidecar, and motor tricycles where the paired wheels are less than 460 mm apart. A divisional court has held that the BMW C1 motor cycle (which has a rigid rider cell in the form of a cab) is a motor cycle for these purposes. The Regulations do not apply to mowing machines, motor cycles being propelled by a person on foot, or followers of the Sikh religion while wearing a turban. Helmets must comply with various British Standard or EEA specifications. Breach of the Regulations is an offence contrary to RTA 1988, s 16(4). However, it is not an offence to aid and abet the failure to wear a crash helmet, unless the other party is under 16.

By virtue of s 18(3), it is an offence to drive or ride on a motor cycle on a road without wearing eye protectors of the type prescribed by the Motor Cycles (Eye Protectors) Regulations 1999. For the purposes of s 18, the Regulations define 'motor cycle' in the same way as in relation to protective helmets. The present requirement does not apply to a person driving or riding on a mowing machine nor does it apply to a person driving or riding on a motor cycle temporarily brought into Great Britain by a foreign resident, if it has been here for less than one year. In addition, the requirement does not apply to a member of the armed forces of the Crown who is driving or riding on a motor cycle on duty, if he is wearing an eye protector which is part of his service equipment. A person propelling a motor cycle on foot is not required to wear an eye protector.

Use of pedal cycles

By RTA 1988, s 24 the carriage of more than one person on a road on a bicycle not propelled by mechanical power is an offence by each of the persons carried, unless it is *constructed* or *adapted* for the carriage of more than one person. A tandem is a cycle *constructed* for the carriage of more than one person, and a cycle which has a seat fitted to permit the carriage of a child has been *adapted* for the carriage of more than one person.

The wilful riding of a pedal cycle (or the driving of any other form of vehicle) on a footpath or causeway by the side of any road made or set apart for the use or accommodation of foot passengers remains an offence contrary to the Highways Act 1835, s 72. A person rides a cycle, even if he merely sits astride it and propels himself with his feet. The offence under s 72 does not apply to an invalid carriage (eg a mobility scooter) if the requirements on p 327 are satisfied (Chronically Sick and Disabled Persons Act 1970, s 20).

Races or speed trials

RTA 1988, s 31 provides that a person who promotes or takes part in a race or speed trial for pedal cycles on a highway commits an offence, unless that race or speed trial is authorised under, and conducted in accordance with, the Cycle Racing on Highways Regulations 1960. Time trials and bicycle races are dealt with separately by the Regulations.

Regulation 2 defines a 'time trial' as a cycle race or trial of speed between bicycles or tricycles involving either single competitors, or groups of not more than four competitors, starting at intervals of not less than one minute. In the case of groups they must not compete against one another. The result must depend upon the time taken by a competitor, or if a group any member of it, to reach a finishing point; or on the distance covered in a fixed time. A time trial is authorised if its promoter gives the specified written notice 28 days in advance.

A 'bicycle race' is defined by reg 2 as a race or trial of speed which is not a time trial.

In order for a bicycle race to be authorised *in England*, the following additional requirements must be satisfied:

(a) the numbers taking part are restricted to, in not more than two races a year selected by the British Cycling Federation, 100 competitors, and in any other approved race, 80;

(b) races must not take place during the hours of darkness;

(c) if races follow a circuitous route, they must travel at least 10 miles before passing the same point on a highway twice (in whichever direction);

(d) no continuous part of the race may be on more than one-and-a-half miles of any road subject to a speed limit of 40 mph or less, and no further continuous part in a 40 mph-restricted section may be within three miles of the previous one; and

(e) the race promoter must give the specified written notice 28 days in advance.

A chief officer of police is empowered to impose conditions on the holding or conduct of a race.

In order for a bicycle race to be authorised *in Wales*, the following requirements must be satisfied:

(a) the promoter of the race must complete a written risk assessment, which must include:

   (i) a suitable and sufficient assessment of the risks to the health and safety of competitors, race officials, spectators and other road users arising out of the holding of the race, having regard to the maximum number of competitors eligible to participate in the race; and

   (ii) details of appropriate actions that will be taken by the promoter of the race to ensure the safe operation of the race;

(b) races must not take place during the hours of darkness;

(c) if races follow a circuitous route, they must travel at least five miles before passing the same point on a highway twice (in whichever direction); and

(d) the promoter of the race must give the specified written notice 28 days in advance.

A chief officer of police is empowered to impose conditions on the holding or conduct of a race. A chief officer who decides to do so must provide written reasons for his decision to the promoter of the race and the British Cycling Federation within five working days of making that decision

Electrically assisted pedal cycles

An 'electrically assisted pedal cycle' is not a motor vehicle for the purposes of the Road Traffic Acts; such a cycle is a pedal cycle with two or more wheels, is fitted with pedals by means of which it is capable of being propelled, and has an electric motor of a rated power not exceeding 250 watts and incapable of propelling the vehicle when it is travelling at more than 15.5 mph. There is no longer a maximum kerbside weight requirement. In other words, an electrically assisted pedal cycle is basically a pedal cycle with an auxiliary electric motor which cuts out when the vehicle is travelling in excess of 15.5 mph. A divisional court has held that, to satisfy the definition of an electrically assisted pedal cycle, the nature of the pedals fitted to such a cycle must be such that they are reasonably capable of propelling the vehicle in a safe manner in normal day-to-day use.

Electrically assisted pedal cycles may be driven by anyone aged 14 or over. Unlike motor vehicles, their use does not require a vehicle licence or insurance. Nor do the requirements of testing, driving licences and protective headgear apply.

Brakes on pedal cycles

The Pedal Cycles (Construction and Use) Regulations 1983, reg 4A provides that no person may ride, or cause or permit to be ridden, on a road, an electrically assisted pedal cycle unless it is fitted with braking systems which comply with para 4.6.8 of the 2014 BS EN Standard or with the standards required when the pedal cycle vehicle was type approved (if applicable). Regulation 5 prohibits a person from riding, or causing or permitting to be ridden, on a road such a cycle when the brakes have not been maintained in efficient working order.

Regulation 6 provides that no person shall ride, or cause or permit to be ridden, a pedal cycle which is not electrically assisted if it does not comply with such of the braking-system requirements in regs 7 or 8 as apply to it.

Regulation 7 requires that at least one braking system be fitted to pedal cycles.

Pedal cycles manufactured on or after 1 August 1984 are subjected by reg 7 to additional braking requirements if the saddle height (fully raised and tyre fully inflated) is 635 mm (about 25 inches). The additional requirements are that fixed-wheel cycles must have a braking system acting on the front wheel or on at least two front wheels if there are more than one. Free-wheel cycles must have two independent systems, one acting upon the front wheel, or at least two front wheels if more than one is fitted, and the other acting upon the rear wheel, or at least two rear wheels if more than one is fitted. In the case of pedal cycles manufactured before 1 August 1984, these additional requirements apply under reg 8 to pedal cycles, any wheel of which exceeds 460 mm (approx 18 inches) in diameter including the fully inflated tyre, except that the braking system acting upon the rear need only act upon one rear wheel even if there is more than one rear wheel fitted. A non-goods tricycle, whenever manufactured, may instead have two independent systems both acting upon the front wheel if it has two rear wheels (and vice versa).

Regulation 9 provides that nothing in regs 7 or 8 applies to pedal cycles on which the pedals act directly on the wheel rather than through a gearing system (eg a penny-farthing) and those temporarily in Great Britain when ridden by a visitor, such a cycle having a braking system or systems complying with provisions of the International Convention on Road Traffic.

Regulation 10 prohibits riding, or causing or permitting to be ridden, on a road a pedal cycle the braking system of which, fitted in accordance with these Regulations, is not in efficient working order.

Breach of regs 4, 5, 6, or 10 is an offence contrary to RTOA 1988, s 91. A constable in uniform is empowered by reg 11 to test and inspect a pedal cycle for the purpose of ascertaining that the braking requirements are satisfied. This may be done on a road, or on any premises where the cycle is if the cycle has been involved in an accident (provided that the test and inspection are carried out within 48 hours of the accident with the consent of the owner of the premises).

OFFENCES RELATING TO SMOKING IN SMOKE-FREE VEHICLES

The enforcement of the smoke-free-places legislation is generally a matter for local authorities and port health authorities but chief officers of police are also enforcement authorities for their areas in respect of private vehicles that are smoke-free by virtue of regs 11(1A) and 4A below.

By the Smoke-free (Exemptions and Vehicles) Regulations 2007, reg 11(1) and the Smoke-free Premises, etc (Wales) Regulations 2007, reg 4, an enclosed vehicle and any enclosed part of a vehicle is smoke-free if it is used:

(a) by members of the public or a section of the public (whether or not for reward or hire); or
(b) in the course of paid or voluntary work by more than one person (even if those persons use the vehicle at different times, or only intermittently).

In addition, by reg 11 (1A) (England) and reg 4A (Wales), a vehicle which is not a smoke-free vehicle by virtue of reg 11(1) or reg 4 (ie a private vehicle) or any part of it is smoke-free if:

(a) it is enclosed;
(b) there is more than one person present in the vehicle; and
(c) a person under the age of 18 is present in the vehicle.

However, regs 11(1A) and 4A do not apply to a caravan or motor caravan that is stationary and not on a road, or to a caravan or motor caravan that is stationary, is on a road and is being used as living accommodation.

For the above purposes, in the provisions about smoke-free vehicles:

(a) 'Vehicle' includes every type of vehicle, including a train or vessel, except that it does not include aircraft, ships and hovercraft. A vehicle or part of a vehicle is enclosed where it has doors or windows which may be opened but it is not enclosed unless it is wholly or partly covered by a roof. Thus, a vehicle is enclosed if it has its windows or sunroof open but not if it is a convertible and has its roof completely down.
(b) 'Smoking' refers to smoking tobacco or anything which contains tobacco, or smoking any other substance, and includes being in possession of lit tobacco or of anything lit which contains tobacco, or being in possession of any other lit substance in a form in which it could be smoked. Thus, 'vaping' (e-cigarettes) is not smoking.

Offence of smoking in smoke-free place

A person who smokes in a smoke-free place commits an offence, contrary to the Health Act 2006 (HA 2006), s 7(2). A 'smoke-free place' includes a 'smoke-free vehicle' and it is on such vehicles that the following text focuses. By s 7(4), it is a defence for D to show that he did not know, and could not reasonably have been expected to know, that it was a smoke-free place. For this purpose, if evidence is adduced which is sufficient to raise an issue with respect to that defence, the court must assume that the defence is satisfied unless the prosecution proves beyond doubt that it is not.

Failing to prevent smoking in smoke-free vehicles

The Smoke-free (Vehicle Operators and Penalty Notices) Regulations 2007, reg 2 provides that the following persons are under a duty to cause any person who is smoking in a smoke-free vehicle to stop smoking:

(a) in respect of a vehicle that is smoke-free by virtue of the Smoke-free (Exemptions and Vehicles) Regulations 2007, reg 11(1): (i) a driver, (ii) any person with management responsibilities for the vehicle, and (iii) any person on a vehicle who is responsible for order or safety on it;

(b) in respect of a vehicle that is smoke-free by virtue of the Smoke-free (Exemptions and Vehicles) Regulations 2007, reg 11(1A), the driver.

These provisions only apply in England.

In Wales, there are corresponding provisions under the Smoke-free Premises, etc (Wales) Regulations 2007, regs 7 and 7A respectively.

A person who fails to comply with the duty to prevent smoking commits an offence, contrary to HA 2006, s 8(4). By s 8(5), it is a defence for D to show:

(a) that he took reasonable steps to cause the person in question to stop smoking; or

(b) that he did not know, and could not reasonably have been expected to know, that the person in question was smoking; or

(c) that on other grounds it was reasonable for him not to comply with the duty.

For this purpose, if evidence is adduced which is sufficient to raise an issue with respect to that defence, the court must assume that the defence is satisfied unless the prosecution proves beyond doubt that it is not.

Penalty notice

An authorised officer of an enforcement authority who has reason to believe that a person has committed an offence under HA 2006, s 7(2) or 8(4) may give him a penalty notice offering the opportunity to discharge liability to conviction for the offence if paid in time. The fixed penalties are £30 if paid within 15 working days or £50 if paid within 29 days.

TESTING AND INSPECTION

Testing vehicles on roads: RTA 1988, s 67

Authorised examiners may test a motor vehicle on a *road* to ascertain whether the requirements relating to its construction and use are being complied with, and also whether there is compliance with the requirement that the condition of the vehicle is not such that its use on a road would involve danger of injury to any person. There are two principal types of authorised examiners for the purposes of s 67: (a) police officers specially authorised by their chief constables for this purpose, and (b) vehicle examiners (ie examiners appointed under RTA 1988, s 66A by the Secretary of State in respect of statutory functions conferred on them in respect of public passenger vehicles, goods vehicles and other vehicles). For the purpose of testing a vehicle an examiner may require the driver to comply with his reasonable instructions and may drive the vehicle. All authorised examiners must produce their authority if required to do so.

The provisions of s 67 do not mean that the requirements of RTA 1988 and RV(C&U)R 1986 may only be enforced on a road by an authorised examiner. Particular offences may still be reported by a constable who is not an authorised examiner. In addition, it has been held by a divisional court that any constable may test a vehicle with the owner's consent. In that case, a constable who was not an authorised examiner tested the efficiency of a handbrake with the driver's consent; evidence of his findings was admitted even though he was not an authorised examiner.

Where an examination of the vehicle under s 67 is required by an authorised examiner, the driver may elect that the test shall be deferred to a time and place to be arranged within the next 30 days.

The right to defer does not apply:

(a) when it appears to a constable that, following an accident on a road, the test must be taken forthwith. If this is so and the constable is not an authorised examiner, he may require that the vehicle is not taken away until the test has been carried out (s 67(7)); or

(b) when the vehicle appears to a constable to be so defective that it ought not to be allowed to proceed (s 67(8)).

Testing vehicles off roads: RV(C&U)R 1986

Regulation 74 empowers any police constable in uniform or vehicle examiner to test and inspect the brakes, silencers, steering gear and tyres of any motor vehicle or trailer on any *premises* where that motor vehicle or trailer is, *subject to the consent of the owner of the premises*. This represents the basic difference between these powers and those set out above.

Because the consent of the *owner of the premises* is necessary, there is no power of entry onto premises for the purpose of inspection under reg 74. In addition, the test and inspection cannot be carried out without the consent of the *owner of the vehicle*, unless notice of it has been served personally upon him at least 48 hours before the test, or 72 hours before it if service is effected by recorded delivery. The consent of the *owner of the vehicle* is not required if it has been involved in an accident within the preceding 48 hours.

Prohibition of unfit vehicles

RTA 1988, s 69 empowers an authorised constable to issue an immediate prohibition notice if, on an inspection under the various powers of testing and inspection under the Act, including ss 45 (below), 49 (goods vehicles: Appendix 2), 67 (above), and 68 (public passenger vehicles and goods vehicles (Appendices 1 and 2)), it appears to him that, owing to any defects in the vehicle, driving it (or driving it for any particular purpose or purposes or for any except one or more particular purposes) would involve a danger of injury to any person. The sections referred to deal with powers in relation to construction and use requirements; test certificates generally; inspections related to plated weights of goods vehicles, public service vehicles, and vehicles adapted to carry more than eight passengers which are not public service vehicles; and the testing of the condition of used vehicles at sale rooms, etc. A notice under s 69 may prohibit use absolutely, or for one or more specified purposes, or except for one or more specified purposes.

Vehicle examiners have a similar power.

The Road Vehicles (Prohibition) Regulations 1992 make provision for a vehicle which is subject to a prohibition issued by an authorised constable, or vehicle examiner, to be driven on a road solely for the purpose of submitting it, by prior arrangement, for test with a view to removal of that prohibition, or for it to be driven in the course of any test for the purpose of the removal of the prohibition, or (within three miles from where it is being, or has been, repaired) for it to be driven solely for the purpose of its test or trial with a view to the removal of the prohibition.

TEST CERTIFICATES

RTA 1988, ss 45 to 47 are concerned with tests of the satisfactory condition of motor vehicles, other than goods vehicles, to which s 49 applies. The relevant provisions with regard to such goods vehicles are discussed in Appendix 2 on the companion website. The Secretary of State is authorised by RTA 1988, s 45 to make regulations for the examination of all vehicles to which ss 45 to 47 apply and the Secretary of State has made the Motor Vehicles (Tests) Regulations 1981.

By RTA 1988, s 47(1), a person commits an offence if he uses, or causes or permits to be used, at any time on a road a motor vehicle to which s 47 applies, and as respects which no test certificate has been issued within the appropriate period before the said time. In relation to 'use', 'cause', or 'permit', see pp 415–16. Once it is proved that D has used, etc a vehicle on a road, the burden shifts to him to prove that there was in force a test certificate for the vehicle.

The vehicles to which s 47 applies

The answer to the question which vehicles must be tested depends on the *type of vehicle* and its *age*.

The following must be examined and receive a test certificate annually, *after the period of three years* defined in the next paragraph:

(a) passenger vehicles with not more than eight seats, excluding the driver's seat;
(b) rigid goods motor cars, the unladen weight of which does not exceed 1,525 kg;
(c) dual-purpose vehicles;
(d) motor cycles (including three-wheelers and mopeds); and
(e) motor caravans.

Section 47 applies to motor vehicles of the above types which were first registered not less than three years before the time in question (ie the time of the alleged use without a test certificate). If, for any reason, a vehicle is used on a road in Great Britain or elsewhere before being registered, a test certificate must be obtained three years from the date of manufacture. Thus, a serviceman returning from duty abroad who brings into this country a vehicle which is more than three years old must have it tested immediately.

RTA 1988 requires annual tests for the following motor vehicles *after one year from first registration* or three years from manufacture if used pre-registration:

(a) motor vehicles used for the carriage of passengers and with more than eight seats, exclusive of the driver's (mainly public service vehicles);
(b) taxis licensed to ply for hire; and
(c) ambulances.

Exemptions

The Motor Vehicles (Tests) Regulations 1981 exempt a range of vehicles including:

(a) goods vehicles with a design gross weight exceeding 3,500 kg;
(b) articulated vehicles other than articulated buses;

(c) invalid carriages not exceeding 306 kg unladen weight (or 510 kg if supplied by the Department of Health);

(d) vehicles temporarily in Great Britain for a 12-month period;

(e) police vehicles maintained in police workshops, or vehicles provided for the purposes of NCA;

(f) electrically propelled goods vehicles with a design gross weight not exceeding 3,500 kg;

(g) some licensed hackney carriages and private hire cars;

(h) any vehicle at a time when it is being used on a public road during any calendar week if it is being used only in passing from land in the occupation of its keeper to other land in his occupation, and it has not been used on public roads for more than an aggregate of six miles in that calendar week;

(i) heavy locomotives, light locomotives, motor tractors, track laying vehicles, agricultural motor vehicles and works vehicles;

(j) vehicles which have a Northern Ireland test certificate; and

(k) vehicles having a manufacture date before 1 January 1960.

The Regulations also permit use without a test certificate when a vehicle is being taken to a testing station by previous arrangement for a test, or when it is being brought away from such a test, or while it is being so tested by an authorised person or under his direction. In circumstances in which a test certificate is refused, the vehicle may be moved without a test certificate for the purpose of work being done (once again, by previous arrangement), or for the purpose of delivering it, by towing, to a place where it is to be broken up. Imported vehicles which need to be tested may be driven on arrival in this country to the place of residence of the owner of the motor vehicle.

Test certificate

The contents of a test certificate are not prescribed. A certificate must be in a form supplied by the Secretary of State. A certificate has a serial number; indicates that the vehicle complied with the requirements on the date of the examination; shows the registration mark of the vehicle, the vehicle testing station number, the date of issue of the certificate, the date of expiry, and bears the signature of the person issuing the certificate. A signature may be a facsimile of the signature of the examiner or of a person so authorised by the Secretary of State. If the previous certificate had expired at the time of the examination, the serial number of the previous certificate may also be shown. Tests can only be conducted at testing stations authorised by the Secretary of State.

Requirement to produce test certificate

RTA 1988, s 165 empowers a constable or vehicle examiner to require a person driving, or reasonably believed by him to have been driving, when an accident occurred or when an offence was committed, to give his name and address and the name and address of the owner of the vehicle and to produce certain documents, including a test certificate (if one is required for the vehicle). As with other types of document, there is a proviso which permits production within seven days at a specified police station; or production as soon as reasonably practicable; or proof that production was not reasonably practicable before the day on which proceedings were commenced. Production in person is not required.

CHAPTER 11

Control of Vehicles

TRAFFIC SIGNS AND DIRECTIONS

These are governed by the Road Traffic Regulation Act 1984 (RTRA 1984) and the Traffic Signs Regulations and General Directions 2016 (TSR&GD 2016).

For the purposes of RTRA 1984, the term 'traffic sign' is defined by s 64 as any object or device (fixed or portable) for conveying, to traffic on roads or any specified class of traffic, warnings, information, requirements, restrictions or prohibitions of any description:

(a) specified by regulations made by the relevant Ministers acting jointly; or
(b) authorised by the Secretary of State,

and any line or mark on a road for so conveying such warnings, information, requirements, restrictions or prohibitions. Traffic signs must be of a prescribed size, colour and type, or of any authorised character.

Powers to place traffic signs

RTRA 1984, s 65 empowers *highway authorities* to cause or permit traffic signs to be placed on or near any road in their area.

Sections 66 and 67 empower *a constable, or a traffic officer in uniform (in the case of s 67), or a person acting under the instructions (whether general or specific) of the chief officer of police*, to place on a road such authorised traffic signs indicating prohibitions, restrictions or requirements relating to vehicular traffic as may be required:

(a) to prevent an obstruction on public occasions or near public buildings or at an authorised cycle race (s 66). Section 66 permits police officers to place emergency signs on the road at special events such as air displays;
(b) to prevent or mitigate congestion or obstruction of traffic, or danger to or from traffic, in consequence of extraordinary circumstances (s 67). Among other things, s 67 empowers the police to place emergency signs on the road at the scene of an accident. Such signs may be maintained for a maximum period of seven days. The time starts when the signs are placed. If the need is a permanent one the matter must be dealt with by the highway authority.

Failure to comply with a sign placed under the provisions of RTRA 1984, s 65 66, or 67 is an offence contrary to the Road Traffic Act 1988 (RTA 1988), s 36 (p 440).

Quite apart from the above, the TSR&GD 2016, Sch 13, Part 7, para 11 authorises the *crew of an emergency or breakdown vehicle* which is causing a temporary obstruction to place a 'keep right sign'. Non-compliance with such a sign is an offence against RTA 1988, s 36.

In addition, TSR&GD 2016, Sch 13, Part 7, para 12 authorises *any person* to place a 'road vehicle sign' (temporary obstruction by stationary vehicle) on a vehicle, and to place on any road:

(a) a 'flat traffic delineator', 'traffic cone' or 'traffic pyramid';
(b) a 'traffic triangle'; or
(c) a 'warning light',

for the purpose of *warning* traffic of a temporary obstruction, other than roadworks. Non-compliance with such a sign is not in itself an offence. A 'road vehicle sign' consists of a flexible sheet on which there is a triangle the outer edges of which are red, the inner part being either reflectorised white or fluorescent yellow. It is designed to be fixed to a stationary vehicle, facing approaching traffic. A 'traffic delineator', 'traffic cone' or 'traffic pyramid' is of the 'lane marker' type of device frequently used by emergency services. A 'traffic triangle' is the type of device frequently used by individual motorists, and a 'warning light' is a flashing amber signal.

The indications given by the signs and the form which they take is prescribed by TSR&GD 2016, Sch 13, Part 6.

The placing of signs otherwise than as prescribed is of no legal effect.

Drivers to comply with traffic signs

RTA 1988, s 36(1) states that an offence is committed by a person driving or propelling a vehicle who fails to comply with a lawfully placed traffic sign of the prescribed size, colour and type, or of another character authorised by the Secretary of State. It is no defence for a driver to allege that he did not see a traffic sign.

A traffic sign is not to be treated as lawfully placed unless (a) it indicates a statutory prohibition, restriction or requirement, or (b) it is expressly provided by or under RTA 1988 or RTRA 1984 that RTA 1988, s 36 applies to the sign; such express provision has been made by the relevant parts of TSR&GD 2016. Examples of signs to which s 36 applies thereunder are described in the next three paragraphs (which deal in turn with signs indicating a prohibition, a restriction and a requirement) and on pp 441–2 (particular signs).

Examples of signs which indicate a *prohibition* are 'No entry', 'No right turn', 'No U turn', 'Lorries prohibited', and 'No overtaking' signs. These signs frequently involve the use of symbols only. Except in the case of a 'No Entry' sign, these consist of a red circle with the enclosed symbol in black on a white background. Thus a sign prohibiting entry to lorries would carry the symbol of a lorry with a red circle around it.

Signs dealing with *restrictions* include those dealing with waiting restrictions. These signs have a red outer circle with a blue background and a red band cutting across the face from the top left to bottom right of the sign as seen by approaching drivers. Information concerning the nature of the restrictions in force is provided on a plate, usually attached to the post supporting the sign. A yellow plate with the words 'at any time' in black indicates a total ban on parking, while the words '8.00 am–6.00 pm' would indicate a restriction upon waiting between those hours. Where waiting is limited rather than prohibited, the sign will be of white lettering on a blue background. Restrictions on waiting may be additionally indicated by signs placed on the roadway but such a sign is only effective to create the restriction if used in conjunction with a restriction sign or plate of the type referred to above. A single continuous yellow line running parallel with the kerb restricts waiting (other than for loading or unloading) for a period of at least eight hours between 7 am and 7 pm on a minimum of four days a week. A double continuous yellow line indicates that no waiting at any time is permitted, unless there are signs specifically indicating seasonal restrictions. Broken yellow lines indicate other waiting restrictions, usually unilateral parking schemes, restricting waiting on particular sides of the road on particular days of the week.

Those signs which deal with *requirements* under the section are those which require a driver, etc to do something. 'Stop', 'Give way', 'Keep right', 'Keep left', 'Traffic lights' are all signs which indicate a requirement. The driver must stop his vehicle, turn it in a particular direction or give way to other traffic. These signs vary in appearance. The modern 'Stop' sign is octagonal and coloured red with 'Stop' in white capitals on it, although variations still exist. Other statutory requirements relating to stopping are red traffic lights and manually operated 'stop' signs at road works. 'Give way' signs consist of a red inverted triangle on a white, circular background with the words 'Give way' inside the triangle. White arrows on a blue background indicate the route which a driver must follow. Another example of a sign making a requirement is one requiring certain drivers to telephone for permission to cross automatic level crossings.

For the purposes of RTA 1988, s 36, traffic signs placed on or near a road are deemed to be of the prescribed size, colour and type, or of another authorised character, and to have been lawfully placed, unless the contrary is proved. Consequently, the prosecution does not normally have to offer evidence of the nature of the sign beyond that which satisfies the court of the nature of the prohibition, restriction or requirement in question. However, if the sign is proved not to be of the prescribed size, etc, or not to have been lawfully placed, it will not be a valid sign and no offence can be committed in relation to it, unless the breach of the requirement is trivial. There is a presumption that automatic traffic lights are in working order, unless the contrary is proved.

Where the provisions of s 36 do not apply to a sign but it is governed by regulations concerning traffic control made by the Secretary of State, the Road Traffic Offenders Act 1998 (RTOA 1988), s 91 states that contravention or failure to comply is an offence under that section.

Particular signs

Certain signs indicate particular requirements. A 'Stop' sign requires that:

(a) every vehicle must, before entering the major road, stop at the transverse lines at the junction, or, if the lines are not visible, at the major road; and

(b) no vehicle may proceed past the transverse line painted nearest to the major road, or, if the lines are not visible, may not enter the major road, in such a manner or at such a time as is likely to cause danger to the driver of any other vehicle on the major road, or such as to necessitate the driver of any such other vehicle to change its speed or course in order to avoid an accident.

The latter provision (ie (b)) also applies to 'Give Way' signs. Thus, it is not sufficient to stop, or give way, and then to proceed, if the results of so proceeding are as described. There should be no interference with traffic on the major road. To emerge in such circumstances also indicates an element of carelessness which might amount to careless driving.

TSR&GD 2016, Sch 9, Part 7, para 9 deals with double white lines, which consist of either two continuous white lines or one continuous white line together with a broken white line painted along the middle of the carriageway itself. Any white unbroken line must be immediately preceded by a white warning arrow painted on the road; otherwise the line is not valid as a sign. If there are two continuous white lines vehicles travelling in both directions are required to keep to the nearside of the nearest continuous white line. A broken line with a continuous line requires vehicles to keep to the near-side of the continuous white line when that line is the nearer of the two to the vehicle. Neither of these rules applies if it is both safe to cross the line and necessary to do so:

(a) to enable the vehicle to enter, from the side of the road on which it is proceeding, roadside property or a side road joining that road;
(b) to pass a stationary vehicle;
(c) owing to circumstances outside the control of the driver;
(d) to avoid an accident;
(e) to pass a road maintenance vehicle which is in use, is moving at a speed not exceeding 10 mph, and is displaying to the rear a specified sign (angled white arrow on blue background within white edged circle, which may be mounted on a square or rectangular background);
(f) to pass a pedal cycle moving, or a horse being ridden or led, at a speed not exceeding 10 mph; or
(g) to comply with any direction of a constable in uniform, or a traffic officer in uniform.

No vehicle may stop on either side of the road with only one traffic lane in each direction where there is a double white line marking of either description unless it is done:

(a) to pick up or set down passengers, to load or unload;
(b) in connection with building operations, the removal of an obstruction to traffic, or road or public utility works;
(c) by a vehicle used for police, traffic officer, fire and rescue, special forces, NCA, bomb disposal, or ambulance purposes or for the purpose of emergency-response at the request of an NHS ambulance service;
(d) by a pedal cycle;
(e) to avoid an accident or because it is impossible to proceed; or
(f) with the permission or at the direction of a constable in uniform or a traffic officer in uniform.

This prohibition on stopping does not apply to a lay-by.

Records produced as evidence

RTOA 1988, s 20 provides that evidence of a fact related to an offence involving a driver's failure to comply with a light signal which is at red, contrary to RTA 1988, s 36(1), may be given by the production of a record produced by a device of a description specified by the Secretary of State. However, evidence may only be so given if (in the same or another document) there is a certificate as to the circumstances in which it was produced, signed by a constable, or by a person authorised by (or on behalf of) the chief police officer for the area. The effect of s 20 is that the record and certificate can be tendered in evidence without the need for a witness to be called to prove them. The device must be of a type approved by the Secretary of State; it has been held that this requirement has been satisfied by the Secretary of State's approval of 'a device designed or adapted for recording by photographic or other image recording means the position of vehicles in relation to light signals' as a prescribed device. The device must be used in accordance with conditions subject to which the approval was given.

For a document of the type referred to above to be admissible under s 20, a copy of it must be served on the defendant (D) not less than seven days before the hearing or trial. If D, not less than three days before the hearing or trial, requires the attendance of the person who signed the document, the evidence of the circumstances in which the record was produced will not be admissible, although the record produced by the device will.

Where the prosecution does not serve the record and certificate on D within the seven days before the trial, a police officer may nevertheless attend as a witness to produce and prove those items as real evidence.

Drivers to comply with traffic directions

RTA 1988, s 35(1) provides that, where a constable or a traffic officer in uniform is for the time being engaged in the regulation of traffic in a road, a person driving or propelling a vehicle who neglects (ie fails) or refuses:

(a) to stop the vehicle; or
(b) to make it proceed in, or keep to, a particular line of traffic,

when directed to do so by a constable in the execution of his duty, is guilty of an offence.

Traffic surveys

RTA 1988, s 35(2) provides that, where a traffic survey is being conducted, a constable or a traffic officer in uniform may direct a person driving or propelling a vehicle to stop or to proceed in a line of traffic or to a particular point, but no requirement to give information may be made; non-compliance is an offence. Section 36(4) provides that signs such as 'Stop at Census Point' and 'Census Point—Stop if required' are traffic signs to which s 36 applies.

Other powers to stop drivers and pedestrians

Apart from the powers given to the police by RTA 1988, s 35, RTA 1988, s 163 requires that a person driving a mechanically propelled vehicle or riding a cycle on a road must stop his vehicle on being required to do so by a constable in uniform or a traffic officer in uniform. Failure to do so is an offence against s 163(3).

In addition, by s 37, a person on foot who fails to comply with the signals of a uniformed constable or traffic officer on traffic control commits an offence. Failure to give a name and address in such circumstances is an offence against s 169.

Under the Fire and Rescue Services Act 2004, s 44 an authorised employee of a fire or rescue authority may close off streets, or stop or regulate traffic in any street, whenever he reasonably believes this is necessary for rescue or fire fighting purposes. It is an offence, contrary to the Emergency Workers (Obstruction) Act 2006, s 1(1), without reasonable excuse to obstruct or hinder a fire and rescue authority employee taking action under s 44.

PEDESTRIAN CROSSINGS

TSR&GD 2016 govern 'Zebra' and 'Puffin' crossings. Zebra crossings are uncontrolled; Puffin crossings are light controlled. TSR&GD 2016 revoked the 'Zebra', 'Pelican' and 'Puffin' Pedestrian Crossing Regulations and General Directions 1997. However, the TSR&GD 2016 provides that the provisions of the 1997 Regulations are to be treated as remaining in force (with some modifications) in relation to Pelican crossings established before the TSR&GD 2016 came into force (22 April 2016) or within the six-month period beginning with that date.

By RTRA 1984, s 25(5), a person who contravenes the relevant regulations relating to pedestrian crossings is guilty of an offence.

'Zebra' crossings

TSR&GD 2016 prescribe the nature of uncontrolled crossings and the rules governing them. The *limits* of the crossing itself (the walking area for the pedestrians) are indicated by lines of square or circular marks or studs between which is an area marked by alternate black and white stripes. Flashing yellow globes indicate the presence of such a crossing to approaching drivers. The globes are mounted on poles which are also marked by black and white stripes. There must be a globe at either side of the crossing; if there is a central reservation or street refuge on the crossing, one or more globes may be placed there. The failure of the lamps does not invalidate a Zebra crossing; the regulations must still be complied with.

The approach to the crossing from each direction is marked out as a 'controlled area'. It is in effect a defensive area and drivers are made aware that they are entering it by white lines situated at each kerb and in the crown of the road on the approaching driver's side. This is known as the 'terminal line' and from it three zig-zag lines stretch to a distance of one metre from the crossing itself where they join a broken white line which is the 'give way' line.

These regulations only apply to Zebra crossings when traffic is not being controlled by a uniformed police constable or traffic officer. Immediately such a person takes control of traffic movements at such a crossing, the crossing ceases to be an uncontrolled one and the regulations cease to apply until that control ceases.

Precedence at a Zebra crossing

TSR&GD 2016, Sch 14, Part 5, para 7 states that every pedestrian on the carriageway within the limits of a Zebra crossing has precedence within these limits over any vehicle. That precedence must be afforded by a driver before any part of his vehicle enters the pedestrian limits of the crossing itself. The vehicle must be stopped at or before the broken white line give-way marking on the approach side of the crossing. Where there is a central refuge each side of it is treated as a separate crossing. A pedestrian only has precedence when he or she is within the limits of the crossing before the vehicle enters the limits of the crossing. A pedestrian waiting at the kerbside is awaiting the courtesy of drivers who care to stop; such a person is not entitled to any precedence until he steps on to the crossing.

The driver of a vehicle must always approach a Zebra crossing in such a manner that he will be able to stop before reaching it unless he can see that there is no one in the vicinity. Evidence of a failure to take reasonable care is unnecessary; the duty to accord precedence is strict and its discharge requires an approach to such crossings that will allow precedence to be given in any circumstances. The only exceptions are where there is a sudden defect in the vehicle or it is pushed on to the crossing by the vehicle behind; in such circumstances a driver is clearly unable through no fault of his to discharge his duty to accord precedence. It is important to recognise that the issue of precedence does not arise until there is the question of who goes first. Clear evidence should be offered that the passage of a pedestrian was interfered with by the passage of a motor vehicle over the limits of the crossing. Taken to extremes, where a crossing spans a very wide street, a vehicle might pass over the limits while a pedestrian was on the crossing without the progress of that pedestrian being in any way interfered with. Alternatively, where a vehicle is stopped at a crossing and the pedestrians have passed the point at which it is waiting, the driver is free to proceed. If another pedestrian then steps on the crossing as the vehicle moves off, the driver commits no offence (provided no issue of 'who goes first' is raised).

'Puffin' and 'Pelican' crossings

By TSR&GD 2016, Sch 14, Part 5, para 5, when a red light is being displayed at a Puffin crossing a driver of a vehicle must not cause it to 'proceed beyond the stop line' or, if that line is not visible, the post on which the light signal is mounted. A red with amber signal denotes an impending change to green, but it conveys the same prohibition as a red signal. A steady amber signal when shown alone conveys the same prohibition as a red signal (with the usual proviso applicable to traffic lights), and there may be a green arrow showing, which signals that traffic may cross the stop line to proceed in a particular direction.

A Puffin crossing will have 'controlled areas' on each side of the crossing (or on one side in the case of one-way traffic), indicated by zig-zag lines stretching from the terminal line to the stop line (a line which is met before the limits of the crossing itself—identified by square or circular marks or studs—are reached). The primary signals shown to both drivers and pedestrians are by synchronised light signals. Whilst a steady green light is shown to drivers, a steady red light is shown to pedestrians, and vice versa. The light signals to pedestrians are by means of red and green figures.

Similar provision is made in relation to Pelican crossings by reg 23 of the 1997 Regulations, which are treated as remaining in force for these purposes, as explained above, except that the light signals to pedestrians are, in the case of Pelican crossings, steady red, steady green and flashing green figures reinforced by the illumination of a sign which reads 'WAIT'. Audible signals may be used at Pelican crossings to indicate to pedestrians when it is safe to cross.

Precedence at a Puffin or Pelican crossing

This is determined to a major extent by the light signals which are showing at the time.

However, at Pelican crossings (but not Puffin crossings) a driver may encounter a flashing amber signal which indicates that pedestrians, who are on the carriageway or a central reservation within the limits of the crossing before any part of the vehicle has entered those limits, must be accorded precedence by the driver of a vehicle.

Prohibition on waiting

TSR&GD 2016, Sch 14, Part 5, para 1 prohibits a driver from stopping his vehicle in the limits of a Zebra or Puffin crossing unless he is prevented from proceeding by circumstances beyond his control or it is necessary to avoid an accident.

Moreover, para 3 prohibits the driver of a vehicle from causing the vehicle or any part of it to stop in a 'controlled area' (the zig-zag area). However, by para 4, this does not apply to a pedal cycle which is not mechanically propelled (unless electrically assisted). Paragraphs 4 and 5 also exempt from para 3 vehicles:

(a) whose drivers have stopped to comply with the requirement to accord precedence, or to avoid an accident; or

(b) whose drivers have stopped to comply with a light signal or the direction of a constable in uniform or a traffic officer in uniform;

(c) whose drivers have been prevented from proceeding by circumstances beyond their control; or

(d) which have stopped for fire and rescue, ambulance, blood service, police, NCA, defence or special forces purposes, or for the purpose of emergency-response at the request of an NHS ambulance service, or in connection with the removal of obstructions, building works, road works or repairs to public utilities.

Vehicles may also halt to make right or left turns. Public service vehicles may stop to pick up or set down passengers but only on the far side of the crossing itself, not on its approach.

Paragraph 2 prohibits a pedestrian remaining within the limits of a Zebra or Puffin crossing longer than necessary for the purposes of crossing with reasonable dispatch.

Similar provision is made in relation to Pelican crossings by regs 18 to 22 of the 1997 Regulations, which are treated as remaining in force for these purposes, as explained above.

Prohibition on overtaking

By TSR&GD 2016, Sch 14, Part 5, para 6, a driver within a 'controlled area' of a Zebra or Puffin crossing must not overtake *on the approach side* to a crossing a moving motor vehicle or a stationary motor vehicle which is according precedence to a pedestrian on a Zebra crossing or obeying a red light signal at a Puffin crossing. For these purposes, a vehicle overtakes another if any part of its foremost part passes ahead of the foremost part of another vehicle. The aim of para 6 is to prevent pedestrians from being struck by overtaking vehicles. It is not surprising, therefore, that para 6 limits the prohibition on overtaking to cases where the vehicle overtaken is the only other vehicle in the controlled area, or is the foremost vehicle. If this was not so, where there were two lines of traffic approaching a crossing, it would not be possible for the traffic on the offside to close up. In relation to the prohibition on overtaking a vehicle which has stopped to accord precedence, such a vehicle includes one which has stopped for this purpose even though a pedestrian intending to cross has not yet stepped on to the crossing.

Because of the drafting of para 6, the ban on overtaking does not apply where the overtaking vehicle was actually on the crossing when it passed ahead of the foremost part of the overtaken vehicle.

Similar provision is made in relation to Pelican crossings by reg 24 of the 1997 Regulations, which are treated as remaining in force for these purposes, as explained above.

Parallel, equestrian and 'Toucan' crossings

A parallel crossing is one where provision is made for pedestrians and cyclists to cross the carriageway. Like a Zebra crossing it does not involve light signals. Its appearance in terms of yellow globes, zig-zag lines, black and white stripes and so on is similar to that of a Zebra crossing but with a parallel crossing route for cyclists marked within the controlled area on one side of the striped crossing for pedestrians. The *limits* of the crossing are indicated by lines of square or round marks or studs. By TSR&GD 2016, Sch 14, Part 1, paras 21 to 24, corresponding rules to those which apply to Zebra crossings are provided in relation to parallel crossings in respect of according precedence, waiting and overtaking.

An equestrian crossing is one where provision is made for equestrian traffic to cross the carriageway. Its presence is indicated by a combination of traffic light signals, light signals for users of the crossing and road markings, including zig-zag lines.

A 'Toucan' crossing is one where provision is made for both pedestrians and pedal cyclists to cross the carriageway. Its presence is indicated in a similar way to an equestrian crossing. By TSR&GD 2016, Sch 14, Part 1, para 14, corresponding rules to those which apply to Puffin crossings apply to equestrian crossings and Toucan crossings in respect of stopping, waiting and overtaking.

Breach of a requirement imposed in respect of one of the above crossings is an offence under RTA 1988, s 36 (TSR&GD 2016, Sch 14, Part 4, para 1).

School crossing patrols

RTRA 1984, s 26 authorises an appropriate local authority to make arrangements for school crossing patrols.

The stopping of vehicles at school crossings is dealt with by RTRA 1984, s 28.

When a vehicle is approaching a place in a road where a person is crossing or seeking to cross the road, a school crossing patrol wearing a uniform approved by the Secretary of State is empowered, by exhibiting a prescribed sign, to require the person driving or propelling the vehicle to stop it. When such a person has been required to stop:

(a) he must cause the vehicle to stop before reaching the place where the person is crossing or seeking to cross and so as not to stop or impede his crossing; and

(b) the vehicle must not be put in motion again so as to reach the place in question so long as the sign continues to be exhibited.

As long as a prescribed sign has been properly exhibited, a driver must stop even if the persons have cleared the road and there are no others seeking to cross. A divisional court has held that the words 'so as not to stop or impede his crossing' in (a), above, merely describe the manner in which a driver should stop (ie he must not halt across the path which those children would take) and are not meant to indicate that drivers can ignore a properly displayed sign if, in doing so, they would not directly impede pedestrians. The duty to stop is absolute.

It is an offence under s 28(2) to fail to comply with (a) or to cause a vehicle to be put in motion contrary to (b). These are separate offences.

The approved uniform is a cap, beret, or yellow turban and a coat with or without a fluorescent overgarment. Alternatively, a high visibility coat may be worn. The stopping of traffic may only be effected by exhibiting a sign prescribed by the TSR&GD 2016, Sch 14, Part 2 sign table. That sign will display the word 'Stop' in black letters with a black bar on a yellow fluorescent background surrounded by a red fluorescent border. The uniform worn, or a sign exhibited, by a patrol is rebuttably presumed to be approved (uniform) or in accordance with the regulations (sign).

A sign is exhibited if an approaching driver can see the words on it; but it need not be proved that it was full face to oncoming traffic.

REMOVAL OF VEHICLES

The police have powers to require the removal of vehicles and to remove them themselves. Local authorities are legally obliged to remove abandoned vehicles.

Police powers

The Removal and Disposal of Vehicles Regulations 1986 (RDVR 1986), reg 3 allows a constable to require the owner, driver or other person in charge or control of a vehicle which:

(a) has broken down, or been permitted to remain at rest, on a road or other land in such a position, condition or circumstances as to cause obstruction to other persons using the road or land concerned, or as to be likely to cause danger to such other persons; or

(b) has been permitted to remain at rest or has broken down and remained at rest on a road or other land in contravention of a prohibition or restriction in or under any enactment mentioned in Sch 1 to the Regulations,

to move it or cause it to be moved. 'Other land' is not limited to land in the open air; the land could, for example, include an underground car park.

'Obstruction' in (a) has been held by the Court of Appeal to have a different meaning from that accorded to it in the Highways Act 1980, s 137 and the Road Vehicles (Construction and Use) Regulations 1986, reg 103 (see pp 408 and 423). 'Obstruction' of the highway in (a), the Court held, means more than simply impeding the free access of members of the public to every part of the highway; what is required is obstructing their passage by hindering or preventing them getting past. That 'obstruction', said the Court, need not be an actual one; it includes obstructing people who might be expected to be using the highway. On the other hand, the Court held, mere unreasonable use of a highway does not make it an obstruction. No doubt a corresponding meaning applies in respect of 'other land'.

The statutory prohibitions or restrictions included in Sch 1, referred to in (b) above, are concerned with parking in 'No waiting' areas, in the controlled areas of pedestrian crossings or in contravention of traffic signs—including police 'No waiting' signs. The constable's requirement may include a requirement to move the vehicle to some other place which may be a road or other land, or a requirement that it shall not be moved to such road or other land as may be specified.

It is an offence against RTOA 1988, s 91 to fail to move or cause a vehicle to be moved as soon as practicable when required under the provisions of reg 3.

RDVR 1986, reg 4 allows a constable to remove, or arrange for the removal of, a vehicle which is on a road or other land in the circumstances outlined in (a) or (b), above. He may also do so if the vehicle, having broken down on a road or other land, appears to have been abandoned without lawful authority, or if the vehicle has been permitted to remain at rest on a road or other land in such a position or circumstances as to appear to have been abandoned without lawful authority.

The power to remove vehicles from land occupied by any person is subject to giving notice as prescribed by RTRA 1984, s 99 and RDVR 1986, reg 8. The power under reg 4 is very useful when the driver, person in charge or owner of a vehicle cannot be found or that person refuses to move the vehicle.

Other powers

RDVR 1986, reg 4A empowers *a community support officer or a person accredited for this purpose under a community safety accreditation scheme* to remove, or arrange for the removal of, a vehicle parked or broken down on a road and causing an obstruction, where it is likely to cause danger to road-users, or where an offence is being committed in relation to a statutory prohibition or restriction included in Sch 1 to the Regulations, referred to above.

Regulation 5A empowers *a parking attendant acting on behalf of a local authority* to remove, or arrange for the removal of, a vehicle parked in contravention of a prohibition or restriction order. Regulation 5C extends such powers to a civil enforcement officer acting within a civil enforcement area who has issued a penalty charge notice. In both cases the power may not be exercised until 15 minutes have passed since the expiry of authorised parking.

The Removal and Disposal of Vehicles (Traffic Officers) (England) Regulations 2008 permit *a uniformed traffic officer* to remove, or require the removal of, vehicles from 'relevant roads' (as defined on p 450) in England, and from other roads if necessary to prevent danger or obstruction on a relevant road. Regulation 3 enables a uniformed traffic officer to require the owner, driver or other person in control or in charge of a vehicle which has broken down or been permitted to remain at rest and is causing an obstruction, is likely to cause danger to others, or is in contravention of certain statutory restrictions or prohibitions to move the vehicle or have it moved.

Regulation 4 enables *a uniformed traffic officer* to remove, or arrange for the removal of, such a vehicle as well as a vehicle which appears to have been abandoned.

The powers under regs 3 and 4 also apply to roads which are not relevant roads, but may only be exercised to avoid danger to persons or other traffic using a relevant road or preventing risks of any such danger arising, or to prevent an obstruction to anything on or near to a relevant road, or for a purpose incidental to either of these purposes (reg 7).

Regulation 8 enables *a uniformed traffic officer* to remove, or arrange for the removal of, any vehicle that appears to have been abandoned without lawful authority on other land which is adjacent to a relevant road.

Associated with the two powers relating to abandoned vehicles are the provisions of RTRA 1984, ss 100–102 (interim and absolute disposal of vehicles and charges for removal, storage and disposal).

Duties of local authorities

The Refuse Disposal (Amenity) Act 1978, s 3(1) obliges local authorities to remove motor vehicles abandoned without lawful authority on any land in the open air or on any other land forming part of the highway within their area. Before removing vehicles from land other than a road the local authority must serve notice on the occupier of the land which is involved; if the occupier objects the authority is not entitled to remove the vehicle.

TRAFFIC OFFICERS APPOINTED UNDER THE TRAFFIC MANAGEMENT ACT 2004

Traffic officers are employed by Highways England (in England) or the Welsh Government (in Wales) to perform duties connected with the management of traffic on the network of 'relevant roads' in England or in Wales, depending on which body employs them. A uniformed traffic officer can exercise his powers over any 'relevant road', ie a road for which one of the following is the relevant traffic authority, unless his designation is limited or subject to conditions which will be specified. In England, Highways England is the relevant traffic authority for all highways for which the Secretary of State was previously the traffic authority, except the M6 toll road and the roads that form part of the Severn Crossings up to the border with Wales (for which the Secretary of State remains the relevant traffic authority). In Wales, the relevant traffic authority is the Welsh Government. In short, most motorways and major trunk roads are 'relevant roads'. The powers of a uniformed traffic officer are referred to on pp 439, 443, and 449. In cases referred to on p 449, a traffic officer has powers exercisable elsewhere than on a relevant road. A traffic officer may also be authorised to perform any other function of the relevant authority (in its capacity as a traffic authority or highway authority).

Traffic officers are required to comply with any directions given by a constable. Subject to that limitation, they must comply with any direction given by the appropriate national authority.

It is an offence to assault, or to resist or wilfully obstruct, a traffic officer in the execution of his duty (TMA 2004, s 10(1) and (2) respectively), or, with intent to deceive, to impersonate such an officer or make a statement or perform an act calculated to suggest that that person is a traffic officer (s 10(3)). A traffic officer commits an offence if he suggests that he has powers which he does not have (s 10(3)).

PARKING GENERALLY

RTRA 1984 permits local authorities to make traffic regulation orders (outside Greater London) and similar orders (Greater London). Most of these will be 'No waiting' orders.

Generally, such orders contain exemptions in favour of particular persons or particular types of vehicles. The offences which are committed when the provisions of such orders are contravened are contained in ss 5 (outside Greater London) and 8 (Greater London).

In addition, s 32 empowers a local authority to provide off-street parking places and to authorise the use as a parking place of any part of a road outside Greater London within their area. Section 35 permits local authorities to make parking place orders in respect of places so provided. Sections 45 and 46 permit local authorities to designate parking places on highways within their areas and permit the imposition of charges in respect of such parking. It is an offence against s 47(1) to fail to comply with the requirements of any order so made.

Sections 104 to 106 deal with the immobilisation of vehicles illegally parked in contravention of any statutory prohibition or restriction. Such vehicles may be immobilised within areas specified by the Secretary of State, following an application by a local authority or the Traffic Director for London. Where a vehicle has been immobilised, a notice must be affixed warning against attempting to release the vehicle and specifying the steps to be taken to secure its release. The vehicle will be released on payment of the appropriate sum. An offence is committed by any person who removes or interferes with any notice attached to such a vehicle (s 104(5)), or who removes or attempts to remove an immobilisation device (s 104(6)). A person who damages an immobilisation device in order to release his vehicle commits an offence of criminal damage.

Civil enforcement of parking and some other contraventions

Under regulations made under the Traffic Management Act 2004 (TMA 2004), Part 6 (ss 72–93) civil enforcement officers can impose penalty charges for parking contraventions (and, in Wales, also for bus lane contraventions and for non-compliance with specified traffic signs) in civil enforcement areas. The vast majority of local authority areas in England and Wales have been designated as civil enforcement areas. The relevant provisions are dealt with in Chapter 11 on the companion website.

Immobilising, etc vehicles

The Protection of Freedoms Act 2012 (PFA 2012), s 54(1) provides that a person commits an indictable (either way) offence who, without lawful authority:

(a) immobilises a motor vehicle by the attachment to the vehicle, or a part of it, of an immobilising device (eg a wheel clamp), or
(b) moves, or restricts the movement of, such a vehicle by any means (eg by a barrier, by towing it away, or by blocking it in with another vehicle),

intending to prevent or inhibit the removal of the vehicle by a person otherwise entitled to remove it. For these purposes, a motor vehicle is a mechanically propelled vehicle or a trailer for it.

A person who immobilises a motor vehicle under a statutory power, for example the powers referred to on pp 346–7 and 450, has lawful authority. On the other hand, express or implied consent (whether or not legally binding) of a person otherwise entitled to remove the vehicle, to the immobilisation, movement or restriction concerned, is not lawful authority for the purposes of s 54(1) (s 54(2)), except that, where the restriction of the movement of the vehicle is by means of a fixed barrier and the barrier was present (whether or not restricting movement) when the vehicle was parked, any express or implied consent of its driver to the restriction is lawful authority (s 54(3)).

A person who is entitled to remove a vehicle cannot commit an offence under s 54 in relation to that vehicle (s 54(4)).

The provisions of PFA 2012 about the immobilisation, etc of vehicles are discussed further in Chapter 11 on the companion website.

FIXED PENALTY OFFENCES

RTOA 1988, Sch 3 lists the offences which are 'fixed penalty offences'. Schedule 2 indicates the offences which carry obligatory endorsement; a matter of considerable importance. To assist the memory of police officers in this respect, aides memoire have been prepared listing the various offences which are non-endorsable fixed penalty offences and those which are endorsable. The aide memoire in relation to endorsable fixed penalty offences also indicates the number of penalty points which apply, and gives a code number for each offence. The aide memoire for non-endorsable fixed penalty offences includes advice concerning enforcement policies existing within a police force, particularly where a vehicle rectification scheme is in operation.

The non-endorsable fixed penalty offences are generally concerned with those involving minor defects in the vehicle or its parts; vehicle registration and trade licence offences; failure to display goods vehicle plates; stopping on the verge or hard shoulder of a motorway; contravention of certain traffic directions (eg 'Give way', 'No entry', 'No U turn', 'One-way' signs, and temporary traffic signs); obstruction; waiting and parking offences; lighting and noise offences; offences relating to loads (other than dangerous loads); use of a vehicle without a test certificate; trailer offences; offences peculiar to motorcycles; offences of carrying more than one person on a pedal cycle and of cycling on a footway; using or keeping HGV on a road without payment of HGV road user levy; and other miscellaneous motoring offences (eg failing to wear a seat belt).

The endorsable fixed penalty offences include those in the Road Vehicles (Construction and Use) Regulations 1986 which are concerned with danger (parts, loads, tyres, etc); driving without due care or attention, or without reasonable consideration; failure to comply with 'Stop' signs, double white lines, traffic lights, directions of a constable; illegal waiting at pedestrian crossings, overtaking a moving or stationary vehicle at such a crossing and failure to accord precedence at a Zebra pedestrian crossing; speeding; stopping or reversing on the carriageway of a motorway; driving on a hard shoulder or central reservation; driving on a motorway by a provisional licence-holder; use of offside lane of three-lane motorway by a large goods vehicle or passenger-carrying vehicle; breaches of conditions of provisional licences; use, etc of a vehicle without insurance; failure to identify the driver; offences relating to motorcycle passengers; leaving a vehicle in a dangerous position; use of a vehicle in a designated play street; and driving with uncorrected defective eyesight.

Up to three penalty notices may be issued for one occurrence but only one may be for an endorsable offence.

Fixed penalty notices should not be given to juveniles as there are other recommended procedures for dealing with juveniles which recognise all the circumstances of each case.

The provisions discussed under this heading are contained in RTOA 1988, unless otherwise indicated.

Issue of a fixed penalty notice on-the-spot: person present

The following provisions of RTOA 1988, s 54 apply where *a constable in uniform, or a vehicle examiner (ie an examiner appointed under RTA 1988, s 66A by the Secretary of State) who produces his authority, has reason to believe that a person he finds is committing or has on that occasion committed a fixed penalty offence.*

Issue of notice for non-endorsable offence: person present

A fixed penalty notice may be issued on-the-spot by the constable or vehicle examiner (RTOA 1988, s 54(2)).

If more than one offence is committed on a particular occasion a constable should either issue a fixed penalty notice for up to three offences and administer a verbal warning in respect of all other offences, or report the offender in the normal way for all offences committed. However, this will not apply when offences are subsequently detected, as would occur when documents which were subsequently produced were found to be defective in some respect. These offences, subsequently detected, will be dealt with by the officer reporting the offender with a view to prosecution, even though a fixed penalty notice has been issued for the original offence(s).

Issue of a fixed penalty notice for endorsable offence: person present

RTOA 1988, s 54 states that, subject to the provisions described below, a fixed penalty notice for an endorsable offence may be issued to the offender on-the-spot by a constable in uniform, or a vehicle examiner who produces his authority, who has reason to believe that a person *is committing or has committed* a fixed penalty offence.

Section 54(3): fixed penalty notice   Section 54(3) provides that, where it appears to the constable or the vehicle examiner that the fixed penalty offence involves obligatory endorsement, the constable or vehicle examiner may only give the offender (O) a fixed penalty notice on the spot in respect of the offence if:

(a) the constable or vehicle examiner is satisfied, on accessing information held on O's driving record, that O would not be liable to be disqualified under the 'totting-up' provisions because the total number of penalty points would number 12 or more if he was convicted of the fixed penalty offence; and

(b) in the case of a person who is the holder of a licence, he produces it for inspection by the constable or vehicle examiner and surrenders it to him to be retained and dealt with in accordance with RTOA 1988.

Part 3 of the fixed penalty notice gives advice on the procedure to be followed if O wishes to request a court hearing. If O contests the issue of a fixed penalty notice, his attention should be drawn to this part of the notice. A fixed penalty notice should, wherever possible, include the full postcode as well as O's address, as this assists the registration of subsequent penalties with O's home court.

Section 56 requires a receipt to be given for a driving licence so surrendered. The receipt given is incorporated in the fixed penalty notice. It is valid for one month from the date of issue (or such longer period as may be prescribed). However, a person to whom the penalty is paid may issue a new receipt on the application of the licence-holder, which will expire on such date as may be specified in it. In any event, a receipt ceases to have effect on the return of the licence to the holder. Section 56 enables the receipt to be produced in place of a licence, subject to the same conditions concerning later production, on a request being made by a constable or examiner under RTA 1988, s 164, provided that, if required to do so, the licence-holder subsequently produces his driving licence at the specified police station immediately it is returned.

Section 54(4)–(5B) provisional fixed penalty notice   Section 54(4) and (5) provide that, where the offence appears to the constable or vehicle examiner to be one involving obligatory endorsement, and:

(a) the constable or vehicle examiner is unable to satisfy himself, by accessing information held on O's driving record, that O would not be liable to a 'totting-up' disqualification because the total number of penalty points would number 12 or more if he was convicted of the fixed penalty offence; or

(b) where O is the holder of a licence, he does not produce it for inspection by the constable or vehicle examiner,

the constable or vehicle examiner may give O a provisional fixed penalty notice.

Such a notice given by a constable must state that *if, within seven days after the notice is given, O personally delivers the notice together with his driving licence to a constable or an authorised person at the police station specified in the notice (being a police station chosen by O)* and the requirements in the next paragraph are met O will then be given a fixed penalty notice in respect of the offence (s 54(5) and 5A(a)). (An 'authorised person' is a person at a police station authorised for this purpose by the chief officer of police.) In the case of a notice given by a vehicle examiner the italicised words are replaced by 'if, within 14 days O (either by post or in person) gives the notice, etc to the Secretary of State at the place specified in the notice' (s 54(5A)(b)).

If O delivers the notice and (if he is the holder of a licence) his licence as required, and the following requirements are met:

(i) the person to whom the notice is delivered is satisfied, on accessing information held on O's driving record, that he would not be liable to a 'totting-up' disqualification (as above); and

(ii) if O is the holder of a licence, it is delivered to be retained and dealt with in accordance with RTOA 1988, the person to whom the notice is delivered must give O a fixed penalty notice in respect of the offence (s 54(5B)).

If O is the holder of a licence and fails to produce it under the provisions of RTOA 1988, or it is found that O's penalty points are such that the issue of disqualification arises, O will be prosecuted for the offence in the normal way and the provisional fixed penalty notice is of no further effect.

General   In determining under s 54 whether O would be liable on conviction to disqualification it must be assumed, where the offence carries a range of penalty points, that the points to be attributed to the offence would be the lowest in the range.

Endorsements of licences without hearing   RTOA 1988, s 57A provides that where a fixed penalty notice under s 54 is given to a person in respect of an offence involving obligatory endorsement, the Secretary of State may endorse the person's driving record accordingly without any order of a court. If the fixed penalty is paid before the end of the suspended enforcement period and the person to whom the payment is made is the fixed penalty clerk, the clerk must send to the Secretary of State notice of the relevant particulars which are to be endorsed on the person's driving record.

A person's driving record may not be so endorsed if at the end of the suspended enforcement period (as to which see p 456):

(a) he has given notice, in the manner specified in the fixed penalty notice, requesting a hearing in respect of the offence to which the fixed penalty notice relates; and
(b) the fixed penalty has not been paid.

Section 83 deals with the case where the appropriate person is deceived into endorsing a driving record under s 57A in circumstances in which the licence-holder should have been disqualified under the totting-up procedure and the deception constituted, or was due to, an offence committed by the licence-holder. It provides that if the licence-holder is convicted of that offence, the court before which he is convicted will have the same powers to disqualify as it would have had if it was convicting him of the endorsable offence.

Driver absent: fixing notices to vehicles

RTOA 1988, s 62(1) provides that where a constable or vehicle examiner has reason to believe that a fixed penalty offence is being or has been committed in respect of a stationary vehicle, he may affix to that vehicle a fixed penalty notice in respect of the offence unless the offence appears to him to involve obligatory endorsement.

Notice to owner

In cases in which a fixed penalty notice is affixed to a vehicle under RTOA 1988, s 62, and the fixed penalty has not been paid within the suspended enforcement period, *a notice to owner* may be served under s 63 by or on behalf of the chief officer of police (Secretary of State, if notice fixed by vehicle examiner) on *any person who appears to him* to be the owner of the vehicle (or a person authorised to act on such person's behalf). Such a notice must give particulars of the offence in question, of the fixed penalty concerned, and of the period allowed for response to the notice. It must also indicate that, if the fixed penalty is not paid before the end of that period, the person on whom the notice is served must furnish, before the end of that period, a statutory statement of ownership. The period allowed for response to such a notice is 21 days from the service of the notice. However, a notice need not be served when a request for a hearing has been made with an admission by the person making the request that he was the driver of the vehicle on that occasion. If a person on whom a notice has been served was not the owner of the vehicle at the relevant time, and he furnishes in time a statutory statement to that effect, he is not liable for the offence in question. Otherwise, where a notice is served within six months of the commission of that offence and the fixed penalty has not been paid within the period allowed, a sum equal to the fixed penalty, plus one-half of that penalty, may be registered against the person on whom the notice to owner was served as a fine.

Where person receiving was not the driver

There will be occasions when the person who receives a notice to owner will not have been the driver at the relevant time. RTOA 1988, s 63 therefore requires that the notice must indicate that, before the end of the period permitted for response, the person on whom it is served may either:

(a) request a hearing; or
(b) if he was not the driver and someone purporting to have been the driver wishes to give notice requesting a hearing, furnish, together with a statutory statement of ownership, a statutory statement of facts which has the effect of the actual driver requesting a hearing. (If such a driver is prepared to accept responsibility for the fixed penalty it is implied that he will do so by paying the penalty on behalf of the person to whom the notice is addressed.)

Once a statutory statement of facts has been supplied, the person named in the notice to owner is relieved of further responsibility and any sums due by way of fixed penalty may not be registered for enforcement.

Once a fixed penalty has been registered for enforcement as a fine against a person on whom a notice to owner has been served, however, no proceedings can be brought against any other person in respect of that offence.

Special provisions are applied to hire vehicles, ie a vehicle hired for temporary use, by RTOA 1988, s 66. Provided a form of agreement has been drawn up between the hire firm and the hirer under the Road Traffic (Owner Liability) Regulations 2000, and provided the hire firm produces a copy of this to the police (together with a statement of hirer liability signed by the hirer under that hiring agreement), liability is removed from the hire firm; and the hirer of the vehicle becomes its owner for the purpose of the fixed penalty provisions.

Fixed penalty offences generally

Discretion

The issue of a fixed penalty notice for an endorsable offence (or a non-endorsable offence) is a matter for the constable's discretion so far as this is permitted by force policy.

Within the limits of such policy, a constable may decide to give a verbal warning for the offence; issue a fixed penalty notice provided that existing penalty points permit such a course of action; or report O with a view to proceedings by way of requisition or single justice procedure notice.

When considering whether to deal with the offence by way of fixed penalty, the constable must ensure that O is aware of the implications of such a procedure.

Whatever form of words is used, O must not be given the impression that he must surrender his licence. There is no power to require this.

Number of penalty points

By RTOA 1988, s 28(3), the number of penalty points to be attributed to an offence where a fixed penalty notice has been issued is:

(a) where both a range of numbers and a number followed by the words '(fixed penalty)' is indicated in Sch 2, that number;

(b) where a range of numbers followed by the words 'or appropriate penalty points (fixed penalty)', the appropriate number of penalty points for the offence (such number imposed by order under s 28(3A) and (3B));

(c) where only a range of numbers is shown, the lower number in that range.

Proceedings

No proceedings may be brought for an offence to which a fixed penalty notice relates until 21 days have passed since the day of the notice (or such longer period as may be specified in the notice). This period of time is referred to as the suspended enforcement period.

Where a fixed penalty notice has been given to an offender (O), no proceedings may be brought unless O has given notice requesting a hearing before the end of the suspended enforcement period.

If no such notice has been received and the fixed penalty has not been paid before the end of the suspended enforcement period, a sum equal to the fixed penalty plus one-half of that amount may be registered against O as a fine.

Evidence in court proceedings in fixed penalty notice cases

RTOA 1988, s 79 permits the service of the statement of evidence of a constable or a vehicle examiner together with a fixed penalty notice or notice to owner. Such a statement will be deemed to have been served for the purposes of the Criminal Justice Act 1967, s 9 (referred to on p 251).

RTOA 1988, s 68 and Sch 4 permit 'statutory statements of ownership or of facts' to be used in evidence. A statutory statement of ownership is one where the declarant states whether or not he was the owner of the vehicle at the relevant time. If he was not, it will state whether he was ever the owner and, if so, when. A statutory statement of facts is one where the declarant states that he was not the driver of the vehicle at the relevant time and states the name and address of the person who was.

Payment of penalties

Fixed penalties must be paid to the designated officer for a magistrates' court in a manner specified within the notice and the money must be dealt with as if it were a fine imposed on summary conviction. Payment may be made by way of a properly addressed, pre-paid letter. The payment is regarded as having been made at the time that the letter would be delivered in the course of normal post. In any proceedings a certificate from a fixed penalty clerk is admissible to prove that a fixed penalty was or was not received by a date specified in the certificate, or that a letter was marked as posted on a date so specified. If a fixed penalty is paid before the end of the suspended enforcement period, no further proceedings may be brought.

By RTOA 1988, s 53, the amount of the fixed penalty to be paid in respect of an offence is such amount as the Secretary of State may by order prescribe, or one-half of the maximum fine for it on summary conviction, whichever is less. The Secretary of State may provide for the fixed penalty for an offence to differ depending on the circumstances.

The amounts prescribed by the Secretary of State are currently contained in the Fixed Penalty Order 2000. The penalty for use, etc of a motor vehicle without insurance is fixed at £300; for failure to identify a driver £200; and for other offences involving obligatory endorsement £100. Where the offence is non-endorsable the penalty is normally £50. However, where the non-endorsable offence consists of a fixed penalty parking offence committed elsewhere than in Greater London it is £30, whereas if it is committed in Greater London the penalty is £60 if it is committed on a red route, or £40 if it is committed otherwise than on a red route. 'Fixed penalty parking offence' means:

(a) an offence under RTRA 1984 which does not involve obligatory endorsement and is committed in respect of a stationary vehicle; and
(b) road obstruction offences under a variety of statutory provisions.

A 'red route' means a length of road on which there are traffic signs bearing the words 'red route' or red lines or marks.

The fixed penalty for offences against RTA 1988, ss 14 and 15(2) and 15(4) (seat belt offences: pp 426–9) and those against VERA 1994, ss 42(1), 43(1), and 59 (registration plate and trade plate offences: pp 337–52) is £100. The fixed penalty for use without a MOT certificate or for not exhibiting a licence is £100. The fixed penalty for an offence under RTA 1988 (careless driving, etc) is £100. The fixed penalty for an offence under the Transport Act 1968, ss 96(11), 96(11A), 97(1), 98(4), 99(4), 99ZD(1), or 99C (Appendix 2 on the companion website), the Road Traffic (Foreign Vehicles) Act 1972, s 3(1), the Public Passenger Vehicles Act 1981, s 12(5) (Appendix 1 on the companion website), RTA 1988, s 71(1), RTOA 1988, s 90D(6) (p 460), Goods Vehicles Licensing of Operators Act 1995, s 2(5), or the HGV Road User Levy Act 2013, s 11(1) (Appendix 2) is £300.

Graduated fixed penalties

RTOA 1988, s 53 permits fixed penalties to be different depending upon the circumstances including (in particular):

(a) the nature of the contravention or failure constituting the offence;
(b) how serious it is;
(c) the area, or sort of place, where it takes place; and
(d) whether the offender appears to have committed any offence or offences of a specified description, during the period so specified.

The Fixed Penalty Order 2000, Sch 2 specifies the fixed penalty to be paid for offences by reference to the matters set out above. Graduated fixed penalties apply to offences under the:

(a) Transport Act 1968 (TA 1968), s 96 (drivers' hours) and vary from £60 to £200 depending upon the number of hours in excess of those permitted or the extent of the failure to take rest;
(b) TA 1968, s 97 (recording equipment) and vary from £60 to £200 depending upon the nature of the contravention or failure;

(c) RTA 1988, s 41A (tyres) and the penalty is £120 (£60 in the case of a motor cycle) for failure to have a tread pattern of at least 1 mm;

(d) RTA 1988, s 41B (weight limit offences) and vary from £60 to £200 depending upon the percentage of the excess weight; and

(e) RTA 1988, s 42 (speed limiters and danger in respect of passengers or load) and vary from £60 to £120.

Fixed penalty notices given by vehicle examiners

RTOA 1988, Part 3 allows vehicle examiners to issue fixed penalty notices in respect of offences which they are empowered to enforce. The system is operated independently of the police by the Secretary of State who is responsible for administering the system, collecting the penalties, and the endorsement of driving records. The Fixed Penalty (Vehicle Examiners) Regulations 2009 prescribe certain information or further information to be included in a fixed penalty notice issued by a vehicle examiner, the receipt for a driving licence (if held), and the registration certificate in the case of non-payment of the fixed penalty. They also provide for the return of a driving licence (if so held) to the licence-holder if the period in which no enforcement proceedings can be brought ('the suspended enforcement period') has expired, the fixed penalty has not been paid, and the recipient of the notice has either requested a hearing or the fixed penalty has not been registered for enforcement.

Penalty registered against person who has no knowledge of the offence

It is obvious that there will be occasions when a penalty is registered against a person who, for some reason, has no knowledge of the offence. This may occur when fixed penalty notices are affixed to vehicles which have changed ownership without DVLA records being amended, or where a driver of someone else's vehicle does not inform the owner of the notice.

RTOA 1988, ss 72 and 73 deal with this issue. By s 72, if registration has followed non-receipt of a request for a hearing and the fixed penalty has not been paid, a statutory declaration may be made to the effect (a) that the declarant was not the person to whom the fixed penalty notice was given or (b) that he had requested a hearing before the end of the suspended enforcement period. Section 73 provides that, where the registration has followed service of 'notice to owner', and the penalty has not been paid, the statutory declaration must state either that:

(i)   the declarant did not know of the penalty, or fixed penalty notice, or notice to owner, until he received notice of the registration; or

(ii) he was not the owner at the time of the offence alleged and that he has reasonable excuse for failing to comply with the notice to owner; or

(iii) he requested a hearing as permitted by the notice to owner.

A declaration must be served on the proper officer of the relevant court, within 21 days of receipt of the notification of registration. With the exception of (b) and (iii) respectively, the effect of the declaration is that the relevant notice, registration or endorsement (as the case may be) is void; in case (b), the declarant will be treated as if he had given notice requesting a hearing. In the case of (iii), the effect is to re-activate the 21-day response period referred to in the notice.

Miscellaneous points

RTOA 1988, s 30 requires that, if a person is convicted of an offence involving obligatory endorsement and the court is satisfied that he is liable to have penalty points endorsed upon his driving record within the fixed penalty procedure for an offence committed on the same occasion as those for which he is convicted, the court must reduce the number of penalty points endorsed on the licence by the number which will be attached in consequence of the fixed penalty offence.

It is an offence contrary to RTOA 1988:

(a) s 62(2), to remove or interfere with a notice affixed to a vehicle under s 62(1) (p 454) unless it is done by or under the authority of the driver or person in charge of the vehicle or the person liable for the offence in question;

(b) s 67, recklessly to furnish a statement which is false in a material particular, in response to a notice to owner, or to furnish such a statement knowing it is false in that particular.

Conditional offer of fixed penalty

RTOA 1988, s 75 provides as follows. Where a constable or vehicle examiner has reason to believe that a fixed penalty offence has been committed and *no fixed penalty notice has been given at the time or fixed to the vehicle concerned*, a notice of 'conditional offer' may be sent to the alleged offender (O) by, or on behalf of, the chief officer of police (by the Secretary of State in the case of a vehicle examiner). Section 75 is of particular importance where speeding or traffic light offences have been detected by automatic devices.

A conditional offer must:

(a) give particulars of the circumstances and reasonable information about the alleged offence;

(b) state the amount of the fixed penalty; and

(c) state that proceedings cannot be commenced for the offence until the end of 28 days following the date of issue of the conditional offer (or such longer period as may be specified in it).

A conditional offer must indicate that if:

(a) within the above 28-day period (or whichever longer period is specified), O:
   (i) pays to the appropriate person the fixed penalty; and
   (ii) where O is the holder of a licence and the offence concerned involves obligatory endorsement, at the same time delivers his licence to the appropriate person; and

(b) the appropriate person is satisfied, on accessing information held on O's driving record, that, if O were convicted of the offence, O would not be liable to disqualification under RTOA 1988, s 35 (disqualification for repeated offences),

any liability to conviction will be discharged. For the purposes of (b), it is assumed (where penalty points awardable for the offence are within a range) that the number to be attributed for the offence would be the lowest in the range. Where the conditional offer was made by a constable, 'the appropriate person' means the fixed penalty clerk; where it was issued by a vehicle examiner the term means the Secretary of State.

Where a conditional offer is issued by or on behalf of a chief officer of police the fixed penalty clerk must be notified.

By RTOA 1988, s 76, if payment is made in accordance with the offer and the licence is delivered, no proceedings will be taken for the offence to which the conditional offer relates, unless:

(a) it appears to the appropriate person, on accessing O's driving record, that O would be liable to be disqualified under RTOA 1988, s 35 if he were convicted of the offence;

(b) the appropriate person returns the payment and licence to O; and

(c) where the appropriate person is not the Secretary of State, the appropriate person notifies the chief officer of police that he has done so.

Where, in pursuance of a conditional offer issued by a constable, O pays the fixed penalty and (if he is the holder of a licence) delivers his licence to the fixed penalty clerk, and proceedings against O are excluded by s 76, the fixed penalty clerk is required by RTOA 1988, s 77A to send to the Secretary of State notice of the relevant particulars for endorsement on O's driving record together with any licence delivered. Where in pursuance of a conditional offer issued by a vehicle examiner, O pays the fixed penalty and (if he is the holder of a licence) delivers his licence to the Secretary of State, and proceedings against O are excluded by s 76, the Secretary of State must likewise endorse O's driving record.

Financial penalty deposits

RTOA 1988, Part 3A (ss 90A–90F) empowers a constable or vehicle examiner, who has reason to believe that a person is committing, or has on that occasion committed, a prescribed motor vehicle offence, to require from him the payment of a financial penalty deposit if he does not provide a satisfactory address in the UK. This power only exists where the person and the circumstances, as well as the offence, are within descriptions specified by regulation. Under the Road Safety (Financial Penalty Deposit) Order 2009, the offences in respect of which financial penalty deposits may be required are specified. The specified person is the person in charge of the vehicle at the time and the specified circumstances are that the offence is being, or has been, committed on a road or other public place. The Road Safety (Financial Penalty Deposit) (Appropriate Amount) Order 2009 provides that the term 'appropriate amount' is that required to be made to the Secretary of State as specified in the Schedules to the Order.

Police and vehicle examiners are empowered to prohibit the moving of the vehicle if the deposit is not paid immediately, although a written direction may be given to remove it to a specified place. The Road Safety (Immobilisation, Removal and Disposal of Vehicles) Regulations 2009 provide for the detention, etc of vehicles prohibited from being driven following the imposition of a prohibition: see Appendix 2 on the companion website. The prohibition continues until the deposit is paid, or (where the offender has received a fixed penalty notice or conditional offer) the offender has paid the fixed penalty, or the offender is convicted or acquitted of the offence or informed that he will not be prosecuted for it, or a 12-month period has elapsed since the deposit requirement. It is an offence to fail to comply with a prohibition, to cause or permit a vehicle to be driven in contravention of it, or to fail to comply within a reasonable time with a direction requiring the person in charge of the vehicle to remove it to a specified place (RTOA 1988, s 90D(6)).

Thus, a means is provided to secure a deposit where an enforcement officer is not satisfied that a penalty or fine could be enforced in the UK. If a person who has paid a financial penalty deposit is subsequently acquitted of the offence, the deposit, with interest, will be returned to him; otherwise it will be set against any penalty imposed.

PARKING BY DISABLED DRIVERS

The Chronically Sick and Disabled Persons Act 1970 (CS&DPA 1970), s 21 requires that a 'blue badge' be issued by local authorities in England, Wales and Scotland for motor vehicles driven by, or used for the carriage of, disabled persons resident within their areas. A 'blue badge' must be 'in valid form', ie of a form specified or approved by the Secretary of State, in the case of a badge issued by an English or Welsh local authority, or of a prescribed form, in the case of a badge issued by a Scottish local authority. The Secretary of State is established as a blue badge issuing authority for disabled persons resident in prescribed places (66 states or territories) outside the UK who are members of the armed forces or are employed in support of those forces, together with members of the same household of such persons. Generally speaking, references in s 21 to a 'local authority' are to be read as including a reference to the Secretary of State.

Badges may also be issued to organisations concerned with the care of the disabled. Badges are normally valid for three years.

The Disabled Persons (Badges for Motor Vehicles) (England) Regulations 2000 and the Disabled Persons (Badges for Motor Vehicles) (Wales) Regulations 2000 (the Badges Regulations) prescribe the forms of the badges to be issued and the Schedule to the regulations shows the contents and various forms of badges. The background on the front and reverse sides of the badge is coloured light blue. Badges are electronically printed and completed and have a unique hologram, a unique serial number and (in the case of an individual's badge) a digital photograph.

CS&DPA 1970, ss 21A and 21C set out a system for the recognition in England and Wales of badges issued under equivalent provisions in Northern Ireland or under corresponding provisions in those foreign jurisdictions set out in regulations. At the time of writing no such regulations have been made. The Badges Regulations provide that badges issued in Scotland are valid in England and Wales.

Exemptions conferred by badge

The Local Authorities' Traffic Orders (Exemptions for Disabled Persons) (England) Regulations 2000 and the Local Authorities' Traffic Orders (Exemptions for Disabled Persons) (Wales) Regulations 2000 (the Exemptions Regulations) require that, except in respect of certain areas in central London, all 'No waiting' orders, etc made by local authorities must contain exemptions in favour of a vehicle displaying a disabled person's badge. The exemptions in favour of a disabled person's vehicle are in respect of orders prohibiting vehicles waiting beyond a specified period of time, orders prohibiting waiting for vehicles at all times of day or during specified periods of the day (whether in relation to some types or all vehicles), and orders prescribing charges or time limit restrictions at parking meters. The only restriction which may apply to disabled persons' vehicles is that, where there is a prohibition on waiting for a period of more than three hours, a vehicle displaying a disabled person's badge is exempt for a maximum of three hours (and must not return to the same road for an hour), and is only so exempt if a parking disc is displayed showing the time of arrival (disc parking scheme). Any exemption required to be made in no waiting orders may be limited to vehicles of the same class as those to which the no waiting order applies.

The badge scheme does not permit parking:

(a) during the time a ban on loading or unloading is in force (indicated by one, two or three yellow marks on a kerb, at a time shown on a post-mounted plate);
(b) where there is a double white line in the centre of the road even if one of the lines is broken;
(c) in a bus or cycle lane when it is in use;

(d) on Zebra, Puffin or other crossings referred to on pp 443–7, or on the zig-zag markings before or after these crossings;

(e) in parking places reserved for specific users, eg loading bays, residents, taxis or cycles; and

(f) in suspended meter bays or when the use of the meter is prohibited.

Display of badge

A badge issued under the CS&DPA 1970, s 21 may be displayed on a vehicle either inside or outside the area of the issuing authority (or a prescribed place outside the UK, referred to on p 461).

The Badges Regulations require that a disabled person's badge be exhibited on the dashboard or fascia of the vehicle, or where the vehicle is not fitted with a dashboard or fascia, the badge is exhibited in a conspicuous position, in either case, so that the front of the badge is clearly legible from outside the vehicle. Similar provisions are made by the Exemptions Regulations for the display of parking discs, so that the quarter-hour period during which the period of waiting begins is legible from outside the vehicle.

The Badges Regulations set out the circumstances in which a disabled person's badge may be displayed while the vehicle is being *driven*. These are:

(a) the holder is either driving or being carried in the vehicle; or

(b) the vehicle is being used solely to collect the holder; or

(c) the vehicle, after being driven by or carrying the holder, is leaving the place where he has got out.

For (b) and (c) to apply, it is necessary (i) that a disabled person's concession (other than one relating to parking) would be (in the case of (b)), or is (in the case of (c)), available to a vehicle displaying such a badge; and (ii) that it would not be practicable for the vehicle to be lawfully driven to, or to stop at, the place where the holder is collected (in the case of (b)), or would not have been practicable for the vehicle to have left the place where the holder got out (in the case of (c)), if the concession did not apply to the vehicle.

By the Badges Regulations, the circumstances in which an individual's disabled person's badge may be displayed while the vehicle is *parked* are:

(a) it has been driven by the holder, or has been used to carry him, to the place where it is parked; or

(b) it is to be driven by the holder, or is to be used to carry him, from that place.

A local authority may cancel a blue badge issued by it if it appears to it that the person to whom the badge was issued no longer holds it because the badge has been lost or stolen or for any other reason. A cancellation will only be effective on notice being given by the authority to the person.

It is an offence under CS&DPA 1970, s 21(4BZA) for a person to drive a motor vehicle on a road at a time when a blue badge is displayed on the vehicle if:

(a) the badge should have been returned to the issuing authority in compliance with the Badges Regulations (eg on expiry, on the death of the holder or, in the case of a replacement badge, on the discovery of the replaced badge);

(b) the issuing authority requires the return of the badge on account that its misuse has led to a badge-related conviction or that the badge was obtained by false representation or has purportedly been transferred to another; or

(c) the badge has been cancelled.

CS&DPA 1970, s 21(4B) makes it an offence for a person to drive a motor vehicle which is displaying a badge purporting to be in valid form otherwise than in a manner or in circumstances prescribed by the Regulations.

Production of badge

CS&DPA 1970, s 21(4BA)–(4BD) makes provision for the inspection of badges. Section 21(4BA) provides that, where it appears to a constable or enforcement officer that there is displayed on any motor vehicle a badge purporting to be in valid form, he may require anyone who:

(a) is in the vehicle, or
(b) appears to have been in, or to be about to get into, the vehicle,

to produce the badge for inspection.
'Enforcement officer' means:

(a) a civil enforcement officer (see p 450);
(b) a local authority parking attendant;
(c) an employee of a local authority in England and Wales, or of a person with whom the authority has made arrangements for the purposes of s 21, authorised in writing by the authority to exercise the requirement power described above and the retention power described below.

The power conferred on an enforcement officer is exercisable only for purposes connected with the discharge of his functions in relation to a stationary vehicle.

A person who, without reasonable excuse, fails to produce a badge when required to do so under s 21(4BA) commits an offence against s 21(4BD). Failure to comply with a requirement imposed by an officer referred to in (d) is not an offence if he does not produce appropriate evidence of authority.

A constable or enforcement officer to whom a person produces a badge purporting to be in valid form may retain the badge if he believes on reasonable grounds that the badge was not issued under s 21, or that it was issued under s 21 and:

(a) it should have been returned to the issuing authority in compliance with the Badges Regulations;
(b) its return has been required by the issuing authority;
(c) it has been cancelled; or
(d) it was being displayed on a vehicle otherwise than in the prescribed circumstances set out on p 462 (s 21(4D)).

Wrongful use of badge

RTRA 1984, s 117 provides that a person who commits a parking offence under the Act is also guilty of an offence under s 117 if the following conditions are satisfied:

(a) there was displayed on the motor vehicle a badge purporting to be in valid form;
(b) he was using the vehicle in circumstances where a disabled person's concession would be available to a disabled person's vehicle,

but he is not guilty of an offence under s 117 if the badge was properly issued and displayed. A 'properly issued' badge does not include a badge which should have been returned to the issuing authority in compliance with the Badges Regulations, a badge whose return has been required by the issuing authority or a badge which has been cancelled.

DRIVING INSTRUCTION

RTA 1988, s 123 prohibits the giving of paid driving instruction (ie for money or money's worth) in the driving of a motor car unless the instructor is a registered approved instructor or the holder of a licence authorising him to give such instruction. There must be fixed to, and exhibited on, the motor car the current licence or certificate of registration, in a similar position to that formerly occupied by the vehicle licence. Free instruction given as a perk when buying a car from a motor trader is deemed to be given for payment. By s 124, s 123 does not apply to police instructors.

Licensed instructor

To enable persons to gain experience with a view to undergoing the practical test of ability and fitness to instruct, which is part of the official driving instructor's examination for registration purposes, RTA 1988, s 129 allows the Registrar to grant a licence to give instruction in the driving of a motor car. An applicant must have passed the written part, and the practical test of driving ability and fitness to drive, of the official driving instructors' examination. Licence-holders may only give instruction from premises named in the licence. If the premises are a driving school the licence-holder may only give instruction if properly employed in accordance with rules that there can be no more than one licence-holder to each registered instructor.

For the first three months of any licence (other than the second of two consecutive ones) the holder either must be under the direct personal supervision of a registered instructor for at least one-fifth of that time and keep a log to that effect, or must undertake a minimum of 20 hours' supplementary training. In the case of the latter alternative he must undertake five further hours of training in a second consecutive period.

Offences

By RTA 1988, s 123(4), a person giving instruction in breach of s 123 commits an offence, as does his employer if he is employed for that purpose. It is a defence to prove that he did not know and had no reasonable cause to believe that his name, or that of his employee, was not in the register.

A person to whom a certificate of registration or a licence has been granted must produce it to a constable or authorised person on being required to do so. Failure to do so is an offence, contrary to s 137(3). However, it is a defence to show that:

(a) the document was produced within seven days at a police station specified by the constable or at a place specified by the authorised person; or
(b) the document was produced at that police station or place as soon as reasonably practicable; or
(c) it was not reasonably practicable for it to be so produced before the day on which proceedings commenced (s 137(4)).

By s 135(2), it is an offence for any unregistered person to wear or display a badge or certificate or to use any name, title or description which is prescribed or which implies that he is registered. Section 135(3) makes it an offence for someone carrying on a driving instruction business to use any such title or description in respect of an unregistered employee, or to issue any advertisement, etc which is misleading in that respect. It is a defence to an offence under s 135(2) or (3) for the defendant to prove that he did not know, and had no reasonable cause to believe, that his name, or that of his employee, was not in the register at the material time.

A registered or licensed instructor commits an offence if he:

(a) fails, without reasonable excuse, to disclose a relevant or prospective disability (s 133C(4)); or

(b) having undergone emergency control assessments, gives paid instruction in the driving of a motor car without a current emergency control certificate (s 133D(2) and (4)); or

(c) having undergone emergency control assessments, gives, in any unauthorised motor car, paid instruction, unless he has a full driving licence which is not limited by virtue of a notice that his disability is such that there is likely to be danger to the public if he drives a vehicle other than one of a particular class (s 133D(3), (3A) and (4)).

If the instructor is employed by another to give the instruction in breach of (b) or (c) that other person is also guilty of an offence (s 133D(4)).

RESTRICTIONS ON THE USE OF MOTORWAYS

The Motorways Traffic (England and Wales) Regulations 1982 impose various restrictions on drivers on motorways of the classes of vehicles permitted to use motorways. Contravention of the Regulations is an offence.

Vehicles which may use motorways

Under the 1982 Regulations, Class I and Class II vehicles are, in normal circumstances, permitted to use motorways. Class I includes heavy and light locomotives, motor tractors, heavy motor cars, motor cars and motorcycles of not less than 50 cc and trailers drawn by such vehicles. (These terms are defined in Chapter 10.) Track-laying vehicles are not within Class I. To be in Class I vehicles must be fitted with pneumatic tyres, must not be agricultural motor vehicles or machines and must not be pedestrian-controlled. All such vehicles must be capable of attaining a speed of 25 mph when unladen.

Class II vehicles are those specially made to transport abnormal, indivisible loads, and large vehicles (eg tank transporters) used by the armed services. In addition, earth movers and similar engineering plant are Class II vehicles if they are capable of attaining 25 mph when unladen.

Other provisions

The 1982 Regulations also contain provisions about:

- the direction of driving;
- stopping;
- reversing;
- the general use, including by provisional licence-holders; and
- exclusion of certain vehicles from the outside lane,

on a motorway.

These provisions, and exceptions and relaxations from the effect of the 1982 Regulations, are set out in Chapter 11 on the companion website.

Offence

A person who uses a motorway in contravention of the 1982 regulations commits an offence under RTRA 1984, s 17(4).

CHAPTER 12

Lights and Vehicles

The lighting requirements for vehicles are set out in the Road Vehicles Lighting Regulations 1989. Unless otherwise indicated, all references in this chapter to 'the Regulations' or to a regulation are to these Regulations or a regulation in them.

The Regulations define certain terms which are used throughout as follows:

Daytime hours   The time between half an hour before sunrise and half an hour after sunset.

Hours of darkness   The time between half an hour after sunset and half an hour before sunrise.

Obligatory lamp, reflector, rear marking or device   A lamp, reflector, rear marking or device with which a vehicle, its load or equipment, is required by the Regulations to be fitted.

Optional lamp, reflector, rear marking or device   A lamp, reflector, rear marking, or device with which a vehicle, its load or equipment, is not required by the Regulations to be fitted.

OBLIGATORY LAMPS, REFLECTORS, REAR MARKINGS, AND DEVICES

Required equipment

By reg 18, a person must not use a vehicle on a road, or cause or permit it to be so used, unless it is equipped with obligatory lamps, reflectors, devices or markings as specified by Sch 1 to the Regulations. Column 1 of Sch 1 lists the type of lamp, reflector, rear marking or device required; column 2 the installation (including height and lateral positioning) and performance requirement (by reference to other Schedules); and column 3 any exceptions to the general rule.

Each of the lamps, reflectors, devices and markings listed below is obligatory for motor vehicles (with exceptions mentioned later) and some of them are obligatory for trailers drawn by motor vehicles and for other vehicles. Such lamps, etc must be fitted in the manner described by the Regulations.

As the requirements have increased, the position of vehicles manufactured before new requirements were made has had to be safeguarded. The various regulations therefore specify the date of application by applying the requirements to vehicles first used on or after a given date. However, reg 4 provides that, even if a motor vehicle is first used on or after that date, it will be exempt from the requirements of the particular regulation if manufactured more than six months in advance of that date. In some instances this provision is expressly repeated in a particular regulation, but generally it must be implied into a particular regulation from reg 4.

For the purpose of the Regulations, a lamp is not treated as being a lamp if it is so painted over or masked that it is not capable of being immediately used or readily put to use, or if it is an electric lamp which is not provided with any system of wiring by means of which that lamp is (or can readily be) connected with a source of electricity.

Front lights

Front position lamps

Vehicles with three or more wheels (other than invalid carriages and pedal tricycles) require two front position lamps, ie front side lamps.

Pedal cycles, solo motor bicycles, hand-propelled vehicles (see exemption on p 000 where width does not exceed 800 mm) and invalid carriages require only one front position lamp, which must be fitted on the centre line or offside of the vehicle. Motorcycle combinations with a headlamp on the motor bicycle require a front position lamp on the centre line of the sidecar, or on the side of the sidecar furthest from the motor bicycle. A solo motor bicycle fitted with a headlamp need not be fitted with a front position lamp.

All front position lamps must be white in colour, unless they are incorporated in a yellow headlamp, in which case they may be yellow. They must be visible from a reasonable distance.

Dipped beam headlamps

Two dipped beam headlamps are required by motor vehicles with three or more wheels in most circumstances. Solo motor bicycles or combinations, and three-wheelers first used before 1 January 1972, or with an unladen weight of not more than 400 kg and an overall width of not more than 1,300 mm, require only one headlamp on the centre line of the motor vehicle itself. A bus first used before 1 October 1969 need only have one dipped beam headlamp.

The light emitted by a dipped beam headlamp must be white or yellow. The lamp itself must be so constructed that the direction of the beam of light can be adjusted whilst the vehicle is stationary. Where two dipped beam headlamps are required to be fitted, they must form a matched pair and be capable of being switched on and off simultaneously and not otherwise.

Main beam headlamps

The provisions concerning the number of obligatory headlamps to be fitted are the same as those relating to dipped beam headlamps, except that a bus must have two main beam headlamps, even if first used before 1 October 1969. The outer edges of the illuminated areas must not be outside those of the dipped beam headlamps; there is no maximum distance which should separate a pair of such lamps.

Main beam headlamps must emit a white or yellow light and must be constructed so that they can be deflected at the will of the driver to become a dipped beam, or so that they can be extinguished by the operation of a device which at the same time switches on a dipped beam or causes another lamp to emit a dipped beam. Thus headlamps of the 'long-range' type are invariably wired so that as they are extinguished a dipped beam is emitted from the normal headlamps. Main beam headlamps must be constructed so that the direction of the beam can be adjusted whilst the vehicle is stationary.

Dim-dip devices

These are devices capable of causing a dipped beam headlamp to operate at reduced intensity. Dim-dip devices must be provided on motor vehicles with three or more wheels first used on or after 1 April 1987. Vehicles having a maximum speed of 40 mph or less and home forces vehicles are exempt, as are vehicles which comply with Community Directive 76/756/EEC. Running lamps in the form of a matched pair of front lamps may be fitted as an alternative. A running lamp is defined as a lamp (not being a front position lamp, an end-outline marker lamp, headlamp or front fog lamp) used to make the presence of a moving motor vehicle readily visible from the front; in effect, a higher intensity front position lamp.

Rear lights

Rear position lamps

Most vehicles with three or more wheels require two rear position lamps, ie rear side lamps. The following vehicles, some of which have three or more wheels, require only one rear position lamp: buses first used before 1 April 1955; solo motor bicycles; pedal cycles with less than four wheels; trailers drawn by pedal cycles; trailers (the overall width of which does not exceed 800 mm) drawn by solo or motorcycle combinations; invalid carriages having a maximum speed not exceeding 4 mph; and vehicles propelled by hand. (See p 474 for the exemption for hand-propelled vehicles not exceeding 800 mm in width.) Some motor vehicles of maximum speed not exceeding 25 mph, and their trailers, require four rear position lamps; the details are in Sch 10 to the Regulations.

In cases in which only one rear position lamp is required it must be fitted on the centre line of the vehicle or on its offside.

All rear position lamps must be red.

Rear fog lamps

If it was first used on or after 1 April 1980, any motor vehicle having three or more wheels, and any trailer drawn by a motor vehicle, must, unless specifically dealt with elsewhere in the Regulations, have at least one rear fog lamp fitted, at or near the rear, on the centre line or offside of the vehicle. If two lamps are fitted there is no requirement concerning the distance these lights are placed from the sides of the vehicle. No more than two lamps may be fitted.

Vehicles first used before 1 April 1980 do not need to be fitted with rear fog lamps. Nor do motor vehicles whose maximum speed is 25 mph or less, nor motor vehicles or trailers which are no more than 1,300 mm in width, nor agricultural vehicles or works trucks first used before 1 April 1986. If one of these exempt vehicles is fitted with such lamps there are no restrictions in relation to the number of lamps which may be fitted.

A rear fog lamp must show a red light. It must not be fitted so that it can be illuminated by the application of any braking system of the vehicle. A tell-tale must be fitted to show that the lights are in operation. If two lamps are fitted to a motor vehicle first used on or after 1 April 1986, or on a trailer manufactured on or after 1 October 1985, they must form a matched pair. If two rear fog lamps are fitted, the rules for obligatory fog lamps apply to both of them.

Stop lamps

Stop lamps must show a red light. Motor vehicles having three or more wheels, and trailers drawn by a motor vehicle, must, unless otherwise stated, be fitted with two stop lamps. Solo motor bicycles, combinations, invalid carriages, and trailers drawn by motor cycles, together with motor vehicles or trailers first used before 1 January 1971, need only be fitted with one stop lamp. Motor bicycles of less than 50 cc first used before 1 April 1986 do not require any stop lamp, nor does any type of motor vehicle first used before 1 January 1936 or a motor vehicle whose maximum speed is 25 mph or less or an agricultural vehicle or works truck first used before 1 April 1986.

If two stop lamps are fitted they should be on each side of the longitudinal axis of the vehicle. If only one is fitted it should be on the centre line or offside.

The lamps must be operated by the application of the service braking system of the motor vehicle, and this also applies to the stop lamps of any trailer attached to that vehicle. Where two stop lamps are required to be fitted, they must form a pair.

Rear registration plate lamp

All vehicles which are required to be fitted with a rear registration plate must have lighting which is capable of adequately illuminating the rear registration plate.

Other obligatory lamps

Direction indicators

The requirements for direction indicators are as follows:

(1) Motor vehicles first used before 1 April 1936 and trailers manufactured before that date *may* have any arrangement of indicators but they are not required to have any at all.

(2) Motor vehicles first used on or after that date and before 1 April 1986, and trailers manufactured between 1 January 1936 and 1 October 1985, *must* be provided with any arrangement of indicators so as to satisfy the requirement of visibility to front and rear (or rear only in the case of a trailer).

(3) Motor vehicles first used on or after 1 April 1986, and trailers manufactured on or after 1 October 1985, are subject to detailed restrictions. Motor vehicles with three or more wheels, other than motorcycle combinations, must have a single front indicator, one side repeater indicator and one rear indicator on each side. One additional optional rear indicator may be fitted and any number of side repeater indicators may be added. Trailers manufactured after the specified date must have a rear indicator on each side. Additional optional indicators may be fitted as above. Motor bicycles and combinations must have a single front and a single rear indicator on each side of the vehicle.

The colour of the light shown by direction indicators is amber in most instances. Motor vehicles first used before 1 September 1965, and the trailer of such a vehicle, may show white or amber to the front or red or amber to the rear. However, if such an indicator is visible from both the front and the back it must show an amber light regardless of the date of first use. All indicators on any side of a vehicle or its trailer must be operated by one switch. There must be a tell-tale to show that the indicators are in operation. Flashing indicators must flash constantly at a rate of not less than 60 and not more than 120 times per minute.

Vehicles whose maximum speed does not exceed 15 mph or invalid carriages having a maximum speed not exceeding 4 mph are not required to have direction indicators fitted, nor are vehicles first used before 1 August 1986 which are agricultural vehicles, industrial tractors or works vehicles.

Agricultural vehicles having an unladen weight not exceeding 255 kg do not require direction indicators.

End-outline marker lamps

These are lamps fitted near the edge of a vehicle in addition to the front and rear position lamps to indicate the presence of a wide vehicle. They are required on motor vehicles first used on or after 1 April 1991, except those with a maximum speed not exceeding 25 mph; those having an overall width not exceeding 2,100 mm; and incomplete vehicles proceeding to works, etc.

There must be two white lights fitted to the front and two red lights to the rear, not more than 400 mm from the side of the vehicle. Each set must be a matched pair. Any number may be fitted.

Hazard warning signals

These signals are obligatory on motor vehicles having three or more wheels and first used on or after 1 April 1986, except vehicles which are not required to be fitted with direction indicators. Hazard warning signals which are optionally fitted to other vehicles must comply with the same provisions. Each device must be operated by one switch which causes all direction indicators with which the vehicle or combination of vehicles is equipped to flash in phase. There must be a tell-tale, and the device must be capable of operation without the ignition being switched on.

Side marker lamps

Such a lamp is a lamp fitted to the side of a vehicle or its load and used to render the vehicle more visible to other road users. Some motor vehicles with three or more wheels, and trailers drawn by motor vehicles are required to have side marker lamps on each side. Most are not, since motor vehicles first used before 1 April 1991 and trailers, the overall length of which does not exceed 6m (or 9.15m if manufactured before 1 October 1990), are not required to have side marker lamps, and nor are the following first used on or after that date:

(a) motor vehicles whose maximum speed does not exceed 25 mph;
(b) passenger vehicles;
(c) incomplete motor vehicles;
(d) those not exceeding 6m in length;
(e) those first used before 1 April 1996 complying with Community Directive 76/756/ EEC (and trailers manufactured before 1 October 1985 which comply with this Directive);
(f) trailers, whose overall length, excluding any drawbar and any fittings for its attachment, exceeds 6m (9.15m if manufactured before 1 October 1990);
(g) agricultural and works trailers;
(h) caravans and boat trailers; and
(i) trailers complying with the Community Directive.

A side marker lamp is a lamp which will show an amber light, if fitted to a vehicle first used on or after 1 October 1990, unless it is placed within 1m of the rear of the vehicle, when it may be red. Trailers manufactured before that date may have lamps which show a white light to the front and a red light to the rear.

The requirements are to have two, on each side, and as many more as are sufficient to ensure that the maximum distance from the front of the vehicle (including any drawbar) to the first lamp is 4m and the maximum distance from the rear in respect of the rearmost side marker lamp is 1m. The maximum separation distance of adjacent obligatory lamps on the same side of the vehicle is 3m or, if this is not practicable, 4m.

A vehicle, or a combination of vehicles whose overall length (including any load) exceeds 18.3m, must have additional side marker lamps, one lamp being no more than 9.5m from the foremost part of the vehicle or vehicles and one lamp no more than 3.05m from the rear (including loads in both circumstances). Other lamps must be placed to ensure that no more than 3.05m separates the lamps.

Where the length exceeds 12.2m but not 18.3m and the load is supported by any two vehicles, lamps must be placed behind the rearmost part of the drawing vehicle, but not more than 1,530 mm to the rear of that point. If the supported load extends more than 9.15m to the rear of the drawing vehicle, the lamp must not be forward of, or more than 1,530 mm to the rear of, the centre of the length of the load. These provisions do not apply to articulated vehicles.

Obligatory reflectors, etc

Rear retro reflectors

Generally, all vehicles must be equipped with two rear retro reflectors, ie reflectors used to indicate the presence and width of a vehicle when viewed from the rear. By way of exception, the following only require one retro reflector: solo motor bicycles; pedal cycles with less than four wheels (with or without a sidecar); trailers drawn by pedal cycles; trailers not exceeding 800 mm drawn by solo motorcycles or combinations; invalid carriages having a maximum speed not exceeding 4 mph; and hand-propelled vehicles. Some restricted vehicles (maximum speed 25 mph) require four reflectors.

Reflectors must be fitted at or near the rear of the vehicle. Where there is only one reflector it must be on the centre line or offside of the vehicle.

The colour of all rear reflectors must be red. A triangular-shaped rear reflector may only be fitted to a trailer or broken-down vehicle under tow.

Side retro reflectors

Side reflectors, ie reflectors fitted to the side of a vehicle or its load and used to render the vehicle more visible from the side, are obligatory on certain motor vehicles with three or more wheels and their trailers. The relevant requirements do not apply to a passenger vehicle (including private cars), nor to an incomplete vehicle travelling to a works for completion, etc, mobile cranes, plant and certain earth-removal vehicles, nor to a vehicle having a maximum speed not exceeding 25 mph. Nor do they apply to a goods vehicle whose overall length does not exceed 6m (if first used on or after 1 April 1986) or 8m (if first used before that date).

The requirements therefore are restricted to long goods vehicles. In the case of such vehicles, first used before 1 April 1986, and trailers manufactured before 1 October 1985, there must be two side retro reflectors on each side of the vehicle. In the case of those first used or manufactured on or after the relevant date, there must be two on each side of the vehicle and as many more as are required by Sch 17 to the Regulations. Side retro reflectors must be amber or, within 1m of the rear of the vehicle, they may be red. They must not be triangular in shape.

Rear markings

The rear markings provisions relate to 'long vehicle' markings, and therefore most vehicles are exempted from them. In the case of those motor vehicles first used before

1 April 1996 which are not exempted, those which do not exceed 13m in length need only carry the marker boards with diagonal lines, whereas those which exceed 13m must carry marker boards with the words 'long vehicle' in black on a yellow background surrounded by a red border or, as an alternative, boards of yellow retro reflective material surrounded by a red fluorescent border. Those used on or after 1 April 1996, which are not exempted, must carry boards of red and yellow diagonal stripes if they do not exceed 13m in length; if they exceed 13m, they must carry boards of yellow retro reflective material surrounded by a red fluorescent border. The same markings are required on certain trailers forming part of a combination of vehicles. In the case of a trailer manufactured on or after 1 October 1995 which does not, in combination, exceed 11m, it must carry a board of red and yellow diagonal stripes; if it exceeds 11m but not 13m it must carry boards of such red and yellow stripes or of yellow surrounded by red; and if it exceeds 13m, the boards must be of yellow surrounded by red. In the case of a trailer manufactured before 1 October 1995, if the overall length does not exceed 11m, the marking must be of the diagonal line variety; if between 11m and 13m the marking may be of any approved variety; and if it exceeds 13m it must be the 'long vehicle' type, or a board of yellow reflective material surrounded by a red fluorescent border.

A vehicle fitted with conspicuity markings to the rear where the fitting complies with the relevant UN Economic Commission for Europe (ECE) conspicuity requirements is exempt from the rear marking requirements.

Conspicuity markings

A goods vehicle which is—

(a) a motor vehicle first used on or after 10 July 2011, or
(b) a trailer manufactured on or after 10 July 2011,

must be fitted with conspicuity markings (devices intended to increase the conspicuity of a vehicle, when viewed from the side or rear, by the reflection of light emanating from a light source not connected to the vehicle, the observer being situated near the source, ie high visibility 'conspicuity marking tape') complying with the relevant ECE conspicuity requirements.

This requirement does not apply to a goods vehicle which is—

(a) a motor vehicle with a maximum gross weight not exceeding 7,500kg;
(b) a trailer with a maximum gross weight not exceeding 3,500kg;
(c) an incomplete vehicle proceeding to a works for completion or to a place where it is to be stored or displayed for sale; or
(d) a motor car or heavy motor car intended to form part of an articulated vehicle.

A goods vehicle to which the above requirement applies is known as a 'relevant goods vehicle'.

If the overall length of a relevant goods vehicle does not exceed 6m, conspicuity markings need not be fitted to the side of that vehicle.

If the overall width of a relevant goods vehicle does not exceed 2.1m, conspicuity markings need not be fitted to the rear of that vehicle.

Pedal retro reflectors

Pedal cycles manufactured on or after 1 October 1985 must be provided with two amber reflectors on each pedal.

Fitting and performance

The Regulations require that obligatory lamps, reflectors, rear markings and devices are fitted and performing satisfactorily at all times. However, there are certain understandable exceptions to this rule. The Regulations do not require any lamp or reflector to be fitted between sunrise and sunset to:

(a) an incomplete vehicle proceeding to a works for completion,
(b) a pedal cycle,
(c) a pedestrian-controlled vehicle,
(d) a horse-drawn vehicle,
(e) a combat vehicle (ie a tank, armoured car, field gun and the like, and vehicles constructed for the carriage of such a thing or of other weapons or ammunition), or
(f) a vehicle being taken to, or removed from, a testing station by an authorised vehicle examiner in order to submit the vehicle for an examination there in order to ensure that the examination carried out at the station is correctly carried out, or a vehicle being removed by an examiner following that examination.

To that list is added a vehicle which is not fitted with any front or rear position lamps, so that if a person is building a kit car and has not yet installed such lights he will not commit an offence by using the vehicle on a road during daylight hours. In addition, the regulations relating to fitting do not apply to a vehicle based outside Great Britain which is on a journey in this country, provided that it has not been here for more than 12 months and that it complies with international requirements. Vehicles going to a port for export are similarly exempt. Hand-drawn or -propelled vehicles whose overall width does not exceed 800 mm do not require lamps or reflectors between sunset and sunrise if used close to the nearside of the carriageway, or to cross the carriageway.

OPTIONAL LAMPS, REFLECTORS, REAR MARKINGS, AND DEVICES

The Regulations do not generally prevent the fitting of optional lamps, etc, ie lamps, etc which are not obligatory under the Regulations. Regulation 20 provides that every optional lamp, etc fitted to a vehicle must comply with provisions set out in the respective Schedules to the Regulations. A table included in the Regulations describes the types of optional lamps, etc and requires compliance with certain parts of the directions given in the relevant Schedule.

Optional lamps, etc can be divided into two categories:

(a) those which are additional to obligatory lamps, etc; and
(b) those which are not additional in that sense; there is no absolute requirement to have any lamp, etc of the particular type.

Additional lamps, etc

The position is:

(1) Any number of optional front position lamps may be fitted (except that a solo motor bicycle first used on or after 1 April 1991 may not be fitted with a total of more than two front position lamps). They must be white or, if incorporated in a yellow headlamp, yellow.

(2) Any number of optional dim-dip devices or additional running lamps may be fitted.

(3) Two optional dipped beam headlamps may be fitted to a vehicle with three or more wheels and a maximum speed exceeding 25 mph first used on or after 1 April 1991; any number may be fitted to other vehicles. These lamps must be white or yellow, comply with maximum and minimum height requirements, and be capable of adjustment while the vehicle is stationary.

(4) Any number of optional main beam headlamps may be fitted. They must be white or yellow, electrically connected so that they deflect or extinguish by the dip switch, and be capable of adjustment while the vehicle is stationary.

(5) Any number of optional rear position lamps may be fitted. They must be red.

(6) The number of optional rear fog lamps is controlled in the case of motor vehicles first used on or after 1 April 1980 (or, in the case of trailers, manufactured on or after 1 October 1979). No more than two such lamps are permitted in such a case. There is no limit in respect of other vehicles. Rear fog lamps must be red.

(7) Any number of stop lamps can be fitted. If additional lamps are fitted they must comply with the provisions for obligatory stop lamps, except those relating to position and angles of visibility. Motor vehicles first used on or after 1 April 1991 are subject to control in relation to the intensity of the light projected through the rear windows. Rear stop lamps must be red.

(8) Any number of side retro reflectors may be fitted. They may not be triangular. They must be amber except that, in respect of a vehicle used for the following purposes, the following colours are permitted:
   - Police—amber, yellow, blue, white*
   - Fire and Rescue Authority—amber, yellow, red
   - Ambulance, or a vehicle providing emergency response at request of an NHS ambulance service (but only if vehicle owned, leased or hired by service)—amber, yellow, green, white*
   - DVSA (Driver and Vehicle Standards Agency)—amber, yellow, silver, white*
   - Traffic officer—amber, yellow, white.
   (*Or, if within 1m of the rear of the vehicle, red.)

(9) Any number of rear retro reflectors may be fitted. Optional rear retro reflectors must be red, except that, in respect of a vehicle used for police, ambulance, fire and rescue authority, DVSA or traffic officer purposes, or in respect of a vehicle providing emergency response at request of an NHS ambulance service (but only if vehicle owned, leased or hired by service), the following colours are permitted: red, yellow or orange (or any combination). Optional rear retro reflectors may not be triangular, except in the cases referred to on p 472.

Non-additional optional lamps, etc

If such lamps are fitted they must comply with the following requirements.

Front fog lamps

These must be white or yellow lamps. Where a pair of front fog lamps is used in conditions of seriously reduced visibility in place of the obligatory dipped beam headlamps, they must not be more than 400 mm from the side of the vehicle.

Motor vehicles (other than motor bicycles) first used on or after 1 April 1991 may not have more than two front fog lamps.

Reversing lamps

Such a lamp must show a white light. Not more than two, facing the rear, may be fitted. In the case of a motor vehicle first used on or after 1 July 1954, they must be such that they cannot be illuminated other than automatically by the selection of the reverse gear or otherwise there must be a tell-tale.

If a vehicle has an overall length in excess of 6m and is a bus or a vehicle which is not a passenger vehicle four reversing lamps may be fitted. If four are fitted to such a vehicle the configuration must be four to the rear or two to the rear and one on each side. If such side lamps are fitted:

(a) it must not be possible for them to be illuminated unless the front and rear position lamps of the vehicle are illuminated; and

(b) they must be switched on and off by the manual operation of one switch which has no other function; but

(c) they must switch off automatically if the vehicle is moving forward at a speed of 10 km/h or more.

Warning beacons

The lights of such warning beacons must flash between 60 and 240 times per minute at constant intervals. Warning beacons, with the colours below, are permitted to be fitted in accordance with reg 11:

(1) Blue—a blue-and-white chequered light is permitted from a chequered domed lamp fitted to a police control vehicle and intended for use at the scene of an emergency; a blue light is permitted from a warning beacon or rear special warning lamp on an emergency vehicle, or on a special forces vehicle used in response to, or for training or practising to respond to, a national security emergency. No other type of vehicle may be fitted with a beacon of these types (or a device resembling one). Where an emergency or special forces vehicle fitted with a warning lamp is used for a purpose other than that to which the permission relates, as where an ambulance is used to take children to school, there is no requirement that the lamp should be covered or removed.

(2) Amber—permitted on road-clearance, refuse or breakdown vehicles; those with an overall width exceeding 2.9m; road-service vehicles; special vehicles carrying abnormal loads; vehicles escorting an abnormal load; vehicles used for escort purposes other than escorting an abnormal load, while they are travelling at a speed not exceeding 25 mph; and vehicles of HMRC (fuel-testing vehicles). Regulation 17 requires motor vehicles with four or more wheels, other than those first used before 1 January 1947, which have a maximum speed which does not exceed 25 mph, or any trailer which they are drawing, to be fitted with, and display, at least one amber warning beacon when being driven on an unrestricted dual carriageway road. The Regulations do not apply to such vehicles when merely crossing such a road in the quickest possible manner.

(3) Green—permitted to be used by registered medical practitioners.

(4) Yellow—permitted to be used by airport vehicles.

Conspicuity markings

To the extent that a relevant goods vehicle (see p 473) is exempt from the requirement to be fitted with conspicuity markings, conspicuity markings may be fitted to the side or rear (as the case may be).

A vehicle, other than:

(a) a passenger vehicle (except a bus);
(b) a trailer with a maximum gross weight not exceeding 750 kg,

which is not a relevant goods vehicle may be fitted with conspicuity markings.

USE OF LAMPS, REFLECTORS, ETC

No red lights to the front

By reg 11(1), no vehicle may be fitted with a lamp or retro reflective material which is capable of showing a red light to the front. The important word is 'capable': the provision is not confined to the hours of darkness, nor is it necessary that the light is actually shown. The exceptions to the provision are obvious; they are (1) red-and-white chequered lamps or beacons fitted to a fire service vehicle for emergency purposes, (2) a red side marker lamp or a red side retro reflector, (3) red retro reflective material or a red side retro reflector fitted to any wheel or tyre of a pedal cycle (or its trailer or sidecar), a motor bicycle or motor-bicycle combination or an invalid carriage, and (4) a traffic sign attached to a vehicle.

Red lights to the rear

Regulation 11(2) provides that no vehicle may be fitted with a lamp or retro reflective material which is capable of showing a light to the rear other than a red light. The same comments apply to 'capable' as made above. The exceptions are plentiful and include direction indicators, reversing lamps, conspicuity markings, interior illumination, rear number plates, public service vehicle route indicators, retro reflective material or side retro reflectors fitted to bicycles (or their sidecar or trailer), motor bicycles (or motor-bicycle combinations) and invalid carriages, and the various emergency lights described above. Pedal cycles may show an amber light to the rear from lamps fitted to their pedals. Pedal cycles, their trailers or sidecars may show a white or amber light to the rear from lamps fitted to their wheels or tyres if the lamp is designed to emit primarily to the side.

Maintenance of lamps, reflectors, rear markings, and devices

Regulation 23(1) prohibits a person using, or causing or permitting to be used, on a road, any vehicle unless every front position lamp, rear position lamp, headlamp, rear registration plate lamp, side marker lamp, end-outline marker lamp, rear fog lamp, retro reflector and rear marking with which it is required to be fitted is in good working order and, in the case of a lamp, clean.

Regulation 23, therefore, requires correct maintenance of all of the lamps, reflectors, markings and devices with which a vehicle is *required* to be fitted. Moreover, reg 23 goes on to require that all stop lamps, running lamps, dim-dip devices, headlamp levelling device, hazard warning signalling devices and direction indicators, even if they are in excess of those required by law, must be maintained at all times. However, reg 23 does not apply to rear fog lamps on a vehicle which is a part of a combination of vehicles, if any part of the combination is not required to have a rear fog lamp. Nor does reg 23 apply to a rear fog lamp on a vehicle drawing a trailer; nor to any defective lamp reflector, dim-dip device or headlamp levelling device where the defect arose in the course of the journey on a vehicle in use in the daytime (ie between sunrise and sunset), or if arrangements have been made to remedy the defect with all reasonable expedition; nor, during the daytime, to a lamp, reflector or rear marking fitted to a combat vehicle.

Driving or parking without lights

Regulation 24 prohibits a person using, or causing or permitting to be used, a vehicle on a road between sunset and sunrise or (while the vehicle is in motion) during daytime hours in seriously reduced visibility unless every obligatory front position lamp, rear position lamp, rear registration plate lamp, side marker lamp and end-outline marker lamp is kept lit and unobscured. Except as indicated below, it also prohibits allowing (or causing or permitting to be allowed) a vehicle to remain at rest (ie parked) in similar circumstances between sunset and sunrise. There are variations to these provisions in respect of motorcycles and trailers not required to be fitted with front position lamps, since the prohibitions are not breached if there are fitted to these vehicles 'ad hoc' front position lamps.

Regulation 24 also provides that vehicles of certain classes may lawfully park between sunset and sunrise on roads subject to speed limits of 30 mph or less, without showing such lights. These are goods vehicles with gross vehicle weight not exceeding 2,500 kg, passenger vehicles other than buses, invalid carriages, and motorcycle, or pedal cycles (in either case with or without a sidecar). The exemption does not apply if the vehicle has a trailer attached or is carrying a load which requires lamps.

The exemption only applies to vehicles parked in:

(a) designated parking places on roads; or

(b) a lay-by which is clearly shown to be such; or

(c) elsewhere, provided, if the vehicle is parked on a one-way road, it is facing in the correct direction on either side of the road as close as possible to the kerb, or, if it is parked on an ordinary road, it is properly parked and facing the correct way, and in either case no part of the vehicle is less than 10m from a junction with the road upon which it is parked, whether the junction is on the same side of the road or not. Where a curving kerb exists, the 'junction' begins where the kerb begins to curve.

The lighting requirements under reg 24 do not apply to a solo motorcycle or pedal cycle, which is being pushed close to the nearside kerb, a pedal cycle which is halted and waiting to proceed (eg at traffic lights) if it is kept to the nearside, or a vehicle which is parked at roadworks and properly outlined by lamps or traffic signs.

Use of headlamps

Regulation 25 provides that a person must not use, or cause or permit to be used, on a road, a vehicle which is fitted with obligatory dipped beam headlamps unless every such lamp is kept lit:

(a) during the hours of darkness, except on a road which is a restricted one by virtue of a system of street lighting, when those lights are lit; and

(b) during daylight hours in seriously reduced visibility.

There are certain permitted variations; for example, motor vehicles with one obligatory dipped beam headlamp are exempt from the above requirement if a main beam or fog lamp is kept lit. Vehicles which are being towed, those which are parked and those propelling snow ploughs are exempt from the above requirement. In addition, in the case of a motor vehicle other than a motor tricycle or motor-bicycle combination, a pair of main beam lamps may be used as an alternative or, in seriously reduced visibility, a pair of front fog lamps may be used, provided that they are not more than 400 mm from the outer edges of the vehicle.

Prohibition of particular use of lamps or devices

Regulation 27 provides that a person must not use, or cause or permit to be used, on a road, any vehicle on which any lamp, hazard signal warning device or warning beacon of a specified type is used in the manner listed below.

Headlamps may not be used so as to cause undue dazzle or discomfort to other persons using the road and shall not be lit when a vehicle is parked. These prohibitions also apply to front fog lamps, with the addition of a prohibition upon use at any time other than in conditions of seriously reduced visibility.

The use of rear fog lamps is similarly restricted but the reference to undue dazzle or discomfort is predictably restricted to following drivers. They must also not be used when a vehicle, other than an emergency vehicle, is parked.

Reversing lamps must not be used for any purpose other than that of reversing. Similarly the use of hazard warning signal devices is restricted to warning road users of a temporary obstruction (or the presence of a school bus which is stationary and loading or unloading school children under 16) when the vehicle is at rest, or, on a motorway or unrestricted dual carriageway, to warn of a temporary obstruction ahead, or, in the case of a bus, to summon assistance for the driver or conductor or an inspector who is on the vehicle.

Blue lamps and special warning lamps may only be used at the scene of an emergency, or to indicate the urgency of the journey or the presence of a hazard on the road. The use of amber lights is similarly restricted but they may also be used in connection with breakdowns or slow-moving vehicles on dual carriageways. Green lights may only be used whilst the vehicle is occupied by a registered medical practitioner and used in an emergency. Yellow light beacons may not be lit on a road. Work lamps must not dazzle, etc and must not be used other than for illuminating a working area, accident, breakdown, or works in the vicinity of the vehicle. No other lamp which is fitted to a vehicle may ever be used so as to cause undue dazzle or discomfort to other persons using the road.

Movement of lamps or reflectors and nature of light

Regulation 12 provides that no person shall use, or cause or permit to be used, on a road, a vehicle fitted with a lamp or reflector capable of being moved (by swivelling, deflecting or otherwise) while the vehicle is in motion. There are some obvious exceptions, for example dipping headlights, lamps which may be adjusted to compensate for loads, retracting headlamps, etc, amber pedal reflectors, and retro reflective material fitted to any wheel or tyre of pedal cycles or their trailer or sidecar.

Steady light

By regulation 13, the light shown by lamps covered by the Regulations must be a steady light, in that flashing lights are not permitted. There are exceptions for warning beacons prescribed for emergency vehicles, etc, and flashing front or rear position lamps fitted to pedal cycles (or their trailer or sidecar).

Projecting trailers and vehicles carrying overhanging or projecting loads

Regulation 21 prohibits a person using, or causing or permitting to be used, on a road:

(a) any trailer projecting laterally beyond the preceding vehicle in the combination; or

(b) any vehicle or combination of vehicles carrying a load or equipment,

which (in either case) does not comply with the following specifications:

(i) a trailer, which (or whose load) projects laterally more than 400 mm from the outermost part of the obligatory front position light on that side of the vehicle in front of it, must have white lights to the front which are not more than 400 mm from the outermost projection of the trailer (or, as the case may be, of the load);

(ii) a vehicle whose load projects laterally more than 400 mm must have lights at the front and rear not more than 400 mm from the outermost projection of the load;

(iii) a vehicle whose load projects more than 1m to the front or to the rear must have a front or rear lamp not more than 1m from the foremost or rearmost projection of the load (except that that distance is 2m in the case of an agricultural vehicle or a vehicle carrying a fire escape); or

(iv) a vehicle carrying a load which obscures any obligatory lamps, reflector or rear markings must show a lamp, etc in the prescribed position.

These requirements only apply when the vehicle/trailer is being used between sunset and sunrise or in circumstances of reduced visibility, except that in relation to obligatory stop lights and direction indicators in (iv) the requirement applies in all circumstances.

TESTING AND INSPECTION OF LIGHTING EQUIPMENT, ETC

Regulation 28 applies the provisions of reg 74 of the Road Vehicles (Construction and Use) Regulations 1986 to lighting equipment and reflectors with which a vehicle is *required* by the Regulations to be fitted. Regulation 74 empowers a constable in uniform to test and inspect lighting equipment on motor vehicles and trailers on any premises, subject to the consent of the owner of the premises.

OFFENCES

Contravention of, or failure to comply with, any regulation contained in the Road Vehicles Lighting Regulations 1989 is an offence contrary to RTA 1988, s 42 except that a breach which relates to a pedal cycle is an offence contrary to the Road Traffic Offenders Act 1988, s 91.

It is also an offence under RTA 1988, s 42 for a person to use on a road a motor vehicle or trailer which does not comply with these Regulations or to cause or permit a vehicle to be so used.

CHAPTER 13

Traffic Accidents

DUTY TO STOP, ETC

Where, owing to the presence of a mechanically propelled vehicle (MPV) on a road or other public place, an accident occurs by which:

(a) personal injury is caused to someone other than the driver of that MPV; or
(b) damage is caused to a vehicle other than that MPV or a trailer drawn by it, or to an animal other than an animal in or on that vehicle or a trailer drawn by it, or to any other property constructed on, fixed to, growing in or otherwise forming part of the land on which the road or other public place in question is situated or land adjacent to such land (Road Traffic Act 1988 (RTA 1988), s 170(1)),

the driver of the MPV is required by RTA 1988, s 170(2) to stop and, if required to do so by any person having reasonable grounds for so requiring, give his name and address, and also the name and address of the owner and the identification marks of the vehicle. If an accident might occur owing to the presence of two or more vehicles on a road, the driver of each vehicle must stop, etc if the consequences set out above occur.

The driver of a MPV, owing to whose presence on a road or other public place an accident occurs, is not obliged by s 170 (or any other provision) to stop, etc if:

(a) no one (besides that driver) is injured; and
(b) no vehicle (besides that vehicle or its trailer) is damaged; and
(c) no animal (other than one in that vehicle or its trailer) is injured; and
(d) no property forming part, etc of the road or land adjacent to it is damaged.

Section 170(2) places duties only upon the *drivers of MPVs*; the rider of a pedal cycle has no obligations to stop, etc under it (or any other provision).

An accident must have occurred owing to the presence of a motor vehicle on a road or other public place

'MPV' and 'road' were defined on (pp 310 and 311). As to 'public place', see p 487.

For an *accident* to have occurred *owing to the presence* of a MPV on a road or other public place, there must be a direct causal connection between the presence of the MPV and the occurrence of the accident. If the driver of a vehicle brakes sharply on approaching a pedestrian who is crossing the road and the noise of that braking so startles the pedestrian that he falls and is injured, there is a direct causal connection between the vehicle and the accident. Likewise, if a cyclist collides with a motor car waiting at traffic lights, there is a direct causal connection between the presence of the vehicle and the accident in that the cyclist was in contact with it.

A divisional court has held that 'accident' bears its ordinary popular meaning (as opposed to any technical meaning) and that the question is whether an ordinary person would say that an accident has occurred. It also held that there can be an accident even though part of the chain of events leading to the injury or damage was a deliberate act on someone's part. For the obligations in s 170 to apply to the driver of a MPV, it is not necessary that his vehicle is involved in an accident in the sense that it is in collision. For example, if D, the driver of a motor car, carelessly drives it across a junction with a major road, causing vehicles on the major road to take avoiding action which causes them to collide with each other, D certainly causes that accident although he is not involved in the collision. In such a case, the obligations in s 170 will have to be discharged by D, as well as by the drivers of the other motor vehicles.

The accident must have caused one of the specified consequences

As we have seen, these specified consequences are:

(1) Personal injury to a person *other than the driver* of the MPV owing to whose presence on a road or other public place the accident occurred.
(2) Damage to a vehicle *other than the MPV, or its trailer*, owing to whose presence on a road or other public place the accident occurred.
(3) Damage to any animal *other than an animal in or on the MPV, or its trailer*, owing to whose presence on a road or other public place the accident occurred.

'Animal' means any horse, cattle, ass, mule, sheep, pig, goat, or dog. Poultry are not included, nor are cats (no matter how valuable they may be).
(4) Damage to any other property constructed on, fixed to, growing in or otherwise forming part of the land on which the road or other public place in question is situated or land adjacent thereto.

It is a question of fact to be determined by the court whether or not property which is damaged forms part of, or is adjacent to, land on which the road or other public place in question is situated. If a car collides with the petrol pumps in a filling station adjacent to the road there is little doubt that a court would consider the petrol pumps to be on land adjacent to land on which a road is situated. Should damage be occasioned to a house which is immediately at the roadside, that house is undoubtedly constructed on land which is at least adjacent to land on which the road is situated. It is probable that, even if a garden exists at the front of the house, a court would consider that the house was constructed on land adjacent to the road. If, because of the presence of a car on a road, an accident occurs and the car crashes through a fence into a field of corn, the accident certainly causes damage to both the fence and the crops which are on land adjacent to the road.

The driver of the motor vehicle must stop and, if required by a person having reasonable grounds for so requiring, must give certain information

'*Driver*' means the person who takes the vehicle out on a road; he remains its 'driver' until that particular journey is over or someone replaces him as 'driver'.

The obligation to stop arises immediately the accident occurs. Thus, in one case, where a bus driver had injured a passenger by braking sharply and had driven on to a rendezvous with an ambulance which he had arranged by radio, a divisional court held that he had failed to stop as required by s 170(2). Because the duty to stop is an immediate one, a driver who leaves the scene and later returns to it does not 'stop' for the purpose of s 170(2).

ce are in attendance at the scene of an accident from which an unconscious driver
ken to hospital.

he obligation to report is to do so at a police station or to a constable as soon as
onably practicable and, in any case, within 24 hours of the occurrence of the acci-
t. 24 hours is, therefore, the maximum period in which the report may be made, so
if the driver does not report until 24 hours or more have elapsed since the accident
s necessarily in breach of his obligation under s 170(3). Even if the report is made
hin 24 hours, the driver will nevertheless be in breach of his obligation if he has not
de it 'as soon as reasonably practicable'. What is 'reasonably practicable' is a matter
the court to decide on in the particular circumstances. If a driver who is not seeking
ent medical attention drives from the scene of an accident and past a police station,
order to go to his home, and only reports the accident 20 hours later, a court is un-
ely to find that he reported the accident as soon as reasonably practicable. On the
er hand, in a case where a motorist's car left the road and collided, causing damage,
23.00 and the driver left his address in his car at the scene and was interviewed by
police at 08.30 the next day (at which point of time he reported the accident), a div-
onal court held that the justices were entitled to conclude that in the circumstances
ere had been no failure to report as soon as reasonably practicable.

The obligation to report can only be performed officially and personally; telling a
end who is a police officer will not do, nor will a telephone message to a police station.

FFENCES

person who fails to comply with any requirement of RTA 1988, s 170(2) or (3) com-
ts an offence against s 170(4). In fact, if he fails to stop (or to give specified informa-
on), contrary to s 170(2), and also fails to report the accident to the police, contrary
s 170(3), he commits two offences. The first offence can be committed in two ways,
ther by failing to stop *or* having stopped, failing to provide the information which is
quired to be given by a person with reasonable grounds; neither failure is excused by
subsequent report to the police.

A divisional court has held that a person charged with an offence under s 170(4) has
defence if he proves that he did not know that an accident had occurred. However, in
le case of the second offence, if, although unaware of the accident at the time of it, he
ubsequently becomes aware of it within the 24-hour period and fails to report it to the
olice, he can be convicted of that offence since he will be obliged to report the accident
nd his failure at that time will be with knowledge of the accident. In addition, a div-
ional court has held that the defence of 'ignorance of accident' is not available where
hat ignorance is due to the defendant's voluntary intoxication.

NJURY ACCIDENTS: DUTY TO PRODUCE INSURANCE

RTA 1988, s 170(5) provides that if, in the case of a *personal injury* accident to which s
70 applies by virtue of (1) on p 482, the driver of a *motor vehicle* (other than an invalid
arriage) does not at the time of the accident produce a certificate of insurance or se-
urity, or other evidence prescribed by regulations:

(a) to a constable; or
(b) to someone who, having reasonable grounds for so doing, has requested him to
    produce it,

The term 'stop' means that the driver should stop and remain where
for a period of time sufficient to enable persons who have reasonable
doing to require of him directly and personally the information which
quired to supply. In determining what that period should be, particular
be paid to the character of the road or the place where the accident occu
is that of the driver and his responsibilities cannot be discharged by som
leaves at the scene. The driver must remain sufficiently near to the vehic
person to make the requests permitted by the section.

As already implied, the duty to stop does not cast on the driver the c
seek persons to whom to give the above information.

Section 170(2) also requires *the driver to provide certain information if*
do by 'any person having reasonable grounds for so requiring'. Such a pe
ally be the driver of any other vehicle involved in the accident, a person i
owner of property or of an animal. However, there are other persons wh
reasonably demand information from the driver of a MPV, for examp
someone who has been injured. It will be a matter for the court to deter
of doubt. It may well look differently upon a demand made by a 'nosey
posed to one made by some person who quite genuinely had the other pa
at heart.

The information which the driver is required by s 170(2) to give is:

(a) his name and address;
(b) the name and address of the owner of the vehicle; and
(c) the identification mark of the vehicle.

Section 170(2) can be satisfied by giving an address other than a home ad
ample the address of the driver's solicitor or the driver's business address,
driver can be contacted via that address reasonably swiftly and easily.

This obligation is absolute in the sense that, if the requirement is made
having reasonable grounds to make it, the driver must supply this i
However, if this information is supplied at the scene the obligations of the
and there is no need to report the accident to the police. (If injury to son
occasioned there is also a need to produce evidence of insurance; see p 484

DUTY TO REPORT TO THE POLICE

RTA 1988, s 170(3) deals with a driver's obligation to report an accident to
Its wording is important: if for any reason the driver of the MPV does not gi
and address as required by s 170(2), he must report the accident. If a drive
name and address to a person reasonably requiring information, but refuses
name and address of the owner or the identification mark of the vehicle, he
obliged to report the accident to the police, although he will commit an offer
in consequence of his refusal to give the other information.

The obligation to report an accident to the police arises whenever the
not given *his* name and address at the scene of the accident, whether or n
requested to do so by anyone there (and indeed, even though he was know
ally to any person with reasonable grounds to request his name and address
divisional court has held, the obligation to report arises even though the dri
not have given his name and address at the scene of the accident because he wa
scious throughout the time he was there. The obligation is not negated by the

the driver must report the accident and produce such a certificate or other evidence. It is, of course, insufficient to wave a certificate of insurance in front of the eyes of a person requesting such information; it must be produced in the sense that he is able to satisfy himself that an effective insurance is in force.

As in the case of the duty to report an accident under s 170(3), the driver must report the accident (and produce his insurance certificate, etc) at a police station or to a constable and must do so as soon as reasonably practicable, within 24 hours (s 170(6)). It is an offence, contrary to s 170(7), to fail to do so. However, the offence is subject to the proviso that a person is not to be convicted of it by reason *only* of a failure to produce a certificate, etc if, within seven days after the accident, the certificate, etc is produced at the police station specified by him when the accident was reported.

CHAPTER 14

Driving Offences

INTRODUCTION

Statutory offences were created in the nineteenth century to deal with carriages and the like. Although these provisions were enacted before the days of mechanically propelled vehicles, they can be applied to such vehicles. The Highways Act 1835 prohibits certain acts in relation to 'carriages', and the Town Police Clauses Act 1847, s 28 deals with the furious driving in a street of any horse or carriage. The Offences Against the Person Act 1861, s 35 still punishes as an offence triable only on indictment the causing of bodily harm by wanton or furious driving on a road or otherwise by a person having charge of a carriage or vehicle; this charge can be useful in circumstances in which the negligent driving of a mechanically propelled vehicle did not take place on a road or other public place. However, for all practical purposes, driving offences that are committed in relation to mechanically propelled vehicles are governed by the Road Traffic Act 1988 (RTA 1988). Those offences contain a number of general terms, which are defined below or elsewhere in this book.

'Driving'

The essence of 'driving' is the use of the driver's controls (or at least one of them) in order to control the movement of the vehicle, however that movement is produced, provided that what occurs can in any sense be regarded as 'driving'. Thus, a person who releases the handbrake and 'coasts' downhill in a car is 'driving' it (even if the steering is locked). Someone who propels a moped by 'paddling' with his feet, sitting astride it and steering it, is driving it. A person in the driving seat of a car which is being towed is driving if he has the ability to control its movements by means of the brakes or steering. This is so even if the vehicle is attached by means of a rigid tow bar which is attached to the towing vehicle by means of a ball hitch, and to the vehicle being drawn by means of a shackle. Such a combination leaves the person holding the steering wheel of the towed vehicle with a substantial potential for directional control because he is able (indeed he is required) to keep the towed vehicle in line with the towing vehicle by means of the steering wheel. It would be irrelevant that the towed vehicle does not have any brakes. On the other hand, a person in the driving seat of a vehicle on a fixed tow is not driving it, since he cannot control its movements by the use of any of the driver's controls. Nor is a person who is pushing a car and steering it with his hand through the window driving it because this cannot in any sense be described as driving.

A divisional court has held that the defendant (D) was 'driving' in circumstances where the vehicle was stationary. D was sitting in the driver's seat of a vehicle on a grass verge engaging in an activity which he described as 'wheel spinning'. This involved the use of the engine, accelerator, clutch and steering wheel with the vehicle in gear but the handbrake applied preventing any form of movement. The court held that the ordinary meaning of the word 'driving' included a situation where someone was ensuring that there was no movement but the wheels were spinning.

Two people may be driving a vehicle at the same time. For example, if A, who is in the driving seat, operates the clutch and brakes and gear shift but allows his passenger, B, to steer the vehicle, both A and B are driving.

The Road Traffic Act 1988 (RTA 1988), s 192 provides that, except for the purposes of the offence of causing death by dangerous driving, where a separate person acts as steersman of a motor vehicle he is driving the vehicle (as well as any other person engaged in driving it). This covers the case where one person is primarily concerned with the propulsion of the vehicle and another acts as its steersman. It is relevant only in the case of traction engines and the like.

An employer cannot be convicted of a driving offence physically committed by an employee.

It must be proved that the person alleged to have been driving was driving at the time of the alleged offence. Difficulties in this respect have arisen in cases in which a witness has reported an incident to a police officer and at the same time has provided, from memory, the registration mark of the vehicle. Even with the modern rules about hearsay evidence, there may be problems if the officer seeks to say in evidence that he was told that the number of the car involved in the incident was that given by the witness. In such cases, it would be good practice for the officer to record the number given to him in his notebook and to have the witness endorse the entry as being correct and sign it. Such a record then becomes 'joint' and may be referred to by either. The witness's statement should also include the fact that he gave that particular number to the officer and that it was the number of the vehicle seen on that occasion.

Other terms

Mechanically propelled vehicle See p 327.
Motor vehicle See p 327.
Road See p 328.

Other public place   This term means a place (other than a 'road') to which the public, whether on payment or otherwise, have access with at least the tolerance of the landowner or proprietor. It is irrelevant whether the public could have access; the question is whether they actually have access to the place in question at the time in question. For example, the car park of a public house is open to the public at large during licensing hours and is therefore a public place during those hours, but the car park of a members' club is restricted to members of that club and their guests and therefore it is never a 'public place'. A car park situated within the business premises of a motor dealer for use by customers has been held to be a public place as members of the public using the car park did not cease to be members of the public and become a special class of persons merely because they used the car park as customers.

A place can be a 'public place' even though access to it is only permitted after a person has been screened, provided that the screening does not relate to a special characteristic or reason personal to the person screened. Thus, if anyone can pass through the screening process and gain access simply by paying an entry fee (eg a site fee at a caravan park), or by satisfying conditions imposed by the landowner (eg access only for private vehicles or the possession of a boarding pass), the place is a public place. It would be different if the screening related to membership of the caravan club or status as a worker at a factory to whose car park access is sought.

The absence of a physical obstruction or of a notice forbidding entry does not of itself mean that the public have access.

DANGEROUS DRIVING, AND CAUSING DEATH OR SERIOUS INJURY BY DANGEROUS DRIVING

Dangerous driving

RTA 1988, s 2 provides that it is an offence for a person to drive a mechanically propelled vehicle dangerously on a road or other public place. The offence is an indictable (either way) offence.

The ways in which driving may be dangerous are set out in RTA 1988, s 2A.

Dangerous manner

RTA 1988, s 2A(1) provides that a person is to be regarded as driving dangerously if:

(a) the way that he drives falls far below what would be expected of a competent and careful driver; and

(b) it would be obvious to a competent and careful driver that driving in that way would be dangerous.

This test in RTA 1988, s 2A(1) is concerned with whether the manner of D's driving falls *far* below what would be expected of a careful and competent driver in circumstances where it would be obvious to a competent and careful driver that driving in that way would be dangerous. The presence of the word '*far*' separates offences of dangerous driving from those which should more appropriately be charged as careless driving.

It would be no defence that D was doing his incompetent best, nor that he did not intend to drive dangerously. This was held by the Court of Appeal in a case where a bus driver unintentionally pressed the accelerator when he meant to press the brake; as a result the bus travelled across a pedestrian island and pedestrians were killed. The court held that the driver's lack of an intention to drive dangerously was no defence.

The objective standards to be applied will vary according to the prevailing conditions and to exceptional circumstances which might have existed. In fog, the competent and careful driver would drive in a manner quite different from that which he would adopt in dry, clear conditions. Whilst driving at a speed of 70 mph in an area restricted to 30 mph might be described as dangerous, it would not often be so on a dual carriageway. If it occurred in the middle of the night when the road was not being used by any other person or vehicle, such driving in a restricted area might not be 'dangerous', whilst driving at that speed on a dual carriageway which is restricted by road works might be.

The opinion of witnesses as to whether or not D drove dangerously is, of course, inadmissible.

Once it has been established that the actual driving fell far below standards of a competent and careful driver, it becomes necessary to consider whether or not it would be 'obvious' to a competent and careful driver that such driving would be dangerous. Section 2A(3) states that 'dangerous' refers to danger either of injury to any person or of serious damage to property. It also states that, for the purposes of s 2A(1) and (2) (see p 489), in determining what would be expected of, or obvious to, a competent and careful driver in a particular case, regard must be had not only to the circumstances of which he could be expected to be aware but also to any circumstances shown to have been within the defendant's knowledge. Regard must not be had to any circumstance which D wrongly believed to exist. Consequently, it has been held that, where a police officer pursued a stolen car at speed through traffic lights at red, his mistaken belief that the junction was being controlled by other officers (so that he could cross safely) was irrelevant to the issue of dangerous driving. The Court of Appeal has held that D's special skill as a driver (eg D had taken a police advanced driving course) is an irrelevant consideration when considering whether driving was dangerous: to take it into account would be inconsistent with the objective test of the competent and careful driver.

A breach of the Highway Code does not necessarily mean that an offence has been committed, but the Code's provisions can be considered by a jury or magistrates, provided that it is clearly explained that they do not provide a 'standard'.

Dangerous state of the vehicle

The second way in which driving may be dangerous is provided by RTA 1988, s 2A(2), which provides that a person is also to be regarded as driving dangerously if it would be obvious to a competent and careful driver that driving the vehicle in its current state would be 'dangerous' (in the sense defined by s 2A(3)). In determining the state of the vehicle, regard may be had to anything carried on or in it, and the manner in which it is attached or carried.

Because the danger involved in driving the vehicle in its current state must be obvious, the offence will not be committed if the defect involved is a latent one. A danger is 'obvious' in this context only if it could be seen or realised at first glance by a competent and careful driver. It is not enough that such a driver would have taken steps to check out whether the vehicle was in a condition which was not dangerous, and by doing so would have discovered the defect, perhaps by examining the underside of the vehicle.

'Current state' in s 2A(2) implies a state different from the original or manufactured state. Thus, where the alleged danger relates solely to something inherent in the original design of the vehicle (eg spikes forming part of a grab unit at the front of an agricultural vehicle) dangerous driving is not committed. It would be different if the original, unaltered state made the *manner* of the driving dangerous.

As with s 2A(1), in determining what would be obvious to a competent and careful driver, regard must be had not only to the circumstances of which he could be expected to be aware but also to any circumstances shown to have been within D's knowledge. Apart from such knowledge, the state of D's mind is irrelevant.

Driving in a dangerously defective state through intoxication or consumption of drugs

Evidence of consumption of alcohol or drugs cannot by itself establish the fact that a driver has committed an offence of dangerous driving. The offence is concerned with the dangerous nature of the driving, not with the dangerous nature of the driver due to drink. The Court of Appeal has held that, while evidence of alcohol consumption is admissible in respect of an offence of dangerous driving if the amount of alcohol is proved or admitted, even though the driver's blood alcohol level is below the legal limit, it cannot be conclusive. The consumption of a drug, even if the amount is unquantified, has been held by the Court of Appeal to be admissible in respect of such an offence, although it cannot be conclusive. In either case, there must be evidence that the vehicle was driven dangerously within the definition in RTA 1988, s 2A.

Dangerous cycling

A person who rides a bicycle or tricycle dangerously on a road commits a separate and less serious offence contrary to RTA 1988, s 28(1). A person is to be regarded as riding dangerously if he rides in a *manner* which equates to the manner of driving described above (s 28(2) and (3)).

Causing death by dangerous driving

RTA 1988, s 1 provides that a person who causes the death of another person by driving a mechanically propelled vehicle dangerously (as defined in s 2A, above) on a road or other public place is guilty of an offence. The offence is triable only on indictment. The victim may be someone else in D's vehicle.

It is not necessary to show that the dangerous driving was the sole cause of death, since it is sufficient that it is a more than minimal cause. The rules about causation referred to on p 690 apply to s 1 and to ss 1A, 2B and 3A (below).

It is not necessary that the driver should have been driving the vehicle (ie it need not have been in motion) at the time that the fatal injury was caused. It is enough that there has been dangerous driving by the driver and that this driving is more than a minimal cause of death. This is shown by a case where a driver took his lorry on to a motorway after having been warned that his brake air-pressure gauges were not working (which constituted dangerous driving), and the handbrake system was activated due to loss of air pressure. The trailer unit blocked the nearside lane of the motorway. Some 12 minutes later a lorry collided with it and the driver of that vehicle was killed. The Court of Appeal held that the consequences of dangerous driving are capable of outlasting the time the driver spends at the wheel. It held that the dangerous driving must have played a part, not simply in creating the occasion of the fatal accident, but in bringing it about. On the facts the consequences of the dangerous driving were not 'spent' and too remote from the accident, and were more than a minimal cause of the death. As a result the driver's conviction for causing death by dangerous driving was upheld.

It is irrelevant that the risk of death resulting from the dangerous driving in question was unforeseen or unforeseeable, as would be the case where the only obvious risk was of damage to property.

Causing death by dangerous driving is a serious offence and it is important that the evidence offered to a court is well presented. Identification of the person fatally injured is of extreme importance. Medical evidence will be given at the Crown Court concerning the cause of death of the person injured in the accident. It is essential that a police officer, who was at the scene of the accident and saw the injured person, identifies that person to the pathologist who carries out the post mortem examination. In the absence of such evidence, there is nothing to connect the person upon whom the post mortem examination was carried out with the person injured in the accident. In addition, a careful note must be made of everything observed at the scene of the accident at the particular time at which it occurred. All fatal traffic accidents must be handled carefully and the possibility of the need for forensic evidence should be considered. There is little purpose in tracing a damaged vehicle suspected of having been involved in a fatal accident if samples of glass and paint, and other vehicle debris were not collected at the scene at the time of the accident.

The ingredients of the offences of manslaughter by gross negligence and of causing death by dangerous driving (a less serious offence in terms of punishment) are similar. CPS policy is to charge manslaughter only if the evidence shows a very high degree of risk, making the case one of the utmost gravity.

Causing serious injury by dangerous driving

A person commits an offence under RTA 1988, s 1A if he causes serious injury to another person by driving a mechanically propelled vehicle dangerously (as defined in s 2A) on a road or other public place. 'Serious' injury means physical harm which amounts to grievous bodily harm for the purposes of the Offences against the Person Act 1861 (p 652). It is irrelevant that serious injury—or indeed any injury—was unforeseen or unforeseeable. The offence under s 1A is an indictable (either way) offence.

CARELESS OR INCONSIDERATE DRIVING, AND CAUSING DEATH BY CARELESS OR INCONSIDERATE DRIVING

Offences of careless or inconsiderate driving

RTA 1988, s 3 creates two separate offences by providing that if a person drives a mechanically propelled vehicle on a road or other public place without due care and attention, or without reasonable consideration for other persons using the road or place, he is guilty of an offence.

Driving without due care and attention

RTA 1988, s 3ZA provides that a person is to be regarded as driving 'without due care and attention' if (and only if) the way he drives falls below what would be expected of a competent and careful driver. In determining what would be expected of a competent and careful driver in a particular case, regard must be had not only to the circumstances of which he could be expected to be aware but also to any circumstances shown to have been within the knowledge of the defendant (D). The definition of driving without due care and attention differs from that relating to dangerous driving in relation to the extent to which D's driving falls below the standard of a competent and careful driver. While dangerous driving requires a fall 'far' below what would be expected of a competent and careful driver, simply 'falling below' that standard, however marginally, suffices for careless driving.

The standard is an objective standard, impersonal and universal, fixed in relation to the safety of the other users of the highway. It is in no way related to the degree of proficiency or degree of experience attained by the individual driver, and it is unaffected by the fact that the driver was driving to an emergency.

Bearing in mind the objective approach to be applied, it is no defence that, as a learner, the driver was doing his best, if that best falls short of the standard which might be expected from a competent and careful driver. There is only one standard of competence and his actions fall short of it. In circumstances where a competent driver wears shoes with smooth leather soles and this causes his foot to slip from the brake pedal, the court will have to consider whether in the circumstances a competent and careful driver would have been aware of the possibility of this happening and would not have driven the car with such shoes. In the same way, it is essential to keep in mind that experienced drivers or specially trained drivers do not in consequence of that experience or training owe some higher standard of care. For example, the driver of a police vehicle owes the ordinary standard of care to other persons on the road.

In applying the appropriate test as to whether D has driven without due care and attention, all the circumstances of the case can be considered, including evidence that D had been affected by drink or that D had taken such an amount of drink as would be likely to affect a driver, since such evidence may indicate a lack of due care on D's part in driving as he did.

Failure to observe a provision of the Highway Code does not of itself establish driving without due care and attention, but any such failure may be relied on as evidence of it.

In some cases the facts are such that, unless D offers some explanation consistent with him having taken due care, which is not disproved, the only proper inference is careless driving, in which case the justices must convict him.

Driving without reasonable consideration

RTA 1988, s 3ZA provides that a person is to be regarded as driving without reasonable consideration for other persons only if those persons are inconvenienced by his driving. Those persons must be shown to have been inconvenienced. Thus, a driver may deliberately drive at speed through a pool of water, but will only commit this offence if other persons were either dampened or forced to flee.

Once again, an objective test should be applied as to whether particular forms of driving are carried out without reasonable consideration for other persons using the road or place. Thus, the question is whether D drove without showing the consideration to other road users which would be shown by a considerate driver. The driver who occupies the fast lane of a motorway, or even the outside lane of a dual carriageway, in circumstances in which there is nothing to prevent him from regaining the nearside lane, is unreasonably interfering with the progress of other drivers. The irresponsible use of full-beam headlamps may also amount to driving without reasonable consideration. A person may drive without reasonable consideration for other persons using the road even where his lack of consideration is to his own passenger.

A point about both offences

Because RTA 1988, s 3 creates two offences, an information or written charge alleging both alternatives is likely to fail for duplicity. It is sufficient to allege that a person drove without due care and attention at a particular time or place, or, as the case may be, to allege that he drove without reasonable consideration at a time and place, since it is not necessary to specify the nature of his negligence in the information or written charge.

Vehicle used in manner causing alarm, distress or annoyance

The Police Reform Act 2002 (PRA 2002), s 59(1) provides that, where a uniformed constable has reasonable grounds for believing that a mechanically propelled vehicle (MPV) *is being used* in a manner which contravenes RTA 1988, s 3 and which is causing, or is likely to cause, alarm, distress or annoyance to members of the public, he has the powers under PRA 2002, s 59(3) set out below.

By s 59(2), a uniformed constable additionally has the powers under s 59(3) where he has reasonable grounds for believing that a MPV *has been used* on any occasion in a manner falling within s 59(1).

The powers set out in s 59(3) are:

(a) if the vehicle is moving, to order the person driving it to stop it;
(b) to seize and remove the vehicle;
(c) for the purposes of exercising a power falling within (a) or (b), to enter any premises other than a 'dwelling house', which term does not include any garage or other structure occupied with the dwelling house, or any land appurtenant to the dwelling house, on which he has reasonable grounds for believing the vehicle to be;
(d) to use reasonable force, if necessary, in the exercise of any power conferred by (a)–(c).

Section 59(4) provides that the power of seizure may not be exercised unless:

(a) the constable has warned the person appearing to be the person whose use falls within s 59(1) that he will seize the vehicle if that use continues or is repeated; and
(b) it appears that the use has continued or been repeated after the warning.

However, a warning need not be given if:

(i) the circumstances make it impracticable;
(ii) the constable has already on that occasion given a warning under s 59(4) in respect of any use of that vehicle or of another MPV by that person or any other person;
(iii) the constable has reasonable grounds for believing that such a warning has been given on that occasion otherwise than by him; or
(iv) the constable has reasonable grounds for believing that the person whose use of that MPV on that occasion would justify the seizure is a person to whom a warning has been given (whether or not by that constable or in respect of the same vehicle or the same or a similar use) on a previous occasion in the previous 12 months.

It is an offence under s 59(6) to fail to comply with an order under s 59(3) to stop a MPV.

The Police (Retention and Disposal of Motor Vehicles) Regulations 2002 provide for the safe keeping, retention, release and disposal of a vehicle seized under s 59(3). They provide that a person who would otherwise be liable to charges is not liable to pay if the use which caused the seizure was not a use by him and he did not know of the use of the vehicle in the manner which led to its seizure, had not consented to its use in that manner and could not, by the taking of reasonable steps, have prevented its use in that manner.

These powers also apply where a uniformed constable reasonably believes that an offence against RTA 1988, s 34 (prohibition of off-road driving, see p 411) is or has been committed in a manner causing, or likely to cause, alarm, distress or annoyance to members of the public.

Causing death by careless or inconsiderate driving

RTA 1988, s 2B provides that a person who causes the death of another person by driving a mechanically propelled vehicle on a road or other public place without due care and attention, or without reasonable consideration for other persons using the road or place, is guilty of an offence. The offence is an indictable (either way) offence. It is not necessary to show that the careless driving was the sole cause, since it is sufficient that it is a more than minimal cause. It is irrelevant that the risk of death resulting from the careless driving was unforeseen or unforeseeable. These points also apply to the next offences.

Causing death by careless or inconsiderate driving when under the influence of drink or drugs

RTA 1988, s 3A(1) provides that it is an offence for a person to cause the death of another person by driving a mechanically propelled vehicle on a road or other public place without due care and attention, or without reasonable consideration for other persons using the road or place, where he:

(a) is, at the time when he is driving, unfit to drive through drink or drugs; or
(b) has consumed so much alcohol that the proportion of it in his breath, blood or urine at that time exceeds the prescribed limit; or

(c) has in his body a specified controlled drug and the proportion of it in his blood or urine at that time exceeds the specified limit for that drug; or

(d) is, within 18 hours after that time, required under s 7 to provide a specimen, but without reasonable cause fails to provide it; or

(e) is required by a constable to give his permission for a laboratory test of a specimen of blood taken from him under s 7A, but, without reasonable excuse, fails to do so.

The offence is triable only on indictment.

In essence, to be guilty of an offence under s 3A(1), D must be proved to have committed one or other of the offences of careless driving and thereby killed another, and to have fallen within one of the drink/drug drive elements in (a)–(e) above.

The term 'unfit to drive through drink or drugs' is explained in Chapter 15, as are other references to drink or drugs, prescribed limits, etc. Other matters concerned with the evidential linking of the driver to the person who received fatal injuries are discussed above.

Despite the wording of s 3A(1), the offences at (b) to (e) apply only to persons driving motor vehicles as opposed to mechanically propelled vehicles.

Careless or inconsiderate cycling

There are separate, and less serious, offences, contrary to RTA 1988, s 29, of riding a bicycle or tricycle on a road without due care and attention, or without reasonable consideration for other persons using the road.

DEFENCES TO OFFENCES INVOLVING DANGEROUS OR CARELESS DRIVING

The defences of duress of circumstances, duress by threats, and automatism, referred to in Chapter 1, apply to the above offences. As seen, the terms of these defences are strict.

It should be noted that a defendant who, for example, falls asleep at the wheel or goes into a hypoglycaemic coma at the wheel can be convicted of dangerous or careless driving under the ordinary principles of liability, not in relation to the time when he was an automaton but in relation to the time when he realised or should have realised that he was about to become unconscious and should have stopped. The reason is clear: to drive in such a case falls below the standard of a reasonable and prudent driver (who would have stopped).

The fact that the driving complained of was due to the sudden mechanical failure of an essential part of a vehicle can provide a defence to charges of dangerous or careless driving, provided that the defect was not known by D to exist prior to the occurrence which forms the basis of the charge, and was not such that it should have been discovered by a reasonably prudent driver. Thus, where a driver knew that the brakes of his vehicle pulled to the off-side but nevertheless drove it, the defence of mechanical defect was held not to be open to him.

Like the defence of automatism, the essence of this defence is that the dangerous situation was caused by a sudden loss of control which was in no way due to the fault of the driver.

SPEEDING

Speeding offences can be divided into those which relate (a) to restricted roads, (b) to roads subject to a speed limit order, (c) to motorways, (d) to roads subject to maximum or minimum speed limits introduced by temporary orders, and (e) to speed limits which affect particular vehicles in particular places.

Restricted roads

By RTRA 1984, s 81 it is not lawful for a person to drive a motor vehicle on a restricted road at a speed exceeding 30 mph. It is an offence contrary to s 89(1) to do so.

A 'restricted road' is basically defined by s 82 as one upon which there is provided a system of street lighting furnished by means of lamps placed not more than 200 yards apart. A divisional court has held that an error of 12 yards between two lamps in a system of 24 does not prevent the road from being restricted. In addition to this basic definition, s 82 provides that a direction may be given by the traffic authority that a specified road with street lighting as described above shall cease to be a restricted road for the purpose of s 81 or that a road which is not provided with such lighting shall be a restricted road for the purpose of s 81. Such directions are made by the traffic authority, ie Highways England (in England) or the Welsh Ministers (in Wales) in the case of trunk roads, and by the local authority in the case of other roads (except that Transport for London is the traffic authority for a GLA road).

Signage

A road with street lighting which has been de-restricted by a direction must show the prescribed de-restriction signs (including repeater signs). Likewise, a road without such lighting which has been made a restricted road (or subjected to some other speed limit) must be provided with the prescribed restriction signs (including repeater signs). If these are not in place on the relevant part of the road, a driver cannot be convicted of exceeding the indicated speed limit. Moreover, even if they are, it is a requirement that the relevant signs can reasonably be expected to indicate the limit to an approaching driver in sufficient time to reduce from the previous lawful limit to a speed within the new limit. Thus, where a driver proved that the restriction sign, because of an overgrowing hedgerow, was not visible until the sign itself was reached, a divisional court allowed his appeal against conviction for speeding. Subject to this qualification, where signs are correctly placed, it is no defence to such a charge that the driver simply did not see the signs. The de-restriction or restriction signs which must be used are prescribed by the Traffic Signs Regulations and General Directions 2016.

The requirement for restriction signs does not apply to a road which is restricted by virtue of having a system of street lighting with lamps not more than 200 yards apart. Consequently, it is no defence for a driver accused of exceeding 30 mph on such a road that no signs were provided.

Roads subject to speed limit orders

Quite apart from 'restricted roads', many other roads are subject to speed limits. RTRA 1984, s 84 empowers a traffic authority to make an order prohibiting the driving of motor vehicles on a specified road at a speed exceeding that specified in the order (either at any time or during specified periods) or at a speed exceeding that indicated by traffic signs in accordance with the order. By s 89(1), a person who drives a motor vehicle at a speed in excess of that specified for the particular road is guilty of an offence. If a speed limit order is made under s 84, the specified road must bear the prescribed restriction signs (including repeater signs). If it does not at the point of enforcement, a person cannot be convicted of driving in excess of the specified limit.

Speed limits on motorways

The Motorways Traffic (Speed Limit) Regulations 1974 impose an overall speed limit of 70 mph on any motor vehicle using a motorway. If a section of motorway is subject to a lesser limit, this is expressly listed and that section must bear the prescribed signs indicating the lower limit (otherwise a driver cannot be convicted of exceeding that limit). Contravention of the Regulations is an offence contrary to RTRA 1984, s 17(4).

Temporary maximum speed limits

RTRA 1984, s 88 permits temporary speed limit orders to be made by the Secretary of State or the Welsh Ministers when it is desirable to do so in the interests of safety or for the purpose of facilitating the movement of traffic. Such orders may impose temporary maximum speed limits.

The 70 mph, 60 mph and 50 mph (Temporary Speed Limit) Order 1977, which was made under the predecessor to s 88 and was continued in force indefinitely in 1978, imposes a maximum limit of 60 mph on single carriageways and of 70 mph on dual carriageways. These are general limits which apply to all roads (other than motorways) unless some other speed limit operates by virtue of the provisions described in this chapter.

The 1977 Order also imposes a limit of 60 mph on certain specified lengths of dual carriageway and of 50 mph on certain specified lengths of single carriageway. Such lengths must be provided with the prescribed restriction signs (including repeaters).

By RTRA 1984, s 89(1), it is an offence for a person to drive a motor vehicle on a road in excess of an applicable temporary speed imposed under the Order.

Temporary minimum speed limits

RTRA 1984, s 88 also permits temporary orders to be made imposing minimum speed limits, subject to such exceptions as may be specified. Signs must be displayed if a minimum speed limit is in force in respect of any road. By s 88(7), breach of such an order is an offence. Neither disqualification nor endorsement can be ordered on a conviction for this offence. Such a minimum speed limit only applies, of course, to motor vehicles.

Temporary speed restrictions in special cases

RTRA 1984, s 14 permits traffic authorities to impose temporary speed limits because of roadworks or work which is being undertaken near a road, or because of the likelihood of danger to the public or of serious damage to the road, or for the purpose of cleaning or clearing litter. Such an order cannot continue in force for more than 18 months unless the Secretary of State or Welsh Ministers consents to its further continuance. A divisional court has held that variable speed limits may be imposed under s 14.

A person who contravenes a speed restriction imposed under s 14 commits an offence contrary to RTRA 1984, s 16, but a divisional court has held that persons committing this offence should be charged under s 89(1).

Maximum speed limits on particular vehicles

Quite apart from the various speed limits which apply to roads, speed limits are also imposed on various types of vehicle. Thus, the driver of such a vehicle must not only observe the *speed limit applying to the road* in question but also the *speed limit applying to his vehicle on that road.* RTRA 1984, s 86 provides that it is unlawful for a person to drive a motor vehicle on a road at a speed in excess of a speed limit applicable to that vehicle. By s 89(1), a person who does so is guilty of an offence.

RTRA 1984, Sch 6 sets out the speed limits applying to particular classes of vehicles as follows:

Class of vehicle	M/ways	Dual carr	Other roads
1 Invalid carriage	n/a	20	20
2 Passenger vehicle, motor caravan, car-derived van or dual purpose vehicle drawing one trailer	60	60	50
3 Vehicle of the type mentioned in 2, drawing more than one trailer	40	20	20
4 Goods vehicle (except car-derived van) up to 7.5 tonnes mlw (maximum laden weight) not drawing a trailer	70	60	50
5 Articulated goods vehicle up to 7.5 tonnes mlw, and goods vehicles drawing one trailer where the combined mlw does not exceed 7.5 tonnes	60	60	50
6 Articulated goods vehicle over 7.5 tonnes mlw, goods vehicle over 7.5 tonnes mlw, and goods vehicles drawing one trailer where the combined mlw exceeds 7.5 tonnes	60	60	50
7 Goods vehicle, other than a car-derived van, drawing more than one trailer	40	20	20
8 Motor tractor, light loco, heavy loco	20	20	20
9 Motor tractor, light loco, heavy loco with certain requirements as to springs and wings being met	40	30	30
10 Works truck	18	18	18
11 Passenger vehicle exceeding 3.05 tonnes unladen weight or adapted to carry more than eight passengers:			
Not exceeding 12 m length	70	60	50
Exceeding 12 m length	60	60	50
12 Agricultural motor vehicle	40	40	40

The term 'car-derived van' means a goods vehicle which is constructed or adapted as a derivative of a passenger vehicle and which has a maximum laden weight not exceeding 2 tonnes. It is treated as if it was a passenger vehicle of the type from which it was derived.

A recovery vehicle equipped with a special boom for lifting vehicles is not a motor tractor. It is constructed to carry a load and is not, therefore, restricted to 40 mph on a motorway.

Exemptions for emergency services

RTRA 1984, s 87 exempts motor vehicles which are being used for fire and rescue, ambulance or police purposes from the statutory provisions imposing speed limits on motor vehicles, if the observance of any such provision would be likely to hinder the use of the vehicle for the purpose for which it is being used on that occasion. The exemption relating to vehicles being used for ambulance purposes has been extended to cover vehicles which, although not being used for ambulance purposes, are being used for the purpose of providing a response to an emergency at the request of an NHS ambulance service. Section 87 also applies in relation to vehicles being used for NCA purposes, or for training drivers for use for NCA purposes, as it applies to a vehicle being driven for police purposes. However, other than in the case of training, s 87 does not apply in relation to a vehicle being driven for NCA purposes unless it is being driven by a person trained to drive vehicles at high speeds.

Exemptions for special forces

The Road Traffic Exemptions (Special Forces) (Variation and Amendment) Regulations 2011 vary statutory provisions which impose speed limits to provide exemptions for drivers who are members of the special forces using vehicles in response to a national security emergency or whilst being trained or practising to do so.

It is a condition of the exemptions that drivers have been trained in the driving of vehicles at high speeds.

Regulation 2 provides that speed limits imposed by or under:

(a) RTRA 1984, s 81 (p 495);
(b) existing orders or notices under RTRA 1984, s 14 (p 496);
(c) existing orders under RTRA 1984, ss 16A (prohibitions or restrictions on road in connection with sporting event, social event or entertainment held on road), 84 (p 495) or 88 (p 496);
(d) motorway speed limits regulations (p 496);
(e) any local Act,

are varied so as to exempt special forces drivers using vehicles in response to a national security emergency or whilst being trained or practising to do so.

Procuring, etc speeding: a special provision

RTRA 1984, s 89(4) provides that, if a person who employs others to drive motor vehicles on roads publishes or issues any timetable or schedule, or gives any directions, under which any journey or part of a journey is required to be completed within a specified time, and it is not practicable for that journey (or part) to be completed in the specified time without the commission of an offence under s 89(1), that publication or issue, or giving of directions, may be produced as evidence that the employer procured or (as the case may be) encouraged or assisted his employees to commit such an offence.

Proof

RTRA 1984, s 89(2) states that a person must not be convicted of an offence of speeding *contrary to s 89(1)* solely on the evidence of one witness to the effect that, in the opinion of the witness, the person prosecuted was driving the vehicle at a speed exceeding the specified limit. A similar provision applies to an offence under s 88(7) of non-compliance with a temporary minimum speed limit.

Section 89(2) requires corroborative evidence; it does not require that there must necessarily be more than one witness. Although, technically, there is no reason why a driver cannot be convicted on the evidence of two witnesses, where one corroborates the other by stating that in his opinion the vehicle was, for example, exceeding a limit of 30 mph, the courts would generally not be satisfied with two such opinions unless the speed was estimated to be far in excess of the limit imposed. Corroboration is therefore usually provided by some mechanical device, which is read by an operator (normally a police officer) who may then give evidence of its reading. The reading will provide corroboration of the operator's opinion of the speed of the vehicle in question.

Corroboration of speed may be obtained by the use of stopwatches to assess speeds over a measured distance, but it is usually provided by a speedometer, fixed camera, radar speed meter, VASCAR or similar prescribed device. Where a speedometer is used, it is important to establish that the police vehicle containing the speedometer maintained an even distance from the vehicle being checked as this is relevant to the issue of speed.

A police officer's opinion of a vehicle's speed may also be corroborated from scientific calculations made by him (or another) based, for example, on damage to the vehicle and skid marks where it has crashed. It has been held by a judge in the Administrative Court that a police officer is entitled to corroborate his own opinion of whether a vehicle was exceeding a speed limit by reference to a prescribed device even if that device is not of a *type* approved by the Secretary of State (so that RTOA 1988, s 20 (below) cannot be relied on).

In instances where two police officers are involved in detecting speeding offences, they may keep one record of the transaction provided that both check and acknowledge the accuracy of that record at the time. This frequently occurs where one officer is engaged in checking the speed of the vehicle, whilst another stops and deals with the offending driver.

Radar meters are extremely accurate devices, and the courts will accept evidence of speed which is based upon meter readings provided that the operator can satisfy the court that he is a trained operator and that there is clear evidence of the identity of the particular motor vehicle alleged to have exceeded the speed limit. The vehicle will have been stopped by another officer and clear proof will be required that the vehicle stopped by the second officer was the one which had exceeded a statutory speed limit.

Hand-held radar guns are accurate, provided the batteries are fully charged or, if they are operating from another source, provided they are properly connected. However, their accuracy is affected if they are operated within a quarter of a mile of powerful VHF or UHF transmissions or within 100 yards of high-voltage cables. Care must also be taken to ensure that the beam is not bounced off metal objects and that it could not have picked up a reading from another moving object. In the case of devices such as the LT1 20.20 which can measure the speed of vehicles at a distance of 1,000 metres, it is essential that the device is aimed at one spot and does not waver. A small movement of the 'spot' directed at the vehicle can lead to a false reading.

VASCAR and similar devices are also in common use within police forces. They record speeds averaged by a vehicle over a specified distance. Operators must be carefully trained as the device is operated by a series of switches. It is essential that the operator is able to satisfy a court that the switches were operated at the right time to ensure that correct distances are recorded, and that the vehicle was properly identified, together with the precise moment when it passes the object which marks the limit of the distance over which it is checked.

The above devices are prescribed devices (see below).

Evidence produced by prescribed devices

RTOA 1988, s 20 provides that a record produced by a prescribed device (ie a device of a description prescribed by the Secretary of State) in an order made by statutory instrument is evidence of a fact related to any offence of speeding. The Road Traffic Offenders (Prescribed Devices) Order 1992 prescribed devices designed or adapted for measuring by radar the speed of motor vehicles. An identically named Order in 1993 prescribed devices designed or adapted for measuring speed by means of sensors or cables on or near the surface of a highway and those activated by means of a light beam or beams. Another identically named Order in 1999 prescribed cameras designed or adapted to record speed by correlating the image of the motor vehicle as it passes two positions, digitally recording each image and the time it is photographed, and calculating the average speed between the two positions. The cameras do not require film but transmit computer images to a computer centre. They are capable of measuring the speed of vehicles in different lanes. Another order with the same title in 2008 approved the use of manually operated devices that record the speed of a vehicle (vehicle A) from another vehicle (vehicle B) by (a) measuring the time it takes for vehicle A to travel between two points, (b) recording the distance between those points by means of the odometer pulses of vehicle B as it travels between the two points, and (c) calculating vehicle A's average speed between the two points by reference to the time in (a) and the distance calculated under (b) or measured manually.

The record must provide (in the same or another document) a certificate as to the circumstances in which the record was produced, signed by a constable or a person authorised by, or on behalf of, a chief police officer for the area in which the offence is alleged to have been committed.

A record produced by a prescribed device is inadmissible unless the device is of a type proved to have been approved by the Secretary of State and was used in accordance with conditions subject to which the approval was given.

The Orders referred to above show that a statutory instrument specifying a 'prescribed device' is drafted in general terms (as permitted by the legislation). On the other hand, approval of a type of device is given specifically in relation to a particular make and model. Evidence of the approval of the particular type of device used may be required and should be offered in the absence of judicial notice having been taken of its existence. This may be done by production of a valid copy of the instrument of approval or oral evidence may be given from a police officer who has knowledge of the approval, but approval may not be inferred merely from the fact that the device is in general use within police forces. A divisional court has held that the fact that a device is not properly used, in particular that a pre-operative test has not been performed, does not mean that the device is not of an approved type. The court went on to uphold a conviction for speeding where the expert evidence indicated that the failure properly to calibrate a laser speed device did not give rise to any material error.

The purpose and effect of RTOA 1988, s 20 is to enable a record relying on an accompanying certificate to be tendered in evidence without the necessity of a witness being called to prove them. A copy of evidence obtained by means of an approved device must be served on the person charged with the offence not less than seven days before the hearing or trial. If, not less than three days before the hearing or trial, the defendant requires the attendance of the person who signed the document, the evidence of the circumstances in which the record was produced will not be admissible, although the record produced by the device will. Where the record and certificate are not served on the defendant seven days before the trial, the magistrates should allow them to be produced by a police officer as real evidence.

Notices under RTA 1988, s 172

Notices may be sent under s 172, requiring the owner of the vehicle to identify the driver within 28 days. See further p 405.

Motor racing and rallies

It is an offence contrary to RTA 1988, s 12(1) to promote or take part in a race or trial of speed between motor vehicles on a highway. Thus, there is a complete ban on racing motor vehicles on a highway.

RTA 1988, s 13(1) creates the offence of promoting or taking part in a 'competition or trial' (other than a race or trial of speed) which involves the use of motor vehicles *on a highway* unless the event is authorised and conducted in accordance with any conditions imposed. The Motor Vehicles (Competitions and Trials) Regulations 1969 deal with such events. Competitions or trials are authorised without the need for an application if:

(a) there are no more than 12 vehicles involved and the event does not take place within eight days of another similar event promoted by the same person or club;

(b) no merit is attached to completing the event with the lowest mileage and, in respect of any part of the event on a public highway, there are no performance tests and no route, competitors are not timed or required to visit the same places, although they may be required to finish at the same place by a specified time;

(c) in respect of any part of the event on the public highway, merit is attached to a competitor's performance only in relation to good road behaviour and compliance with the Highway Code; or

(d) all competitors are members of the armed forces of the Crown and the event is designed solely for the purpose of service training.

Regulation 6 permits the authorisation of other events by the Royal Automobile Club Motor Sports Association Ltd. Applications for such events must be made not less than two months before the event is due to be held (or, if it is to be held on more than one date, the date the event is due to begin). Except in the case of a specified event, which is an event which is run not more than once a year, for example the 'Veteran Car Run', and is specified in the schedule to the Regulations, the application must not be made more than six months before the event.

RTA 1988, s 13A states that a person is not guilty of an offence under s 1, 1A, 2, 2B or 3 by virtue of driving a vehicle *in a public place other than a road* if he shows that he was driving in accordance with an authorisation for a motoring event given under regulations. The Motor Vehicles (Off Road Events) Regulations 1995 authorise a number of bodies to issue such authorisations.

Section 33(1) prohibits the promoting or taking part in a trial of any description between motor vehicles on a footpath, bridleway or restricted byway unless the holding of it has been authorised by the local authority. Contravention of s 33(1), or breach of a condition of an authorisation, is an offence under s 33(3).

As from a day to be appointed, RTA 1988, s 12 will be subject to RTA 1988, ss 12A–12F, added by the Deregulation Act 2015, s 73, which makes provision to allow the holding of races or trials of speed between motor vehicles on a highway. RTA 1988, ss 12A–12F are described in Chapter 14 on the companion website.

NOTICE OF INTENDED PROSECUTION

If not interviewed by the police at the time of a driving offence, a driver may experience considerable difficulty in recalling the circumstances some weeks after the event. For this reason, RTOA 1988, s 1 states that, in relation to certain named offences, a person may not be convicted unless:

(a) he was warned at the time of the possibility of prosecution for the offence; or

(b) he was served with a requisition, single justice procedure notice or summons for the offence within 14 days of its commission; or

(c) a notice of intended prosecution specifying the nature of the alleged offence and the time and place where it is alleged to have been committed was served within 14 days on him or the person, if any, registered as the keeper of the vehicle at the time of the commission of the offence. (In the case of dangerous or careless cycling the notice must be served on the rider.)

These requirements are deemed to have been complied with unless and until the contrary is proved.

The following offences require notice in one of these forms:

(a) RTA 1988, ss:
    2   Dangerous driving
    3   Careless, or inconsiderate, driving
    22 Leaving vehicle in a dangerous position
    28 Dangerous cycling
    29 Careless, or inconsiderate, cycling
    35 Failing to conform with traffic directions
    36 Failing to comply with traffic signs

(b) RTRA 1984, ss:
    16   Exceeding temporary speed restrictions imposed under s 14
    17(4) Exceeding speed restriction on special road (ie a motorway)
    88(7) Breach of temporary minimum speed limit
    89(1) Speeding offences generally

(c) Aiding and abetting any of the above offences.

However, such notice need not be given in relation to an offence in respect of which a full or provisional fixed penalty notice has been given or fixed under RTOA 1988.

Warning at the time of the offence

The words 'at the time of the offence' mean at the *time of the incident and not the moment of the offence*. In one case, a warning, given by a police officer at the scene of an incident 35 minutes after its occurrence and while it was still being dealt with, was held to have been given 'at the time'. In other circumstances, where the police immediately traced the driver but the process took two-and-a-half hours, the notice was held to have been given 'at the time'. However, there is obviously a limit, and the matter should be judged in the context of the warning being given as a part of the continuous process of initial investigation, a question of fact and degree. If there has been any delay at the scene, it is best to send a written notice.

The warning must be heard and understood by the person concerned, and it must be to the effect that the question of prosecuting him for one or other of the above offences will be taken into consideration. There is no prescribed form of words and any clear statement to the above effect will do. It is appreciated that it is not always possible to decide whether the prosecution might be for dangerous or merely careless driving but a warning that it might be for either will suffice as the evidence upon which the charge will be based will be similar.

Service of requisition, single justice procedure notice, summons or notice of intended prosecution

Where a warning is not given at the time, either a requisition, single justice procedure notice, summons or written notice of intended prosecution must be served within 14 days. The day on which the offence was committed is ignored.

A notice of intended prosecution may be served by delivering it to the person or addressing it to him and leaving it at his last known address. In addition, a notice may be served by sending it to the person by registered post, recorded delivery service or first class post addressed to him at his last known address. There is a difference between the first two postal methods and the third. A notice sent by registered post or recorded delivery service is irrebuttably deemed to have been served on someone if addressed to him at his last known address, and this includes being irrebuttably deemed to have been served within the period of 14 days. On the other hand, there is no such irrebuttable presumption in respect of a notice sent by first class post; consequently, if it is proved that a letter so sent was delivered after the end of the 14-day period it will not have been effectively served.

In the absence of personal service, it is obviously advisable to serve a notice by sending it by registered post or recorded delivery since in such a case the addressee is deemed to have been served if the notice was addressed to him at his last known address, notwithstanding that the notice is returned as undelivered or is for some other reason not received by him.

As to service of a requisition, single justice procedure notice or summons see p 17.

It has been held that service of a notice on D's wife by handing her the notice was valid, since she was authorised to accept and deal with D's mail. It would be different if the notice was left with a hall porter, as he would not be so authorised.

Circumstances where non-compliance is no bar to conviction

By RTOA 1988, s 2(3), a failure to comply with the above requirements is no bar to conviction if the court is satisfied that the defendant's or the vehicle's registered keeper's name and address could not with reasonable diligence have been ascertained in time for service of a requisition, single justice procedure notice, summons or notice of intended prosecution or that the defendant by his own conduct contributed to the failure.

Section 2(1) waives the requirements of s 1 in relation to any offence if, at the time of the offence or immediately thereafter, an *accident occurs owing to the presence on a road of the vehicle* in respect of which the offence was committed. This exemption exists because, in such circumstances, the offender will normally be aware of the circumstances surrounding the offence and the risk of prosecution. It does not apply, therefore, if the accident was so trivial that the driver was unaware that the accident had occurred. Here, the requirements of s 1 apply. On the other hand, the waiver of the requirements of s 1 does apply if the driver was unaware of the circumstances of an accident owing to the severity of his injuries, because subsequently the driver will be only too aware that the accident has occurred.

'Accident' in s 2(1) is given a commonsense meaning and is not restricted to un-intended consequences having an adverse physical effect. It is for the prosecution to prove beyond reasonable doubt that an 'accident' has occurred. The words 'owing to the presence on a road of the vehicle' require there to be a direct causal link between the vehicle on the road and the accident.

CHAPTER 15

Drinking or Drug-Taking and Driving

The Road Traffic Act 1988 (RTA 1988), ss 4 to 11 contain various offences relating to drinking and driving. The principal types of offence are driving or attempting to drive a motor vehicle with an alcohol concentration in excess of the prescribed limit (s 5), and driving or attempting to drive a mechanically propelled vehicle when unfit to drive through drink or drugs (s 4). In addition, s 5A makes driving or attempting to drive a motor vehicle with a concentration of a specified controlled drug in excess of the specified limit an offence.

Where a case could be prosecuted under s 5, or under s 4, it is normally preferable to prosecute for an offence under s 5, as appropriate, rather than one under s 4. This is because s 5 lays down an objective test; whereas under s 4 it is necessary for the prosecution to prove that the ability of the defendant (D) to drive properly was for the time being impaired by drink or drugs, which is a question of fact for the justices. The same comments apply in respect of s 5A as in respect of s 5.

DRIVING, ETC WITH EXCESS ALCOHOL

Under RTA 1988, s 5(1) it is an offence for a person:

(a) to drive or attempt to drive a motor vehicle on a road or other public place; or
(b) to be in charge of a motor vehicle on a road or other public place,

after consuming so much alcohol that the proportion of it in his breath, blood or urine exceeds the prescribed limit.

The charge must state whether the person was driving, attempting to drive or in charge of the vehicle and the nature of the specimen in which the prescribed limit was exceeded. If it does not it is likely to fail for duplicity.

Road or other public place

See pp 328 and 487, respectively.

Driving, attempting to drive, or in charge of motor vehicle

Driving
See p 486.

Attempting to drive
As explained in Chapter 39, what is required is the doing of an act which is more than merely preparatory to the commission of the full offence, coupled with the intention

to commit the full offence. For example, if someone gets no further than sitting in the driving seat of a motor car on a road and searching his pockets for the ignition key, the justices would find that his acts were merely preparatory and that he was not attempting to drive (although he could be convicted of the offence of being in charge with excess alcohol). On the other hand, if he gets as far as placing the key in the ignition switch and turning it it is almost certain that the justices would find that the act was more than merely preparatory, and that therefore he was attempting to drive.

The offence of 'attempting to drive' is convenient where a driver with excess alcohol is stopped in a private place, for example a private car park, as he drives towards a road. In such circumstances he can be convicted of an attempt to drive on a road with excess alcohol.

Being in charge

A divisional court has held that there are broadly two distinct classes of cases:

(a) If the defendant is the owner or lawful possessor or has recently driven the vehicle, he will have been 'in charge' of it and the question will be whether he is still in charge or has relinquished his charge. Usually such a defendant will be prima facie in charge unless he had put the vehicle in someone else's charge. However, he would not be so if in all the circumstances he had ceased to be in actual control and there was no realistic possibility of his resuming actual control while unfit, for example if he was home in bed for the night or a great distance from the car or if it was taken by another.

(b) If the defendant is not the owner, lawful possessor or recent driver, but is sitting in the vehicle or otherwise involved with it, the question will be whether he has assumed being in charge of it. He will have if he is voluntarily in actual control of the vehicle or if, in the circumstances, including his position, his intentions and his actions, he may be expected imminently to assume control. Usually this will involve his having gained entry to the car and having indicated an intention to take control. But gaining entry may not be necessary if he manifests that intention in some other way, for example by stealing the keys of a car in circumstances which show that he means to drive it.

Because more than one person can be in charge of a vehicle, someone sitting in a passenger seat supervising a learner driver is in charge of the vehicle.

The defence under s 5(2)   RTA 1988, s 5(2) provides that it is a defence for a person charged with 'being in charge of a motor vehicle', etc to prove that, at the time he is alleged to have committed the offence, the circumstances were such that there was no likelihood of his driving the vehicle whilst the proportion of alcohol in his breath, blood or urine remained likely to exceed the prescribed limit. In determining whether there was such a likelihood the court may disregard any injury to him and any damage to the vehicle (s 5(3)). Normally, the defendant (D) will only succeed in proving this defence if there is expert evidence as to the rate of alcohol destruction by the body which indicates that his alcohol level would not have been above the limit at the time he was likely to drive.

A divisional court has held that the defence is not primarily concerned with D's intentions, although they might be a factor to be considered. D's subjective intentions cannot be decisive in circumstances where he was affected by alcohol at a level well over the prescribed limit and had no means of knowing or proving when his alcohol levels had fallen below that limit.

The House of Lords has ruled that D bears a persuasive burden of proof of the s 5(2) defence (ie on the balance of probabilities).

Motor vehicle

See p 327.

Driving motor vehicle on a road or other public place

A divisional court has held that for a vehicle to be driven 'on' a road or other public place it is not necessary that its wheels should be on the road, etc or for the entirety of the vehicle to be on the road, etc. It is enough that the vehicle materially encroaches on the road. The court, therefore, upheld a conviction where the boot of a car being manoeuvred in a private driveway had projected into a road and collided with a car parked there.

After consuming so much alcohol that the proportion of it in breath, blood or urine exceeds the prescribed limit

'Consuming' is a wide enough term to include other methods of ingestion than through the mouth. Thus, for example, an alcohol level which may have, in part, resulted from the injection of a substance, comes about through 'consumption'.

The prescribed limits

These are defined by RTA 1988, s 11 which states that the 'prescribed limit' means, as the case may require:

(a) 35 microgrammes of alcohol in 100 millilitres of breath;
(b) 80 milligrammes of alcohol in 100 millilitres of blood; or
(c) 107 milligrammes of alcohol in 100 millilitres of urine,

or such other proportion as may be prescribed by regulations made by the Secretary of State. So far, the Secretary of State has not prescribed any other proportion.

The 35 microgrammes is roughly equivalent to the 80 and 107 milligrammes of the two other levels.

DRIVING, ETC WITH CONCENTRATION OF SPECIFIED CONTROLLED DRUG ABOVE SPECIFIED LIMIT

RTA 1988, s 5A(1) and (2) provides that it is an offence for a person:

(a) to drive or attempt to drive a motor vehicle on a road or other public place; or
(b) to be in charge of a motor vehicle on a road or other public place,

and there is in his body a specified controlled drug, if the proportion of the drug in his blood or urine exceeds the specified limit for that drug. 'Specified' means specified by regulation. The following controlled drugs and limits (expressed in microgrammes (µg) per litre (l) of blood) have been specified:

(i) Illicit drugs:
    Amphetamine, 250 µg/l
    Benzoylecgonine, 50 µg/l
    Cocaine, 10 µg/l
    Delta–9–Tetrahydrocannabinol (Cannabis and Cannabinol), 2 µg/l

Ketamine, 20 µg/l
Lysergic Acid Diethylamide (LSD), 1 µg/l
Methylamphetamine, 10 µg/l
Methylenedioxymethaphetamine (MDMA—Ecstasy), 10 µg/l
6-Monoacetylmorphine (6-MAM—Heroin and Diamorphine), 5 µg/l
(ii) Generally prescription drugs:
Clonazepam, 50 µg/l
Diazepam, 550 µg/l
Flunitrazepam, 300 µg/l
Lorazepam, 100 µg/l
Methadone, 500 µg/l
Morphine, 80 µg/l
Oxazepam, 300 µg/l
Temazepam, 1000 µg/l

It is a defence to a charge under s 5A for D to show that:

(a) the specified controlled drug had been prescribed or supplied to him for medical or dental purposes;
(b) he took the drug in accordance with any directions given by the person by whom the drug was prescribed or supplied, and with any accompanying instructions (so far as consistent with any such directions) given by the manufacturer or distributor of the drug; and
(c) his possession of the drug immediately before taking it was not unlawful under the Misuse of Drugs Act 1971, s 5 (restriction of possession of controlled drugs: p 869) because of an exemption under the Misuse of Drugs Regulations 2001 (s 5A(3)).

This defence is not available if D's actions were:

(i) contrary to any advice, given by the person by whom the drug was prescribed or supplied, about the amount of time that should elapse between taking the drug and driving a motor vehicle; or
(ii) contrary to any accompanying instructions about that matter (so far as consistent with any such advice) given by the manufacturer or distributor of the drug (s 5A(4)).

If evidence is adduced that is sufficient to raise an issue with respect to the above defence, the court must assume that the defence is satisfied unless the prosecution proves beyond reasonable doubt that it is not (s 5A(5)).

It is a defence to a charge of 'being in charge with an excess drug level' to prove that at the time that D is alleged to have committed the offence the circumstances were such that there was no likelihood of him driving the vehicle whilst the proportion of the specified controlled drug in his blood or urine remained likely to exceed the specified limit for that drug (s 5A(6)). In determining whether there was such a likelihood, the court may disregard any injury to D and any damage to the vehicle (s 5A(7)).

DRIVING, ETC UNDER INFLUENCE OF DRINK OR DRUGS

RTA 1988, s 4(1) and (2) provides that:

(1) A person who, when driving or attempting to drive a mechanically propelled vehicle on a road or other public place, is unfit to drive through drink or drugs is guilty of an offence.

(2) Without prejudice to subsection (1), a person who, when in charge of a mechanically propelled vehicle which is on a road or other public place, is unfit to drive through drink or drugs is guilty of an offence.

The charge must state whether the person was driving, attempting to drive or in charge.

Many of the elements of these offences have been dealt with already in relation to s 5. It is worth noting that s 4 applies to a mechanically propelled vehicle (see p 327), whereas ss 5 and 5A are limited to a motor vehicle, and that s 4(3) provides a similar defence for persons charged with 'being in charge' to that provided by ss 5(2) and 5A(7) for those charged with the corresponding offences under ss 5 and 5A, namely that it is a defence for the defendant to prove that there was no likelihood of his driving the vehicle while he remained unfit through drink or drugs.

It remains to be added that 'drink' means alcoholic drink and 'drug' means any intoxicant other than alcohol, including medicines and glue.

Unfitness to drive

Section 4(5) provides that a person is to be taken to be unfit to drive if his ability to drive properly is for the time being impaired. The evidence before the court on this point will normally include evidence of the defendant's driving before his vehicle was stopped; any evidence of driving apparently outside the pattern of normal driving is relevant in that it may show some impairment of the ability to drive properly. In addition, the evidence of the defendant's speech after he was stopped, together with his general manner and demeanour and any apparent lack of co-ordination or control over bodily movements, may be important. So may the result of a preliminary impairment test. The evidence before the court will also normally include the report of a medical examination by a medical practitioner, which is extremely important since the practitioner will have required the defendant to carry out a series of tests indicative of his ability (or lack of ability) to drive properly. Lastly, the evidence may include the result of the analysis of a specimen of breath, blood or urine required under s 7. The procedure relating to such specimens, and the rules relating to the use of their analysis as evidence, are essentially the same as for the offences of driving, etc with excess alcohol. It must be remembered that the presence of a drug can be detected by a blood or urine test, but not by a breath test.

PROCEDURE

The procedures which precede a person being charged with an offence under RTA 1988, s 5 are regulated by RTA 1988. These procedures may begin with a constable requiring a preliminary test, usually at the roadside, followed by an arrest (whether as a result of a positive test or of a failure to provide a breath specimen for it) which then must be followed by a requirement for a specimen of breath (for an evidential breath test) or, in limited cases, a specimen of blood or urine (for analysis) in order to get an indication of the proportion of alcohol in the person's breath, blood or urine. In such a case the specimen is required to be provided at a police station or hospital. However, amendments made in 2015 allow a constable to move directly to an evidential breath test at the roadside *when* a portable breath-testing device is available (as to which see p 518). Thus, although a constable can still administer a preliminary test as a means of establishing grounds for arrest, he will not have to do so if a portable testing device is available.

A charge under s 3A (causing death by careless driving when unfit through drink or drugs or with excess alcohol (p 493)) or s 4 will also normally be preceded by a preliminary test requirement, followed by an arrest and requirement for a breath, blood or urine specimen, except that in the case of a suspected drink-driver a constable can go straight to an evidential breath test. The same also applies where the suspected offence is drug-driving, with the variation that only a blood or urine specimen can be required.

PRELIMINARY TESTS

Under RTA 1988, s 6, there are three types of preliminary test whose purpose is to give an indication as to a defendant's 'impairment' in consequence of consumption of alcohol and/or of taking drugs, by means of a breath test, an impairment test or a drugs test.

Power to require preliminary tests

RTA 1988, s 6(1) provides that where any of s 6(2) to (5) applies, a constable may require a person to co-operate with one or more preliminary tests administered to that person by that constable or another.

Section 6(2) provides that such a test may be required *if a constable reasonably suspects that the person*:

(a) *is driving, is attempting to drive or is in charge of* a motor vehicle on a road or other public place; and
(b) *has alcohol or a drug in his body or is under the influence of a drug.*

Section 6(3) authorises a test where a constable *reasonably suspects* that the person:

(a) *has been driving, attempting to drive or in charge of* a motor vehicle on a road or other public place *while having alcohol or a drug in his body or while unfit to drive because of a drug*; and
(b) *still has alcohol or a drug in his body or is still under the influence of a drug.*

Section 6(4) authorises a test where a constable *reasonably suspects* that the person:

(a) *is or has been driving or attempting to drive or in charge of* a motor vehicle on a road or other public place; and
(b) *has committed a traffic offence while the vehicle was in motion.*

The type of traffic offence which the constable must reasonably suspect to have been committed is defined by s 6(8), which provides that 'traffic offence' in this context means an offence under any provision of the Public Passenger Vehicles Act 1981, Part II (fitness of vehicles and PSV operator's licence), the Road Traffic Regulation Act 1984 (RTRA 1984), the Road Traffic Offenders Act 1988 (RTOA 1988) except Part III (offences relating to fixed penalty procedures), or any provision of RTA 1988 except Part V (driving instruction for payment without being licensed or registered and other driving instructor offences). This effectively covers the range of road traffic offences which could be described as 'moving traffic offences'. All offences which are set out in regulations made under those Acts are also included within this description, for example offences contrary to the Road Vehicles (Construction and Use) Regulations 1986 or the Road Vehicles Lighting Regulations 1989.

Section 6(5) authorises a test if:

(a) *an accident occurs* owing to the presence of a motor vehicle on a road or other public place; and

(b) a constable *reasonably believes* that the person *was driving, attempting to drive or in charge of the vehicle at the time* of the accident.

The tests required (other than in the case of a test under s 6(5) (road traffic accidents)) may only be administered by a constable in uniform. Whether or not a constable was in uniform is a question of fact in each case. A constable wearing his uniform except for his helmet has been held to be in uniform so long as he is easily identifiable as a constable. A court is entitled to assume that a constable was in uniform unless this point is disproved.

The necessary suspicion or belief need not arise while the vehicle is in motion. Indeed, a uniformed constable may stop motorists, under his common law or statutory powers to do so, in order to see whether there is a reasonable suspicion that they have consumed alcohol, and if a reasonable suspicion then emerges of such consumption, go on to require a preliminary test. Thus, random stopping of motorists is not prohibited, although random preliminary tests are.

A constable does not have to administer a caution before requiring a preliminary test. It is only where the motorist has failed such a test (or failed to take it) that a caution needs to be administered.

Special circumstances which apply where an accident has occurred

As already stated, there is a power, under RTA 1988, s 6(5), to require a 'preliminary' test if an accident occurs owing to the presence of a motor vehicle on a road or other public place. A constable may require any person whom he has *reasonable cause to believe* was driving or attempting to drive or in charge of the vehicle at the time of the accident to provide a preliminary test, subject to s 9 (hospital procedure: p 525).

'Accident' in this context bears its ordinary meaning, and it has been held that a crash which is deliberately caused falls within that meaning. The person's vehicle need not have been physically involved but there must have been a direct causal connection between his vehicle being on the road and the accident occurring. Where a sequence of events begins on a road and leads to a vehicle leaving the road and colliding with an object some distance from the road, there is an accident for the purposes of s 6(5).

Of course, the fact that an accident has occurred owing to the presence of a motor vehicle on a road or other public place does not entitle a constable to require a specimen of breath under s 6(5) from anyone; that provision only empowers him to make such a requirement of any person whom he has *reasonable cause to believe was driving or attempting to drive or in charge of* the vehicle at the time of the accident.

The reader will remember that the power to require a breath specimen under the other provisions of s 6 is framed in terms of a constable having *reasonable cause to suspect* the specified things. In contrast, s 6(5) uses the term '*has reasonable cause to believe*', which requires more than 'reasonable suspicion' since 'believe' requires more than mere suspicion and refers to being virtually certain (ie having no substantial doubt) about the facts.

The nature of preliminary tests

Preliminary breath test

RTA 1988, s 6A provides that a preliminary breath test is a procedure whereby the person to whom the test is administered provides a specimen of breath to be used for the purpose of obtaining, by means of a device approved by the Secretary of State, an indication whether the proportion of alcohol in the person's breath or blood is likely to exceed the prescribed limit.

A preliminary breath test may be administered under s 6(2) to (4) only at or near the place where the requirement to co-operate with the test is imposed; where it is administered under s 6(5) (ie following an accident), it may be administered at or near that place or, if the constable who imposes the requirement thinks it expedient, at a police station specified by him.

Preliminary breath test devices used by police officers must be approved by the Secretary of State. Currently, the Secretary of State has approved two types of device, one which might be described as the 'blow in the bag' type of device and the other 'electronic'.

Approved devices of the 'blow in the bag' type are the Draeger Alcotest 80, the Alcotest R80A, and the Lion Alcolyser.

A number of electronic devices have been approved by the Secretary of State. There are various types of some of these devices (because new models have been approved as a particular device has been developed). In the following list the latest model of devices currently available is given: the Lion Alcolmeter 500 B, the Draeger Alcotest 6810 GB, the Intoximeter Alcosensor FST and the Envitec AlcoQuant 6020.

PACE Code C: The Code of Practice for the Detention, Treatment and Questioning of Persons by Police Officers, referred to in Chapter 4, excludes the 'specimens for analysis' procedures under RTA 1988, s 7 (p 516) from the provisions of the Code which relate to 'interviews'; no similar exclusion is made in relation to s 6 procedures. It is therefore advisable that, where there is conversation between an officer and a suspect which relates to his condition, that conversation is recorded and read and signed by the suspect. A divisional court, however, refused to interfere with a decision of the justices not to exclude evidence subsequently obtained following an officer's inquiry as to whether a suspect had been drinking, to which the suspect replied, 'Yes, I've had a couple of pints'. It said that the justices, although recognising that there had been a breach of Code C, were entitled to find that this breach had not been sufficiently 'significant and substantial' to merit exclusion of the evidence.

Nevertheless, care must be taken when engaging in conversation with drivers suspected of drink/drive offences. In one case police officers spoke to a man on three occasions, at his home prior to arrest and before caution; after his arrest and caution at his home; and in a police car, in the course of which he admitted that he had been to a funeral and had taken alcohol afterwards, that his last drink ('a couple of cans') had been taken at about 4 pm and that he had last driven his car at 5 pm and had not since taken a drink. It was held that these three conversations were 'interviews' for the purpose of Code C.

The preliminary impairment test

Such a test is designed to indicate whether a person is unfit to drive, and, if he is, whether or not this is due to drink or drugs.

RTA 1988, s 6B provides that a preliminary impairment test is a procedure whereby the constable administering the test observes the person to whom the test is administered in his performance of tests specified by the constable, and makes such other observations of the person's physical state as the constable thinks expedient. Section 6B requires that such tests may only be administered by a constable approved for the purpose by his chief officer of police. It may be administered at or near the place where the requirement to co-operate with the test is imposed or, if the constable who imposes the requirement thinks it expedient, at a police station specified by him.

Under s 6B the Secretary of State has issued the Code of Practice for Preliminary Impairment Tests for the use of constables trained and authorised to carry out such tests, to which a constable administering a preliminary impairment test must have regard. The Code of Practice sets the kind of task that may be specified for the purpose of such a preliminary impairment test, the kind of observation of physical state that may be made in the course of it, the manner in which it should be administered and the inferences that may be drawn from observations made in the course of it.

The preliminary test procedure set out in the Code of Practice comprises:

(a) a pupillary examination;
(b) the modified Romberg balance test;
(c) the walk and turn test;
(d) the one-leg stand test;
(e) the finger-to-nose test.

Details about these tests and their execution are set out in Chapter 15 on the companion website.

A constable may decide, in consequence of these tests, that there is sufficient evidence to justify an arrest on reasonable suspicion of an offence under RTA 1988, ss 3A or 4 (pp 493 and 508). There is no pass/fail standard, nor a scoring system. A decision must be based upon overall observation during the tests and the records made of those performances.

The preliminary drugs test

This is dealt with by RTA 1988, s 6C. A preliminary drugs test is a procedure by which a specimen of sweat or saliva is obtained and used for the purpose of obtaining, by means of a device of a type approved by the Secretary of State, an indication whether the person to whom the test is administered has a drug in his body and if so:

(a) whether it is a specified controlled drug;
(b) if it is, whether the proportion of it in the person's blood or urine is likely to exceed the specified limit for that drug.

It may be administered at or near the place where the requirement to co-operate with the test is imposed or, if the constable who imposes the requirement thinks it expedient, at a police station specified by him.

Up to three preliminary drug tests may be administered.

The Secretary of State has approved two devices for the purposes of s 6C: the Draeger DrugTest 5000 and Securetec DrugWipe 3S S303G, both of which test a saliva sample. Both types of device have been approved for use to administer a mobile preliminary drug test, either in a police station or at or near the place where the test-requirement is made, for the purpose of obtaining an indication whether a person has THC (the active ingredient in cannabis) or cocaine in his body.

Arrest

Positive preliminary breath test or drug test

RTA 1988, s 6D(1) provides that a constable may arrest a person without warrant if as a result of a preliminary breath test or preliminary drug test the constable reasonably suspects that:

(a) the proportion of alcohol in the person's breath or blood exceeds the prescribed limit; or

(b) the person has a specified controlled drug in his body and the proportion of it in the person's blood or urine exceeds the specified limit for that drug.

The suspect must be requested co-operate with a preliminary breath test before he can be arrested under s 6D, even if his conduct makes this difficult. Where an officer is assaulted by the suspect and thus prevented from making a proper request, the suspect should be arrested under another appropriate provision. The fact that evidential specimens of breath have been provided under s 7 (see p 516) by the person concerned does not prevent s 6D(1) having effect if the constable who imposed on him the requirement to provide the specimens has reasonable cause to believe that the device used to analyse the specimens has not produced a reliable indication of the proportion of alcohol in the breath of that person (s 6D(1A)).

Failure to co-operate

By RTA 1988, s 6D(2), a constable may arrest a person without warrant if:

(a) the person fails to co-operate with a *preliminary test* in pursuance of a requirement imposed under s 6, and
(b) *the constable reasonably suspects that the person has alcohol or a drug in his body or is under the influence of a drug.*

Section 11(2) provides that 'fails' includes 'refusal'. If a person is given an opportunity to do something and does not do it, there is a failure to comply with that request. Where a person refuses to reply to such a clear request, there has been a failure and it is no defence to allege that the refusal to reply was consequent upon a previous caution. It is essential that the constable makes it clear to the person concerned that he is required to co-operate in the test.

In a case where a driver refused to wait until a preliminary breath test device arrived at the scene, having been properly required to provide a specimen, it was held that he had failed to provide a specimen of breath. A demand that a test be deferred until the arrival of a solicitor amounts to a refusal. There can be no acceptance subject to conditions.

Section 11(3) provides that a person does not co-operate with a preliminary test unless his co-operation is sufficient to enable the test to be carried out, and is provided in such a way as to enable the objective of the test to be satisfactorily achieved. The importance of this can be shown by reference to the preliminary breath test. The various preliminary breath test devices require breath to be supplied in various ways to allow a sufficient sample to be obtained. If sufficient breath has not been supplied there has been a failure. Where a preliminary breath test device requires the illumination of two lights before a satisfactory specimen has been obtained, there is a 'failure' where only one of those lights is illuminated and a police officer is not required to 'read' such a specimen.

An important point to note about the power to arrest after a failure to co-operate is that, before effecting an arrest, the constable must have reasonable cause to suspect that the person has alcohol or a drug in his body or is under the influence of a drug.

General

Section 6D(2A) provides that a person arrested under s 6D, instead of being taken to a police station, be detained at or near the place where the preliminary test was, or would have been administered, with a view to imposing on him there a requirement for an evidential test under RTA 1988, s 7. Thus, a means is provided to carry out an evidential test at the roadside as an alternative to taking the person concerned to a police station.

Clear words must be used in all cases to indicate the reason for arrest and that the person concerned is being compulsorily taken to a police station in consequence of such a failure.

Normally, a constable will exercise his power of arrest but this is not a pre-condition of further steps in the procedure being adopted and is unnecessary if the person concerned is quite happy to proceed to the next stage in the procedure.

No arrest of hospital patient

A person may *not* be arrested under s 6D *while at hospital as a patient* (RTA 1988, s 6D(3)).

Power of entry

By RTA 1988, s 6E a constable may enter any place (using reasonable force if necessary) for the purpose of:

(a) imposing a preliminary test requirement by virtue of s 6(5) following an accident in a case where the constable reasonably suspects that the accident involved injury of any person; or

(b) arresting a person under s 6D following an accident in a case where the constable reasonably suspects that the accident involved injury of any person.

It must be emphasised that, with the one exception in (a), police officers do not have power to enter a place without the express or implied consent of the occupier for the purpose of requiring a preliminary breath, impairment or drug test. Likewise, police officers, with the one exception in (b), do not have power to enter a place without the express or implied consent of the occupier for the purpose of making an arrest under s 6D.

Offence of failure to co-operate with a preliminary test under s 6

RTA 1988, s 6(6) provides that a person commits an offence if without reasonable excuse he fails to co-operate with a preliminary test in pursuance of a requirement imposed under s 6. This offence can be committed notwithstanding that the defendant has not been warned that refusal to co-operate will be an offence. Such warning is not required.

As to what constitutes a 'failure to co-operate', see p 514. There cannot be a conviction for this offence unless the co-operation has been required under s 6, and it will not have been so required if the requirement made is invalid for some reason. For example, if the constable is a trespasser at the time of requiring a preliminary breath test he will be behaving unlawfully and his requirement will not be valid.

In addition, where there is a preliminary breath test, there cannot be a conviction for failing to provide a specimen if the requisite procedure is not validly administered, as will be the case if the device used is not an approved one, or if it is defective or if the constable fails to comply with the manufacturer's instructions as to *assembly*. However, if the constable realises the defect or mistake he may validly require another breath test to be taken on another device. Provided the constable acts in good faith and not negligently, non-compliance by him with the manufacturer's instructions as to the use of the device does not invalidate the test unless the non-compliance is prejudicial to the defendant.

A person cannot be convicted of failing to co-operate with a preliminary test unless his failure was without reasonable excuse. It is not a reasonable excuse that the defendant (D) did not think that he had consumed any alcohol, nor that he mistakenly believed that the test requirement was invalid, nor that he had consumed alcohol after driving.

It has been stated in a number of cases that no excuse can be adjudged reasonable unless D was physically or mentally unable to provide the specimen or its provision would entail a substantial risk to his health, as where D was unable to supply a sufficient specimen of breath because of a medical condition, or where he was concussed and unable to appreciate the requirement made of him. However, it has also been held that a foreigner who is unable to understand the purpose of the requirement and the penal consequence of a failure to comply has a reasonable excuse. Not surprisingly, someone who has made himself too drunk to understand these matters does not have a reasonable excuse, nor does someone who fails to provide a specimen because he is in a state of self-induced agitation. See also p 529.

PROVISION OF SPECIMEN FOR ANALYSIS

RTA 1988, s 7(1) provides that, in the course of an investigation into whether a person has committed an offence under ss 3A, 4 or 5, a constable may, subject to the other provisions of s 7 (below) and of s 9 (p 525), require him to provide:

(a) two specimens of breath for analysis by means of a device of an approved type, known as an 'evidential breath test' (s 7(1)(a)); or
(b) a specimen of blood or urine for a laboratory test (s 7(1)(b)).

Section 7(1A) provides that, in the course of an investigation into whether a person has committed an offence under s 5A, a constable may, subject to ss 7(3)–(7) and 9, require the person to provide a specimen of blood or urine for a laboratory test.

No need for prior preliminary test or arrest

The fact that a requirement under ss 7(1) or 7(1A) can be made 'in the course of an investigation' into whether a person has committed an offence under ss 3A, 4, 5 or 5A indicates that it is not necessary that a preliminary test should have been required (indeed, as indicated on p 509, it may well not have been required where the investigation relates to drink-driving and a portable evidential breath-testing device is available (as to which see p 518)) and that, if there has been such a test, it is irrelevant that there has been some breach in the procedure relating to it.

For the procedure under s 7 to apply it is irrelevant that the person concerned has not been arrested, or that he has been arrested on reasonable suspicion of driving, etc while unfit through drink or drugs or on reasonable suspicion of a non-drink/drive offence, or that he has been unlawfully arrested. Thus, if a driver reports an accident at a police station, and it is suspected that he has drugs in his body, he may be required to provide specimens for analysis. If someone is the subject of an investigation into whether an offence under ss 3A, 4, 5 or 5A has been committed by him, a specimen may be required under s 7. In addition, a person who alleges that he was a passenger, not the driver of a car, at the time in question, may lawfully be required to provide a specimen as a person under an investigation for an offence under ss 3A, 4, 5 or 5A. It is not necessary to show that he was driving or in charge. Although, of course, liability for an offence under ss 3A, 4, 5 or 5A will depend on proof that he was driving, attempting to drive, or in charge at the material time, he can be convicted under s 7 of failing to provide a specimen even if he was not driving, etc.

As already stated, the procedure under s 7 does not constitute an 'interview' for the purposes of PACE Code C. However, under PACE, s 78, the evidence obtained from the analysis of a specimen can be excluded if it appears to the court that, having regard to all the circumstances, including non-compliance with the preliminary test procedure under s 6, the admission of that evidence would have such an adverse effect on the fairness of the proceedings that the court ought not to admit it. Section 78 was so applied in a case where a preliminary test was improperly required (because the officer did not have one of the requisite reasonable suspicions specified by RTA 1988, s 6). A divisional court held that, since D had been denied the protection afforded by s 6, the prosecutor had obtained evidence which he would not otherwise have obtained and, as a result, D was significantly prejudiced in resisting the charge. The magistrates, it held, were therefore entitled to exclude the evidence.

We now turn to the procedure to be adopted under s 7; it should be noted that where the person in question is a patient at a hospital a special procedure, governed by s 9 (p 525), must be followed. It should also be noted that, because time is of the essence, it is only where the delay would be very short that the procedure can be delayed to enable the person to obtain legal advice. The courts have held that, except in such a case: (a) evidence obtained under the procedure will not have been obtained in breach of PACE, s 58, and (b) there will be no reasonable excuse should the person fail to provide a specimen.

Breath specimens

In terms of an investigation into whether an alcohol-related offence under RTA 1988, s 3A or 4, or an offence under s 5, has been committed, the important part of the procedure under s 7(1) is s 7(1)(a) whereby a constable may require two specimens of *breath*. It is only in exceptional circumstances that alternative samples may be required under s 7(1)(b).

Where breath specimens can be required

Section 7(2) provides that a constable may make a requirement under s 7 to provide specimens of breath only if:

(a) the requirement is made at a police station or a hospital;
(b) the requirement is imposed in circumstances where s 6(5) (p 510: after an accident) applies; or
(c) the constable is in uniform.

By s 7(2C), where a constable has imposed a requirement on the person concerned to co-operate with a preliminary breath test *at any place*, he is entitled to remain at or near that place in order to impose on him there a requirement under s 7.

Section 7(2D) provides that if a requirement under s 7(1)(a) has been made at a place other than a police station, such a requirement may subsequently be made at a police station if (but only if):

(a) a device or a reliable device of the type mentioned in s 7(1)(a) was not available at that place or it was for any other reason not practicable to use such a device there, or

(b) the constable who made the previous requirement has reasonable cause to believe that the device used there has not produced a reliable indication of the proportion of alcohol in the breath of the person concerned.

The result of the analysis of a roadside evidential breath specimen is admissible in evidence to the same extent as the analysis of a specimen at a police station.

By s 7(5A), a constable may arrest a person without warrant if:

(a) the person fails to provide a specimen of breath when required to do so in pursuance of s 7; and

(b) the constable reasonably suspects that the person has alcohol in his body.

This is of obvious importance where there has not been a preliminary test followed by an arrest.

A constable requiring a person to provide a breath specimen under s 7 is required by s 7(7) to warn him that a failure to supply it may result in his prosecution. The results of a breath test under s 7 taken in the absence of a warning are inadmissible, even if no prejudice to the person results from the lack of a warning.

Specimen of breath

RTA 1988, s 7 requires that the two specimens of breath which have been required under it be analysed by means of a device approved by the Secretary of State. Someone who has provided one specimen of breath which exceeded the prescribed limit but has failed to provide a second specimen cannot, on the basis of that specimen, be convicted of driving with excess alcohol. He can, however, be convicted of failing to provide a specimen of breath (p 529).

Section 11(3) provides that a person does not provide a specimen of breath for analysis unless his co-operation is sufficient to enable the analysis to be carried out, and is provided in such a way as to enable the objective of the analysis to be satisfactorily achieved. This is an important provision, as it is necessary for the person providing the specimen to continue blowing until the indicator lights signify that sufficient breath has been obtained for analysis. If sufficient is not provided, there has been a 'failure'.

For the purposes of the legislation relating to the provision of 'specimens of breath', 'breath' does not mean deep-lung air but should be given its ordinary dictionary definition, ie 'air exhaled from anywhere'; therefore there is no need for the prosecution to prove that the reading from an approved device related solely to deep-lung alcohol and was not related to mouth alcohol.

The following are approved evidential breath testing devices: Camic Datamaster; Lion Intoxilyzer 6000 UK; Intoximeter EC/IR. At the time of writing no portable evidential breath testing device had been approved.

Analysis of breath by approved devices

Procedure   The devices have been designed to overcome the problems likely to arise from an evidential viewpoint. At the outset the devices are correctly calibrated but in actual use the devices check themselves for accuracy. They check their correct calibration both before and after each of the two breath samples and a record is made of those calibration checks on the eventual print-out slip. The slip therefore shows two separate readings of alcohol levels sandwiched between records of calibration checks to ensure that the devices are operating correctly. The defendant is present throughout the procedure and has the opportunity to see the device at work. The officer carrying out the test is not obliged to explain to the defendant that the second specimen must be provided within three minutes of the first, or the test will abort.

The devices provide a timed and dated print-out which gives evidence of two separate readings of alcohol content in the breath of the defendant. The normal procedure thereafter is that the constable who has operated the device certifies all copies of the print-out, which shows, in addition to the readings, the particulars of the person from whom the sample is obtained, the signature of the officer, and the signature of the person (or a record that such a signature was refused). The constable's statement declares the lower of the two readings given by the device to be at the specified level and certifies that copies of the statement were signed by him and by the defendant, or that the defendant refused. Where a print-out is not produced in evidence and no oral evidence is given in relation to correct calibration, it is open to a court to find that calibration was correct where there is evidence that the machine was used by a trained operator.

The devices are computers. In the absence of evidence to the contrary, courts will presume that the computer system was working correctly. If there is evidence that it might not have been, the party seeking to introduce the evidence will need to prove that it was working. It is therefore desirable that police officers record on the appropriate procedural forms the fact that the computer was operating correctly, together with any appropriate observations.

The officer also certifies that he handed a copy of the statement to the defendant who accepted, or declined to accept it. The mere fact that the copy handed to the defendant is not signed by the officer does not affect the validity of the original. RTOA 1988, s 16(3) requires that a copy is either 'handed to' a defendant at the time, or is served upon him not later than seven days before the hearing. Where a defendant signed all the copies of the statement but refused to accept one, a divisional court held that s 16(3) had been complied with when the defendant was offered a copy although there had been no physical transfer of possession of the document. Nevertheless, it will be good practice in such circumstances subsequently to serve a copy of the statement upon the defendant in accordance with s 16(3).

Evidence, however, of the test is not restricted to documentary evidence. Oral evidence may be given of the results of a test should the prosecutor, for some reason, choose not to use the simplified procedure. If this is done, oral evidence of calibration should also be given. It will be advisable, in such cases, to serve a copy of the evidence of the police operator on the defendant in accordance with the Criminal Justice Act 1967, s 9. A divisional court has said that, where an officer is giving oral evidence of the result of an analysis, there is no difference between those results having been seen on the screen, and seen on a print-out.

Defence lawyers have no right to obtain documents kept in relation to breath-analysis devices, such as the log, repair reports and memory roll, with a view to searching for material which might support a submission that the device was defective. They must rely upon the prosecution to carry out its duty to disclose material evidence which might be of assistance to the defence. The reliability of the approved device which has been used can be challenged either by direct evidence of some malfunctioning or by evidence from which the inference of unreliability can reasonably be drawn. On the other hand, the reliability of the device used cannot be challenged on grounds relating to all devices of the prescribed type because the type of device has been approved by the Secretary of State.

Only the lower reading is evidence RTA 1988, s 8 provides that it is only the lower of the two readings given by the machine which may be used as evidence; the other must be disregarded. Where one of the two required readings is not obtained within the same operating cycle of the machine, a second cycle must be commenced. In such a case it is the lower specimen in the first cycle taken and the first of the second cycle which should be recognised. However, where neither of the specimens in the first cycle is valid, a second cycle is undertaken and third and fourth specimens are, effectively, the first and second specimens recognised by the machine.

Where only one satisfactory specimen of breath has been obtained due to a failure of the breath-analysis machine and, in consequence, an alternative blood or urine specimen has been obtained and a charge has been preferred alleging an excess of alcohol in that alternative specimen, evidence of the proportion of alcohol found in the one specimen of breath is inadmissible, as it is not relevant to a charge of excess alcohol in another specimen. However, where the accuracy of the analysis of the alternative specimen is challenged, the prosecution is required to prove beyond reasonable doubt that the blood/urine analysis was reliable and if the breath test result is broadly equivalent to the analysis of the alternative specimen then, notwithstanding the reason for requiring the alternative specimen, such evidence is at least capable of tending to support the reliability of the analysis of the alternative specimen. Provided that the significance of the relationship between the two analyses is explained by an expert, the evidence may be relevant.

Blood or urine specimens

RTA 1988, s 7(3) provides that a requirement (p 516) to provide a specimen of *blood* or *urine* can only be made at a *police station* or at a *hospital*; and that it cannot be made at a police station unless:

(a) the constable making the requirement has reasonable cause to believe that for medical reasons a specimen of breath cannot be provided (because of inability) or should not be required (for some other reason, such as the taking of a drug which affects blood/alcohol levels). Provided that a reasonable cause to believe that there are medical reasons exists, it is irrelevant that the constable himself does not believe that for medical reasons a breath specimen cannot be provided or should not be required. The constable is not required to seek medical advice; the question is whether on the facts before the constable he had reasonable cause to believe that medical reasons exist;

(b) specimens of breath have not been provided elsewhere and, at the time the requirement is made, an approved device or a reliable approved evidential breath testing device is not available at the police station or it is then for any other reason not practicable to use such a device there;

(c) an approved evidential breath testing device has been used (at the police station or elsewhere) but the constable who required the specimen of breath has reasonable cause to believe that the device has not produced a reliable indication of the proportion of alcohol in the breath of the person concerned;

(d) as a result of the administration of a preliminary drug test, the constable making the requirement has reasonable cause to believe that the person required to provide a specimen of blood or urine has a drug in his body; or

(e) the suspected offence is one under ss 3A, 4 or 5A and the constable making the requirement has been advised by a medical practitioner or registered health care professional (as defined on p 522), hereafter 'practitioner or health care professional', that the condition of the person required to provide the specimen might be due to some drug;

but may then be made notwithstanding that the person required to provide the specimen has already provided or been required to provide two specimens of breath.

The fact that the constable has been advised by a practitioner or health care professional that the person's condition may be due to some drug may be proved by oral evidence from the practitioner or health care professional or by the police officer testifying to what the practitioner or health care professional said to him. In addition, where unchallenged evidence has been given by the custody officer as to what the practitioner or health care professional said and did and as to his completion of a procedural form recording the signed observations of the practitioner or health care professional, justices are entitled to find that this advice had been given. While an endorsement signed by the practitioner or health care professional is, in its contents, hearsay, the fact that a practitioner had signed the endorsement and said things which led the officer to complete the remainder of the form in a particular way, indicating that it was concerned with impairment through drugs after medical advice, has been held to be a matter to which the justices were entitled to have regard.

Reliable approved device not available or not practicable to use it

A 'reliable device' referred to in (b) is one which the police officer concerned reasonably believes to be reliable. The police officer must reasonably believe that no approved, reliable device *is* available. Where a police officer thought that the available device might be unreliable, because the defendant did not appear to be as badly affected as the device indicated, and required an alternative specimen, the conviction was quashed on the grounds that a belief that the device might be unreliable is insufficient. It is 'not practicable to use a device' if there is no officer available at the station who has been trained to use the device.

Where a suspect has provided two specimens of breath on a machine which is then found to be defective, he may lawfully be required to provide two further specimens of breath for analysis by another device instead of being required to provide blood or urine. Where this involves a suspect being taken to another police station, a divisional court has said that it might be wise, *as a matter of an abundance of caution*, to repeat, at the second police station, the statutory warning that failure may render him liable to prosecution.

Unreliable indication reasonably believed

Under (c) an alternative specimen may be required where a breath-analysis device has been used and the constable who required the specimens has reasonable cause to believe that the device has not produced a *reliable indication* of the proportion of alcohol in the breath of the person concerned. Thus, if a device produces two readings which indicate significant differences in the levels of alcohol, it is open to the constable to require an alternative specimen if he reasonably believes that the device has not produced a reliable indication of alcohol in the breath. The latest breath-analysis devices incorporate new software which enables them to identify and flag up automatically where it is suspected an interfering substance may be present, or the alleged offender produces mouth alcohol, or the difference between the readings of two specimens is greater than 15 per cent. In such situations a constable will be able to require blood or urine as an alternative.

Reliance on the guidance contained in procedural instructions about the use of breath-analysis devices, which leads to the conclusion that an indication is unreliable, will mean that the constable has reasonable grounds to believe that the device has not produced a reliable reading.

It has been held that, where the constable has reasonable cause to suspect that the unreliable indication is due not to the unreliability of the device but to the way in which the individual provided the breath specimens, the officer may offer the individual the opportunity to provide further breath specimens (instead of requiring him to provide a blood or urine specimen).

Decision as to blood or urine

RTA 1988, s 7(4) provides that, if the provision of a specimen other than a specimen of breath may be required in pursuance of s 7, the question whether it is to be a specimen of blood or a specimen of urine and, in the case of a specimen of blood, the question who is to be asked to take it shall be decided (subject to s 7(4A)) by the constable making the requirement. The limitation in s 7(4A) is that there must be no requirement to provide a blood specimen if:

(a) the medical practitioner who is asked to take the specimen is of the opinion that, for medical reasons, it cannot or should not be taken; or

(b) the registered health care professional who is asked to take it is of that opinion and there is no contrary opinion from a medical practitioner.

A 'registered health care professional' is a registered nurse, or a registered member of a health care profession designated by an order made by the Secretary of State. A registered paramedic is so designated. If the constable knows of a medical reason affecting this issue he must pass on that knowledge.

Section 7(4A) also provides that where, by virtue of s 7(4A), there can be no requirement to provide a specimen of blood, the constable may require a specimen of urine instead.

Where a constable requires blood as an alternative and the person required to give blood refuses but offers urine as an alternative, there is a 'failure' to provide a specimen as required under s 7 unless a medical reason exists.

Information to be given to suspect

On requiring a person to provide a specimen of blood or urine, a constable:

(a) must warn him that a failure to provide it may render him liable to prosecution; and

(b) state the reason why a breath specimen cannot be taken or used.

Both requirements (the first made by s 7(7) and the second by the House of Lords) are mandatory; non-compliance with either of them renders the analysis of a blood or urine specimen inadmissible, even if no prejudice to the person results from the absence of a warning.

In addition, in order to ensure that the person is aware of the role of the medical practitioner or registered health care professional, the constable should tell him that it is for the constable to decide whether the specimen is to be of blood or urine and, if (as is usually the case) the constable decides to require blood, ask the person if there are any medical reasons why a blood specimen cannot or should not be taken from him by a medical practitioner or registered health care professional. Failure to do so will not lead to a dismissal of the charge unless the court has a reasonable doubt as to whether or not the person was prejudiced by not being told about the role of the practitioner or professional. Thus, for example, if he was aware that a practitioner would take the blood specimen, the charge will not be dismissed.

The House of Lords has held that there is no statutory requirement, nor any consideration of fairness, which requires a police officer to ask a suspect if any non-medical reason exists in consequence of which a specimen of blood should not be taken. Any such matter might support 'a reasonable excuse for failure to provide a specimen' but that is a matter for a court.

There is no need to give the person a chance to indicate his preference as to the alternatives of blood or urine.

Where a medical reason is given (for example that the suspect is taking tablets) there must be evidence that the police officer took this into account or had considered whether it could be a medical reason. Although medical possibilities might appear to be far-fetched, it is impossible to *know* that this is so. There must be evidence that the officer has asked questions. Where a 'medical reason' offered is capable of being valid the officer must refer the matter to a medical practitioner or registered health care professional. If he does not, a requirement will not have been made pursuant to the Act and evidence of the resulting analysis will be inadmissible.

Taking of blood specimen

RTA 1988, s 11(4) provides that a person supplies a specimen of blood if and only if:

(a) he consents to the taking of such a specimen from him; and
(b) the specimen is taken from him by a medical practitioner or by a registered health care professional.

Specimens of blood taken from a person incapable of consenting

RTA 1988, s 7A deals with the taking of blood specimens from a person who has been involved in an accident and is, for some reason, incapable of giving a valid consent to the taking of a specimen of blood.

Section 7A(1) provides that a constable may request a medical practitioner or registered health care professional (hereafter 'practitioner') to take a specimen of blood from a person ('the person concerned') irrespective of whether that person consents if:

(a) that person is a person from whom the constable would (in the absence of any incapacity of that person and of any objection under s 9 referred to on p 525) be entitled under s 7 to require the provision of a specimen of blood for a laboratory test;
(b) it appears to that constable that this person has been involved in an accident which constitutes or is comprised in the matter that is under investigation or the circumstances of that matter;
(c) it appears to that constable that this person is or may be incapable (whether or not he has purported to do so) of giving a valid consent to the taking of a specimen of blood; and
(d) it appears to that constable that this person's incapacity is attributable to medical reasons.

Section 7A(2) provides that a request under s 7A:

(a) must not be made to a practitioner who for the time being has any responsibility (apart from the request) for the clinical care of the person concerned; and
(b) must not be made to a practitioner other than a police practitioner unless:
    (i) it is not reasonably practicable for the request to be made to a police practitioner; or

(ii) it is not reasonably practicable for such a practitioner (assuming him to be willing to do so) to take the specimen.

A 'police practitioner' is a medical practitioner or registered health care professional who is engaged under any agreement to provide medical or health care services for purposes connected with the activities of a police force.

By s 7A(3), it is lawful for a practitioner (as defined above) to whom a request is made:

(a) to take a specimen of blood from the person concerned irrespective of whether that person consents; and
(b) to provide the sample to a constable.

Section 7A(4) states that, if a specimen is taken pursuant to a request under s 7A, the specimen must not be subjected to a laboratory test unless the person from whom it was taken:

(a) has been informed that it was taken; and
(b) has been required by a constable to give his permission for a laboratory test of the specimen; and
(c) has given his permission.

On requiring a person to give permission for the purposes of s 7A for a laboratory test of a specimen, a constable is required by s 7A(5) to warn him that a failure to give the permission may render him liable to prosecution.

It is an offence under s 7A(6) for a person, without reasonable excuse, to fail to give permission for a laboratory test of a specimen of blood taken from him under s 7A. It is a defence that a warning was not given under s 7A(5) or has not been understood by the person in question.

Other provisions about blood or urine specimens

Blood   If a specimen of blood is taken, RTOA 1988, s 15(4) provides that a specimen of blood must be disregarded unless:

(a) it was taken from the defendant (D) with his consent by a medical practitioner or a registered health care professional (hereafter a 'practitioner'); or
(b) it was taken from D by a practitioner under RTA 1988, s 7A and D subsequently gave his permission for a laboratory test of the specimen.

Evidence that a specimen of blood was taken from D with his consent by a practitioner may be given by the production of a document purporting to certify that fact and to be signed by a practitioner.

Urine   A urine specimen must, by RTA 1988, s 7(5), be provided within one hour of the requirement and after the provision of a previous specimen. This means that a specimen must be taken and discarded, and another provided (for analysis) within one hour of the requirement. A police officer is not obliged to extend the time but, if he does accept a second specimen of urine outside the time limit, the result of the analysis of that specimen is nevertheless admissible. It has been held that a constable is entitled to require a specimen of urine where, the breath-analysis device being inoperable, he had required blood but a doctor was unable to obtain such a specimen when the defendant's vein collapsed. The rule is that an unproductive request for one specimen (ie the specimen is not provided) does not prevent a subsequent request for another specimen from being valid.

A divisional court has held that, where a urine sample is taken from someone who is catheterised, a specimen is provided for the purposes of s 7(5) each time the catheter bag is emptied, rather than at the point the urine leaves the body.

Providing D with part of specimen   RTOA 1988, s 15(5) provides that, where (at the time a blood or urine specimen was provided by D) D asked to be provided with such a specimen, evidence of the proportion of alcohol or any drug found in the specimen is inadmissible on behalf of the prosecution unless:

(a) the specimen is one of two parts into which the specimen was divided at the time it was provided; and
(b) the other part was supplied to D.

'At the time' does not mean 'then and there' nor 'in the presence of D'. It suffices that the division is closely linked in time and part of the same event as the taking of the sample. It is, however, desirable that the division takes place in D's presence. There is no obligation to inform D that he may request part of the specimen. Provided that at his request the specimen has been divided and one part has been offered to him, it is irrelevant that he does not take up the offer; the statutory requirement is satisfied, and evidence of the alcohol level in the part retained by the police is admissible. Where someone is not in a position to take receipt of the second part of a sample, it may be provided to him for present purposes by handing it to someone else for safe-keeping.

RTOA 1988, s 15(5A) provides that, where a specimen was taken under RTA 1988, s 7A, evidence of the proportion of alcohol or any drug found in the specimen is not admissible on behalf of the prosecution unless:

(a) the specimen in which the alcohol or drug was found is one of two parts into which it was divided at the time it was taken; and
(b) any request to be supplied with the other part of the specimen taken from D, which was made by him when he gave his permission for a laboratory test of the specimen, was complied with.

Labelling   When a specimen of blood or urine has been obtained, the labels identifying it with that person must be carefully made out and attached securely to the specimen which must then be sent to the forensic science laboratory.

HOSPITAL PATIENTS

RTA 1988, s 9 lays down a special procedure which applies while a person is at a hospital as a patient.

Section 9(1) states that, while a person is at a hospital as a patient, he must not be required to co-operate with a preliminary test or to provide a specimen under RTA 1988, s 7 unless the medical practitioner in immediate charge of his case has been notified of the proposal to make the requirement, and:

(a) if the requirement is made, it must be for co-operation with a test administered, or for the provision of a specimen, at the hospital; but
(b) if the medical practitioner objects on the ground specified in s 9(2) (below), the requirement must not be made.

This procedure is concerned with whether the practitioner objects to a preliminary test of, or a specimen being provided by, a patient, and not whether the practitioner objects to a particular type of test or specimen.

Section 9(1A) provides that, while a person is at a hospital as a patient, no specimen of blood may be taken from him under s 7A (person incapable of consenting) and he must not be required to give his permission for a laboratory test of a specimen taken under s 7A unless the medical practitioner in immediate charge of his case:

(a) has been notified of the proposal to take the specimen or to make the requirement; and
(b) has not objected on the ground specified in s 9(2).

By s 9(2), the ground on which the medical practitioner may object is:

(a) in a case within s 9(1), that the requirement or the provision of the specimen or (if one is required) the warning required by s 7(7) (p 518) would be prejudicial to the proper care and treatment of the patient; and
(b) in a case within s 9(1A), that the taking of the specimen, the requirement or the warning required by s 7A(5) (p 524) would be so prejudicial.

If the medical practitioner objects on the ground that the requirement, or the provision of a specimen, or the warning about the consequences of failing to provide it would be prejudicial to the proper care and treatment of the patient, the requirement in question must not be made.

It should be noted that if a preliminary test undergone by a patient proves positive, or he fails to undergo it, he may not be arrested, but this does not prejudice the rest of the procedure being followed (s 6D(3)).

It is not strictly necessary to obtain a preliminary test before requiring a specimen for analysis but an explanatory circular states that it is assumed that this will be done. It is good practice to give a person the opportunity quickly to clear himself of suspicion.

Where a requirement to provide a specimen of blood has been made at a hospital but the patient is discharged before the specimen can be taken, that requirement is not varied or discharged by the mere fact that the person to whom the requirement was made is then taken to a police station. The specimen of blood may be taken there. The only exception is if a police officer abrogates the procedure started at the hospital by asking for breath specimens and thereby setting in train the procedure under s 7.

EVIDENCE IN PROSECUTIONS UNDER ROAD TRAFFIC ACT 1988, ss 3A, 4, 5 OR 5A

By RTOA 1988, s 15(2), evidence of the proportion of alcohol or any drug in a specimen of breath, blood or urine provided by or taken from D must, in all cases, be taken into account and it *must be assumed*:

(a) that the proportion of alcohol in D's breath, blood or urine at the time of the alleged offence was not less than in the specimen;
(b) that the proportion of a drug in D's blood or urine at the time of the alleged offence was not less than in the specimen.

Evidence of a breath, blood or urine specimen is not the only admissible evidence. The result is, for example, that, if the analysis or test reveals a proportion of alcohol below the prescribed limit, but the magistrates are sure from expert evidence that, given the lapse of time between the alleged offence and the provision of the specimen, the proportion of alcohol at the time of the alleged offence was over the prescribed limit, they may convict D of an offence under ss 3A, 4 or 5. On the other hand, since D's alcohol level *must be assumed to be not less* than that found in the sample, he is not permitted to adduce evidence at trial that, although above the limit when the specimen was taken, he was below it when actually driving.

The assumption made by s 15(2) does not apply if there is evidence that the evidential device was unreliable or that a blood or urine specimen is unreliable (eg because analysis of the part given to D is below the limit). A divisional court held that justices can assume that a device was reliable unless there is evidence that it was not, and that if there is evidence that a device was unreliable the prosecution are obliged to prove its reliability. Presumably, the same approach as taken in that case applies where the challenge is to the reliability of a blood or urine specimen. Evidence relating to unreliability may be direct evidence, but—depending on the disparity between the claimed consumption and the analysis—evidence of the unreliability may be provided by reference to the amount of alcohol allegedly consumed before the specimen was provided. Expert evidence of the reading which could be produced in the circumstances by D is not essential.

Although s 15 says that the proportion of alcohol or any drug in a specimen provided by D must in all cases be taken into account, there are exceptions. This is because s 15(4) expressly states that evidence derived from a specimen of blood must be disregarded unless:

(a) it was taken with D's consent by a 'practitioner' (ie a medical practitioner or a registered health care professional); or
(b) it was taken from D by a practitioner under RTA 1988, s 7A (without consent) and D subsequently gave his permission for a laboratory test of the specimen.

In addition, as seen on p 525, in the case of a blood or urine specimen, the evidence derived from it is inadmissible if D's request for one of the parts into which it was divided was not properly complied with.

Breaches of the procedure laid down by RTA 1988, ss 7 to 9 will render the evidence obtained from the specimen inadmissible under s 15(2), because a specimen obtained in breach of that procedure cannot be said to have been obtained under the Act, as RTOA 1988, s 15(2) requires.

Hip-flask defence

RTOA 1988, s 15(3) allows D what is often described as the 'hip-flask' defence. It provides that, in cases under RTA 1988, ss 3A, 4, 5 or 5A:

(a) the assumption as to alcohol level must not be made if D proves that:
  (i) he consumed alcohol before he provided the specimen or had it taken from him and,
   (a) in relation to an offence under s 3A, after the time of the alleged offence; and
   (b) otherwise, after he had ceased to drive, attempt to drive or be in charge of a vehicle on a road or other public place; and
  (ii) had he not done so the proportion of alcohol in his breath, blood or urine would not have exceeded the prescribed limit and, if the proceedings are for an offence under RTA 1988, s 4, would not have been such as to impair his ability to drive properly; and
(b) the assumption as to drug level must not be made if D proves:
  (i) that he took the drug before he provided the specimen or had the specimen taken from him and,
   (a) in relation to an offence under s 3A, after the time of the alleged offence; and

(*b*) otherwise, after he had ceased to drive, attempt to drive or be in charge of a vehicle on a road or other public place; and

(ii) that had he not done so the proportion of the drug in his blood or urine:

(*a*) in the case of a specified controlled drug, would not have exceeded the specified limit for that drug; and

(*b*) if it is alleged that he was unfit to drive through drugs, would not have been such as to impair his ability to drive properly.

It has been held by the Court of Appeal that the burden of proof placed on D is a persuasive one, ie proof on the balance of probabilities.

In such cases it will almost invariably be necessary for D to call expert medical or scientific evidence in order to discharge this burden of proof, unless in rare cases the non-expert evidence which is called is such that a layman would reliably and confidently say that the subsequent drinking was the explanation for the excess level.

Defendants who are able to prove the hip-flask defence may nevertheless be liable for the offence of wilfully obstructing a constable in the execution of his duty. In any event, such deliberate consumption is liable to be self-defeating since D will often still be in charge of the vehicle at the time of the additional imbibing. It is therefore good practice, in instances in which D drinks from a bottle before submitting to testing procedures, to charge D with an offence of 'being in charge, etc' should tests prove to be positive.

Use of certificates

RTOA 1988, s 16(1) provides that evidence of the proportion of alcohol in a specimen of breath may be given by the production of the print-out produced by the breath-analysis device together with the certificate signed by a constable (normally the operator) (which certification may be made on the print-out). As already explained, that certification is to the effect that the print-out relates to a specimen provided by D at the date and time shown in it. The print-out and certificate are only admissible in evidence on behalf of the prosecution if a copy of it (or both) has been handed to D when the print-out was produced, or has been served on him not later than seven days before the hearing. Moreover, the certificate is not so admissible if D, not later than three days before the hearing or within such further time as the court may allow, has served notice on the prosecution requiring the attendance at the hearing of the constable who signed the certificate. While the Act makes specific provision for print-outs to be offered in evidence, it does not require that this be done. Consequently, a constable may give oral evidence of the readings obtained on the screen of the device, provided that he is able to testify that the device was working properly and was accurately self-calibrating.

Section 16(1) also provides that evidence of the proportion of alcohol or a drug in a specimen of blood or urine may be given by the production of a certificate signed by an authorised analyst as to the proportion of alcohol or any drug found in the specimen identified in the certificate. However, such a certificate is only admissible in evidence on behalf of the prosecution if a copy of it has been served on D not later than seven days before the hearing. In default of this, evidence of the analysis can be given by the authorised analyst attending as a witness. In addition, the certificate is not admissible under s 16(1) if, not later than three days before the hearing or within such further time as the court may allow, D has served notice on the prosecutor requiring the attendance at the hearing of the analyst who signed the certificate. However, a divisional court has held that, if the analyst is unable to attend, a court is entitled to admit the evidence of a certificate of analysis as hearsay under CJA 2003, s 116.

A divisional court has held that the s 16(1) requirement for an analyst to be authorised only applies to the giving of a certificate under s 16 and does not apply to, or prevent, the giving of oral evidence or a statement under CJA 1967, s 9 (p 251).

OFFENCE OF FAILING TO PROVIDE A SPECIMEN REQUIRED UNDER s 7

RTA 1988, s 7(6) makes it an offence for a person, without reasonable excuse, to fail
to provide a specimen when required to do so in pursuance of s 7. Where a person is
charged with failure to provide a specimen of blood for laboratory analysis in circumstances in which an approved breath-analysis device was not available, and the validity
of the request for a sample of blood is challenged, the non-availability of the device
must be proved in accordance with the laws of evidence. However, where D contended
that there was no direct evidence to prove that there was no approved device available
at the police station, as there could have been a second machine there, a divisional
court ruled that evidence that the device failed to operate together with evidence that D
was told that it was not therefore possible to take specimens of breath was sufficient. As
in the case of the offence under s 6(6), there cannot be a conviction under s 7(6) if the
requirement made for a specimen is invalid for some reason; the fact that the person
was brought to the police station after a wrongful arrest or after a trespass by the police
does not render the requirement invalid.

Fail

As already said, 'fail' includes 'refuse'. However, where D refused to supply a specimen
of breath, but within five seconds said that he wanted to change his mind, there was
no refusal. A divisional court said that the justices had ignored the motorist's words
five seconds after his refusal. Regard must be had to all words and conduct in reaching a conclusion. It is submitted that, in the light of this and other rulings, the right to
change one's mind will exist until the constable has moved on to the next stage of the
procedure. Where a person declines to provide a specimen of breath, alleging a medical
reason which is discounted by a medical practitioner or registered health care professional, there is a failure to provide a specimen without reasonable excuse. The police
officer is not obliged to start the procedure all over again. If it were otherwise, recalci-
trant persons could play the system to gain some delay. Once D is required to provide a
specimen an offence is committed if, without reasonable excuse, D does not provide it.

A person fails to provide a specimen of breath if the specimen is insufficient for analysis, or is so provided that it cannot be analysed.

Reasonable excuse

A foreigner who is unable to understand the purpose of the requirement and the penal
consequences of a failure to comply has a reasonable excuse. In addition, there would
be a reasonable excuse for failing to provide a specimen of blood where D has refused
to sign a form of consent (to providing a specimen of blood) until he has read it. Apart
from these instances an excuse cannot be adjudged reasonable unless D was physically
or mentally unable to provide the specimen requested, or its provision would entail a
substantial risk to his health. Where D refuses to supply specimens of breath and it
is subsequently found that, because of his limited lung capacity, he would have been
unable to supply specimens, this cannot amount to a reasonable excuse. There must

be a causative link between the refusal and the excuse and this cannot be so where the condition was not known to exist at the time of the refusal. While an invincible repugnance, amounting to a medically recognised phobia, to blood being taken is a reasonable excuse, the fear of the sight of blood is not; D can always close his eyes or look away.

A divisional court has held that D's non-communication of a medical condition of which he was aware at the time of the request but only belatedly proffered will normally result in the court concluding that there was no reasonable excuse for a failure to provide a specimen.

It has been held by divisional courts that stress caused by self-precipitated agitation cannot amount to a reasonable excuse for failure to provide breath, nor can mental anguish caused by a constable's conduct which D considered to be oppressive. There would have to be a causal connection between such anguish and the failure.

The fact that D was so drunk that he could not understand the procedure which was being followed does not amount to a reasonable excuse because it does not relate to his *capacity* to supply a specimen. However, where D failed to provide two specimens of breath and two police officers gave evidence that he appeared to be too drunk to do so, a divisional court refused to overturn a decision of the justices that he had had a reasonable excuse for not providing a specimen due to stress resulting from adverse personal and family circumstances which had led to recent breathlessness, although no medical evidence was offered. The justices had reached their decision on unimpeachable findings of fact and the divisional court would not interfere.

While a fear of AIDS is not a reasonable excuse for not providing a specimen of blood, a medically recognised *phobia* in relation to contracting AIDS is, as stated above. The wording of the relevant provisions is such that a person who fails to provide a specimen under s 7 on the grounds that he has been unlawfully arrested also does not have a reasonable excuse.

Someone who has not been given time to read PACE Code C, or to refer to a law book, does not have a reasonable excuse for not providing a specimen in consequence of that lack of opportunity, nor does someone who has been advised by his solicitor not to provide a specimen. Nor does someone who refuses to supply a specimen unless he can first consult a solicitor, unless the consultation will only cause a very short delay to the taking of the specimen.

D does not have the burden of proving reasonable excuse. There must, however, be evidence in support of facts which could constitute a reasonable excuse, otherwise the prosecution does not have to prove that there was no reasonable excuse. In almost every imaginable case of alleged physical or mental incapacity, that evidence must be medical evidence; in exceptional cases, however, other evidence—even that of D—can suffice. An example of such an exceptional case was where D had provided one specimen of breath but began to lose composure, sobbing continuously and experiencing difficulty in breathing. She was unable to provide a second specimen. A divisional court ruled that the justices were entitled to conclude that D was physically incapable of providing a specimen, whilst accepting that the case was close to the borderline. The need for medical evidence on such a point could not be accepted in absolute terms.

Other points

As already indicated, on requiring a person to provide a specimen in pursuance of RTA 1988, s 7, a constable must warn him that a failure to provide it may render him liable to prosecution (s 7(7)). Although an omission to warn is no defence to a charge of failing to co-operate with a preliminary test, contrary to s 6(4), it is a defence to a charge under s 7(6) that such a warning has not been given or has not been understood by the person from whom the specimen is required.

In terms of available punishment, an offence under s 7(6) is as serious as one under ss 4 or 5 or 5A in respect of which the specimen was sought (but less serious than one under s 3A).

Because there is only one offence under s 7(6), an information or written charge framed in terms of s 7(6) alone, without reference to the circumstances in which the requirement was made, is unlikely to fail for duplicity. It would be *good practice* to inform D of the circumstances surrounding the charge as soon as they have been established. In most cases, the issue of whether he was driving, attempting to drive, or in charge of the vehicle will be known at the time of his arrest. It is therefore preferable that the charge should specify the offence in relation to which the investigation was being carried out.

DETENTION OF PERSONS AFFECTED BY ALCOHOL OR A DRUG

RTA 1988, s 10(1) provides that a person who has been required under ss 7 or 7A to provide a specimen of breath, blood or urine may be detained at a police station (or, if the specimen was provided otherwise than at a police station, arrested and taken to and detained at a police station) if a constable has reasonable grounds for believing that, if he was released and drove or attempted to drive, he would commit an offence against ss 4, 5 or 5A. In practice this may often involve detention until a negative preliminary test. On any question under s 10 whether a person's ability to drive properly is or might be impaired through drugs, a constable must consult a medical practitioner and must act on his advice (s 10(3)).

Section 10(1) does not apply to a person if it ought reasonably to appear to the constable that there is no likelihood of his driving or attempting to drive whilst his ability to drive properly is impaired, or whilst the proportion of alcohol in his breath, blood or urine exceeds the prescribed limit, or whilst the proportion of a specified controlled drug in his blood or urine exceeds the specified limit for that drug (s 10(2)).

A hospital patient may not be arrested and taken to a police station if it would prejudice his proper care and treatment (s 10(2A)).

OTHER OFFENCES

Cycling while unfit

By RTA 1988, s 30, it is an offence to ride a cycle with two or more wheels on a road or other public place while unfit to ride through drink or drugs. Being in charge of such a cycle in such circumstances is not an offence under RTA 1988, but it is an offence under the Licensing Act 1872, s 12, which is described in the next paragraph.

Drunk in charge of a carriage, horse, etc

By the Licensing Act 1872, s 12 (p 575) it is an offence for a person to be drunk while in charge on any highway or other public place of any carriage, horse, cattle or steam engine. A mechanically propelled vehicle, trailer, bicycle, or tricycle is a 'carriage' for this purpose, but a person liable to be charged with an offence of driving or being in charge of a mechanically propelled vehicle when unfit to drive through drink or drugs should not be charged with the present offence since its maximum punishment is far less severe than that for the appropriate offence under RTA 1988.

Persons involved in guided public transport systems, shipping or aviation

The Transport and Works Act 1992 provides offences involving drink or drugs which apply to specified workers on guided transport systems which are used, or are intended to be used, wholly or partly for the carriage of members of the public. The relevant provisions are restricted to railways, tramways and other *guided transport systems* specified by the Secretary of State. The guided transport systems at Birmingham International Airport; Merry Hill Centre, West Midlands; and Gatwick and Stansted Airports have been so specified.

The Railways and Transport Safety Act 2003 provides offences involving the consumption of alcohol or drugs by those involved in marine activities (currently only if in a professional capacity) or aviation activities.

The above provisions are dealt with in Chapter 15 on the companion website.

CHAPTER 16

Children and Young Persons

The various statutes dealing with children and young persons are partly concerned with punishing adults, particularly those under a duty to care for a child or young person, whose conduct is physically or mentally harmful to him or otherwise harmful to his proper development. They are also concerned with the responsibilities of local authorities to receive a child or young person into their care; with the power of civil courts to put a child or young person into care, when this is necessary on specified grounds for his welfare; with the power of a court to make a child safety order or parenting order; and with barring unsuitable people from working in a range of activities with children.

MEANING OF TERMS

Child and young person

Unless otherwise indicated, in this chapter, a 'child' means a person under 14, and a 'young person' means a person who has reached 14 and is under 18.

For the purposes of law, a person attains an age on the relevant anniversary of his birth. The Children and Young Persons Act 1933 (CYPA 1933), s 99 states that when a person is brought before a court, other than as a witness, the issue of whether or not he is a child or young person must be decided upon inquiry by the court as to the age of the person. If it is later found that the age was different from that established by the court, any judgment or order will not be invalidated.

Guardian

Generally, the CYPAs are concerned with 'guardians' in the wide sense of including any person who, in the opinion of the court, has for the time being the care of the child or young person. This covers a much wider range of people than 'legal guardian'. A 'legal guardian' is a person appointed to have parental responsibility by a signed and witnessed document (including a will) or by order of a court.

RESPONSIBILITIES OF PARENT OR GUARDIAN

By CYPA 1933, s 34A, where a child or young person is charged with an offence or is, for any other reason, brought before a court, the court may in any case, and must in the case of a child or young person who is under 16, require a person who is a parent or guardian of his to attend court during all stages of the proceedings, unless and to the extent that the court is satisfied that it would be unreasonable to require such attendance. 'Parent or guardian' in this context includes a local authority which has parental responsibility for a child or young person, and which has him in its care, or in accommodation which it provides under the Children Act 1989 (ChA 1989).

Where a child or young person under 16 is convicted of an offence, the court is obliged by the Powers of Criminal Courts (Sentencing) Act 2000 (PCC(S)A 2000), s 137, to order that a fine, a surcharge, costs or compensation be paid by the parent or guardian (or by a local authority with parental responsibility for the child or young person if it is in the authority's care or accommodation), unless the court is satisfied that such parent or guardian cannot be found, or it would be unreasonable to make an order for payment, having regard to the circumstances of the case. In the case of a young person of 16 or more, the court may make such an order. These provisions also apply to circumstances in which such fines result from failure to comply with a community order.

Except where a referral order is made, PCC(S)A 2000, s 150 empowers a court, where a child or young person is convicted of an offence, to order a parent or guardian to enter into a recognisance not exceeding £1,000 to take proper care of him and to exercise proper control over him. In the case of a child or young person under 16, the court must exercise these powers where it is satisfied that it is desirable in the interests of preventing him from committing further offences to do so. Where it does not exercise these powers, it must state in open court that it is not so satisfied and give its reasons for so finding. Such a recognisance must not exceed three years. The order must not extend beyond the date upon which the person becomes 18. A parent or guardian must consent to the making of such an order. If he refuses and the court considers his refusal unreasonable, it may order him to pay a fine not exceeding £1,000.

OFFENCES OF CRUELTY TO PERSON UNDER 16

Responsibilities are placed upon social agencies by various Acts of Parliament and this has had the effect of relieving the police of some of their burdens. 'Child abuse' is dealt with by the criminal law by the offences of cruelty towards children and young persons which are governed by CYPA 1933, s 1. Section 1(1) provides that someone *of age 16 or over who has the responsibility for any child or young person under that age* commits an indictable (either way) offence, if he wilfully:

(a) *assaults,*
(b) *ill-treats (whether physically or otherwise),*
(c) *neglects,*
(d) *abandons,* or
(e) *exposes him;* or
(f) *causes or procures him to be assaulted, ill-treated (whether physically or otherwise), neglected, abandoned or exposed,*

in a manner likely to cause him unnecessary suffering or injury to health (whether the suffering or injury is of a physical or a psychological nature).

CYPA 1933, s 1(1) does not prevent a parent, or other person with the right to do so, administering punishment to a child or young person. As explained in Chapter 23, the right to administer corporal punishment is now very limited.

Key elements

Responsibility for a child

In this context a person is presumed to have responsibility for a child or young person if:

(a) he has parental responsibility for him under ChA 1989 (which the mother and father will both have if they were married to each other when the child or young person was born, or which only the mother will have if the mother and father were not so married, or which another person (including the father in the instance just given) or a local authority may acquire by operation of law); or

(b) he is otherwise liable to maintain him; or

(c) he has care of him.

Wilfully

'Wilfully' makes it clear that any offence under s 1 requires mens rea on the part of the defendant (D) as to the risk of unnecessary suffering or injury to health. For example, on a charge of wilfully neglecting, D must be aware of the risk of unnecessary suffering or injury to health resulting from the neglect, and if (to continue the example) that charge involves failure to provide adequate medical aid, the requirement of wilfulness can only be satisfied where D was aware that the child or young person's health might be at risk if he was not provided with medical aid or where D's non-awareness of this risk was due to his not caring whether the child's health was at risk or not.

Assault

'Assault' for the purpose of s 1 requires more than a mere common assault or battery. An assault or battery may amount to no more than frightening a person or giving him a light slap, but this could hardly be done 'in a manner likely to cause unnecessary suffering or injury to health'. Although consent can be an issue in some minor assaults, it must be remembered that, particularly in the case of children, mere submission to a person in authority does not signify consent.

Ill-treat

This signifies a continuous course of conduct leading to unnecessary suffering. A series of assaults, each of which, if considered on its own, would not amount to an offence against s 1, might together form ill-treatment over a period of time. Likewise, persistent frightening or bullying will suffice if it is likely to cause unnecessary suffering.

Neglect

This signifies a want of adequate care. The likelihood of causing unnecessary suffering or injury to health can be caused by a deliberate omission to supply medical or surgical aid. Direct proof of such likelihood is not always strictly necessary as this may be inferred from the evidence of neglect and its actual effect.

Section 1(2) provides that a parent or other person legally liable to maintain a child or young person or his legal guardian is deemed to have neglected him in a manner likely to cause injury to health if he has failed to provide adequate food, clothing, medical aid or lodging for him or if, having been unable to provide such food, clothing, medical aid or lodging, he has failed to take steps to procure it to be provided under the enactments applicable in that behalf.

Section 1(2) also declares that if the death of an infant under three years of age is caused by suffocation (other than by disease or a foreign body in the throat or air passage) while the infant was in bed with a person of 16 or over, that person, if he was, when he went to bed or at any later time before the suffocation, under the influence of drink or a prohibited drug, will be deemed to have neglected the infant in a manner likely to cause injury to health. The reference to the infant being 'in bed' with another ('the adult') includes a reference to the infant lying next to the adult in or on any kind of furniture or surface being used by the adult for the purpose of sleeping (and the reference to the time when the adult 'went to bed' is to be read accordingly). A drug is a prohibited drug for the above purposes in relation to a person if the person's possession of the drug immediately before taking it constituted an offence under the Misuse of Drugs Act 1971, s 5(2) (p 869).

Abandon or expose

It is helpful to consider these terms together since an abandonment frequently leads to exposure. To abandon a child means leaving it to its fate. If a woman separated from her husband takes her child to her husband's home and leaves the child at his door, she abandons that child. From the moment of abandonment the child is exposed and, if that exposure leads to suffering, the child has been abandoned and exposed in a manner likely to cause unnecessary suffering. If the husband becomes aware that the child has been left on his doorstep and allows it to remain there, he cannot then disclaim his custodial responsibilities. 'Exposure' does not cover exposure to risk. A father, who took his son and other boys on to a baulk of timber and floated the timber into deep water in London Docks, was not guilty of an offence under s 1, because this was not the type of exposure to which the section refers.

Police action in cruelty cases

It is now standard procedure to refer reports of cruelty to children to officers of the National Society for the Prevention of Cruelty to Children. The NSPCC attempts, through a process of encouragement, persuasion and warnings, to remedy the situation without recourse to the law whenever possible.

In all cases of non-accidental injury to children the police are likely to become involved at the outset when carrying out their role as one of the emergency services. Local authorities, social services, the NSPCC and the police have the power to initiate civil proceedings in the family court when a child appears to be in need of care. The police have power to detain children who appear to be in need of care and to take them to safe places. We deal with these matters later in this chapter. Police officers must never feel that the other social agencies have assumed responsibility for these matters. It is still the duty of the police to take some initial action to ensure the safety of any child in circumstances where a report of child abuse is received. Such cases may, in appropriate circumstances, be referred to other agencies later.

OTHER OFFENCES

There are a number of offences under CYPA 1933 which require little explanation. These offences are committed in relation to children of a specified age, which varies from offence to offence.

Brothels

By CYPA 1933, s 3(1), it is an offence for any person who has responsibility for a child or young person who has attained the age of four, but is under 16, to allow that child or young person to reside in or frequent a brothel. What is and what is not a brothel is discussed in Chapter 30. It is important to remember that a woman who is a prostitute and receives men in her own room, but does not allow other women to use her room, is not keeping a brothel. This is the most likely situation to come to the notice of the police. Although an offence is not committed in these circumstances, care proceedings (see later) could perhaps be considered (as they should in the case of a brothel).

Begging

Causing or procuring a child or young person under 16 to be in any street, premises or place for the purpose of begging or receiving alms, or of inducing the giving of alms (whether or not there is any pretence of singing, playing, performing, offering anything for sale or otherwise), is an offence contrary to CYPA 1933, s 4(1). There is a similar offence under the Vagrancy Act 1824, s 3.

It is an offence under CYPA 1933, s 4(1) for the person having the responsibility for such a child or young person to allow him so to act. Such a person allows a child or young person to beg in the street if he fails to prevent this when he could and should have prevented it. If it is proved that a child or young person was in a street, etc for the purpose of begging, etc and that a person with responsibility for him allowed him to be in the street, etc, that person is presumed to have allowed him to be there for that purpose, until the contrary is proved.

Intoxicating liquor

It is an offence, contrary to CYPA 1933, s 5, to give, or cause to be given, intoxicating liquor to a child under the age of five, otherwise than on the orders of a duly qualified medical practitioner or in an emergency.

Risk of burning

If a person of 16 or over, having responsibility for a child under 12, allows the child to be in a room containing an open fire grate or any heating appliance liable to cause injury to a person by contact with it and not sufficiently guarded against the risk of the child being burnt or scalded, without taking reasonable precautions against that risk, and in consequence the child is killed or seriously injured, that person commits an offence contrary to CYPA 1933, s 11.

It will be noted that death or serious injury must result from the unguarded fire or appliance and it is almost certain that civil proceedings for a 'care order' (see below) would result from any incident likely to be charged as an offence under s 11, which is punishable only by a fine.

Section 11 adds that a prosecution under s 11 will not affect a person's liability to prosecution for any indictable offence, for example for manslaughter.

Safety at entertainments

CYPA 1933, s 12(1) provides that, wherever an entertainment is provided in a building for an audience mainly of children, then, if there are more than 100 children attending the entertainment, there must be a sufficient number of adult attendants, properly stationed and instructed in their duties, to prevent more people being admitted than can properly be accommodated and to control the movement of those entering and leaving and general safety. If these provisions are not complied with, the person providing the entertainment is guilty of an offence under s 12(2). A constable may enter any building in which he has reason to believe that such an entertainment is taking place, or is about to take place, to ensure that this is being done. Section 12 does not apply to any entertainment in a dwelling house.

Dangerous performances

By CYPA 1933, s 23, no person aged 16 or under may take part in any performance in which his life or limbs are endangered without a local authority licence. Anyone who causes or procures this to be done, or a parent or guardian who allows it, commits an offence. No proceedings may be brought under s 23 except by or with the authority of a chief officer of police. The types of performance referred to are those in respect of which a charge is made, or which take place in licensed premises or registered clubs, or which are live or recorded broadcast performances, or performances filmed for public exhibition.

CARE AND PROTECTION OF CHILDREN

The Children Act 1989 (ChA 1989) makes various provisions for children to be brought into the care of a local authority (ie the council of a county (including a unitary authority) or a metropolitan district or London borough council or the Common Council of the City of London (in England) or a county or county borough council (in Wales)). *For the purposes of provisions under the Children Act 1989 mentioned in this chapter, a 'child' is a person under 18.* ChA 1989 emphasises that the child's welfare is paramount in all matters, particularly those concerned with his upbringing, and that delay in deciding such matters is likely to prejudice the child's welfare. The guiding principle of ChA 1989 is that the court should not make an order unless to do so is considered better for the child than making no order. Most of the Act's provisions relate to the functions of local authorities and the social service agencies. Those matters which most directly affect the police are considered later. ChA 1989, s 21 requires local authorities to make provisions for the reception and accommodation of children, including a child who is in police protection (see p 540). A child whom a custody officer has authorised to be kept in police detention after arrest must be received by a local authority where that officer so requests.

Care and supervision orders

ChA 1989, s 31 provides that, on the application of a local authority or authorised person (NSPCC or other body authorised by the Secretary of State), the family court may make an order:

(a) placing the child with respect to whom the application is made in local authority care; or
(b) putting him under local authority supervision or the supervision of a probation officer.

A court may only make a care or supervision order if it is satisfied:

(a) that the child concerned is suffering, or is likely to suffer, significant harm; and
(b) that the harm, or likelihood of harm, is attributable to:
  (i) the care given to the child, or likely to be given to him if the order were not made, not being what it would be reasonable to expect a parent to give him; or
  (ii) the child being beyond parental control.

'Harm' means ill-treatment or the impairment of health or development, including, for example, impairment suffered from seeing or hearing the ill-treatment of another.

Such an order may not be made with respect to a child who has reached the age of 17 (or 16 in the case of a child who is married). A care order may not be made until the court has considered a care plan. On an application for a care order the court may make a supervision order, and vice versa.

List entry (b)(ii) supplies a means of obtaining a care order where a child who is below the age of criminal responsibility (10) habitually commits a crime, or where a child receives adequate care from his parents but is so out of control that he is likely to harm himself.

A temporary, interim order can be made when an application for a care or supervision order is adjourned.

Care and supervision orders are civil orders, as are the other orders under ChA 1989 mentioned below. In consequence, the standard of proof required of an applicant for one of these orders is only proof on the balance of probabilities.

Child assessment orders

ChA 1989, s 43 permits a local authority or authorised person to apply to the family court for such an order where difficulties are being experienced in making an assessment of the needs of such a child. This may be due to lack of co-operation by those who have parental responsibility for the child. Such an order permits assessment to be made over a period not exceeding seven days and may require any person to produce the child to a person named in the order and to comply with specified instructions. However, the court should not make such an order if it is satisfied that there are grounds for making an emergency protection order and that it ought to do so rather than make a child assessment order.

Emergency protection order

ChA 1989, s 44 empowers a court, on the application of any person, to make an emergency order for the protection of a child. It may do so if it is satisfied that:

(a) there is reasonable cause to believe that the child is likely to suffer significant harm if:
   (i) he is not removed to accommodation provided by or on behalf of the applicant, or
   (ii) he does not remain in the place in which he is then being accommodated;
(b) in the case of an application made by a local authority:
   (i) inquiries are being made with respect to the child under the authority's duty to investigate where it reasonably suspects that a child is suffering, or is likely to suffer, significant harm, and
   (ii) these inquiries are being frustrated by access to the child being unreasonably refused to a person authorised to seek access and that the applicant has reasonable cause to believe that access to the child is required as a matter of urgency; or
(c) in the case of an application made by an authorised person:
   (i) the applicant has reasonable cause to suspect that the child is suffering, or is likely to suffer, significant harm,
   (ii) the applicant is making inquiries with respect to the child's welfare, and
   (iii) those inquiries are being frustrated by access to the child being unreasonably refused to a person authorised to seek access and the applicant has reasonable cause to believe that access to the child is required as a matter of urgency.

An emergency protection order directs any person in a position to do so to produce the child, and authorises the child's removal to accommodation provided by or on behalf of the applicant or the prevention of the removal of the child from a hospital or other place. It also gives the applicant parental responsibility for the child. An emergency protection order has effect for such period, not exceeding eight days, as is specified by the court, but the court has power (on one occasion only) to extend it for up to a further seven days. An emergency protection order can include an exclusion requirement in specified circumstances. Such a requirement enables the child to stay in its home by excluding someone else, such as a suspected child abuser, from it.

By s 44(15), it is an offence intentionally to obstruct a person exercising the power (under an order) to remove or prevent the removal of a child.

Removal and accommodation of children by police in emergencies

ChA 1989, s 46 empowers police officers to take a child into 'police protection' in prescribed circumstances. It also places responsibilities upon 'designated police officers', that is officers designated by chief officers of police to conduct inquiries into such cases.

Where a constable has reasonable cause to believe that a child would otherwise be likely to suffer significant harm, he may:

(a) remove the child to suitable accommodation and keep him there; or
(b) take such steps as are reasonable to ensure that the child's removal from any hospital, or other place, in which he is then being accommodated is prevented.

The courts have held that, in cases of emergency too pressing to obtain an interim care order, the preferable procedure is to apply for an emergency protection order under s 44, where this is practicable, rather than proceed under s 46; but the police must always have regard to the paramount need to protect children from significant harm. Where a police officer knows that an emergency protection order is in force in respect of a child, he should not exercise the power of removal under s 46, unless there are compelling reasons to do so.

As soon as is reasonably practicable after taking a child into police protection under s 46, as above, the constable must:

(a) inform the local authority within whose area the child was found of the steps that have been, or are proposed to be, taken with respect to the child and the reasons for taking them;
(b) give details to the local authority within whose area the child is ordinarily resident ('the appropriate authority') of the place at which the child is being accommodated;
(c) inform the child (if he appears capable of understanding):
   (i) of the steps that have been taken and of the reasons for taking them, and
   (ii) of the further steps which may be taken with respect to him under s 46;
(d) take such steps as are reasonably practicable to discover the wishes and feelings of the child;
(e) secure that the case is inquired into by a designated officer; and
(f) where the child was taken into police protection by being removed to accommodation which is not provided:
   (i) by or on behalf of a local authority, or
   (ii) as a refuge (ie a voluntary home or registered children's home certified as a refuge),

secure that he is moved to accommodation which is so provided.

The constable must also, as soon as reasonably practicable, inform:

(a) the child's parents;
(b) any other person who has parental responsibility for him; and
(c) any other person with whom the child was living immediately before being taken into police protection,

of the steps that he has taken under s 46 with respect to the child, the reasons for taking them and the further steps that may be taken with respect to him under the section.

When the case has been inquired into by the designated officer, he must release the child from police protection unless he considers that there is still reasonable cause for believing that the child would be likely to suffer significant harm if released.

No child may be kept in police protection for more than 72 hours. However, at any time while the child is in police protection, the designated officer may apply *on behalf of the appropriate local authority* for an emergency protection order to be made with respect to the child. Such an application may be made whether or not the local authority knows of it or agrees to its being made.

Whilst a child is in police protection, the designated officer must do what is reasonable in all the circumstances of the case for the purpose of safeguarding or promoting the child's welfare (having regard in particular to the length of the period during which the child will be so protected).

The designated officer must allow:

(a) parents;
(b) any other person with parental responsibility;
(c) any person with whom the child was living immediately before he was taken into police protection;
(d) any person named in a child arrangements order as someone with whom the child is to spend time or otherwise have contact;
(e) where the child is in local authority care, any person allowed to have contact with the child by virtue of a court order; and
(f) any person acting on behalf of any of these persons,

to have such contact (if any) with the child as, in the opinion of the designated officer, is both reasonable and in the child's best interest. However, if a child taken into police protection is in accommodation provided by, or on behalf of, the appropriate authority, these contact responsibilities are those of the authority rather than the designated officer.

Abduction of children in care, etc

It is an offence against ChA 1989, s 49(1) for any person, knowingly and without lawful authority or reasonable excuse, to take a child to whom s 49 applies from the responsible person, or to keep such a child away from the responsible person, or to induce or assist or incite such a child to run away or stay away from the responsible person. Section 49 applies to a child who is in care, the subject of an emergency protection order or in police protection. A 'responsible person' means any person who for the time being has care of him by virtue of the care order, the emergency protection order or ChA 1989, s 46 (p 540), as the case may be.

Where such abduction has occurred, s 50 permits a court to issue a 'recovery order'.

Police powers

By ChA 1989, s 48, an emergency protection order may include a requirement directed to a person to disclose the whereabouts of the child and may authorise an applicant to enter premises specified by the order and search for the child. Such a warrant may authorise a constable to assist an applicant where entry is being, or is likely to be, denied. It may also direct that a constable be accompanied by a registered medical practitioner, registered nurse or registered midwife.

If a child or young person is absent without the consent of the responsible person:

(a) from a place of safety to which he has been taken under PCC(S)A 2000, Schs 1 or 8 (pending court appearance after referral by youth offender panel, or after breach of reparation order or for revocation or amendment of order), CJIA 2008, Sch 2 (pending court appearance for breach of youth rehabilitation order);

(b) from local authority accommodation:
  (i)   in which he is required to live by a youth rehabilitation order,
  (ii) to which he has been remanded after an arrest for referral back to the appropriate court, or for breach of a reparation order; or

(c) from a place in which he has been accommodated pursuant to a remand otherwise than on bail after conviction or in extradition proceedings,

CYPA 1969, s 32 authorises a constable to arrest such a child or young person without a warrant. When so arrested he must be conducted to the place of safety, local authority accommodation, the place mentioned in (c), or such other place as the responsible person may direct.

Arrest of young offenders in breach of remand conditions

The Legal Aid, Sentencing and Punishment of Offenders Act 2012, s 97 provides that a constable may arrest without warrant someone under 18 who has been remanded to local authority accommodation in respect of any breach of a condition of that remand if the constable has reasonable grounds for suspecting that the offender has broken any of those conditions.

The arrested person must be brought before a justice as soon as is practicable and in any event within 24 hours of his arrest. In reckoning any period of 24 hours, no account is taken of Christmas Day, Good Friday or any Sunday.

CHILD SAFETY ORDERS

These are governed by the Crime and Disorder Act 1998 (CDA 1998), ss 11 to 13.

A child safety order is an order which:

(a) places a child under 10, for a period specified in the order, under the supervision of the responsible officer; and

(b) requires the child to comply with such requirements as are so specified.

The permitted maximum period of supervision for the above purposes is 12 months.

The requirements that may be specified under (b) are those which the court considers desirable in the interests of:

(a) securing that the child receives appropriate care, protection and support and is subject to proper control; or

(b) preventing any repetition of the kind of behaviour which led to the child safety order being made.

The main responsibility of the responsible officer will be to the child and paramount to that will be the need to supervise the child and to ensure full compliance with the requirements of the order. However, the officer also has an important role to play in relation to the child's family circumstances.

The 'responsible officer' will be one of the following who is specified in the order:

(a) a social worker of a local authority; and
(b) a member of a youth offending team.

The child safety order is directed to the child and requires or prohibits conduct specified in it. Where it is linked with a parenting order (below) that order could make associated requirements of the parent. For example, if the child safety order requires a child to be home by 7 pm, the associated parenting order could require the parent to ensure that the child is home by then.

Child safety orders are made by the family court. A court can make an order only if it is convinced that, with respect to a child under 10, one or more of the following conditions is satisfied:

(a) the child has committed an act which, if he had been 10 or over, would have constituted an offence;
(b) a child safety order is necessary to prevent the child committing such an act; or
(c) the child has acted in a manner that caused or was likely to cause harassment, alarm or distress to one or more persons not of the same household as himself.

A child safety order cannot be made without an application by a local authority (defined in the same way as on p 538).

Breach of a child safety order

Proceedings for breach of a child safety order must be brought by the responsible officer.

If on such an application it is proved that the child has failed to comply with any requirement in the order, the family court may make an order varying the order in the same way as on a variation after an application for discharge.

Breach of a child safety order may also result in the making of a parenting order; it is one of the triggers of such an order.

PARENTING ORDERS

Parenting orders

A parenting order can be made under CDA 1998, s 8, or under the Anti-social Behaviour Act 2003 (A-sBA 2003), ss 20, 26, 26A or 26B.

A parenting order is a court order requiring a parent or guardian (ie the person for the time being with care):

(a) to comply, for a period not exceeding 12 months, with such requirements ('the compliance requirements') as are specified in the order; and
(b) to attend, for a concurrent period not exceeding three months, such counselling and guidance programme as may be specified in directions given by the responsible officer.

A parenting order need not include a counselling and guidance-session requirement under (b) if the parent has previously been made subject to a parenting order, although it may do so.

The 'responsible officer', for example a probation officer, social worker or youth offending team member, who is to specify the counselling or guidance sessions to be attended will be specified in the order.

The responsible officer's role is also to ensure that parents attend whatever sessions are specified in his directions and to ensure compliance with the order and any requirements under it.

The compliance requirements which may be specified are those which the court considers desirable in the interest of preventing any repetition of the kind of conduct which 'triggers' the making of a parenting order or (as the case may be) the commission of any further offence of the type which is a 'trigger'. Examples of compliance requirements are a requirement to exercise control over the child and a requirement to ensure that he is home by a certain time of night.

Parenting orders under CDA 1998, s 8

When can an order be made under s 8?

By CDA 1998, s 8, a parenting order may be made in any court proceedings where:

(a) a child safety order is made in respect of a child or the court determines that a child has failed to comply with such an order;

(b) an injunction under the Anti-social Behaviour, Crime and Policing Act 2014 (AsB,C&PA 2014), s 1 is granted, a criminal behaviour order is made, or a sexual harm prevention order is made, in respect of a child or young person;

(c) a child or young person is convicted of an offence;

(d) a person is convicted of an offence under the Education Act 1996, s 443 (failure to comply with a school attendance order) or s 444 (failure to secure regular attendance at school of registered pupil); or

(e) a parental compensation order is made in relation to a child's behaviour.

If the court is satisfied that 'the relevant condition' is met, it may (or must, see below) make a parenting order in respect of a person who is the parent or guardian of the child or young person or (as the case may be) the person convicted of an offence referred to in (d).

The 'relevant condition' is that the parenting order would be desirable in the interests of preventing:

(a) in a case falling within (a), (b) or (e) above, any repetition of the kind of behaviour which led to the order, etc referred to there being made;

(b) in a case falling within (c) above, the commission of any further offence by the child or young person; and

(c) in a case falling within (d) above, the commission of any further offence referred to there.

CDA 1998 provides that a court is not normally obliged to make a parenting order if one of the relevant conditions under s 8 is satisfied; it simply has the power to do so. There are two exceptions, both provided by s 9, in relation to a child or young person under 16. If it is satisfied that the relevant condition is satisfied, a court must make a parenting order (a) where it has convicted such a person of an offence; and

(b) where it grants an injunction under A-sB,C&PA 2014, s 1 or makes a criminal behaviour order against such a person. If such a person is convicted or subjected to an injunction under A-sB,C&PA 2014, s 1 or a criminal behaviour order but the court is not so satisfied, it must say so in open court and give its reasons why it is not so satisfied. Exception (a) does not apply where the court makes a referral order in respect of the offence.

Parenting orders in cases of exclusion or potential exclusion from school

The provisions about parenting orders for parents convicted of a school attendance offence are complemented by the provisions of A-sBA 2003, s 20. These enable applications for a parenting order to be made to a magistrates' court in relation to the parent of a pupil who has been excluded (or whose behaviour warrants his exclusion) from school on disciplinary grounds, provided any prescribed conditions (below) are satisfied. A local authority (or, in England, the school governors) may apply for a parenting order as a first measure, or where a parent refuses to sign a 'parenting contract'.

Conditions have been prescribed for England by the Education (Parenting Contracts and Parenting Orders) (England) Regulations 2007, and for Wales by the Education (Parenting Contracts and Parenting Orders) (Wales) Regulations 2010.

The court may make such an order in respect of a pupil's parent if the relevant prescribed condition is met and the court is satisfied that an order is desirable in the interests of improving the pupil's behaviour.

In deciding whether to make a parenting order under A-sBA 2003, ss 20 or 26 (below), a court must consider any refusal by a parent to enter into a parenting contract, or a failure by the parent to comply with any requirement of a contract. In the case of a person under 16, it must consider the pupil's family circumstances and the order's likely effect upon them.

Parenting orders in respect of criminal conduct and anti-social behaviour: youth offending teams

Similar provision is made by A-sBA 2003, s 26 for a parenting order where a youth offending team applies to a magistrates' court for such an order in respect of a child or young person who has been referred to the team. If the court is satisfied that such a child or young person has engaged in criminal conduct or anti-social behaviour and that the making of the order is desirable in preventing further criminal conduct or anti-social behaviour, it may make such an order. Only a member of a youth offending team can be the responsible officer in respect of an order under s 26.

Parenting orders in respect of anti-social behaviour: local authorities and registered social landlords

A-sBA 2003, ss 26A and 26B respectively enable a local authority or registered social landlord to apply to a magistrates' court for a parenting order against a parent in respect of anti-social behaviour by his or her child or young person. Such an application may also be made to a county court as an adjunct to other proceedings in that court.

General points about parenting orders

As long as a parenting order of any type is in force, it is an offence for a parent to fail without reasonable excuse to comply with any requirement included in a parenting order, or specified in directions given by the responsible officer (CDA 1998, s 9(7)).

The process of enforcement envisaged is that the responsible officer will report to the police an alleged breach of a parenting order. The police will investigate the allegation, taking statements, etc and proceed from there. This can be contrasted with breach of a community order where it is the National Probation Service which brings proceedings and conducts them.

A-sBA 2003, s 28A makes provision for the Secretary of State (in Wales, the Welsh Assembly) to enable, by order, a local authority to 'contract out', to a person specified in the order, its functions in respect of parenting orders.

REMOVAL OF TRUANTS AND EXCLUDED PUPILS TO SCHOOLS OR DESIGNATED PREMISES

CDA 1998, s 16 provides that when a local authority has designated premises in a police area to which children and young persons of compulsory school age may be removed under s 16, and has notified the chief constable of the designation, a police superintendent (or above) may direct that the powers set out in the next paragraph are to be exercisable as respects any area falling within the police area that is specified in the direction. The powers will only be exercisable during the period specified in the direction. A British Transport Police superintendent (or above) has power to make such a direction but in such a case the powers set out below are only exercisable in any area or in the vicinity of any premises policed by the British Transport Police or in the premises themselves.

Section 16 provides that, where a police officer has reasonable cause to believe that a child or young person found by him in a public place in a specified area during a specified period:

(a) is of compulsory school age; and
(b) is absent from a school without lawful authority, or has been excluded from school on disciplinary grounds and has no justification for being in a public place,

he may remove the child or young person to designated premises, or to the school from which he is so absent. Condition (b) only applies to an excluded juvenile where he is so found during school hours.

The constable does not have to be in uniform. The child must be 'found in a public place' by a police officer. There is no power to enter private premises (eg the child's home) nor to remove a truant found on private premises on which the police officer is already lawfully present. 'Public place' means any highway and any place to which at the material time the public or any section of the public has access, on payment or otherwise, as of right or by virtue of express or implied permission, for example shopping centres, local authority parks, recreation grounds and amusement arcades.

For the purpose of the requirement of a reasonable belief in the juvenile's absence from a school without lawful authority, a child's absence is deemed to be without lawful authority unless the absence is (a) with leave, or (b) because attendance at school is prevented by sickness or any unavoidable cause, or (c) because the absence is on a day exclusively set aside for religious observance by the religious body to which his parent belongs.

PENALTY NOTICE FOR AN OFFENCE OF FAILURE TO SECURE REGULAR ATTENDANCE AT SCHOOL

The offence of failure to secure regular attendance at a relevant school of a registered pupil under the Education Act 1996, s 444 is one in respect of which a penalty notice may be given in England by an authorised officer. An 'authorised officer' for these purposes is a constable, a community support officer, an accredited person, an authorised local authority officer or an authorised staff member (head teacher or staff member authorised by the head teacher). A relevant school is a maintained school, a pupil referral unit, an Academy, an alternative provision Academy, a city technology college or a city college for the technology of the arts.

The Education (Penalty Notices) (England) Regulations 2007 prescribe the form of the notice and allow a period of 28 days during which no proceedings will be taken. The Regulations require that a code of conduct be drawn up by each local authority in consultation with other parties, to ensure consistency in the issuing of penalty notices. Records of the issue of notices must be kept by the authority. The penalty to be paid is £60 where payment is made within 21 days of receipt of the notice and £120 where paid within 28 days of receipt of the notice. The Education (Penalty Notices) (Wales) Regulations 2013 make similar provision in Wales but specify 28 and 42 days in place of 21 and 28 respectively.

DISQUALIFICATION FROM WORKING WITH CHILDREN

The Safeguarding of Vulnerable Groups Act 2006 (SVGA 2006) and regulations under it provide the framework for a central vetting and barring scheme for a range of people whose activities give them significant access to children (ie persons under 18). The Scheme is operated by the Disclosure and Barring Service (DBS).

Those subject to the previous system of barring have been included or considered for inclusion in the barred lists under SVGA 2006. There is a similar system in respect of those whose work gives them access to vulnerable adults.

How the SVGA 2006 scheme works

Regulated activity

SVGA 2006 refers to a 'regulated activity', a term which covers a range of activities, such as being a teacher or registered child-minder, or a range of paid or voluntary activities involving close contact with children. The DBS maintains two barred lists, the 'children's barred list' (CBL) listing those barred from engaging in regulated activity with children, and the 'adults' barred list' listing those barred from engaging in such activity with vulnerable adults.

The children's barred list

SVGA 2006, Sch 3 contains provisions for determining whether an individual is included in the CBL.

Automatic inclusion   If the DBS is satisfied that any of the prescribed criteria for automatic inclusion is met by a person it must include him in the CBL.

Inclusion subject to consideration of representations   If it appears to the DBS that any of the criteria for this type of inclusion is met by a person and that he is or has been, or might in future be, engaged in regulated activity relating to children, it must give him the opportunity to make representations as to why he should not be included in the CBL. If the person does not make representations in the prescribed time, or his whereabouts cannot reasonably be ascertained, and the DBS has reason to believe that the person is or has been, or might in future be, engaged in regulated activity relating to children, it must include him in the CBL. If the person does make representations in the prescribed time, the DBS must include him in the CBL if it has reason to believe that he is or has been, or might in future be, engaged in regulated activity relating to children, and is satisfied that it is appropriate to include him in the CBL.

Inclusion on grounds of relevant conduct   Where it appears to the DBS that the person has (at any time) engaged in relevant conduct, and is or has been, or might in future be, engaged in regulated activity relating to children, and the DBS proposes to include him in the CBL, it must give him the opportunity to make representations as to why he should not be included in the list. The DBS must include the person in the CBL if it is satisfied that the person has engaged in relevant conduct, it has reason to believe that the person is or has been, or might in future be, engaged in regulated activity relating to children, and it is satisfied that it is appropriate to include the person in the list.

'Relevant conduct' is defined as follows:

(a) conduct which endangers a child, or is likely to endanger a child;
(b) conduct which, if repeated against or in relation to a child, would endanger that child or would be likely to endanger him;
(c) conduct involving sexual material relating to children (including possession of such material);
(d) inappropriate conduct of a sexual nature or involving sexually explicit images or depicting violence against human beings (including possession of such images).

Inclusion on grounds of risk of harm   Where it appears to the DBS that a person may:

(a) harm a child;
(b) cause a child to be harmed;
(c) put a child at risk of harm;
(d) attempt to harm a child; or
(e) incite another to harm a child;

and is or has been, or might in future be, engaged in a regulated activity relating to children, and the DBS proposes to include him in the CBL, the DBS must give the person opportunity to make representations as to why he should not be included in the list. The DBS must include the person in the CBL if it is satisfied that the person falls within (a)–(e), it has reason to believe that the person is or has been, or might in future be, engaged in regulated activity relating to children, and it is satisfied that it is appropriate to include the person in the list.

Supplementary

Having included a person's name in the CBL, the DBS must take all reasonable steps to notify an individual of his inclusion.

SVGA 2006, s 50A empowers the DBS to provide information it holds to the chief officer of police for use in the prevention, detection and investigation of crime, the apprehension and prosecution of offenders, the appointment of persons under his direction and control, or any prescribed purpose. It must provide to a chief officer on request, for use for any of these purposes, a barred list or information as to whether a person is barred.

Effect of inclusion in barred list

A person included in the CBL, or the corresponding lists in Scotland and Northern Ireland, is barred from regulated activity relating to children.

After the specified minimum barred period, which varies depending on the circumstances, has elapsed, and provided he has made no other such application in the prescribed period ending with the time when he does so, a barred individual may apply to the DBS for permission to apply for a review of his inclusion. The DBS must not grant permission unless it thinks that the applicant's circumstances have changed since he was included in the list or last applied for permission and that the change is such that permission should be granted.

Offences

By SVGA 2006, s 7(1), an individual commits an indictable (either way) offence if he:

(a) seeks to engage in regulated activity from which he is barred;
(b) offers to engage in regulated activity from which he is barred;
(c) engages in regulated activity from which he is barred.

It is a defence for the defendant to prove that he did not know, and could not reasonably be expected to know, that he was barred from that activity. It is also a defence for the defendant to prove that:

(a) he reasonably thought that it was necessary for him to engage in the activity for the purpose of preventing harm to a child;
(b) he reasonably thought that there was no other person who could engage in the activity for that purpose; and
(c) he engaged in the activity for no longer than was necessary for that purpose.

Indictable (either way) offences are also committed by employers who use, or employment agencies who supply, a barred person for a regulated activity.

CHAPTER 17

Licensed Premises, Licensed Persons, Clubs, Places of Entertainment, and Offences of Drunkenness

INTRODUCTION

The Licensing Act 2003 (LA 2003) introduced a system of licensing operated by licensing authorities, essentially local authorities. The 'licensable activities' and 'qualifying club activities' to which the provisions of the Act apply are not restricted to matters involving the sale or supply of alcohol; they also include various forms of entertainment and (in the case of licensable activities) the provision of late-night refreshment.

The key to understanding the regime under LA 2003 is that a *licensable activity* must be carried on (a) under and in accordance with a premises licence, or (b) in circumstances where it is carried out in accordance with a temporary event notice (TEN) and the relevant conditions are met. By way of qualification, as from a day to be appointed, the licensable activity of selling alcohol by retail may be carried on if each sale is a permitted sale by virtue of LA 2003, Part 5A (sale of alcohol at community events, etc and ancillary business sale of alcohol). In addition, a personal licence is required by a person selling alcohol by retail, or supplying it by, or on behalf of, a club to, or to the order of, a member of the club, on premises which have a premises licence. A *qualifying club activity* must be carried on under and in accordance with a club premises certificate.

On certain occasions it is an offence under LA 2003 intentionally to obstruct an authorised person (ie an officer of a licensing authority or a person with a health, safety or environmental role appointed or authorised by certain bodies). These officers share powers with a constable in relation to the enforcement of many provisions of the Act. On each of these occasions it will also, of course, be an offence against the Police Act 1996, s 89(2) wilfully to obstruct a constable in the execution of his duties.

By LA 2003, s 4, a licensing authority must carry out its functions under LA 2003 with a view to promoting the licensing objectives under that section:

(a) the prevention of crime and disorder ('and' has been held to mean 'and/or');
(b) public safety;
(c) the prevention of public nuisance; and
(d) the protection of children from harm.

TERMINOLOGY

Licensable activities and qualifying club activities

These are the activities which are regulated by LA 2003 and require authorisation by the relevant licensing authority.

Licensable activities

By LA 2003, s 1(1), the following are licensable activities:

(a) the sale by retail of alcohol;
(b) the supply of alcohol by or on behalf of a club to, or to the order of, a member of the club, otherwise than a sale by retail;
(c) the provision of regulated entertainment; and
(d) the provision of late-night refreshment.

The reference to 'sale by retail' in (a) means that 'business-to-business' wholesale sales are outside the provisions of the Act. The reference to 'otherwise than a sale by retail' in para (b) of this definition can be explained as follows. In the case of a members' club (as opposed to a proprietary one) the property of the club belongs to its members for the time being jointly in equal shares. Consequently, if alcohol is supplied to a member at a price, this is not a sale by retail but a release by the other members of their interest in the drink supplied. This would not be covered by para (a), although a supply at a price to a guest of a member of the club would be.

Section 173 excludes activities which would otherwise be licensable activities from being so if they are carried on in particular places, for example aboard an aircraft, hovercraft or train on a journey, at an approved wharf at a designated port or hoverport, on board a vessel on an international journey, or at an examination station at a designated international airport (area beyond security check-in). Premises permanently or temporarily used for the purpose of the armed forces are also exempted.

Section 175 provides that the promotion of an incidental lottery will not constitute a licensable activity by reason only of one or more of the prizes in the lottery consisting of or including alcohol, provided that the alcohol is in a sealed container.

Qualifying club activities

By LA 2003, s 1(2), the following licensable activities are also qualifying club activities:

(a) the supply, otherwise than a sale by way of retail, of alcohol by or on behalf of a club to, or to the order of, a member of the club;
(b) the sale by retail of alcohol by or on behalf of a club to a guest of a member of the club for consumption on the premises where the sale takes place; and
(c) the provision of regulated entertainment where that provision is by or on behalf of a club for members of the club or members of the club and their guests.

A number of terms in the above definitions are defined as follows.

Alcohol

'Alcohol' in LA 2003 means spirits, beer, wine, cider or any other fermented, distilled or spirituous liquor, except alcohol with a strength not exceeding 0.5 per cent and obvious exceptions like perfume, medicinal or veterinary products, and liqueur confectionery.

Regulated entertainment

LA 2003, Sch 1 provides that 'the provision of regulated entertainment' means 'entertainment' of a type described below where the following two conditions are satisfied:

(a) that the entertainment is provided:
  (i)   to any extent for members of the public or a section of the public;
  (ii) exclusively for members of a club (or members and their guests) which is a qualifying club in relation to the provision of regulated entertainment; or
  (iii) in any case not falling within (i) or (ii), for consideration and with a view to profit;
(b) that the premises on which the entertainment is provided are made available for the purpose, or for purposes which include the purpose, of enabling the entertainment concerned.

The descriptions of 'entertainment' are:

(a) a performance of a play;
(b) an exhibition of a film;
(c) an indoor sporting event ('sporting event' means any contest, exhibition or display of any sport other than a boxing or wrestling entertainment);
(d) a boxing or wrestling entertainment (ie any contest, exhibition or display of boxing or wrestling, or which combines boxing or wrestling with one or more martial arts);
(e) a performance of live music;
(f) any playing of recorded music;
(g) a performance of dance; or
(h) entertainment of a similar description to that falling within (e), (f), or (g),

where the following conditions are satisfied (so far as relevant).

The first condition is that the entertainment takes place in the presence of an audience, and is provided for the purpose, or for purposes which include the purpose, of entertaining that audience.

The second condition is relevant only to a performance of a play or dance, or an indoor sporting event, and is that one or more of the following applies:

(i)   the audience consists of more than 500 persons (play or dance) or 1,000 (indoor sporting event);
(ii) the entertainment takes place before 08.00 on any day;
(iii) the entertainment takes place after 23.00 on any day; or
(iv) (dance only) the entertainment is a 'relevant entertainment' (defined as any live performance, or live display of nudity, whose sole or principal purpose, other than financial gain, is sexually stimulating any member of the audience).

So much of any entertainment of a description specified in paragraphs (a) to (h) above as does not satisfy these conditions (so far as relevant) is not 'entertainment'.

Exemptions   The following are not regulated entertainments:

(a) playing of live TV and radio programmes;
(b) music or films incidental to an activity which is not itself 'entertainment', for example background music in a shop, or a piano in a restaurant;
(c) films used for product demonstration, advertisement, information, education or instruction, or in an exhibition in a museum or art gallery;

(d) films at community premises if the following conditions (i) to (v) are satisfied:
- (i) prior written consent for the entertainment to take place at the community premises must have been obtained, by or on behalf of an organiser or manager of the above entertainment:
  - (*a*) from the management committee of the community premises, or
  - (*b*) where there is no management committee, from:
    - (*i*) a person who has control of the community premises in connection with the carrying on by that person of a trade, business or other undertaking (for profit or not), or
    - (*ii*) where there is no such person, an owner of the community premises;
- (ii) the entertainment must not be provided with a view to profit;
- (iii) the entertainment must take place in the presence of an audience of no more than 500;
- (iv) the entertainment must take place between 08.00 and 23.00 on the same day
- (v) the film classification body or the relevant licensing authority must have made a recommendation concerning the admission of children to an exhibition of the film and the admission of children is subject to such restrictions (if any) as are necessary to comply with the recommendation of that body or authority (or of that authority, if they have both made recommendations);

(e) entertainment incidental to a religious service or at a place of religious worship;
(f) entertainment at a garden fete;
(g) Morris dancing or dancing of similar type;
(h) entertainment provided on vehicles in motion;
(i) 'relevant entertainment' (p 552 (iv)) at premises for which a sex establishment licence is required (or waived) by virtue of the Local Government (Miscellaneous Provisions) Act 1982, Sch 3, or would be required but for the infrequency of the relevant entertainment;
(j) any entertainment provided by or on behalf of health care providers, local authorities and school proprietors, if:
- (i) it takes place:
  - (*a*) if it is provided by or on behalf of a health care provider, on any premises forming part of a hospital in which that provider has a relevant property interest (freeholder or lessor of a lease of three years or more), or which are lawfully occupied by that provider,
  - (*b*) if it is provided by or on behalf of a local authority, on any premises in which that authority has a relevant property interest or which are lawfully occupied by that authority, and
  - (*c*) if it is provided by or on behalf of a school proprietor, on the premises of the school;
- (ii) the premises are not domestic premises (ie premises occupied as a private dwelling, including any garden, yard, garage, outhouse or other appurtenance of such premises whether or not used in common by the occupants of more than one such dwelling);
- (iii) the entertainment takes place between 08.00 and 23.00 on the same day (or, where a special occasion order (p 554) has effect, between the hours specified in that order); and
- (iv) the entertainment is not a 'relevant entertainment' for the purposes of the Local Government (Miscellaneous Provisions) Act 1982, Sch 3 (licensing of sex establishments);

(k) entertainment consisting of a performance of live music and/or the playing of re-corded music if the following conditions are satisfied:
  (i) that the entertainment takes place at:
    (*a*) community premises that are not authorised, by a premises licence or club premises certificate, to be used for the supply of alcohol for consumption on the premises,
    (*b*) the premises of a hospital or of a school, or
    (*c*) premises in which a local authority has a relevant property interest (as above) or which are lawfully occupied by a local authority;
  (ii) that the premises are not domestic premises (as above);
  (iii) that the entertainment takes place in the presence of an audience of no more than 500 persons;
  (iv) that the entertainment takes place between 08.00 and 23.00 on the same day (or, where a special occasion order has effect, between the hours specified in that order); and
  (v) that a person concerned in the organisation or management of the entertain-ment has obtained the prior written consent of a relevant person for the enter-tainment to take place.
  Where the entertainment takes place at community premises, a 'relevant person' means the management committee of the premises, or, if there is none, a person who has control of the premises in connection with the carrying on by that per-son of a trade, business or other undertaking (for profit or not) or (in the absence of such a person) a person with a relevant property interest in the premises. Where the entertainment takes place at the premises of a hospital, it means a health care provider which has a relevant property interest in or lawfully occupies those prem-ises. Where the entertainment takes place at premises in which a local authority has a relevant property interest or which are lawfully occupied by a local authority, it means that authority. Where the entertainment takes place at school premises, it means the school proprietor;
(l) live music or recorded music on premises authorised to be used for the supply of alcohol for consumption on the premises by a premises licence or club premises certificate, provided:
  (i) the premises are then open for the supply of alcohol for consumption on the premises;
  (ii) if the music is amplified, it takes place in the presence of an audience of no more than 500 persons;
  (iii) the music takes place between 08.00 and 23.00 on the same day (or, where a special occasion order has effect, between the hours specified in that order); and
  (iv) conditions have not been included in the licence or certificate by virtue of LA 2003, s 177A(3) or (4) (referred to on p 574));
(m) live music at a workplace provided:
  (i) the place is not licensed under LA 2003 (or is so licensed only for the provision of late night refreshment);
  (ii) the audience does not exceed 500; and
  (iii) the live music takes place between 08.00 and 23.00 on the same day;
(n) subject to s 177A(3) and (4), live unamplified music which takes place between 08.00 and 23.00 on the same day;
(o) any entertainment that consists of or forms part of a performance by a travelling circus, if:

(i) the entertainment is not an exhibition of a film or a boxing or wrestling entertainment (as defined on p 552);

(ii) it takes place between 08.00 and 23.00 on the same day;

(iii) it takes place wholly within a moveable structure, inside which the audience is also wholly accommodated; and

(iv) the travelling circus has not been located on the same site for more than 28 consecutive days;

(p) entertainment consisting of a boxing or wrestling entertainment, if:

(i) it is a contest, exhibition or display of Greco-Roman wrestling, or of freestyle wrestling, between two participants (regardless of their sex);

(ii) it takes place in the presence of no more than 1000 spectators;

(iii) it takes place between 08.00 and 23.00 on the same day; and

(iv) it takes place wholly inside a building, inside which the spectators are wholly accommodated.

Late-night refreshment

LA 2003, Sch 2 provides that 'late-night refreshment' means the supply on or from any premises at any time between 23.00 and 05.00 of hot food or hot drink for consumption on or off the premises: (a) to members of the public (or a section of it), or (b) when members of the public (or a section of it) are admitted to any premises, to any persons (or to a person of a particular type) on or off those premises. 'Hot' for the purposes of the Act means food or drink which is heated on the premises or elsewhere or that which, after it is supplied, may be heated on the premises.

The following are not the provision of late-night refreshment for the purposes of LA 2003:

(a) supply on or from premises to persons staying at hotels, camping sites or other premises supplying accommodation as their main purpose;

(b) supply on or from premises to members of recognised clubs;

(c) supply on or from premises to employees of particular employers (works canteens, etc);

(d) supply on or from premises already licensed under other Acts, for example 'near beer' premises in London;

(e) supply free of charge provided no charge has been made for admission to the premises or some other item;

(f) supply by a registered charity;

(g) supply by means of a vending machine;

(h) supply on a vehicle not permanently or temporarily parked;

(i) supply on or from premises which are wholly situated in an area designated by the relevant licensing authority;

(j) supply on or from premises which are of a description designated by the relevant licensing authority; or

(k) supply during a period (beginning no earlier than 23.00 and ending no later than 05.00) designated by the relevant licensing authority.

A licensing authority may designate a description of premises for the purposes of (i), (j) or (k) only if the description is prescribed by the Licensing Act 2003 (Late Night Refreshment) Regulations 2015, ie motorway service areas; filling stations; licensed premises authorised to sell by retail alcohol for consumption on the premises between 23.00 and 05.00; and (with exceptions) local authority premises, school premises, hospital premises or community premises.

PREMISES LICENCES, CLUB PREMISES CERTIFICATES AND TEMPORARY EVENT NOTICES

Premises licence

Premises licences are governed by LA 2003, Part 3 (ss 11 to 59). They authorise premises to be used for one or more licensable activities.

A premises licence is granted by the licensing authority for the area and authorises its holder to use the premises to which the licence relates for one or more licensable activities (see p 551).

In addition to the general right to apply for a review of a premises licence, an involved process, a chief officer of police may apply for an expedited review of a premises licence. A chief officer may do so where a superintendent (or above) has certified that he considers that premises which are licensed are associated with serious crime or disorder. A serious crime is one defined by the Regulation of Investigatory Powers Act 2000, s 81 (generally, those crimes for which a sentence of imprisonment for at least three years may be imposed and offences involving violence, resulting in substantial gain or involving a large number of persons in pursuit of a common purpose). Interim steps may be taken in accordance with regulations without the licence-holder being given an opportunity to make representations.

Where it is intended to build or extend premises a person may apply to the relevant licensing authority for a provisional statement about whether, if the work is done as proposed, it would be appropriate to attach conditions to the premises licence, exclude a licensable activity, refuse to accept a specified person as premises supervisor, or refuse a premises licence.

By s 59, a constable or authorised person (see p 550) may enter the premises to which an application for a premises licence or provisional statement relates, before that application has been determined, in order to assess the likely effect on the promotion of the licensing objectives of the grant of the application. An authorised person must produce evidence of his authority, if requested. It is an offence against s 59(5) intentionally to obstruct an authorised person exercising such a power.

A licence will be granted subject to conditions consistent with the operating schedule and any mandatory conditions which are appropriate.

The premises licence-holder must ensure that the licence (or a certified copy) and a list of relevant mandatory conditions is kept on the premises in his custody or control or that of an employee there nominated in writing, and that the summary of the licence (or a certified copy) and the position of any nominee referred to above are prominently displayed on the premises. Non-compliance by the premises licence-holder, without reasonable excuse, is an offence under s 57(4). A constable or authorised person may require production of the premises licence (or a certified copy) or a list of relevant mandatory conditions. An authorised person must, on request, produce evidence of his authority. Non-compliance without reasonable excuse with such a request is an offence under s 57(8).

Club premises certificates

These are dealt with by LA 2003, Part 4 (ss 60 to 97).

Club premises certificates will be granted to a qualifying club by the licensing authority for the area and will authorise the use of club premises for qualifying club activities specified in the certificate (see p 538).

A club may wish to provide entertainment to members of the public on certain occasions and, in consequence, it may hold a club premises certificate in respect of its day-to-day activities and a premises licence authorising the provision of entertainment.

A club premises certificate will be subject to conditions in the same way as a premises licence.

A club premises certificate may authorise the supply of alcohol to its *members* for consumption off the premises. In general:

(a) a club premises certificate may not authorise the supply of alcohol for consumption off the premises unless it also authorises its supply to members for consumption on the premises;

(b) a club premises certificate authorising the supply of alcohol for consumption off the premises must include three conditions as to such supply. The supply must be:

    (i) made at a time when the premises are open for the purposes of supplying alcohol, in accordance with the club premises certificate, to members of the club for consumption on the premises,

    (ii) in a sealed container, and

    (iii) to a member of the club in person.

Sale of alcohol by retail to a guest for such consumption is not authorised by the certificate.

No conditions attached to a club premises certificate may prevent the sale by retail of alcohol or the provision of regulated entertainment to associate members of a club or their guests if those are permitted activities.

A constable or authorised person may require production of a certificate (or certified copy) or a list of relevant mandatory conditions. Failure to comply, without reasonable excuse, is an offence against s 94(9). The club secretary must ensure that the certificate (or certified copy) is held on the club's premises by a person nominated by him, and the nominated person must ensure that a summary of the certificate and notice of the nominated individual responsible for it on the premises are prominently displayed. Failure to comply with one of these requirements, without reasonable excuse, is an offence against s 94(5) (failure by secretary to ensure holding) or (6) (failure to ensure display).

By s 96, on production of his authority a constable authorised by the chief officer of police or an authorised person may enter and inspect premises in respect of which an application has been made for the grant of a certificate. 48 hours' notice must have been given to the club. It is an offence against s 96(5) intentionally to obstruct an authorised person exercising these powers.

By s 97 a constable may enter and search club premises (by force, if necessary) where he has reasonable cause to believe that an offence in respect of the supply of controlled drugs or psychoactive substances has been, is being, or is about to be, committed or that there is likely to be a breach of the peace.

Temporary event notices

Sometimes, a person wishes to carry out licensable activities at premises which are not licensed, eg to provide bar facilities at a wedding reception on premises not licensed for the sale of alcohol, or to set up a disco constituting regulated entertainment in premises which, although licensed for the sale of alcohol, are not licensed for the provision of entertainment. This can be achieved under the provisions of LA 2003, Part 5 (ss 98 to 110) which deals with permitted temporary activities. Under Part 5, licensable activities can occur on premises which do not have a premises licence or club premises certificate on a temporary basis (for a period not exceeding 168 hours) subject to conditions and limitations.

A licensable activity is a 'permitted temporary activity' if:

(a) it is carried out in accordance with:
  (i) a temporary events notice (TEN) given, no later than 10 working days before the event starts and with the prescribed fee, to the relevant licensing authority; and
  (ii) where relevant, any conditions imposed; and
(b) it satisfies the following conditions:
  (i) the TEN has been duly acknowledged (if required (no requirement if licensing authority has issued counter-notice following police objection or if permitted limits already exceeded)) by the licensing authority;
  (ii) the TEN has not been subsequently withdrawn by the individual giving the notice; and
  (iii) no counter-notice has been issued by the relevant licensing authority.

The individual who gives the TEN is called the 'premises user'.

The temporary event notice

A TEN must contain details including:

(a) the licensable activities to be carried out;
(b) the date(s) when the licensable activities are to be carried out (and the total length of the event);
(c) the times during the event at which the licensable activities are to be carried out;
(d) the maximum number of people to be allowed on the premises at any one time, which must be less than 500;
(e) whether any alcohol sales are to be made for consumption on or off the premises (or both).

If the proposed licensable activities include the supply of alcohol, the notice must include the condition that all supplies will be made by, or under the authority of, the premises-user.

Objections and counter-notices

Where a 'relevant person' (a chief officer of police or local authority with an environmental or health function) considers that if the temporary event should proceed it would undermine a licensing objective, the premises-user, the relevant licensing authority and every other relevant person must be informed by an objection notice, setting out the reasons, before the end of the second working day following the day on which the TEN was received. If there is such an objection there must be a hearing unless all parties agree that it is unnecessary. Where the licensing authority accepts the objection it must give the premises-user a counter-notice preventing the event from taking place; this must be done at least 24 hours before the proposed event. If the counter-notice is not given as required, the premises-user may proceed with the event.

Where there has been an objection by a relevant person, at any time before a hearing that person may, with the consent of the premises-user, modify the terms of the TEN. If this is done the notice takes effect with those modifications.

In addition to the case where an objection is accepted, a licensing authority must give a counter-notice in certain cases; the effect is to prevent the event taking place.

Rights of entry, production of notice, etc

LA 2003, s 108 provides that a constable or an authorised officer of the licensing authority may, at any reasonable time, enter premises to assess the probable impact of the proposed event upon the crime prevention objective. An authorised officer must produce evidence of his authority, if requested. It is an offence intentionally to obstruct such an officer (s 108(3)).

The premises-user must ensure:

(a) that a copy of the TEN together with any statement of conditions is prominently displayed on the premises; or

(b) that the TEN and such statement are kept there in his custody or that of a nominated person. Where the TEN and any statement of conditions are in the custody of a nominated person, the premises-user must ensure that a notice to that effect is prominently displayed on the premises.

It is an offence against s 109(4) for a premises-user, without reasonable excuse, to fail to comply with one or other of these requirements.

Where a TEN or any statement of conditions is not prominently displayed and there is no notice displayed as to its whereabouts, a constable or authorised officer may require the premises-user to produce the TEN or statement of conditions. Where a notice relating to a 'nominated person' is displayed on the premises a constable or authorised officer may require the nominated person to produce the actual notice or statement of conditions. It is an offence under s 109(8) for a person to fail, without reasonable excuse, to produce a TEN or statement of conditions when requested to do so.

Sale of alcohol at community events, etc and ancillary business sale of alcohol—Licensing Act 2003, Part 5A

LA 2003, Part 5A (ss 110A–110N), which will come into force on a day to be appointed, enables prescribed bodies (eg community organisations or small businesses which sell alcohol as an ancillary part of a wider service) to sell alcohol without having to use one of the existing forms of authorisation under LA 2003. Its purpose is to create a lighter touch authorisation to reduce burdens on those persons or bodies.

Part 5A provides as follows.

General conditions for permitted sales

A sale by retail of alcohol is a permitted sale by virtue of Part 5A if:

(a) the community event conditions (below) or the ancillary business sales conditions (below) are satisfied in relation to it; and

(b) the following conditions are satisfied in relation to it:

   (i) the sale must take place on premises specified in a notice that complies with s 110D (below) (a 'Part 5A notice');

   (ii) no counter-notice (below) must have been given in relation to the Part 5A notice;

   (iii) the sale must take place during the period of 36 months beginning with the date when the Part 5A notice takes effect; and

   (iv) the sale must take place between 07.00 and 23.00.

Community event conditions and ancillary business sales conditions

The *community event conditions*, in relation to a sale by retail of alcohol, are those set out in (a) to (e) below and any additional conditions set out in regulations:

(a) the sale must be made by or on behalf of a body that is of a prescribed description, does not trade for profit, and meets any prescribed criteria;
(b) the sale must be ancillary to an event that:
   (i) is taking place on the premises;
   (ii) is organised by the body by or on whose behalf the sale is made;
   (iii) has been advertised in advance; and
   (iv) meets any prescribed criteria;
(c) the sale must take place on the premises during the course of the event;
(d) the alcohol must be sold for consumption on the premises during the course of the event; and
(e) the number of persons present on the premises at the time of the sale must not exceed 300.

The *ancillary business sales conditions*, in relation to a sale by retail of alcohol, are those set out in (a) to (d) below and any additional conditions set out in regulations:

(a) the sale must be made by or on behalf of a body that is of a prescribed description, and meets any prescribed criteria;
(b) the sale must take place on premises that:
   (i) are managed by the body by or on whose behalf the sale is made;
   (ii) are of a prescribed description; and
   (iii) meet any prescribed criteria;
(c) the sale must be ancillary to the provision of goods or services to a person on the premises where the sale takes place;
(d) except in prescribed circumstances, the alcohol must be sold for consumption on those premises.

Part 5A notices

A notice must:

(a) contain the requisite information in the prescribed form;
(b) be given, on behalf of the body by or on whose behalf the sale of alcohol on the premises would take place, by someone concerned in the management of the body;
(c) be given to the relevant licensing authority at least 10 working days (but no more than three months) before the event.

Where a Part 5A notice is given on behalf of a body, and a counter-notice is given in relation to the notice, no further Part 5A notice may be given in respect of any premises specified in the notice, whether on behalf of that body or an associate of it, for a year after the counter-notice is given. However, this restriction ceases to apply if the counter-notice is revoked or quashed by a court.

If the licensing authority is of the opinion that the notice does not comply with s 110D, it must as soon as possible give to the person who gave the notice written notification of its reasons.

Objections and counter-notices

Where a relevant person (as defined on p 558) given a Part 5A notice considers that allowing alcohol to be sold on the premises in question would undermine a licensing objective, the relevant licensing authority, the person who gave the Part 5A notice and every other relevant person must be informed.

An objection notice may be given only during the period beginning with the day of the giving of the Part 5A notice and ending with the third working day following that day ('the three-day period'). However, this restriction does not apply to an objection notice based on:

(a) things occurring after the end of the three-day period, or
(b) information that the relevant person was unaware of, and could not with reasonable diligence have discovered, until after the end of that period.

Where there is an objection, a relevant licensing authority may:

(a) give the person who gave the notice a counter-notice; and
(b) give a copy of the counter-notice to each relevant person.

Rights of entry, production of notice, etc

By LA 2003, s 110L, a constable or an authorised officer of the licensing authority may, at any reasonable time, enter premises to which a Part 5A notice relates to assess the likely effect of the notice on the promotion of the crime prevention objective. An authorised officer exercising this power must, if requested, produce evidence of his authority to exercise the power. It is an offence, contrary to s 110L(3), intentionally to obstruct an authorised officer exercising a power conferred by s 110L.

Whenever premises are being used for permitted sales by virtue of Part 5A, the person who gave the Part 5A notice must secure that a copy of it is either:

(a) prominently displayed at the premises; or
(b) kept there in his custody or that of a nominated person.

Where a copy of the Part 5A notice is kept in the custody of a nominated person, the person who gave the Part 5A notice must secure that a notice stating that a copy of the Part 5A notice is in the nominated person's custody is prominently displayed at the premises.

It is an offence, contrary to s 110M(4), for the person who gave the Part 5A notice to fail, without reasonable excuse, to comply with one or other of these requirements.

Where a copy of the Part 5A notice is not prominently displayed and no notice is displayed as to its whereabouts, a constable or authorised officer may require the person who gave the Part 5A notice to produce a copy of it for examination. Where a 'nominated person notice' is displayed as mentioned above, a constable or authorised officer may require the nominated person to produce a copy of the Part 5A notice. It is an offence for a person to fail, without reasonable excuse, to produce a copy of a Part 5A notice when required to do so (s 110M(8)).

Opening hours of premises in respect of which there is a premises licence or club premises certificate

LA 2003 does not prescribe 'permitted hours' within which alcohol may be sold or supplied for consumption on or off the premises. In addition, there are no general restrictions placed upon any other licensable activity. An applicant for a premises licence or a club premises certificate may choose the hours within which it would like to be authorised to carry out the licensed activities. The licence will be granted on those terms unless, following representations, the authority considers it necessary to reject the application or alter its terms bearing in mind the licensing objectives set out on p 550.

The Secretary of State is empowered by LA 2003, s 172 to make an order to permit premises with a premises licence or a club premises certificate to open for specified, generally extended hours, on special occasions of international, national or local significance.

Early morning alcohol restriction orders

LA 2003, s 172A empowers a licensing authority to make an early morning alcohol restriction order if it considers it appropriate for the promotion of the licensing objectives.

An order will provide that premises licences and club premises certificates granted by the authority, and TENs given to the authority, do not have effect to the extent that they authorise the sale or supply of alcohol during the period specified in the order. The period that may be specified in the order must begin no earlier than 24.00 and end no later than 06.00. The order would, therefore, apply not only to pubs, bars and nightclubs but also to non-profit clubs such as sports, political and working men's clubs, supermarkets and convenience stores, and temporary events. An order may have effect:

(a) in relation to the same period of every day on which the order is to apply, or in relation to different periods of different days;
(b) every day or only on particular days (eg particular days of the week or year);
(c) in relation to the whole or part of the licensing authority's area; or
(d) for a limited or unlimited period.

The Licensing Act 2003 (Early Morning Restriction Orders) Regulations 2012 prescribe exceptions from the effect of an early morning alcohol restriction order. The prescribed exceptions are:

(a) premises which are a hotel, guest house, lodging house or hostel at which the supply of alcohol between 00.00 and 06.00 on any day may only be made to persons staying at the premises for consumption in their rooms (eg alcohol supplied by room service or by virtue of a mini-bar);
(b) premises which are authorised to supply alcohol for consumption on the premises between 00.00 and 06.00 only on 1 January in every year.

Thus, premises of these descriptions may continue to supply alcohol notwithstanding that they are situated in an area to which an early morning alcohol restriction order applies. An order made under s 172A is subject to an order made under s 172 (unless the s 172 order provides otherwise).

PERSONAL LICENCES

A personal licence is a licence granted by a licensing authority to an individual which authorises him to supply alcohol, or to authorise the supply of alcohol, in accordance with a premises licence. Supplying alcohol in this context means selling it by retail, or supplying it by or on behalf of a club to, or to the order of, a member of the club. On any premises with a premises licence authorising their use for the sale or supply of alcohol, the person nominated for the day-to-day running of the premises must hold a personal licence and is known as the 'designated premises supervisor'. There may be more than one personal licence-holder on the licensed premises, but it is not necessary for all members of staff to have personal licences. However, all supplies of alcohol under a premises licence must be made by or under the authority of a personal licence-holder.

A personal licence is one which relates solely to the supply of alcohol. A personal licence is not required in respect of the other activities regulated by LA 2003.

Personal licences are dealt with by LA 2003, Part 6 (ss 111 to 135). The licensing authority must grant a personal licence if it appears to it that:

(a) the applicant is aged 18 or over;
(b) as from a day to be appointed, he is entitled to work in the UK;
(c) he possesses a recognised qualification or is a person of a prescribed description;
(d) no personal licence held by him has been forfeited in the five-year period ending with the date of application; and
(e) he has not been convicted of any 'relevant offence' (a long list of offences ranging from theft to possession of drugs) or any 'foreign offence' (an offence (other than a relevant offence) under the law of any country outside England and Wales) or—as from a day to be appointed—required to pay an immigration penalty.

A licensing authority must reject an application if the applicant fails to meet the condition in (a), (b) (when in force), (c) or (d).

If an applicant meets the conditions in (a), (b) (when in force), (c) and (d), but fails to meet condition (e), the authority must notify the chief officer of police for its area. If the chief officer is satisfied, by reference (i) to any conviction for a relevant offence, or (ii) any conviction for a foreign offence which he considers comparable to a relevant offence, or (iii) (prospectively) to a requirement to pay an immigration penalty, that granting a personal licence to the applicant would undermine the crime prevention objective of LA 2003, he must within 14 days give the authority an objection notice.

As from a day to be appointed, if the applicant meets conditions (a) to (d) but fails to meet condition (e) by virtue of having been convicted of a specified immigration offence or of a foreign offence comparable to an immigration offence, or required to pay an immigration penalty, the authority must inform the Secretary of State. Where, having regard to such a conviction or requirement, the Secretary of State is satisfied that granting the licence would be prejudicial to the prevention of illegal working in licensed premises, the Secretary of State must, within 14 days of being informed, give the authority the reasons for being so satisfied in an 'immigration objection notice'.

If no objection notice or (prospectively) immigration objection notice is given in the requisite time, the authority must grant the personal licence. If such a notice is given in the requisite time, the authority must hold a hearing to consider the notice; having regard to the notice, the authority must:

(i) where the notice is an objection notice, reject the application if it considers it appropriate for the promotion of the crime prevention objective to do so; or
(ii) where the notice is an immigration objection notice, reject the application if it considers it appropriate to the prevention of illegal working in licensed premises to do so,

otherwise the application must be granted.

A licence specifies the holder's name and address, the authority which granted it, and convictions for relevant or foreign offences. The holder must notify the authority of any change in name or address. It is an offence to fail, without reasonable excuse, to do so (s 127(4)).

The system of personal licences permits licensed persons to move from one set of premises to another, regardless of area.

Where the holder of a personal licence is on premises to sell or authorise the sale of alcohol by virtue of a premises licence or TEN, he may be required by a constable or an authorised officer of the licensing authority to produce his licence; if requested an authorised officer must produce his authority. Failure to comply with such a request, without reasonable excuse, is an offence against s 135(5).

LICENSING OFFENCES

Unauthorised licensable activities

It is an offence against LA 2003, s 136(1)(a) for a person to carry on, or attempt to carry on, or against s 136(1)(b) for a person knowingly to allow to be carried on, a licensable activity on or from any premises otherwise than under or in accordance with an authorisation provided by a:

(a) premises licence;
(b) club premises certificate; or
(c) TEN.

In addition, as from a day to be appointed, the licensable activity of selling alcohol by retail is under and in accordance with an authorisation if each sale is a permitted sale by virtue of LA 2003, Part 5A described earlier.

A divisional court has held that the offence under s 136(1)(a) is directed at persons who *actually* carry on, or attempt to carry on, a licensable activity otherwise than in accordance with such authorisation. Thus, for example, where premises subject to a premises licence are used in breach of a condition under the premises licence the premises licence-holder is not automatically guilty of the offence. This is of obvious importance where (as in the case referred to) the premises licence-holder owns the licensed premises but lets them to someone else who actually carries out the licensable activity there and who breaches a condition of the licence unknown to the licence-holder.

Exposing alcohol for unauthorised sale

It is an offence against LA 2003, s 137(1) to expose, on any premises, alcohol for sale by retail in circumstances where the actual sale by retail of that alcohol would be an unauthorised licensable activity. As can be seen, a sale, or an attempted sale, is not necessary.

Keeping alcohol on premises for unauthorised sale

LA 2003, s 138(1) creates the offence of possessing, or having under control, alcohol, with the intention of selling it by retail, or supplying it, where that sale or supply would be an unauthorised licensable activity.

Defence of due diligence

By LA 2003, s 139, it is a defence to an offence under ss 136(1)(a), 137 or 138 that the defendant's act was due to a mistake, or to reliance on information given to him, or to an act or omission of another person, or to some cause beyond his control, and he took all reasonable steps and exercised all due diligence to avoid committing the offence.

DRUNKENNESS AND DISORDERLY CONDUCT

Where it is referred to in the various offences under the above heading, 'relevant premises' are premises in respect of which there is a premises licence, or a club premises certificate, or premises which may be used for a permitted temporary activity, or premises that (by reason of being specified in a Part 5A notice) are premises on which a sale by retail of alcohol is capable of being a permitted sale by virtue of Part 5A.

Allowing disorderly conduct on licensed premises, etc

LA 2003, s 140(1) and (2) makes it an offence knowingly to allow disorderly conduct on licensed premises, premises in respect of which a club premises certificate is in force or premises which may be used for a permitted temporary activity. The offence can be committed by any person who works on the premises in a capacity, paid or unpaid, which gives him the authority to prevent such conduct. On premises with a premises licence, the offence can also be committed by the premises licence-holder or designated premises supervisor. In the case of a club, the offence can also be committed by an officer or member of the club who is present when the disorderly conduct takes place and who has the authority to prevent it. Members of a club committee would obviously be in such a position. In the case of a temporary event the offence can also be committed by the premises-user. As from a day to be appointed, in the case of premises specified in a Part 5A notice, the offence can also be committed by the person who gave the notice.

Sale of alcohol to a person who is drunk or obtaining alcohol for such a person

By LA 2003, s 141, it is an offence, on relevant premises, knowingly to sell, or attempt to sell, alcohol to a person who is drunk, or to allow alcohol to be sold to such a person. The offence also applies to the supply of alcohol by or on behalf of a club.

The offence may be committed by the same category of persons to which s 140 applies.

The s 141 offence is a 'penalty offence' for the purposes of CJPA 2001: see p 31.

By s 142(1), it is an offence for a person knowingly to obtain, or attempt to obtain, alcohol for consumption on relevant premises by a person who is drunk.

Failure to leave licensed premises, etc

A person commits an offence against LA 2003, s 143(1) and (2) if he is drunk and disorderly and fails, without reasonable excuse, to leave relevant premises at the request of a police constable or:

(a) any person who works at the premises in a capacity, paid or unpaid, which gives him the authority to make that request;
(b) a premises licence-holder or designated premises supervisor;
(c) an officer or member of a club who is present at the time and has authority to make that request;
(d) a premises-user who has given a TEN in respect of the event; and
(e) as from a day to be appointed, in the case of premises specified in a Part 5A notice, the person who gave the notice.

A person who is drunk and disorderly also commits an offence under s 143(1) and (2) if, without reasonable excuse, he enters, or attempts to enter, such premises when requested not to do so by any such persons.

Section 143(4) requires a constable to assist in the expulsion of persons who are drunk and disorderly from such premises, or to help prevent such a person from entering, if requested to do so by any of the persons described above.

OFFENCES IN RELATION TO CHILDREN

Where it is referred to in the various offences under LA 2003 in relation to children, 'relevant premises' are premises in respect of which there is a premises licence, or a club premises certificate, or premises which may be used for a permitted temporary activity, or (as from a day to be appointed, except in ss 145 and 152 (below and p 569), premises that (by reason of being specified in a Part 5A notice) are premises on which a sale by retail of alcohol is capable of being a permitted sale by virtue of part 5A.

Unaccompanied children prohibited from certain premises

It is an offence against LA 2003, s 145(1) for a person, knowing that 'relevant premises' are within s 145(4), to allow a child under 16 to be on certain categories of relevant premises if he is not accompanied by an adult (18 or over) and the premises are open for the supply of alcohol for consumption on the premises. 'Relevant premises' are within s 145(4) if:

(a) they are exclusively or primarily used for the supply of alcohol for consumption on the premises; or
(b) they are open for the purpose of being used for the supply of alcohol for consumption on the premises by virtue of LA 2003, Part 5 (permitted temporary activities) and, at the time the TEN in question has effect, they are exclusively or primarily used for such supplies.

It is also an offence against s 145(1) to allow an unaccompanied child under 16 to be on 'relevant premises' at a time between the hours of 00.00 and 05.00 when the premises are open for the supply of alcohol for consumption there.

By s 145(3), these offences may be committed by a person working on the premises in any capacity, paid or unpaid, with the authority to ask the child to leave; the premises licence-holder or designated premises supervisor; an officer or member of a club with that authority; or the premises-user who has given a TEN in respect of the premises.

No offence is committed where the unaccompanied child is merely passing through the premises, where this is the convenient route.

A person charged with an offence under s 145 by reason of his own conduct has a defence if he believed the child to be 16 or over, or that an individual accompanying him was 18 or over, and had either taken all reasonable steps to establish the individual's age, or no one could reasonably have suspected from the individual's appearance that he was aged under 16 or 18, as the case may be. A person will be treated as having taken all reasonable steps to establish an individual's age if he asked for evidence of it and the evidence would have convinced a reasonable person. Where a person is charged because of the default of some other person, it is a defence to show that he had exercised all due diligence to avoid committing the offence.

Sale of alcohol to children

LA 2003, s 146(1) prohibits the sale of alcohol to an individual aged under 18 *anywhere*. Section 146(2) provides that a club commits an offence if alcohol is supplied by or on its behalf to, or to the order of, a member under 18, or to a person under 18 to the order of a member of a club. A person who supplies alcohol on behalf of a club in such circumstances commits an offence contrary to s 146(3).

Section 146(4) provides a defence where D (the person charged with an offence under s 146) believed that the purchaser was 18 or over and either:

(a) D took all reasonable steps to establish the purchaser's age; or
(b) no one could reasonably have suspected from the purchaser's appearance that he was under 18.

D will be deemed to have taken all reasonable steps if he asked the individual for evidence of his age and the evidence would have convinced a reasonable person. In the latter respect, the prosecution may show that the evidence of age produced was such that no reasonable person would have been convinced by it (it might be an obvious forgery or obviously belong to some other person).

Where a sale or supply was made by some other person than D (as where a barman supplies a drink on behalf of the holder of the premises licence) it is a defence to show that D exercised all due diligence to avoid committing the offence (s 146(5)).

An offence under s 146(1) or (3) is a 'penalty offence' for the purposes of CJPA 2001: see p 31.

It is an offence against s 147(1) for a person knowingly to allow the sale of alcohol to a person under 18 on 'relevant premises' as defined on p 566. The persons who can commit this offence are those workers, paid or unpaid, with authority to prevent sale or supply. An officer or member of a club, or a worker in it, with that authority commits an offence under s 147(3) if he allows alcohol to be supplied to or to the order of a member under 18, or to someone under 18 to the order of such a member.

Persistently selling alcohol to children

LA 2003, s 147A(1) provides that an offence is committed if, on two or more different occasions in a period of three consecutive months, alcohol is unlawfully sold to an individual who is under 18 on the same premises, which *at the time of each sale* were licensed premises, premises authorised to be used for a permitted temporary activity, or (as from a day to be appointed) premises specified in a Part 5A notice. The offence is committed by a person who was a 'responsible person' in relation to the premises *at each such time*. A person is a 'responsible person' for the purposes of s 147A(1) if, *at that time,* he is the person (or one of the persons) who holds the premises licence or who is the premises-user in respect of a TEN or who is a giver of a Part A notice. For the purposes of s 147A, alcohol is unlawfully sold to an individual under 18 if the person making the sale believed the individual to be under 18 or did not have reasonable grounds for believing him to be 18 or over. A person has reasonable grounds for so believing only if he asked for evidence of age and the evidence produced was such that it would have convinced a reasonable person, or if no person could reasonably have suspected from the individual's appearance that he was less than 18. The sales mentioned in s 147A(1) might, but need not, be to the same individual. The same sale may not be counted in respect of different offences for the purpose of enabling the same person to be convicted of more than one offence under s 147A, or for the purpose of enabling the same person to be convicted under s 147A and an offence under s 146 (sale of alcohol to children) or s 147 (allowing such a sale) referred to above. The purpose of s 147A is to provide a much larger penalty for persistent sales by responsible persons.

For the purposes of establishing the offence under s 147A, evidence in respect of a conviction, caution or fixed penalty notice for an offence under s 146 in respect of a sale to *that individual on those premises on that occasion* is admissible as evidence that there has been an unlawful sale of alcohol to an individual under 18 on any premises on any occasion.

On conviction of a premises licence-holder for an offence against s 147A, the court may suspend the premises licence for up to three months in respect of retail sales of alcohol.

As an alternative to a prosecution under LA 2003, s 147A, LA 2003, s 169A permits a 'relevant officer' (superintendent (or above) or an inspector of weights and measures) to issue a closure notice in the prescribed form in relation to any premises if:

(a) there is evidence of the commission of an offence against s 147A;
(b) the relevant officer considers that the evidence provides a realistic prospect of a conviction; and
(c) the offender is still the premises licence-holder (or one of them) in respect of the premises in question.

Such a notice proposes a prohibition of the sale of alcohol at the premises in question for a period specified in the notice and offers the offender the chance to discharge all criminal liability for the alleged offence against s 147A by the acceptance of the prohibition proposed by the notice. The length of the prohibition specified in the order must not exceed 336 hours. The period specified in the notice as the *start time* for closure must not be less than 14 days following service of the notice. Service of a notice must take place when licensable activities are taking place. The notice has the effect of temporarily suspending the premises licence. If sales take place during the period of prohibition, those sales will be unlawful in terms of s 136 referred to on p 564.

Purchase of alcohol by children or on their behalf

LA 2003, s 149(1) makes it an offence for a person under 18 (a) to buy or attempt to buy alcohol, or (b) if he is a member of a club, for him to have alcohol supplied to him by the club in circumstances in which he initiates the supply, or for him to attempt to do so. Test purchasing on behalf of a constable or trading standards officer is excepted from these provisions.

Section 149(3) makes it an offence for a person to act as an agent for a child in purchasing, or attempting to purchase, alcohol.

Section 149(4) provides an offence which is committed on 'relevant premises' (see p 566) by prohibiting a person from buying or attempting to buy alcohol for consumption by a person under 18 on those premises. This would cover any relative or friend of a child who buys a drink for a child, or tries to do so, on 'relevant premises'. However, the offence is not committed by an adult who buys beer, wine or cider for a person aged 16 or 17 to consume with a table meal (ie a meal eaten by a person seated at a table, counter or other structure used as a table by seated persons) taken on those premises in the company of an adult.

The offences under s 149(3) and (4) also apply in respect of the *supply* of alcohol in premises in respect of which there is in force a club premises certificate.

A s 149 offence is a 'penalty offence' for the purposes of CJPA 2001: see p 31.

Consumption of alcohol by children

It is an offence against LA 2003, s 150(1) for an individual under 18 knowingly to consume alcohol on 'relevant premises'. Because of the presence of 'knowingly' the offence will not be committed where a child accidentally consumes alcohol, being unaware of the nature of his drink, or where something has been furtively added to it.

Section 150(2) makes it an offence for a person knowingly to allow such consumption to take place on 'relevant premises'. This offence can be committed by a worker at the premises who has authority to prevent the consumption or by a member or officer of a club in a capacity to do so.

These offences do not apply to a person of 16 or 17 who consumes beer, wine or cider with a table meal on licensed, etc premises and is accompanied by a person of 18 or over.

An offence under s 150 is a 'penalty offence' for the purposes of CJPA 2001: see p 31.

Delivering alcohol to children

LA 2003, s 151(1) is concerned with the delivery of alcohol to a person under 18. Delivery is a term which avoids 'sale or supply'. The offence lies in a person who works on 'relevant premises', knowingly delivering to a person under 18, alcohol which is sold on the premises or supplied by a club. It may be that his mother has bought and paid for a quantity of drink and has left it at the off-licence to be picked up. If a child goes to pick up the alcohol and it is handed over to that child, there has been a delivery. It is an offence (by s 151(2)) for a person working on the premises with the necessary authority to prevent the delivery to allow it to take place. A similar offence under s 151(4) applies to clubs.

None of the offences under s 151 is committed if alcohol is delivered to a home or workplace, nor does it apply where the job of a minor involves the delivery of alcohol, nor where alcohol is sold or supplied for consumption on the 'relevant premises' (as other offences are committed in this circumstance).

An offence under s 151 is a 'penalty offence' for the purposes of CJPA 2001: see p 31.

Sending child to obtain alcohol

In view of the offences involving delivery to a person under 18, it is not surprising to find that 'sending' such a person to obtain alcohol sold, or to be sold, on 'relevant premises', or supplied or to be supplied by a club, is an offence against LA 2003, s 152(1). Thus where a parent orders by telephone from an off-licence and sends a child to seek the order, an offence against the section is committed. Section 152 provides that the offence is committed whether the child is sent to the licensed premises, etc or to some other delivery point. Thus, if the 'order' has been sent to a distribution centre and it is collected from those premises, the offence is still committed. No offence is committed where the minor works at the premises in a capacity involving the delivery of alcohol, nor if the child is assisting a constable or trading standards officer.

Unsupervised sales by children

It is an offence against LA 2003, s 153(1) for a responsible person knowingly to allow on 'relevant premises' a person under the age of 18 to sell or, in the case of a club, supply alcohol, unless each sale or supply has been specifically approved by a responsible person. A 'responsible person' means:

(a) in the case of licensed premises, the holder of the premises licence or the designated premises supervisor or an adult authorised by such a person to prevent the sale; or
(b) in the case of club certificate premises, any member or officer present in a capacity to prevent the supply; or
(c) at a temporary permitted activity, the premises-user or an adult authorised by him to prevent the sale; or
(d) as from a day to be appointed, in relation to a sale by retail that is a permitted sale by virtue of Part 5A, the person who gave the Part 5A notice or an adult authorised by him to prevent the sale,

as appropriate. Many of the checkout personnel in supermarkets which are authorised to sell for off-consumption are under 18, but provided that each sale is specifically approved no offence is committed. Such youngsters are seen to gain the approval of more senior personnel. Section 153 exempts sales in a restaurant of alcohol to be taken with a table meal. Thus waiters and waitresses under 18 may serve drinks in such a part of the premises.

Offence of persistently possessing alcohol in a public place

The Policing and Crime Act 2009, s 30(1) provides that a person under 18 is guilty of an offence if, without reasonable excuse, he is in possession of alcohol in any relevant place on three or more occasions within a period of 12 consecutive months.

'Relevant place', in relation to a person, means any public place, other than excluded premises, or any place, other than a public place, to which the person has unlawfully gained access. 'Excluded premises' means:

(a) premises which may by virtue of LA 2003, Parts 3 or 5 (see pp 556 and 557) be used for the supply of alcohol;
(b) premises which may by virtue of Part 4 (see p 556) be used for the supply of alcohol to members or guests.

CONFISCATION OF ALCOHOL—YOUNG PERSONS

The Confiscation of Alcohol (Young Persons) Act 1997 (CA(YP)A 1997), s 1 provides that, where a constable reasonably suspects that P, a person in any public place other than licensed premises, or any place (other than a public place) to which P has unlawfully gained access, is in possession of alcohol and that either:

(a) P is under 18; or
(b) P intends that any of the alcohol should be consumed by a person under the age of 18 in that or another similar place; or
(c) a person under the age of 18 who is, or has recently been, with P, has recently consumed alcohol in that or another similar place,

the constable may require P to surrender anything which P possesses which is, or the constable reasonably believes to be, alcohol or a container for it. A constable who imposes such a requirement on a person must also require him to state his name and address and may, if the constable reasonably suspects that he is under 16, remove him to his place of residence or to a place of safety. A person who, without reasonable excuse, fails to comply with a surrender of alcohol requirement or a name and address requirement commits an offence under s 1(3). A constable who makes a surrender requirement must inform the person concerned of his suspicion and that failing without reasonable excuse to comply with either type of requirement is an offence.

Section 1 provides a means by which the nuisance caused by youngsters assembling in public places and drinking may be removed. It effectively embraces all persons likely to be in such a group, including those who are 18 or over if, as they are almost certain to be, they are associated with drinking by those who are under age.

A constable may dispose of anything surrendered to him under CA(YP)A 1997 in such a manner as he considers appropriate.

OTHER PROHIBITIONS UPON THE SALE OR CONSUMPTION OF ALCOHOL

Prohibition of sale of alcohol on moving vehicles

LA 2003, s 156(1) creates the offence of selling alcohol by retail on or from a vehicle which is not permanently or temporarily parked. It is a defence where the sale was mistaken; was due to the seller relying on information given to him; was the fault of another person; or was due to some cause beyond the seller's control, provided (in each case) that he took all reasonable precautions and exercised due diligence to avoid committing the offence.

Power to prohibit sale of alcohol on trains

LA 2003, s 157 provides for a magistrates' court to make an order prohibiting the sale of alcohol at specified stations or on trains travelling between specified stations for a particular period. A prohibition order may be made on the application of a police officer of at least the rank of inspector, if the magistrates are satisfied that an order is necessary for the prevention of disorder. A copy of the order must be served by the police upon the operator or operators concerned. Thus, provision is made for 'dry' soccer specials, at least so far as the operating companies are concerned. A sale, or attempted sale, in breach of a prohibition order is an offence under s 157(3), as is allowing such a sale.

MAKING FALSE STATEMENTS IN APPLICATIONS FOR LICENCES AND CERTIFICATES AND IN NOTICES

It is an offence against LA 2003, s 158(1) for a person knowingly or recklessly to make a false statement in or in connection with (a) an application for the grant, variation, transfer or review of a premises licence or club premises certificate, (b) an application for a local authority provisional statement in respect of a premises licence, (c) a TEN or any other notice under the Act, or (d) an application for the grant or renewal of a personal licence. For the purposes of s 158 a person is treated as making a false statement if he produces, furnishes, signs or otherwise makes use of a document that contains a false statement.

CLOSURE OF LICENSED PREMISES DUE TO DISORDER, ACTUAL OR ANTICIPATED

LA 2003, s 160 deals with situations in which there is, or there is expected to be, disorder in a local justice area. In such cases, a magistrates' court acting for that area may make a closure order for a period not exceeding 24 hours, in relation to all premises situated at or near the place of the disorder or expected disorder and in respect of which a premises licence or a TEN has effect. Application for such an order must be made by a superintendent (or above) and the order must not be made unless the court is satisfied that it is necessary to prevent disorder.

It is an offence under s 160(4) for a manager of premises, the holder of a premises licence, the designated premises supervisor or the premises-user in the case of a temporary event, knowingly to keep open premises to which the order relates, or to allow any such premises to be kept open, during the currency of that order.

By s 160(7), a constable may use such force as may be necessary to close such premises.

CLOSURE OF UNLICENSED PREMISES UNDER PROVISIONS OF CJPA 2001

Where a constable or a local authority is satisfied that premises are being, or within the last 24 hours have been, used for unauthorised sale of alcohol for consumption on, or in the vicinity of, the premises, CJPA 2001, s 19 provides that he or it may serve a closure notice on a person having control of, or responsibility for, the activities carried on at the premises. A closure notice must also be served on any person occupying any other part of the building whose access would be impeded by the order. It may also be served on any other person with control of, or responsibility for, the activities on the premises, or any person with an interest in the premises. A closure notice must specify the nature of the alleged use of the premises, state the effect of s 20 (below), and set out the steps which may be taken to ensure that the alleged use of the premises ceases or (as the case may be) does not recur. Closure notices issued by a constable or a local authority may be cancelled at any time.

Section 20 provides that when a closure notice has been served the constable or local authority may seek an order from the justices, not less than seven days, and not more than six months, after the service of the notice. An order should not be sought where the constable or local authority is satisfied that the offending use of the premises has ceased and that there is no reasonable likelihood of resumption. Where the justices on hearing the case are satisfied that a notice was properly served under s 19, and that the premises and/or the vicinity of those premises continue to be used for the offending purpose or that there is a reasonable likelihood that there will be such use, they may make a closure order under s 21, requiring in particular:

(a) immediate closure of the premises to the public until the constable or local authority (as the case may be) has certified that the need for the order has ceased (such an order may include conditions relating to admission and access to other parts of the building);

(b) any offending use to be discontinued immediately; and

(c) any defendant to pay into court a sum of money which will not be released until the other requirements of the order have been complied with.

The constable or local authority (as the case may be) must fix a copy of the order to the premises.

Affected persons may seek discharge of the order. If the justices are satisfied that the need for the order has ceased, they may discharge it.

A person who, without reasonable excuse, permits premises to be open in contravention of a closure order, or who otherwise fails to comply with it, commits an offence against s 25(4) or (5) respectively.

Police powers

By CJPA 2001, s 25(1) and (2), where a closure order has been made a constable or an authorised person, who identifies himself if so required, may enter the premises at any reasonable time, if need be by reasonable force, and do anything reasonably necessary to secure compliance with the order.

It is an offence contrary to s 25(3) for a person intentionally to obstruct a constable or an authorised person in the exercise of these powers.

MISCELLANEOUS MATTERS

Exclusion of persons convicted of offences of violence from licensed premises

The Licensed Premises (Exclusion of Certain Persons) Act 1980, s 1 permits courts to make exclusion orders in respect of someone convicted by or before them of offences of violence or threats of violence on premises in respect of which a premises licence authorising the supply of alcohol for consumption on the premises is in force, prohibiting such a person from entering specified licensed premises without the express consent of the licensee, his employee or agent. Entry in breach of an exclusion order is an offence under s 2(1). By s 3, the licensee, his employee or agent may expel a person who has entered, or whom he reasonably suspects of entering, in breach of an order. A constable must, on the demand of a licensee, his employee or agent, help to expel any person whom the constable reasonably suspects of being in breach of an exclusion order.

Prohibition of sales of alcohol at service areas, garages, etc

LA 2003, s 176 provides that no premises licence, club premises certificate or TEN has effect to authorise the sale by retail or supply of alcohol on or from excluded premises. These are premises on the land of a motorway authority being used for the provision of facilities at motorway service stations or premises used primarily as a garage or which form part of such premises. The definition of excluded premises may be altered by the Secretary of State.

Dancing in certain small premises

LA 2003, s 177 is concerned with the situation where (a) a premises licence or a club premises certificate authorises dancing and the sale of alcohol for consumption on the premises, and (b) the premises are used primarily for the sale of alcohol for consumption on the premises and have a capacity limit of up to 200. Section 177 provides that, at any time when the premises are open for the supply of alcohol for consumption on the premises and are being used for dancing, any conditions imposed in respect of music entertainment (ie live music or dancing) by the licensing authority, other than those set out in the licence-holder's operating schedule, will be suspended unless they were imposed for public safety or the prevention of crime and disorder.

Section 177 may be disapplied in relation to conditions in respect of particular premises following a review of the licence or certificate.

Licence review for live and recorded music

Section 177A provides that, where music (whether live or recorded) takes place on premises authorised to be used for the supply of alcohol for consumption on the premises by a premises licence or club premises certificate, and:

(a) at the time of the music, the premises are open for the purposes of being used for the supply of alcohol for consumption on the premises;

(b) if the music is amplified, it takes place in the presence of an audience of no more than 500 persons;

(c) the music takes place between 08.00 and 23.00 on the same day (or, where a special occasion order (p 562) has effect, between the hours specified in that order),

any condition of the premises licence or club premises certificate which relates to live music, recorded music or both does not have effect in relation to the music, unless, on a review of the licence or certificate, s 177A is disapplied in relation to that condition (s 177A(3)) or a condition is added relating to the music as if it were regulated entertainment and the licence or certificate licensed the music (s 177A(4)). For the purposes of s 177A, 'condition' means a condition included in a premises licence or club premises certificate, other than one which is a mandatory one, including one added by way of variation at the request of the licence-holder or the club, as the case may be.

Section 177A does not apply to music which, by virtue of a provision in Sch 1, other than the exemption relating to licensed venues (exemption (l) on p 554) or the exemption relating to live unamplified music (exemption (n) on p 554), is not regarded as the provision of regulated entertainment for the purposes of LA 2003.

Police powers

LA 2003, s 179(1) provides for a police officer or authorised person (see p 550) to enter premises where he has reason to believe that the premises are being, or are about to be, used for a licensable activity to ensure that the activities are being carried on under and in accordance with an authorisation. As from a day to be appointed, an immigration officer may enter premises where he has reason to believe that they are being used for the retail sale of alcohol or the provision of late night refreshment to see whether an offence under the Immigration Acts is being committed in connection with the carrying on of such an activity (s 179(1A)). An authorised person or immigration officer must produce his authority if requested. Reasonable force may be used if necessary. By s 179(4), it is an offence intentionally to obstruct an authorised person or immigration officer acting under s 179.

Section 180 provides that a police officer may enter and search premises where there is reason to believe an offence under the Act has been, is being or is about to be committed, and may use reasonable force to gain entry.

OFFENCES OF DRUNKENNESS AND POLICE POWERS

Drunkenness is not in itself an offence but becomes so in certain circumstances, which are described below. Drunkenness in this context is limited to intoxication through drink and does not include intoxication through drugs or through glue-sniffing. A divisional court has held that 'drunkenness' requires that the defendant has voluntarily consumed alcohol and that this has resulted in his becoming drunk. 'Drunk' bears its ordinary natural meaning; whether a defendant was drunk is a question of fact in each case.

The offence of being drunk at a designated sports ground is dealt with in Chapter 27.

Drunk on highway or other public place

The Licensing Act 1872 (LA 1872), s 12 provides that a person is guilty of an offence if he is found drunk on any highway or other public place, whether a building or not, or on any licensed premises. The offence is often described as one of 'simple drunkenness' to distinguish it from other offences dealing with aggravated forms of drunkenness. It is particularly worth remembering that PACE, s 24 permits an arrest if it is necessary to prevent the person from suffering physical injury. Such injury would be likely if he was left unconscious in the open.

This offence under LA 1872, s 12 is a 'penalty offence' for the purposes of CJPA 2001: see p 31.

Drunk and disorderly

The Criminal Justice Act 1967, s 91 states that any person who in any public place is guilty, while drunk, of disorderly behaviour commits an offence. A divisional court has held that whether the defendant's behaviour was disorderly is a simple question of fact. What is required is that his behaviour, viewed objectively, was disorderly. 'Disorderly behaviour' does not involve any element of mens rea. Where there is an intercom system and locks on the entrance to a block of flats, so that only those admitted by the occupiers are given access to the area, the landing area outside the flats is not a public place for the purposes of this offence. Nor would it be for the purposes of the offence of simple drunkenness.

An offence under s 91 is a 'penalty offence' for the purposes of CJPA 2001: see p 31.

Drunk in charge of particular things

LA 1872, s 12 also makes it an offence for a person to be drunk while in charge on any highway or other public place, of a carriage, a horse, cattle, or a steam engine, or to be drunk when in possession of a loaded firearm. 'Carriage' includes a motor vehicle, but if a person is drunk in charge of such a vehicle the appropriate offence is that under RTA 1988, s 4 (discussed in Chapter 15) and not the present one, since it is a more serious offence which reflects the gravity of the situation. Although a bi-cycle is a 'carriage', *riding* a cycle while unfit through drink is also an offence under RTA 1988, s 30, and if a person rides while unfit he should be dealt with under that section. However, a person *in charge*, for example pushing a pedal cycle, in such a condition commits an offence only against LA 1872, s 12. The Act does not define the term 'firearm' for the purposes of the section, but that term bears its everyday meaning and includes an airgun.

Drunk in charge of a child

The Licensing Act 1902, s 2 creates the offence of being found drunk on any highway or other public place, whether a building or not, or on any licensed premises, while having the charge of a child apparently under the age of seven.

CHAPTER 18

Dogs

CONTROL OF DOGS

Collars

The Control of Dogs Order 1992 requires that while on a highway or in a place of public resort every dog must wear a collar with the owner's name and address inscribed upon it, or on a plate or badge attached to it. This does not apply to:

(a) any pack of hounds;
(b) any dog while being used:
    (i) for sporting purposes;
    (ii) for the capture or destruction of vermin;
    (iii) for the driving or tending of cattle or sheep;
    (iv) on official duties by a member of the armed forces or Revenue and Customs or by the police force for any area; or
    (v) in emergency rescue work; or
(c) any dog registered with the Guide Dogs for the Blind Association.

The owner or the person in charge of a dog who, without lawful authority or excuse, the proof whereof is on him, causes or permits the dog to be in a highway or place of public resort without the requisite collar is guilty of an offence under reg 3.

Leads and muzzles

The Road Traffic Act 1988, s 27 empowers local authorities to make orders designating lengths of roads within their areas as roads upon which dogs must at all times be kept on a lead. The chief officer of police must be consulted before such an order is made and the local authority is required to publish it and to place signs on the designated length of road subject to the order. When such an order is in force, it is an offence under s 27(1) to cause or permit a dog to be on such a length of road if it is not held on a lead. The offence does not apply to dogs tending cattle or sheep in the course of a business nor to those being used for sporting purposes. Further exceptions may be made by the order.

STRAY DOGS

The Environmental Protection Act 1990, s 149 requires every local authority to appoint an officer to deal with stray dogs found in its area. Where the appointed officer has reason to believe that any dog found in a public place or on any other land or premises is a stray dog, he must, where possible, seize it and detain it. Where the place concerned is not a public place, he may only seize and detain the dog with the consent of the owner or occupier of the place. Where the dog wears a collar on which appears a person's name and address, or its owner is known, a notice must be served on that person, stating that the dog will be liable to be disposed of if it is not claimed within seven clear days and the expenses of its detention met. After the dog has been detained for seven clear days (or, where a notice has been served, if it has not been claimed and the expenses paid within seven clear days after service of the notice) the dog may be disposed of by way of sale, gift or destruction. The ownership of a dog so sold or given is vested in the buyer if he acts in good faith.

The officer must keep a register giving particulars of all dogs so seized and disposed of. The register must be available for inspection by the public without charge.

Section 150 requires the finder of a stray dog to:

(a) return it to its owner; or
(b) take the dog to the appointed local authority officer for the area or to the nearest police station;

and to inform that officer or the police officer in charge of where the dog was found. Failure to do so is an offence (s 150(5)). Where a dog has been taken to an appointed officer, the finder may keep the dog, if he wishes, on informing the officer of this and his name and address. In such a case the finder must keep the dog for at least a month; he commits an offence if he fails to do so (s 150(5)).

DANGEROUS DOGS

Order to keep under control

If it appears to a magistrates' court that a dog is dangerous and not kept under proper control, it may, under the Dogs Act 1871, order the owner to keep it under control or order the dog's destruction. The proceedings must be by way of complaint. Complaints may be preferred by a police officer.

Such an order may be made whether or not the dog is shown to have injured any person. It may specify the measures to be taken for keeping the dog under control, whether by muzzling it, keeping it on a lead or excluding it from specified places, or otherwise. Such an order may also require the neutering of a male dog.

Divisional courts have held that it is not necessary that the dog is dangerous to mankind; it is enough that it is dangerous to other animals of whatever kind, even another dog. In an old case, a dog which killed two pet rabbits was held by a divisional court not to be dangerous as it was within the natural instincts of a dog to chase, wound or kill other small animals.

The Dangerous Dogs Act 1989 (DDA 1989), s 1(1) empowers a magistrates' court, when it makes a destruction order under the 1871 Act, to appoint a person to undertake the destruction and to require the custodian to deliver it up, and to disqualify the owner from having custody for a specified period.

DDA 1989, s 1(3) provides offences of failing to keep a dog under proper control as ordered under the 1871 Act, and failing to deliver up a dog for destruction. The punishment can include disqualification from having custody of a dog for a specified period. An owner who has custody of a dog while disqualified under s 1(1) or (3) commits an offence under s 1(6).

Specific offences in relation to dangerous dogs

The Dangerous Dogs Act 1991 (DDA 1991), ss 1 and 3 make further provisions in relation to dangerous dogs.

Possession or control of dogs bred for fighting

DDA 1991, s 1(3) provides that no person may have in his possession or control a dog to which s 1 applies, except under a power of seizure or destruction or (by s 1(5)) under the provisions relating to the exemption schemes referred to on this page and pp 580–2. Section 1 applies to any dog of the type known as pit bull terrier, Japanese tosa, and any other type of dog designated by order of the Secretary of State, currently the dogo Argentino and the Fila Braziliero. 'Type' has a wider meaning than 'breed'. Determining the limits of a type is a question of fact for determination by the court. The court is entitled to look at the American Dog Breeders' Association (ADBA) breed standard as a guide. The fact that a dog does not meet that standard in every respect is not conclusive that it is not one of the specified types. Thus, for example, it has been held that the fact that a dog is near to, or has a substantial number of, characteristics of a pit bull terrier as set out in the ADBA standard is sufficient for the dog to be found to be of the pit bull terrier type. It is relevant to consider whether the dog exhibited the behavioural characteristics of a pit bull terrier but that evidence would not be conclusive.

In any proceedings under s 1, it is presumed that a dog is of such a type unless D proves the contrary. Breach of s 1(3) is an offence under s 1(7).

Court-ordered exemption scheme

The Dangerous Dogs Exemption Schemes (England and Wales) Order 2015 (DDES(E&W)O 2015), Part 2 (arts 4–11) deals with this. The prohibition in DDA 1991, s 1(3) does not apply to a dog provided that:

(a) a court has determined under s 4(1A) or 4B (pp 583 and 584) that the dog is not a danger to public safety and has made the dog subject to a contingent destruction order under s 4A (p 584) or 4B;

(b) the following 'exemption conditions' are met in respect of that dog within the 'specified time period':
   (i)   the dog is neutered;
   (ii) the dog is microchipped;
   (iii) third-party insurance in respect of the dog is obtained; and
   (iv) a certificate of exemption is issued,
   in each case in accordance with DDES(E&W)O 2015; and

(c) the requirements attached to the certificate of exemption are complied with throughout the lifetime of the dog.

Subject to any extension granted by the court, the conditions in (b) must be complied with:

- in the case of an adult dog, within two months of the contingent destruction order; and
- in the case of a dog under the age of six months at the time of the contingent destruction order, within one month of the dog attaining six months.

A dog is not exempt from the prohibition in s 1(3):

(a) if the conditions referred to in (b) (above) are not met within the time period just specified; or

(b) if the requirements attached to the certificate of exemption are not complied with at any time after the certificate is issued.

The Index of Exempted Dogs, the Agency designated to discharge functions under DDES(E&W)O 2015 (hereafter 'the Agency'), must issue a certificate of exemption in respect of the dog if it is satisfied that:

(a) the court, in determining that the dog is not a danger to public safety, has decided the person to whom the certificate is to be issued is a fit and proper person to be in charge of the dog and has made the dog subject to a contingent destruction order;

(b) the relevant fee plus VAT has been paid to the Agency; and

(c) conditions (i) to (iii) above have been met.

A certificate of exemption must contain requirements:

(a) to keep the dog at the same address as the person to whom the certificate is issued save for any 30 days in a 12-month period;

(b) to notify the Agency: (i) of any proposed change of address (not to include any changes of address in the 30 days mentioned in (a)), and (ii) of the death or export of the dog;

(c) to satisfy the Agency that a policy of third-party insurance is in force;

(d) to keep the dog: (i) muzzled and on a lead when in a public place, and (ii) in sufficiently secure conditions to prevent its escape;

(e) to provide access to the dog for the purpose of reading a microchip on request by a constable (or authorised local authority officer);

(f) to produce to such a person the certificate of exemption and confirmation that third-party insurance is in force within five days of being requested to do so by him.

Substitution of person in charge of dog exempted

DDES(E&W)O 2015, Part 3 (arts 12–19) deals with this.

When a dog has been exempted from the prohibition in DDA 1991, s 1(3), a person may apply to a magistrates' court to be substituted as the person in charge of the dog only if the person determined by the court as being a fit and proper person to be in charge of the dog is unable to continue to be in charge of it by reason of the death of that person, or serious illness rendering him unable to be in charge. Subject to any extension by the court, the application must be made within six weeks of the death of the person in charge, or of an official letter from a medical practitioner confirming the serious illness of the person in charge. Non-compliance results in the dog no longer being exempted.

At least two weeks before making an application to the court, the applicant must provide to the chief officer of police for the area in which he lives:

(a) his name, address and date of birth; and

(b) details of the exempted dog and of the person to whom the certificate of exemption was issued.

The court may only grant the application for substitution of the applicant as the person in charge of the exempted dog if satisfied that the dog does not constitute a danger to public safety. In determining whether the dog constitutes a danger to public safety the court must consider (i) the temperament of the dog including its past behaviour, and (ii) whether the applicant is a fit and proper person to be in charge of the dog, and may consider any other relevant circumstances.

Until the application is determined by the court the dog may be kept at the applicant's address with the applicant on and after the date of the death of the person in charge, or of the official medical letter, as the case may be. Requirements (b)–(f) which apply to a certificate of exemption also apply in relation to the applicant until a new certificate of exemption is issued to the applicant.

If the court is satisfied that the applicant is a fit and proper person to be substituted as the person in charge of the exempted dog the court must notify the Agency of:

(a) the name, address and contact details of the applicant; and
(b) details of the exempted dog and of the person to whom the original certificate of exemption was issued.

The Agency must issue a new certificate of exemption to the applicant in respect of the dog if it is satisfied that:

(a) the court has determined the person to be substituted as the person in charge of the dog as a fit and proper person to be in charge of the dog;
(b) the relevant fee plus VAT has been paid to the Agency; and
(c) the third-party insurance required has been obtained.

The provisions attached to a certificate of exemption apply to a new certificate of exemption so issued.

A dog is not exempt from the prohibition in s 1(3) if there is a failure to comply with the requirements attached to the new certificate of exemption, or to comply with the requirements in (b)–(f) of the original certificate pending the issue of the new certificate.

Interim exemption scheme

DDES(E&W)O 2015, Part 4 (arts 20–26) provides as follows.

Where a dog suspected of being a dog to which DDA 1991, s 1 applies is seized under a statutory power conferred prior to the court's final determination in respect of whether the dog should be destroyed under s 4 or 4B (pp 583 and 584), the chief officer of police for the area may release the dog to the person intending to apply for exemption of the dog under the DDES(E&W)O 2015 ('the person in interim charge') only in accordance with Part 4.

The chief officer of police may only release the dog under Part 4 if satisfied that it does not constitute a danger to public safety. The same test applies to the determination of this as in relation to the substitution of the person in charge (above).

Where the chief officer of police is satisfied that the dog is not a danger to public safety, the dog is exempt on an interim basis from the prohibition in s 1(3) provided that:

(a) the chief officer of police is satisfied that *exemption conditions* (i), (ii) and (iii) (p 579) have been met;
(b) the additional requirements referred to below are met throughout the period of interim exemption; and
(c) the person in interim charge confirms in writing that he understands the conditions mentioned and the continuing additional requirements and the consequences of any failure to comply with those conditions or requirements.

If there is a failure to comply with the additional requirements, or if the chief officer of police is no longer satisfied that the danger to public safety test is met, the dog may be seized under DDA 1991, s 5 and the dog is not exempt under DDES(E&W)O 2015, Part 4 from the prohibition in DDA 1991, s 1(3).

The seized dog may only be released when the neutering and insurance exemption conditions have been met. Where a dog is under six months when the chief officer of police determines that the dog may be released the *exemption conditions* in (i), (ii) and (iii) must be met within one month of the dog attaining six months.

Where a dog is released to the person in interim charge, that person must comply with the following additional requirements:

(a) to keep the dog at the same address as that person;
(b) to notify the police of any proposed change of address;

(c) to satisfy the police on request that a policy of third-party insurance is in force;

(d) to provide access to the dog for the purpose of reading a microchip on request by a constable or authorised local authority officer;

(e) to keep the dog in sufficiently secure conditions to prevent its escape, and muzzled and on a lead when in a public place;

(f) any other requirement for the purpose of preventing the dog being a danger to public safety considered appropriate by the chief officer of police;

(g) to produce to a constable (or authorised local authority officer) the certificate of exemption and confirmation that third-party insurance is in force within five days of being requested to do so by that person.

Miscellaneous

When a dog has been released under the interim exemption scheme and is subsequently made subject to a contingent destruction order by the court under DDA 1991, s 4A or 4B:

(a) additional requirements under the interim exemption scheme continue to apply until a certificate of exemption is issued; and

(b) if the exemption conditions are not met within the specified time limits the dog may be seized under s 5 with a view to its destruction in accordance with the contingent destruction order.

Subject to the above, an interim exemption ceases when a court makes a final determination in respect of the dog under s 4 or 4B or determines that the dog is not one to which s 1 applies, or a decision is taken not to commence or continue with proceedings in respect of the dog.

Breeding, selling, etc of dogs bred for fighting

DDA 1991, s 1(2) and (7) makes it an offence to breed, sell, exchange, give or offer to give, advertise or expose for sale, exchange or gift, a dog specified above in relation to s 1(3).

Section 1(2) and (7) also makes it an offence for the owner (p 584) to abandon such a dog, or for the owner or person in charge of it to allow it to stray.

Finally, s 1(2) and (7) makes it an offence for the owner, or person for the time being in charge, of such a dog to allow it to be in a public place (p 585) without being muzzled and kept on a lead. This prohibition in s 1 is a strict one. If a dog of the requisite type is in a public place, it must not be allowed to be unmuzzled and must be kept on a lead. There are no circumstances in which the necessity of a situation, eg avoiding cruelty to the dog, can overtake the prohibition.

Keeping dogs under proper control

Where any dog is dangerously out of control in a place (whether or not a public place), the owner or the person for the time being in charge of it is guilty of an offence under DDA 1991, s 3(1). There is an aggravated, indictable (either way) offence if the dog, whilst so out of control, injures any person or 'assistance dog'. Because there are different maximum sentences on conviction on indictment for an aggravated offence under s 3(1), depending on whether a person is injured and dies, a person is simply injured, or an assistance dog is injured, there are three separate offences under s 3(1), distinguished in this way.

Section 3(1A) provides that a person (D) is not guilty of an offence under s 3(1) in a case which is a 'householder case', ie a case where:

(a) the dog is dangerously out of control while in or partly in a building, or part of a building, that is a dwelling or is forces accommodation (or is both), and

(b) at that time (i) the person in relation to whom the dog is dangerously out of control (V) is in, or is entering, the building or part as a trespasser, or (ii) D (if present at that time) believed V to be in, or entering, the building or part as a trespasser.

The provisions set out on p 656 apply equally here.

The Court of Appeal has held that a person who is the owner, or for the time being in charge, of a dog which is dangerously out of control is not guilty of an offence under s 3(1) unless the prosecution proves an act or omission on his part which to some more than minimal degree contributed to the dog being in the place in question, dangerously out of control. Thus, for example, if a dog escapes from D's house as a result of the unauthorised action of a third party, for example a burglar, and as a result is dangerously out of control in the place in question, D is not guilty of an offence under s 3(1).

Strict liability is imposed by s 3(1) on the owners or handlers of such dogs. The test is objective and the state of mind of the owner is irrelevant. However, an owner has a defence if he can prove that at the time of the offence the dog was in the charge of a person whom he reasonably believed to be a fit and proper person to be in charge of it. A divisional court has held that the defence only applies if there is plain evidence that 'charge' has been transferred to an identified person.

Police powers

By DDA 1991, s 5(1), a constable (or authorised local authority officer) may seize any dog:

(a) which appears to be a dog to which s 1 applies and which is in a public place (p 585); or

(b) which is in a public place and which appears to be dangerously out of control.

Section 5(1A) provides that a constable or authorised local authority officer may seize any dog in any place which is not a public place, if the dog appears to the constable or officer to be dangerously out of control.

If a justice of the peace is satisfied by information on oath that there are reasonable grounds to believe that one of the above offences has been committed, or that evidence of such an offence is to be found on any premises, he may issue a warrant authorising a constable to enter and search them and to seize any dog or other thing which is evidence of such an offence (s 5(2)). The additional powers of seizure provided by the Criminal Justice and Police Act 2001, s 50 apply to this power of seizure.

Destruction and disqualification orders

These are dealt with by DDA 1991, ss 4, 4A and 4B.

Immediate destruction order

Section 4(1)(a) provides that, where a person is convicted of an offence against s 1 or 3(1), the court may order destruction of the dog concerned. Indeed, it must do so in the case of an offence under s 1 or an aggravated offence contrary to s 3(1), unless (by s 4(1A)) it is satisfied that the dog would not constitute a danger to public safety.

Dogs may not be destroyed during the period allowed for notice of, and determination of, any appeal.

Where a court makes a destruction order under s 4(1)(a) or s 4B (below), it may appoint a person to undertake the destruction of the dog and require it to be delivered up for that purpose.

Contingent destruction order

Section 4A, as interpreted by a judge in the Administrative Court, provides that where:

(a) a person is convicted of an offence under s 1;
(b) the court does not order destruction of the dog under s 4; and
(c) in the case of an offence under s 1, the dog is subject to the prohibition under
     s 1(3),

the court must order the dog to be destroyed, *unless* the dog is exempted from that prohibition within the requisite period. That period, two months, may be extended by the court.

Section 4A also provides that, where a person is convicted of an offence under DDA 1991, s 3, the court may order that, unless its owner keeps it under proper control, the dog must be destroyed. Such an order may specify the measures to be taken to keep the dog under control, whether by muzzling, keeping on a lead, excluding it from specified places, or otherwise, and, if it appears to the court that the dog is a male and would be less dangerous if neutered, may require that the dog be neutered.

Destruction order otherwise than on conviction

DDA 1991, s 4B makes provision for an order of destruction which may be made by a justice of the peace in respect of a dog which has been seized under s 5(1) or (2) or under any other statutory power (a) where there is no prosecution, or (b) where the dog cannot be released without contravention of s 1(3). A justice is not required to make such an order if he is satisfied that the dog would not be a danger to public safety. Where, in a case falling within (b), a justice does not order the destruction of the dog, he must order that, *unless* the dog is exempted from that prohibition in s 1(3) within the requisite period, it must be destroyed. That period, two months, may be extended by the court. It has been held in the Administrative Court that, if the dog is exempted within the requisite period, the police cannot subsequently summarily destroy the dog because they believe that the exemption has ceased to exist. It would seem that this decision, made in relation to an order under s 4B, could also apply to an order under s 4A.

Disqualification order

By s 4(1)(b), where a person is convicted of an offence under s 1 or 3(1) a court may also order him to be disqualified from keeping a dog for such a period as it thinks fit. Offences are committed against s 4(8) where a person has custody of a dog while disqualified, or where he fails to deliver up a dog for destruction as ordered.

Dogs owned by young persons

Where a dog is owned by a person who is under 16, the term 'owner' in DDA 1991, ss 1 or 3 includes a reference to the head of the household, if any, of which that person is a member (s 6).

Public place

'Public place' in DDA 1991 means any street, road, or other place (whether or not enclosed) to which the public have or are permitted to have access whether for payment or otherwise, including the common parts of a building containing two or more separate dwellings (eg a block of flats) (s 10(2)). A front garden or driveway is not a public place in this context and neither is any other type of place which people enter by express or implied invitation. On the other hand, a dog in a private car on a public highway is in a public place.

DOGS WORRYING LIVESTOCK

The Dogs (Protection of Livestock) Act 1953 (D(PL)A 1953), s 1(1) declares that the owner of a dog, and, if it is in the charge of a person other than the owner, that person also, is guilty of an offence if the dog worries livestock on any agricultural land.

By s 1(2), 'worry livestock' covers attacking livestock, or chasing livestock in such a way as might reasonably be expected to cause injury or suffering to it, or, in the case of females, abortion, or loss of or diminution in their produce. It also covers a dog being at large (ie not on a lead or under close control) in a field or enclosure in which there are sheep, but not where the dog is owned by, or in the charge of, the occupier of the field or is a police dog, guide dog, trained sheepdog, working gun dog or, perhaps unexpectedly, a pack of hounds.

'Livestock' means cattle, sheep, goats, swine, horses (including asses and mules) or poultry. Thus 'livestock' can generally be described as farm animals. 'Agricultural land' means land used as arable, meadow or grazing land or for the purposes of poultry farming, pig farming, market gardens, allotments, nursery grounds or orchards.

Defences

If the dog which attacks the livestock is owned by, or in the charge of, the occupier of that land or a person authorised by him, a defence is open to that person provided that he did not cause the dog to attack the livestock (s 1(3)).

The dog's owner has a defence if he proves that at the time in question it was in the charge of some other person, whom he reasonably believed to be a fit and proper person to be in charge (s 1(4)), as where he has allowed a reliable person to take the dog for a walk.

Police powers

By D(PL)A 1953, s 2(2), a constable is empowered to seize a dog, found anywhere, which he reasonably believes to have been worrying livestock on agricultural land and to retain it until the owner is found and has paid the expenses of its detention. This power cannot be exercised if there is a person present who admits to being the owner of the dog or in charge of it.

If, on an application by a constable, a justice is satisfied that there are grounds for believing that:

(a) an offence under the Act has been committed; and
(b) the dog in question is on premises specified in the application,

he may issue a warrant under s 2A authorising a constable to enter and search the premises in order to identify the dog.

GUARD DOGS

It is an offence under the Guard Dogs Act 1975, ss 1(1) and 5(1) to use or permit the use of a guard dog on any premises unless a person ('the handler') who is capable of controlling the dog is present on the premises and the dog is under the direct control of the handler at all times while it is being so used except while it is secured so that it is not at liberty to go freely about the premises. A 'guard dog' is one which is used either to protect the premises or property on them, or to protect a person guarding the premises or property.

The handler of a guard dog must keep the dog under his control at all times while it is being used as a guard dog at any premises except:

(a) while another handler has control over the dog; or
(b) while the dog is secured so that it is not at liberty to go freely about the premises (s 1(2)).

Failure to do so is an offence under s 5(1).

The Act excludes from the term 'premises' agricultural land and land in the curtilage of a dwelling house, thus exempting farm dogs and those confined within a dwelling house or its yard or garden.

When guard dogs are kept upon 'premises' warning notices must be clearly displayed at all entrances to the premises (s 1(3)); failure to display such notices is an offence under s 5(1).

WELFARE OF DOGS

The welfare of dogs is dealt with in Appendix 4 on the companion website.

CHAPTER 19

Firearms and Weapons

The Firearms Act 1968 (FiA 1968) controls the possession, use, manufacture, transfer and acquisition of firearms or ammunition. Other Acts punish the possession or use of firearms in particular circumstances and deal with other forms of weapon.

FIREARMS: DEFINITIONS

FiA 1968, s 57 defines 'firearm' for the purposes of that Act as a *lethal barrelled weapon* of any description *from which any shot, bullet or other missile can be discharged*. This is the basic definition. Section 57 also provides that 'firearm' includes any *prohibited weapon*, whether or not it is such a lethal weapon, and any *component part* of such a lethal or prohibited weapon, and any *accessory* to any such weapon designed or adapted to *diminish the noise or flash caused by firing the weapon*.

With one exception (p 598), nothing in the FiA 1968 relating to firearms applies to an antique firearm which is sold, transferred, purchased, acquired or possessed as a curiosity or ornament. 'Antique' is not defined. Basically, it is a question of fact and degree for the court to decide; it is unlikely that a court will consider that anything made in this or the last century is an antique.

Firearms: the basic definition

Lethal weapon

It is clear from judicial decisions that a 'lethal weapon' means a weapon which in itself is capable of causing injury from which death might result. It need not be designed or manufactured for the purpose of causing such injury; if it is not, it is enough that it is capable of causing such injury if misused. Consequently, even though the purpose of its designer and manufacturer was to produce a toy, a spring pistol which can fire pellets through a barrel will be a firearm if, albeit only through misuse, it is capable of causing an injury from which death might result. By way of further example, a signalling pistol which fired an explosive flare, and which was capable of killing at short range, has been held to be lethal; the fact that the manufacturer did not produce it for the purpose of killing or injuring was immaterial. Many air guns would normally only cause a trivial injury but they may be classed as lethal since they could cause death by a pellet striking an extremely vulnerable part of the body, for example an eye.

Whether or not a weapon is lethal must be assessed in relation to the particular weapon in question, and not to weapons of its type. If the particular weapon is not in working order and is therefore incapable of causing injury from which death might result *it* is not a lethal weapon, even though a weapon of its type is so capable when in working order.

Under the *basic* definition of a 'firearm', the 'lethal weapon' must be *barrelled* and capable of *discharging* any shot, bullet or other *missile*.

Barrelled

A barrel, in relation to a gun, is a tube through which a bullet or shot is discharged.

Shot, bullet or other missile

The terms 'shot' and 'bullet' are self-explanatory, and the term 'other missile' should be taken to relate to some similar solid object which can be discharged from some form of 'barrelled weapon'.

Prohibited weapon

As already indicated, such weapons are firearms, whether or not they are lethal barrelled weapons from which any shot, bullet or other missile can be discharged. See pp 593–5 for the definition of a prohibited weapon.

Changes in type

A weapon which at any time has been classified as a prohibited weapon (or as a FiA 1968, s 1 firearm (p 589) or as a shotgun) remains so classified notwithstanding anything done to convert it into a weapon of another type (eg prohibited weapon into a s 1 firearm).

Component parts and accessories

The fact that any *component part* of a lethal barrelled weapon or prohibited weapon is stated by FiA 1968, s 57 to be a firearm in itself is of importance.

The only *accessories* which are included within the term 'firearm' by FiA 1968, s 57, and are therefore controlled by the Act, are those designed or adapted to diminish noise or flash, ie silencers and flash eliminators. Any other accessory to a firearm is not included. A telescopic sight is an accessory but it is not an 'accessory' for the purposes of FiA 1968.

Imitation firearms

Under the Firearms Act 1982, s 1 the provisions of FiA 1968 concerned with a FiA 1968, s 1 firearm are widened so as to apply (with limited exceptions) to an imitation firearm which has the appearance of being a s 1 firearm and which is so constructed or adapted as to be readily convertible into such a firearm. The limited exceptions are indicated in the text. An imitation firearm is '*readily* convertible' if it can be converted into a firearm without special skill and without equipment or tools not in common use. '*Convertible*' refers to converting an item from which a missile could not be discharged into one from which a missile could be discharged. It does not matter whether that process would involve the permanent alteration of the item (eg by drilling) or some more temporary result; an item can be converted by altering its construction or by adapting the way it could be used (eg by making it capable of discharging a missile by the use of an external implement). Where an alleged offence involves an imitation firearm which is readily convertible into a s 1 firearm, it is a defence for the defendant (D) to prove that he did not know and had no reason to suspect that it was readily convertible.

Ammunition

For the purposes of FiA 1968, 'ammunition' is defined by s 57 as meaning ammunition for any firearm; a blank cartridge is ammunition. Section 57 provides that the term also includes grenades, bombs and other missiles, whether capable of use with a firearm or not, and also that it includes prohibited ammunition. A 'bomb' is any explosive substance in a case, or a case containing poison gas, smoke or inflammable material which might be dropped from an aircraft, fired from a gun, or thrown or placed by hand.

POSSESSION, PURCHASE OR ACQUISITION OF FIREARMS OR AMMUNITION

Section 1 firearms and ammunition

FiA 1968, s 1(1) states that, subject to any exemption under FiA 1968, it is an offence for a person to have in his possession, or to purchase or acquire:

(a) a firearm to which s 1 applies; or
(b) any ammunition to which s 1 applies,

without holding a firearm certificate, or otherwise than as authorised by such a certificate, or (ammunition only) in quantities in excess of those so authorised.

The offence is an indictable (either way) offence.

Section 1 applies to every firearm except:

(a) a shotgun, as defined below; and
(b) an air weapon (ie an air rifle, air gun or air pistol which does not fall within FiA 1968, s 5(1) (p 593) and is not of a type declared by rules made by the Secretary of State under FiA 1968 to be specially dangerous (p 590)).

FiA 1968, s 1(1) applies to ammunition for a firearm except:

(a) cartridges containing five or more shot, none of which exceeds .36 inch in diameter;
(b) ammunition for any air gun, air rifle or air pistol; and
(c) blank cartridges not more than one inch in diameter.

A person can be in possession of a firearm or ammunition even though he does not have physical custody of it nor keeps it in his home; it is enough that he knowingly has more than momentary control of it (as where he stores a firearm at the home of a relative for safe-keeping). Indeed, someone can be in possession of a firearm or ammunition even though he does not know or suspect that the thing under his control is a firearm or ammunition, as the case may be. For example, if someone has custody of a firearm in a holdall which he knows contains something without giving thought to the nature of its contents, he is in possession of the firearm. The fact that possession was brief, or that he did not know or could not reasonably have been expected to know that it contained a firearm, affords no defence. Because the defendant (D) need not know or suspect that the article possessed was a firearm or ammunition within the relevant meaning of those terms, an honest and reasonable mistaken belief that the article is not a firearm or is an antique firearm is no defence.

It is an indictable (either way) offence under s 3(2) for a person to sell or transfer a s 1 firearm or ammunition to a person other than a registered firearms dealer or person who has a firearm certificate authorising its purchase or acquisition.

Shotguns and ammunition

For the purposes of FiA 1968, a 'shotgun' is a smooth-bore gun (not being an airgun) which:

(a) has a barrel not less than 24 inches in length and does not have any barrel with a bore exceeding two inches in diameter;
(b) either has no magazine or has a non-detachable magazine incapable of holding more than two cartridges; and
(c) is not a revolver gun.

If the barrel of a shotgun is shortened to less than 24 inches it is no longer a shotgun, but becomes a s 1 firearm.

Shotguns are excepted from the provisions of FiA 1968, s 1 but FiA 1968, s 2 states that, subject to any exemption under FiA 1968, it is an indictable (either way) offence for a person to have in his possession, or to purchase or acquire, a shotgun without holding a certificate under FiA 1968 authorising him to possess shotguns. Shotgun ammunition, other than s 1 ammunition, does not require a firearm certificate, shotgun certificate or any other form of certificate for its possession, acquisition or purchase.

What was said about possession and D's state of mind in relation to FiA 1968, s 1 is equally applicable here.

It is an indictable (either way) offence under s 3(2) for a person to sell or transfer a shotgun to a person other than a registered firearms dealer or person who has a shotgun certificate authorising its purchase or acquisition.

Air weapons and ammunition

Air weapons essentially operate by the release of compressed air. However, the Firearms (Amendment) Act 1997, s 48 provides that any reference in the firearms legislation to an air rifle, air pistol or air gun also includes a reference to a rifle, pistol or gun powered by compressed carbon dioxide. An 'air weapon' (ie an air rifle, air gun or air pistol) which is not a prohibited weapon and which has not been declared by the Secretary of State to be specially dangerous does not require a firearm certificate or any other form of certificate for its possession, acquisition or purchase. Nor does ammunition for any air weapon, even if declared especially dangerous. The Secretary of State has declared that an air weapon will be specially dangerous (and therefore a s 1 firearm) if:

(a) on discharge from the muzzle there is a kinetic energy in excess of 6 ft/lb in the case of an air pistol, or 12 ft/lb in the case of a weapon other than a pistol; or
(b) it is disguised as another object.

Firearm certificates and shotgun certificates

Firearm certificates

To obtain a firearm certificate an applicant must apply to the chief officer of police of the area in which he resides and must state such particulars as may be required by the application form ('Application for the grant or renewal of a firearm or shotgun certificate'). Information concerning previous names, residence, and convictions and written cautions (other than those for parking offences) must be given, and a personal health and medical declaration must be made. The applicant must sign a statement to the effect that the statements are true, rather than believed to be true. It is an indictable offence under FiA 1968, s 28A(7) knowingly or recklessly to make a statement false in a material particular. An applicant must provide four photographs and the names and addresses of two persons who have agreed to act as referees.

FiA 1968, s 27 states that a firearm certificate must be granted by the chief officer of police if he is satisfied that the applicant:

(a) is fit to be entrusted with a firearm to which FiA 1968, s 1 applies and that he is not prohibited by FiA 1968 (see p 598) from possessing such a firearm;

(b) has good reason for having in his possession, or for purchasing or acquiring, the firearm or ammunition in respect of which the application is made;

(c) can, in all the circumstances, be permitted to have the firearm or ammunition in his possession without danger to the public safety or peace.

The certificate must specify the nature and number of firearms to which it relates and certain other matters. A chief officer may impose conditions subject to which the firearm certificate is held. These conditions may refer to the nature of the storage of the weapons or their use. Conditions can be varied at any time by notice in writing to the holder, who may be required to return his certificate for variation. Failure to comply with a condition may have the effect of depriving the holder of the certificate of a statutory exemption that would otherwise be available to him (eg humane killing of animals) or even deprive him of legal authority to possess the weapon.

Someone under 18 who applies for such a certificate is capable of having a good reason for possessing or acquiring it *only* if he has no intention of using it, before that age, for a purpose other than an authorised purpose under the European Weapons Directive. An authorised purpose is a sporting purpose, the shooting of vermin, a purpose related to estate management activities, competition shooting, or target shooting, and use as or with a slaughtering instrument. Such purposes are likely to be specified in the certificate.

Police officers are required to carry out inquiries on behalf of the chief officer and, with these provisions in mind, they are required to check upon the intended usage of the weapon. The officer conducting the inquiry should always check the secure place in which the weapon will be stored.

Shotgun certificates

The rules relating to applications for shotgun certificates are not quite so strict. An application must be made to the chief officer of police on the application form referred to on p 590. There are similar requirements in respect of the submission of photographs and the name and address of *one* referee. The 'false statement offence' under FiA 1968, s 28A(7) also applies to an applicant for a shotgun certificate.

By FiA 1968, s 28, such a certificate must be granted by the chief officer of police if he is satisfied that the applicant can be permitted to possess a shotgun without danger to the public safety or to the peace, unless he has reason to believe that the applicant is prohibited by FiA 1968 from possessing a shotgun (see p 598), or is satisfied that the applicant does not have a good reason for possessing, purchasing or acquiring one.

A sporting or competitive purpose is declared by FiA 1968 to be a good reason. A person under 18 is deemed not to have a good reason for possessing or acquiring a shotgun if it is his intention to use the shotgun, before he attains that age, for a purpose not authorised by the European Weapons Directive.

A shotgun certificate must specify the description of the shotguns to which it relates including, if known, the identification numbers of the guns.

General

The Firearms Rules 1998, r 3 provides as follows. If a firearm or shotgun certificate is granted, the holder must on receipt sign it in ink. He must inform the chief officer of the theft or loss of the certificate (within seven days) or a change of address (without undue delay).

Transfer of firearms, etc between authorised persons

The Firearms (Amendment) Act 1997 (Fi(A)A 1997), s 32 requires that where:

(a) a s 1 firearm or ammunition is sold, let on hire, lent or given; or
(b) a shotgun is sold, let on hire, lent or given for a period of more than 72 hours,

by any person, to a person who is not a firearms dealer nor exempt from holding a cer-tificate, the following requirements must be complied with:

(i)   the transferee must produce to the transferor the appropriate firearm or shotgun certificate or a visitor's permit (p 597);
(ii) the transferor must comply with any instructions contained in the certificate, etc; and
(iii) the transferor must hand the firearm to the transferee personally.

Failure to comply with these requirements is an offence under s 32(3).

Each party to the transfer (as described above) of a s 1 firearm or ammunition or of a shotgun who is the holder of a firearm or shotgun certificate must give notice of the transfer within seven days to the chief officer of police by registered post, the recorded delivery service or permitted electronic means. It is an offence under s 33(4) to fail to do so.

In the case of a s 1 firearm or ammunition, the offences under s 32(3) or 33(4) are indictable (either way) offences.

De-activation, destruction or loss of firearms or shotguns

Fi(A)A 1997, s 34 requires that where a firearm to which a firearm certificate or shotgun certificate relates is de-activated, destroyed or lost (by theft or otherwise), the certificate holder must give notice to the chief officer of police within seven days by registered post, the recorded delivery service or permitted electronic means. It is an offence under s 34(4) to fail to do so without reasonable excuse; in the case of a s 1 firearm, the offence is an indictable (either way) offence.

Grant, refusal, revocation, etc

There is a right of appeal to the Crown Court against a refusal to grant a person a firearm or shotgun certificate or to vary a certificate or condition therein.

A firearm certificate may be revoked if the chief officer of police has reason to believe that the holder:

(a) is of intemperate habits or unsound mind or is otherwise unfitted to be entrusted with a firearm; or
(b) can no longer be permitted to have the firearm or ammunition to which the certifi-cate relates without danger to the public safety or peace;
(c) is prohibited from possessing a s 1 firearm (p 598); or
(d) no longer has a good reason for possessing, purchasing or acquiring the firearm or ammunition which the certificate authorises him to have, etc.

A firearm certificate may also be revoked if the holder has failed to comply with a notice requiring him to deliver up his certificate.

In addition, a chief officer may partially revoke a firearm certificate in relation to any particular firearm or ammunition held under its authority if satisfied that the holder no longer has a good reason for possessing, purchasing or acquiring it.

A shotgun certificate may be revoked only if the holder becomes a 'prohibited person', or cannot be permitted to possess a shotgun without danger to the public safety or to the peace. It has been held that a chief officer, in deciding whether to revoke a shotgun licence, is entitled to take into account irresponsible conduct by the licence holder which does not involve the use of a shotgun. It is a matter for the chief officer's discretion to what extent he should investigate a particular offence.

Where a certificate is revoked the holder must be notified in writing and required to surrender his certificate. It is an offence to fail to comply with such a notice within 21 days of the date of the notice.

POSSESSION, PURCHASE OR ACQUISITION OF PROHIBITED WEAPONS OR AMMUNITION

Because prohibited weapons and ammunition can only properly be regarded as suitable for official use, FiA 1968, s 5(1) and (1A) provide that a person commits an offence if he has in his possession, or purchases or acquires, any prohibited weapon or ammunition to which s 5(1) or (1A) respectively apply without the written authority of the Secretary of State. An offence under s 5(1) or s 5(1A) is one of strict liability as to the fact that the weapon or ammunition is prohibited, so that it is no defence that the possessor is reasonably unaware of the characteristic which makes the weapon or ammunition prohibited. The offence under s 5(1) (except in relation to a prohibited weapon within (h) below) and the offence under s 5(1A) (in relation to a firearm disguised as another object) are triable only on indictment; otherwise the above offences are triable either way.

The controls under s 5(1) and (1A) apply over and above the need for a firearm certificate.

Prohibited weapons

For the purposes of the offence under FiA 1968, s 5(1), a prohibited weapon is:

(a) any firearm which is so designed or adapted that two or more missiles can be successively discharged without repeated pressure on the trigger;

(b) any self-loading or pump-action rifled gun other than one chambered for .22 inch rim-fire cartridges;

(c) any firearm which either has a barrel less than 30 cm in length or is less than 60 cm in length overall, other than an air weapon, a muzzle-loading gun, or a firearm designed as a signalling apparatus;

(d) any self-loading or pump-action smooth-bore gun which is not an air weapon or chambered for .22 inch rim-fire cartridges and either has a barrel of less than 24 inches in length or is less than 40 inches in length overall;

(e) any smooth-bore revolver gun other than one which is chambered for 9 mm rim-fire cartridges or a muzzle-loading gun;

(f) any rocket launcher, or any mortar, for projecting a stabilised missile, other than a launcher or mortar designed for line-throwing or pyrotechnic purposes or as signalling apparatus;

(g) any air rifle, air gun or air pistol which uses, or is designed or adapted for use with, a self-contained gas cartridge system; and

(h) any weapon of whatever description designed or adapted for the discharge of any noxious liquid, gas or other thing.

In relation to (a) above, the Court of Appeal has held that the words 'so designed or adapted that two or more missiles can be successively discharged without repeated pressure on the trigger' relate to what is objectively possible and not to the intention of the designer of the weapon. Thus, if that effect could be brought about, even if only in expert hands, the weapon is designed as a prohibited weapon.

For the purposes of (c) and (d), any detachable, folding, retractable or other movable butt-stock is disregarded in measuring the length of any firearm.

References to muzzle-loading guns in (c) and (e) are references to guns which are designed to be loaded at the muzzle end of the barrel or chamber with a loose charge and a separate ball (or other missile).

An air weapon referred to at (g) possessed on 30 April 2004 may be retained subject to the need to obtain a firearm certificate. A chief officer may not refuse an application for a firearm certificate in such circumstances, nor an application for renewal, on the ground that the person does not have a good reason for having the weapon.

List entry (h) covers a wide variety of weaponry including a flamethrower and a high-voltage electric stunning device. The fact that a stun-gun designed for an electrical charge is not working due to some unknown fault does not change its character as a prohibited weapon. The words 'designed or adapted' mean that any other type of weapon which is converted in any way for these purposes is a prohibited weapon as it has been 'adapted'. These weapons do not need to be either lethal or barrelled *provided* they are capable of discharging noxious liquid, gas or other thing. If the weapon is capable of discharging such a substance, and was either designed or adapted for that purpose, it is prohibited. A water pistol used to discharge gas would not be a prohibited weapon if it was used in an unaltered state, since it would not have been designed or adapted to discharge one of the prohibited substances. The same applies to a washing-up liquid bottle filled with hydrochloric acid. The container was neither designed nor adapted for the discharge of a noxious liquid. 'Noxious' before 'liquid, gas or other thing' must apply to all three things. A substance is noxious if it is harmful, hurtful or injurious. A weapon which has not been designed for the purpose of discharging a noxious gas but is capable of doing so falls within list entry (h), at least (according to the Court of Appeal) if it has a 'deliberate design capability'.

Slaughtering instruments, humane killers, shot pistols used for killing vermin, starting pistols, trophies of war, firearms of historic interest and weapons used for treating animals are exempted from the prohibitions imposed upon weapons falling within (c) above (or, in the case of weapons used for treating animals, within (c) or (g)) subject to conditions set out in the Fi(A)A 1997.

For the purposes of s 5(1A), the following are prohibited weapons:

(a) any firearm which is disguised as another object; and

(b) any launcher or other projecting apparatus, not a prohibited weapon under s 5(1), which is designed to be used with any rocket or ammunition designed to explode on or immediately before impact and is prohibited ammunition under s 5(1) or s 5(1A).

In relation to s 5(1) and (1A), there are a number of exemptions in terms of weapons and of ammunition. They relate principally to collectors and to possession, purchase or acquisition for use for slaughtering animals, shooting vermin, or estate management purposes.

Prohibited ammunition

Prohibited ammunition for the purposes of FiA 1968, s 5(1) is:

(a) any cartridge with a bullet designed to explode on or immediately before impact (eg a 'dum-dum' bullet);

(b) any ammunition which contains, or is designed or adapted to contain, any noxious liquid, gas or other thing; and

(c) if capable of being used with a firearm of any description, any grenade, bomb (or other like missile), rocket or shell designed to explode on or immediately before impact,

other than ammunition used for treating animals.

Therefore containers designed or adapted to contain any noxious gas, etc for use as a missile or bomb are prohibited ammunition, whether filled or not. The other types of prohibited ammunition are explosive bullets and (if capable of being used with a firearm) grenades, bombs, rockets and shells.

Prohibited ammunition for the purposes of s 5(1A) is:

(a) any rocket or ammunition which is not prohibited ammunition (under (c) above) for the purposes of s 5(1) which consists in or incorporates a missile designed to explode on or immediately before impact and is for military use;

(b) any ammunition for military use which consists in or incorporates a missile designed so that a substance contained in the missile will ignite on or immediately before impact;

(c) any ammunition for military use which consists in or incorporates a missile designed, on account of its having a jacket and hard-core, to penetrate armour plating, armour screening or body armour;

(d) any ammunition which incorporates a missile designed or adapted to expand on impact;

(e) anything which is designed to be projected as a missile from any weapon and is designed to be, or has been incorporated in:

(i) any ammunition falling within any of the above definitions; or

(ii) any ammunition which would fall within any of those definitions but for its being specified in s 5(1).

LAWFUL POSSESSION WITHOUT A FIREARM CERTIFICATE OR SHOTGUN CERTIFICATE

Permits

Persons who hold a permit under FiA 1968, s 7 from the chief officer of police of the area in which they reside may, without holding a certificate, possess a firearm (including a shotgun) and ammunition in accordance with the terms of the permit. Such permits are frequently issued where the holder of a certificate dies and a relative requires some form of authority to possess the firearm pending its sale or disposal. It is unusual for such permits to be valid for more than one month.

Exemptions

Firearms dealers (if registered: see p 606) and their employees may possess firearms and ammunition without a certificate.

Other people may lawfully possess firearms and ammunition without holding a certificate. The principal exemptions provided by FiA 1968, ss 9 to 15 and 54 and the Firearms (Amendment) Act 1988 (Fi(A)A 1988), ss 15 and 16 are as follows:

(a) an auctioneer, carrier, warehouseman, or the employee of such a person, is frequently required to handle other people's firearms and ammunition in the course of his duties. Sensibly this is permitted, but it is necessary for such persons to take reasonable precautions for safe custody and to report loss or theft forthwith to the police;

(b) a slaughtering instrument and its ammunition may be possessed by a licensed slaughterman;

(c) a person carrying a firearm or ammunition belonging to another person who is the holder of a certificate may possess that firearm or ammunition under instructions from, and for the use of, that other person for sporting purposes only. The person carrying the firearm, etc can best be described as a 'gun bearer'. However, where the person carrying the firearm or ammunition is under 18, this exemption only applies if the other person is 18 or over;

(d) if aged 18 or over, a starter at an athletic meeting may possess a firearm for the purpose of starting races only. The exemption does not allow a starter to possess ammunition, so that he is restricted to blanks not exceeding one inch in diameter (which do not, of course, require a certificate);

(e) subject to any exclusion of the club or restriction to specified types of rifle by the Secretary of State, a member of an approved rifle club (including a miniature rifle club) or of an approved muzzle-loading pistol club may possess a firearm and ammunition when engaged as such a member in connection with target shooting. An approval of a club may be limited to specified weapons;

(f) a person conducting or carrying on a miniature rifle range (whether for a rifle club or otherwise) or a shooting gallery at which no firearms are used other than air weapons or miniature rifles not exceeding .23 inch calibre may possess such miniature rifles and ammunition suitable for them;

(g) a person may use any such miniature rifle as is described in (f) above at such a range or gallery;

(h) a person who does not hold a shotgun certificate may borrow a shotgun from the occupier of private premises and use it on those premises, provided the occupier is present, but if the borrower is under 18 the occupier must be 18 or over;

(i) a person of 17 or over may, without holding a firearm certificate, borrow a rifle from the occupier of private premises and use it on the premises in the presence of the occupier or an employee of the occupier, if that person holds a firearm certificate in respect of that rifle, the borrower's possession and use complies with any conditions in the certificate, and, where the borrower is 17, the person present is 18 or over;

(j) a person may, without holding a shotgun certificate, use a shotgun at a time and place approved by the chief officer of police for shooting at artificial targets. This exemption is designed to cover a person who is interested in shooting or wishes to receive instruction, but has not got a shotgun certificate. Commonly approved places at which the exemption permits him to shoot include agricultural shows and permanent shooting grounds run by firearms dealers;

(k) a person taking part in a theatrical performance, rehearsal or film may possess a firearm during the performance, etc. This exception does not extend to ammunition, so that any ammunition used would have to be blanks not more than one inch in diameter;

(l) signalling apparatus or ammunition for it may be possessed on board an aircraft or at an aerodrome as a part of its equipment. It may also be transferred at an aerodrome from one aeroplane to another, or from or to an aeroplane at an aerodrome to or from an appointed place of storage there;

(m) a firearm and ammunition may be possessed on board a ship as a part of its equipment. However, if it is to be removed from or to a ship a permit to do so must be obtained from a constable (a similar permit is required if the signalling apparatus described at (l) is to be removed from or to an aeroplane or aerodrome);

(n) a Northern Ireland shotgun certificate authorises possession of a shotgun in Great Britain; and

(o) any 'person in the service of the Crown', a term which includes a member of a police force (or civilian officer) who is in possession of a firearm or ammunition in his capacity as such does not require a certificate. Nor does such a person require the Secretary of State's authority to possess a prohibited weapon or prohibited ammunition.

Fi(A)A 1988, s 17 makes provision for 'visitors permits' issued by a chief officer of police in relation to both s 1 firearms and shotguns. A firearm permit permits a person to possess a firearm and ammunition and to acquire ammunition for it, and a shotgun permit permits a person to possess or acquire a shotgun (although there are exceptions in the case of a shotgun with a magazine). 'Group' applications may be made for not more than 20 permits. These will cover persons visiting Great Britain to take part in competitions.

Fi(A)A 1988, ss 16A and 16B authorise, respectively, persons under the supervision of a member of the armed forces to possess a firearm and ammunition on service premises without holding a firearm certificate, and persons being trained or assessed under the supervision of a member of the Ministry of Defence Police to do so on premises used for any purpose of the Ministry of Defence Police. The sections also authorise such persons in such circumstances to possess a prohibited weapon or prohibited ammunition without obtaining the Secretary of State's authority.

Museum licences

By virtue of Fi(A)A 1988, s 19 and Sch 1 specified museums do not need to have a firearm certificate, shotgun certificate or s 5 authority, as the case may be, in relation to exhibits displayed or stored at the museum if they have a museum firearm licence granted under those provisions. Specified museums are those registered with the Museums and Galleries Commission for the purpose of making them eligible for a museum firearm certificate.

European Firearms Pass

The Firearms Act 1968, s 32A governs the issue of a European Firearms Pass. Persons holding such passes are entitled to acquire in another EU member state firearms to which the pass relates. Such 'passes' are issued in Great Britain by the chief officer of police to holders of an appropriate firearm certificate. A European Firearms Pass must be produced on demand by a constable.

PERSONS PROHIBITED FROM POSSESSING A FIREARM

FiA 1968, s 21 prohibits the possession of any firearm or ammunition by a person who has been convicted of a crime and been sentenced to:

(a) custody for life or preventive detention, or to imprisonment, corrective training, youth custody, or detention in a young offender institution for three years or more. Such a person is banned for life;

(b) imprisonment or youth custody or detention in a young offender institution from three months to three years, or subject to a secure training order or a detention and training order. Such a person is banned for five years from the date of his release; or

(c) a suspended sentence of imprisonment for three months or more. Such a person is banned for five years beginning with the second day after the sentence was passed.

Where a person was in possession of a firearm immediately before 14 July 2014, and by reason of a suspended sentence imposed before that date would otherwise be subject to a ban under s 21, and his possession immediately before that date was authorised by a firearm (or shotgun) certificate, the prohibition under s 21 does not apply while the certificate remains in force.

Air weapons are included in the prohibition. The exemption in respect of antique firearms referred to on p 587 does not apply to an offence under s 21.

Contravention of these provisions is an offence under s 21(4). So is supplying a firearm or ammunition to someone (X) prohibited from possessing it, or repairing, testing or proving it for him, if D knows or has reasonable grounds to believe that X is so prohibited (s 21(5)). Both offences are indictable (either way) ones.

A person subject to a prohibition under s 21 can apply to the Crown Court for its removal.

POSSESSION OR ACQUISITION BY YOUNG PERSONS

FiA 1968, ss 22 to 24 deal with the possession or acquisition of all types of firearms by juveniles.

Section 1 firearms

If a person under 18 wishes to have a s 1 firearm, or ammunition for it, he cannot buy or hire it himself; if he does so he commits an offence under FiA 1968, s 22(1). Under s 24(1), the seller or person letting it on hire also commits an offence, unless (by s 24(5)) he can prove that he reasonably believed that the other person was 18 or over. However, provided that someone is 14 or over he may receive a firearm, together with ammunition, by way of a gift or loan. Where an adult wishes to buy a firearm as a gift for such a youth, he must obtain a firearm certificate and so must the youth. The seller may then sell to the adult, who may then transfer the weapon to the youth, both notifying the chief officer of police of the transaction by registered post, recorded delivery or permitted electronic means within 48 hours. Certificates granted to persons under 18 are endorsed to the effect that firearms or ammunition cannot be sold or hired to them until the specified date, which is the date of their 18th birthday.

It is an offence under s 24(2)(a) to give or lend a s 1 firearm or ammunition to a person under 14 years of age. It is an offence under ss 22(2) and 24(2)(b) respectively for such a person to possess such a thing, or for someone to part with possession of such a thing to such a person, with certain exceptions. In recalling these exceptions it is helpful to consider those persons who are permitted to possess s 1 firearms without a certificate and to identify the exceptions which might apply to persons under 14. The exceptions are when he:

(a) is carrying the firearm or ammunition for another for sporting purposes, and that other person is 18 or over and the holder of a firearm certificate; or
(b) is using the firearm or ammunition at a shooting gallery or miniature rifle range where the only weapons used do not exceed .23 inch calibre; or
(c) as a member of an approved rifle club, is engaged in connection with target shooting.

If proved, a reasonable belief that the other person was 14 or over is a defence to a charge under s 24(2)(a) or (b) (s 24(5)).

It is an offence under FiA 1968, s 22(1A) for a firearm certificate holder under 18 to use a firearm covered by it for a purpose not authorised by the European Weapons Directive referred to on p 591.

Shotguns

It is an offence under FiA 1968, s 22(1) for a person under 18 to purchase or hire any shotgun or ammunition. Likewise, someone who sells or lets it on hire to such a person commits an offence under s 24(1). It is an offence under s 24(3) to make a gift of a shotgun to a person under 15. (These rules also apply to ammunition for a shotgun.) It is, of course, possible for a person of 15, 16, or 17 lawfully to acquire a shotgun by the same process as that outlined in relation to s 1 firearms. If proved, a reasonable belief that the other person was 18 or over, or 15 or over, is a defence to a charge under s 24(1) or (3) respectively (s 24(5)).

All young persons in possession of shotguns must have a shotgun certificate. Although FiA 1968 does not prescribe a minimum age at which a shotgun certificate may be granted, control is exercised by the chief officer of police who must consider the grant of such a certificate in the context of public safety.

Even if he has a shotgun certificate, it is an offence under s 22(3) for a person under 15 to 'have with him' an assembled shotgun, except while:

(a) under the supervision of a person of 21 or more; or
(b) it is so securely fastened with a gun cover that it cannot be fired.

In addition, a holder of a shotgun certificate who is under 18 may not use the weapon for a purpose which is not authorised by the European Weapons Directive; to do so is an offence under s 22(1A).

Air weapons

The same general rule applies. By FiA 1968, s 22(1), it is an offence for a person under 18 to purchase or hire an air weapon or ammunition. The seller or person who lets on hire in such a case also commits an offence under s 24(1); if proved, a reasonable belief that the other person was 18 or over is a defence. There are, however, restrictions in relation to possession and they are predictable.

By s 22(4) a person under 18 commits an offence if he has with him an air weapon or ammunition for it except when:

(a) he is under the supervision of someone aged 21 or over (s 23(1)), but the supervisor commits an offence under s 23(1) if he allows the juvenile to fire a missile beyond the premises. The supervisor will have a defence if he shows that the only premises into or across which the missile was fired were premises occupied by a person who had consented to this;

(b) as a member of an approved club, he is engaged in connection with target shooting (s 23(2)(a));

(c) he is using the weapon or ammunition at a shooting gallery or miniature range where the only firearms used are either air weapons or miniature rifles not exceeding .23 inch calibre (s 23(2)(b)); or

(d) he is aged 14 or over and is on private premises with the consent of the occupier (s 23(2)(c)).

In relation to the exception under (a), it may be noted that a person of any age commits an offence under s 21A if he fires a missile from an air weapon beyond the premises where he is, unless he shows that the occupier of the premises into or across which the missile is fired had consented to this.

It is an offence under s 24(4)(a) for any person to make a gift of an air weapon or ammunition to a person under 18. By s 24(4)(b), it is an offence to part with the possession of an air weapon or ammunition to a person under 18 except where that person is not prohibited from having it with him by virtue of one of the exceptions in s 23. If proved, a reasonable belief that the person was 18 or over is a defence (s 24(5)).

By s 24ZA(1) and (2), it is an offence for a person in possession of an air weapon to fail to take reasonable precautions to prevent any person under the age of 18 from having the weapon with him, unless, by virtue of s 23, that person is not prohibited from having the weapon with him. *It is a defence to show that D reasonably believed that the other person was 18 or over. A person is taken to have shown these matters if sufficient evidence of them is adduced to raise an issue with respect to them, and the contrary is not proved beyond reasonable doubt.*

Purchase of imitation firearm by or sale to minors

FiA 1968, s 24A(1) and (2) respectively make it an offence for a person under 18 to purchase an imitation firearm, or for anyone to sell an imitation firearm to such a person. In relation to 'selling', the defence italicised above applies. In this offence, 'imitation firearm' is defined by FiA 1968, s 57 (and not by the Firearms Act 1982, s 1); see p 601 for that definition.

FIREARMS OFFENCES RELATING TO PREVENTION OF CRIME AND PUBLIC SAFETY

Conversion of firearms

It is an indictable (either way) offence under FiA 1968, s 4(1) to shorten the barrel of a shotgun within the meaning of FiA 1968 (see p 590) to a length of less than 24 inches. It is not an offence for a registered firearms dealer to shorten a barrel for the sole purpose of replacing a defective part so as to produce a barrel not less than 24 inches in length.

It is an indictable (either way) offence under s 4(3) for anyone other than a registered firearms dealer to convert into a firearm anything which, though having the appearance of a firearm, cannot discharge a missile through its barrel. Section 4(3) does not apply to an imitation firearm to which the Firearms Act 1982 (p 588) applies.

Possession with intent to endanger life

Under FiA 1968, s 16 it is an offence triable only on indictment to possess a firearm or ammunition with intent by means thereof to endanger life, or to enable another person by means thereof to endanger life, whether an injury has been caused or not.

Possession of a firearm, etc with intent to enable another person, by means thereof, to endanger life, means more than merely making it available to known criminals who might endanger life. An intention to endanger the life of a person abroad is sufficient for s 16; consequently, it covers possession by terrorist groups who might intend their mischief elsewhere. Possession with intent to commit suicide is not covered by s 16; an intent to endanger life must relate to the life of another.

The present offence is not committed by a person who intends to endanger life for a lawful purpose, as where a person whose house is besieged by an armed gang threatens them with his firearm in self-defence. This defence, however, is only available in circumstances where there is a specific risk of imminent attack: it does not apply where there is only a potential risk.

Possession with intent to cause fear of violence

By FiA 1968, s 16A, a person commits an offence triable only on indictment if he has in his possession any firearm or imitation firearm with intent:

(a) by means thereof to cause; or
(b) to enable any other person by means thereof to cause,

any person to believe that unlawful violence will be used against him or another.

In this offence, 'imitation firearm' is defined by FiA 1968, s 57 (and not by the Firearms Act 1982, s 1), as meaning anything which at the material time has the appearance of being a firearm (other than a weapon for the discharge of a noxious liquid, gas or other thing) whether or not it is capable of discharging any shot, bullet or other missile. An automatic pistol with the firing pin removed has been held to be such an imitation firearm; clearly, it fell within the definition. So may things which have the appearance of being firearms in particular circumstances on specific occasions, but not in others. A piece of roughly fashioned wood held in the hand in a darkened room might certainly have the appearance of being a firearm. It would be a matter for the jury to decide whether something actually did have the appearance of being a firearm in the circumstances in question. The House of Lords has held that fingers positioned in a jacket so as to appear to be a gun are not in law capable of constituting a firearm.

The Court of Appeal has held that s 16A is not limited to cases where the intent specified in s 16A was formed before the material time. It held that, provided there is a coincidence of possession and intent, s 16A also embraces the situation where D forms an intention to cause fear of violence at or immediately before the time of his actions which were designed to cause such fear.

Use of firearms to resist arrest

It is an offence by FiA 1968, s 17(1) for a person to make, or attempt to make, any use whatsoever of a firearm or imitation firearm with intent to resist or prevent the lawful arrest or detention of himself or another person. The offence is triable only on indictment. If a firearm or imitation firearm is used in resisting lawful arrest or detention, whether of the person using the firearm, or some other person, the offence is complete. The important words are 'to make, or attempt to make, any use' of the firearm and the issue of in whose possession the firearm was before that moment does not arise. Someone who grabbed a gun from the person arresting him and made use of it in this way would be guilty. It must be proved that the firearm was used intentionally for such a purpose. The offence would not be made out, for example, if the firearm was used with the intention of preventing a search of premises and an arrest was not intended at that time.

Section 17(2) creates a second indictable-only offence of possessing a firearm or imitation firearm *at the time of committing or being arrested* for an offence specified in Sch 1, unless D can show that he possessed it for a lawful object. The offences in Sch 1 include theft, robbery, burglary, blackmail, taking a conveyance, assaulting a constable in the execution of his duty, rape, assault by penetration, causing a person to engage in sexual activity without consent where the activity caused involved penetration, rape of a child under 13, assault of a child under 13 by penetration, causing or inciting a child under 13 to engage in a sexual activity where any activity involving penetration was caused, sexual activity with a person with a mental disorder impeding choice where the touching involved penetration, causing or inciting a person with a mental disorder impeding choice to engage in sexual activity where penetration was caused, criminal damage, malicious wounding, assault occasioning actual bodily harm, and assault with intent to resist arrest.

By way of example, a person who takes a conveyance whilst in possession of an air pistol, or even an imitation firearm, commits the s 17(2) offence. Even if he had not possessed the firearm at the time of taking the conveyance, he would be equally liable if he was in possession of it at the time of his arrest. Where the case is one of possession *at the time of arrest*, there is no requirement that the prosecution prove that D actually committed the specified offence. It is only necessary to prove that D was in possession of the firearm when lawfully arrested for a specified offence. The physical possession of the firearm is not essential. The Court of Appeal has said that 'possession' in s 17(2) simply refers to 'custody and control'. Consequently, for example, a person remains in possession of a firearm for the purposes of s 17(2) if he has left it in a nearby van at the time of committing a specified offence elsewhere.

For the purposes of both subsections of s 17, a 'firearm' does not include a component part or accessory. Subject to this, 'imitation firearm' in s 17(1) and (2) has the same meaning as in s 16A (see p 601).

Having firearm with criminal intent

FiA 1968, s 18(1) deals with the offence committed by a person who has with him a firearm or imitation firearm with intent to commit an indictable offence, or to resist arrest or prevent the arrest of another, in either case while he has the firearm or imitation firearm with him. The offence is triable only on indictment.

'Imitation firearm' has the same meaning as in FiA 1968 s 16A (see p 601). As to 'has with him', see p 603.

The intent required by s 18 is a particular one. It is not sufficient that D intended to commit an indictable offence or to resist, etc the arrest. D must also intend to have a firearm or imitation firearm with him at the time of that commission or resistance. On the other hand, D does not have to intend to use or carry the gun in furtherance of the indictable offence. Section 18(2) provides that proof that D had a firearm or imitation firearm with him and intended to commit an offence, or to resist or prevent arrest, is evidence that he intended to have it with him while doing so.

Having firearm in a public place

A person commits an offence contrary to FiA 1968, s 19 if, without lawful authority or reasonable excuse (the proof whereof lies on him), he has with him in a public place:

(a) a loaded shotgun;
(b) an air weapon (whether loaded or not);
(c) any other firearm (whether loaded or not) together with ammunition suitable for use in that firearm; or
(d) an imitation firearm (same meaning as in ss 16A to 18: see p 601).

Such an offence is an indictable (either way) offence with the following exceptions. If it is committed in relation to a prohibited weapon under s 5(1) (on pp 593–4) (other than that at (h)), or a prohibited weapon of type (a) under s 5(1A) (p 594), the offence is triable only on indictment. If the offence relates to an air weapon it is a summary offence.

A shotgun which has a loaded magazine is loaded, even though there is no round in the breach.

This is another offence which refers to 'having with him' rather than 'possessing'. The former term is a narrower one. As we have seen, a person can be in possession of a firearm if he has control of it, even though it is not in his physical custody and is not immediately available to him, as where it is in his home in Norwich while he is in London. In contrast, although a person can have a firearm with him, even though he is not carrying it, he must have a close physical link with it and it must be readily accessible to him. Someone who has a gun in his pocket clearly has it with him, and the same is true if it is in a bag which he is carrying or in the glove compartment of the car which he is driving. Provided that the firearm is readily accessible to him, a person may even have with him at the time a firearm which he has left in his car which he has parked down the street. A person does not 'have with him' something of whose presence he is unaware, such as a firearm which has been slipped into his bag; but once he knows of its presence it is no excuse that, at the material time, he has forgotten about it, as where he puts a firearm in the glove compartment of his car but has forgotten about it when he is stopped by a patrol car a month later.

'Public place' has the same meaning as given on p 609.

The offence under s 19 is one of strict liability as to the nature of the item in question as defined above. Thus, knowledge or suspicion as to its nature is not required, and even a reasonably mistaken belief that it is not of that nature will not excuse.

It is difficult to imagine circumstances in which someone could, with lawful authority or reasonable excuse, have with him a loaded shotgun in a public place. The possession of a shotgun certificate certainly does not authorise this. Depending on the circumstances, a gamekeeper, crossing a public highway in the course of his duties, might be considered to have a reasonable excuse for having a loaded shotgun with him. Someone going to his rifle club carrying a .22 rifle and ammunition in a rifle-case would doubtless be able to prove a reasonable excuse for having the rifle and ammunition with him, provided that he possessed a firearm certificate.

Trespassing with a firearm

An indictable (either way) offence is committed against FiA 1968, s 20(1) if a person, while he has any firearm or imitation firearm with him, enters or is in any building or part of a building as a trespasser and without reasonable excuse (the proof whereof lies on him). A less serious offence is committed under s 20(2) where the trespass is on land; the other ingredients of this offence are identical to those in s 20(1). 'Imitation firearm' bears the same meaning as in s 16A (see p 601).

'Enters' requires the bodily presence of D to some degree. As to 'trespasser', 'trespass' requires the absence of lawful authority or of permission (express or implied) from the occupier or someone on his behalf. 'Building' refers to a structure which has a roof and is of a reasonably permanent nature; the term 'part of a building' covers instances where a person might have a right to be in a building, for example a hotel, but is a trespasser in someone else's room, which would be a part of that building. For the purposes of s 20(2), the expression 'land' includes land covered with water, so that a person with a firearm trespassing in a boat on a lake is guilty of this offence.

POLICE POWERS

Stop and search in certain cases

FiA 1968, s 47(1) authorises a constable to require any person whom he has reasonable cause to suspect:

(a) of having a firearm, with or without ammunition, with him in a public place; or
(b) to be committing or about to commit, elsewhere than in a public place, an offence of 'having with him' a firearm or imitation firearm with intent to commit an indictable offence or to resist arrest (contrary to s 18, above), or an offence of trespassing with a firearm (contrary to s 20, above),

to hand over the firearm or ammunition for examination. Failure to comply with such a demand is an offence (s 47(2)). 'Imitation firearm' bears the same meaning as on p 601.

Section 47(3) also provides that a constable who has reasonable cause to suspect the existence of one of the above circumstances (ie (a) or (b)) may search that person and may detain him for the purpose of doing so. This power extends to the search of vehicles and the constable may require a driver to stop for that purpose (s 47(4)).

A constable may enter any place to exercise his powers under s 47.

Production of certificates

FiA 1968, s 48(1) states that a constable may demand, from any person whom he believes to be in possession of a firearm or ammunition to which s 1 applies, or of any shotgun, the production of his firearm certificate or (as the case may be) his shotgun certificate.

Section 48(1A) provides that, where a constable has made a demand under s 48(1) and the person to whom it is made fails:

(a) to produce a firearm certificate or (as the case may be) a shotgun certificate; or

(b) to show that he is a person who is not entitled to be issued with a document identifying that firearm under any provisions which in the other EU states correspond to the provisions under FiA 1968 for the issue of European Firearms Passes; or

(c) to show that he is in possession of the firearm only in his capacity as a recognised firearms collector of another EU state,

the constable can demand from that person the production of a valid European Firearms Pass issued to that person in another EU state relating to the firearm in question. Failure to comply with such a demand is an offence (s 48(4)).

If a person on whom a demand has been made under s 48 fails to produce the certificate or document or to permit the constable to read it, or to show that he is exempt from the requirement to have a certificate, the constable may seize and detain the firearm, ammunition or shotgun and may require the person immediately to declare his name and address (s 48(2)). It is an offence under s 48(3) to refuse or fail to give a true name and address.

Search warrant

By FiA 1968, s 46(1), a justice, who is satisfied by information on oath that there is reasonable ground for suspecting that:

(a) an offence relevant for the purposes of s 46 has been, is being or is about to be committed; or

(b) in connection with a firearm or ammunition, there is a danger to the public safety or to the peace,

may grant a search warrant. The warrant will authorise a constable or civilian officer:

(a) to enter at any time any premises or place specified, if necessary by force, and to search them and every person found there;

(b) to seize and detain anything found on the premises or place, or on any such person, in respect of which or in connection with which he has reasonable grounds for suspecting that:
   (i) a relevant offence has been, is being or is about to be committed, or
   (ii) in connection with a firearm, imitation firearm or ammunition there is a danger to the public safety or to the peace (s 46(2)).

A 'relevant offence' is any offence under FiA 1968 except that under s 22(3) (person under 15 having assembled shotgun otherwise than under supervision) or an offence relating specifically to air weapons (ie under ss 22(4), 22(5), 23(1), 24(4) or 24ZA).

The power of seizure and detention includes power to require information which is stored in any electronic form and is accessible from the premises or place to be produced in a form in which it is visible and legible (or from which it can readily be produced in such form) and can be taken away. The additional powers of seizure provided by the Criminal Justice and Police Act 2001, ss 50 and 51 apply where a search warrant is executed under FiA 1968, s 46.

The Court of Appeal has held that the police may use reasonable force to restrain or detain the occupants of premises when executing a warrant under s 46.

It is an offence intentionally to obstruct a constable or civilian officer in the exercise of these powers (s 46(5)).

Entry into rifle clubs

By Fi(A)A 1988, s 15(7), a constable duly authorised in writing by a chief officer of police, on producing (if required) his authority, may enter any premises occupied or used by an approved rifle club and inspect them, and anything on them, for the purpose of ascertaining whether the provisions about such a club and any limitations in the approval are being complied with.

FIREARMS OFFENCES UNDER OTHER ACTS

Drunk in possession

It is an offence contrary to the Licensing Act 1872, s 12 to be drunk when in possession on any highway or other public place of any loaded firearm (including a loaded air rifle).

Discharge near the highway

By the Highways Act 1980, s 161(2)(b), a person commits an offence if, without lawful authority or excuse, he discharges any firearm within 50 feet of the centre of any highway which consists of or comprises a carriageway, *and in consequence thereof* a user of the highway is injured, interrupted (eg by being forced to make a detour) or endangered. For the meaning of 'highway', see p 328.

Wanton discharge in a street

By the Town Police Clauses Act 1847, s 28, it is an offence wantonly to discharge a firearm in any street to the obstruction, annoyance or danger of residents or passengers.

BUSINESS AND OTHER TRANSACTIONS RELATING TO FIREARMS AND AMMUNITION

Section 1 firearms and ammunition, shotguns and air weapons

It is an indictable (either way) offence under FiA 1968, s 3(1), for a person to:

(a) manufacture, sell, transfer, repair, test or prove any s 1 firearm or ammunition, or a shotgun,
(b) expose for sale or transfer, or possess for sale, transfer, repair or proof, any such firearm or ammunition, or a shotgun, or
(c) sell or transfer, or expose for sale or transfer, an air weapon, or possess such a weapon for sale or transfer,

without being registered under FiA 1968 as a firearms dealer.

By way of exception, it is not an offence for an auctioneer to sell by auction a firearm or ammunition without being registered as a firearms dealer, provided he holds a police permit for that purpose (s 9(2)).

A 'firearms dealer' is defined by FiA 1968, s 57 as a person who, by way of trade or business, *manufactures, sells, transfers, repairs, tests or proves firearms or ammunition to which FiA 1968, s 1 applies, or shotguns, or sells or transfers air weapons.*

The Violent Crime Reduction Act 2006 (VCRA 2006), s 32(1) and (2) makes it an offence to sell an air weapon by way of trade or business to a person who is not a registered firearms dealer when this is not done face to face.

The sale or transfer of a s 1 firearm or ammunition or of a shotgun to a person other than a registered firearms dealer is an indictable (either way) offence under FiA 1968, s 3(2), unless that person produces the necessary certificate, or shows he is legally entitled to purchase or acquire the firearm or ammunition without a certificate.

The chief officer of police must keep a register of firearms dealers. An applicant must provide details of every place of business (including storage places) in the area, at which he proposes to carry on business as a firearms dealer, and details of the precise nature of the business which he intends to conduct. A registered firearms dealer or his employee is permitted to keep, purchase or acquire firearms and ammunition in the ordinary course of his business without holding firearm certificates in respect of them, and this is so even though the place where the firearm or ammunition is possessed, purchased or acquired by the dealer or employee is not the dealer's place of business or has not been registered as his place of business.

Except on certain specified grounds, the chief officer of police must enter the applicant's name and place(s) of business in the register and grant him a certificate of registration. The chief officer of police may, however, impose conditions upon registration. These conditions are generally concerned with ensuring the safe-keeping of firearms. They usually include the following conditions; that:

(a) the dealer must, on being given reasonable notice, allow a police officer authorised in writing by the chief officer to enter and inspect his premises;
(b) hand-guns must be kept in a locked safe;
(c) other weapons must be chained together by the trigger guards and locked in a rack;
(d) ammunition is to be stored separately and locked up;
(e) rifle bolts must be removed and kept separately;
(f) the windows of cabinets for storage must be illuminated at night; and
(g) glass door panels and windows must be barred.

In addition, conditions are usually imposed concerning notification of dealings in various types of weapon.

All certificates of registration are renewable every three years. A new place of business must be notified to the chief officer and must be registered by him, unless the use of those premises for firearms dealing would endanger the public safety or the peace. A registered dealer may be removed from the register if he ceases to deal in firearms, or to have a business place within the area, or if he cannot be permitted to continue in business without danger to the public safety or the peace. Failure to comply with conditions also provides reason for removal from the register. Particular premises may be removed from the register on safety grounds.

Additional rules for prohibited weapons or ammunition

Under FiA 1968, s 5(2A), a person commits an offence, triable only on indictment, if without the written authority of the Secretary of State:

(a) he manufactures any prohibited weapon or ammunition *specified in s 5(1)*;
(b) he sells or transfers *any* prohibited weapon or prohibited ammunition,
(c) he has in his possession for sale or transfer *any* prohibited weapon or prohibited ammunition, or

(d) he purchases or acquires for sale or transfer any prohibited weapon or prohibited ammunition.

Dealer to keep records

A registered dealer must keep a register of transactions. He must within 24 hours enter in his register the particulars of persons to whom firearms and ammunition (excluding those to which FiA 1968, s 1 does not apply: see p 589) are sold or transferred.

Registered dealers must allow police officers or civilian officers, authorised in writing by the chief officer of police, to enter and inspect all stock in hand, and must produce their registers for inspection. It is an offence to fail to do so, or knowingly or recklessly to make any false entry in a register (FiA 1968, s 40(5)). A police officer who is authorised in writing by his chief officer of police to carry out these duties must produce that written authority if required to do so.

Manufacture, import and sale of realistic imitation firearms

VCRA 2006, s 36(1) makes it an offence to manufacture, import or sell a realistic imitation firearm (ie an imitation firearm which has an appearance that is *so realistic as to make it indistinguishable*, for all practical purposes, from a real firearm, and is neither a de-activated firearm nor itself an antique). Such an imitation firearm is not to be regarded as '*so distinguishable*' if it is distinguishable only by an expert, on close examination or by attempting to load or to fire it. Defences are provided by s 37 in relation to things done for specified legitimate purposes.

The Violent Crime Reduction Act 2006 (Realistic Imitation Firearms) Regulations 2007 specify the sizes and colours of imitation firearms which are to be regarded as unrealistic for the purposes of the definition of 'realistic imitation firearm'. The Regulations provide that an imitation firearm is not a 'realistic' one if:

(a) it is less than 38 mm high and 70 mm in length; or
(b) it is of one of the following colours: bright
    (i)   red,
    (ii) orange,
    (iii) yellow,
    (iv) green,
    (v) pink,
    (vi) purple, or
    (vii) blue;
    or is made of transparent material.

The Regulations provide a defence to a charge under s 36 for D to show that his conduct was for the purpose only of making the imitation firearm available for the organisation and holding of permitted activities in respect of which there were insurance arrangements in respect of third-party liabilities, or for the purpose of display at a permitted event. 'Permitted activities' means the acting-out of military or law enforcement scenarios for the purpose of recreation (eg historical re-enactments of battles); and 'permitted events' means a commercial event at which firearms or realistic imitation firearms (or both) are offered for sale or displayed. D will have shown such a matter if there is sufficient evidence to raise an issue and the contrary is not proved beyond reasonable doubt.

OFFENSIVE WEAPONS IN PUBLIC PLACES

The Prevention of Crime Act 1953 (PCA 1953), s 1(1) provides that any person who without lawful authority or reasonable excuse, the proof whereof lies on him, has with him in any public place any offensive weapon is guilty of an indictable (either way) offence. The court may make an order as to the disposal of a weapon following conviction.

'Has with him' was defined on p 603. D need not know of the facts which render the article an offensive weapon within the meaning of the statute.

An offensive weapon is defined by s 1(4) as any article made or adapted for use for causing injury to the person, or intended by the person having it with him for such use by him or by some other person. This definition includes two classes of offensive weapon.

Articles made or adapted for causing injury to the person

Examples of articles *made* for causing injury to the person are petrol bombs, bayonets, coshes, knuckledusters, swords, flick knives and butterfly knives. These weapons are described as offensive per se (ie in themselves). The Court of Appeal has held that an article which has all the characteristics of one made for causing injury to the person (in the instant case a flick knife) is a weapon offensive per se despite the fact that it has a harmless secondary characteristic, eg of being a lighter.

Examples of articles *adapted* for causing injury to the person are a piece of chain whose links have been sharpened and someone's cap in the peak of which a razor blade has been inserted with the cutting edge exposed. In such cases, articles which are harmless in themselves are made offensive weapons by their deliberate adaptation for use for causing personal injury.

Articles intended to be used for causing injury to the person

This class covers articles which are inoffensive per se (ie in themselves), because they have not been made or adapted for causing personal injury, but which are rendered offensive by D's intention to use them for causing injury to the person. Such articles include belts, shoes, umbrellas and dog leads, provided it can be shown that there was an intention to use the article for causing injury to the person. The difficulty of proving such an intention increases in proportion to the generally non-offensive character of the article in question.

It is not enough that someone, who is in innocent possession of an article in a public place, suddenly uses it for an offensive purpose. Thus, where a carpenter took a hammer from his tool bag during a fight at a railway station and used it, a divisional court held that he was not guilty of an offence under PCA 1953, s 1, as he did not have the hammer with him for causing injury to the person. This is a stricter rule than applies to similar wording in the offence of aggravated burglary (see p 911).

Public place

D must have with him the offensive weapon in a public place; this can include having it with him in a vehicle which is in a public place. 'Public place' includes any highway, and any other premises or place to which at the material time the public have or are permitted (ie invited or tolerated) to have access, whether on payment or otherwise.

The issue is generally whether the public have access, or are permitted to have it if they wish. Public access is a matter of fact and if access is restricted to certain classes of person, it must be restricted to some considerable degree before it will be accepted that the public are not admitted.

The fact that a person is found with an offensive weapon in a private place may lead to a conviction for the present offence. For example, if a visitor to a dwelling house produces an offensive weapon, this gives rise to a strong inference that he brought it with him through the streets and therefore had it with him in a public place.

Lawful authority or reasonable excuse

A person does not commit the offence if he has lawful authority or reasonable excuse for having with him the offensive weapon; D has the onus of proving such authority or excuse.

Those who may have offensive weapons with lawful authority include members of the armed services, or police forces, who may carry weapons which are offensive in themselves as part of their duty. On the other hand, it has been held that private security guards do not have lawful authority to carry truncheons or the like.

In terms of 'reasonable excuse', the appeal courts have held as follows. Carrying a weapon for self-protection against imminent attack can amount to a reasonable excuse; whether it is or not depends on how imminent, how likely and how specific the perceived threat, and how serious the anticipated attack. A person who has with him a weapon in order to commit suicide does not have a reasonable excuse, nor does a security guard who carries a truncheon 'as a deterrent' and 'as part of his uniform'. A claim by a person who has been proved to be in possession of a weapon which is offensive per se that he did not know that the article in question was an offensive weapon cannot amount to a reasonable excuse. Nor can the fact that D had forgotten that the article was in his possession in itself amount to a reasonable excuse.

Threatening with offensive weapon in public

Under PCA 1953, s 1A(1), a person is guilty of an indictable (either way) offence if he:

(a) has an offensive weapon (as defined on p 609) with him in a public place (as defined on p 609),
(b) unlawfully and intentionally threatens another person with the weapon, and
(c) does so in such a way that there is an immediate risk of serious physical harm to that other person.

For these purposes, physical harm is serious if it amounts to grievous bodily harm for the purposes of the Offences Against the Person Act 1861 (p 652).

ANCILLARY OFFENCES TO THOSE UNDER PCA 1953

Having article with blade or point in a public place

The Criminal Justice Act 1988 (CJA 1988), s 139 provides an ancillary offence which is useful where a knife or the like cannot be proved to have been made, adapted or intended to cause injury to the person. Section 139(1) makes it an indictable (either way) offence for a person to have with him in a public place an article which is sharply pointed or with a blade, other than a folding pocket knife with a blade not exceeding three inches. 'Has with him' has, and 'public place' essentially has, the same meaning as under PCA 1953.

A butter knife without a handle and with no cutting edge and no point has been held to be a bladed article within CJA 1988, s 139. A folding knife which is secured in an open position by a locking device and can only be released from the open position by the pressing of a release button is not a folding pocket knife within the meaning of s 139.

D has a defence if he proves lawful authority or good reason for having the article with him in a public place, or that he had it with him there for use at work, for a religious reason or as part of any national costume (s 139(4) and (5)). Whether D was in possession of such a knife 'for use at work' is a matter for the court or jury as the statute uses ordinary, everyday language. Whether D had a good reason is a matter for the court or jury. A judge should not tell a jury what 'good reason' means, but in a clear case the judge can rule that D's explanation cannot amount to a good reason. The Court of Appeal has held that D's forgetfulness that he has the article is not a good reason, but that forgetfulness combined with another reason may be. A fear of attack may be a good reason, depending on how imminent, how likely, how specific the perceived threat, and how serious the anticipated attack.

Having article with blade or point (or offensive weapon) on school premises

CJA 1988, s 139A(1) makes it an indictable (either way) offence for a person to have any article to which s 139 applies with him on school premises. Section 139A(2) creates a similar either-way offence in relation to an offensive weapon to which PCA 1953 applies. The term 'school premises' means land used for the purpose of a school excluding any land occupied solely as a dwelling by a person employed at the school. Similar defences exist; a person who proves that he had good reason or lawful authority for having the article or weapon with him on the premises has a defence (s 139A(3)). So has a person who proves that he had the article or weapon with him for the purposes set out above in relation to s 139 (s 139A(4)). In addition, he may show possession 'for educational purposes' (s 139A(4)).

Threatening with article with blade or point (or offensive weapon)

Under the Criminal Justice Act 1988, s 139AA(1), a person is guilty of an indictable (either way) offence if he:

(a) has an article to which s 139AA applies with him in a public place (as defined for s 139: above) or on school premises (as defined for s 139A: above),
(b) unlawfully and intentionally threatens another person with the article, and
(c) does so in such a way that there is an immediate risk of serious physical harm (as defined on 610) to that other person.

In relation to a public place, s 139AA(1) applies to an article to which s 139 applies (above). In relation to school premises, s 139AA(1) applies to an article to which s 139 applies, and to an offensive weapon within the meaning of PCA 1953, s 1.

Power of entry to search for articles with a blade or point and offensive weapons

CJA 1988, s 139B provides a constable with a power of entry, using reasonable force if necessary, into school premises and the power to search those premises and any person on those premises for articles to which CJA 1988, s 139 applies, or to which PCA 1953, s 1 applies, if he has reasonable grounds for suspecting that an offence under CJA 1988, s 139A or s 139AA (above) is being, or has been, committed. He may seize any articles or weapons discovered in the course of such a search which he reasonably suspects to be such articles or weapons.

RESTRICTION OF OFFENSIVE WEAPONS

Manufacture, sale, etc of flick knives and gravity knives

The Restriction of Offensive Weapons Act 1959 is concerned with the manufacture and distribution of flick knives and gravity knives. It is an offence under s 1(1) for any person to manufacture, sell, hire, offer for sale or hire, or to expose or have in his possession for the purpose of sale or hire, or to lend or give to any person, either of these weapons.

A 'flick knife' is any knife which has a blade which opens automatically by hand pressure applied to a button, spring or other device in or attached to the handle of the knife. A 'gravity knife' is one which has a blade which is released from the handle or sheath thereof by the force of gravity or the application of centrifugal force and which, when released, is locked in place by means of a button, spring, lever or other device. The flick knife is therefore one with an up-and-over blade and a gravity knife is one which allows the blade to be shaken from the handle.

Manufacture, sale, etc of specified weapons

By CJA 1988, s 141(1), a person who manufactures, sells or hires, or offers for sale or hire, exposes or has in his possession for the purpose of sale or hire, or lends or gives to any other person, any weapon specified by order by the Secretary of State commits an offence.

The specified weapons

The Secretary of State has made the Criminal Justice Act 1988 (Offensive Weapons) Order 1988 which provides that s 141(1) applies to the following weapons, other than those which are antiques (ie ones manufactured more than 100 years before the alleged offence under s 141(1)). The specified weapons are: a knuckleduster, a swordstick, a handclaw, a belt buckle knife, a push dagger, a hollow kubotan (small truncheon with spikes), a footclaw, a death star, a butterfly knife, a telescopic truncheon, a blow-pipe, a kusari gama (sickle and chain), a kyoketsu shoge (hooked knife and chain), a manrikigusari or kusari (weights joined by chain), a disguised knife (any knife which has a concealed blade or concealed sharp point and is designed to appear to be an everyday object of a kind commonly carried on the person or in a handbag, briefcase or other hand luggage (such as a comb, brush, writing instrument, cigarette lighter, key, lipstick or telephone)), a stealth knife (a knife or spike, which has a blade or a sharp point, made from a material that is not readily detectable by apparatus used for detecting metal, and which is not designed for domestic use or for use in the processing, preparation or consumption of food or as a toy), a straight, side-handled or friction-lock truncheon (sometimes known as a baton), a zombie knife, zombie killer knife or zombie slayer knife (a blade with a cutting edge, a serrated edge and images or words (whether on the blade or otherwise) suggesting that it is to be used for the purposes of violence), and a sword with a curved blade 50 cm or more in length (for which purpose the length of the blade is the straight line distance from the top of the handle to the tip of the blade). It is a defence to a charge under s 141 in relation to the last-named to show:

(a) that the sword was made before 1954 or was made at any other time according to traditional methods of making swords by hand;
(b) that the conduct was for the purpose of making the weapon available for the purposes of the organisation and holding of a permitted activity (historical re-enactment or a sporting activity) in respect of which public liability insurance is held; or
(c) that D's conduct was for the purpose only of making the weapon available for the purposes of use in religious ceremonies.

D shows (a), (b) or (c) if sufficient evidence as to it is adduced to raise an issue with respect to it and the contrary is not proved beyond reasonable doubt.

General defences

It is a defence to a charge under CJA 1988, s 141 to show that the conduct in question was only for the purpose of making the weapon available to a public museum or gallery or for theatrical performances (or rehearsals) or the production of films or television programmes. D shows this if sufficient evidence of the matter is adduced to raise an issue with respect to it and the contrary is not proved beyond reasonable doubt.

Police powers

A justice may issue a warrant under CJA 1988, s 142 authorising entry and search on the application of a constable if he is satisfied that there are reasonable grounds for believing that there are on those premises knives such as are mentioned in the Restriction of Offensive Weapons Act 1959, s 1(1) or weapons to which CJA 1988, s 141 applies, that an offence under either of these provisions has been or is being committed in relation to them, and that one of the normal essential conditions for a search warrant exists.

Sale of knives, etc to persons under 18

By CJA 1988, s 141A(1), it is an offence to sell to a person under the age of 18 a knife, knife blade or razor blade, any axe, and any other article which has a blade or which is sharply pointed and which is made or adapted for use for causing injury to the person. Section 141A does not apply to articles already controlled by the Restriction of Offensive Weapons Act 1959 or CJA 1988, s 141, or described in an order made by the Secretary of State under s 141A. The Secretary of State has made an order in respect of a folding pocket knife with a blade which does not exceed three inches and razor blades permanently enclosed in a cartridge or housing.

It is a defence if D proves that he took all reasonable precautions and exercised all due diligence to avoid commission of the offence.

Marketing, etc of combat knives

Marketing

The Knives Act 1997 (KA 1997), s 1(1) provides that it is an indictable (either way) offence to market a knife in a way which:

(a) indicates, or suggests, that it is suitable for combat; or
(b) is otherwise likely to stimulate or encourage violent behaviour involving the use of the knife as a weapon.

The term 'market' includes selling or hiring, offering or exposing for sale or hire, or possession for the purpose of sale or hire. 'Suitable for combat' means suitable for use as a weapon for inflicting injury on a person or causing a person to fear injury; and 'violent behaviour' means an unlawful act inflicting injury on a person or causing a person to fear injury.

Publication

KA 1997, s 2(1) provides the indictable (either way) offence of publishing any written, pictorial or other material in connection with the marketing of any knife, which:

(a) indicates, or suggests, that the knife is 'suitable for combat'; or
(b) is otherwise likely to stimulate or encourage 'violent behaviour' involving the use of the knife as a weapon.

Defences

In relation to the offence under KA 1997, s 1, proof that the knife was marketed for use by the armed forces of any country, or as an antique or curio is a defence.
In relation to the offence under s 2, it is a defence to prove that:

(a) the material was published in connection with marketing a knife for use by the armed forces of any country or as an antique or curio; and
(b) it was reasonable for the knife to be marketed in that way; and
(c) there were no reasonable grounds for suspecting that a person into whose possession the knife might come in consequence of the way in which it was marketed would use it for an unlawful purpose.

It is also a defence to a charge under KA 1997, s 1 or s 2 for D to prove that he did not know or suspect, and had no reasonable grounds for suspecting, that the way the knife was marketed (s 1), or the material (s 2), amounted to an indication or suggestion that the knife was 'suitable for combat', or was likely to stimulate or encourage 'violent behaviour' involving the use of the knife as a weapon. Lastly, it is a defence to either offence for D to prove that he took all reasonable precautions and exercised due diligence to avoid committing the offence.

Police powers

KA 1997, s 5 provides for the issue of search warrants authorising entry, search and seizure in respect of knives and publications. Reasonable force may be used in exercising the powers under the warrant. The additional powers of seizure provided by the Criminal Justice and Police Act 2001, s 50 apply where such a search warrant in respect of publications is executed.

USING SOMEONE TO MIND A WEAPON

VCRA 2006, s 28 provides that a person is guilty of an offence triable only on indictment if:

(a) he uses another to look after, hide or transport a dangerous weapon for him; and
(b) he does so under arrangements or in circumstances that facilitate, or are intended to facilitate, the weapon being available to him for an unlawful purpose.

For this purpose, the cases where a dangerous weapon is to be regarded as available to a person for an unlawful purpose include any case where it is available for him to take possession of it at a time and place at which his possession of the weapon would constitute, or be likely to involve or to lead to, the commission by him of an offence. A 'dangerous weapon' is a firearm (other than an air weapon or a component part of, or accessory to, an air weapon) or a weapon to which CJA 1988, s 141 or 141A applies (specified offensive weapons, knives and bladed weapons: see pp 612–13).

CROSSBOWS

The Crossbows Act 1987 creates specific offences in respect of crossbows with a draw weight of at least 1.4 kg.

By s 1, it is an offence for any person to sell or let on hire such a crossbow or part of a crossbow to a person under the age of 18. No offence is committed if the seller or hirer believes the person so acquiring to be 18 or older, provided he has reasonable ground for that belief. Similarly, by s 2, it is an offence for a person under 18 to purchase or hire a crossbow or part of a crossbow.

Section 3 provides that, unless he is under the supervision of a person who is 21 or older, a person under 18 who has with him a crossbow which is capable of discharging a missile, or parts of a crossbow which together (and without any other parts) can be assembled to form a crossbow capable of discharging a missile, is guilty of an offence.

Where a constable suspects with reasonable cause that a person is committing or has committed an offence under s 3, he may:

(a) search that person for a crossbow or part of a crossbow; or
(b) search any vehicle, or anything in or on a vehicle, in or on which the constable reasonably suspects there is a crossbow or part of a crossbow connected with the offence.

A person or vehicle may be detained by the constable for the purpose of such a search and anything appearing to be a crossbow (or part) may be seized. The constable may enter any land other than a dwelling house to exercise these powers. These powers are provided by s 4.

CHAPTER 20

Explosives

FIREWORKS

Offences under the Fireworks Act 2003

The Fireworks Regulations 2004 (FR 2004), made under the Fireworks Act 2003, contain a number of prohibitions. FR 2004, reg 12 requires chief officers of police to enforce the prohibitions (below) relating to possession or use. Enforcement of the prohibitions relating to unlicensed supply is a matter for the local weights and measures authority, except that in a metropolitan county licensing enforcement is a matter for that county's fire and rescue authority.

The Fireworks Act 2003, s 11 provides that any person who contravenes a prohibition imposed by fireworks regulations, or who fails to comply with a requirement imposed by or under such regulations, is guilty of an offence. The defence of 'due diligence' provided by the Consumer Protection Act 1987, s 39 applies to these offences. The offence is a 'penalty offence' for the purposes of the Criminal Justice and Police Act 2001 (p 31).

Prohibition on possession

FR 2004, reg 4 provides that no person under 18 may possess an adult firework in a public place, ie any place to which at the material time the public have or are permitted access (whether on payment or otherwise).

Regulation 5 prohibits anyone from possessing a 'category 4 firework'. This is a firework classified as category 4 under Part I of BS 7114.

However, reg 6 provides that nothing in regs 4 and 5 prohibits the possession of any firework by any person:

(a) employed by, or in business as, a professional organiser or operator of firework displays who possesses the firework for such purposes;

(b) employed in, or whose trade or business (wholly or partly) is, the manufacture of fireworks or assemblies containing fireworks who possesses the firework for the purposes of his trade, employment or business;

(c) employed in, or whose trade or business (wholly or partly) is, the supply of fireworks or such assemblies in accordance with the Pyrotechnic Articles (Safety) Regulations 2015;

(d) employed by a local authority, or a UK government department, or in a naval, military or air force establishment, who, in the course of his employment, possesses the firework for the purpose of a firework display, in connection with a national public celebration or a national commemorative event, or (government employee only) for research or investigation;

(e) employed by or otherwise acting on behalf of a local authority, enforcement authority or other body, where the authority or body has enforcement powers applying to the firework in question, and the person possesses that firework for the purposes of the exercise of those powers;

(f) for use, in the course of a trade, business or employment, for special effects purposes in the theatre, on film or on television; or

(g) in business as or employed by a supplier of goods designed and intended for use in conjunction with fireworks or assemblies containing fireworks who possesses the firework for testing those goods in connection with safety.

Prohibition of use at night

FR 2004, reg 7 prohibits the use of an adult firework during 'night hours' (23.00 to 07.00) otherwise than on a permitted fireworks night or by a local authority employee in the course of a local authority display or at a national public celebration or commemorative event. Permitted fireworks nights are Chinese New Year (23.00 to 01.00); 5 November (23.00 to 24.00); the day of Diwali (23.00 to 01.00); and 31 December (23.00 to 01.00).

Throwing fireworks

It is an offence to throw, cast or fire any fireworks in or onto any highway, street, thoroughfare or public place. This offence, provided by the Explosives Act 1875 (EA 1875), s 80, is extremely useful. Although there are other offences in relation to the use of fireworks in streets and public places, for example under the Highways Act 1980, s 161 and the Town Police Clauses Act 1847, s 28, this offence is the most easily proved. There are no exceptions to the offence.

The offence under EA 1875, s 80 is a 'penalty offence' for the purposes of the Criminal Justice and Police Act 2001 (p 31).

EXPLOSIVE SUBSTANCES ACT 1883

The Explosive Substances Act 1883 (ESA 1883) deals with many offences which can be committed in relation to 'explosive substances'.

Explosive substance

The term is defined by ESA 1883, s 9, which declares that an explosive substance is deemed to include:

(a) any material for making any explosive substance;

(b) any apparatus, machine, implement or materials used, or intended to be used, or adapted for causing, or aiding in causing, any explosion in or with any explosive substance; and

(c) any part of any such apparatus, machine or implement.

This wide definition covers, for example, an ingredient which would go into the making of an explosive substance, an empty bomb case and a detonator for a bomb.

ESA 1883 does not define the essential term 'explosive' but the Court of Appeal has held that 'explosive' should be interpreted in the light of the definition of 'explosive' in EA 1875, s 3, which states that the term means:

(a) gunpowder, nitro-glycerine, dynamite, gun-cotton, blasting powder, fulminate of mercury or of other metals, coloured fires, and every other substance, whether similar to those already mentioned or not, used or manufactured with a view to producing a practical effect by explosion or a pyrotechnic effect; and

(b) includes fog-signals, fireworks, fuses, rockets, percussion caps, detonators, cartridges, ammunition of all descriptions, and every adaptation or preparation of an explosive as above defined.

'Explosive substance' is, therefore, a wide term. A petrol bomb has been held to be an 'explosive substance'.

Causing an explosion likely to endanger life

ESA 1883, s 2 makes it an offence for any person unlawfully and maliciously to cause by an explosive substance any explosion of a nature likely to endanger life or to cause serious injury to property, whether such injury or damage occurs or not.

'Unlawfully' means without lawful justification, ie otherwise than in self-defence, prevention of crime, or the like, which will rarely be the case. 'Maliciously' simply means an intention to cause some unlawful harm to another or to property, or recklessness as to the risk of this resulting from the explosion. It does not mean or require spite or ill-will.

Attempt to cause explosion; making or keeping explosives with intent

ESA 1883, s 3(1) creates two offences. The first offence is concerned with acts done with the specified intent to cause an explosion, and the second with making or possessing an explosive substance with the specified intent.

The offences are unlawfully and maliciously:

(a) to do any act with intent to cause by an explosive substance an explosion of a nature likely to endanger life or cause serious injury to property; or
(b) to make or have in one's possession or under one's control an explosive substance with intent by means thereof to endanger life or cause serious injury to property, or to enable any other person to do so.

The intended consequences may be in the UK or elsewhere. 'Unlawfully' has the same meaning as in s 2. 'Maliciously' is redundant in this offence because of the specific nature of the required intent.

In examining circumstances which might lead to the identification of offences contrary to s 3, one should think in terms of those who have not yet caused an explosion (and are therefore not caught by ESA 1883, s 2) but are doing some act with that intention in mind. Section 3 extends to acts which are merely preparatory to causing an explosion and therefore could not amount to an attempt to commit a s 2 offence.

Making or possessing an explosive under suspicious circumstances

There will often be practical difficulties associated with proving that explosive substances were made or possessed for the purpose of causing explosions likely to endanger life, etc. On occasions, the circumstances of the finding, any admissions and the nature of the explosive device itself may tend to support a charge under ESA 1883, s 3, but on other occasions there may be difficulties in proving a particular intention. ESA 1883, s 4(1) is useful in such cases.

Section 4(1), as interpreted by the Court of Appeal, provides that any person who knowingly makes or knowingly has in his possession or under his control any explosive substance, under such circumstances as to give rise to a reasonable suspicion that he is not making it or does not have it in his possession or under his control for a lawful object, commits an offence. If the defendant claims that he made, possessed or controlled it for a lawful object, he must prove that this was so, in which case the offence is not committed.

Section 4 does not define what constitutes a 'lawful object' but it has been held that it requires a positive object which is lawful, and not simply the absence of a criminal purpose. Thus, it has been held, making a bomb with no intention of exploding it would not be making an explosive substance for a lawful object. On the other hand, it has been held that self-defence or the like against an imminent attack would be a lawful object if the defendant intended to use the explosive in a way which was no more than reasonably necessary to meet the imminent attack.

General

An offence under ESA 1883 is triable only on indictment. A prosecution for such an offence may not be instituted without the consent of the Attorney General.

OTHER OFFENCES IN RELATION TO EXPLOSIVES

Police officers should always remember, when considering charges which can be preferred in relation to the activities of bombers, that more general offences under OAPA 1861 and the Criminal Damage Act 1971 may also be relevant. These offences are described in Chapters 23 and 37.

GENERAL POLICE POWERS AND DUTIES IN RESPECT OF EXPLOSIVES

By EA 1875, s 73, a constable may enter at any time, by force if necessary, any place (including a building, vehicle or vessel) upon reasonable cause for believing that any offence has been or is being committed in that place with respect to an explosive if he is in possession of:

(a) a justices' warrant granted following information on oath; or
(b) a written order from a superintendent (or above), which may be issued if the case is one of emergency and delay in obtaining a warrant would be likely to endanger life,

and search for explosives, and take samples of any explosives and ingredients of an explosive.

There are certain duties which must be carried out by the police when thefts of explosives are reported. The Hazardous Substances Division of the Health and Safety Executive should be informed of the exact nature and quantity of explosives stolen, the circumstances of the theft, whether the explosives have been stolen from a store or conveyance, and the use to which the explosives are normally put. The Division also requires the identity of the caller and details of place, time and date of the theft, together with details of any explosives left behind by the thieves. Where explosives are found, similar notification should be given to the Division.

The HSE Explosives Inspectorate requires details of all cases of illegal manufacture of explosives, even in the case of trivial experimentation by children. The usual details of the person, time, date, etc, of offence are required together with details of police action or court action and of any forensic report on the substance. The Inspectorate also likes to know where the persons concerned obtained their knowledge of the manufacture of explosives.

BOMB HOAXES

The offences which generally attract the description of bomb hoaxes are those dealt with by the Criminal Law Act 1977 (CLA 1977), s 51.

Placing or dispatching an article

CLA 1977, s 51(1) creates two indictable (either way) offences.

The first is committed by any person who places an article in any place whatsoever with the intention of inducing some other person to believe that it is likely to explode or ignite and thereby cause personal injury or damage to property. Section 51(1) states that the term 'article' includes any substance. Someone who deposits a fake bomb at a railway station, for example, commits the offence because he clearly intends to induce others to believe that it is an explosive device.

The second offence is dispatching any article by post, rail or any other means from one place to another with the intention to induce in some other person a belief that it is likely to explode or ignite and thereby cause personal injury or damage to property. If someone sends through a post office sorting office a number of false devices with the intention of causing fear of an explosion to be aroused in the staff of that office, the offence is complete.

Neither offence requires the defendant to have any particular person in mind as the person in whom he intends to induce the relevant belief.

False messages

CLA 1977, s 51(2) is concerned with false messages to the effect that an explosive device has been planted. It states that it is an indictable (either way) offence for a person to communicate any information, which he knows or believes to be false, to another person, with the intention of inducing in him or any other person a false belief that a bomb or other thing liable to explode or ignite is present in any place or location whatever. The use of the words 'there is a bomb' by a hoaxer is sufficient to give rise to the offence. It is not necessary that the person communicating the false information should identify a location.

When police officers receive such a call, it is essential to gain as much information as possible from the caller, or from the person who is passing on a message received from such a caller. The details should include sex, estimated age, urgency in voice, emotion, and accent, together with details of the time, date, duration of call, whether from a private telephone or a call box, and any background voices. All information given by the caller must be established: where, when and why the bomb is likely to explode, description of the type of bomb and its appearance, and as many of the actual words used as can be recalled.

Although the offence is most commonly committed by means of a telephone call, it can be committed by any form of communication. It is not necessary that the defendant had any particular person in mind in whom he intends to induce the relevant belief.

CHAPTER 21

Railways

RAILWAY TRESPASS

Trespass offence

Under the British Transport Commission Act 1949 (BTCA 1949), s 55, an offence is committed by any person who trespasses upon any of the lines of railway or sidings, or in any tunnel, or upon any railway embankment, cutting, or similar work belonging, leased to or worked by Network Rail or by Transport for London, or trespasses upon any other lands of such a body in dangerous proximity to any such lines of railway or other works or to any electrical apparatus used for, or in connection with, the working of the railway.

A person trespasses in the above places if he is there without a right by law to do so or express or implied permission of the occupier, whether this is so (for example) because he has climbed over a fence onto the track or, having lawfully entered a railway station, has unauthorisedly gone onto the track. However, a person may not be convicted of the offence under s 55 unless it is proved to the satisfaction of the court that public warning has been given to persons not to trespass upon the railway by a notice clearly exhibited at the station on the railway nearest to the place where the offence is alleged to have been committed. The notice must be renewed as often as it is obliterated or destroyed; if it is not, a person cannot be convicted of the offence.

The offence only applies to trespassing on the track, land, etc. Thus, it does not apply where a person who is not trespassing on such land jumps onto (and thereby trespasses on) a passing train, nor does it apply where the trespass is on the track, land, etc of one of the various companies running restored steam trains. It is useful to police officers to be aware of the provisions of BTCA 1949, but it is preferable to leave enforcement to the British Transport Police and to railway officials. However, in the interests of the safety of such trespassers it may be necessary for any police officer to take action in such cases. A refusal by a trespasser to leave railway property on such an occasion will amount to an obstruction of a police officer in the execution of his duty, contrary to the Police Act 1996, s 89(2).

The offence under BTCA 1949, s 55 is a 'penalty offence' for the purposes of the Criminal Justice and Police Act 2001 (see p 31).

Offence of refusal to quit

The Railway Regulation Act 1840, s 16 states that it is an offence for any person wilfully to trespass upon the railway or any station or premises connected therewith and to refuse to quit upon request by any officer or agent of the railway company. This offence is not restricted to the operational areas of a railway system, unlike the offence under BTCA 1949. It can occur anywhere on railway property but the offence is not complete until there is a refusal to quit at the request of any officer or agent of the railway company. Police officers, other than officers of the British Transport Police, are not 'officers of the company'. There is no need to prove that notices are displayed in such a case.

ENDANGERING THE SAFETY OF PASSENGERS

Interfering with the railway system with intent

Under the Offences Against the Person Act 1861 (OAPA 1861), s 32, it is an offence triable only on indictment unlawfully and maliciously to carry out certain acts *with intent to endanger the safety of any person travelling or being on a railway*. Basically, these acts involve interference with the railway system itself by doing or causing something to be done, for example the placing of obstructions on a railway, the displacing of parts of it, the moving of points and similar fittings, the showing of a false signal, or the concealment of a real one.

Throwing things with intent

OAPA 1861, s 33 provides that it is an offence triable only on indictment unlawfully and maliciously to throw, or cause to fall or strike, any wood, stone, or other matter or thing, at, against, into or upon any engine, tender, carriage or truck used upon any railway *with intent to injure or endanger the safety of any person on the train*.

Endangering passengers

OAPA 1861, s 34 creates a less serious indictable (either way) offence which can be committed by any person who, by any unlawful act, or by any wilful omission or neglect, endangers or causes to be endangered the safety of any person conveyed or being in or upon a railway. An intent to endanger is not required; indeed, it is irrelevant whether or not the defendant ever considered the consequences of his conduct.

The reference to any wilful omission or neglect is of importance to railwaymen. A driver who neglected to keep a lookout for signals would certainly be guilty of this offence.

Stone-throwing on railway

BTCA 1949, s 56 creates an offence of throwing stones and other objects at locomotives, carriages and other things on railways belonging or leased to or worked by one of the organisations referred to in relation to s 55. This is a 'penalty offence' for the purposes of the Criminal Justice and Police Act 2001 and may be dealt with under a fixed penalty procedure: see p 31.

OBSTRUCTION, ETC OF ENGINES AND THE LIKE

The Malicious Damage Act 1861 (MDA 1861), ss 35 and 36 deal with this. With some variations, they mirror OAPA 1861, ss 32 and 34.

Interfering with the railway system with intent

MDA 1861, s 35 is almost identical to OAPA 1861, s 32. The only difference is in relation to intent. The intention required by MDA 1861 must be to obstruct, upset, overthrow, injure or destroy an engine, tender, carriage, or truck using such railway. An offence under MDA 1861, s 35 is triable only on indictment.

Obstructing engines or carriages

MDA 1861, s 36 parallels the offence previously described in OAPA 1861, s 34. There must have been an unlawful act, or a wilful omission or neglect, which led to the obstruction of an engine or carriage using a railway (as opposed to endangering the safety of passengers as required by OAPA 1861, s 34). If, therefore, someone unlawfully obstructs a line, he commits an offence of the same gravity, whether he does so in such a way that the safety of passengers is threatened, or merely in such a way that an engine, etc was obstructed. A person who causes a train to stop or to slacken speed by altering signals or by making unauthorised signals with the arms is guilty of obstructing a train contrary to MDA 1861, s 36. The offence is also committed by those who cause an obstruction to take place. It is an indictable (either way) offence.

TICKET OFFENCES

Travelling without a ticket

The Regulation of Railways Act 1889 (RRA 1889), s 5(1) provides that every passenger on a railway, on request by an officer or agent or servant of the railway company, must either produce, and if requested deliver up, a ticket showing that his fare is paid, or pay his fare from the place where his journey started, or give his name and address (ie his true name and address), so that the fare may be recovered from him by civil process, if necessary. In default of doing so, the passenger commits an offence.

Travelling with intent to avoid paying fare

RRA 1889, s 5(3) provides two offences.

First, if any person travels, or attempts to travel, on a railway without having previously paid his fare, and with intent to avoid payment thereof, he commits an offence. The intention to avoid payment may be proved by showing that the passenger has ignored opportunities to pay his fare or has taken measures to avoid a ticket inspector. A person who leaves a train without paying his fare when there has been an opportunity to do so indicates such an intention. In addition, a person who travels on a ticket issued to another person, which is not transferable, clearly indicates an intention to avoid payment. A person, therefore, who produces a concessionary ticket issued to a young person or a senior citizen to which he is not entitled clearly shows an intention to avoid payment of his true fare. In this respect the term 'fare' means the correct fare for the particular journey and the class of carriage by which the person travels. A person who travels in a first-class carriage with a standard-class ticket may be convicted of travelling without having previously paid his fare, if an intention to avoid payment of the correct fare is indicated by his refusal to pay the excess. The offence is a wide one because a divisional court has held that an intent to defraud is not required, and that a passenger who mistakenly believes his ticket is valid would intend to avoid payment of the fare which should have been paid for the journey.

Second, it is also an offence under s 5(3) knowingly and wilfully to proceed by train beyond the distance for which a fare has been paid. Opportunities exist on all trains to obtain an additional ticket for the excess journey, and if opportunities to do so are ignored on the journey this may be taken to indicate a knowing and wilful act.

Railway Byelaws

The Railway Byelaws provide as follows.

By byelaw 17(1), no person shall enter a compulsory ticket area on the railway unless he has with him a valid ticket. Byelaw 18(1) provides that, in any area not designated as a compulsory ticket area, no person shall enter any train for the purpose of travelling on the railway unless he has with him a valid ticket entitling him to travel.

A person is not in breach of byelaw 17(1) or 18(1)) if:

(a) there were no facilities in working order for the issue or validation of any ticket at the time when, and the station where, he began his journey; or
(b) there was a notice at the station where he began his journey permitting journeys to be started without a valid ticket; or
(c) an authorised person gave him permission to travel without a valid ticket (byelaw 17(3) and 18(3)).

Breach of byelaw 17 or 18 is an offence.

The Railway Byelaws do not apply to Transport for London. Instead, the TfL Byelaws apply to London Underground, Docklands Light Railway and London Overground.

Penalty fares

The Railways (Penalty Fares) Regulations 1994 provide for the charging of penalty fares for failure to produce, when required to do so, a ticket or other authority authorising a person to travel by train or to be present in a compulsory ticket area at a station. The Regulations apply to all train operators.

By reg 3, subject to the provisions of the regulations, and to any rules made under them:

(a) any person travelling by, present on, or leaving a train must, if required by or on behalf of the train operator, produce a ticket or other authority authorising his travelling by or his being present on that train, as the case may be; and
(b) any person present in or leaving a compulsory ticket area must, if so required, produce a ticket or other authority authorising him to be present in or leave that area.

Failure to produce a ticket or other authority when so required renders the person liable to be charged a penalty fare by the train operator or someone acting on its behalf. A person is not liable to pay a penalty fare in a case covered by (a) if, when he boarded the train (or a preceding train on his journey, which was operated by the same operator):

(i)   there were no ticket facilities in operation available for the journey in question;
(ii) there was no notice in a prescribed form indicating the penalty fare scheme;
(iii) at the station where and when he commenced his journey, a notice was displayed indicating that it was permissible to travel without having such ticket or authority; or
(iv) a person in authority (or apparently in authority) at the originating station gave permission to travel without a ticket, etc.

These exemptions do not exempt a person who had the opportunity to obtain a fare ticket while on the train (or one of them used on the journey).

There are similar exemptions from liability to pay a penalty fare in respect of a case covered by (b) above.

A person who fails to pay a penalty fare at once must provide his name and address on being required to do so by an authorised person.

In an action to recover a penalty fare, which is a civil action, a defendant may provide the claimant with a 'relevant statement' explaining his failure to produce a ticket, etc and including particulars of his journey, which must be submitted within 21 days. Where this has been done it will be for the claimant to show that any of the facts in the relevant statement is not true. In any other case it is for the defendant to show that the facts of the case fall within those exemptions.

If a person has been charged a penalty fare in respect of his failure to produce a ticket or other authority when required and he is then prosecuted under RRA 1889, s 5(3) or for breach of a railway byelaw (above) in respect of the lack of a ticket, etc, he ceases to be liable to pay the penalty fare. If he has already paid it, it must be refunded.

CHAPTER 22

Nuisances, Collections, Vagrancy, Peddling and Scrap Metal

NUISANCES

Common law offence of public nuisance

It is a common law indictable (either way) offence to cause a public nuisance. A public nuisance is an act not warranted by law, or an omission to discharge a legal duty, whose effect is to endanger the life, health, property or comfort of the public, or to obstruct a substantial section of the public in the exercise or enjoyment of rights common to all members of the public. An act which is specifically authorised by law cannot be a public nuisance if carried out as prescribed. Despite its width, this common law offence is little used as most 'nuisances' are covered by statutes.

Nuisances related to noise

Because of difficulties experienced by local authorities and police officers in dealing with 'noise' nuisances, the Noise Act 1996 (NA 1996) provides powers for local authorities to serve warning notices in respect of a dwelling ('the offending dwelling') or premises in respect of which a premises licence or a temporary event notice (see p 557) has effect ('the offending premises') from which excessive noise is emanating, such noise being heard during the night. For these purposes, 'night' is the period between 23.00 and 07.00. Local authorities are equipped with approved measuring devices which establish noise levels. A local authority which receives a relevant complaint must secure that an officer of the authority takes reasonable steps to investigate the complaint.

Where a warning notice has been served in respect of an offending dwelling, it is an offence under NA 1996, s 4(1) for any person responsible for the noise to emit from it, within a period specified in the notice, noise which exceeds the permitted level, as measured from within the complainant's dwelling or premises. This offence is subject to a defence of 'reasonable excuse', the onus of proving which is on the defendant.

Where a warning notice has been served in respect of other premises and noise is emitted from them, within a period specified in the notice, which exceeds the permitted level as measured from within the complainant's dwelling, the responsible person in respect of the offending premises commits an offence under s 4A(1).

If an authorised local authority officer has reason to believe that a person has committed or is committing one of the above offences, he may give that person a fixed penalty notice. Where this has been done, no proceedings may be instituted for the offence within 14 days following the date of the notice. Payment of the fixed penalty within that period is a bar to conviction of the offence in question.

Local authority officers have a power of entry to a dwelling or other premises in respect of which a warning notice has been issued. It is an offence to obstruct such an officer. NA 1996 provides powers of seizure and disposal of equipment causing such a noise nuisance.

Depositing litter

The Environmental Protection Act 1990 (EPA 1990), s 87, which deals with land 'in the open air' (a term including a covered place open to the air on at least one side), provides that a person commits an offence if he *throws down, drops or otherwise deposits,* any litter in *any* place open to the air in the area of a principal litter authority, *and leaves it* (s 87(1)). However, s 87 does not apply to a covered place open to the air on at least one side if the public does not have access to it, with or without payment. The offence of depositing litter is committed whether the litter is deposited on land or on water.

No offence is committed where the depositing of litter is authorised by law or is done with the consent of the owner or occupier or other person having control of the place where it is deposited. Consent may only be given to the depositing of litter in a lake, pond or watercourse by the owner, occupier or other person having control of all of the land adjoining that lake, pond or watercourse and all of the land into which water from those places directly or indirectly discharges, otherwise than by means of a public sewer.

The term 'litter' includes the discarded ends of cigarettes and like products and discarded chewing gum and the like.

A divisional court has held that 'leave' for these purposes does not mean abandon, and that an article deposited with no intention to remove it can be 'left' after only a short period of time. Someone who throws down fish wrappers, and refuses to pick them up immediately, commits an offence under s 87. He has no intention of removing the wrappers and this is evidenced by his refusal.

The offence under s 87 is a 'penalty offence' for the purposes of the Criminal Justice and Police Act 2001 (see p 31).

Where the offence under s 87 is dealt with by a local authority 'litter warden' (who must be authorised in writing so to act on behalf of a litter authority), s 88 permits the use of a fixed penalty procedure under *that* section.

Abandonment of property

Things other than motor vehicles

The Refuse Disposal (Amenity) Act 1978 (RD(A)A 1978), s 2(1)(b) provides the offence of abandoning, without lawful authority, on any land in the open air, or on any other land forming part of a highway, anything other than a motor vehicle which has been brought to the land for the purpose of being abandoned there. This deals with instances where someone takes refuse quite deliberately into the countryside and abandons it there.

Motor vehicles

RD(A)A 1978, s 2(1)(a) punishes the abandonment of motor vehicles in similar circumstances. The difference is that it is not necessary to prove that a motor vehicle was brought to the land for the purpose of abandonment. The offence is committed by someone who, without lawful authority, abandons on any land in the open air, or on any other land forming part of a highway, a motor vehicle or anything which formed part of a motor vehicle and was removed from it in the course of dismantling the vehicle on the land. Section 2A provides for the offence under s 2(1)(a) to be dealt with as a fixed penalty offence by an authorised local authority officer.

General

Section 2(2), which applies to s 2(1)(a) and (b), deals with a person who leaves anything on land in such circumstances or for such a period that he may reasonably be assumed to have abandoned it or to have brought it to the land for the purpose of abandoning it there. It provides that such a person is deemed to have abandoned it there or, as the case may be, to have brought it to the land for that purpose, unless the contrary is shown.

Nuisance on educational premises

These offences are provided by the Education Act 1996, s 547 (which deals with schools) and the Further and Higher Education Act 1992, s 85A (which deals with further education colleges and 16 to 19 Academies). Both sections create an offence which may be committed by a person who is present on educational premises to which they apply, without lawful authority, who causes or permits nuisance or disturbance to the annoyance of persons who lawfully use those premises (whether or not any such persons are present at the time). 'Premises' includes playgrounds, playing fields and other premises for outdoor recreation. A constable or a person authorised by the appropriate authority may remove a person from the premises if he has reasonable cause to suspect that that person is committing or has committed such an offence.

COMMUNITY PROTECTION NOTICES

These notices are governed by the Anti-social Behaviour, Crime and Policing Act 2014 (A-sB,C&PA 2014), Part 4, Ch 1 (ss 43–58). The community protection notice (CPN) is intended to deal with unreasonable, ongoing problems or nuisances which negatively affect the community's quality of life by targeting the person responsible. The CPN has replaced measures such as litter clearing notices, defacement removal notices and street litter control notices which were issued only by local authorities. It has not replaced the statutory nuisance regime operated by local authorities under the Environmental Protection Act 1990 (EPA 1990), Part 3 (ss 79–82) in respect (a) of the state of premises, or things emitted from them (eg smoke, fumes or smell), (b) of accumulations, deposits or animals, or (c) of noise, provided in each case that it is prejudicial to health or a nuisance. However, there is no legal bar to a CPN being issued where behaviour is such as to amount to a statutory nuisance. For example, a local authority could issue a CPN to address anti-social behaviour while investigating whether it constitutes statutory nuisance. The issue of a CPN does not relieve the local authority of its obligation under EPA 1990, Part 3 to serve an abatement notice where the relevant test is met.

A CPN is a notice imposing any of the following requirements on an individual or body issued with it, namely a requirement:

(a) to stop doing specified things;
(b) to do specified things;
(c) to take reasonable steps to achieve specified results.

Power to issue notices

By A-sB,C&PA 2014, s 43, an authorised person may issue a CPN to an individual aged 16 or over, or a body, if satisfied on reasonable grounds that:

(a) the conduct ('conduct' includes a failure to act) of the individual or body is having a detrimental effect, of a persistent or continuing nature, on the quality of life of those in the locality, and
(b) the conduct is unreasonable.

The only requirements that may be imposed are ones that are reasonable to impose in order to prevent the detrimental effect referred to in (a) and (b) from continuing or recurring, or to reduce that detrimental effect or to reduce the risk of its continuance or recurrence.

An 'authorised person' means:

(a) a constable (or a community support officer designated for the purposes of s 43);
(b) the relevant local authority;
(c) a social housing provider designated by the relevant local authority for these purposes.

For the purposes of CPNs, 'local authority' means, in relation to England, a district council, a county council for an area for which there is no district council, a London borough council, the Common Council of the City of London, or the Council of the Isles of Scilly; or in relation to Wales, a county council or a county borough council. 'The relevant local authority' means the local authority (or, as the case may be, any of the local authorities) within whose area the conduct specified in the CPN has, according to the notice, been taking place. For a fixed penalty notice (below), 'the relevant local authority' means the local authority (or, as the case may be, any of the local authorities) within whose area the offence in question is alleged to have taken place.

A person (A) may issue a CPN to an individual or body (B) only if:

(a) B has been given a written warning that the notice will be issued unless B's conduct ceases to have the detrimental effect referred to above; and
(b) A is satisfied that, despite B having had enough time to deal with the matter, B's conduct is still having that effect.

Before issuing a community protection notice, A must inform any body or individual he thinks appropriate.

A CPN must identify the conduct referred to above, and explain the effect of ss 46 to 51 below. It may specify periods within which, or times by which, requirements to do things or take reasonable steps are to be complied with.

For the purposes of s 43, conduct on, or affecting, premises ('premises' includes any land) that a particular person owns, leases, occupies, controls, operates or maintains, is treated as conduct of that person, except that conduct on, or affecting, premises occupied for the purposes of a government department is treated as conduct of the Minister in charge of that department. An individual's conduct is not treated as that of another person if that person cannot reasonably be expected to control or affect it.

Where:

(a) an authorised person has power to issue a CPN;
(b) the detrimental effect referred to above arises from the condition of premises or the use to which premises have been put; and

(c) the authorised person has made reasonable enquiries to find out the name or
     proper address of the occupier of the premises (or, if the premises are unoccupied,
     the owner) but without success,

that person may post the CPN on the premises, and enter the premises, or other premises, to the extent reasonably necessary for that purpose. 'Owner' means a person
(other than a mortgagee not in possession) entitled to dispose of the fee simple of the
premises, whether in possession or in reversion, or a person who holds or is entitled to
the rents and profits of the premises under a lease that (when granted) was for a term
of not less than three years.

The CPN is treated as having been issued to the occupier of the premises (or, if the
premises are unoccupied, the owner) at the time the notice is posted.

A person issued with a CPN may appeal, within 21 days, to a magistrates' court
against the notice on specified grounds. While an appeal is in progress, a requirement imposed by the notice to stop doing specified things remains in effect, unless
the court orders otherwise, but any other requirement imposed by the notice is of no
effect (s 46).

Failure to comply with notice

Remedial action by local authority

Where a person issued with a CPN ('the defaulter') fails to comply with a requirement of the notice, the relevant local authority (RLA) may take action as follows under
A-sB,C&PA 2014, s 47.

The RLA may have work carried out to ensure that the failure is remedied, but only
on land that is open to the air.

As regards premises other than land open to the air, if the RLA issues the defaulter
with a notice:

(a) specifying work it intends to have carried out to ensure that the failure is remedied;
(b) specifying the estimated cost of the work; and
(c) inviting the defaulter to consent to the work being carried out,

the RLA may have the work carried out if the necessary consent is given. 'The necessary
consent' means the consent of the defaulter, and (unless the RLA has made reasonable
but unsuccessful efforts to contact the owner of the premises) of the owner of the premises on which the work is to be carried out (if that is not the defaulter). If work is carried
out and the RLA issues a notice to the defaulter detailing that work, and specifying an
amount that is no more than the cost to the authority, the defaulter is liable to the authority for that amount (subject to the outcome of any appeal to a magistrates' court,
within 21 days, on the ground that the amount specified is excessive).

For the above purposes, the 'RLA' means:

(a) the local authority that issued the CPN;
(b) if the CPN was not issued by a local authority, the local authority (or, as the case
     may be, one of the local authorities) that could have issued it.

Offence of failing to comply with notice

A person issued with a CPN who fails to comply with it commits an offence under
s 48(1), unless he took all reasonable steps to comply with the notice, or there is some
other reasonable excuse for the failure to comply with it (s 48(2)). On conviction for
such an offence, the court may make a remedial order to ensure that what the notice

requires to be done is done, and may also make a forfeiture order in respect of any item used in the commission of the offence (ss 49 and 50).

Seizure of item used in commission of offence

A justice of the peace who is satisfied on information on oath that there are reasonable grounds for suspecting that an offence under s 48 has been committed, and that there is an item used in the commission of the offence on premises specified in the information, may issue a warrant authorising any constable or designated community support officer (see above) to enter the premises within 14 days from the date of issue of the warrant to seize the item (s 51). A constable or designated officer may use reasonable force, if necessary, in executing such a warrant.

A constable or designated officer who has seized an item under such a warrant:

(a) may retain the item until any criminal proceedings for the s 48 offence in whose commission the item was allegedly used have been finally determined, if such proceedings are started before the end of the period of 28 days following the day of the seizure;

(b) otherwise, must before the end of that period return the item to the person from whom it was seized.

Fixed penalty notices

Section 52 provides that an authorised person (above) may issue a fixed penalty notice to anyone who that person has reason to believe has committed an offence under s 48. A fixed penalty notice offers the person to whom it is issued the opportunity of discharging any liability to conviction for the offence by payment of a fixed penalty to a local authority specified in the notice (ie the local authority that issued the CPN to which the fixed penalty notice relates or, if that was not issued by a local authority, the local authority (or, as the case may be, one of the local authorities) that could have issued it).

Where a person is issued with a fixed penalty notice:

(a) no proceedings may be taken for the s 48 offence before the end of the period of 14 days following the date of the notice;

(b) the person may not be convicted of the offence if the person pays the fixed penalty before the end of that period.

The amount of fixed penalty specified in the notice must not exceed £100. The notice may specify two amounts and specify that, if the lower of those amounts is paid within a specified period (of less than 14 days), that is the amount of the fixed penalty.

Issuing of notices

A CPN or related fixed penalty notice may be issued by handing it to the person, leaving it at his proper address, or sending it by post to him at that address. A notice to a body corporate may be issued to the secretary or clerk of that body; and, to a partnership, to a partner or a person who has the control or management of the partnership business.

For these purposes, the proper address of a person is the person's last known address, except that:

(a) in the case of a body corporate or its secretary or clerk, it is the address of the body's registered or principal office;

(b) in the case of a partnership or person having the control or the management of the partnership business, it is the principal office of the partnership.

The principal office of a company registered outside the UK, or of a partnership carrying on business outside the UK, is its principal office within the UK. If a person has specified an address in the UK, other than the person's proper address, as the one at which the person or someone on the person's behalf will accept notices of the same description as a notice under the above provisions, that address is also treated as the person's proper address.

Guidance

Ministerial guidance has been issued to chief officers of police and local authorities about the exercise of functions under the above provisions.

PUBLIC SPACES PROTECTION ORDERS

These orders were introduced by the A-sB,C&PA 2014, Part 4, Ch 2 (ss 59–76).

The public spaces protection order (PSPO) is intended to deal with a particular nuisance or problem in a particular area that is detrimental to the local community's quality of life, by imposing conditions on the use of that area. The order can also be used to deal with likely future problems. It has replaced orders under the Criminal Justice and Police Act 2001 banning the consumption of alcohol in designated public places, gating orders under the Highways Act 1980 (which restricted public right of way over a highway to assist in the reduction of crime or anti-social behaviour) and dog control orders under the Clean Neighbourhoods and Environment Act 2005.

Power to make a PSPO

A-sB,C&PA 2014, s 59 provides that a local authority may make a PSPO if satisfied on reasonable grounds that two conditions are met:

(a) that activities carried on in a public place within the authority's area have had a detrimental effect on the quality of life of those in the locality, or it is likely that activities will be carried on in a public place within that area and that they will have such an effect; and

(b) that the effect, or likely effect, of the activities:

    (i)   is, or is likely to be, of a persistent or continuing nature,

    (ii)   is, or is likely to be, such as to make the activities unreasonable, and

    (iii) justifies the restrictions imposed by the notice.

'Public place' is defined as meaning any place to which the public or any section of the public has access, on payment or otherwise, as of right or by virtue of express or implied permission.

A PSPO must identify the public place referred to in (a) ('the restricted area') to which it applies. It must also identify the activities referred to in (a), explain the effect of s 63 below (where it applies) and s 67 below, and specify the period for which it has effect.

A PSPO can prohibit specified things in respect of a specified public place (for example, drinking alcohol (other than on licensed premises), unauthorised busking, urinating (other than in a public toilet) or loitering in groups), require specified things to be done there (for example, keeping dogs on leashes), or both. For instance, a single order could be used to prohibit drinking, or loitering in groups, in a specified public place as well as ensuring dogs were kept under control there, through either being kept on a leash or limiting the number of dogs an individual can walk at one time. The only prohibitions or requirements that may be imposed are ones that are reasonable to impose in order to prevent the detrimental effect referred to in (a) above from continuing, occurring or recurring, or to reduce that detrimental effect or to reduce the risk of its continuance, occurrence or recurrence.

A prohibition or requirement may be framed so as to apply:

(i)   to all persons, or only to persons in specified categories, or to all persons except those in specified categories;
(ii) at all times, or only at specified times, or at all times except those specified;
(iii) in all circumstances, or only in specified circumstances, or in all circumstances except those specified.

A PSPO must be published on the local authority's website, and by a notice (or notices) on or adjacent to the public place to which the order relates drawing attention to the order and its effect.

A PSPO will last for up to three years before requiring a review; there is no limit on the number of times a PSPO can be reviewed and renewed.

There is power for a PSPO to be made by a body (other than a local authority) if it is designated by the Secretary of State in respect of land that it has a statutory power to regulate.

The following matters relating to a PSPO are of particular relevance to the police.

Failure to comply with a PSPO

Under A-sB,C&PA 2014, s 67, it is an offence for a person without reasonable excuse:

(a)   to do anything that he is prohibited from doing by a PSPO, or
(b)   to fail to comply with a requirement to which he is subject under a PSPO.

A person does not commit such an offence by failing to comply with a prohibition or requirement that the local authority did not have power to include in the PSPO (s 67(3)).

Consuming alcohol in breach of a PSPO is not an offence under s 67 (s 67(4)). As to such conduct, see s 63 below.

Prohibition on consuming alcohol

Special powers are given by A-sB,C&PA 2014, s 63 to a constable or an authorised person who reasonably believes that a person (P) is or has been consuming alcohol in breach of a prohibition in a PSPO, or intends to consume alcohol in circumstances in which doing so would be a breach of such a prohibition. 'Authorised person' means a person authorised for the purposes of s 63 by the local authority that made the order, or a community support officer designated for those purposes.

The constable or authorised person may require P:

(a)   not to consume, in breach of the order, alcohol or anything which the constable or authorised person reasonably believes to be alcohol;
(b)   to surrender anything in P's possession which is, or which the constable or authorised person reasonably believes to be, alcohol or a container for alcohol.

A constable or an authorised person may dispose of anything surrendered under (b) in whatever way he or she thinks appropriate.

As can be seen, it is not essential in order for a requirement to be made that a person is seen consuming alcohol. If a person has alcohol in a glass or open container this raises the inference that he intends to drink it. Where alcohol is in a sealed container, notice must be taken of the circumstances. Possession of a 'four-pack' by someone walking home differs from possession by a group of persons assembled at that place for the purpose of drinking.

A constable or an authorised person who imposes such a requirement must tell P that failing without reasonable excuse to comply with the requirement is an offence.

A requirement imposed by an authorised person is not valid if he or she is asked by P to show evidence of his or her authorisation, and fails to do so.

A person who fails without reasonable excuse to comply with a requirement commits an offence contrary to s 63(6).

By s 62, a PSPO on consuming alcohol does not apply to:

(a) premises (other than council-operated licensed premises) authorised by a premises licence to be used for the supply of alcohol;

(b) premises authorised by a club premises certificate to be used by the club for the supply of alcohol;

(c) a place within the curtilage of premises within (a) or (b);

(d) premises which by virtue of the Licensing Act 2003, Part 5 (permitted temporary activities (p 557)) may at the relevant time be used for the supply of alcohol or which, by virtue of that Part, could have been so used within the 30 minutes before that time;

(e) a place where facilities or activities relating to the sale or consumption of alcohol are at the relevant time permitted by virtue of a permission granted under the Highways Act 1980, s 115E (council permission to set up objects and structures on a highway for income-producing purposes).

A prohibition in a PSPO on consuming alcohol does not apply to council-operated licensed premises (ie premises in respect of which a local authority holds the premises licence, or which are occupied by such an authority or managed by it or on its behalf) when the premises are being used for the supply of alcohol, or within 30 minutes thereafter.

Fixed penalty notices

Section 68 provides that a constable or an 'authorised person' may issue a fixed penalty notice to anyone he or she has reason to believe has committed an offence under s 63 or 67 in relation to a PSPO. 'Authorised person' means a person authorised for the purposes of s 68 by the local authority that made the order, or a community support officer designated for those purposes.

Such a fixed penalty notice is a notice offering the person to whom it is issued the opportunity of discharging any liability to conviction for the offence by payment of a fixed penalty to a local authority specified in the notice, ie the one that made the PSPO. The provisions relating to a PSPO fixed penalty notice are the same as mentioned above in relation to those which apply to a fixed penalty notice under the community protection notice provisions (p 631).

Guidance

Ministerial guidance has been issued to chief officers of police and local authorities about the exercise of functions under the above provisions.

STREET AND HOUSE-TO-HOUSE COLLECTIONS
Street collections

The Police, Factories, etc (Miscellaneous Provisions) Act 1916, s 5 permits local authorities or the Mayor's Office for Policing and Crime to make regulations with respect to the places where and the conditions under which persons may be permitted, in any street or public place within their area, to collect money or sell articles for the benefit of charitable or other purposes. It also provides that a contravention of any regulations so made is an offence.

House-to-house collections

The House to House Collections Act 1939 (HHCA 1939) prohibits house-to-house collections for charitable purposes unless the collection is authorised. Such a collection may be authorised by a licence (issued by a district council, the Commissioner of the Metropolitan Police or the Common Council of the City of London), or an order of exemption (granted by the Minister for the Cabinet Office where the charitable purpose is to be pursued throughout the whole of England or a substantial part of it), or a certificate of exemption (granted by a chief officer of police in respect of a collection which is local in character and likely to be completed within a short period of time).

The House to House Collections Regulations 1947 deal with such matters as badges, certificates of authority, collecting boxes and receipt books, and duties of collectors and promoters. They prescribe a minimum age of 16 in respect of collectors. The 1947 Regulations do not apply to a collection under a certificate of exemption. Breach of the regulations is an offence under HHCA 1939, s 4(3).

HHCA 1939, s 5 punishes the unauthorised use of prescribed badges or certificates of authority, or a thing so closely resembling those articles as to be calculated to deceive.

A constable may require any person whom he believes to be acting as a collector for the purposes of a collection for charitable purposes to declare to him his name and address and to sign his name. Failure to comply with such a requirement is an offence under s 6.

Charities Act 2006

The provisions above about street collections and house-to-house collections are prospectively repealed. When their repeal takes effect, they will be replaced by the following provisions in the Charities Act 2006.

The Charities Act 2006, Part 3, Ch 1 (ss 45–66), the substantive provisions of which are not in force at the time of writing, establishes a regime for the conduct and regulation of public charitable collections. It defines two types: collections in a public place, and door-to-door collections. Its provisions are set out in Chapter 22 on the companion website.

VAGRANCY OFFENCES
Begging

The Vagrancy Act 1824 (VA 1824), s 3 punishes persons who wander abroad, or place themselves in any public place, street, highway, court or passage, to beg or gather alms, or who cause, procure or encourage any child to do so. A divisional court has held that the offence does not cover those who collect alms in an orderly manner for a specific purpose, eg striking workers who seek assistance by asking for contributions towards their cause.

VA 1824, s 4 deals with the aggravated forms of begging by the exposure of wounds or deformities in public or by going about seeking charitable contributions of any kind by false pretences.

Sleeping out, etc

It is an offence contrary to VA 1824, s 4 for any person, wandering abroad and lodging in any barn or outhouse, or in any deserted or unoccupied building, or in the open air, or under a tent, or in any cart or waggon, not to give a good account of himself.

People holidaying at a static caravan site and genuine hikers who, being tired and hungry, rest in a barn or outhouse are not guilty of this offence because they can easily give a good account of themselves by explaining their presence. In contrast, a tramp found sleeping in a barn would find it much more difficult to give a good account of himself, particularly if he has made a temporary home in that building.

Two important limits were imposed on the offence by the Vagrancy Act 1935. First, the Act amended VA 1824, s 4 by providing that the reference to a person lodging under a tent or in a cart or waggon does not include a person lodging under a tent, cart or waggon with or in which he travels. It was thereby made quite clear that the present offence was not concerned with gypsies travelling in their own waggons, nor with persons sleeping out in their own tents.

The Vagrancy Act 1935 also requires that, before a person can be guilty of the present offence, it must be proved either that:

(a) on the occasion in question, he had been directed to a reasonably accessible place of free shelter and that he failed to apply for, or refused, accommodation there; or

(b) he is a person who persistently wanders abroad and, notwithstanding that a place of free shelter is reasonably accessible, lodges or attempts to lodge in a way described above; or

(c) by, or in the course of, lodging in a way described above he caused damage to property, infection with vermin, or other offensive consequence, or he so lodged in such circumstances as to appear to be likely to do so.

As a result, the present offence is of little practical significance to police officers. The reason is that there are few places of free shelter to which people may be directed, or which are reasonably accessible to the person who persistently sleeps out. The provision of greatest practical significance is that at (c), which can apply to the roadster who destroys hay or feed in a barn by his presence, or who causes the barn or outbuilding to become verminous by his presence.

PEDLARS

The Pedlars Act 1871 (PA 1871) still exists to provide some element of control over those who engage in some forms of door-to-door trading. Not the least of the reasons for this control is that peddling provides for those who commit crime a convenient cover or excuse to visit houses, where they may take advantage of opportunities to steal.

'Pedlar'

'Pedlar' is defined by PA 1871, s 3 as meaning a hawker, pedlar, petty chapman (another name for a pedlar), tinker, caster of metals, or other person who, without any horse or other beast bearing or drawing burden, travels and trades on foot, and goes from town to town or to other men's houses, carrying to sell, or exposing for sale, any goods, wares, or merchandise, or procuring orders for goods, etc immediately to be delivered. A judge in the Administrative Court has held that the reference to 'without any horse or beast' should be read as 'without any motor van or car'.

An important part of this definition is 'travels and trades on foot', which has been held to require that, to be a pedlar, a person must *go round* selling things; he must *trade as he travels on foot*, although he may stop to conduct a particular sale, rather than simply selling from a stall or pitch. Thus, a door-to-door salesman is a pedlar, but someone who stands in one place with a pitch, soliciting custom, is not. Nor is a person who moves a barrow from place to place, waiting at each place for customers to come to him. Provided the words of the definition are satisfied, it is irrelevant that the trade is carried out on the basis that the proceeds of sale will go (wholly or partly) to a charity.

Pedlar's certificate

A person who acts as a pedlar without a pedlar's certificate commits an offence, contrary to PA 1871, s 4, subject to certain exceptions. A pedlar's certificate is obtained from the chief officer of police of the district in which the applicant has resided during the month preceding his application. Before granting a certificate the chief officer must be satisfied that the applicant is above 17, is of good character, and in good faith intends to carry on the trade of a pedlar.

The certificate is renewable annually and authorises the holder to carry on the trade of a pedlar in any part of the UK. It also permits the pedlar to sell vegetables and fruits within the limits of a market, but only in the district in which it was granted. A chief officer of police may not deprive a pedlar of his certificate during its currency. The only way in which a pedlar may be deprived of a certificate is by order of a court in circumstances set out in s 16.

Chief officers of police must maintain a register of certificates.

PA 1871 permits a chief officer to delegate his functions under PA 1871. In practice, certificates are usually issued within police divisions and signed by the divisional commander on behalf of the chief officer.

An applicant may appeal to the justices against a refusal to issue a pedlar's certificate; the applicant must give to the chief officer, within one week of the refusal, written notice of his wish to appeal.

Exemption from need for a certificate

PA 1871, s 23 states that it is not necessary for certain persons to obtain a pedlar's certificate, and these are:

(a) commercial travellers or other persons selling or seeking orders for goods, wares or merchandise, to or from dealers therein, and who buy to sell again;

(b) those who sell or seek orders for books as agents authorised in writing by the publishers of such books;

(c) sellers of vegetables (a term which has been held to include lavender), fish, fruit or victuals; and

(d) persons selling or exposing for sale goods, etc in any public market or fair which is legally established.

The exemption in (d) appears to be unnecessary as market traders do not go to other men's houses in any case.

Other offences

It is an offence for a pedlar to refuse on demand to show his pedlar's certificate to a justice or constable or to a person to whom he offers his goods for sale (or upon whose private grounds or premises he is found), or to refuse to allow it to be read (PA 1871, s 17).

It is an offence to make a false representation with a view to obtaining a pedlar's certificate (s 12).

SCRAP METAL DEALERS

The relevant provisions are contained in the Scrap Metal Dealers Act 2013 (SMDA 2013).

Scrap metal dealer

For the purposes of SMDA 2013:

(a) 'scrap metal dealer (SMD)' means a person who is for the time being carrying on business as a scrap metal dealer, whether or not authorised by a licence; and
(b) 'scrap metal' includes any old, waste or discarded metal or metallic material, and any product, article or assembly which is made from or contains metal and is broken, worn out or regarded by its last holder as having reached the end of its useful life. However, gold, silver, and any alloy of which 2 per cent or more by weight is attributable to gold or silver are not scrap metal.

Licensing of SMDs

By SMDA 2013, s 1(1), no person may carry on business as a SMD unless authorised by a scrap metal licence under the Act. It is an offence to do so (s 1(3)).

A person carries on business as a SMD if he:

(a) carries on a business which consists wholly or partly in buying or selling scrap metal, whether or not the metal is sold in the form in which it was bought; or
(b) carries on business as a motor salvage operator (so far as that does not fall within (a)).

For the purposes of (a), a person who manufactures articles is not to be regarded as selling scrap metal if he sells scrap metal only as a by-product of manufacturing articles or as surplus materials not required for manufacturing them.

For the purposes of (b), a person carries on business as a motor salvage operator if he carries on a business which consists *wholly or partly* (in (i)) *or wholly or mainly* (in (ii)–(iv)) in:

(i) recovering salvageable parts from motor vehicles for re-use or sale and subsequently selling or otherwise disposing of the rest of the vehicle for scrap;
(ii) buying written-off vehicles and subsequently repairing and reselling them;

(iii) buying or selling motor vehicles which are to be the subject (whether immediately or on a subsequent re-sale) of any of the activities mentioned in (i) and (ii); or
(iv) activities falling within (ii) and (iii).

Form and effect of licence

Local authorities are responsible for issuing scrap metal licences. Such a licence must be a site licence, or a collector's licence. For these purposes, 'local authority' means, (in England) a district council, a London borough council, or the Common Council of the City of London, and (in Wales) a county council or a county borough council.

A site licence authorises the licensee to carry on business at any site in the authority's area which is identified in the licence. It must:

(a) name the licensee,
(b) name the authority,
(c) identify all the sites in the authority's area at which the licensee is authorised to carry on business,
(d) name the site manager of each site, and
(e) state the expiry date of the licence.

'Site manager' means the individual who exercises day-to-day control and management of activities at the site, and 'site' means any premises used in the course of carrying on business as a SMD (whether or not metal is kept there).

A collector's licence authorises the licensee to carry on business as a mobile collector in the authority's area. It must:

(a) name the licensee,
(b) name the authority, and
(c) state the expiry date of the licence.

'Mobile collector' means someone who:

(i) carries on business as a SMD otherwise than at a site, and
(ii) regularly engages, in the course of that business, in collecting waste materials and old, broken, worn out or defaced articles by means of visits from door to door.

A person may hold more than one licence issued by different local authorities, but may not hold more than one licence issued by any one authority.

By s 8(1), an applicant for a scrap metal licence, or for the renewal or variation of a licence, must notify the authority to which the application was made of any changes which materially affect the accuracy of the information which the applicant has provided in connection with the application. A licensee who is not carrying on business as a SMD in the area of the authority which issued the licence must notify the authority of that fact within 28 days of the beginning of the period in which the licensee is not carrying on business in that area while licensed (s 8(2) and (3)). If a licensee carries on business under a trading name, ie a name other than that stated in the licence, the licensee must, within 28 days of the change, notify the authority which issued the licence of any change to that name (s 8(4) and (5)). An applicant or licensee who fails to comply with s 8 is guilty of an offence (s 8(9)), but he has a defence if he proves that he took all reasonable steps to avoid committing the offence (s 8(10)).

Closure of unlicensed sites

SMDA 2013, Sch 2 deals with this.

For the purposes of Sch 2, a person has an interest in premises if he is the owner, leaseholder or occupier of the premises. In the case of a local authority, the powers conferred by Sch 2 are exercisable only in relation to premises in the authority's area. In SMDA 2013, 'premises' includes any land or other place (whether enclosed or not).

Closure notice

If a constable or the local authority is satisfied:

(a) that premises (other than residential premises) are being used by a SMD in the course of business; and
(b) that the premises are not a licensed site,

the constable or authority may issue a closure notice which:

(i)   states that the constable or authority is so satisfied;
(ii) gives the reasons for that;
(iii) states that the constable or authority may apply to the court for a closure order; and
(iv) specifies the steps which may be taken to ensure that the alleged use of the premises ceases.

The constable or authority must give the closure notice to:

(a) the person who appears to the constable or authority to be the site manager of the premises, and
(b) any person (other than the person in (a)) who appears to the constable or authority to be a director, manager or other officer of the business in question, and may also give the notice to any person who has an interest in the premises.

Where:

(a) a person occupies another part of any building or structure of which the premises form part, and
(b) the constable or authority reasonably believes that the person's access to that other part would be impeded if a closure order were made in respect of the premises,

the constable or authority must give the notice to that person.

A closure notice may be cancelled by a notice issued by a constable or the local authority, which takes effect when it is given to any one of the persons to whom the closure notice was given. The cancellation notice must also be given to any other person to whom the closure notice was given.

Application for closure order

Where a closure notice has been given, a constable or the local authority may make a complaint to a justice of the peace for a closure order not less than seven days after the date on which the closure notice was given, nor more than six months after that date. On such a complaint, the justice may issue a summons to answer to the complaint; the summons must be directed to any person appearing to be the site manager or to be a director, etc of the business, to whom the closure notice was given. If a summons is so issued, notice of the date, time, and place at which the complaint will be heard must be given to all other persons to whom the closure notice was given.

Closure order

If, on hearing the complaint, the court is satisfied that the closure notice was given to any person appearing to be the site manager or to be a director, etc of the business and that:

(a) the premises continue to be used by a SMD in the course of business; or
(b) there is a reasonable likelihood that the premises will be so used in the future,

the court may make such order as it considers appropriate for the closure of the premises (a 'closure order').

A closure order may, in particular, require:

(a) that the premises be closed immediately to the public and remain closed until a constable or the local authority makes a certificate of termination (below);
(b) that the use of the premises by a SMD in the course of business be discontinued immediately;
(c) that any defendant pay into court such sum as the court determines and that the sum will not be released by the court to that person until the other requirements of the order are met.

A closure order including a requirement mentioned in (a) may, in particular, include such conditions as the court considers appropriate relating to:

(i)   the admission of persons onto the premises;
(ii) the access by persons to another part of any building or other structure of which the premises form part.

A closure order may include such provision as the court considers appropriate for dealing with the consequences if the order should cease to have effect under a certificate of termination.

As soon as practicable after a closure order is made, the complainant must fix a copy of it in a conspicuous position on the premises in respect of which it was made.

Termination of closure order by certificate of constable or authority

Where a closure order has been made, but a constable or the local authority is satisfied that the need for the order has ceased, the constable or authority may make a certificate to that effect, whereupon the closure order ceases to have effect. Any sum paid into court under the closure order must be released by the court to the defendant. As soon as practicable after making a certificate, the constable or authority must:

(a) give a copy of it to any person against whom the closure order was made;
(b) give a copy of it to the designated officer for the court which made the order; and
(c) fix a copy of it in a conspicuous position on the premises in respect of which the order was made.

The constable or authority must also give a copy of the certificate to any person who requests one.

Discharge of closure order by court

Any person to whom the closure notice was given, and any other person who has an interest in the premises, may make a complaint to a justice of the peace for an order that a closure order be discharged (a 'discharge order'). The court may not make a discharge order unless it is satisfied that there is no longer a need for the closure order.

Where a complaint seeking a discharge order has been made, the justice may issue a summons directed to such constable as the justice considers appropriate, or the local authority, requiring that constable or authority to appear before the magistrates' court to answer to the complaint. If a summons is so issued, notice of the date, time and place at which the complaint will be heard must be given to all the persons to whom the closure notice was given (other than the complainant).

Enforcement of closure order

A person is guilty of an offence under SMDA 2013, Sch 2, para 9(1) if, without reasonable excuse, he permits premises to be open in contravention of a closure order, or otherwise fails to comply with, or does an act in contravention of, a closure order.

If a closure order has been made in respect of any premises, a constable or an authorised person may (if necessary using reasonable force) enter the premises at any reasonable time, and, having entered the premises, do anything reasonably necessary for the purpose of securing compliance with the order. A constable or an authorised person seeking to exercise these powers in relation to any premises must produce evidence of his identity, or of his authority to exercise those powers, if the owner, occupier or other person in charge of the premises requires him to produce it. A person who intentionally obstructs a constable or an authorised person in the exercise of these powers is guilty of an offence under Sch 2, para 9(5). An 'authorised person' is a person authorised for the above purposes by the local authority.

Conduct of business

Display of licence

A SMD who holds a site licence must display a copy of the licence at each site identified in the licence; the copy must be displayed in a prominent place in an area accessible to the public.

A SMD who holds a collector's licence must display a copy of the licence on any vehicle being used in the course of the dealer's business; the copy must be displayed in a manner which enables it easily to be read by a person outside the vehicle.

A SMD who fails to comply with these provisions commits an offence under SMDA 2013, s 10(5).

Verification of supplier's identity

A SMD must not receive scrap metal from a person without verifying the person's full name and address (SMDA 2013, s 11(1)). That verification must be by reference to documents, data or other information obtained from a reliable and independent source (s 11(2)). The SMDA 2013 (Prescribed Documents and Information for Verification of Name and Address) Regulations 2013 prescribe documents, data or other information which are sufficient for these purposes.

The Regulations provide that, in order to verify a person's name and address, it is sufficient for the SMD to refer to either:

(a) a document listed below which bears the person's full name, photograph and residential address; or
(b) both of:
  (i) a document listed below which bears the person's full name, photograph and date of birth, and
  (ii) a supporting document listed below which bears the person's full name and residential address.

The documents which apply for the purposes of (a) or (b)(i) are a valid:

(a) UK passport; or
(b) passport issued by an EEA state; or
(c) Great Britain or Northern Ireland photo-card driving licence; or
(d) UK biometric immigration document.

The supporting documents which apply for the purposes of (b)(ii) are:

(a) a bank or building society statement;
(b) a credit or debit card statement;
(c) a council tax demand letter or statement; or
(d) a utility bill, but not a mobile telephone bill,

provided that the date on which the document in question was issued is not more than three months before the date when the scrap metal is received by the SMD.

If a SMD receives scrap metal in breach of the above provision, each of the following is guilty of an offence under s 11(4):

(a) the SMD;
(b) if the metal is received at a site, the site manager;
(c) any person who, under arrangements made by a person within (a) or (b), has responsibility for verifying the name and address.

It is a defence for a person within (a) or (b) to prove that he made arrangements to ensure that the metal was not received without the necessary verification, and that he took all reasonable steps to ensure that those arrangements were complied with (s 11(5)).

A person who, on delivering scrap metal to a SMD, gives a false name or false address commits an offence (s 11(7)).

Offence of buying scrap metal for cash, etc

By SMDA 2013, s 12(1), a SMD must not pay for scrap metal except:

(a) by a cheque which is not transferable, or
(b) by an electronic transfer of funds (authorised by credit or debit card or otherwise).

'Paying' includes paying in kind (with goods or services).

If a SMD pays for scrap metal in breach of s 12(1), each of the following is guilty of an offence under s 12(4):

(a) the SMD;
(b) if the payment is made at a site, the site manager;
(c) any person who makes the payment acting for the dealer.

It is a defence for a person within (a) or (b) to prove that he made arrangements to ensure that the payment was not made in breach of s 12(1), and that he took all reasonable steps to ensure that those arrangements were complied with (s 12(5)).

Records: receipt of metal

The following provisions set out in SMDA 2013, s 13 apply if a SMD receives any scrap metal in the course of his business.

The dealer must record the following information:

(a) the description of the metal, including its type (or types if mixed), form, condition, weight, any marks identifying previous owners, and any other distinguishing features;

(b) the date and time of its receipt;
(c) if the metal is delivered in or on a vehicle, the registration mark of the vehicle;
(d) if the metal is received from a person, the full name and address of that person;
(e) if the dealer pays for the metal, the full name of the person who makes the payment acting for the dealer (s 13(2)).

If the dealer receives the metal from a person, he must keep a copy of any document which he uses to verify the name or address of that person (s 13(3)). If the dealer pays for the metal by cheque, he must keep a copy of the cheque (s 13(4)). If the dealer pays for the metal by electronic transfer he must keep the receipt identifying the transfer, or (if no such receipt was obtained) he must record particulars identifying the transfer (s 13(5)).

Records: disposal of metal

SMDA 2013, s 14 requires records to be kept in respect of the disposal of scrap metal by a SMD in the course of his business. For these purposes metal is disposed of:

(a) whether or not it is in the same form in which it was received;
(b) whether or not the disposal is to another person;
(c) whether or not the metal is dispatched from a site (s 14(2)).

Where the disposal is in the course of business under a site licence, the dealer must record the following information:

(a) the description of the metal, including its type (or types if mixed), form and weight;
(b) the date and time of its disposal;
(c) if the disposal is to another person, the full name and address of that person;
(d) if the dealer receives payment for the metal (whether by way of sale or exchange), the price or other consideration received (s 14(3)).

Where the disposal is in the course of business under a collector's licence, the dealer must record the following information:

(a) the date and time of the disposal;
(b) if the disposal is to another person, the full name and address of that person (s 14(4)).

Records: supplementary

The information mentioned in SMDA 2013, ss 13(2) and (5) and 14(3) and (4) must be recorded in a manner which allows the information and the scrap metal to which it relates to be readily identified by reference to each other (s 15(1)).

The records mentioned in s 13(3) and (4) must be marked so as to identify the scrap metal to which they relate (s 15(2)). The dealer must keep the information and other records mentioned in ss 13(2) to (5) and 14(3) and (4) for a period of three years beginning with the day on which the metal is received or (as the case may be) disposed of (s 15(3)).

If a SMD fails to fulfil a requirement under ss 13, 14 or 15, each of the following is guilty of an offence under s 15(4)):

(a) the SMD;
(b) if the metal is received at or (as the case may be) dispatched from a site, the site manager;

(c) any person who, under arrangements made by a person within (a) or (b), has responsibility for fulfilling the requirement.

It is a defence for a person within (a) or (b) to prove that he made arrangements to ensure that the requirement was fulfilled, and took all reasonable steps to ensure that those arrangements were complied with (s 15(5)).

Right to enter and inspect

SMDA 2013, s 16 provides the following rights of entry and inspection.

A constable or an officer of a local authority (hereafter 'officer') may enter and inspect a licensed site at any reasonable time on notice to the site manager (s 16(1)). A constable or an officer may enter and inspect a licensed site at any reasonable time, otherwise than on such notice, if:

(a) reasonable attempts to give such notice have been made and have failed, or
(b) entry to the site is reasonably required for the purpose of ascertaining whether the provisions of SMDA 2013 are being complied with or investigating offences under it and (in either case) the giving of notice would defeat that purpose (s 16(2)).

Section 16(1) and (2) do not apply to residential premises (s 16(3)). There is no entitlement to use force to enter premises in the exercise of the powers under s 16(1) and (2) (s 16(4)).

By s 16(5), a justice of the peace may issue a warrant authorising entry (in accordance with s 16(7) below) to any premises within s 16(6) if he is satisfied by information on oath that there are reasonable grounds for believing that entry to the premises is reasonably required for the purpose of securing compliance with the provisions of SMDA 2013, or ascertaining whether those provisions are being complied with. Premises are within s 16(6) if they are a licensed site, or they are not a licensed site but there are reasonable grounds for believing that the premises are being used by a SMD in the course of business. A warrant is in accordance with s 16(7) if it is a warrant signed by the justice which specifies the premises concerned and authorises a constable or an officer to enter and inspect the premises at any time within one month from the date of the warrant. A constable or an officer may, if necessary, use reasonable force in the exercise of the powers under a warrant under s 16(5) (s 16(8)).

A constable or an officer may:

(a) require production of, and inspect, any scrap metal kept at any premises mentioned in s 16(1) or (2) or in a warrant under s 16(5);
(b) require production of, and inspect, any records kept in accordance with ss 13 or 14 and any other records relating to payment for scrap metal;
(c) take copies of or extracts from any such records (s 16(9)).

If a constable or an officer seeks to exercise powers under s 16 in relation to any premises, and the owner, occupier or other person in charge of the premises requires him to produce evidence of his identity, or of his authority to exercise those powers, he must produce that evidence (s 16(10) and (11)).

It is an offence to obstruct the exercise of a right of entry or inspection under s 16 or to fail to produce a record required to be produced under s 16 (s 16(13)).

CHAPTER 23

Non-Fatal Offences Against the Person

COMMON ASSAULT AND BATTERY

Common assault and battery are offences contrary to the Criminal Justice Act 1988, s 39. They are separate offences. Rather confusingly, the word 'assault' is used in some other statutes to refer to assault or battery.

Assault

A person is guilty of the separate offence of assault if he intentionally or recklessly causes another person to apprehend the immediate application to himself of unlawful force.

Any act, even mere words, can suffice if it has the requisite result. An example would be where, during an argument in a pub, someone holding a beer glass loses his temper and shouts out to his antagonist, 'I'll glass you for that'. Although words alone can constitute an assault, threatening words are more likely to be prosecuted as an offence under the Public Order Act 1986, ss 4, 4A or 5.

The requirement that the immediate application of unlawful force must be apprehended means that it is an assault to aim a blow at V, whether or not that blow hits him, unless V is blind, or the blow is aimed from behind him, or for some other reason he does not apprehend force. The requirement of 'immediacy' has been given a liberal interpretation by the courts. In one case, where a woman (V) had been caused psychiatric harm after repeated telephone calls and letters from the defendant (D), the last two of which contained threats, the Court of Appeal held that the jury were entitled to find that the last letter had caused V fear of immediate force. It emphasised that D, who was known to V, lived near her and she thought that something could happen at any time. The Court of Appeal, albeit accepting the requirement of the apprehension of immediate force, said that it was enough for the prosecution to prove fear of force 'at some time not excluding the immediate future', which seems to require a fear of the application of force at some time in the future, including the immediate future. Cases involving repeated conduct such as that just described are now better dealt with by bringing a prosecution for an offence under the Protection from Harassment Act 1997, described later in this chapter.

If V is put in fear of immediate force, it is irrelevant that D could not in fact carry out his threat; for example, pointing an unloaded gun at someone who is unaware of its harmlessness can be an assault.

The force apprehended must be unlawful; see p 653.

The mens rea required for an assault is an intention to cause the other person to apprehend the immediate application of unlawful force or recklessness as to whether he might so apprehend.

Battery

A person is guilty of battery if he intentionally or recklessly applies unlawful force to another person. Most batteries are preceded by an assault, but this is not always so. If a person is clubbed down from behind there is certainly a battery but, if he was unaware that the blow was coming, there cannot be an assault, because there would have been no apprehension by him of the immediate application of unlawful force.

A battery requires some conduct on D's part which results in unlawful force being applied to another (V). Technically, the slightest degree of force, even a mere touching, suffices, but a prosecution is most unlikely unless some harm has been caused. The force can be applied directly, as where D hits V with his fist or an instrument, or indirectly, as where D puts a tripwire across an alley over which V trips or D puts acid in a hand drier which is blown onto the hands of the next user. The fact that a battery requires an application of force means that causing someone psychiatric harm by a threat does not involve a battery.

Normally, the force must be applied as a result of an act by D. However, liability can also be based on an omission (with the appropriate mens rea) to take such steps as are in D's power to counteract a dangerous situation created by him, even if inadvertently. This was held by a divisional court in a case where V, a police officer, approached D and told him that she intended to carry out a full body search. V asked D to turn out his pockets. D did so and produced some syringes without needles. V asked D if he had any needles on him and he replied 'No'. When V searched one of D's pockets her finger was pierced by a hypodermic needle, at which D smirked. Clearly, D had failed to counteract a danger, which his assurance had created, by not warning V not to put her hand in the pocket. As a result, force (the needle) had been applied to V's finger and there could be a conviction for battery since D had the mens rea for that offence.

The force applied must be unlawful; see p 653.

The mens rea required for a battery is an intention to apply unlawful force to the other or recklessness as to whether unlawful force might be so applied. It follows that, if D punches V mistakenly believing that V is attacking him, there is no battery because, as we shall see, he will not have intended, nor been reckless as to, the application of *unlawful* force.

Clearly, it is not a battery to hit someone accidentally (since there is no intention to apply force to another), unless D can be proved to have realised the risk that his act, for example of swinging his arm, might possibly result in unlawful force being applied to another and unreasonably run that risk (in which case he would be proved to have been reckless as to the risk).

Procedural matters

Where the person has been merely 'put in fear' (ie assault) D must be charged that he 'did assault' that person. If force has been applied (ie battery), the charge should allege 'did assault by beating'.

AGGRAVATED ASSAULTS

There are a number of offences of aggravated assault. Among them are assault with intent to rob, and racially or religiously aggravated assault, discussed later. Like the aggravated assaults discussed below, they require an assault or battery which is accompanied either by a particular intention or by a special circumstance or consequence.

Assault occasioning actual bodily harm

It is an indictable (either way) offence, contrary to the Offences Against the Person Act 1861 (OAPA 1861), s 47, to assault any person, thereby occasioning him actual bodily harm (ABH). What is required is an assault or battery which has occasioned ABH. 'Harm' is a synonym for 'injury'. 'Actual' indicates that the injury should not be so trivial as to be wholly insignificant. Harm which is both transient and trifling is not ABH. 'Bodily harm' refers to injury to any part of the body (including a person's hair) or an identifiable psychiatric injury brought about by psychological factors (eg post-traumatic stress disorder, or battered wife syndrome, or reactive depression) but not mere emotions such as fear, distress or panic which are not themselves evidence of an identifiable clinical condition. Consequently, to cause someone psychiatric injury by a threat of 'immediate' force can amount to an offence under s 47. Where V claims to have suffered psychiatric injury as a result of a non-physical assault, there must be psychiatric evidence as to whether the symptoms alleged by V amount to a psychiatric injury. It has been held that loss of consciousness falls within the meaning of 'harm', because it involves an injurious impairment to the victim's sensory functions.

There must be a causal connection between the 'assault' and the bodily harm occasioned and in most circumstances this will be apparent. If D punches V in the face and causes ABH, for example cuts or bruises, there has been a battery and the harm has been occasioned thereby. Cases where the assault is not the only cause of the ABH are governed by the same principles of causation as apply to murder and manslaughter (p 690), substituting 'ABH' for 'death'.

The mens rea required for this offence is the mens rea required for an assault or battery (as the case may be). It is not necessary to establish that D intended to cause some bodily harm or was reckless as to the risk of doing so.

Assault with intent to resist arrest

It is an indictable (either way) offence under OAPA 1861, s 38 for someone to assault (ie by an assault or by a battery) any person with intent to resist or prevent the lawful apprehension or detaining of himself, or any other person, for any offence. Section 38 deals with assaults on any person effecting an arrest, and therefore protects members of the public who are making 'citizens' arrests'. It does not apply, however, if the arrest is for a breach of the peace (which is not itself an offence) or in civil process; it is limited to an arrest for an offence.

An offence under s 38 is proved if it is established that the arrest was lawful; that D intended to resist it; and that he knew that the person whom he assaulted was seeking to arrest him. The issue of whether or not an offence which merited arrest had been committed is irrelevant as is an alleged belief on D's part that he had not committed the offence.

Assault on a constable in the execution of his duty

The Police Act 1996 (PA 1996), s 89(1) makes it an offence for a person to assault (by an assault or by a battery) a constable in the execution of his duty. While, of course, D must have the necessary mens rea for the assault or battery which he commits, it is irrelevant that he does not know that V was a constable acting in the execution of his duty. However, if D, ignorant that V is a constable, applies force to V who is exercising one of his powers, and that force would have been reasonable on the ground of self-defence if V had not been a constable, D does not commit an offence. He will not have intentionally or recklessly applied unlawful force (the mens rea for a battery) because of his ignorance of V's status.

The key point about this offence is that the constable must be acting in the execution of his duty. At first sight the offence seems to be quite straightforward as there is a tendency to assume that police officers are in the execution of their duty at all times while they are carrying out duties in the course of their routine work. This is not so, and it is important to remember that on every occasion upon which it is alleged that this offence has been committed the particular duty which was being executed at the time will be examined by the courts.

To be acting in the execution of his duty, a constable must be acting within the general scope of a duty imposed on him by law (such as his duties to protect life and property, to keep the peace, to prevent and investigate crimes and to prevent obstruction of the highway) and he must not be acting unlawfully at the time. Thus, even if a constable is acting within the general scope of one of his duties, he is not acting in the execution of his duty if he has no power to do the thing in question (and is, therefore, committing a trespass against a person or his property). The courts have held that, since a constable does not have the power without arresting someone to physically detain him for questioning, he will not be acting in the execution of his duty if he does, even if the detention is only for a few seconds. It would be different if the constable is exercising a power of arrest. Where a constable arrests a person and it is not practicable to give the reason for that arrest at the time, the arrest will be lawful and an assault upon the constable will, at that time, be committed while he is in the execution of his duty. This is so even if the arrest is subsequently made unlawful by a failure to give the reason for arrest as soon as it is practicable to do so.

It has been held by a judge in the Administrative Court that, as a constable has the power to ask someone to stop and answer questions if he does not physically detain him or threaten to do so, a constable who so asks is acting in the execution of his duty at that time, even if he intends unlawfully to detain the person asked to stop.

A constable does not act outside the execution of his duty if what he does involves no more than a trivial touching; so to act is lawful because the conduct would be generally acceptable in the ordinary conduct of daily life (see p 655). In one case, for example, a constable, who touched a man on the shoulder to attract his attention because he wished to speak to him in relation to an offence, was held to have been acting in the execution of his duty. On the other hand, where a police officer restricted a person's movements (blocking him) in a doorway for a few seconds, without having intended or purported to arrest him, in order to question him, the Court of Appeal held that this went beyond conduct which was generally acceptable in the ordinary conduct of daily life and was unlawful. The constable was therefore not acting in the execution of his duty at the time.

The test whether a police officer is acting in the execution of his duty is judged objectively. Thus, for example, an officer who makes an unlawful arrest is not acting in the execution of his duty even though he believes that he has the necessary reasonable grounds for making an arrest. Officers who arrive on the scene and assist a colleague in what turns out to be an unlawful arrest will also not be acting in the execution of their duty.

Assaults upon constables frequently occur in police stations and, once again, the nature of the duties being undertaken at the time must be examined before a charge under s 89(1) is preferred. A person who has not been arrested is entitled to leave a police station at any time unless he is detained under particular provisions which allow detention. An officer who attempts to prevent him from leaving a police station is not acting in the execution of his duty. In one case, two policewomen, in searching a prisoner in accordance with their interpretation of the chief constable's instructions, removed her brassiere and were assaulted by the prisoner. It was held that, regardless of those instructions, they were not acting in the execution of their duty if they had not personally considered whether such a search was necessary for a lawful purpose, or whether the removal of that garment was necessary for that particular person's protection. This is an interesting decision which clearly places responsibility for lawful search upon the officer conducting it.

Police officers are frequently asked to assist with the expulsion of persons from premises, where the owner of the premises considers them to be intruders or for some other reason they are unwelcome. An officer may lawfully assist the owner of property in these circumstances, but he is not bound to do so. Unless there are particular circumstances which demand such expulsion, for example the removal of violent, quarrelsome, disorderly persons from various premises as required by law (see, eg, p 566), or where a breach of the peace is taking place or apprehended, it is unlikely that he will be considered to have been acting in the execution of his duty.

On occasions constables are given the authority to enter premises, and if they enter under such an authority they are acting in the execution of their duty. For example, the common law authorises a constable to enter premises to deal with a breach or reasonably apprehended breach of the peace (and it also authorises him to remain for this purpose if he is already on the premises); such a constable is acting in the execution of his duty. Response to a burglar alarm gives police an implied permission to enter premises for a reasonable time for the purpose of a search, but there is no legal right to enter premises found insecure at night. Where a constable is invited to enter premises by a member of the family and is later told to leave by the occupier, and he is assaulted by the occupier while he is immediately complying with that request, it is an assault upon him in the execution of his duty. On the other hand, he would no longer be in the execution of his duty if he did not comply with the request within a reasonable time because he would become a trespasser; if he was assaulted after the expiry of such a time an offence under s 89(1) would not be committed.

A divisional court has held that, where a constable has acted unlawfully (eg by using unlawful force) during a sequence of events, this does not mean that the constable's previous or subsequent exercise of his powers is also outside the execution of his duty.

Where a constable does something mistakenly believing that the subject of his action is committing a particular offence whereas that person is committing another offence, and the constable would have power to act as he did in either event, he will be acting in the execution of his duty if he has a reasonable basis for his mistaken belief and is acting in good faith.

Obstructing or resisting a constable in the execution of his duty

It is an offence under PA 1996, s 89(2) for a person to resist or wilfully obstruct a constable in the execution of his duty, or a person assisting him.

To '*obstruct*' is to do any conduct which prevents or makes it more difficult for a constable to carry out his duty, and in this sense those who give warning of police speed checks may obstruct the constables in the execution of their duty. It has been held that someone who warns motorists of a police speed check is only guilty of obstructing a constable in the execution of his duty if the prosecution proves that the motorists warned were in fact speeding or were likely to be speeding at that location. Someone who deliberately drinks alcohol after an accident to negate the breath-testing procedure is also guilty of this offence.

The obstruction must be 'wilful', which in this context means that:

(1) D's conduct which has resulted in the obstruction must have been deliberate and intended by him to bring about a state of affairs which, in fact, prevented or made it more difficult for the constable to carry out his duty, whether or not D realised that that state of affairs would have that effect.

(2) Also, D must have had no lawful excuse. Police officers often experience difficulty in obtaining names and addresses from offenders but a refusal to give such information will not amount to a wilful obstruction unless that person has a duty to give that information, because otherwise he will have a lawful excuse for his refusal. Nor, for the same reason, is it a wilful obstruction to advise someone not to answer police questions which he is not obliged to answer, even if the advice is given in an abusive way. Much of the traffic legislation imposes a duty to give particular types of information, but there is no such requirement in relation to most offences. Just as in the case of a failure to provide information, so in the case of other failures to assist the police (eg by failing to accord entry to a constable), there is only a wilful obstruction if the constable has the right to require the assistance in question, so that D is under a legal duty to provide it. An example would be where a constable has a statutory right of entry. A refusal to admit the constable in breach of the duty to admit him would be a wilful obstruction.

It has been held that a defendant who believed that the person obstructed was not a constable could not be convicted of the present offence.

Like obstruction, *resistance* does not require an assault or battery. Probably, any resistance is also an obstruction, but resistance is a more appropriate word in certain cases (such as where a person arrested by a constable tears himself away).

What was said above about 'acting in the execution of his duty' is equally applicable to the offences of obstruction and resistance. Thus, for example, where a person seeks to prevent an arrest which, in the circumstances, is not a lawful arrest, he is not guilty of a wilful obstruction of a police officer acting in the execution of his duty since the officer will not be acting *in the execution of his duty*.

Other points

By PA 1996, s 89(3) the offences under s 89 may also be committed against constables of the Police Service of Scotland or Northern Ireland who are executing warrants or acting in England and Wales by virtue of any enactment. Section 89 also applies to a constable of the British Transport Police Force or a member of the Civil Nuclear Constabulary (Railways and Transport Safety Act 2003, s 68; Energy Act 2004, s 68). A foreign police or customs officer carrying out surveillance in England and Wales under the Regulation of Investigatory Powers Act 2000, s 76A is treated as if he were acting as a constable in the execution of his duty (Crime (International Co-operation) Act 2003, s 84).

Under s 89(1) and (2) it is also an offence to assault, obstruct, or resist a person assisting a constable in the execution of his duty. The reference in s 89 to 'a person assisting a constable in the execution of his duty' includes reference to any person who is neither a constable nor in the company of a constable but who is carrying out his functions as a member of an international joint investigation team led by a member of a police force.

The Police Reform Act 2002, s 46 creates similar offences in relation to assaults on, or the obstruction of, a designated or accredited person acting in the execution of his duty, or someone assisting such a person.

OFFENCES INVOLVING WOUNDING OR GRIEVOUS BODILY HARM

Malicious wounding or infliction of grievous bodily harm

OAPA 1861, s 20 provides two indictable (either way) offences: malicious wounding and malicious infliction of grievous bodily harm. Section 20 provides that a person who unlawfully and maliciously wounds or inflicts any grievous bodily harm on any other person, either with or without any weapon or instrument, is guilty of an offence.

Both offences have two elements in common: 'unlawfully' and 'maliciously'. The difference between them relates to their actus reus: 'wounding' and 'infliction of grievous bodily harm', and these terms will be discussed first.

Wounding or infliction of grievous bodily harm

The term 'wound' indicates a breaking of the continuity of all layers of the skin. Consequently, all injuries involving broken bones are excluded unless the bone pierces the skin. However, such injuries will normally amount to grievous bodily harm.

'Grievous bodily harm' (GBH) means really serious harm, but 'really serious' appears to mean no more than 'actually serious'; 'bodily harm' can include psychiatric injury or loss of consciousness but, of course, such injury must be serious in order to be grievous. It is not necessary that the nature of the harm should be either permanent or dangerous.

A wound can be caused or grievous bodily harm can be 'inflicted' even though it does not result from the application of force; it is enough, instead, that it is caused by something done by D. The same principles of causation apply as apply to murder and manslaughter (p 690), substituting 'GBH' or 'wounding' for 'death'.

Unlawfully

This means 'without lawful justification' and is merely intended to except from the offence, in certain circumstances, acts done with a justification rendering the harm lawful, for example harm lawfully caused in self-defence.

Maliciously

The mens rea of an offence under OAPA 1861, s 20 is that D should have wounded or inflicted GBH 'maliciously'. This does not mean that D must have acted out of spite or ill-will. Instead, what is required is that D must have intended his act to cause some unlawful harm to another, or been reckless as to whether some unlawful harm might result from his act. It must be emphasised that it is not necessary that D should have intended or foreseen a wound or really serious harm; foresight that *some* harm, albeit of a minor character, might result, is enough.

Because D must have been aware that his act might cause some *unlawful* bodily harm, someone who mistakenly believes that he is acting in self-defence or has some other legal justification is not guilty under s 20 if he wounds or inflicts grievous bodily harm on someone.

Wounding or causing grievous bodily harm with intent to do grievous bodily harm or to resist or prevent arrest

OAPA 1861, s 18 provides that a person who unlawfully and maliciously by any means whatsoever wounds or causes GBH to any person with intent to do GBH to any person, or with intent to resist or prevent the lawful apprehension or detainer of any person, is guilty of an offence triable only on indictment.

An offence under s 18 is a very serious one; the nature of the maximum punishment (life imprisonment) is a factor to bear in mind when deciding which of the various non-fatal offences against the person to charge.

OAPA 1861, s 18 provides two offences: wounding with intent to do GBH or with intent to resist the lawful apprehension or detaining of any person, and causing GBH with one of these intents.

What was said in relation to OAPA 1861, s 20 in relation to 'unlawfully', 'wound', and 'GBH' is equally applicable to OAPA 1861, s 18. However, s 18 specifies that GBH must be 'caused' (as opposed to 'inflicted'). This difference in terminology between s 18 and s 20 raises the question of whether there is a difference of substance. GBH can be 'caused' by a deliberate and culpable omission to act; but opinions differ as to whether GBH can be 'inflicted' by a deliberate and culpable omission to act.

Mens rea

If D is charged with wounding with intent to do GBH, or with causing GBH with such intent, the word 'maliciously', the meaning of which was explained above, is rendered redundant by the stricter requirement of an intent to do GBH. The GBH intended need not be GBH to the particular victim. D may be convicted of wounding V with intent, even though D thought that V was X, or even though D fired at X and hit V by accident. If a person fires a gun into a group of people without taking particular aim, but intending to harm someone, he may be charged with a s 18 offence against the person whom he hits.

The basic distinction between wounding or causing GBH with intent to do GBH and attempted murder is that, in the former offences, only an intent unlawfully to do GBH is required, while the latter requires an intent unlawfully to kill.

Where D is charged with wounding with intent to resist or prevent the lawful apprehension or detaining of any person (whether himself or another), or with causing GBH with such intent, 'maliciously' is relevant. It must be proved that D intended his conduct to cause *some* unlawful harm to another (or was reckless as to this occurring), ie that he was 'malicious', *and* that he intended to resist or prevent the lawful apprehension or detaining of himself or another. The lawful arrest which D intends to resist or prevent need not be for an offence; it could be for a breach of the peace or in civil process.

UNLAWFUL FORCE OR HARM

It is an integral part of the offences referred to above that the requisite force (apprehended or applied) or harm (as the case may be) must be unlawful. In this context, the essential point is that, if the victim has given a valid consent to the force or harm, or if D has acted in self-defence, prevention of crime or the like, it is lawful.

Consent

Consent can validly be given to an act which does not cause actual bodily harm. 'Actual bodily harm' means any injury which is not so trivial as to be wholly insignificant. See, further, p 648.

Consent cannot validly be given if an act causes actual bodily harm which D intended or foresaw *unless the case falls within one of a number of recognised exceptions or a new exception is recognised on public interest grounds.* The result of all this is that if a person intentionally causes another actual bodily harm or the actual bodily harm caused was foreseen, it is generally irrelevant whether or not the latter has consented, since, generally, he cannot give a valid consent in such a case. Thus, assuming the other elements of the offence are proved, there can generally be a conviction for an assault occasioning actual bodily harm or some other offence involving harm to the person in such a case, despite the victim's apparent consent. For example, men who fight each other to 'settle a score' and cause actual bodily harm commit an assault occasioning actual bodily harm when they fight each other, despite their consent to such harm since actual bodily harm is clearly intended or foreseen. For the same reason, willing and enthusiastic participants in harmful sado-masochistic acts of violence for the sexual pleasure engendered in the giving and receiving of pain can be convicted of an assault occasioning actual bodily harm (or a more serious non-fatal offence).

The recognised exceptions

A person can give a valid consent to 'any actual bodily harm' caused by reasonable surgical operations or procedures; if he could not, the surgeon would commit a battery or an assault occasioning actual bodily harm or some more serious offence against the person.

It has been held that a valid consent can be given to ear piercing, to being tattooed or, even, to being branded with one's spouse's initials, since the bodily harm caused by these activities is not contrary to public policy.

Those who agree to take part in a lawful sport consent to the rules of that sport and, if those rules allow forms of physical contact, they validly consent to the risk of actual bodily harm which is likely to result from physical contact which is within the rules or is a minor infringement of them. For example, a blow struck in a boxing match under the Queensberry Rules (in which boxers wear approved gloves) is not a battery or any other offence, regardless of the injury caused, unless the blow is struck in circumstances far outside the rules (eg hitting an opponent when he is lying unconscious on the floor, or hitting an opponent with a glove in which is concealed a heavy object). Likewise, in soccer and rugby, the participants consent to the risk of actual bodily harm resulting from something within the rules of the game or not too far removed from them, but not to the risk of such harm resulting from something which is far outside the rules, such as a head-butt or deliberately kicking a player who is on the ground.

Not all sports are lawful. For example, a prize-fight, where gloves are not worn and the fight continues until one of the participants can no longer continue, is an unlawful sport. Thus, the participants cannot give a valid consent to the actual bodily harm intended or foreseen, with the result that the force which they apply to each other is always unlawful.

Other points on consent

Sometimes when a person has consented to the application of force, his consent is invalid, even though actual bodily harm is not caused by the force. This occurs where he is so young or mentally impaired as not to be able to make a rational decision whether or not to consent, or where his apparent consent has been procured by duress or has been given under a mistake as to the identity of the other party or as to the nature of the act or its purpose.

When considering a claim of consent one must consider what it is that is supposed to have been consented to. A person does not consent to something if he does not give an 'informed consent' to it. Suppose that someone consents to have intercourse with an AIDS sufferer in ignorance of that person's disease. While he will have consented to the intercourse (bodily contact) involved, this does not mean that he will have consented to run the risk of becoming diseased with the HIV virus (grievous bodily harm). In such a case, the consent to contact means that there will not be a battery but there can be liability for a more serious offence (see pp 652–3) based on the infliction or causing of grievous bodily harm.

Assuming it is valid, a consent need not be express; it can be implied from the circumstances. Everyday living demands a certain amount of physical contact. People are often touched in order to attract their attention, and there are constant collisions in shopping precincts, and the consent of people to such things can normally be implied. It is, of course, different if the person touched has indicated that he does not want to be touched. If V tells D, who has been pestering him, to go away, V clearly does not impliedly consent to D touching him soon after in order to attract his attention. Of course, there is a limit to what a person impliedly consents to. There is certainly no consent to a violent blow, allegedly to attract attention, perhaps as a person walked away after an argument. Similarly, one does not impliedly consent to collisions in a shopping precinct caused by hooligans charging about.

Another way of expressing cases based on implied consent is that they fall within a general exception embracing all physical contact which is generally acceptable in the ordinary conduct of daily life.

Other factors which render force lawful

Disciplinary use of force and corporal punishment

Subject to the limitations below, parents and other people in loco parentis are entitled as a disciplinary measure to apply a reasonable degree of force to their children or charges old enough to understand its purpose. In relation to the following offences:

(a) wounding or causing grievous bodily harm with intent, or unlawful wounding or infliction of grievous bodily harm;
(b) assault occasioning actual bodily harm; or
(c) cruelty to a person under 16,

battery of a child cannot be justified on the ground that it constituted reasonable punishment.

Teachers are no longer entitled by virtue of their position as such to apply reasonable corporal punishment as a disciplinary measure. However, the prohibition on corporal punishment by teachers does not affect the power of members of school staff to use reasonable force to restrain a pupil from:

(a) committing an offence or continuing to do so;
(b) causing or continuing to cause personal injury or damage to property; or
(c) behaving or continuing to behave in a way prejudicial to good order and discipline at school or among the pupils.

Prevention of crime or effecting arrest

The Criminal Law Act 1967 (CLA 1967), s 3 provides that it is lawful to use such force as is reasonable in the circumstances in the prevention of crime or in effecting (or assisting in) the lawful arrest of offenders, suspected offenders, or persons unlawfully at large. The effecting of an arrest will almost always involve some form of restraint, even if it is only symbolic, and this would be a battery but for the present defence. It must be emphasised that, if the force used to prevent a crime or to make an arrest is unreasonable in the circumstances, it will be unlawful and the person using it will not have a defence to a charge of battery or of another offence against the person. Like anyone else, a police officer has no defence, even though he uses reasonable force, if he is acting in furtherance of an unlawful arrest. Nor does he have a defence if he uses force to restrain someone whom he does not intend or purport to arrest, even though an arrest would have been justified.

Self-defence and defence of property or of another

Self-defence and the defence of property or of another are common law defences. They are limited to defence against an actual or imminent unlawful (ie criminal or tortious) act. However, a person who acts in defence of himself or another or of property is almost invariably acting in the prevention of crime, in which case he also has the defence under CLA 1967, s 3. For practical purposes, the terms of both the common law and the statutory defences are identical in their requirements.

Use of force against an innocent person

The Court of Appeal has held that self-defence and the defence under CLA 1967, s 3 extends to the use of force against an innocent third party where such force is used to prevent a crime being committed by someone else. Two examples of cases where the defence is capable of arising include a police constable bundling a man out of the way to get to another man who is about to detonate an explosive device, and where a person knocks car keys out of the hands of a third party to prevent the keys being given to a drunk person who is attempting to drive.

Applicable principles

The Criminal Justice and Immigration Act 2008, s 76, which applies to the common law defences of self-defence, defence of another and defence of property, and to the defences under CLA 1967, s 3(1) of the use of force in the prevention of crime or making of a lawful arrest, provides that the question whether the degree of force used by D was reasonable in the circumstances is to be decided by reference to the circumstances as D believed them to be, and that in connection with deciding that question:

(a) if D claims to have held a particular belief as regards the existence of any circumstances:
    (i) the reasonableness or otherwise of that belief is relevant to the question whether he genuinely held it, but
    (ii) if it is determined that D did genuinely hold it, he is entitled to rely on it, whether or not it was mistaken or (if it was mistaken) the mistake was a reasonable one to have made;
    but (ii) does not enable D to rely on any mistaken belief attributable to intoxication that was voluntarily induced;
(b) in a householder case, the degree of force used by D is not to be regarded as having been reasonable in the circumstances as D believed them to be if it was grossly disproportionate in those circumstances. This provision does not direct that any degree of force less than grossly disproportionate is reasonable. Whether it was or

not reasonable will depend on the particular facts and circumstances of the case. 'A householder case' is a case where:

(i) the defence concerned is the common law defence of self-defence or defence of another;

(ii) the force concerned is force used by D while in or partly in a building, or part of a building, that is a dwelling or is 'forces accommodation' (armed services living accommodation), or is both;

(iii) D is not a trespasser at the time the force is used; and

(iv) at that time D believed the victim to be in, or entering, the building or part as a trespasser.

Where a part of a building is a dwelling where D dwells, another part of it is a place of work for D or another person who dwells in the first part, and that other part is internally accessible from the first part, that other part, and any internal means of access between the two parts, are each treated for the above purposes as a part of a building that is a dwelling. There is a similar provision in respect of 'forces accommodation'.

For the above purposes, 'building' includes a vehicle or vessel.

(c) in a case other than a householder case, the degree of force used by D is not to be regarded as having been reasonable in the circumstances as D believed them to be if it was disproportionate in those circumstances. Although this means that force which is disproportionate is automatically unreasonable, it does not mean that force which is proportionate is necessarily reasonable. In almost all cases if the degree of force is proportionate it will also be reasonable, but the two terms are not to be equated;

(d) in deciding whether the degree of force used by D was reasonable in the circumstances, a possibility that D could have retreated is to be considered (so far as relevant) as a factor to be taken into account, rather than as giving rise to a duty to retreat;

(e) in deciding whether the degree of force used by D was reasonable in the circumstances, the following considerations are to be taken into account (so far as relevant in the circumstances of the case):

(i) that a person acting for the purpose of crime prevention, effecting a lawful arrest, self-defence, defence of another or defence of property ('a legitimate purpose') may not be able to weigh to a nicety the exact measure of any necessary action, and

(ii) that evidence of a person's having only done what the person honestly and instinctively thought was necessary for a legitimate purpose constitutes strong evidence that only reasonable action was taken by that person for that purpose.

For the avoidance of doubt, it must be stated that the mere fact that a person who has used force against another was provoked to lose self-control (as opposed to acting in self-defence, etc) is no defence.

RACIALLY OR RELIGIOUSLY AGGRAVATED NON-FATAL OFFENCES AGAINST THE PERSON

The Crime and Disorder Act 1998 (CDA 1998), s 29 provides that a person is guilty of an indictable (either way) offence under this section if he commits:

(a) an offence under OAPA 1861, s 20;

(b) an offence under OAPA 1861, s 47;

(c) common assault (or battery),

which is racially or religiously aggravated for the purposes of this section.

On a charge of an offence under CDA 1998, s 29, the prosecution must prove that D has committed one of the relevant specified basic offences and that it (the basic offence) was racially or religiously aggravated.

Racially or religiously aggravated

By CDA 1998, s 28, an offence is racially or religiously aggravated if:

(a) at the time of committing the offence, or immediately before or after doing so, the offender demonstrates towards the victim of the offence hostility based on the victim's membership (or presumed membership) of a racial or religious group (s 28(1)(a)); or

(b) the offence is motivated (wholly or partly) by hostility towards members of a racial or religious group based on their membership of that group (s 28(1)(b)).

In (a), 'membership', in relation to a racial or religious group, includes association with members of that group; 'presumed' means presumed by the offender.

Religious group

'Religious group' means a group of persons defined by reference to religious belief or lack of religious belief. Muslims and Rastafarians are religious groups, for instance.

Racial group

'Racial group' means a group of persons defined by reference to race, colour, nationality (including citizenship), or ethnic or national origins. These words are given a broad, non-technical interpretation.

A group of people will be a racial group defined by reference to race if, in ordinary speech, those people would be regarded as belonging to a named race. In one case, for example, it was held by a divisional court that 'African' described a racial group defined by reference to race because in ordinary language 'African' denotes a limited group of people regarded as common stock and as one of the major divisions of humankind having distinct physical features in common; it 'denotes a person characteristic of the blacks in Africa'. This was said to be so despite the fact that, strictly, 'African' is capable of covering Egyptians and white South Africans who would not fit the 'common stock' definition of 'Africans'. This broad, non-technical approach has been taken further where the victims of the words 'bloody foreigners' were Spanish. The House of Lords considered that these words were capable of satisfying the requirements of s 28(1)(a). It held that people who are not of British origin constitute a racial group for the purposes of the definition of 'racial group'. Thus, a racial group can be defined exclusively by reference to what its members are not in terms of race, colour, nationality, or ethnic or national origins, for example non-British or non-white, as well as inclusively by reference to what they are in such terms, for example Spanish or black.

Section 28(1)(a)

Because s 28(1)(a) does not require D's conduct to be motivated by racial or religious hatred, but simply requires the demonstration of such hatred (as defined), it is possible for D to fall within s 28(1)(a) even though he is of the same colour, etc as the victim of his conduct. This was held by a divisional court in a case where it upheld the conviction of D whose conduct had demonstrated hostility based on the victim's membership of a racial group which was the same as D's.

For the test under s 28(1)(a) to be satisfied, D must have formed the view that the victim was a member of a racial group (or religious group, as the case may be) and D must have done or said something which demonstrated hostility towards the victim (V) based on that membership. Words used need not expressly identify the racial or religious group to which the victim belongs. This was held by the Court of Appeal in a case where V was Indian and brown-skinned. He was called an 'immigrant doctor' by D immediately before D assaulted him. The Court of Appeal held that it was open to the jury to conclude that D had identified V as falling within the racial groups 'Indian' and 'brown-skinned' and that the use of 'immigrant' demonstrated hostility based on the victim's membership of such groups.

Section 28(1)(a) does not require the hostility demonstrated to be based only on V's membership of a racial or religious group, or even principally on it. However, the more incidental the words or other conduct with a racial or religious content, the more difficult it will be to prove that D has demonstrated racial or religious hostility.

The word 'immediately' in s 28(1)(a) qualifies 'after' as well as 'before'; s 28(1)(a) strikes at words uttered or acts done in the immediate context of the basic substantive offence. Thus, a divisional court held that a racially aggravated offence was not made out where D demonstrated racial hostility to the victim only 20 minutes after committing the basic offence, while being questioned by the police.

Section 28(1)(b)

Section 28(1)(b) requires that the offence is motivated (wholly or partly) by hostility towards members of a racial or religious group based on their membership of that group. Section 28(1)(b) does not require D to be motivated by racial or religious hostility towards the victim of the offence but 'merely' by hostility 'towards members of a racial or religious group'. Hostility towards one member of a racial or religious group based on his membership of that group is sufficient to qualify so long as it forms part of the motivation for the conduct. Normally the victim will be a member of that group (and thus included within the ambit of that hostility) or at least be associated with it, but this is not a requirement of s 28(1)(b). For example, a person who, motivated by hostility towards members of the Jewish religious community, attacked a bricklayer whom he knew was not Jewish who was building a synagogue would fall foul of s 28(1)(b).

Although s 28(1)(a) requires proof of what D did at the time of committing the offence, s 28(1)(b) can be established by evidence relating to what D might have said or done on other occasions (since such evidence may be relevant to D's motivation at the time of the offence).

PROTECTION FROM HARASSMENT ACT 1997

Prohibitions of harassment

The Protection from Harassment Act 1997 (PHA 1997) sets out two prohibitions of harassment. The first, contained in s 1(1), prohibits a person from pursuing a course of conduct:

(a) which amounts to harassment of another person; and
(b) which he knows or ought to know amounts to harassment of the other person.

The second prohibition of harassment, contained in s 1(1A), prohibits a person from pursuing a course of conduct:

(a) which involves harassment of two or more persons; and
(b) which he knows or ought to know involves harassment of those persons; and
(c) by which he intends to persuade any person (whether or not one of those mentioned above),
    (i)   not to do something that he is entitled or required to do, or
    (ii) to do something that he is not under any obligation to do.

Section 1(1A) was added to protect company employees from harassment by animal rights groups. Section 1(1) does not protect such employees if they are only harassed on one occasion.

Course of conduct

In the case of conduct relating to a single person (see PHA 1997, s 1(1)), a 'course of conduct' must involve conduct on at least two occasions in relation to that person. In the case of conduct in relation to two or more persons (see s 1(1A)), a 'course of conduct' must involve conduct on at least one occasion in relation to each of those persons. Publishing a series of articles in a newspaper can constitute a course of conduct.

The term 'conduct' in PHA 1997 includes speech. By s 7(3A), a person's (X's) conduct on any occasion which is aided, abetted, counselled or procured by another (Y) is taken:

(a) also to be on that occasion the conduct of Y; and
(b) to be conduct in relation to which Y's knowledge and purpose (and what Y ought to have known) are the same as they were in relation to what was contemplated or reasonably foreseeable at the time of the aiding, abetting, etc.

This means in relation to the wording in s 1(1) that there can be a breach of the prohibition on harassment by Y if, for example, on one occasion the harassing conduct is by X aided and abetted by Y and on the second occasion is by Y himself, provided that the two pieces of conduct can be regarded as a 'course' and that part (b) of s 7(3A) is satisfied. The same principle will apply to conduct aimed at different company employees so far as s 1(1A) is concerned.

By s 1(2), for the purposes of ss 1 and 2A (see p 661) the person whose course of conduct is in question ought to know that his conduct amounts to or involves harassment of another if a reasonable person in possession of the same information would think the course of conduct amounted to or involved harassment of the other. The reasonable person in this context is not imbued with any mental illness or other characteristic which the defendant has.

Although, a company cannot be harassed for the purposes of PHA 1997, it can be liable for harassment.

Harassment

By s 7(2), 'harassment' in PHA 1997 *includes* alarming another person or causing that person distress. However, the Court of Appeal has held that it does not necessarily follow that any course of conduct which causes alarm or distress therefore amounts to harassment; s 7(2) does not equate harassment with causing alarm or distress. Many actions that cause alarm or distress will not amount to harassment. By way of example, the Court of Appeal has stated that a person who habitually drives too fast in a built-up area may cause alarm to other road-users, but his conduct would not amount to harassment.

The Court of Appeal has held that s 7(2) does not provide a comprehensive definition of harassment. The Court of Appeal has also held that, in addition to the statutory requirement, the conduct must be unacceptable and oppressive, either physically or mentally, such that it would sustain criminal liability; it must be targeted at an individual, and must result in fear or distress. The Court also stated that, when considering whether conduct amounts to or involves harassment, it is right to have regard to what the ordinary person would understand by harassment.

While s 1 was fashioned with 'stalkers' in mind (in this respect note s 2A below), its terms are wide enough to embrace situations in which harassment is caused to neighbours or to persons living in a particular area in which unruly juveniles tend to congregate. Section 1 can also cover the activities of political protesters and members of the 'paparazzi', and more mundane things like sending a series of letters demanding payment of a debt, if the other elements are established.

Exceptions

By PHA 1997, s 1(3), the prohibitions of harassment in s 1(1) and (1A) do not apply to a course of conduct if the person who pursued it shows that it was pursued for the purpose of preventing or detecting crime; or that it was pursued under any enactment or rule of law or to comply with a condition or requirement lawfully imposed; or that, in the particular circumstances, the pursuit of the course of conduct was reasonable. It has been stated by a divisional court that whether conduct was reasonable involves balancing the interests of the victim against the purpose and nature of the course of conduct pursued, including the right to peaceful protest.

Offence of harassment

PHA 1997, s 2(1) makes it an offence to break either of the prohibitions of harassment.

Civil remedy

PHA 1997, s 3 makes provision for an actual or apprehended breach of the prohibition of harassment under s 1(1) to be the subject of a civil claim in the High Court or county court by the victim. Damages may be awarded against the person in breach of the prohibition of harassment (or against his employer if he was acting in the course of his employment). The court may grant an injunction for the purpose of restraining a defendant from pursuing any course of conduct which amounts to harassment.

Section 3A permits an injunction to be sought where there is an actual or apprehended breach of s 1(1A). It permits a person who is or might be the victim of the course of conduct in question, or anyone who is or might be a person falling within s 1(1A)(c), to apply to the High Court or county court for an injunction to forbid such conduct.

Victims should be made aware of these possibilities. Breach of an injunction under s 3 or s 3A is an indictable (either way) offence.

Offence of stalking

PHA 1997, s 2A(1) provides that a person is guilty of an offence if (a) he pursues a course of conduct *in breach of the prohibition of harassment in s 1(1)*, and (b) the course of conduct amounts to stalking. For the purposes of (b), a person's course of conduct amounts to stalking of another person if:

(a) it amounts to harassment (pp 660–1) of that person,
(b) the acts or omissions involved are ones associated with stalking, and
(c) the person whose course of conduct it is knows or ought to know that the course of conduct amounts to harassment of the other person (s 2A(2): see p 660).

Section 2A is a more appropriate offence than that under s 2 to deal with stalkers. However, the offence of stalking may alternatively be dealt with by a prosecution under PHA 1997, s 2.

Section 2A(3) gives the following examples of acts or omissions which, in particular circumstances, are ones associated with stalking:

(a) following a person,
(b) contacting, or attempting to contact, a person by any means,
(c) publishing any statement or other material:
    (i)   relating or purporting to relate to a person, or
    (ii) purporting to originate from a person,
(d) monitoring the use by a person of the internet, email or any other form of electronic communication,
(e) loitering in any place (whether public or private),
(f) interfering with any property in the possession of a person,
(g) watching or spying on a person.

Power of entry in relation to offence of stalking

PHA 1997, s 2B provides that a justice of the peace may, on an application by a constable, issue a warrant authorising a constable to enter and search premises (as defined on p 66) if the justice of the peace is satisfied that there are reasonable grounds for believing that:

(a) an offence under s 2A has been, or is being, committed,
(b) there is material on the premises which is likely to be of substantial value (whether by itself or together with other material) to the investigation of the offence,
(c) the material is likely to be admissible in evidence at a trial for the offence, and does not consist of, or include, items subject to legal privilege, excluded material or special procedure material (as defined on pp 73–4), and
(d) either entry to the premises will not be granted unless a warrant is produced, or the purpose of a search may be frustrated or seriously prejudiced unless a constable arriving at the premises can secure immediate entry to them.

A constable may seize and retain anything for which a search has been so authorised. The additional powers of seizure provided by the Criminal Justice and Police Act 2001, s 50 apply to this power of seizure. A constable may use reasonable force, if necessary, in the exercise of any power conferred by virtue of PHA 1997, s 2B.

Putting people in fear of violence

PHA 1997, s 4 creates the indictable (either way) offence of putting people in fear of violence. Section 4(1) provides that a person whose course of conduct causes another to fear, on at least two occasions, that violence will be used against him, is guilty of an offence if he knows or ought to know that his course of conduct will cause that other person so to fear on each of those occasions. The Court of Appeal has held that the course of conduct must amount to harassment of another. Direct evidence from the victim that he was caused to fear such violence is not essential, because a court may infer such fear if there is other evidence entitling it to do so, but without direct evidence from the victim proof may be difficult.

For the purposes of s 4, the person whose course of conduct is in question ought to know that it will cause another to fear that violence will be used against him on any occasion if a reasonable person in possession of the same information would think the course of conduct would cause the other so to fear on that occasion.

Section 4 provides similar defences to those under s 1(3) with the substitution of 'circumstances in which the pursuit of his course of conduct was reasonable for the protection of himself or another or for the protection of his or another's property', for 'the pursuit of the course of conduct being reasonable in the circumstances'.

Stalking involving fear of violence or serious alarm or distress

PHA 1997, s 4A(1) provides that a person (D) whose course of conduct:

(a) amounts to stalking, and
(b) either:
  (i) causes another (V) to fear, on at least two occasions, that violence will be used against V, or
  (ii) causes V serious alarm or distress which has a substantial adverse effect on V's usual day-to-day activities,

is guilty of an indictable (either way) offence if D knows or ought to know that D's course of conduct will cause V so to fear on each of those occasions or (as the case may be) will cause such alarm or distress.

For the purposes of s 4A, D ought to know that his course of conduct will cause V to fear that violence will be used against V on any occasion if a reasonable person in possession of the same information would think the course of conduct would cause V so to fear on that occasion; and D ought to know that his course of conduct will cause V serious alarm or distress which has a substantial adverse effect on V's usual day-to-day activities if a reasonable person in possession of the same information would think the course of conduct would cause V such alarm or distress.

The same defences are available as apply to an offence under s 4.

The offence under s 4A may alternatively be dealt with by a prosecution under s 4.

Breach of restraining order

PHA 1997, s 5, which empowers a court to make a restraining order when sentencing a convicted person for *any* offence, is of particular importance in respect of cases under PHA 1997. It provides that, in addition to any other sentence imposed, the court may make an order protecting the victim(s) of the offence, or any other person mentioned in the order, from further conduct which amounts to harassment or will cause a fear of violence.

Section 5A permits a court before which D is acquitted of an offence under PHA 1997 or otherwise, if it considers that it is necessary to do so to protect a person from harassment by D, to make an order prohibiting D from doing anything specified in the order.

If, without reasonable excuse, a person does anything which is prohibited by a restraining order, he commits an indictable (either way) offence (ss 5(5) and 5A(2)).

Police directions stopping the harassment, etc of a person at his home

The Criminal Justice and Police Act 2001 (CJPA 2001), s 42 provides that a constable who is at the scene may give a direction to a person if:

(a) this person is present outside, or in the vicinity of, premises used by someone (the resident) as a dwelling;
(b) that constable believes, on reasonable grounds, that this person is there for the purpose (by his presence or otherwise) of representing to the resident or another individual, or of persuading the resident or other individual that:
    (i) he should not do something which he is entitled or required to do, or
    (ii) he should do something which he is not under any obligation to do; and
(c) the constable also believes on reasonable grounds that the presence of this person (either alone or together with others who are likely to be present):
    (i) amounts to, or is likely to result in, the harassment of the resident, or
    (ii) is likely to cause alarm or distress to the resident.

A direction under s 42 is one which requires its addressee to do things which the constable considers to be necessary to prevent the harassment of the resident or the causing of alarm or distress to the resident. It may be given orally, either to an individual or a group. Requirements that may be made under s 42 include:

(a) a requirement to leave the vicinity of the premises in question; and
(b) a requirement to leave that vicinity and not to return to it within such period as the constable may specify, not being longer than three months.

A requirement to leave may be to do so immediately or after a specified period. A direction may include exceptions and may make exceptions subject to conditions, including conditions as to the distance from the premises in question at which, or the location where, those who do not leave must remain, and conditions as to the numbers, or identity, of the persons who are authorised by the exception to remain in the vicinity.

When there is more than one officer at the scene, only the senior officer present may give the direction. The power to give a direction under s 42 does not include the power to direct a person to refrain from activity which is lawful under the Trade Union and Labour Relations (Consolidation) Act 1992, s 220 (see p 770). Any direction given may be varied or withdrawn.

A person who knowingly fails to comply with a requirement in a direction (other than a requirement not to return under (b) above) commits an offence (s 42(7)). A person who in breach of a requirement under (b) returns to the vicinity of the premises within the period specified for the purpose of persuading the resident or another individual as described above also commits an offence (s 42(8)).

Offence of harassment, etc of a person in his home

CJPA 2001, s 42A provides that a person also commits an offence if:

(a) he is present outside or in the vicinity of any premises that are used by any individual (the resident) as a dwelling; and

(b) he is there to represent to the resident or another individual, or to persuade the resident or other person, that he should not do something which he is entitled or required to do, or should do something he is not obliged to do;

(c) he intends his presence to amount to harassment, alarm or distress to the resident, or knows or ought to know that his presence is likely to do so; and

(d) his presence amounts to, or is likely to result in, harassment of, or alarm or distress to, the resident, a person in the resident's building or a person in another dwelling in the vicinity of the resident's dwelling.

RACIALLY OR RELIGIOUSLY AGGRAVATED HARASSMENT OR STALKING OFFENCES

A person commits an indictable (either way) offence under CDA 1998, s 32 if he commits an offence under PHA 1997, ss 2 to 4A, which is racially or religiously aggravated. CDA 1998, s 32 does not create one offence which can be committed in more than one way; it creates separate aggravated offences based on the offences under PHA 1997, ss 2, 2A, 4 and 4A. For the meaning of 'racially or religiously aggravated' see p 658.

ATTEMPTED CHOKING, AND POISONING, TORTURING, ETC

OAPA 1861, ss 21 to 24 include other offences which are associated with the causing, or attempted causing, of forms of bodily harm. These offences, which are all triable only on indictment, should be considered when circumstances are presented involving actual or attempted harm to a person.

Attempting to choke, etc

This offence, provided by OAPA 1861, s 21, consists of:

(a) an attempt by D, by any means whatsoever, to choke, suffocate or strangle any other person, or

(b) an attempt by D, by any means calculated to choke, suffocate or strangle, to render any other person insensible, unconscious or incapable of resistance,

with intent thereby to enable D or another person to commit any indictable offence, or with intent to assist another to do so.

Using chloroform, etc to commit an indictable offence

By OAPA 1861, s 22, D commits an offence if he unlawfully applies or administers to, or causes to be taken by, any person a stupefying or overpowering drug, matter or thing, with intent thereby to enable himself or another person to commit any indictable offence, or with intent to assist another to do so.

Administering poison, etc so as thereby to endanger life, etc or with intent to injure, etc

OAPA 1861, s 23 provides that a person is guilty of an offence if he unlawfully and maliciously administers to, or causes to be administered to or taken by, any other person any poison, or other destructive or noxious thing, *so as thereby to endanger the life of such person, or so as thereby to inflict upon such person any grievous bodily harm.*

OAPA 1861, s 24 provides that a person is guilty of an offence if he unlawfully and maliciously administers to, or causes to be administered to or taken by, any other person any poison, or other destructive or noxious thing, *with intent to injure, aggrieve or annoy such person.*

A 'poison' means a recognised poison, in whatever quantity it may be administered, etc; a 'noxious thing' is any other drug or thing which is harmful in the dosage in which it was administered, etc. 'Administer' does not necessarily involve the application of direct physical force and covers, for example, the spraying of tear gas from a distance. Where D acts in concert with V who self-injects a drug (for example by holding a tourniquet around V's arm while V self-injects or by preparing and giving V the drug for immediate self-injection), D does not *thereby* administer the drug. If the act of self-injection by V was not free, or not deliberate or not informed, as where V was forced to self-inject, D would cause the thing to be administered by V.

A poison, or other destructive or noxious thing, is caused to be taken if it is left for a person who then drinks it in ignorance of what it is or under duress. To leave it for the purpose of it being taken would be to attempt to cause it to be taken.

The consent of the person to whom the poison is given is no defence to charges under s 23 or 24. For example, heroin can be a noxious substance for the purposes of these offences. If a shot of heroin is administered to another with his consent, this will amount to an administration for the purposes of this section.

The distinction between the offences under ss 23 and 24 lies partly in the fact that the offence under s 23 requires the additional element that the administration must be such as thereby to endanger life or to inflict grievous bodily harm, and partly in the fact that the requirement of mens rea is not the same for each offence. The differences between the two offences are shown by the words italicised in the definitions given above.

The mens rea required is as follows. In the case of the offence under s 23, the Court of Appeal has held that where endangering of life or grievous bodily harm is caused directly (eg by injection) the requirement of malice is satisfied by its deliberate administration; no mens rea is required to be proved as to the risk of injury. The Court stated that where the endangering of life, etc was caused indirectly (eg by causing the victim to inhale gas) foresight of injury must be proved. In the case of an offence under s 24 not only must an intentional or reckless administration, etc of a poison or other destructive or noxious thing be proved but also an intention to injure, aggrieve or annoy.

Torture

The offence of torture, which is triable only on indictment, is governed by the Criminal Justice Act 1988, s 134.

By s 134(1), a public official or person acting in an official capacity, whatever his nationality, commits the offence of torture if he intentionally inflicts severe physical or mental pain or suffering on another in the performance or purported performance of his official duties.

By s 134(2), a person not acting in such an official capacity commits the offence of torture if he intentionally inflicts severe physical or mental pain or suffering on another at the instigation or with the consent or acquiescence of a public official or person acting in that capacity, and the official or other person is performing or purporting to perform his official duties when he instigates the commission of the offence or consents to or acquiesces in it.

It is immaterial whether the pain or suffering is physical or mental and whether it is caused by an act or omission. It is a defence for a person to prove that he had lawful authority, justification or excuse for that conduct.

The consent of the Attorney General is required for a prosecution for the offence of torture.

ILL-TREATMENT OR NEGLECT

In addition to the offences of cruelty under the Children and Young Persons Act 1933 (CYPA 1933), s 1 (p 534), there are the following offences involving ill-treatment or neglect.

Ill-treatment or neglect: persons lacking (or apparently lacking) capacity

The Mental Capacity Act 2005 (MCA 2005), s 44(1) and (2) provides that if D:

(a) has the care of a person (P) *who lacks, or whom D reasonably believes to lack, capacity*;

(b) is the donee of a lasting power of attorney or an enduring power of attorney created by P; or

(c) is a deputy appointed by the court to make decisions for P,

D is guilty of an offence if he ill-treats or wilfully neglects P.

For the purposes of (a), P lacks capacity in relation to a matter if at the material time he is unable to make a decision for himself in relation to the matter because of an impairment of, or a disturbance in the functioning of, the mind or brain, whether permanent or temporary. P is unable to make a decision for himself if he is unable to understand the information relevant to the decision, to retain, use or weigh it as part of the decision-making process, or to communicate his decision (whether by talking, sign language or otherwise).

Ill-treatment or wilful neglect: care worker offence

By the Criminal Justice and Courts Act 2015 (CJCA 2015), s 20(1), it is an offence for an individual who has the care of another individual by virtue of being a care worker to ill-treat or wilfully to neglect that individual. 'Care worker' means an individual who, as paid work, provides:

(a) health care for an adult or child, other than excluded health care (ie health care at an educational institution, children's home or residential family centre); or

(b) social care for an adult,

including an individual who, as paid work, supervises or manages individuals providing such care or is a director or similar officer of an organisation which provides such care.

Ill-treatment or wilful neglect: care provider offence

A care provider commits an offence under CJCA 2015, s 21(1) if:

(a) an individual who has the care of another individual by virtue of being part of the care provider's arrangements ill-treats or wilfully neglects that individual;

(b) the care provider's activities are managed or organised in a way which amounts to a gross breach of a relevant duty of care owed by the care provider to the individual who is ill-treated or neglected; and

(c) in the absence of this breach, the ill-treatment or wilful neglect would not have occurred or would have been less likely to occur.

'Care provider' means:

(a) a body corporate or unincorporated association which provides or arranges for the provision of:
   (i) health care for an adult or child, other than excluded health care, or
   (ii) social care for an adult, or
(b) an individual who provides such care and employs, or has otherwise made arrangements with, other persons to assist him or her in providing such care,

except that a local authority, or a person or body carrying out certain functions for a local authority, or a registered adoption society or adoption support agency, is not a care provider.

A 'relevant duty of care' means a duty owed under the law of negligence, but only to the extent that the duty is owed in connection with providing, or arranging for the provision of, health care or social care.

A breach of a duty of care by a care provider is a 'gross' breach if the conduct alleged to amount to the breach falls far below what can reasonably be expected of the care provider in the circumstances.

General

Ill-treatment and neglect have the same meaning as in the Children and Young Persons Act 1933, s 1, but unlike that section, MCA 2005, s 44 does not include the words 'in a manner likely to cause unnecessary suffering or injury to health'.

The above offences are indictable (either way) offences.

CHILD ABDUCTION

Two indictable (either way) offences of child abduction are provided by the Child Abduction Act 1984 (CAA 1984). These offences contain a number of common features; these will be dealt with after the separate offences have been outlined.

Abduction from the United Kingdom by parent, etc

By CAA 1984, s 1(1), a person connected with a child under 16 commits an offence if he takes or sends the child *out of the UK* without the appropriate consent. A person is regarded as 'sending' a child if he causes the child to be sent. A person connected with a child does not commit an offence if the appropriate consent has been given for a child to be removed from the UK for a defined period but the child is kept out of the UK after the end of that period and the appropriate consent no longer exists.

For the purposes of the offence, a person is 'connected with' a child if:

(a) he is the child's parent; or
(b) in the case of a child whose parents were not married to each other at the time of his birth, there are reasonable grounds for believing that he is its father; or
(c) he is a guardian or special guardian of the child; or

(d) he is a person named in a child arrangements order as a person with whom the child is to live; or

(e) he has custody of the child.

Only persons falling within these categories can commit the present offence.

The reference to the 'appropriate consent', in relation to the removal or sending of the child out of the UK, means:

(a) the consent of *each* of the following:
    (i)   the child's mother,
    (ii) the child's father, if he has parental responsibility for him,
    (iii) any guardian or special guardian of the child,
    (iv) any person named in a child arrangements order as a person with whom the child is to live, and
    (v) any person who has custody of the child; or

(b) the leave of the court granted under or by virtue of the Children Act 1989, Part II (ss 8–16A) (orders with respect to children in family proceedings); or

(c) if any person has custody of the child, the leave of the court which granted custody to him.

It is irrelevant that the child consents to what occurs.

A person does not commit the present offence by taking or sending a child out of the UK without the appropriate consent:

(a) if he is a person named in a child arrangements order as a person with whom the child is to live and he takes or sends the child out of the UK for a period of less than one month; or

(b) if he is a special guardian of the child and takes or sends it out of the UK for a period of less than three months,

unless he is in breach of an order under the Children Act 1989, Part II.

A person does not commit the present offence by doing anything without the consent of another person whose consent is required if:

(a) he does it in the belief that the other person has consented or would consent if he was aware of all the relevant circumstances; or

(b) he has taken all reasonable steps to communicate with the other person but has been unable to communicate with him; or

(c) the other person has unreasonably refused to consent.

However, condition (c) does not apply where the person who refused consent is a person named in a child arrangements order as a person with whom the child is to live, or who has custody of the child; or where the taking or sending out of the UK is in breach of an order made by a court in the UK.

There are special provisions where the child is in the care of a local authority or a voluntary organisation, detained in a place of safety, remanded to local authority accommodation, or the subject of proceedings (or an order) for adoption, or is in a place of safety.

The offence under CAA 1984, s 1 cannot be prosecuted without the DPP's consent.

The Court of Appeal has held that the defence of duress of circumstances is not available on a charge under s 1; the remedy where serious bodily harm to the child is believed to be imminent is, it said, to seek the protection of the courts.

Abduction of child by other persons

This offence is governed by CAA 1984, s 2. It can be committed by anyone other than:

(a) the father or mother (if they were married when the child was born) or the mother (if they were not); or
(b) the child's guardian or special guardian;
(c) a person within (a)(iv) on p 669; or
(d) a person with custody of the child.

Other important differences from the offence under s 1 are that the child need not be abducted from the UK and that the offence can be committed by taking *or detaining* a child.

Section 2(1) provides that anyone, other than someone mentioned above, commits an offence if, without lawful authority or reasonable excuse, he takes or detains a child under 16 so as either to remove him from the lawful control of anyone having lawful control of him or to keep him out of the lawful control of any person entitled to it. Removal from control does not require any removal in a geographical sense; it suffices to deflect the child from what, with the consent of those having lawful control of him, he would be otherwise doing into some activity induced by D, as where D finds a child in a park pursuing a particular activity (eg playing football) and induces it to go elsewhere in the park for another activity (eg to look for an alleged lost bicycle).

There can be a 'taking' for the purposes of s 2 despite the fact that a child consents provided that D's acts were a cause of the child accompanying him and such acts are more than just peripheral or inconsequential. If D's acts are an effective cause of the child accompanying him, that is sufficient.

A person is regarded as detaining a child if he causes him to be detained or induces the child to remain with him or another.

Although it must be proved that there was an intentional or reckless taking by D, the objective consequence of which was to remove or keep the child from the lawful control of anyone having lawful control of the child, it does not have to be proved that D intended or was reckless as to this consequence occurring.

It is a defence for D to prove that, at the time of the alleged offence, he believed the child was 16 or over. Alternatively, in the case where the father and mother of 'the child in question' (ie the child taken or detained) were not married to each other at the time of birth, it is a defence for D to prove that he is the father of the child taken or detained or that he had reasonable grounds to believe he was that child's father. Lastly, D is not guilty of an offence under s 2 if he mistakenly believed, reasonably or not, in facts which—if they had been as he believed—would have given him a lawful authority or reasonable excuse. On this basis, a man who takes a child, thinking that it is his child whereas in truth it is another child, will not be guilty if, on the facts as he believes them to be, he would have a lawful authority or reasonable excuse for taking the child.

General

For the purposes of both offences, a person is regarded as taking a child if he causes or induces the child to accompany him or any other person, or causes the child to be taken.

KIDNAPPING

The offence involves four requirements:

(a) The taking or carrying away of one person by another

This can include the case where a person is induced to walk or drive away himself, if the other elements of the offence are fulfilled (as where his car is hijacked and he drives away under the instructions of the hijackers). Although the person taken or carried away is often secreted thereafter, this is not a requirement of the offence.

(b) The taking or carrying away must be by force or by fraud

'Force' is not limited to physical force or the threat of it. It encompasses any conduct which, coupled with the taking or carrying away (requirement (a)), overrides the true consent of the person taken or carried away (requirement (c)). Thus, the exercise of mental or moral power or influence to compel another to do something against his will can suffice if it overcomes his will. Any fraud which induces the victim to consent to being taken or carried away will suffice, and will invalidate the victim's apparent consent.

(c) The taking or carrying away must be without the consent of the person taken or carried away

This requirement must be satisfied whatever the age of that person. However, there can be a kidnapping, even though the person carried away consents at first, if he changes his mind and ceases to consent while still being carried away. A very young child does not have the understanding or intelligence to give consent so that the absence of consent will be a necessary inference from its age. In the case of an older child, it is a question of fact for the jury whether the child had sufficient understanding or intelligence to give consent and, if so, whether absence of consent has been proved. Unlike child abduction, the presence or absence of consent on the part of the person having custody or care and control of a child victim is immaterial (except that such consent may support a defence of lawful excuse). Likewise the presence or absence of consent on the part of other people, such as the spouse of a person who is taken, is immaterial.

It must be proved that a person charged with kidnapping knew or was reckless that he did not have the victim's consent.

(d) The taking or carrying away must be without lawful excuse

Clearly, for example, someone with custody of a child will often have a lawful excuse for taking or carrying away the child. An exception would be where this contravenes a court order in relation to the child.

Procedural points

Kidnapping is triable only on indictment. The House of Lords has held that the conduct of a parent who snatches his own child in defiance of a court order relating to its custody or care and control (such as one making the child a ward of court) should normally be dealt with as a contempt of court rather than as the subject matter of a prosecution for kidnapping, unless the parent's conduct was particularly bad.

The Court of Appeal has held that where both child abduction and kidnapping have been committed by a parent, it does not necessarily follow that for policy reasons a charge of kidnapping is always inappropriate.

The consent of the Director of Public Prosecutions to the institution of a prosecution for kidnapping is required wherever the victim is under 16 or where the prosecution is against a person connected with the child (parent or guardian, etc).

SLAVERY AND TRAFFICKING

Slavery, servitude and forced or compulsory labour

A person commits an indictable (either way) offence under the Modern Slavery Act 2015 (MSA 2015), s 1(1) if:

(a) he holds another person in slavery or servitude and the circumstances are such that he knows or ought to know that the other person is held in slavery or servitude; or

(b) he requires another person to perform forced or compulsory labour and the circumstances are such that he knows or ought to know that the other person is being required to perform forced or compulsory labour.

In determining whether a person is being held in slavery or servitude or required to perform forced or compulsory labour, regard may be had to all the circumstances, including (i) any of his personal circumstances (such as his being a child, his family relationships, and any mental or physical illness) which may make him more vulnerable than other persons, and (ii) any work or services provided by the person, including work or services provided in circumstances which constitute exploitation within s 3(3) to (6) (below).

The consent of a person (whether an adult or a child) to any of the acts alleged to constitute holding the person in slavery or servitude, or requiring the person to perform forced or compulsory labour, does not preclude a determination that the person is being held in slavery or servitude, or required to perform forced or compulsory labour.

Human trafficking

A person commits an indictable (either way) offence under MSA 2015, s 2(1) if he arranges or facilitates the travel of another person (V) with a view to V being exploited. It is irrelevant whether V consents to the travel (whether V is an adult or a child). A person may in particular arrange or facilitate V's travel by recruiting V, transporting or transferring V, harbouring or receiving V, or transferring or exchanging control over V.

A person arranges or facilitates V's travel with a view to V being exploited only if:

(a) he intends to exploit V (in any part of the world) during or after the travel; or

(b) he knows or ought to know that another person is likely to exploit V (in any part of the world) during or after the travel.

'Travel' means arriving in, or entering, any country, departing from any country, or travelling within any country. In relation to the repealed trafficking provisions of the Sexual Offences Act 2003, the Court of Appeal has held that the key factor was that travel, a journey, was contemplated. The fact that the journey might be short did not affect whether there had been travel for the purposes of the offence.

'Country' includes territory or other part of the world.

A person who is a UK national commits an offence under s 2(1) regardless of where the arranging or facilitating takes place, or where the travel takes place. 'UK national' means a British citizen, a person who is a British subject by virtue of the British Nationality Act 1981, and who has a right of abode in the UK, or a person who is a British overseas territories citizen by virtue of a connection with Gibraltar.

A person who is not a UK national commits an offence under s 2(1) if any part of the arranging or facilitating takes place in the UK, or the travel consists of arrival in or entry into, departure from, or travel within, the UK.

The Electronic Commerce Directive (Trafficking People for Exploitation) Regulations 2013 makes special provision in connection with an offence under s 2 in relation to information society service providers in order to ensure compatibility with the EU's E-Commerce Directive where such an offence has an international element relating to an EEA member state. As to 'EEA member state', see p 334.

Meaning of exploitation

For the purposes of MSA 2015, s 2, a person is exploited only if one or more of the following provisions apply in relation to him.

Slavery, servitude and forced or compulsory labour   The person is the victim of behaviour which involves the commission of an offence under s 1, or which would involve the commission of an offence under s 1 if it took place in England and Wales (s 3(2)).

Sexual exploitation   Something is done to or in respect of the person which involves the commission of an offence under the Protection of Children Act 1978, s 1(1)(a) (indecent photographs of children) or the Sexual Offences Act 2003, Part 1, or which would involve the commission of such an offence if it were done in England and Wales (s 3(3)).

Removal of organs, etc   The person is encouraged, required or expected to do anything which involves the commission, by him or another person, of an offence under the Human Tissue Act 2004, s 32 or 33 (prohibition of commercial dealings in organs and restrictions on use of live donors), or which would involve the commission of such an offence, by him or another person, if it were done in England and Wales (s 3(4)).

Securing services, etc by force, threats or deception   The person is subjected to force, threats or deception designed to induce him to provide services of any kind, to provide another person with benefits of any kind, or to enable another person to acquire benefits of any kind (s 3(5)).

Securing services, etc from children and vulnerable persons   Another person uses or attempts to use the person for a purpose within s 3(5), having chosen him or her for that purpose on the grounds that (a) he is a child (if under 18), is mentally or physically ill or disabled, or has a family relationship with a particular person, and (b) an adult, or a person without the illness, disability or family relationship, would be likely to refuse to be used for that purpose (s 3(6)).

Anonymity of complainant

An offence under MSA 2015, s 2 is subject to the anonymity rules set out on p 835.

Committing offence with intent to commit offence under MSA 2015, s 2

A person commits an offence under MSA 2015, s 4 if he commits any offence ('the index offence') with the intention of committing an offence under s 2 (including an index offence committed by aiding, abetting, counselling or procuring an offence under s 2). An offence under s 4 is an indictable (either way offence) unless the index offence is kidnapping or false imprisonment, in which case it is triable only on indictment.

Police powers

MSA 2015, s 12 provides that, if a person (P) has been arrested for an offence under s 2, a constable or senior immigration officer may detain a relevant land vehicle, ship (any vessel, including a hovercraft, used in navigation) or aircraft:

(a) until a decision is taken as to whether or not to charge P with the offence,
(b) if P has been charged, until P is acquitted, the charge is dismissed or the proceedings are discontinued, or
(c) if P has been charged and convicted, until the court decides whether or not to order forfeiture of the vehicle, ship or aircraft.

A land vehicle, ship or aircraft is relevant if the constable or officer has reasonable grounds to believe that an order for its forfeiture could be made under s 11 (forfeiture on conviction on indictment of an offence under s 2) if P were convicted of the offence.

A person (other than P) may apply to the court for the release of the land vehicle, ship or aircraft on the grounds that he:

(a) owns the vehicle, ship or aircraft,
(b) was, immediately before the detention of the vehicle, ship or aircraft, in possession of it under a hire-purchase agreement, or
(c) is a charterer of the ship or aircraft.

Preventive orders

MSA 2015, ss 14–22 make provision for 'slavery and trafficking prevention orders' (much like sexual harm prevention orders described on p 840). MSA 2015, ss 23–29 make provision for 'slavery and trafficking risk orders' (much like sexual risk orders described on p 843). Breach of an order made under one of these sets of provisions is an indictable (either way) offence (s 30).

Special provisions about protection of complainants in investigations into a 'human trafficking offence'

The Trafficking People for Exploitation Regulations 2013 provide measures aimed at the protection of complainants where there is a police investigation into a 'human trafficking offence', ie:

(a) an offence under the Sexual Offences Act 2003, ss 57–59A (repealed) (trafficking for sexual exploitation);
(b) an offence under the Asylum and Immigration (Treatment of Claimants, etc) Act 2004, s 4 (repealed) (trafficking people for exploitation);
(c) an offence under MSA 2015, s 2;
(d) attempting or conspiring to commit an offence under (a), (b) or (c), or aiding, abetting, counselling or procuring the commission of such an offence, or an offence of assisting or encouraging such an offence under the Serious Crime Act 2007, Part 2.

Regulation 3 provides that, without prejudice to the rights of the defendant (D: someone who is alleged to have committed, or has committed, a 'human trafficking offence'), and in accordance with an individualised assessment of the personal circumstances of the complainant (C: someone against or in relation to whom a human trafficking offence is alleged to have been committed, or has been committed), the relevant chief officer of police (the chief officer of police for the police area in which an investigation of a human trafficking offence takes place) must ensure that C receives specific treatment aimed at preventing secondary victimisation by avoiding, as far as possible, during an investigation of a human trafficking offence:

(a) unnecessary repetition of interviews;
(b) visual contact between C and D, using appropriate means including communication technologies;
(c) unnecessary questioning concerning C's private life.

By reg 4, where C is under 18, and without prejudice to D's rights, during an investigation of a human trafficking offence, the relevant chief officer of police must ensure that:

(a) interviews with C take place without unjustified delay after the facts have been reported;
(b) interviews with C take place, where necessary, in premises designed or adapted for the purpose;
(c) interviews with C are carried out, where necessary, by or through professionals trained for the purpose;
(d) if possible and where appropriate, the same persons conduct all the interviews with C;
(e) the number of interviews with C is as limited as possible and interviews are carried out only where strictly necessary for the purposes of the investigation;
(f) C may be accompanied by an adult of C's choice, unless a reasoned decision has been made to the contrary in respect of that adult.

Duty to notify Secretary of State about suspected victims of slavery or human trafficking

If a 'public authority', eg a chief officer of police or the NCA, has reasonable grounds to believe that a person may be a victim of slavery or human trafficking it is required by MSA 2015, s 52 to notify:

(a) the Secretary of State; or
(b) if regulations made by the Secretary of State require it to notify a public authority other than the Secretary of State, that public authority.

The information to be included in a notification is specified in the Modern Slavery Act 2015 (Duty to Notify) Regulations 2015. No regulations have been made under (b).

A person is a victim of slavery if he is a victim of conduct which constitutes an offence under s 1, or conduct which would have constituted an offence under s 1 if s 1 had been in force when the conduct occurred. A person is a victim of human trafficking if he is the victim of:

(a) conduct which constitutes an offence under s 2, or would constitute an offence under s 2 if the person responsible for the conduct were a UK national, or

(b) conduct which would have been within (a) if s 2 had been in force when the conduct occurred.

Defence for slavery or trafficking victims who commit an offence

MSA 2015, s 45(1) provides that a person (D) is not guilty of an offence if:

(a) D is 18 or over when he does the act which constitutes the offence;
(b) D does that act because he is compelled to do it;
(c) the compulsion is attributable to slavery or to 'relevant exploitation' (defined below); and
(d) a reasonable person in the same situation and having D's 'relevant characteristics' (defined below) would have no realistic alternative to doing that act.

D may be compelled to do something by another person or by D's circumstances (s 45(2)). Compulsion is attributable to slavery or to relevant exploitation only if:

(i) it is, or is part of, conduct which constitutes an offence under s 1 or conduct which constitutes relevant exploitation; or
(ii) it is a direct consequence of a person being, or having been, a victim of slavery (p 675) or a victim of relevant exploitation (s 45(3)).

'Relevant exploitation' is exploitation (within the meaning of s 3, see p 673) that is attributable to the exploited person being, or having been, a victim of human trafficking (p 675) (s 45(5)).

Section 45(4) provides that a person (D) is not guilty of an offence if:

(a) D is under 18 when he does the act which constitutes the offence;
(b) D does that act as a direct consequence of being, or having been, a victim of slavery or a victim of relevant exploitation; and
(c) a reasonable person in the same situation and having D's relevant characteristics would do that act.

For the above purposes, 'relevant characteristics' means 'age, sex and any physical or mental illness or disability' (s 45(5)). References to an act include an omission (s 45(6)).

Section 45(1) and (4) do not apply in respect of any of the long list of serious offences in Schedule 4. These offences include murder; manslaughter; false imprisonment; kidnapping; perverting the course of justice; offences under: the Infanticide Act 1938, s 1; the Domestic Violence, Crime and Victims Act 2005, s 5; the Infant Life (Preservation) Act 1929, s 1; the Road Traffic Act 1968, ss 1 or 3A; the Offences Against the Person Act 1861, ss 4, 16, 18, 20, 21–23, 28–30, 32, 33 and 38; the Crime and Disorder Act 1998, ss 29 or (if based on the Public Order Act 1986, s 4 or 4A) 31; the Female Genital Mutilation Act 2003, ss 1–3; the Taking of Hostages Act 1982, s 1; the Protection from Harassment Act 1997, ss 4 or 4A; the Child Abduction Act 1984, ss 1 or 2; the Children and Young Persons Act 1933, s 1; the Explosive Substances Act 1883, ss 2–4; the Firearms Act 1968, ss 5, 16, 16A, 17(1) or (2) or 18; the Public Order Act 1936, s 2; the Public Order Act 1986, ss 1 or 2; the Terrorism Act 2000, ss 54–57 or 59; the Terrorism Act 2006, ss 5, 6 or 9–11; the Anti-terrorism, Crime and Security Act 2001, ss 47, 50 or 113; the Sexual Offences Act 2003, ss 1–10,13–15, 16–19, 25, 26, 30–41, 47–50, 61–67 or 70; the Modern Slavery Act 2015, ss 1 or 2; the

Theft Act 1968, ss 8, 9, 10, 12A or 21; the Criminal Damage Act 1971, s 1 (if arson or offence under s 1(2) other than arson); Immigration Act 1971, s 25 (assisting unlawful immigration to EU member state); encouraging or assisting, attempting or conspiring to commit one of these offences, or aiding, abetting, counselling or procuring one of them.

In the case of these offences, or indeed any offence, a prosecutor will still be able to decide not to prosecute a slavery or trafficking victim who may have committed an offence as a direct consequence of his slavery or trafficking, if it would not be in the public interest to do so.

HOSTAGE TAKING

The Taking of Hostages Act 1982, s 1 provides that a person of any nationality commits an offence triable only on indictment if he detains any other person ('the hostage') and, in order to compel any state, international governmental organisation, or person to do or abstain from doing any act, he threatens to kill, injures or continues to detain the hostage. The consent of the Attorney General is required before a prosecution may be brought for this offence.

CONTAMINATION OF GOODS, ETC WITH INTENT

The Public Order Act 1986 (POA 1986), s 38(1) provides that it is an indictable (either way) offence for a person to contaminate or interfere with goods, or make it appear that goods have been contaminated or interfered with, or to place goods which have been contaminated or interfered with, or which have that appearance, in a place where goods of that description are consumed, used, sold or otherwise supplied, with the intention:

(a) of causing public alarm or anxiety;
(b) of causing injury to members of the public consuming or using the goods;
(c) of causing economic loss to any person by reason of (i) the goods being shunned by members of the public, or (ii) steps taken to avoid any such alarm or anxiety, injury or loss.

Section 38(2) makes it an indictable (either way) offence for a person to threaten that he or another will do, or claim that he or another has done, any of the acts referred to in s 38(1) with such intention as is mentioned in (a) or (c) above. This does not include someone who, in good faith, reports or warns that such acts have been, or appear to have been, committed. Thus, the broadcast of a warning received, if carried out in good faith, is excused.

By s 38(3), possession of contaminated goods, apparently contaminated goods, or materials with which to contaminate goods or to make it appear that goods have been contaminated, is also an indictable (either way) offence.

Thus, the activities of groups, calculated to hit at businesses with which they are not in sympathy, are made punishable. However, it must be remembered that such activities may also amount to attempts to commit offences (for example, attempted murder, if poisons are placed in foodstuffs with an intention of killing). In addition, if someone actually consumes a contaminated product and suffers harm, there will be liability for the relevant 'full' offence against the person, depending on the degree of harm.

GUNPOWDER, ETC OFFENCES

The Offences Against the Person Act 1861 (OAPA 1861), ss 28 to 30 and 64 create a number of offences triable only on indictment related to the use or possession of explosives.

Section 28 provides that anyone who unlawfully and maliciously, by the *explosion* of gunpowder or other explosive substance, *burns, maims, disfigures, disables, or does any grievous bodily harm to any person* is guilty of an offence.

Section 29 provides that anyone who unlawfully and maliciously *causes an explosion, or sends or delivers to any person an explosive substance (or any other dangerous or noxious thing), or places or throws at any person any corrosive fluid or any destructive or explosive substance, with intent to burn, maim, disfigure, or disable any person, or to do some grievous bodily harm to any person*, is guilty of an offence, whether or not any bodily injury is effected.

Section 30 provides that it is an offence unlawfully and maliciously to *place or throw in, into, upon, against or near any building or vessel an explosive substance with intent to do any bodily injury to any person, whether or not any explosion occurs and whether or not anyone is injured.*

It has been held that a petrol bomb is an explosive substance under s 29. This decision is equally applicable to the meaning of 'explosive substance' in ss 28 and 30.

Section 64 makes it an offence to make, manufacture or knowingly possess any explosive substance or machine, engine or instrument with intent to commit any offence under OAPA 1861, or for the purpose of enabling others to do so.

CHAPTER 24

Disputes

Quite a large part of a police officer's time is spent in advising members of the public of action which they may take in relation to disputes involving them and their spouses, cohabitants, other members of their families, landlords, and the like. On occasion it is appropriate to have recourse to the criminal law, but on most occasions the most useful approach may be to put them in touch with one of the various agencies which are equipped to deal with such situations. In many cases civil remedies are available and particularly appropriate.

DOMESTIC VIOLENCE AND ABUSE

The government's definition of domestic violence and abuse is: any incident or pattern of incidents of controlling, coercive, threatening behaviour, violence or abuse between those aged 16 or over who are, or have been, intimate partners or family members, regardless of gender or sexuality. The abuse can encompass, but is not limited to, psychological, physical, sexual, financial or emotional abuse.

Reference is made below to the victim of domestic violence or abuse as a woman but—as the previous paragraph recognises—it must not be forgotten that sometimes the victim is a man. A woman who has been injured by her husband, civil partner or cohabitant is competent and compellable to give evidence against that person in a criminal court in relation to the offence in question, and may wish to do so. Likewise, a family member who has been subject to domestic violence or abuse is competent and compellable. However, it will be appreciated that this is frequently an extremely difficult decision for a wife, partner or family member to make. Many women, for example, feel trapped and helpless and, being unable to face up to life on their own, prefer to remain with a man who treats them badly. In such circumstances they will not wish to give evidence against him because of their fear that this will lead to a final breakdown of the relationship. The social services are experienced in the handling of these situations and will help if the woman will accept such aid.

Domestic violence or abuse, particularly domestic violence, can result in civil proceedings (pp 680–6) or in liability for one of the various offences under the criminal law which are not limited to such conduct. In addition, it may constitute the following offence.

Controlling or coercive behaviour in an intimate or family relationship

Under the Serious Crime Act 2015, s 76(1), a person (A) commits an indictable (either way) offence if:

(a) A repeatedly or continuously engages in behaviour towards another person (B) that is controlling or coercive;

(b) at the time of the behaviour, A and B are personally connected;

(c) the behaviour has a serious effect on B; and

(d) A knows or ought to know that the behaviour will have a serious effect on B.

For the purposes of (d), A 'ought to know' that which a reasonable person in possession of the same information would know.

A and B are 'personally connected':

(a) if A is in an intimate personal relationship with B; or

(b) if A and B live together and they are members of the same family, or they have previously been in an intimate personal relationship with each other.

A and B are members of the same family if:

(a) they are, or have been, married to each other;

(b) they are or have been, civil partners of each other;

(c) they are relatives;

(d) they have agreed to marry one another (whether or not the agreement has been terminated);

(e) they have entered into a civil partnership agreement (whether or not the agreement has been terminated);

(f) they are both parents of the same child (ie someone under 18);

(g) they have, or have had, parental responsibility for the same child.

Examples of coercive or controlling behaviour can include violence, threats, humiliation and intimidation or other abuse used to harm, punish or frighten the victim (coercive behaviour); or acts designed to make a person subordinate and/or dependent, for example by limiting someone's access to family, friends or finances, by controlling someone's access to social media accounts, by surveillance through apps, by dictating what someone wears, or by threats to reveal or publish private information.

A does not commit an offence under s 76(1) if at the time of the behaviour in question:

(a) A has parental responsibility for B, or is otherwise legally liable to maintain B, or has care of him; and

(b) B is under 16 (s 76(3)).

A's behaviour has a 'serious effect' on B if it causes B to fear, on at least two occasions, that violence will be used against B, or if it causes B serious alarm or distress which has a substantial adverse effect on B's usual day-to-day activities.

It is a defence for A to show that:

(a) in engaging in the behaviour in question, A believed that he or she was acting in B's best interests; and

(b) the behaviour was in all the circumstances reasonable (s 76(8)).

A is to be taken to have shown these facts if sufficient evidence of the facts is adduced to raise an issue with respect to them, and the contrary is not proved beyond reasonable doubt (s 76(9)). This defence is not available to A in relation to behaviour that causes B to fear that violence will be used against B (s 76(10)).

The Secretary of State has issued guidance about the investigation of offences under s 76.

Non-molestation orders

Where a woman (or member of a family who is a child) has been subjected to domestic violence, she can seek assistance by applying in civil family proceedings for a non-molestation order under the Family Law Act 1996 (FLA 1996), s 42, which is not limited to proceedings between current or former spouses, civil partners or cohabitants.

A non-molestation order is an order containing either or both of the following provisions:

(a) prohibiting a person (the respondent, R) from molesting another person who is associated with R; and

(b) prohibiting R from molesting a relevant child.

A non-molestation order may be made:

(a) on the application (whether in other family proceedings or without any other family proceedings being instituted) of a person who is associated with R; or

(b) during family proceedings to which R is a party, if the court considers that such an order will benefit any other party or a relevant child even though no application has been made.

The Court of Appeal has held that 'molestation' in the present context implies some deliberate conduct aimed at a high degree of 'harassment' (as defined on p 660) of the other party, sufficient to call for the intervention of the court.

By FLA 1996, s 62, a person is 'associated with' R if they are spouses (or ex-spouses), civil partners (or ex-civil partners), or cohabitants (or ex-cohabitants), or members (or ex-members) of the same household, or relatives, or are or have been engaged, or have or have had an intimate personal relationship which is or was of significant duration, or are parties to family proceedings other than proceedings for a non-molestation order. In addition, in relation to a child (ie someone under 18), a person is associated with R if each of them is a parent of the child or has had parental responsibility for it. Where a child has been adopted or freed for adoption, two persons are associated with each other if one is its natural parent (or a parent of such a natural parent) and the other is the child or someone who is its adoptive parent (or an applicant for adoption) or with whom the child has been placed for adoption.

A 'relevant child' in relation to such proceedings is any child who is living with or might reasonably be expected to live with either party to the proceedings, or any child in relation to whom an order under the Adoption Act 1976, the Adoption and Children Act 2002 or the Children Act 1989 is in question in the proceedings, or any other child whose interests the court considers relevant.

In deciding whether to make a non-molestation order, the court must consider all the circumstances, including the need to secure the health, safety and well-being of the applicant or any relevant child.

A non-molestation order may refer to molestation in general, to particular acts of molestation, or both. It may be made for a specified period, or until a further order is made. An order which is made in other family proceedings ceases to have effect if those proceedings are withdrawn or dismissed.

Application without notice to the other party

Where it appears to be just and convenient to do so a court may, under FLA 1996, s 45(1), make a non-molestation order even though the party against whom the complaint is made (the respondent, R) has not been given notice of the proceedings. In such cases, the court must consider:

(a) the risk of significant harm if the order is not made immediately;

(b) whether if such an order is not made the applicant is likely to be deterred or prevented from pursuing the application; and

(c) whether there is reason to believe that R is aware of the proceedings but is deliberately evading service of the notice and the applicant, or a relevant child, will be seriously prejudiced by the delay involved in effecting service (or substituted service) of the proceedings.

Where an order is made on an application without notice to R, it must afford R an opportunity to make representations as soon as just and convenient at a full hearing.

Arrest warrant

Where a non-molestation order has been made, and the applicant considers that R has failed to comply with it, the applicant may apply to the court for a warrant to arrest R.

Offence of breaching non-molestation order

Under FLA 1996, s 42A(1), a person who without reasonable excuse does anything that he is prohibited from doing by a non-molestation order is guilty of an indictable (either way) offence. In the case of an order made without notice to the other party, a person can be guilty of the offence only in respect of conduct engaged in when he was aware of the existence of the order. Where a defendant has adduced evidence which raises the issue of reasonable excuse, the prosecution must disprove reasonable excuse beyond reasonable doubt.

Undertakings

Where a non-molestation order could be made, a court may accept an undertaking from any party to the proceedings. Breach of such an undertaking is not an offence. However, the undertaking is enforceable in civil law in the same way as a court order, except that no power of arrest attaches to its breach.

Domestic violence protection notices and orders

The Crime and Security Act 2010 empowers a superintendent (or above) to issue a domestic violence protection notice (DVPN). A DVPN prohibits a suspected perpetrator (P) from molesting a victim of domestic violence (V) and, where they cohabit, may require P to leave those premises. Sections 24 to 26 deal with DVPNs.

The issue of a DVPN triggers an application for a domestic violence protection order (DVPO), which is an order lasting between 14 and 28 days. A DVPO prohibits P from molesting V and may also make provision about access to shared accommodation by P and V. Sections 27 to 30 deal with DVPOs.

Under the scheme the police and courts can protect V when V is most vulnerable, in the immediate aftermath of an attack, by preventing P from contacting V or returning home for up to 28 days. This helps victims who may otherwise have had to flee their home and gives them the space and time to access the support they need and to consider their options.

The scheme is intended to plug a gap in protection for victims of domestic violence due to either the police being unable to charge the perpetrator due to lack of evidence (so V cannot be protected through strict bail conditions) or the process for granting longer-term non-molestation orders taking several days or weeks to apply for.

DVPN

A DVPN may be issued to P, if P is aged 18 or over, where the authorising officer (superintendent (or above)) has reasonable grounds for believing that:

(a) P has been violent, or has threatened violence, towards an associated person, V, and

(b) the issue of a notice is necessary in order to protect V from violence or the threat of violence by P.

An 'associated person' has the same meaning as in FLA 1996, s 62 (see p 681).

Before issuing a DVPN, the authorising officer must consider the welfare of any child whose interests the officer considers relevant. He must take reasonable steps to find out the opinion of V as to whether the DVPN should be issued. Consideration must also be given to any representation P makes in relation to the issuing of the DVPN. Where the DVPN is to include conditions in relation to the occupation of premises shared by P and V, reasonable steps must also be taken to find out the opinion of any other associated person who lives in the premises. The issue of the DVPN does not require V's consent, as the authorising officer may nevertheless have reason to believe that V requires protection from P.

A DVPN must contain provision to prohibit P from molesting V for the duration of the DVPN, which may be expressed so as to refer to molestation in general, particular acts of molestation, or both.

Where P and V share living premises, the DVPN may explicitly:

(a) require P to leave the premises; or

(b) prohibit P from evicting or excluding V from the premises, from entering the premises, or from coming within a certain distance of the premises (as specified in the DVPN) for the duration of the DVPN.

It does not matter for these purposes whether the premises are owned or rented in the name of P or V.

Where a DVPN is issued which prevents P from entering (or requires P to leave) premises, and the authorising officer believes that P is subject to service law and the premises are service living accommodation, he must make reasonable efforts to inform P's commanding officer that the notice has been issued.

The DVPN must state the grounds for issuing a DVPN; that a constable may arrest without warrant if he has reasonable grounds to believe that P is in breach of the DVPN; that the police will make an application for a DVPO which will be heard in court within a 48-hour period and a notice of the hearing will be given to P; that the DVPN will continue to be in effect until the DVPO application is determined; and the provision that may be included in a subsequent DVPO. A DVPN must be in writing and only be served on P personally by a constable. The constable serving the DVPN must ask P to supply an address in order to enable P to be given notice of the hearing for the DVPO.

If he has reasonable grounds to believe that P is in breach of the DVPN, a constable may arrest P without warrant as set out above. P must then be held in custody and brought within a period of 24 hours before the magistrates' court that will hear the application for the DVPO. In calculating the end of that period, a Sunday, Christmas Day, Good Friday or a Bank Holiday is disregarded. However, if the DVPO hearing has already been arranged to take place within that 24-hour period, then P must be brought before the court for *that* hearing. If P is brought before the court in advance of the DVPO hearing, the court may remand P; it may also remand P if it adjourns the hearing.

DVPO

Once a DVPN has been issued, a constable must apply by complaint to a magistrates' court for a DVPO. The magistrates' court hearing must be no later than 48 hours (calculated as for a DVPN) after the time when the DVPN was served. Notice of the hearing must be given to P. Where no address has been given by P, the court must be satisfied that reasonable efforts have been made to give P the notice of the hearing.

If the hearing of the application is adjourned, the DVPN continues in effect until the application is determined by the court. V is not compelled to attend the hearing of an application for a DVPO, or to answer questions (unless V has given oral or written evidence at the hearing).

Two conditions must be met for a DVPO to be made:

(a) the court must be satisfied on the balance of probabilities that P has been violent, or threatened violence, towards an associated person, V;

(b) the court must think that the DVPO is necessary to secure the protection of V from violence, or the threat of violence, by P.

Before making a DVPO, the court must consider: the welfare of any person under 18 whose interests the court considers relevant to the DVPO; the opinion (if known) of V; and, where the DVPO is to include conditions in relation to the occupation of premises shared by P and V, the opinion (if known) of any other associated person who lives in the premises. The court may issue a DVPO regardless of whether or not V consents.

A DVPO must contain provision explicitly prohibiting P from molesting V for the duration of the DVPO. The prohibition may be expressed so as to refer to molestation in general, particular acts of molestation, or both. Where P and V share living premises, the DVPO may explicitly: prohibit P from evicting or excluding V from the premises; prohibit P from entering the premises; require P to leave the premises; or prohibit P from coming within a certain distance of the premises (as specified in the DVPO). The DVPO must state that a constable may arrest P without warrant if he has reasonable grounds for believing that P is in breach of the DVPO.

A DVPO may be in force for a minimum of 14 days, and a maximum of 28 days, from the day on which it is made. It must state the period for which it is to be in force.

If P is arrested for breach of a DVPO, P must be held in custody and brought before a magistrates' court within a 24-hour period (calculated as for a DVPN). If the matter is not disposed of when P is brought before the court, the court may remand P.

General

Like various other orders, a DVPO is a civil order. As the proceedings are civil in nature the law of civil evidence applies. Under that law, the court can also take into account evidence of bad character untrammelled by the conditions for doing so in criminal proceedings under the Criminal Justice Act 2003, s 101. In determining whether the conditions are met the court can also take into account hearsay evidence admissible under the Civil Evidence Act 1995 (CEA 1995).

Under CEA 1995, s 1, subject to certain safeguards in later sections, hearsay evidence is admitted in civil cases.

CEA 1995, s 1 does not give a party to a civil action an unfettered right to introduce hearsay evidence in proceedings. In particular, a statement is not admissible at all if the maker of it (not the witness but the person whose words it is sought to admit) would not have been a competent witness. In addition a number of sections provide specific safeguards as follows.

CEA 1995, s 4 provides that in estimating the degree of weight which is given to the statement the court 'shall have regard to any circumstances from which any inference can reasonably be drawn as to the reliability or otherwise of the evidence'. Section 4(2) lists a number of factors to which the court should have regard in assessing weight but does not restrict the court to these factors. Factors listed include whether it would have been reasonable and practicable to call the maker of the statement, whether the statement was contemporaneous with events narrated in it, and whether the statement involved multiple hearsay.

CEA 1995, s 5 allows the credibility of the maker of the statement to be impeached and also allows the admission of inconsistent statements made by the maker of the statement. With the leave of the court the maker of the statement, if available, may be called as a witness.

Normally, CEA 1995, s 2 provides that a party proposing to adduce hearsay evidence must give notice to that effect and provide further details if requested to do so by the other party to the action. The Magistrates' Courts (Hearsay Evidence in Civil Proceedings) Rules 1999 require a party who desires to give hearsay evidence to serve a hearsay notice not less than 21 days before the date fixed for the hearing. Failure to give notice (or provide further details if requested) does not affect the admissibility of the evidence but may affect the weight that is given to it. CEA 1995, s 2 does not, however, apply to DVPO proceedings.

If what are relied on are oral statements to a police officer, the officer should give direct evidence of what was said and the circumstances in which it was said.

Rights associated with the matrimonial home

Where domestic disputes occur, regardless of whether or not a non-molestation order or a DVPO has been sought, there is the issue of rights of occupation in relation to the home. FLA 1996 deals with this.

Where one spouse has no estate, etc

FLA 1996, s 30 provides that, where one spouse or civil partner (X) is legally entitled to occupy a dwelling house and the other spouse or civil partner (Y) has no such legal entitlement, Y has 'home rights' which means that:

(a) if Y is in occupation, Y has a right not to be evicted or excluded from the dwelling house or any part of it by X without the leave of the court under FLA 1996, s 33 (occupation order provisions); and

(b) if Y is not in occupation, Y has a right with the leave of the court under FLA 1996, s 33 to enter and occupy the dwelling house.

There is, therefore, no lawful way by which one party to a marriage or civil partnership can be removed from the home without the circumstances being examined by a civil court.

Occupation orders

FLA 1996, s 33 provides for the making of an occupation order where the applicant (A) has an estate or interest, etc entitling him to occupy a dwelling house or has home rights in it and the dwelling house is or has been the home of A and of someone else (the respondent, R) with whom he is associated (or was intended by both such people to be their home). If an occupation order is made it may:

(a) enforce A's occupation rights as against R;
(b) require R to permit A to enter and remain in that dwelling house or part of it;
(c) regulate the occupation by either or both parties;

(d) if R is entitled via an estate or interest, etc to occupy, prohibit, restrict or suspend the exercise by him of his occupation rights;

(e) if R has home rights and A is the other spouse or civil partner, restrict or terminate those rights;

(f) require R to leave the dwelling house or part of it; or

(g) exclude R from a defined area in which the dwelling house is included.

In deciding whether to make an occupation order and (if so) in what manner, the court must have regard to all of the circumstances including the housing needs and housing resources of both parties and any relevant child (as defined on p 681), the financial resources of both parties, the likely effect of any order (or of a failure to make an order) on the health, safety or well-being of each party and any relevant child, and the conduct of the parties in relation to each other and otherwise.

Former spouse, etc not entitled to occupy, and situations in which neither spouse, former spouse, etc entitled to occupy

FLA 1996 makes similar provisions for occupation orders in relation to former spouses or civil partners, and cohabitants or former cohabitants, where one of them is legally entitled to occupy a dwelling house, and the other is not. It also makes provision for occupation orders in circumstances in which neither spouse or civil partner or cohabitant (or ex-spouse or ex-civil partner or ex-cohabitant) has a legal entitlement to occupy a dwelling house which is (or was) the matrimonial home. These provisions are set out in ss 35 to 38.

Breaches of occupation order and other points

Under FLA 1996, s 47, there is a power to arrest without warrant for breach of an occupation order where such a power has been attached to the order; otherwise an application must be made for an arrest warrant. 'Undertakings' and orders without notice to the other party may be made in respect of these orders in the same way as in the case of non-molestation orders.

EVICTION AND HARASSMENT

The Protection from Eviction Act 1977 (PEA 1977), s 1 provides three indictable (either way) offences whose aim is to protect tenants: the offence of eviction and two offences of harassment. The Act specifically authorises district councils to institute proceedings for these offences.

The offences use the term 'residential occupier'. In relation to any premises, the term means a person occupying the premises as a residence, whether under a contract or by virtue of any enactment or rule of law giving him the right to remain in occupation or restricting the right of any other person to recover possession of the premises. Therefore, a tenant, or even a lodger who is living in a furnished room under an agreement with the owner, is a residential occupier. However, someone like a lodger who simply had a contractual licence which has expired is not a residential occupier. A squatter is not a residential occupier of the premises.

Eviction

PEA 1977, s 1(2) provides that if any person unlawfully deprives the residential occupier of any premises of his occupation of the premises or any part thereof, or attempts to do so, he is guilty of an offence unless he proves that he believed, and had reasonable cause to believe, that the residential occupier had ceased to reside in the premises.

It is not necessary that any form of violence or intimidation is used; it would be sufficient if the residential occupier was tricked into leaving so that the owner could regain occupation, or that the owner entered by stealth during the residential occupier's absence. The deprivation of occupation need not be permanent. Consequently, a person who unlawfully excludes a residential occupier from his premises, intending the exclusion to be permanent, can be convicted under s 1(2) even though he repents almost immediately and lets the occupier back in.

The commission of the offence is not restricted to the owner or any person having an interest in the property; it can be committed by anyone (eg an employee of the owner) who unlawfully deprives, or attempts to deprive, a residential occupier of his premises.

It is a defence to prove a reasonable belief that the residential occupier has ceased to reside in the premises.

Harassment

PEA 1977, s 1(3) deals with harassment and provides that if any person with intent to cause the residential occupier of any premises:

(a) to give up the occupation of the premises or any part thereof; or
(b) to refrain from exercising any right or pursuing any remedy in respect of the premises or part thereof;

does any act likely to interfere with the peace or comfort of the residential occupier or members of his household, or persistently withdraws or withholds services reasonably required for the occupation of the premises as a residence, he is guilty of an offence.

Provided that it is likely to interfere with the peace or comfort of the residential occupier, any *act*, such as intimidation, threats, or even interference with the building, perhaps by removing window frames or doors on the pretence that they are to be replaced, will do; the House of Lords has held that it is irrelevant that the act in question was not wrongful in civil law. Alternatively the offence can consist of a *lack of action* which results in services reasonably required for the occupation of the premises being persistently withdrawn or withheld, as where the landlord fails to pay for essential services to the premises occupied by the tenant. The use of the word 'persistently' which is used as an adverb to both 'withdraws' and 'withholds' indicates that this must be done for some period of time.

The intention must be to cause the *residential occupier* to give up permanently occupation of the premises or to refrain from exercising any right or pursuing any remedy in respect of the premises or part of them.

Proof of the requisite intention under s 1(3) may not always be easy. Consequently, s 1(3A) provides that the landlord of a residential occupier or an agent of the landlord commits an offence if he does acts likely to interfere with the peace or comfort of the residential occupier or members of his family, or if he persistently withdraws or withholds services reasonably required for the occupation of the premises, and (in either case) *he knows or has reasonable cause to believe that this conduct is likely to cause* the residential occupier to give up occupation of the whole or part of the premises or to refrain from exercising any right or pursuing any remedy in respect of the whole or any part of the premises. A person is not guilty under s 1(3A) if he proves that he had reasonable grounds for doing the acts or withdrawing or withholding the services in question.

Caravans: eviction and harassment

The Caravan Sites Act 1968 (CSA 1968), s 3 provides similar indictable (either way) offences to those under PEA 1977 in relation to a residential caravan on a protected site. The Act only applies in England. The Mobile Homes (Wales) Act 2013 makes similar provision in Wales. See Chapter 24 on the companion website.

Police action

The primary duty of police officers will always be the prevention of a breach of the peace. When allegations are made concerning a dispute affecting a landlord and tenant a police officer should make all inquiries which are possible at that time at the scene of the dispute. If it appears that there might have been an offence in relation to the provisions outlined above in respect of dwellings or caravans, the officer should explain the provisions to the landlord and should warn him of the possibility of prosecution. However, whether or not such a warning is issued at the time, a comprehensive report of the circumstances should be sent to the local housing authority immediately. In appropriate cases, the police should inform the complainant in writing that the complaint has been referred to the housing authority.

CHAPTER 25

Homicide and Related Offences

The following homicide offences are dealt with in this chapter: murder, manslaughter, infanticide, and corporate manslaughter. The various 'death by driving' offences were dealt with in Chapters 9 and 14.

MURDER

Murder is a common law offence triable only on indictment. It is committed where someone unlawfully kills another human being, who is under the Queen's peace, with intent unlawfully to kill or cause grievous bodily harm.

In three types of exceptional case a person is not guilty of murder, but only of voluntary manslaughter, even though the definition of murder is satisfied. Those exceptions are where the defendant (D) was suffering from diminished responsibility, has the defence of loss of control or was acting in pursuance of a suicide pact.

With the exception of the reference to D's intent, the terms of the definition of murder also apply to involuntary manslaughter, which is discussed later in this chapter.

Unlawfully

A killing is unlawful unless it falls within one of the following categories:

Prevention of crime or effecting arrest

It is lawful to use such force as is *reasonable* in the circumstances as D believed them to be in the prevention of a crime under the law of England and Wales or in effecting (or assisting in) the lawful arrest of offenders, suspected offenders or persons unlawfully at large. See, further, pp 655–7.

Self-defence and defence of another or of property

Self-defence and defence of another or of property render a killing lawful if the force used is *reasonable* in the circumstances as D believed them to be. See, further, pp 656–7.

Misadventure

Death is caused by misadventure where the killing is not murder, manslaughter or any other offence of homicide. As an example, if a patient dies as a result of a lawful operation carried out by a surgeon with proper care, the killing is by misadventure, and so not unlawful, and therefore the surgeon is not guilty of any offence of homicide.

Kills

Generally, some form of action is required which proves to be a substantial cause of death. However, 'substantial' in this context simply means 'more than minimal'. Although generally some 'act' is required, if D is under a legally recognised duty to act (as where a parent or similar person has the care of a child or helpless person), and fails to act, that failure being a substantial cause of death, he may be convicted of an offence of homicide.

If D's original act was a substantial cause of death it does not matter that some other intervening event finally caused the death, provided that this intervening event (as opposed to its details) was reasonably foreseeable in the ordinary course of things. If D knocks V unconscious on the beach and V is killed by the incoming tide, D's act is regarded in law as the cause of V's death because the incoming tide was clearly reasonably foreseeable. On the other hand, if two men (D and V) fight in a park and D leaves V unconscious but not seriously hurt and V is later killed by a tree which falls upon him when it is blown down by a gale, the fact that the fall of the tree was not reasonably foreseeable means that D's act is not regarded in law as a cause of V's death. A similar rule applies where D threatens someone who takes evasive action and is killed in doing so, as where a woman jumps out of a first-floor window to avoid rape. Provided that the evasive action is likely, the threat will be a cause of death if it was a substantial cause (as almost inevitably it will be).

If the injuries inflicted by D are an operating cause of death it is irrelevant that an intervening act by a third party also contributed to the death, provided that D's act was a substantial contribution. Suppose that D causes such serious injuries to V that V can only be kept alive by a life-support machine. If, subsequently, because there is no hope of recovery, doctors switch off that machine, D has still killed that person as his act was a substantial and operating cause of death. Suppose, on the other hand, that D's act is not an operating cause of death but merely provides the setting in which an intervening act by a third party is the immediate cause of death. D's act will not be a legal cause of death unless the third party's act is not free or not deliberate or not informed. In one case D, in attempting to evade arrest, snatched a girl in front of him as he fired at police officers. The officers fired back instinctively, killing the girl. Although the officers' act resulted in the girl's death, it was held that D's act was in law a cause of the girl's death; the officers' reaction was instinctive (and therefore not deliberate) and was done in self-defence (and therefore not free).

Even where negligence in the treatment of a victim was the immediate cause of death, this does not exclude D's responsibility, unless the original injury had ceased to be an operative cause of death and the negligent treatment was so independent of D's acts and itself so potent in causing death that D's contribution was insignificant.

Sometimes a victim contributes to his death by doing something (other than taking evasive action, dealt with above) after D's act. The normal rule here is that if the victim's intervening act is not free, or is not deliberate, or is not informed, D's act will be a legal cause of death, whereas if the victim's act was free, deliberate and informed D's act will not be a legal cause of death.

If an act is committed which leads to death, it is legally immaterial that the person injured had a medical condition rendering him more susceptible to death (eg haemophilia or a weak heart) or refused medical treatment. A person who commits violent acts must take his victim as he finds him, including the victim's mental condition or, even, the victim's religion. Where a girl, who was a Jehovah's witness, was stabbed by an assailant and refused a blood transfusion required before surgery and died, the act of her attacker was held to be a cause of her death.

The victim

Any human being, however deformed or subnormal, is protected by the law of homicide.

This raises the question of the point of time at which a foetus becomes a human being. The law of homicide only protects those who have been born alive, and this requires that a child must have completely emerged into the world and have a separate existence from its mother. To have had that separate existence it is not essential that the cord has been severed or even that the afterbirth has been expelled, but it must have breathed.

The wilful destruction of a child capable of being born alive before it is born alive may amount to the offence of child destruction, while the intentional procuring of a miscarriage may constitute the offence of abortion; see p 700. If someone injures a pregnant woman, and as a result of the attack she goes into premature labour and her child, although born alive, subsequently dies owing to its prematurity, the assailant is guilty of manslaughter but cannot be convicted of murder despite the fact that he intended to kill the woman or seriously harm her. It would make no difference that he intended also to destroy the foetus in the womb because such an intent does not suffice for murder.

Under the Queen's peace

For the purposes of homicide offences, all persons are under the Queen's peace whether they are Her Majesty's subjects or not, with the exception of alien enemies (and possibly rebel subjects) in the actual heat and exercise of war.

Lapse of time between act and death

An offence of homicide may be committed by a person who carries out an appropriate act with the necessary mens rea regardless of the time which has passed since the injury, etc was inflicted. However, where the injury alleged to have caused the death was sustained more than three years before the death occurred, or where the person whom it is intended to prosecute for an offence of homicide has already been convicted of an offence in circumstances alleged to be connected with the death, no prosecution for an offence of homicide may be brought without the consent of the Attorney General. These provisions also apply to the offences of encouraging or assisting suicide and of causing or allowing the death of a child or vulnerable adult.

Intent unlawfully to kill or cause grievous bodily harm

The mens rea required for murder is an intent unlawfully to kill another human being or unlawfully to cause grievous bodily harm to another human being. This is described as 'malice aforethought'. 'Malice' is a misleading term because an intentional killing motivated by compassion (a mercy killing) is murder unless reduced to manslaughter on grounds of diminished responsibility. 'Aforethought' is also misleading because it suggests that the killing must have been premeditated, which is certainly not a legal requirement. Provided that D's fatal act was done with intent unlawfully to kill or cause grievous bodily harm, it is irrelevant that he acted on the spur of the moment, the intention only being formed a brief second before the killing. A person who intends to kill or cause grievous bodily harm will not intend to do so unlawfully if on the facts, as he believes them, his use of force is reasonable to prevent crime or in self-defence.

MANSLAUGHTER

Manslaughter is a term which covers a variety of unlawful homicides which do not amount to murder. Manslaughter continues to be a common law offence triable only on indictment. There are two varieties: voluntary and involuntary manslaughter.

Voluntary manslaughter

Voluntary manslaughters embody all the characteristics of murder including the necessary malice aforethought. It is the presence of particular circumstances acting upon the mind of the defendant, which has the effect of reducing the nature of the crime to voluntary manslaughter. These circumstances are: where the person was acting under 'loss of control' at the material time; where the person was suffering from 'diminished responsibility' at that time; and where a killing occurred in consequence of a suicide pact. Each of these circumstances operates as a partial *defence* to a charge of murder, reducing liability to manslaughter. A person cannot, for example, be charged with manslaughter under loss of control.

Loss of control

The Coroners and Justice Act 2009 (C&JA 2009), s 54(1) provides that where a person (D) kills or is a party to the killing of another (V), D is not to be convicted of murder if:

(a) D's acts and omissions in doing or being a party to the killing resulted from D's loss of self-control,
(b) the loss of self-control had a qualifying trigger, and
(c) a person of D's sex and age, with a normal degree of tolerance and self-restraint and in the circumstances of D, might have reacted in the same or in a similar way to D.

D does not have to prove the defence. If sufficient evidence is adduced to raise an issue with respect to the defence under s 54(1), the jury must assume that the defence is satisfied unless the prosecution proves beyond reasonable doubt that it is not.

The fact that one party to a killing is by virtue of the defence of loss of control not liable to be convicted of murder does not affect the question whether the killing amounted to murder in the case of any other party to it.

Section 54(2) provides that it does not matter whether or not the loss of self-control was sudden. However, by s 54(4) the defence does not apply if, in doing or being a party to the killing, D acted in a considered desire for revenge.

Qualifying trigger   D's loss of self-control must have had a qualifying trigger. By s 55(2)–(5), a loss of self-control would have a qualifying trigger if D's loss of self-control was attributable to:

(a) D's fear of serious violence from V against D or another identified person; or
(b) a thing or things done or said (or both) which:
   (i)   constituted circumstances of an extremely grave character, and
   (ii) caused D to have a justifiable sense of being seriously wronged; or
(c) a combination of the above matters.

There are two limits to the first trigger (ie (a)):

- the fear of serious violence must be of violence from V, the person killed; and
- the fear must be of such violence to D or some other identified person.

In determining whether a loss of self-control had a qualifying trigger, D's fear of serious violence must be disregarded to the extent that it was caused by a thing which D incited to be done or said for the purpose of providing an excuse to use violence.

The second trigger (ie (b)) deals with cases of gross provocation. In determining whether a loss of self-control had a qualifying trigger:

- a sense of being seriously wronged by a thing done or said is not justifiable if D incited the thing to be done or said for the purpose of providing an excuse to use violence;
- the fact that a thing done or said constituted sexual infidelity must be disregarded. (However, the Court of Appeal has held that, although sexual infidelity must be disregarded where it is the only element in support of a qualifying trigger, sexual infidelity may be relied on when it is not the only element relied on in support and is integral to and forms an essential part of the context.)

Objective requirement   Assuming the other two requirements in s 54(1) are satisfied, D is not guilty of murder if a person of D's sex and age, with a normal degree of tolerance and self-restraint and in the circumstances of D, might have reacted in the same or in a similar way to D. As can be seen this requirement is not wholly objective. It is not simply concerned with whether someone with a normal degree of tolerance and self-restraint might have reacted as D did (ie might he have reacted, and if so might he have reacted as D did?) but also whether a person of D's sex and age (the latter in particular may be relevant to tolerance and self-restraint) and in D's circumstances might have reacted as D did. However, not all D's circumstances can be taken into account. This is because s 54(3) provides that the reference in s 54(1)(c) to 'the circumstances of D' is a reference to all of D's circumstances other than those whose only relevance to D's conduct is that they bear on D's general capacity for tolerance or self-restraint. The closing words of s 54(3) make it clear that characteristics or other circumstances whose only relevance to D's conduct is that they bear on D's general capacity for tolerance or self-restraint cannot be referred to in applying the present requirement. Thus, the fact that D was intoxicated or intolerant or irritable or excessively jealous or had problems in controlling his impulses or otherwise had impaired powers of self-control must be ignored.

Diminished responsibility

The Homicide Act 1957, s 2 governs this defence. Section 2(1) provides that a person (D) who kills or is a party to the killing of another is not to be convicted of murder if D proves that he was suffering from an abnormality of mental functioning which:

(a) arose from a recognised medical condition;
(b) substantially impaired D's ability to do one or more of the things mentioned below; and
(c) provides an explanation for D's acts and omissions in doing or being a party to the killing.

The things referred to in (b) are set out in s 2(1A). They are:

(i)   to understand the nature of D's conduct;
(ii) to form a rational judgement;
(iii) to exercise self-control.

As regards (c), by s 2(1B), an abnormality of mental functioning provides an explanation for D's conduct if it causes, or is a significant contributory factor in causing, D to carry out that conduct. This means that abnormality of mental functioning need not be the sole cause of D's conduct. Thus, for example, the fact that other explanations or causes were also operative does not in itself negate the defence of diminished responsibility.

Although acute intoxication is a recognised medical condition, the Court of Appeal has held that the defence of diminished responsibility cannot be based on it.

Suicide pacts

The Homicide Act 1957, s 4 declares that it is manslaughter, and not murder, for a person to kill another or be party to someone else killing another, if he was acting in pursuance of a suicide pact between himself and the person killed. This is a matter for the defence to prove.

A 'suicide pact' is a common agreement between two or more persons, having for its object the death of them all, whether or not each is to take his own life. Nothing done by a person entering into a suicide pact may be treated as in pursuance of such a pact unless it is done while he has the settled intention of dying in pursuance of the pact.

Involuntary manslaughter

This category covers cases where D, who has unlawfully killed another (ie has committed the actus reus of murder), is not guilty of murder because he lacked malice aforethought but acted with some lesser degree of mens rea.

There are three types of involuntary manslaughter, between which there is a degree of overlap:

(a) killing by an unlawful and dangerous act;
(b) killing by gross negligence; and
(c) killing with recklessness as to death or serious bodily harm.

Killing by an unlawful and dangerous act

This mode of committing manslaughter is commonly known as 'constructive manslaughter'. It cannot be committed by an omission to act; an unlawful act by D is required. Three elements must be proved by the prosecution:

(1) *That D has committed the actus reus of an offence (other than homicide) with the mens rea required for that offence*; proof of this is proof of the 'unlawful act'. In most cases the offence will be a battery, but constructive manslaughter is certainly not limited to that offence; for example it is not unusual for a constructive manslaughter conviction to be based on an offence of administering a noxious thing (see p 665). However, the mere supplying of a noxious thing to another who then freely, deliberately and voluntarily injects himself with it will not amount to an offence of administration of a noxious thing and therefore is not an unlawful act and cannot make the supplier guilty of constructive manslaughter. Dangerous driving or careless driving which results in death can never constitute constructive manslaughter.

(2) *That the unlawful act was dangerous.* For an unlawful act to be dangerous it must be such that all sober and reasonable people would inevitably recognise that it must subject another person to the risk of some physical harm (including physical harm—for example, a heart attack—resulting from shock), albeit not serious harm. This element is applied on the basis of the facts known to D at the time of his unlawful act and of any other facts of which a reasonable person would have been aware

or, if the act continues over a period of time, of facts which became known during that period.

(3) *That the unlawful and dangerous act was a cause of death*. It is not enough that some other act by D caused the death. As to the requirement of causation, see p 690.

Killing by gross negligence

This type of manslaughter may be committed by an act or by a failure to act (if D has failed in breach of a legal obligation to do an act); it is irrelevant whether or not D's act or omission would have constituted an offence if death had not resulted. It can no longer be committed by an organisation, to which the offence of corporate manslaughter applies.

The requirements of manslaughter by gross negligence are:

(1) *The existence of a duty of care*. Such a duty arises when it is foreseeable to D that negligence will cause injury to the victim (V); there is a relationship of sufficient proximity between D and V, and it would be 'just and reasonable' to impose liability.

(2) *A gross breach of duty*. Normally, proof of negligence simply involves proof that, whether or not he realised the risk (of which he should have been aware), the person subject to the duty did something, or failed to do something, in a way which fell below the standard of conduct expected of a reasonable person in all the circumstances (including D's expertise and training, if they are relevant in the context). This is not enough in the case of gross negligence. For there to be gross negligence, D's conduct must have involved an obvious and serious risk of death to another and in respect of that risk his conduct must have fallen so far below the standard to be expected of a reasonable person, ie be so bad, that it should be judged criminal.

(3) *The breach must cause death*. This simply repeats the requirement of causation.

Killing with recklessness as to death or serious bodily harm

In this context, a person is reckless as to a risk of death or serious bodily harm if he himself foresees that risk as a highly probable consequence of the fatal act or omission and he takes that risk, and in all circumstances it is unreasonable for him to do so.

The present type of involuntary manslaughter will often overlap with constructive manslaughter and manslaughter by gross negligence, but it will not do so where the fatal act is not otherwise unlawful and there is no risk of death.

CORPORATE MANSLAUGHTER

The offence

The Corporate Manslaughter and Corporate Homicide Act 2007 (CMCHA 2007) creates the offence of 'corporate manslaughter' which is triable only on indictment. CMCHA 2007, s 1(1) provides that an organisation to which s 1 applies is guilty of an offence if the way in which its activities are managed or organised:

(a) causes a person's death; and
(b) amounts to a gross breach of a relevant duty of care owed by the organisation to the deceased.

By s 1(3), an organisation is guilty of corporate manslaughter only if the way in which its activities are managed or organised by its senior management is a substantial element in the breach referred to in s 1(1). Because the offence requires a gross breach of a duty of care this offence is one requiring proof of gross negligence within its terms.

The DPP's consent is required before proceedings may be instituted.

Organisations to which CMCHA 2007, s 1 applies

Section 1 applies to:

(a) a corporation;
(b) a government department or other public body listed in CMCHA 2007, Sch 1;
(c) a police force; and
(d) a partnership, or a trade union or employers' association, that is an employer (s 1(2)).

Senior management

'Senior management', in relation to an organisation, means the persons who play significant roles in: (a) the making of decisions about how the whole or a substantial part of its activities are to be managed or organised; or (b) the actual managing or organising of the whole or a substantial part of those activities.

Relevant duty of care

Section 2 states that, subject to the exclusions referred to below, a 'relevant duty of care', in relation to an organisation, means any of the following duties owed by it under the law of negligence:

(a) a duty owed to employees to provide safety at work;
(b) a duty owed as occupier of buildings or land to provide for the safety of persons on the premises;
(c) a duty owed in connection with the use or keeping of any plant, vehicle or other thing;
(d) a duty owed in connection with supplying goods or services;
(e) a duty owed in connection with carrying on any other activity on a commercial basis;
(f) a duty owed in connection with carrying on construction or maintenance operations; or
(g) a duty owed to a person who is held in detention. 'Detention' means detention in a prison or similar establishment, or in a custody area at a court, police station or customs premises, or detention in service custody premises, or detention in immigration detention facilities, or transportation under escort to such places, or placement in secure accommodation for children and young persons, or detention under mental health provisions.

Whether or not a duty of care was owed to a particular individual is a matter of law to be decided by a judge.

Exclusions

Sections 3 to 7 set out exclusions from the 'relevant duty of care'.

Decisions relating to public policy taken by public authorities such as government departments and local authorities are excluded, as are activities involved in carrying out statutory inspections unless the duty is connected to the organisation's duty as an employer or occupier of premises.

Other exclusions include those relating to policing and law enforcement. Section 5 provides that any duty of care owed by the police and other enforcement agencies in respect of:

(a) operations for dealing with terrorism, civil unrest or serious disorder, which involve policing or law enforcement activities in the course of which officers or employees of the authority come under attack or face the threat of attack or violent resistance;

(b) activities carried on in preparation for, or directly in support of, such operations; or

(c) training of a hazardous nature, or training carried out in a hazardous way, which it is considered needs to be carried out, or carried out in that way, in order to improve or maintain the effectiveness of officers or employees of the public authority with respect to such operations,

is not a 'relevant duty of care'. Section 5 also provides that any duty of care owed by the police and other law enforcement agencies in respect of policing and law enforcement is not a 'relevant duty of care' unless it falls within (a), (b) or (g) on p 696.

Exclusions from the relevant duty of care exist for fire and rescue services, NHS bodies, ambulance services and the armed forces in respect of the way in which they respond to emergencies, and for child-protection and probation functions.

Gross breach of duty

By s 1(4)(b), a breach of a duty of care by an organisation is 'gross' if the conduct alleged to amount to a breach of that duty falls far below what can reasonably be expected of the organisation in the circumstances.

INFANTICIDE

The Infanticide Act 1938, s 1 states that where a woman by any wilful act or omission causes the death of her child, being a child under the age of 12 months, but at the time of that act or omission the balance of her mind was disturbed by reason of not having fully recovered from the effect of giving birth to the child, or by reason of the effect of lactation consequent on the birth of her child, then if the circumstances were such that, but for the Infanticide Act 1938, the offence would have amounted to murder or manslaughter, she is guilty of infanticide.

The basis of the law on infanticide is that depression after childbirth, or the effect of breast-feeding a child, are factors which can cause a mother to act out of character by committing some wilful act, or omitting to do something which a caring mother would do, that act or omission leading to the death of a child.

Infanticide may be charged in the first instance as an offence triable only on indictment or may be raised as a defence to a charge of murder or manslaughter.

CAUSING OR ALLOWING A CHILD OR VULNERABLE ADULT TO DIE OR SUFFER SERIOUS PHYSICAL HARM

In cases of child abuse, or of abuse of a vulnerable adult, where the victim has died or been injured as a result of the act or default of someone in the same household, it is sometimes difficult to prove who perpetrated the crime, or to prove that either A aided and abetted B to do so or B aided and abetted A to do so (so that both can be convicted of an offence of homicide described above or a non-fatal offence, as the case may be).

This problem is resolved by the Domestic Violence, Crime and Victims Act 2004, s 5. Section 5(1) provides that a person (D) is guilty of an offence triable only on indictment if:

(a) a child under 16 or vulnerable adult (V) dies or suffers serious physical harm as a result of the unlawful act of a person who:
   (i) was a member of the same household as V, and
   (ii) had frequent contact with him;
(b) D was such a person at the time of that act;
(c) at that time there was a significant risk of serious physical harm being caused to V by the unlawful act of such a person; and
(d) either D was the person whose act caused the death or serious physical harm, or:
   (i)   D was, or ought to have been, aware of the risk mentioned in para (c),
   (ii) D failed to take such steps as he could reasonably have been expected to take to protect V from the risk, and
   (iii) the act occurred in circumstances of the kind that D foresaw or ought to have foreseen.

The prosecution does not have to prove whether it is the first alternative in (d) or the second ((i)–(iii)) that applies.

There are two offences under s 5(1), one where death has occurred, and one where only serious physical harm has occurred.

If D was not the mother or father of V:

(a) D may not be charged with an offence under s 5 if he was under 16 at the time of the act that caused the death or serious physical harm;
(b) for the purposes of (d)(ii), D could not have been expected to take any such step as is referred to there before attaining 16.

For the purposes of s 5:

- 'act' includes a course of conduct and also includes omission;
- an 'unlawful' act is one that constitutes an offence, or (except where the act is by D) would constitute an offence but for being the act of a person under 10 or of a person who has the defence of insanity;
- 'vulnerable adult' means a person aged 16 or over whose ability to protect himself from violence, abuse or neglect is significantly impaired through physical or mental disability or illness, through old age or otherwise; and
- a person is to be regarded as a 'member' of a particular household, even if he does not live in that household, if he visits it so often and for such periods of time that it is reasonable to regard him as a member of it.

It is important to note that s 5 is not limited to the case where it is unclear which of two defendants killed or seriously harmed the vulnerable person. Thus, it can apply to make D guilty under it where it is clear that another person killed or seriously harmed a vulnerable person and that D failed to protect that person.

THREATS TO KILL

By the Offences Against the Person Act 1861 (OAPA 1861), s 16 it is an indictable (either way) offence for any person, without lawful excuse, to make to another person a threat to kill him or a third person, intending that that other person would fear that it would be carried out. An unborn child is not 'a third person' for the purposes of s 16.

Self-defence can amount to lawful excuse for a threat provided that the threatened force is reasonable in the circumstances as the maker of the threat believes them to be.

SOLICITING ANOTHER TO COMMIT MURDER

It is an offence contrary to OAPA 1861, s 4 for a person to solicit, encourage, persuade or endeavour to persuade, or to propose to any person, to murder any other person. There must be some form of communication and this may be in any form. It is not essential that the person solicited, etc was affected by the communication. The offence is triable only on indictment.

ENCOURAGING OR ASSISTING SUICIDE

The Suicide Act 1961 (SA 1961) provides as follows.

By SA 1961, s 2(1) a person (D) commits an offence if:

(a) D does an act capable of encouraging or assisting the suicide or attempted suicide of another person; and
(b) D's act was intended to encourage or assist suicide or an attempt at suicide.

Section 2(1A) provides that the person referred to in (a) need not be a specific person (or class of persons) known to, or identified by, D. Thus, provided the necessary mens rea can be proved, a person who posts information about how to commit suicide to a suicide chat room may be convicted of the present offence. By s 2(1B), D may commit an offence under s 2 whether or not a suicide, or an attempt at suicide, occurs.

Section 2A elaborates on what constitutes an 'act capable of encouraging or assisting the suicide or attempted suicide of another person'. It provides that:

(a) if D arranges for D2 to do an act that is capable of encouraging or assisting the suicide or attempted suicide of another person and D2 does that act, D is also to be treated as having done it. Thus, if D tells D2 to assist in the commission of suicide by T, and D2 does so, D is treated as having done the act of assistance done by D2. Both of them can be convicted of an offence of encouraging or assisting suicide;
(b) where the facts are such that an act is not capable of encouraging or assisting suicide or attempted suicide, it is to be treated as so capable:
   (i)   if the act would have been so capable had the facts been as D believed them to be at the time of the act (as where D wrongly believes that the harmless drugs which he supplies to assist another's suicide are lethal); or
   (ii) had subsequent events happened in the manner D believed they would happen (as where D posts a lethal drug to another to assist the other's suicide but this is lost in the post); or
   (iii) both;
(c) a reference to a person (D) doing an act that is capable of encouraging the suicide or attempted suicide of another person includes a reference to D doing so by threatening another person or otherwise putting pressure on another person to commit or attempt suicide.

A reference to an act in SA 1961 includes a reference to a course of conduct, and a reference to doing an act is to be read accordingly.

A prosecution for the offence requires the DPP's consent. The DPP has published a policy outlining public interest factors for and against such a prosecution. The offence is triable only on indictment.

Information society services providers

In order to ensure that SA 1961, s 2 is compatible with the UK's obligations under the EU's E-Commerce Directive, the Coroners and Justice Act 2009, Sch 12 makes special provision in connection with the operation of SA 1961 in relation to information society services providers.

CHILD DESTRUCTION

The Infant Life (Preservation) Act 1929 (ILPA 1929), s 1(1) provides that an offence triable only on indictment is committed by a person who, with intent to destroy the life of a child capable of being born alive, by any wilful act causes a child to die before it has an existence independent of its mother.

A child is capable of being born alive when it has reached a state of development in the womb in which it is capable, if born then, of living and breathing through its own lungs without any connection with its mother. ILPA 1929 provides a presumption that a child is capable of being born alive at any time after the 28th week of pregnancy. However, the offence can be committed in relation to a younger child if it is proved that it was capable of being born alive. Provided that the child was capable of being born alive, it is irrelevant that it is not capable of sustained survival.

There is a proviso to the offence, namely that a person is not guilty of it unless it is proved by the prosecution that D did not act in good faith for the purpose only of preserving the life of the mother. This proviso has been construed by the judges as including acting to preserve the mother's physical or mental health. In addition, the Abortion Act 1967 (AA 1967), s 5(1) provides that no offence under ILPA 1929 is committed by a registered medical practitioner who terminates a pregnancy in accordance with the provisions of AA 1967, explained on p 701.

ABORTION

The OAPA 1861, s 58 makes it an offence to do one of a number of specified acts with intent to procure a miscarriage, ie the expulsion of an ovum implanted in the uterus (whether or not this occurs). Because there must be such an intent, someone who does something to *prevent* the implantation of a fertilised ovum in the uterus (as where the 'morning-after' pill is used) does not commit an offence under s 58 because a pregnancy only begins, and a miscarriage can only occur, after implantation. An offence under s 58 is triable only on indictment. The common description of such an offence as abortion is somewhat misleading because the relevant offence does not require the abortion (miscarriage) of a foetus.

The woman herself

Section 58 states that it is an offence for a woman, *being with child* and with intent to procure her own miscarriage, unlawfully to administer to herself any poison or other noxious thing, or unlawfully to use any instrument or other means whatsoever.

Any other person

Section 58 goes on to provide that anyone (other than the woman herself) who, with intent to procure the miscarriage of any woman, unlawfully administers to her, or causes to be taken by her, any poison or other noxious thing, or who, with the same intent, unlawfully uses any instrument or other means whatsoever, commits an offence, *whether or not the woman is pregnant*.

The means

'Poison' has been defined as a recognised poison. If such a thing is taken, etc, it is irrelevant that the quantity is too small to cause harm. The term 'noxious thing' means any substance, other than a recognised poison, which is harmful in the dosage in which it was administered even though it might be harmless in smaller quantities. Clearly 'noxious thing' is a wide term. If a dosage is insufficient to render a substance a noxious thing, although D believes it is, there can be a conviction for an attempt to commit an offence under s 58. The term 'instrument' covers the range of surgical instruments usually associated with medical operations and also instruments such as knitting needles. The phrase 'other means whatsoever' embraces any other way in which a person may seek to bring about an abortion, such as manual manipulation with the fingers.

Unlawfully: the effect of the Abortion Act 1967

By AA 1967, s 5(2) anything done with intent to procure a woman's miscarriage (or, in the case of a woman carrying more than one foetus, her miscarriage of any foetus) is unlawfully done unless authorised by s 1.

Section 1 legalises abortions (including abortion operations which are unsuccessful or not completed) carried out by a registered medical practitioner where two registered medical practitioners are of the opinion formed in good faith that:

(a) the pregnancy has not exceeded its 24th week and that the continuance of the pregnancy would involve risk, greater than if the pregnancy was terminated, of injury to the physical or mental health of the pregnant woman or any existing children of her family (a question in the determination of which account may be taken of the pregnant woman's actual or reasonably foreseeable environment); or

(b) the termination is necessary to prevent *grave* permanent injury to the physical or mental health of the pregnant woman (a question in the determination of which account may be taken of the woman's actual or reasonably foreseeable environment); or

(c) the continuance of the pregnancy would involve risk to the life of the pregnant woman, greater than if the pregnancy was terminated; or

(d) there is a substantial risk that if the child were born it would suffer from such physical or mental abnormalities as to be seriously handicapped.

In order to be lawful, any treatment for the termination of pregnancy must be carried out in a NHS hospital, NHS Trust hospital (in Wales), NHS Foundation Trust hospital, or other approved place.

In an emergency any treatment for the termination of pregnancy may be carried out by a registered medical practitioner without complying with the above requirements if it is necessary to do so immediately to save the life of a pregnant woman, or to prevent grave permanent injury to her physical or mental health. This might occur during an operation upon the woman or at the scene of, or immediately following, a serious road accident.

The person supplying or procuring the means

OAPA 1861, s 59 punishes those who unlawfully supply or procure any poison or other noxious thing, or any instrument or physical thing whatsoever, knowing that it is intended to be unlawfully used or employed with intent to procure the miscarriage of any woman, whether she be or be not with child. The offence is triable only on indictment. 'Supply' should be given its ordinary meaning of transferring physical control of something from one person to another. 'Procure' in s 59 means to obtain possession of something for some other person. As to 'intent to procure miscarriage', see p 700.

CONCEALMENT OF BIRTH

OAPA 1861, s 60 provides that, if any woman is delivered of a child, every person who, by any secret disposition of the dead body of that child, endeavours to conceal its birth is guilty of an indictable (either way) offence. It is irrelevant whether the child died before, at or after its birth. However, in the case of a stillborn child, it must have reached a sufficient state of maturity that, but for some accidental circumstance, it might have been born alive.

The secret disposition may be done by anyone, but typically it is done by the mother following an unattended birth. In such a case, the offence is of importance where it cannot be proved how and/or when a child died, so that the mother cannot be convicted of an offence of homicide or of child destruction.

The abandonment of the child's body is not enough. There must be a secret disposition of it in an endeavour to conceal its birth from the world at large, but there can be such an endeavour even though some of the defendant's confidantes know of the birth. Clearly, a secret disposition in an endeavour to conceal the birth from a particular person does not constitute the offence.

CHAPTER 26

Public Order other than Offences Related to Sporting Events or Industrial Disputes

BREACH OF THE PEACE

There is a breach of the peace whenever and wherever (even on private premises):

(a) harm is *actually done*, or is *likely* to be done, to a person, whether by the conduct of the person against whom a breach of the peace is alleged or by someone whom it provokes; or

(b) harm is *actually* done, or is *likely* to be done, to a person's property in his presence; or

(c) a person is genuinely in fear of harm to himself or to his property in his presence as a result of an assault, affray, riot or other disturbance.

Mere agitation or excitement does not amount to a breach of the peace where there is no question of harm or threat of harm.

A breach of the peace is not in itself a criminal offence, but it can result in an arrest without warrant being lawfully made or in other steps being lawfully taken or in a binding-over order being made.

A police officer (and, indeed, every citizen) has power to arrest without a warrant or to take other reasonable preventive steps where:

(a) a breach of the peace occurs in his presence; or

(b) he reasonably believes that such a breach is about to occur, whether or not there has yet been a breach.

The House of Lords has confirmed that the power to prevent a breach of the peace does not arise when it is believed (however reasonably) that a breach of the peace is *likely to become imminent* and that it is reasonable to take action to prevent it; it must be believed that the breach of the peace is *actually imminent*.

An example of the exercise of the power to take preventive steps in relation to a reasonably apprehended imminent breach of the peace is 'kettling' (containment of people within a police cordon during a violent demonstration). The European Court of Human Rights, affirming a decision of the House of Lords, has held that 'kettling' does not amount to a deprivation of the right to liberty, guaranteed by art 5 of the European Convention on Human Rights, of those kettled so long as it is rendered unavoidable as a result of circumstances beyond the control of the authorities, is necessary to avert a real, imminent risk of serious injury or damage, and is kept to the minimum required for that purpose. The Court of Appeal has held that kettling of a group of relatively peaceful demonstrators to prevent another group of protesters, who were violent, taking over the former demonstration was legally permissible because there had been a reasonably believed risk of imminent and serious breaches of the peace. On the other hand, a divisional court has held that police who had lawfully kettled demonstrators had exceeded their powers by requiring them to be filmed and provide their personal details for identification purposes as the price for release.

Where a person's conduct is lawful but provocative, preventive steps cannot be taken against him if his behaviour is reasonable; if it is, preventive steps can be taken against opponents who are likely to react violently to the provocation if this reaction would be unreasonable. For example, where a person concerned in a lawful activity, eg a demonstration against neo-fascists, acts reasonably in making a reasoned but impassioned speech against neo-fascism, which is likely to produce violence from his opponents, preventive steps can be taken not against him but against them if their violent reaction would be unreasonable. It would be different if it is the speaker's conduct which is unreasonable.

A constable is entitled to enter private premises (or to remain on them if he is already there) to deal with a breach of the peace or reasonably apprehended breach of the peace.

BINDING OVER

'Binding over' is a precautionary measure; it is not a conviction or punishment. It should not be ordered for some act that is past and not likely to be repeated.

The powers of a magistrates' court to bind over a person may be exercised either on a complaint (under the Magistrates' Courts Act 1980, s 115) or on the court's own motion, at any stage of court proceedings, under the Justices of the Peace Act 1361 and common law powers. Other courts can also bind over on their own motion, but we shall limit ourselves to the powers of a magistrates' court.

The importance of the fact that a magistrates' court can bind over of its own motion is that a person can be bound over in criminal proceedings whether or not he has been convicted of an offence; if he has been so convicted, the binding over may be in addition to any punishment imposed.

Where the magistrates act on a complaint they can only bind a person over if the facts complained of have been proved beyond reasonable doubt. If they act of their own motion, it must be proved beyond reasonable doubt that there is a risk of a breach of the peace or of an offence in the future.

The process of binding over is effected by requiring the individual to enter into a recognisance, with or without sureties, to keep the peace.

A person enters into a recognisance if he undertakes to pay a sum of money fixed by the court if he fails within the time specified by the court to comply with the terms of the recognisance, and a person becomes a surety if he agrees to pay a sum so specified if that other person so fails to comply.

The court cannot impose a binding over if the person does not consent but, in the event of a refusal to be so bound, or to find sureties, the person concerned may be committed to prison for a fixed term not exceeding six months or until he complies with the requirements of the court, if sooner.

RIOT

The Public Order Act 1986 (POA 1986), s 1(1) provides that, where 12 or more persons who are present together use or threaten unlawful violence for a common purpose and the conduct of them (taken together) is such as would cause a person of reasonable firmness present at the scene to fear for his personal safety, each of the persons using unlawful violence for the common purpose is guilty of riot. Riot is triable only on indictment. It is the most serious offence against public order.

Riot may be committed in private as well as in public places. Thus, a riot can take place at factory premises, in a club, in a college, or—even—in someone's home.

Use of unlawful violence

A person does not perpetrate the offence of riot merely by threatening unlawful violence; he must actually use violence in the prescribed circumstances. If 12 or more people simply threaten violence for a common purpose in a frightening way, but none of them uses violence, riot is *not* committed.

On the other hand, provided one of 12 or more people actually uses violence for the common purpose, the offence of riot is perpetrated by him (or by all those who so use violence if more than one does). Those who merely threaten violence for the common purpose can, however, be convicted as accomplices to riot if they aid, abet, counsel or procure the use of violence by another (like anyone else who does so).

'Violence' is defined by POA 1986, s 8 as 'violent conduct'. It is not limited to violent conduct towards a person or persons since it includes violent conduct towards property (for example, smashing shop windows or overturning cars). Nor is it limited to conduct causing or intended to cause personal injury or damage to property, since it includes any other violent conduct (for example, throwing at or towards a person a missile of a kind capable of causing injury which does not hit or falls short). Swinging a knife at someone or firing a gun in his direction is violence under the definition in s 8, even though he is not hit.

The requirement that the violence be unlawful excludes from riot the use of violence which is justified by law (for example, under the rules relating to the use of reasonable force in self-defence, the prevention of crime or the effecting of an arrest).

Use or threat of unlawful violence for a common purpose by 12 or more present together

The 12 or more people need not form a cohesive group or be present pursuant to an agreement to come together.

The same comments apply to 'violence' as have been made above. If, during public disorder, the residents of a street use or threaten reasonable violence for the common purpose of defending themselves or their property from attack, their use or threat of violence does not constitute a riot because their violence is not unlawful.

In relation to threats, they may be by gestures alone (eg the brandishing of a weapon or the pointed display of it) or be by words alone, or be by a combination of both.

POA 1986, s 1(2) provides that it is immaterial whether or not the 12 or more use or threaten violence simultaneously. Equally, it is immaterial whether or not *any* of the others used or threatened violence at the time of the use of violence by the defendant (D). Provided that 12 or more persons who use or threaten violence are present *together* throughout, and that the violence is used or threatened by 12 or more for a common purpose, the offence of riot can be committed. Thus, it covers the situation where violence is used or threatened in one part of a crowd, then dies away, only to break out in another part at a later time.

It must be proved that the use or threat of violence by the 12 or more present together was for a purpose common to them (or at least to 12 of them). The question is not whether the 12 or more were present for a common purpose but whether they threatened or used violence for a common purpose. The common purpose need not be violence and it need not be an unlawful purpose (although, no doubt, it will normally be so). The common purpose may be inferred from the conduct of those involved.

Conduct such as would cause fear

The question is not whether the conduct of an individual defendant would cause fear but whether the conduct of the '12 or more present together …' is such as would, *taken together,* cause fear (ie alarm or apprehension). The conduct of the 12 or more must be such as *would* cause a person (ie a third-party bystander) of reasonable firmness present at the scene to fear for his *personal safety*; it does not matter whether it actually caused fear to a person present at the scene or even *might* have.

No person of reasonable firmness need actually be, or be likely to be, present at the scene; in fact, no one else (besides the 12 or more) need be present or likely to be present at the scene. No doubt the case where there are no bystanders will be exceptional; where it occurs, proof of the riot may be particularly difficult.

Mens rea

By POA 1986, s 6(1), a person is guilty of riot only if he intends to use violence or is aware that his conduct may be violent. Section 6(5) provides that, for the purposes of the offence of riot, a person whose awareness is impaired by intoxication shall be taken to be aware of that of which he would be aware if not intoxicated, unless he shows either that his intoxication was not self-induced (as where his drink has been 'laced') or that it was caused solely by the taking or administration of a substance in the course of medical treatment. 'Intoxication' here means any intoxication, whether caused by drink, drugs, or other means (eg glue), or by a combination of means.

VIOLENT DISORDER

POA 1986, s 2(1) provides that, where three or more people who are present together use or threaten unlawful violence and their conduct (taken together) is such as would cause a person of reasonable firmness present at the scene to fear for his personal safety, each of the persons using or threatening unlawful violence is guilty of violent disorder, an indictable (either way) offence. No person of reasonable firmness need actually be, or be likely to be, present at the scene.

As in the case of riot, violent disorder may be committed in private as well as in public places.

The prohibited conduct for this offence is substantially the same as that of riot (and the comments made when discussing the identical elements in riot are equally applicable here) with the exceptions that:

(a) D is guilty if he uses or *threatens* unlawful violence;
(b) only three persons (including D) who are present together are required to use or threaten unlawful violence;
(c) neither D nor the other participants are required to use or threaten unlawful violence for a common purpose.

The operation of the above can be illustrated as follows. If a racist march or static demonstration takes place in the centre of an immigrant community, accompanied by threats of immediate violence which would make a person of reasonable firmness fear for his personal safety, the offence is committed; but not if the taunts are merely of a racist nature highly offensive to local inhabitants, although they might give rise to an offence under POA 1986, ss 4A, 5 or 18 or the Crime and Disorder Act 1998, s 31 (pp 711, 713 and 737).

By POA 1986, s 6(2) a person is guilty of violent disorder only if he intends to use or threaten violence or is aware that his conduct may be violent or threaten violence.

As in the case of riot, a person whose awareness is impaired by intoxication is to be taken to be aware of that of which he would be aware if not intoxicated, unless he shows either that his intoxication was not self-induced or that it was caused solely by the taking or administration of a substance in the course of medical treatment.

AFFRAY

POA 1986, s 3(1) provides that a person is guilty of affray, an indictable (either way) offence, if he uses or threatens unlawful violence towards another and his conduct is such as would cause a person of reasonable firmness present at the scene to fear for his personal safety.

The prohibited conduct is that:

(a) D must use or threaten violence *towards* another; and
(b) his conduct must be such as would cause a person of reasonable firmness present at the scene to fear for his personal safety.

Like riot and violent disorder, affray may be committed in private as well as in public places. One result is that, if a fight breaks out at a party in someone's home, those who participate in it can be guilty of affray if the terms of the offence are satisfied. In fact any assault—even a domestic one—wherever committed, accompanied by the use or threat of violence, is an affray if it would cause a person of reasonable firmness present at the scene to fear for his personal safety. *Most* of the elements of the actus reus are common to riot and violent disorder.

Use or threat of unlawful violence towards another

Unlike the position in riot and violent disorder, 'violence' here does not include violent conduct towards property.

Another important difference between affray and riot and violent disorder is that a threat of violence cannot be made by the use of words alone. Of course, an affray can be committed where a threat of violence is made by a combination of words and gestures (such as shouting out, 'I'll get you for that', while brandishing a weapon or even shaking a fist) as well as by gestures alone. A threat or use of violence must be directed towards a person or persons actually present at the scene.

An affray, like riot and violent disorder, can only be committed if the violence is 'unlawful' as defined on p 705. Thus, a person who fights another in self-defence cannot be guilty of an affray, although his assailant can be if his use of violence would make a person of reasonable firmness fear for his personal safety.

Where two people use or threaten unlawful violence there is no need for them to do so for a common purpose.

Conduct such as would cause a person of reasonable firmness present at the scene to fear for his personal safety

This requirement provides an important limit on the offence, and excludes many fights from it. For example, it is most unlikely that a fight between two people, arising out of a personal quarrel but without any danger of the involvement of others, would constitute an affray.

Where two or more people use or threaten the unlawful violence, it is the conduct of them taken together that must be considered for the purpose of ascertaining whether the conduct would have the required effect.

As in the case of riot and violent disorder no one besides the participants (ie no bystander) need be present, or be likely to be present, at the scene, and it is expressly provided by POA 1986, s 3(4) that no person of reasonable firmness need actually be, or be likely to be, present at the scene. The offence of affray is, in reality, concerned with *three* persons: a person using or threatening unlawful violence (D), a person towards whom the violence or threat is directed (V), and a notional person of reasonable firmness. It is not enough that the victim of the violence or threat is put in fear for his personal safety. The question is whether, *if the notional person of reasonable firmness* had been so present, he would have been caused to fear for *his* personal safety (as opposed to that of D or V or someone else).

Mens rea

By POA 1986, s 6(2), a person is guilty of affray only if he intends to use or threaten violence or is *aware* that his conduct may be violent or threaten violence. As in the case of riot, a person whose awareness is impaired by intoxication—whether by drink, drugs, or other means (or a combination of these)—must be taken to be aware of what he would have been aware of if not intoxicated, unless he shows that his intoxication was not self-induced or that it was caused solely by the taking or administration of a substance in the course of medical treatment.

FEAR OR PROVOCATION OF VIOLENCE

POA 1986, s 4(1) provides that a person is guilty of an offence if he:

(a) uses towards another person threatening, abusive or insulting words or behaviour; or
(b) distributes or displays to another person any writing, sign or other visible representation which is threatening, abusive or insulting,

with intent to cause that person to believe that immediate unlawful violence will be used against him or another by any person, or to provoke the immediate use of unlawful violence by that person or another, or whereby that person is likely to believe that such violence will be used or it is likely that such violence will be provoked.

Threatening, abusive or insulting

The words 'threatening, abusive or insulting' do not bear an unusual legal meaning. Instead, the magistrates will decide as a question of fact whether D's conduct was threatening, abusive or insulting in the ordinary meaning of those terms, and this is to be judged according to the impact which the conduct would have on a reasonable member of the public. Behaviour is not threatening, abusive or insulting merely because it gives rise to a risk that immediate violence will be feared or provoked, nor simply because it gives rise to anger, disgust or distress.

If conduct is threatening, abusive or insulting, it does not matter whether or not anyone who witnessed it felt himself to be threatened, abused or insulted.

Use, distribution or display

The distribution or display of any writing, sign or other visible representation which is threatening, abusive or insulting covers handing out leaflets (distribution) or holding up a banner or placard (display).

POA 1986, s 4 requires that threatening, abusive or insulting words or behaviour must be used *towards another person* or that threatening, etc written material be distributed or displayed *to another*. In relation to the use of threatening, abusive or insulting words or behaviour, 'towards another' imports a requirement that the words or behaviour in question must be directed towards (ie deliberately aimed at) another particular person or persons; if they are not, one must rely on the offence under s 4A or the lesser offence under s 5. Conduct is not used towards another if he is not present, in the sense that he can perceive with his own senses the threatening words or behaviour, etc. Thus, a person who makes a threat against a person who is out of earshot and only learns of it through a third party who is not under the control or direction of the maker of the threat cannot be convicted of an offence under s 4. However, whilst the person towards whom the behaviour was aimed must have been present to perceive it, this does not mean that the only means of proving that the victim perceived the behaviour is by hearing evidence from that person. Justices may rely solely on evidence from a bystander and may draw the inference that the victim did perceive what was said and done by an accused.

The insertion of 'to another' after 'displays' requires that the display of written material be directed towards another particular person or persons (ie deliberately brought to his attention), rather than simply being displayed (eg as a poster).

Public or private place

With one exception, an offence under POA 1986, s 4 can be committed in private places, as well as in public places. Thus, an offence can be committed by pickets who threaten working colleagues, whether the pickets are inside or outside factory premises, or by protesters who invade a military base.

The exception is that, in order to exclude domestic disputes, s 4 has the effect of providing that the use of words or behaviour inside a dwelling is only an offence if the addressee (ie another person towards whom the words or behaviour are used or the writing, etc is displayed) is not inside that dwelling or any other dwelling. Thus, to use threatening, abusive or insulting words towards someone else in the same house cannot be an offence under s 4, and the same is true if such words are shouted to someone in the house next door. On the other hand, if such words are shouted in a house at a next-door neighbour who is in his back garden, an offence under s 4 will be committed, provided that the other elements of the offence are satisfied.

For the above purpose, 'dwelling' means any structure or part of a structure occupied as a person's home or as other living accommodation (whether the occupation is separate or shared with others) but does not include any part not so occupied, such as a garage, a shop with accommodation over, or the communal parts of a block of flats. Thus, if threatening words are shouted from a flat to a shop below, an offence under s 4 may be committed, and so may it if the words are shouted from the shop to the flat upstairs. 'Structure' here includes a tent, caravan, vehicle, vessel or other temporary or movable structure. A police cell is not a home or other living accommodation and is therefore not a dwelling for these purposes.

Mens rea

D must either intend the words, behaviour or writing, etc to be threatening, abusive or insulting or be aware that they or it might be. The result of this requirement is that a person who uses words which are seemingly innocuous but which are addressed to, or heard by, persons to whom (unknown to him) they are highly insulting is not guilty of the present offence.

A person whose awareness is impaired by intoxication must be taken to be aware of that of which he would be aware if not intoxicated, unless he shows either that his intoxication was not self-induced or that it was caused solely by the taking or administration of a substance in the course of medical treatment.

POA 1986, s 4 also requires that D's use of the words or behaviour towards another (hereafter described as 'an addressee'), or D's distribution or display to an addressee of the writing, etc, must be intended by D or be likely (whether or not D realises this) either:

(a) to provoke the immediate use of unlawful violence by an addressee or another; or
(b) to cause an addressee to believe that immediate unlawful violence will be used against him or another.

It will be noted, under para (a), that it is not necessarily an addressee who must be intended or likely to be provoked to immediate violence. It is sufficient that someone else present, towards whom the threatening, etc behaviour, etc was not directed, was intended or likely to be provoked. Thus, if X shouts at an Asian person whom he knows cannot speak English, 'Paki bastard, go home', intending that this should provoke immediate violence on the part of a group of racists who are in the near vicinity, the present offence is committed. On the other hand, for the purposes of para (b) (fear of immediate violence, intended or likely), the fear must be felt by an addressee (although it need not be fear of violence against himself, nor of violence by D).

It is important to note that the offence under s 4, unlike those under ss 1 to 3, is not concerned with the reactions of a hypothetical person of reasonable firmness. Instead, for example, a speaker must take his audience as he finds it. If he uses insulting words at a meeting, he is guilty of the present offence if they are likely to provoke the immediate use of violence by the particular audience he is addressing, even though he does not intend to provoke this and even though his words would not be likely to cause a reasonable person so to react, provided that he intends his words to be insulting or is aware that they might be.

It has been held that, since constables are under a common law duty to preserve the peace, they are unlikely to respond to threatening, abusive or insulting conduct by using violence. Nevertheless, such conduct directed towards a constable will constitute an offence under s 4 if it is intended or likely to put him in fear of immediate unlawful violence or is intended to provoke him to such violence. If the conduct is so serious as to amount to a breach of the peace and make it likely that a constable to whom it is addressed will have to use violence in the exercise of his common law power to arrest for a breach of the peace, an offence under s 4 will not be committed because the violence likely to be provoked will not be unlawful.

The fact that the unlawful violence which is intended or likely to be feared or provoked must be *immediate* must be emphasised. However, that term has been given a liberal interpretation by a divisional court. 'Immediate' does not mean 'instantaneous'. Instead violence will be 'immediate' if it is likely to result in a relatively short period of time and without any intervening occurrence.

As indicated above, the immediate violence which is intended or likely to be feared or provoked will not be unlawful if it is reasonable force in self-defence, or is otherwise legally justified.

In the reference to an intention to cause, or the likelihood of causing, the apprehension of immediate unlawful violence or the provocation of it, 'violence' has the same meaning as in riot and related offences: see p 705.

HARASSMENT, ALARM OR DISTRESS

POA 1986, s 4 does not deal with many minor acts of hooliganism or other anti-social behaviour which are prevalent, particularly in inner city areas. It is at problems such as these, in particular, that the offences under POA 1986, ss 4A and 5 are aimed.

Section 4A provides that a person is guilty of an offence if, *with intent to cause a person harassment, alarm or distress,* he:

(a) uses *threatening, abusive or insulting* words or behaviour, or *disorderly* behaviour; or
(b) displays any writing, sign or other visible representation which is *threatening, abusive or insulting,*

thereby causing that or another person harassment, alarm or distress.

POA 1986, s 5 provides that a person is guilty of an offence if he:

(a) uses *threatening or abusive* words or behaviour, or *disorderly* behaviour; or
(b) displays any writing, sign or other visible representation which is *threatening or abusive,*

within the hearing or sight of a person *likely to be caused harassment, alarm or distress thereby.* It will be noted that 'insulting' does not appear in s 5.

'Threatening', 'abusive' and 'insulting' have already been discussed and what is said there is equally applicable here. A similar approach applies to 'disorderly'. Thus, it is a question of fact for the magistrates whether D's conduct was disorderly in the ordinary meaning of the term. A divisional court, in confirming this, has held that an element of 'violence' is not essential for there to be disorderly behaviour, and that neither is any feeling of insecurity, in an apprehensive sense, on the part of a member of the public.

In relation to the requirement that harassment, alarm or distress must be caused (s 4A) or be likely (s 5), 'harassment, alarm or distress' are not defined by POA 1986, but it has been held as follows for the purposes of ss 4A and 5.

Divisional courts have held that:

(1) 'Harassment' does not require any apprehension about one's personal safety, nor (probably) does 'distress'.
(2) A person can be harassed without experiencing emotional disturbance or upset.
(3) The words or behaviour in question must be likely to cause some real, as opposed to trivial, harassment.
(4) 'Distress' requires emotional disturbance or upset. That emotional disturbance does not have to be grave but the requirement should not be trivialised. There must be something amounting to real emotional disturbance or upset.

In relation to any threatening, abusive or insulting writing, sign or other visible representation, the offences are limited to displaying and cannot (unlike an offence under s 4) also be committed by distribution. One result is that handing out threatening, abusive or insulting leaflets is not caught by s 4A or s 5, unless the leaflets are so printed, and so held, that their contents can be said to be displayed in the sight of another.

Another distinction between the offences under s 4A and s 5 and that under s 4 is that the words or behaviour need not be used towards another person (nor need writing, etc be displayed to another). It follows that words or behaviour need not be directed towards another, nor need written material be deliberately brought to the attention of another. The display of graffiti or slogans can therefore suffice.

An offence under s 4A or s 5 may be committed in a public or a private place, except that no offence is committed where the words or behaviour are used, or the writing, sign or other visible representation is displayed, by a person inside a dwelling (p 709) and the other person who is harassed, alarmed or distressed thereby (s 4A), or within whose sight or hearing it occurs and who is likely to be harassed, alarmed or distressed thereby (s 5), is also inside that or another dwelling.

The separate elements: POA 1986, s 4A

While D's conduct need not be directed towards another (and written material need not be displayed by him to another), there must be a victim in the sense that someone else is actually caused harassment, alarm or distress.

D must either intend his words or behaviour, or the writing, etc, to be threatening, abusive or insulting or be aware that they or it may be threatening, abusive or insulting, or (as the case may be) intend his behaviour to be or be aware that it may be disorderly.

D must also intend his threatening, etc words or behaviour or his display of threatening, etc, writing, etc to cause a person harassment, alarm or distress; it is irrelevant that the person who was actually caused the harassment, etc was not the intended victim.

Section 4A(3) provides two defences. Section 4A(3)(a) provides a defence for a defendant who alleges that he was inside a dwelling at the material time. It states that it is a defence for him to prove that he was inside a dwelling and had no reason to believe that the words or behaviour used, or the writing, sign or other visible representation displayed, would be heard or seen by a person outside that or any other dwelling.

Section 4A(3)(b) provides that it is a defence for a defendant to prove that his conduct was reasonable, reasonableness being judged objectively. It would be reasonable, for example, to shout a threat at a pickpocket across the street to deter him. This is an exceptionally vague defence and proving it may often be difficult.

The separate elements: POA 1986, s 5

While D's conduct need not be directed towards another (and written material need not be displayed by him to another), there must be a victim in the sense that what D does must be within the hearing or sight of a person likely to be caused harassment, alarm or distress thereby, although no likelihood of violence being provoked or feared is required. Whilst there must be evidence that someone was able to see or hear the words or behaviour complained of, the prosecution does not have to call evidence that the words or behaviour were actually heard or seen. However, if it does call a witness who says nothing in giving evidence about experiencing harassment, alarm or distress it cannot be inferred that he was likely to be caused harassment, etc.

It is not necessary that a person who is likely to be alarmed should be alarmed for his own safety; it suffices that he is likely to be alarmed about the safety of someone unconnected with him.

D must either intend his words or behaviour, or the writing, etc, to be threatening or abusive or be aware that it may be threatening or abusive, or (as the case may be) intend his behaviour to be or be aware that it may be disorderly. Consequently, a person who gives no thought to the nature of his conduct, or who honestly believes that there is no risk of it being threatening or abusive, does not commit this offence. The provisions of s 6(5) concerning intoxication, discussed on p 706, apply equally to an offence under s 5.

Although D's conduct must be in the hearing or sight of a person likely to be caused harassment, alarm or distress thereby, D is not required to intend this or to be aware that it might occur. On the other hand, s 5(3)(a) provides that it is a defence for D to prove that he had no reason to believe that there was any person within hearing or sight who was likely to be caused harassment, alarm or distress.

Section 5(3)(b) provides a defence identical to that under s 4A(3)(a) above.

Section 5(3)(c) provides a defence (conduct reasonable) identical to that under s 4A(3)(b) above. A divisional court has held that if the prosecution proves, as it must, that D's conduct was threatening, abusive or disorderly, and that he intended it to be, or was aware that it might be, it would in most cases follow that his conduct was objectively unreasonable. The court also stated that, in considering whether conduct was reasonable, the court must have regard to all the circumstances, and to the European Convention on Human Rights, art 10(2), which sets out the grounds on which the freedom of expression may be interfered with. See, further p 756.

Offences against POA 1986, s 5 are 'penalty offences' for the purpose of the Criminal Justice and Police Act 2001, as explained on p 31.

RACIALLY OR RELIGIOUSLY AGGRAVATED PUBLIC ORDER OFFENCES

A person commits an offence under the Crime and Disorder Act 1998 (CDA 1998), s 31 if he commits an offence under POA 1986, ss 4, 4A or 5 which is racially or religiously aggravated. There are three separate offences under s 31, each based on one of the three basic offences under POA 1986. Those based on ss 4 or 4A are indictable (either way) offences.

CDA 1998, s 28(1) defines when an offence is racially or religiously aggravated for the purposes of s 31 in the same way as for the purposes of s 29 (see p 658).

PROTECTION OF ACTIVITIES OF ANIMAL RESEARCH ORGANISATIONS

Interference with contractual relationships so as to harm animal research organisation

The Serious Organised Crime and Police Act 2005 (SOCPA 2005), s 145 provides that a person (A) commits an offence if, with the intention of harming an animal research organisation, he:

(a) does a relevant act; or

(b) threatens that he or someone else will do a relevant act,

in circumstances in which that act or threat is intended or likely to cause a second person (B):

(i)   not to perform any contractual obligation owed by B to a third person (C) (whether or not such non-performance amounts to a breach of contract);

(ii) to terminate any contract B has with C; or

(iii) not to enter into a contract with C.

The offence is an indictable (either way) offence.

A 'relevant act' is an act amounting to a *criminal offence*, or to a *tortious act* (ie an act giving rise to liability for damages) causing B to suffer loss or damage of any description. For these purposes, a tortious act does not include an act which is actionable on the ground *only* that it induces another person to break a contract with B.

'Contract' includes any other arrangement, and to 'harm' an animal research organisation means to cause the organisation to suffer loss or damage *of any description*, or to prevent or hinder the carrying-out by the organisation of any of its activities.

Section 145 does not apply to any act done wholly or mainly in contemplation or furtherance of a trade dispute within the meaning of the Trade Union and Labour Relations (Consolidation) Act 1992 (TULR(C)A 1992) which deals with similar acts committed in contemplation or furtherance of trade disputes (see pp 769–71).

Section 145 seeks to plug gaps in other legislation dealing with forms of harassment and disorder which were exploited by those who engaged in activities of various kinds aimed at 'persuading' animal research organisations to abandon research involving the use of animals. Targeting was not restricted to the actual animal research establishments, since it was also directed at other organisations alleged to have business dealings with such establishments or with organisations which had such dealings.

Intimidation of persons connected with animal research organisation

Many animal research establishments, and the business premises of organisations with a connection with such establishments, are able to take effective measures to protect their property, to a large extent, but their employees and others associated with them present an easier target to protesters.

SOCPA 2005, s 146 therefore provides that a person (D) commits an offence if, with the intention of causing a second person (V) to abstain from doing something which V is entitled to do (or do something which V is entitled to abstain from doing):

(a) D threatens V that D or somebody else will do a relevant act; and
(b) D does so wholly or mainly because V is:
  (i)   an employee or officer of an animal research organisation,
  (ii)   a student at an educational establishment that is an animal research organisation,
  (iii)   a lessor or licensor of premises occupied by an animal research organisation,
  (iv)   a person who has a financial interest in, or who provides financial assistance to, such an organisation,
  (v)   a customer or supplier of such an organisation,
  (vi)   a person contemplating becoming someone within (iii), (iv) or (v),
  (vii)   a person who is, or is contemplating becoming, a customer or supplier of someone within (iii), (iv), (v) or (vi),
  (viii) an employee or officer of someone within (iii), (iv), (v), (vi) or (vii),
  (ix)   a person with a financial interest in, or who provides financial assistance to, someone within (iii), (iv), (v), (vi) or (vii),
  (x)   a spouse, civil partner, friend or relative of, or a person known personally to, someone within (i)–(ix),
  (xi)   a person who is, or is contemplating becoming, a customer or supplier of someone within (i), (ii), (viii), (ix) or (x), or
  (xii)   an employer of someone within (x).

The offence is an indictable (either way) offence.

The provisions in s 146 do not apply to trade disputes within the meaning of TULR(C)A 1992 (p 000).

'Relevant act' has the same meaning as in s 145, except that the limitation whereby a tortious act does not include an act actionable only because it induces a breach of contract does not apply.

General

Proceedings for an offence under SOCPA 2005, ss 145 or 146 may not be taken without the consent of the DPP.

'Animal research organisation' means any person or organisation which or who:

(a) is the owner, lessee or licensee of premises constituting or including a place specified in a licence granted under the Animals (Scientific Procedures) Act 1986;
(b) is the employer of, or engages under a contract of service, a person who is the holder of a licence under that Act or who is specified by it; or
(c) holds a licence under the provisions for the licensing of undertakings involving the use of animals for scientific procedures.

PUBLIC PROCESSIONS

Advance notice

POA 1986, s 11 requires that, where it applies, written notice specifying the date a procession is intended to be held, the time when it is intended to start, its proposed route, and the name and address of the person (or one of the persons) proposing to organise it, must be given to a police station in the police area in which it is proposed the procession will start. Section 11 applies if the procession is public and it is intended:

(a) to demonstrate support for or opposition to the views or actions of any person or body of persons;
(b) to publicise a cause or campaign; or
(c) to mark or commemorate an event.

If such a procession starts in Scotland, it is the first police area in England along the proposed route which must be given notice. The notice may be given by hand not less than six clear days before the date upon which the procession is intended to be held or, if that is not reasonably practicable (as where there is an unexpected event following which a group wishes to demonstrate immediately), as soon as delivery is reasonably practicable.

Section 11 permits delivery of the notice by recorded delivery service, if the notice is delivered not less than six clear days in advance. The provisions of the Interpretation Act 1978 under which a document sent by post is deemed to have been served when posted and to have been delivered in the ordinary course of post do not apply to the service of such notices.

Section 11 does not apply to processions commonly or customarily held (for example, a procession connected with an annual gala, a Remembrance Day parade, or a monthly campaigning mass cycle ride), or to funeral processions organised by funeral directors (as opposed to processions which suddenly appear in protest at a death). The House of Lords has held that a monthly campaigning cycle ride through central

London which took a different route each time, although it set off from a fixed starting point, was a commonly or customarily held procession and therefore no prior notice needed to be given to the police.

Each of the persons organising a public procession is guilty of an offence if notice has not been so given, or if the details given in the notice differ from the actuality of the procession (s 11(7)). It is a defence for D to prove that he did not know of, and neither suspected nor had reason to suspect, the failure to give such notice, or that differences in the time, date or route occurred due to circumstances beyond his control, or with the agreement of a police officer or by his direction (s 11(8) and (9)).

Conditions

By POA 1986, s 12, the senior police officer may impose conditions in relation to any public procession, having regard to its time, place or circumstances, including its route or proposed route, if he reasonably believes that:

(a) it may result in serious public disorder, serious damage to property, or serious disruption to the life of the community; or
(b) the purpose of the persons organising it is the intimidation of others with a view to compelling them not to do an act they have a right to do, or to do an act they have a right not to do.

These conditions may include any measures which appear necessary to prevent such disorder, damage, disruption or intimidation, including conditions as to the route or proposed route of the procession or prohibiting it from entering any specified public place.

For these purposes, the 'proposed route' of a public procession is not limited to a specifically planned route; it can also cover one which is spontaneously chosen by the participants from time to time. Thus, conditions can be imposed in respect of what is reasonably believed might be the potential route.

In the case of a procession which is actually being held, the senior police officer is the police officer most senior in rank present at the scene; in such a case, it is not necessary for the notice to be in writing. In the case where people are assembling for a procession, the senior police officer is the chief officer of police; in such a case the chief officer must give the notice in writing.

Offences are committed by an organiser (s 12(4)) or participant (s 12(5)) who knowingly fails to comply with a condition. A divisional court has held that the participants in a procession (a protest march) where conditions under s 12 had been imposed designating its route were in breach of those conditions when they diverted from the designated route to join another protest, because they remained part of the original procession. The court added that there would not have been a breach if the participants in the procession had left it to go home or for some similar purpose, because they would no longer be part of the procession. It is a defence for D to prove that the failure arose from circumstances beyond his control. A person who incites another to participate in a procession and to fail to comply with a condition also commits an offence (s 12(6)).

Prohibition

A chief officer of police may apply under POA 1986, s 13 to the council of the district for an order prohibiting for a period, not exceeding three months, the holding of all public processions (or any class of procession specified) within that district. The chief officer must reasonably believe that, because of particular circumstances existing, his power to impose conditions will not be sufficient to prevent serious public disorder. Such an order may be made by the council with the consent of the Secretary of State. The Commissioners of the Metropolitan and City of London Police Forces may themselves make such an order in respect of their police areas with the consent of the Secretary of State.

A person who organises (s 13(7)), or takes part in (s 13(8)), a public procession commits an offence if he knows that it has been prohibited. Those who incite others to participate in a prohibited procession are also guilty of an offence (s 13(9)).

Delegation

A chief officer of police may delegate any of his functions under ss 12 or 13 to an assistant chief constable or an assistant commissioner of police (as the case may be).

ANTI-SOCIAL BEHAVIOUR: INJUNCTIONS

The Anti-social Behaviour, Crime and Policing Act 2014 (A-sB,C&PA 2014), Part 1 (ss 1–21) contains provisions for an injunction to deal with actual or threatened anti-social behaviour. Such an injunction, like injunctions in general, is a purely civil order. It has replaced the anti-social behaviour order on application, the intervention order and the individual support order (under the Crime and Disorder Act 1998), as well as the anti-social behaviour injunction (under the Housing Act 1996, s 153A: housing-related anti-social behaviour) and the drinking banning order on application (under the Violent Crime Reduction Act 2006).

Power to grant injunctions

A-sB,C&PA 2014, s 1(1) provides that a court may grant an injunction (commonly referred to as a 'Part 1 injunction') against a person aged 10 or over (the respondent, R) if two conditions are met:

(a) the court is satisfied, on the balance of probabilities, that R has engaged or threatens to engage in anti-social behaviour. In relation to this the civil rules of evidence (see p 684) apply;

(b) the court considers it just and convenient to grant the injunction for the purpose of preventing R from engaging in anti-social behaviour. This is an exercise of judgment and does not involve a standard of proof.

For these purposes, 'anti-social behaviour' is defined by s 2(1) as meaning:

(i) conduct that has caused, or is likely to cause, harassment, alarm or distress to any person;

(ii) (which, by s 2(2), applies only where the injunction is applied for by a housing provider, local authority or chief officer of police) conduct capable of causing nuisance or annoyance to a person in relation to that person's occupation of residential premises; or

(iii) conduct capable of causing housing-related nuisance or annoyance to any person ('housing-related' means directly or indirectly relating to the housing management functions of a housing provider or local authority).

Prohibitions and requirements

A Part 1 injunction may, for the purpose of preventing R from engaging in anti-social behaviour, *prohibit* him from doing, or *require* him to do, anything described in the injunction (s 1(4)). Examples of requirements are attendance on an alcohol or drug awareness course, undergoing anger management training, or receiving help from a support (eg mental health) service.

Prohibitions and requirements in a Part 1 injunction must, so far as practicable, be such as to avoid:

(a) any interference with the times, if any, at which R normally works or attends school or any other educational establishment;

(b) any conflict with the requirements of any other court order or injunction to which R may be subject (s 1(5)).

Section 1(6) provides that a Part 1 injunction must specify the period for which it has effect, or state that it has effect until further order; in the case of an injunction granted before R has reached 18, a period must be specified and it must be no more than 12 months.

Under s 3, a Part 1 injunction that includes a requirement must specify the person (an individual or organisation) who is to be responsible for supervising compliance with the requirement. A person specified (P) must:

(a) make any necessary arrangements in connection with the requirements for which P has responsibility (the 'relevant requirements');

(b) promote R's compliance with the relevant requirements;

(c) if P considers that R has complied with all the relevant requirements, or has failed to comply with a relevant requirement, inform the applicant for the injunction and the appropriate chief officer of police.

A respondent subject to a requirement included in a Part 1 injunction must, as a requirement of the injunction, keep in touch with P about that requirement, in accordance with any instructions given by P from time to time, and notify P of any change of address.

A Part 1 injunction may have the effect of excluding R from the place where he normally lives ('the premises') only if:

(a) R is 18 or over,

(b) the injunction is granted on the application of:

    (i)   a local authority;

    (ii) the chief officer of police for the police area that the premises are in; or

    (iii) if the premises are owned or managed by a housing provider, that housing provider, and

(c) the court thinks that the anti-social behaviour in which R has engaged or threatens to engage consists of or includes the use or threatened use of violence against other persons, or that there is a significant risk of harm to other persons from R (s 13).

Power of arrest

By s 4, a court granting a Part 1 injunction may attach a power of arrest to a prohibition or requirement (other than one requiring participation in particular activities) of the injunction if it thinks that the anti-social behaviour in which R has engaged or threatens to engage consists of or includes the use or threatened use of violence against other persons, or that there is a significant risk of harm to other persons from R. The court may specify a period for which the power of arrest is to have effect which is shorter than that of the prohibition or requirement to which it relates.

Applications for injunctions

An application for a Part 1 injunction must be made to a youth court, in the case of a respondent under 18, and (subject to the following exception) to the High Court or the county court, in any other case. The exception, provided by the Magistrates' Courts (Injunctions: Anti-Social Behaviour) Rules 2015, is that a youth court may on application permit an application for a Part 1 injunction against a respondent aged 18 *or over* to be made to the youth court if:

(a) an application to the youth court has been, or is to be, made for a Part 1 injunction against a person under 18, and the application *for permission* includes details of the application for a s 1 injunction relating to the person aged under 18; and

(b) the youth court thinks that it would be in the interests of justice for the applications for a Part 1 injunction to be heard together, and for this purpose the application *for permission* must include a statement of the reasons why it is in the interests of justice for the applications for a Part 1 injunction to be heard together.

Where a respondent attains 18 after the commencement of proceedings for a Part 1 injunction, the proceedings must remain in a youth court, unless the court in which the proceedings were continuing when the respondent attained 18 directs that the proceedings be transferred to the High Court or county court.

By A-sB,C&PA 2014, s 5, the injunction may be granted only on the application of:

(a) a local authority,

(b) a housing provider,

(c) the chief officer of police for a police area,

(d) the chief constable of the British Transport Police Force,

(e) Transport for London,

(f) the Environment Agency,

(g) the Natural Resources Body for Wales,

(h) the Secretary of State exercising security management functions, or a Special Health Authority exercising security management functions on the direction of the Secretary of State, or

(i) the Welsh Ministers exercising security management functions, or a person or body exercising security management functions on the direction of the Welsh Ministers or under arrangements made between the Welsh Ministers and that person or body.

A chief officer of police can delegate his functions in respect of an application for an order to an officer or officers in his force judged suitable by him. In practice, applications under (h) and (i) will be made by NHS Protect and NHS Protect (Wales) respectively.

Ministerial guidance has been issued to the persons and bodies listed above about the exercise of their functions under A-sB,C&PA 2014, Part 1.

Applications without notice

An application for a Part 1 injunction may be made without notice being given to R. If such an application is made the court must either adjourn the proceedings and grant an interim injunction (below), or adjourn the proceedings without granting an interim injunction, or dismiss the application (s 6).

Consultation, etc

By s 14, a person applying for a Part 1 injunction on notice must before doing so:

(a) consult the local youth offending team about the application, if R will be aged under 18 *when the application is made*;
(b) inform any other body or individual the applicant thinks appropriate of the application.

Where the court adjourns a without-notice application, before the date of the first on-notice hearing, the applicant must comply with (a) and (b) just mentioned, except that 'on that date' is substituted for the words italicised.

Interim injunctions

Section 7 provides as follows. Where the court adjourns the hearing of an application (whether made with notice or without) for a Part 1 injunction, it may grant an interim Part 1 injunction lasting until the final hearing of the application or until further order if it thinks it just to do so. An interim injunction made at a 'without-notice hearing' may not have the effect of requiring participation in particular activities.

Protection of witnesses

The provisions about special measures under the Youth Justice and Criminal Evidence Act 1999 (see p 236) apply to vulnerable and intimidated witnesses in the context of proceedings under A-sB,C&PA 2014, Part 1.

Variation or discharge

The court may vary or discharge a Part 1 injunction on the application of the person who applied for the injunction, or the respondent (s 8).

Breach of injunction

Arrest without warrant

A-sB,C&PA 2014, s 9 provides as follows.

Where a power of arrest is attached to a provision of a Part 1 injunction, a constable may arrest R without warrant if he has reasonable cause to suspect that R is in breach of the provision. The constable must inform the applicant for the injunction. The arrested person must, within the period of 24 hours beginning with the time of the arrest, be brought before:

(a) a judge of the High Court or a judge of the county court, if the injunction was granted by the High Court;
(b) a judge of the county court, if the injunction was granted by the county court or the injunction was granted by a youth court but R is aged 18 or over;
(c) a justice of the peace, if neither (a) nor (b) applies.

In calculating when the period of 24 hours ends, Christmas Day, Good Friday and any Sunday are disregarded.

The judge before whom a person is brought under (a) or (b) may remand the person if the matter is not disposed of straight away. The justice of the peace before whom a person is brought under (c) must remand the person to appear before the youth court that granted the injunction. A remand under s 9 or under s 10 below may be in custody or on bail. In the case of someone under 18 it must normally be on bail.

Issue of arrest warrant

Section 10 deals with this.

If the applicant for a Part 1 injunction thinks that R is in breach of any of its provisions, the applicant may apply for the issue of a warrant for his arrest. The application must be made to:

(a) a judge of the High Court, if the injunction was granted by the High Court;
(b) judge of the county court, if:
   (i) the injunction was granted by the county court, or
   (ii) the injunction was granted by a youth court but R is aged 18 or over;
(c) a justice of the peace, if neither (a) nor (b) applies.

A judge or justice may issue such a warrant only if the judge or justice has reasonable grounds for believing that R is in breach of a provision of the injunction.

A warrant issued by a judge of the High Court, or of the county court, must require R to be brought before the High Court or county court, as the case may be. A warrant issued by a justice of the peace must require R to be brought before the youth court that granted the injunction, if the person is aged under 18, and before the county court, if he is aged 18 or over.

A constable who arrests a person under a warrant issued under s 10 must inform the applicant for the injunction.

If R is brought before a court by virtue of such a warrant but the matter is not disposed of straight away, the court may remand R.

Contempt of court

Because an injunction is a civil order, breach of a Part 1 injunction is not a criminal offence. Where the person in breach of a Part 1 injunction is 18 or over, the breach is dealt with as a civil contempt of court (which is imprisonable). The breach is dealt with by the High Court or the county court, as appropriate. The breach must be proved beyond reasonable doubt.

Supervision orders and detention orders

A-sB,C&PA 2014, Sch 2 deals with cases where a person alleged to be in breach of a Part 1 injunction is under 18. It provides that, on the application of the person who applied for the injunction, a youth court can make one of the following orders, where it is satisfied beyond reasonable doubt that a person under 18 is in breach of that injunction:

(a) a supervision order;
(b) if the person is aged 14 to 17 inclusive, a detention order.

A person making an application for such an order must before doing so:

(a) consult the youth offending team specified in the injunction or, if none is specified, the local youth offending team; and
(b) inform any other body or individual the applicant thinks appropriate.

In determining the application the court must consider any representations made by the youth offending team.

A supervision order is an order imposing on the person in respect of whom it is made ('the defaulter') one or more of the following: a supervision requirement; an activity requirement; a curfew requirement.

The maximum period of any requirement is six months. A supervision order containing a curfew requirement may also contain an electronic monitoring requirement.

A detention order is an order that the person in respect of whom it is made (the defaulter) be detained for a period (not exceeding three months) specified in the order in youth detention accommodation.

PERSONS ACTING IN ANTI-SOCIAL MANNER: REQUIREMENT TO GIVE NAME AND ADDRESS

The Police Reform Act 2002, s 50(1) provides that, if a constable in uniform has reasonable grounds to believe that a person has been acting in an anti-social manner, he may require that person to give his name and address.

For these purposes, 'anti-social behaviour' means:

(a) conduct that has caused, or is likely to cause, harassment, alarm or distress to any person;
(b) conduct capable of causing nuisance or annoyance to a person in relation to that person's occupation of residential premises; or
(c) conduct capable of causing housing-related nuisance or annoyance to any person ('housing-related' means directly or indirectly relating to the housing management functions of a housing provider or local authority).

Failure to give a name and address when required do so under s 50(1), or the provision of a false or inaccurate name or address, is an offence contrary to s 50(2).

CRIMINAL BEHAVIOUR ORDERS

Under A-sB,C&PA 2014, Part 2 (ss 22–33), following a conviction for any criminal offence in the Crown Court, a magistrates' court or a youth court, the court may make a criminal behaviour order (CBO). The CBO has replaced the anti-social behaviour order on conviction and an individual support order associated with such an order (under the Crime and Disorder Act 1998), and the drinking banning order on conviction (under the Violent Crime Reduction Act 2006). A CBO can be made where the court is satisfied beyond reasonable doubt that the offender (O) has engaged in behaviour that caused or was likely to cause harassment, alarm or distress to any person, and considers that the CBO will help in preventing O engaging in such behaviour. The provisions about special measures under the Youth Justice and Criminal Evidence Act 1999 (p 236) apply to vulnerable and intimidated witnesses in the context of the proceedings for a CBO (below). A CBO is an order which, for the purpose of preventing the offender from engaging in such behaviour, prohibits O from doing anything described in the order and requires O to do anything described in the order. The CBO must be additional to a sentence in respect of the offence, or an order of conditional discharge. It may be made only on the application of the prosecution. A CBO may be varied or discharged by the court which made it on the application of the offender or the prosecution. An interim order may be made where a court adjourns the hearing of an application for a CBO. Where the CBO is made against someone under 18 the operation of the CBO is subject to a system of annual review as long as he under 18.

By s 30(1), a person who without reasonable excuse

(a) does anything he or she is prohibited from doing by a CBO, or
(b) fails to do anything he or she is required to do by a CBO,

commits an indictable (either way) offence.

ANTI-SOCIAL BEHAVIOUR, ETC: THE COMMUNITY REMEDY

A-sB,C&PA 2014, s 102 deals with the case where:

(a) a constable, an investigating officer or a person authorised by a relevant prosecutor to give a conditional caution or youth conditional caution (P) has evidence that an individual (A) has engaged in anti-social behaviour (as defined below) or committed an offence,
(b) A admits to P that he has done so,
(c) P thinks that the evidence is enough for taking proceedings against A for an injunction under A-sB,C&PA 2014, s 1, or taking other court proceedings, but decides that it would be appropriate for A to carry out action of some sort instead, and
(d) if the evidence is that A has committed an offence, P does not think that it would be more appropriate for A to be given a conditional caution, youth conditional caution or a fixed penalty notice.

For the purposes of s 102, anti-social behaviour is defined as (i) conduct that has caused, or is likely to cause, harassment, alarm or distress, (ii) conduct capable of causing nuisance or annoyance to a person in relation to his occupation of residential premises, or (iii) conduct capable of causing housing-related nuisance or annoyance to anyone. 'Housing related' means directly or indirectly relating to the management functions of a housing provider or local authority.

For the purposes of s 102, 'action' includes the making of a payment to the victim (but does not include the payment of a fixed penalty).

Section 102 provides that, before deciding what action to invite A to carry out, P must make reasonable efforts to obtain the views of the victim (if any) of the anti-social behaviour or the offence, and in particular the victim's views as to whether A should carry out any of the actions listed in the community remedy document (see p 285).

If the victim expresses the view that A should carry out a particular action listed in the community remedy document, P must invite A to carry out that action unless it seems to P that it would be inappropriate to do so. Where there is more than one victim and they express different views, or for any other reason the italicised words do not apply, P must nevertheless take account of any views expressed by the victim (or victims) in deciding what action to invite A to carry out.

If A does not agree to carry out the particular action which he is invited to carry out, this can lead to a more formal sanction.

REVIEW OF RESPONSE TO COMPLAINTS ABOUT ANTI-SOCIAL BEHAVIOUR

A-sB,C&PA 2014, s 104 provides for the 'community trigger'. The community trigger is a mechanism for victims of persistent anti-social behaviour to request that relevant bodies undertake a case review. An anti-social behaviour (ASB) case review entails the relevant bodies sharing information in relation to the case, discussing what action has previously been taken and collectively deciding whether any further action could be taken. 'Relevant bodies' means *the relevant district council comprised within a county, or any type of unitary authority (or in Wales a county or county borough council); the chief officer of police for that body's area; each clinical commissioning group (Local Health Board in Wales)*; and any co-opted local provider of social housing. Any individual, community or business can make an application for a case review, and the relevant bodies must carry out an ASB case review if the threshold is met. The threshold is set by the relevant bodies. The threshold may be set with reference to the persistence of the behaviour, the potential for harm to the victim and the adequacy of response from agencies. The threshold should be set no higher than three complaints, but the relevant bodies may choose to set a lower threshold.

The ASB review mechanism is intended as a backstop safety net for the victims of anti-social behaviour who consider that there has not been an appropriate response to their complaints about such behaviour.

The relevant bodies in each local government area must make and publish arrangements for ASB case review procedures. Joint arrangements may be made for a larger area such as the police force area. The bodies carrying out the ASB case review must inform the applicant of their decision on whether or not the threshold for review is met, the outcome of the review and any recommendations made as a result of the review. In addition, they may make recommendations to a person who carries out public functions, including any of the bodies that have taken part in the review, and that person must have regard to the recommendations.

Relevant bodies must publish information about the number of ASB case review applications received, the number of times the threshold was not met, the number of reviews carried out and the number of reviews that resulted in further action.

Schedule 4 makes additional provisions for ASB case reviews. Review procedures must include:

(a) what happens when the applicant is dissatisfied with the way their application was dealt with or the review carried out;
(b) an assessment of the effectiveness of the procedures and revising them.

In making and revising the procedures, the relevant bodies must consult the local policing body (eg the PCC), and such local providers of social housing as they consider appropriate.

Schedule 4 also requires the bodies italicised above to make arrangements for co-opting local providers of social housing to be included among the relevant bodies. Those bodies must consult such other local providers of social housing as they consider appropriate in carrying out ASB reviews.

VIOLENT OFFENDER ORDERS

Nature of orders and applications for such orders

CJIA 2008, Part 7 (ss 98 to 117) provides that a 'violent offender order' (VOO) may be made in respect of a qualifying offender imposing prohibitions, restrictions or conditions for the purpose of protecting the public from the risk of serious violent harm caused by the offender. The minimum term of a VOO is two years and the maximum, five. The reference to protecting the public includes the public in the UK, or any particular members of the public in the UK, from the risk of serious physical or psychological harm caused by that person committing one or more 'specified offences'.

'Specified offences' are:

(a) manslaughter;
(b) an offence under OAPA 1861, ss 4, 18 or 20 (soliciting murder, wounding with intent to cause grievous bodily harm or malicious wounding);
(c) attempting to commit murder or conspiracy to commit murder; or
(d) a corresponding service offence.

A 'qualifying offender' is a person aged 18 or over who has been convicted of a specified offence and given a custodial sentence of at least 12 months or a hospital order, or a person found not guilty of such an offence by reason of insanity but made subject to a hospital order or a supervision order, or a person found to be under a disability to be tried and to have done the act charged who has been made subject to such an order. A person is also a qualifying offender if the above terms are satisfied in respect of proceedings outside England and Wales in respect of equivalent offences or murder under the corresponding foreign law.

A chief officer of police may apply by way of complaint to a magistrates' court for a VOO in respect of a person who resides in his area, or who he believes is in, or intends to come to, that area, if it appears that: (a) that person is a qualifying offender; and (b) he has acted in such a way as to give reasonable cause to believe that it is necessary for such an order to be made. That application may be made to any magistrates' court whose area includes any part of the chief officer's police area, or any place in which it is alleged that the person so acted. An order may be made if conditions (a) and (b) above are satisfied. It may not be made so as to come into force at any time when the offender is subject to a custodial sentence, on licence, or subject to a hospital order or supervision order, in respect of an offence.

A VOO may contain prohibitions, restrictions or conditions preventing the offender from going to specified premises or places (whether at all or at specified times), attending specified events or having any (or specified) contact with a specified individual.

Provision is made for interim VOOs which apply before determination of an application.

Notification requirements

Offenders who are for the time being subject to VOOs (or interim VOOs) must notify the police, within three days of the making of the order, of particulars specified in CJIA 2008, s 108 (personal particulars including date of birth, name(s) on the relevant date, National Insurance number, home address and other addresses at which the offender may be found) and any other information to be prescribed by regulations. Changes must be notified within three days of the change in circumstances occurring. In addition, the offender must renotify the police annually of the information required to be given on initial notification; in respect of renotification of addresses (other than a home address) at which the offender may be found, provision is made for some other renotification period to be prescribed in regulations. The periodic renotification requirement does not apply in the case of an interim order. In addition, the time periods referred to above are suspended while a person is remanded in custody, in prison, or detained in hospital. The Criminal Justice and Immigration Act 2008 (Violent Offender Orders) (Notification Requirements) Regulations 2009 impose notification requirements in respect of travel outside the UK.

Offences

It is an indictable (either way) offence against CJIA 2008, s 113 for a person to fail, without reasonable excuse, to comply with any prohibition, restriction or condition contained in a VOO or interim VOO, or with any notification requirement, or to fail to provide fingerprints and/or a photograph if requested when making a notification. Knowingly providing false information when making a notification is also an indictable (either way) offence under s 113.

INJUNCTIONS TO PREVENT GANG-RELATED VIOLENCE AND DRUG-DEALING ACTIVITY

These injunctions are dealt with by the Policing and Crime Act 2009 (P&CA 2009), Part 4 (ss 34–50).

Those involved in gang-related violence or drug-dealing activity should be prosecuted for a criminal offence if there is sufficient evidence and it is in the public interest, but there may be instances where criminal proceedings have not yet been brought and applying for an injunction under the above provisions may be an appropriate response.

Power to grant injunctions to prevent gang-related violence and drug-dealing activity

P&CA 2009, s 34 empowers a youth court (if the respondent is under 18), and the High Court or a county court (in any other case), to grant an injunction in civil proceedings against a respondent aged 14 or over to prevent gang-related violence or gang-related drug-dealing activity if two conditions are met:

(a) that the court is satisfied on the balance of probabilities that the respondent has engaged in, or has encouraged or assisted, gang-related violence or gang-related drug-dealing activity; and

(b) that the court thinks it is necessary to grant the injunction for either or both of the following purposes:

   (i) to prevent the respondent from engaging in, or encouraging or assisting, gang-related violence or gang-related drug-dealing activity;

   (ii) to protect the respondent from gang-related violence or gang-related drug-dealing activity.

Something is 'gang-related' if it occurs in the course of, or is otherwise related to, the activities of a group that consists of at least three people, and has one or more characteristics that enable its members to be identified by others as a group. A judge in the Administrative Court has held, in reference to the requirement of a characteristic of a group that enables it to be identified by others as a group, that it is not sufficient that a police officer piecing together the available information is able to draw the conclusion of a link between members of the gang if there is no common characteristic that would enable others generally to be able to make that identification. Dealing with a gang composed of family members, he accepted that it is possible that such a gang might communicate to others that they have a cohesive characteristic of common family membership and they might indeed be known as a family gang but, he held, it is not sufficient if the group in question is an assortment of individuals who happen to have familial relationships if that is not an important badge of identification communicated to others and explains how others see them.

'Violence' includes a threat of violence.

'Drug-dealing activity' means the unlawful production, supply, importation or exportation of a controlled drug or a psychoactive substance, as defined in the Misuse of Drugs Act 1971 or the Psychoactive Substances Act 2016.

An injunction under s 34 may (for either or both of purposes (i) and (ii) above) prohibit the respondent from doing anything described in the injunction, or require the respondent to do anything described in the injunction.

The prohibitions and requirements included in the injunction must, so far as practicable, be such as to avoid any conflict with the respondent's religious beliefs and any interference with the times at which the respondent normally works or attends any educational establishment.

An injunction under s 34 may not include a prohibition or requirement that has effect after the end of the period of two years beginning with the day on which the injunction is granted.

The court may attach a power of arrest in relation to any prohibition in the injunction, or to any requirement in the injunction (other than a requirement which has the effect of requiring the respondent to participate in particular activities).

Applications for injunctions

By P&CA 2009, s 37, an application for an injunction under s 34 may be made by:

(a) the chief officer of police for a police area,
(b) the chief constable of the British Transport Police Force, or
(c) a local authority.

A chief officer of police can delegate the application for an injunction to an officer in his force.

An application can be made 'with notice' or 'without notice'.

Applications with notice

These require the applicant to notify the respondent of the application for the injunction. In addition, before applying for an injunction, the applicant must consult:

(a) any local authority, and any chief police officer, that the applicant thinks it appropriate to consult,
(b) the youth offending team(s) in the area(s) where it appears to the applicant that the respondent resides if the respondent is under 18 (and will be under 18 when the application is made), and
(c) any other body or individual that the applicant thinks it appropriate to consult.

If the court adjourns the hearing of a 'with notice' application for an injunction, it may grant an interim injunction if it thinks that it is just and convenient to do so.

Applications without notice

By s 39, an application under s 37 may be made without the respondent being given notice, in which case the above consultation requirement does not initially apply. If such an application is made the court must:

(a) dismiss it, or
(b) adjourn the proceedings until a full hearing, in which case the applicant must comply with the consultation requirement before the date of the first full hearing (ie a hearing of which notice has been given to the applicant and respondent).

If an application without notice is made, and the proceedings are adjourned, the court may grant an interim injunction if it thinks that it is necessary to do so (s 41). Such an interim injunction may not have the effect of requiring the respondent to participate in particular activities.

Applications without notice should not be routine but may be appropriate if an injunction is urgently required, if there is a risk that the respondent may flee if given prior notice of an injunction application, or if giving notice would endanger witnesses.

Variation and discharge of injunctions

An injunction may be varied or discharged after a review hearing, or on an application made by the applicant for the injunction or the respondent. If such an application is dismissed, no further application may be made by anyone without the court's consent.

Breach of injunction and enforcement

Arrest without warrant

This is governed by P&CA 2009, s 43, which applies if a power of arrest is attached to a provision of an injunction. Its provisions mirror those which apply to a breach of a 'Part 1 injunction' (p 718).

Issue of warrant of arrest

If the applicant for the injunction considers that the respondent is in breach of any of its provisions, he may apply under P&CA 2009, s 44 to a relevant judge for the issue of a warrant for the arrest of the respondent. A relevant judge may only issue a warrant if he has reasonable grounds for believing that the respondent is in breach of any provision of the injunction.

Punishment

Breach of an injunction granted under s 34 is punishable by the High Court or county court as a civil contempt of court where the person in breach is 18 or over. Where that person is under 18, special provision is made by P&CA 2009, Sch 5A (power to make a supervision order or a detention order). The provisions of Sch 5A correspond to those on pp 721–2. Breach of an injunction must be proved beyond reasonable doubt. If the respondent's behaviour constitutes a criminal offence, it should be dealt with as such.

Miscellaneous

The Secretary of State has published guidance on the use of gang-related injunctions. A chief officer of police or a local authority must have regard to the guidance published.

CLOSURE OF PREMISES ASSOCIATED WITH NUISANCE OR DISORDER, ETC

A-sB,C&PA 2014, Part 4, Ch 3 (ss 76–93) sets out provisions for the closure of premises associated with nuisance or disorder, etc, which replaced various provisions for closure in respect of licensed or non-licensed premises contained in the Licensing Act 2003 and the Anti-social Behaviour Act 2003.

Closure notices

Power to issue closure notices

A-sB,C&PA 2014, s 76 provides as follows.

A police inspector (or above), or the local authority, may issue a closure notice if satisfied on reasonable grounds that:

(a) the use of particular premises has resulted, or (if the notice is not issued) is likely soon to result, in nuisance to members of the public; or

(b) there has been, or (if the notice is not issued) is likely soon to be, disorder near those premises associated with the use of those premises,

and that the notice is necessary to prevent the nuisance or disorder from continuing, recurring or occurring.

A closure notice is a notice prohibiting access to the premises for a period specified in the notice. A closure notice may prohibit access:

(a) by all persons except those specified, or by all persons except those of a specified description;

(b) at all times, or at all times except those specified;

(c) in all circumstances, or in all circumstances except those specified.

A closure notice may not prohibit access by people who habitually live on the premises, or by the owner of the premises, and accordingly they must be specified under list entry (a) just mentioned.

A closure notice must:

(a) identify the premises;

(b) explain the effect of the notice;

(c) state that failure to comply with the notice is an offence;

(d) state that an application will be made under s 80 for a closure order;

(e) specify when and where the application will be heard;

(f) explain the effect of a closure order;

(g) give information about the names of, and means of contacting, persons and organisations in the area that provide advice about housing and legal matters.

A closure notice may be issued only if reasonable efforts have been made to inform:

(a) people who live on the premises (whether habitually or not), and

(b) any person who has control of or responsibility for the premises or who has an interest in them,

that the notice is going to be issued.

Before issuing a closure notice the police officer or local authority must ensure that any body or individual the officer or authority thinks appropriate has been consulted.

Duration

By A-sB,C&PA 2014, s 77, the maximum period that may be specified in a closure notice is 24 hours, except that the maximum period is 48 hours:

(a) if, in the case of a notice issued by a police officer, the officer is a superintendent (or above); or

(b) if, in the case of a notice issued by a local authority, the notice is signed by its chief executive officer (CEO) or a person designated by him for this purpose.

In calculating when the period of 48 hours ends, Christmas Day is disregarded.
    The 24-hour period may be extended by up to 24 hours if:

(a) in the case of a notice issued by a police officer, an extension notice is issued by a
     superintendent (or above), or
(b) in the case of a notice issued by a local authority, the authority issues an extension
     notice signed by its CEO or a person designated by him for this purpose.

An extension notice is a notice which identifies the closure notice to which it relates,
and specifies the period of the extension.

Cancellation or variation

A-sB,C&PA 2014, s 78 deals with this. It applies where the relevant officer or authority is no longer satisfied as mentioned in s 76, either (a) as regards the premises
as a whole, or (b) as regards a particular part of the premises. Section 78 provides
that, in a case within (a) the relevant officer or authority must issue a cancellation
notice (a notice cancelling the closure notice), and that in a case within (b) the relevant officer or authority must issue a variation notice (a notice varying the closure
notice so that it does not apply to the part of the premises referred to in (b)). Such
a notice issued by a local authority must be signed by the person who signed the
closure notice (or extension notice) (or, if unavailable, by another person qualified
to sign it).
    For these purposes, 'the relevant officer or authority' means:

(a) in the case of a closure notice issued by a police officer and not extended,
     that officer (or, if that officer is not available, another officer of the same or
     higher rank);
(b) in the case of a closure notice issued by a police officer and extended, the officer
     who issued the extension notice (or, if that officer is not available, another officer of
     the same or higher rank);
(c) in the case of a closure notice issued by a local authority, that authority.

Service

By A-sB,C&PA 2014, s 79, a closure notice, an extension notice, a cancellation notice,
or a variation notice must be served by a constable (notice issued by a police officer),
or by a representative of the authority (notice issued by a local authority). That person
must, if possible, (a) fix a copy of the notice to at least one prominent place on the
premises, to each normal means of access to the premises, and to any outbuildings
apparently used with or as part of the premises; and (b) give a copy of the notice to at
least one person apparently having control of or responsibility for the premises, to the
residents on the premises, and to anyone not living there who was informed (under
s 76) that the notice was going to be issued.
    If the constable or local authority representative reasonably believes, at the time of
serving the notice, that there are persons occupying another part of the building or
other structure in which the premises are situated whose access to that part will be impeded if a closure order is made under s 80 (below), he must also if possible serve the
notice on those persons.
    The constable or local authority representative may enter any premises, using rea-
sonable force if necessary, for the purposes of fixing a notice on the premises.

Closure orders

Power of court to make closure orders

A-sB,C&PA 2014, s 80 provides that whenever a closure notice is issued an application must be made to a magistrates' court for a closure order (unless the notice has been cancelled under s 78). Such an application must be made:

(a) by a constable, if the closure notice was issued by a police officer;
(b) by the authority that issued the closure notice, if the notice was issued by a local authority.

The application must be heard by the magistrates' court not later than 48 hours after service of the closure notice. In calculating that period, Christmas Day is disregarded.

The court may make a closure order if it is satisfied that:

(a) a person has engaged, or (if the order is not made) is likely to engage, in disorderly, offensive or criminal behaviour on the premises; or
(b) the use of the premises has resulted, or (if the order is not made) is likely to result, in serious nuisance to members of the public; or
(c) there has been, or (if the order is not made) is likely to be, disorder near those premises associated with the use of those premises,

and that the order is necessary to prevent the behaviour, nuisance or disorder from continuing, recurring or occurring.

A closure order is an order prohibiting access to the premises for a period specified in the order. The period may not exceed three months. A closure order may prohibit access:

(a) by all persons, or by all persons except those specified, or by all persons except those of a specified description;
(b) at all times, or at all times except those specified;
(c) in all circumstances, or in all circumstances except those specified.

A closure order may be made in respect of the whole or any part of the premises, and may include provision about access to a part of the building or structure of which the premises form part. The court must notify the relevant licensing authority if it makes a closure order in relation to premises in respect of which a premises licence is in force.

Proceedings for a closure order (or interim order, below) are civil in nature; for the implications of this, see pp 684–5.

Temporary orders

Where an application has been made for a closure order, and the court does not make a closure order, it may (under A-sB,C&PA 2014, s 81) order that the closure notice continues in force for a specified further period of not more than 48 hours, if satisfied that:

(a) the use of particular premises has resulted, or (if the notice is not continued) is likely soon to result, in nuisance to members of the public, or
(b) there has been, or (if the notice is not continued) is likely soon to be, disorder near those premises associated with the use of those premises,

and that the continuation of the notice is necessary to prevent the nuisance or disorder from continuing, recurring or occurring.

The court may adjourn the hearing of the application for not more than 14 days to enable the occupier of the premises, the person with control of or responsibility for them, or any other person with an interest in them to show why a closure order should not be made. On an adjournment, the court may order that the closure notice continues in force until the end of the adjournment period.

Extension of closure orders

At any time before the expiry of a closure order, an application may be made to a justice of the peace for an extension (or further extension) of the period for which the order is in force (A-sB,C&PA 2014, s 82). The application may be made by an inspector (or above) where the closure order was made on the application of a constable, and by the local authority where the closure order was made on its application. Such a police officer or local authority may apply only if satisfied on reasonable grounds that it is necessary for the period of the order to be extended to prevent the occurrence, recurrence or continuance of:

(a) disorderly, offensive or criminal behaviour on the premises;
(b) serious nuisance to members of the public resulting from the use of the premises, or
(c) disorder near the premises associated with the use of the premises,

and also satisfied that the appropriate consultee has been consulted about the intention to make the application. The 'appropriate consultee' means the local authority, in the case of an application by an inspector (or above), and the chief officer of police, in the case of an application by a local authority.

Where an application is made for an extension, the justice may issue a summons directed to any person on whom the closure notice was served, or any other person who appears to have an interest in the premises but on whom the closure notice was not served, requiring him to appear before the magistrates' court to respond to the application. A notice stating the date, time and place of the hearing of the application must be served on the persons to whom the summons is directed.

If the magistrates' court is satisfied that it is necessary for the period of the order to be extended to prevent the occurrence, recurrence or continuance of a matter mentioned in (a), (b) or (c) above, it may make an order extending (or further extending) the period of the closure order by a period not exceeding three months. The period of a closure order may not be extended so that the order lasts for more than six months.

Discharge of closure orders

A constable (where the order was made on the application of a constable), the local authority (on whose application the order was made), a person on whom the closure notice was served, and anyone else who has an interest in the premises but on whom the closure notice was not served, may apply for the closure order to be discharged by a magistrates' court (A-sB,C&PA 2014, s 83). The court may not discharge the order unless satisfied that the closure order is no longer necessary to prevent the occurrence, recurrence or continuance of disorderly, offensive or criminal behaviour on the premises, serious nuisance to members of the public resulting from the use of the premises, or disorder near the premises associated with the use of the premises.

Enforcement

By A-sB,C&PA 2014, s 85, an authorised person may enter premises in respect of which a closure order is in force, and do anything necessary to secure the premises against entry. An 'authorised person' is, in relation to an order made on the application of a constable, a constable or person authorised by the chief officer of police; and, in relation to an order made on the application of a local authority, a person authorised by the authority. A person so acting may use reasonable force. A person seeking to enter premises under s 85 must, if required to do so by or on behalf of the owner, occupier or other person in charge of the premises, produce evidence of his identity and authority before entering the premises. An authorised person may also enter the premises during the order to carry out essential maintenance or repairs to the premises.

Offences

A person who without reasonable excuse remains on or enters premises in contravention of a closure notice (including a notice continued in force under A-sB,C&PA 2014, s 81) commits an offence contrary to s 86(1).

A person who without reasonable excuse remains on or enters premises in contravention of a closure order commits an offence contrary to s 86(2).

A person who without reasonable excuse obstructs a person acting under s 79 or under the power to enter and secure in s 85 commits an offence contrary to s 86(3).

Guidance

Ministerial guidance has been issued to chief officers of police and local authorities about the exercise of the above functions under A-sB,C&PA 2014, Part 4, Ch 3.

DISPERSAL POWERS

A-sB,C&PA 2014, Part 3 (ss 34–42) introduced new dispersal powers which replace those under the Anti-social Behaviour Act 2003, Part 4 and the Violent Crime Reduction Act 2006, s 27.

Authorisations to use powers

By A-sB,C&PA 2014, s 34, an inspector (or above) may authorise the use in a specified locality, during a specified period of not more than 48 hours, of the powers given by s 35 (below). 'Specified' means specified in the authorisation.

An officer may give such an authorisation only if satisfied on reasonable grounds that the use of those powers in the locality during that period may be necessary for the purpose of removing or reducing the likelihood of:

(a) members of the public in the locality being harassed, alarmed or distressed, or
(b) the occurrence in the locality of crime or disorder.

In deciding whether to give such an authorisation an officer must have particular regard to the rights of freedom of expression and freedom of assembly set out in the European Convention on Human Rights, arts 10 and 11 (pp 756–7).

An authorisation must be in writing, must be signed by the officer giving it, and must specify the grounds on which it is given.

Directions under s 35 excluding a person from an area

A-sB,C&PA 2014, s 35 provides that if the following conditions are met and an authorisation is in force under s 34, a constable in uniform may direct a person who is in a public place in the locality specified in the authorisation:

(a) to leave the locality (or part of the locality), and
(b) not to return to the locality (or part of the locality) for the period specified in the direction (the exclusion period).

'Public place' means a place to which at the material time the public or a section of the public has access, on payment or otherwise, as of right or by virtue of express or implied permission. The exclusion period may not exceed 48 hours. Provided it begins during the period specified in the authorisation, the exclusion period may expire after that period.

The first condition is that the constable has reasonable grounds to suspect that the behaviour of the person in the locality has contributed or is likely to contribute to:

(i)   members of the public in the locality being harassed, alarmed or distressed, or
(ii) the occurrence in the locality of crime or disorder.

The second condition is that the constable considers that giving a direction to the person is necessary for the purpose of removing or reducing the likelihood of the events mentioned in (i) or (ii).

A direction:

(a) must be given in writing, unless that is not reasonably practicable;
(b) must specify the area to which it relates;
(c) may impose requirements as to the time by which the person must leave the area and the manner in which the person must do so (including the route).

Unless it is not reasonably practicable, the constable must tell the person to whom the direction is given that failing without reasonable excuse to comply with the direction is an offence. If the constable reasonably believes that the person to whom the direction is given is under 16, he may remove the person to a place where the person lives or a place of safety.

Any constable may withdraw or vary a direction, but a variation must not extend the duration of a direction beyond 48 hours from when it was first given. Notice of such a withdrawal or variation must be given to the person to whom the direction was given, unless that is not reasonably practicable, and, if given, must be given in writing unless that is not reasonably practicable.

By s 36, a constable may not give a direction:

(a) to a person who appears to him to be under 10;
(b) that prevents the person to whom it is given (P) having access to a place where P lives; or
(c) that prevents P attending at a place which P is required to attend for the purposes of his employment, or a contract of services, or by an obligation imposed by or under an enactment or by the order of a court or tribunal, or expected to attend for educational, training or medical treatment purposes, at a time when P is required or expected (as the case may be) to attend there.

A constable may not give a direction to a person if the person is one of a group of persons who are:

(a) engaged in conduct that is lawful under the Trade Union and Labour Relations (Consolidation) Act 1992, s 220 (p 770), or
(b) taking part in a public procession to which the Public Order Act 1986, s 11 applies (p 715) in respect of which written notice has been given in accordance with s 11 or is not required to be given under s 11.

In deciding whether to give a direction a constable must have particular regard to the rights of freedom of expression and freedom of assembly set out in the European Convention on Human Rights, arts 10 and 11.

Surrender of property

A-sB,C&PA 2014, s 37 provides that a constable who gives a person (P) a direction under s 35 may also direct P to surrender to the constable any item in P's possession or control that the constable reasonably believes has been used or is likely to be used in behaviour that harasses, alarms or distresses members of the public. Such a direction (a s 37 direction) must be given in writing, unless that is not reasonably practicable. A constable giving a s 37 direction must (unless it is not reasonably practicable) tell P that failing without reasonable excuse to comply with it is an offence, and give P written information about when and how P may recover the surrendered item.

The surrendered item must not be returned to P before the end of the exclusion period. If after the end of that period P asks for the item to be returned, it must be returned (unless there is some other statutory power to retain it). However, if it appears to a constable that P is under 16 and is not accompanied by a parent or other responsible adult, the item may be retained until P is so accompanied. If P has not asked for the return of the item before the end of 28 days beginning with the day on which the direction was given, the item may be destroyed or otherwise disposed of.

Record-keeping

A constable who gives a direction under A-sB,C&PA 2014, s 35 is required by s 38 to make a record of:

(a) the individual to whom the direction is given,
(b) the time at which the direction is given, and
(c) the terms of the direction (including in particular the area to which it relates and the exclusion period).

A constable who withdraws or varies a direction under s 35 must make a record of:

(a) the time at which the direction is withdrawn or varied,
(b) whether notice of the withdrawal or variation is given to the person to whom the direction was given and if it is, at what time, and
(c) if the direction is varied, the terms of the variation.

A constable who gives a direction under s 37 must make a record of:

(a) the individual to whom the direction is given,
(b) the time at which the direction is given, and
(c) the item to which the direction relates.

Offences

A person given a direction under A-sB,C&PA 2014, s 35 who fails without reasonable excuse to comply with it commits an offence under s 39(1).

A person given a direction under s 37 who fails without reasonable excuse to comply with it commits an offence under s 39(3).

Guidance

Ministerial guidance has been issued to chief officers of police about the exercise by their officers of those officers' functions under the above provisions.

RACIAL OR RELIGIOUS HATRED OR HATRED ON THE GROUNDS OF SEXUAL ORIENTATION

POA 1986, Part III (ss 17 to 29) provides indictable (either way) offences relating to racial hatred. POA 1986, Part IIIA (ss 29A to 29N) provides indictable (either way) offences relating to religious hatred and to hatred on grounds of sexual orientation.

To a large extent, the offences of religious hatred and hatred on the grounds of sexual orientation mirror those under ss 17 to 29 which forbid threatening, abusive or insulting words, behaviour or material intended or likely to cause racial hatred, *but they are limited to words, behaviour or material which is 'threatening' and D must intend thereby to stir up religious hatred or hatred on grounds of sexual orientation*. It is convenient to deal with these matters together within the parallel offences.

Section 17 provides that '*racial hatred*' means hatred against a group of persons defined by reference to colour, race, nationality (including citizenship) or ethnic or national origins (as to these words see p 658). Hereafter, such a group is described for convenience as a 'racial group'.

Section 29A provides that '*religious hatred*' means hatred against a group of persons defined by reference to religious belief or lack of religious belief.

Section 29AB defines '*hatred on the grounds of sexual orientation*' as meaning hatred against a group of persons defined by reference to sexual orientation (whether towards persons of the same sex, the opposite sex or both).

Other introductory points

The comments about 'threatening' and (POA 1986, Part III only) 'abusive' and 'insulting' on p 708 are equally applicable to the present offences.

POA 1986, s 29J provides that nothing in Part IIIA of the Act should be read or given effect in a way which prohibits or restricts discussion, criticism, or expressions of antipathy, dislike, ridicule, insult or abuse of particular religions or the beliefs or practices of their adherents, or of any other belief system or the beliefs or practices of its adherents, or proselytising or urging adherents of a different religion or belief system to cease practising their religion or belief system. Section 29JA provides that, for the avoidance of doubt, discussion or criticism of:

(a) sexual conduct or practices or the urging of persons to refrain from or modify such conduct or practices; or

(b) marriage which concerns the sex of the parties to the marriage,

shall not be taken of itself to be threatening or intended to stir up hatred.

Use of words or behaviour or display of written material

POA 1986, s 18(1) provides that a person who uses threatening, abusive or insulting words or behaviour, or displays any written material which is threatening, abusive or insulting, is guilty of an offence if:

(a) he intends thereby to stir up racial hatred; or
(b) having regard to all the circumstances, racial hatred is likely to be stirred up thereby.

The parallel offence created by s 29B relating to religious hatred or hatred on grounds of sexual orientation requires the use of *threatening* words or behaviour, or the display of written material which is *threatening*, and an *intention* thereby to stir up religious hatred or hatred on the grounds of sexual orientation.

'Written material' includes any sign or other visible representation. POA 1986, ss 18 and 29B do not apply to words or behaviour used, or written material displayed, solely for the purpose of being included in a television or sound broadcasting or cable service. In such a case, however, an offence might be committed under s 22 (or s 29F) when the programme is transmitted.

These offences may be committed in a public place or a private place. There is one limit in relation to private places. As with similar offences under POA 1986, ss 4 to 5 an offence is not committed by the use of words or behaviour, or the display of written material, by a person inside a dwelling which is not heard or seen except by other persons in that or another dwelling.

It is a defence for D to prove that he was inside a dwelling and had no reason to believe that the words or behaviour used, or the written material displayed, would be heard or seen by a person outside that or any other dwelling.

As already seen, the prosecution must prove in the case of s 18 offences, that D intended to stir up racial hatred by his threatening, abusive or insulting words, behaviour or display or that such hatred was likely to be stirred up thereby. Where an offence against s 29B is alleged, there must be proof that D intended by his threatening words, behaviour, or display to stir up religious hatred or hatred on grounds of sexual orientation.

Section 18(5) provides that a person who is not shown to have intended to stir up racial hatred is not guilty of an offence under s 18 if he did not intend his words or behaviour or the written material to be, and was not aware that it might be, threatening, abusive or insulting. Unlike comparable provisions in other offences in POA 1986, Part III, D does not have the burden of proving this lack of intent or awareness. There is no parallel provision to s 18(5) under s 29B as that section is limited to cases where D intended to stir up religious hatred or hatred on grounds of sexual orientation.

Racial or religious abuse or harassment unaccompanied by the mental element just described might, nevertheless, result in liability for an offence under CDA 1998, ss 31 (p 713) or 32 (p 665).

Publishing or distributing

POA 1986, s 19(1) provides that a person who publishes or distributes written material which is threatening, abusive or insulting is guilty of an offence if:

(a) he intends thereby to stir up racial hatred; or
(b) having regard to all the circumstances, racial hatred is likely to be stirred up thereby.

'Written material' includes any sign or other visible representation. Articles in electronic form are written material.

There must be a publication or distribution to the public or to a section of the public. 'The public' and 'section of the public' are not defined by the Act. There is no minimum number of persons to whom publication or distribution must be made in order for it to be to 'the public'. Ultimately, the question must be solved by common sense, the question being whether the publication or distribution has been on a scale and on a basis such as to be describable as being to 'the public'.

The Court of Appeal has held that a family living together in one house is not a 'section of the public'. The Court stated that 'section of the public' refers to some identifiable group, 'in other words members of a club or association'.

Although the prosecution must prove that D intended to stir up racial hatred by the publication or distribution or that such hatred was likely to be stirred up thereby, it does not have to prove any knowledge on D's part in relation to the content of the written matter which he has published, or distributed, although he will almost inevitably have had such mens rea if he is proved to have intended to stir up racial hatred. However, under s 19(2), it is a defence for a defendant who is not proved to have intended to stir up racial hatred to prove that he was not aware of the content of the matter and neither suspected nor had reason to suspect it of being threatening, abusive or insulting. The defence under s 19 is of obvious importance to innocent publishers or distributors, like newsagents.

Section 29C provides that a person who publishes or distributes written material which is threatening is guilty of an offence if he intends thereby to stir up religious hatred, or hatred on the grounds of sexual orientation. The publication or distribution of written material must be to the public or a section of the public.

Possession of material

POA 1986, s 23(1) provides that a person who has in his possession written material which is threatening, abusive or insulting, with a view to its being displayed, published, distributed, or included in a television or radio broadcast or in a cable service (whether or not by himself) is guilty of an offence if:

(a) he intends racial hatred to be stirred up thereby; or
(b) having regard to all the circumstances, racial hatred is likely to be stirred up thereby.

Section 23(1) also makes similar provision in relation to a recording of visual images or sounds.

For the above purposes, regard must be had to such display, publication, distribution, showing, playing or inclusion in a programme service, as D has, or it may reasonably be inferred that he has, in view.

The intended publication or distribution need not be by the person in possession. The result is that, if racially inflammatory pamphlets printed by X are deposited with Y for safekeeping in his warehouse until X wishes to collect and distribute them, the present offence can be committed by X and by Y (as long as the pamphlets are in the warehouse) because, since Y (as well as X) is in control of the pamphlets, Y and X are in possession of them.

As with s 19, the prosecution does not have to prove any mens rea on the part of a person charged with possession contrary to s 23 in relation to the content of the material possessed by him. Likewise, it need not necessarily be proved that D intended racial hatred to be stirred up by the publication or distribution, since it is enough that, if the material were published or distributed, racial hatred would be likely (having regard to all the circumstances) to be stirred up as a result of the publication or distribution. However, under s 23(3), it is a defence for a defendant who is not proved to have intended to stir up racial hatred to prove that he was not aware of the content of the material, and neither suspected nor had reason to suspect it of being threatening, abusive or insulting. This is of obvious importance to 'innocent' possessors of racialist material, such as warehousemen.

The person in possession of the material must have been in possession with a view to its publication or distribution. If there is a dispute about this, the magistrates or jury will have to draw such inferences as seem reasonable from the quantity and nature of the material possessed.

Section 29G parallels this offence in relation to religious hatred or hatred on the grounds of sexual orientation. In this case, however, the material must be 'threatening' and intended to stir up religious hatred or hatred on the grounds of sexual orientation.

A justice of the peace, if satisfied by information on oath laid by a constable that there are reasonable grounds to suspect that a person has possession of written material or a recording in contravention of s 23 or s 29G, may issue a warrant authorising the entry and search of premises where it is suspected the material or recording is situated. A constable executing such a warrant may use reasonable force if necessary.

Other offences

POA 1986, ss 20, 21 and 22 respectively provide offences relating to threatening, abusive or insulting words, behaviour or material in public plays, visual or sound recordings, and programmes in radio or television broadcasts or cable services, which are intended or likely to stir up racial hatred. A detailed explanation of these offences is outside the scope of this book.

Sections 29D, 29E and 29F respectively provide offences corresponding to those under ss 20, 21 and 22 in relation to threatening words, behaviour or material in public plays, visual or sound recordings, and programmes in broadcasts or cable services. In all these cases the play, recording, programme or broadcast must be intended to stir up religious hatred or hatred on the grounds of sexual orientation.

General

None of the above offences applies to a fair and accurate report of:

(a) proceedings in Parliament, the Scottish Parliament, or the National Assembly of Wales; or
(b) proceedings publicly heard before a court or tribunal exercising judicial authority.

However, in the case of a report of the proceedings of a court or tribunal, the exemption *only* applies if the report is published *contemporaneously* with those proceedings or, if it is not reasonably practicable or would be unlawful to publish a report of them contemporaneously (because of the law of contempt of court), is published *as soon as publication is reasonably practicable and lawful.*

No prosecution for an offence under POA 1986, Part III or Part IIIA may be instituted except by or with the consent of the Attorney General.

INDECENT, GROSSLY OFFENSIVE, THREATENING OR FALSE COMMUNICATIONS

Two statutes are relevant under this heading.

Malicious Communications Act 1988

The Malicious Communications Act 1988 (MCA 1988), s 1 makes it an indictable (either way) offence for any person to send to another:

(a) a letter, electronic communication or article of any description which conveys:
   (i)   a message which is indecent or grossly offensive,
   (ii) a threat, or
   (iii) information which is false and known or believed to be false by the sender; or
(b) any other article or electronic communication which is wholly or partly of an indecent or grossly offensive nature,

if his purpose or one of his purposes in sending it is that the message, threat or information should cause distress or anxiety to the recipient or to any other person to whom he intends that it, or its content or nature, should be communicated (s 1(1)).

A divisional court has held that the fact that a communication is political or educational in nature has no bearing on whether it is indecent or grossly offensive. The court added that it is possible to interpret s 1 in a way that is compatible with the European Convention on Human Rights, arts 9 and 10 (freedom of thought, conscience and religion and freedom of expression), by giving a heightened meaning to the terms 'grossly offensive' and 'indecent' or by reading into s 1 a provision to the effect that s 1 will not apply where to create an offence would be a breach of a person's Convention rights.

In relation to the sending of a threat, a defence exists if D shows that the threat is to reinforce a demand made by him on reasonable grounds and that he believed and had reasonable grounds for believing that it was a proper means of reinforcing the demand.

For the purposes of the MCA 1988 the term 'electronic communication' includes any oral or other communication by means of an electronic communication network, and any communication (however sent) that is in electronic form.

Communications Act 2003

The Communications Act 2003, s 127(1) provides that a person commits an indictable (either way) offence who:

(a) sends, by means of a *public* electronic communications network, a message or other matter which is grossly offensive or of an indecent, obscene or menacing character; or
(b) causes any such message or matter to be so sent.

A divisional court has held that a tweet is a message sent by means of a public electronic communications network because, although the twitter social networking platform is owned by a private company, it operates through the internet, a public electronic network provided for the public and paid for by the public through internet service providers.

The House of Lords has held that whether a message or other matter is grossly offensive for the purposes of s 127 must be judged by the standards of an open and just multiracial society; the words must be judged taking account of their context and all other relevant circumstances. To be guilty of a 'grossly offensive offence' under s 127, D must intend his words to be grossly offensive to those to whom they relate, or be aware that they might be taken to be so. If D has such a state of mind, it is irrelevant that a recipient of the message was not offended.

A divisional court has held that a message or other matter which does not create fear or apprehension in those to whom it is communicated, or who may reasonably be expected to see it, is not menacing; thus, if the person or persons who receive or read a message containing a threat would brush it aside as a silly joke or empty bombastic banter or would regard it as no more than merely 'nasty', it is not menacing. In deciding whether a message is menacing, its precise terms, and inferences to be drawn from it, need to be examined in the context in which (and the means by which) it was sent. The Court added that, to be guilty of a 'menacing offence' under s 127, D must intend that the message should be of a menacing character, or be aware that it may create fear or apprehension in any reasonable member of the public who reads or sees it.

In addition, it is an offence against s 127(2) to send, *for the purpose of causing annoyance, inconvenience or needless anxiety to another*, by means of a *public* electronic communications network, a message which is known to be false, or to cause such a message to be sent, or persistently to make use of such a network for such a purpose.

An offence under s 127 is a 'penalty offence' for the purposes of CJPA 2001 and may be dealt with under a fixed penalty procedure: see p 31.

SQUATTING IN A RESIDENTIAL BUILDING

A person commits an offence under the Legal Aid, Sentencing and Punishment of Offenders Act 2012, s 144(1) if:

(a) he is in a *residential building* as a trespasser having entered it as a trespasser,
(b) he knows or ought to know that he is a trespasser, and
(c) he is living in the building or intends to live there for any period.

The offence is not committed by someone holding over after the end of a lease or licence (even if he leaves and re-enters the building).

For the purposes of s 144:

(a) 'building' includes any structure or part of a structure (including a temporary or movable structure);
(b) a building is 'residential' if it is designed or adapted, before the time of entry, for use as a place to live; and
(c) the fact that a person derives title from a trespasser, or has the permission of a trespasser, does not prevent him from being a trespasser.

ENTERING AND REMAINING ON PROPERTY

The Criminal Law Act 1977 (CLA 1977), Part 2 (ss 6–13) provides certain offences relating to entering and remaining on premises. Although these offences are often associated with 'squatters', the relevant provisions extend to situations beyond those involving squatting.

For the purposes of these offences, 'premises' is defined as any building, any part of a building under separate occupation (eg a flat), any land ancillary to a building, and the site comprising any building or buildings together with any land ancillary thereto, and 'building' includes any immovable structure, and any movable structure, vehicle or vessel designed or adapted for use for residential purposes (eg a residential caravan or houseboat).

Violence for securing entry

By CLA 1977, s 6(1), it is an offence for any person, without lawful authority, to use or threaten violence for the purpose of securing entry into *any premises* either for himself or for any other person, provided that:

(a) there is someone present on those premises at the time who is opposed to the entry which the violence is intended to secure; and
(b) the person using or threatening the violence knows that this is the case.

Use or threat of violence

The essence of this offence is the use or threat of violence against a person or property for the purpose of securing entry into premises on which a person opposed to the entry is present: actual entry is not required. It is immaterial whether the entry which the violence is intended to secure is for the purpose of acquiring possession of the premises or for some other purpose. People who use or threaten violence in order to secure entry to a dance are guilty of the present offence if they know that someone inside is opposed to their entry; so are would-be squatters who, with such knowledge, seek to enter a house by such means; and so are protesters who likewise seek to enter a public building or a factory.

The violence used or threatened may be against a person or property (whether he or it is on or off the premises). It is important to recognise that the offence is to use 'violence', not 'force'. Although the difference may seem to be small, it is considerable in certain circumstances. It would no doubt amount to violence against the property to set fire to it to drive out those inside and thereby gain entry, but the degree of force necessary to insert a key and to secure entry does not amount to violence. It would be different if the lock were burst open by using violence against the door.

Someone on the premises opposed to the entry

Someone must be physically present on the premises who is opposed to the entry to them which the violence is intended to secure. He might equally be the owner of the premises or a trespasser who is opposed to the owner's re-entry. Clearly, the present offence is not committed where someone breaks into an empty house.

Mens rea

D must not only use or threaten violence for the purpose of securing entry into any premises but he must also know that there is someone on the premises at the time who is opposed to the entry in question.

Without lawful authority

An offence is not committed under CLA 1977, s 6(1) if the person using or threatening violence has lawful authority for acting in the prescribed way. This exemption is essential to protect the violent entries which might have to be made by police officers or bailiffs in executing warrants or orders of courts. However, the only entries so protected will be those where the form of violence used to secure entry is authorised by law.

Section 6(2) states that the fact that a person has any interest or right to possession or occupation of any premises does not give him lawful authority to use or threaten the use of violence for the purpose of securing his entry onto those premises. This means that landlords and other non-residential occupiers must seek to recover possession of their premises by an action in the civil courts, unless it is possible for them to effect a peaceful re-entry. If an occupier does succeed in re-entering his premises, he does not commit any offence by proceeding to eject any trespasser, whatever liability he may incur by virtue of his entry.

Displaced residential occupiers and protected intending occupiers

Special provision is made for people falling within the definition of a 'displaced residential occupier' or 'protected intending occupier' of premises or any access to them.

The offence under s 6(1) does not apply to a person who is a *displaced residential occupier* or a *protected intending occupier* of the premises in question or who is acting on behalf of such an occupier. This exemption does not have to be proved by D. Instead, if he adduces sufficient evidence (ie evidence which raises a reasonable doubt) that he was, or was acting on behalf of, such an occupier he is presumed to be, or to be acting on behalf of, such an occupier unless the contrary is proved by the prosecution.

By s 12, any person who was occupying any premises as a residence immediately before being excluded from occupation by anyone who entered those premises, or any access to those premises, as a trespasser is a *displaced residential occupier* of the premises as long as he continues to be excluded from occupation of the premises by the original trespasser or by any subsequent trespasser. A person who is a displaced residential occupier of premises by virtue of this provision is regarded as such an occupier also of any access to those premises. Section 12 also provides that a person who was himself occupying the premises as a trespasser before being excluded is not a displaced residential occupier. The obvious example of a displaced residential occupier is the householder who discovers squatters in his house when he returns from work or from holiday.

An involved definition of '*protected intending occupier*' is provided by s 12A.

The first type is an individual who, at the time of the request to leave:

(a) has in the premises in question a freehold interest or leasehold interest with not less than two years still to run;
(b) requires the premises for his own occupation as a residence;
(c) is excluded from occupation of them by a person who entered them, or any access to them, as a trespasser; and
(d) holds, or a person acting on his behalf holds, a written statement, signed by him and witnessed by a magistrate or commissioner for oaths, which:
  (i) specifies his interest in the premises, and
  (ii) states that he requires the premises for occupation as a residence for himself.
The purpose of the statement is to enable the police to identify the protected intending occupier and thereby prevent abuse of the protection given by the Act.

The second type of protected intending occupier is an individual who, at the time of the request to leave:

(a) has a tenancy of the premises (other than a tenancy falling within the other two definitions) or a licence to occupy them granted by a person with a freehold interest or a leasehold interest with not less than two years still to run in the premises;
(b) requires the premises for his own occupation as a residence;
(c) is excluded from occupation of the premises by a person who entered them, or access to them, as a trespasser; and

(d) holds, or a person acting on his behalf holds, a written statement:
   (i) which specifies that he has been granted a tenancy of those premises or a licence to occupy them,
   (ii) which specifies the interest in the premises of the person who granted that tenancy or licence to occupy (the landlord),
   (iii) which states that he requires the premises for occupation as a residence for himself, and
   (iv) which is signed by the landlord and by the tenant or licensee and witnessed by a magistrate or commissioner for oaths.

The third type of protected intending occupier is an individual who, at the time of the request to leave:

(a) has a tenancy of the premises in question (other than a tenancy falling within the other two definitions) or a licence to occupy them granted by a local authority, the Regulator of Social Housing, or a registered housing association or certain other bodies;
(b) requires the premises for his own occupation as a residence;
(c) is excluded from occupation of them by a person who entered them, or any access to them, as a trespasser; and
(d) has been issued by or on behalf of the authority, Regulator or association with a certificate stating that the authority, etc is one to which these provisions apply and that he has been granted a licence or tenancy to occupy the premises as a residence.

Adverse occupation of residential premises

CLA 1977, s 7(1) creates an offence of 'adverse occupation'. It provides that any person who is on any premises (including any access to them whether or not any such access constitutes premises within the meaning of CLA 1977) as a trespasser, after having entered as such, is guilty of an offence if he fails to leave those premises on being required to do so by or on behalf of a *displaced residential occupier, or a person who is a protected intending occupier of the premises.*

Section 7 gives a displaced residential occupier or a protected intending residential occupier of premises (eg a buyer or tenant who has not yet taken up occupation) who has been excluded from them by trespassers a swifter remedy for recovering possession of them than the available civil remedy. He may require the trespassers to leave and they commit an offence if they fail to do so.

There is no time set upon departure and it is submitted that this indicates that the requirement is immediate.

Three defences are provided by s 7(3), the burden of proof in each case being on D:

(1) It is a defence that D believed that the person requiring him to leave was not a displaced residential occupier or a protected intending occupier of the premises, or someone acting on his behalf (s 7(2)). This plea will rarely succeed, particularly in the light of the requirement in the case of a protected intending occupier of a written statement or certificate to this effect.
(2) It is a defence that the premises in question are or form part of premises used mainly for non-residential purposes and that D was not on any part of the premises used wholly or mainly for residential purposes (s 7(3)). This means, for instance, that people involved in a factory sit-in do not commit the present offence if they fail to leave when required by a resident owner, so long as they are not in his flat or

in part of the premises used wholly or mainly for access to, or in connection with, the flat.

(3) Where D was requested to leave by a person claiming to be (or to act on behalf of) a protected intending occupier, it is a defence for D to prove that, although asked to do so by D at the time that he was requested to leave, the person requesting him to leave failed at that time to produce a written statement, or certificate, complying with CLA 1977 (s 12A(9)).

Trespassing with weapon of offence

CLA 1977, s 8(1) provides that a person who is on any premises as a trespasser, after having entered as such, is guilty of an offence if, without lawful authority or reasonable excuse, he has with him on the premises any weapon of offence. As to 'has with him' see p 603.

The term 'weapon of offence' means any article made or adapted for use for causing injury to or incapacitating a person, or intended by the person having it with him for such use. An identical definition is discussed on p 911.

INTERIM POSSESSION ORDERS IN RELATION TO PREMISES

Obtaining a final possession order in respect of premises can take rather longer than desirable. As a result an interim possession order, which can be obtained more speedily, has been introduced by rules of court. By the Criminal Justice and Public Order Act 1994 (CJPOA 1994), s 76(2), it is an offence for a person to be present on premises as a trespasser at any time during the currency of such an order. However, no offence is committed if such a person leaves within 24 hours of the time of service of the order and does not return, or if a copy of the order was not affixed to the premises in accordance with the rules of court. A person in occupation at the time of service, who leaves the premises, commits an offence under s 76(4) if he re-enters the premises as a trespasser or attempts to do so after the expiry of the order but within a period of one year from service of the order.

By s 75(1), a person commits an indictable (either way) offence if, for the purpose of obtaining an interim possession order, he makes a statement which he knows to be false or is misleading in a material particular, or recklessly makes such a statement. Likewise, a person commits an indictable (either way) offence under s 75(2) if he knowingly or recklessly makes such a statement to resist the making of an interim possession order.

POWER TO REMOVE TRESPASSERS

Direction to leave

CJPOA 1994, s 61 provides that if the senior police officer (the most senior in rank of the police officers present at the scene) reasonably believes that two or more persons are trespassing on land, that they are present with the common purpose of residing there for any period, that reasonable steps have been taken by or on behalf of the occupier to ask them to leave and that:

(a) any of those persons has caused damage to property on the land or used threatening, abusive or insulting words or behaviour towards the occupier, a member of his family or an employee or agent of his; or

(b) those persons have between them brought six or more vehicles onto the land, he may direct those persons, or any of them, to leave the land and to remove any vehicles or other property they have with them on the land. The direction must be to leave immediately or as soon as reasonably practicable, rather than at a future time.

Where the persons in question are reasonably believed by the senior officer present to be persons who were not originally trespassers but have become trespassers on the land, he must reasonably believe that the other conditions above are satisfied after those persons became trespassers before he can exercise these powers.

The senior officer must reasonably believe that two or more persons are present on the land as trespassers with the common purpose of residence, no matter how brief that intended period of residence may be. A person can have a purpose of residing in a place notwithstanding that he has a home elsewhere. 'Land' does not include buildings other than agricultural buildings, nor does it include scheduled monuments or land forming part of a highway unless it is a footpath, bridleway, byway open to all traffic, restricted byway, or cycle track. The term includes 'common land', whether public or privately owned common land.

The senior officer must also reasonably believe that reasonable steps have been taken by or on behalf of the occupier (the person entitled to possession of the land by virtue of an estate or interest held by him) to require the trespassers to leave.

The senior officer, reasonably believing these facts, may require such persons to leave without further reason if he reasonably believes they have brought six or more vehicles onto the land. If they have not, he must reasonably believe that any of those persons has caused damage to the land or to property on the land (eg crops or trees), or has used threatening, abusive or insulting words or behaviour towards the persons specified (the occupier of the land, a member of his family or an employee or agent of his). Thus overnight campers are outside these provisions, provided that they have not caused damage to property on the land or used such words or behaviour. 'Damage' includes the deposit of any substance capable of polluting the land.

Where the land in question is common land, the references in s 61 to trespassing and trespassers include acts and persons doing acts which constitute a trespass as against the occupier or an infringement of the commoners' rights, and references to 'the occupier' include the commoners or any of them or, where the public has access to the common, the local authority as well as any commoner.

For the purposes of s 61, the term 'vehicle' includes any vehicle, whether or not it is in a fit state for use on roads, and includes any chassis or body, with or without wheels, appearing to have formed part of such a vehicle, and any load carried by, and anything attached to, such a vehicle, and a caravan.

The purpose of s 61 is to give the occupier of the land a swifter remedy for recovering possession of it than the available civil remedy.

Offences

If a trespasser directed to leave complies with that direction, he commits no offence. On the other hand, he commits an offence under CJPOA 1994, s 61(4) if, knowing that a direction has been given which applies to him:

(a) he fails to leave the land (with any vehicle or other property he is required to remove), as soon as reasonably practicable; or

(b) having left, he again enters the land as a trespasser within a three-month period beginning on the day on which the direction is given.

(a) and (b) above are separate offences. By s 61(6), it is a defence for D to prove that:

(a) he was not trespassing on the land; or
(b) he had a reasonable excuse for failing to leave the land as soon as reasonably practicable or, as the case may be, for again entering the land as a trespasser.

The defence of 'not trespassing' refers to not trespassing at the time that the senior police officer forms his reasonable belief, and not the time of the prohibited conduct.

Police powers

By CJPOA 1994, s 62, where a direction under s 61 has been given, a constable may seize and remove a vehicle if he reasonably suspects that a person to whom the direction applies has, without reasonable excuse, failed to remove the vehicle which appears to belong to him or be in his possession or control. The same powers apply where such a person has, without reasonable excuse, re-entered the land within a period of three months from the date of the direction.

POWER TO REMOVE TRESPASSERS WHERE AN ALTERNATIVE SITE IS AVAILABLE

Direction to leave

CJPOA 1994, s 62A provides that, where the senior police officer present at the scene reasonably believes that certain conditions are satisfied in relation to a person and land, he may direct the person to leave the land and to remove any vehicle and other property which he has with him on the land. The conditions are:

(a) that the person and one or more others ('the trespassers') are trespassing on land;
(b) that the trespassers have between them at least one vehicle on the land;
(c) that the trespassers are there for the common purpose of residing there for any period;
(d) if it appears to the officer that the person has one or more caravans in his possession or control on the land, that there is a suitable pitch on a relevant caravan site (ie a site in the same local authority area managed by that authority, a private registered provider of social housing, or a registered social landlord) for the caravan(s); and
(e) that the occupier of the land or someone acting on his behalf has asked the police to remove the trespassers.

Such a direction may be communicated to the person to whom it applies by any constable at the scene. 'Land' does not include buildings other than agricultural buildings or scheduled monuments. A person may be regarded as having a purpose of residing in a place even if he has a home elsewhere, as would be the case where there is a 'sited' residential caravan. 'Occupier' and 'vehicle' have the same meaning as in CJPOA 1994, s 61. Section 62D makes the same provision in respect of common land as applies to s 61.

Where a police officer proposes to give such a direction he must consult every local authority within whose area the land is situated as to whether there is a suitable pitch for the caravan or each of the caravans on a relevant caravan site situated in their area.

Offences

By CJPOA 1994, s 62B(1), a person commits an offence if he knows that a direction under s 62A has been given which applies to him and (a) he fails to leave the land as soon as reasonably practicable, or (b) he enters any land within the area of the relevant local authority as a trespasser within a period of three months with the intention of residing there. Section 62B(5) provides defences where D can show:

(a) that he was not trespassing on land in respect of which he is alleged to have committed the offence; or

(b) that he had a reasonable excuse for failing to leave as soon as reasonably practicable, or for entering land in the area of the relevant local authority as a trespasser with the intention of residing there; or

(c) that at the time the direction was given he was under 18 and was residing with his parent or guardian.

Police powers

CJPOA 1994, s 62C provides that, where a constable reasonably suspects that a person subject to such a direction has, without reasonable excuse, failed to remove any vehicle which appears to belong to him or to be under his possession or control, or that such a person has entered any land in the area of the relevant local authority as a trespasser with a vehicle within the period of three months from the day of the direction, he may seize and remove the vehicle.

UNAUTHORISED CAMPING WITH A VEHICLE

CJPOA 1994, s 77 empowers a county council, district council or London borough council to direct persons residing in a vehicle or vehicles to leave:

(a) any land forming part of a highway;

(b) any other unoccupied land in the open air; or

(c) any occupied land in the open air where they are camping without the consent of the occupier of the land.

Such a direction may be addressed to a particular person or persons or to all of the occupants of vehicles on the land. It is not necessary for the local authority to show that there has been any form of nuisance caused by their presence.

Where such notice of a direction has been served, any person who knows that the direction has been given, and that it applies to him, commits an offence under s 77(3):

(a) if he fails, as soon as practicable, to leave the land or remove from the land any vehicle or any other property which is a subject of the direction; or

(b) if, having removed any such vehicle or property, he again enters the land with a vehicle within a period of three months from the day upon which the direction was given.

Section 77(5) provides a defence where such failure to leave or remove a vehicle or other property as soon as practicable, or the re-entry with a vehicle, was due to illness, mechanical breakdown, or other immediate emergency. The onus is upon D to show such a defence.

If a direction under s 77 is not complied with, the local authority can make an application to a magistrates' court under s 78 for an order for the removal by local authority officers and employees of persons and vehicles on the land in contravention of the direction. Wilful obstruction of someone acting under such an order is an offence under s 78(4). Although police officers do not actually execute an order under s 78, they will often be in attendance in view of the risk to public order.

AGGRAVATED TRESPASS

Offence of aggravated trespass

CJPOA 1994, s 68(1) states that a person commits the offence of aggravated trespass if he trespasses on land and, in relation to any lawful activity which persons are engaged in, or are about to engage in, on that land or adjoining land, does there anything which is intended by him to have the effect:

(a) of intimidating those persons or any of them so as to deter them or any of them from engaging in that activity;
(b) of obstructing that activity; or
(c) of disrupting that activity.

For this purpose, an activity on the part of a person or persons on land is 'lawful' if he or they may engage in the activity on that land on that occasion without committing an offence against English law or trespassing on the land. The Supreme Court has held that an activity is not rendered unlawful by some unlawful act or event incidental or collateral to, or remote from, it; the unlawfulness must be integral to the activity in question.

The persons engaged, or about to engage, in the relevant lawful activity must physically be present on the land in question at the time of the alleged trespass.

Some act is required in addition to trespass. It must be specified in the charge and must be shown to be intended to have one of the effects set out at (a)–(c). Thus a trespasser who gives drugged meat to gundogs commits such an act, as does someone who immobilises a bulldozer on a construction site. Indeed, a divisional court has held that a trespasser commits an offence under s 68 if he does an act with intent to commit a further act, which is not committed, and thereby to intimidate, obstruct or disrupt a lawful activity, if the act done is sufficiently closely connected with the intended intimidation, etc as to be more than merely preparatory to it. On this basis, the court upheld the conviction under s 68 of a person who had trespassed on land and run after a hunt with the intention of getting close enough to do something to disrupt it. In a case concerned with a demonstration in a shop by trespassers, a divisional court dealt with the question of whether continued occupation of land by the trespassers could amount in itself to a further act distinct from the act of trespass for the purposes of s 68(1). It held that it could. It stated that whether or not continued occupation of land by trespassers in a particular case did amount in itself to a further act distinct from the act of trespass depended on the circumstances in which the occupation had taken place. If those who trespassed continued to remain on land 'in force', they might be guilty of aggravated trespass if they continued to occupy the land with the necessary intent that that continued occupation should have one of the effects (a) to (c) above. On the other hand, it said, if that occupation was not 'in force' or 'mass occupation', it would be difficult, if not impossible, to prove the necessary intent.

The act must be committed on land. 'Land' does not include land forming part of a highway unless it is a footpath, bridleway, etc. A divisional court has held that 'land' in s 68 includes buildings.

A failure to do something is not enough. Trespassers who were already at a particular spot, who refused on an impulse to move to allow other persons to pass, would not commit an offence under s 68; whereas it would be an offence if they deliberately placed themselves there with the intention of disrupting the activity.

The offence is one requiring 'intent' to create one of these specified effects. The trespassing rambler who walks through grouse moors will not commit this offence even though he disrupts a shoot, if that was not his intention. Those who protest at the building of a new road will commit the offence if they deliberately sit down on private land in front of the machines because they intend to obstruct or disrupt the lawful activity of the developers.

Since they are not acting to prevent an unlawful act, protesters who are otherwise guilty under s 68 cannot rely on the common law defence of defence of property as a defence to a charge of aggravated trespass, because that defence is limited to defence against an act which is criminal or tortious (see p 656).

Direction to leave

By CJPOA 1994, s 69, where the senior police officer present at the scene reasonably believes that:

(a) a person is committing, has committed or intends to commit the offence of aggravated trespass on land; or
(b) two or more persons are trespassing on land and are present there with the common purpose of intimidating persons so as to deter them from engaging in a lawful activity or of obstructing or disrupting a lawful activity,

he may direct that person, or those persons (or any of them), to leave the land. 'Land' has the same meaning as in s 68.

A person who, knowing that such a direction has been given which applies to him, fails to leave the land as soon as practicable or, having left, again enters the land as a trespasser within the period of three months beginning with the day on which the direction was given, commits an offence under s 69(3).

It is a defence to a charge of an offence under s 69(3) for D to prove that he was not trespassing on the land, or that he had a reasonable excuse for failing to leave the land as soon as practicable or, as the case may be, for again entering the land as a trespasser (s 69(4)).

TRESPASSING ON PROTECTED SITE

The Serious Organised Crime and Police Act 2005 (SOCPA 2005), s 128(1) provides that a person commits an offence if he enters, or is on, any protected site in England or Wales as a trespasser.

A 'protected site' is either a nuclear site (ie the outer perimeter (fences, etc) of premises in respect of which a nuclear site licence exists and other premises within that perimeter) or a 'designated site'. A 'designated site' is one specified or described by order by the Secretary of State. A site may only be designated if:

(a) it is comprised in Crown land;
(b) it is comprised in land belonging to Her Majesty in Her private capacity or to the immediate heir to the Throne in his private capacity; or
(c) this is considered appropriate in the interests of national security.

SOCPA 2005 (Designated Sites) Order 2005 designates HM Naval Base, Clyde; Northwood Headquarters; RAF Brize Norton; RAF Croughton; RAF Fairford;

RAF Feltwell; RAF Fylingdales; RAF Lakenheath; RAF Menwith Hill; RAF Mildenhall; RAF Welford; Royal Navy Armaments Depot Coulport; and Sea Mounting Centre Marchwood as designated sites. SOCPA 2005 (Designated Sites under s 128) Order 2007 designates the following sites: 85 Albert Embankment; Buckingham Palace; the Ministry of Defence Main Building, Whitehall; the Old War Office Building, Whitehall; Thames House, Millbank; St James's Palace Site; the Chequers Estate Site; the Downing Street Site; the GCHQ Hubble Road Site; the GCHQ Scarborough Site; the GCHQ Bude Site; the Highgrove House Site; the Palace of Westminster and Portcullis House Site; the Sandringham House Site; the Windsor Castle Site; the Kensington Palace Site; and the Anmer Hall Site as designated sites.

It is a defence for a person charged with an offence under s 128 to prove that he did not know, and had no reasonable cause to suspect, that the site was protected (s 128(4)). No proceedings for such an offence may be instituted without the consent of the Attorney General.

CONTROLS ON ACTIVITIES IN THE PARLIAMENT SQUARE AND PALACE OF WESTMINSTER CONTROLLED AREAS

The Police Reform and Social Responsibility Act 2011, Part 3 deals with these matters. Its provisions are dealt with in Chapter 26 on the companion website.

PUBLIC ASSEMBLIES

Generally

POA 1986, s 14 authorises the senior police officer, on the basis of the same grounds of reasonable belief as in the case of conditions on public processions (p 716), to impose such conditions in relation to the place at which any public assembly (an assembly of two or more persons in a public place which is wholly or partly open to the air) may be (or continue to be) held, its maximum duration, or the maximum number of persons who may constitute it, as appear to him to be necessary to prevent serious public disorder, serious damage to property, serious disruption to the life of the community, or intimidation. A divisional court has held that conditions may be imposed under this provision requiring those assembled to disperse by a specified route and to stay in a specified place as long as necessary to enable dispersal to take place safely and without disorder.

In the case of an assembly which is actually being held, the senior police officer is the police officer most senior in rank present at the scene; in such a case it is not necessary for the notice to be in writing. In the case of an assembly which is intended to be held, the senior police officer is the chief officer of police; in such a case the chief officer must give the notice in writing. Although extensive detail is not required, the chief officer's notice must provide sufficient detail of the reasons for his belief in the ground (or grounds) for a demonstrator to understand why a direction is being given.

A chief officer of police may delegate any of his functions under ss 14 or 14A (below) to an assistant chief constable or an assistant commissioner of police (as the case may be).

Offences under s 14 are committed by the same classes of persons as in relation to a breach of a public procession condition (s 14(4), (5) and (6)): see p 716.

Trespassory assemblies

These are dealt with by POA 1986, ss 14A, 14B and 14C.

Section 14A is concerned with the prohibition of a trespassory assembly before it has taken place. Where a trespassory assembly has already commenced, police involvement is limited to the prohibition of its continuance if an officer believes that this is necessary to prevent a breach of the peace.

Section 14A provides that where a chief officer of police reasonably believes that an assembly of 20 or more people is intended to be held in any district at a place on land in the open air to which the public has no right of access or only a limited right of access and that the assembly:

(a) is likely to be held without the permission of the occupier of the land or to conduct itself in such a way as to exceed the limits of any permission of his or the limits of the public's right of access; and
(b) may result:
    (i)   in serious disruption to the life of the community, or
    (ii) where the land, or a building or monument on it, is of historical, architectural, archaeological or scientific importance, in significant damage to the land, building or monument,

he may apply to the council of the district for an order prohibiting for a specified period the holding of all trespassory assemblies in the district, or a part of it as specified. An order may only be made by a council with the Secretary of State's consent. In London the relevant Commissioner may make an order with such consent. Where such an order is made, it will operate to prohibit any assembly of 20 or more which is held on land in the open air to which the public has no right of access or only a limited right of access and takes place without the permission of the occupier, or in excess of his permission or the public's right of access. Such an order may not prohibit such an assembly for a period exceeding four days or in an area exceeding a circle with a radius of five miles from a specified centre.

It is irrelevant that the anticipated assembly is open to the public or is a private ceremony, but it must be held on land in the open air. This can be contrasted with the power to impose conditions on a public assembly under s 14; there the assembly may be held wholly or partly in the open air. 'Land' in s 14A includes land forming part of the highway. It follows, for example, that an intended obstructive assembly of 20 or more on the highway (which is by definition trespassing, since the public only have a right to pass and repass on it and make other reasonable use of it) can be the trigger for an order under s 14A.

It is important to understand that these powers are restricted to assemblies which are reasonably believed to be trespassory in nature. Assemblies *with permission* are not covered by the legislation unless there is a reasonable belief that they will be conducted in such a way as to exceed that permission.

Offences

A person who organises an assembly which he knows to be prohibited under s 14A commits an offence against s 14B(1). So does a person who takes part (s 14B(2)), or who incites another to do so (s 14B(3)).

Central to these offences is that the assembly must be prohibited under s 14A, and an assembly is prohibited only if, within the area and duration of the prohibition order, it:

(a) is held on land in the open air to which the public has no right of access or only a limited right of access; and

(b) takes place in the prohibited circumstances, ie without the permission of the occupier of the land or so as to exceed the limits of any permission of his or the limits of the public's right of access.

In the case of assemblies on the highway, the public's right of access to the highway has been held by the House of Lords to include the right to hold a public assembly which is peaceful and non-obstructive of the rights of passage of other users of the highway provided the assembly is a reasonable use of the highway.

Police powers

By s 14C, if a constable in uniform reasonably believes that a person is on his way to an assembly within the area to which such an order under s 14A applies, which the constable reasonably believes is likely to be an assembly which is prohibited by that order, he may, within the area specified in the order:

(a) stop that person; and
(b) direct him not to proceed in the direction of the assembly.

A person who fails to comply with such a direction which he knows has been given to him commits an offence under s 14C(3).

Raves

CJPOA 1994, ss 63 to 65 provide the police with certain powers to deal with 'raves'. Section 63 is the main provision. It applies to a gathering *on land in the open air* of 20 or more persons *(whether or not trespassers)* at which amplified music is played during the night (with or without intermissions) and is such as, by reason of its loudness and the duration and the time at which it is played, is likely to cause serious distress to the inhabitants of the locality; and for this purpose:

(a) such a gathering continues during intermissions in the music and, where the gathering extends over several days, throughout the period during which amplified music is played at night (with or without intermissions); and
(b) 'music' includes sounds wholly or predominantly characterised by the emission of a succession of repetitive beats.

'Land in the open air' includes a place partly open to the air. Thus, both an aircraft hangar without doors, or a Dutch barn, would be such a place. The Act does not define the term 'during the night'.

Section 63 also applies to a gathering if:

(a) it is a gathering on *land* of 20 or more persons who are *trespassing* on the land; and
(b) the gathering would be of a kind described above if it took place on land in the open air.

Section 63 does not apply to a gathering which is licensed by a local authority entertainments licence.

Where a superintendent (or above) reasonably believes, in respect of any land, that:

(a) two or more persons are making preparations for the holding there of a gathering to which s 63 applies;
(b) 10 or more are waiting for such a gathering to begin there; or
(c) 10 or more are attending such a gathering which is then in progress,

he may give a direction that those persons and any other persons who come to prepare or wait for or to attend the gathering are to leave the land and remove any vehicles or other property which they have with them on the land. The direction may be conveyed to the gathering by any constable. If reasonable steps have been taken to convey the direction, it is deemed to have been given.

Persons occupying or working on the land and their families are exempt from a direction under s 63.

A person who knows that such a direction has been given which applies to him who:

(a) fails to leave the land as soon as reasonably practicable; or
(b) having left, again enters the land within a period of seven days beginning with the day on which the direction is given,

commits an offence under s 63(6). It is a defence for D to show that he had a reasonable excuse for failing to leave the land as soon as reasonably practicable or, as the case may be, for again entering the land (s 63(7)).

A person commits an offence under s 63(7A) if:

(a) he knows that a s 63 direction has been given which applies to him; and
(b) he makes preparations for or attends a gathering to which s 63 applies within the 24-hour period starting when the direction was given.

This means that those who have been given a direction to leave a rave cannot simply move to another site (and carry on raving) with impunity.

Police powers

Section 64 provides that, where a superintendent (or above) reasonably believes that circumstances exist which would justify giving such a direction, he may authorise a constable to enter the land without warrant to ascertain that these circumstances exist and to exercise powers conferred upon him. Where such a direction has been given, and a constable reasonably suspects that any person to whom the direction applies has, without reasonable excuse:

(a) failed to remove any vehicle or sound equipment on the land which appears to the constable to belong to him or to be in his possession or under his control; or
(b) entered the land as a trespasser with a vehicle or sound equipment within the period of seven days beginning with the day on which the direction was given,

the constable may seize and remove that vehicle or sound equipment.

Section 66 permits a court to order the forfeiture of sound equipment but also allows the owner of the equipment (if he is not the person from whom it was seized) to claim it by applying to the court within six months. The Police (Disposal of Sound Equipment) Regulations 1995 provide for the disposal of the equipment where a forfeiture order has been made and any such claim has been unsuccessful.

Where a constable in uniform reasonably believes that a person is on his way to such a gathering in respect of which a direction has been given, he may, by s 65, stop that person and direct him not to go in the direction of the gathering. This power may only be exercised within five miles of the boundary of the site of the gathering. It does not apply to occupiers of the land, etc. A person who, knowing that such a direction has been given, fails to comply with such a direction commits an offence under s 65(4).

PUBLIC MEETINGS

It is an offence, contrary to the Public Meeting Act 1908, s 1(1), for any person at a lawful public meeting to act in a disorderly manner for the purpose of preventing the transaction of the business for which the meeting was called together. It is also an offence to incite others to do so (s 1(2)).

'Public meeting' means a meeting open to the public and not restricted to members of a particular organisation or club. Meetings which are open to the public but held on private premises are therefore public meetings. A police officer who reasonably suspects a breach of the peace may enter and/or remain on the private premises.

Section 1 only applies to a lawful public meeting. The fact that a meeting is held on a highway does not render it unlawful merely because it is so held. However, the circumstances in which the meeting is held may make the participants liable for other offences, such as obstructing the highway.

Section 1(3) empowers a constable who reasonably suspects a person of committing an offence under s 1(1) or (2) to require him immediately to give his name and address. However, a constable may only execute this power if requested to do so by the chairman of the meeting. The constable must decide whether or not the person to whom his attention is directed is merely asking questions and making points which the chairman and platform party do not like, or is acting in a disorderly manner for the purpose of preventing the transaction of the business. Refusal or failure to give a name or address, or the giving of a false name and address, is an offence under s 1(3).

PUBLIC ORDER ACT 1936

POA 1936 governs the wearing of political uniforms and participation in quasi-military organisations.

Political uniforms

It is an offence under s 1(1) for any person to wear uniform, in any public place or at any public meeting, which signifies his association with any political organisation or with the promotion of any political object. By way of exception, a chief officer of police, with the consent of the Secretary of State, may by order permit the wearing of such uniforms at a ceremonial, anniversary or other special occasion. The consent of the Attorney General is required for the continuation of the prosecution of a person charged with this offence.

For these purposes, a 'meeting' is a meeting held for the purpose of discussing matters of public interest and a 'public meeting' includes any meeting in a public place and any meeting in a private place if the public (or a section of the public) are permitted to attend (whether on payment or otherwise). There are many organisations (whose objectives are quite harmless) whose members wear some form of identifying clothing within their organisation. This would be within the scope of s 1, but for the fact that it only deals with cases where the uniform signifies association with a political organisation or the promotion of a political object *and* it is worn in a public place or a public meeting. It must be emphasised that even members of a political organisation may wear uniforms in private, even in meetings if these are restricted to their own membership.

The term 'uniform' includes any particular article of clothing which is worn by each member of a group and which is intended to indicate his association with such an organisation or object. The article does not have to cover any major part of the body and it is sufficient to prove that the article has been commonly used by members of a political organisation, for example the berets, dark glasses and dark pullovers which have been used by the IRA.

Quasi-military organisations

Section 2 is concerned with the preparation of private quasi-military forces of any description. A person who takes part in the control or management of any association, or in its training, commits an indictable (either way) offence under s 2(1) if its members or adherents are:

(a) organised, trained or equipped for the purpose of enabling them to usurp the functions of the police or armed forces; or
(b) organised and trained or organised and equipped either to promote a political object by the use or display of physical force, or to arouse reasonable apprehension of that purpose.

In relation to the last words in (b), it has been held that the fact that there was no evidence of actual attacks on opponents, or of plans to attack them, did not necessarily remove grounds for 'reasonable apprehension of that purpose'.

Where a person is charged with taking part in the control or management of such an association, as opposed to training, he has a defence if he proves that he neither consented to nor connived at the organisation, training or equipment in contravention of s 2.

The provision of a reasonable number of stewards to assist in the preservation of order at a public meeting held on private premises is permitted, as is the provision of badges and insignia for them. The instruction of such persons in their lawful duties is also permitted.

The institution of a prosecution for an offence under s 2 requires the Attorney General's consent.

PUBLIC ORDER OFFENCES AND HUMAN RIGHTS

Public order law can interfere with the exercise of Convention rights, particularly those under arts 10 and 11 referred to below.

Article 10 is concerned with freedom of expression. It declares that:

(1) Everyone has the right to freedom of expression. This right shall include freedom to hold opinions and to receive and impart information and ideas without interference by public authority and regardless of frontiers. This Article shall not prevent states from requiring the licensing of broadcasting, television or cinema enterprises.
(2) The exercise of these freedoms, since it carries with it duties and responsibilities, may be subject to such formalities, conditions, restrictions or penalties as are prescribed by law and are necessary in a democratic society, in the interests of national security, territorial integrity, or public safety, for the prevention of disorder or crime, for the protection of health or morals, for the protection of the reputation or rights of others, for preventing the disclosure of information received in confidence, or for maintaining the authority or impartiality of the judiciary.

The following provisions of art 11, which are concerned with the freedoms of assembly and association, are likely to lead to challenges. It provides:

(1) Everyone has the right to freedom of peaceful assembly and to freedom of association with others, including the right to form and join trade unions for the protection of his interests.

(2) No restriction shall be placed on the exercise of these rights other than such as are prescribed by law and are necessary in a democratic society in the interests of national security or public safety, for the prevention of disorder or crime, for the protection of health or morals or for the protection of the rights and freedoms of others. This Article shall not prevent the imposition of lawful restrictions upon the exercise of these rights by members of the armed forces, of the police or of the administration of the State.

It is not sufficient that an interference, prescribed by law, with one of these rights is reasonable or desirable in the interests of a specified legitimate aim; there must be a pressing social need. An interference within a law must be proportionate to the legitimate aim pursued.

Some of the matters listed as legitimate aims can be described as 'essential', for example matters affecting national security or public safety, where the limitation is necessary in a democratic society for such a purpose. Some of the other limitations, such as the prevention of disorder or the protection of the rights of others, are particularly likely to arise in public order situations. Where, for example, D raises the defence that his conduct was reasonable at a trial for an offence under POA 1986, s 4A or 5, or D challenges a condition on a public procession or public assembly or a ban on a public procession or trespassory assembly (the lawfulness of the condition or ban depends on its reasonableness), arts 10 and 11 are relevant to the determination of the issue. The question will be whether any interference with freedom of expression or of assembly or association is prescribed by law and necessary in a democratic society for such a purpose.

CHAPTER 27

Public Order Offences Related to Sporting Events and Those Connected with Industrial Disputes

PUBLIC ORDER AND SPORTING EVENTS

Alcohol on coaches, trains, etc

The Sporting Events (Control of Alcohol, etc) Act 1985 (SE(CA)A 1985), ss 1 and 1A provide offences designed to prevent drunken behaviour by football fans en route to or from matches, and to prevent them arriving at grounds drunk. These offences are offences of:

(a) causing or permitting the carriage of alcohol on a specified vehicle;
(b) being in possession of alcohol on such a vehicle; and
(c) being drunk on a specified vehicle.

Specified vehicles

The offences under SE(CA)A 1985, s 1 apply to public service vehicles (ie coaches, buses, and the like: see Appendix 1 on the companion website) and passenger trains *which are being used for the principal purpose of carrying passengers for the whole or part of a journey to or from a 'designated sporting event'*. Section 1, therefore, does not apply to a bus or train on a normal scheduled service because it is not being used for the principal purpose of carrying passengers to or from a designated sporting event, even if the majority of the passengers are travelling to or from a match, since the words 'used' and 'principal purpose' must refer to use by, and the principal purpose of, the operator. On the other hand, s 1 does apply to a 'football special' or to a chartered coach or train, provided that it is travelling to or from a designated sporting event.

The offences under s 1A apply to a motor vehicle which:

(a) is not a public service vehicle but is adapted to carry more than eight passengers; and
(b) is being used for the principal purpose of carrying *two or more* passengers for the whole or part of a journey to or from a designated sporting event.

Designated sporting event

'Designated sporting event' in SE(CA)A 1985 means a sporting event or proposed sporting event designated by the Sports Grounds and Sporting Events (Designation) Order 2005.

The Sports Grounds and Sporting Events (Designation) Order 2005 designates as sporting events to which SE(CA)A 1985 applies:

(a) association football matches, at any sports ground in England or Wales, in which one or both of the participating teams represents a club which is for the time being a member (whether a full or associate member) of the Football League, the Football Association Premier League, the Football Conference National Division, the Scottish Professional Football League or Welsh Premier League, or whose home ground is situated outside England and Wales, or represents a country or territory;

(b) association football matches, at any sports ground in England and Wales, in competition for the Football Association Cup (other than in a preliminary or qualifying round); and

(c) association football matches at a sports ground outside England and Wales in which one or both of the participating teams represents a club which is for the time being a member (whether a full or associate member) of the Football League, the Football Association Premier League, the Football Conference National Division, the Scottish Professional Football League or Welsh Premier League, or represents the Football Association or the Football Association of Wales.

SE(CA)A 1985 does not apply to any sporting event or proposed sporting event where all competitors are to take part otherwise than for reward, and to which all spectators are to be admitted free of charge.

Causing or permitting carriage of alcohol on a vehicle

SE(CA)A 1985, s 1(2) provides that a person who knowingly causes or permits alcohol to be carried on a vehicle to which s 1 applies is guilty of an offence:

(a) if the vehicle is a public service vehicle and he is the operator of the vehicle or the employee or agent of the operator; or

(b) if the vehicle is a hired vehicle and he is the person to whom it is hired or the employee or agent of that person. Thus, an organiser of the supporters' club (or his agent) can be convicted if he permits alcohol to be carried on a chartered train, but a train guard who fails to prevent this cannot because, although he permits it, he is not a person to whom the train is hired (nor the employee or agent of such a person).

Section 1A(2) provides that a person who knowingly causes or permits alcohol to be carried on a motor vehicle to which s 1A applies is guilty of an offence:

(a) if he is its driver; or

(b) if he is not its driver but its keeper, the employee, or agent of its keeper, a person to whom it is made available (by hire, loan or otherwise) by its keeper or the keeper's employee or agent, or the employee or agent of a person to whom it is so made available.

Possession of alcohol on a vehicle

Section 1(3) makes it an offence for a person to have alcohol in his possession while on a vehicle to which s 1 applies. There is a corresponding offence under s 1A(3) in relation to motor vehicles to which s 1A applies.

Being drunk on a vehicle

Section 1(4) provides that a person who is drunk on a vehicle to which s 1 applies is guilty of an offence. There is a corresponding offence under s 1A(4) in relation to motor vehicles to which s 1A applies.

Police powers

By s 7(3), a constable may stop a public service vehicle to which s 1 applies or a motor vehicle to which s 1A applies and may search *such a vehicle or a railway passenger vehicle* if he has reasonable grounds to suspect that an offence under s 1 or s 1A is being or has been committed in respect of that vehicle.

As to search of a person see p 761.

Alcohol, containers, fireworks, etc at designated sports grounds

Possession of alcohol, etc at designated ground

SE(CA)A 1985, s 2(1) provides that a person who has alcohol or an article to which s 2 applies in his possession:

(a) at any time during the period of a designated sporting event when he is in any area of a designated sports ground from which the event may be directly viewed (s 2(1)(a)); or

(b) while entering or trying to enter a designated sports ground at any time during the period of a designated sporting event at that ground (s 2(1)(b)),

is guilty of an offence.

Section 2(3) states that an article to which s 2 applies is any article capable of causing injury to a person struck by it, being:

(a) a bottle, can or other portable container (including such an article when crushed or broken) which is for holding any drink and is of a kind which, when empty, is normally discarded or returned to, or left to be recovered by, the supplier; or

(b) part of an article falling within (a).

However, the definition expressly does not apply to anything that is for holding any medicinal product.

The container need not be made specifically to hold alcohol, and it is irrelevant that it has never contained alcohol or that it is broken. An empty soft drink bottle or can is caught. On the other hand, a re-usable plastic drinks container, a mug, a thermos flask or a hip flask is not, since it is not of a kind normally discarded or returned to, or left to be recovered by, the supplier.

Possession of fireworks, etc

SE(CA)A 1985, s 2A(1), which is essentially aimed at reducing the risk of fire, makes identical provision in relation to the possession of a firework or of distress flares, fog signals, canisters of smoke or visible gas, and similar articles. Matches and cigarette lighters are expressly excluded.

It is a defence for the defendant (D) to prove that he had possession with lawful authority.

Being drunk at a designated sports ground

By SE(CA)A 1985, s 2(2), a person who is drunk in a designated sports ground at any time during the period of a designated sporting event at that ground, or who is drunk while entering or trying to enter such a ground at any time during the period of a designated sporting event at that ground, is guilty of an offence.

Period of a designated sporting event

Normally, the 'period of a designated sporting event' in SE(CA)A 1985 is the period beginning two hours before the start of the event or (if earlier, as where the start is delayed) two hours before the time at which it is advertised to start, and ending one hour after the end of the event. Where a match is postponed to a later day or cancelled, the period ends one hour after the advertised start time. In respect of a room in a designated sports ground from which the designated sporting event may be directly viewed and to which the public are not admitted (eg the directors' box), there is a different period in relation only to an offence of possession of alcohol, etc under s 2(1)(a) (above). This is a 'restricted period' beginning 15 minutes before the start of the event (or advertised start) and ending 15 minutes after the end of the event or 15 minutes after the advertised start (if the event is postponed to a later day or cancelled).

Designated sports ground

A 'designated sports ground' is any sports ground in England or Wales where accommodation is provided for spectators.

Sporting events: general police powers

By SE(CA)A 1985, s 7(1), a constable may, at any time during the period of a designated sporting event at any designated sports ground, enter *any* part of the ground for the purpose of enforcing SE(CA)A 1985.

By s 7(2), a constable may search a person he has *reasonable grounds to suspect* is committing or has committed an offence under SE(CA)A 1985. The provisions of PACE, s 2 and PACE Code A apply to stop and search under s 7. See pp 40–4 and 47–52.

Code A provides that its requirement that a person must not be searched, even with his consent, except under a specific power of search does not affect the searching of persons entering sports grounds or other premises with their consent given as a condition of entry.

Misbehaviour at a designated football match

The Football (Offences) Act 1991 (F(O)A 1991) creates a number of offences. They can only be committed at a 'regulated football match'. Such matches are designated by the Football (Offences) (Designation of Football Matches) Order 2004. They are association football matches:

(a) in which one or both of the participating teams represents:
   (i) a club which is for the time being a member (whether a full or associate member) of the Football League, the Football Association Premier League, the Football Conference, the Welsh Premier League or the Scottish Professional Football League; or

(ii) a club whose home ground is situated outside England and Wales; or

(iii) a country or territory; or

(b) which are played in the FA Cup, other than a preliminary or qualifying round.

References to things done at a designated football match include anything done there in the period beginning two hours before the start of the match or (if earlier) two hours before the advertised start time and ending one hour after the end of the match. If the match does not take place, the period is two hours before the advertised start time until one hour after that time.

Throwing objects

By F(O)A 1991, s 2, it is an offence to throw anything at or towards:

(a) the playing area or any area adjacent to the playing area to which spectators are not generally admitted; or

(b) any area in which spectators or other persons are or may be present,

without lawful authority or excuse (which it is for D to prove).

Thus, those who throw objects onto the pitch, into the players' tunnel, etc, or into spectator areas will commit offences. Those who may prove 'lawful authority or excuse' would include vendors who throw packets of crisps, etc into the crowd, or spectators who throw money to such persons.

Chanting

F(O)A 1991, s 3(1) makes it an offence to engage or take part in chanting of an indecent or racist nature at a designated football match. 'Chanting' means the repeated uttering of words or sounds (whether alone or in concert with one or more others), and 'racist nature' means consisting of or including matter which is threatening, abusive or insulting to a person by reason of his colour, race, nationality (including citizenship) or ethnic or national origin.

Pitch invasion

By F(O)A 1991, s 4, it is an offence for a person to go onto the playing area, or any area adjacent to the playing area to which spectators are not generally admitted, without lawful authority or lawful excuse (which it is for D to prove).

It is not easy to obtain a conviction where spectators surge forward onto the pitch. Most will contend that they were carried forward unwillingly by the momentum of the crowd. If this is not disproved, a conviction for an offence under s 4 will not be possible, since a person cannot generally be convicted if his conduct was beyond his control. Those who would have lawful excuse for going onto the pitch include trainers and official first aiders.

BANNING ORDERS

The Football Spectators Act 1989 (FSA 1989), Part II deals with these. The relevant provisions only apply in respect of a regulated football match.

Regulated football match

A 'regulated football match' is an association football match (whether in the UK or elsewhere) which is a prescribed match or a match of a prescribed description. The

Football Spectators (Prescription) Order 2004 prescribes 'regulated football matches in England and Wales' and 'regulated football matches outside England and Wales'.

Regulated football match in England and Wales

This is an association football match:

(a) in which one or both of the participating teams represents:
  (i) a club which is for the time being a member (whether a full or associate member) of the Football League, the Football Association Premier League, the Football Conference, the Welsh Premier League or the Scottish Professional Football League;
  (ii) a club whose home ground is situated outside England and Wales; or
  (iii) a country or territory; or
(b) which is played in the FA Cup, other than a preliminary or qualifying round.

Regulated football match outside England and Wales

This is an association football match involving:

(a) a national team appointed by the Football Association to represent England or by the Football Association of Wales to represent Wales;
(b) a team representing a club which is for the time being a member (whether a full or associate member) of the Football League, the Football Association Premier League, the Football Conference, the Welsh Premier League or the Scottish Professional Football League (SPFL);
(c) a team representing any country or territory whose football association is for the time being a member of FIFA where the match is part of a competition or tournament organised by or under the authority of FIFA or UEFA and the competition is one in which a national team referred to in (a) is eligible to participate, or has participated; or
(d) a team representing a club which is for the time being a member (whether a full or associate member) of, or affiliated to, a national football association which is a member of FIFA, where the match is part of a competition or tournament organised by, or under the authority of, FIFA or UEFA and the competition is such that a club from the Football League, the Football Association Premier League, the Football Conference, the Welsh Premier League or the SPFL is eligible to participate, or has participated.

When can a banning order be made?

A banning order may be made under FSA 1989, s 14A, s 14B or s 22.

Banning orders following a conviction for a relevant offence

FSA 1989, s 14A is concerned with a situation in which an offender is convicted of a 'relevant offence'. The relevant offences are set out in FSA 1989, Sch 1. They are:

(a) any offence contrary to FSA 1989, ss 14J(1) or 19(6) or 20(10) or 21C(2), (failure to comply with banning order requirement or requirement under s 14(2B) or (2C), or failure to comply with a requirement made at initial reporting at a police station or, being subject to a banning order, knowingly or recklessly providing false or misleading information in support of his application for exemption from requirements imposed under FSA 1989, or non-compliance with a notice under s 21B);

(b) an offence under the Police, Public Order and Criminal Justice (Scotland) Act 2006, s 68(1) or (5) (corresponding offences to those in (a));

(c) any offence contrary to SE(CA)A 1985, ss 2 or 2A committed at a regulated football match or while entering or trying to enter the ground;

(d) any offence involving harassment, alarm or distress contrary to the Public Order Act 1986 (POA 1986), ss 4A or 5, or racial or religious hatred or hatred on the ground of sexual orientation contrary to POA 1986, Part III or IIIA, or any offence involving the use of violence or threat of violence towards another person or property:

    (i) committed during a 'period relevant to a regulated football match' (the period from 24 hours before the start or advertised start of the match (whichever is earlier) to 24 hours after its end, or the period from 24 hours before the advertised start of a cancelled game or one postponed to another day to 24 hours after that time) while at, entering or leaving the ground (or trying to do so), or

    (ii) if the court makes a declaration of relevance (ie declares that the offence related to regulated football matches), while on a journey to or from a regulated football match;

(e) any offence involving harassment, alarm or distress (POA 1986, ss 4A or 5) or racial or religious hatred or hatred on the ground of sexual orientation (POA 1986, Part III or IIIA), or any offence involving the use or threat of violence towards another person or property which does not fall within (d), which was committed during a period relevant to a regulated football match and as respects which the court declares that the offence related to that match or that match and other regulated football matches during that period;

(f) any offence of drunkenness (ie being found drunk, or being drunk and disorderly, in a public place), committed while on such a journey, as to which offence the court makes a declaration of relevance;

(g) any offence contrary to SE(CA)A 1985, s 1 or the Road Traffic Act 1988, ss 4, 5, or 5A (drink or drugs and driving, etc) committed on a journey to or from a regulated match, as to which offence the court makes a declaration of relevance;

(h) any offence contrary to F(O)A 1991;

(i) any offence involving the use, carrying or possession of an offensive weapon or firearm:

    (i) committed during a period relevant to a regulated football match while at, or entering or leaving the ground (or trying to do so), or

    (ii) if the court makes a declaration of relevance, committed while on a journey to or from a regulated football match;

(j) any offence involving the use, carrying, or possession of an offensive weapon or firearm which does not fall within (i)(i) or (i)(ii), which was committed during a period relevant to a regulated football match and as respects which the court declares that the offence related to that match or to that match and any other football offence during that period;

(k) ticket touting contrary to the Criminal Justice and Public Order Act 1994, s 166.

Attempting, conspiring, encouraging or assisting, or aiding, abetting, counselling or procuring, the commission of any such offence is included within these provisions.

A person may be regarded as having been on a journey to or from a football match whether or not he attended or intended to attend the match. A journey includes breaks (including overnight breaks).

If, upon conviction for such an offence, a court is satisfied that there are reasonable grounds to believe that making a banning order would help to prevent violence or disorder at, or in connection with, any regulated football match, it *must* make such an order in respect of the offender. If it is not so satisfied, it must state its reasons in open court. A divisional court has held that a football banning order under s 14A should be made only where there are strong grounds for concluding that the offender has a propensity for taking part in football hooliganism. However, it added that the court is entitled to give weight to deterrence; there are clear benefits in it being widely known that someone who assaults a match official is liable to be made subject to a football banning order even if the incident was, for that person, an isolated one.

A banning order is in addition to a sentence or order of conditional discharge.

Banning orders made on complaint

Under FSA 1989, s 14B, the chief officer of police of an area in which a person resides, or appears to reside, the chief constable of the British Transport Police or the DPP may make a complaint to a magistrates' court that the respondent has at some time contributed to violence or disorder in the UK or elsewhere.

If the court is satisfied as to the substance of the complaint and has reasonable grounds for believing that making a banning order would help to prevent violence or disorder at or in connection with any regulated football match it *must* make a banning order. In deciding whether to make an order a court may take into account (among other things):

(a) any decision of a court or tribunal outside the UK;
(b) deportation or exclusion from a country outside the UK;
(c) removal or exclusion from football grounds in the UK or elsewhere; or
(d) conduct recorded by video or by any other means.

However, a court may only take note of matters occurring within the 10 years preceding the application. It must also consider the reasons given by a court when, in relation to a relevant offence, it did not make a banning order.

The Court of Appeal has described the standard of proof as to the substance of the complaint as an exacting one which would be hard in practice to distinguish from the criminal standard of proof beyond reasonable doubt. This high standard is justified because of the serious restraints on an individual's freedom which a banning order imposes.

Banning order under FSA 1989, s 22

FSA 1989, s 22 governs the making of a banning order as a result of a conviction outside England and Wales for a 'corresponding offence'. A 'corresponding offence' is an offence under the law of a country specified outside England and Wales in an Order in Council. At the time of writing, there are no such orders in force. This is because FSA 1989, s 22 has fallen out of use, given that there is an alternative route to securing a banning order under the FSA 1989 via s 14B (above).

The effect of a banning order

A 'banning order' means an order made by a court under FSA 1989, Part II which:

(a) in relation to regulated football matches in the UK, prohibits the person who is subject to the order from entering premises for the purpose of attending such matches; and

(b) in relation to regulated football matches outside the UK, requires that person to report at a police station in accordance with Part II.

An order will apply to the whole range of matches which are prescribed, whatever the venue and whatever the club; a court cannot limit it to particular matches or teams. This is sensible. Clearly, a banning order would not be very effective if it barred a person only from the ground at which the offence was committed.

A banning order must require the person subject to the order to report to a police station specified in the order, within five days beginning with the day upon which the order is made.

A banning order must require the person subject to the order to notify the enforcing authority of the following events:

(a) a change of any of his names, of his home address, or of his temporary address (or of his ceasing to have one);
(b) his first use after the order of a name that was not disclosed at the time of the making of the order;
(c) his acquisition of a temporary address;
(d) his becoming aware of the loss of his passport;
(e) his receipt of a new passport;
(f) an appeal in relation to the order or against the making of a declaration of relevance in respect of an offence of which he has been convicted; and
(g) an application for termination of the order.

The notification must be given before the end of the seven-day period beginning with the day on which the event in question occurs and:

(a) in the case of a change of a name or address or the acquisition of a temporary address, must specify the new name or address;
(b) in the case of a first use of a previously undisclosed name, must specify that name; and
(c) in the case of a receipt of a new passport, must give details of that.

A banning order must contain a requirement as to the surrender, in accordance with the Act (below), in connection with regulated football matches outside the UK, of the passport of the person subject to the order.

The court may impose additional requirements on a person subject to such an order and may subsequently vary an order so as to impose, replace or omit requirements on the application of the person subject to the order or the person who applied for the order or the prosecutor. In addition, the court has power to require a constable to photograph the person or cause him to be photographed.

Duration of banning order

Where a banning order is made under s 14A and is in addition to a sentence of imprisonment (any form of detention) taking immediate effect, the maximum duration is 10 years and the minimum, six. In any other case following conviction the maximum is five years and the minimum, three. Orders which are made under s 14B or s 22 may be for a maximum of five years and a minimum of three.

Termination of an order

After two-thirds of the period of the ban has passed, the person subject to it may apply to the court by which the order was made to terminate it. The court, in considering whether or not to terminate the ban, must have regard to a person's character; conduct since the order was made; the nature of the offence or conduct concerned; and any other relevant circumstances.

Functions of the enforcing authority and local police forces

FSA 1989, s 19(2) provides that, when a banned person initially reports at a police station, the officer responsible for that station may make such requirements of that person as are determined by the enforcing authority to be necessary or expedient for giving effect to the banning order, so far as matters are related to regulated football matches outside the UK. The 'enforcing authority' is the Football Banning Orders Authority established by the Secretary of State.

If, in connection with any regulated football match outside the UK, that authority considers that a requirement to report is necessary or expedient to reduce the likelihood of violence or disorder at or in connection with the match, the authority is required by s 19(2B) to give the person subject to the order a notice in writing to report as instructed and to surrender his passport as instructed. Under s 19(2B), the notice may also require compliance with additional requirements.

In the case of any regulated football match, the enforcing authority may by notice in writing require the person subject to the order to comply with any additional requirements of the order in the manner specified in the notice (s 19(2C)).

A notice under s 19 may not require the person subject to it to report except in the 'control period' in relation to a regulated football match outside the UK or an external tournament which includes such matches and may not require him to surrender a passport except in such a control period. The 'control period' in relation to such a regulated football match outside the UK is the period commencing five days before the day of the match and ending when the match is finished or cancelled. In relation to an external tournament the 'control period' means any period described in an order made by the Secretary of State beginning five days before the first match outside the UK and ending when the last match outside the UK has been finished or cancelled. However, qualifying matches do not count in determining the start of the tournament.

If the Secretary of State considers it necessary or expedient to do so in order to secure the effective enforcement of these provisions, the 'control period' may be extended by order in relation to any regulated football match to a maximum of not more than 10 days before the day of the match (or the day of the first match in the external tournament, as the case may be).

Failure to comply with a requirement

It is an offence, contrary to FSA 1989, s 19(6), to fail, without reasonable excuse, to comply with a requirement imposed under s 19(2).

It is an offence, contrary to s 14J(1), for a person subject to a banning order to fail to comply with any requirement imposed by the order or by s 19(2B) or s 19(2C).

Summary measures

FSA 1989, ss 21A and 21B underpin the procedure for the application by way of complaint for a banning order. They provide for a constable in uniform to exercise powers of detention and of reference to a court in specified circumstances. The powers under ss 21A and 21B may be exercised only in relation to a British citizen.

Section 21A provides a constable in uniform with the power to detain a person in his custody if, during any 'control period' in relation to a regulated football match outside the UK or an external tournament:

(a) he has reasonable grounds to suspect that the person has at any time caused or contributed to any violence or disorder in the UK or elsewhere; and
(b) he has reasonable grounds to believe that making a banning order in his case would help to prevent violence or disorder at, or in connection with, any regulated football matches.

Such a person may be detained until the constable has decided whether or not to issue a notice under s 21B requiring him:

(a) to appear before a magistrates' court at a specified time;
(b) not to leave England and Wales before that time; and
(c) if the control period relates to a regulated football match outside the UK or to an external tournament which includes such matches, to surrender his passport to the constable,

and stating the grounds upon which his decision is based.

Such detention may not exceed four hours or, with the authority of an inspector (or above), six hours. A person so detained may not be further detained within the same control period unless new information becomes available.

The notice referred to above may be issued where the officer is authorised to do so by an inspector (or above). The time at which such a person must appear before a magistrates' court must be within 24 hours of receiving the notice or that person's detention, whichever is the earlier. Such a notice will be treated as an application for a banning order by way of complaint.

Where a person to whom such a notice has been given appears before a magistrates' court, the court may remand him. If he is remanded on bail, he may be required not to leave England and Wales before his appearance before the court and, if the control period relates to a regulated football match outside the UK or to an external tournament which includes such matches, he may be required to surrender his passport to a constable.

It is an offence under s 21C to fail to comply with a notice under s 21B.

Enforcement in England and Wales of corresponding Scottish provisions

The following provisions of the Police, Public Order and Criminal Justice (Scotland) Act 2006 extend to England and Wales:

(a) s 68(1) and (2) (offences of failing to comply with a requirement imposed by a football banning order, under s 61(1) or by a notice under s 61(4), and defence of reasonable excuse);
(b) s 68(5) (offence of making a false statement, etc in connection with an application for exemption from a notice under s 61(4)).

TICKET TOUTS

The Criminal Justice and Public Order Act 1994, s 166 makes it an offence for an unauthorised person to sell, or otherwise dispose of to another person, a ticket for a designated football match. 'Selling' includes offering or exposing a ticket for sale, making it available for sale by another, advertising it as available for purchase, and giving it to a person who pays or agrees to pay for some other goods or services or offers to do so.

The only persons who are 'authorised' are those authorised in writing by the organisers of the match. 'Ticket' includes anything which purports to be a ticket, so that false tickets are included. However, where a false ticket is involved a charge of fraud would be more appropriate where knowledge of such falsity can be proved. A 'designated football match' has the same meaning as 'regulated football match' (pp 762–3), except that it does not cover the Scottish Professional Football League or matches in the FA Cup between clubs which are not members of the Leagues specified on p 763.

Internet touting is dealt with by special rules under s 166A.

Police powers

The provisions of PACE 1984, s 32 (search of an arrested person and his vehicle) are extended to the case where the vehicle is reasonably believed to have been used for any purpose connected with an offence under s 166.

LABOUR LAWS

The primary piece of legislation dealing with trade disputes is the Trade Union and Labour Relations (Consolidation) Act 1992 (TULR(C)A 1992).

Acts of 'interference' with workers

TULR(C)A 1992, s 241 deals with such acts. It is not confined to trade disputes. However, that is its normal application. It deals with acts which might or might not be committed away from the picket line but which nevertheless amount to attempts to prevent a worker from exercising his own freedom of choice.

An offence is committed under TULR(C)A 1992, s 241(1) by any person who, *with a view to compelling (as opposed simply to persuading) any other person to abstain from doing or to do any act which that other person has a legal right to do or abstain from doing, wrongfully and without legal authority does one of the following things*:

(a) *uses violence to or intimidates such other person or his spouse, civil partner or children, or injures his property;*

(b) *persistently follows such other person about from place to place.*
'Persistently' is not meant to convey any form of permanence in this activity and it is sufficient if a person, or part of the mob outside a works, doggedly follows someone from the works through the streets;

(c) *hides any tools, clothes, or other property owned or used by such other person or deprives him of or hinders him in the use thereof;*

(d) *watches or besets the house or other place where such other person resides, or works, or carries on business, or happens to be, or the approach to such a house or place.*
'Watching or besetting' merely describes certain forms of picketing. It must be remembered that all the various types of conduct covered by s 241 are only criminal if they are done wrongfully. As a result, a person engaged in lawful picketing is not guilty under s 241 by virtue of the present provision. What constitutes 'lawful picketing' is described below. This mode of the offence is designed among other

things to prevent the removal of picket lines or single persuaders from the works to a dwelling house or its approaches;

(e) *follows such other person with two or more other persons in a disorderly manner in or through any street or road.*

This conduct differs from that of persistently following in that there is no need to prove any form of persistence. The aggravation by being accompanied by two or more persons and the incidence of disorderly conduct are sufficient. This mode of committing the offence can only be committed in a street or road.

Peaceful picketing: Trade Union and Labour Relations (Consolidation) Act 1992

TULR(C)A 1992, s 220(1) states that it shall be lawful for a person in contemplation or furtherance of a trade dispute to attend:

(a) at or near his own place of work; or
(b) if he is an official of a trade union, at or near the place of work of a member of that union whom he is accompanying and whom he represents,

for the purpose only of peacefully obtaining or communicating information, or peacefully persuading any person to work or abstain from working. These words contain key requirements for lawful picketing. They are concerned with *the place* where a person attends in contemplation or furtherance of a trade dispute and with *the purpose* for which he attends.

The place

Section 220(1) provides that it is lawful for a person in contemplation or furtherance of a trade dispute to attend at or near *his own place of work*; it does not, of course, authorise access to private premises without the consent of their owner. Except in the case of a trade union official accompanying a member whom he represents at or near the latter's place of work, picketing at some place other than the picket's own place of work is not declared to be lawful. Thus, picketing by 'flying pickets' or by other people who do not work at the place in question is not declared to be lawful by s 220(1); such a picket may be guilty from the outset of an offence against s 241 on the ground of 'watching or besetting', however peaceful the picket may be.

Whether or not picketing is *at or near* the picket's place of work depends upon a common-sense approach. In one case the Court of Appeal held that pickets, who stood at the entrance to a trading estate 1,200 yards away from their employer's premises on that estate and would have been trespassing if they had picketed on the estate, were attending (picketing) near their place of work.

Section 220(2) and (3) make special provision about the meaning of 'his own place of work'. Section 220(2) deals with the case of a worker who does not work at any one particular place (eg a service engineer or train driver) or whose place of work is so located that it is impracticable for him to attend there to picket. It provides that the place of work of such a person is *any premises* of his employer *from* which he works or *from* which his work is administered.

There are occasions when the above provisions of s 220 would act unfairly against a worker who, having been dismissed from his employment, would be excluded from the right to protest because he would no longer have a place of work at or near which he could attend. Section 220(3) protects such a worker, by stating that where:

(a) his last employment was terminated in connection with a trade dispute; or

(b) the termination of his employment was one of the circumstances giving rise to the dispute,

his former place of work shall be treated as if it was his place of work.

Trade dispute

By s 244(1), 'trade dispute' means a dispute between workers and their employer relating wholly or mainly to one or more of the following:

(a) terms and conditions of employment, or the physical conditions of work;

(b) engagement or non-engagement, or termination or suspension of employment or the duties of employment;

(c) allocation of work;

(d) discipline;

(e) membership or non-membership of a trade union;

(f) facilities for trade union officials; and

(g) machinery for negotiation or consultation, and other procedures, relating to any of the above matters, including the recognition of the right of a trade union to represent workers in such negotiation, etc.

The purpose

Even if the requirement that the picket must be obtaining or communicating information, or peacefully picketing, at or near the place of work is satisfied, his conduct is *only declared to be lawful by s 220(1) if his attendance is for the purpose only of peacefully persuading any person to work or abstain from working*. A person who attends for some other purpose, for example forcibly to prevent workers or deliveries entering premises, is not protected by s 220(1) and is liable for any criminal offence which he may commit; he might also, of course, be liable to pay damages under the civil law for any harm which he causes by molesting a worker or interfering with his right to work. Thus, pickets who link arms and form a physical barrier to prevent movement in and out of works are criminally liable, even though they work there, for an offence against s 241 and for any other offence which they may commit, since it cannot be said that they are there *only* for fulfilling one of the specified purposes peacefully.

The physical presence of lawful pickets on a highway must represent some form of obstruction and this is permitted to the extent that it is reasonably necessary for such pickets to carry out their task of speaking to their colleagues. However, this right is restricted to those who are lawful pickets in accordance with the provisions of s 220. It is a question of fact as to whether or not the degree of obstruction has passed beyond that reasonably required. Mass picketing clearly goes beyond what is reasonably required and is therefore illegal. So is the total obstruction of an entrance, and so are other measures which have the same effect. Where pickets kept moving by walking around in a circle outside the main entrance to a factory and were required to stop doing so by a police officer, they were held to have obstructed him in his duty by their refusal, as they were carrying out an illegal act.

The police have a duty to limit the size of lawful pickets to a number which appears to be reasonable in the circumstances, and a refusal by the organisers to comply with reasonable requests made by the police may amount to a wilful obstruction contrary to the Police Act 1996, s 89(2).

The role of the police

The police must not be concerned with the merits of any trade dispute. Their role is the impartial preservation of the peace. It is no part of a police officer's duty to assist with civil remedies; if an employer wishes to identify persons on picket lines or outside his works with a view to civil process, that is his responsibility and police officers should not attempt to identify such persons on his behalf. The enforcement of any orders made in favour of employers is the responsibility of court officers, and police participation must be restricted to ensuring the maintenance of the peace.

The Picketing Code of Practice issued for the guidance of pickets (which recommends that in general the number of pickets at any entrance to a workplace should not exceed six) is not a part of the criminal law. The number of pickets in particular circumstances is a matter for police discretion bearing in mind their primary purpose of maintaining the peace.

CHAPTER 28

Terrorism Generally

This chapter refers to the offences and powers under the Terrorism Acts 2000 and 2006, the Anti-terrorism, Crime and Security Act 2001, the Counter-Terrorism Act 2008 and the Counter-Terrorism and Security Act 2015. Reference is also made to the power to impose terrorism prevention and investigation measures under the Terrorism Prevention and Investigation Measures Act 2011 to protect the public from terrorism. These Acts can be described as the 'terrorism legislation'.

All the offences described in this chapter are indictable (either way) offences, unless otherwise indicated.

MEANING OF 'TERRORISM' IN TERRORISM LEGISLATION

For the purposes of this legislation, 'terrorism' is defined by the Terrorism Act 2000 (TA 2000), s 1, as meaning the use or threat of action (inside or outside the UK) which:

(a) (i)   involves serious violence against a person wherever he is,
    (ii) involves serious damage to property wherever situated,
    (iii) endangers a person's life, other than that of the person committing the action,
    (iv) creates a serious risk to the health and safety of the public or a section of the public, or
    (v)   is designed seriously to interfere with or seriously to disrupt an electronic system;
(b) is designed to influence the government of the UK (or part thereof), or the government of any other country, or an international governmental organisation, or to intimidate the public or a section of the public anywhere; *and*
(c) is made for the purpose of advancing a political, religious, racial or ideological cause.

The Court of Appeal has held that it is not enough that the use or threat of action unwittingly or accidentally has an effect within (a)(i)–(v); it must have been done or made with intention or recklessness as to having such effect.

The use or threat of action falling within (a) which includes the use of firearms or explosives is terrorism whether or not (b) is satisfied.

The Court of Appeal has also held that the reference in (b) to the government of any other country is not limited to a representative or democratic government. The Supreme Court has held that, provided (b) and (c) are satisfied, military attacks by a non-state armed group against any state or inter-governmental armed forces in the context of a non-international conflict fall within the above definition.

There is no exemption from criminal liability for terrorist activities motivated by the alleged nobility of the terrorist cause.

PROSCRIBED ORGANISATIONS

TA 2000 contains a number of offences which can be committed in relation to a 'proscribed organisation' listed in TA 2000, Sch 2:

(1) Belonging or professing to belong to a proscribed organisation, subject to a defence on 'proof' (interpreted by the House of Lords as only imposing an evidential burden) by the defendant (D) that he joined the proscribed organisation before it was proscribed and he has not taken part in the activities of the organisation since it became proscribed (TA 2000, s 11). The Court of Appeal has held that membership of a proscribed organisation depends on the nature of the organisation in question. Membership of a loose and unstructured organisation may not require an express process, whereas a more structured organisation may have an express process whereby a person becomes a member. The core elements of membership within s 11 will frequently be voluntary and knowing association with others with a view to furthering the aims of the proscribed organisation. Unilateral sympathy with the aims of an organisation, even coupled with acts designed to promote similar objectives, whilst being clear evidence of belonging, will not always be sufficient.

(2) Inviting support for a proscribed organisation, other than support with money or property (s 12(1)).

(3) Arranging, managing or assisting in arranging or managing a meeting of three or more people (whether or not the public are admitted) which D knows is:
   (a) to support a proscribed organisation,
   (b) to further the activities of a proscribed organisation, or
   (c) to be addressed by a person who belongs or professes to belong to a proscribed organisation, subject to a defence (where the offence relates to a private meeting) if D adduces sufficient evidence that he had no reasonable cause to believe that such an address would support a proscribed organisation or further its activities, whereupon the prosecution must disprove this (s 12(2)).

(4) Addressing a meeting where the purpose is to encourage support for a proscribed organisation or to further its activities (s 12(3)).

(5) Wearing in a public place any item of clothing, or wearing, carrying or displaying any article, in such a way or in such circumstances as to arouse reasonable apprehension of being a member or supporter of a proscribed organisation (s 13). This is a summary offence.

The proscribed organisations associated with terrorism in Northern Ireland are at present:

the Irish Republican Army; Cumann na mBan; Fianna na hEireann; the Red Hand Commando; Saor Eire; the Ulster Freedom Fighters; the Ulster Volunteer Force; the Irish National Liberation Army; the Irish People's Liberation Organisation; the Ulster Defence Association; the Loyalist Volunteer Force; the Continuity Army Council; the Orange Volunteers; and the Red Hand Defenders.

Other proscribed organisations are:

Al-Qa'ida (also known as al-Nusrah Front and as Jabhat al Nusrah li-ahl al Sham); Egyptian Islamic Jihad; Al-Gama'at al-Islamiya; Armed Islamic Group (Groupe Islamique Armée) (GIA); Salafist Group for Call and Combat (Groupe Salafiste pour la Prédication et le Combat) (GSPC); Babbar Khalsa; Harakat Mujahideen; Jaish e Mohammed; Lashkar e Tayyaba (also known as Jama'at ud Da'wa); Liberation Tigers of Tamil Eelam (LTTE); the military wing of Hizballah, including the Jihad Council and all units reporting to it (including the Hizballah External Security Organisation);

Hamas-Izz al-Din al-Qassem Brigades; Palestinian—Islamic Jihad—Shaqaqi; Abu Nidal Organisation; Islamic Army of Aden; Kurdistan Workers' Party (Partiya Karkeren Kurdistan) (PKK) (also known as Kongra Gele Kurdistan, and KADEK); Revolutionary Peoples' Liberation Party—Front (Devrimci Halk Kurtulus Partisi-Cephesi) (DHKP-C); Basque Homeland and Liberty (Euskadi ta Askatasuna) (ETA); 17 November Revolutionary Organisation (N17); Abu Sayyaf Group; Asbat Al-Ansar; Islamic Movement of Uzbekistan; Jemaah Islamiyah; Al Ittihad Al Islamia; Ansar Al Islam; Ansar Al Sunna; Groupe Islamique Combattant Marocain; Harakat-ul-Jihad-ul-Islami; Harakat-ul-Jihad-ul-Islami (Bangladesh); Harakat-ul-Mujahadeen/Alami; Hezb-e Islami Gulbuddin; Islamic Jihad Union; Jamaat ul-Furquan; Jundallah; Khuddam ul-Islam; Lashkar-e Jhangvi (also known as Ahle Sunnat wal Jamaa); Libyan Islamic Fighting Group; Sipah-e Sahaba Pakistan (also known as Ahle Sunnat wal Jamaa); Baluchistan Liberation Army; Teyrebaz Azadiye Kurdistan; Jammat-ul Mujahideen Bangladesh; Tehrik Nefaz-e Shari'at Muhammadi; Al-Shabaab; Tehrik-e Taliban Pakistan; Indian Mujahideen; Ansarul Muslimina Fi Biladis Sudan (Vanguard for the Protection of Muslims in Black Africa) (Ansaru); Jama'atu Ahli Sunna Lidda Awati Wal Jihad (Boko Haram) and Minbar Ansar Deen (Ansar Al Sharia UK); Imarat Kavkaz (Caucasus Emirate); Ansar Bayt al-Maqdis (Ansar Jerusalem), Al Murabitun; Ansar al Sharia—Tunisia; Islamic State of Iraq and the Levant (Islamic State of Iraq and al-Sham) (Dawat al Islamiya fi Iraq wa al Sham (DAISh)) (also known as Islamic State (Dawlat al Islamiya)); Turkiye Halk Kurtulus Partisi-Cephesi (Turkish People's Liberation Party) (The Hasty Ones) (Mukavamet Suriye); Kateeba al-Kawthar (Ajnad al-sham) (Junud ar-Rahman al Muhajireen); Abdallah Azzam Brigades, including the Ziyad al-Jarrah Battalions; Popular Front for the Liberation of Palestine—General Command; Ansar al-Sharia-Benghazi (Partisans of Islamic Law); Ajnad Misr (Soldiers of Egypt); Jaysh al Khalifatu Islamiya (Army of the Islamic Caliphate) (Majahideen of the Caucasus and the Levant); Jund Al-Aqsa (Soldiers of Al-Aqsa); Jund al Khalifa—Algeria (Soldiers of the Caliphate in Algeria); Jamaat ul-Ahrar; The Haqqani Network; Global Islamic Media Front (including GIMF Bangla Team (Ansarullah Bangla Team) (Ansar-al Islam)); Mujahedeen Indonesia Timur (East Indonesia Mujahedeen); Turkestan Islamic Party (East Turkestan Islamic Party) (East Turkestan Islamic Movement) (East Turkestan Jihadist Movement) (Hizb al-Islami al-Turkistani); Jamaah Anshorut Daulah; Al-Ghurabaa; and The Saved Sect. Al Muhajiroun (ALM); Call to Submission; Islam4UK; Islamic Path; London School of Sharia; Muslims against Crusades; Need4Khilafah; the Shariah Project; and Islamic Dawah Association, are treated as alternative names for both Al-Ghurabaa and The Saved Sect.

The Secretary of State has the power to add to, remove or amend a name included in TA 2000, Sch 2.

As can be seen, the provisions of TA 2000, ss 11 to 13 create a wide range of offences dealing with membership or professed membership of proscribed organisations, with the promotion of them, and meetings in support of them.

TERRORIST PROPERTY

Fund-raising

TA 2000, s 15 provides that a person is guilty of an offence if he:

(a) invites any other person to provide money or other property, and intends that it should be used, or has reasonable cause to suspect that it may be used, for the purposes of terrorism (s 15(1)); or

(b) receives money or other property, and intends that it should be used, or has reasonable cause to suspect that it may be used, for the purposes of terrorism (s 15(2)); or

(c) provides money or other property, and knows or has reasonable cause to suspect that it will or may be used, for the purposes of terrorism (s 15(3)).

The references to the 'provision' of money or other property are references to its being given, lent or otherwise made available, whether or not for consideration.

A person does not commit an offence under s 15 (or under ss 16 to 18 below) in the circumstances set out in ss 21, 21ZA, 21ZB or 21ZC (p 777).

Use and possession

TA 2000, s 16(1) prohibits as an offence the use of money or property for the purposes of terrorism. Section 16(2) creates a further offence of possessing money or other property intending that it should be used, or having reasonable cause to suspect that it might be used, for the purposes of terrorism.

Funding arrangements

TA 2000, s 17 makes it an offence for a person to enter into, or become concerned in, an arrangement as a result of which money or other property is made (or is to be made) available to another, knowing or having reasonable cause to suspect that it might be used for terrorism.

Insurance against payments made in respect to terrorist demands

TA 2000, s 17A(1) provides that the insurer under an insurance contract commits an offence if:

(a) the insurer makes a payment under the contract, or purportedly under it;

(b) the payment is made in respect of any money or other property that has been, or is to be, handed over in response to a demand made wholly or partly for the purposes of terrorism; and

(c) the insurer or the person authorising the payment on the insurer's behalf knows or has reasonable cause to suspect that the money or other property has been, or is to be, handed over in response to such a demand.

Money laundering

TA 2000, s 18(1) prohibits as an offence money laundering of terrorist property by concealment, removal from jurisdiction, transfer to nominees, or in any other way. Section 18(2) provides a defence if D proves lack of knowledge or reason to suspect that the arrangement was concerned with terrorist property.

Disclosure of information: duty

TA 2000, s 19(1) and (2) provides that a person commits an offence if he does not disclose to a constable, as soon as reasonably practicable, a belief or suspicion, and the information upon which it is based, where he:

(a) believes or suspects that another person has committed an offence under any of TA 2000, ss 15 to 18; and

(b) bases his belief or suspicion on information which came to his attention in the course of his employment (whether or not in a trade, profession or business).

However, s 19 does not apply if the information came to the person in the course of a business in the regulated sector. A business is in the regulated sector to the extent that it engages in accepting deposits, operating a bureau de change, dealing in, advising in relation to, or managing investments, accountancy business, estate agency or casino, or a range of other financially related activities listed in Sch 3A for the purposes of s 21A (set out below), which provides offences which can be committed in those circumstances.

It is a defence to prove reasonable excuse for non-disclosure. In the case of an employee, where there is an established procedure concerning disclosure, it is a defence for him to prove that disclosure was made within that procedure. Section 19 does not require disclosure by a professional legal adviser of legally privileged information or of a belief or suspicion based on such information.

Co-operation with the police

TA 2000, s 21 provides that a person does not commit an offence under ss 15 to 18 if he is acting with the express consent of a constable.

Exceptions

In order to implement a Community Directive, TA 2000, ss 21ZA, 21ZB and 21ZC provide exceptions which apply to the offences against ss 15 to 18. Section 21ZA provides an exception if D has made a disclosure to an authorised officer before becoming involved in a transaction or an arrangement and acts with the consent of the authorised officer. 'Authorised officer' means an NCA officer authorised for the purposes of s 21ZA by the Director General of the NCA. Section 21ZB provides a further exception to cover those who become involved in a transaction or an arrangement and then make a disclosure, so long as there is a reasonable excuse for failure to make a disclosure in advance. Finally, s 21ZC provides a defence if D proves that he intended to make a disclosure under s 21ZA or 21ZB and has a reasonable excuse for failing to do so.

Failure to disclose: regulated sector

TA 2000, s 21A is aimed at preventing money laundering by terrorist organisations. Section 21A(1) to (4) creates an offence of failure by D to disclose certain information or other matter to a constable or a nominated officer as soon as is practicable after that information comes into his possession. The offence occurs where:

(a) D knows or suspects or has reasonable grounds for knowing or suspecting that another person (X) has committed or attempted to commit an offence under any of TA 2000, ss 15 to 18; and

(b) that information or other matter, on which D's knowledge or suspicion is based or which gives reasonable grounds for such knowledge or suspicion, came to him in the course of a business in the regulated sector (see above).

X will be taken to have committed an offence against ss 15 to 18 for these purposes if:

(a) he has taken action or been in possession of a thing; and
(b) he would have committed the offence if he had been in the UK at the time when he took the action or was in possession of the thing.

D does not commit an offence under s 21A if:

(a) he has a reasonable excuse for not disclosing the information or other matter;
(b) he is a professional legal adviser or relevant professional adviser (a qualified accountant, auditor or tax adviser) and the information or other matter came to him in privileged circumstances; or
(c) (i)   he is employed by, or in partnership with, such an adviser to provide the adviser with assistance or support,
     (ii) the information or other matter comes to him in connection with the provision of such assistance or support, and
     (iii) the information or other matter comes to him in privileged circumstances.

In deciding whether D has committed an offence under s 21A, a court must consider whether D had followed any relevant Treasury approved guidance issued by a supervisory authority and properly brought to the attention of affected persons.

A disclosure to a 'nominated officer' is one made to a person nominated by D's employer to receive such disclosures and is made in the course of D's employment in accordance with established procedures.

Protected disclosures

By TA 2000, s 21B a disclosure will not be taken to have breached any restriction upon the disclosure of information (however imposed) if (a) the information came to the discloser in the course of a business in the regulated sector, (b) the information is such that it causes him to know or suspect, or gives him reasonable grounds for knowing or suspecting, that another person has committed an offence under ss 15 to 18, and (c) the disclosure is made to a constable or nominated officer as soon as is practicable.

Disclosures to the NCA

Where a disclosure is made under the above provisions to a constable, the constable must disclose it in full as soon as practicable to a member of staff of the NCA authorised for this purpose by the Director General of the NCA; where a disclosure is made to a constable under TA 2000, s 21, this duty to disclose is a duty to disclose to an NCA officer specifically authorised to receive s 19 disclosures (s 21C).

TERRORIST INVESTIGATIONS

Police cordons

TA 2000, ss 33 to 36 provide powers to impose a police cordon for the purposes of a 'terrorist investigation'. A 'terrorist investigation' means an investigation of:

(a) the commission, preparation or instigation of acts of terrorism (see p 773);
(b) an act which appears to have been done for the purposes of terrorism;
(c) the resources of a proscribed organisation (as to which see p 774);

(d) the possibility of making an order proscribing an organisation; or

(e) the commission, preparation or instigation of an offence under the Act or under the Terrorism Act 2006 (pp 802–5) other than an offence under TA 2006, s 1 or s 2 (encouragement of terrorism and dissemination of terrorist publications).

TA 2000, s 34 permits a superintendent (or above), where he considers it expedient for the purpose of a terrorist investigation, to authorise a cordon to be imposed on an area specified by him in that authorisation. (An officer below that rank may do so where there is great urgency. He must, as soon as reasonably practicable, make a written record of the time of the designation of the area and ensure that an officer of at least the rank of superintendent is informed. Such an officer must confirm the designation or cancel it from a specified time, in which case his reason for doing so must be stated.)

The area on which a cordon is imposed must, so far as is reasonably practicable, be indicated by means of police tape or in such other manner as appears appropriate to the police officer responsible for carrying out the arrangements for applying the cordon. The period of time initially specified must not exceed 14 days, but may be extended by a superintendent (or above) by one or more written variations; however, the overall period must not exceed 28 days.

Persons must leave the area immediately when ordered to do so by a constable in uniform and persons must also leave premises which are wholly or partly in or adjacent to a cordoned area when so ordered. Drivers or persons in charge of vehicles must move them out of the area when ordered by such a constable (who also has power to remove such vehicles). A constable in uniform may prohibit or restrict vehicular or pedestrian access to a cordoned area. A summary offence is committed under s 36(2) by someone who does not comply with the constable's order, prohibition or restriction. It is a defence to prove a reasonable excuse.

Offences relating to terrorist investigations

Information about acts of terrorism

By TA 2000, s 38B, a person who has information which he knows or believes might be of material assistance:

(a) in preventing the commission by another person of an act of terrorism; or

(b) in securing the apprehension, prosecution or conviction of another person, in the UK, for an offence involving the commission, preparation or instigation of an act of terrorism,

commits an offence if he does not disclose the information as soon as reasonably practicable to a constable.

This offence may be treated as having been committed in any place where the person to be charged is, or has at any time been, since he first knew or believed that the information might be of material assistance, and proceedings may be taken in any such place.

Offences relating to disclosure

By TA 2000, s 39(2), an offence is committed by a person who knows or has reasonable cause to suspect that a constable is conducting, or proposes to conduct, a terrorist investigation (as defined on p 778 and above) and who:

(a) discloses to another anything which is likely to prejudice the investigation; or

(b) interferes with material which is likely to be relevant to the investigation.

Where a person knows or has reasonable cause to believe that a disclosure has been or will be made under ss 19 to 21B (pp 776–8) or 38B (p 779), he commits an offence under s 39(4) if he:

(a) discloses to another anything which is likely to prejudice an investigation resulting from the disclosure under one of these sections; or
(b) interferes with material which is likely to be relevant to an investigation resulting from the disclosure under that section.

It is a defence to a charge under s 39(2) or (4) for a person to adduce evidence that he did not know and had no reasonable cause to suspect that the disclosure was likely to affect a terrorist investigation (whereupon the prosecution must disprove this) or to prove that he had a reasonable excuse for the disclosure or interference.

COUNTER-TERRORIST POWERS

Search of premises

By TA 2000, s 42, a justice of the peace may issue a warrant on the application of a constable in relation to the search of specified premises if satisfied that there are reasonable grounds for suspecting that a person, whom the constable reasonably suspects to be a person who is or has been concerned in the commission, preparation or instigation of acts of terrorism, is to be found there. Such a warrant authorises entry and search for the purpose of the arrest of a person subject to arrest under the provisions of s 41 (p 791). This power of search includes a power to search a container on the premises.

Search warrants may also be granted under Sch 5, described on p 76.

Code of practice relating to searches of persons and vehicles

Acting under TA 2000, s 47AB, the Secretary of State has issued a Code of Practice for the Exercise of Stop and Search Powers under ss 43 and 43A of TA 2000 and the Authorisation and Exercise of Stop and Search Powers relating to s 47A of, and Sch 6B to, TA 2000 (hereafter 'the Terrorism Search Powers Code'). These statutory provisions are dealt with below. A constable must have regard to the Terrorism Search Powers Code when exercising any powers to which it relates. A failure on the part of a constable to act in accordance with any provision of the Code does not of itself make him liable to criminal or civil proceedings. However, the Code is admissible in evidence in any such proceedings, and a court may, in particular, take into account a failure by a constable to have regard to it in determining a question in any such proceedings. The references to a constable include, in relation to any of the above functions exercisable by a community support officer by virtue of the Police Reform Act 2002, Sch 4 (see p 291), references to that person.

The Code provides that chief officers and 'police authorities' (police and crime commissioners, the Mayor's Office for Policing and Crime, and police authorities) must have regard to it when discharging a function to which it relates. The Code must be followed by them unless there is good reason not to do so, in which case the decision not to follow it should be recorded in writing.

Search of persons

A constable is given power by TA 2000, s 43(1) to stop and search *a person* whom he *reasonably suspects* to be a terrorist to discover whether he has in his possession anything which might constitute evidence that he is a terrorist. A 'terrorist' is defined as a person:

(a) who has committed an offence under s 11 (membership of a proscribed organisation); s 12 (support for it); ss 15 to 18 (fund-raising, etc and money laundering); s 54 (weapons training); or ss 56 to 63 (directing terrorist organisation, possession for terrorist purposes, collecting information, inciting terrorism overseas, and foreign terrorist bombing and finance offences); or
(b) who is, or has been, concerned in the commission, preparation or instigation of acts of terrorism.

This power to stop a person includes the power to stop a vehicle.

By s 43(2), a constable may also search anyone arrested under s 41 (p 791) to discover whether he has anything in his possession which may constitute such evidence. Reasonable suspicion that such evidence may be found is not required.

The powers to search a person under s 43 include the power to search anything carried by the person, eg a bag. Anything found in a search under s 43(1) or (2) may be seized and retained if the constable reasonably suspects that it is evidence that the person is a terrorist (s 43(4)). The additional powers of seizure under the Criminal Justice and Police Act 2001, s 51 are available.

Where a constable exercising the power under s 43(1) to stop a person stops a vehicle he may:

(a) search the vehicle and anything in or on it to discover whether there is anything which may constitute evidence that the person concerned is a terrorist (but he may not search someone in the same vehicle as the suspected terrorist solely on the basis that that person is with the suspected terrorist); and
(b) seize and retain anything which he discovers in the course of such a search, and reasonably suspects may constitute evidence that the person is a terrorist (s 43(4A) and (4B)).

A 'vehicle' includes an aircraft, hovercraft, train or vessel. The additional powers of seizure under the Criminal Justice and Police Act 2001, s 50 are available. A constable stopping a vehicle must be in uniform.

The grounds for stopping and searching a person under s 43(1) are the same as the grounds for arrest under s 41 (p 791): reasonable suspicion that the person is a terrorist. Stop and search is a less intrusive power than arrest and will be more appropriate in many situations, for example in encounters with individuals where a stop and search may help to allay suspicions. Stop and search should not be used in any situation where it is more appropriate to arrest or where an officer believes it may put him, or members of the public, in danger.

Powers to stop and search must be exercised fairly, responsibly and in accordance with the Equality Act 2010 (referred to on p 35).

The same provisions apply to the removal of clothing in conducting a search as apply under PACE Code A: Stop and Search Code (see p 49). Although there is no longer a statutory requirement for the constable conducting the search to be of the same sex as the person searched, where such a constable is readily available, that constable should carry out the search. Otherwise, searches may be carried out by a constable of the opposite sex unless the removal of clothes other than an outer coat or jacket is required. Particular regard should be paid to the sensitivities of some religious communities in respect of being searched by a member of the opposite sex.

For a prospective power of a constable to remove and retain a document to ascertain whether it is one that may be seized under TA 2000, s 43 (or s 43A below), see Chapter 28 on the companion website.

Search of vehicles

By TA 2000, s 43A, if a constable *reasonably suspects* that a *vehicle* is being used for the purposes of terrorism, he may stop and search:

(a) the vehicle,
(b) the driver of the vehicle,
(c) a passenger in the vehicle,
(d) anything in or on the vehicle or carried by the driver or a passenger,

to discover whether there is anything which may constitute evidence that the vehicle is being used for the purposes of terrorism (s 43A(1) and (2)). An unattended vehicle can be searched under s 43A.

'Driver', in relation to an aircraft, hovercraft or vessel, means the captain, pilot or other person with control of the aircraft, hovercraft or vessel, or any member of its crew, and, in relation to a train, includes any member of its crew. A constable stopping a vehicle must be in uniform.

Searches may be undertaken of anything in or on the vehicle, but care should be taken not to damage a vehicle as part of a search or, in the case of an unattended vehicle, in order to gain entry into it. Vehicles stopped under s 43A and persons in those vehicles may be detained only for so long as is necessary to carry out the searches—at or near the place the vehicle was stopped.

A constable may seize and retain anything which he:

(a) discovers in the course of such a search, and
(b) reasonably suspects may constitute evidence that the vehicle is being used for the purposes of terrorism (s 43A(3)).

A person who has the powers of a constable in one part of the UK may exercise a power under s 43A in any part of the UK.

The additional powers of seizure under the Criminal Justice and Police Act 2001, ss 50 and 51 are available.

Power to give an authorisation to stop and search in specified areas or places: TA 2000, s 47A

By TA 2000, s 47A(1), a senior police officer may give a stop and search authorisation under s 47A(2) or (3) (below) in relation to a specified area or place if the officer:

(a) reasonably suspects that an act of terrorism will take place; and
(b) reasonably considers that:
    (i)   the authorisation is necessary to prevent such an act;
    (ii) the specified area or place is no greater than is necessary to prevent such an act; and
    (iii) the duration of the authorisation is no longer than is necessary to prevent such an act.

Those parts of the Code of Practice referred to on p 780 which relate to the exercise of a senior police officer's functions under s 47A are set out in Chapter 28 on the companion website.

Senior police officer

'Senior police officer' for the purposes of s 47A and Sch 6B means an assistant chief constable (or above), or a commander (or above) in the case of the two London police forces. Authorising officers must be either substantive or on temporary promotion to the qualifying rank. Officers who are acting in the rank may not give authorisations.

Specified areas or places

An authorisation given by a senior police officer who is not a member of the British Transport Police, the Ministry of Defence Police or the Civil Nuclear Constabulary may specify an area or place in his police area together with the internal waters (ie waters such as a bay, estuary of a large river, or the sea near larger islands) which are not covered in any police area but are adjacent to that area or place, or a specified area of those internal waters. Police force areas do not cover the sea below the low water mark.

An authorisation by an assistant chief constable (or above) of the British Transport Police, the Ministry of Defence Police or the Civil Nuclear Constabulary may only be given in respect of specified areas or places policed by his force. An authorisation given by a senior police officer of the Civil Nuclear Constabulary does not have effect except in relation to times when the specified area or place is a place where members of that Constabulary have the powers and privileges of a constable.

Authorised conduct

An authorisation under TA 2000, s 47A(2) authorises any constable in uniform to stop a vehicle in the area or place specified in the authorisation and to search:

(a) the vehicle;
(b) the driver of the vehicle;
(c) a passenger in the vehicle;
(d) anything in or on the vehicle or carried by the driver or a passenger.

For these purposes, 'vehicle' includes an aircraft, hovercraft, train or vessel, and 'driver', in relation to an aircraft, hovercraft or vessel, means the captain, pilot, or other person with control of it or any member of its crew and, in relation to a train, includes any member of its crew.

An authorisation under s 47A(3) authorises any constable in uniform to stop a pedestrian in the area or place specified in the authorisation and to search:

(a) the pedestrian;
(b) anything carried by the pedestrian.

Written authorisation or confirmation

Authorisations should, where practicable, be given in writing. A senior police officer who gives an authorisation under s 47A orally must confirm it in writing as soon as reasonably practicable (TA 2000, Sch 6B).
Where:

(a) a vehicle or pedestrian is stopped by virtue of s 47A(2) or (3), and
(b) the driver of the vehicle or the pedestrian applies for a written statement that the vehicle was stopped, or that the pedestrian was stopped, by virtue of s 47A(2) or (as the case may be) (3),

the written statement must be provided. Such an application must be made within the period of 12 months beginning with the date on which the vehicle or pedestrian was stopped.

Duration of authorisation

TA 2000, Sch 6B provides that an authorisation under s 47A has effect during the period:

(a) beginning at the time when the authorisation is given, and
(b) ending with the date or at the time specified in the authorisation.

The power under (b) includes power to specify different dates or times for different areas or places.

The specified date or time in (b) must not occur after the end of the period of *14 days* beginning with the day on which the authorisation is given.

Confirmation of authorisation

The senior police officer who gives an authorisation must inform the Secretary of State (the relevant Secretary of State is the Home Secretary) of it as soon as reasonably practicable; the police should aim to have provided the written authorisation (or written confirmation of an oral authorisation) within two hours of an authorisation being given. Where practicable, notification of an intention to give an authorisation and (unless the authorisation is for less than 48 hours) a draft of that authorisation should be given before the authorisation is given. If the authorisation is not confirmed by the Secretary of State within 48 hours of being given it will automatically cease to have effect at the end of that period, but this will not affect the lawfulness of things done in reliance on the authorisation before then.

When confirming an authorisation, the Secretary of State may substitute an earlier date or time for the specified date or time, or substitute a more restricted area or place for the specified area or place, or both. Where an authorisation specifies more than one area or place, the latter power includes a power to remove areas or places from the authorisation.

The Secretary of State may cancel an authorisation which has been confirmed.

Cancellation or variation of authorisation by senior police officer

By TA 2000, Sch 6B, a senior police officer may cancel an authorisation, or substitute an earlier date or time, or a more restricted area or place, for that specified in the authorisation. Where an authorisation specifies more than one area or place this power of substitution includes a power to remove areas or places from the authorisation. Any cancellation or substitution by a senior officer in relation to an authorisation confirmed by the Secretary of State must be notified to the Secretary of State but does not require confirmation by the Secretary of State. If, during the currency of an authorisation, the authorising officer:

(a) no longer reasonably suspects that an act of terrorism of the description given in the authorisation will take place or no longer considers that the powers are necessary to prevent such an act, he must cancel the authorisation immediately; or
(b) believes that the duration or geographical extent of the authorisation is no longer necessary for the prevention of such an act of terrorism, he must substitute a shorter period, or more restricted geographical area.

New authorisation

The existence, expiry or cancellation of an authorisation does not prevent the giving of a new authorisation (Sch 6B).

Exercising the stop and search powers under s 47A

By TA 2000, s 47A(4), a constable in uniform may exercise the power conferred by an authorisation under s 47A(2) or (3) only for the purpose of discovering whether there is anything which may constitute evidence that the vehicle concerned is being used for the purposes of terrorism or (as the case may be) that the person concerned is or has been concerned in the commission, preparation or instigation of acts of terrorism. The search can therefore only be carried out to look for anything that would link the vehicle or the person to terrorism.

The power conferred by such an authorisation may be exercised whether or not the constable reasonably suspects that there is such evidence.

When exercising s 47A powers, officers should have a basis for selecting individuals or vehicles to be stopped and searched. This basis will be set by the tactical briefing which has been given. Constables should still consider whether powers requiring reasonable suspicion are more appropriate and should only use the powers conferred by a s 47A authorisation if they are satisfied that they cannot meet a threshold of reasonable suspicion sufficient to use other police powers.

When selecting individuals to be stopped and searched, officers should consider the following:

Deciding which power to use   If a s 47A authorisation is in place, the powers conferred by that authorisation may be used. However, if there is a reasonable suspicion that a person is a terrorist, then powers requiring reasonable suspicion in TA 2000, s 43 (p 780) or s 43A (p 782) should be used as appropriate instead.

Selecting an individual or vehicle using indicators   What are the *geographical limits* of the authorisation and what are the parameters within which the briefing allows stops and searches to be conducted? *Behaviour*: Is the person to be stopped and searched acting in a manner that gives cause for concern, or is a vehicle being used in such a manner? Could the person's *clothing* conceal an article of concern, which may constitute evidence that a person is a terrorist? Could an *item being carried* conceal an article that could constitute evidence that a person is a terrorist or a vehicle is being used for the purposes of terrorism?

Selecting individuals 'at random'   What are the geographical and other parameters of the operation as set out in the authorisation?

Explanation   Officers should be reminded of the need to explain to people why they or their vehicles are being searched.

Equality   The powers to stop and search must be used fairly, responsibly and in accordance with the Equality Act 2010: see p 35. Officers should take care to avoid any form of racial or religious profiling when selecting people to search under s 47A powers. Racial or religious profiling is the use of racial, ethnic, religious or other stereotypes, rather than individual behaviour or specific intelligence, as a basis for making operational or investigative decisions about who may be involved in criminal activity. Profiling in this way may amount to an act of unlawful discrimination, as would selecting individuals for a search on the grounds of any of the other protected characteristics. Profiling people from certain ethnicities or religious backgrounds may also lose the confidence of communities.

Great care should be taken to ensure that the selection of people is not based solely on ethnic background, perceived religion or other protected characteristic. A person's appearance or ethnic background will sometimes form part of a potential suspect's description, but a decision to search a person under powers conferred by s 47A should be made only if such a description is available.

Removal of clothing

A constable may not require a person to remove any clothing in public except for headgear, footwear, an outer coat, a jacket or gloves. Officers should be aware of the cultural sensitivities that may be involved in the removal of headgear.

Photography/film

It is important that police officers are aware, in exercising their counter-terrorism powers, that:

(a) members of the public and media do not need a permit to film or photograph in public places;
(b) it is not an offence for a member of the public or journalist to take photographs/ film of a public building; and
(c) the police have no power to stop the filming or photographing of incidents or police personnel.

Under s 47A, police officers can stop and search someone taking photographs/film within an authorised area just as they can stop and search any other member of the public in the proper exercise of their discretion in accordance with the legislation and provisions of the Code. However, an authorisation itself does not prohibit the taking of photographs or digital images.

On the rare occasion that an officer reasonably suspects that photographs/film are being taken as part of hostile terrorist reconnaissance, a search under TA 2000, s 43 (p 780) or an arrest should be considered. It is important that police officers do not automatically consider photography/filming as suspicious behaviour. The size of the camera/video equipment should not be considered as a risk indicator.

Health and safety

When undertaking any search, officers should always consider their own safety and the health and safety of others. Officers should have an appropriate level of personal safety training and be in possession of personal protective equipment. Officers carrying out searches should use approved tactics to keep themselves and the public safe.

If, during the course of a stop and search there is a suspicion that a person is in possession of a hazardous device or substance, an officer should immediately request the assistance of officers appropriately trained and equipped to deal with the situation.

Seizure

Section 47A(6) provides that a constable may seize and retain anything which he:

(a) discovers in the course of a search under an authorisation under s 47A(2) or (3); and
(b) reasonably suspects may constitute evidence that the vehicle concerned is being used for the purposes of terrorism or (as the case may be) that the person concerned is a person who is or has been concerned in the commission, preparation or instigation of acts of terrorism.

Film and memory cards may be seized as part of the search if the officer reasonably suspects they are evidence that the person is a terrorist, or a vehicle is being used for the purposes of terrorism, but officers do not have a legal power to delete images or destroy film. Cameras and other devices should be left in the state they were found and forwarded to appropriately trained staff for forensic examination. The person being searched should never be asked or allowed to turn the device on or off because of the danger of evidence being lost or damaged.

Seizures of cameras, etc may only be made, following a stop and search, where the officer reasonably suspects that they constitute evidence that the person is a terrorist or that the vehicle is being used for the purposes of terrorism as the case may be.

Anything seized may be retained for as long as necessary in all the circumstances. This includes retention for use as evidence at a trial for an offence.

A record should be made of any item seized or retained and made available with a copy of the record of the stop and search. If the reasonable suspicion referred to in (b) above ceases to apply, the item should be returned to the individual from whom it was seized, or the person in charge of the vehicle from which it was seized, unless there are other grounds for retaining it (eg in respect of the investigation of a separate offence). If there appears to be a dispute over the ownership of the article, it may be retained for as long as necessary to determine the lawful owner.

Use of powers by community support officers

Where an authorisation under s 47A is in place, community support officers who are in the company of a constable who is supervising them may stop any pedestrian or vehicle, search anything carried by the pedestrian, the driver or a passenger, the vehicle or anything carried in or on it, and exercise the power of seizure under s 47A(6). They may not, however, search people or people's clothing under the s 47A powers. Authorising officers may consider whether to include community support officers within a stop and search operation authorised by s 47A. If community support officers are to use the powers available, they should be properly briefed on the limitations on their powers, as well as being briefed on the appropriate use of their powers.

Points general to TA 2000, ss 43, 43A, and 47A

Given that they require reasonable suspicion in order to be exercised, the use of powers under ss 43(1) and 43A should be prioritised for the purposes of stopping and searching individuals for the purposes of preventing or detecting terrorism. The authorisation of the no suspicion powers under s 47A should only be considered as a last resort, where reasonable suspicion powers are considered inadequate to respond to the threat. Use of the search powers under s 47A should only be made (in an authorised area) when the powers in ss 43 and 43A are not appropriate.

The Terrorism Search Powers Code provides guidance as to 'reasonable suspicion' which corresponds with that under PACE Code A: the Stop and Search Code (p 40).

Steps to be taken prior to a search

Before any search of a detained person or attended vehicle takes place the officer must take reasonable steps to give his identification number and name of police station (subject to the endangerment exception below) to the person to be searched or to the person in charge of the vehicle to be searched and to give that person the following information:

(a) that he is being detained for the purposes of a search;
(b) the legal search power which is being exercised;

(c) a clear explanation of:
   (i)   the object of the search (ie to search for evidence that the person is a terrorist or that a vehicle is being used for the purposes of terrorism); and
   (ii) in the case of s 47A, the nature of the powers conferred by s 47A, the fact an authorisation has been given and the reason why he has been selected for a stop and search, or, in the case of ss 43 or 43A, the grounds for suspicion;
(d) that he is entitled to a copy of the search record if he asks within three months of the search;
(e) that if he is not arrested and taken to a police station as a result of the search and it is practicable to make the record on the spot, that immediately after the search is completed he will be given (subject to the officer being called to an incident of higher priority), if he requests, either:
   (i)   a copy of the record, or
   (ii) a receipt which explains how he can obtain a copy of the full record or access to an electronic copy of the record. A receipt may take the form of a simple business card which includes sufficient information to locate the record should the person ask for a copy, for example the date and place of the search, or a reference number;
(f) that if he is arrested and taken to a police station as a result of the search, that the record will be made at the station as part of his custody record and he will be given, if he requests, a copy of his custody record which includes a record of the search as soon as practicable whilst he is at the station.

A person who is not provided with an immediate copy of a search record may request a copy within three months of being stopped and searched. In addition a person is also entitled, on application, to a written statement that he was stopped by virtue of the powers conferred by s 47A(2) or (3) (p 783), if requested within 12 months of the stop taking place.

If the person to be searched, or person in charge of a vehicle to be searched, does not appear to understand what is being said, or there is any doubt about the person's ability to understand English, the officer must take reasonable steps to bring information regarding that person's rights to his attention. If he is deaf or cannot understand English and is accompanied by someone, then the officer may try to establish whether that person can interpret or otherwise help the officer to give the required information. This does not preclude an officer from conducting a search once he has taken reasonable steps to explain the person's rights.

Conduct of stops and searches

The constable may detain the person or vehicle for such time as is reasonably required to permit the search to be carried out at or near the place where the person or vehicle is stopped. The length of time must be kept to a minimum. A person or vehicle may be detained under the stop and search powers at a place other than where the person or vehicle was first stopped, only if that place, be it a police station or elsewhere, is nearby. Such a place should be located within a reasonable travelling distance using whatever mode of travel (on foot or by vehicle) is appropriate.

All stops and searches must be carried out with courtesy, consideration and respect for the person concerned. Every reasonable effort must be made to minimise the embarrassment that a person being searched may experience. The co-operation of the person to be searched must be sought in every case, even if the person initially objects to the search. A forcible search may be made only if it has been established that the person is unwilling to co-operate or resists. Reasonable force may be used as a last resort if necessary to conduct a search or to detain a person or vehicle for the purposes of a search.

Recording requirements

Searches which do not result in an arrest   When an officer carries out a search under TA 2000, s 43(1) or 43A or in the exercise of powers conferred by s 47A and the search does not result in the person searched, or person in charge of the vehicle searched, being arrested and taken to a police station, a record must be made of it at the time, electronically or on paper, unless there are circumstances which make this wholly impracticable. If a record is not made at the time of the stop and search, the officer must make the record as soon as practicable after the search is completed. There may be situations in which it is not practicable to obtain the information necessary to complete a record, but the officer should make every reasonable effort to do so. If it is not possible to complete a record in full, an officer must make every reasonable effort to at least record details of the date, time and place where the stop and search took place, the power under which it was carried out, and the officer's identification number.

If the record is made at the time, the person who has been searched or who is in charge of the vehicle that has been searched must be asked if he wants a copy of the record, and, if he does, he must be given immediately, either:

(a)   a copy of the record, or
(b)   a receipt which explains how he can obtain a copy of the full record or access to an electronic copy of the record.

There is an exception: an officer is not required to provide a copy of the full record or a receipt at the time if he is called to an incident of higher priority.

Where it is not practicable to provide a written copy of the record or immediate access to an electronic copy of the record or a receipt at the time, the officer should give the person details of the police station at which he may request a copy of the record.

Searches which result in an arrest   If a search conducted under s 43, 43A or 47A results in a person being arrested and taken to a police station, the officer who carried out the search is responsible for ensuring that a record of the search is made as part of that person's custody record. The custody officer must then ensure that the person is asked if he wants a copy of the custody record and, if he does, that he is given a copy as soon as practicable.

Record of search

The record of a search must always include the following information:

(a)   a note of the self-defined ethnicity, and, if different, the ethnicity as perceived by the officer making the search, of the person searched or of the person in charge of the vehicle searched (as the case may be);
(b)   the date, time and place the person or vehicle was searched;
(c)   the object of the search;
(d)   in the case of:
   (i)   the powers under s 47A, the nature of the powers, the fact that an authorisation has been given and the reason the person or vehicle was selected for the search;
   (ii)   the powers under s 43 or 43A, the grounds for suspicion;
(e)   the officer's warrant number or other identification number (subject to the endangerment exception).

Officers should record the self-defined ethnicity of every person stopped according to the same categories as used in PACE Code A (the Stop and Search Code): see p 51. The procedure is identical to that set out on pp 51–2.

For the purposes of completing the search record, there is no requirement to record the name, address and date of birth of the person searched or the person in charge of a vehicle which is searched and the person is under no obligation to provide this information. An officer may remind a person that providing these details will ensure that the police force is able to provide information about the stop and search in future should the person request that information or if it is otherwise required.

The names of police officers are not required to be shown on the search record in the case of operations linked to the investigation of terrorism or otherwise where an officer reasonably believes that recording names might endanger the officers; this is the 'endangerment exception' referred to in (e) above. In such cases the record must show the officer's warrant or other identification number and duty station.

A record is required for each person and each vehicle searched. However, if a person is in a vehicle and both are searched, and the object and grounds of the search are the same, only one record need be completed. If more than one person in a vehicle is searched, separate records for each search of a person must be made. If only a vehicle is searched, the self-defined ethnic background of the person in charge of the vehicle must be recorded, unless the vehicle is unattended.

The record of the grounds for making a search must, briefly but informatively, explain the reason for suspecting the person concerned, by reference to the person's behaviour and/or other circumstances, or, in the case of searches under s 47A, the reason why a particular person or vehicle was selected.

After searching an unattended vehicle, or anything in or on it, an officer must leave a notice in it (or on it, if things on it have been searched without opening it) recording the fact that it has been searched. The notice must include the name of the police station to which the officer concerned is attached and state where a copy of the record of the search may be obtained and how (if applicable) an electronic copy may be accessed and where any application for compensation should be directed. The vehicle must if practicable be left secure.

Monitoring and supervising the use of stop and search powers

The Terrorism Search Powers Code contains provisions in this respect which correspond to those in PACE Code A (the Stop and Search Code): see p 52. Statistical data on the use of powers should be provided quarterly to the Home Office.

Community engagement

Ongoing community engagement is essential in improving relationships with the community. Use may be made, for example, of existing community engagement arrangements. However, where stop and search powers affect sections of the community with whom channels of communication are difficult or non-existent, these should be identified and steps taken to engage. For example, if s 47A authorisations have primarily been made around transport hubs, effort should be made to engage with people using those hubs.

When planning a counter-terrorism search operation, police authorities and the local CONTEST Prevent strategic partnership should be involved at the earliest opportunity to provide advice and assistance in identifying mechanisms for engaging with communities.

If it is not possible to carry out community engagement prior to authorisation, police forces should carry out a retrospective review of the use of the powers, including stakeholders. Police forces should continue to monitor the use of s 47A powers for the duration of an authorisation, both in discussion with community representatives and by explaining how and why the powers are being used to individuals who are stopped and searched. Officers should be ready to explain to individuals why the powers are in place, insofar as this can be communicated without disclosing sensitive intelligence or causing undue alarm. Stop and search operations should form part of wider counter-terrorism policing, and public awareness of the powers should be considered as part of any wider communications strategy associated with an operation.

Seizure of passports, etc from persons suspected of involvement in terrorism

The Counter-Terrorism and Security Act 2015, Sch 1 provides powers to seize passports, etc from persons at ports who are reasonably suspected of involvement in terrorism. For these purposes, 'port' means an airport, a sea port, a hoverport, a heliport, a railway station where passenger trains depart to, or arrive from, places outside the UK, or any other place at which a person is able, or attempting, to get on or off any craft, vessel or vehicle in connection with entering or leaving Great Britain. See Chapter 28 on the companion website for details about these provisions.

Prohibitions or restrictions on parking

TA 2000, s 48 permits a police officer of or above the rank of assistant chief constable (or commander), where it appears to him to be expedient in order to prevent acts of terrorism, to give an authorisation to any constable to prohibit or restrict the parking of vehicles on a specified road. This is to be done by the placing of traffic signs. A constable exercising his powers under s 48 may suspend a parking place and this will have the effect of permitting the removal of vehicles. Such an authorisation remains in force for a period, not exceeding 28 days, specified in it. It may be renewed subject to the same rules.

Failing to move a vehicle when ordered to do so by a constable is an offence under s 51(2). Parking in contravention of such a prohibition or restriction is an offence under s 51(1). It is a defence to either offence to prove a reasonable excuse. Current disabled persons' badge-holders are not exempt from these requirements and have no reasonable excuse for failure to comply on those grounds. The powers to impose these restrictions are additional to any other powers available to a constable.

The offences under s 51 are summary offences.

Arrest without warrant

TA 2000, s 41 provides that a constable may arrest without warrant a person whom he reasonably suspects to be a terrorist (as defined on p 781).

A person who has been so detained may be held for 48 hours. Continued detention beyond that period is subject to a warrant of further detention granted in accordance with the procedures prescribed by TA 2000, Sch 8 (described on p 800).

Treatment of persons detained under Terrorism Act 2000, s 41 (or Sch 7)

The following rules, set out in TA 2000, Sch 8, relate to someone detained under TA 2000, s 41 or Sch 7 (special powers of 'examining officers'—ie constables, immigration officers and designated customs officers—to stop, question and detain a person at seaports and airports to determine whether he appears to be someone concerned in the commission, preparation or instigation of acts of terrorism). The relevant code of practice in relation to those detained under s 41 is not PACE Code C (the Detention Code) but is PACE Code H: the Code of Practice in Connection with the Detention, Treatment and Questioning by Police Officers of Persons under s 41 of, and Sch 8 to, the Terrorism Act 2000 and the Treatment and Questioning of Detained Persons in Respect of whom an Authorisation to Question after Charge has been given under C-TA 2008, s 22. In relation to the first part of its subject matter, Code H generally mirrors Code C (see Chapters 4 and 5). A separate Code of Practice for Examining Officers and Review Officers applies to those detained under Sch 7.

Except in relation to the special powers to question under Sch 7, TA 2000, s 114 empowers a constable to use reasonable force to exercise any power relating to the treatment of those detained under s 41 (or Sch 7).

Place of detention

The Secretary of State is required to designate places at which persons may be detained under s 41 or Sch 7. A reference in Sch 8 to a police station includes a place so designated. Under Sch 8, a person arrested by a constable under s 41 must be taken, as soon as practicable, to the police station which the constable considers to be the most appropriate. If the person was arrested as a result of a search in which PACE Code A (the Stop and Search Code) or the Terrorism Search Powers Code applies, the officer carrying out the search is responsible for ensuring that the record of that stop and search is made as part of the person's custody record. The custody officer must then ensure that the person is asked if he wants a copy of the search record and, if he does, that he is given a copy as soon as practicable. The person's entitlement to a copy of the search record which is made as part of his custody record is in addition to, and does not affect, his entitlement to a copy of his custody record.

Identification

An 'authorised person' (which term includes a constable) may take any steps which are reasonably necessary for photographing, measuring or identifying the detained person. However, these initial measures do not include the taking of fingerprints, non-intimate samples or intimate samples.

Interviews

Acting under a power in TA 2000, Sch 8, the Secretary of State has made an order requiring the video recording with sound of an interview at a police station by a constable of a person detained under TA 2000, s 41 or Sch 7. 'Police station' includes any place designated as a place where a person may be detained under TA 2000, s 41. Such an interview must be conducted in accordance with the Code of Practice for the Video Recording with Sound of Interviews with Persons Detained and Post-Charge Questioning of Persons Authorised under C-TA 2008, s 22.

The Code provides in relation to such an interview that it may be necessary to delay an interview to make arrangements to overcome any difficulties that might otherwise prevent the record being made, for example non-availability of suitable re-cording equipment and interview facilities. If a person refuses to go into or remain in a suitable interview room, and the custody officer considers, on reasonable grounds, that the interview should not be delayed, the interview may, at the custody officer's discretion, be conducted in a cell using portable recording equipment. The reasons must be recorded.

Before any interview starts, the person and any appropriate adult and interpreter must be given a written notice which explains that the interview must be video re-corded with sound. At the same time, the person, the appropriate adult (as defined on p 97) and interpreter must be informed verbally of the content of the notice.

If the person interviewed or the appropriate adult raises objections to the interview being recorded, the interviewing officer must explain that the interview is being re-corded in order to protect both the person being interviewed and the interviewing officer and that there is no opt-out facility.

The provisions of the Code about the procedure relating to the recording mirror those under PACE Code F, described on p 132.

Rights

A person detained at a place under TA 2000, s 41 (or Sch 7) is entitled, if he so requests, to have a named person who is a friend, relative, or person known to him who is likely to take an interest in his welfare informed, as soon as is reasonably practicable, that he is being detained there. If the detained person is transferred to another place, he is en-titled to exercise that right at the second place.

In addition, the detained person is entitled, if he so requests, to consult a solicitor as soon as is reasonably practicable, privately and at any time. A record must be made of such a request.

Where a person detained under Sch 7 requests to consult a solicitor, the examining officer may not question him to determine whether he appears to be someone con-cerned in the commission, preparation or instigation of acts of terrorism ('the relevant matters') until the detainee has consulted a solicitor (or no longer wishes to do so). This does not apply if the examining officer reasonably believes that postponing the ques-tioning until then would be likely to prejudice determination of the relevant matters. The detained person is entitled to consult a solicitor in person, unless the examining officer reasonably believes that the time it would take to consult a solicitor in person would be likely to prejudice determination of the relevant matters, in which case he may require any consultation to take place in another way.

A superintendent (or above) may authorise a delay in informing the person named by the detained person or in permitting the detained person to consult a solicitor, but he must be permitted to exercise these rights within 48 hours. Such an officer may give an authorisation only if he has reasonable grounds for believing that informing the named person or solicitor of the detained person's detention at the time when the person wishes this to be done, will lead to:

(a) interference with or harm to evidence of an indictable offence;
(b) interference with or physical injury to any person;
(c) alerting persons who are suspected of having committed an indictable offence but who have not been arrested for it;
(d) hindering the recovery of property obtained as a result of an indictable offence or in respect of which a forfeiture order in respect of the terrorist property offences in TA 2000, ss 15–18 or other terrorism offences could be made under the Act;

(e) interference with the gathering of information about the commission, preparation or instigation of acts of terrorism;
(f) alerting a person and thereby making it more difficult to prevent an act of terrorism; and
(g) alerting a person and thereby making it more difficult to secure a person's apprehension, prosecution or conviction in connection with the commission, preparation or instigation of an act of terrorism.

In addition, a similar authorisation may be given where a superintendent (or above) has reasonable grounds for believing that the offence concerned is one in which there exist powers of confiscation in respect of the proceeds of an offence, and that the detained person has benefited from the offence and that, by informing the named person, or exercising the right to see a solicitor, the recovery of the value of that benefit will be hindered.

Where any delay is authorised the detained person must be told of the reason for the delay as soon as reasonably practicable and the reason must be recorded.

A direction may be made that a person may only consult a solicitor, under the above right, in the sight and hearing of a qualified officer. Such a direction may only be given by an assistant chief constable or commander (or above) and only if he has reasonable grounds for believing that:

(a) unless the direction is given, the exercise of the right of the detained person will have any of the consequences specified in (a)–(g) above; or
(b) the detained person has benefited from his criminal conduct and that, unless the direction is given, the exercise of the right by the detained person will hinder the recovery of the value of the property constituting the benefit.

A 'qualified officer' must be a uniformed inspector (or above) who has no connection with the case. Such a direction will cease to exist when the reason for it ceases to exist.

Fingerprinting, non-intimate and intimate samples

Taking fingerprints or non-intimate samples   Fingerprints or non-intimate samples may be taken from a person detained under s 41 or Sch 7 by a constable:

(a) with the written appropriate (p 208) consent of the detainee; or
(b) without such consent:
   (i) where he is detained at a police station and a superintendent (or above) gives an authorisation, or
   (ii) where the detainee has been convicted of a recordable offence (and, in the case of a non-intimate sample, he was so convicted on or after 10 April 1995). As to 'recordable offence', see p 209.

A superintendent (or above) may make an authorisation under (b)(i) *if a person is detained under TA 2000, s 41, where the officer reasonably suspects that the person has been involved in an offence specified under TA 2000, ss 11 and 12 (see p 774), ss 15–18, (see pp 775–6), s 54 (see p 805), s 56 (directing terrorist operations), s 57 (see p 800), s 58 (see p 801), s 58A (see p 802), s 59 (inciting terrorism overseas), ss 62 or 63 (terrorist bombing or finance offences outside the UK), and the officer reasonably believes that the fingerprints or sample will tend to confirm or disprove his involvement, or, in any other case, the officer is satisfied that taking the fingerprints or sample is necessary to assist in determining whether the person has been concerned in the preparation, commission or instigation of acts of terrorism.*

A superintendent (or above) may also authorise the taking under (b)(i) of fingerprints from a person detained at a police station if he is satisfied that this person's fingerprints will facilitate the ascertainment of his identity, and that person has refused to identify himself or the officer has reasonable grounds for suspecting that that person is not who he claims to be. References to ascertaining a person's identity include references to showing that he is not a particular person.

If non-intimate samples of hair are taken, they may be taken by cutting or plucking provided that no more are plucked than is reasonably necessary to provide a sufficient sample.

Taking intimate samples An intimate sample (p 204) may be taken by a constable from a person detained under TA 2000, s 41, but only if he is detained at a police station, with the written appropriate consent and the authorisation of a superintendent (or above). However, an intimate sample other than a sample of urine or a dental impression may be taken only by a registered medical practitioner acting on the authority of a constable. A dental impression may be taken only by a registered dentist acting on the authority of a constable. An authorisation for the consensual taking of an intimate sample may only be given in the above two cases if the conditions italicised on p 794 are satisfied.

Where two or more non-intimate samples suitable for the same means of analysis have been taken from a person and these samples have proved insufficient, and the person concerned has been released from detention, an intimate sample may be taken with written appropriate consent and the authorisation of a superintendent (or above). Where appropriate, if written consent to the taking of an intimate sample is refused without good cause, in any proceedings for an offence, the court may draw such inferences from the refusal as appear proper.

General Before fingerprints or samples are taken, the person must be informed that they may be used for the purpose of checking against other fingerprints or samples held on behalf of police forces (speculative search) and, where taken with consent or in consequence of having been convicted of a recordable offence, of the reason for the fingerprints or samples being taken. All such matters must be recorded.

Destruction and retention of fingerprints and DNA profiles, etc TA 2000, Sch 8, para 20A provides that paragraph 20A material, ie:

(a) fingerprints taken under Sch 8;
(b) a DNA profile derived from a DNA sample taken under Sch 8;
(c) relevant physical data taken or provided by virtue of provisions which deal with the retention, destruction and use of biometric material taken in Scotland;
(d) a DNA profile derived from a DNA sample taken by virtue of specified Scottish provision,

must be destroyed if it appears to the responsible chief officer of police that:

(i) the taking or providing of the material or, in the case of a DNA profile, the taking of the sample from which the DNA profile was derived, was unlawful, or
(ii) the material was taken or provided, or (in the case of a DNA profile) was derived from a sample taken, from a person in connection with that person's arrest under TA 2000, s 41 and the arrest was unlawful or based on mistaken identity.

'Responsible chief officer of police' means, in relation to fingerprints or samples taken in England or Wales, or a DNA profile derived from a sample so taken, the chief officer of police for the police area in which the material concerned was taken.

In any other case, para 20A material must be destroyed unless it is retained under any power conferred by paras 20B to 20E (below).

Para 20A material which ceases to be retained under a power mentioned below may continue to be retained under any other such power which applies to it.

Nothing in para 20A prevents a relevant search, in relation to para 20A material, from being carried out within such time as may reasonably be required for the search if the responsible chief officer of police considers the search to be desirable. A 'relevant search' is a search carried out for the purpose of checking the material against:

(a) other fingerprints or samples taken under the above provisions or a DNA profile derived from such a sample;
(b) any of the relevant physical data (as defined by the Criminal Procedure (Scotland) Act 1995, s 18(7A)), samples or information mentioned or held by virtue of specified corresponding Scottish legislation;
(c) material to which the Counter-Terrorism Act 2008, s 18 applies (see p 222);
(d) any of the fingerprints, data or samples obtained under the Terrorism Prevention and Investigation Measures Act 2011, Sch 6 or the corresponding Scottish legislation or information derived therefrom;
(e) any of the fingerprints, samples and information mentioned in PACE, s 63A(1)(a) and (b) (see p 213); and
(f) any of the fingerprints, samples and information mentioned in the corresponding Northern Irish legislation about checking of fingerprints and samples.

Any copies of the fingerprints or relevant physical data required to be destroyed by para 20A which are held by a police force must also be destroyed. No copy of a DNA profile required by para 20A to be destroyed may be retained by a police force except in a form which does not identify the person to whom the profile relates.

Retention of para 20A material   By TA 2000, Sch 8 para 20B, the following provisions apply.

Para 20A material relating to a person who is detained under TA 2000, s 41:

(a) in the case of a person previously convicted of a recordable offence (see p 209) (other than a single exempt conviction (p 797)), or an imprisonable offence in Scotland, or a person so convicted before the end of the period within which the material may be retained by virtue of para 20B, may be retained indefinitely;
(b) in the case of a person who has no previous convictions, or only one exempt conviction, may be retained until the end of the relevant retention period. The retention period is:
   (i) in the case of fingerprints or relevant physical data, the period of *three years* beginning with the date on which the fingerprints or relevant physical data were taken or provided, and
   (ii) in the case of a DNA profile, the period of *three years* beginning with the date on which the DNA sample from which the profile was derived was taken (or, if the profile was derived from more than one DNA sample, the date on which the first of those samples was taken).

Para 20C makes identical provision to that under (a) and (b) above in relation to para 20A material relating to a person detained under Sch 7, except that 'six months' is substituted for 'three years' in both places italicised.

For the purposes of paras 20B and 20C, para 20D(1) provides that a person is to be treated as having been convicted of an offence if:

(a) in relation to a recordable offence in England and Wales or Northern Ireland:
  (i) he has been given a caution in respect of the offence (or has been warned or reprimanded under the Crime and Disorder Act 1998, s 65 (repealed)),
  (ii) he has been found not guilty by reason of insanity or to be under a disability and to have done the act charged,
(b) in relation to an imprisonable offence in Scotland:
  (i) he has accepted or has been deemed to accept a conditional offer, a compensation offer, a combined offer, or a work offer,
  (ii) he has been acquitted on account of insanity or committed to hospital for inquiry into his mental condition,
  (iii) having been given a fixed penalty notice, he has paid the fixed penalty, or the sum which he is liable to pay, or
  (iv) he has been discharged absolutely.

For the purposes of the above provisions relating to the retention of para 20A material, 'spent convictions' count as convictions but a conviction in respect of the repealed offences of buggery and gross indecency with a man is not to be treated as a conviction if it is to be disregarded by virtue of a 'disregard decision' by the Secretary of State. In addition:

(a) a person has no previous convictions if he has not previously been convicted in England and Wales or Northern Ireland of a recordable offence (p 209), or, in Scotland, of an imprisonable offence, and
(b) a conviction for a recordable offence is exempt if it is in respect of a such offence, other than a qualifying offence (p 203), committed when the person was under 18.

If a person is convicted of more than one offence arising out of a single course of action, those convictions are treated as a single conviction for the purposes of calculating under para 20B or 20C whether the person has been convicted of only one offence.

The responsible chief officer of police (p 795) or a specified chief officer of police may apply to a District Judge (Magistrates' Courts) for an order extending the retention period for two years. Such an application must be made within a three-month period ending on the last day of the retention period. The responsible chief officer of police, a specified chief officer of police, or the person from whom the material was taken may appeal to the Crown Court against an order, or a refusal to make such an order. A 'specified chief officer of police' means the chief officer of the police force of the area in which the person from whom the material was taken resides, or a chief officer of police who believes that the person is in, or is intending to come to, the chief officer's police area. Nothing in para 20B or 20C prevents the start of a new retention period in relation to para 20A material if a person is detained again under TA 2000, s 41 or (as the case may be) Sch 7 when an existing retention period (whether or not extended) is still in force in relation to that material.

Retention of para 20A material: national security determination   Paragraph 20A material may be retained for as long as a national security determination made by the responsible chief officer of police has effect in relation to it. A national security determination is made if the responsible chief officer of police determines that it is necessary for any para 20A material to be retained for the purposes of national security.
  A national security determination:

(a) must be made in writing,
(b) has effect for a maximum of two years beginning with the date on which it is made, and
(c) may be renewed.

Destruction of samples   Paragraph 20G deals with para 20G material, ie samples taken under the provisions of TA 2000, Sch 8 referred to on pp 794–5, or by virtue of corresponding Scottish provisions. Paragraph 20G is not yet in force for the purposes of its application to samples which are, or may become, disclosable under the Criminal Procedure and Investigations Act 1996 (CPIA 1996) or the CPIA 1996 (s 23(1)) Code of Practice (pp 274–8).

Samples to which para 20G applies must be destroyed if it appears to the responsible chief officer of police that:

(a) the taking of the sample was unlawful, or
(b) the sample was taken from a person in connection with that person's arrest under TA 2000, s 41 and the arrest was unlawful or based on mistaken identity.

Subject to this, the following rules apply to a sample so taken.
A DNA sample must be destroyed:

(a) as soon as a DNA profile has been derived from the sample, or
(b) if sooner, before the end of the period of six months beginning with the date on which the sample was taken.

Any other sample must be destroyed before the end of the period of six months beginning with the date on which it was taken.

The responsible chief officer of police may apply to a District Judge (Magistrates' Courts) for an order to retain a sample beyond the date on which it would otherwise be required to be destroyed by the above two paragraphs if the sample was taken from a person detained under s 41 in connection with the investigation of a qualifying offence, and the responsible chief officer considers that, *having regard to the nature and complexity of other material that is evidence in relation to the offence, the sample is likely to be needed in any proceedings for the offence for the purposes of*:

(a) *disclosure to, or use by, a defendant, or*
(b) *responding to any challenge by a defendant in respect of the admissibility of material that is evidence on which the prosecution proposes to rely.*

'Qualifying offence' has the meaning given on p 203. Such an application must be made before the date on which the sample would otherwise be required to be destroyed by virtue of the above two paragraphs.

If the District Judge is satisfied that the italicised condition is met, he may make an order which:

(a) allows the sample to be retained for a period of 12 months beginning with the date on which the sample would otherwise be required to be destroyed, and
(b) may be renewed (on one or more occasions) for a further period of not more than 12 months from the end of the period when the order would otherwise cease to have effect.

An application for such an order (other than an application for renewal):

(a) may be made without notice of the application having been given to the person from whom the sample was taken, and
(b) may be heard and determined in private in his absence.

A sample retained by virtue of such an order may only be used for the purposes of proceedings for the offence in connection with which it was taken. A sample that ceases to be retained by virtue of such an order must be destroyed. Nothing in para 20G prevents a relevant search (as defined above in relation to para 20A) in relation to the above types of samples from being carried out within such time as may reasonably be required for the search if the responsible chief officer of police considers the search to be desirable.

Use of para 20A or 20G material Any para 20A or 20G material must not be used other than:

(a) in the interests of national security,
(b) for the purposes of a terrorist investigation (as defined on p 778),
(c) for purposes related to the prevention or detection of crime, the investigation of an offence, or the conduct of a prosecution, or
(d) for purposes related to the identification of a deceased person or of the person to whom the material relates.

The reference to crime includes a reference to any conduct which:

(i) constitutes one or more criminal offences (whether under the law of a part of the UK or of a country or territory outside the UK), or
(ii) is, or corresponds to, any conduct which, if it all took place in any one part of the UK, would constitute one or more criminal offences.

Subject to the above paragraph, a relevant search (as defined above) may be carried out in relation to material to which para 20A or 20G applies if the responsible chief officer of police considers the search to be desirable.

Material which is required by para 20A or 20G to be destroyed must not at any time after it is required to be destroyed be used:

(a) in evidence against the person to whom the material relates, or
(b) for the purposes of the investigation of any offence.

The references above to using material include a reference to allowing any check to be made against it and to disclosing it to any person. The references to an investigation and to a prosecution include references, respectively, to any investigation outside the UK of any crime or suspected crime and to a prosecution brought in respect of any crime in a country or territory outside the UK.

Limit The above provisions about the destruction, use and retention of fingerprints, DNA profiles and samples do not apply to para 20A material relating to a person detained under s 41 which is, or may become, disclosable under CPIA 1996 or the CPIA 1996 (s 23(1)) Code of Practice.

Where a sample falls within the above paragraph, and would otherwise be required to be destroyed under para 20G (p 798), it must not be used for the purposes of any proceedings for the offence in connection with which the sample was taken. A sample that once fell within the above paragraph but no longer does, and so becomes a sample to which para 20G applies, must be destroyed immediately if the time specified for its destruction under para 20G has already passed.

Review of detention under s 41

The detention of a person arrested under TA 2000, s 41 must be periodically reviewed by a review officer. The first review must be as soon as reasonably practicable after the arrest; thereafter reviews must be carried out at intervals of no more than 12 hours. A review officer may authorise continued detention only if he does so:

(a) to obtain relevant evidence whether by questioning the detainee or otherwise;
(b) to preserve relevant evidence;

(c) while awaiting the result of an examination or analysis of relevant evidence;

(d) for the examination or analysis of anything with a view to obtaining relevant evidence;

(e) pending a decision to apply to the Secretary of State for a deportation notice to be served on the detainee, the making of any such application, or the consideration of any such application by the Secretary of State; and

(f) pending a decision to charge the detainee with an offence.

The review officer may not authorise continued detention unless satisfied that the relevant matter is being dealt with diligently and expeditiously. The detainee may not be held for more than 48 hours unless a warrant of further detention is granted.

Under Sch 8, a Crown Prosecutor or a superintendent (or above) may apply within the 48-hour period just mentioned or the six-hour period after its end to a designated District Judge (Magistrates' Courts) for a warrant of further detention for a period of seven days from the time of the arrest under s 41, unless the person was being detained by an examining officer under Sch 7 (port and border controls) at the time of arrest (in which case time runs from the start of his examination under Sch 7). The judge may issue a warrant for a shorter period where the application is for a shorter period or he is satisfied that there are circumstances that would make it inappropriate for the specified period to be as long as seven days. This may be extended or further extended, on application to a designated District Judge (Magistrates' Courts), if the extension would not extend the period for more than 14 days after the person's arrest (or examination commencement) or a shorter period. Thus, the maximum period of detention of a person arrested under s 41 is 14 days. The grounds for a warrant of further detention or an extension are that there are reasonable grounds for believing that the further detention of the person concerned is necessary to obtain relevant evidence and the investigation is being conducted diligently and expeditiously. The Secretary of State has an emergency power to make an order temporarily extending the maximum period of detention of a person arrested under s 41 when Parliament is dissolved or when Parliament has met after a dissolution but before the first Queen's Speech. Such an order would extend the maximum period of detention to 28 days for a period of three months.

An application for a warrant of further detention or an extension may be made orally or in writing depending upon the circumstances of the case and fairness to the detainee. It may not be heard unless notice of it has been given to the detainee. Applications may make use of video conferencing facilities. A judge may require the physical presence of the detainee.

TA 2000, Sch 8 makes provision about the review of a person's detention under Sch 7. See Chapter 28 on the companion website.

MISCELLANEOUS OFFENCES UNDER TA 2000

Possession of articles for terrorist purposes

Under TA 2000, s 57(1), a person commits an offence if he possesses an article in circumstances giving rise to a reasonable suspicion that the article is in his possession for a purpose connected with the commission, preparation or instigation of acts of terrorism. According to the Court of Appeal, the reasonable suspicion must be that the person intends the article to be used for the specified purpose. Section 57(3) provides that, where it is proved that at the time of the commission of such an alleged offence, the person and the article were both present in any premises, or the article was in the premises of which he was the occupier, or which he habitually used other than as a member of the public, the court may assume that the person possessed the article, unless he adduces sufficient evidence to raise the issue that he did not know of the presence on the premises or that he had no control over it, whereupon the prosecution must disprove this.

A document or record in electronic or printed form is an article for the purposes of s 57.

The Court of Appeal has held that the offence can only be committed if there is a direct connection between the article and an intended act of terrorism.

It is a defence for D to prove that possession of an article was not for a purpose connected with the commission, preparation or instigation of an act of terrorism.

Unlawful collection, recording or possession of information

TA 2000, s 58 provides that a person commits an offence if he collects or makes a record of information of a kind likely to be useful to a person committing or preparing an act of terrorism, or possesses a document or record containing information of that kind. 'Record' includes a photographic or electronic record. It has been held by the Court of Appeal that 'information of a kind likely to be useful to a person committing or preparing an act of terrorism' is broad enough to potentially include a series of suggestions as to the avoidance of detection or surveillance. On the other hand, the House of Lords has held, if a document containing information is one in everyday use (eg a published timetable or map) it cannot be treated as falling within s 58; the aim of s 58 is to catch information which would typically be of use to terrorists, as opposed to ordinary members of the public. The information collected or possessed must, of its very nature, be designed to provide practical assistance to someone committing or preparing an act of terrorism.

The House of Lords has also held as follows in this paragraph. In order for D to be convicted of an offence of possession contrary to s 58, the prosecution must prove beyond reasonable doubt that:

(a) he had control of a record which contained information that was likely to provide practical assistance to a person committing or preparing an act of terrorism;
(b) he knew he had the record;
(c) he knew the kind of information which it contained.

If these elements are established, D falls to be convicted subject to the defence of reasonable excuse. While s 57 focuses on the circumstances of D's possession of the article, s 58 focuses on the nature of the information which D collected, recorded or possessed in a document or record. Section 58 does not require proof that D had a terrorist purpose for doing what he did. Unless it amounts to a reasonable excuse, D's purpose in doing what he did is irrelevant. There is an overlap between ss 57 and 58. The possession of a document can, in an appropriate case, fall within both sections.

It is a defence under s 58 for D to adduce sufficient evidence to raise the issue that he had a reasonable excuse for his action or possession, whereupon the prosecution must disprove this. The House of Lords has held that, if D adduces such evidence of something which could be a reasonable excuse, the defence succeeds unless the prosecution disproves the explanation advanced or proves that, even if D's explanation is true, it does not amount to a reasonable excuse. If it does disprove that thing, the defence fails and D is guilty under s 58. The prosecution does not have to prove that D did not have a reasonable excuse at all.

The provisions of s 58 are wide enough to embrace the failure of close relatives of terrorists to disclose information in their possession as soon as reasonably practicable. It is recommended that relatives of a terrorist, who are not themselves involved in terrorism, should not be investigated with a view to obtaining evidence of offences by them against this section, unless particular extreme circumstances make this desirable. An example of such circumstances would be where the withholding of information could lead to death, serious injury or the escape of a terrorist offender.

The courts have provided the following guidance about 'reasonable excuse' in s 58. For these purposes 'reasonable excuse' means an objectively reasonable excuse; possessing a document for purposes of carrying out a bank raid is a purpose not connected with terrorism, but it is not a reasonable excuse. The Court of Appeal has held that it cannot be a reasonable excuse to a charge of possessing documents, etc contrary to s 58 that the documents, etc originated as part of an effort to change an illegal and undemocratic regime.

Eliciting, publishing or communicating information about members of the armed forces, etc

A person commits an offence under TA 2000, s 58A who:

(a) elicits or attempts to elicit information about an individual who is or has been:
  (i) a member of Her Majesty's forces,
  (ii) a member of any of the intelligence services, or
  (iii) a constable,
  which is of a kind likely to be useful to a person committing or preparing an act of terrorism; or
(b) publishes or communicates any such information.

It is a defence for D to prove that he had a reasonable excuse for his action. If D adduces evidence sufficient to raise an issue with respect to the defence it is assumed that the defence is satisfied unless the prosecution prove beyond reasonable doubt that it is not.

ENCOURAGEMENT, ETC OF TERRORISM

Encouragement of terrorism

TA 2006, s 1(2) provides that a person (D) commits an offence if:

(a) D publishes a statement to which s 1 applies or causes another to publish such a statement; and
(b) at that time, D intends members of the public to be directly or indirectly encouraged or otherwise induced by the statement to commit, prepare or instigate acts of terrorism or Convention offences, or is reckless as to whether they will be.

Section 1 applies to a statement likely to be understood by some or all of the public to whom it is published as a direct or indirect encouragement or inducement to commit, prepare or instigate acts of terrorism or Convention offences. In TA 2006, an 'act of terrorism' includes anything constituting an action taken for the purposes of terrorism, within the meaning of TA 2000 (see p 773) (including a reference to action taken for the benefit of a proscribed organisation). A 'Convention offence' means an offence listed in TA 2006, Sch 1 (eg specified explosives offences, biological, chemical or nuclear weapons offences, hijacking, hostage taking, offences relating to terrorist funds or directing terrorist organisations, and offences directed at a nuclear facility or interference with the operation of such a facility) or an equivalent offence under the law of a country or territory outside the UK.

For the purposes of s 1, the statements that are likely to be understood by members of the public as indirectly encouraging the commission of acts of terrorism or Convention offences include every statement which glorifies the commission or preparation (whether in the past, future or generally) of such acts or offences (whether or not in particular), and is a statement from which those members of the public could reasonably be expected to infer that what is being glorified is conduct that should be emulated by them. 'Glorification' includes any form of praise or celebration.

Where it is not proved that D intended the statement directly or indirectly to bring about the commission, preparation or instigation of acts of terrorism or Convention offences, he has a defence if he proves that the statement neither expressed his view nor had his actual endorsement, and that it was clear that this was so. In the case of electronic material, the defence will not be available where there has been a failure to comply with a notice under s 3 (p 804).

Dissemination of terrorist publications

TA 2006, s 2(1) makes it an offence to sell or otherwise disseminate terrorist publications, including information on the internet, if (a) D intends his conduct to encourage or induce people to engage in the commission, preparation or instigation of acts of terrorism, (b) D intends it to assist in the commission or preparation of such acts, or (c) D is reckless as to whether his conduct will have either effect.

By s 2(2), the offence can be committed by distributing or circulating a terrorist publication; giving, selling or lending a terrorist publication; offering such for sale or loan; providing a service which enables a person to obtain, read, listen to or look at such material; transmitting it by electronic means, or possessing it with a view to it being dealt with in one of these ways. Where D within the UK possesses terrorist material with the relevant mens rea, it is irrelevant that the dissemination of the material is to take place abroad.

A publication is a terrorist publication if it contains matter (a) likely to be understood by some or all of the persons to whom it might become available as an encouragement or inducement to them to the commission, preparation or instigation of acts of terrorism, or (b) likely to be useful in the commission or preparation of such acts or offences and likely to be understood (by some or all of such persons) as contained in the publication, or made available, for the purpose of being so useful.

Where the publication is a terrorist publication by virtue of (a) and it is not proved that D acted with the intention of encouraging or inducing the commission, preparation or instigation of acts of terrorism, it is a defence for D to show that the material which encourages terrorism did not express his views, nor had his actual endorsement, and that it was clear, in all of the circumstances, that this was so. In the case of electronic material, the defence will not be available where there has been a failure to comply with a notice under s 3.

TA 2006, s 28 gives a justice of the peace power to issue a warrant authorising a constable to enter and search premises and seize any article on those premises if it is likely to be subject of conduct falling within s 2(2) and it would be treated as a terrorist publication, where he is satisfied that there are reasonable grounds for suspecting that such an article is on the premises. Reasonable force may be used in effecting entry.

Bulk material may be removed in such circumstances under CJPA 2001, s 50 (p 68) for later examination. Notice must be given by the constable responsible for the seizure to every person whom he believes to be the owner of any material. In the event of there being no such person, notice must be given to the person believed to be the occupier of the premises.

For a prospective power of removal and retention of a document to ascertain whether it may be seized, see Chapter 28 on the companion website.

Internet activity

TA 2006, s 3 applies for the purposes of ss 1 and 2 in relation to cases where a statement is published or caused to be published in the course of, or in connection with, the provision or use of a service provided electronically, or where conduct falling within s 2(2) was in the course of, or in connection with, the provision or use of such a service. Section 3 provides that the cases where a statement, or the article or record to which the conduct is related, is to be regarded as having the endorsement of a person at any time, include a case where:

(a) that person has been given a notice by a constable which
  (i) declares that in the constable's opinion the statement, article or record concerned is unlawfully terrorism-related,
  (ii) requires him to secure that the statement, etc (so far as so related) is not available to the public,
  (iii) warns him that a failure to comply with the notice within two working days will result in the statement, etc being regarded as having his endorsement, and
  (iv) explains how he may become liable by virtue of the notice if the statement, etc becomes available to the public after he has complied with the notice;
(b) that time falls more than two working days after the notice was given; and
(c) that person has failed without reasonable excuse to comply with the notice.

The procedures relating to the giving of such notices are set out in s 4.

PREPARATION OF TERRORIST ACTS AND TERRORIST TRAINING

Preparation of terrorist acts

TA 2006, s 5 bites at an earlier stage than the offences of conspiracy or attempt by prohibiting anyone intentionally preparing to commit, or assist others to commit, one or more acts of terrorism, wherever it is to take place. The offence is triable only on indictment.

Training for terrorism

TA 2006, s 6(1) prohibits knowingly giving training to a would-be terrorist in the making or handling of noxious substances or the use of terrorist methods or techniques (including design or adaptation of methods or techniques for the purposes of terrorism). For these purposes, a 'noxious substance' means a pathogen or toxin, or any other substance which is hazardous or noxious or which may be or become hazardous or noxious only in certain circumstances. Section 6(2) makes it an offence for a would-be terrorist to receive such training.

Unless he proves that his purpose was not assisting, preparing for or participating in terrorism, a person who gives or receives weapons training commits an offence under TA 2000, s 54(1) or (2).

Attendance at a place used for terrorist training

TA 2006, s 8 prohibits attending any place in the UK or elsewhere at which terrorist training is taking place. It must be proved that D knew or believed that training for those purposes was taking place, or that D could not reasonably have failed to understand that this was so.

OFFENCES INVOLVING RADIOACTIVE DEVICES AND MATERIALS AND NUCLEAR FACILITIES AND SITES

TA 2006, s 9(1) creates offences related to the making or possession of radioactive devices or the possession of radioactive material, for use in the commission or preparation of an act of terrorism or for purposes of terrorism.

Section 10(1) prohibits the use of such items in the course of or in connection with the commission of an act of terrorism, or for the purposes of terrorism. Section 10(2) creates an offence of using or damaging a nuclear facility in the course of or in connection with acts of terrorism, in such a manner that radioactive material is released, or that the risk that such material will be released is created or increased.

Section 11(1) provides that it is an offence, in the course of or in connection with the commission of an act of terrorism or for the purposes of terrorism, to demand the supply of a radioactive device or radioactive material, or that a nuclear facility, or access to a nuclear facility, be made available, if such a demand is supported by a threat of action if the demand is not met. The threat must be a credible one.

Section 11(2) makes it an offence to make a credible threat to use a radioactive device or material, or to use or damage a radioactive facility, in the course of or in connection with the commission of an act of terrorism or for the purposes of terrorism.

The offences under ss 9 to 11 are triable only on indictment.

OFFENCES INVOLVING THE USE OF NOXIOUS SUBSTANCES OR THINGS TO CAUSE HARM AND INTIMIDATE

The Anti-terrorism, Crime and Security Act 2001, s 113(1) creates the offence committed by any person who takes any action which:

(a) involves the use of a noxious substance or other noxious thing;
(b) has or is likely to have an effect which:
  (i) causes serious violence against a person, or serious damage to property, anywhere in the world,
  (ii) endangers human life or creates a serious risk to the health or safety of the public or a section of the public, or
  (iii) induces in members of the public the fear that the action is likely to have the effect in (ii); and
(c) is designed to influence the government or an international governmental organisation or to intimidate the public or a section of the public.

By s 113(3), an offence is committed by someone who:

(a) threatens that he or another will take any action constituting an offence under s 113(1); and
(b) intends thereby to induce anyone anywhere in the world to fear that the threat is likely to be carried out.

Under s 114(1), a person commits an offence if he:

(a) places any substance or other thing in any place; or
(b) sends any substance or other thing from one place to another,

with the intention of inducing in a person anywhere in the world a belief that it is likely to be (or contain) a noxious substance or other noxious thing and thereby endanger human life or create a serious risk to human health.

A person is guilty of an offence under s 114(2) if he communicates any information which he knows or believes to be false with the intention of inducing in a person anywhere in the world a belief that a noxious substance or other noxious thing is likely to be present in any place and thereby endanger human life or create a serious risk to human health.

For these purposes, 'substance' includes any biological agent and any other natural or artificial substance (whatever its form, origin or method of production). In the case of ss 113(3) or 114 the person concerned need not have any particular person in mind as the person in whom he intends to induce the belief in question.

GENERAL

Consent of DPP

The consent of the DPP is required for any proceedings in relation to any of the above offences under the Terrorism Acts 2000 and 2006. Where an offence appears to have been committed outside the UK or for a purpose wholly or partly connected with the affairs of a country other than the UK, the DPP's consent may only be given with the consent of the Attorney General. Proceedings for an offence committed under the Anti-terrorism, Crime and Security Act 2001, s 113 outside the UK require the Attorney General's consent.

Post-charge questioning

The Counter-Terrorism Act 2008 (C-TA 2008), s 22 permits a judge of the Crown Court to authorise questioning of a person concerning an offence with which he has been charged or informed that he may be prosecuted, where that offence is a 'terrorism offence' or where the judge considers the offence to have a terrorist connection. A judge must not authorise such questioning unless he is satisfied that:

(a) further questioning is necessary in the interests of justice;
(b) the investigation for the purposes of which the further questioning is being proposed is being conducted diligently and expeditiously; and

(c) the questioning would not interfere unduly with the preparation of the person's defence to the charge or any other criminal charge that he may be facing.

'Terrorism offence' includes specified offences, mainly against TA 2000 (eg ss 11 to 13, 15 to 19, 21A, 21D, 38B, 39, 54, and 56 to 58A) and TA 2006 (ss 1, 2, 5, 6, and 8 to 11) and the Anti-terrorism, Crime and Security Act 2001, s 113. An offence has a 'terrorist connection' if the offence is, or takes place in the course of, an act of terrorism, or is committed for the purpose of terrorism.

PACE Code H applies to the treatment and questioning of the detainee.

Access to a solicitor may not be delayed, nor may the person be required to consult a solicitor within the sight and hearing of a police officer.

Unless the restriction on drawing adverse inferences from silence applies (see Chapter 4), before post-charge questioning begins the caution must be given in the terms set out in Chapter 4. The only restriction on drawing adverse inferences from silence applies where a person has asked for legal advice and is questioned before receiving such advice on grounds of urgency.

An interview by virtue of C-TA 2008, s 22 must be video recorded with sound in accordance with the Code of Practice for the Video Recording with Sound of Interviews with Persons Detained and Post-Charge Questioning of Persons Authorised under C-TA 2008, s 22.

NOTIFICATION REQUIREMENTS

C-TA 2008, Part 4 and associated Schedules:

(a) set out a system of notification requirements (initial notification, notification of change, periodic re-notification, and notification of return after absence from UK) for persons convicted of a terrorism offence or of a non-terrorism offence with a terrorist connection;

(b) make provision to apply notification requirements to persons convicted of equivalent offences outside the UK; and

(c) make provision for the making of foreign travel restriction orders against persons subject to the above notification requirements.

See Chapter 28 on the companion website for details.

IMPOSITION OF TERRORISM PREVENTION AND INVESTIGATION MEASURES

The Terrorism Prevention and Investigation Measures Act 2011 (TPIMA 2011) provides for the making of terrorism prevention and investigation measures against individuals suspected of being involved in terrorism-related activity.

Such measures may be imposed by the Secretary of State, normally with the prior permission of the High Court. Breach of such a measure without reasonable excuse is an indictable (either way) offence. The details about the regime under TPIMA 2011 are in Chapter 28 on the companion website.

TEMPORARY EXCLUSION FROM THE UNITED KINGDOM

The Counter-Terrorism and Security Act 2015, Part 1, Ch 2 (ss 2–15) and Schs 2–4 provide for the imposition of temporary exclusion orders.

A 'temporary exclusion order' is an order which requires an individual who has the right of abode in the UK and is suspected of terrorism-related activity outside the UK not to return to the UK unless the return is in accordance with a permit to return issued by the Secretary of State before the individual began the return, or the return is the result of the individual's deportation to the UK. 'Return to the UK' includes, in the case of an individual who has never been in the UK, a reference to coming to the UK for the first time.

Such an order may be imposed by the Secretary of State, normally with the prior permission of the High Court. Breach of such an order without reasonable excuse is an indictable (either way) offence. The details about the regime under the Counter-Terrorism and Security Act 2015 are in Chapter 28 on the companion website.

CHAPTER 29

Sexual Offences

INTRODUCTION

The law in relation to sexual offences is principally governed by the Sexual Offences Act 2003 (SOA 2003).

Sexual

For the purposes of the various offences in SOA 2003, s 78 provides that, except in relation to the offences of sexual activity in a public lavatory and (from a day to be appointed) sexual communication with a child, penetration, touching or any other activity is sexual if a reasonable person would consider that:

(a) whatever its circumstances or any person's purpose in relation to it, it is because of its nature sexual; or

(b) because of its nature it *may* be sexual and because of its circumstances or the purpose of any person in relation to it (or both) it *is* sexual.

The Court of Appeal has held that (b) contains two requirements. The first is whether a reasonable person would consider that because of its nature the actual act could be sexual. In relation to this requirement, the circumstances before or after the act took place, or any evidence as to the purpose of any person in relation to it are irrelevant. If the answer to the question posed by this requirement is 'No', the act is not sexual. If the answer to the question is 'Yes', the second requirement comes into play, and requires the jury or magistrates to ask themselves whether because of the circumstances of the activity and/or the purpose of *any* person in relation to it (not just the person who does the act, but—for example—someone who encourages the act to be done), the activity *is* sexual.

Consent

For the purposes of the offences under SOA 2003 involving the absence of consent, 'consent' is defined by SOA 2003, s 74 as follows: a person consents if he agrees by choice, and has the freedom and capacity to make that choice.

An agreement can be express or implied, and may be evidenced by words or conduct, past or present.

Consent to sex can take many forms, ranging from willing enthusiasm to reluctant acquiescence. An example of reluctant consent would be where someone who has the capacity and freedom to make a choice nevertheless submits to a demand that he or she feels unable to resist.

If the complainant has made it clear that he or she will only agree to the relevant activity if a factual precondition (eg the use of a condom) relating to it is satisfied by the defendant before or during the activity, there will be no agreement by choice, and therefore no consent under s 74 if, without the complainant's agreement, the defendant deliberately does not fulfil the condition.

Capacity to choose

The SOA 2003, s 74 does not lay down a test of capacity. However, reference to the offences under ss 30 and 31 against persons with a mental disorder impeding choice shows that a person lacks capacity if that person lacks the capacity to choose whether to agree (whether because that person lacks sufficient understanding of the nature or reasonably foreseeable consequences if what is being done, or for any other reason). The words 'for any other reason' are clearly capable of encompassing a wide range of circumstances in which a person's mental disorder may rob that person of the ability to make an autonomous choice, even though he or she may have sufficient understanding of the information relevant to making it. It has been held in the High Court that capacity is not only 'issue-specific' in relation to different types of transaction (so that someone may have capacity for one purpose but not for another), but it is also issue-specific in relation to different transactions of the same type (so that a vulnerable adult (B) may have the capacity to consent to one type of sexual activity whilst lacking the capacity to consent to some other (and, to B, unfamiliar) type of sexual activity). In addition, the House of Lords has held, capacity to choose can be 'person-specific' or 'situation-specific' as well as 'issue-specific'. Thus, for example, B can have capacity vis-à-vis C but not vis-à-vis A.

Speaking in the context of rape, the Court of Appeal has held that if through drink (or for any other reason) the complainant (B) has temporarily lost capacity to choose whether to have intercourse on the relevant occasion, B is not consenting and, subject to questions about whether the defendant had mens rea, if intercourse takes place, this will be rape. However, it said, where B has voluntarily consumed even substantial quantities of alcohol, but nevertheless remains capable of choosing whether or not to have intercourse, and in drink agrees to do so, this will not be rape.

Freedom to choose

A person might not have freedom to make a choice whether or not to agree if violence is being used or threatened against him or another at the material time or immediately beforehand. A person may also lack freedom of choice for other reasons, as where someone agrees because he is unlawfully detained or where there was the use, or threat, of violence to destroy property which was of special value, financially or emotionally, or threat of dismissal by an employer to an employee, or threat to remove children. It would all depend on the nature of the threat and the other circumstances, the perception of the complainant, and whether in the light of these factors the complainant was not in reality free to agree or disagree.

Another example where there may not be freedom of choice is provided by a Court of Appeal case where A's conviction for rape of B, a young adult, who had from childhood been sexually abused, dominated and controlled by A, was upheld. The Court held that from such conduct an apparent consent might be found not to be a real consent. Likewise, the fact that B has been groomed may mean that an apparent consent is not a real consent. The Court of Appeal has stated that one of the consequences of grooming is that it has a tendency to limit or subvert the alleged victim's capacity to make free decisions.

Deception and mistake

Some mistakes may invalidate an apparent agreement, especially if induced by deception.

Irrebuttable presumptions as to absence of consent

Two kinds of deception are specifically addressed in SOA 2003, s 76, by means of irrebuttable presumptions, but only in the context of alleged offences under SOA 2003, ss 1 to 4 (rape, sexual assault, etc).

Section 76 provides that if in proceedings for an offence under ss 1 to 4 it is proved that the defendant did the '*relevant act*' and that either of the *specified circumstances* existed, it is to be conclusively (ie irrebuttably) presumed:

(a) that the complainant (B) did not consent to the relevant act; and
(b) that the defendant did not believe that the complainant consented to the relevant act.

The *specified circumstances* are: that the defendant intentionally deceived the complainant as to the nature or purpose of the relevant act; and that the defendant intentionally induced the complainant to consent to the relevant act by impersonating a person known personally to B.

By the SOA 2003, s 77, in relation to an offence to which ss 75 (below) and 76 apply, references to the *relevant act* and to the complainant are to be read as follows:

Offence	*Relevant act*
Under s 1 (rape)	The defendant intentionally penetrating, with his penis, the vagina, anus or mouth of the complainant
Under s 2 (assault by penetration)	The defendant intentionally penetrating, with a part of his body or anything else, the vagina or anus of the complainant where the penetration is sexual
Under s 3 (sexual assault)	The defendant intentionally touching the complainant, where the touching is sexual
Under s 4 (causing person to engage in sexual activity without consent)	The defendant intentionally causing the complainant to engage in an activity, where the activity is sexual

Deception or mistake not covered by s 76

Whether or not there is an effective consent in cases of deception falling outside SOA 2003, s 76, or in cases of self-induced mistake, must be determined by the jury by applying the terms of s 74. The statement in s 74 that a person consents if he agrees by choice and has the freedom to make that choice requires an informed choice. A deception about the use of a condom or about the intent to pay for sex, for example, are factors which can be considered by a jury when assessing whether the complainant (B) freely agreed to the act.

Where one party to sexual activity has a sexually transmissible disease which is not disclosed to the other party any consent that may have been given to that activity by the other party is not thereby invalidated. The sexual act remains a consensual act. However, the party suffering from the sexually transmissible disease will not have any defence to any charge of an offence against the person which may result from harm created by that sexual activity, merely by virtue of that consent, because such consent does not include consent to infection by the disease.

Rebuttable presumptions as to absence of consent

Section 75 provides that if in proceedings for an offence to which s 75 applies (those under ss 1–4) it is proved:

(a) that A did the *relevant act* (see table on p 811);
(b) that any of the *specified circumstances* below existed; and
(c) that A *knew* that those circumstances existed,

B is to be taken (ie presumed) not to have consented to the relevant act unless sufficient evidence is adduced to raise an issue as to whether B consented, and A is to be taken not to have reasonably believed that B consented *unless* sufficient evidence is adduced to raise an issue as to whether he *reasonably* believed it. Evidence is not sufficient if it is fanciful or speculative.

The *specified circumstances* are that:

(a) any person was, at the time of the relevant act or immediately before it began, using violence against B or causing B to fear that immediate violence would be used against him;
(b) any person was, at the time of the relevant act or immediately before it began, causing B to fear that violence was being used, or that immediate violence would be used, against another person;
(c) B was, and A was not, unlawfully detained at the time of the relevant act;
(d) B was asleep or otherwise unconscious at the time of the relevant act;
(e) because of B's physical disability, B would not have been able at the time of the relevant act to communicate to A whether B consented;
(f) any person had administered to or caused to be taken by B, without B's consent, a substance which, having regard to when it was administered or taken, was capable of causing or enabling B to be stupefied or overpowered at the time of the relevant act.

If sufficient evidence is adduced to raise an issue as to one (or both) of the two matters, the matter must be determined in the normal way.

Penetration, touching and parts of the body

By SOA 2003, s 79, 'penetration' is a continuing act from entry to withdrawal. It has long been established by the courts that the slightest degree of penetration is enough. SOA 2003, s 79 also provides that references to a part of the body include references to a part surgically constructed (in particular through gender re-assignment surgery); that 'vagina' includes vulva (external female genital organs); and that 'touching' includes touching with any part of the body, or with anything else, or through anything, and in particular includes touching through penetration. The Court of Appeal has held that 'touching' includes touching a person's clothing without applying any force to his body.

NON-CONSENSUAL SEXUAL OFFENCES

Rape

By SOA 2003, s 1(1), a person (A) commits an offence triable only on indictment if:

(a) he intentionally penetrates the vagina, anus or mouth of another person (B) with his penis;

(b) B does not consent to the penetration; and

(c) A does not reasonably believe that B consents.

The absence of consent does not have to be demonstrated by offering resistance or by communicating it to the defendant. As noted on p 809, if a woman has made it clear that she would only consent to sexual intercourse if the man uses a condom, there would be no consent to the sexual intercourse if, without her consent, he deliberately does not use a condom, or removes or tears the condom without her consent.

Section 1(2) provides that whether a belief in consent is reasonable is to be determined having regard to all the circumstances, including any steps A has taken to ascertain whether B consents. The words 'all the circumstances' must refer to those which might be relevant to the issue, including any characteristic of the defendant, permanent or transient, which might affect his ability to perceive or understand whether or not the victim is consenting. However, the Court of Appeal has held that account may not be taken of voluntary intoxication, or of mental disorder if it leads to an irrational belief in consent.

Proof of lack of consent and of the absence of reasonable belief is assisted by the rebuttable and irrebuttable presumptions in ss 75 and 76 (pp 811 and 812).

Rape of a child under 13

By SOA 2003, s 5(1), a person (A) commits an offence triable only on indictment if:

(a) he intentionally penetrates the vagina, anus or mouth of another person (B) with his penis; and

(b) B is under 13.

Whether or not the other person consents to the penetration is irrelevant; a child under 13 is legally incapable of giving a legally significant consent.

The House of Lords has confirmed that the need for a mental element is negatived by necessary implication, as evidenced by the express references to reasonable belief of age in other sections of the Act. Thus, not even a reasonable belief that B was 13 or over will excuse A.

Exceptions

The offence is one of the offences in respect of which there are exceptions from criminal liability under SOA 2003, s 73, on the basis of aiding, abetting or counselling the commission of the offence if a person acts for the purpose of:

(a) protecting the child from sexually transmitted infection;

(b) protecting the physical safety of the child;

(c) preventing the child from becoming pregnant; or

(d) promoting the child's emotional well-being by the giving of advice,

and not for the purpose of obtaining sexual gratification or for the purpose of causing or encouraging the activity constituting the offence or the child's participation in it.

Assault by penetration

By SOA 2003, s 2(1), a person (A) commits an offence triable only on indictment if:

(a) he intentionally penetrates the vagina or anus of another person (B) with a part of his body (eg a finger or tongue) or anything else;

(b) the penetration is sexual;

(c) B does not consent to the penetration; and

(d) A does not reasonably believe that B consents.

Section 2(2) provides that whether a belief is reasonable must be determined having regard to all the circumstances, including whether A has taken reasonable steps to ascertain whether B consents.

Proof of lack of consent and of the absence of reasonable belief is assisted by the rebuttable and irrebuttable presumptions in ss 75 and 76.

Assault of a child under 13 by penetration

By SOA 2003, s 6(1), a person commits an offence triable only on indictment if:

(a) he intentionally penetrates the vagina or anus of another person with a part of his body or anything else;

(b) the penetration is sexual; and

(c) the other person is under 13.

The absence of consent by the other person is not an element of this offence. The above exceptions under s 73 from liability for aiding, abetting or counselling apply to this offence.

Sexual assault

By SOA 2003, s 3(1), a person (A) commits an indictable (either way) offence if:

(a) he intentionally touches another person (B);

(b) the touching is sexual;

(c) B does not consent to the touching; and

(d) A does not reasonably believe that B consents.

Section 3(2) provides that whether a belief is reasonable must be determined with regard to all the circumstances, including any steps A has taken to ascertain whether B consents.

The Court of Appeal has held that the 'intentional touching' element of this offence simply requires a deliberate touching. It has also held that this intent is a basic intent, with the result that evidence of voluntary intoxication cannot be relied upon to negate it. These points are equally applicable to other offences under SOA 2003 involving intentional penetration or touching.

Proof of lack of consent and of the absence of reasonable belief is assisted by the rebuttable and irrebuttable presumptions in ss 75 and 76.

Sexual assault of a child under 13

By SOA 2003, s 7(1), a person commits an indictable (either way) offence if:

(a) he intentionally touches another person;

(b) the touching is sexual; and

(c) the other person is under 13.

The absence of the other person's consent is not an element of the offence. The exceptions under s 73 (p 813) from liability for aiding, abetting or counselling apply to this offence.

Causing a person to engage in sexual activity without consent

By SOA 2003, s 4(1) and (5), a person (A) commits an indictable (either way) offence if:

(a) he intentionally causes another person (B) to engage in an activity;
(b) the activity is sexual;
(c) B does not consent to engaging in the activity; and
(d) A does not reasonably believe that B consents.

A more serious offence triable only on indictment is committed under s 4(1) and (4) if the activity caused involves one of four circumstances:

(a) penetration of B's anus or vagina;
(b) penetration of B's mouth with a person's penis;
(c) penetration of a person's anus or vagina with a part of B's body or by B with anything else; or
(d) penetration of a person's mouth with B's penis.

Section 4(2) provides that whether a belief is reasonable must be determined with regard to all the circumstances, including any steps A has taken to ascertain whether B consents.

Proof of lack of consent and of the absence of reasonable belief is assisted by the rebuttable and irrebuttable presumptions in ss 75 and 76.

Causing or inciting a child under 13 to engage in sexual activity

By SOA 2003, s 8(1) and (3), a person commits an indictable (either way) offence if:

(a) he intentionally causes or incites another person (B) to engage in an activity;
(b) the activity is sexual; and
(c) B is under 13.

A more serious offence triable only on indictment is committed under s 8(1) and (2) if the activity caused or incited involved one of the four circumstances set out above in relation to s 4.

The absence of B's consent is not an element of an offence under s 8.

An offence of intentionally inciting a child under 13 to engage in sexual activity can be committed even though it is not possible to identify any specific or identifiable child to whom the incitement was addressed. It matters not whether the incitement was directed at a particular child or a very large group of children. These points are equally applicable to the other offences of incitement to sexual activity in SOA 2003.

The Court of Appeal has held that 'intentional' causing or inciting for the purposes of s 8 means deliberate causing or inciting; recklessness will not do. This is equally applicable to the other offences of intentionally causing or inciting under SOA 2003.

CHILD SEX OFFENCES

In these offences, it is irrelevant that the child may have consented.

Sexual activity with a child

By SOA 2003, s 9(1) and (3), a person aged 18 or over (A) commits an indictable (either way) offence if:

(a) he intentionally touches another person (B);
(b) the touching is sexual; and
(c) either:
    (i) B is under 16 and A does not reasonably believe that B is 16 or over; or
    (ii) B is under 13.

A more serious offence triable only on indictment is committed under s 9(1) and (2) if the touching involves one of the following four circumstances:

(a) penetration of B's anus or vagina with a part of A's body or anything else;
(b) penetration of B's mouth with A's penis;
(c) penetration of A's anus or vagina with a part of B's body; or
(d) penetration of A's mouth with B's penis.

The exceptions under s 73 (p 813) from liability for aiding, abetting or counselling apply to an offence under s 9.

Causing or inciting a child to engage in sexual activity

By SOA 2003, s 10(1) and (3), a person aged 18 or over (A) commits an indictable (either way) offence if:

(a) he intentionally causes or incites another person (B) to engage in an activity;
(b) the activity is sexual; and
(c) either:
    (i) B is under 16 and A does not reasonably believe that B is 16 or over; or
    (ii) B is under 13.

A more serious offence triable only on indictment is committed under s 10(1) and (2) if the activity caused or incited involves:

(a) penetration of B's anus or vagina;
(b) penetration of B's mouth with a person's penis;
(c) penetration of a person's anus or vagina with a part of B's body or by B with anything else; or
(d) penetration of a person's mouth with B's penis.

Engaging in sexual activity in the presence of a child

By SOA 2003, s 11(1), a person aged 18 or over (A) commits an indictable (either way) offence if:

(a) he intentionally engages in an activity;
(b) the activity is sexual;
(c) for the purpose of obtaining sexual gratification, he engages in it:
    (i) when another person (B) is present or is in a place from which A can be observed; and

(ii) knowing or believing that B is aware, or intending that B should be aware, that he is engaging in it; and

(d) either:

(i) B is under 16 and A does not reasonably believe that B is 16 or over; or

(ii) B is under 13.

'Observed' in (c) and elsewhere in SOA 2003 means observation whether direct or by looking at an image produced by any means.

Causing a child to watch a sexual act

By SOA 2003, s 12(1), a person aged 18 or over (A) commits an indictable (either way) offence if:

(a) for the purpose of obtaining sexual gratification, he intentionally causes another person (B) to watch a third person engaging in an activity, or to look at an image of any person engaging in an activity;

(b) the activity is sexual; and

(c) either:

(i) B is under 16 and A does not reasonably believe that B is 16 or over, or

(ii) B is under 13.

'Image' in (a), and elsewhere in the Act, includes a moving or still image, however produced, and, where—as here—the context permits, a three-dimensional image. It does not include written material. References to an image of a person include references to an image of an imaginary person.

The purpose of obtaining sexual gratification need not relate to immediate gratification (eg from seeing the victim watch the images). The Court of Appeal has held that the offence under s 12 can be committed where A's purpose involves immediate, or deferred, or immediate and deferred, gratification. Thus, the offence can be committed, for example, where A causes a child to watch a sexual act to put the child in the mood for future sexual abuse, as well as where he does so because he derives enjoyment at the time from seeing the child watch the sexual act. This decision is equally applicable to other offences under SOA 2003 in which the phrase 'for the purpose of obtaining sexual gratification' appears.

Child sex offences committed by children or young persons

By SOA 2003, s 13(1), a person under 18 commits an indictable (either way) offence if he does anything which would be an offence under SOA 2003, ss 9 to 12 if he were aged 18. It is, however, a less serious offence than those offences. The exceptions under s 73 (p 813) from liability for aiding, abetting or counselling apply to this offence if what is done would be an offence under s 9 if the offender were aged 18 or over.

Arranging or facilitating the commission of a child sex offence

By SOA 2003, s 14(1), a person commits an indictable (either way) offence if:

(a) he intentionally arranges or facilitates something that he intends to do, intends another person to do or believes that another person will do, in any part of the world; and

(b) doing it will involve the commission of an offence under ss 9 to 13.

Section 14(2) and (3) provides exceptions for people who seek to protect a child from pregnancy or sexually transmitted disease, to protect a child's physical safety or to give it advice, where they do not intend an offence under ss 9 to 13 to be committed but believe that it will. They provide that a person does not commit an offence under s 14 if:

(a) he arranges or facilitates something that he believes another person will do, but that he does not intend to do or intend another person to do; and

(b) any offence within ss 9 to 13 which the doing of that thing would involve would be an offence against a child for whose protection he acts.

In this context, a person acts for the protection of a child if he acts for the purpose of:

(a) protecting the child from sexually transmitted infection;
(b) protecting the child's physical safety;
(c) preventing the child from becoming pregnant; or
(d) promoting the child's emotional well-being by the giving of advice,

and not for the purpose of obtaining sexual gratification or for the purpose of causing or encouraging the activity constituting an offence within ss 9 to 13 or the child's participation in it.

The Court of Appeal has stated that s 14 covers taking preparatory steps (with the necessary intent) to commit an offence under ss 9 to 13. It has also stated that an arrangement may be made without the agreement or acquiescence of anyone else.

Meeting a child following sexual grooming, etc with a view to engaging in sexual activity with it

SOA 2003, s 15(1) deals with sexual grooming by providing that a person aged 18 or over (A) commits an indictable (either way) offence if:

(a) having met or communicated with another person (B) anywhere in the world on one or more occasions:
  (i) A subsequently intentionally meets B, or
  (ii) A subsequently travels with the intention of meeting B in any part of the world or arranges to meet B in any part of the world, or
  (iii) B travels with the intention of meeting A in any part of the world;

(b) A intends to do anything to or in respect of B, during or after the meeting mentioned in (a)(i)–(iii) above, and in any part of the world, which if done will involve the commission by A of a relevant offence;

(c) B is under 16; and

(d) A does not reasonably believe that B is 16 or over.

Sexual communication with a child

As from a day to be appointed, a person aged 18 or over (A) will commit an indictable (either way) offence under the SOA 2003, s 15A(1) if:

(a) for the purpose of obtaining sexual gratification, A intentionally communicates with another person (B);

(b) the communication is sexual or is intended to encourage B to make (whether to A or another) a communication that is sexual; and

(c) B is under 16 and A does not reasonably believe that B is 16 or over.

For these purposes, a communication is sexual if:

(i)   any part of it relates to sexual activity, or
(ii) a reasonable person would, in all the circumstances but regardless of any person's purpose, consider any part of the communication to be sexual, and

in (i) 'sexual activity' means an activity that a reasonable person would, in all the circumstances but regardless of any person's purpose, consider to be sexual.

The offence is intended to criminalise a defendant at the very start of the grooming process.

ABUSE OF POSITION OF TRUST

All the offences under this heading are indictable (either way) offences.

Abuse of position of trust: sexual activity with a child

Provided that he has any necessary mens rea, a person aged 18 or over (A) commits an offence under SOA 2003, s 16(1) if:

(a) he intentionally touches another person (B);
(b) the touching is sexual;
(c) A is in a position of trust in relation to B; and
(d) B is under 18.

B's consent is, of course, irrelevant in offences involving abuse of a position of trust. The exceptions under s 73 (p 813) from liability for aiding, abetting or counselling apply to this offence if B is under 16.

Abuse of position of trust: causing or inciting a child to engage in sexual activity

Provided that he has any necessary mens rea, a person aged 18 or over (A) commits an offence under s 17(1) if:

(a) he intentionally causes or incites another person (B) to engage in an activity;
(b) the activity is sexual;
(c) A is in a position of trust in relation to B; and
(d) B is under 18.

Abuse of position of trust: sexual activity in the presence of a child

Provided that he has any necessary mens rea, a person aged 18 or over (A) commits an offence under SOA 2003, s 18(1) if:

(a) he intentionally engages in an activity;
(b) the activity is sexual;
(c) for the purpose of obtaining sexual gratification, he engages in it:
  (i)   when another person (B) is present or is in a place from which A can be observed, and
  (ii) knowing or believing that B is aware, or intending that B should be aware, that he is engaging in it;

(d) A is in a position of trust in relation to B; and

(e) B is under 18.

Abuse of position of trust: causing a child to watch a sexual act

Provided that he has any necessary mens rea, a person aged 18 or over (A) commits an offence under SOA 2003, s 19(1) if:

(a) for the purpose of obtaining sexual gratification, he intentionally causes another person (B) to watch a third person engaging in an activity, or to look at an image of any person engaging in an activity;

(b) the activity is sexual;

(c) A is in a position of trust in relation to B; and

(d) B is under 18.

Position of trust

For the purposes of the above offences, a person (A) is, by SOA 2003, s 21, in a position of trust in relation to another person (B) if:

(a) any of paras (1)–(11) below apply; or

(b) any condition specified in an order made by the Secretary of State is met. No order has yet been made.

(1) If A looks after persons under 18 who are detained in an institution by virtue of a court order or under an enactment, and B is so detained in that institution.

(2) If A looks after persons under 18 who are resident in a home or other place for children in residential care, and B is in residential care there.

(3) If A looks after persons under 18 who are accommodated and cared for in a hospital, an independent clinic (in Wales), a care home, residential care home or private hospital, a community home, voluntary home or children's home, or the like, and B is accommodated and cared for in that institution.

(4) If A looks after persons under 18 who are receiving education at an educational institution and B is receiving, and A is not receiving, education at that institution.

(5) If A is engaged in the provision of a careers service or similar service and, in that capacity, looks after B on an individual basis.

(6) If A regularly has unsupervised contact with B (whether face to face or by any other means) in the provision of accommodation for children in need thereof, or in police protection or detention, or on remand.

(7) If A, as a person who is to report to the court on matters relating to the welfare of B, regularly has unsupervised contact with B (whether face to face or by any other means).

(8) If A is a personal adviser appointed for B under the Children Act 1989, or under the Social Services and Well-being (Wales) Act 2014 in respect of category 1 or category 2 young persons, and, in that capacity, looks after B on an individual basis.

(9) If:

  (a) B is subject to a care order, a supervision order or an education supervision order, and

  (b) in the exercise of functions conferred by virtue of the order on an authorised person or the authority designated by the order, A looks after B on an individual basis.

(10) If A is an officer of the Children and Family Court Advisory Support Service (CAFCASS) appointed for B, or is appointed children's guardian or guardian ad litem of B under the relevant rules, and, in that capacity, regularly has unsupervised contact with B (whether face to face or by any other means).

(11) If:
- (a) B is subject to requirements imposed by or under an enactment on his release from detention for a criminal offence, or is subject to requirements imposed by a court order made in criminal proceedings, and
- (b) A looks after B on an individual basis in pursuance of the requirements.

For the purposes of paras (1), (2), (3) and (4), a person looks after persons under 18 at an institution or the like if he is regularly involved in caring for, training, supervising or being in sole charge of such persons there, not necessarily the child abused.

Paragraphs (5), (8), (9) and (11) refer to a person looking after another on an individual basis. A person (A) looks after another (B) on such a basis if:

- (a) A is regularly involved in caring for, training or supervising B; and
- (b) in the course of his involvement, A regularly has unsupervised contact with B (whether face to face or by any other means).

Mens rea

In addition to requiring A intentionally to do the thing specified by each individual section, ss 16 to 19 make further provision as to the mens rea required in respect of the child's age and the existence of a position of trust.

In terms of the mens rea as to the age of the child (B), A must not reasonably believe that B is 18 or over. However, this provision does not apply if B is under 13 at the material time; in such a case the offences are undoubtedly ones of strict liability as to age. Although the prosecution ultimately has the persuasive burden of proof of the absence of reasonable belief that B is 18 or over where B is aged 13 to 17, the prosecution is assisted by the provision that, where in proceedings for an offence under ss 16 to 19 it is proved that B was under 18, A is to be taken not to have reasonably believed that B was 18 or over unless sufficient evidence is adduced to raise an issue as to whether A reasonably believed it.

Where A is in a position of trust in relation to B by virtue of circumstances within paras (1), (2), (3) or (4) above, and, in each case, A is not also in a position of trust by virtue of other circumstances, it must be proved that A knew or could reasonably be expected to know of the circumstances by virtue of which he is in a position of trust in relation to B. Proof of this is aided by the provision that, where it is proved that A was in a position of trust in relation to B by virtue of the four circumstances just referred to, and it is not proved that he was in such a position of trust by virtue of other circumstances, it is to be presumed that A knew or could reasonably have been expected to know of the circumstances by virtue of which he was in such a position of trust unless sufficient evidence is adduced to raise an issue as to whether A knew or could reasonably have been expected to know of those circumstances.

Where a position of trust arises wholly or partly by virtue of the other categories of circumstance referred to above, the Act does not require proof of any mens rea as to the position of trust.

Exceptions: marriage, civil partnership and existing sexual relationships

Conduct by a person (A) which would otherwise be one of the offences under SOA 2003, ss 16 to 19 against another person (B) is not such an offence if:

- (a) B was 16 or over, and the defendant proves that A and B were lawfully married (or civil partners) at the time of the conduct; or

(b) the defendant proves that, immediately before the position of trust arose, a sexual relationship existed between A and B, but this exception does not apply if at that time sexual intercourse between A and B would have been unlawful, for example because B was under 16.

FAMILIAL SEXUAL OFFENCES

Offences involving a child family member

Sexual activity with a child family member

A person (A) commits an indictable (either way) offence under SOA 2003, s 25(1) if:

(a) he intentionally touches another person (B);
(b) the touching is sexual;
(c) the relation of A to B is within the specified relationships;
(d) A knows or could reasonably be expected to know that his relation to B is of a description falling within those relationships; and
(e) either:
    (i) B is under 18 and A does not reasonably believe that B is 18 or over; or
    (ii) B is under 13.

SOA 2003 has the effect of distinguishing between two offences. The more serious is committed where A is 18 or over at the time of the offence. If the touching involves:

(f) penetration of B's anus or vagina with a part of A's body or anything else;
(g) penetration of B's mouth with A's penis;
(h) penetration of A's anus or vagina with part of B's body (but not with anything else); or
(i) penetration of A's mouth by B's penis,

the offence is triable only on indictment (s 25(1) and (4)(a)); otherwise it is an indictable (either way) offence (s 25(1) and (4)(b)).

The less serious offence is where A was not 18 or over at the material time, whatever type of activity was involved (s 25(1) and (5)). It is an indictable (either way) offence.

Where it is proved that the relation of A to B was of a description falling within the specified relationships, it is to be taken that A knew or could reasonably have been expected to know that his relation to B was of that description unless sufficient evidence is adduced to raise an issue as to whether A knew or could reasonably have been expected to know that it was.

In respect of the mens rea in (e)(i) (no reasonable belief (where B is not under 13) that B is 18 or over), where it is proved that B was under 18, A is to be taken not to have reasonably believed that B was 18 or over unless sufficient evidence is adduced to raise an issue as to whether A reasonably believed it.

The exceptions under s 73 (p 813) from liability for aiding, abetting or counselling apply to an offence under s 25 if B is under 16.

Inciting a child family member to engage in sexual activity

A person (A) commits an offence under SOA 2003, s 26(1) if:

(a) he intentionally incites another person (B) to touch, or allow himself to be touched by, A;

(b) the touching is sexual;

(c) the relation of A to B is within the specified relationships;

(d) A knows or could reasonably be expected to know that his relation to B is of a description falling within those relationships; and

(e) either:

(i) B is under 18 and A does not reasonably believe that B is 18 or over; or

(ii) B is under 13.

There are two offences under s 26: by s 26(4) and (5) they are distinguished (and triable) in a similar way as in s 25.

The mens rea in respect of the fact that the relation of A to B is within the specified relationships is the same as that in the offences described in relation to s 25. Thus, where it is proved that the relation of A to B was of a description falling within the specified relationships, it is to be taken that A knew or could reasonably have been expected to know that his relation to B was of that description unless sufficient evidence is adduced to raise an issue as to whether A knew or could reasonably have been expected to know that it was.

Likewise, in respect of the mens rea in para (e)(i) (no reasonable belief (where B is not under 13) that B is 18 or over), where it is proved that B was under 18, A is to be taken not to have reasonably believed that B was 18 or over unless sufficient evidence is adduced to raise an issue as to whether A reasonably believed it.

Family relationships

For the purposes of SOA 2003, ss 25 and 26, the relation of A and B must be within s 27. The relation of A to B is within the specified relationships if it is within paras (a)–(c) below, including an adoptive relationship (as well as a biological one).

The relation of A and B is within the specified relationships if:

(a) one of them is the other's parent, grandparent, brother, sister, half-brother, half-sister, aunt or uncle, or A is or has been B's foster parent;

(b) A and B live or have lived in the same household, or A is or has been regularly involved in caring for, training, supervising or being in sole charge of B, and:

(i) one of them is or has been the other's step-parent,

(ii) A and B are cousins,

(iii) one of them is or has been the other's stepbrother or stepsister, or

(iv) the parent or present or former foster parent of one of them is or has been the other's foster parent;

(c) A and B live in the same household, and A is regularly involved in caring for, training, supervising or being in sole charge of B, for example a nanny or au pair. It will be noted that (c) only applies while A is living in the same household.

A 'step-parent' includes someone who is neither married to, nor the civil partner of, a parent, if that person is a parent's 'partner'. In (b)(iii), the reference to a stepbrother or stepsister is to be read as follows: X's stepbrother or stepsister includes someone who is the son/daughter of the civil partner of X's parent (but not the son/daughter of either of X's parents).

Exceptions: marriage, civil partnership and existing sexual relationships

By SOA 2003, ss 28 and 29, conduct by A which would otherwise be an offence under s 25 or s 26 against B is not an offence thereunder if:

(a) B is 16 or over, and A and B are lawfully married (or civil partners); or

(b) (i) the relation of A to B is not within (a) of the specified relationships above, either biologically or adoptively; and

    (ii) immediately before the relation of A to B first became such as to fall within the specified relationships, a sexual relationship existed between A and B (as where, when A's mother marries B's father, A and B were already in a sexual relationship).

The defence in (b) does not apply if at the time referred to in (b)(ii) sexual intercourse between A and B would have been unlawful, eg because one of them was under 16.

It is for the defendant to prove the relationship mentioned in (a) or (b).

Sex with an adult relative

A person aged 16 or over (A) (subject to SOA 2003, s 64(3A)—see below) commits an indictable (either way) offence under s 64(1) if:

(a) he intentionally penetrates another person's vagina or anus with a part of his body or anything else, or penetrates another person's mouth with his penis;

(b) the penetration is sexual;

(c) the other person (B) is aged 18 or over;

(d) A is related to B in a specified way; and

(e) A knows or could reasonably be expected to know that he is related to B in that way.

A person aged 16 or over (A) (subject to s 65(3A)—see below) commits an indictable (either way) offence under s 65(1) if:

(a) another person (B) penetrates A's vagina or anus with a part of B's body or anything else, or penetrates A's mouth with B's penis;

(b) A consents to the penetration;

(c) the penetration is sexual;

(d) B is aged 18 or over;

(e) A is related to B in a specified way; and

(f) A knows or could reasonably be expected to know that he is related to B in that way.

The specified ways that A may be related to B are as a parent, grandparent, child, grandchild, brother, sister, half-brother, half-sister, uncle, aunt, nephew or niece.

Where a child has been adopted, not only are the biological parent and child related to each other for the purposes of ss 64 and 65, whenever the child was adopted, but 'parent' also includes an adoptive parent and 'child' includes an adopted person. However, where ss 64(1) or 65(1) apply in a case where A is related to B as B's child by virtue of being B's adopted child, A does not commit an offence under ss 64(1) or 65(1), as the case may be, unless A is 18 or over. This is provided by ss 64(3A) and 65(3A). It remains the case that other adoptive relationships, for example that of adoptive brother and sister, are excluded from the application of ss 64 or 65.

These references to an adoptive relationship are to be read as including a corresponding relationship arising by virtue of a parental order under the Human Fertilisation and Embryology Act 2008 (the 'test tube babies' Act).

In terms of the requirement that the prosecution must prove that A knew or could reasonably be expected to know that he is related to B in a specified way, it is to be taken that A knew or could reasonably have been expected to know that he was related in that way unless sufficient evidence is adduced to raise an issue as to whether A knew or could reasonably have been expected to know that he was.

OFFENCES AGAINST PEOPLE WITH A MENTAL DISORDER
Meaning of mental disorder

For the purposes of these offences, 'mental disorder' means any disorder or disability of the mind. A person with a learning disability falls within this definition.

Offences against persons with a mental disorder impeding choice

Sexual activity with a person with a mental disorder impeding choice

A person (A) commits an indictable (either way) offence under SOA 2003, s 30(1) if:

(a) he intentionally touches another person (B);
(b) the touching is sexual;
(c) B is unable to refuse because of or for a reason related to a mental disorder; and
(d) A knows or could reasonably be expected to know that B has a mental disorder and that because of it or for a reason related to it B is likely to be unable to refuse.

Under s 30(1) and (3), A commits a more serious offence triable only on indictment if the touching involves:

(i)   penetration of B's anus or vagina with a part of A's body or anything else;
(ii)   penetration of B's mouth with A's penis;
(iii) penetration of A's anus or vagina with a part of B's body (but not with anything else); or
(iv)   penetration of A's mouth with B's penis.

B is unable to refuse if:

(a) he lacks the capacity to choose (see p 810) whether to agree to the touching (whether because he lacks sufficient understanding of the nature or reasonably foreseeable consequences of what is being done, or for any other reason); or
(b) he is unable to communicate such a choice to A.

In relation to the first type of inability, the House of Lords has held that the words 'for a reason related to mental disorder' in the definition of the offences were clearly capable of encompassing a wide range of circumstances in which a person's mental disorder might rob him or her of the ability to make an autonomous choice, even though he or she might have sufficient understanding of the information relevant to making it. Those circumstances could include the kind of compulsion which drove a person with anorexia to refuse food, the delusions which drove a person with schizophrenia to believe that she had to do something, or the phobia or irrational fear which drove a person to refuse a life-saving injection. Irrational fear plainly was capable of depriving a person of capacity; the question was whether it did in a particular case.

The second type of inability to refuse covers people who might be able to make a choice but are unable to communicate it. The House of Lords has held that it is not limited to cases where B was *physically* unable to communicate because of his mental disorder, and that it also includes cases of an inability to communicate which was the result of or associated with a disorder of the mind. Thus, inability to communicate includes someone with such a degree of learning difficulty that he has never acquired the gift of speech, so that it is impossible to discover whether or not he can understand or make a choice.

The exceptions under s 73 (p 813) from liability for aiding, abetting or counselling apply to an offence under s 30 if B is under 16.

Causing or inciting a person with a mental disorder impeding choice to engage in sexual activity

A person (A) commits an indictable (either way) offence under SOA 2003, s 31(1) if:

(a) he intentionally causes or incites another person (B) to engage in an activity;
(b) the activity is sexual;
(c) B is unable to refuse because of or for a reason related to a mental disorder; and
(d) A knows or could reasonably be expected to know that B has a mental disorder and that because of it or for a reason related to it B is likely to be unable to refuse.

Under s 31(1) and (3), A commits a more serious offence triable only on indictment if the activity caused or incited involves:

(a) penetration of B's anus or vagina;
(b) penetration of B's mouth with a person's penis;
(c) penetration of a person's anus or vagina with a part of B's body or by B with anything else; or
(d) penetration of a person's mouth with B's penis.

B is unable to refuse if:

(a) he lacks the capacity to choose whether to agree to engaging in the activity caused or incited (whether because he lacks sufficient understanding of the nature or reasonably foreseeable consequences of the activity, or for any other reason); or
(b) he is unable to communicate such a choice to A.

Engaging in sexual activity in the presence of a person with a mental disorder impeding choice

A person (A) commits an indictable (either way) offence under SOA 2003, s 32(1) if:

(a) he intentionally engages in an activity;
(b) the activity is sexual;
(c) for the purpose of obtaining sexual gratification, he engages in it:
    (i)   when another person (B) is present or is in a place from which A can be observed, and
    (ii) knowing or believing that B is aware, or intending that B should be aware, that he is engaging in it;
(d) B is unable to refuse because of or for a reason related to a mental disorder; and
(e) A knows or could reasonably be expected to know that B has a mental disorder and that because of it or for a reason related to it B is likely to be unable to refuse.

B is unable to refuse if:

(a) he lacks the capacity to choose whether to agree to being present (whether because he lacks sufficient understanding of the nature of the activity, or for any other reason); or
(b) he is unable to communicate such a choice to A.

Causing a person with a mental disorder impeding choice to watch a sexual act

A person (A) commits an indictable (either way) offence under SOA 2003, s 33(1) if:

(a) for the purpose of obtaining sexual gratification, he intentionally causes another person (B) to watch a third person engaging in an activity, or to look at an image of any person engaging in an activity;
(b) the activity is sexual;
(c) B is unable to refuse because of or for a reason related to a mental disorder; and
(d) A knows or could reasonably be expected to know that B has a mental disorder and that because of it or for a reason related to it B is likely to be unable to refuse.

B is unable to refuse if:

(a) he lacks the capacity to choose whether to agree to watching or looking (whether because he lacks sufficient understanding of the nature of the activity, or for any other reason); or
(b) he is unable to communicate such a choice to A.

Inducements, etc to persons with a mental disorder

Inducement, threat or deception to procure sexual activity with a person with a mental disorder

A person (A) commits an indictable (either way) offence under SOA 2003, s 34(1) if:

(a) with the agreement of another person (B) he intentionally touches that person;
(b) the touching is sexual;
(c) A obtains B's agreement by means of an inducement offered or given, a threat made or a deception practised by A for that purpose;
(d) B has a mental disorder; and
(e) A knows or could reasonably be expected to know that B has a mental disorder.

Under s 34(1) and (2), A commits a more serious offence triable only on indictment if the touching involves:

(a) penetration of B's anus or vagina with a part of A's body or anything else;
(b) penetration of B's mouth with A's penis;
(c) penetration of A's anus or vagina with a part of B's body; or
(d) penetration of A's mouth with B's penis.

It is not necessary in either of these offences or in the case of the related offences under ss 35 to 37 that B's mental disorder made B unable to refuse. These offences are concerned with gaining the consent of a mentally vulnerable person by inducement (eg a reward), a threat (eg 'I won't tell on you if you agree') or a deception (eg 'This is what everyone does').

The exceptions under s 73 (p 813) from liability for aiding, abetting or counselling apply to an offence under s 34 if B is under 16.

Causing a person with a mental disorder to engage in, or agree to engage in, sexual activity by inducement, threat or deception

A person (A) commits an indictable (either way) offence under SOA 2003, s 35(1) if:

(a) by means of an inducement offered or given, a threat made or a deception practised by him for this purpose, he intentionally causes another person (B) to engage in, or to agree to engage in, an activity;
(b) the activity is sexual;

(c) B has a mental disorder; and
(d) A knows or could reasonably be expected to know that B has a mental disorder.

A more serious offence triable only on indictment is committed under s 35(1) and (2) if the activity caused or agreed involves:

(a) penetration of B's anus or vagina;
(b) penetration of B's mouth with a person's penis;
(c) penetration of a person's anus or vagina with a part of B's body or by B with anything else; or
(d) penetration of a person's mouth with B's penis.

Engaging in sexual activity in the presence, procured by inducement, threat or deception, of a person with a mental disorder

A person (A) commits an indictable (either way) offence under SOA 2003, s 36(1) if:

(a) he intentionally engages in an activity;
(b) the activity is sexual;
(c) for the purpose of obtaining sexual gratification, he engages in it:
   (i) when another person (B) is present or is in a place from which A can be observed, and
   (ii) knowing or believing that B is aware, or intending that B should be aware, that he is engaging in it;
(d) B agrees to be present or in the place referred to in (c)(i) because of an inducement offered or given, a threat made or a deception practised by A for the purpose of obtaining that agreement;
(e) B has a mental disorder; and
(f) A knows or could reasonably be expected to know that B has a mental disorder.

Causing a person with a mental disorder to watch a sexual act by inducement, threat or deception

A person (A) commits an indictable (either way) offence under SOA 2003, s 37(1) if:

(a) for the purpose of obtaining sexual gratification, he intentionally causes another person (B) to watch a third person engaging in an activity, or to look at an image of any person engaging in an activity;
(b) the activity is sexual;
(c) B agrees to watch or look because of an inducement offered or given, a threat made or a deception practised by A for the purpose of obtaining that agreement;
(d) B has a mental disorder; and
(e) A knows or could reasonably be expected to know that B has a mental disorder.

Offences by care workers with persons with mental disorder

Sexual activity by a care worker with a person with mental disorder

A person (A) commits an indictable (either way) offence under SOA 2003, s 38(1) if:

(a) he intentionally touches another person (B);
(b) the touching is sexual;
(c) B has a mental disorder;
(d) A knows or could reasonably be expected to know that B has a mental disorder; and

(e) A is involved in B's care in a way that falls within the provisions described on p 830.

A more serious offence triable only on indictment is committed under s 38(1) and (3) if the touching involves:

(a) penetration of B's anus or vagina with a part of A's body or anything else;
(b) penetration of B's mouth with A's penis;
(c) penetration of A's anus or vagina with a part of B's body; or
(d) penetration of A's mouth with B's penis.

The exceptions under s 73 (p 813) from liability for aiding, abetting or counselling apply to an offence under s 38 if B is under 16.

Offences under s 38, and the other 'care worker offences' referred to below, are designed to protect a mentally disordered person with the capacity to refuse consent from exploitation by a care worker of his or her relationship with that person.

Care worker causing or inciting a person with mental disorder to engage in sexual activity

A person (A) commits an indictable (either way) offence under SOA 2003, s 39(1) if:

(a) he intentionally causes or incites another person (B) to engage in an activity;
(b) the activity is sexual;
(c) B has a mental disorder;
(d) A knows or could reasonably be expected to know that B has a mental disorder; and
(e) A is involved in B's care in a way that falls within the provisions described on p 830.

A more serious offence triable only on indictment is committed under s 39(1) and (3) if the sexual activity caused or incited involves:

(a) penetration of B's anus or vagina;
(b) penetration of B's mouth with a person's penis;
(c) penetration of a person's anus or vagina with a part of B's body or by B with anything else; or
(d) penetration of a person's mouth with B's penis.

Sexual activity by care worker in presence of person with mental disorder

A person (A) commits an indictable (either way) offence under SOA 2003, s 40(1) if:

(a) he intentionally engages in an activity;
(b) the activity is sexual;
(c) for the purpose of obtaining sexual gratification, he engages in it:
   (i) when another person (B) is present or is in a place from which A can be observed, and
   (ii) knowing or believing that B is aware, or intending that B should be aware, that he is engaging in it;
(d) B has a mental disorder;
(e) A knows or could reasonably be expected to know that B has a mental disorder; and
(f) A is involved in B's care in a way that falls within the provisions described on p 830.

Care worker causing person with mental disorder to watch a sexual act

A person (A) commits an indictable (either way) offence under SOA 2003, s 41(1) if:

(a) for the purpose of obtaining sexual gratification, he intentionally causes another person (B) to watch a third person engaging in an activity, or to look at an image of any person engaging in an activity;

(b) the activity is sexual;

(c) B has a mental disorder;

(d) A knows or could reasonably be expected to know that B has a mental disorder; and

(e) A is involved in B's care in a way that falls within the provisions described below.

Rebuttable presumption of mens rea as to mental disorder

If it is proved at a trial for an offence under ss 38 to 41 that B had a mental disorder, it is to be taken that A knew or could reasonably have been expected to know that B had a mental disorder unless sufficient evidence is adduced to raise an issue as to whether A knew or could reasonably have been expected to know it (ss 38(2), 39(2), 40(2) and 41(2)).

Definition of care worker

For the purposes of the offences described in ss 38 to 41, a person (A) is involved in the care of another (B) ('care worker' for short) if para (a), (b) or (c) below applies, that is:

(a) if:
   (i) B is accommodated and cared for in a care home, community home, voluntary home or children's home, and
   (ii) A has functions to perform in the home in the course of employment which have brought him or are likely to bring him into regular face-to-face contact with B;

(b) if B is a patient for whom services are provided:
   (i) by a National Health Service body or an independent medical agency, or
   (ii) in an independent clinic (in Wales) or an independent hospital,
   and A has functions to perform for the body or agency or in the clinic or hospital in the course of employment which have brought him or are likely to bring him into regular face-to-face contact with B;

(c) if:
   (i) A is, whether or not in the course of employment, a provider of care, assistance or services to B in connection with B's mental disorder, and
   (ii) as such, has had or is likely to have regular face-to-face contact with B.

Exceptions: marriage, civil partnership and existing sexual relationships

By SOA 2003, ss 43 and 44, conduct by a person (A) which would otherwise be an offence under ss 38 to 41 against another person (B) is not such an offence if respectively:

(a) B was 16 or over at the time of the conduct and the defendant proves that A and B were lawfully married (or civil partners) at that time; or

(b) the defendant proves that immediately before A became involved in B's care in a way described above, a sexual relationship existed between A and B. This exception does not apply if at that time sexual intercourse between A and B would have been unlawful, for example because B was under 16.

PREPARATORY OFFENCES

Administering a substance with intent

A person (A) commits an indictable (either way) offence under SOA 2003, s 61(1) if he intentionally administers a substance to, or causes a substance to be taken by, another person (B):

(a) knowing that B does not consent; and
(b) with the intention of stupefying or overpowering B, so as to enable any person to engage in a sexual activity that involves B.

Although the nature of the substance administered is not restricted provided that it is intended to have the specified effect, this offence is aimed at the activity which has become known as 'date rape' which is frequently carried out following the 'spiking' of a drink with a stupefying drug. However, it would also include circumstances where a person's drink was spiked with strong alcohol if that person believed that he or she was drinking a non-alcoholic drink or where a person was given an injection or caused to inhale chloroform. It would not, of course, cover circumstances in which a person was merely encouraged to drink alcoholic drinks where that person was aware that he or she was drinking alcohol.

A need not carry out the act so that *he* may thereby be enabled to engage in sexual activity; it will be sufficient if he does so to enable some other person to so engage in that activity. The nature of the sexual activity envisaged by s 61 would include sexual intercourse, masturbation, oral sex and any other associated activity. It does not matter whether sexual activity actually takes place; it is sufficient that A administered the substance, knowing that there was no consent and with the appropriate intention.

Committing an offence with intent to commit a sexual offence

A person commits an offence under SOA 2003, s 62(1) if he commits any offence with the intention of committing a relevant sexual offence. A 'relevant sexual offence' is any offence under SOA 2003, Part 1 (ss 1 to 79), as described in this chapter and, in terms of child sexual exploitation and prostitution and sex trafficking, Chapter 30, including an offence of aiding, abetting, counselling or procuring such an offence. Generally, an offence under s 62 is an indictable (either way) offence. A person who commits an offence under s 62 by kidnapping or false imprisonment is guilty of a more serious offence triable only on indictment (s 62(1) and (3)).

Trespass with intent to commit a sexual offence

A person commits an indictable (either way) offence under SOA 2003, s 63(1) if:

(a) he is a trespasser (whether or not he entered as a trespasser) on any premises;
(b) he intends to commit a relevant sexual offence (as defined in the last paragraph) on the premises; and
(c) he knows that, or is reckless as to whether, he is a trespasser.

MISCELLANEOUS SEXUAL OFFENCES

All the offences under this heading besides the last are indictable (either way) offences.

Exposure

A person commits an offence under SOA 2003, s 66(1) if:

(a) he intentionally exposes his genitals; and
(b) he intends that someone will see them and be caused alarm or distress.

The indecent exposure of any part of the body in a place to which the public has access though not necessarily as of right, or a place where what is done is capable of public view, can constitute the common law offence of outraging public decency, if it is capable of being seen by at least two people who are actually present (even if they do not actually see it). This offence is rarely charged and should not be invoked in a case covered by s 66 unless there is good reason for doing so.

Voyeurism: observing

A person commits an offence under SOA 2003, s 67(1) if:

(a) for the purpose of obtaining sexual gratification, he observes another person doing a private act; and
(b) he knows that the other person does not consent to being observed for his sexual gratification.

For the purposes of s 67, a person is doing a private act if the person is in a place which, in the circumstances, would reasonably be expected to provide privacy, and:

(a) the person's genitals, buttocks or breasts are exposed or covered only with underwear;
(b) the person is using a lavatory; or
(c) the person is doing a sexual act of a kind not ordinarily done in public.

The Court of Appeal has held that the reference to breasts in (a) is limited to female breasts. The Court has also held that in the context of communal showers or changing rooms there is no reasonable expectation of privacy from casual observation by other users of the communal showers or changing rooms, whereas there is a reasonable expectation of privacy from being spied on in such places by someone who has drilled a hole in the wall for this purpose. Thus, casual observation of other users of communal showers or changing rooms does not amount to the offence of voyeurism, even if the observer gains sexual gratification from what he sees.

A person commits an offence under s 67(4) if he installs equipment, or constructs or adapts a structure or part of a structure, with the intention of enabling himself or another person to commit the above offence. 'Structure' includes a tent, vehicle or vessel or other temporary or movable structure.

Voyeurism: operating equipment

A person commits an offence under SOA 2003, s 67(2) if:

(a) he operates equipment with the intention of enabling another person to observe, for the purpose of obtaining sexual gratification, a third person (B) doing a private act (as defined above); and
(b) he knows that B does not consent to his operating equipment with that intention.

'Observation' means any observation, whether direct or by looking at a moving or still image (eg by installing a webcam).

Voyeurism: recording

A person commits an offence under SOA 2003, s 67(3), if:

(a) he records another person (B) doing a private act (as defined above);
(b) he does so with the intention that he or a third person will, for the purpose of obtaining sexual gratification, look at a moving or still image of B doing the act; and
(c) he knows that B does not consent to his recording the act with that intention.

Intercourse with an animal

A person commits an offence under SOA 2003, s 69(1) if:

(a) he intentionally performs an act of penetration with his penis;
(b) what is penetrated is the vagina or anus of a living animal; and
(c) he knows that, or is reckless as to whether, that is what is penetrated.

   In relation to an animal, references to the vagina or anus include references to any similar part.
   A person (A) commits an offence under s 69(2) if:

(a) A intentionally causes, or allows, A's vagina or anus to be penetrated;
(b) the penetration is by the penis of a living animal; and
(c) A knows that, or is reckless as to whether, that is what A is being penetrated by.

Sexual penetration of a corpse

A person commits an offence under SOA 2003, s 70 if:

(a) he intentionally performs an act of penetration with a part of his body or anything else;
(b) what is penetrated is a part of the body of a dead person;
(c) he knows that, or is reckless as to whether, that is what is penetrated;
(d) the penetration is sexual.

Sexual activity in a public lavatory

A person commits an offence under SOA 2003, s 71 if:

(a) he is in a lavatory to which the public or a section of the public has, or is permitted to have access, whether on payment or otherwise;
(b) he intentionally engages in an activity; and
(c) the activity is sexual.

   For the purposes of s 71, an activity is sexual if a reasonable person would, in all the circumstances but regardless of any person's purpose, consider it to be sexual.
   This offence is not indictable.

RESTRICTIONS ON EVIDENCE OR QUESTIONS ABOUT COMPLAINANT'S SEXUAL HISTORY

The Youth Justice and Criminal Evidence Act 1999 (YJCEA 1999), s 41 imposes such restrictions where a person is charged with (a) any sexual offence under SOA 2003,

Part 1 (ss 1 to 79), ie all the offences discussed so far in this chapter, as well as those under SOA 2003 relating to child sexual exploitation or prostitution see (the next chapter); (b) the offence at (d) on p 836; or (c) aiding, abetting, counselling or procuring the commission of such an offence, conspiracy or attempt to commit such an offence, or encouraging or assisting the commission of such an offence.

YJCEA 1999, s 41 requires that, where someone is charged with a sexual offence then, except with the leave of the court, no evidence may be adduced, and no questions may be asked in cross-examination, by or on behalf of any defendant about the 'sexual behaviour' of the complainant. 'Sexual behaviour' means any sexual behaviour or other sexual experience, whether or not involving any defendant or other persons, but excluding (except as specified in italics in (a)(iii) and (b) below) anything alleged to have taken place as part of the event which is the subject matter of the charge.

If the defence wishes to introduce evidence or ask questions about such matters, it must apply to the court for leave to do so. The court will decide the application in private and in the absence of the complainant, after the prosecution has had the chance to oppose the application. The court can only grant leave when two conditions are satisfied. The first is that a refusal of leave might have the result of rendering unsafe a conclusion of the jury or (as the case may be) of the court on any relevant issue in the case. The second condition is that:

(a) the evidence in question relates to a relevant issue in the case and either:
   (i)   that issue is not an issue of consent (for example, if the defence is that the defendant *believed* the complainant was consenting, evidence of recent consensual activity between them is admissible in relation to the issue of the defendant's belief, but not as to whether the complainant had consented), or
   (ii) it is an issue of consent and the complainant's sexual behaviour to which the evidence or question relates is alleged to have occurred at or about the same time as the event which is the subject matter of the charge against the defendant (for example, that the complainant had consented to intercourse with the defendant a couple of hours earlier), or
   (iii) it is an issue of consent and the complainant's sexual behaviour to which the evidence or question relates is so similar either to *any sexual behaviour of the complainant which (according to the defence's version) took place as part of the event which is the subject matter of the charge*, or to any other sexual behaviour of the complainant which (according to the defence's version) took place at or about the same time as that event, that the similarity cannot reasonably be explained as a coincidence; or
(b) the evidence or question relates to *any evidence adduced by the prosecution about any sexual behaviour of the complainant*, and would go no further than necessary to enable the evidence adduced by the prosecution to be rebutted or explained by the defendant.

To be admitted under the above provisions, the evidence must relate to a specific instance, or instances, of sexual behaviour. If the court considers that the purpose (or main purpose) of the evidence which the defence seeks to have admitted is to undermine or diminish the complainant's credibility, it will not allow the evidence to be given.

The House of Lords has held that under (a)(iii) the test of admissibility is whether the evidence, and questioning relating to it, was so relevant to the issue of consent that to exclude it would endanger the fairness of the trial, contrary to the defendant's right to a fair trial under the European Convention on Human Rights, art 6. If that test was satisfied, the sexual behaviour evidence should not be excluded.

ANONYMITY OF COMPLAINANTS

The Sexual Offences (Amendment) Act 1992 provides for the anonymity of complainants in the case of any offence under the provisions of SOA 2003, Part 1, except ss 64 and 65 (sex with an adult relative), 69 (intercourse with an animal), and 71 (sexual activity in a public lavatory). The same restrictions apply to similar offences against legislation which existed before SOA 2003. They also apply to the offence of human trafficking, contrary to the Modern Slavery Act 2015, s 2.

Where an *allegation* is made that one of these offences has been committed against a person, no matter relating to that person may, during that person's lifetime, be included in any publication if it is likely to lead members of the public to identify that person as the person against whom the offence was committed. These matters include particularly (if their inclusion in any publication is likely to have such a result):

(a) the person's name or address;
(b) the identity of any educational establishment attended by the person or of any place of work; and
(c) any still or moving picture of the person.

For the purpose of the anonymity provisions, 'publication' is widely defined. It includes any communication, for example, a radio programme, a film, a written communication, or a speech, addressed to the public at large or a section of the public.

This prohibition ceases to apply once a person has been accused of one of the above offences. Thereafter, a corresponding provision applies whereby, where a person has been accused of one of the above offences, no matter whatsoever (including (a)–(c) above) which is likely to lead to the identification of the complainant may be included in any publication during the complainant's lifetime. Provision is made for this prohibition to be set aside or relaxed on application being made to the trial judge where it is considered necessary to induce persons to come forward as witnesses and that the applicant's defence will be substantially prejudiced if the direction is not given. The judge also has a 'public interest' discretion to set aside the prohibition.

If any matter is published in breach of the above rules, an offence is committed:

(a) in the case of a newspaper or periodical, by any proprietor, editor or publisher of it;
(b) in the case of any other publication, by its publisher; or
(c) in the case of a programme, by any body corporate engaged in providing the service and by anyone involved in the programme corresponding to an editor of a newspaper.

INFORMATION ABOUT GUESTS AT HOTELS BELIEVED TO BE USED FOR CHILD SEXUAL EXPLOITATION

Under the Anti-social Behaviour, Crime and Policing Act 2014, s 116 an inspector (or above) may issue a written notice to the owner, operator or manager of a hotel which he reasonably believes has been or will be used for child sexual exploitation purposes, or conduct that is preparatory to, or otherwise connected with, such sexual exploitation.

'Child sexual exploitation' means conduct that constitutes an offence listed in (a) or (b), or an offence in (c) or (d) against someone under 18, namely:

(a) an offence under any of SOA 2003, ss 5 to 13, 16 to 19, 25 and 26 (all dealt with previously), and 47 to 50 (sexual exploitation of children: pp 849–50);

(b) an offence under the Protection of Children Act 1978, s 1 (indecent photographs of children);
(c) against someone under 18, an offence under any of SOA 2003, ss 1 to 4, 30 to 41, 61, 66 and 67 (all dealt with previously), and s 59A (trafficking people for sexual exploitation) (repealed), and
(d) against someone under 18, an offence under the Modern Slavery Act 2015, s 2 (human trafficking) committed with a view to sexual exploitation within s 3(3) (pp 672–3).

The notice must specify the hotel to which it relates and the dates on which it comes into effect and expires (not more than six months after it comes into effect), and explain the effect of: the provisions in the following paragraph, the provisions about the right of appeal to a magistrates' court against a notice within 21 days of its issue, and the provisions of s 118 (below).

A constable may require someone issued with a notice to provide him with information about guests at the hotel. The only information that may be required is: (a) guests' names and addresses; (b) other information about guests that is specified in regulations (yet to be made), and can be readily obtained from one or more of the guests themselves.

A requirement must be in writing, and specify the period to which it relates and the date(s) on or by which the required information must be provided. The period specified must end no later than the expiry of the notice.

'Guest' means someone who, for a charge payable by him or another, has the use of a guest room at the hotel in question; and 'hotel' includes any guest house or similar establishment at which accommodation is provided for a charge.

A person who fails, without reasonable excuse, to comply with a requirement imposed under s 116 commits an offence (s 118(1)). A person commits an offence if, in response to a requirement imposed under s 116, he provides incorrect information which he did not take reasonable steps to verify or to have verified, or knows to be incorrect (s 118(2)). A person does not commit an offence under s 118(2) on grounds of failure to take reasonable steps to verify it or to have it verified if there were no steps that he could reasonably have taken to verify the information or to have it verified (s 118(3)).

NOTIFICATION REQUIREMENTS

SOA 2003, Part 2 requires a 'relevant offender' (a person subject to the notification requirements under the Act: hereafter RO) to make an initial notification to the police of his date of birth, his National Insurance number, his name and home address (and any other name and any other address which he uses), and any other information which has been prescribed. The Sexual Offences Act 2003 (Notification Requirements) (England and Wales) Regulations 2012 prescribe the following additional information:

(a) where an RO resides, or stays for a period of at least 12 hours, at a relevant household (a place where a child resides or stays, and to which the public do not have access), he must notify:
    (i) the date on which he begins to reside or stay at a relevant household,
    (ii) the address of the relevant household, and
    (iii) where he holds such information, the period or periods for which he intends to reside or stay at the relevant household;
(b) where an RO solely or jointly holds an account with a banking institution (defined as a bank, building society or any other institution providing banking services), a

debit card in relation to such an account, a credit card account, or a credit card, he must notify specified details relating to it;

(c) where an RO holds any passport, other identity document, or (in a case where he does not hold any passport or other identity document) any other document in which his full name appears, he must notify the number and his full name as it appears in the document and (except in the case of a passport) describe the document. If he holds a passport the information must be given in relation to it. If he does not, the information must be given in relation to another identity document if he holds one. If he does not, it must be given in relation to any other document.

Notification by the RO must be made within three days of the relevant date and must be made by attending at any prescribed police station in his local police area, and giving an oral notification to any police officer, or to any person authorised for the purpose by the officer in charge of the station. The relevant date is the date of conviction, finding or caution but the three-day period does not include any time when the RO is in custody by a court order or in prison, detained in hospital, or outside the UK. On giving notification, the RO may be required by the police officer or authorised person to have his fingerprints and a photograph taken.

After such an original notification, an RO must give notice, within a three-day period of the change, of a new (ie unnotified) name; of a change of home address; of a new (ie unnotified) place of residence in the UK where he has resided for a qualifying period of seven days, or periods amounting to seven days in a 12-month period; of his release from custody, imprisonment or detention in hospital; or of any prescribed change of circumstances. The 2012 Regulations prescribe the following changes of circumstance:

(a) where the RO resides, or stays for a period of at least 12 hours, at a relevant household in relation to which there has been no initial notification, or ceases to reside or stay at a relevant household in relation to which there has been an initial notification. A notification of such a change must disclose the date from which he resides or stays, or the date on which he ceases to reside or stay, at a relevant household;

(b) where the RO's account is opened or closed, a debit or credit card is obtained, no longer held, or has expired and information previously notified by him has altered or become inaccurate or incomplete. A notification of such a change must give the same specified details about the account or card as an initial notification;

(c) where the RO obtains a passport, other identity document or other document in relation to which there has been no initial notification, or ceases to hold a passport, other identity document or other document in relation to which there has been an initial notification.

Although notification is permitted before use of the new name or the change of address, if the change subsequently takes place more than two days before the date notified that notification is invalid. Moreover, if the event to which an advance notification relates has not occurred within three days of the date notified, the offender must within six days of the notified date notify the police that it did not occur within that period.

An RO must notify the police of his intention to leave the UK, and of his return, in accordance with the Sexual Offences Act 2003 (Travel Notification Requirements) Regulations 2004.

An RO must also annually re-notify the police of the information required to be given on initial notification. By way of exception, where the home address initially notified, or notified as a change, was a location where the RO can regularly be found in the absence of his having a fixed abode in the UK, the duty to re-notify is not an annual one but is to re-notify every seven days. Where an RO is in custody by a court order, in prison, detained in hospital, or outside the UK at the relevant time, the re-notification period is three days from release, or return to the UK.

The persons subject to the notification requirements under SOA 2003, Part 2 (ie ROs) are those convicted of an offence listed in SOA 2003, Sch 3; those found not guilty of such an offence by reason of insanity; those found to be under a disability (ie unfit to plead) and to have done the act charged in respect of such an offence; and those cautioned in respect of such an offence. Persons previously convicted of offences which made them subject to the Sex Offenders Act 1997, Part 1 remain subject to the notification requirements then imposed, until the completion of the period for which notification was required.

Schedule 3 offences

The schedule includes offences under SOA 2003 of rape, assault by penetration, most sexual assaults, child sex offences, sexual grooming, (prospectively) sexual communication with a child, offences involving an abuse of trust in relation to children, familial child sexual offences, offences against persons with a mental disorder including offences by care workers, sexual exploitation of children offences, administering substances with intent, trespassing with intent to commit a sexual offence, sex with an adult relative, exposure, voyeurism, intercourse with an animal and sexual penetration with a corpse. In brief, this list includes every offence under SOA 2003, Part 1 (ss 1 to 79) besides those relating to prostitution (other than prostitution involving sexual exploitation of a child), or to sexual activity in a public lavatory. The listed offences also include offences relating to an indecent photograph or pseudo-photograph of a child, possession of a paedophile manual, possession of an extreme pornographic image, and possession of a prohibited image of a child. Encouraging or assisting, attempting, conspiring to commit, and aiding and abetting, such offences are also Sch 3 offences. Reference should be made to the Schedule as the offences often only give rise to the notification requirements in particular circumstances or in the case of particular sentences.

Duration of notification requirement

Relevant offenders (ROs) sentenced to life imprisonment, or to 30 months' imprisonment or more, or persons sentenced to imprisonment for public protection under the Criminal Justice Act 2003, s 225, or persons admitted to hospital under a restriction order, are indefinitely subject to the notification requirement; ROs sentenced to more than six months but less than 30 months are subject for a period of 10 years; ROs sentenced to less than six months or admitted to a hospital without a restriction order are subject for a period of seven years; and ROs of any other description, for a period of five years. However, where ROs are under 18, the periods of ten, seven, and five years are halved. ROs who are cautioned are subject to the requirements for two years. Those who are conditionally discharged are subject to the requirements during the period of conditional discharge.

The Court of Appeal has held that the whole of the term of an extended sentence (ie the aggregate of the appropriate custodial term and the extension period for which the offender is to be subject to a licence) constitutes the term for which a person is 'sentenced to imprisonment' for the purposes of determining the notification period.

In the case of a young offender the court may direct a person with parental responsibility for the offender to comply with the notification requirements until the offender reaches the age of 18 or until an earlier date specified in the order.

The indefinite notification requirement referred to above was initially incompatible with the European Convention on Human Rights, art 8 (right to private and family life) because there was no possibility of review. To cure this defect, the Sexual Offences Act 2003 (Remedial) Order 2012 provides that an RO subject to an indefinite notification requirement, and not subject to a sexual harm prevention order (or an interim order), may apply in writing to the relevant chief officer of police for the area in which he is residing or staying (according to his latest notification) for a determination that he is no longer subject to the indefinite notification requirements. Such an application must be made on or after the qualifying date or, as the case may be, the further qualifying date. Where the qualifying RO was 18 or over when the notification requirement began, the qualifying date is the day after the end of the 15-year period beginning with the day on which the RO gives the first notification after release from prison or other detention in relation to the conviction giving rise to the indefinite requirement. Where he was under 18 when the requirement began, it is the day after the end of the eight-year period beginning with that day. As to the further qualifying date, see below.

For the purposes of the determination of an application for review, the RO must satisfy the chief officer of police on the balance of probabilities that it is not necessary for the purpose of protecting the public or any particular members of the public from sexual harm for him to remain subject to the indefinite notification requirements.

If the chief officer determines that the RO should not remain subject to the indefinite notification requirements, the RO ceases to be subject to them on the date of receipt of the notice of determination.

If the chief officer determines that the RO should remain subject to the indefinite notification requirements, the notice of the determination must:

(a) state the reasons for the determination; and
(b) inform the RO of his right to appeal within 21 days to a magistrates' court.

In the event of such a determination, the further qualifying date (ie for another review) will be eight years from the determination, or up to 15 years (as determined by the chief officer) if he considers that the risk of sexual harm posed by the RO is sufficient to justify a continuation of those requirements after the end of the eight-year period beginning with the day on which the determination is made.

A divisional court has held that a chief officer's functions under SOA 2003 can be delegated to an officer of an appropriate level: a superintendent (or above) in the present context.

Offences relating to notification requirements

It is an indictable (either way) offence under SOA 2003, s 91(1) for a person:

(a) to fail without reasonable excuse to comply with the notification requirements;
(b) to notify to the police, in purported compliance with these requirements, any information which he knows to be false.

PREVENTIVE ORDERS

Notification orders

SOA 2003, s 97 provides that a chief officer of police (see p 839) may apply to a magistrates' court for a civil order (a notification order) in respect of a defendant who resides in his police area, or whom he believes is in, or is intending to come to, his police area, where it appears to him that the following conditions are satisfied with respect to the defendant:

(a) under the law in force in a country outside the UK:
  (i) he has been convicted of a relevant offence (whether or not he has been punished for it),
  (ii) a court exercising jurisdiction under that law has made in respect of a relevant offence a finding equivalent to a finding that he is not guilty by reason of insanity,
  (iii) such a court has made in respect of a relevant offence a finding equivalent to a finding that he is under a disability and did the act charged against him in respect of that offence, or
  (iv) he has been cautioned in respect of the relevant offence;
(b) condition (a) above is met because of a conviction, finding or caution which occurred on or after 1 September 1997 (or although a person was convicted before that date he was dealt with after it) or because, although there was a conviction before that date, the person concerned was detained in the foreign country, or subject to supervision or a community sentence; and
(c) the notification requirement period specified in respect of the relevant offence has not expired.

If it is proved that these conditions exist the court must make a notification order. A 'relevant offence' means an act which constituted an offence under the law in force in the country concerned and would have constituted an offence listed in SOA 2003, Sch 3 if it had been done in any part of the UK.

The effect of a notification order is to subject the defendant to the notification requirements under SOA 2003, Part 2 for a period corresponding to that which would apply if he had been convicted in the UK. The notification period runs from the date of the foreign conviction, etc. The initial notification must be made within three days of the service of the order.

Provision is made for an 'interim notification order' pending determination of an application for a notification order. Where a relevant offence has been committed abroad it may take some time to obtain the necessary documentation to put before the court. A person subject to an interim order is subject to the notification requirements while the order is in force and must make that notification within three days of service of the order.

Sexual harm prevention orders

Sexual harm prevention orders (SHPOs) have replaced sexual offences prevention orders (SOPOs) and foreign travel orders (FTOs). SHPOs are governed by SOA 2003, ss 103A to 103K.

Effect of SHPO

By SOA 2003, s 103C, a SHPO prohibits the defendant (D) from doing anything described in the order. With one exception, a prohibition contained in a SHPO has effect for a fixed period, specified in the order, of at least five years, or until further order. The exception is that a prohibition on foreign travel contained in a SHPO must be for a fixed period of not more than five years, although it may be extended for a further such period (s 103D).

Section 103C provides that a SHPO:

(a) may specify that some of its prohibitions have effect until further order and some for a fixed period;

(b) may specify different periods for different prohibitions.

The only prohibitions that may be included in a SHPO are those necessary for the purpose of:

(a) protecting the public in the UK or any particular members of the public from sexual harm from D, or

(b) protecting children (persons under 18) or vulnerable adults generally, or any particular children or vulnerable adults, from sexual harm from D outside the UK.

'Vulnerable adult' means someone aged 18 or over whose ability to protect himself from physical or psychological harm is significantly impaired through physical or mental disability or illness, through old age or otherwise.

By s 103D, a 'prohibition on foreign travel', referred to above, means a prohibition on travelling:

(a) to any country outside the UK named or described in the order;

(b) to any country outside the UK other than a country named or described in the order; or

(c) to any country outside the UK (in which case the order must require D to surrender all his passports at a police station specified in the order on or before the date when the prohibition takes effect, or within a period so specified).

Any passports surrendered under (c), other than a non-UK passport returned to its issuing authority, must be returned as soon as reasonably practicable after D ceases to be subject to a SHPO containing a prohibition within (c).

A person subject to a SHPO (or interim order) is subject to the notification requirements of SOA 2003, Part 2 for the duration of the order.

When can a SHPO be made?

SOA 2003, s 103A provides that a court may make a SHPO in respect of D in two cases:

(a) by a criminal court as part of disposal after a conviction, etc; and

(b) by a magistrates' court (or youth court) on application by the police or NCA.

SHPO as part of disposal

Where:

(a) a court deals with D after conviction for an offence listed in SOA 2003, Sch 3 or Sch 5 (see pp 838 and 842), or after a finding that D is not guilty of such an offence by reason of insanity, or a finding of being under a disability and to have done the act charged in respect of such an offence; and

(b) the court is satisfied that it is necessary to make a SHPO for the purpose of protecting the public or any particular members of the public in the UK from sexual harm from D, or protecting children or vulnerable adults (above) generally, or any particular children or vulnerable adults, from sexual harm from D outside the UK, the court may make a SHPO.

'Sexual harm' means physical or psychological harm caused by D committing a Sch 3 offence or offences, or (in the case of harm outside the UK) by D doing, outside the UK, anything which would constitute a Sch 3 offence if done in any part of the UK.

SHPO on application

A chief officer of police or the Director General of the NCA (the Director General) may apply by complaint (ie in civil proceedings) to a magistrates' court (or youth court) for a SHPO in respect of D if it appears to him that D is a qualifying offender and has since the appropriate date acted in such a way as to give reasonable cause to believe that it is necessary for a SHPO to be made. As in the case of applications for other preventive orders, a chief officer or the Director General can delegate this function to an officer of an appropriate level.

On such an application, the court may make a SHPO if it is proved that D is a 'qualifying offender', and the court is satisfied that D's behaviour since the 'appropriate date' makes it necessary to make a SHPO, for the purpose of protecting the public or any particular members of the public from sexual harm (as defined above) from D, or protecting children or vulnerable adults generally, or any particular children or vulnerable adults, from sexual harm from D outside the UK.

Where the Director General has made such an application, he must as soon as practicable notify the chief officer of police for a relevant police area of the application.

A person is a 'qualifying offender' for these purposes if he has been:

(a) convicted of a Sch 3 or Sch 5 offence;
(b) found not guilty of such an offence by reason of insanity;
(c) found to be under a disability and to have done the act charged against him in respect of such an offence; or
(d) cautioned in respect of such an offence.

Schedule 3 offences have been described on p 838, but it should be noted that any restrictions referred to in Sch 3 in terms of particular circumstances or penalties do not apply where a Sch 3 offence is in issue for the purpose of a SHPO. Schedule 5 offences include offences of child cruelty or neglect, etc, child abduction, outraging public decency, as well as murder and other offences of serious violence, harassment, stalking, exploitation of prostitution offences and human trafficking.

A person is also a 'qualifying offender' for these purposes if, under the law of a country outside the UK:

(a) he has been convicted of a relevant offence;
(b) a court exercising jurisdiction under that law has made, in respect of a relevant offence, a finding equivalent to a finding of not guilty by reason of insanity, or a finding equivalent to a finding that he is under a disability and did the act charged against him in respect of the offence; or
(c) he has been cautioned in respect of a relevant offence.

A 'relevant offence' means an act which constituted an offence under the law in force in the country concerned, and would have constituted a Sch 3 or Sch 5 offence if it had been done in any part of the UK.

For these purposes, the 'appropriate date', in relation to a qualifying offender, means the date or (as the case may be) the first date on which he was convicted, found or cautioned as mentioned above.

Under s 103F, interim SHPOs may be made in appropriate circumstances by the magistrates' court to which an application for a SHPO is or has been made pending determination of the application for a SHPO. The applicant or D may apply to the court that made the interim SHPO for the order to be varied, renewed or discharged. On an application for an interim SHPO, the court may, if it considers it just to do so, make an interim notification order (either in addition to or instead of an interim SHPO).

On an application for a SHPO made by a chief officer of police, the court must make a notification order in respect of D (either in addition to or instead of a SHPO) if the applicant invites the court to do so, and it is proved that the three conditions ((a)–(c) on p 840) for such an order are met.

The Secretary of State is required to issue guidance to chief officers of police and the Director General about the exercise of their powers relating to SHPOs and interim SHPOs.

Variation, renewal and discharge

A SHPO may be varied, renewed or discharged but (unless its only prohibition is one on foreign travel) it may not be discharged before the end of five years beginning with the day on which the order was made, without the consent of D and (a) where the application is made by a chief officer of police, that chief officer, or (b) in any other case, the chief officer of police for the area in which D resides.

Breach

Breach of a prohibition in a SHPO or interim SHPO without reasonable excuse is an indictable (either way) offence under SOA 2003, s 103I(1). This offence also applies to breach of a sexual offences prevention order, interim sexual offences prevention order or foreign travel order.

Failure, without reasonable excuse, to comply with the passport-surrender condition in a prohibition on foreign travel is an offence under s 103I(2).

D only has an evidential burden in respect of these defences of reasonable excuse.

Sexual risk orders

Sexual risk orders (SROs) replaced risk of sexual harm orders (RSHOs). SROs are governed by SOA 2003, s 122A to 122K.

Effect of order

By SOA 2003, s 122A(7), a SRO prohibits D from doing anything described in the order; it has effect for a fixed period (not less than two years) specified in the order or until further order. A prohibition on foreign travel contained in a SRO must not be for a period of more than five years, although it may be extended for a further such period. It may specify different periods for different prohibitions. The only prohibitions that may be imposed are those necessary for the purpose of protecting the public in the UK or any particular members of the public from physical or psychological harm caused by D doing an act of a sexual nature, or protecting children or vulnerable adults generally, or any particular children or vulnerable adults, from such harm from D outside the UK (s 122A(9)). 'Child' and 'vulnerable adult' mean the same as for a SHPO.

By s 122C, the same rules apply to a 'prohibition on foreign travel', referred to earlier, as apply to such a prohibition in relation to a SHPO.

Section 122F provides that a person in respect of whom a court makes a SRO (other than one that replaces an interim SRO), or an interim SRO, must, within three days beginning with the date of service of the order, notify to the police his name (and, where he uses more than one, each of his names), and his home address, unless he is already subject to the notification requirements. If he uses a name which has not been notified, or changes his address, he must notify the police of this within three days beginning with the date on which this happens.

Applications

By SOA 2003, s 122A(1), a chief officer of police or the Director General of NCA may apply by complaint to a magistrates' court (or youth court) for a SRO in respect of D if it appears to him that D has done an act of a sexual nature as a result of which there is reasonable cause to believe that it is necessary for a SRO to be made. As in the case of applications for other preventive orders, a chief officer or the Director General can delegate this function to an officer of an appropriate level.

The Director General must as soon as practicable notify the chief officer of police for a relevant police area of any application that he has made.

On such an application, the court may make a SRO if satisfied that D has done an act of a sexual nature as a result of which it is necessary to make such an order for the purpose of protecting the public or any particular members of the public from harm from D, or protecting children or vulnerable adults generally, or any particular children or vulnerable adults, from harm from D outside the UK.

Under s 122E, interim SROs may be made. The rules about interim SROs are identical to those which apply to an interim SHPO.

The Secretary of State is required to issue guidance to chief officers of police and the Director General about the exercise of their powers relating to SROs and interim SROs.

Variation, etc

A SRO may be varied, renewed or discharged but (unless its only prohibition is one on foreign travel) it may not be discharged before the end of two years beginning with the day on which the order was made, without the consent of D and (a) where the application is made by a chief officer of police, that chief officer, or (b) in any other case, the chief officer of police for the area in which D resides.

Breach

Breach of a prohibition in a SRO or interim SRO without reasonable excuse is an indictable (either way) offence under SOA 2003, s 122H(1). This offence also applies to breach of a risk of sexual harm order (RSHO) or interim risk of sexual harm order.

Failure, without reasonable excuse, to comply with the passport-surrender condition in a prohibition on foreign travel is an offence under s 122H(2).

D only has an evidential burden in respect of these defences of reasonable excuse. Where:

(a) D is convicted of an offence under s 122H or 128 (breach of RSHO or interim RSHO), or is found not guilty of such an offence by reason of insanity or to be under a disability and to have done the act charged, or is cautioned for such an offence; and
(b) D was subject to the notification requirements under SOA 2003, Part 2; and
(c) D would otherwise cease to be subject to those requirements while the relevant order has effect,

D remains subject to the notification requirements.

Where D was not subject to the notification requirements at the time of such conviction, 'finding' or caution, D becomes subject to the notification requirements and remains so until the relevant order ceases to have effect. In such a case, the 'relevant date' for the purposes of those requirements is the date when this provision first applies to D.

Application of orders throughout UK

SOA 2003, s 136ZA provides that, for the purposes of the offences relating to their breach, the prohibitions imposed by a SHPO, interim SHPO, SRO or interim SRO (or one of the orders which have been replaced) made in one part of the UK apply (unless expressly confined to a particular location) throughout that and every other part of the UK.

Where a court in England and Wales makes a SHPO in relation to someone already subject to a SOPO or foreign travel order (FTO), or a SRO in relation to someone already subject to a risk of sexual harm order (RSHO) or FTO, the earlier order ceases to have effect (whichever part of the UK it was made in) unless the court orders otherwise (s 136ZB). There are corresponding provisions in relation to Scottish or Northern Irish courts.

CHAPTER 30

Offences Relating to Prostitution, Obscenity and Indecent Photographs

PROSTITUTION

Prostitute

For the purposes of legislation other than the Sexual Offences Act 2003 (SOA 2003), the term 'prostitute' is defined by case law. This establishes that a *prostitute* is a woman (or a man) who offers her (or his) body commonly for sexual intercourse or acts of a sexual nature, in return for payment. It has been held by the Court of Appeal that it is immaterial that the woman (or man) is dishonest and intends simply to pocket advance payment and not to provide sexual services. The reference to other acts of a sexual nature extends the definition of 'prostitute'. Masseuses, for example, who carry out acts of masturbation on request are engaging in such acts. So are women who engage in sado-masochistic sessions for the sexual pleasure of their partner. Since sexual intercourse is not required, even a virgin can be a prostitute. If a person offers intercourse for payment regularly to one person, the offeror is not a prostitute as services are restricted to one person. If the offer is made to a number of persons because of the promiscuous nature of the offeror and no payment is required for the services, the offeror is not a prostitute as no payment is received in return.

For the purposes of SOA 2003, 'prostitute' is defined as a person (A) who, on at least one occasion and whether or not compelled to do so, offers or provides sexual services to another person in return for payment or a promise of payment to A or a third person; 'prostitution' in SOA 2003 is interpreted accordingly. 'Payment' for the purposes of SOA 2003 means any financial advantage, including the discharge of an obligation to pay or the provision of goods or services (including sexual services) gratuitously or at a discount. Thus, any form of financial arrangement will be classified as payment. The settlement of a debt by the provision of sexual services, or the supply of drugs, or their provision at a discounted price will be sufficient. There is no doubt that a similar approach will be followed in relation to other statutes.

It is not an offence in itself to be a prostitute, but there are a number of offences which can only be committed by, or in respect of, prostitutes.

Persistent loitering or soliciting by a prostitute

The Street Offences Act 1959 (StOA 1959), s 1(1) creates the offence committed by a prostitute (whether male or female) who persistently loiters or solicits in a street or public place for the purposes of prostitution. The offence can only be committed by someone aged 18 or over.

Persistently loitering or soliciting for the purposes of prostitution

Loitering or soliciting is persistent if it takes place on two or more occasions in any period of three months.

Loitering by a prostitute does not need to be for the purpose of making approaches to others; it is sufficient that there is loitering for the purpose of being approached by potential clients (as where a prostitute loiters in an area noted as a haunt of prostitutes). Loitering need not be on foot. It can, for example, be done in a slowly moving vehicle.

Soliciting need not be by words. Movements of the body, arms, hands, as well as facial expressions and gestures can be equally compelling forms of solicitation. Tapping on window panes, leaning out of windows with signals to indicate price, signalling the position of the entry door with the fingers are all forms of solicitation. The test to be applied should be, 'Is it clear to the reasonable man that he is being offered sex for money?'

Street or public place

'Street' for the purpose of StOA 1959 includes any bridge, road, lane, footway, subway, square, court, alley or passage, whether a thoroughfare or not, which is for the time being open to the public. In addition, the doorways and entrances to premises abutting on a street and the ground adjoining and open to a street are treated as forming part of the street.

The definition is quite wide. As the courts have confirmed, it includes places which are upon private property if they are open to a street, eg a balcony or a room whose window faces onto a street.

'Public place' is not defined but generally the courts have accepted that a public place is one where the public go, no matter whether they have a right to go or not. What is a public place may vary from time to time; the question is whether the place was public at the material time. The point has not been tested whether places such as public houses, restaurants or similar places can be public places for the purpose of the Act.

Orders requiring attendance at meetings

Under the StOA 1959, s 1(2A), the court may deal with someone convicted of an offence contrary to s 1(1) by making an order requiring the offender to attend three meetings with the person for the time being specified in the order ('the supervisor') or with such other person as the supervisor may direct. If the court makes such an order it may not impose any other penalty in respect of the offence.

Failure to comply with such an order without reasonable excuse can result in a magistrates' court revoking the order and dealing with the offender, for the offence in respect of which the order was made, as if the offender had just been convicted of the offence (StOA 1959, Sch 1).

Soliciting to obtain a prostitute's sexual services

Under SOA 2003, s 51A(1), it is an offence for a person in a street (as defined by the StOA 1959) or public place to solicit another (B) for the purpose of obtaining B's sexual services as a prostitute. The reference to a person in a street or public place includes a person in a vehicle in a street or public place.

Placing of advertisements relating to prostitution

The Criminal Justice and Police Act 2001 (CJPA 2001), s 46(1) creates an offence of placing on, or in the immediate vicinity of, a public telephone, an advertisement relating to prostitution, with intent that the advertisement should come to the attention of any other person. An advertisement is covered by s 46 if it is for the services of a prostitute, whether male or female, or indicates that premises are premises in which such services are offered. Any advertisement which a reasonable person would consider to be an advertisement relating to prostitution is presumed to be so, unless shown not to be.

For these purposes, 'public telephone' means any telephone located in a public place for use by the public (or a section of the public) together with any structure in which it is housed. A 'public place' means any place to which the public have, or are permitted to have, access, whether on payment or otherwise, other than (a) any place to which children under the age of 16 are not permitted to have access, whether by law or otherwise, and (b) any premises which are wholly or mainly used for residential purposes.

Exploitation of prostitution

The offences under this heading are indictable (either way) offences.

SOA 2003, s 52(1) provides that it is an offence for a person intentionally to cause or incite another person to become a prostitute in any part of the world if he does so for or in the expectation of gain for himself or for a third person. Section 53(1) makes it an offence for a person intentionally to control any of the activities of another person relating to that person's prostitution in any part of the world for or in the expectation of gain for himself or a third person. 'Control' is not limited to conduct which forces another to carry out the relevant activity; it can be exercised in various ways. It is enough if a defendant instructed or directed a prostitute to carry out the relevant activity or do it in a particular way.

For the purposes of these offences the term 'gain' means:

(a) any financial advantage, including the discharge of an obligation to pay or the provision of goods or services (including sexual services) gratuitously or at a discount; or

(b) the goodwill of any person which is or appears likely, in time, to bring financial advantage.

This definition makes it clear that there is no requirement that money is intended to change hands from the prostitute to the defendant (D). It may be that D wants no more than an occasional 'freebee' for himself or another, or intends that the prostitute should pay for his drug habit out of her earnings.

Sections 52 and 53 are of particular importance in relation to the protection of persons aged 18 or over, because ss 47 to 50 (pp 849–50) specifically protect those under 18.

Paying for sexual services of a prostitute subjected to force, etc

By SOA 2003, s 53A, a person (A) commits an offence if:

(a) A makes or promises payment for the sexual services of a prostitute (B),
(b) a third person (C) has engaged in exploitative conduct of a kind likely to induce or encourage B to provide the sexual services for which A has made or promised payment, and
(c) C engaged in that conduct for or in the expectation of gain for C or another person (apart from A or B).

It is irrelevant where in the world the sexual services are to be provided or whether those services are provided. It is also irrelevant whether A is, or ought to be, aware that C has engaged in exploitative conduct.

For the purposes of s 53A:

(a) C engages in exploitative conduct if C uses force, threats (whether or not relating to violence), or any other form of coercion, or C practises any form of deception; and
(b) 'payment' and 'gain' have the meanings as given on pp 846 and 848 respectively.

Sexual exploitation of children

All the offences under this heading are indictable (either way) offences, besides that under s 47(1) and (3) (which is triable only on indictment).

Paying for the sexual services of a child

SOA 2003, s 47(1) and (5) makes it an offence for a person (A) intentionally to obtain for himself the sexual services of another person (B) under 18 where, in advance, such services have been paid for by A or (to A's knowledge) another or where payment has been promised by A or (to A's knowledge) another.

A more serious offence is committed under s 47(1) and (4)(a) if the offence involved penetration, as defined below, or s 47(1) and (4)(b) if it does not, and in either case B is under 16.

An even more serious offence is committed under s 47(1) and (3) if B is under 13 and the offence involved:

(a) penetration of B's anus or vagina with a part of A's body or anything else,
(b) penetration of B's mouth with A's penis,
(c) penetration of A's anus or vagina with a part of B's body or by B with anything else, or
(d) penetration of A's mouth with B's penis.

The payment or promise may be made to B or to someone else. Where B is under 13 an offence will be committed regardless of any belief which A might have concerning age. However, where B is 13 or over A is only guilty if he did not reasonably believe that the victim was 18 or over; it will be for the prosecution to prove that such a belief did not exist.

Causing or inciting sexual exploitation of a child

SOA 2003, s 48(1) makes it an offence for a person (A) intentionally to cause or incite another person (B) under 18 to be *sexually exploited* (see below) in any part of the world. Where B is under 13, it is irrelevant what belief A (however reasonably) might have had as to B's age. If B was 13 or over, the prosecution must prove that A did not reasonably believe that B was under 18. Section 48 does not require proof that A acted for gain. Nor do ss 49 and 50 below.

Controlling a child in relation to sexual exploitation of a child

SOA 2003, s 49(1) makes it an offence if a person (A) intentionally controls any of the activities of another person (B) relating to B's *sexual exploitation* (see below) in any part of the world, and either B is under 18 and A does not reasonably believe that B is 18 or over, or B is under 13. As to 'control' see p 848.

Arranging or facilitating sexual exploitation of a child

SOA 2003, s 50(1) makes it an offence for a person (A) intentionally to arrange or facilitate the *sexual exploitation* in any part of the world of another person (B), where either B is under 18 and A does not reasonably believe that B is 18 or over, or B is under 13.

This offence covers, for example, those who 'convey' young persons to places or premises where sexually exploitative activities are intended to take place and those who merely make the administrative arrangements for such activities.

Sexually exploited

For the purposes of ss 48–50, B is sexually exploited if:

(a) on at least one occasion and whether or not compelled to do so, B offers or provides sexual services to another person in return for payment (p 846) or a promise of payment to B or a third person; or

(b) an indecent image of B is recorded,

and 'sexual exploitation' is to be interpreted accordingly.

CLOSURE ORDERS

SOA 2003, Part 2A gives the courts the power to make premises closure orders where there is evidence of the premises being used for activities relating to certain prostitution or child sex offences. See Chapter 30 on the companion website.

OFFENCES RELATING TO BROTHELS

Keeping a brothel

By the Sexual Offences Act 1956 (SOA 1956), s 33, it is an offence for a person to keep a brothel, or to manage it, or to act or assist in its management. Premises are a brothel if they are used by persons for illicit heterosexual or homosexual intercourse or other indecent behaviour. It is not necessary to show that some of the people resorting to the premises are prostitutes or that they received payment for their services, but there must be at least three people who use the premises in this way. It does not matter that one of them is the occupier, and it does not matter that only two people at a time ever use the premises for sexual activities.

Keeping a brothel for prostitution

By SOA 1956, s 33A(1), it is an indictable (either way) offence for a person to keep, or to manage, or to act or assist in the management of, a brothel *to which people resort for practices involving prostitution* (whether or not also for other practices).

If separate and self-contained flats are separately let, each to one prostitute, it is likely that the building in its entirety will not be classed as a brothel as there is only one prostitute in each of the flats. However, if single rooms are let to prostitutes in one building, it may be sufficient if the rooms are sufficiently close to constitute what might be described as a nest of prostitutes.

Where a brothel is used for prostitution, SOA 1956, s 33A catches the keeper of the premises, who is most likely to be the residential landlord, a manager, who looks after the maintenance and day-to-day needs of the building and its tenants, the 'madame' of the trade, and those who act or assist in the management of the brothel. 'Assisting in the management of a brothel' covers any conduct which contributes to the management of the brothel. It does not require proof that the person actively exercised some control over the brothel or carried out some specific act of management. A person who takes advertisements to a post office and pays for them assists in the management of the brothel. So does a person who discusses with a potential customer the nature of the sexual activities on offer, or who negotiates the price. On the other hand, it has been held that a cleaner at a brothel does not assist in its management.

Related offences

SOA 1956, ss 34, 35(1), and 36 go further and add offences to cover other possibilities in relation to responsibility for the brothel. First, a lessor or landlord of premises (or his agent) who has knowledge of their intended or actual use as a brothel is guilty of an offence (s 34). In addition, the tenant or occupier, or person in charge, of premises who knowingly permits the whole or part of them to be so used is also guilty of an offence (s 35). Lastly, by s 36, it is an offence for the tenant or occupier of any premises knowingly to permit the whole or part of the premises to be used for the purposes of habitual prostitution (whether any prostitute involved is male or female).

OBSCENE PUBLICATIONS

These are governed in general by the Obscene Publications Act 1959 (OPA 1959).

Under OPA 1959, s 2, an indictable (either way) offence is committed by a person who:

(a) publishes an obscene article, whether for gain or not; or
(b) has an obscene article for publication for gain, whether for himself or another.

Writing or otherwise creating an obscene article is not an offence under OPA 1959, nor is simply possessing it or possessing it to give as a gift.

Obscene publication via a broadcast or cable service is a rather specialised type of obscene publication, and is not dealt with further in this book.

What is an 'obscene article'?

An 'article' for present purposes means any article containing or embodying matter to be read or looked at or both, any sound record, and any film or other record of a picture or pictures (such as a photograph, video cassette or computer disc). OPA 1959 also applies to things like negatives from which an article may be reproduced or manufactured.

An article is deemed to be obscene if its effect, or (where the article comprises two or more distinct items) the effect of any of its items is, taken as a whole, such as to tend to deprave and corrupt a significant proportion of persons who are likely, having regard to all the circumstances, to read, see or hear the matter contained in it.

Though a novel may be considered as a whole, a magazine must be considered item by item and, if any one of the items is obscene, this suffices. 'Deprave and corrupt' are strong words; to lead morally astray is not necessarily to deprave and corrupt. Obscenity is not confined to that which has a tendency to corrupt sexual morals; a book depicting the career of a drug addict has been held to be obscene because of its likely effect. On occasions, articles may be directed at persons who may already be considered to have become depraved and corrupted but this might still amount to an offence if the object is to maintain that state of depravity and corruption and to prevent escape from it. Whether an article is obscene because it is likely to deprave and corrupt is essentially a matter for the jury or magistrates.

Publication, etc

To 'publish' means to distribute, circulate, sell, let on hire, give, or lend, or to offer for sale or hire. 'Publishing' also includes 'making available', as where X gives Y a key to a library containing obscene articles. Additionally, in the case of a record, a film, etc 'publish' includes showing, playing or projecting it. A person who enables another to access electronically stored obscene matter on a computer 'shows' the other that matter, and therefore 'publishes' it. Where the matter is data stored electronically, a person publishes it if he transmits that data.

As implied above, there can be a publication for the purposes of OPA 1959 even if the obscene material has been communicated only to one person.

Defences

Under OPA 1959, s 2(5), it is a defence for D to prove he had not examined the article and had no reasonable cause to suspect that it was such that his publication of it, or possession, as the case may be, would make him liable under OPA 1959.

Section 4 provides a defence of 'public good'. If it is proved that publication was justified as being for the public good on the grounds that it is in the interests of science, literature, art or learning, or of other objects of general concern, a person must not be convicted of the above offences. Expert evidence may be given to establish or negative such a defence.

Police powers

By OPA 1959, s 3, if an information on oath is laid before a justice that there are reasonable grounds for suspecting that obscene articles are kept on any premises, stall or vehicle for publication for gain, he may issue a warrant authorising a constable to search for and seize any articles which he has reason to believe to be obscene and to be kept for publication for gain. The additional powers of seizure provided by the Criminal Justice and Police Act 2001, s 50 apply where such a search warrant is executed. If the justice considers that any articles seized are obscene the justice may issue a summons to the occupier of the premises, etc to appear before a magistrates' court and show cause why the articles should not be forfeited. If the court is satisfied that the articles seized are obscene and kept for publication for gain, it must order their forfeiture, unless the 'public good defence' applies.

INDECENT PHOTOGRAPHS OR PSEUDO-PHOTOGRAPHS OF CHILDREN

The Protection of Children Act 1978 (PCA 1978), s 1 and the Criminal Justice Act 1988 (CJA 1988), s 160 provide a range of indictable (either way) offences relating to such photographs or pseudo-photographs.

General definitions

Photographs or pseudo-photographs

References in the offences to an indecent photograph include an indecent film, a copy of an indecent photograph or film, and an indecent photograph comprised in a film. References to photographs also include the negative as well as the positive version, and data stored on a computer disc or by other electronic means which is capable of conversion into a photograph. References to a photograph also include (a) a tracing or other image whether made by electronic or other means (of whatever nature) which is not itself a photograph or pseudo-photograph, but which is derived from the whole or part of a photograph or pseudo-photograph (or a combination of either or both); and (b) data stored on a computer disc or by other electronic means which is capable of conversion into an image within (a). Such items could be described as 'derivative photographs'. Such derivatives will include line-traced and computer-traced images such as might be taken on a mobile telephone.

A 'pseudo-photograph' is an image, whether made by computer graphics or otherwise howsoever, which appears to be a photograph. The term includes:

(a) a copy of an indecent pseudo-photograph; and
(b) data stored on a computer disc or by other electronic means which is capable of conversion into an indecent pseudo-photograph.

An exhibit obviously consisting of parts of two different photographs taped together cannot be said to 'appear to be a photograph' and is therefore not a pseudo-photograph, although, if it was itself photocopied, it could be.

Indecent

The term 'indecent' is an objective one. The test is whether the image was indecent according to recognised standards of propriety, as judged by the ordinary person. A photograph or pseudo-photograph can be indecent even though it is not obscene. The child's age (or in the case of a pseudo-photograph, apparent age) is a relevant factor as to whether or not the photograph or pseudo-photograph is indecent, but the circumstances in which it was taken or made, or the motivation of the photographer (or the maker of a pseudo-photograph), is not. Something abstracted from a decent set of images is capable of being indecent if the abstracted matter satisfies the test of indecency. This was held by the Court of Appeal in a case where D copied a television programme of a medical examination of a boy's genitals and subsequently removed the commentary and slowed down the filming. The Court of Appeal held that the jury were entitled to look at the images independently of the original decent television programme in order to decide whether they were indecent.

The Court of Appeal has emphasised that the categorisation of images into various levels for sentencing purposes is irrelevant to the question of whether an image is indecent.

Child

A photograph or pseudo-photograph must be of a child. In the case of a photograph, a child is someone under 18. A person in a photograph is taken to have been a child at the material time if it appears from the evidence as a whole that he was then under 18. It is for a jury or magistrates to decide whether an unknown person in an indecent photograph was under 18 without the assistance of expert evidence. Since a pseudo-photograph will not be an image of a real person with a real age, it is provided that, if the impression conveyed by the pseudo-photograph is that the person shown is a child under 18, the pseudo-photograph is to be treated for all purposes as showing such a child, and so is a pseudo-photograph where the predominant impression conveyed is that the person shown is a child under 18 notwithstanding that some of the physical characteristics shown are those of an adult.

Taking or making

PCA 1978, s 1(1)(a) provides that, subject to ss 1A and 1B, it is an offence for a person to take, or permit to be taken, or to make any indecent photograph or pseudo-photograph of a child.

A person who deliberately downloads an indecent image of a child from a web page on to a computer screen 'makes' a photograph or pseudo-photograph. If he does this knowing that the image was, or was likely to be, an indecent photograph or pseudo-photograph of a child, he commits an offence. It is irrelevant whether or not his motive is sexual gratification.

Even if the images originated outside England and Wales, the downloading or printing of them in England and Wales creates new material which has been *made* inside England and Wales.

Defences

PCA 1978, s 1A provides a defence (to a charge of *taking or making an indecent photograph or pseudo-photograph*) of consent by the child or reasonable belief in consent. It states that, where in such proceedings, D proves that the photograph or pseudo-photograph was of the child *aged 16 or over*, and that at the time of the offence charged the child and he were married or civil partners of each other, or lived together as partners in an enduring family relationship, and sufficient evidence is adduced to raise an issue as to whether the child consented to the photograph or pseudo-photograph being taken or made, or as to whether D reasonably believed that the child so consented, D is not guilty of the offence unless it is proved that the child did not so consent and that D did not reasonably believe that the child so consented. Section 1A applies whether the photograph or pseudo-photograph showed the child alone or with D, but not if it showed any other person.

In addition, s 1B provides that in respect of a charge of *making an indecent photograph or pseudo-photograph*, for example downloading of an image from the internet, or copying a photograph from a computer hard drive, a person will not be guilty of an offence if he proves that it was done for the purpose of the prevention, detection or investigation of crime, or for the purpose of criminal proceedings. A similar defence also applies to a member of the Security Service, the Secret Intelligence Service, or GCHQ who is able to prove that it was necessary to make the photograph or pseudo-photograph for the exercise of any functions of that Service or GCHQ.

Distributing or showing or possession with a view to distribution or showing

By PCA 1978, s 1(1)(b) it is an offence to distribute or show indecent photographs or pseudo-photographs of a child. Section 1(1)(c) provides that it is an offence for a person to have in his possession such a photograph or pseudo-photograph with a view to its distribution or showing by himself or others.

'Showing' includes 'making available', as where a person gives another access to a computer or cupboard containing indecent photographs. The same would be so where a person makes available a password which enables someone to download a 'photograph' stored on a computer to his own computer. The offence of possession with a view to showing' under s 1(1)(c) requires D to be in possession with a view to showing the indecent photographs to a third party; a view to showing them to himself is insufficient.

A person possesses indecent photographs, etc with a view to their being distributed or shown by him to others only if one reason (not necessarily the primary reason) for possessing them is that they would be distributed or shown to others.

Defences

PCA 1978, s 1(4) provides a defence to charges *of distributing or showing or possession with a view to distribution or showing* if D proves either that:

(a) he had a legitimate reason for distributing or showing the photographs or pseudo-photographs or (as the case may be) having them in his possession; or
(b) he had not seen the photographs or pseudo-photographs and did not know, nor had any reason to suspect, them to be indecent.

In respect of proceedings for *distributing or showing an indecent photograph or pseudo-photograph*, PCA 1978, s 1A provides an additional defence for the case where D proves that the photograph or pseudo-photograph was of the child *aged 16 or over*, and that at the time of the offence charged (ie the distributing or showing), or at the time when he obtained the photograph or pseudo-photograph, the child and he were married or civil partners of each other, or lived together as partners in an enduring family relationship. Section 1A states that in such a case D is not guilty of the offence unless it is proved that the showing or distributing was to someone other than the child.

In respect of proceedings for *possessing an indecent photograph or pseudo-photograph of a child with a view to its being distributed or shown*, s 1A provides a defence where the child consents to D's possession of the photograph or pseudo-photograph (or that D reasonably believed in such consent) and D intended to distribute or show the photograph or pseudo-photograph only to the child. It states that where, in such proceedings, D proves the photograph or pseudo-photograph was of the child *aged 16 or over*, and that at the time of the offence (ie the possession) charged, or at the time when he obtained the photograph or pseudo-photograph, the child and he were married or civil partners of each other, or lived together as partners in an enduring family relationship, and sufficient evidence is adduced to raise an issue both:

(a) as to whether the child consented to the photograph or pseudo-photograph being in D's possession, or as to whether D reasonably believed that the child so consented; and
(b) as to whether D had the photograph or pseudo-photograph in his possession with a view to its being distributed or shown to anyone other than the child,

D is not guilty of the offence unless it is proved either that the child did not so consent and that D did not reasonably believe that the child so consented, or that D had the photograph or pseudo-photograph in his possession with a view to its being distributed or shown to a person other than the child.

The above defences under s 1A apply whether the photograph or pseudo-photograph showed the child alone or with D, but not if it showed any other person.

Publishing, or causing to be published, advertisements

PCA 1978, s 1(1)(d) provides that it is an offence for a person to publish or cause to be published any advertisement likely to be understood as conveying that the advertiser distributes or shows indecent photographs or pseudo-photographs of a child, or intends to do so.

Simple possession

CJA 1988, s 160(1) makes it an offence for a person to have any indecent photograph or pseudo-photograph of a child in his possession.

For the purposes of an offence under PCA 1978 or under CJA 1988, s 160, 'possession' means custody or control. It follows, for example, that an assistant in a sex shop containing indecent photographs of children is, like his employer, in possession of them. Where the image concerned is a computer file, D is in possession of it at the relevant time if it is within his control (as where, for example, he can produce it on his screen, make a hard copy of it or send it to someone else). Thus, images which have been emptied from the computer's recycle bin may be considered to be within the control of a defendant who is skilled in the use of computers and owns the software necessary to retrieve the images; whereas the images may not be considered to be within the control of a defendant who does not possess the requisite skill, and does not own the necessary software.

The offence is not committed unless D knew that he had, or once had, the photograph or pseudo-photograph in his possession.

Defences

By CJA 1988, s 160(2), a person charged under s 160 has a defence if he proves:

(a) that he had a legitimate reason for having the photograph or pseudo-photograph in his possession; or
(b) that he had not himself seen the photograph or pseudo-photograph and did not know, nor had any reason to suspect, it to be indecent; or
(c) that the photograph or pseudo-photograph was sent to him without any previous request made by him or on his behalf and that he did not keep it for an unreasonable time.

The Court of Appeal has held that it is implicit in (b) that a defendant who had not seen the photograph or pseudo-photograph but had cause to suspect that it was indecent has a defence if he proves that he had no reason to suspect that it was an indecent photograph or pseudo-photograph *of a child*.

By s 160A, if D proves that the photograph or pseudo-photograph was of the child *aged 16 or over*, and that at the time of the offence charged, or at the time when he obtained the photograph or pseudo-photograph, the child and he were married or civil partners of each other, or lived together as partners in an enduring family relationship, and sufficient evidence is adduced to raise an issue as to whether the child consented to the photograph or pseudo-photograph being in D's possession, or as to whether D reasonably believed that the child so consented, D is not guilty of the offence unless it is proved either that the child did not so consent or that D did not reasonably believe that the child so consented. Section 160A applies whether the photograph or pseudo-photograph showed the child alone or with D, but not if it showed any other person.

Prosecution

Proceedings for the above offences may only be instituted by or with the consent of the DPP.

The Court of Appeal has stated that, where photographs are contained in books available from reputable outlets, the proper course (if it is claimed that they are indecent) is to prosecute the publisher or retailer under PCA 1978, and not an individual purchaser under CJA 1988, s 160.

Police powers

Under PCA 1978, s 4, on information laid on oath by a constable or by or on behalf of the DPP, a justice may issue a warrant to authorise entry, search for, and seizure of indecent photographs or pseudo-photographs of a child. The additional powers of seizure provided by CJPA 2001, s 50 apply where a search warrant under PCA 1978, s 4 is executed.

PCA 1978, Sch permits forfeiture of indecent photographs or pseudo-photographs of children, and the devices that hold them. Forfeiture is automatic (ie without the involvement of a court) unless the owner or some other person with an interest in the material objects. Computer hard drives which contain indecent photographs or pseudo-photographs of children may be forfeited where it is not technically possible to separate them. PCA 1978, Sch applies irrespective of the power under which material was seized. Thus, a computer seized during an investigation into fraud and found to contain indecent photographs of children may be forfeited.

POSSESSION OF PROHIBITED IMAGES OF CHILDREN

The Coroners and Justice Act 2009, s 62(1) provides that it is an offence for a person to be in possession of a prohibited image of a child, other than an excluded image. An offence under s 62(1) is an indictable (either way) offence. The institution of proceedings requires the DPP's consent.

Prohibited image

A prohibited image is an image which:

(a) is pornographic;
(b) focuses solely or principally on a child's genitals or anal region, or portrays any of the following acts:
   (i) the performance by a person of an act of intercourse or oral sex with or in the presence of a child;
   (ii) an act of masturbation by, of, involving or in the presence of a child;
   (iii) an act which involves penetration of the vagina or anus of a child with a part of a person's body or with anything else;
   (iv) an act of penetration, in the presence of a child, of the vagina or anus of a person with a part of a person's body or with anything else;
   (v) the performance by a child of an act of intercourse or oral sex with an animal (whether dead or alive or imaginary);
   (vi) the performance by a person of an act of intercourse or oral sex with an animal (whether dead or alive or imaginary) in the presence of a child; and
(c) is grossly offensive, disgusting or otherwise of an obscene character.

An 'image' includes (a) a moving or still image (produced by any means), or (b) data (stored by any means) which is capable of conversion into an image within (a), but it does not include an indecent photograph, or indecent pseudo-photograph, of a child within the meaning of PCA 1978. References to an image of a person (or child) include references to an image of an imaginary person (or child).

'Child' means a person under 18. An image of a person is treated as an image of a child if the impression conveyed by the image is that the person shown is a child, or the predominant impression conveyed is that the person shown is a child.

Exclusion of classified film

Section 63 provides that the offence under s 62 does not apply to an 'excluded image', ie an image which forms part of a series of images contained in a recording of the whole or part of a classified work. But such an image is not an 'excluded image' if it is contained in a recording (including a device for storing data electronically and from which images may be produced) of an extract from a classified work and it is of *such a nature that it must reasonably be assumed to have been extracted (whether with or without other images) solely or principally for the purpose of sexual arousal*. 'Classified work' means a video work in respect of which a classification certificate has been issued under the Video Recordings Act 1984 by a designated authority.

Where an extracted image is one of a series of images contained in the recording, the question whether the image is of the nature italicised above is to be determined in the same way as the determination of whether an image which forms part of a series of images is pornographic (see below).

Pornographic

An image is 'pornographic' if it is of such a nature that it must reasonably be assumed to have been produced solely or principally for the purpose of sexual arousal. The Court of Appeal has held that the assumed purpose (of production) of sexual arousal refers to the sexual arousal of anyone who came to have the image, whether he was the producer of the image, a distributor or the ultimate recipient.

Where an image forms part of a series of images, which as a whole might not be of a nature to be assumed to have been produced for the purpose of sexual arousal, the question whether it is pornographic is to be determined by reference to:

(a) the image itself; and
(b) (if the series of images is such as to be capable of providing a context for the image) the context in which it occurs in the series of images.

So, for example, where:

(a) an image forms an integral part of a narrative constituted by a series of images; and
(b) having regard to those images as a whole, they are not of such a nature that they must reasonably be assumed to have been produced solely or principally for the purpose of sexual arousal,

the image may, by virtue of being part of that narrative, be found not to be pornographic, even though it might have been found to be pornographic if taken by itself. For the purposes of this provision it is irrelevant that the series was created by someone other than the creator of the individual image or images in issue.

Defences

Section 64 provides three defences to an offence under s 62. The terms of s 64 are identical to those of CJA 1988, s 160(2) (p 856), with the substitution of 'image' for 'photograph or pseudo-photograph' and 'prohibited' for 'indecent'.

General

By s 67, the provisions of PCA 1978 relating to entry, search and seizure, and to forfeiture apply in relation to prohibited images of children as they apply in relation to indecent photographs of children.

Special rules relating to information society services providers

See p 861.

POSSESSION OF PAEDOPHILE MANUAL

It is an indictable (either way) offence under the Serious Crime Act 2015, s 69(1) to be in possession of any 'item' (which term includes anything in which information of any description is recorded) that contains advice or guidance about abusing children sexually. 'Abusing children sexually' means doing anything that constitutes:

(a) an offence under the Sexual Offences Act 2003, Part 1 (ss 1–79), or a corresponding Northern Irish offence, against a person under 16;
(b) an offence under the Protection of Children Act 1978, s 1, or a corresponding Northern Irish offence, involving indecent photographs (but not pseudo-photographs); or
(c) an offence under the Modern Slavery Act 2015 (MSA 2015), s 2 (human trafficking) committed with a view to sexual exploitation within s 3(3) (pp 672–3).

By s 69(2), it is a defence for the defendant:

(a) to prove that he had a legitimate reason for being in possession of the item;
(b) to prove that—
    (i) he had not read, viewed or (as appropriate) listened to the item, and
    (ii) he did not know, and had no reason to suspect, that it contained advice or guidance about abusing children sexually; or
(c) to prove that the item was sent to him without any request made by him or on his behalf, and that he did not keep it for an unreasonable time.

Proceedings for an offence under s 69(1) may be brought only by or with the consent of the Director of Public Prosecutions. The police powers set out p 857 in relation to indecent photographs of children also apply in relation to the offence.

For special provision in connection with the operation of s 69 in relation to information society services providers see p 861.

POSSESSION OF EXTREME PORNOGRAPHIC IMAGES

The Criminal Justice and Immigration Act (CJIA) 2008, s 63 created the indictable (either way) offence of possession of an extreme pornographic image. The institution of proceedings requires the DPP's consent.

The definitions of 'image' and 'pornographic' are identical to those in the first and last three paragraphs on p 858.

An image is 'extreme' if:

(a) it portrays, in an explicit and realistic way:
   (i) an act which threatens a person's life,
   (ii) an act which results, or is likely to result, in serious injury to a person's anus, breast or genitals,
   (iii) an act which involves sexual interference with a human corpse, or
   (iv) a person performing an act of intercourse or oral sex with an animal (whether dead or alive),
   and a reasonable person looking at the image would think that any such person or animal was real; and
(b) it is grossly offensive, disgusting or otherwise of an obscene character.

These references to parts of the body include references to any part which is surgically reconstructed (in particular through gender reassignment surgery).

In addition, an image is also 'extreme' if:

(a) it portrays, in an explicit and realistic way, either of the following:
   (i) an act which involves the non-consensual penetration of a person's vagina, anus or mouth by another with the other person's penis, or
   (ii) an act which involves the non-consensual sexual penetration of a person's vagina or anus by another with a part of the other person's body or anything else,
   and a reasonable person looking at the image would think that the persons were real; and
(b) it is grossly offensive, disgusting or otherwise of an obscene character.

For these purposes, penetration is a continuing act from entry to withdrawal, and 'vagina' includes vulva.

Exclusion of classified films, etc

Section 64 excludes from s 63 an image forming part of a series of images contained in films which have been classified by a designated authority under the Video Recordings Act 1984. The terms of s 64 are identical to those under C&JA 2009, s 63 (p 858).

Defences

Section 65 provides three defences which are identical to those under CJA 1988, s 160(2) (p 856), with the substitution of 'image' for 'photograph or pseudo-photograph' and 'extreme pornographic' for 'indecent'.

In addition, where:

(a) a person (D) is charged with an offence under s 63; and
(b) the offence relates to an image that portrays an act or acts constituting an extreme image within either definition of 'extreme image' (but does not portray a person performing intercourse or oral sex with an animal),

it is a defence under s 66 for D to prove:

(i) that he directly participated in the acts portrayed; and

(ii) that the act or acts did not involve the infliction of any non-consensual harm on any person; and

(iii) if the image portrays an act involving sexual intercourse with a human corpse, that what is portrayed as a human corpse was not in fact a corpse, and if the image portrays an act within the second definition of 'extreme image', that what is portrayed as non-consensual penetration was in fact consensual.

For these purposes, harm inflicted on a person (P) is non-consensual harm if:

(*a*) the harm is of such a nature that P cannot, in law, consent to it being inflicted on himself; or

(*b*) where P can, in law, consent to it being so inflicted, P does not in fact consent to it being so inflicted.

SPECIAL RULES RELATING TO INFORMATION SOCIETY SERVICES PROVIDERS

The Coroners and Justice Act 2009 (C&JA 2009), Sch 13, Serious Crime Act 2015 (SCA 2015), Sch 3, Criminal Justice and Immigration Act 2008 (CJIA 2008), Sch 14, and the Criminal Justice and Courts Act 2015 (CJCA 2015), Sch 8 make special provision in essentially the same terms in connection with the operation of C&JA 2009, s 62, SCA 2015, s 69, CJIA 2008, s 63 and CJCA 2015, s 33 (below) respectively in relation to information society services providers in order to ensure compatibility with the EU's E-Commerce Directive where an offence has an international element relating to an EEA member state.

DISCLOSING PRIVATE SEXUAL PHOTOGRAPHS AND FILMS WITH INTENT TO CAUSE DISTRESS

It is an indictable (either way) offence under the Criminal Justice and Courts Act 2015, s 33(1) for a person to disclose a private sexual photograph or film if the disclosure is made:

(a) without the consent of an individual (V) who appears in the photograph or film; and

(b) with the intention of causing V distress.

Disclosure to V is not an offence under s 33 (s 33(2)).

A person charged with an offence under s 33 is not to be taken to have disclosed a photograph or film with the intention of causing distress merely because that was a natural and probable consequence of the disclosure (s 33(8)).

Defences

It is a defence for a defendant (D) to prove that he reasonably believed that the disclosure was necessary for the purposes of preventing, detecting or investigating crime (s 33(3)).

It is a defence for D to show that:

(a) the disclosure was made in the course of, or with a view to, the publication of journalistic material; and

(b) he reasonably believed that, in the particular circumstances, the publication of the journalistic material was, or would be, in the public interest (s 33(4)).

It is a defence for D to show that:

(a) he reasonably believed that the photograph or film had previously been disclosed for reward, whether by V or another person; and
(b) he had no reason to believe that the previous disclosure for reward was made without the consent of V (s 33(5)).

D is taken to have shown the matters mentioned in s 33(4) or (5) if sufficient evidence of the matters is adduced to raise an issue with respect to it, and the contrary is not proved beyond reasonable doubt (s 33(6)).

General

The following definitions apply for the purposes of s 33.

A person '*discloses*' something to a person if, by any means, he gives or shows it to the person or makes it available to the person. Something that is given, shown or made available to a person is disclosed whether or not it is given, shown or made available for reward, and whether or not it has previously been given, shown or made available to the person.

'*Photograph or film*' means a still or moving image in any form that:

(a) appears to consist of or include one or more photographed or filmed images;and
(b) in fact consists of or includes one or more photographed or filmed images.

References to a photograph or film include a negative version of, or stored data capable of conversion into, an image. The reference in (b) to photographed or filmed images includes photographed or filmed images that have been altered in any way.

'*Photographed or filmed image*' means a still or moving image that was originally captured by photography or filming, or is part of an image originally captured by photography or by filming on any medium, from which a moving image may be produced.

'*Consent*' to a disclosure includes general consent covering the disclosure, as well as consent to the particular disclosure.

A photograph or film is '*private*' if it shows something that is not of a kind ordinarily seen in public.

A photograph or film is '*sexual*' if:

(a) it shows all or part of an individual's exposed genitals or pubic area;
(b) it shows something that a reasonable person would consider to be sexual because of its nature; or
(c) its content, taken as a whole, is such that a reasonable person would consider it to be sexual.

In the case of a photograph or film that:

(a) consists of or includes a photographed or filmed image that has been altered in any way;
(b) combines two or more photographed or filmed images; and
(c) combines a photographed or filmed image with something else,

the photograph or film is not private and sexual if:

(i)   it does not consist of or include a photographed or filmed image that is itself private and sexual,

(ii) it is only private or sexual by virtue of the above alteration or combination, or

(iii) it is only by virtue of the above alteration or combination that V is shown as part of, or with, whatever makes the photograph or film private and sexual.

'*Publication*' of journalistic material means disclosure to the public at large or to a section of the public.

SENDING INDECENT, ETC MATTER THROUGH POST

Under the Postal Services Act 2000, s 85(1) it is an indictable (either way) offence to send a postal packet which encloses any indecent or obscene matter, or which has on the packet indecent or obscene words, marks, or designs. So far as this offence is concerned the words 'indecent' and 'obscene' are directed at offending against the recognised standards of propriety. It is for a court or jury to decide, applying these standards, whether the material is indecent or obscene.

INDECENT DISPLAYS, ETC

The Indecent Displays (Control) Act 1981 (ID(C)A 1981), s 1(1) provides that it is an indictable (either way) offence to make a public display of indecent matter, or cause or permit such a display.

Matter is deemed to be publicly displayed if displayed in, or visible from, a public place. For these purposes, 'public place' means any place to which the public have access (whether on payment or otherwise) while that matter is displayed, except:

(a) a place to which the public are permitted to have access only on payment which is for, or includes payment for, that display, or

(b) a shop, or any part of a shop, to which public access can only be gained by passing beyond an adequate warning notice,

but the exclusions in (a) and (b) only apply where persons under 18 are not allowed to enter while any such display is actually taking place. The 'adequate warning notice' should read as set out below and this notice should be looked for in premises where it is known that such displays are held:

'WARNING

Persons passing beyond this notice will find material on display which they may consider indecent. No admittance to persons under 18 years of age.'

'Matter', for the purposes of ID(C)A 1981, includes anything capable of being displayed, but does not include the actual human body or a part of it. Thus ID(C)A 1981 is not concerned with strippers. This is a useful Act to police officers as it can be applied to everything from the display of obscene graffiti scrawled on a wall to indecent film shows, etc which are open to the public.

Official TV programmes, art galleries, museums, Crown buildings, local authority buildings, theatres, and arenas controlled by other legislation are totally outside the provisions of the Act.

Police powers

Under ID(C)A 1981, s 2, a constable may seize articles which he has reasonable grounds for believing to be indecent, or to contain indecent matter, or to have been used in the commission of an offence under the Act.

In addition, a justice may grant a search warrant, on information on oath, authorising entry within 14 days and seizure of material reasonably suspected to have been used in an offence under the Act. The additional powers of seizure provided by CJPA 2001, s 50 apply where a search warrant under ID(C)A 1981 is executed.

CHAPTER 31

Drugs

CONTROLLED DRUGS

Introduction

The Misuse of Drugs Act 1971 (MDA 1971) provides a number of offences intended to control the misuse of drugs. All the offences under MDA 1971 described below, with the exception of an offence under s 9A, are indictable (either way) offences. Drugs which are subject to the Act are designated as 'controlled drugs'.

A 'controlled drug' is any substance or product for the time being specified:

(a) in MDA 1971, Sch 2, Part I, II or III; or
(b) in a temporary class drug order as a drug subject to temporary control.

Part I of Sch 2 lists 'Class A drugs'; Part II, 'Class B drugs'; and Part III, 'Class C drugs'. Drugs can be added to the lists contained in Sch 2 by Order in Council, or moved from one class to another. One of the points of the classification of controlled drugs is that it affects the punishment of some of the offences under MDA 1971. As a result of a House of Lords decision, what may appear to be one offence (eg unlawful supply) is in law divisible into distinct offences depending on the maximum penalty for the drug in question.

Class A drugs include narcotic drugs, such as cocaine, morphine, opium, pethidine, and heroin, and hallucinogenic drugs, such as mescaline, LSD, MDMA (ecstasy) however the MDMA is produced, or fungus of any kind which contains psilocin or an ester of psilocin. A recent addition to the list of Class A drugs is 4.4'-DMAR, a former 'legal high', which is a stimulant. Class B drugs include amphetamines, cannabis, cannabis resin, cannabis derivatives and ketamine. Class C drugs include benzyphetamine, GHB (often called the 'date rape' drug), khat, pipradol and temazepam.

There are more than 100 drugs listed in Class C and a similar number are listed in Class A. There are fewer Class B drugs. Only an analysis of the substance will prove its nature, but the forms of drug in popular usage on the street are generally Classes A and B.

'Cannabis' and 'cannabis resin' are defined by MDA 1971. 'Cannabis' (except in the expression 'cannabis resin') means any part of the genus *Cannabis* or any part of any such plant (by whatever name designated) except that it does not include cannabis resin, or any of the following products, after separation from the rest of the plant, namely:

(a) mature stalk of any such plant;
(b) fibre produced from mature stalk of any such plant; and
(c) seed of any such plant.

'Cannabis resin' means the separated resin, whether crude or purified, obtained from any plant of the genus *Cannabis*.

As indicated, a 'controlled drug' is a specified substance or *product*. In addition 'controlled drug' includes any 'preparation or other product' containing a specified substance or product. Some growing things, such as certain types of mushroom, contain a specified substance. In their natural state such things are not a specified substance or product, but if they are picked and subjected to some process to enable them to be used as a drug, they become a 'preparation' containing a specified substance and become a controlled drug. If they are picked, packed and frozen they become a 'product' containing a specified substance and become a controlled drug.

'*Temporary class drug*' means any substance or product which is for the time being a controlled drug by virtue of a temporary class drug order. Where the punishment depends on the class of the controlled drug a temporary class drug is treated in the same way as a Class B drug. The Secretary of State may make a temporary class drug order specifying any substance or product (other than one specified in Sch 2) as a drug subject to temporary control. A temporary class drug order must be made by statutory instrument and ceases to have effect unless approved by each House of Parliament. A substance or product specified in a temporary class drug order ceases to be a controlled drug by virtue of the order:

(a) at the end of one year beginning with the commencement day of the order; or
(b) if earlier, upon the coming into force of an Order in Council by virtue of which the substance or product is specified as a controlled drug in Sch 2.

This is without prejudice to the power of the Secretary of State to vary or revoke a temporary class drug order.

A temporary class drug order may provide for the exception of a temporary class drug from the prohibitions on the import, export, production or supply of controlled drugs, and for circumstances in which a person's possession of the drug is to be treated as excepted possession for the purposes of MDA 1971.

Unlawful import and export

MDA 1971, s 3 prohibits the import or export of a Class A, B or C controlled drug, otherwise than as authorised by regulations made under the Act or by a licence issued by the Secretary of State. MDA 1971, s 3 also prohibits the import or export of a temporary class drug unless the drug has been excepted in the circumstances from s 3 by a provision in the temporary class drug order.

Breach of s 3 is not an offence under the Act but it is an indictable (either way) offence under the Customs and Excise Management Act 1979, ss 50 and 68.

Unlawful production

MDA 1971, s 4(2) states that it is an offence for any person unlawfully to produce a controlled drug or to be concerned in the production of a controlled drug. An offence under s 4(2) is subject to the defence provided by s 28 (see p 872).

Unlawful

The production of any Class A, B or C controlled drug, otherwise than as authorised by regulations, is an unlawful production. The Misuse of Drugs Regulations 2001 authorise production by drug companies, by research establishments for experimental purposes, and by chemists in the course of their business. The production of a temporary class drug is an unlawful production unless a provision of a temporary class drug order excepts the drug from the provisions of s 4 or authorises its production in the circumstances in question.

Produce

'Produce' means to produce a controlled drug by manufacture, cultivation or any other method, and 'production' has a corresponding meaning.

The Court of Appeal has held that the conversion of cocaine hydrochloride into freebase cocaine, in which form it would vaporise and be capable of being inhaled, by dissolving cocaine hydrochloride in water and either baking powder or household ammonia, amounts to production of a Class A drug 'by any other method' than manufacture or cultivation since the drug, in these two forms, is chemically different. It did not matter that the cocaine hydrochloride was already a Class A drug before the process began. By way of further example, where cannabis plants are stripped to take out those parts which could be used for smoking, it has been held that this amounts to production of a Class B drug (cannabis) as a controlled drug is produced by some 'other method'. 'Any other method' has also been held by the Court of Appeal to include the making of an infusion from a controlled drug which, although it does not alter the drug's chemical make-up, has been put into a form which enables it to be consumed.

Since the offence is to produce a controlled drug, it is essential that a controlled drug is actually produced before the offence can be committed.

Concerned in the production

The effect of these words is that criminal liability is not limited to those who actually participate in the production of a controlled drug, since those who arrange for the delivery of ingredients to the place of manufacture of such a drug, knowing the purpose for which they are required, are concerned in its production, as is someone who knowingly allows his premises to be used.

Unlawful supply

If a controlled drug is unlawfully imported or produced it must then have a distribution network. MDA 1971, s 4(3) states that it is an offence for a person unlawfully to supply a controlled drug to another or to be concerned in the supplying of such a drug to another, or to offer to supply a controlled drug to another, or to be concerned in the making to another of an offer to supply such a drug.

The defence provided by s 28 (see p 872) applies to an offence under s 4(3).

Unlawful

The supply of a Class A, B or C controlled drug is unlawful unless authorised by regulations. The circumstances in which a Class A, B or C controlled drug may be supplied lawfully are set out in the Misuse of Drugs Regulations 2001 made under the Act. They are not difficult to imagine. For example, doctors may issue drugs direct from their own dispensaries; pharmacists may supply them upon prescription; nurses may supply patients in hospital; laboratory analysts, inspectors, and quality controllers may also handle drugs and pass them from one to another. The inclusion of the term 'unlawfully' ensures that all circumstances in which Class A, B or C controlled drugs are supplied to a person outside any exception amount to offences under MDA 1971.

A 'supply' of a temporary class drug is not unlawful if a provision of a temporary class drug order excepts the drug from s 4 or authorises its supply in the circumstances in question.

To supply to another

'Supply' means more than the mere transfer of physical control from one person to another; it means furnishing to another the drug in order to enable the other to use it for his own purposes, whether this is done by an importer, producer, 'drug mule', pusher or anyone else in the distribution chain. The person who distributes drugs at a party supplies the drugs to another. So does someone who returns a drug to a person who already owns it so that he can use it, or who hands a 'joint' to someone so that he can take a puff. On the other hand, a person who hands a drug to another for safe-keeping or to an employee of a professional courier service does not supply it to him. Nor does a person who injects another if that drug is already in the other's control.

Although a person who makes a joint purchase of drugs for consumption by himself and another, paying with their joint funds, supplies the other when he hands over the latter's share of the drugs, the Court of Appeal has stated that a charge of supplying the latter is undesirable.

Before an offence of supplying can be committed the substance supplied must be a controlled drug. It is not sufficient that the supplier believed that the substance was a drug, when in fact it was not, although he could be convicted of an attempt to supply in such a case or, depending on the circumstances, of an offer to supply.

Direct evidence of supply is not required; circumstantial evidence can suffice.

To be concerned in the supply

The wide meaning given to the term 'concerned' when discussed in its application to offences of production should be applied. Proof that the defendant (D) was concerned in the supply of a controlled drug does not require proof that he physically supplied it to another. The Court of Appeal has stated that D's participation can take other forms, for example setting up a meeting, being a middle man, providing the finance or arranging the contacts.

The Court of Appeal has held that the word 'supply' *in the present context* is not confined to an 'actual delivery', but refers to the entire process of supply. Thus, the Court upheld convictions of defendants who had been concerned in transporting controlled drugs (heroin) from London to Portsmouth to be delivered to others in that area. That, said the Court, fell plainly within 'supply' for the purposes of the offence of being concerned in the supply of a controlled drug.

To offer to supply or to be concerned in the offer

It is the making of an offer which is the important factor here; the extension of the offence to those who may be concerned in the making of such an offer gives it considerable width. If an offer is made to supply a controlled drug, an offence is committed even though the thing offered is not intended to be supplied, or is not in fact a controlled drug as the offeror knows. Likewise, the offence of offering to supply a controlled drug is committed if the offeror does not intend to supply anything.

Supply or offer to supply article

MDA 1971, s 9A makes it an offence to supply or offer to supply an article which may be used or adapted to be used (whether by itself or in combination with another article) in the administration by a person of a controlled drug (s 9A(1)), or which may be used to prepare a controlled drug for administration (s 9A(3)), in either case believing it would be so used in circumstances which would be unlawful.

It is not an offence under s 9A(1) to supply or offer to supply a hypodermic syringe. In addition, under the Misuse of Drugs Regulations 2001, it is lawful for someone employed or engaged in the lawful provision of drug treatment services to supply or offer to supply aluminium foil as part of structured steps to engage a patient in a drug treatment plan, or which form part of such a plan. Aluminium foil can be used to warm some drugs and inhale them; inhaling is safer than injecting.

The offences under s 9A are the only offences under MDA 1971 described in this book which are not indictable.

Unlawful possession

The offences of unlawful possession of controlled drugs are those with which police officers are most commonly involved. MDA 1971, s 5(2) states that it is an offence for a person unlawfully to have a controlled drug in his possession. The defence under s 28 (p 872) applies to these offences. Possession of various forms of cannabis and cannabis derivatives or of khat (or any preparation or other product containing one of these things) is a 'penalty offence' for the purposes of the Criminal Justice and Police Act 2001: see p 31.

The offences under MDA 1971, s 5(2) do not apply in relation to a temporary class drug (s 5(2A)).

Unlawful

The Misuse of Drugs Regulations 2001 specify when possession of a controlled drug is lawful. They provide that such possession is lawful if it is under the authority of a licence issued by the Secretary of State or under a doctor's, first-level nurse's, nurse independent prescriber's, pharmacist's, pharmacist independent prescriber's, or registered midwife's prescription. In addition, a constable who comes into possession of controlled drugs in the course of his duties is in lawful possession of them, and so are carriers, postal workers, despatchers, workers in forensic laboratories who examine drugs on behalf of the police, medical personnel, ship's masters, etc, in circumstances properly connected with their duties.

Possession

Physical custody of the drug is not necessary for possession but physical control over it is. It follows that a person who has bought a controlled drug is not in possession of it if it is still hidden in the seller's car or stored at the seller's home. On the other hand, a person who leaves a drug in his car or at home while he is away remains in possession of the drug since he retains physical control over it.

Possession can be joint: for example, if two people share a car which they know contains cannabis, they are both in possession of the cannabis if each shares with the other the right to control what is done with it. Moreover, MDA 1971, s 37(3) states that for the purposes of the Act the things which a person has in his possession shall be taken to include anything subject to his control which is in the custody of another. Therefore there may be a number of persons in possession of a particular controlled drug. If a man imports cannabis and hands it to his business manager to store pending distribution, both are in possession as the drug is subject to their control. If the business manager then passes it on to the warehouseman to keep pending its distribution, all three are in possession of it.

Possession cannot begin until the person with control is aware that the thing is under his control; if a drug is slipped into a person's pocket, unknown to him, he is not in possession of it. (As an exception, a person is in possession of a drug delivered to his home, even if he is unaware that it has arrived, provided it is delivered in response to a request by him.)

Knowledge of a thing's quality is not required. It follows that a mere mistake by D as to the quality of the thing under his control (as where D thinks some heroin tablets are aspirins) is not enough to prevent him being in possession.

In the case of drugs in a parcel, packet or other container in D's physical control, D is in possession of those drugs if he knows that he is in control of that container and that it contains something, even though he thinks that the thing is something different in kind from a drug and even though he has no right to open the container to check its contents.

Possession, once begun, continues as long as the thing is in the person's control, even though he has forgotten about it or mistakenly believes it has been destroyed or disposed of.

Although it is not necessary to prove that a minimum or usable quantity of a controlled drug was unlawfully in D's possession, D must have been in possession of a quantity of it which was visible, tangible and measurable. Persons who are found under the influence of a drug are not then in possession of it for the purposes of this offence, even though traces of it are found in a blood or urine sample. This is because, once consumed, the thing changes its character and can no longer be considered a controlled drug. However, evidence of the presence of a drug in a blood or urine sample can be given to support an allegation of possession of the drug in its true state at some earlier time, ie before it was taken into the body.

Defence

A person is not criminally liable for the unlawful possession of a controlled drug contrary to MDA 1971, s 5(2) in the circumstances outlined by s 5(4).

Section 5(4) provides that if it is proved that D had a controlled drug in his possession it is a defence for D to prove that:

(a) knowing or suspecting it to be a controlled drug, he took possession of it for the purpose of preventing another from committing or continuing to commit an offence in connection with that drug and that as soon as possible after taking possession he took all such steps as were reasonably open to him to destroy the drug or to deliver it into the custody of a person lawfully entitled to take custody of it; or

(b) knowing or suspecting it to be a controlled drug, he took possession of it for the purpose of delivering it into the custody of a person lawfully entitled to the custody of it and that as soon as possible after taking possession of it he took all such steps as were reasonably open to him to deliver it into the custody of such a person.

Despite the fact that MDA 1971, s 5(4) requires D to 'prove' a defence under it, it would seem likely from a House of Lords decision that all D has to do is to adduce sufficient evidence to raise the defence, whereupon it will be for the prosecution to prove beyond reasonable doubt that the defence is not made out.

Possession with intent to supply

MDA 1971, s 5(3) provides offences of having a controlled drug in one's possession, whether lawfully or not, with intent to supply it unlawfully to another. It need not be proved that D knew the identity of the substance. The defence under s 28 (p 872) applies to such an offence.

The Court of Appeal has held that the intended supply must be a supply in the UK.

The Court of Appeal has also held that, to come within s 5(3), the intention to supply (of someone in possession of a controlled drug) has to be an intention to supply *the* thing of which he was then in possession. Thus, it held that where D intended to supply cannabis plants then in his possession when they reached maturity in a few months' time there was no offence under s 5(3).

An offence of possession with intent to supply may be committed by persons who are lawfully in possession in the first instance. For example, it can be committed by a doctor who is in possession of drugs lawfully, but forms an intention to supply them unlawfully (eg merely for profit, as opposed to bona fide treatment). However, the offence is usually committed by drug pushers and the like.

In terms of proving that possession was with intent unlawfully to supply, evidence of drug-related paraphernalia, evidence of an extravagant lifestyle, and evidence of the possession of large amounts of cash *which are prima facie explicable only if derived from drug dealing* are relevant—but not conclusive—to the issue of *intent to supply* but not normally to the issue of possession. A case where such evidence might be relevant to possession, as well as to intent to supply, is where there is evidence of frequent brief visits by different young people, who then leave carrying small packages, and when the premises (whose occupant is long-term unemployed) are searched large sums of money and some drugs are found. Such evidence may be admitted as evidence that the occupant knew of the drugs and was in control of them (ie in possession) as well as of an intent to supply them.

Whilst evidence in the form of documents relating to transactions and cash in D's possession is relevant, the relevance of the cash in D's possession must be related to evidence of ongoing (and not merely previous) drug transactions in order for it to be admissible. Evidence which shows that D has supplied drugs in the past is potentially admissible under the 'bad character' provision in the Criminal Justice Act 2003, s 101(1)(d) (see condition (d) on p 264).

Cultivation of cannabis

MDA 1971, s 6(2) states that it is an offence unlawfully to cultivate any plant of the genus *Cannabis*. The only lawful cultivation of cannabis is that authorised by a licence issued by the Secretary of State. The defence under s 28 (p 872) applies to an offence under s 6(2).

'Cultivate' indicates some form of attention to the plant during the process of its growth. A person who puts seeds in the ground cultivates, as does he who hoes, waters, prunes or generally cares for a plant during the process of its growth. It is doubtful if a person could be held to have cultivated plants merely because he failed to remove those which were growing wild but this would depend upon the circumstances. If they were deliberately preserved, by caring for the ground in which they were growing, this would amount to the type of care which could be described as cultivation.

Medical necessity

The defence of duress of circumstances is not available to a defendant in relation to offences of cultivation, production, possession, or possession with intent to supply cannabis or resin, where his purpose is to alleviate pain arising from an illness.

Smoking of opium

MDA 1971, s 9 prohibits a person from:

(a) smoking or otherwise using prepared opium; or
(b) frequenting a place used for the purpose of opium smoking; or
(c) having in his possession:
(i) any pipes or other utensils made or adapted for use in connection with the smoking of opium, being pipes or utensils which have been used by him or with his knowledge and permission in that connection or which he intends to use or permit others to use in that connection; or
(ii) any utensils which have been used by him or with his knowledge or permission in connection with the preparation of opium for smoking.

The defence under s 28 (below) applies to an offence under s 9.

'Prepared opium' is opium prepared for smoking and includes dross and any other residue remaining after opium has been smoked.

'Frequenting a place' means to go there often. There is no requirement that a person who frequents a place used for opium smoking must have been shown to have been involved in opium smoking. The place does not need to be a building. Proof that it is used as an opium den will be necessary.

Statutory defence

MDA 1971, s 28 provides a defence in relation to charges contrary to s 4(2) (unlawful production), s 4(3) (unlawful supply), s 5(2) (unlawful possession), s 5(3) (possession with intent to supply), s 6(2) (unlawful cultivation of cannabis), and s 9 (smoking opium, etc). For convenience, the defence will be explained in relation to the offence of unlawful possession but what is said will be equally applicable (with the appropriate changes of words) to the other offences just mentioned.

Assuming that the prosecution has proved that D was in unlawful possession of a controlled drug, he can be convicted of that offence, even though it is not proved that he knew that what was in possession was a controlled drug. However, s 28 provides D with a defence in the circumstances outlined below. Although s 28 says that D has to prove the defence, the House of Lords has held that s 28 should be read as simply imposing an evidential burden on D so as to make it compatible with the presumption of innocence under the European Convention on Human Rights, art 6(2). The result is that, provided that sufficient evidence is adduced to raise a defence under s 28, the defence will succeed unless the prosecution proves beyond reasonable doubt that its terms are not satisfied.

The basic definition of the defence is contained in s 28(2), which states that it is a defence for D to 'prove' that *he neither knew of, nor suspected, nor had reason to suspect* the existence of some fact alleged by the prosecution which it is necessary for the prosecution to prove if he is to be convicted of the offence charged. (This does not affect the need for the prosecution to prove the element of knowledge required to establish 'possession'.)

This provision is subject to a qualification, provided by s 28(3), where D alleges, and 'proves', that he did not know, suspect or have reason to suspect that the thing in question was the controlled drug alleged, and proved, by the prosecution to have been involved. In this case, such 'proof' by D is not enough to give him a defence. In order to be acquitted D must also 'prove' one of two things:

(a) that he neither believed nor suspected, nor had reason to suspect, that the thing in question was a controlled drug at all; or

(b) that he believed that the thing in question was a controlled drug which he was, in fact, legally entitled to possess (or supply or produce, etc as the case may be).

Controlled drugs on premises

A person commits an offence under MDA 1971, s 8 if, being the occupier or concerned in the management of any premises, he knowingly permits or suffers any of the following activities to take place on those premises:

(a) unlawfully producing or attempting to produce a controlled drug;

(b) unlawfully supplying or attempting to supply a controlled drug to another, or offering to supply a controlled drug unlawfully to another;

(c) preparing opium for smoking; or

(d) smoking cannabis, cannabis resin or prepared opium.

There must be proof that the conduct in (a), (b), (c) or (d) actually occurred; merely giving tacit approval in advance is insufficient.

The occupier

To be 'the occupier' a person does not have to be a tenant or have an estate in the premises. A person is the occupier of premises if he is entitled to exclusive possession of them, in the sense that he has the requisite degree of control over them to exclude from them those who might otherwise carry on one of the forbidden activities there. Thus, a student who had a room in a college hostel was held to be the occupier of it because his contractual licence gave him such exclusivity of possession, whether or not he was entitled to exclude the college authorities. If there is drug-taking in a house, and it is knowingly permitted by the householder (ie 'the occupier'), he commits an offence under s 8. However, he would not commit that offence if, in his absence and unknown to him, his teenage son knowingly permitted drug-taking on the premises. Nor would the son be guilty of an offence under s 8 on the basis of being 'the occupier' of the premises since he would not have that status. Nevertheless, depending on the circumstances, the son might be guilty of an offence under s 8 on the basis of 'being concerned in the management of the premises', to which phrase we now turn.

Concerned in management

A person 'concerned in the management of premises' is anyone who is concerned in exercising control over the premises or in running or organising them on a day-to-day basis. It is possible that such a person will have some control over who shall be permitted to enter the premises and who shall not, but this is not a prerequisite for a person to be concerned in their management. If drug-taking was generally permitted on the premises of a club, it is possible that only the general manager would have the right to permit entry but other officials of the club might control activities in different rooms. If drug use is generally and knowingly permitted, then all who are concerned in any way in the management of the premises (ie the general manager and other officials) would be guilty of this offence.

Persons who occupy premises as trespassers (and are therefore not 'occupiers' for the purpose of the offence) might nevertheless be concerned in the management of those premises. For example, if drug-taking activities are organised upon premises by squatters, all concerned in that organisation are guilty of the present offence.

Premises

MDA 1971 does not define the term 'premises'. The term should be given its normal, everyday meaning, and in this sense 'premises' includes any form of building and the grounds in which a building stands and also land without any building on it. Therefore, the organiser of an open-air pop festival who knowingly permitted one of the activities described above would (as a person concerned in the management of the premises) be guilty of the present offence, as would the occupier of the site if he knowingly permitted one of these activities.

Knowingly permits or suffers

'Permit' and 'suffer' are synonymous. In law, a person only permits or suffers something to occur if, physically and legally, he could prevent it but does not do so. The Court of Appeal has held that 'permit' (and presumably 'suffer') require proof of unwillingness to prevent the prohibited activity, which can be inferred from failure to take reasonable steps readily available to prevent it. The fact that D believed that he had taken reasonable steps to prevent the prohibited activity is irrelevant.

The inclusion of the word 'knowingly' is an important point. As mentioned in Chapter 1, 'knowledge' may (not must) be inferred from wilful blindness, ie suspecting what is going on but deliberately refraining from making inquiries.

On a charge of permitting the premises to be used for producing or supplying a controlled drug, it is not necessary for the prosecution to prove more than that D 'knew' of the production or supply of a controlled drug; it need not be proved that D knew that it was the particular type of controlled drug supplied. It remains to be seen whether, on a charge of permitting the smoking of cannabis, D could be convicted even if he thought that cannabis resin or opium was being smoked, and so on.

Powers

Inspection

MDA 1971, s 23(1) empowers a constable, or other person authorised by the Secretary of State, to enter the premises of a business producing or supplying controlled drugs and to demand and inspect any books or documents relating to dealings in them and to inspect any stocks of them. By s 23(4), it is an offence to conceal from such a person any such books, documents, stocks or drugs, or to fail without reasonable excuse to produce such books or documents when demanded.

Search, seize and detain

MDA 1971, s 23(2) provides that, if a constable has reasonable grounds to suspect that any person (P) is in *possession of a controlled drug in contravention of MDA 1971 or of any regulations or temporary class drug orders thereunder*, the constable may:

(a) search P, and detain him for the purpose of searching him;
(b) search any vehicle or vessel in which the constable suspects that the drug may be found, and for that purpose require the person in control to stop it;
(c) seize and detain, for the purpose of proceedings under MDA 1971, anything found in the course of the search which appears to the constable to be evidence of an offence under MDA 1971.

It must be emphasised that the exercise of these powers depends upon there being reasonable grounds to suspect possession of a controlled drug in contravention of MDA 1971 or regulations or orders. As to this requirement of reasonable suspicion, see p 40.

As noted on p 869, simple possession of a temporary class drug is not a contravention of MDA 1971. Therefore, s 23(2) does not apply to it. For this reason, s 23A provides a further power to search, seize and detain in relation to temporary class drugs which applies where a constable has reasonable grounds to suspect that a person (P) is in *possession of a temporary class drug*, and it does not appear to the constable that a power under s 23(2) applies to the case. Section 23A provides that in such a case the constable may exercise the powers under (a) and (b) above and may seize and detain anything found in the course of the search *which appears to the constable to be a temporary class drug* or to be evidence of an offence under MDA 1971. If a constable reasonably believes that anything so detained is a temporary class drug but is not evidence of any offence under MDA 1971, the constable may dispose of the drug in such manner as he thinks appropriate.

A temporary class drug order may provide for circumstances where a person's possession of a temporary class drug is to be treated as 'excepted possession' for the purposes of MDA 1971. If any provision has been made about excepted possession by a temporary class drug order that applies to the temporary class drug in question, the powers in s 23A apply only if the constable has no reason to believe that P's possession of the drug is to be treated as excepted possession.

The above powers to search a person must extend to searching things in his immediate possession, for example a suitcase or a holdall. If this was not so the power to search persons would be totally ineffective.

In a case where there had been forcible use of emetics to induce vomiting by a man suspected of swallowing 'bubble wraps' of cocaine, the European Court of Human Rights held that forcible medical intervention to obtain evidence had to be *necessary* otherwise the European Convention on Human Rights, art 3 (prohibition of inhuman or degrading treatment) will be contravened. The court considered that in the circumstances it would have been possible to wait for the natural discharge of the 'bubbles'.

Search warrant

MDA 1971, s 23(3) authorises a justice to grant a search warrant if satisfied by information on oath that there is a reasonable ground for suspecting that controlled drugs are, in contravention of MDA 1971 or any regulations or temporary class drug orders thereunder, in the possession of a person on any premises, or that a document directly or indirectly relating to drug dealing is in the possession of persons on any premises. The warrant will name the particular premises, and it is only those premises (and persons in them) which may be searched on its authority. If necessary, force may be used to enter the premises.

If there is reasonable ground for suspecting that an offence has been committed in relation to any controlled drugs found on the premises or in the possession of anyone there, or that a document so found directly or indirectly relates to drug dealings, the drugs or document may be seized and detained.

A divisional court has held that, where a search warrant has been issued under both MDA 1971 and PACE, and the warrant refers to both persons and premises, MDA, s 23 provides the power to detain persons for the purpose of a search and PACE, s 117 provides the power to use reasonable force for the purpose of executing the warrant, including moving persons to one room while another is searched.

Additional powers of seizure

The additional powers of seizure provided by the Criminal Justice and Police Act 2001, ss 50 and 51 apply where a search is made under the power in MDA 1971, s 23(2) or where a search warrant under s 23(3) is executed.

Obstruction

It is an offence intentionally to obstruct a person, or a constable, in the execution of his powers under MDA 1971, s 23 or s 23A, respectively (s 23(4), s 23A(6)).

Seizure and forfeiture of drug-cutting agents

The Serious Crime Act 2015, Part 4 (ss 52–65) and Sch 2 sets out provisions relating to the seizure and forfeiture of drug-cutting agents. A substance is a 'drug-cutting agent' if it is added to a controlled drug in connection with the supply or exportation of the drug. Drug cutting agents are dealt with in Chapter 31 on the companion website.

Travel restrictions on drug trafficking offenders

The Criminal Justice and Police Act 2001, s 33 empowers a court to make a 'travel restriction order' where a person has been convicted of a 'drug-trafficking offence' relating to a controlled drug and he is sentenced to four years' or more imprisonment. Such an order prohibits the offender from leaving the UK at any time after his release from prison until such date as is set out in the order. It is an indictable (either way) offence, contrary to s 36(1), to leave the UK while subject to a travel restriction.

For further detail see Chapter 31 on the companion website.

PSYCHOACTIVE SUBSTANCES

Introduction

The Psychoactive Substances Act 2016 (PSA 2016) creates a blanket ban on the production, distribution, sale and supply of psychoactive substances.

PSA 2016, s 2 defines a 'psychoactive substance' for the purposes of the Act as any substance which:

(a) is capable of producing a psychoactive effect in a person who consumes it; and
(b) is not an exempted substance (see below).

For these purposes, a substance produces a psychoactive effect in a person if, by stimulating or depressing his central nervous system, it affects his mental functioning or emotional state.

Schedule 1 excludes the following 'exempted substances' from the definition: controlled drugs; medicinal products; alcohol or alcoholic products; nicotine; tobacco products; caffeine or caffeine products; any substance which is ordinarily consumed as food or drink, and does not contain a prohibited ingredient (ie any psychoactive substance which is not naturally occurring in the substance, and the use of which in or on food is not authorised by an EU instrument). In the case of the alcoholic, nicotine and caffeine products mentioned, the relevant exemption does not apply if they contain any psychoactive substance other than alcohol, nicotine or caffeine, as the case may be.

The list of exempted substances can be amended by regulations.

For the purposes of PSA 2016, a person consumes a substance if he causes or allows the substance, or fumes given off by the substance, to enter his body in any way.

Offences

PSA 2016, ss 4 and 5 and 7–9 contain the following provisions about indictable (either way) offences relating to psychoactive substances. Exceptions to those offences are provided by s 11.

Production

A person commits an offence contrary to PSA 2016, s 4(1) if:

(a) he intentionally produces a psychoactive substance;
(b) he knows or suspects that the substance is a psychoactive substance; and
(c) he intends to consume the psychoactive substance for its psychoactive effects, or knows, or is reckless as to whether, it is likely to be consumed by some other person for its psychoactive effects.

For the purposes of PSA 2016, any reference to producing a substance is a reference to producing it by manufacture, cultivation or any other method.

Supply

A person commits an offence contrary to PSA 2016, s 5(1) if:

(a) he intentionally supplies a substance to another person;
(b) the substance is a psychoactive substance;
(c) he knows or suspects, or ought to know or suspect, that the substance is a psychoactive substance; and
(d) he knows, or is reckless as to whether, the psychoactive substance is likely to be consumed by the person to whom it is supplied, or by some other person, for its psychoactive effects.

A person (D) commits an offence contrary to s 5(2) if:

(a) D offers to supply a psychoactive substance to another person (R); and
(b) D knows or is reckless as to whether R, or some other person, would, if D supplied a substance to R in accordance with the offer, be likely to consume the substance for its psychoactive effects.

For the purposes of (b), the reference to a substance's psychoactive effects includes a reference to the psychoactive effects which the substance would have if it were the substance which D had offered to supply to R.

For the purposes of PSA 2016, any reference to supplying a substance includes a reference to distributing.

Possession with intent to supply

A person commits an offence contrary to PSA 2016, s 7(1) if:

(a) he is in possession of a psychoactive substance;
(b) he knows or suspects that the substance is a psychoactive substance; and
(c) he intends to supply the psychoactive substance to another person for its consumption, whether by any person to whom it is supplied or by some other person, for its psychoactive effects.

For the purposes of PSA 2016, the items which are in a person's possession include any items which are subject to his control, but in the custody of another person.

With the exception of the following offence, 'simple possession' of a psychoactive substance is not an offence.

Possession of a psychoactive substance in a custodial institution

A person commits an offence contrary to PSA 2016, s 9(1) if:

(a) he is in possession of a psychoactive substance in a custodial institution;
(b) he knows or suspects that the substance is a psychoactive substance; and
(c) he intends to consume the psychoactive substance for its psychoactive effects.

A 'custodial institution' means a prison, young offender institution, secure training centre, secure college, juvenile justice centre, remand centre, removal centre, short-term holding facility or pre-departure accommodation, or similar custodial accommodation.

Importing or exporting a psychoactive substance

A person commits an offence contrary to PSA 2016, s 8(1) if:

(a) he intentionally imports a substance;
(b) the substance is a psychoactive substance;
(c) he knows or suspects, or ought to know or suspect, that the substance is a psychoactive substance; and
(d) he intends to consume the psychoactive substance for its psychoactive effects, or knows, or is reckless as to whether, the psychoactive substance is likely to be consumed by some other person for its psychoactive effects.

A person commits an offence contrary to s 8(2) if he intentionally exports a substance, and (b), (c) and (d) just mentioned are satisfied.

Where a person imports or exports a controlled drug suspecting it to be a psychoactive substance, he is treated for the purposes of s 8 as if he had imported or exported a psychoactive substance suspecting it to be such a substance. 'Controlled drug' has the same meaning as in the Misuse of Drugs Act 1971.

Exceptions to above offences

PSA 2016, s 11 provides that it is not an offence for a person to carry on any listed activity if, in the circumstances in which it is carried on by him, the activity is an exempted activity. The listed activities are producing, supplying, offering to supply, possessing with intent to supply, possessing in a custodial institution, or importing or exporting, a psychoactive substance.

An 'exempted activity' means an activity listed in Sch 2, ie:

(a) any activity carried on by a person who is a health care professional and is acting in the course of his profession;
(b) any activity carried on for the purpose of, or in connection with the supply to, or the consumption by, any person of a substance prescribed for that person by a health care professional acting in the course of his profession or in accordance with the directions of a health care professional acting in the course of his profession;
(c) any activity carried on in respect of an active substance by a person who is registered in accordance with the Human Medicines Regulations 2012, reg 45N, or is exempt from any requirement to be so registered;

(d) any activity carried on in the course of, or in connection with, approved scientific research.

Powers for dealing with prohibited activities

PSA 2016, ss 12–35 contain powers for dealing with prohibited activities in respect of psychoactive substances. These are powers for a 'senior officer' or a local authority to give prohibition notices or premises notices and for a court to make prohibition orders or premises orders.

In PSA 2016, 'senior officer' means a police inspector (or above), a designated NCA officer of grade 3 (or above) or a general customs official of the grade of higher officer (or above), and 'local authority' means a county council, district council or the like.

Meaning of 'prohibited activity'

The following are a 'prohibited activity':

(a) producing a psychoactive substance that is likely to be consumed by individuals for its psychoactive effects; or
(b) supplying, offering to supply, importing or exporting such a substance; or
(c) assisting or encouraging the carrying on of a prohibited activity referred to in (a) or (b),

unless the carrying on of that activity would not be an offence under PSA 2016 by virtue of s 11.

Prohibition notices (s 13)

A prohibition notice is a notice requiring the person (P) to whom it is given not to carry on any prohibited activity or a prohibited activity of a description specified in the notice. A prohibition notice may not be given to someone under 10.

A senior officer or a local authority may give a prohibition notice if the senior officer or local authority reasonably believes:

(a) that P is carrying on, or is likely to carry on, a prohibited activity; or
(b) that it is necessary and proportionate to give the notice to prevent P from carrying on any prohibited activity.

A notice given to someone under 18 must specify the period for which it has effect, and may not have effect for more than three years.

Premises notices (s 14)

A premises notice is a notice requiring the person (P) to whom it is given to take all reasonable steps to prevent any prohibited activity, or a prohibited activity of a description specified in the notice, from being carried on at any premises specified in the notice that are owned, leased, occupied, controlled or operated by P.

For the purposes of s 14 (and ss 20 and 22 (p 881)), a person (other than a mortgagee not in possession) 'owns' premises if he is the freeholder or the lessor of them under a lease of three years or more.

'Premises' in PSA 2016 has the same meaning as in PACE (see p 66).

A premises notice may not be given to an individual who is under 18.

A senior officer or a local authority may give a premises notice to P if:

(a) (i) the senior officer or local authority reasonably believes that a prohibited activity is being, or is likely to be, carried on at particular premises, and

(ii) P owns, leases, occupies, controls or operates the premises; and
(b) that officer or authority reasonably believes that it is necessary and proportionate to give the premises notice to prevent any prohibited activity from being
carried on at any premises owned, leased, occupied, controlled or operated by P.

General points about prohibition notices and premises notices

A notice must set out the grounds for giving it, and explain the possible consequences
of not complying with the notice.

A prohibition or premises notice, or notice that it has been withdrawn, takes effect
when it is given. It may be given to a person by handing it to him, leaving it at his proper
address, posting it to him at that address or (in specified circumstances) sending it to the
person by electronic means.

Prohibition orders

A prohibition order is an order prohibiting the person (P) against whom it is made
from carrying on any prohibited activity or a prohibited activity of a description specified in the order (s 17). A prohibition order may be made on application or by a court
dealing with someone following conviction of an offence under any of PSA 2016, ss 4,
5, 7 and 8 or a related offence.

Prohibition orders on application (s 18)

An adult magistrates' court (youth court if P is under 18) may make a prohibition order
against P if:

(a) the court is satisfied on the balance of probabilities that P has failed to comply with
a prohibition notice; *or*
(b) where no prohibition notice has been given (or one has been withdrawn), the court
is satisfied on the balance of probabilities that P is carrying on, or is likely to carry
on, a prohibited activity, and considers that P would fail to comply with a prohibition notice; and in either case
(c) the court considers it necessary and proportionate to make the order to prevent P
from carrying on any prohibited activity.

If a prohibition order is based on (a) having been met, the prohibition notice is deemed
withdrawn.

A prohibition order under s 18 may not be made against someone under 10. An
order against someone under 18 at the time of the order must specify the period for
which it has effect, and may not take effect for more than three years.

Prohibition orders following conviction (s 19)

Where a court is dealing with a person who has been convicted of a relevant offence, it
may add a prohibition order to the sentence if it considers that it is necessary and proportionate to prevent him from carrying on any prohibited activity.

If a court makes a prohibition order under s 19, any prohibition notice given to
the person against whom the order is made is deemed withdrawn. A s 19 prohibition
order against someone under 18 must specify its period of effect (maximum three
years).

In s 19, 'relevant offence' means an offence under any of ss 4, 5, 7 or 8 (pp 877–8),
an offence of being an accomplice to such an offence, or an offence of encouraging or
assisting, conspiring, or attempting, to commit such an offence.

Premises orders (s 20)

A premises order is an order against an adult that requires the person (P) against whom it is made to take all reasonable steps to prevent any prohibited activity, or a prohibited activity of a description specified in the order, from being carried on at any premises specified in the order that are owned (p 879), leased, occupied, controlled or operated by P. A magistrates' court may make a premises order against a person if:

(a) the court is satisfied on the balance of probabilities that P has failed to comply with a premises notice; *or*

(b) where no premises notice has been given (or one has been withdrawn):
   (i) the court is satisfied on the balance of probabilities that a prohibited activity is being, or is likely to be, carried on at particular premises,
   (ii) P owns, leases, occupies, controls or operates the premises, and
   (iii) the court considers that P would fail to comply with a premises notice if given; and in either case

(c) the court considers it necessary and proportionate to make the premises order for the purpose of preventing any prohibited activity from being carried on at any premises owned, leased, occupied, controlled or operated by P.

If a court makes a premises order based on (a) having been met, the premises notice is deemed withdrawn.

Applications for prohibition orders and premises orders

An application for a prohibition order under s 18 or a premises order may be made only by the chief officer of police for a police area, by the chief constable of the British Transport Police Force, by the Director General of the NCA, by the Secretary of State by whom general customs functions are exercisable, or by a local authority. However, where an application is made based on a failure to comply with a prohibition notice or a premises notice given by a senior officer (or by a local authority), the application must be made by the chief officer, etc, Director General, Secretary of State or local authority of whose force, organisation, etc the senior officer is a member (or by that authority, as the case may be).

Provision that may be made by a prohibition order or premises order

Under s 22, a court making a prohibition order or a premises order, or varying such an order, may impose any prohibitions, restrictions or requirements that it considers appropriate (in addition to the prohibition referred to in s 17 or the requirement referred to in s 20, as the case may be).

The prohibitions that may be imposed on a person by a prohibition order or a premises order include, for example, an 'access prohibition', ie a prohibition prohibiting access to premises owned (p 879), occupied, leased, controlled or operated by the person for a 'specified' period (ie specified in the order) not exceeding three months (or six months if subsequently extended by the court). An access prohibition may prohibit access:

(a) by all persons, or by all persons except those specified, or by all persons except those of a specified description;

(b) at all times, or at all times except those specified;

(c) in all circumstances, or in all circumstances except those specified.

By s 23, an authorised person (a constable, a person authorised by the chief officer of police or the BTP chief constable, a general customs official, or a person authorised by the Director General of the NCA, by a local authority or by the Secretary of State with a customs function) may enter premises in respect of which an access prohibition is in effect, and do anything necessary to secure the premises against entry; reasonable force may be used.

Someone seeking to enter premises under the above power must, if required to do so by the occupier of the premises or by another person appearing to be in charge of the premises in the occupier's absence, give his name, and (if not a uniformed constable) produce documentary evidence that he is an authorised person. An authorised person may also enter premises in respect of which an access prohibition is in effect to carry out essential maintenance or repairs to the premises.

Offence of failing to comply with a prohibition order or premises order

A person (D) against whom a prohibition order or a premises order is made commits an offence contrary to s 26(1) by failing to comply with the order. D does not commit the offence if he took all reasonable steps to comply with the order, or there is some other reasonable excuse for the failure to comply (s 26(3)).

Offence of failing to comply with an access prohibition, etc

Where a prohibition order or a premises order imposes an access prohibition:

(a) a person (D), other than the person against whom the order was made, who without reasonable excuse remains on or enters premises in contravention of the prohibition commits an offence contrary to s 27(1) and (2);

(b) a person who without reasonable excuse obstructs a person enforcing (under s 23) the prohibition commits an offence contrary to s 27(1) and (3).

Variation and discharge

A prohibition order or a premises order may be varied or discharged by a court, normally the one which made the order.

Nature of proceedings

Proceedings before a court arising by virtue of the above provisions, including those relating to a prohibition order following conviction, are civil proceedings, and the standard of proof to be applied by the court in the proceedings is the balance of probabilities (s 32(1) and (2)). The court is not restricted to considering evidence that would have been admissible in the criminal proceedings in which the person concerned was convicted (s 32(3)). See further p 684.

Special measures

The Youth Justice and Criminal Evidence Act 1999 (YJCEA 1999), ss 16–33C (special measures directions in the case of vulnerable and intimidated witnesses: p 236) applies with necessary modifications to relevant proceedings under PSA 2016, ss 18, 20 and variation and discharge proceedings as it applies to criminal proceedings.

Information society services providers

PSA 2016, Sch 4 contains special rules to ensure that the provisions relating to the offence of offering to supply a psychoactive substance under s 5(2) and the prohibition notices and orders provisions (insofar as they impact on such providers) are compatible with the EU's E-Commerce Directive where an international element relating to an EEA member state is involved.

Powers of entry, search and seizure

PSA 2016, ss 36–54 contain enforcement powers.

Power to stop and search persons

By PSA 2015, s 36, a constable, designated NCA officer or general customs official who has reasonable grounds to suspect that a person has committed, or is likely to commit, an offence under any of PSA 2016, ss 4, 5 and 7–9 or 26 (failing to comply with prohibition order or premises order) may search the person for evidence that such an offence has been committed, and stop and detain him for that purpose. These powers may be exercised in any place to which the constable, etc lawfully has access (even if the public does not).

Power to enter and search vehicles

PSA 2016, s 37 provides that a constable, general customs official or designated NCA officer (C) who has reasonable grounds to suspect that there is evidence in a vehicle that an offence under any of PSA 2016, ss 4, 5 and 7–9 or 26 has been committed may at any time enter the vehicle and search it for such evidence, and for this purpose may stop and detain the vehicle. This power does not apply if the vehicle is a dwelling.

Where a vehicle has been stopped under this power, and C considers that it would be impracticable to search the vehicle in the place where it has stopped, C may require the vehicle to be taken to such place as he directs to be searched. In addition, C may require anyone travelling in a vehicle, or its registered keeper, to afford such facilities and assistance with respect to matters under that person's control as C considers would facilitate the exercise of any of the above powers.

These powers under s 37 may be exercised in any place to which C lawfully has access (even if the public does not).

In s 37, 'vehicle' does not include any vessel or aircraft.

Section 38 contains similar powers in respect of boarding and searching vessels and aircraft.

Power to enter and search premises

PSA 2016, s 39 provides that, where a justice is satisfied that the requirements below are met in relation to any premises (p 879), he may issue a search warrant authorising *a relevant enforcement officer* (a constable, designated NCA officer, general customs official or local authority officer) to enter the premises, and to search them for 'relevant evidence' (evidence that an offence under any of PSA 2016, ss 4, 5, 7–9 or 26 has been committed).

As in the case of a warrant under PACE (p 72), such a warrant may be either a 'specific-premises warrant' or an 'all-premises warrant'.

The requirements referred to above are met in relation to premises if there are reasonable grounds to suspect that there are items on the premises that are relevant evidence, and, in a case where the premises are specified in the application, that any of the following conditions is met:

(a) that it is not practicable to communicate with any person entitled to grant entry to the premises;

(b) that it is not practicable to communicate with any person entitled to grant access to the items;

(c) that entry to the premises is unlikely to be granted unless a warrant is produced;

(d) that the purpose of entry may be frustrated or seriously prejudiced unless a relevant enforcement officer arriving at the premises can secure immediate entry to them.

Section 40 and Sch 3 contain provisions about a search warrant under PSA 2016 which correspond with the provisions of PACE, ss 15 and 16 (see pp 77–81). The only notable differences are that entry and search must be within one month from its date of issue, that it refers to a relevant enforcement officer wherever those sections refer to a constable, and that the reference to an inspector (or above) in PACE, s 16 (p 879) is replaced by a reference to a 'senior officer' (as defined on p 80). As a result of this correspondence, for example, s 40 provides that the warrant may authorise persons to accompany any relevant enforcement officer who executes it.

Powers of examination, etc

Where a relevant enforcement officer is exercising a power of search conferred by s 37, 38 or 39 in relation to any premises, he has power under PSA 2016, s 41 to examine anything that is in or on the premises, and to measure or test (including taking a sample from a live plant) anything which he has such power to examine.

For the purpose of exercising a power of search conferred by s 37, 38 or 39, or any power conferred by s 41, the officer may, so far as is reasonably necessary for that purpose, break open any container or other locked thing.

The officer may require any person in or on the premises to afford such facilities and assistance with respect to matters under that person's control as the officer considers would facilitate the exercise of a power of search conferred by s 37, 38 or 39, or any power conferred by s 41.

Power to require production of documents, etc

Where a relevant enforcement officer is exercising a power of search conferred by PSA 2016, s 37, 38 or 39 in relation to any premises, he has power under s 42 to require any person in or on the premises to produce any document or record that is in the person's possession or control. 'Produce any document' includes a reference to the production of a hard copy of information recorded otherwise than in hard copy form, or information in a form from which a hard copy can be readily obtained.

Powers of seizure, etc

A constable, general customs official or designated NCA officer who is exercising the power of search conferred by PSA 2016, s 36 may seize and detain anything found in the course of the search. Where a relevant enforcement officer is exercising such a power of search in relation to any premises, or is otherwise lawfully on premises, he may seize and detain or remove any item found on the premises, and take copies of or extracts from any document or record found on them.

A relevant enforcement officer to whom any document or record has been produced in accordance with a requirement under s 42 may seize and detain or remove that document or record, and take copies of or extracts from it.

These powers, provided by s 43, may only be exercised for the purposes of determining whether an offence under any of ss 4, 5, 7–9 or 26 has been committed, or in relation to an item which a relevant enforcement officer reasonably believes to be (a) evidence that such an offence has been committed, or (b) a psychoactive substance (whether or not it is relevant evidence).

There is no power under s 43 to seize an item which is an excluded item, ie items subject to legal privilege, excluded material and special procedure material (all of which are defined on pp 73–4) (s 44).

Further provision about seizure under s 43

Where:

(a) any items which a relevant enforcement officer wishes to seize and remove are in a container; and

(b) the officer reasonably considers that it would facilitate the seizure and removal of the items if they remained in the container for that purpose,

any power to seize and remove the items conferred by s 43 includes power under s 45 to seize and remove the container.

If a container is seized under s 45, reasonable efforts must be made to return it to the person from whom it was seized, or (if different) a person to whom it belongs, unless the container appears to be of negligible value, or if it is not practicable for the container to be returned, or while the container is or may be needed for use as evidence at a criminal trial.

If, in the opinion of a relevant enforcement officer (O), it is not for the time being practicable for O to seize and remove any item, O may require:

(a) the person from whom the item is being seized; or

(b) where O is exercising a power of search conferred by s 37, 38 or 39 in relation to any premises, any person in or on the premises,

to secure that the item is not removed or otherwise interfered with until such time as O may seize and remove it.

Where a relevant enforcement officer, or a person accompanying a relevant enforcement officer, seizes any item under s 43, s 46 provides as follows. When the item is seized, the officer (O) must make reasonable efforts to give written notice to each of the following persons:

(a) in the case of an item seized from a person, the person from whom it was seized;

(b) in the case of an item seized from premises, any person who appears to O to be their occupier or otherwise to be in charge of them;

(c) if O thinks that the item may belong to any person not falling within (a) or (b), that other person.

If the item is seized from premises, and at that time it is not reasonably practicable to give a notice to any affected person (ie a person falling within any of (a)–(c)), O must leave a copy of the notice in a prominent place on the premises. The notice must state what has been seized and the reason, specify any offence which O believes has been committed, and explain the effect of ss 49–51 and 53 (p 886). O must make a record of what has been seized. If a person appearing to a relevant enforcement officer to be an affected person asks for a copy of that record, the officer must, within a reasonable time, provide a copy of that record to that person.

Powers of entry, search and seizure: supplementary provisions

A relevant enforcement officer (or a person authorised under s 40 to accompany him) may use reasonable force, if necessary, for the purpose of exercising any power conferred by ss 36–45 (or ss 39–45) respectively (s 47).

Offences in relation to enforcement officers

A person commits an offence contrary to PSA 2016, s 48(1) if, without reasonable excuse, he intentionally obstructs a relevant enforcement officer in the performance of any of the officer's functions under ss 36–45.

A person commits an offence contrary to s 48(2) if:

(a) he fails without reasonable excuse to comply with a requirement reasonably made, or a direction reasonably given, by a relevant enforcement officer in the exercise of any power conferred by ss 37–45; or
(b) he prevents any other person from complying with any such requirement or direction.

The above references to a relevant enforcement officer include a reference to a person authorised under s 40 to accompany a relevant enforcement officer.

Retention and disposal of items

Retention of seized items

By PSA 2016, s 49, an item seized under s 43 may be retained so long as is necessary in all the circumstances. In particular, it may be retained for use as evidence at a trial for an offence under PSA 2016, or for forensic examination or for investigation in connection with an offence under PSA 2016, unless a photograph or a copy would suffice.

Power of police, etc to dispose of seized psychoactive substances

PSA 2016, s 50 provides that, if:

(a) a constable, general customs official or designated NCA officer (C) has seized an item found during the course of a search under s 36, 37 or 38;
(b) the search was carried out in a place to which C lawfully had access without a warrant;
(c) C reasonably believes that the item (i) is a psychoactive substance which, if it had not been seized, was likely to be consumed by an individual for its psychoactive effects, but (ii) is not evidence of any offence under this Act; and
(d) C has no reason to believe that, at the time of the seizure, the item was being used for the purposes of, or in connection with, an 'exempted activity' (see s 11 (p 878)) carried on by the person from whom it was seized or, (if different) any person to whom it belongs,

C may dispose of the item in whatever way C thinks suitable.

Forfeiture of seized items by court on application

A relevant enforcement officer may apply under PSA 2016, s 51 to an adult magistrates' court (or youth court where the individual to whom the application relates is under 18) for the forfeiture of an item retained under s 49. See, further, Chapter 31 on the companion website.

Return of item to person entitled to it, or disposal if return impracticable

PSA 2016, s 53 deals with this.

Where the retention of an item has been, but is no longer, authorised under PSA 2016, the item must normally be returned to a person entitled to it, and a magistrates' court (or youth court, as the case may be) must, if asked to do so by a person entitled to the item, order it to be returned to him. See, further, Chapter 31 on the companion website.

CHAPTER 32

Theft and Related Offences, Robbery, and Blackmail

THEFT

The Theft Act 1968 (TA 1968), s 1(1) provides that a person is guilty of theft if he dishonestly appropriates property belonging to another with the intention of permanently depriving the other of it. Theft is an indictable (either way) offence, except that low-value shoplifting (goods not in excess of £200 in value) is triable only summarily unless the defendant (D) is 18 or over and elects trial in the Crown Court. Any reference in PACE to an indictable offence has effect as if it included low-value shoplifting.

By TA 1968, s 30, the leave of the DPP is required for the institution of proceedings for the theft by one spouse or civil partner of the other's property, unless, by virtue of any judicial decree or order, the spouses were not obliged to cohabit at the material time or an order is in force providing for the separation of the civil partners, as the case may be.

Theft is a 'penalty offence' for the purposes of the Criminal Justice and Police Act 2001: see p 31. This may be an appropriate course of action in cases of low-level shoplifting.

It is immaterial whether the appropriation is made with a view to gain, or is made for the thief's own benefit. Thus, a postman who flushes postal packets down the lavatory to avoid delivering them, or who takes them to give to his son, is as guilty of theft as if he had taken them for his own benefit. The terms of the definition of theft in TA 1968, s 1(1) are defined, in whole or part, by ss 2 to 6.

For the purposes of exposition, it is best to start by noting that to be guilty of theft D must be proved:

(a) to have appropriated property belonging to another; and
(b) to have done so dishonestly and with the intention of permanently depriving the other of it.

Appropriation

TA 1968, s 3(1) describes appropriation as any assumption by a person of the rights of an owner, and this includes, where he has come by the property (innocently or not) without stealing it, any later assumption of a right to it by keeping or dealing with it as owner.

The essence of this definition is an 'assumption of the rights of an owner'. An owner of property has many rights in relation to it, including the rights to use it, to destroy it, to give it away, to sell it and so on. The House of Lords has held that, despite the use of the words 'the rights' at the beginning of s 3(1), s 3 as a whole indicates that an appropriation does not require an assumption of all the rights of an owner and that it is enough that there has been an assumption of any of the rights of the owner.

The House of Lords has ruled that an act amounting to an assumption of a right of the owner done with the authority or consent of the owner can amount to an appropriation of goods for the purposes of TA 1968.

An appropriation can occur even though the assumption is only momentary. It has been held, for example, that there was an appropriation where a man wrested a bag from a woman's grasp, even though he then dropped it on the ground and did not make off with it.

A shopper who removes goods from a shelf in a supermarket and conceals them in his shopping bag thereby appropriates them (because this amounts to an assumption of one of the rights of the owner of the goods), and so does someone who simply puts goods in a supermarket basket without concealing them. In both cases, however, the person concerned would not be guilty of theft if he intended to pay at the checkout because he would not appropriate the goods dishonestly.

Switching the price labels on articles in a shop, so that a lesser price than the true price is paid at the cash desk, amounts to an assumption of the owner's right to fix the price, and therefore to an appropriation.

Someone can appropriate property even though he never possesses it, as where, pretending to be the owner, he points to another's car and offers to sell it (because he has assumed the owner's right to sell). On the other hand, the Court of Appeal has held, a person who has never had possession or control of property but who deceives his victim into transferring it to a third party does not thereby appropriate it.

There may also be an appropriation through an innocent agent. If a person in authority signs a false invoice, intending that innocent people take further steps which result in money being debited and thus appropriated from a bank account, he is guilty of theft.

Appropriation by those already in possession

A person can appropriate property even though he is already in possession or control of it. This is made clear by the latter part of TA 1968, s 3(1), which provides that 'appropriation' includes, where D 'has come by the property (innocently or not) without stealing it, any later assumption of a right to it by keeping or dealing with it as owner'. It follows that a shop assistant who sells goods at less than the marked price thereby appropriates them because he has assumed the owner's right to fix the price. A car-hirer who sells, or—even—offers to sell, the car thereby appropriates the car because he assumes the right of the owner to sell it.

The latter part of s 3(1) can lead to the conviction of a person who originally came by the property dishonestly without stealing it. Suppose that D helps himself to V's umbrella in order to go out during a shower but intending to return it. D does not steal the umbrella at that stage because, although he has appropriated it, he did not then intend permanently to deprive V. However, if D subsequently decides to keep the umbrella or to sell it, and does so, he is then guilty of theft because his later assumption of a right to it by keeping or dealing with it as owner constitutes an appropriation which is accompanied by an intent permanently to deprive V.

An express exception

TA 1968, s 3(2) excludes a particular type of case, which falls within the definition in s 3(1), from being an appropriation. It provides that, where property or a right or interest in property is or purports to be *transferred for value* to a person *acting in good faith*, no later assumption by him of rights which he believed himself to be acquiring shall, by reason of any defect in the transferor's title, amount to theft of the property. The effect of s 3(2) is that, if X steals goods from V and sells them to D who neither knows nor suspects that they are stolen, a refusal by D to restore the goods (or his actual disposal of them) after his discovery of the theft by X is not theft by him from V.

Property

By TA 1968, s 4(1), 'property' includes money and all other property, real or personal, including things in action and other intangible property.

'Real property' means land and things forming part of the land, such as plants and buildings, and rights in it. Although land and things forming part of the land are 'property' for the purposes of theft, there are special provisions (below) restricting the theft of them.

'Personal property', in its tangible sense, means movable things which can be owned, such as cars, computers and television sets.

A 'thing in action' is intangible property. It is a personal right of property which can only be enforced by a legal action, and not by taking possession. Its inclusion in the definition of 'property' means that someone who dishonestly assumes a right of ownership over a thing in action, such as a debt, copyright or trade mark, with the intention of permanently depriving the person entitled to it, is guilty of theft. Thus, if D dishonestly assigns to X a debt owed to D and his partner, V, in order to defeat V's rights, D is guilty of the theft of a thing in action belonging to V. Where a bank account is in credit the bank owes a debt to its customer for the amount of that credit. Consequently, if D dishonestly draws cheques on V's account and uses the proceeds for his own purposes, D can be convicted of the theft of property belonging to V because he will have appropriated a thing in action (the debt) owned by V when he presents the cheque.

'Other intangible property' covers such things as gas stored in pipes, which is undoubtedly capable of being stolen, and patents.

Despite the wide terms of s 4(1), there are some things which do not, or may not, come within the definition and hence cannot be stolen. A live human body is not property because it can never be owned. The same is true in relation to a human corpse. However, where a corpse (or part of a corpse) has undergone the application of human skill (such as embalming or dissecting) it becomes property. Thus, for example, an anatomical or pathological specimen which has been embalmed or dissected for exhibition or teaching purposes is property for the purposes of s 4.

It has been held that confidential information, such as a trade secret, is not property for the purposes of theft, so that the mere abstraction of the information is not theft, and it has also been held that electricity is not property for such purposes and cannot be stolen. There is, however, a separate offence of abstracting electricity (see p 897).

Land and things forming part of the land

TA 1968, s 4(2) provides that a person cannot steal land, or things forming part of land and severed from it by him or by his directions, except in the following cases:

(a) when he is a trustee or personal representative, or is authorised by power of attorney, or as liquidator of a company, or otherwise, to sell or dispose of land belonging to another, and he appropriates the land or anything forming part of it by dealing with it in breach of the confidence reposed in him; or

(b) when he is not in possession of the land and appropriates anything forming part of the land by severing it or causing it to be severed, or after it has been severed; or

(c) when, being in possession of the land under a tenancy, he appropriates the whole or any part of any fixture or structure let to be used with the land.

TA 1968, s 4(3) goes on to provide that a person who picks mushrooms growing wild on any land, or who picks flowers, fruit or foliage from a plant growing wild on any land, does not (although not in possession of the land) steal what he picks, unless he does it for reward or for sale or other commercial purposes. For these purposes, 'mushroom' includes any fungus, and 'plant' includes any shrub or tree.

These provisions can be explained as follows:

(1) Land as a whole cannot be stolen except where the appropriator is of a defined class and acts in a defined way. The class of appropriators comprises a trustee or personal representative, or a person authorised by power of attorney, or as a liquidator of a company, or otherwise, to sell or dispose of land belonging to another. The defined mode of appropriation is dealing with the land in breach of the confidence reposed in the appropriator. The result of the rule that land as a whole cannot be stolen except by a trustee, etc is that a person cannot steal land as a whole by moving a boundary fence or by occupying it as a squatter. The appropriation of land in such a way must be dealt with by civil process, or in the case of a residential building by a prosecution for the offence of squatting in such a building (see p 741).

(2) Things forming part of the land, such as soil, houses, bricks in a wall, and fixtures, can only be stolen in the following cases:

(a) As for land as a whole, by the defined persons in the defined way.

(b) Where a person not in possession of the land appropriates the thing by severing it or causing it to be severed. If a trespasser digs up gravel, removes bricks from a building, digs up growing things, picks flowers from a cultivated plant, cuts hay, or cuts down trees or their branches, or causes such severance to be done, he may be convicted of theft (although it will generally be more appropriate to charge him with, and convict him of, criminal damage).

The present provision (s 4(2)(b)) does not apply to the picking of *wild* mushrooms or fungi nor to picking *from wild* plants and the like, notwithstanding that there has been a severance. Such conduct is dealt with by s 4(3), whereby picking wild mushrooms or other fungi, or picking flowers, fruit or foliage *from* a plant, shrub or tree growing wild, by a person not in possession of the land cannot amount to theft unless it is done for reward or for sale or other commercial purpose.

Thus, wild mushroom gathering cannot amount to theft if it is done by a person who picks the mushrooms for his own use, but it can if done for sale. Likewise, picking a few sprigs of holly for use at home cannot be theft, but it can if done for reward (eg payment by a florist). The term 'pick from' does not include uprooting or sawing off the top of a Christmas tree; both are clear cases of severance covered by s 4(2)(b) and unaffected by s 4(3).

As Christmas approaches, police officers become increasingly involved in the protection of growing things which are a traditional part of Christmas decorations. Vehicles carrying Christmas trees should be accompanied by delivery notes issued by the Forestry Commission or the landowner in question. If they are not, there is reason to suspect that the trees have been stolen.

It should be noted that a person who gathers or plucks any part of a 'protected' wild plant without uprooting thereby commits an offence under the Wildlife and Countryside Act 1981, s 13. These matters are referred to in Appendix 4 on the companion website.

(c) Generally, a person in possession of land under a tenancy cannot steal things forming part of the land. Thus, he cannot be convicted of theft if he digs up a plant on the land, or picks blackberries from wild plants on the land in order to sell them. The only exception relates to the whole or part of any structure or fixture let to be used with the land; such is stealable by the tenant. The obvious example of a 'structure' is a building but the term also includes a wall or bridge. A 'fixture' is an article, such as a washbasin or fireplace, which is attached to the land or to a building so as to make a permanent improvement to the land or building; by law it becomes part of the land.

The result of all this is that a tenant may be convicted of theft if he demolishes the garage on the land of which he is a tenant, or if he removes a fireplace there in order to sell it.

For the above purposes, 'tenancy' means any tenancy regardless of whether it is a long lease or a weekly tenancy, and includes an agreement for such a tenancy. A person who remains as a statutory tenant after the end of his tenancy is treated as being in possession under a tenancy.

Of course, once a thing has been severed from the land it ceases to be part of the land and may thereafter be the subject of theft in the same way as any other piece of personal property, which it has become. In other words, the special provisions of TA 1968, s 4(2) and (3) no longer apply to it.

Wild creatures

TA 1968, s 4(4) states that wild creatures, whether tamed or untamed, are to be regarded as property, but that a person cannot steal a wild creature, not tamed or ordinarily kept in captivity, or the carcase of any such creature, unless either it has been reduced into possession by or on behalf of another person and possession of it has not since been lost or abandoned or another person is in course of reducing it into possession.

Section 4(4) distinguishes two groups of wild creatures:

Wild creatures which have been tamed or are ordinarily kept in captivity   Such a creature can be stolen in the same ways as any other property. Thus a person may be guilty of theft by dishonestly appropriating a tamed fox or a bear from a zoo.

Wild creatures neither tamed nor ordinarily kept in captivity   Such a creature or its carcase cannot normally be stolen but becomes 'stealable':

(a) if reduced into possession by or on behalf of another (in which case it remains 'stealable' so long as possession has not subsequently been lost or abandoned); or
(b) if another person is in course of reducing it into possession.

Thus, it is not theft to poach game on another's land, unless for instance the game is taken from a sack into which another, even another poacher, has put the product of his own shooting (because there has been a reduction into possession by another) or is picked up from the ground where it is lying after it has been shot by another but not yet picked up by him (because another is in the course of reducing it into his possession). For the above purposes, possession of a live wild creature is abandoned if the possessor allows it to escape from his possession; it is lost if a wild creature not ordinarily kept in captivity escapes of its own volition. Possession of the carcase of a wild creature is not lost by a person who mislays it. Although s 4(4) means that poachers are not normally thieves, there are other offences which they commit, mentioned in Appendix 5 on the companion website.

Belonging to another

The property appropriated must belong to another when appropriated.

The basic rule

TA 1968, s 5(1) states that property is regarded as belonging to any person having possession or control of it, or having in it any proprietary right or interest (not being an equitable interest arising only from an agreement to transfer or grant an interest). Possession or control need not be lawful. Thus, the appropriation of a drug in the unlawful possession of V can amount to theft.

Normally, it is obvious whether the property appropriated belonged to another person. If a wallet is taken from V's pocket it quite clearly belongs to V, since he will almost certainly be its owner (and complete ownership is the clearest example of a proprietary right) and, anyway, it will be in his possession. If goods are taken from a shop they clearly belong to the proprietor of the shop for the same reasons. When there are joint owners of property, one of them will steal from the other if he dishonestly assumes one of the rights of the owner, because the property will also belong to the other co-owner under s 5(1).

Someone who leaves his clock to be repaired still owns it and therefore it still belongs to him. The repairer now has possession of the clock, and, if it is then handed to one of his assistants to effect the repair, that assistant has control of it. The clock can now be stolen from either the owner, the repairer, or his assistant, and it can be stolen by one of these from the other. For example, if the assistant takes the clock to the pub at lunchtime and sells it, he thereby appropriates property belonging to another (to the owner and to the repairer, since the clock is technically still in the repairer's possession). Likewise, if the owner sneaks into the repairer's shop and takes away the clock without paying for the repair he appropriates property belonging to another.

A person who mislays property nevertheless still retains ownership of it, and he also retains possession until the property comes into the possession of another. Thus, 'lost property' is still capable of being stolen. This must be contrasted with the situation where the property has been abandoned. When a person throws away his old bicycle, not caring what happens to it (ie he abandons it), he loses ownership and possession of it. Since the property has no owner or possessor, it cannot thereafter be stolen unless and until it comes into the possession or control of another. It would be different if a tyre punctured and the owner placed the cycle behind a hedge before setting off for a repair kit. The bicycle would not be abandoned because the owner cares about what may happen to it, and it therefore still belongs to him.

Property subject to a trust

Where property is subject to a trust, it is regarded as belonging to the beneficiaries (who have a proprietary interest in it) as well as to the trustees, with the result that trustees who appropriate trust property can be convicted of stealing it from the beneficiaries.

Charitable trusts and certain other types of trust do not, in law, have beneficiaries, with the result that under s 5(1) the trust property belongs only to the trustees. To prevent trust property being unprotected in such a case against appropriations by the trustees, s 5(2) provides that, where property is subject to a trust, the persons to whom it belongs shall be regarded as including any person having a right to enforce the trust, and that an intention to defeat the trust shall be regarded accordingly as an intention to deprive of the property any person having that right. In the case of a charitable trust, the Attorney General, although not a beneficiary, has the right to enforce the trust, so that appropriation of a charitable trust fund by the trustees is capable of amounting to theft since the fund belongs to the Attorney General under s 5(2).

Property received under an obligation to retain and deal with it in a particular way

TA 1968, s 5(3) provides that, where a person receives property from or on account of another and is under an *obligation* (ie a legal obligation) to the other to *retain* and *deal* with that property, or *its* proceeds (ie things into which it has been converted), *in a particular way*, the property or proceeds shall be regarded (*as against him*) as belonging to the other. This is important where ownership, possession and control of the property have been transferred to the recipient.

The essence of s 5(3) is that property (usually money) or its proceeds is regarded (as against the defendant (D)) as belonging to another from or on whose account D has received the property if D is under a *legal obligation* to that person *to retain and deal* with the property or its proceeds *in a particular way*. Section 5(3) is clearly satisfied where D receives money from V which he is legally obliged to V to use in a particular way (eg to pay it into a Christmas Club which D runs), or where D is legally obliged to V to use in a particular way the proceeds of money received from V (eg to use the money to get some goods for V and bring them to V). In the latter case, both the money and the goods (its proceeds) will belong to another (V) under s 5(3). Section 5(3) is also satisfied if a shop assistant receives money from a customer for some of his employer's goods, since he has received the money on account of another (the employer) and is under a legal obligation to deal with it in a particular way (to put it in the till); as against D, the money will belong to the employer. On the other hand, s 5(3) is not satisfied where D, a decorator, is given a down-payment on a job by a customer. D is obliged to the customer to do the job, but not to retain and deal with the money in a particular way.

Property got by another's mistake

TA 1968, s 5(4) states that where a person gets property by another's mistake, and is under an obligation to make restoration (in whole or in part) of the property or its proceeds or of the value thereof, then to the extent of that obligation the property or proceeds shall be regarded (as against him) as belonging to the person entitled to restoration, and an intention not to make restoration shall be regarded accordingly as an intention to deprive that person of the property or proceeds.

The important point about this provision is that it only applies where the recipient of property transferred under a mistake is thereby under an immediate *legal obligation* to restore it (or its proceeds or value). For practical purposes, this provision is only of importance where the recipient was ignorant of the mistake when he got the property and he has acquired ownership, possession and control of the property to the exclusion of anyone else. If he was aware of the mistake when he got the property he could be convicted of theft on the basis that his appropriation at that time was accompanied by mens rea. On the other hand, if the recipient only discovers the mistake later, but decides not to return the property his appropriation with mens rea will be of property which is then in his ownership, possession and control. Section 5(4) provides that if the recipient is under an obligation to restore the property, its proceeds or value, the property is regarded (as against him) as belonging to the person entitled to restoration.

The best example of a case of a legal obligation to make restoration, where a person has received ownership, possession and control of property under a mistake, is where money is paid under a mistake which leads the transferor to believe that the transferee is legally entitled to the money. Thus, if V, by a mistake as to the number of hours of overtime worked, overpays his employee, D, and D, realising the mistake, appropriates the excess amount, D has appropriated money which by s 5(4) belongs to another. If D in such a case is paid by cheque and cashes the cheque and appropriates the cash received, he will appropriate property belonging to another under s 5(4) because the cash will be the proceeds of the cheque and D would be obliged to make restoration of it to V. On the other hand, if V is induced to give D some money as a gift by a self-induced mistaken belief that D is destitute, D cannot be convicted of theft if he appropriates the money on discovering V's mistake because, the requirements of s 5(4) not having been met (since D is not legally obliged to make restoration of the money), the money will not belong to another (ie other than D) when D appropriates it.

Property of a corporation sole

TA 1968, s 5 contains one other provision, s 5(5), which can be disposed of briefly. Section 5(5) provides that the property of a 'corporation sole', such as a bishop, a chief constable or a police and crime commissioner in his official capacity, shall be regarded as belonging to the corporation notwithstanding a vacancy in the corporation. Thus, the property of a police and crime commissioner 'belongs to another', and is therefore capable of being stolen, even though the commissioner has just died and not yet been replaced by a successor.

Dishonesty

The appropriation of property belonging to another must be committed dishonestly.

TA 1968, s 2(1)

Section 2(1) expressly and as a matter of law excludes appropriations carried out with certain states of mind from being dishonest. Section 2(1) provides that a person's appropriation of property belonging to another is *not* to be regarded as dishonest:

(a) if he appropriates the property in the belief that he has in law the right to deprive the other of it, on behalf of himself or a third person; or

(b) if he appropriates the property in the belief that he would have had the other's consent if the other knew of the appropriation and the circumstances of it; or

(c) (except where the property came to him as a trustee or personal representative) if he appropriates the property in the belief that the person to whom the property belongs cannot be discovered by taking reasonable steps.

These provisions are concerned with the defendant's belief. *It is legally irrelevant that a belief in this context is unreasonable*, although, of course, magistrates or a jury are less inclined to accept an alleged belief as truly held if it is an unreasonable one.

Belief in legal right to deprive   By s 2(1)(a), the element of dishonesty is excluded if a person appropriating property belonging to another *believes* that he has a *right in law* to deprive the other of it, whether on behalf of himself or a third person. If D, who is owed money by V, takes some of V's property to the equivalent value, mistakenly believing that he has a legal right to do so to recoup the debt, he is not guilty of theft.

Where a person acts under a belief in a *moral* right to deprive, the question of his dishonesty depends on the two-stage test described below.

Belief that the 'owner' would have consented if he had known   Section 2(1)(b) (belief that the person to whom the property belongs would have consented if he had known of the appropriation and its circumstances) clearly covers the case, for example, of someone who takes a bottle of lager from a flatmate's room, leaving the price behind him and believing that his flatmate would have consented had he known all the circumstances.

Belief that the 'owner' cannot be discovered by taking reasonable steps Section 2(1)(c) is primarily concerned with those who find property belonging to another. It exempts D from dishonesty if he appropriates another's property under a *belief* that the person to whom the property belongs cannot be discovered by taking reasonable steps. The question is not whether the 'owner' could not be found by taking reasonable steps, but whether D believed this.

If D finds a £5 note in the street and appropriates it, it will be almost impossible to disprove a claim by him that he believed the owner could not be found by taking reasonable steps. It will be different if the note is contained in a purse bearing the owner's name and address (or containing other material identifying the owner); in that case it will be much easier to disprove a claimed belief that the owner could not be found by taking reasonable steps.

The exemption is not restricted to things which are found. Suppose that D's friend, on emigrating, left property under D's care until he should return to this country. If, after many years, during which D has not heard from his friend, D sells the property, honestly believing that he will not return and that he cannot be traced by taking reasonable steps, D will not be guilty of theft.

Section 2(1)(c) expressly does not apply to a person who received the property as a trustee of property or a personal representative. This is sensible in view of the special obligations of such a person.

Dishonesty in cases outside s 2(1)

The negative definition of dishonesty in TA 1968, s 2(1) is only a partial definition; consequently, a defendant's appropriation may not have been made dishonestly even though the case falls outside s 2(1). Whether or not a defendant who appropriated property with some alleged state of mind other than one of the three referred to in s 2(1) did so dishonestly is a question of fact for the jury. This means that, unlike the situation in which a belief of the type referred to in s 2(1) is pleaded (where the judge must tell the jury that in law an appropriation with such a belief is not dishonest), it is not for the judge to tell the jury whether or not an appropriation with the alleged state of mind is dishonest but for the jury to decide this according to the following two-stage test.

In deciding this, the jury must first see whether, given his state of mind, D's actions were dishonest according to the ordinary standards of reasonable and honest people. If his actions were not dishonest according to those standards, the matter ends there and the prosecution fails. However, if his actions were dishonest by those standards, the jury must go on to decide whether D must have realised that what he was doing would be considered dishonest according to the standards of reasonable and honest people. If D did not realise this, his appropriation will not have been dishonest; if he did it will have been.

Where a theft charge is tried in a magistrates' court the two-stage test is, of course, applied by the justices.

TA 1968, s 2(2)

For the sake of completeness, it should be mentioned that TA 1968, s 2(2) says what has already been implied, by providing that an appropriation may be dishonest notwithstanding that D intends to pay for what he took. If a collector fails to purchase a valuable antique at an auction, his appropriation would almost certainly be found to be dishonest if he took the antique from the home of the successful bidder and left money in payment, even if that money represented a reasonable purchase price. It has been held that an appropriation can be dishonest even though the original owner of goods or money is not the poorer because of D's conduct.

Intention permanently to deprive

The dishonest appropriation of property belonging to another must be accompanied by an intention permanently to deprive the other of that property.

An intent permanently to deprive will usually be proved by evidence of what D did with the property appropriated. If D takes V's £5 note and spends it on drink this clearly indicates an intent permanently to deprive V of the note as D has passed the note into circulation. It is no use D alleging that he intended to pay it back. Although this may prevent him being found to have been dishonest, and lead to an acquittal on that ground, D will nevertheless have intended permanently to deprive V of the thing (the actual £5 note) which he has appropriated. If a car is appropriated and a false registration book is produced, and the engine and chassis numbers are altered, this is clear evidence of an intent permanently to deprive.

In certain limited cases a person can be convicted of theft even though he did not mean permanently to deprive, and even though he positively intended to return the property at some future date (or did actually return it). A conviction in such a case is possible if the case falls within TA 1968, s 6, which extends the meaning of 'intention of permanently depriving'.

Section 6(1) provides that a person appropriating property belonging to another without meaning the other permanently to lose the thing itself is nevertheless to be regarded as having the intention of permanently depriving the other of it if his *intention is to treat the thing as his own to dispose of regardless of the other's rights;* and a borrowing or lending of it may amount to so treating it if, but only if, the borrowing or lending is for a period and in circumstances making it equivalent to an outright taking or disposal.

Treating as one's own to dispose of regardless of other's rights

The first part of s 6(1) is the key part. It operates to 'deem' a person to have intended permanent deprivation if he intended to treat the thing as his own to dispose of regardless of the other's rights.

One type of case which may be caught by the first part of s 6(1) is that where D takes V's property, intending to return it to V only if a condition is fulfilled by V. In such a case, this does not automatically mean that D intends to treat the property as his own to dispose of regardless of V's rights, but depending on the facts he may do so. The position is that, if the condition attached by D to the return of the property is one which would not be fulfilled or would not be fulfilled in the foreseeable future, the circumstances may well amount to an intention to treat the property as D's own to dispose of regardless of V's rights, and hence to an intention permanently to deprive. On the other hand, if the condition can readily be fulfilled and may be fulfilled in the near future, this may well not amount to an intention to treat the property as D's own to dispose of regardless of V's rights, and therefore not be an intention permanently to deprive.

Another type of case which may fall within s 6(1) is where D abandons the property and is indifferent as to whether it is recovered by the person to whom it belongs. If, by the circumstances of the abandonment and/or the nature of the property, it is (to D's knowledge) extremely unlikely that the property will be recovered, D can be said to intend to dispose of it regardless of the rights of the other. If V's car is taken and driven a distance of 200 miles by D then abandoned, the justices or jury are most unlikely to find that there was an intention to treat it as D's own to dispose of regardless of V's rights, as a car is easily identifiable and will certainly be returned to V. It would be different if what was taken and so abandoned was a watch.

Borrowing or lending

The second part of s 6(1) goes on to provide that a borrowing or lending may amount to treating property as one's own to dispose of regardless of the other's rights, if the borrowing or lending is for a period and in circumstances which make it equivalent to an outright taking or disposal. The Court of Appeal has ruled that this provision is only satisfied by a borrower if his intention is to return the thing only when 'all its goodness or virtue has gone'.

Suppose that D takes V's monthly season ticket, intending to return it at the end of the month. D's borrowing is clearly for a period and in circumstances making it equivalent to an outright taking since, when it is returned, the season ticket will be a virtually worthless piece of paper. Because the borrowing is equivalent to an outright taking or disposal, D's intention so to act is regarded by s 6(1) as an intent to treat as his own to dispose of regardless of V's rights and, hence, as an intent permanently to deprive.

On the other hand, a cinema projectionist who borrows a film in order to make pirate copies does not intend to treat the film as his own to dispose of regardless of the owner's rights because on its return the film would not have lost all of its goodness or virtue.

An example of a case where a lending would satisfy the present provision would be where D, an assistant in a florist's, lends some cut flowers to X for a week for a flower display, knowing that they will have died by the time of their return. D intends to treat the flowers as his own to dispose of because, as he knows, the lending is for a period and in circumstances making it equivalent to an outright disposal.

Parting with property subject to a condition

Section 6(2) provides a further explanation of 'treating as one's own to dispose of regardless of the other's rights'. It states that, where a person having possession or control (lawfully or not) of property belonging to another, parts with the property under a condition as to its return which he may not be able to perform, this (if done for purposes of his own and without the other's authority) amounts to treating the property as his own to dispose of regardless of the other's rights. Thus, where D, who is in possession of V's property, pawns it, intending to redeem it and return it if he wins a bet, this amounts to treating as his own to dispose of regardless of the rights of the other (V) and his intention to do so is deemed by s 6(1) to be an intention permanently to deprive V of it.

ABSTRACTING ELECTRICITY

As already indicated, it has been held that electricity is not property and therefore cannot be stolen. However, a special indictable (either way) offence is provided by TA 1968, s 13, which states that a person who dishonestly uses without due authority, or dishonestly causes to be wasted or diverted, any electricity is guilty of an offence.

The offence will usually be encountered when a person, who has had his electricity supply disconnected, reconnects it, and thus uses electricity without authority; or when evidence is found that a consumer has by-passed his meter, since his authority to use electricity supplied by the electricity company is conditional upon that electricity having passed through the meter before use.

Section 13 covers wasting or diverting in addition to using, as where D diverts electricity for use by another. It seems that the person who by-passes his meter could be charged with either dishonest use or dishonest diversion, as he does not have authority to use in that way and he has certainly caused electricity to be diverted.

Section 13 is not restricted to mains electricity.

It is important not to forget that the element of dishonesty must be proved. The provisions of TA 1968, s 2 are limited to theft, and therefore do not apply to an offence under s 13, but the rest of the above explanation of dishonesty for the purposes of theft applies equally to an offence under s 13.

DISHONESTLY OBTAINING ELECTRONIC COMMUNICATIONS SERVICE, AND POSSESSION OR SUPPLY OF APPARATUS FOR DOING SO

It is an offence under the Communications Act 2003 (CA 2003), s 125 dishonestly to obtain an electronic communications service with the intention of avoiding payment of a charge in respect of that service. However, s 125 exempts the dishonest obtaining of a broadcasting or cable programme service provided from a place in the UK.

It is an offence under CA 2003, s 126(1) to possess or have under one's control anything that may be used for obtaining an electronic communications service, or in connection with obtaining such a service, with certain specified intentions. The specified intentions are an intent: to use the thing to obtain such a service dishonestly; to use it for a purpose connected with the dishonest obtaining of such a service; dishonestly to allow it to be so used; or to allow it to be used for a purpose connected with the dishonest obtaining of such a service. Once again, s 126 exempts dishonestly obtaining a broadcasting or cable programme service provided from a place in the UK. Section 126(2) also prohibits the supply, or offer to supply, of anything which may be used to commit the above offence where the supplier knows or believes that the person supplied, etc has one of the above intentions.

These offences are indictable (either way) offences.

ROBBERY

Under TA 1968, s 8(1), a person is guilty of robbery (an offence triable only on indictment) if he steals, and immediately before or at the time of doing so, and in order to do so, he uses force on any person, or puts or seeks to put any person in fear of being then and there subjected to force.

No theft: no robbery

Robbery is an aggravated form of theft, the theft being aggravated by the use of force or threat of force. If there is no theft, there is no robbery. Where a person uses or threatens force in order to steal but has not achieved the appropriation of any property, and is therefore not guilty of robbery, he can be convicted of the offence of assault with intent to rob, which is triable only on indictment. There can be no conviction for robbery if it is found that the person who used or threatened force in order to appropriate the property believed that he had a legal right to it, even though he did not believe he was entitled to use force to obtain it, because the essential ingredient for theft, 'dishonesty', is missing. Of course, there can be a conviction for some offence of assault (other than assault with intent to rob).

Use or threat of force immediately before or at time of theft

To constitute robbery, the force must be used or threatened 'immediately before or at the time of' the theft. There can be no robbery if force is only used or threatened after 'the time' of the theft. A person who pushes a woman to the ground in order to steal her handbag, and does so, commits robbery; so does someone who approaches her and steals her handbag by threatening to punch her in the face unless she hands it over. The first uses force at the time of the theft and the other threatens force immediately before the theft. However, a man who steals a woman's handbag without force but, being discovered by her in possession of the bag several minutes afterwards, assaults her, cannot be convicted of robbery. This is because the time of the theft will have elapsed when the force is used. He could, of course, be convicted of theft and assault. The 'time' of the theft is not limited to the split second during which the appropriation with mens rea initially occurs, since an act of appropriation may be a continuing one. The 'time' of the theft lasts as long as the theft can be said still to be in progress in commonsense terms, ie so long as the defendant is 'on the job'. On this basis, there can be a robbery, for example, where a shoplifter takes goods from a supermarket shelf and, when approached by a store security guard, uses force on him in order to remove the goods.

Use of force on a person or threat then and there to subject to force

Where force is used, it must be used 'on' a person, but it has been held that the force need not be used directly against the person. Consequently, it is enough to use force to obtain possession of property in the physical possession of another. For example, the use of force to wrest a handbag from a woman's grasp is robbery. Minimal force, such as that used to snatch a cigarette from another's fingers, will not suffice.

In the case of a threat of force, a threat of future force is insufficient; the threat must be 'then and there' to subject another to force. A threat of force to property will not suffice, nor will the actual use of force against it.

The references above to threats of force are a shorthand way of referring to the requirement that D 'puts or seeks to put any person in fear of being then and there subjected to force'. These words must not be forgotten. If D threatens violence to a month-old baby in a pram unless the mother parts with her money, this is not robbery because D cannot be said to have put or sought to put the mother in fear of immediate force to herself.

Although the force must be used or threatened on a person, it is not essential that the theft is carried out in his presence, provided that it is used or threatened for the purpose of stealing. It is robbery, for example, where a security guard is tied up so that property may be removed from some other part of the warehouse in which he is on duty.

The theft need not be from the person against whom the force is used or threatened. Thus, if D threatens a married couple that he will stab the wife unless the husband hands over his wallet, D can be convicted of robbery.

Use or threat of force in order to steal

The force used or threatened must be used in order to steal. If a man during an argument with another, threatens to give him a beating and the man threatened gives money to him not to do so, this cannot be robbery as the threat of force was not made with the intention of stealing. Likewise, a man who knocks a woman to the ground to rape her, but who then changes his mind and instead takes the handbag which she has dropped, is not guilty of robbery or of assault with intent to rob.

REMOVAL OF ARTICLES FROM PLACES OPEN TO THE PUBLIC

Because theft requires an intention permanently to deprive another of his property, a charge of theft would fail against an art lover who takes a painting from a public gallery, intending to enjoy its presence in his home for a year and thereafter to return it. For this reason, TA 1968, s 11 creates an indictable (either way) offence to cover cases such as this. Section 11(1) provides that, where the public have access to a building in order to view the building or part of it, or a collection or part of a collection housed in it, any person who without lawful authority removes from the building or its grounds the whole or part of any article displayed or kept for display to the public in the building, or that part of it, or in its grounds, is guilty of an offence.

The removal of an article must be either from a building to which the public have access in order to view the building or part of it, or a collection or part of a collection housed in it, or from the grounds of such a building. The offence is therefore concerned with removals of articles from stately homes, galleries, historic buildings, etc which are open to the public in the above sense, or from their grounds. A person who removes the portrait of an Edwardian mayor from the entrance of the town hall does not commit the present offence because, although the public have access to the town hall, it is only for the purpose of paying council tax, making inquiries or seeing their councillors; they do not have access in order to view the building, or any collection in it, or any part of the building or collection. If someone removes a painting from a collection in a stately home, access to which is limited to members of the Women's Institute, he does not commit the present offence because the public do not have access to the building in question.

The offence is not committed if the collection has been made or exhibited for the purposes of effecting sales or other commercial dealings. Thus, removals of paintings from commercial art galleries are not caught by s 11. Subject to this, it does not matter that the collection in question is one got together for a temporary purpose. The annual art exhibition in the village hall is therefore caught by s 11.

Generally, an offence under s 11 can be committed whether or not the building is open to the public at the time of the removal. There is one exception: if the thing removed is there otherwise than as forming part of, or being on loan for exhibition with, a collection intended for permanent exhibition to the public, it must be removed on a day when the public has access to the building or grounds. Thus, if a painting is removed from the collection at the National Gallery it is irrelevant that the Gallery is then closed over the Christmas period, whereas it is not an offence to remove a painting from the annual art exhibition in the village hall on a day when the hall is closed.

The offence under s 11 only applies where the thing removed is the whole or part of any article displayed or kept for display to the public in the building, or part of it, to which the public have access or in its grounds. If a visitor takes an old vase which forms a part of the display, he commits this offence. If he takes the attendant's coat on the way out he does not, as the coat is not a part of the display.

There must be a removal from the building or its grounds. A visitor who moves the vase from one room to another does not commit the offence, but one who takes it out of the building does.

Section 11(1) makes it clear that no offence is committed where the person removing an article covered by it has lawful authority for doing so.

There is no need to prove dishonesty in respect of the act of removal but s 11(3) exempts someone who believes that he has lawful authority, or that he would have it if the person entitled to give it knew of the removal and its circumstances. Therefore, a furniture-remover who was removing articles on behalf of their owner would not commit an offence if he took one of the exhibited articles, believing that it was one of the items to remove. Likewise, a picture-restorer who carried out work for the owner from time to time would not commit an offence if in the owner's absence he took a painting for its five-yearly restoration, believing that, had the owner been present, he would have consented.

TAKING VEHICLES OR OTHER CONVEYANCES

TA 1968, s 12(1) provides that a person is guilty of an offence if, without having the consent of the owner or other lawful authority, he takes any conveyance for his own or another's use, or, knowing that any conveyance has been taken without such authority, drives it or allows himself to be carried in or on it.

There are two offences under s 12(1): taking a conveyance without authority, and driving or allowing oneself to be carried in or on a conveyance which one knows has been so taken. Neither offence requires proof of an intent permanently to deprive. Section 12 is aimed at 'joy-riders'.

'Conveyance' is defined to include any conveyance constructed or adapted for the carriage of a person or persons whether by land, water or air, but it does not include a conveyance constructed or adapted for use only under the control of a person not carried in or on it, and 'drive' is construed accordingly. 'Conveyance' therefore covers almost all motor vehicles, as well as aeroplanes, hovercraft, boats and ships, but it does not cover pedestrian-controlled vehicles, such as prams and trolleys. Nor does it cover pedal cycles. Pedal cycles are covered by a separate offence (see p 903).

Taking without authority

Taking

The mere unauthorised assumption of possession or control is not enough to constitute a 'taking' of a conveyance; *there must be some movement of it, however small.* Consequently, a person who gets into a car and drives it a few feet takes a conveyance, as does a person who climbs into a boat on a boating lake and rows it to the other bank. On the other hand, people who unlawfully occupy a conveyance, either to shelter or to make love in it, do not take it. Of course, someone who gets into another's car and starts it is attempting to take a conveyance, but as the taking would amount to a summary offence there can be no charge of attempting to take it. In such a case there may be a conviction for the offence of interfering with vehicles (see p 904).

Unauthorised use of a conveyance by a person already in lawful possession or control of a conveyance may amount to a 'taking'. A lorry driver who uses his employer's lorry for his own purposes 'out of hours', or who appropriates it for his own use during the working day in a manner which is inconsistent with the rights of the employer and shows that he has assumed control for his own purposes, thereby 'takes' it. A similar principle applies to a person who has borrowed a conveyance if he uses it for a purpose other than that for which he has been given permission or after the time he is permitted to have the conveyance. By so using the conveyance, he takes it.

For the defendant's or another's use

Section 12(1) also requires that the taking be for D's own or another's use, and this means that either the conveyance must be used as a conveyance or it must be taken for later use as a conveyance. It follows that a person who cuts the mooring rope of a boat and allows it to drift away empty does not commit this offence, whereas he would if he was aboard or if he towed it away for later use as a boat.

Without consent or other authority

The taking must be without the consent of the owner or other lawful authority. An apparent consent to a taking obtained by intimidation is not a true consent, so that the taking will be without consent. On the other hand, a consent which has been obtained by fraud is nevertheless valid and prevents the offence being committed, however fundamental (eg as to the identity of the deceiver) the mistake which is induced.

In relation to a conveyance subject to a hiring or hire-purchase agreement, 'owner' means the person in possession of it under that agreement. It follows that, during the currency of the agreement, such a person cannot commit the present offence in relation to that conveyance since he can hardly be said to take it without the consent of the owner.

The addition of the words 'or other lawful authority' excuses lawful takings, such as the removal by a constable of a vehicle which is causing an obstruction. Finance companies on occasion reclaim vehicles which are on hire-purchase from them when the terms of the agreement have been broken by the hirer, and they will usually have lawful authority to do so under the terms of the agreement.

A mistaken belief in the existence of lawful authority or a mistaken belief that the owner would, if asked, have consented is also a defence.

Driving or allowing self to be carried

In relation to the taking of motor vehicles in particular, but not exclusively, it is frequently the case that, after a conveyance has been taken by one person, it is used to convey a number of persons, each of whom may take a turn at driving. The second offence in s 12(1) deals with this situation, by providing that an offence is committed by anyone who, *knowing* that a conveyance has been taken without the consent of the owner or other lawful authority, drives it or allows himself to be carried in or on it. In circumstances where a vehicle, known to have been 'taken' contrary to s 12(1), is seen to be moving (for it is essential that there is movement in order that a person can be said to be 'carried'), and all the occupants are seen to step out of the vehicle but all deny driving it, the issue of who was driving is unimportant because all have allowed themselves to be 'carried' in the vehicle (since that expression covers a person who was driving).

Where a person takes a vehicle without consent and later picks up a friend and takes him for a drive, his friend commits no offence unless he knows that the vehicle has been so taken. Should the driver disclose that the vehicle has been unlawfully taken in the course of the journey, the passenger is guilty if he continues to allow himself to be carried.

Pedal cycles

Pedal cycles are separately dealt with by s 12(5). Section 12(5) provides that a person commits an offence if, without having the consent of the owner or other lawful authority, he takes a pedal cycle for his own or another's use, or rides a pedal cycle knowing it to have been taken without such authority. What was said earlier about the various elements of the offence under s 12(1) is equally applicable to the present offences.

Aggravated vehicle-taking

TA 1968, s 12A provides indictable (either way) offences of aggravated vehicle-taking. An offence is committed under s 12A(1) where a person has committed *either of the offences under TA 1968, s 12(1)* (the basic offence) in any way in relation to a *mechanically propelled vehicle* and it is proved that, at any time after the vehicle was unlawfully taken (whether by himself or another) and before it was recovered, the vehicle was driven, or injury or damage was caused, in one or more of the following circumstances:

(a) the vehicle was driven in a dangerous manner on a road or other public place; the test of such driving in the Road Traffic Act 1988, s 2A(1) (pp 488–9) applies here;
(b) owing to the driving of the vehicle, an accident occurred by which injury was caused to any person;
(c) owing to the driving of the vehicle, an accident occurred by which damage was caused to any property other than the vehicle; or
(d) damage was caused to the vehicle.

The prosecution does not have to prove that the dangerous driving was by D, or that the injury, damage or accident was caused by D's driving or by D at all. The Supreme Court has held that it is implied in (b) or (c) that it must be proved that there was some element of fault in the driving of the vehicle, whether or not amounting to careless or inconsiderate driving, which contributes in some more than minimal way to the injury or damage. 'Accident' in (b) and (c) includes a situation where a person has deliberately caused injury or damage. Once it is proved that the driving, injury or damage was caused during the period between the taking of the vehicle contrary to s 12(1) and its recovery, D is fixed with liability for an offence contrary to s 12A, unless he has one of the defences referred to in the next paragraph. A vehicle is 'recovered' when it is returned to its owner or other lawful possession or custody.

It is a defence for D to prove that the relevant driving, accident or damage occurred before he committed the basic offence, or that he was neither in, nor on, nor in the immediate vicinity of the vehicle when such driving, accident or damage occurred.

Since the maximum penalty is greater where death is caused, s 12A(1) creates two offences: one where death is caused, and the other for other situations. It has been held that there is nothing to prevent both aggravated vehicle-taking (involving an allegation that the vehicle was driven dangerously) and dangerous driving being charged.

INTERFERENCE WITH VEHICLES

The Criminal Attempts Act 1981 (CAA 1981), s 9(1) provides that D is guilty of the offence of vehicle interference if he interferes with a motor vehicle (p 327) or trailer or with anything carried in or on a motor vehicle or trailer with the intention that an offence of:

(a) theft of the motor vehicle or trailer or part of it;
(b) theft of anything carried in or on the motor vehicle or trailer; or
(c) taking a conveyance, contrary to TA 1968, s 12(1),

shall be committed by himself or some other person. If it can be proved that D intended that one of these offences should be committed, it is immaterial that it cannot be shown which offence it was.

If a group of rowdy youths rock a vehicle in order to set off its intruder alarm, they do not commit an offence under s 9. They certainly interfere with the vehicle but they lack the intention to commit any of the specified offences. On the other hand, if they start to unscrew the aerial or a wing mirror with the intention of stealing it, they commit an offence under s 9. The removal of tarpaulins from goods vehicles carrying loads indicates an interference with the intention to steal part of the load.

If someone is seen trying to open the door of someone else's motor vehicle this is certainly an interference with that vehicle. However, it is unlikely to satisfy a court that he intends to steal or take the vehicle, or to steal anything contained in it, unless there are further circumstances which point to such an intention. Such an intention becomes more apparent as attention is paid by the interferer to more than one vehicle, or he is seen to examine the interior of the vehicle through its windows to check its contents, or even to try a number of doors on the same vehicle. The further the interference extends, the more likely it becomes that there is an appropriate criminal intent.

GOING EQUIPPED TO STEAL

Under TA 1968, s 25(1), a person commits an indictable (either way) offence if, when not at his place of abode, he has with him any article for use in the course of or in connection with any burglary or theft.

The offence can be committed anywhere besides D's place of abode. It has been decided that, where a person lives in a motor vehicle, it is his place of abode whilst on the site where he intends to abide, but that as soon as the vehicle leaves the site he is no longer at his place of abode.

Although the offence is described in the marginal note to s 25 as 'going equipped for stealing, etc', and is commonly so described, it is not limited to conduct which could be described as 'going equipped'. The term 'has with him' has the same meaning as in the Prevention of Crime Act 1953 (PCA 1953) (p 603).

D must intend the article to be used in the future in the course of or in connection with any burglary or theft; it is not necessary to prove that the articles are to be used in connection with any particular burglary or theft. 'Possession' to enable someone else to use the article is sufficient for the purposes of s 25. For the purposes of the present offence, an offence under s 12(1) of taking a conveyance is treated as theft.

If D is found with an article made or adapted for use in committing burglary or theft, proof of the offence under s 25 is assisted by s 25(3), which states that where there is proof that D had with him such an article that is evidence that he had it with him for such use. Of course, this can be rebutted by evidence of a contrary intention. The result of s 25(3) is that, if D is found trespassing in the grounds of a dwelling house with a bunch of skeleton keys in his pocket, this is evidence that he had those articles with him for use in committing burglary.

BLACKMAIL

Blackmail is triable only on indictment. It is dealt with by TA 1968, s 21(1) which provides that a person is guilty of blackmail if, with a view to gain for himself or another or with intent to cause loss to another, he makes any unwarranted demand with menaces; and for this purpose a demand with menaces is unwarranted unless the person making it does so in the belief:

(a) that he has reasonable grounds for making the demand; and
(b) that the use of the menaces is a proper means of reinforcing the demand.

It is irrelevant that D obtained nothing as a result of his demand.

Demand with menaces

The nature of the act or omission demanded is immaterial. An oral demand is made when the words are said; if it is made by letter, it is made when that letter is posted. A demand need not be made in terms of an express demand or requirement, since (taken together with the menaces) it may be implied by a suggestion or other conduct which is by no means aggressive or forceful.

'Menaces' are not limited to threats of violence, since they include 'threats of action detrimental to or unpleasant to the person addressed'. It is immaterial whether the menaces do or do not relate to action to be taken by the person making the demand. The man who says, 'Pay me £5,000 or my daughter will tell the world that you seduced her' is as guilty of blackmail as the man who reinforces his demand with threats of action by himself.

Trivial threats will not suffice. The threat must be of 'such a nature and extent that the mind of an ordinary person of normal stability and courage might be influenced or made apprehensive so as to accede unwillingly to the demand'. By way of exception, if, although they would not have affected the mind of an ordinary person of normal stability, the threats affected the addressee's mind, they will amount to menaces if D was aware of the likely effect of his actions on the addressee, for example because D knew of an unusual susceptibility on the addressee's part.

If, on the facts known to D, his threats might have affected the mind of a person of ordinary stability, they will amount to menaces, even though they did not affect the addressee.

It is irrelevant whether D intends to carry out his menaces or is in any position to effect them.

With a view to gain or intent to cause loss

D must make his demand with menaces with a view to gain for himself or another, or with an intent to cause loss to another. The terms 'gain' and 'loss' are defined by s 34 as extending only to gain or loss in money or other property, whether temporary or permanent. Section 34 also provides that:

(a) 'gain' includes a gain by keeping what one has, as well as a gain by getting what one has not; and

(b) 'loss' includes not getting what one might get, as well as a loss by parting with what one has.

Unwarranted

Section 21 provides that a demand with menaces *is unwarranted unless* the person making it does so in the *belief* that he has reasonable grounds for making the demand *and* that the use of the menaces is a proper means of reinforcing the demand. If D has sex with a girl after promising payment of £500 and then refuses to pay, a demand by her for the money supported by a threat to inform D's wife will not be blackmail by the girl if she *believes* that she has reasonable grounds for making such a demand *and* that her threat is a proper means of reinforcing the demand.

D does not have to prove these beliefs, but this does not mean that the prosecution must negative the existence of a belief for which there is no evidence, since the prosecution need only negative the existence of one of the specified beliefs if there is evidence before the court in support of both types of belief; otherwise the jury is obliged to find that the demand with menaces was unwarranted.

CHAPTER 33

Burglary

The Theft Act 1968 (TA 1968), s 9(1) states that a person is guilty of burglary if:

(a) he enters any building or part of a building as a trespasser and with intent to commit any such offence as is mentioned in s 9(2); or

(b) having entered any building or part of a building as a trespasser he steals or attempts to steal anything in the building or that part of it or inflicts or attempts to inflict upon any person therein any grievous bodily harm.

It has been held that TA 1968, s 9(1) creates two types of offence, the first being set out by s 9(1)(a) and the second by s 9(1)(b). Because in each type of offence there is a higher maximum penalty if the building entered as a trespasser is a dwelling, each of the two types of offence has in it two offences, one committed if it is alleged and proved that the building was a dwelling and the second if it is not alleged and proved that the building was a dwelling. The definitions of the offences under s 9(1)(a) and (b) include many common terms which require explanation. These are given below as s 9(1)(a) is described, but what is said will be equally applicable to s 9(1)(b). Burglary offences are triable only on indictment where an offence triable only on indictment is committed or intended, or where the burglary is in a dwelling and either a person there is subjected to, or threatened with, violence or the defendant (D) is 18 or over and has two previous convictions for domestic burglary at the time of the burglary; otherwise, they are triable either way.

BURGLARY CONTRARY TO THEFT ACT 1968, s 9(1)(a): ENTRY WITH INTENT

A person is guilty of burglary under s 9(1)(a) if he enters any building or part of a building as a trespasser and with intent to commit one of the offences listed in s 9(2), namely to steal anything in the building or part of a building in question, or to inflict on any person therein grievous bodily harm, or to do unlawful damage to the building or anything therein.

Enters

The Court of Appeal has adopted the test of an 'effective entry'. This test excludes minimal intrusions, as where D's fingers are inserted through a gap between a window and its frame in order to open the window. However, where D was found stuck in a downstairs window of a house with his head and right arm inside but trapped by the window itself, which rested on his neck, the Court of Appeal held that there had been an entry. The issue of whether D was able, from that position, to steal anything was irrelevant.

Under pre-TA 1968 law, an entry could be effected merely by the insertion of an instrument without the intrusion of any part of the body *provided it was inserted to commit a relevant further offence*, but not if it was inserted merely to facilitate access by a person's body. Assuming that this remains the law, someone who, whilst remaining outside a building, inserts his walking stick in order to hook and steal a handbag inside enters the building for the purposes of burglary. On the other hand, someone who inserts a rod through a window which has been left ajar in order to release its catch does not enter the building because the insertion of the rod is merely to facilitate access by his body, not to commit an offence inside.

As a trespasser

A person enters a building or part of a building as a trespasser if it is in the possession of another and he enters without a right by law or permission to do so; the entry need not involve any force at all.

Rights of entry are granted by statute to certain people, such as the police and public health inspectors, for an authorised purpose. Such a person is not a trespasser if he enters for such a purpose. However, he enters as a trespasser if he enters premises for an unauthorised purpose, eg to steal something inside.

Likewise, a permission to enter will be given for a particular purpose or purposes. A person who enters for a purpose other than one for which he has permission enters as a trespasser. For example, the Court of Appeal has held that a man, who had permission to enter his father's house, entered it as a trespasser when he entered to steal his father's television set because he entered in excess of his permission.

Permission to enter for a particular purpose or purposes may be given by the occupier or by someone with the express or implied authority of the occupier. For example, a member of the family has authority to invite someone into her parents' house for a cup of tea but does not have authority to invite that person in in order to steal her parents' property.

Permission to enter may be implied, instead of express. For instance, in the case of a shop there is an implied permission for members of the public to enter the public parts of the shop for the purposes of inspecting goods on display or making purchases, and a person who enters for such a purpose is not a trespasser.

A permission to enter might not necessarily extend to every part of the building. Thus a person might lawfully enter a building such as a hotel or shop, but trespass in the manager's office or the stockroom; equally, he might be a lawful guest at a meal in a private house, but enter a bedroom as a trespasser. In both of these cases the entry as a trespasser will be into a 'part of a building'.

The 'owner' of a building may trespass in part of it if that part is in the exclusive possession of someone else. For example, if a householder rents out the rooms in his attic to X, on terms whereby X obtains exclusive possession of them, the householder will enter them as a trespasser if he enters without X's permission.

Building or part of a building

'Building' should be given its everyday meaning of a structure with walls and a roof and of a permanent or semi-permanent nature. Dwelling houses, warehouses, shops and the like are all buildings; so are outhouses and greenhouses (provided they are at least semi-permanent) and substantial portable structures with most of the attributes normally found in buildings, provided that there is an element of permanence in their site.

Section 9(4) states that references to a building also apply to an inhabited vehicle or vessel, and this is so whether or not the person having a habitation in it is there at the time. Clearly, a caravan or houseboat which is someone's permanent home is an 'inhabited vehicle or vessel', even though he is not there at the time but, say, abroad on holiday; so is a caravan or boat which is used as a holiday home in the summer during those weeks or weekends in which it is being so used, but not at other times in the summer and not at all in the rest of the year when it is closed up.

'Part of a building' refers to a particular area of a building. An obvious example of 'part of a building' is a separate room but the term is not limited to this. It also includes a physically marked-out area in a room, such as the area behind a counter in a shop, from which D is plainly excluded, whether expressly or impliedly.

Mens rea

The mens rea required for burglary contrary to s 9(1)(a) is that, when entering the building or part of a building, D must satisfy two requirements.

First, D must know he is entering the building, or part, as a trespasser (ie he must know the facts which make him a trespasser), or at least be reckless as to whether he is so entering.

Second, D must enter with intent to commit one of the offences listed in TA 1968, s 9(2):

(a) to 'steal' (ie to commit theft in respect of) anything in the building or, as the case may be, the part trespassed in;
(b) to inflict grievous (ie serious) bodily harm on any person in the building or, as the case may be, the part trespassed in; or
(c) to do unlawful (ie criminal) damage to the building or anything therein (whether or not D has trespassed in the part in which the damage is intended to occur).

It is, of course, irrelevant that it might be impossible for D to carry out his intent.

General point

In most instances, unless there is an admission by D, the only way in which one of the requisite intentions will be apparent is if there has been some act almost amounting to an attempt to commit the intended offence.

BURGLARY CONTRARY TO THEFT ACT 1968, s 9(1)(b): HAVING ENTERED AS A TRESPASSER, STEALING OR INFLICTING GRIEVOUS BODILY HARM, OR ATTEMPTING TO DO SO

Section 9(1)(b) provides that a person is guilty of burglary if having entered a building or part of a building as a trespasser he steals or attempts to steal anything in the building or that part of it or inflicts or attempts to inflict on any person therein any grievous bodily harm.

What was said in relation to s 9(1)(a) applies equally to the corresponding terms in this definition.

TA 1968, s 9(1)(a) distinguished

An important distinction between an offence of burglary under TA 1968, s 9(1)(a) and that under TA 1968, s 9(1)(b) is that the latter requires D, having entered a building or part of a building as a trespasser, actually to have committed or attempted to commit in the building or part trespassed in:

(a) the offence of theft (contrary to TA 1968, s 1); or
(b) an offence involving the infliction of grievous bodily harm contrary to the Offences
      Against the Person Act 1861 (OAPA 1861), ss 18, 20 or 23.

Another important distinction is that, unlike the offence under s 9(1)(a), the offence
under s 9(1)(b) does not require D to have intended to commit one of the above offences when he entered as a trespasser. Consequently if D enters a building as a trespasser, but without one of the intents specified in s 9(2) (so that he is not guilty under
s 9(1)(a)), he can only be guilty of burglary (under s 9(1)(b)) if he then steals or inflicts
grievous bodily harm in the building or attempts to do either.

Mens rea

Apart, of course, from having the mens rea required for theft, or an offence involving
the infliction of grievous bodily harm, or an attempt to commit such, as the case may
be, D must know or be reckless that he has entered as a trespasser when he commits
one of these offences. It is irrelevant whether or not he realised at the time of entry that
he was entering as a trespasser. Thus, if a person enters a building, thinking that he has
permission, and later realises that he has not and then steals something inside or inflicts grievous bodily harm on someone inside (eg the occupier who is trying to eject
him) he is guilty of burglary of the present type.

Examples of TA 1968, s 9(1)(b) offence

A person who enters an empty house as a trespasser to sleep in it for the night does not
commit burglary contrary to s 9(1)(b), nor does he if he switches on the electric fire
(because electricity is not property and cannot be stolen). But if he turns on a gas fire,
he commits burglary contrary to s 9(1)(b) because gas is property and can be stolen.
Likewise, he would be guilty of burglary contrary to s 9(1)(b) if, being discovered there
by a security guard, he then deliberately strikes the guard with a piece of wood lying
nearby and inflicts grievous bodily harm, whether he intended to or not, since he will
have committed the offence of unlawfully and maliciously inflicting grievous bodily
harm, contrary to OAPA 1861, s 20.

Of course, there is some overlap between the two types of offence of burglary. Where
a person enters a building (or part) as a trespasser with intent to steal or to inflict
grievous bodily harm therein, and he commits the intended offence or attempts to do
so, he can be charged with either offence. It is normally preferable to charge burglary
contrary to s 9(1)(b) in such a case since it is easier to prove.

AGGRAVATED BURGLARY

TA 1968, s 10(1) states that a person is guilty of aggravated burglary if he commits any
burglary and at the time has with him any firearm or imitation firearm, any weapon of
offence, or any explosive. Offences of aggravated burglary are triable only on indictment.

Firearm, imitation firearm, weapon of offence, or explosive

TA 1968, s 10(1) provides as follows.
  'Firearm' includes an air gun or an air pistol. 'Firearm' is not otherwise defined. It is
clear that the definition of a firearm given in the Firearms Act 1968 was not included in

TA 1968 because it includes component parts. Aggravated burglary is aimed at burglars who are 'tooled up' and therefore pose a particular threat of injury. There is very little threat of injury posed by the possession of a magazine case for a rifle.

'*Imitation firearm' means anything which has the appearance of being a 'firearm' whether or not capable of being discharged.*

'*Weapon of offence' means any article made or adapted for use for causing injury to or incapacitating a person, or intended by the person having it with him for such use.* Thus, 'weapon of offence' covers not only articles which would be offensive weapons for the purposes of the Prevention of Crime Act 1953, such as coshes, knuckledusters or even pickaxe handles, but also articles made, adapted or intended to be used for incapacitating a person. Articles made for incapacitation include handcuffs, leg irons or a straitjacket; those adapted would include a scarf or pair of tights adapted for use for tying-up; and those intended for such use would include drugs to induce sleep or handkerchiefs or pads for use with chloroform.

If the article in question is made or adapted for causing injury to, or incapacitating, a person, it will be necessary to prove no more than that a burglary was committed by D and that he was in possession of such a weapon of offence at the time. If it is alleged he was in possession of an article which he intended to use to cause injury or to incapacitate, it will be necessary to prove D's intention so to use it. In the absence of an admission, this is only likely to occur where D threatens someone in the building in such a way that he indicates an intention to use that weapon. For the purposes of aggravated burglary, an article not made or adapted to injure or incapacitate can be a weapon of offence, even if the necessary intent is only formed an instant before it is used to injure or incapacitate (which makes an interesting contrast to the different rule which applies to other offences (see, eg, p 609). Thus, a trespasser who, hearing someone coming downstairs, takes a screwdriver from his bag, having decided to use it to injure, commits aggravated burglary if he causes serious injury.

'*Explosive' means any article manufactured for the purpose of producing a practical effect by explosion, or intended by the person having it with him for that purpose.* This definition makes clear that a thing which simply causes a 'pyrotechnic effect' (and is therefore an 'explosive substance' under the Explosive Substances Act 1883) is not an 'explosive substance' for present purposes.

It is not essential that D should intend to use one of the above articles in the course of the burglary; it suffices that he had it with him for such use on another occasion (as where D intends to use a cosh to enable him to hijack a get-away car).

Has with him at time of burglary

In order to 'have with him' a firearm, etc, D must be armed with it; it is not enough that it is readily accessible to D. Thus, if the firearm, etc is carried not by the burglar but by an accomplice waiting outside the building, aggravated burglary is not committed. This is a stricter approach than is taken to the phrase 'has with him' in other offences where the term appears. In addition, D must know that he has the thing with him: a burglar does not have with him a cosh which somebody has slipped into his swag bag, unknown to him, for example.

D must have had with him a relevant article *at the time of committing* the offence of burglary.

Where the burglary is alleged to have been committed by stealing or inflicting grievous bodily harm, or attempting to do so, after entry as a trespasser, the possession must be proved at the time at which the theft, etc was committed or attempted, because that is the time at which the offence of burglary will have been committed. Where the burglary is alleged to have been committed by an entry with intent to commit one of the offences specified for s 9(1)(a), D must be proved to have been in possession at the time of entry, because that is the time at which the offence of burglary will have been committed. For example, if D enters a workshop without a weapon, merely intending to trespass there (and is therefore not guilty of an offence of burglary under s 9(1)(a) at that stage), but when confronted by a security guard he picks up a hammer stored in the workshop and uses it to strike the guard, causing him grievous bodily harm, D will be guilty of aggravated burglary. This is because he had the hammer with him at the time of committing burglary under s 9(1)(b) and the hammer was clearly intended by him for use for causing injury (and was therefore a weapon of offence).

CHAPTER 34

Fraud and Related Offences

THE OFFENCE OF FRAUD

The Fraud Act 2006 (FA 2006), s 1(1) and (2) provides that a person is guilty of the offence of fraud if he is in breach of ss 2, 3 or 4 (which provide different ways of committing the offence). Section 2 is concerned with fraud by false representation; s 3 with fraud by failing to disclose information; and s 4 with fraud by abuse of position.

The offence of fraud is an indictable (either way) offence.

Fraud by false representation

Under FA 2006, s 2, a person is in breach of s 1 if he:

(a) dishonestly makes a false representation; and
(b) intends by making the representation to make a gain for himself or another, or to cause loss to another, or to expose another to a risk of loss.

This is the widest of the three ways of committing fraud.

Making false representation

Representation   FA 2006, s 2(3) provides that 'representation' means any representation as to fact or law, including a representation as to the state of mind of:

(a) the person making the representation, or
(b) any other person.

By s 2(4), a representation may be express or implied.

An obvious example of a representation of fact would be a statement that a worthless ring was a diamond ring. A statement as to the meaning of a statute is clearly a representation of law.

Because 'representation' includes a representation as to the state of mind of the representor or another, the making of a false statement of the present intentions of the person making the statement or another person (eg a false promise) can amount to a false representation. The intention may, of course, be implied from the nature of the transaction in which the defendant engages. A request for a loan of money implies an intention to repay, and the ordering of a meal in a restaurant implies a representation that the representor (or, possibly, another) intends to pay for it.

The requirement that the representation must be as to fact (ie a past or present verifiable thing) or law, or as to a state of mind, means that a statement which merely expresses an opinion does not in itself constitute a false representation if the opinion turns out to be unjustified. By way of example, if a statement that a picture is worth £1,000 turns out to be unjustified there is no false representation. However, if the person making the statement is aware that the opinion is unjustified, he will at the same time by his conduct make a false representation as to his state of mind, because he will impliedly represent that he believes the opinion is justified when in fact he does not so believe.

There is no limit on how an express representation may be made. Thus, it can be stated by words, whether oral or written. It can be communicated by conduct (as where a rogue dresses up in a security guard's uniform in order to convey the impression that he is a security guard).

An implied representation may be made by words or by conduct, such as the implied representation by conduct, referred to above, made by someone who orders a meal in a restaurant, that he intends to pay for it, or such as that made by someone who sells property, that he has a right to sell.

A common example of an implied false representation by conduct concerns 'bouncing cheques'. The giver of a cheque normally impliedly represents that the state of facts existing at the date of delivery of the cheque is such that the cheque will be honoured in the ordinary course of events on presentation for payment on or after the date specified on the cheque. If the facts are not as represented, a false representation is made.

If a credit card or debit card is used, provided any conditions referred to by the card are complied with, the card company is legally obliged to honour the transaction, because a contract to this effect is brought into being between the payee and the card company. It is irrelevant that the user has no authority to use the card. In such a case, there will not be a false representation about payment. However, a person who uses a credit card or debit card impliedly represents by his conduct that he has actual authority from the card company to use the card to make a contract with the payee on behalf of the card company. If he has no such authority the representation as to it is false.

By s 2(5), a representation may be regarded for the purposes of s 2 as made if it (or anything implying it) is submitted in any form to any system or device designed to receive, convey or respond to communications (with or without human intervention). Thus, s 2 can be breached where the false representation is submitted to a computer or other machine rather than being addressed to a human being, as where a person unauthorisedly enters someone else's number into a 'CHIP and PIN' machine.

False representation   By s 2(2), a representation is false if:

(a) it is untrue or misleading; and
(b) the person making it knows that it is, or might be, untrue or misleading.

A false representation may involve a half-truth. A representation is a half-truth where, although it is literally true, it omits a material matter, as where an applicant for a job correctly states that he does not have a criminal record but fails to state that he has been charged with theft to which he intends to plead guilty.

No one is required to have been deceived by a false representation.

Mens rea

In addition to knowing that his representation is, or might be, untrue or misleading:

(a) D must make the false representation dishonestly. 'Dishonesty' in ss 2 to 4 involves a two-stage test: whether D's behaviour would be regarded as dishonest by the ordinary standards of reasonable and honest people; and, where this is so, whether D was aware that his conduct would be regarded as dishonest by reasonable and honest people. The answer to both tests must be 'yes';

(b) D must intend, by making the representation, to make a gain for himself or another, or to cause loss to another or to expose another to a risk of loss. 'Gain' and 'loss' have the same meaning as in blackmail (p 905).

Fraud by failing to disclose information

FA 2006, s 3 provides that a person is in breach of s 1 if he:

(a) dishonestly fails to disclose to another person information which he is under a legal duty to disclose; and
(b) intends, by failing to disclose the information, to make a gain for himself or another, or to cause loss to another or to expose another to a risk of loss.

A 'legal duty to disclose' means one in civil law. It may be one prescribed by statute; from the fact that the transaction is one of good faith (such as a contract of insurance); from the express or implied terms of a contract; from the custom of a trade or market; or from the existence of a relationship (such as that of a solicitor and client, trustee and beneficiary, or agent and principal). By way of example, a person in a position of trust has a duty to disclose material information when entering into a contract with a beneficiary.

Fraud by abuse of position

By FA 2006, s 4, a person is in breach of s 1 if he:

(a) occupies a position in which he is expected to safeguard, or not to act against, the financial interests of another person;
(b) dishonestly abuses that position; and
(c) intends, by means of the abuse of that position, to make a gain for himself or another, or to cause loss to another or to expose another to the risk of loss.

A person may be regarded as having abused his position even though his conduct consisted of an omission rather than an act.

The Court of Appeal has held that, to establish an abuse of position under FA 2006, s 4, the prosecution must demonstrate a breach of fiduciary duty or an obligation akin to a fiduciary duty. Accordingly, it held, s 4 did not apply in the general commercial arena where individuals or businesses competed in the market of one kind or another, including labour markets where participants were entitled to or expected to look after their own interests.

ARTICLES FOR USE IN FRAUD

Possession of articles for use in fraud

By FA 2006, s 6, a person commits an indictable (either way) offence if he has in his possession or under his control any article for use in the course of or in connection with any fraud.

The Court of Appeal has stated that D must have 'actual control or possession' of the article, and that an 'ability to control' is insufficient. A person would be in possession or control of data held on a computer in his possession or control. Two (or more) people can be in joint possession or control of an article if they each have possession or control of it.

D must intend the article to be used in the future in the course of or in connection with a fraud. A general intention to commit fraud is sufficient.

The term 'articles' in this section and s 7 below includes any program or data held in electronic form. Computer programs can generate credit card numbers; computer templates can be used for producing blank bills; and computer files may contain credit card details of persons.

Making or supplying articles for use in fraud

A person commits an indictable (either way) offence against FA 2006, s 7 if he makes, adapts, supplies or offers to supply any article:

(a) knowing that it is designed or adapted for use in the course of or in connection with fraud; or
(b) intending it to be used to commit, or assist in the commission of, fraud.

Where payment is made based upon energy consumed by a customer and consumption is measured by a meter, a person who makes or supplies a device intended to interfere with the record made by the device will intend it to be used to commit fraud.

OBTAINING SERVICES DISHONESTLY

A person commits an indictable (either way) offence against FA 2006, s 11(1) if he obtains services for himself or another:

(a) by a dishonest act; and
(b) in breach of the provisions of s 11(2).

By s 11(2), a person obtains services in breach of s 11 if:

(a) they are made available on the basis that payment has been, is being or will be made for or in respect of them;
(b) he obtains them without any payment having been made for or in respect of them or without payment having been made in full; and
(c) when he obtains them he knows:
    (i)   that they are being made available on the basis described in (a), or
    (ii) that they might be,
    but intends that payment will not be made, or will not be made in full.

The offence does not require a false representation. There must be an 'obtaining' of a service. An example would be where a film is exhibited in a cinema and D sneaks in to watch it. Obtaining services by the dishonest use of false credit card details or personal information would similarly amount to an offence against s 11. Trespassory entry into premises to view a free event is not an offence against s 11 as the service provided is not one for which a person is expected to pay.

Dishonesty bears the same meaning as described on p 914.

MAKING OFF WITHOUT PAYMENT

The Theft Act 1978, s 3(1) provides that a person who, knowing that payment on the spot for any goods supplied or service done is required or expected from him, dishonestly makes off without having paid as required or expected, and with intent to avoid payment of the amount due, is guilty of an offence. The offence is an indictable (either way) offence. These provisions are useful in that they cover cases, such as leaving a restaurant or self-service petrol station without paying, in which it may be difficult to prove that any particular intention existed at the time that the goods were supplied or the service was done.

Because D must make off 'without having paid as required or expected', an offence is not committed if the creditor (or his agent) has agreed that payment would be postponed (as where goods or services are supplied on credit), even if that postponement has been procured by a dishonest deception.

The Court of Appeal has held that 'making off without payment' involves a departure without paying from the place where payment would normally be made; for example, in the case of a taxi, payment might be made while sitting in it or standing at the window. Subsequently, the Court of Appeal has indicated that this statement about the taxi should not be applied too literally; if a taxi-passenger (D) honestly explained that he had to enter his house to get the fare, the moment of payment would be deferred and a decision not to return to the taxi would mean that, from that moment, D would make off without payment.

'Payment on the spot' includes payment at the time of collecting goods on which work has been done or in respect of which a service has been provided.

Section 3 does not apply if the payment required or expected is not legally due (eg because the person demanding it is seriously in breach of contract). Nor does the section apply to the supplying of goods or the doing of services which is contrary to the law, nor where the service done is such that payment is not enforceable. Consequently, for example, the offence is not committed by the man who makes off without paying a prostitute for services rendered.

The term 'knowing that payment on the spot is required or expected' relates to the knowledge D must have of when payment must be made (s 3(2)).

Dishonesty needs to be shown to have existed at the time of 'making off'. Dishonesty is a question of fact for the jury or justices and is approached in the same way as in the offence of fraud (p 914).

It has been held by the House of Lords that the requisite intention to evade payment is an intention permanently to evade payment; an intention to postpone (ie temporarily evade) payment is insufficient.

FALSE ACCOUNTING

The indictable (either way) offences of false accounting contrary to the Theft Act 1968 (TA 1968), s 17 are not restricted to clerks and other people who are employed in the traditional sense for the purpose of bookkeeping. The falsity need not necessarily be with a view to gain since it is sufficient that the falsity is accompanied by an intent to cause loss to another.

TA 1968, s 17(1) states that a person is guilty of an offence where he dishonestly, with a view to gain for himself or another or with intent to cause loss to another:

(a) destroys, defaces, conceals or falsifies any account or any record or document made or required for any accounting purpose, or
(b) in furnishing information for any purpose produces or makes use of any account, or any such record or document as aforesaid, which to his knowledge is or may be misleading, false or deceptive in a material particular.

Section 17(1) creates two quite separate and distinct offences which might be described as the falsification of accounts (s 17(1)(a)) and the use of false or deceptive accounts (s 17(1)(b)). Before examining these offences separately a number of points can be made which apply to both of them.

Mens rea

For the purposes of either type of offence, D's conduct must be carried out dishonestly and with a view to gain for himself or another or with intent to cause loss to another. 'Dishonesty' in this context is understood in the same way as in the offences of fraud (p 914). 'With a view to gain … or with intent to cause loss …' bears the same meaning as in blackmail (pp 905–6). There is no need for any gain or loss actually to be caused.

Account, record or document made or required for any accounting purpose

The acts specified by s 17(1)(a) and (b) must be done in relation to 'any account, record or document made or required for any accounting purpose'. These terms should be given their ordinary meaning. An accounts book, balance sheet or a payroll record is made for an accounting purpose. That is the reason for its existence; it has no other real purpose as it can be used for little other than the keeping of accounts. Documents may be required for an accounting purpose, even though they have other purposes as well as an accounting purpose. For example, a housing benefit claim form which contained the only information used to calculate housing benefit has been held by a divisional court to be a document required for an accounting purpose, despite the fact that it is also used to determine entitlement to benefit.

The terms 'account' or 'record' are wide enough to cover an account or record produced by a mechanical device, such as a taxi meter or the turnstile at a soccer ground which records the number of persons admitted so that the entries may be related to the money collected.

The separate requirements of the two offences are as follows.

Falsification of accounts (s 17(1)(a))

What is required here is the destruction, defacement, concealment or falsification of any account, etc. If entry to a cinema is recorded by the issue of a ticket by a process which produces a duplicate copy on a roll, the destruction of any part of that record, if carried out with the necessary intent, would be an offence. If some of the duplicate copies were not handed over to the manager so that a false total figure could be shown to cover deficiencies, those copies would be 'concealed' for the purposes of s 17(1)(a). If, to cover deficiencies in the accounts, a corrosive liquid or other damaging agent, was applied to the duplicate records, this would amount to a defacement. However, the most common offence is always likely to be the falsification of figures in an account, record or document. 'Falsification' covers the preparation of false accounts, as well as the falsification of existing ones.

Section 17(2) states that a person who makes or concurs in making in an account or other document an entry which is or may be misleading, false or deceptive in a material particular, or who omits or concurs in omitting a material particular from an account or other document, is to be treated as falsifying the account or document. However, this is not an exclusive definition of falsification. In one case, it has been held that a turnstile operator, who allowed two people through the turnstile while only recording one of them, falsified the record. It might be that the falsification was within s 17(2) (by omitting a material particular) but, if not, there was a 'falsification' within the ordinary meaning of that term.

Somewhat surprisingly, the Court of Appeal has held that a person can falsify an accounting document by completely failing to fill in a blank form required for an accounting purpose, and even though the particular document so falsified cannot be identified. The Court of Appeal therefore upheld the conviction of an international telephone operator who had failed to log calls on the forms provided for this purpose. The court held that, as soon as a call was made, it was the operator's duty to fill in one of the forms in a pile in front of him and that thereby one of them became a document required for an accounting purpose and the fact that the particular form could not be identified (since the operator might not have chosen to use the first form) did not matter.

Use of false or deceptive account (s 17(1)(b))

Whereas TA 1968, s 17(1)(a) is concerned with those who falsify or destroy, etc any account, etc, s 17(1)(b) deals with those who, in furnishing information for any purpose, produce or make use of any account or any record or document made or required for any accounting purpose, *knowing* it is or might be misleading, false or deceptive in a material particular (ie liable to mislead in a significant way).

Of course, a person who has falsified an account contrary to TA 1968, s 17(1)(a) might go on to use it contrary to s 17(1)(b), in which case he will have committed both offences. However, an offence under s 17(1)(b) may also be committed by a person who has not falsified the document in question, for it is not uncommon for persons with a view to gain to use in a dishonest way documents which have been made out erroneously by someone else. If a person, who is entitled to receive payment for money which he has spent on petrol for use in his firm's car, receives a receipt which he knows has been wrongly made out for a higher amount, he commits an offence against s 17(1)(b) if, when making out his claim (furnishing information), he makes use of that receipt, since, to his *knowledge*, it is or may be misleading, false or deceptive in a material particular.

BRIBERY

Bribery is another form of fraudulent conduct. The Bribery Act 2010 sets out the following offences which are described in Chapter 34 on the companion website: offences of bribing another person (s 1); offences relating to being bribed (s 2); bribery of public officials (s 6); and failure of commercial organisations to prevent bribery (s 7).

CHAPTER 35

Handling Stolen Goods and Related Offences

HANDLING STOLEN GOODS

If stolen goods had no sales outlet the incidence of theft would undoubtedly diminish significantly. Many thefts, especially where the appropriator engages in widespread offences of burglary, are committed in the knowledge that there is a ready market for certain types of article. The law concerning the indictable (either way) offence of handling stolen goods is concerned with punishing not only the ultimate receiver, in the sense that he is the buyer of the goods, but anyone who handles them en route to him or afterwards.

The Theft Act 1968 (TA 1968), s 22(1) states that a person handles stolen goods if (otherwise than in the course of the stealing) knowing or believing them to be stolen goods he dishonestly receives the goods, or dishonestly undertakes or assists in their retention, removal, disposal or realisation by or for the benefit of another person, or if he arranges to do so.

Goods

'Goods' are defined by TA 1968, s 34(2)(b), as including money and every other description of property except land, and includes things severed from the land by stealing.

Stolen

For the offence to be committed, the goods handled must be 'stolen goods' at that point of time. By TA 1968, s 24, 'stolen goods' are goods which have been:

(a) stolen, contrary to TA 1968, s 1;
(b) obtained as a result of blackmail, contrary to TA 1968, s 21;
(c) obtained by fraud, contrary to the Fraud Act 2006 (FA 2006), s 1; or
(d) 'stolen' abroad contrary to the law of that land, provided that had the 'stealing' occurred in England or Wales an offence contrary to TA 1968, ss 1 or 21 or FA 2006, s 1 would have been committed.

In addition, references to stolen goods also include money which is dishonestly withdrawn from an account to which a 'wrongful credit' has been made, but only to the extent that the money derives from the credit. 'Wrongful credit' is defined on p 927.

If a child below the age of criminal responsibility appropriates property in circumstances which would amount to theft by someone over that age, a person who dishonestly handles that property is not guilty of this offence as the goods are not 'stolen goods'. However, that person would normally be guilty of theft.

The fact that goods were stolen goods when handled can be proved by evidence of the conviction of someone for their prior theft. Another way is by offering evidence of ownership, the owner identifying the goods and describing the circumstances of their loss. It is not necessary to prove that goods were stolen by any particular person; merely that they were stolen by someone. The acquittal of an alleged thief does not prevent the goods being found to be stolen.

When goods cease to be stolen

TA 1968, s 24(3) provides that no goods shall be regarded as having continued to be stolen goods after they have been restored to the person from whom they were stolen or to other lawful possession or custody. Clearly, this goes further than repossession by the owner, since it includes cases in which goods have been restored to other lawful possession or custody. When a police officer in the course of his duties takes possession of stolen goods, they are thereby restored to 'other lawful possession or custody' and are no longer stolen; consequently, it is not an offence to handle them thereafter.

The issue is whether or not the stolen goods have been taken into possession or custody on the owner's account so that they may be returned to him. Where a security guard marked cartons of stolen cigarettes so that they would more easily be identified in the hands of a handler, they were not restored to lawful possession or custody. If a police officer sees property inside a parked car which he suspects might be stolen and immobilises the car to ensure that he will have an opportunity of questioning the driver, he does not take possession of the stolen goods unless he immobilises the car with the intention of taking charge of those goods so that they cannot be removed. If he has retained an open mind as to whether he should take possession, and merely immobilises the car to prevent the driver getting away without questioning, he does not reduce the goods into his possession or custody. It is the state of mind of the officer which is the deciding factor in each case.

Section 24(3) also provides that goods cease to be stolen goods where the person from whom they were stolen and any other person claiming through him have ceased to have rights of restitution in respect of the theft. The right to restitution of property is a matter of civil law. There are various ways in which the right to restitution might have been lost. An example is where X obtains goods from Y by fraud. If Y, on discovering the fraud, nevertheless affirms the transaction he thereby ceases to have any right to restitution of the goods, which therefore cease to be stolen goods at that point of time.

Goods representing those originally stolen

TA 1968, s 24(2) provides that references to stolen goods include, in addition to the goods originally stolen and parts of them (whether in their original state or not):

(a) any other goods which directly or indirectly represent or have at any time represented the stolen goods in the hands of *the thief* as being the proceeds of any disposal or realisation of the whole or part of the goods stolen or of goods so representing the stolen goods; and

(b) any other goods which directly or indirectly represent or have at any time represented the stolen goods in the hands of *a handler of the stolen goods or any part of them* as being the proceeds of any disposal or realisation of the whole or part of the stolen goods handled by him or of goods so representing them.

'The thief' means the person by whose conduct the goods were originally stolen. 'A handler' means any person who has committed the actus reus of handling with the appropriate mens rea. The Court of Appeal has held that goods are in the hands of the thief or of a handler if they are in his possession or under his control; physical custody is not required.

The rule can be illustrated as follows. A steals a car. He sells it to B for £1,000 and receives that sum in cash. The car and the cash are now both stolen goods, the cash because it *directly represents the original goods (the car) in the hands of the thief—as the proceeds of the car's disposal or realisation.* Therefore, if A then gives the £1,000 (or part of it) to C, who receives it knowing it has represented the original stolen goods in A's hands and C buys a camera with the £1,000, the camera becomes stolen goods once it is in C's hands because *it indirectly represents the original stolen goods in the hands of a handler as the proceeds of the disposal or realisation of goods representing the original stolen goods.* Consequently if D receives the camera from C, knowing it has represented the stolen goods in C's hands, D can be convicted of handling stolen goods. However, if E receives the camera from D, unaware that it represents the original stolen goods, and then sells it for cash, the cash which he receives will not become stolen goods because, lacking mens rea, he is not a handler and therefore *that* cash does *not represent the original stolen goods in the hands of a handler as the proceeds of their disposal or realisation.*

Various forms of handling

TA 1968, s 22 defines 'handling' as receiving stolen goods, or undertaking or assisting in their retention, removal, disposal or realisation by or for the benefit of another person, or arranging to do one of these things.

It must not be forgotten that s 22 excludes from its provisions those who handle in one of these ways in the course of the original stealing. This is a commonsense approach to offences of handling. We are not concerned with thieves (and their accomplices) who handle stolen goods in the course of the original theft as they are punishable in respect of the theft, whatever form that theft may take.

The charge

Although an examination of the definition of 'handling' shows that there are 18 different ways in which handling can be committed, it is unnecessary to make exclusive selections of a particular variant of the offence. Section 22 provides a single offence of handling stolen goods, which can be committed by receiving or by any of the other ways specified. Consequently, an information or written charge or indictment which simply alleges handling of stolen goods is unlikely to fail for duplicity.

Nevertheless, in order to be fair and clear to the defendant (D), the better practice is to particularise the form of handling relied on, and, if there is any uncertainty about the form of handling in question, it is advisable to have more than one information or written charge (or more than one count in the indictment). But only two informations or written charges (or counts) should generally be used in such a case: one charging receiving, and the other charging the various forms of 'undertaking or assisting in' by or for the benefit of another (or such forms of these as are clearly the only ones relevant).

The forms of handling can be explained as follows.

Receiving

This requires proof that D obtained possession or control of stolen goods from someone else; a finder of goods does not receive them. The presence of stolen goods on the premises of another does not necessarily mean that they are in the possession or control of the owner of the premises. To be a 'receiver' a person need not have contact with the goods in any physical sense, since a person can have control of goods without any physical contact with them, as where an employee or agent acting on his orders received them (in which case the employee or agent is also a receiver).

It is unnecessary that a receiver should act to gain any profit or even advantage from his possession of stolen goods.

Arranging to receive

This requires preparation by D, or a concluded agreement between D and another (eg the thief), for the receiving of stolen goods by D. It is essential that the goods are stolen goods at the time the arrangement to receive is made. Thus, D does not commit handling where he agrees to receive goods which are to be stolen. However, in such a case, he and any other party to the agreement could be convicted of conspiracy to handle.

The other forms of handling set out below differ in a vital respect from receiving, or arranging to receive, in that they must be done 'by or for the benefit of' a person other than the alleged handler (or, the Court of Appeal has held, a co-defendant on the same charge of handling). The other person should be named in the charge if his identity is known. If it is not, the charge should indicate that the acts were done, as appropriate, 'by or for the benefit of' some person unknown and such a charge will have to be supported by strong evidence that that other person existed.

Undertaking the retention, removal, disposal or realisation of stolen goods for the benefit of another

These four forms of handling cover the case where D, either alone or with another, retains, removes, disposes or realises the stolen goods for the benefit of another.

'Retention' means 'keeping possession of, not losing, continuing to have'. 'Removal' refers to the movement of stolen goods from one place to another, for example transporting stolen goods to a hideout for the benefit of the thief or another. 'Disposal' covers dumping, giving away or destroying stolen goods, for example melting down candlesticks for the thief. 'Realisation' means the exchange of stolen goods for money or some other property. A person who sells stolen goods as agent for a third party (eg the thief) undertakes their realisation for the benefit of another. However, the House of Lords has held that a person who sells stolen goods on his own behalf does not undertake their realisation for the benefit of another because the buyer benefits from the purchase and not from the realisation (which benefits only the seller).

Of course, a person who undertakes one of these four activities will often be in possession or control of the stolen goods. If he knew or believed they were stolen when he acquired possession or control, he is guilty of handling anyway on the basis of receiving. However, if he lacked such a state of mind at that point of time but realised the goods were stolen when he undertook one of the four activities, he can be convicted of handling on that basis, provided that his 'undertaking' was for the *benefit of another*.

Assisting in the retention, removal, disposal or realisation of stolen goods by another

These four forms of handling are appropriate to cover cases where D provides assistance to another person, the thief or another handler, who is going to undertake the retention, removal, disposal or realisation of stolen goods.

For there to be 'assistance', D must do something for the purpose of enabling the goods to be retained, etc, whether or not he succeeds.

There is some overlap with cases of 'undertaking'. For example, a person who joins with another in removing stolen goods not only undertakes their removal for the benefit of another but also assists in their removal by another.

A person *assists in the retention* of stolen goods by another if he puts the thief in touch with a warehouse-keeper, or provides tarpaulins to conceal stolen goods, or tells lies so as to make it more difficult for the police to find stolen goods retained by the thief or a handler. On the other hand, the Court of Appeal has held, a refusal to answer police questions as to the whereabouts of stolen goods does not amount to handling, although it might well assist in their retention by another. A person who innocently allows goods to be left on his premises, but later discovers that they are stolen, assists in their retention by another if he nevertheless permits them to continue to remain on the premises. Merely to use stolen goods does not suffice, since it does not in itself amount to assistance in their retention.

A person *assists in the removal* of stolen goods by another if he lends a lorry for their removal. He *assists in their disposal* by another if he advises the thief as to how to get rid of the goods. He *assists in their realisation* by another if he puts a 'fence' in touch with the thief.

Arranging to undertake or assist in the retention, removal, disposal or realisation of stolen goods by or for the benefit of another

The effect of TA 1968, s 22 is further extended by the addition of the words 'or arranging to do so'. Any arrangement to undertake or assist in one of the activities described above can suffice; it is irrelevant that nothing further is done. However, as mentioned in relation to the offence of 'arranging to receive', it must be proved that the arrangements in respect of these other forms of handling relate to goods which were stolen goods at the time of the arrangements.

Mens rea

It must be proved that, when he handled the stolen goods, D knew or believed that they were stolen, and acted dishonestly.

Knowledge or belief

Wilful blindness, ie deliberately turning a blind eye to the question of whether or not goods are stolen, does not suffice for 'knowledge' or 'belief', but it has been held that, if wilful blindness as to the goods being stolen is proved, knowledge or belief *may* (not must) be inferred from it. This is important since, in the absence of an admission by the handler, knowledge or belief (at the time of the handling) that the goods were stolen can be difficult to prove, particularly in the common case of sales, at bargain prices, of goods which 'fell off a lorry' and which turn out to have been stolen.

D need not be aware of the precise nature of the goods. If D receives boxes believing them to contain stolen whisky, it is immaterial that the boxes actually contained stolen wine.

Proof   Frequently, knowledge or belief is proved by reference to the surrounding circumstances. If stolen goods have been carefully concealed on private premises, this suggests not only that the occupier of the premises did not wish to be found in possession of them but also that he knew that the goods were stolen.

In general, where D is found in possession of property which has been recently stolen, a judge may direct a jury that they may infer knowledge or belief if D fails to offer an explanation for his possession, or if they are satisfied beyond reasonable doubt that any explanation which is offered is false. This rule is merely an application of the ordinary rules of circumstantial evidence. In addition, TA 1968, s 27, which applies where D is being prosecuted at the trial in question only for handling stolen goods, recognises the difficulties which may exist in proving knowledge in handling offences by allowing special evidence to be offered in certain circumstances. It provides that, if evidence has been given of an act of handling by D in relation to the goods in question, the following evidence may be given to assist proof of knowledge or belief that the property was stolen:

(a) evidence that D has had in his possession, or has undertaken or assisted in the retention, removal, disposal or realisation of, stolen goods from any theft taking place not earlier than 12 months before the offence charged; and
(b) provided that seven days' notice in writing have been given to D of the intention to prove the conviction, evidence that he has, within the five years preceding the date of the offence charged, been convicted of theft or of handling stolen goods.

Section 27 supplements the general rules about admissibility of 'bad character' evidence (see p 264). It must be emphasised that it only permits the evidence described in (a) and (b) to be given to prove knowledge or belief that the goods were stolen. It does not enable such evidence to be used for any other purpose, for example to prove dishonesty on D's part or an act of handling by him.

The provisions in (b) must be read with PACE, s 73(2), which provides that where evidence of a previous conviction on indictment is admissible by means of a certificate of conviction the certificate must give 'the substance and effect of the indictment and conviction'. The House of Lords has held that, when (b) is so read, a certificate of previous conviction for theft or handling should:

(a) where the conviction was on indictment, state the substance and effect of the indictment and conviction, including the nature of the property concerned; and
(b) where the conviction was in summary proceedings, record the nature of the property concerned.

Dishonestly

Dishonesty is always a question of fact for the jury or justices, and the same approach is to be taken by them, as it is in relation to the offence of fraud (p 914). It follows, for example, that if a person knowingly receives stolen goods, but does so in order to restore them to their owner, or to hand them over to the police, his handling is not likely to be found to be dishonest by the jury or justices.

MONEY LAUNDERING OFFENCES

The offence of handling stolen goods is, strictly, no longer necessary in virtually every case covered by it because of the wider money laundering provisions of the Proceeds of Crime Act 2002 (PCA 2002), Part 7 (ss 327–340). Stolen goods in all their forms fall within the definition of 'criminal property' within PCA 2002, s 340(3), which provides that property is criminal property if:

(a) it constitutes a person's benefit from criminal conduct or it represents such a benefit (in whole or part and whether directly or indirectly), and
(b) the alleged offender knows or suspects that it constitutes or represents such a benefit.

PCA 2002, s 327(1) makes it an offence to conceal, disguise, convert or transfer criminal property, or to remove it from England and Wales.

Section 328(1) provides that it is an offence for a person to enter into or become concerned in an arrangement which he knows or suspects facilitates (by whatever means) the acquisition, retention, use or control of criminal property by or on behalf of another person.

By s 329(1), it is an offence for a person to acquire, use or possess criminal property, unless he does so for adequate consideration or certain other exceptions apply.

Although many instances of handling fall outside the popular conception of money laundering, the offences in ss 327–329 are, between them, capable of covering virtually anything which constitutes handling stolen goods. In addition, the mens rea requirement for these offences is less demanding since D is not required to know or believe that the property constitutes or represents the benefit from criminal conduct, but is simply required to know or suspect this. In addition, there is no requirement of 'dishonesty'.

The offences under PCA 2002, ss 327–329 (all of which are indictable (either way) offences) clearly have the potential to be more attractive to a prosecutor than that of handling stolen goods. However, they were created in the context of legislation directed primarily at money laundering and matters of serious criminality, and the courts have discouraged any practice of prosecuting inappropriate cases under PCA 2002, ss 327–329 instead of charging handling stolen goods under TA 1968, s 22.

ADVERTISING REWARDS FOR RETURN OF STOLEN OR LOST GOODS

TA 1968, s 23 punishes the public advertisement of a reward for the return of any lost or stolen goods which uses any words to the effect that no questions will be asked, or that the person producing the goods will be safe from apprehension or inquiry, or that any money paid for the purchase of the goods or advanced by way of loan on them will be repaid. The printer and publisher of such an advertisement are liable, as well as the advertiser.

SEARCH WARRANTS

By TA 1968, s 26, a justice may grant a warrant, upon information being received on oath that there is reasonable cause to believe that any person has in his custody or possession or on his premises any stolen goods, to search for and seize those goods.

A Crown Court judge has power to make a search and seizure warrant under PCA 2002, s 352 where someone is subject to a money laundering investigation.

The additional powers of seizure provided by the Criminal Justice and Police Act 2001, s 50 apply where a search warrant under one of these two provisions is executed.

DISHONESTLY RETAINING A WRONGFUL CREDIT

The offence of handling is not committed by someone into whose bank account a 'wrongful credit', as defined below, has been received because that credit itself is not stolen goods.

This gap is filled by TA 1968, s 24A, which provides that a person (D) is guilty of an offence if:

(a) a wrongful credit has been made to an account kept by him or in respect of which he has any right or interest;

(b) he knows or believes that the credit is wrongful; and
(c) he dishonestly fails to take such steps as are reasonable in the circumstances to secure that the credit is cancelled.

The offence is an indictable (either way) offence.

What is required is a failure by D to take such steps as are reasonable in the circumstances to secure the cancellation of a wrongful credit made to an account kept by D or in respect of which D has any right or interest. Nothing need be done by D.

A 'credit' refers to a credit of an amount of money in an account. 'Money' includes currencies other than sterling. A credit to an account is wrongful to the extent that it derives from theft, blackmail, fraud (contrary to FA 2006, s 1) or stolen goods. An 'account' is an account kept with:

(a) a bank;
(b) a person carrying on a business:
  (i) in the course of which money is received by way of deposit which is lent to others; or
  (ii) of which any other activity is financed, wholly or to any material extent, out of the capital of, or the interest on, money received by way of a deposit; or
(c) an issuer of electronic money (as defined by the Electronic Money Regulations 2011).

In determining whether a credit to an account is wrongful, it is immaterial whether the account is overdrawn before or after the credit is made.

D must know or believe that the credit is wrongful; he must know or believe the facts which make the credit 'wrongful' in law, although he need not know that they have this effect (since ignorance of the criminal law is no defence).

D must dishonestly fail to take such steps which are reasonable in the circumstances to secure that the wrongful credit is cancelled. The approach to this question is the same as in handling and fraud.

Section 24A covers a range of situations. Suppose that X commits an offence of fraud and thereby causes a money transfer to be made to D's account, unknown to D. If D dishonestly fails to take reasonable steps to cancel the credit on discovering the truth, D commits an offence under s 24A because the credit is wrongful. Another example is where Y pays money which he has stolen into his bank account, and then transfers the credit thereby created to D's bank account. If D dishonestly fails to take reasonable steps to cancel that credit he can be convicted of an offence under s 24A, because the credit is wrongful.

CHAPTER 36

Forgery and Counterfeiting

The law relating to forgery and counterfeiting is governed by the Forgery and Counterfeiting Act 1981 (FCA 1981). Part I of the Act is concerned with forgery and related offences, and Part II with counterfeiting and related offences.

Offences under the Identity Documents Act 2010 are also dealt with in this chapter.

With three exceptions (p 934 and p 938), all the offences described in this chapter are indictable (either way) offences.

FORGERY AND RELATED OFFENCES: GENERAL POINTS

Meaning of 'instrument'

By FCA 1981, s 8, 'instrument' is:

(a) any document, whether of a formal or informal character (other than a currency note);
(b) any stamp issued or sold by a postal operator (or a metered postage mark);
(c) any Inland Revenue stamp denoting any duty or fee; and
(d) any disc, tape, soundtrack or other device on or in which information is *recorded or stored* by mechanical, electronic or other means. To be 'recorded' or 'stored' the information must be preserved for an appreciable time with the object of subsequent retrieval. Examples of items covered are microfilm records and information on computers or discs and tachograph record sheets, but not electronic impulses in a computer or its 'user segment' (which stores information momentarily while the computer searches its memory, eg to check a password). Thus, computer hacking is not forgery although it is an offence under the Computer Misuse Act 1990, s 1.

The Court of Appeal has held that a thing is only a document within (a) if it conveys two messages: a message about the thing itself (eg that it is a cheque) and a message to be found in the words or other symbols that is to be accepted and acted on (eg the message in a cheque to the banker to pay a specified sum). Thus, cheques, wills and building society passbooks are examples of documents (and are therefore instruments), but paintings (even if falsely signed), false autographs, and any writing on manufactured articles or their wrappings indicating the name of the manufacturer or country of origin are not.

Meaning of 'false'

FCA 1981, s 9(1) states that an instrument is false if it purports to have been:

(a) *made in the form* in which it is made by *a person who did not in fact make it* in that form; or
(b) *made in the form* in which it is made on *the authority of a person who did not in fact authorise its making* in that form; or

(c) *made in the terms* in which it is made *by a person who did not in fact make it* in those terms; or

(d) *made in the* terms in which it is made *on the authority of a person who did not in fact authorise its making* in those terms; or

(e) *altered* in any respect *by a person who did not in fact alter it* in that respect; or

(f) *altered* in any respect *on the authority of a person who did not in fact authorise the alteration* in that respect; or

(g) *made* or *altered* on a *date* on which, or at a *place* at which, or *otherwise in circumstances* in which, it was *not in fact made or altered*; or

(h) *made* or *altered* by an *existing person* but he did not *in fact exist*.

The key point is that it is not enough that the document tells a lie (ie contains a false statement); what is required is that it should tell a lie about itself in relation to the person who made the instrument, or authorised its making, or altered it, or if it purports to have been made or altered on a date, or in a place, or otherwise in circumstances in which it was not in fact made or altered, or if it represents itself as having been made or altered by an existing person who in fact did not exist.

If D writes an application for a job and falsely alleges that he has a degree, that instrument is not a forgery although its contents are untrue. It was made by the applicant, it has not been altered in any way or falsely dated, and it is made by an existing person. Should D make out a reference which is allegedly from his tutor that would be a false instrument, as it alleges that it was made by a person who did not make it or authorise its making.

If D finds a cheque book and signs the name of the person who holds the account, the cheque is a false instrument as it lies about itself by alleging that it was signed by another who did not make the instrument or authorise its making. On the other hand, someone who opens an account in a false name, in order to pay in a stolen cheque, does not make a false instrument when he completes a withdrawal form in that name. The drawer's name is the same as the depositor's (although false) and the withdrawal form does not purport to be made by a person who did not make it.

A cheque, made out quite properly by the holder of the bank account for the sum of £100, becomes a false instrument when another person alters that cheque to show a sum of £1,000 by adding another zero to the figure shown on the face of the cheque and writing alongside it the initials of the account holder without that person's authority.

FORGERY

A person is guilty of forgery, contrary to FCA 1981, s 1(1), if he makes a false instrument, with the intention that he or another shall use it to induce somebody to accept it as genuine, and by reason of so accepting it to do or not to do some act to his own or any other person's prejudice.

D must make the false instrument with the intention that he or another person shall use it to induce somebody to accept it as genuine, and with the intention to induce that person by reason of so accepting it to do or not to do some act to his own or any other person's prejudice. Consequently, it is not enough simply to intend to induce someone to believe that an instrument is genuine. For example, making a false birth certificate solely to induce a belief that one comes from a noble family is not forgery. If D acts with the necessary double intent, it is irrelevant whether the instrument is communicated to anyone, whether anyone is induced to accept the instrument as genuine or whether prejudice (within the meaning set out below) is caused. D need not intend to induce another human being, it suffices that he intends to induce a machine to respond to the instrument as if it were genuine.

The act or omission intended to be induced must be to the prejudice of the person induced or of someone else (besides D). FCA 1981, s 10(1) provides that, for the purposes of forgery and related offences, an act or omission intended to be induced is only to a person's prejudice if it is one which, if it occurs:

(a) will result:
  (i) in his temporary or permanent loss of property (including a loss by not getting what he might get as well as a loss by parting with what he has), as where a false cheque or will is made to cause him either to part with property or not to get property he might have got; or
  (ii) in his being deprived of an opportunity to earn remuneration or greater remuneration or to gain a financial advantage otherwise than by way of remuneration, as where a letter, falsely purporting to come from someone asked to give a reference for a job applicant or a person tendering for a contract, states that the applicant or tenderer is incompetent; or
(b) will result in somebody being given an opportunity:
  (i) to earn remuneration or greater remuneration from him (the person induced), as where a false degree certificate is made in order to obtain a job or better pay; or
  (ii) to gain a financial advantage from him otherwise than by way of remuneration, as where a false airline ticket is made in order to get a free flight; or
(c) will be the result of his having accepted a false instrument as genuine (or—and this is only relevant to offences under FCA 1981, ss 2 and 4 below—a copy of a false instrument as a copy of a genuine one) in connection with his performance of a duty, as where a false pass is made to induce a doorkeeper to admit an unauthorised person to premises. As this example shows, the intended prejudice under (c) need not be financial.

Where the intended inducement is of a machine (eg a cash dispenser), the act or omission intended to be induced by the machine responding to the instrument is treated as an act or omission to a person's prejudice.

By virtue of s 10(2), it is not forgery where the maker of a false instrument intends to induce someone to do something which he is under an enforceable legal duty to do (or to induce someone not to do something he is not legally entitled to do).

Provided that the requirements of s 10(1) are satisfied, an honest and reasonable belief in a legal or moral claim to the gain which D intended to make as a result of falsifying the instrument is no defence (unless s 10(2) applies). Indeed, it is not a defence in itself that D might actually have been entitled to have property transferred to him if he had made a true claim.

COPYING A FALSE INSTRUMENT

FCA 1981, s 2 is concerned with the separate offence of copying a false instrument. It provides that it is an offence for a person to make a copy of an instrument which is, and which he knows or believes to be, a false instrument, with the intention that he or another will use it to induce somebody to accept it as a copy of a genuine instrument, and with the intention to induce that person by reason of so accepting it to do some act to the prejudice of himself or some other person.

The essential points to prove are that the original instrument is a false instrument; that the person who made the copy knew or believed this to be so; and that the copy was made with intent to induce a belief that it is a copy of a genuine instrument and to induce someone to act, etc.

USING A FALSE INSTRUMENT OR COPY OF IT

FCA 1981, s 3 makes it an offence for a person to use an instrument which is false, and which he knows or believes to be false, with the intention of inducing somebody to accept it as genuine, and with the intention of inducing that person by reason of so accepting it to do or not to do some act to his own or any other person's prejudice.

Section 4 provides a similarly worded offence of using a copy of a false instrument which is, and which he knows or believes to be, a false instrument, with the intention of inducing somebody to accept it as a copy of a genuine instrument, and by reason of so accepting it to do or not to do some act to his own or any other person's prejudice.

Any use of a false instrument (or, as the case may be, a copy of a false instrument) with the necessary intent suffices. The verb 'use' is wide in meaning and covers, for example, a person who offers, delivers, tenders in payment or exchange, or exposes for sale, a false instrument (or a copy of one).

CUSTODY OR CONTROL OF MONEY ORDERS, SHARE CERTIFICATES, ETC

FCA 1981, s 5 provides a number of offences under this heading, which are concerned with the following instruments:

(a) money orders or postal orders;
(b) UK postage stamps;
(c) Inland Revenue stamps;
(d) share certificates;
(e) cheques or other bills of exchange;
(f) travellers' cheques;
(g) bankers' drafts;
(h) promissory notes;
(i) credit cards or debit cards;
(j) certified copies relating to an entry in a register of births, adoptions, marriages, civil partnerships, conversions (of a civil partnership into a marriage) or deaths and issued by the Registrar General, the Registrar General for Northern Ireland, a registration officer or a person lawfully authorised to issue such certified copies; and
(k) certificates relating to entries in such registers.

Any such instrument is hereafter referred to as a 'specified instrument'.

Custody or control of such instruments

By FCA 1981, s 5(1), it is an offence for a person to have in his custody or under his control a specified instrument which is, and which he knows or believes to be, false, with the intention that he or another shall use it to induce somebody to accept it as genuine, and by reason of so accepting it to do or not to do some act to his own or any other person's prejudice.

This 'possession' offence completes the cycle of offences which are likely to be committed if a false instrument is made for the purposes previously described. If D makes out a false cheque with intent to induce someone to accept it as genuine, and by reason of so accepting it to do something to his prejudice, D commits forgery contrary to s 1. If D walks through the streets to a bank, with the false cheque, in order to cash it, he commits the present offence under s 5(1). If D then passes the cheque to a bank official in order to induce him to part with money, D commits the offence of 'using' contrary to s 3. Of course, it might be that different people will commit different offences in the cycle, as where the person who makes the false instrument gets other people to engage in the use of such false instruments.

If the intent required for an offence under s 5(1) cannot be proved, one can fall back on s 5(2). This makes it an offence for a person merely to have in his custody or control, without lawful authority or excuse, a specified instrument which is, and which he knows or believes to be, false. 'Lawful authority or excuse' is likely to be limited to such matters as possession by a police officer after seizure of a specified instrument or possession by some other person who is in the course of handing over to the police such an instrument.

Making, custody or control of equipment or materials

FCA 1981, s 5(3) and (4) is aimed at the tools of a forger's trade. Section 5(3) provides that it is an offence for a person to make or to have in his custody or under his control a machine or implement, or paper or any other material, which to his knowledge is or has been specially designed or adapted for the making of a specified instrument, with the intention that he or another shall make a specified instrument which is false and that he or another shall induce somebody to accept it as genuine, and by reason of so accepting it to do or not to do some act to his own or another's prejudice. In this way the Act strikes at a would-be forger even before he starts to make a false instrument. Whether or not the necessary intent for an offence under s 5(3) can be proved will often depend, in part, on the amount of forging equipment, etc in D's custody or control.

If the intent required under s 5(3) cannot be proved, one can fall back on s 5(4), which makes it an offence for a person to make or to have in his custody or control any such machine, implement, paper or material, without lawful authority or excuse.

FORGERY, ETC: DEFENCE FOR REFUGEES

It is a defence under the Immigration and Asylum Act 1999, s 31, for a refugee charged with an offence under FCA 1981, Part I or the Identity Documents Act 2010, s 4 or 6 (below), or an attempt to commit such an offence, to prove that, having come to the UK directly from a country where his life or freedom was threatened (within the meaning of the Refugee Convention), he:

(a) presented himself to the authorities in the UK without delay;

(b) showed good cause for his illegal entry or presence; and

(c) made a claim for asylum as soon as was reasonably practicable after his arrival in the UK.

If, in coming from the country where his life or freedom was threatened, the refugee stopped in another country outside the UK, the defence applies only if he proves that he could not reasonably have expected to be given protection under the Refugee Convention in that other country.

FORGERY, ETC: POLICE POWERS

See p 938.

FALSE IDENTITY DOCUMENT OFFENCES: GENERAL POINTS

Identity document

'Identity document' means any document that is, or purports to be:

(a) an immigration document;
(b) a UK passport;
(c) a passport issued by or on behalf of the authorities of a country or territory outside the UK or by or on behalf of an international organisation;
(d) a document that can be used (in some or all circumstances) instead of a passport;
(e) a UK driving licence; or
(f) a driving licence issued by or on behalf of the authorities of a country or territory outside the UK (Identity Documents Act 2010 (IDA 2010), s 8).

For the above purposes, 'immigration document' means a document used for confirming the right of a person under the EU Treaties in respect of entry or residence in the UK, or a document which is given in exercise of immigration functions and records information about leave granted to a person to enter or to remain in the UK, or a registration card (within the meaning of the Immigration Act 1971, s 26A). A 'document' includes a stamp or label.

False identity document

An identity document is false only if it is false within the meaning given by FCA 1981 (see pp 928–9) (IDA 2010, s 9).

Improperly obtained identity document

An identity document is improperly obtained if false information was provided, in or in connection with, the application for its issue or an application for its modification, to the person who issued it or (as the case may be) to a person entitled to modify it. For these purposes:

(a) 'false' information includes information containing any inaccuracy or omission that results in a tendency to mislead;
(b) 'information' includes documents (including stamps and labels) and records; and
(c) the 'issue' of a document includes its renewal, replacement or re-issue (with or without modifications) (s 9).

Personal information

'Personal information', in relation to an individual, means:

(a) his full name;
(b) other names by which he is or has previously been known;
(c) his gender;
(d) his date and place of birth;

(e) his external characteristics that are capable of being used for identifying him;

(f) the address of his principal place of residence in the UK;

(g) the address of every other place in the UK or elsewhere where he has a place of residence;

(h) where in the UK and elsewhere he has previously been resident;

(i) the times at which he was resident at different places in the UK or elsewhere;

(j) his current residential status;

(k) residential statuses previously held by him; and

(l) information about numbers allocated to him for identification purposes and about the documents (including stamps or labels) to which they relate.

'Residential status' means:

(i) an individual's nationality;

(ii) an individual's entitlement to remain in the UK; and

(iii) if that entitlement derives from a grant of leave to enter or remain in the UK, the terms and conditions of that leave (s 8).

POSSESSION OF FALSE IDENTITY DOCUMENTS, ETC

Possessing false identity documents, etc with improper intent

It is an offence, triable only on indictment, against IDA 2010, s 4(1) for a person (D) with the improper intention to have in his possession or under his control:

(a) a false identity document he knows or believes to be false;

(b) an improperly obtained identity document which he knows or believes to have been improperly obtained; or

(c) an identity document relating to someone else.

The improper intention is:

(i) the intention of using the document for establishing personal information about D; or

(ii) the intention of allowing or inducing another to use it for establishing, ascertaining or verifying personal information about D or about any other person (with the exception, in the case of an identity document that relates to someone else, of the individual to whom it relates).

Possession of apparatus with prohibited intention

Under IDA 2010, s 5(1), it is an offence triable only on indictment for D with the prohibited intention to make or to have in his possession or under his control:

(a) any apparatus which, to his knowledge, is or has been specially designed or adapted for use in making false identity documents; or

(b) any article or material which, to D's knowledge, is or has been specially designed or adapted for use in making false identity documents.

The prohibited intention is the intention:

(i) that D or another will make a false identity document; and

(ii) that the document will be used by somebody for establishing, ascertaining or verifying personal information about a person.

The references to the making of a false identity document include references to the modification of an identity document so that it becomes false (s 9).

Possession without reasonable excuse

It is an indictable (either way) offence against IDA 2010, s 6(1) for D to have in his possession or under his control, without reasonable excuse:

(a) a false identity document;
(b) an improperly obtained identity document;
(c) an identity document relating to someone else; or
(d) any apparatus, or article or material which, to his knowledge, is or has been specially designed or adapted to make false identity documents, or to be used to make such documents.

The Court of Appeal has held that the mere fact that D did not know or believe that the document was false cannot of itself and without more amount to a reasonable excuse, but (it held) lack of such knowledge or belief can be relevant to a defence of reasonable excuse by way of explanation of D's possession—it might explain why the document had not been thrown away or handed to the police. Possession of a document for an innocent purpose cannot in itself amount to 'reasonable excuse'. Subject to these limits, 'reasonable excuse' is a matter for the jury or magistrates.

Defence for refugees

See p 932.

COUNTERFEITING AND RELATED OFFENCES: GENERAL POINTS

Counterfeit

By FCA 1981, s 28(1), a thing is a counterfeit of a currency note or of a protected coin:

(a) if it is not a currency note or a protected coin, but *resembles a currency note or protected coin* (whether on one side only or on both) *to such an extent that it is reasonably capable of passing for a currency note or protected coin of that description*; or
(b) if it is a currency note or protected coin which has been *so altered that it is reasonably capable of passing for a currency note or protected coin of some other description*.

For the avoidance of any doubt on the matter, s 28(2) goes on to provide that a thing consisting of one side only of a currency note, with or without the addition of other material, is a counterfeit of such a note, and that a thing consisting of parts of two or more currency notes (or of parts of such note(s) and other material) is capable of being a counterfeit of a currency note. Thus, for example, a supposed currency note composed of parts of true currency notes and other materials is a counterfeit, as is a thing which consists of one side only of a currency note as a result of that note being 'split'.

For the purposes of FCA 1981, 'currency note' means:

(a) any note which has been lawfully issued in the UK, the Channel Islands, the Isle of Man or the Irish Republic, *is or has been* customarily used as money in the country of issue, and is payable on demand; or

(b) any note which has been lawfully issued in some other country, and *is* customarily
used as money in that country.

Thus, a £20 note, a €20 note and a 100 dinar note are all 'currency notes'; so is an old
style £5 note, which is no longer legal tender, but not a note which is no longer valid
currency in the foreign country where it was issued.

A 'protected coin' is defined as any coin which is customarily used as money in any
country, ie any coin which *is still* valid tender at the time. It also includes a sovereign,
half-sovereign, krugerrand (or a coin denominated as a fraction thereof), a Maria-
Theresia thaler dated 1780, and any euro coin.

Passing or tendering

In the offences below, references to 'passing or tendering' a note or coin are not confined to passing or tendering it as legal tender, so that (for example) passing or tendering a note or coin to a coin dealer or as a collector's item is a 'passing or tendering' for
the purpose of these offences. A person 'passes' a note or coin to somebody when the
latter actually accepts it from him; a person 'tenders' a note or coin when he offers to
pass it to somebody. On the other hand, simply to produce a bundle of counterfeit notes
to impress a lady friend does not constitute a tender of them, since it does not involve
any offer to pass them to her or anyone else.

COUNTERFEITING

FCA 1981, s 14(1) states that it is an offence for a person to make a counterfeit of a
currency note or protected coin, intending that he or another shall pass or tender it as
genuine. Section 14(2) makes it an offence for a person to make a counterfeit of a currency note or protected coin without lawful authority or excuse.

Both offences punish those who make a counterfeit currency note or protected coin;
the difference between them is this. If the maker's intention is that he or another shall
pass it into circulation, he commits an offence under s 14(1). If he did not so intend,
or that intent cannot be proved, he can be convicted of the lesser offence under s 14(2)
unless he had a lawful authority or excuse for making the thing (which will be rare).

PASSING OR TENDERING COUNTERFEIT CURRENCY

Passing or tendering counterfeit as genuine

By FCA 1981, s 15(1)(a), it is an offence for a person to pass or tender as genuine any
thing which is, and which he knows or believes to be, a counterfeit of a currency note
or of a protected coin.

Someone who sells to another counterfeit notes or coins, having declared them to be
such, does not pass or tender them as genuine.

Delivering counterfeit

FCA 1981, s 15(1)(b) makes it an offence for someone to deliver to another any thing
which is, and which he knows or believes to be, a counterfeit of a currency note or
protected coin, intending that the person to whom it is delivered or another shall
pass or tender it as genuine. Section 15(1)(b) deals, for example, with the person who
knowingly takes counterfeits from the maker and delivers them to a second person,

intending that the second person should pass or tender them as genuine. It is irrelevant whether or not the second person is an innocent recipient.

Where it cannot be proved that the person who delivered the counterfeit intended that the recipient or another should pass or tender it as genuine, he may be convicted of the offence of delivery without lawful authority or excuse, which is dealt with by s 15(2).

CUSTODY OR CONTROL OF COUNTERFEIT CURRENCY AND COUNTERFEITING IMPLEMENTS

The offences of 'possession' under FCA 1981, s 5 of false instruments and of materials and implements for their making dealt with above have their counterparts in ss 16 and 17 in relation to people who have counterfeit currency or counterfeiting materials or implements in their custody or under their control.

Custody or control of counterfeit currency

By FCA 1981, s 16(1), it is an offence for a person to have in his custody or control a counterfeit of a currency note or of a protected coin, knowing or believing it to be so and intending either to pass or tender it as genuine or to deliver it to another with the intention that he or another shall pass or tender it as genuine. Section 16(2) makes it an offence for a person to have such custody or control, with such knowledge or belief, without lawful authority or excuse. On a charge under s 16(2) D's intention is irrelevant. Whilst a settled intention to hand in counterfeit currency may amount to a lawful excuse, the fact that a person has not yet decided what to do with it cannot amount to such an excuse.

The offences of 'possession' in respect of currency may be committed even though the coin or note is not in a fit state to be passed or tendered or even though its making or counterfeiting has not been finished or perfected. Consequently, these offences may be committed, for example, in relation to the part-finished efforts of a counterfeiter.

Making, custody or control of counterfeiting materials and implements

FCA 1981, s 17(1) makes it an offence for a person to make, or to have in his custody or under his control, any thing *which he intends to use, or to permit any other person to use, for the purpose of making a counterfeit of a currency note or of a protected coin with the intention that it be passed or tendered as genuine.* The words 'any thing which he intends to use' include *any thing used as a part of the process of counterfeiting.* This includes chromolins (printers' proofs used to check the quality of an aluminium plate produced from a film) of a currency note, special papers and inks, and reprographic equipment.

Section 17(2) provides that it is an offence for a person without lawful authority or excuse to make or to have in his custody or under his control any thing which, to his knowledge, is or has been specially designed or adapted for the making of a counterfeit of a currency note. The intentions italicised above are not required.

By s 17(3), it is an offence for a person to make or have in his custody or under his control, any implement which, to his knowledge, is capable of imparting to any thing a resemblance to the whole or part of either side of a protected coin, or of the reverse of the image on either side of a protected coin. A person charged with this offence has a defence if he proves that he had the written consent of the Treasury, or some other lawful authority or excuse. This is the only offence in the Act where the defendant has the burden of proving a lawful authority or excuse.

REPRODUCING BRITISH CURRENCY

FCA 1981, ss 18 and 19 deal respectively with the reproduction of British currency notes without written consent to do so from the relevant authority, and with the making, sale or distribution of imitation British coins in connection with a scheme intended to promote the sale of any product or service.

These offences are neither serious (since, although triable either way, they are punishable only by way of a fine) nor do they require any counterfeiting in its strict sense (ie notes and coins reasonably capable of passing as currency notes or protected coins), but set out to prevent the use of reproductions in any form, even though the copy reproduced would not fool any reasonable person. If there was no legislation to prevent the production of good quality 'stage money', this could lead to abuse. Colour supplement magazines could print a reproduction of one side of a currency note as a voucher entitling the holder to a price reduction in certain stores. This would no doubt be done innocently, but the reproduction might be used falsely by some other person. Section 18 goes to the extent of prohibiting copies of notes which are not reproduced on the correct scale, in order to prevent 'blow-ups' being produced which may be of assistance to a counterfeiter.

POLICE POWERS

FCA 1981, ss 7 and 24 authorise a justice who is satisfied upon information on oath that there is reasonable cause to believe that a person has in his *custody* or under his *control*:

(a) any thing which has been used, or is intended to be used, for the making of a false instrument or copy of a false instrument, contrary to ss 1 or 2;

(b) any false instrument or copy which has been used, or is intended to be used, contrary to ss 3 or 4;

(c) any thing which it is unlawful to possess without authority, etc, under s 5 (false money orders, stamps, etc);

(d) any thing which is a counterfeit currency note or protected coin, or a reproduction made in breach of ss 18 or 19; or

(e) any thing which has been used, or is intended to be used, for the making of such counterfeit or reproductions,

to issue a warrant authorising a constable to enter premises, search for and seize such objects. The additional powers of seizure provided by the Criminal Justice and Police Act 2001, s 50 apply where a search warrant under FCA 1981 is executed.

A constable may, at any time after seizure, apply to a magistrates' court for an order for the forfeiture and destruction or disposal of objects seized.

SUPPLYING SPECIALIST PRINTING EQUIPMENT

It has been found difficult to prosecute those who knowingly supply specialist printing equipment to criminals for use in the manufacture of false documents, because of the absence of a targeted offence. The Specialist Printing Equipment and Materials (Offences) Act 2015, s 1(1) has created a specific criminal offence of supplying specialist printing equipment, knowing it will be used for criminal purposes. The offence is triable only on indictment.

CHAPTER 37

Criminal Damage and Computer Misuse

CRIMINAL DAMAGE: INTRODUCTION

The Criminal Damage Act 1971 (CDA 1971) deals with most offences concerned with damage to property but other legislation still exists in this area. The Malicious Damage Act 1861 still deals with offences of obstructing railways or interfering with them (see Chapter 21) and of concealing or removing navigation marks or buoys. If damage is caused by an explosion the offence under the Explosive Substances Act 1883, s 2 (p 618) should be considered.

All the offences under CDA 1971 described in this chapter are indictable (either way) offences, except the offences under CDA 1971, s 1(2) or s 1(2) and (3), which are triable only on indictment.

CRIMINAL DAMAGE

CDA 1971, s 1(1) provides what is known as the simple offence of criminal damage. It states that a person who without lawful excuse destroys or damages any property belonging to another intending to destroy or damage any such property, or being reckless as to whether any such property would be destroyed or damaged, is guilty of an offence.

If the destruction or damage is by fire, there is a separate offence under s 1(1) and (3), required to be charged as arson, which carries a higher maximum punishment. As a result there are technically two offences: criminal damage otherwise than by fire contrary to s 1(1) and criminal damage committed by fire, contrary to CDA 1971, s 1(1) and (3).

By the Theft Act 1968 (TA 1968), s 30, the leave of the DPP is required for the institution of proceedings for criminal damage by one spouse or civil partner to the other's property, unless, by virtue of any judicial decree or order, the spouses were not obliged to cohabit at the material time or an order is in force providing for the separation of the civil partners.

Criminal damage contrary to CDA 1971, s 1(1) (but not s 1(1) and (3)) is a 'penalty offence' for the purposes of the Criminal Justice and Police Act 2001, and may be dealt with under a fixed penalty procedure: see p 31. This may be an appropriate course of action in minor cases.

What is said below about the elements of an offence of criminal damage is equally applicable to the other offences under the Act, unless the contrary is indicated.

Destroy or damage

Property may be damaged if it suffers physical harm which involves permanent or temporary impairment of the property's use or value. If a motor car is scratched when a coin is scraped along its side it is damaged thereby, because its value is impaired; likewise a wall is damaged if slogans are painted on it, as is beer if water is poured into it. If part of a machine is removed, without which it cannot work, the machine may be damaged, even though neither it nor the part suffers actual physical injury, because its use is impaired. Consequently, a car may be damaged if the rotor arm is removed from its engine.

The fact that what is done is rectifiable does not prevent the property being damaged but the amount and cost of rectification are relevant factors in determining whether there has been damage; if they are minimal it may be found that the property has not been damaged.

By CDA 1971, s 10(5), any modification of the contents of a computer is not to be regarded as damaging any computer or computer storage medium (eg a hard disc), unless its effect on the computer or medium impairs its *physical* condition. Unauthorised acts with intent to impair the operation of a computer are dealt with by the Computer Misuse Act 1990, s 3, see p 947.

The destruction of property involves something which goes beyond damage, such as the demolition of a machine, the pulling down of a wall or other structure, or the killing of an animal.

If arson is charged, it must also be proved that the destruction or damage was caused by fire.

Property

CDA 1971, s 10(1) defines property as being property of a tangible nature, whether real or personal, including money and:

(a) including wild creatures which have been tamed or are ordinarily kept in captivity, and any other wild creatures or their carcasses *if,* but only if, they have been reduced into possession which has not been lost or abandoned, or are in the course of being reduced into possession; but
(b) *not* including mushrooms growing wild on any land or flowers, fruit or foliage of a plant growing wild on any land.

The term 'mushroom' includes any fungus and 'plant' includes shrubs and trees.

Thus, 'property' is defined by s 10 in a similar way to the definition of that term in TA 1968 for the purposes of theft. One difference is that land itself, which generally cannot be stolen, is not subjected to any limits on when it can be the subject of criminal damage. A man who moves his fence to capture a little of his neighbour's lawn cannot be convicted of theft of that piece of lawn, but he would be guilty of criminal damage if he damaged it. Another difference is that intangible things, such as copyright, cannot be the subject of criminal damage although they may be stolen. A third difference is that wild mushrooms and wild flowers, etc can never be the subject of *criminal* damage, although they can be stolen in certain circumstances. The provisions of the Wildlife and Countryside Act 1981 (see Appendix 4 on the companion website) offer protection to some wild creatures and plants in circumstances which would include forms of damage.

Belonging to another

The class of persons to whom property is treated for the purposes of CDA 1971 as belonging by s 10(2) to (4) is by no means limited to the owners of property, but includes a range of other people with a connection with it.

Section 10(2) provides that property is to be treated as belonging to any person:

(a) having the custody or control of it;
(b) having in it any proprietary right or interest (not being an equitable interest arising only from an agreement to transfer or grant an interest); or
(c) having a charge on it.

Co-owners of property each have a proprietary right or interest in the property and if one damages the property he may be convicted of criminal damage since the property 'belongs to another'. The adjective 'proprietary' excludes those, such as insurance companies, which, although they have an interest in the property, do not have a proprietary interest.

Finally, persons having a charge on property have a proprietary interest in it. The best example of a charge is where, to buy his house, a house owner mortgages it by way of charge to a building society. As a result of s 10(2), the house will belong to the building society, as well as to the house owner, and if he intentionally or recklessly damages it without lawful excuse he can be convicted of criminal damage, since the house will 'belong to another'.

Section 10(3) and (4) provides that, as in the case of theft, where property is subject to a trust, the person to whom it belongs shall include any person having the right to enforce the trust; and that property belonging to a corporation sole (see p 894) is to be treated as belonging to the corporation notwithstanding a vacancy in the corporation.

Mens rea

To do an act deliberately, for example deliberately throwing a stone, is not enough; D must have intended his conduct to result in property belonging to another being destroyed or damaged, or been reckless as to the risk of such destruction or damage resulting from his conduct.

Without lawful excuse

In order to commit an offence under CDA 1971, s 1(1) or s 1(1) and (3), D must destroy or damage another's property 'without lawful excuse'. D does not have the burden of proof in respect of a lawful excuse, only an evidential burden. For these purposes, s 5(2) provides that a person is to be treated as having a lawful excuse if he acted with one of two types of belief, neither of which need be reasonable (although the more reasonable an alleged belief the more likely that it will be found to have been held).

Belief in consent

Section 5(2)(a) provides that a person has a lawful excuse if, at the time of the act or acts alleged to constitute the offence, he believed that the person or persons whom he believed to be entitled to consent to the destruction of or damage to the property had so consented, or would have so consented if he or they had known of the destruction or damage and its circumstances.

An employee who demolished a shed in his employer's yard, wrongly believing that his foreman had instructed him to do so by saying 'Clear that yard at the back', would have a lawful excuse. If no such direction had been given, but the worker honestly believed that he would have been given permission by the foreman had he asked, this would still amount to lawful excuse.

Belief in defence of property

Section 5(2)(b) provides that a person is to be treated as having a lawful excuse if he destroyed or damaged the property in question in order to protect his own property or that of some other person, or a right or interest (such as a right of way) in property which was or which he believed to be vested in himself or another, *and* at the time of the act he believed that the property, right or interest was in immediate need of protection, and at that time he believed that the means of protection adopted or proposed to be adopted were reasonable having regard to all the circumstances. It is immaterial whether or not the threatened harm which the defendant sought to prevent was unlawful or lawful.

The property intended to be protected, unlike that damaged, need not be tangible; it can also consist of a right or privilege in or over land, whether created by grant, licence or otherwise. Just as a person is entitled in appropriate circumstances to shoot a dog attacking his sheep, so he is entitled to demolish a wall barring a right of way which he has (or believes he has). Because a person is not 'property', breaking down a door to recover a child who is being unlawfully detained does not fall within the defence of 'lawful excuse' under s 5(2).

The defence under s 5(2)(b) involves the following four elements:

(1) *D must have destroyed or damaged the property in question in order to protect property or a right or interest in it.* Whether or not he did so depends on an objective test: 'Whatever D's state of mind and assuming an honest belief, can it be said that what D did was done in order to protect particular property?' This was stated by the Court of Appeal in a case where D had set fire to bedding in an isolated part of a sheltered accommodation in order, D said, to demonstrate that the fire alarm was not working and thereby to protect the building from the risk posed to it. Applying the above test, the Court of Appeal held that it admitted of only one answer: D's act was not done to protect the building; it was not an act which in itself protected or was capable of protecting property.

(2) *The property must belong to D or another.* D cannot rely successfully on s 5(2)(b) if what he seeks to protect is neither property belonging to himself or another nor a right or interest in property which is (or which he believes is) vested in himself or another. Thus, where D went onto farmland and destroyed badger traps in order to protect wild badgers, a divisional court held that D could not rely on s 5(2)(b) because the badgers, being wild and not reduced into possession, did not belong to anyone.

(3) *D must believe that the property or right or interest is in need of immediate protection.* The Court of Appeal has held that whether D believes that the property, etc is in need of protection is a subjective question. On the other hand, it has been held that whether the property, etc is in need of 'immediate' protection is an objective question, to be determined by the court or jury in the light of all the circumstances as D believed them to be.

(4) *D must believe that the means adopted were reasonable.* A divisional court has held that this is a purely subjective question. The question is not whether the means adopted by D were objectively reasonable having regard to the circumstances, but whether D believed them to be so.

Lawful excuse in a general sense

Quite apart from the statutory instances of lawful excuse provided by CDA 1971, s 5, any other defence recognised by law amounts to a lawful excuse. A police officer, in executing a search warrant, may, if denied entry, break a lock, thereby committing damage. He would have a lawful excuse for his actions because the statutes under which search warrants may be granted authorise entry by force, if necessary. Other examples of lawful excuses besides those provided by s 5 are self-defence and the defence of another.

On the other hand, a belief in a moral entitlement is not a lawful excuse, nor is a belief that the destruction or damage was reasonable in pursuit of some political objective.

RACIALLY OR RELIGIOUSLY AGGRAVATED CRIMINAL DAMAGE

A person commits an offence under the Crime and Disorder Act 1998, s 30(1) if he commits an offence under CDA 1971, s 1(1) which is racially or religiously aggravated.

An offence of criminal damage is racially or religiously aggravated if:

(a) at the time of committing it, or immediately before or after doing so, the offender demonstrates towards the person to whom the property belongs or is treated as belonging for the purposes of CDA 1971 hostility based on that person's membership (or presumed membership) of a racial or religious group; or

(b) the offence is motivated (wholly or partly) by hostility towards members of a racial or religious group based on their membership of that group.

See pp 658–9 for explanation of the terms of (a) and (b).

DESTROYING OR DAMAGING PROPERTY WITH INTENT TO ENDANGER LIFE OR RECKLESSNESS AS TO LIFE BEING ENDANGERED

CDA 1971, s 1(2) declares that it is an offence for a person without lawful excuse to destroy or damage any property, whether belonging to himself or another:

(a) intending to destroy or damage any property or being reckless as to whether any property would be destroyed or damaged; *and*

(b) intending the destruction or damage to endanger the life of another or being reckless as to whether the life of another would thereby be endangered.

An offence under s 1(2) is generally described as aggravated criminal damage.

By s 1(3), an offence committed under s 1(2) by destroying or damaging property by fire is required to be charged as arson and is charged as contrary to s 1(2) and (3).

There are four separate aggravated offences:

(a) criminal damage with intent to endanger life;
(b) criminal damage reckless as to whether life would be endangered;
(c) arson with intent to endanger life; and
(d) arson reckless as to whether life would be endangered.

It is, of course, open to the prosecution to charge more than one count, alleging different offences in the above list, for example one alleging offence (a) and another offence (b).

An offence under s 1(2) (or s 1(2) and (3)) can be committed in respect of property which 'belongs' only to the defendant (D), and the reason for this can easily be appreciated. If D sets fire to his house which 'belongs' only to him with his wife asleep inside it, D can be charged under s 1(2) and (3).

Except for the fact that the property need not belong to another, the actus reus of an offence under s 1(2) is the same as under s 1(1).

D must either have intended to destroy or damage the property or been reckless in that respect. D must additionally have intended that the destruction or damage would endanger someone's life, or been reckless as to whether human life would be endangered by the destruction or damage, depending on the terms of the indictment.

D must have intended to endanger life, or been reckless as to whether life would be endangered, *by the destruction or damaging* of property which he intentionally or recklessly caused; it is not enough that he merely intended to endanger life, or was reckless as to whether life would be endangered, by the act which caused the destruction or damage. Consequently, a person who fires a gun from outside a house at a person standing behind a window in it cannot be convicted under s 1(2), even though he intended to endanger that person's life, if he did not intend the damaging of the window to endanger life (and was not reckless as to that damage doing so).

The provisions in s 5(2) about lawful excuse do not apply to the present offences. 'Lawful excuse' for an offence under s 1(2), or s 1(2) and (3), is therefore restricted to those defences recognised under the general law, such as self-defence and defence of another.

THREATS TO DESTROY OR DAMAGE PROPERTY

Threats to destroy or damage property are dealt with under CDA 1971, s 2, which states that a person who without lawful excuse makes to another a threat, intending that that other would fear that it *would be* carried out:

(a) to destroy or damage any property belonging to that other or a third person; or
(b) to destroy or damage his own property in a way which he knows is likely to endanger the life of that other or a third person,

is guilty of an offence. The Court of Appeal has held that the italicised words 'would be' include as an alternative the notion of a fear that the threat *might* be carried out.

The threat must be to do something which would be an offence against CDA 1971, s 1. It must be carried out with the intention of inducing a fear in the mind of the recipient that it would be carried out. It does not matter how the threat is communicated, nor that the person who offers the threat does not intend to carry it out (provided that he intends the recipient to fear that he would do so), nor that the recipient is not actually put in fear by the threat.

Someone who communicates the threat of an explosion to another person, intending that the recipient will fear that the threat will be carried out, commits the present offence if the threat is concerned with destruction or damage to property, etc. There is often confusion with the bomb hoax offences created by the Criminal Law Act 1977, s 51(2) (see p 620), which deals with the offence of communicating false information to induce such a fear. That offence is distinguished from the one under CDA 1971, s 2 by its limitations to false information whereas the offence under s 2 can be committed whether or not the threat involves false information.

The provisions of s 5(2) relating to 'lawful excuse' apply (with a minor modification) to threats to destroy or damage another's property but do not apply to threats to destroy or damage the threatener's own property in a way likely to endanger the life of some person.

POSSESSING THING WITH INTENT TO DESTROY OR DAMAGE PROPERTY

The possession of things to be used for the purpose of causing damage is dealt with by CDA 1971, s 3, which states that a person who has anything in his custody or under his control intending without lawful excuse to use or cause or permit another to use it:

(a) to destroy or damage any property belonging to some other person; or
(b) to destroy or damage his own or the user's property in a way which he knows is likely to endanger the life of some other person

is guilty of an offence.

As can be seen, the possession of the 'thing' must be for the purpose of doing something (or causing or permitting something to be done) which would be an offence under s 1. There must be a clear intention to use the thing in such a way or to cause or permit another to do so; it is not sufficient to prove that D realised that it 'might' be so used. Provided that such an intention does exist it is immaterial that there is no immediate intention to use it but only a conditional one. A terrorist group which possesses explosives in a warehouse, intending to use them to destroy or damage property if, and when, the opportunity arises, can therefore be convicted of the present offence.

'Possession' is covered in s 3 by the use of 'in his custody or under his control'. These precise terms cover the same situations as possession but their use avoids the technicalities of the concept of 'possession'. The explosives contained in a warehouse might be in the custody of the keeper of that warehouse but they might also be under the control of the leaders of the terrorist group, who can order their removal and use at any time.

The offence is sufficient to include instances of possession of a terrorist arsenal, the possession of pickaxe handles by protection racketeers, or even the possession of paint by those who intend to endorse graffiti on the walls of buildings.

Where the offence involves an intent falling within (a), ie to destroy or damage another's property, 'without lawful excuse' is subject to s 5(2) (with a minor modification), but where the intent falls within (b), ie to destroy or damage property in a way known to be likely to endanger life, it is not.

POLICE POWERS

CDA 1971, s 6 empowers a justice, following information given on oath, to grant a search warrant if there is reasonable cause to believe that a person has in his custody or under his control or on his premises anything which there is reasonable cause to believe *has been* used, or is *intended for use*, without lawful excuse to destroy or damage property belonging to another or to destroy or damage property in a way likely to endanger the life of another.

If such a search warrant is granted, a constable may enter (if need be by force) any premises and search for the thing in question. He may seize anything which he believes to have been used or to be intended to be used as aforesaid.

SALE OF AEROSOL PAINT TO A CHILD

For convenience, this offence is dealt with here. The Anti-social Behaviour Act 2003, s 54(1) makes it an offence for a person to sell an aerosol paint container to a person under the age of 16.

It is a defence for D to show that he took all reasonable steps to determine the purchaser's age and that he reasonably believed that the purchaser was not under 16. Where the sale was effected by another person, for example an assistant, it is a defence to prove that D took all reasonable steps to avoid the commission of the offence.

COMPUTER MISUSE

The misuse of computer hardware or software may involve one or more of four offences under the Computer Misuse Act 1990 (CMA 1990), ss 1 to 3ZA set out below. The offences under ss 1 to 3 are indictable (either way) offences. An offence under s 3ZA is triable only on indictment.

Unauthorised access to computer material

By CMA 1990, s 1(1), a person commits an offence if:

(a) he causes a computer to perform any function with intent to secure access to any program or data held in any computer;
(b) the access he intends to secure or to enable to be secured is unauthorised; and
(c) he knows at the time when he causes the computer to perform the function that this is the case.

This offence covers all forms of computer hacking, including hacking by someone who simply seeks access because of the challenge of breaking through a security system. On the other hand, the offence does not cover computer eavesdropping; mere surveillance of data displayed on a VDU screen does not trigger it, since D must cause the computer to perform a function if he is to be guilty.

Actual access to any program or data held in a computer is not required, since it is enough that D simply causes a computer to perform a function with intent to secure access to a program or data held in it, such intended access being unauthorised to his knowledge.

A person intends to secure access to a program or data if he intends, by causing a computer to perform any function, to:

(a) alter or erase the program or data;
(b) copy or move it to any storage medium other than that in which it is held or to a different location in the storage medium in which it is held;
(c) use it; or
(d) have it output from the computer in which it is held (whether by having it displayed or in any other manner).

The intended access need not relate to any particular program or data, nor any particular type of program or data, nor to a program or data held in any particular computer. It is immaterial whether the program or data is unauthorisedly accessed directly from the computer containing it or indirectly via another computer.

Access of any kind by any person to a program or data held in a computer is unauthorised if:

(a) he is not himself entitled to control access of the kind in question to the program or data; and
(b) he does not have consent to access by him of the kind in question to the program or data from any person who is so entitled.

Because the definition refers to 'access of the kind' in question, a person who has authority to view data may nevertheless unauthorisedly access it if he accesses it to alter or copy it if he has no authority to access for such a purpose.

Unauthorised access with intent to commit or facilitate further offence

By CMA 1990, s 2(1), a person commits an offence if he commits the unauthorised access offence under s 1 with intent:

(a) to commit an offence to which s 2 applies; or
(b) to facilitate the commission of such an offence (whether by himself or by any other person).

Section 2 applies to any offence whose sentence is fixed by law (essentially, murder), and to any offence for which an offender of 21 or over may be sentenced to imprisonment for five years (eg fraud, theft, and forgery).

It is immaterial whether the further offence is to be committed on the same occasion as the unauthorised access offence or on any future occasion, and it is also immaterial that the facts are such that the commission of the further offence is impossible.

Unauthorised acts with intent to impair, or with recklessness as to impairing, operation of computer, etc

By CMA 1990, s 3(1), a person is guilty of an offence if:

(a) he does any unauthorised act in relation to a computer;
(b) at the time when he does the act he knows that it is unauthorised; and
(c) either s 3(2) or s 3(3) (below) applies.

For the purposes of s 3:

(a) a reference to doing an act includes a reference to causing an act to be done;
(b) 'act' includes a series of acts.

An act is unauthorised if the person doing the act (or causing it):

(a) is not himself a person who has responsibility for the computer and is entitled to determine whether the act should be done; and
(b) does not have consent to the act from any such person.

Although the owner of a computer which is able to receive email is ordinarily to be taken to consent to the sending of emails to the computer, such implied consent is not without limits. For example, a divisional court has held, it does not extend to emails which are not sent for the purpose of communicating with the owner, but are sent as a 'mail bombing campaign' for the purpose of interrupting the proper operation and use of the system.

Section 3(2) applies if the person intends by doing the act:

(a) *to impair the operation of any computer;*
(b) *to prevent or hinder access to any program or data held in the computer; or*
(c) *to impair the operation of any such program or the reliability of any such data.*

'Impairing, preventing or hindering' something includes doing so temporarily.

An example of s 3(2) would be where someone, by misusing or bypassing a password, places in the files of a computer a bogus email pretending that the password holder was the author; such an addition would result in an unauthorised alteration of the contents of the computer and would clearly be done with intent to cause an alteration of the contents, and by so doing to impair the reliability of the data on the computer.

Section 3(3) applies if the person is reckless as to whether the act will do any of the things italicised above.

The intention or recklessness referred to in s 3(2) or (3) above need not relate to any particular computer or any particular program or data, or a program or data of any particular kind.

Unauthorised acts causing, or creating risk of, serious damage

A person is guilty of an offence under CMA 1990, s 3ZA(1) if:

(a) he does any unauthorised act in relation to a computer;
(b) at the time of doing the act he knows that it is unauthorised;
(c) the act causes, or creates a significant risk of, serious damage of a material kind; and
(d) he intends by doing the act to cause serious damage of a material kind or is reckless as to whether such damage is caused.

By s 3ZA(2), damage is of a 'material kind' if it is damage to human welfare in any place, to the environment of any place, to the economy of any country or to the national security of any country. For these purposes an act causes damage to human welfare only if it causes:

(i)   loss to human life;
(ii) human illness or injury; or
(iii) disruption of a supply of money, food, water, energy or fuel, of a system of communication, of facilities for transport or of services relating to health.

It is immaterial for the purposes of s 3ZA(2) whether or not an act causing damage does so directly, or is the only or main cause of the damage.

A reference above to doing an act includes a reference to causing an act to be done, 'act' includes a series of acts, and a reference to a country includes a reference to a territory, and to any place in (or part or region of) a country or territory.

Where an offence under s 3ZA(1) is committed as a result of causing or creating a significant risk of serious damage to human welfare or serious damage to national security, a more serious offence is committed under s 3ZA(1) and (7).

Making, supplying or obtaining articles for use in an offence against CMA 1990, s 1, 3 or 3ZA

CMA 1990, s 3A provides indictable (either way) offences preparatory to an offence under s 1, 3 or 3ZA. It states that a person commits an offence in the following three cases if:

(a) he makes, adapts, supplies or offers to supply any article intending it to be used to commit, or to assist in the commission of, an offence against s 1, 3 or 3ZA;
(b) he supplies or offers to supply any article believing that it is likely to be so used; or
(c) he obtains any article:

   (i) intending to use it to commit, or to assist in the commission of, an offence under s 1, 3 or 3ZA, or

  (ii) with a view to it being supplied for such use.

'Article' includes any program or data held in electronic form, and therefore includes a computer password or other means by which a computer system may be accessed.

These offences are aimed at 'hacker tools' which are increasingly being used in connection with organised crime.

CHAPTER 38

Offences Against Administration of Justice

With two exceptions indicated at the appropriate points, the offences referred to in this chapter are indictable. Besides perjury and perverting the course of justice, all these indictable offences are triable either way.

ASSISTING OFFENDERS

The Criminal Law Act 1967 (CLA 1967), s 4(1) provides that, where a person has committed a relevant offence, another person is guilty of an offence if (knowing or believing him to be guilty of the offence, or of some other relevant offence) without lawful authority or reasonable excuse that person does any act with intent to impede his apprehension or prosecution. A 'relevant offence' is: (a) an offence for which the sentence is fixed by law (essentially, murder); (b) an offence for which a person of 18 years or over (not previously convicted) may be sentenced to a term of imprisonment for a term of five years.

Such a person is not guilty, as an accomplice, of the relevant offence which has been committed, because this conduct occurs after its commission; the offence under s 4(1) is a separate offence.

Although the *commission* of the 'relevant offence' by the principal offender (E) must be proved, it is not necessary that E should have been convicted of it. Indeed, the acquittal of E does not prevent a conviction of D for assisting that person; the commission of the relevant offence by E may be established in the case of D, even though it is not established against E himself, for example because evidence admissible against D was not admissible against E, or because, after E's acquittal, but before D's trial, the discovery of further evidence puts the commission of the offence by E beyond doubt.

CONCEALING OFFENCES

This offence is governed by CLA 1967, s 5(1), which provides that, where a person has committed a relevant offence (as defined above), another person is guilty of an offence if he, knowing or believing that the offence or some other relevant offence has been committed, and that he has information which might be of assistance in securing the prosecution or conviction of an offender for it, accepts or agrees to accept for not disclosing it any consideration other than the making good of loss or injury caused by the offence, or the making of reasonable compensation for it.

Prosecutions for offences contrary to CLA 1967, ss 4 or 5 may only be instituted by or with the consent of the DPP.

WASTEFUL EMPLOYMENT OF POLICE

The CLA 1967, s 5(2) states that it is an offence for a person to cause any wasteful employment of the police by knowingly making to any person a false report tending to show that an offence has been committed or that the informant has any information material to any police inquiry, or giving rise to apprehension for the safety of any persons or property. The offence is not indictable.

The Criminal Justice and Police Act 2001 provides that this is a 'penalty offence' in respect of which a 'penalty notice' may be given: see p 31.

PERJURY

The Perjury Act 1911 (PA 1911), s 1(1) provides that it is an offence for any person, lawfully sworn as a witness or interpreter in a judicial proceeding, to wilfully make a statement material in that proceeding which he knows to be false or does not believe to be true.

A 'person lawfully sworn' includes a person who has made an affirmation or declaration that he will tell the truth. A 'judicial proceeding' is a proceeding before any court, tribunal or person having by law power to hear, receive and examine evidence on oath. The presence of the word 'wilfully' means that it must be proved that the person concerned made that statement deliberately. A 'material statement' is one which might affect the decision of the court.

By the Youth Justice and Criminal Evidence Act 1999 (YJCEA 1999), s 29, this offence applies to an intermediary (see p 241) as it applies to an interpreter lawfully sworn in a judicial proceeding.

PA 1911, s 13 states that a person shall not be convicted of perjury or any other offence under PA 1911 solely on the evidence of one witness as to the falsity of any statement alleged to be false, so that there is a requirement of corroboration in this respect.

Subornation of perjury

PA 1911, s 7(1) provides that a person who aids, abets, counsels, procures or suborns (ie procures by bribery or other corrupt means another to commit perjury) is liable for perjury 'as if he were a principal offender'. This provision is redundant since it adds nothing to the criminal liability which would otherwise be imposed under the general principle relating to accomplices.

OFFENCES AKIN TO PERJURY

Offences relating to false unsworn statement (YJCEA 1999, s 57 (not indictable)), false written statements tendered in evidence in criminal proceedings (Criminal Justice Act 1967, s 89), false statements on oath made otherwise than in a judicial proceeding (PA 1911, s 2) and false statutory declarations and other false statements without oath (PA 1911, s 5) are dealt with in Chapter 38 on the companion website.

PERVERTING THE COURSE OF JUSTICE

The common law offence of perverting the course of justice may be committed by any act or series of acts which has a tendency to pervert the course of justice and is intended to do so.

For the purposes of the offence, it has been held that the course of justice may be perverted by, for example: discontinuing a criminal prosecution in return for payment; making false claims about an offence; making false statements to police officers investigating an offence; making a false complaint to the police capable of being taken seriously, whether or not it identifies particular individuals; retracting a truthful allegation of an offence, or truthful evidence; interfering with a witness or a juror; producing fabricated evidence; and destroying evidence of an offence to hamper an investigation (actual or potential). The Court of Appeal has stated that there is no closed list of acts which may give rise to the offence, but that any extension by the judges in the range of recognised acts should take place with caution. The requisite acts are not limited to those giving rise to some other independent criminal wrongdoing.

INTIMIDATION OF WITNESSES, JURORS AND OTHERS

Intimidation, etc before or during a criminal trial

The Criminal Justice and Public Order Act 1994 (CJPOA 1994), s 51(1) provides that a person commits an offence if:

(a) he does an act which intimidates, and is intended to intimidate, another person (the victim);
(b) he does the act knowing or believing that the victim is assisting in the investigation of an offence or is a witness or potential witness, or a juror or potential juror, in proceedings for an offence; and
(c) he does it thereby intending to cause the investigation or the course of justice to be obstructed, perverted or interfered with.

In respect of the requirement of the doing of an act which intentionally results in another person being intimidated, it is immaterial that the act is done otherwise than in the presence of the victim, or to a person other than the victim.

The Court of Appeal has held that 'intimidation' requires that a person is actually put in fear by violence or a threat. Threatened harm may be physical (to the person or a person's property) or financial.

Section 51(1) does not require that the person who is intimidated be actually assisting in the investigation of an offence at the time, or be a witness or potential witness, or a juror or potential juror, in proceedings for an offence. It is sufficient that D believes that the person so intimidated is involved in that way. There must, however, be an investigation in progress; it is insufficient that D believed that such an investigation was taking place. An 'investigation into an offence' in s 51 means an investigation by the police or other persons charged with the duty of investigating offences or charging offenders.

In respect of (c), CJPOA 1994, s 51(7) provides that if it is proved that the intimidating act was done with the required knowledge or belief, it must be presumed, unless the contrary is proved, that D did the act with the required intention. Thus, in such circumstances, the onus is upon D to show that he did not have such an intention.

Reprisals against witnesses, jurors and others in criminal cases

CJPOA 1994, s 51(2) provides that a person commits an offence if:

(a) he does an act which harms, and is intended to harm, another person or, intending to cause another person to fear harm, he threatens to do an act which would harm that other person;
(b) he does or threatens to do the act knowing or believing that the person harmed or threatened to be harmed (the victim), or some other person, has assisted in the

investigation into an offence or has given evidence or particular evidence in proceedings for an offence, or has acted as a juror or concurred in a particular verdict in proceedings for an offence; and

(c) he does or threatens to do it because of that knowledge or belief.

For the purposes of (a), it is immaterial that the act is or would be done, or that the threat is made, otherwise than in the presence of the victim, or to a person other than the victim. There is no requirement that the other person is actually intimidated thereby.

The harm which may be done or threatened may be physical (whether to the person or a person's property) or financial.

In respect of (c), s 51(8) provides that if it is proved that within the 'relevant period':

(i) D did an act which harmed, and was intended to harm, another person; or
(ii) intending to cause another person fear of harm, he threatened to do an act which would harm that other person,

and that he did the act, or (as the case may be) threatened to do the act, with the knowledge or belief required by s 51(2)(b), then D is presumed, unless the contrary is proved, to have done the act, or (as the case may be) threatened to do the act, because of that knowledge or belief.

For the purposes of this presumption, the 'relevant period', in relation to:

(a) *a witness or juror*, begins with the institution of proceedings and ends with the first anniversary of the conclusion of the trial, or of any appeal;
(b) *a person who has assisted in the investigation of an offence (or is believed by D to have done so) but who was not a witness in proceedings for an offence*, is the period of one year beginning with the act (or believed act) which assisted the investigation; and
(c) *a person who has assisted in the investigation of an offence (or is believed by D to have done so) and was also a witness in proceedings for an offence*, is the period beginning with the act (or believed act) which assisted in the investigation and ending with the first anniversary of the conclusion of the trial, or of any appeal.

General

CJPOA 1994, s 51(5) provides that the intention/motive required (in either case) need not be the only or predominating intention/motive with which the act is done or threatened. This excludes defences based upon the fact that the primary intention of the perpetrator was to avoid a miscarriage of justice.

CORRESPONDING PROVISIONS IN RESPECT OF CIVIL PROCEEDINGS

The Criminal Justice and Police Act 2001, ss 39 and 40 provide for the protection of witnesses in civil proceedings before the Court of Appeal, the High Court, the Crown Court, the county court or a magistrates' court. The relevant provisions are dealt with in Chapter 38 on the companion website.

CHAPTER 39

Preventive Justice

This chapter deals with the general statutory offences of encouraging or assisting crime, conspiracy to commit an offence, and attempt to commit an offence. The statutory offence of participating in an organised crime group and the common law offence of conspiracy are also dealt with.

ENCOURAGING OR ASSISTING CRIME

The Serious Crime Act 2007 (SCA 2007), Part 2 (ss 44 to 67) provides three offences of encouraging or assisting crime.

Intentionally encouraging or assisting an offence

A person commits an offence against SCA 2007, s 44 if:

(a) he does an act capable of encouraging or assisting the commission of an offence other than encouraging or assisting suicide; and
(b) he intends to encourage or assist its commission.

In s 44 (and ss 45 and 46, below), the reference to the doing of an act includes a reference to a failure to act, the continuation of an act already begun and an attempt to do an act (except an act amounting to the commission of the offence of attempting to commit another offence).

Encouraging or assisting an offence believing it will be committed

A person commits an offence against SCA 2007, s 45 if:

(a) he does an act (see above) capable of encouraging or assisting the commission of an offence; and
(b) he believes that the offence will be committed and that his act will encourage or assist its commission.

For this offence, it need not be proved that the defendant (D) intended to encourage or assist the commission of the offence which his act is capable of assisting or encouraging. Instead, it is sufficient to prove that D believed that an act would be done which would amount to the commission of that offence and that his act would encourage or assist the doing of that act.

In reckoning whether (for the purposes of s 45) an act is capable of encouraging or assisting the commission of an offence, specified offences are to be disregarded. As a result, a person cannot be guilty under s 45 of encouraging or assisting a specified offence. The offences specified are:

(a) an offence under SCA 2007, ss 44, 45 or 46, and
(b) an offence listed in SCA 2007, Sch 3, Parts 1, 2 or 3 (mainly various statutory offences of incitement already referred to in this book). They also include the following offences:
  (i) solicitation of murder (Offences Against the Person Act 1861, s 4);
  (ii) encouraging or assisting suicide (Suicide Act 1961, s 2(1));
  (iii) assisting an offender (Criminal Law Act 1967, s 4(1));
  (iv) concealing an offence for reward (Criminal Law Act 1967, s 5(1));
  (v) participating in an organised crime group (Serious Crime Act 2015, s 45);
  (vi) statutory conspiracy (Criminal Law Act 1977, s 1(1));
  (vii) common law conspiracy; and
  (viii) criminal attempt (Criminal Attempts Act 1981, s 1(1)).

It is sufficient if D believes that the offence will be committed once certain conditions are met. Thus, if D encourages E to beg some money from V and tells him that, if V refuses, E should take some money from V by force, D can be convicted under s 45 of encouraging or assisting robbery because D believes that the offence (of robbery) will be committed if certain conditions are met (ie V refuses to hand over money).

If it is alleged under s 45 that D believed that an offence would be committed and that his act would encourage or assist its commission, it is sufficient to prove that D believed:

- that an act would be done which would amount to the commission of that offence; and
- that his act would encourage or assist the doing of that act.

Encouraging or assisting an offence believing one or more will be committed

By SCA 2007, s 46, a person commits an offence if:

(a) he does an act (see p 954) capable of encouraging or assisting the commission *of one or more of a number of offences*; and
(b) he believes:
  (i) that one or more of those offences will be committed (but has no belief as to which), and
  (ii) that his act will encourage or assist the commission of one or more of them.

It is immaterial for the purposes of (b)(ii) whether the person has any belief as to which offence will be encouraged or assisted. The Court of Appeal has held that s 46 should only be used when it may be that D, at the time of doing the act, believes that one or more of, for example, *either* offence X, *or* offence Y *or* offence Z will be committed, but has no belief as to which one or ones of the three will be committed.

An offence under ss 44, 45 or 46, or an offence under Sch 3, Parts 1, 2 or 3 (above), is to be disregarded in reckoning whether an act is capable of encouraging or assisting the commission of one or more of a number of offences.

If it is alleged under (b) that D believed that one or more of a number of offences would be committed and that his act would encourage or assist the commission of one or more of them, it is sufficient to prove that D believed that one or more of a number of acts would be done which would amount to the commission of one or more of those offences, and that his act would encourage or assist the doing of one or more of those acts.

Points relating to ss 44 to 46 in general

Act capable of encouraging or assisting

SCA 2007, s 65 provides that the reference to a person's doing an act that is capable of encouraging the commission of an offence includes a reference to his doing so by:

(a) threatening another person or otherwise putting pressure on another person to commit the offence;
(b) taking steps to reduce the possibility of criminal proceedings being brought in respect of that offence; or
(c) failing to take reasonable steps to discharge a duty.

However, it also provides that a person is not to be regarded as doing an act that is capable of encouraging or assisting the commission of an offence merely because he fails to respond to a constable's request for assistance in preventing a breach of the peace.

Further provisions about mens rea

SCA 2007, s 47(5) sets out the mens rea that must be proved under ss 44, 45 or 46 if an offence that it is alleged D intended or believed would be committed requires proof of mens rea or of circumstances or consequences. It provides that, in proving whether an act or omission is one which, if done, would amount to the commission of an offence:

(a) if the offence is one requiring proof of fault, it must be proved that:
    (i)   D believed that, were the act to be done, it would be done with that fault,
    (ii) D was reckless as to whether or not it would be done with that fault, or
    (iii) D's state of mind was such that, were he to do it, it would be done with that fault; and
(b) if the offence is one requiring proof of particular circumstances or consequences, it must be proved that:
    (i)   D believed that, were the act to be done, it would be done in those circumstances or with those consequences, or
    (ii) D was reckless as to whether or not it would be done in those circumstances or with those consequences.

In the case of an offence under s 44, (b)(i) is to be read as if the reference to 'D believed' were a reference to 'D intended or believed'.

It follows from (a) that, if an offence that D is alleged to have intended or believed would be encouraged or assisted requires mens rea, D must believe or be reckless to the possible consequence that, if the act encouraged or assisted is done, it would be done with the necessary mens rea by the person encouraged or assisted, or (by (a)(iii)) D must have the necessary mens rea for that offence. The latter point is important where D thinks that the other person will lack the mens rea. Thus, the offences under ss 44, 45 or 46 apply to the encouragement or assistance of an innocent agent. Section 47(6) provides that, for the purposes of (a)(iii), D is assumed to be able to do the act in question. Thus, D cannot escape liability in respect of (a)(iii) simply because it is impossible for him to commit the offence encouraged or assisted.

It follows from (b) that a requirement to prove mens rea on D's part applies in respect of any circumstances or consequences of the actus reus of the offence that D is alleged to have intended or believed would be encouraged or assisted, and that this is so even though that offence is one of strict liability as to that particular element. For example, the offence of driving a motor vehicle on a road or other public place with excess alcohol, contrary to the Road Traffic Act 1988, s 5, is one of strict liability, for which no mens rea is required. If D asks E to drive him to the station, in ignorance that E has been drinking and is 'over the limit', D cannot be convicted of an offence of encouraging or assisting crime (the only relevant one would be that under s 44) because he neither believes that E is over the limit, nor is he reckless as to the consequence that if E complies with his request he would prove to be over the limit, despite the fact that if E did drive D as requested E would commit the substantive offence.

In the case of an offence under s 46 it is sufficient to prove the matters referred to in s 47(5) by reference to one offence only.

Commission of offence encouraged or assisted not required

SCA 2007, s 49 provides that D may be guilty of offences under ss 44, 45 or 46 whether or not any offence capable of being encouraged or assisted is in fact committed. Thus, an offence under ss 44, 45 or 46 is complete on the giving of the encouragement or assistance.

Where, however, the offence encouraged or assisted by D is *committed*, an offence under ss 44, 45 or 46 exists alongside D's liability for that offence as a party to it, referred to in Chapter 1.

Defence of acting reasonably

SCA 2007, s 50 provides that D is not guilty of an offence under ss 44, 45 or 46 if he proves that (a) he knew certain circumstances existed, and that it was reasonable for him to act as he did in those circumstances; or (b) he reasonably believed certain circumstances to exist, and it was reasonable for him to act as he did in the circumstances as he believed them to be.

The factors which might be considered, in determining whether it was reasonable for a person to act as he did, include: the seriousness of the anticipated offence; any purpose for which he claims to have been acting; and any authority by which he claims to be acting. However, there might be other factors which would be equally relevant.

Protective offences: victims not liable

In the case of 'protective offences' D does not commit an offence under SCA 2007, ss 44, 45 or 46 if he falls within the category of a 'protected person' and he is the person in respect of whom the offence is committed or would have been committed. A 'protective offence' is one that exists (wholly or partly) for the protection of a particular category of persons, for example the child sex offences included in the Sexual Offences Act 2003. Thus, where a child encourages a man to commit a child sex offence against her, that child is not guilty of an offence of encouraging or assisting that offence, as it was fashioned to protect her. Nor could she be convicted as an accomplice to the sex offence itself if it was committed.

Mode of trial

An offence under ss 44 or 45 is triable in the same way as the anticipated offence. An offence under s 46 is only triable on indictment.

Application of other provisions

By SCA 2007, s 54 any provision in other legislation which:

(a) requires the consent to a prosecution of the DPP or some other person;
(b) confers a power to prosecute;
(c) confers a power of seizure;
(d) confers a power of forfeiture of property,

in relation to a substantive offence, also applies to the offence of encouraging or assisting that offence.

OFFENCE OF PARTICIPATING IN ACTIVITIES OF ORGANISED CRIME GROUP

The Serious Crime Act 2015, s 45(1) provides that a person (D) who participates in the criminal activities of an organised crime group commits an offence triable only on indictment. For this purpose, D participates in the criminal activities of an organised crime group if he takes part in any activities that he knows or reasonably suspects (a) are criminal activities of an organised crime group, or (b) will help an organised crime group to carry on criminal activities.

'Criminal activities' are activities carried on with a view to obtaining (directly or indirectly) any gain or benefit, which are activities:

(a) carried on in England and Wales, and which constitute an offence in England and Wales punishable on conviction on indictment with imprisonment for seven years or more; or
(b) carried on outside England and Wales, and which constitute an offence under the law of the country where they are carried on, and would constitute an offence in England and Wales of the kind mentioned in (a) if the activities were carried on in England and Wales.

'Organised crime group' means a group that has as its purpose (or as one of its purposes) the carrying on of criminal activities, and consists of three or more persons who act (or agree to act) together to further that purpose.

For D to be guilty of an offence under s 45(1) it is not necessary:

(a) for D to know any of the persons who are members of the organised crime group;
(b) for all of the acts or omissions comprising participation in the group's criminal activities to take place in England and Wales (so long as at least one of them does); or
(c) for the gain or benefit referred to above to be financial in nature.

By s 45(8), it is a defence for D to prove that his participation was necessary for a purpose related to the prevention or detection of crime.

CONSPIRACY: INTRODUCTION

There are two offences of conspiracy:

(1) It is a *statutory* offence to agree with any other person or persons to commit an offence. Statutory conspiracy is governed by the Criminal Law Act 1977 (CLA 1977).
(2) It is a *common law* offence to agree to defraud or, to the extent that the conduct agreed on would not amount to or involve an offence if carried out by a single person, to engage in conduct which tends to corrupt public morals. Prior to CLA 1977, an agreement to commit an offence or an agreement to do certain other things was a common law conspiracy but that Act abolished common law conspiracy except to the extent just stated.

Both types of conspiracy are only triable on indictment. They require a concluded agreement between two or more people. It is not sufficient for one person to have spoken in the presence of another of his intention to commit a crime, for example; that other person must agree with him that the crime be committed. Immediately such an agreement has been reached, the offence of conspiracy is complete; no steps need be taken in furtherance of it, although it will usually be most unlikely that the conspiracy will be discovered or capable of proof if no further steps are taken. A party cannot escape liability for conspiracy by withdrawing from the agreement.

STATUTORY CONSPIRACY

CLA 1977, s 1(1) provides that if a person agrees with any other person or persons that a course of conduct shall be pursued which, if the agreement is carried out in accordance with their intentions, either:

(a) will necessarily amount to or involve the commission of any offence or offences by one or more of the parties to the agreement (s 1(1)(a)); or
(b) would do so but for the existence of facts which render the commission of the offence or any of the offences impossible (s 1(1)(b)),

he is guilty of conspiracy to commit the offence or offences in question.

The effect of s 1(1)(a) is that a person commits statutory conspiracy if he agrees with any other person or persons *that a course of conduct shall be pursued which, if the agreement is carried out in accordance with their intentions, will necessarily amount to or involve the commission of an offence or offences by one or more of the parties to the agreement*. Special provision is made by CLA 1977, s 1(1)(b) for the case where the criminal objective is impossible, and this is dealt with shortly.

The key issue under s 1(1)(a) is whether, when the agreement is made, the course of conduct agreed on by the parties will necessarily amount to or involve the commission of an offence by one or more of them if it is carried out in accordance with their intentions. Thus, if D1 and D2 agree to have intercourse with a woman without her consent, there is a statutory conspiracy to rape because the course of conduct agreed on—penile penetration—will necessarily amount to the commission of rape if it is carried out in accordance with their intentions, namely to have penile penetration with a woman without her consent.

The offence which the agreed course of conduct will necessarily amount to or involve may be of any type, including (with one exception) a summary offence. By CLA 1977, s 1A, s 1(1) applies in certain cases to an agreement to pursue a course of conduct outside England and Wales which would amount to an offence under the law of the country concerned.

The exceptional case referred to above is provided by the Trade Union and Labour Relations (Consolidation) Act 1992, s 242. It is that where, in pursuance of any agreement, the acts constituting the offence are to be done in contemplation or furtherance of a trade dispute, that offence is not an 'offence' for the purposes of conspiracy if it is triable only summarily and *not* punishable with imprisonment. This exemption is provided to remove the potential danger of conspiracy charges in relation to the many minor offences which might be committed by union members in the course of a dispute, for example simple obstructions of highways.

Impossibility

CLA 1977, s 1(1)(b) deals with agreements which are impossible of fulfilment. It provides that an agreement on a course of conduct which, if the agreement is carried out in accordance with the parties' intentions, would necessarily amount to or involve the commission of an offence or any offences by one or more of the parties *but for the existence of facts which render the commission of the offence or any of the offences impossible* is a statutory conspiracy. This is a sensible provision; the essence of the offence is hatching a plot to commit a crime and this is not made less blameworthy because the actual commission of that crime is rendered impossible because of some fact.

As a result of s 1(1)(b), it is clear, for example, that D1 and D2 can be convicted of conspiracy to murder even though their intended victim was already dead when they agreed to kill him.

Mens rea

At least two parties to the agreement must share the mens rea set out below.

If the actus reus of the substantive offence (ie the agreed offence) requires the existence of a fact or circumstance, a defendant and at least one other party to the agreement (X) must intend or know that it shall or will exist.

There cannot be a statutory conspiracy unless there are at least two parties to an agreement who intend that the agreement be carried out and that the offence they are alleged to have conspired to commit be committed. Surprisingly, because it does violence to the wording of CLA 1977, s 1(1), the House of Lords has held that an individual party to an agreement can be convicted of conspiracy, even though he did not intend that it be carried out and the offence intended by the other parties be committed. In practice this ruling has been ignored and the courts require an intention that the agreement be carried out and that the offence be committed to be proved against an individual defendant.

A defendant and at least one other party (X) must have any additional mens rea (eg dishonesty and an intent permanently to deprive on a charge of conspiracy to steal) required for the substantive offence.

Exemptions from liability for statutory conspiracy

CLA 1977, s 2 provides the following exemptions:

(a) a person cannot be guilty of a conspiracy to commit any offence if he or she is the intended victim of that offence;
(b) a person is not guilty of a conspiracy to commit any offence if the *only* other person or persons with whom he or she agrees (both initially and at all times during the currency of the agreement) is or are:
  (i)   his or her spouse or civil partner,
  (ii) under the age of criminal responsibility (ie under 10), or
  (iii) an intended victim or victims of the substantive offence.

The Court of Appeal has held that, for the purposes of (i), 'spouse' includes a party to a polygamous marriage which is valid under the law of the place of celebration and is not regarded as void under English law.

COMMON LAW CONSPIRACY

As already explained, the only types of common law conspiracy which now exist are conspiracy to defraud and, to the extent that the conduct agreed on would not in itself amount to or involve an offence, conspiracy to engage in conduct which tends to corrupt public morals. Spouses (but not civil partners) are not guilty of common law conspiracy if they are the only parties to the agreement.

Conspiracy to defraud requires further explanation. There can be a conspiracy to defraud without any element of deception since it is sufficient to prove an agreement by dishonesty to deprive a person of something which is his (or to which he is or would be or might be entitled) or an agreement by dishonesty to injure some proprietary right of his. Where the intended victim of an agreement is a public official performing public duties, as distinct from a private individual, there can also be a conspiracy to defraud if the agreement is dishonestly to deceive such a person into acting contrary to his duty (eg in granting a licence or giving information). The causing of economic loss or prejudice, or (as the case may be) the deceiving of a public official into acting contrary to his duty, need not be the purpose of the parties to the agreement, since it suffices if they have dishonestly agreed to bring about a state of affairs which they realised would or might have such a result.

To be a conspiracy to defraud an agreement must incorporate some unlawfulness in its object or means.

Clearly, the definition of conspiracy to defraud is wide enough to cover cases where the object or means of the agreement would itself be an offence as well as those where the object or means would not be criminal but would otherwise be unlawful (eg as a tort). Agreements to steal, or to forge, and so on, may, of course, be prosecuted as statutory conspiracies to steal, etc but, by virtue of the Criminal Justice Act 1987, s 12, they may instead be charged as common law conspiracies to defraud. However, they should ordinarily be charged as a statutory conspiracy unless there is good reason otherwise.

ATTEMPT

The Criminal Attempts Act 1981 (CAA 1981), s 1(1) provides that if, with intent to commit an offence to which CAA 1981, s 1 applies, a person does an act which is more than merely preparatory to the commission of the offence, he is guilty of attempting to commit the offence. The offence under s 1(1) is triable in the same way as the offence attempted.

The offences to which CAA 1981, s 1 applies are described by s 1(4), which provides that s 1 applies to any offence which, if completed, would be triable in England and Wales as an indictable offence, except:

(a) conspiracy (whether common law or statutory);
(b) aiding, abetting, counselling, procuring or suborning the commission of an offence;
(c) offences under the Criminal Law Act 1967, s 4(1) (assisting offenders) or s 5(1) (concealing offences); and
(d) encouraging or assisting suicide under the Suicide Act 1961, s 2(1).

It follows that all attempts to commit indictable offences, other than those specified above, are offences contrary to s 1 but attempts to commit summary offences are not. However, by way of special exception, attempted low-value shoplifting is an offence under s 1. It should be noted that a number of statutes providing summary offences also provide specific offences of attempt in relation to them.

Mens rea

The requirement of mens rea plays a particularly important role in the crime of attempt because whether or not a particular act amounts to an attempt might well hinge on the intent with which it is done. For example, to strike a match near a haystack might or might not be attempted arson of a haystack, depending on whether there is an intent to set fire to the haystack or to light a cigarette: the intent colours the act.

The mens rea specified by CAA 1981, s 1(1) is an 'intent to commit an offence to which this section [ie s 1] applies' and which the defendant (D) is alleged to have attempted. This apparently straightforward statement needs further explanation since 'an intent to commit the offence attempted' may involve a number of mental states.

D must, of course, intend to commit an act or to continue with a series of acts which, when successfully completed, will amount to or lead to an offence. In addition, if the crime attempted requires some consequence to result from his conduct, D must *intend* to cause that consequence. This is so even though some other type of mens rea (eg recklessness) is required or suffices for the full offence. This requirement of mens rea in attempt can be illustrated as follows:

(1) On a charge of attempted murder, it must be proved that D intended the unlawful death of another human being. By way of comparison, if D had actually killed someone he could be convicted of murder merely because he intended his act unlawfully to cause grievous bodily harm to another person.

(2) On a charge of attempted criminal damage, it must be proved that D intended the destruction or damaging of property belonging to another, even though if D had actually destroyed or damaged that property he could have been convicted of criminal damage if he was reckless as to the risk that his act might possibly have this effect.

Where the actus reus of the crime attempted includes some circumstance, such as the fact that the goods handled are stolen in handling stolen goods, D will have sufficient mens rea as to that circumstance on a charge of attempt if he intends that it will exist, or knows or believes that it does. Moreover, although there are conflicting Court of Appeal decisions, there is authority that, where some lesser mental state as to a circumstance suffices for the full offence or no mental state as to it is required at all, recklessness as to it suffices on a charge of attempt.

The requirement that D must intend to commit the offence attempted means that D must have any other mental element, additional to mens rea as to the elements of the actus reus of the crime attempted, required for that crime. Thus, to be convicted of attempted theft D must not only have intended to appropriate the property belonging to another but have acted dishonestly and with intent permanently to deprive the 'owner' of it.

Actus reus

CAA 1981, s 1(1) requires 'an act that is *more than merely preparatory* to the commission of the offence', ie the full offence which D intends to commit.

The 'more than merely preparatory' formula is not limited to 'last act' cases, ie cases where D has done the last act towards the commission of the full offence which, to his knowledge, it was necessary for him to do in order to commit the full offence, even though something more remains to be done by another, innocent, person, since it *can* be satisfied where D still has to take some further step or steps himself before the full offence can be committed by him. In this context it must be emphasised that the question is not whether D has done an act which was more than preparatory but whether D has done an act which was *more than merely* preparatory. Appeal courts have held that if D has got as far as having embarked on the commission of the offence (ie is 'on the job'), there is sufficient evidence to leave to the jury of an act *more than merely* preparatory to the commission of the intended crime.

Impossibility

CAA 1981, s 1(2) provides that a person may be guilty of attempting to commit an offence to which s 1 applies, even though the facts are such that the commission of the offence is impossible. Therefore, a person who attempts to murder by an inadequate dosage of poison is guilty of attempted murder.

Section 1(3) purports to reinforce the rule in s 1(2), by declaring that where:

(a) apart from s 1(3) a person's intention would not be regarded as having amounted to an intent to commit an offence; but

(b) if the facts of the case had been as that person believed them to be, his intention would have been so regarded,

he is to be regarded as having an intent to commit that offence.

By virtue of s 1(2) and (3), a person who intends to kill another by shooting him in a bed, but who discovers after he has fired the shot that the assumed and intended victim was a pillow, can be convicted of attempted murder. Likewise, a person who handles some goods mistakenly believing that they are stolen can be convicted of attempting to handle stolen goods.

Other statutory offences of attempt

CAA 1981, s 3 applies the provisions of the Act to other existing statutory attempts to commit offences, by stating that the same provisions apply to those attempts. Section 3 therefore ensures a common approach to all offences of attempted crime, even where the specific offence of attempt is created by a particular statute and even where that specific offence relates to a summary offence.

Online Supplements

As a result of the large amount of legislation which continues to be made, the increasing size of *Police Law* edition by edition has become a concern. A further increase in size is not sustainable. It has been necessary to exclude from the body of the book a few topics of marginal importance to police officers. However, those excluded topics, revised as necessary, will be dealt with on the companion website to *Police Law* <http://www.oup.com/>.

The online supplements available for *Police Law* are:

Appendix 1 Public Service Vehicles
Appendix 2 Goods Vehicles
Appendix 3 Immigration
Appendix 4 Animals, Birds, and Plants
Appendix 5 Game, Deer, and Fish

Please visit the companion website to sign up for access to these supplements, as well as any additional information to which reference is made in the text and legislative and case law updates available during the course of the 15th edition.

Index